THE
BOOK
OF THE
STATES

1986-87 EDITION

Volume 26

The Council of State Governments
Lexington, Kentucky

Copyright 1986
The Council of State Governments
Iron Works Pike
P.O. Box 11910
Lexington, Kentucky 40578

Manufactured in the United States of America

ISBN 0-87292-062-3
Price: $42.50

CONTENTS

A review of constitutional revision and actions on proposals in the states during 1984-85, along with general information on state constitutions, amendment procedures, and constitutional commissions and conventions.

An overview of the states' chief executives, other officials, and executive branch activities in 1984-85, as well as current information on the office of the governor—including qualifications for office, compensation, powers, cabinet systems, transition provisions—and the powers, duties, qualifications for office, annual salaries, methods of selection, and length of terms for selected executive branch officials.

A review of the evolution of the legislature, with special emphasis on changes in the last two years. Basic information on the state legislatures—including the legal provisions for legislative sessions and a variety of legislative procedures—is presented, along with legislative compensation, statistics on bill introductions and enactments for 1983, 1984, and 1985, and membership turnover in the legislatures.

An exploration of the state of the judiciary, with information on the courts of last resort, intermediate appellate courts, and general trial courts, as well as the compensation and methods of selection and removal of state judges.

Chapter Nine
INTERGOVERNMENTAL AFFAIRS
A review of recent developments in the relationships between the federal
government and the states and the states and their local governments, and
cooperative efforts among the states themselves. Statistics on federal aid and
state intergovernmental revenue and expenditures for 1983 and 1984 are
included.

Chapter Ten
STATE PAGES
A variety of statistics and information about the states—including capitals,
population sizes, land areas, historical data, elected executive branch officials,
legislative leaders, and judges of the courts of last resort. State mottos, flowers,
songs, birds, and other items unique to the states and other U.S. jurisdictions
also are presented.

INDEX

TABLES

FOREWORD

This book is about the state of the states. It contains a wealth of facts, figures, insights, and information pertaining to all aspects of state government. For over 50 years, *The Book of the States* has chronicled the structure, functions, finances, and personnel of each state, documenting significant trends and changes. The Council of State Governments is committed to providing in-depth, timely information about state government in all aspects of its work. Through the biennial series, *The Book of the States*, the Council continues to demonstrate its role as the source of information for and about the states.

May 1986

Carl W. Stenberg
Executive Director

STAFF

Deborah A. Gona
Editor-in-Chief
Research and Information Development

Lisa L. Brewer
Assistant to the Editor-in-Chief

Karen Pinches
Compositor

Nancy C. Pickens
Indexer

Proofreaders
Melissa L. Silvestri
Jan Lobitz
Louise B. Curry

Production
David Jackson
Charles Haspel

ACKNOWLEDGEMENTS

Many thanks to the hundreds of individuals in the states who provided data and information; to the authors who graciously shared their expertise; and to the thousands of state officials who, through their daily work, contributed to the story of state government that is presented in this volume.

THE STATE OF THE STATES

—remarks of former Governor Charles S. Robb, Virginia, 1985
President of The Council of State Governments, at the CSG Annual
Governing Board Meeting, Stateline, Nevada, December 5, 1985.

A revolution is occurring in America. The battle is not with the British—but over the budget—and I believe the consequences will change the course of government in this country.

The federal government—once the source of financial support and the impetus for social change—is in retreat. Just as the Great Depression brought the federal government into the center of American life, the deficit has diminished federal influence in improving our way of life.

There is, however, one important difference between the government's response to the Depression and its reaction to the deficit. In the 1930s, the federal government made a major effort to resolve the nation's financial crisis; in the 1980s, the federal government helped create it.

But the news isn't all bad.

America's $200 billion deficits have forced us to ask fundamental questions about how much government will do and which level of government will do it. Although the federal budget is still in the birthing process more than two months into the fiscal year, we can make some long-term observations.

First—The shift in responsibilities from Washington to the states will continue regardless of which party is in power.

I don't know if the decision to let deficits soar in the early 1980s was part of an undercover plan to reorder the nation's government. But plan or no plan, the arithmetic now leaves the administration and the Congress with no choice but to unload substantial responsibilities. For the rest of the decade, decisions will be more fiscal than political—and the tide won't easily be turned, even with a general tax increase.

Second—States should prepare for the possibility that federal funding—with the exception of income support programs—may be completely shut off.

Federal funds to states have been drastically reduced. Apart from income support programs, state grants have been reduced by 40 percent since 1981. And more cuts are coming. On the endangered list, I would place community development programs, transportation and transit aid, environmental and housing programs. It is not farfetched to project that by the end of the century, if not before, the federal government will be responsible for the national defense, the national debt, social security and income maintenance programs—and little else.

If such steps were taken today, it would mean an annual loss of more than $35 billion to state and local governments. . .

Third—While there will be fewer federal dollars, don't expect a decrease in federal regulation.

In light of their diminished domestic duties, some might expect that the Congress will return to its 18th century habit of meeting for several months and retiring to plant the crops. Well, perhaps.

I think that state and local governments are more likely to find that the federal government will attempt to do with mandates what it can no longer do with money. And when the carrots are all gone, the sticks usually become clubs.

What can the states expect besides less money and more regulation? We can bank on the fact that the nation's needs will continue to grow. By 1990, states will have more than $64 billion in additional annual needs for schools, highways, prisons, waste water treatment, hazardous waste, and health care.

I don't believe we will be able to meet these needs with the current division of labor. If the deficit dilemma has done one thing, it has helped point out problems in the federal-state system that have persisted for decades:

• Our federal system of government is inefficient, ineffective, poorly designed, and expensive.

• It lacks accountability and encourages allegiances to programs, rather than solving problems for people.

• It perpetuates regulations that often are costly, out-dated, and counter-productive.

The bottom line is that we have three levels of government, and two of them still work fairly well. The other is deep in debt and isn't working very well at all. This isn't any secret, and doesn't come as any real surprise.

The danger, however, is that once the federal government finishes throwing programs over the side for the states and locals to rescue, we'll all go down together.

The story doesn't have to end that way, though. We can turn the current chaos to our advantage. We can begin a principled assessment of who will do what. I would join those urging the president to convene a domestic summit—a summit that not only determines how we will deal with the deficit, but how we address America's domestic agenda.

Such a summit would include meetings not only with the administration and members of Congress, but also with state and local leaders who can sit down and look at the fundamental issue of which level of government can best deliver particular services to the American people. . .

However the duties are divided, one thing is certain: the states are no longer the Third World of the federal system or a way station that wastes federal money en route to localities.

We can do more. Certainly the federal government is going to do less. This can either be an exercise in damage control or an opportunity to set a new course for the country. I hope it will be the latter.

CHAPTER ONE

STATE
CONSTITUTIONS

STATE CONSTITUTIONS AND CONSTITUTIONAL REVISION: 1984-85

By Albert L. Sturm and Janice C. May

General Overview:
Use of Authorized Methods

The diminished pace of state constitutional change during the early 1980s, noted in the last volume of *The Book of the States*, continued in 1984-85. During this period, a total of 238 proposed changes were submitted to voters in 45 states; 158, including two amendments adopted in Delaware by legislative action only, were approved. As Table A indicates, the total number of proposed changes by all methods was substantially smaller in 1984-85 than in the two preceding bienniums. This reduction is attributable mainly to fewer local amendments; statewide proposals remained at approximately the same level as in the early 1980s. The percentage of voter adoptions for all proposed changes dropped off considerably during 1984-85 as compared with the preceding biennium—from 73 to 65.5 percent—but the adoption rate of the 1980s remained substantially higher than that of 1970-71.

No new or revised state constitutions were adopted or became effective during the past biennium, but New Hampshire's 17th Constitutional Convention convened and adjourned in 1984, and Rhode Island voters approved a convention call on November 6, 1984. The New Hampshire convention did not propose a general revision of the constitution, but did submit a series of amendments to the voters.

Tables 1.2, 1.3, and 1.4 summarize the procedures associated with three methods used in 1984-85 to initiate constitutional change: proposal by the state legislature, available in all states; the constitutional initiative, authorized in 17 state constitutions; and the constitutional convention, available in all states (although not expressly authorized in nine state constitutions). A fourth method of initiating and submitting proposed constitutional changes to the electorate, the constitutional commission (expressly authorized only in the Florida constitution) was not used in 1984-85, nor in any of the bienniums shown in Table A.

Legislative proposal, the most commonly used method of initiating constitutional change, accounted for 88.7 percent of the 238 proposed changes submitted to the voters in 1984-85. Historically, the adoption rate of legislative proposals has been much higher than that of other methods; however, in 1984-85 there was a substantially lower percentage of such adoptions than in the early 1980s—67.3 percent as compared with 75.5 and 73.2 percent in 1982-83 and 1980-81, respectively. The decrease in the number of local amendments (which are usually adopted) accounts for a large part of the lower adoption rate evidenced during the past biennium.

As Table 1.3 indicates, 17 states authorize use of the constitutional initiative, which is appropriate only for making limited constitutional change. During 1984, 17 constitutional initiative proposals were submitted to voters in 10 states, and of these, 47.1 percent were adopted. One additional proposed initiative was removed from the ballot before the election in each of three states—Arkansas, Florida, and Montana. As Table A indicates, the adoption rate for initiatives is far lower than that of legislative proposals. The numbers of constitutional initiatives proposed and adopted in the 10 states during the biennium were as follows: Arizona (1-0), Arkansas (3-1), California (3-1), Colorado (2-1), Michigan (1-0), Missouri (1-1), Nevada (1-0), North Dakota (1-1), Oklahoma (1-1), and Oregon (3-2). The constitutional initiative was not used in 1985.

Constitutional conventions

The constitutional convention is the oldest, best known, and most traditional method for extensively revising an old constitution or

Albert L. Sturm is Professor Emeritus, Center for Public Administration and Policy, Virginia Polytechnic Institute and State University, Blacksburg, Virginia, and Janice C. May is Associate Professor of Government, The University of Texas at Austin.

writing a new one. Through 1985, more than 230 such constituent assemblies have been convened in the states. This method is usually initiated by the state legislature after the voters have approved a convention call. An increasing number of state constitutions require periodic submission to the voters of the question of calling a constitutional convention. As Table 1.4 indicates, 14 state constitutions contain such a provision: eight states provide for submission of the convention question to the voters every 20 years; one state, every 16 years; four states, every 10 years; and one, every nine years.

One state constitutional convention—the first to be convened in the states in the 1980s—was operative during 1984-85. New Hampshire's 17th Constitutional Convention convened on May 9, 1984 and adjourned June 28, 1984, having held 14 plenary sessions during the 50 calendar days it was in session. Its 400 delegates were elected on a non-partisan basis from lower house districts on February 28, 1984, following the electorate's approval of the convention call by a vote of 115,351 to 105,027 on November 2, 1982. Of the 175 resolutions proposing change that were introduced, only 10 were approved by the required three-fifths majority for submission to the voters. At the election on November 6, 1984, the electorate approved six of the 10 proposed changes. In comparison, the referendums on proposals submitted by two 1980 constitutional conventions resulted in the adoption of only two of eight proposed changes (in Arkansas, two proposed, none adopted; and in New Hampshire, six proposed, two adopted).

Like New Hampshire, Rhode Island is one of four states whose constitution requires a referendum on the convention question every 10 years unless one has convened. On November 6, 1984, the Rhode Island electorate approved a convention call by a vote of 155,337 to 131,648. The enabling act, approved June 19, 1985, provided for an unlimited constitutional convention with 100 delegates, one elected from each lower house district. These delegates were elected on a non-partisan basis at the general election on November 5, 1985. Supported by an appropriation of $50,000 for expenses, Rhode Island's 12th Constitutional Convention was scheduled to convene on January 6, 1986.

Our summary in the last volume of *The Book of the States* included a brief account of constitutional developments in the District of Columbia where a proposed "Constitution of the State of New Columbia," drafted by a constitutional convention and approved by the voters in 1982, was transmitted to the U.S. Congress in the fall of 1983. On September 12, 1983, D.C. Delegate Walter C. Fauntroy introduced H.R. 3861, the New Columbia Admissions Act, on which initial hearings were held May 15, 1984. An informal task force was organized by Delegate Fauntroy to study the constitution and make recommendations for change based upon the hearing record, comments received from members of Congress, D.C. officials, and other sources. A hearing on changes proposed by the task force, rescheduled for November 14, 1985, was postponed until early 1986. Major criticism has focused on some new guarantees in the bill of rights, and various other provisions have been challenged as illegal, unconstitutional, or impractical. Some critics believe that the document is too seriously flawed and politically unorthodox to win necessary congressional approval.

Table A

State Constitutional Changes by Method of Initiation
1970−71, 1980−81, 1982−83 and 1984−85

Method of Initiation	Number of states involved				Total proposals				Total adopted				Percentage adopted			
	1970 −71	1980 −81	1982 −83	1984 −85	1970 −71	1980 −81	1982 −83	1984 −85	1970 −71	1980 −81	1982 −83	1984 −85	1970 −71	1980 −81	1982 −83	1984 −85
All methods	48	46	45	45	403	388	345	238	224	272	258	158	55.6	70.1	73.0*	65.5*
Legislative proposal	47	46	45	45	392	362	330	211	222	265	255	144	55.6	73.2	75.5*	67.3*
Constitutional initiative	4	11	9	10	5	18	15	17	1	5	3	8	20.0	27.8	20.0	47.1
Constitutional convention	2	2	−	1	6	8	−	10	1	2	−	6	16.7	25.0	−	60.0
Constitutional commission	−	−	−	−	−	−	−	−	−	−	−	−	−	−	−	−

*In calculating these percentages, the amendments adopted in Delaware (where proposals are not submitted to the voters) are excluded.

5

Constitutional commissions

Constitutional commissions generally serve two major purposes: (1) to study the constitution and propose needed changes; and (2) to prepare for a constitutional convention. As shown in Table 1.5, constitutional commissions were operative in Mississippi, New Hampshire, Rhode Island, and Utah during 1984-85.

Mississippi Governor William A. Allain created the Governor's Constitutional Study Commission in mid-November 1985. Acting on his own initiative and without an appropriation for commission expenses, Allain invited a widely representative group of citizens to serve on the commission. (Members will serve without compensation or per diem expense allowance, but the commission's expenses will be paid from resources in the governor's office.) As of early 1986, 362 individuals—representing all branches of state and local government, numerous social, economic, professional, and political organizations, geographical areas, minorities, and other components of the state's citizenry—had accepted the invitation to serve. James P. Coleman, former governor and retired federal judge, was designated to chair the commission, which held its first plenary session on December 12, 1985.

Initially, nine substantive committees were appointed: executive branch, county government, economic development, legislative branch, municipal government, higher education, judicial branch, elementary/secondary education, and agriculture and forestry. Three additional substantive committees on elections and franchise, the bill of rights, and general provisions were designated later. The second plenary session of the commission was scheduled for April 9, 1986. The commission is expected to submit its recommendations to the governor by mid-October 1986; proposed revisions will be submitted to the legislature in January 1987.

As reported in the last volume of *The Book of the States*, the New Hampshire General Court created a 10-member Constitutional Convention Task Force in 1983 to prepare for the 1984 constitutional convention. During November 1983, the task force held five public hearings and received over 60 suggestions for constitutional change. Its report, submitted in January 1984, addressed 11 major issues and proposed nine changes in the constitution.

In 1983, the Rhode Island General Assembly created the bi-partisan Preparatory Commission for a Constitutional Convention to assemble information on constitutional questions for voters prior to the 1984 referendum on calling the state's 12th constitutional convention. This bi-partisan body had 13 members, including four representatives appointed by the speaker of the house, three senators appointed by the senate majority leader, and six public members named by the majority and minority leaders in the two chambers. In its report, dated July 5, 1984, the commission recommended that the voters approve calling a constitutional convention and submitted a list of specific issues for consideration by a convention, if approved by the electorate.

The Utah Constitutional Revision Commission, a permanent body since 1977, is mandated to submit recommendations for constitutional revision to the legislature at least 60 days before each legislature convenes. Voter action on the commission's proposals through 1985 has included adoption of revised articles on labor, revenue and taxation, and the executive, legislative, and judicial branches. Proposed revisions of the articles on education, local government, and public debt will be submitted to the legislature in 1986. Total appropriations to the commission through 1985 were $483,000, including $55,000 for each year of the 1984-85 biennium.

In Georgia, the Select Committee on Constitutional Revision, which coordinated the drafting of the state's 10th constitution, continued in existence officially, but was inactive during the biennium. However, the work of reviewing the estimated 1200 local amendments ratified by Georgia voters over the years, and of listing those currently in effect with a limited analysis, has been completed by the Office of Legislative Counsel. The new constitution provides for the repeal of all existing local amendments unless they are specifically continued in effect prior to July 1, 1987, and prohibits the adoption of any additional local amendments. In early 1985, the General Assembly created a Local Constitutional Amendments Overview Committee to coordinate the study and disposition of the local amendments, but this body still had not been activated by the end of the year.

In summary, during 1984-85, a total of 45 states took some official action to amend or revise their constitutions. All 45 states used the method of legislative proposal to initiate one or more proposed changes; 10 states used the constitutional initiative, and only one convened a constitutional convention during the biennium. The five states that took no action toward constitutional revision during the period were: Kansas, Massachusetts, Tennessee, Vermont, and Wisconsin.

Substantive Changes

Piecemeal rather than comprehensive constitutional change characterized the 1984-85 biennium. No new constitution was adopted, nor was comprehensive constitutional revision approved in any state. Only two extensively revised articles and three new ones were proposed, and relatively little editorial revision was attempted.

Table B provides an overview of the general subject matter of constitutional changes during the first three bienniums of the 1980s and in 1970-71. All proposals are grouped into two major categories: (1) those of general statewide application, which are by far the most numerous and involved 45 states during both 1982-83 and 1984-85; and (2) proposed local amendments, submitted by six state legislatures in 1982-83, but by only two (Alabama and Texas) in 1984-85. Of the 228 statewide proposals in 1984-85, 67.1 percent were adopted—a percentage somewhat higher than during the two preceding bienniums of the 1980s and substantially greater than in 1970-71. The adoption rate of local

amendments (40 percent) was far lower than that for statewide proposals and less than half the adoption percentage of the two preceding bienniums of the 1980s—a reduction due in large measure to the elimination of local amendments under the new Georgia constitution.

In Table B, statewide amendments proposed during each biennium are further classified under the principal subject matter areas of state constitutions, identified for convenience by the titles of articles found in virtually all state constitutions.

By far the largest number of proposals during 1984-85 and the other bienniums related to finance, encompassing taxation, borrowing and debt, and fiscal administration. In 1984-85, proposed changes in suffrage and elections and amendment and revision, received 100 percent voter approval. Adoption percentages for proposals relating to state bills of rights, the judicial branch, local government, state and local debt, and miscellaneous proposals exceeded 70 percent. Proposals relating to the legislative branch and state functions ranked the lowest, hovering just above the 50 percent approval mark.

The bill of rights, suffrage, and elections

Proposals affecting individual rights enjoyed a high approval percentage (77.7) in 1984-85. North Dakota and Utah approved guarantees of the right to keep and bear arms. Equal rights and anti-discrimination proposals were on the ballot in Connecticut

Table B

Substantive Changes in State Constitutions:
Proposed and Adopted, 1970−71, 1980−81, 1982−83 and 1984−85

Subject Matter	Total Proposed				Total Adopted				Percentage Adopted			
	1970 −71	1980 −81	1982 −83	1984 −85	1970 −71	1980 −81	1982 −83	1984 −85	1970 −71	1980 −81	1982 −83	1984 −85
Proposals of statewide applicability	300	254	226	228	176	160	149	154	58.4	63.0	65.9*	67.1*
Bill of rights	13	13	13	9	11	10	13	7	84.6	76.9	100.0	77.7
Suffrage and elections	39	5	5	5	23	5	4	5	59.0	100.0	80.0	100.0
Legislative branch	42	43	32	37	19	21	18	19	45.2	48.8	56.3	51.4
Executive branch	27	21	19	30	22	10	9	20	81.5	47.6	47.4	66.7
Judicial branch	17	23	26	19	11	17	21	16	64.7	73.9	80.8	78.9*
Local government	21	11	13	16	15	4	9	13	71.4	36.4	69.2	75.0*
Finance and taxation	50	77	48	67	29	52	28	43	58.0	67.5	58.3*	64.2
State and local debt	25	20	26	21	10	13	19	16	40.0	65.0	73.1	76.2
State functions	46	23	31	17	26	16	18	9	56.5	69.6	58.1	52.9
Amendment and revision	13	9	2	2	7	7	1	2	53.8	77.8	50.0	100.0
General revision proposals	7	1	1	−	3	0	1	−	42.9	0.0	100.0	−
Miscellaneous proposals	N.A.	8	10	5	N.A.	5	8	4	N.A.	62.5	80.0	80.0
Local amendments	103	134	123	10	48	112	107	4	46.6	83.6	87.0	40.0

*In calculating these percentages, the changes adopted in Delaware (where proposals are not submitted to the voters) are excluded.
Key:
N.A.—Not available.

and Maine, with approval in the former and rejection in the latter. The Connecticut proposal extended protections to the disabled. Voters in West Virginia approved a requirement that public schools set aside a time for students' voluntary contemplation, meditation, or prayer.

Most of the remaining proposals concerned criminal justice, an area that has attracted a great deal of voter interest and concern in recent years. Although there were somewhat fewer than in the preceding biennium, the ballot propositions continued to mark the trend toward limiting the rights of the accused. Oregon, for example, reinstated the death penalty in 1984 for the second time since 1914. Other changes included lowering standards of evidence required of the state in criminal proceedings (New Hampshire) and altering rules pertaining to admissibility of confessions (Pennsylvania). Also of significance was the rejection by Rhode Island voters of the restoration of ex-felons' voting rights. In Texas, a ban on the out-of-state transportation of offenders was revised to permit interstate exchange of prisoners for incarceration purposes.

Proposals concerning suffrage were adopted in five states. Colorado approved a language change requiring that voters for state elective executive officers and signers of petitions on specified matters be registered voters. Voters in Maryland adopted a requirement that elective constitutional officers be registered voters. One of the convention proposals adopted in New Hampshire requires that voter registration and polling places be easily accessible to all qualified persons. In Pennsylvania, additional provisions for absentee voting were adopted, and in Oregon, voters changed the number of signatures required on a recall petition. Also of importance to elections was the adoption by California voters of a "truth in campaigning" measure under which elected officials can be removed from office if, in a civil suit, it is proved that their libelous or slanderous statements contributed substantially to their election.

The three branches of state government

Collectively, proposed constitutional changes relating to the three branches of government numbered approximately the same as those in the general area of finance and debt—86 as compared to 88. Proposals

concerning the legislative branch (37) outnumbered executive proposals (30) and proposed changes in the judicial branch (19), but with an adoption percentage of 78.9 in 1984-85, judicial proposals were relatively more successful with the voters. In 1984-85, however, the number of executive proposals surpassed those in the two previous bienniums, and the approval rate was high, second only to that of 1970-71.

Proposed changes for the legislative branch related mainly to legislative powers, members' privileges, reapportionment and redistricting, and various aspects of organization and procedure. In 1984, North Dakota adopted two amendments providing for a general revision of the legislative article, the first dealing with structure and organization, and the second with procedure. Of four redistricting proposals, only two passed. California voters again rejected a major change to a reapportionment commission (Proposition 39). Idaho voters also rejected changes, but voters in Montana passed a provision for a 90-day period for congressional redistricting, and the Indiana electorate approved some language alterations. New Hampshire voters rejected convention proposals to reduce the size of their House of Representatives (from 400 to 388) and increase Senate membership (from 24 to 36), and to reduce the minimum age qualification for state senators and executive councilors from 30 to 25. Authority to review administrative regulations was approved in Iowa, but rejected in Alaska, Michigan, and New Jersey. In Texas, the legislature gained power over budget execution for the first time.

As a result of proposal actions involving legislative sessions, New Hampshire joined the ranks of states with annual legislative sessions, Utah equalized the number of days of its annual sessions, and Alaska limited the length of each session to 120 days (subject to an extension by an extraordinary legislative majority). Louisiana voters rejected an organizational session, and Hawaii electors opposed changes in recess provisions (as did New Hampshire voters who rejected expansion of the recess power of the governor and the council). Of two legislative compensation proposals, a change in the manner of payment was authorized in Hawaii, but an increase in per diem pay for Texas legislators was defeated.

One of the more controversial issues involving legislative powers concerned establishment of a state lottery. Authorization for a state lottery was approved in California, Missouri, Oregon, and West Virginia. In California, the lottery proposition also prohibited casino gambling. Other proposals for legalizing games of chance and wagering were on the ballot in Arkansas, Colorado, New Jersey, and New York.

Colorado voters adopted an initiative proposal prohibiting the use of public funds to pay for any induced abortion, but authorized the General Assembly to appropriate funds for medical services necessary to save lives under specified conditions. Oklahoma authorized its legislature to set statutory limits on damages for injuries resulting in death when brought against the state or a political subdivision.

State electorates approved two-thirds of the proposals concerning the executive branch. Among the reforms adopted were: a four-year term of office for the governor and other elected state officers in Arkansas; a provision for the appointment of a commissioner of insurance in Colorado; the establishment of a division of criminal justice and a procedure to determine gubernatorial incapacity in Connecticut; and creation of a state department of economic development in Missouri. New Hampshire voters rejected a four-year term for their governor, North Dakota voters rejected a proposal to remove the state treasurer as an elected constitutional officer, and the Wyoming electorate defeated a proposal that state officers appointed by the governor serve at the governor's pleasure unless otherwise provided by law.

Among the successful propositions affecting administrative agencies and public employees was a South Carolina amendment designed to limit the number of government employees hired annually to the state's average annual population growth. Arizona voters rejected a proposal prohibiting public employees' right to strike. Public employee retirement systems were the subject of several other propositions.

In 1984-85, as in the preceding biennium, more than three-fourths of the proposed changes in state judiciaries met with the voters' approval. These proposals dealt mainly with juries, court jurisdiction, conditions of judicial service, discipline of judges, procedure, and court organization. The Utah electorate adopted a comprehensive revision of the judicial article that included changes in organization and administration, judicial selection and discipline, and jurisdiction and appeals. Voters in South Carolina approved the establishment of an intermediate appellate court, and a requirement that all Supreme Court rules and procedures must be submitted to the legislature during its regular sessions (if not vetoed by the legislature, they become effective in 90 days). Texas voters adopted a significant and long-sought judicial redistricting reform. Montana joined Texas in revising judicial discipline sections of the constitution. The jurisdiction of the courts of last resort in New York and Texas was expanded to permit ruling on certified questions from federal courts (and in New York, from other state courts). Proposals regarding jury changes generally failed.

Local government, finance

During 1984-85, the General Assembly of Delaware and voters in 13 states approved three-fourths of the proposed changes relating to local government—a higher rate of adoptions than in any other biennium shown in Table B. As in the preceding biennium, the office of sheriff was the subject of a number of proposed changes, all of which were approved: Kentucky deleted limitations on the number of terms; Maine extended the length of the term from two to four years; and New York authorized the legislature to determine whether sheriffs should be elected every three or every four years. Other changes relating to local offices included: deletion of the requirement for at-large election of county commissioners in Florida; approval of specified conditions for tenure in office in Georgia; removal from the North Dakota constitution of references to two county offices; abolition of the office of county treasurer in certain Texas counties; and authorization for a member of a local governing body in Virginia to be elected or appointed to fill a vacancy in the office of mayor or board chairman if permitted to do so by general or special act. Extension of authority or other modification of existing powers of local government units and the establishment of standards of performance for various functions were the subjects of other proposed changes.

Voters in New Mexico and New Hampshire adopted the principle that state-mandated programs for local governments must be funded by the state, or in the case of New Hampshire, approved by local voters. "Tax increment" funding at the local level was rejected in Washington, but certain property tax incentives for new manufacturing were accepted in South Carolina.

Proposed changes in articles on finance and taxation and on state and local debt, which comprised 38.6 percent of the 228 statewide proposals in 1984-85, enjoyed a 67 percent approval rate. During the biennium, voters considered a variety of proposed fiscal changes, including tax levies, assessments and exemptions, bonds and trust funds, spending limits, financial administration and policy, and other related subjects.

Of special interest was the defeat in four states (California, Michigan, Nevada, and Oregon) of initiative propositions that would have imposed stringent limitations on state and local taxing powers. This post-Proposition 13 trend was observed in the preceding biennium and suggests that the taxpayers' revolts spawned by California in 1978 have ended. In Oregon, voters rejected two fiscal initiatives: one, a 1984 proposal similar to Proposition 13, was concerned with the property tax and required popular votes for new or increased taxes; the other, in 1985, would have established limitations on conditions for any state general retail sales tax and use tax, prohibited the imposition of such taxes by local governments, regulated school property taxes, and required the legislature to limit expenditure growth. The propositions defeated in California (Proposition 36), Michigan, and Nevada were noteworthy for including fees (service charges in Nevada) within the limitations. The Michigan proposal centered on popular votes to restrict taxes or, as an alternative in some cases, a four-fifths vote of the legislative body.

Property taxes continued to draw the most proposals, with a good share of the total concerned with exemptions. Most of these proposals, including those benefiting senior citizens in New Jersey, passed. Proposed increases in sales taxes and motor fuels taxes, however, did not fare so well. Nevada voters rejected a sales tax on food.

Other fiscal provisions concerned spending limits, borrowing, and trust funds. As for spending limitations, South Carolina joined those states that tie state expenditure increases to the state's economic growth. Loui-

siana voters, however, rejected a limit on growth in state general fund expenditures. Both South Carolina and Virginia approved a "balanced budget" amendment. New bonds for water development, conservation, veterans housing, and the purchase of farm and ranch lands in Texas, and for coal technology research in Ohio, were passed by the voters. Alabama voters approved a new permanent trust fund from oil proceeds, and a new Higher Education Assistance Fund was approved in Texas. Louisiana voters rejected a proposal for a permanent trust.

State functions, constitutional revisions, miscellaneous

Proposed alterations in the major policy provisions of state constitutions may be classified under legislative powers, since determination of public policy is a principal ingredient of lawmaking. However, most operating state constitutions include separate articles on the major substantive functional areas of state policymaking, such as education, conservation, corporations, and health and welfare. During 1984-85, only 17 proposed changes in state functional areas (the fewest by far in the four bienniums shown in Table B) were submitted to voters in five states; of these, 52.9 percent (the lowest rate of the years shown in Table B) were adopted. Principal changes during the biennium concerned corporations, education, conservation and natural resources, and welfare.

The process of state constitutional amendment and revision was the subject of only two proposals submitted to voters in two states during the biennium. The Indiana electorate adopted a restatement of some constitutional provisions and removed antiquated language in the constitution to reflect current conditions, practices, and requirements. In South Carolina, the voters approved a temporary provision (for the 1986 and 1988 general elections) authorizing revision of an entire article of the constitution, addition of a new article, and changes in related provisions in other articles by the submission of a single question to the voters. In the preceding analysis, we noted that during the biennium entirely new or extensively revised articles were adopted in North Dakota (legislative branch) and Utah (judiciary), and one was rejected in Oregon (establishing limitations and conditions for general sales and use taxation). New articles also were added to the constitutions of Missouri (benefits for dependents of government employees) and Oklahoma (alcoholic beverage control).

Of the five proposals in the miscellaneous category shown in Table B, four were adopted in 1984. Florida voters approved extension to any natural person (not just the head of a family) of the exemption of homesteads and personal property from forced sale and certain liens. In New Jersey, the electorate extended to senior citizen associations and clubs the privilege of conducting raffles and using the proceeds to support such organizations. On September 18, 1984, Oklahoma voters adopted a constitutional initiative proposal providing for an alcoholic beverage control commission, approval of liquor-by-the-drink by popular vote in a county election, and enactment of implementing legislation by the state legislature. At the following general election, however, the electorate rejected a proposal authorizing the legislature to set statutory limits on damages for personal injuries resulting in death that can be covered on claims against the state or its political subdivisions. Finally, in Oregon, voters adopted an initiative proposal to establish a state lottery commission to operate a state lottery, the profits from which are to be used to create jobs and to further economic development.

In conclusion, probably the most significant contrast between 1984-85 and the other bienniums shown in Table B is the small number of local amendments—those which apply to only one or a few political subdivisions, and have long been acknowledged to be a problem by constitution makers. Two southern states accounted for the 10 local proposals in 1984-85—Alabama (eight proposed, two adopted) and Texas (two proposed, two adopted). Prior to July 1, 1983, when its new constitution became effective, Georgia had originated many, if not most, local amendments.

State Constitutional Sources and Resources

The resource highlight of 1984-85 was the new literature on state constitutional law generated by the "rediscovery" of state constitutions by the legal profession. By one count, the number of law review articles on the subject from 1969 to 1984 totaled 70. In addition to numerous individual articles and several symposia on specific state constitutions—including articles on the Ohio constitution in the *University of Toledo Law Review*, 10 (Winter 1985) and the Washington constitution in the *University of Puget Sound Law Review*, 8 (Winter 1985)—several book-length compilations of articles from state constitutional law conferences were produced. Co-sponsored by the Conference of Chief Justices, the National Center for State Courts, and the Marshall-Wythe School of Law, a national conference held in Williamsburg, Virginia in March 1984 resulted in the 1985 book, *Developments in State Constitutional Law*, edited by Bradley D. McGraw. The publication incorporates 11 articles and a bibliography. Conferences at the University of Texas Law School in January 1985 resulted in a special two-part issue of the *Texas Law Review*, 63 (June 1985). A third publication, *Recent Developments in State Constitutional Law*, edited by Phylis Skloot Bamberger, was published in 1985 by the Practising Law Institute which sponsored two conferences.

A significant addition to the body of literature on state constitutional conventions was the 1985 book, *Behind the Scenes, The Politics of a Constitutional Convention*, written by Philip G. Schrag, a Georgetown University law professor who was elected a delegate to the D.C. Constitutional Convention of 1982. (For information on the convention, see *The Book of the States 1984-85*, page 212.) This volume combines a personal and political diary of events with a more traditional account of the convention. Also in 1985, the U.S.House Committee on the District of Columbia published a history of the D.C. statehood convention as a committee print.

In recognition of the role that state constitutions play in the changing intergovernmental system, the U.S. Advisory Commission on Intergovernmental Relations incorporated a chapter on "State Constitutions" in a 1985 volume, *The Question of State Government Capability*.

The selected list of references at the end of this summary analysis includes several works of particular significance: *Sources and Documents of United States Constitutions* (edited and annotated by the late William F. Swindler), designed to integrate national and state constitutional documents into a reference collection on American constitutional developments; *Model State Constitution*, first published in 1923 by the National Municipal

League and since revised six times; and *Index Digest of State Constitutions*, prepared by the Legislative Drafting Research Fund at Columbia University. The collections on state constitutions and associated material by the Congressional Information Service are also very valuable. During the biennium, a new basic reference on state bills of rights, "Bills and Declarations of Rights Digest," appeared in the third edition of *The American Bench, 1985-86.* Compiled and edited by Ronald K.L. Collins, the digest contains notes, and comparative charts and tables.

The selected list necessarily excludes many specific items on constitutional reform efforts in particular states and numerous special studies. Students, planners, and participants in constitutional revision should consult the official proceedings, debates, and reports of state constitutional conventions and state constitutional commissions, and the special studies prepared for constitution-making in given states, as well as publications of The Council of State Governments, the U.S. Advisory Commission on Intergovernmental Relations, the Citizens Forum on Self-Government, and the League of Women Voters. Particularly useful are the complete, annotated, and comparative analyses of the Illinois and Texas constitutions prepared for the delegates to the constitutional conventions in those states. In addition, a vast quantity of ephemeral material is stored in the archives and libraries of states where major constitutional reform efforts have occurred. Excepting the holdings of the Library of Congress, probably the most extensive collections of fugitive and published materials on state constitutions are those of the Citizens Forum on Self-Government and The Council of State Governments.

Sources of periodic reviews and updates of state constitutional developments are the biennial summaries of official actions in *The Book of the States* and the annual surveys in the *National Civic Review* (which have appeared in the January or February issue each year since 1970). Written by one of the authors, the latter contains state-by-state accounts of substantive changes during the year. The 1982-83 volume of the former included a 50-year review of state constitutional materials. Since 1982, Ronald K.L. Collins has authored articles on developments in state constitutional law, which have appeared periodically in *The National Law Journal.*

Selected References

Bamberger, Phylis Skloot, ed. *Recent Developments in State Constitutional Law.* New York, N.Y.: Practising Law Institute, 1985.

Brown, Cynthia E., comp. *State Constitutional Conventions: From Independence to the Completion of the Present Union. A Bibliography.* Westport, Conn.: Greenwood Press, 1973.

Clem, Alan L., ed. *Contemporary Approaches to State Constitutional Revision.* Vermillion, S.D.: Governmental Research Bureau, University of South Dakota, 1970.

Collins, Ronald K.L., comp. and ed. "Bills and Declarations of Rights Digest." *The American Bench, Judges of the Nation.* 3rd ed. Minneapolis, Minn.: Reginald Bishop Forster and Associates, Inc., 1985, 2483-2655.

Constitutions of the United States: National and State. 2nd ed. 2 vols. Dobbs Ferry, N.Y.: Oceana Publications, 1974. Loose leaf. Updated periodically.

Cornwell, Elmer E., Jr., et al. *Constitutional Conventions: The Politics of Revision.* New York, N.Y.: National Municipal League, 1974. (In second series of the National Municipal League's *State Constitution Studies.*)

Dishman, Robert B. *State Constitutions: The Shape of the Document.* Rev. ed. New York, N.Y.: National Municipal League, 1968. (In first series of the National Municipal League's *State Constitution Studies.*)

Edwards, William A., ed. *Index Digest of State Constitutions.* 2nd ed. Dobbs Ferry, N.Y.: Oceana Publications, 1959. Prepared by the Legislative Drafting Research Fund, Columbia University.

Elazar, Daniel J., ed. Series of articles on American state constitutions and the constitutions of selected foreign states. *Publius: The Journal of Federalism* 12, 2 (Winter 1982): entire issue.

Grad, Frank P. *The State Constitution: Its Function and Form for Our Time.* New York, N.Y.: National Municipal League, 1968. Reprinted from *Virginia Law Review* 54, 5 (June 1968). (In first series of the National Municipal League's *State Constitution Studies.*)

Graves, W. Brooke. "State Constitutional Law: A Twenty-five Year Summary." *William and Mary Law Review* 8, 1 (Fall 1966): 1-48.

_____, ed. *Major Problems in State Constitutional Revision.* Chicago: Public Administration Service, 1960.

Leach, Richard H., ed. *Compacts of Antiquity: State Constitutions.* Atlanta, Ga.: Southern Newspaper Publishers Association Foundation, 1969.

May, Janice C. "Texas Constitutional Revision: Lessons and Laments." *National Civic Review* 66, 2 (February 1977): 64-69.

Selected References—Continued

_____. *The Texas Constitutional Revision Experience in the Seventies.* Austin Tx.: Sterling Swift Publishing Company, 1975.

McGraw, Bradley D., ed. *Developments in State Constitutional Law, The Williamsburg Conference.* St. Paul, Minn.: West Publishing Co., 1985.

Model State Constitution. 6th ed. New York, N.Y.: National Municipal League, 1963. Revised 1968.

Pisciotte, Joseph P., ed. *Studies in Illinois Constitution Making.* 10 vols. Urbana, Ill.: University of Illinois Press, 1972-1980.

Sachs, Barbara Faith, ed. *Index to Constitutions of the United States: National and State.* London, Rome and New York: Oceana Publications, 1980. Prepared by the Legislative Drafting Research Fund, Columbia University. The first two in the series are: *Fundamental Liberties and Rights: A Fifty-State Index* (1980), and *Laws, Legislatures and Legislative Procedures: A Fifty-State Index* (1982).

Schrag, Philip G. *Behind the Scenes: The Politics of a Constitutional Convention.* Washington, D.C.: Georgetown University Press, 1985.

Southwick, Leslie H. "State Constitutional Revision: Mississippi and the South." *The Mississippi Lawyer* 32, 3 (November-December 1985): 21-25.

State Constitutional Convention Studies. 11 vols. New York, N.Y.: National Municipal League, 1969-1978.

State Constitution Studies. 10 vols. in two series. New York, N.Y.: National Municipal League, 1960-1965.

State Constitutional Conventions, Commissions, and Amendments, 1959-1978: An Annotated Bibliography. 2 vols. Washington, D.C.: Congressional Information Service, 1981. This bibliography incorporates the contents of the following two supplements to the Browne bibliography:

Yarger, Susan Rice, comp. *State Constitutional Conventions, 1959-1975: A Bibliography.* Westport, Conn.: Greenwood Press, 1976.

Canning, Bonnie, comp. *State Constitutional Conventions, Revisions, and Amendments, 1959-1976: A Bibliography.* Westport, Conn.: Greenwood Press, 1977.

State Constitutional Conventions, Commissions, and Amendments on Microfiche. 4 pts. [Microform]. Westport, Conn.: Greenwood Press, 1972-1976; Washington, D.C.: Congressional Information Service, 1977-1981.

Sturm, Albert L. *A Bibliography on State Constitutions and Constitutional Revision, 1945-1975.* Englewood, Colo.: The Citizens Conference on State Legislatures, August 1975.

_____. Annual summary analyses of state constitutional developments. Published in the January or February issues of the *National Civic Review* since 1970.

_____. "The Development of American State Constitutions." *Publius: The Journal of Federalism* 12, 2 (Winter 1982): 57-98.

_____. *Thirty Years of State Constitution Making, 1938-1968.* New York, N.Y.: National Municipal League, 1970.

Swindler, William F., ed. *Sources and Documents of United States Constitutions.* 10 vols. Dobbs Ferry, N.Y.: Oceana Publications, Inc., 1973-1979.

_____. ed. *Sources and Documents of United States Constitutions.* Second Series. 3 vols. Dobbs Ferry, N.Y.: Oceana Publications, Inc. 1982-1983.

Wheeler, John P., Jr. *The Constitutional Convention: A Manual on Its Planning, Organization and Operation.* New York, N.Y.: National Municipal League, 1961.

_____. ed. *Salient Issues of Constitutional Revision.* New York, N.Y.: National Municipal League, 1961.

Table 1.1
GENERAL INFORMATION ON STATE CONSTITUTIONS
(As of December 31, 1985)

State or other jurisdiction	Number of constitutions*	Dates of adoption	Effective date of present constitution	Estimated length (number of words)	Number of amendments Submitted to voters	Number of amendments Adopted
Alabama	6	1819, 1861, 1865, 1868, 1875, 1901	Nov. 28, 1901	174,000	656	452
Alaska	1	1956	Jan. 3, 1959	13,000	28	20
Arizona	1	1911	Feb. 14, 1912	28,876(a)	187	104
Arkansas	5	1836, 1861, 1864, 1868, 1874	Oct. 30, 1874	40,720(a)	156	71(b)
California	2	1849, 1879	July 4, 1879	33,350	756	449
Colorado	1	1876	Aug. 1, 1876	45,679	227	108
Connecticut	4	1818(c), 1965	Dec. 30, 1965	9,564	24	23
Delaware	4	1776, 1792, 1831, 1897	June 10, 1897	19,000	(d)	115
Florida	6	1839, 1861, 1865, 1868, 1886, 1968	Jan. 7, 1969	25,100	63	41
Georgia	10	1777, 1789, 1798, 1861, 1865, 1868, 1877, 1945, 1976, 1982	July 1, 1983	25,000	11(e)	10
Hawaii	1(f)	1950	Aug. 21, 1959	17,453(a)	85	77
Idaho	1	1889	July 3, 1890	21,500	183	103
Illinois	4	1818, 1848, 1870, 1970	July 1, 1971	13,200	7	3
Indiana	2	1816, 1851	Nov. 1, 1851	9,377(a)	65	36
Iowa	2	1846, 1857	Sept. 3, 1857	12,500	48	45(g)
Kansas	1	1859	Jan. 29, 1861	11,865	107	80(g)
Kentucky	4	1792, 1799, 1850, 1891	Sept. 28, 1891	23,500	54	26
Louisiana	11	1812, 1845, 1852, 1861, 1864, 1868, 1879, 1898, 1913, 1921, 1974	Jan. 1, 1975	36,146(a)	24	15
Maine	1	1819	March 15, 1820	13,500	181	153(h)
Maryland	4	1776, 1851, 1864, 1867	Oct. 5, 1867	41,134	227	195
Massachusetts	1	1780	Oct. 25, 1780	36,690(a,i)	141	116
Michigan	4	1835, 1850, 1908, 1963	Jan. 1, 1964	20,000	41	15
Minnesota	1	1857	May 11, 1858	9,500	203	109
Mississippi	4	1817, 1832, 1869, 1890	Nov. 1, 1890	23,500	124	54
Missouri	4	1820, 1865, 1875, 1945	March 30, 1945	42,000	100	62
Montana	2	1889, 1972	July 1, 1973	11,866(a)	17	10
Nebraska	2	1866, 1875	Oct. 12, 1875	20,048(a)	276	183
Nevada	1	1864	Oct. 31, 1864	20,770	165	100(g)
New Hampshire	2	1776, 1784	June 2, 1784	9,200	271(j)	141(j)
New Jersey	3	1776, 1844, 1947	Jan. 1, 1948	17,086	48	36
New Mexico	1	1911	Jan. 6, 1912	27,200	213	104
New York	4	1777, 1822, 1846, 1894	Jan. 1, 1895	80,000	270	203
North Carolina	3	1776, 1868, 1970	July 1, 1971	11,000	30	24
North Dakota	1	1889	Nov. 2, 1889	31,000	208(k)	119(k)
Ohio	2	1802, 1851	Sept. 1, 1851	36,900	241	142
Oklahoma	1	1907	Nov. 16, 1907	68,800	254(l)	114(l)
Oregon	1	1857	Feb. 14, 1859	25,965	347	174
Pennsylvania	5	1776, 1790, 1838, 1873, 1968(m)	1968(m)	21,675	24(m)	19(m)
Rhode Island	2	1842(c)	May 2, 1843	19,026(a,i)	84	44
South Carolina	7	1776, 1778, 1790, 1861, 1865, 1868, 1895	Jan. 1, 1896	22,500(n)	638(o)	454(o)
South Dakota	1	1889	Nov. 2, 1889	23,300	178	92
Tennessee	3	1796, 1835, 1870	Feb. 23, 1870	15,300	55	32
Texas	5	1845, 1861, 1866, 1869, 1876	Feb. 15, 1876	62,000	430	283
Utah	1	1895	Jan. 4, 1896	17,500	121	73
Vermont	3	1777, 1786, 1793	July 9, 1793	6,600	206	49
Virginia	6	1776, 1830, 1851, 1869, 1902, 1970	July 1, 1971	18,500	19	16
Washington	1	1889	Nov. 11, 1889	29,400	139	76
West Virginia	2	1863, 1872	April 9, 1872	25,600	96	59
Wisconsin	1	1848	May 29, 1848	13,500	161	118(g)
Wyoming	1	1889	July 10, 1890	31,800	90	51
American Samoa	2	1960, 1967	July 1, 1967	6,000	13	7
No. Mariana Is.	1	1977	Oct. 24, 1977	. . .	. . .	. . .
Puerto Rico	1	1952	July 25, 1952	9,281(a)	6	6

GENERAL INFORMATION ON STATE CONSTITUTIONS—Continued

*The constitutions referred to in this table include those Civil War documents customarily listed by the individual states.

(a) Actual word count.

(b) Eight of the approved amendments have been superseded and are not printed in the current edition of the constitution. The total adopted does not include five amendments that were invalidated.

(c) Colonial charters with some alterations served as the first constitutions in Connecticut (1638, 1662) and in Rhode Island (1663).

(d) Proposed amendments are not submitted to the voters in Delaware.

(e) The new Georgia constitution eliminates the need for local amendments, which have been a long-term problem for state constitution makers.

(f) As a kingdom and a republic, Hawaii had five constitutions.

(g) The figure given includes amendments approved by the voters and later nullified by the state supreme court in Iowa (three), Kansas (one), Nevada (six) and Wisconsin (two).

(h) The figure does not include one amendment approved by the voters in 1967 that is inoperative until implemented by legislation.

(i) The printed constitution includes many provisions that have been annulled. The length of effective provisions is an estimated 24,122 words (12,490 annulled) in Massachusetts and 11,399 words (7,627 annulled) in Rhode Island.

(j) The constitution of 1784 was extensively revised in 1792. Figures show proposals and adoptions since the constitution was adopted in 1784.

(k) The figures do not include submission and approval of the constitution of 1889 itself and of Article XX; these are constitutional questions included in some counts of constitutional amendments and would add two to the figure in each column.

(l) The figures include five amendments submitted to, and approved by the voters which were, by decisions of the Oklahoma or U.S. Supreme Courts, rendered inoperative or ruled invalid, unconstitutional, or illegally submitted.

(m) Certain sections of the constitution were revised by the limited constitutional convention of 1967-68. Amendments proposed and adopted are since 1968.

(n) Of the estimated length, approximately two-thirds is of general statewide effect; the remainder is local amendments.

(o) Of the 626 proposed amendments submitted to the voters, 130 were of general statewide effect and 496 were local; the voters rejected 83 (12 statewide, 71 local). Of the remaining 543, the General Assembly refused to approve 100 (22 statewide, 78 local), and 443 (96 statewide, 347 local) were finally added to the constitution.

Table 1.2
CONSTITUTIONAL AMENDMENT PROCEDURE: BY THE LEGISLATURE
Constitutional Provisions

State or other jurisdiction	Legislative vote required for proposal(a)	Consideration by two sessions required	Vote required for ratification	Limitation on the number of amendments submitted at one election
Alabama	3/5	No	Majority vote on amendment	None
Alaska	2/3	No	Majority vote on amendment	None
Arizona	Majority	No	Majority vote on amendment	None
Arkansas	Majority	No	Majority vote on amendment	3
California	2/3	No	Majority vote on amendment	None
Colorado	2/3	No	Majority vote on amendment	None(b)
Connecticut	(c)	(c)	Majority vote on amendment	None
Delaware	2/3	Yes	Not required	No referendum
Florida	3/5	No	Majority vote on amendment	None
Georgia	2/3	No	Majority vote on amendment	None
Hawaii	(d)	(d)	Majority vote on amendment(e)	None
Idaho	2/3	No	Majority vote on amendment	None
Illinois	3/5	No	(f)	3 articles
Indiana	Majority	Yes	Majority vote on amendment	None
Iowa	Majority	Yes	Majority vote on amendment	None
Kansas	2/3	No	Majority vote on amendment	5
Kentucky	3/5	No	Majority vote on amendment	4
Louisiana	2/3	No	Majority vote on amendment(g)	None
Maine	2/3(h)	No	Majority vote on amendment	None
Maryland	3/5	No	Majority vote on amendment	None
Massachusetts	Majority(i)	Yes	Majority vote on amendment	None
Michigan	2/3	No	Majority vote on amendment	None
Minnesota	Majority	No	Majority vote in election	None
Mississippi	2/3(j)	No	Majority vote on amendment	None
Missouri	Majority	No	Majority vote on amendment	None
Montana	2/3(h)	No	Majority vote on amendment	None
Nebraska	3/5	No	Majority vote on amendment(e)	None
Nevada	Majority	Yes	Majority vote on amendment	None
New Hampshire	3/5	No	2/3 vote on amendment	None
New Jersey	(k)	(k)	Majority vote on amendment	None(l)
New Mexico	Majority(m)	No	Majority vote on amendment(m)	None
New York	Majority	Yes	Majority vote on amendment	None
North Carolina	3/5	No	Majority vote on amendment	None
North Dakota	Majority	No	Majority vote on amendment	None
Ohio	3/5	No	Majority vote on amendment	None
Oklahoma	Majority	No	Majority vote on amendment	None
Oregon	(n)	No	Majority vote on amendment	None
Pennsylvania	Majority(o)	Yes(o)	Majority vote on amendment	None
Rhode Island	Majority	No	Majority vote on amendment	None
South Carolina	2/3(p)	Yes(p)	Majority vote on amendment	None
South Dakota	Majority	No	Majority vote on amendment	None
Tennessee	(q)	Yes(q)	Majority vote in election(r)	None
Texas	2/3	No	Majority vote on amendment	None
Utah	2/3	No	Majority vote on amendment	None
Vermont	(s)	Yes	Majority vote on amendment	None
Virginia	Majority	Yes	Majority vote on amendment	None
Washington	2/3	No	Majority vote on amendment	None
West Virginia	2/3	No	Majority vote on amendment	None
Wisconsin	Majority	Yes	Majority vote on amendment	None
Wyoming	2/3	No	Majority vote in election	None
American Samoa	3/5	No	Majority vote on amendment(t)	None
Puerto Rico	2/3(u)	No	Majority vote on amendment	3

(a) In all states not otherwise noted, the figure shown in the column refers to the proportion of elected members in each house required for approval of proposed constitutional amendments.

(b) Legislature may not propose amendments to more than six articles of the constitution in the same legislative session.

(c) Three-fourths vote in each house at one session, or majority vote in each house in two sessions between which an election has intervened.

(d) Two-thirds vote in each house at one session, or majority vote in each house in two sessions.

(e) Majority vote on amendment must be at least 50 percent of the total votes cast at the election; or, at a special election, a majority of the votes tallied which must be at least 30 percent of the total number of registered voters.

(f) Majority voting in election or three-fifths voting on amendment.

(g) If five or fewer political subdivisions of the state are affected, majority in state as a whole and also in affected subdivision(s) is required.

(h) Two-thirds of both houses.

(i) Majority of members elected sitting in joint session.

(j) The two-thirds must include not less than a majority elected to each house.

(k) Three-fifths of all members of each house at one session, or majority of all members of each house for two successive sessions.

(l) If a proposed amendment is not approved at the election when submitted, neither the same amendment nor one which would make substantially the same change for the constitution may be again submitted to the people before the third general election thereafter.

(m) Amendments concerning certain elective franchise and education matters require three-fourths vote of members elected and approval by three-fourths of electors voting in state and two-thirds of those voting in each county.

(n) Majority vote to amend constitution, two-thirds to revise ("revise" includes all or a part of the constitution).

(o) Emergency amendments may be passed by two-thirds vote of each house, followed by ratification by majority vote of electors in election held at least one month after legislative approval.

(p) Two-thirds of members of each house, first passage; majority of members of each house after popular ratification.

(q) Majority of members elected to both houses, first passage; two-thirds of members elected to both houses, second passage.

(r) Majority of all citizens voting for governor.

(s) Two-thirds vote senate, majority vote house, first passage; majority both houses, second passage. As of 1974, amendments may be submitted only every four years.

(t) Within 30 days after voter approval, governor must submit amendment(s) to U.S. Secretary of the Interior for approval.

(u) If approved by two-thirds of members of each house, amendment(s) submitted to voters at special referendum; if approved by not less than three-fourths of total members of each house, referendum may be held at next general election.

Table 1.3
CONSTITUTIONAL AMENDMENT PROCEDURE: BY INITIATIVE
Constitutional Provisions

State	Number of signatures required on initiative petition	Distribution of signatures	Referendum vote
Arizona............	15% of total votes cast for all candidates for governor at last election.	None specified.	Majority vote on amendment.
Arkansas	10% of voters for governor at last election.	Must include 5% of voters for governor in each of 15 counties.	Majority vote on amendment.
California..........	8% of total voters for all candidates for governor at last election.	None specified.	Majority vote on amendment.
Colorado	5% of total legal votes for all candidates for secretary of state at last general election.	None specified.	Majority vote on amendment.
Florida	8% of total votes cast in the state in the last election for presidential electors.	8% of total votes cast in each of 1/2 of the congressional districts.	Majority vote on amendment.
Illinois(a)	8% of total votes cast for candidates for governor at last election.	None specified.	Majority voting in election or 3/5 voting on amendment.
Massachusetts(b).....	3% of total votes cast for governor at preceding biennial state election (not less than 25,000 qualified voters).	No more than 1/4 from any one county.	Majority vote on amendment which must be 30% of total ballots cast at election.
Michigan	10% of total voters for governor at last gubernatorial election.	None specified.	Majority vote on amendment.
Missouri	8% of legal voters for all candidates for governor at last election.	The 8% must be in each of 2/3 of the congressional districts in the state.	Majority vote on amendment.
Montana............	10% of qualified electors, the number of qualified electors to be determined by number of votes cast for governor in preceding general election.	The 10% to include at least 10% of qualified electors in each of 2/5 of the legislative districts.	Majority vote on amendment.
Nebraska	10% of total votes for governor at last election.	The 10% must include 5% in each of 2/5 of the counties.	Majority vote on amendment which must be at least 35% of total vote at the election.
Nevada	10% of voters who voted in entire state in last general election.	10% of total voters who voted in each of 75% of the counties.	Majority vote on amendment in two consecutive general elections.
North Dakota	4% of population of the state.	None specified.	Majority vote on amendment.
Ohio	10% of total number of electors who voted for governor in last election.	At least 5% of qualified electors in each of 1/2 of counties in the state.	Majority vote on amendment.
Oklahoma	15% of legal voters for state office receiving highest number of voters at last general state election.	None specified.	Majority vote on amendment.
Oregon	8% of total votes for all candidates for governor at last election at which governor was elected for four-year term.	None specified.	Majority vote on amendment.
South Dakota	10% of total votes for governor in last election.	None specified.	Majority vote on amendment.

(a) Only Article IV, The Legislature, may be amended by initiative petition.
(b) Before being submitted to the electorate for ratification, initiative measures must be approved at two sessions of a successively elected legislature by not less than one-fourth of all members elected, sitting in joint session.

Table 1.4
PROCEDURES FOR CALLING CONSTITUTIONAL CONVENTIONS
Constitutional Provisions

State or other jurisdiction	Provision for convention	Legislative vote for submission of convention question(a)	Popular vote to authorize convention	Periodic submission of convention question required(b)	Popular vote required for ratification of convention proposals
Alabama	Yes	Majority	ME	No	Not specified
Alaska	Yes	No provision(c,d)	(c)	10 years(c)	Not specified(c)
Arizona	Yes	Majority	(e)	No	MP
Arkansas	No		No		
California	Yes	2/3	MP	No	MP
Colorado	Yes	2/3	MP	No	ME
Connecticut	Yes	2/3	MP	20 years(f)	MP
Delaware	Yes	2/3	MP	No	No provision
Florida	Yes	(g)	MP	No	Not specified
Georgia	Yes	(d)	No	No	MP
Hawaii	Yes	Not specified	MP	9 years	MP(h)
Idaho	Yes	2/3	MP	No	Not specified
Illinois	Yes	3/5	(i)	20 years	MP
Indiana	No		No		
Iowa	Yes	Majority	MP	10 years; 1970	MP
Kansas	Yes	2/3	MP	No	MP
Kentucky	Yes	Majority(j)	MP(k)	No	No provision
Louisiana	Yes	(d)	No	No	MP
Maine	Yes	(d)	No	No	No provision
Maryland	Yes	Majority	ME	20 years; 1970	MP
Massachusetts	No			No	Not specified
Michigan	Yes	Majority	MP	16 years; 1978	MP
Minnesota	Yes	2/3	ME	No	3/5 voting on proposal
Mississippi	No		No		
Missouri	Yes	Majority	MP	20 years; 1962	Not specified(l)
Montana	Yes(m)	2/3(n)	MP	20 years	MP
Nebraska	Yes	3/5	MP(o)	No	MP
Nevada	Yes	2/3	ME	No	No provision
New Hampshire	Yes	Majority	MP	10 years	2/3 voting on proposal
New Jersey	No		No		
New Mexico	Yes	2/3	MP	No	Not specified
New York	Yes	Majority	MP	20 years; 1957	MP
North Carolina	Yes	2/3	MP	No	MP
North Dakota	No		No		
Ohio	Yes	2/3	MP	20 years; 1932	MP
Oklahoma	Yes	Majority	(e)	20 years	MP
Oregon	Yes	Majority	(e)	No	No provision
Pennsylvania	No		No		
Rhode Island	Yes	Majority	MP	10 years	MP
South Carolina	Yes	(d)	ME	No	No provision
South Dakota	Yes	(d)	(d)	No	(p)
Tennessee	Yes(q)	Majority	MP	No	MP
Texas	No		No		
Utah	Yes	2/3	ME	No	MP
Vermont	No		No		
Virginia	Yes	(d)	No	No	MP
Washington	Yes	2/3	ME	No	Not specified
West Virginia	Yes	Majority	MP	No	Not specified
Wisconsin	Yes	Majority	MP	No	No provision
Wyoming	Yes	2/3	ME	No	Not specified
American Samoa	Yes	(r)	No	No	ME(s)
Puerto Rico	Yes	2/3	MP	No	MP

PROCEDURES FOR CALLING CONSTITUTIONAL CONVENTIONS—Continued

Key:

MP—Majority voting on the proposal.

ME—Majority voting in the election.

(a) In all states not otherwise noted, the entries in this column refer to the proportion of members elected to each house required to submit to the electorate the question of calling a constitutional convention.

(b) The number listed is the interval between required submissions on the question of calling a constitutional convention; where given, the date is that of the first required submission of the convention question.

(c) Unless provided otherwise by law, convention calls are to conform as nearly as possible to the act calling the 1955 convention, which provided for a legislative vote of a majority of members elected to each house and ratification by a majority vote on the proposals. The legislature may call a constitutional convention at any time.

(d) In these states, the legislature may call a convention without submitting the question to the people. The legislative vote required is two-thirds of the members elected to each house in Georgia, Louisiana, South Carolina and Virginia; two-thirds concurrent vote of both branches in Maine; three-fourths of all members of each house in South Dakota; and not specified in Alaska, but bills require majority vote of membership of each house. In South Dakota, the question of calling a convention may be initiated by the people in the same manner as an amendment to the constitution (see Table 1.3) and requires a majority vote on the question for approval.

(e) The law calling a convention must be approved by the people.

(f) The legislature shall submit the question 20 years after the last convention, or 20 years after the last vote on the question of calling a convention, whichever date is last.

(g) The power to call a convention is reserved to the people by petition.

(h) The majority must be 50 percent of the total votes cast at a general election or at a special election, a majority of the votes tallied which must be at least 30 percent of the total number of registered voters.

(i) Majority voting in the election, or three-fifths voting on the question.

(j) Must be approved during two legislative sessions.

(k) Majority must equal one-fourth of qualified voters at last general election.

(l) Majority of those voting on the proposal is assumed.

(m) The question of calling a constitutional convention may be submitted either by the legislature or by initiative petition to the secretary of state in the same manner as provided for initiated amendments (see Table 1.3).

(n) Two-thirds of all members of the legislature.

(o) Majority must be 35 percent of total votes cast at the election.

(p) Convention proposals are submitted to the electorate at a special election in a manner to be determined by the convention. Ratification by a majority of votes cast.

(q) Conventions may not be held more often than once in six years.

(r) Five years after effective date of constitutions, governor shall call a constitutional convention to consider changes proposed by a constitutional committee appointed by the governor. Delegates to the convention are to be elected by their county councils.

(s) If proposed amendments are approved by the voters, they must be submitted to the U.S. Secretary of the Interior for approval.

Table 1.5
STATE CONSTITUTIONAL COMMISSIONS
(Operative during January 1, 1984-December 31, 1985)

State	Name of commission	Method and date of creation and period of operation	Membership: number and type	Funding	Purpose of commission	Proposals and action
Mississippi	Governor's Constitutional Study Commission	Executive; appointed by a letter of invitation from Governor in mid-November 1985	362 (to date). Members are widely representative of all branches of government, state and local, and of social, economic, professional, and political organizations in the state	No appropriation. Members receive no compensation or per diem. Expenses are paid from resources of Governor's office	To study the constitution and submit recommendations for revision to Governor by mid-October 1986	The Governor will submit commission recommendations, either a series of proposed amendments or a proposed new or revised constitution, to the legislature in January 1987
New Hampshire	Constitutional Convention Task Force	Statutory; N.H. Laws, 1983, Ch. 469, 125-129. Organized in October 1983, the task force completed its mission when its recommendations were submitted to the convention, which convened May 9, 1984	10 members; appointed by the Speaker of the House (3), the President of the Senate (3), the Governor (2), and the Supreme Court (2)	Appropriation of $15,000 for the fiscal year 1984	Study the constitution and recommend needed amendments to the next constitutional convention	The task force held 5 public hearings in November 1983 and received over 60 suggestions for change. In its report, dated Jan. 1, 1984, the task force addressed 11 major issues (under 6 broad categories) and made 9 recommendations for constitutional change
Rhode Island	Bipartisan Preparatory Commission for a Constitutional Convention	Legislative; R255, 83-H5907, effective May 21, 1983. Created pursuant to requirement of Art. XLII of the state constitution	13 (bipartisan); including 7 legislators appointed by the Speaker of the House (4 representatives) and the Majority Leader of the Senate (3 senators), and 6 public members appointed by the majority leader (2 each) and minority leader (1 each) in the two houses	No appropriation	To assemble information on constitutional questions for the electors	In its report, dated July 5, 1984, the commission recommended that the voters approve calling a constitutional convention and submitted a list of specific issues for consideration by the convention

STATE CONSTITUTIONAL COMMISSIONS—Continued

State	Name of commission	Method and date of creation and period of operation	Membership: number and type	Funding	Purpose of commission	Proposals and action
Utah	Utah Constitutional Revision Commission	Statutory: Ch. 89, Laws of Utah, 1969; amended by Ch. 107, Laws, 1975; amended by Ch. 159, Laws, 1977, which made the commission permanent as of July 1, 1977. (Codified at Ch. 54, Title 63, Utah Code Annotated, 1953)	16; 1 ex officio; 9 appointed by Speaker of House (3), President of Senate (3), and Governor (3)—no more than 2 of each group to be from same party; and 6 additional members appointed by the 9 previously appointed members	Appropriations through 1985 totaled $483,000. (The 1985 appropriation was $55,000, the same as for 1984)	Study constitution and recommend desirable changes, including proposed drafts	Mandated to report recommendations at least 60 days before legislature convenes. Voter action on the commission's recommendations through 1985 included: approval of revised articles on labor, the executive branch, revenue and taxation, the judicial branch, and the legislative branch. Proposed revisions of the articles on education, local government and public debt will be submitted to the legislature in 1986

Table 1.6
STATE CONSTITUTIONAL CONVENTIONS
1984-85

State	Convention dates	Type of convention	Referendum on convention question	Preparatory bodies	Appropriations	Convention delegates	Convention proposals	Referendum on convention proposals
New Hampshire	May 9-June 28, 1984 (14 plenary sessions during the 50 calendar days).	Unlimited	Nov. 2, 1982 Vote: 115,351 105,027	Constitutional Convention Task Force	$400,000	400 (elected Feb. 28, 1984 from lower house districts; non-partisan)	10 proposed amendments were approved by the required 3/5 majority for submission to the voters	Nov. 6, 1984: 6 of the 10 proposed amendments were adopted.

CHAPTER TWO

STATE EXECUTIVE BRANCH

THE GOVERNORS, 1984-85

By Thad L. Beyle

Throughout the 1980s, the importance of the states and their elected leaders has grown, especially as the federal government has sought to reduce its involvement in and responsibility for domestic programs and issues. This trend has helped push the governorship ever more into the leading position in the states—if for no other reason than as the one state official who must take the lead in sorting out the responsibilities the states will continue to perform and determining at what level of effort. Further, the governors have continued to become more active in the traditional functions of the states, such as education and health.

Gubernatorial Elections

Fifteen governorships were up for election in 1984-85; in seven of these contests the incumbent stood for an additional term, with five winning reelection. Both of the defeated incumbents, Allen Olson of North Dakota and John Spellman of Washington, were Republicans who lost the 1984 general elections in their states. Incumbent governors Bill Clinton (D-Arkansas), Robert Orr (R-Indiana), Ted Schwinden (D-Montana), John Sununu (R-New Hampshire), and Thomas Kean (R-New Jersey) all won their attempts to serve an additional term.

Four incumbent governors were constitutionally ineligible to seek another term: Pierre duPont (R-Delaware), Christopher Bond (R-Missouri), James Hunt (D-North Carolina), and Charles Robb (D-Virginia); while four other incumbents opted to retire from office: Joseph Garrahy (D-Rhode Island), Scott Matheson (D-Utah), Richard Snelling (R-Vermont), and John Rockefeller (D-West Virginia). These eight out-going governors, five Democrats and three Republicans, had served a combined total of 60 years in the governorship, all serving for eight years (except Robb, who served under a one-term constitutional limitation).

There has been a general trend in the 1980s for fewer gubernatorial incumbents to seek reelection: in 1980-81, there were 15 races, and 12 incumbents (80 percent) sought reelection; in 1982-83, there were 39 races,

and 26 (67 percent) sought reelection; and in 1984-85, there were 15 races and seven (47 percent) sought another term. Preliminary estimates for the 1986 elections, in which 36 seats will be open, indicate that only 50 percent of the incumbents will seek reelection, continuing the trend noted.[1] However, those seeking reelection in the 1980s generally have fared well, with 31 of the 45 (69 percent) winning—increasing from a 58 percent win rate (seven of 12) in the first two years, to a 73 percent rate (24 of 33) in the last four years.

Gubernatorial campaign costs continued to escalate in 1984-85. As shown in Table A, in the 15 races of the biennium, candidates spent about $65 million as officially reported—led by North Carolina at $13.7 million and New Jersey at $10.7 million—for an average of $4.3 million per race. There was a significant difference between races for an open seat ($40.5 million for an average $5.1 million) and races in which the incumbent or a former governor was seeking reelection ($24.5 million for an average of $3.5 million).

Four years earlier, in the 1980-81 elections for governor in these states, the total spent was $49 million. Thus, there has been an increase of $16 million between the two time periods; controlling for inflation, the increase was $1.6 million (in 1967 dollars) or 8 percent, still an indication that the cost of becoming governor continues to rise.

Clearly, the road to the governorship in the 1980s continues to have stops at elected state offices. Of the 15 governors elected in 1984-85, 10 (67 percent) had run successfully in previous state races and had held a visible state-level office. Of the 10, five previously held statewide office: two moved up from the lieutenant governor's office (Michael Castle, Delaware and Madeleine Kunin, Vermont), two from the attorney general's office (John Ashcroft, Missouri and Gerald Baliles, Virginia), and one from previous service as governor (Arch Moore, West Virginia). Two others moved from the state legislature (Nor-

Thad L. Beyle is Professor of Political Science at the University of North Carolina, Chapel Hill.

State	Year		Total campaign expenditures(a)			Winner's vote percentage	Cost per total vote(b)
			All candidates	Winner	Percent		
Total			$64,972,549	$25,949,017	40	57	$4.10
Arkansas(c)...........	1984	D	1,944,113	874,592	45	63	2.19
Delaware(d)	1984	D	1,057,759	656,711	62	56	4.34
Indiana(c)	1984	R	4,199,264	2,701,965	64	52	1.92
Missouri(d)	1984	R	7,014,292	2,940,503	42	57	3.33
Montana(c)	1984	D	482,113(e)	370,744	77	70	1.31
New Hampshire(c)	1984	R	1,097,918	646,298	59	67	2.86
New Jersey(c)	1985	R	10,725,190	3,398,989	32	70	5.61
North Carolina(d)	1984	R	13,727,628(f)	2,935,176	21	54	6.19
North Dakota(g,h).....	1984	D	630,000(g)	300,000	48	55	2.00
Rhode Island(d).......	1984	R	3,475,483	1,401,091	40	60	8.51
Utah(d,i).............	1984	R	2,621,289	894,551	34	56	4.18
Vermont(d)	1984	D	1,609,917	580,586	36	50	6.99
Virginia(d)............	1985	D	7,417,270	3,569,913	48	55	5.54
Washington(h)	1984	D	5,388,163	2,925,898	54	53	2.85
West Virginia(d)	1984	R	3,582,150	1,752,000	49	53	4.83

Sources: State campaign finance filing offices; Diana Blair, University of Arkansas; Theodore Pedeliski, University of North Dakota; and John Patrick Hagan, University of West Virginia.
Key:
D—Democratic candidate won.
R—Republican candidate won.
(a) Includes primaries and general elections.
(b) Determined by dividing total campaign expenditures by total general election votes for the office.
(c) Incumbent ran and won.
(d) Open seat.

(e) Includes expenditures for lieutenant governors' campaigns; state has joint nomination and election of governor and lieutenant governor.
(f) Includes expenditures for Democratic runoff primary.
(g) Expenditure reports not required by law; estimates are by the candidates.
(h) Incumbent ran and lost in general election.
(i) August gubernatorial primaries for both the Democratic and Republican parties were held as a result of inconclusive state party conventions.

man Bangerter, Utah, and George Sinner North Dakota); two were local government leaders (Edward DiPrete, former mayor of Cranston, Rhode Island, and Booth Gardner, former county executive in Washington); and one was a former congressman (James Martin, North Carolina).

The importance of previous statewide electoral experience in winning the governorship, however, is down somewhat from the 1980-81 period when 80 percent had such experience, and the 1982-83 period when 85 percent had come from state offices. The positions from which to launch a winning gubernatorial race over the six-year period were lieutenant governor (nine of 10, for a 90 percent win rate), attorney general (eight of 13, for 62 percent), and former governor (seven of 11, for 64 percent).

Republicans began to show more parity in their ability to hold and win gubernatorial seats, as they won nine of the 15 races in 1984-85. They captured four governorships previously held by Democrats in North Carolina, Rhode Island, Utah, and West Virginia, while continuing their hold on five seats in Delaware, Indiana, Missouri, New Hampshire, and New Jersey. But Democrats captured three formerly Republican-held spots in North Dakota, Vermont, and Washington,

while continuing to hold onto seats in Arkansas, Montana, and Virginia. The net of this electoral activity is that Democrat governors still hold more than a two-to-one ratio (34-16) of the governorships as of January 1986.

Investigations

In 1985, two gubernatorial incumbents were the focus of investigations in their states. In February 1985, a grand jury indicted Governor Edwin Edwards (D-Louisiana) on 51 counts of fraud and racketeering, in which he was charged with influence peddling by steering state hospital permits to companies in which he was alleged to have had a secret interest. He argued the monies received were for legal fees earned while he was out of the governor's office between terms, and that the secrecy was necessary as then-Governor David Treen, a Republican, would have thrown out any application with Edward's name on it. The first trial ended with a hung jury; the second is underway at this writing.[2]

On July 1, 1985, an Alaskan grand jury issued a 69-page report on alleged favoritism by Governor Bill Sheffield (D-Alaska) in the signing of a $9.1 million, 10-year lease by the state, in which one of his major political supporters was the beneficiary. The allegation was that the governor personally changed the specifications necessary for the leasing of a building by the state so that only one building fit—that owned by his 1982 campaign fund raiser. The grand jury did not issue any indictments in its report, but recommended the state legislature call a special session to consider impeaching the governor for actions which the jury felt were "a hairbreadth above the criminal level."[3] After a highly publicized set of hearings, the Republican-dominated Senate refused to impeach the governor, and the process stopped.

Gubernatorial Impeachment

The Sheffield situation marked the first serious threat of impeachment since the late 1930s when Governor Richard Leche of Louisiana was threatened with impeachment and resigned. While counts vary, there appear to have been 15 gubernatorial impeachments and seven convictions across the 50 states.[4]

Threats of gubernatorial impeachment are more than events concerning the activities of individual governors. They are constitutional crises which pit one branch of state government against another—the legislative versus the executive. Moreover, these crises often broaden to the judicial branch which must reluctantly take sides with one of the other branches—usually the legislative—to settle legal and constitutional questions (even though the very involvement by the courts has itself raised legal questions under the separation of powers clause of most state constitutions).

Among the questions the courts have had to address are whether a state legislature can call itself into special session for the purpose of impeaching the governor (23 states can do so), and whether a legislature, once called into special session by the governor with a specific agenda to address, can go beyond the call to include the consideration of impeachment. Moreover, the courts have had to address the question of what exactly an "impeachable offense" is: Do the actions involved have to be criminal or can governors be impeached for non-criminal acts?

All state constitutions, except Oregon's, provide for the impeachment of elected officials. (For more information, see Table 2.8.) In Oregon, elected officials are tried in the same manner as criminal offenders. Impeachment proceedings are initiated in the lower houses of 47 states, the unicameral

legislature in Nebraska, and the upper house in Alaska. Ten states require a two-thirds vote to impeach, as is suggested in the Model State Constitution, developed by the National Municipal League,[5] 17 require a majority, and 22 have no provision for the vote to impeach.

Impeachment trials are held in the upper houses in 45 states, the lower house in Alaska, a court of impeachment in Nebraska, a special commission elected by the Senate in Missouri (for impeachment of a governor or Supreme Court member), and the Senate and judges of the Court of Appeals (court of last resort) in New York. Most state constitutions require an extraordinary majority vote to convict an official: 29 require a two-thirds vote of the members, and 15 require a two-thirds vote of those members present and voting. In Missouri, a five-sevenths vote of the court of special commission is necessary to convict, and in Nebraska, a two-thirds vote of the court of impeachment. Alabama, Massachusetts, and New Hampshire do not specify the number of votes necessary for conviction.

Although the provisions and procedures for impeachment are in place in the states, they are seldom used. Since the American Revolution, 2,096 governors have served in the states; only 15 (0.7 percent) were impeached, and seven (0.3 percent) were convicted. Impeachment is more of an unlikely threat than a reality.

Gubernatorial Powers

Gubernatorial succession

This question still remains a political issue in some states. In 1984, Arkansas voters adopted a constitutional initiative replacing the two-year, unlimited terms provision with four-year terms for the governor and other elected executive branch officials. Governor William Allain of Mississippi, in his 1985 message to the legislature, called for a study of the state constitution and gubernatorial succession.

In 1984, New Hampshire voters rejected a constitutional amendment that would have provided the governor with a four-year term limited to two consecutive terms, instead of the current two-year unlimited terms provision. The electorate did, however, adopt an amendment which provides for the filling of the governor's seat in the event of a vacancy or incapacity. In the same year, Connecticut voters adopted a constitutional amendment to establish procedures for declaring the governor unable to hold office. The 1985 North Carolina General Assembly has placed a constitutional amendment on the 1986 ballot that, beginning in 1992, would prevent the governor and lieutenant governor from seeking two consecutive terms—a right that was just obtained in a 1977 constitutional amendment.

In a unique transition squabble, the defeated governor of North Dakota refused to leave office until January 5, 1985—exactly four years from the day he took office. The newly-elected governor sought to take office on January 1, but was thwarted in his attempt. Although previous governors had taken office on the first day of the legislative session (which would have been January 8 in 1985), the state Supreme Court ruled with the new governor. The real issues in the transition, however, centered on which governor would appoint two Supreme Court justices, as well as the need for a hiring freeze, and bonuses for state employees.[6]

Finally, in 1984, Georgia voters adopted a constitutional amendment banning retirement benefits for governors based on involuntary separation from office; that action stemmed from a 1983 case in which the outgoing governor filed for retirement benefits arguing that he was involuntarily separated from office by the constitutional provision restricting a governor to two consecutive terms. He later removed his request because of the political reaction it received.

Gubernatorial veto

In North Carolina—the only state that does not provide the governor with veto power—the 1985 General Assembly again refused to honor the governor's request that a constitutional amendment granting veto power be added to the 1986 general election ballot.

Gubernatorial vetoes were also the subject matter of two court actions in 1984: the Kentucky Supreme Court ruled that the state budget must be passed by the legislature as a bill rather than as a joint resolution immune to the line item veto of the governor; and the New Jersey Supreme Court ruled in favor of the governor's use of veto power to reduce or eliminate items in the budget passed during the 1984 legislative session.

Gubernatorial appointments

In 1984, Wyoming voters rejected a constitutional amendment that would have allowed the governor to remove officers he or she appoints, unless otherwise provided by law.

Other activity in the appointments area concerned gubernatorial-legislative relations, which will be discussed later in this analysis.

Governors and Lieutenant Governors

In 1984-85, there were few indications of the problems that so often characterized the relationship between these two state officials in the past. Instead, during this period, there were more positive trends apparent in the lieutenant governorship in the states.

First, was the increasing political importance of the office, at least from an electoral standpoint; as noted earlier, nine of 10 lieutenant governors who sought the governorship won their races. Moreover, Massachusetts Lieutenant Governor John Kerry stepped directly from the office into a U.S. Senate seat in the 1984 elections. In some states, however, there were indications that the office still suffers from a lack of prominence and substance. In 1984, New York Lieutenant Governor Alfred Del Bello resigned from the office to pursue a career in private industry.

Nevertheless, several occupants of the lieutenant governor's office continued to become more active in policy questions facing their states. In 1984, the Iowa incumbent sponsored a major two-day conference—"Iowa and the Future"—in an attempt to take the lead in state planning. In 1985, his counterpart in Kentucky also formed and chaired a conference—"Kentucky Tomorrow: The Commission on Kentucky's Future." In 1985, legislation provided for a "main street program" in the New Mexico lieutenant governor's office—a program designed to assist in the revitalization of central business districts through the preservation of historic and unique architectural structures and economic development. And the governor of Minnesota sent his lieutenant on a series of trade missions to Sweden and Egypt.

The question of whether the office of lieutenant governor is executive or legislative in nature continued to receive attention during the biennium. In his 1985 address to the legislature, the governor of Oklahoma called for the team election of the governor and lieutenant governor. In November 1986, voters in South Dakota will have the opportunity to consider a constitutional amendment removing the lieutenant governor as the presiding officer of the senate, and requiring the governor to assign executive duties to the occupant.

However, these few efforts were offset by other actions during 1984-85. In 1984, Texas voters approved a constitutional amendment authorizing the state Senate to fill a vacancy in the office of lieutenant governor. Events in 1985 pointed to the inability of governors to fill the office when the lieutenant governor dies (as in Ohio) or resigns (as in New York) and the majority leader of the Senate (a member of the opposite party) becomes the next in line of succession to the governorship. The governor of Massachusetts faced a similar problem when his lieutenant governor moved on to the U.S. Senate, thereby placing the separately-elected secretary of state next in line of succession.

Governors and the State Legislatures

Despite an underlying need for the state's chief executive and the legislature to work in harmony, particularly when setting policy and budgetary priorities in the states, the relationship between these political actors continued to show evidence of stress during the biennium.

Politics and powersplits

Partisan politics are always afoot in the relationship between governors and state legislatures. The most obvious problem occurs when the governor is a member of one party and the opposing party controls one or both houses of the legislature. Political power is shared, with neither party completely controlling both branches (or in some states, even controlling both houses of the legislature).

Power sharing is becoming more of a fact of life in the states, with more than half facing this situation during the 1980s. As of January 1986, 28 states were divided, with 16 Democrat and 12 Republican governors facing legislatures partially or totally dominated by the opposition party. The result can be healthy—forcing compromise and workable legislation—or disastrous, with continual stalemate and partisan bickering.[7] The trend is indicative of the effect of split ticket voting in the states, as well as the continual decline in the strength of political parties.

Separation of powers

Conflicts over constitutionally-based separation of powers issues continued to mark relations between the governors and legislatures. As the governors have grown stronger, so too have the legislatures. However, these reforms and changes have done little to reduce the natural executive-legislative conflict built into state constitutions; in fact, they may have heightened the strain as the two branches have continued to vie for power—each one with more weapons at its disposal.

The principal of separation of powers is expressly contained in the constitutions of 38 states. Twenty-nine include some exceptions to a strict interpretation principal. Only 12 constitutions do not include any separation of powers provisions.[8] Hence, conflicts over the "turf" type of issue are often left to the state courts to decide.

Legislative veto

The legislative veto is a procedure legislatures have adopted to permit them to review proposed executive branch regulations or actions, and then block or modify those with which they disagree. After a series of national- and state-level court cases which consistently ruled against legislatures exercising this power based on the constitutional separation of powers concept, several state legislatures tried other means to achieve the same goal.[9]

In 1984, Iowa voters approved a constitutional amendment allowing the legislature to void state agency rules via a joint resolution; and legislation enacted in Virginia calls for executive and legislative review of regulations replacing the legislative veto. In response to the Kansas Supreme Court's voiding of the legislative veto, legislation was adopted in 1985 to allow the legislature to express concern over rules or regulations and to ask that rules be amended or revoked via the adoption of concurrent resolutions.

Taking another route entirely, the 1985 North Carolina General Assembly rewrote the Administrative Procedures Act to restrain the rule-making authority of state agencies, and set up an Office of Administrative Hearings with administrative law judges to settle disputes between state agencies and citizens. This office was to be activated upon the approval of the state's Supreme Court, but the Court refused to give an advisory opinion with no actual case or controversy involved, and did not want to take a step placing itself "directly in the stream of the legislative process."

This non-action by the Court raised a legal cloud over implementing the act, and placed into limbo the proposed eight-person Administrative Rules Review Commission to be appointed by the legislature. However, the chief justice did appoint a director, and hearings judges were hired. Now, the governor has challenged the constitutionality of the revised act, charging that the regulatory authority of the executive branch has been infringed upon by not authorizing gubernatorial appointment of the director.[10]

In the 1984 general election, Alaska voters defeated a constitutional amendment permitting a legislative veto, and in Michigan, the electorate defeated an amendment that would have allowed a joint legislative committee to review agency rules prior to adoption. In 1985, New Jersey voters refused to affirm legislative veto power for their legislature.

Appointments

A related area of conflict between the executive and legislative branches involves appointments to office, and particularly the role of the legislature in this process. Legislatures have the constitutional authority to confirm gubernatorial appointments, and in some states, have the constitutional or statutory authority to make appointments to executive branch boards and commissions—sometimes even appointing legislators to those positions. In 1983, four states strictly banned legislators from being appointed to boards and commissions, and 11 others allowed them to serve only if the body was advisory in nature. More importantly, however, 20 states permitted legislators to sit on boards and commissions exercising management responsibilities.[11]

Such actions are viewed as "legislative intrusion" into the executive branch, and have been successfully challenged in Kentucky, Mississippi, and North Carolina by both governors and citizen members of boards. A 1984

Mississippi court decision led to major statutory changes in appointment powers, and to a constitutional convention for additional changes. In Pennsylvania, however, the 1984 legislature added four of its members to the State Board of Education.

In 1985, in a more traditional type of dispute, Hawaii's governor and state Senate argued over what "advice and consent" by the legislature meant. The governor had nominated the acting attorney general to become attorney general, but the Senate Judiciary Committee, after holding four hearings, refused to report out the name. When the governor kept the nominee, Senate leaders argued the action was improper as the individual had been "rejected" by that body. The governor countered that the nominee had not been "rejected," since the nomination had not gone before the full chamber. Before the constitutional question of legislative "advice and consent" could be decided however, the nominee resigned.[12]

Since 1929, under the constitutional executive budget provision, New York governors have been exercising discretion in authorizing the filling of state positions. More recently, however, the legislature became disenchanted with the governor's failure to authorize the filling of vacancies (with 1983-appropriated funds) in four state agencies. The 1984 appropriations bill specifically provided funds for additional positions, and instructed the budget director to follow a plan that would insure staffing levels were achieved, and to periodically report to the legislature's fiscal committees.[13]

The budgetary process

Considerable executive-legislative stress still exists in the budget process and in determining the role each branch should play in the development and implementation of the budget. The conflicts have been over who controls the creation and implementation of the budget, and the desire of the legislatures to gain more control over federal grant monies coming into the state. The trend during 1984-85, albeit slight, has been in the governors' favor.

In a major shift increasing gubernatorial budgetary power in Mississippi, 1984 legislation moved the budget initiative authority from the Commission of Budget and Accounting to the governor's office, which is to submit the budget to the Legislative Budget Office. Once adopted, a new Fiscal Management Board, consisting of the governor and two of his appointees will oversee daily budget operations. The former Board of Budget and Control was a mixed executive-legislative body consisting of the governor, president of the Senate, chairman of the Senate Finance Committee, and the chairman of the House Ways and Means Committee.

During the biennium, two other states also made changes in their budgetary processes. In 1984, Virginia voters adopted a constitutional amendment requiring a balanced budget, and Alabama voters approved a "budget isolation" amendment, which ties the passage of other legislation to the appropriations bill. The amendment requires a three-fifths vote for any legislation passed prior to the approval of the major appropriations measures—education and the general fund.

Also in 1984, Arizona voters rejected a constitutional amendment that would have provided for legislative control over federal monies received by executive branch agencies.

Executive-legislative budget problems of another sort were reported in North Carolina where the governor lacks the "policing power" of a veto. Recently, there has been an increase in the state legislature's use of special provisions in the budget bill which go beyond the normal instructions to the executive branch on how monies are to be spent. The provisions have been used to amend, repeal, and change laws outside the budget act; to establish new programs or alter powers and duties of existing agency programs; to establish new executive branch boards, commissions, and councils, or alter the powers of existing boards; to change program eligibility requirements; and to change funding formulas and tax laws. In the 1981 regular session, there were 36 special provisions; in the 1985 session, 118—an increase of 328 percent in four years.[14]

Legislative sessions

New Hampshire voters rejected a 1984 constitutional amendment that would have eliminated the power of the governor and the Executive Council to extend a legislative recess without the legislature's consent.

Notes

1. Rhodes Cook, et al., "The 1986 Governors' Elections: Despite History, Opportunity Knocks for GOP," *Congressional Quarterly Weekly Report* 44:1 (January 4, 1986): 3.

2. Since the 1920s, six governors, including Edwards, have been indicted while in office: Warren T. McCray (Indiana, 1924) and Marvin Mandel (Maryland, 1977) were convicted; Arch Moore (West Virginia, 1975) and William Langer (North Dakota, 1934) were found not guilty, and later successfully sought reelection; and Edward L. Jackson (Indiana, 1928) never came to trial. See "Indictment of Governors in Office, Historical," *State Policy Reports* 3:6 (March 1985): 29.

3. Bruce Scandling, "Alaska Impeachment Hearing Delayed," *USA Today* (July 15, 1985): 3A.

4. Those governors convicted and removed were: William Holden (North Carolina, 1870); David Butler (Nebraska, 1871); Adelbert Ames (Mississippi, 1876); William Sulzer (New York, 1913); James Walton (Oklahoma, 1923); Henry Johnston (Oklahoma, 1929); and James Ferguson (Texas), who resigned a day before his conviction in 1917. Another governor's term ended before the impeachment trial took place (Henry Clay Warmoth, Louisiana, 1872), and two other incumbents resigned under the threat of impeachment (Ames of Mississippi and Leche of Louisiana).

Six other governors were impeached, but won acquittal in their trials: Charles Robinson (Kansas, 1862); Harrison Reed (Florida, 1868 and 1873); Powell Clayton (Arkansas, 1871); Johnston (Oklahoma, 1928) who was later impeached and removed from office; Huey Long (Louisiana, 1929); and Henry Horton (Tennessee, 1931).

For an analysis of gubernatorial impeachment, see Thad L. Beyle, "1985: It Was A Great Year for Governor Watchers," unpublished ms., Department of Political Science, University of North Carolina at Chapel Hill.

5. Thad L. Beyle, *State Government: CQ's Guide to Current Issues and Activities, 1985-86* (Washington, D.C.: Congressional Quarterly Press, Inc., 1985): 197.

6. Theodore Pedeliski, "North Dakota's Gubernatorial Transition 1984-85: Battling It Out in the Budgetary Badlands," unpublished ms., Department of Political Science, University of North Dakota.

7. Sharon Sherman, "Powersplit: When Legislatures and Governors Are of Opposing Parties," *State Legislatures* 10:5 (May/June 1984): 9-12.

8. Jody George and Lacy Maddox, "Separation of Powers Provisions in State Constitutions," in *Boards, Commissions, and Councils in the Executive Branch of North Carolina State Government* (Raleigh: North Carolina Center for Public Policy Research, 1984): 51.

9. The U.S. Congress lost the power in *Immigration and Naturalization Service v. Jadish Rai Chandha* (1983); state legislatures in Alaska, Connecticut, Kansas, Kentucky, Montana, New Hampshire, and West Virginia lost the power between 1982 and 1984.

10. "Executive and Legislative Power," *State Policy Reports* 4:2 (January 29, 1986): 28. See also, Rob Christensen, "Martin Plans to Challenge Law on Rules," *The* (Raleigh, N.C.) *News and Observer* (March 18, 1986): 1A; 9A.

11. "Legislators Serving on Boards and Commissions," *State Legislative Report* (Denver: National Conference of State Legislatures, 1983).

12. Anne F. Lee, "Hawaii Legislative Report: 1985 Session," *Comparative State Politics Newsletter* (October 1985): 15.

13. Joseph F. Zimmerman, "New York Legislature Mandates the Filling of Vacancies," *Comparative State Politics Newsletter* (June 1985): 7-8.

14. Ran Coble, "Special Provisions in Budget Bills: A Pandora's Box for North Carolina's Citizens," (Raleigh: North Carolina Center for Public Policy Research, 1986).

Table 2.1
THE GOVERNORS
1986

State or other jurisdiction	Name and party	Length of regular term in years	Date of first service	Present term ends	Number of previous terms	Maximum consecutive terms allowed by constitution	Joint election of governor and lieutenant governor (a)	Official who succeeds governor	Birthdate	Birthplace
Alabama	George C. Wallace (D)	4	1/63	1/87	3(b)	2	No	LG	8/25/19	Ala.
Alaska	Bill Sheffield (D)	4	12/82	12/86		2	Yes	LG	6/26/28	Wash.
Arizona	Bruce Babbitt (D)	4	3/78	1/87	1(c)		(d)	SS	6/27/38	Calif.
Arkansas	Bill Clinton (D)	2(e)	1/79	1/87	2(f)	(e)	No	LG	8/19/46	Ark.
California	George Deukmejian (R)	4	1/83	1/87			No	LG	6/6/28	N.Y.
Colorado	Richard D. Lamm (D)	4	1/75	1/87	2		Yes	LG	8/3/35	Wis.
Connecticut	William A. O'Neill (D)	4	12/80	1/87	(g)		Yes	LG	8/11/30	Conn.
Delaware	Michael N. Castle (R)	4	1/85	1/89		2(h)	No	LG	7/2/39	Del.
Florida	Bob Graham (D)	4	1/79	1/87	1	2	Yes	LG	11/9/36	Fla.
Georgia	Joe Frank Harris (D)	4	1/83	1/87		2	No	LG	2/26/36	Ga.
Hawaii	George R. Ariyoshi (D)	4	10/73	12/86	2(i)	2(j)	Yes	LG	3/12/26	Hawaii
Idaho	John V. Evans (D)	4	1/77	1/87	1(k)		No	LG	1/18/25	Idaho
Illinois	James R. Thompson (R)	4	1/77	1/87	2(l)		Yes	LG	5/8/36	Ill.
Indiana	Robert D. Orr (R)	4	1/81	1/89	1	2	Yes	LG	11/17/17	Ind.
Iowa	Terry Branstad (R)	4	1/83	1/87			No	LG	11/17/46	Iowa
Kansas	John Carlin (D)	4	1/79	1/87	1		Yes	LG	8/3/40	Kan.
Kentucky	Martha Layne Collins (D)	4	12/83	12/87		(m)	No	LG	12/7/36	Ky.
Louisiana	Edwin W. Edwards (D)	4	3/72	3/88	2(n)	2	Yes	LG	8/7/27	La.
Maine	Joseph E. Brennan (D)	4	1/79	1/87	1	2	(d)	PS	11/2/34	Maine
Maryland	Harry R. Hughes (D)	4	1/79	1/87	1	2	Yes	LG	11/13/26	Md.
Massachusetts	Michael S. Dukakis (D)	4	1/75	1/87	1(o)		Yes	LG	11/3/33	Mass.
Michigan	James J. Blanchard (D)	4	1/83	1/87			Yes	LG	8/8/42	Mich.
Minnesota	Rudy Perpich (DFL)	4	12/76	1/87	(p)		Yes	LG	6/27/28	Minn.
Mississippi	William A. Allain (D)	4	1/84	1/88		(m)	No	LG	2/14/28	Miss.
Missouri	John Ashcroft (R)	4	1/85	1/89		2(h)	No	LG	5/9/42	Mo.
Montana	Ted Schwinden (D)	4	1/81	1/89	1		Yes	LG	8/31/25	Mont.
Nebraska	Robert Kerrey (D)	4	1/83	1/87		2	Yes	LG	8/27/43	Neb.
Nevada	Richard H. Bryan (D)	4	1/83	1/87		2	No	LG	6/16/37	D.C.
New Hampshire	John H. Sununu (R)	2	1/83	1/87	1		(d)	PS	7/2/39	Cuba
New Jersey	Thomas H. Kean (R)	4	1/82	1/90		2	(d)	PS	4/21/35	N.Y.
New Mexico	Toney Anaya (D)	4	1/83	1/87		(m)	Yes	LG	4/29/41	N.M.
New York	Mario M. Cuomo (D)	4	1/83	1/87			Yes	LG	6/15/32	N.Y.
North Carolina	James G. Martin (R)	4	1/85	1/89		2(h)	No	LG	12/11/36	Ga.
North Dakota	George A. Sinner (D)	4	1/85	1/89			Yes	LG	5/29/28	N.D.
Ohio	Richard F. Celeste (D)	4	1/83	1/87		2	Yes	LG	11/11/37	Ohio

THE GOVERNORS—Continued

State or other jurisdiction	Name and party	Length of regular term in years	Date of first service	Present term ends	Number of previous terms	Maximum consecutive terms allowed by constitution	Joint election of governor and lieutenant governor (a)	Official who succeeds governor	Birthdate	Birthplace
Oklahoma	George Nigh (D)	4	1/63	1/87	1(q)	2	No	LG	6/9/27	Okla.
Oregon	Victor G. Atiyeh (R)	4	1/79	1/87	1	2	(d)	SS	2/20/23	Ore.
Pennsylvania	Richard L. Thornburgh (R)	4	1/79	1/87	1	2	Yes	LG	7/16/32	Pa.
Rhode Island	Edward D. DiPrete (R)	2	1/85	1/87			No	LG	7/8/34	R.I.
South Carolina	Richard W. Riley (D)	4	1/79	1/87	1	2	No	LG	1/2/33	S.C.
South Dakota	William J. Janklow (R)	4	1/79	1/87	1	2	Yes	LG	9/13/39	Ill.
Tennessee	Lamar Alexander (R)	4	1/79	1/87	1	2	No	SpS(r)	7/3/40	Tenn.
Texas	Mark White (D)	4	1/83	1/87			No	LG	3/17/40	Texas
Utah	Norman H. Bangerter (R)	4	1/85	1/89			Yes	LG	1/4/33	Utah
Vermont	Madeleine Kunin (D)	2	1/85	1/87			No	LG	9/28/33	Switz.
Virginia	Gerald L. Baliles (D)	4	1/86	1/90		(m)	No	LG	7/8/40	Va.
Washington	Booth Gardner (D)	4	1/85	1/89			No	LG	8/21/36	Wash.
West Virginia	Arch A. Moore, Jr. (R)	4	1/69	1/89	2(s)	2	(d)	PS	4/16/23	W.V.
Wisconsin	Anthony S. Earl (D)	4	1/83	1/87			Yes	LG	4/12/36	Mich.
Wyoming	Ed Herschler (D)	4	1/75	1/87	2		(d)	SS	10/27/18	Wyo.
American Samoa	A.P. Lutali (t)	4	1/85	1/89	1(v)	2(u)	Yes	LG	12/24/19	A.S.
Guam	Ricardo J. Bordallo (D)	4	1/75	1/87		2	Yes	LG	12/11/27	Guam
No. Mariana Is.	Pedro P. Tenorio (R)	4	1/82	1/90		3(w)	Yes	LG	4/18/34	Saipan
Puerto Rico	Rafael Hernandez-Colon (PDP)	4	1/73	1/89	1(x)		(d)	SS	10/24/36	P.R.
Virgin Islands	Juan F. Luis (I)	4	1/78	1/87	1(y)	2	Yes	LG	7/10/40	P.R.

Key:
D—Democrat
DFL—Democrat-Farmer-Labor
I—Independent
PDP—Popular Democratic Party
R—Republican
LG—Lieutenant governor
SS—Secretary of state
PS—President of the senate
SpS—Speaker of the senate

(a) The following also choose candidates for governor and lieutenant governor through a joint nomination process: Florida, Kansas, Maryland, Minnesota, Montana, North Dakota, Ohio, Utah, American Samoa, and Guam.
(b) Served 1963-67, 1971-75, and 1975-79.
(c) Succeeded to governor's office March 1978. Elected to first full term November 1978.
(d) No lieutenant governor.
(e) In 1984, a constitutional amendment passed which changes to four years the length of the governor's term, with a maximum of two terms (effective with the 1986 election).
(f) Served 1979-81, and 1983-85.
(g) Succeeded to governor's office December 1980. Elected to first full term November 1982.
(h) Absolute two-term limit, but not necessarily consecutive.

(i) Became acting governor in 1973. Elected to first full term November 1974.
(j) Restriction became effective with November 1978 election. Incumbent allowed to serve out three consecutive terms.
(k) Succeeded to governor's office January 1977. Elected to first full term November 1978.
(l) First term was for two years, four years thereafter.
(m) Successive terms forbidden.
(n) Served 1972-76, and 1976-80.
(o) Served 1975-79.
(p) Succeeded to governor's office December 1976 to serve remainder of unexpired term. Elected to first full term November 1982.
(r) Filled two unexpired terms of former governors. Elected to first full term November 1978. Official bears the additional statutory title of "lieutenant governor."
(s) Served 1969-73, and 1973-77.
(u) American Samoa has no political party system.
(v) Limit is statutory.
(w) Served 1975-79.
(x) Absolute three-term limitation, but not necessarily consecutive.
(y) Served 1973-77.
(y) Succeeded to governor's office January 1978. Elected to first full term in November 1978.

Table 2.2
THE GOVERNORS: QUALIFICATIONS FOR OFFICE

State or other jurisdiction	Minimum age	State citizen (years)	U.S. citizen (years)	State resident (years)	Qualified voter (years)
Alabama	30	7	10	7	...
Alaska	30	...	7	7	★
Arizona	25	5	10	...	...
Arkansas	30	...	★	7	★
California	18	...	5	5	★
Colorado	30	...	★	2	...
Connecticut	30	...	...	...	★
Delaware	30	...	12	6	...
Florida	30	...	...	7	★
Georgia	30	6	15	6	...
Hawaii	30	...	★	5	★
Idaho	30	...	★	2	...
Illinois	25	...	★	3	...
Indiana	30	...	5	5	...
Iowa	30	...	★	2	...
Kansas	...	...	...	...	...
Kentucky	30	6	★	6	...
Louisiana	25	5	5	...	★
Maine	30	...	15	5	...
Maryland	30	...	(a)	5	5
Massachusetts	...	...	...	7	...
Michigan(b)	30	...	...	...	4
Minnesota	25	...	★	1	...
Mississippi	30	...	20	5	...
Missouri	30	...	15	10	...
Montana(c)	25	★	★	2	...
Nebraska	30	5	5	5	...
Nevada	25	2	...	2	★
New Hampshire	30	...	...	7	...
New Jersey	30	...	20	7	...
New Mexico	30	...	★	5	★
New York	30	...	★	5	...
North Carolina	30	...	5	2	...
North Dakota	30	...	★	5	★
Ohio(d)	...	...	...	...	★
Oklahoma	31	...	★	...	10
Oregon	30	...	★	3	...
Pennsylvania	30	...	★	7	...
Rhode Island(e)	...	...	...	...	★
South Carolina	30	5	★	5	...
South Dakota	...	...	2	2	...
Tennessee	30	7	★	...	...
Texas	30	...	★	5	...
Utah	30	5	...	5	★
Vermont	...	...	...	4	...
Virginia	30	...	★	5	5
Washington	18	...	★	...	★
West Virginia	30	5	★	★	★
Wisconsin	...	...	★	...	★
Wyoming	30	...	★	5	★
American Samoa	35	...	★(f)	5	...
Guam	30	...	5	5	★
No. Mariana Is.	30	...	...	7	...
Puerto Rico	35	5	5	5	...
Virgin Islands	30	5	5	5	★

Note: This table includes constitutional and statutory qualifications.
Key:
★—Formal provision; number of years not specified.
. . .—No formal provision.
(a) *Crosse v. Board of Supervisors of Elections* 243 Md. 555, 221A.2d431 (1966)—opinion rendered indicated that U.S. citizenship was, by necessity, a requirement for office.
(b) A person convicted of felony or breach of public trust is not eligible to the office for a period of 20 years after conviction.
(c) A person convicted of a felony is not eligible to hold office until his final discharge from state supervision.
(d) A person convicted of embezzlement of public funds is not eligible to hold office.
(e) A person convicted of bribery is not eligible to hold office.
(f) U.S. citizen or U.S. national.

34

Table 2.3
THE GOVERNORS: COMPENSATION

State or other jurisdiction	Salary	Governor's office staff(a)	Access to state transportation			Travel allowance	Official residence
			Automobile	Airplane	Helicopter		
Alabama	$63,839	30	★	★	...	(b)	★
Alaska	85,728	73	★	...	...	(c)	★
Arizona	62,500	23	★	★	...	(c)	...
Arkansas	35,000	48	★	...	...	(d)	★
California	49,100	82 (e)	★	...	...	(d)	(f)
Colorado	60,000	42	★	★	...	(b)	★
Connecticut	65,000	30	★	...	(g)	(b)	★
Delaware	70,000	22	★	...	★	$ 18,500(d)	★
Florida	78,757	55 (h)	★	★	...	(c)	★
Georgia	79,356	49	★	★	★	(b)	★
Hawaii	59,400	33	★	...	...	45,000(d)	★
Idaho	50,000	15 (i)	★	★	...	(b)	★
Illinois	58,000	144	★	★	★	173,400(d)	★
Indiana	65,988	32	★	★	★	0	★
Iowa	64,000	19	★	★	...	(b)	★
Kansas	65,000	33	★	★	...	(b)	★
Kentucky	61,200	67	★	★	★	(c)	★
Louisiana	73,400	56	★	★	★	27,000(d)	★
Maine	35,000	11	★	★	...	(b)	★
Maryland	75,000	109 (j)	★	★	★	(b)	★
Massachusetts	75,000	100	★	★	★	(b)	...
Michigan	85,800	45	★	★	★	(d)	★
Minnesota	84,560	26	★	★	★	(b)	★
Mississippi	63,000	27	★	★	★	24,017(d)	★
Missouri	81,000	33	★	★	...	(d)	★
Montana	50,452	25. 68	★	★	★	(c)	★
Nebraska	40,000	15	★	★	★	(c)	★
Nevada	65,000	17	★	...	...	(d)	★
New Hampshire	62,880	25	★	...	...	(b)	★(k)
New Jersey	85,000	60	★	...	★	(l)	★(k)
New Mexico	60,000	46	★	★	★	(d)	★
New York	100,000	216	★	★	★	(c)	★
North Carolina	98,196	84	★	★	★	11,500	★
North Dakota	60,862	15. 25	★	★	...	(b)	★(k)
Ohio	65,000	30	★	★	★	(b)	★
Oklahoma	70,128	40	★	★	...	(b)	★
Oregon	72,000	27	★	...	...	0	(f)
Pennsylvania	75,000	54	★	★	...	(c)	★
Rhode Island	49,500	47	★	★	★	8,500(d)	★(k)
South Carolina	60,000	25	★	★	...	17,000	★
South Dakota	55,120	30.9	★	★	...	(b)	★
Tennessee	68,200	35	★	★	★	(b)	★
Texas	94,350	215	...	★	★	(c)	★
Utah	60,009	15. 5	★	★	...	(d)	★
Vermont	60,000	12	★	...	...	(b)	...
Virginia	75,000	27	★	★	★	(c)	★
Washington	63,000	37	★	★	...	N.A.	★
West Virginia	72,000	39	★	★	★	(l)	★
Wisconsin	75,337	33. 5	★	★	...	(m)	★
Wyoming	70,000	7	★	★	...	(d)	★
American Samoa	50,000	N.A.	★	...	...	N.A.	★
Guam	50,000	N.A.	★	...	...	N.A.	★
Puerto Rico	35,000	N.A.	★	...	★	N.A.	★
Virgin Islands	52,400	N.A.	★	...	...	N.A.	★

THE GOVERNORS: COMPENSATION—Continued

(a) Definitions of "governor's office staff" vary across the states—from general office support to staffing for various operations within the executive office.

(b) Travel allowance included in office budget.

(c) Reimbursed for travel expenses. Alaska—governor is reimbursed per diem. Arizona—reimbursed for actual expenses to a maximum of $40/d in state and $75/d out of state. Florida—reimbursed at same rate as other state officials: in state, choice between per diem or actual expenses; out of state, actual expenses. Kentucky—mileage at same rate as other state employees. Montana—reimbursed for actual and necessary expenses in state up to $55/d, and actual lodging plus meal allowance up to $30/d out of state (no annual limit). Nebraska—reasonable and necessary expenses. New York—reimbursed for actual and necessary expenses. Pennsylvania—reimbursed for reasonable expenses. Texas—although governor is reimbursed, all travel expenses for governor and state staff are paid from political officeholders account.

(d) Amount includes travel allowance for entire staff. Arkansas, Mich-

igan, Missouri, Wyoming—amount not available. California—$130,000 in state; $27,000 out of state. Nevada—$24,593 in state, $8,750 out of state. New Mexico—$10,000 in state, $22,000 out of state. Utah—$9,600 in state, $26,000 out of state.

(e) Statutorily authorized to have 82.

(f) In California—provided by Governor's Residence Foundation, a non-profit organization which provides a residence for the governor of California. No rent is charged; maintenance and operational costs are provided by California Department of General Services. In Oregon—state-owned house is provided rent-free for the governor.

(g) Emergency authorization for use of National Guard's.

(h) Does not include Office of Planning and Budgeting and a number of state commissions located within executive office of governor for budget purposes.

(i) Number on staff varies from 12 to 20 during the year.

(j) Includes positions added when Criminal Justice Coordinating Council moved into governor's office.

(k) Governor does not occupy residence.

(l) Included in general expense account.

(m) Averages $32,000/y.

Table 2.4
THE GOVERNORS: POWERS

State or other jurisdiction	Budget-making power — Full responsibility	Budget-making power — Shares responsibility	Veto power(a) — No item veto	Veto power(a) — Item veto-2/3 legislators present to override	Veto power(a) — Item veto-majority legislators elected to override	Veto power(a) — Item veto-3/5 legislators elected to override	Veto power(a) — Item veto-at least 2/3 legislators elected to override	Authorization for reorganization through executive order(b)	Other statewide elected officials(c) — Number of officials	Other statewide elected officials(c) — Number of agencies
Alabama	★				★				17	8
Alaska	★						★	C	1	0(d)
Arizona	★						★		8	6
Arkansas	★				★				6	6
California	★						★	S	10	7
Colorado	★						★		18	6
Connecticut	★						★	C	5	5
Delaware	★					★		C	5	5
Florida	★						★	C	7	7
Georgia	★						★	S	12	8
Hawaii	★						★	(e)	14	2
Idaho	★		★						6	6
Illinois	★						★	C	14	6(f)
Indiana	★						★		6	6
Iowa	★					★			6	6
Kansas	★				★			C	15	6
Kentucky		★					★	S	10	8
Louisiana		★	★					S	21	10
Maine	★		★						0	0
Maryland	★					★		C	3	3
Massachusetts	★			★				C	13	6
Michigan	★						★	C	35	7
Minnesota		★					★	S	5	5
Mississippi	★			★				S	13	9
Missouri	★						★	C	5	5
Montana	★						★		10	6
Nebraska	★					★		S	26	8
Nevada	★		★						23	7
New Hampshire	★		★						0	1
New Jersey	★		(g)						0	0
New Mexico	★			★				S	19	8
New York	★	★					★		3	3
North Carolina		★						C	9	9
North Dakota	★						★		13	11
Ohio	★					★			28	6

37

THE GOVERNORS: POWERS—Continued

State or other jurisdiction	Budget-making power		Veto power(a)					Authorization for reorganization through executive order(b)	Other statewide elected officials(c)	
	Full responsibility	Shares responsibility	No item veto	Item veto 2/3 legislators present to override	Item veto majority legislators elected to override	Item veto 3/5 legislators elected to override	Item veto at least 2/3 legislators elected to override		Number of officials	Number of agencies
Oklahoma	★			★			★	S	9	7
Oregon	★						★		5	5
Pennsylvania	★						★		4	4
Rhode Island		★	★						4	4
South Carolina		★		★					8	8
South Dakota	★						★	C	9	7
Tennessee	★	★			★				3	1
Texas	★	★							33	8
Utah	★						★		14	4
Vermont	★		★					S	5	5
Virginia	★			★				S	2	2
Washington	★			★				S	8	8
West Virginia	★			★	★(h)				5	5
Wisconsin	★			★					5	5
Wyoming	★						★		4	4
American Samoa		★					★	S	1	1
Guam	★						★		36	3
No. Mariana Is.	★						★	C	1	1
Puerto Rico	★						★		0	0
Virgin Islands	★						★		1	1

Sources: The National Governors' Association 1985 survey of governors' offices; The Council of State Governments; and state constitutions and statutes.

Key:
C—Constitutional
S—Statutory

(a) In all states, except North Carolina, governor has the power to veto bills passed by the state legislature. The information presented here refers to the governor's power to item veto—veto items within a bill—and the votes needed in the state legislature to override the item veto. For additional information on vetoes and veto overrides, as well as the number of days the governor is allowed to consider bills, see Table 3.14, "Enacting Legislation: Veto, Veto Overrides and Effective Date."
(b) For additional information on executive orders, see Table 2.5, "Gubernatorial Executive Orders: Authorization, Provisions, Procedures."
(c) Includes only executive branch officials who are popularly elected either on a constitutional or statutory basis (elected members of state boards of education, public utilities commissions, university regents, or other state boards or commissions are also included); the number of agencies involving these officials is also listed.
(d) Lieutenant governor's office is part of governor's office.
(e) Implied through a broad interpretation of gubernatorial authority; no formal provision.
(f) Governor has administrative control over agencies.
(g) Governor has no veto power.
(h) For budget and supplemental appropriations bills, 2/3 legislators elected necessary to override.

Table 2.5
GUBERNATORIAL EXECUTIVE ORDERS: AUTHORIZATION, PROVISIONS, PROCEDURES

State or other jurisdiction	Authorization for executive orders	Provisions: Civil defense disasters, public emergencies	Energy emergencies and conservation	Other emergencies	Executive branch reorganization plans and agency creation	Create advisory, coordinating, study or investigative committees/commissions	Respond to federal programs and requirements	State personnel administration	Other administration	Procedures: Filing and publication procedures	Subject to administrative procedure act	Subject to legislative review
Alabama	S,I(a)	·	·	★(b)	·	·	·	·	·	★(c,d)	·	★
Alaska	C	★(a)	★(a)	★(a)	★	·	★	·	·	★(c)	·	·
Arizona	S,I	★(a)	★(a)	★(a)	★	★	★	★	★	★(c)	·	·
Arkansas	S,I(e)	★	★	★	★	★	★	★	·	·	·	·
California	S	★	★	★(f)	★	·	★	·	·	★	·	·
Colorado	S	★	★	·	·	·	★	★	·	★	·	·
Connecticut	S	★	★	·	★	★	★	★	·	·	·	·
Delaware	C	★	★	★(i)	·	★	★	★	(g,h)	★·	★	·
Florida	C,S	★	★	★(i)	★	★	★	★	(g,h)	·	·	·
Georgia	S,I(e)	★	·	·	★	★	★	·	·	·	·	·
Hawaii	I(a)	·	·	·	·	·	·	·	★(h,j)	★(c)	·	·
Idaho	S	★	·	·	·	·	★	·	·	★(c)	·	★
Illinois	C	★	·	·	★	·	★	·	·	·	★	·
Indiana	I	·	·	·	·	·	★	·	·	·	·	·
Iowa	S	★	★	·	★	·	★	·	·	·	·	·
Kansas	S	★	·	★(m)	★	·	★	★	★(k), (k,n,o,p)	★(c,d,l)	·	★(r,s)
Kentucky	S	★	·	·	★	·	·	·	★(j,r,s)	★(c)	★	★(w)
Louisiana	S(q)	★	·	·	★	·	·	·	·	★(l)	·	·
Maine	S	★	·	★(t,u)	★	★	★	·	★(v)	★(d)	★	·
Maryland	C,S	★	★	·	·	★	★	★	·	·	·	·
Massachusetts	C,I	★	★	★(f,t)	★	★	★	★	★(l)	★(l)	★	·
Michigan	C,S	★	·	·	★	★	★	★	★(p)	★(c)	★	★(x)
Minnesota	S	★	·	·	★	★	★	★	★(y)	★(c,l)	★	★(w)
Mississippi	S	★	·	·	★	★	★	★	★(aa,bb)	·	·	★(w,cc)
Missouri	S	★	·	·	★	·	★	★	(w,cc)	★(w,cc)	·	★(w,cc)
Montana	S	★	·	·	★	·	★	·	★(p)	★(c,dd)	·	·
Nebraska	S	★	·	·	·	·	★	·	·	·	·	·
Nevada	I	·	★(a)	·	·	·	·	·	·	·	·	·
New Hampshire	S	·	★	★(a)	★	·	★	·	(p)	(p)	★	·
New Jersey	S	★	★	★(ee)	★	·	★	·	(bb)	·	·	·

Key:
C—Constitutional
S—Statutory
I—Implied

★—Formal provision
·—No formal provision

(a) Broad interpretation of gubernatorial authority.
(b) To activate or veto environmental improvement authorities.
(c) Executive orders must be filed with secretary of state or other designated officer.
(d) Governor required to keep record in office.
(e) Some or all provisions implied from constitution.
(f) To regulate distribution of necessities during shortages.

Sources: Massachusetts, Legislative Research Council, "Report Relative to Gubernatorial Executive Orders," House Document No. 6557, April 3, 1981, pp. 89-94; E. Lee Burnick, Department of Political Science, University of North Carolina at Greensboro; The Governors Center at Duke University (Survey, March 1984); The National Governors' Association 1985 survey; The Council of State Governments.

GUBERNATORIAL EXECUTIVE ORDERS—Continued

State or other jurisdiction	Authorization for executive orders	Provisions								Procedures		
		Civil defense, public disasters, emergencies	Energy emergencies and conservation	Other emergencies	Executive branch reorganization plans and agency creation	Create advisory, coordinating, study or investigative committees/commissions	Respond to federal programs and requirements	State personnel administration	Other administration	Filing and publication procedures	Subject to administrative procedure act	Subject to legislative review
New Mexico	S	★	★		★							
New York	I								★(s,r)	★(ff)	★	★(w)
North Carolina	S,I					★			★(bb)			
North Dakota	C											★(w)
Ohio	S					★						
Oklahoma	S	★	★	★(t)	★			★	★(gg)	★(c)		★(w)
Oregon	S	★	★	★(i,m,t,v)	★				★(hh)	★(c,l)		★
Pennsylvania	S(a)	★							★(k)			
Rhode Island	I(e)	★(bb)		★(h,i)								
South Carolina					★			★		★(c,d,ii)		★
South Dakota	C	★							★(r)	★(c)		★
Tennessee	S	★			★			★		★	★	★★
Texas	S	★						★★				★
Utah	S											
Vermont	S											
Virginia	I	★		★(q)	★			★	★(h,jj,kk)	★(l)		
Washington	S	★		★	★			★	★(ll)	★(c,l)	★	
West Virginia	S,I(e)	★							★(bb,jj,o)	★(c)		
Wisconsin	S											
Wyoming	I											
American Samoa	C,S	★	★	★	★			★	★	★(mm)	★(mm)	
No. Mariana Is.	C											

(g) To reassign state attorneys and public defenders.
(h) To suspend certain officials and/or other civil actions.
(i) To declare water, crop and refugee emergencies.
(j) To designate game and wildlife areas or other public areas.
(k) To transfer allocated funds.
(l) Included in state register or code.
(m) To give immediate effect to state regulations in emergencies.
(n) To control administration of state contracts and procedures.
(o) To impound or freeze certain state matching funds.
(p) To reduce state expenditures in revenue shortfall.
(q) Broad grant of authority.
(r) Appointive powers.
(s) To suspend rules and regulations of the bureaucracy.
(t) For fire emergencies.
(u) For financial institution emergencies.
(v) To control procedures for dealing with public.

(w) Reorganization plans only.
(x) Legislative appropriations committees must approve orders issued to handle a revenue shortfall.
(y) To assign duties to lieutenant governor, issue writ of special election.
(aa) To control prison and pardon administration.
(bb) To administer and govern the armed forces of the state.
(cc) For meeting federal program requirements.
(dd) Filed with legislature.
(ee) To declare air pollution emergencies.
(ff) Included as appendix to sessions law volume.
(gg) Relating to local governments.
(hh) To transfer funds in an emergency.
(ii) Must be published in register if they have general applicability and legal effect.
(jj) To transfer functions between agencies.
(kk) To control state-owned motor vehicles.
(ll) Regarding annual reports of state agencies.
(mm) If executive order fits definition of rule.

Table 2.6
STATE CABINET SYSTEMS

State	Authorization for cabinet system				Criteria for membership			Number of members in cabinet (including governor)	Frequency of cabinet meetings	Open cabinet meetings
	Statute	Constitution	Governor	Tradition	Appointed to specified office	Elected to specified office	Gubernatorial appointment regardless of office			
Alabama	...	...	...	★	...	...	★	24	Gov.'s discretion	★
Alaska	...	...	★	...	★	...	...	17	Regularly	★(a)
Arizona	...	...	★	...	★	...	...	15	Weekly	...
Arkansas	★	...	...	★	...	...	...	17	Regularly	...
California	...	...	★	...	★	...	★	11	Every two weeks	...
Colorado	...	★	...	...	★	...	...	20	Gov.'s discretion	★
Connecticut	★	...	...	...	★	...	...	24	Gov.'s discretion	...
Delaware	★	...	...	...	...	...	★(b)	16	Gov.'s discretion	★
Florida	...	★	...	...	...	★	...	7	Every two weeks	★
Georgia	------------------------------------(c)------------------------------------									
Hawaii	★	...	...	...	★	...	...	18	Gov.'s discretion	...
Idaho	------------------------------------(c)------------------------------------									
Illinois	...	...	...	★	★(b)	...	...	36	Gov.'s discretion(d)	★
Indiana	------------------------------------(c)------------------------------------									
Iowa	★	...	...	...	...	★	...	5	Weekly	★
Kansas	...	...	★	...	...	...	★	13	Monthly(e)	...
Kentucky	...	...	★	...	★	...	...	18	Weekly	...
Louisiana	★	★	...	...	★	★	...	21	Bi-annually	...
Maine	...	...	...	★	...	...	★(b)	20	Gov.'s discretion	(f)
Maryland	★	...	...	...	★(b)	...	...	23	Gov.'s discretion	...
Massachusetts	★	...	...	...	★	...	...	12	Twice monthly	...
Michigan	...	...	★	...	★	...	...	25	Gov.'s discretion	(g)
Minnesota	...	...	★	...	★	...	...	24(h)	Every two weeks	★
Mississippi	------------------------------------(c)------------------------------------									
Missouri	...	★	...	★	★	...	...	16	Gov.'s discretion	...
Montana	...	...	★	...	★	...	...	15	6 times a year	★
Nebraska	...	...	★	...	★	...	...	27	Weekly	...
Nevada	------------------------------------(c)------------------------------------									
New Hampshire	------------------------------------(c)------------------------------------									
New Jersey	★	★	...	...	★	...	...	21	Once or twice monthly	...
New Mexico	★	...	...	...	★	...	...	12	Monthly	★
New York	...	...	...	★	★	...	...	22	Gov.'s discretion	...
North Carolina(i)	...	...	★	...	...	...	★	10	Monthly	...
North Dakota	------------------------------------(c)------------------------------------									
Ohio	★	...	...	...	★	...	★	27	Gov.'s discretion	(f)
Oklahoma	...	...	★	...	...	...	★	8(j)	Gov.'s discretion	...
Oregon	...	...	★	...	★	...	...	11	Weekly	...
Pennsylvania	★	...	...	...	★	...	...	20	Gov.'s discretion	★
Rhode Island	------------------------------------(c)------------------------------------									
South Carolina	------------------------------------(c)------------------------------------									
South Dakota	...	...	★	...	★	...	★	18	Gov.'s discretion	...
Tennessee	...	...	...	★	★	...	...	25	Gov.'s discretion(e)	(k)
Texas	------------------------------------(c)------------------------------------									
Utah	...	...	★	(l)	★	...	...	26	Monthly	...
Vermont	...	...	★	...	...	...	★	6	Monthly	...
Virginia	★	...	...	...	...	...	★	9	Gov.'s discretion(e)	...
Washington	...	...	★	...	★	...	...	26	Monthly	...
West Virginia	------------------------------------(c)------------------------------------									
Wisconsin	------------------------------------(c)------------------------------------									
Wyoming	------------------------------------(c)------------------------------------									

Key:
★—Yes
...—No
(a) Except when in executive session.
(b) With the consent of the Senate.
(c) No formal cabinet system. In Idaho, however, sub-cabinets have been formed, by executive order; the chairmen report to the governor when requested.
(d) Sub-cabinets meet monthly.
(e) More often during legislative sessions. Kansas—bi-weekly. Tennessee—weekly.
(f) In practice, the media and others do not attend, but cabinet meetings have not been formally designated closed.
(g) Open cabinet meetings in the past; however, not all are open.
(h) Five sub-cabinets have been formed.
(i) Constitution provides for a Council of State made up of elective state administrative officials, which makes policy decisions for the state while the cabinet acts more in an advisory capacity.
(j) Each cabinet member is chair of a sub-cabinet (each state agency). These sub-cabinets meet quarterly.
(k) In Tennessee, closed with some exceptions.
(l) State Planning Advisory Committee, composed of all department heads serves as an informal cabinet. Committee meets at discretion of state planning coordinator.

Table 2.7

THE GOVERNORS: PROVISIONS AND PROCEDURES FOR TRANSITION

State or other jurisdiction	Legislation pertaining to gubernatorial transition	Appropriations available to gov-elect	Provision for: Gov-elect's participation in state budget for coming fiscal year	Gov-elect to hire staff to assist during transition	State personnel to be made available to assist gov-elect	Office space in buildings to be made available to gov-elect	Acquainting gov-elect staff with office procedures and routine office functions	Transfer of information (files, records etc.)
Alabama	...	...	•	(a)	•	•	•	...
Alaska	...	...				•	•	...
Arizona	...		•	...	•	•	•	•
Arkansas	★	60,000(b)	★	★	•	•	...	...
California	★	288,000(c)	★	★	★	★	...	•
Colorado	★	10,000(d)	★	★	★	★	★	★
Connecticut	★	25,000	•	★	•	★	...	★
Delaware	★	49,000(e)	...	...	•	★	•	★
Florida	•	75,000	...	•	•	•	•	•
Georgia	★	★	•	★	★	★	•	★
Hawaii	★	50,000	★	★	★	★	★	★
Idaho	★	30,000	★	★	★	★	...	•
Illinois	★	...	★	★(f)	★	★	★	★
Indiana	★	40,000	★	★	★	★	★	★
Iowa	★(g)	10,000	★	★	•(h)	•	•	★(i)
Kansas	★	100,000	★	★	★	★	★	★
Kentucky	★	Unspecified	★	★	★	★	★	★
Louisiana	★	10,000	★	★	...	★	•	★
Maine	★	5,000	★	★	★(j)	...	★	•
Maryland	★	50,000	★	★	★	★	★	★
Massachusetts	...	★	•	•	★	★	•	•
Michigan	★	1,000,000(c)	•	★	★	•	★	★
Minnesota	★	29,600	★	★	★	★	•	•
Mississippi	★	25,000	★	★	★	★	★	★
Missouri	★	100,000	★	★	•	•	•	•
Montana	★	(k)	★	★	•	•	★	★
Nebraska	...	30,000(l)	•	★	•	•	•	•
Nevada	...	5,000(m)	★	...	•	★	•	•
New Hampshire	★	5,000	★	★	•	★	★	•
New Jersey	★	150,000	★	★	★	★	•	★
New Mexico	★	(k)	★	★	•	★	•	•
New York	...	...	•	•	•	•	•	•
North Carolina	★	51,000(e)	•(n)	★	★	★	•	•
North Dakota	...	★	...	•	•	...	•	★
Ohio	★	(k)	...	★	★	★	...	
Oklahoma	★	10,000	★	★	...	•	•	
Oregon	★	20,000	★	★	★	★	★	★
Pennsylvania	★	100,000	...	★	•	★	★	•
Rhode Island	...	...	★	...	•	•	...	
South Carolina	★	50,000	★	★	...	★	•	★
South Dakota	★	10,000(o)	...	•	•	★	•	★
Tennessee	★	(p)	•	★	★	★	•	★
Texas	...	...	★	★	•	•	...	•
Utah	...	...	...	...	...	...	...	...
Vermont	...	18,000	★(q)	★	★	★	★	(r)
Virginia	...	52,000	...	★	★	★	★	★
Washington	★	80,000	•	•	•	•	•	•
West Virginia	...	...	...	...	•	•	•	•
Wisconsin	★	Unspecified	★	★	★	★	★	★
Wyoming	...	(k)	★	★	•	•	•	•
American Samoa	...	Unspecified	★(s)	•	•	•	...	•
Guam	...	...	...	...	...	...	...	...
No. Mariana Is.	...	...	...	...	...	...	...	...
Puerto Rico	...	250,000(e)	...	•	•	•	...	•
Virgin Islands	...	...	...	...	...	...	...	...

Sources: The National Governors' Association 1985 survey, and The Council of State Governments.

Key:
. . .—No provisions or procedures
★—Formal provisions or procedures
•—No formal provisions, occurs informally
(a) Governor usually hires several incoming key staff during transition.
(b) Made available in 1983.
(c) Made available in 1982.
(d) Minimum.
(e) Inaugural expenses are paid from this amount.
(f) On a contractual basis.
(g) Pertains only to funds.
(h) Provided on irregular basis.

(i) Arrangement for transfer of criminal files.
(j) Budget personnel.
(k) Legislature required to make appropriation; no dollar amount stated in legislation. In Montana, $30,000 was made available in 1979. In New Mexico, $40,000 was made available in 1981.
(l) Determined prior to each election by legislature.
(m) Is not adequate and is augmented by legislature.
(n) New governor can submit supplemental budget.
(o) Made available for 1987.
(p) Money made available from emergency and contingency funds.
(q) Responsible for the preparation of the budget; staff made available.
(r) Not transferred but use may be authorized.
(s) Can submit reprogramming or supplemental appropriation measure for current fiscal year.

Table 2.8
IMPEACHMENT PROVISIONS IN THE STATES

State or other jurisdiction	Governor and other state executive and judicial officers subject to impeachment	Legislative body which holds power of impeachment	Vote required for impeachment	Legislative body which conducts impeachment trial	Chief justice presides at impeachment trial(a)	Vote required for conviction	Official who serves as acting governor	Legislature may call special session for impeachment
Alabama	★(b)	H	...	S	(c)	2/3 mbrs.	LG	★
Alaska	★	S	2/3 mbrs.	H	★	2/3 mbrs.	SS	★
Arizona	★(d)	H	maj. mbrs.	S	★	2/3 mbrs.	...	★
Arkansas	★	H	...	S	...	2/3 mbrs.	...	...
California	★	H	...	S	★	2/3 mbrs.	LG	...
Colorado	★(d)	H	maj. mbrs.	S	★	2/3 mbrs.	LG	★
Connecticut	★	H	...	S	★	2/3 mbrs. present	LG	...
Delaware	★	H	2/3 mbrs.	S	★	2/3 mbrs.	LG	...
Florida	★	H	2/3 mbrs.	S	★	2/3 mbrs. present	LG	...
Georgia	★(e)	H	...	S	★	2/3 mbrs. present	LG	★★
Hawaii	★(f)	H	...	S	★	2/3 mbrs.	LG	★
Idaho	★	H	maj. mbrs.	S	★	2/3 mbrs.	LG	...
Illinois	★	H	maj. mbrs.	S	★	2/3 mbrs.	...	★
Indiana	★	H	2/3 mbrs.	S	...	2/3 mbrs.	...	...
Iowa	★	H	...	S	...	2/3 mbrs. present	LG	...
Kansas	★	H	...	S	...	2/3 mbrs.	LG	★
Kentucky	★	H	...	S	...	2/3 mbrs. present	LG	...
Louisiana	★	H	...	S	...	2/3 mbrs.	LG	★★
Maine	★	H	maj. mbrs.	S	...	2/3 mbrs. present	PS	...
Maryland	★	H	2/3 mbrs. present	S	...	2/3 mbrs.	...	...
Massachusetts	★	H	maj. mbrs.	S	...	2/3 mbrs.	LG	★
Michigan	★	H	maj. mbrs.	S(g)	★	2/3 mbrs.	LG	...
Minnesota	★	H	maj. mbrs.	S	...	2/3 mbrs. present	...	...
Mississippi	★	H	2/3 mbrs. present	S	...	2/3 mbrs.	...	...
Missouri	★	H	...	(h)	(h)	(h)	...	...
Montana	★	H	2/3 mbrs.	S	...	2/3 mbrs.	LG	★
Nebraska	★	S(i)	maj. mbrs.	(j)	(j)	(i)	...	...
Nevada	★(d)	H	maj. mbrs.	S	★	2/3 mbrs.	LG	...
New Hampshire	★	H	maj. mbrs.	S	★	...	LG	...
New Jersey	★(k)	H	maj. mbrs.	S	★	2/3 mbrs.	PS	★

IMPEACHMENT PROVISIONS—Continued

State or other jurisdiction	Governor and other state executive and judicial officers subject to impeachment	Legislative body which holds power of impeachment	Vote required for impeachment	Legislative body which conducts impeachment trial	Chief justice presides at impeachment trial(a)	Vote required for conviction	Official who serves as acting governor	Legislature may call special session for impeachment
New Mexico	★	H	maj. mbrs.	S	★	2/3 mbrs.	LG	★
New York	★	H	maj. mbrs.	S (l)	. . .	2/3 mbrs. present	LG	★
North Carolina	. . .	H	maj. mbrs.	S	★	2/3 mbrs. present	LG	★
North Dakota	★(d)	H	maj. mbrs.	S	. . .	2/3 mbrs.	. . .	. . .
Ohio	★	H	maj. mbrs.	S	. . .	2/3 mbrs.	LG	★
Oklahoma	★(b)	H	. . .	S (m)	★	2/3 mbrs. present	LG	★
Oregon	. . .	. . .	. . .	(m)	. . .	. . .	. . .	. . .
Pennsylvania	★	H	(n)	S	★	2/3 mbrs. present	LG	★
Rhode Island	★	H	. . .	S	★	2/3 mbrs.	LG	. . .
South Carolina	★	H	2/3 mbrs.	S	. . .	2/3 mbrs.	. . .	. . .
South Dakota	★(d)	H	maj. mbrs.	S	★	2/3 mbrs.	LG	★
Tennessee	★	H	. . .	S	★	2/3 mbrs.(o)	LG	. . .
Texas	★	H	2/3 mbrs.	S	. . .	2/3 mbrs. present	LG	★
Utah	★(d)	H	2/3 mbrs.	S	★	2/3 mbrs.	. . .	. . .
Vermont	★	H	2/3 mbrs.	S	. . .	2/3 mbrs. present	. . .	. . .
Virginia	★(d)	H	maj. mbrs.	S	. . .	2/3 mbrs. present	. . .	★
Washington	★(d)	H	. . .	S	. . .	2/3 mbrs.	. . .	★
West Virginia	★	H	maj. mbrs.	S	. . .	2/3 mbrs.	. . .	★
Wisconsin	★(d)	H	maj. mbrs.	S	. . .	2/3 mbrs. present	LG	. . .
Wyoming	★(d)	H	maj. mbrs.	S	★	2/3 mbrs.	SS	. . .
Dist. of Col.	. . .	H	2/3 mbrs.	(p)	. . .	. . .	. . .	. . .
American Samoa	(q)	H	2/3 mbrs.	S	★	2/3 mbrs.	. . .	. . .
Guam	★	H	2/3 mbrs.	S	. . .	2/3 mbrs.	. . .	. . .
No. Mariana Is.	(r)	. . .	2/3 mbrs.	. . .	. . .	3/4 mbrs.	. . .	★
Puerto Rico	. . .	. . .	. . .	S	. . .	. . .	. . .	. . .
Virgin Islands	. . .	. . .	. . .	(p)	. . .	. . .	. . .	. . .

Sources: Legislative Drafting Research Fund, Columbia University, *Constitutions of the United States: National and State* (Dobbs Ferry, N.Y.: Oceana Press, 1982, 1985); *The Book of the States, 1984-85*; and state statutes. Information compiled by Joe Farrell, Public Administration Program, University of North Carolina at Chapel Hill; and The Council of State Governments.

Note: The information in this table is based on a literal reading of the state constitutions and statutes. For information on other methods for removing state officials, see Table 4.5, "Methods for Removal of Judges and Filling of Vacancies," and Table 5.16, "Provisions for Recall of State Officials."

Key:
★ —Yes; provision for
. . . —Not specified, or no provision for
H—House or Assembly (lower chamber)
S—Senate
LG—Lieutenant governor
PS—President of the Senate
SS—Secretary of state

(a) Presiding justice of state court of last resort. In many states, provision indicates that chief justice presides only on occasion of impeachment of governor. Other judicial officers not subject to impeachment.
(b) Includes justices of Supreme Court. Other judicial officers not subject to impeachment.
(c) A Supreme Court justice designated by the court.
(d) With exception of certain judicial officers. In Arizona, Washington, and Wyoming—justices of courts not of record. In Colorado—county judges and justices of the peace. In Nevada and Utah—justices of the peace. In North Dakota and South Dakota—county judges, justices of the peace, and police magistrates.
(e) All persons who have been or may be in office.
(f) Governor, lieutenant governor, and any appointive officer for whose removal the consent of the Senate is required.
(g) House elects three members to prosecute impeachment.
(h) All impeachments are tried before the state Supreme Court, except that the governor or a member of the Supreme Court is tried by a special commission of seven eminent jurists to be elected by the Senate. A vote of 5/7 of the court of special commission is necessary to convict.
(i) Unicameral legislature; members use the title "senator."
(j) Court of impeachment is composed of chief justice and all district court judges in the state. A vote of 2/3 of the court is necessary to convict.
(k) All state officers while in office and for two years thereafter.
(l) Court for trial of impeachment composed of president of the Senate, senators (or major part of them), and judges of Court of Appeals (or major part of them).
(m) No provision for impeachment. Public officers may be tried for incompetency, corruption, malfeasance, or delinquency in office in same manner as criminal offenses.
(n) Vote of 2/3 members required for an impeachment of the governor.
(o) Vote of 2/3 of members sworn to try the officer impeached.
(p) Removal of elected officials by recall procedure only.
(q) Governor, lieutenant governor.
(r) Governor and Supreme Court justices.

THE EXECUTIVE BRANCH: ORGANIZATION AND ISSUES 1984-85

By Thad L. Beyle

State Government Organization

States tend to be cautious when it comes to making major revisions in their governmental structures; it is never entirely clear that something new will be better than the status quo or that the structure is the cause of the problems. But when major changes in state organizational configurations do occur, they often occur in several states at approximately the same time. For example, a major wave of state government reorganizations took place between the mid-1960s and the mid-1970s—the fourth such wave in this century. However, in the 1980s, there have been no major state government reorganizations.

While many reorganization efforts are undertaken for economy and efficiency purposes, evidence that these goals actually are achieved is lacking. In fact, it may be that governmental reorganization is more of a political—rather than an administrative—tool.[1] Nevertheless, Oklahoma is considering major reorganization into a cabinet system, following the recommendations of its governor and the Commission on Reform of State Government, and the governor of Iowa also is proposing major reorganization in that state.

Partial reorganization

During the biennium, most reorganization activity in the states was of a partial nature, as has been the pattern over the past decade. The major reorganization activity was in the area of economic development: Arizona established a Department of Commerce to replace the Governor's Office of Economic Planning and Development (1985); Idaho and West Virginia each created a Department of Commerce (1984); Missouri changed the name of its Department of Consumer Affairs to the Department of Economic Development (1984); Rhode Island set up a Small Business Advocacy Council (1985); Washington created a Department of Trade and Economic Development (1985); West Virginia set up a Governor's Office of Commerce and Indus-

trial Development in the Department of Commerce; and Wyoming created an Economic Development and Stabilization Board (1985).

Several states took steps to enhance the exporting ability of small- and medium-sized businesses: Illinois created an Export Development Authority (1983); Minnesota established an Export Finance Authority in the Department of Agriculture (1983); North Dakota set up an Export Trading Company in conjunction with the Industrial Commission (fully operational in 1985); and Oklahoma created an International Development Division within its Department of Economic Development (1985).

A number of other states established agencies and funds designed to provide financial assistance to economic development efforts: Arkansas created a Finance Development Authority, which may sell tax-exempt bonds for industrial development loans or for capital improvements, and converted a private agency, First Arkansas Development Corporation, into the Arkansas Capital Corporation to provide financial assistance to financial institutions and businesses (1985); Hawaii set up a Capital Loan Revolving Fund for small local businesses (1985); Iowa created a new authority to make grants to lending institutions for lower interest rates on operating loans to farmers and small businesses (1985); Nebraska established the Investment Finance Authority for making loans to companies planning to construct office buildings in the state, and a Small Business Development Authority to provide financial and technical assistance (1984); Vermont set up a State Industrial Development Fund to make loans available to financially-troubled farmers (1985); and Virginia created the Statewide Certified Development Company and a Small Business Financing Act to assist small businesses with capital needs,

Thad L. Beyle is Professor of Political Science at the University of North Carolina at Chapel Hill.

the Statewide Development Company to use federal Small Business Administration funds to assist small businesses, and a Rural Development Foundation for economic programs in rural areas (1984).

In 1984-85, some states took steps to foster closer ties between economic development efforts and higher education: Arkansas took action to provide matching grants to spur university/industry cooperation in research, product development, and production processes (1985); Kentucky established the Office of Business and Technology in the Commerce Cabinet to expedite the transfer of technology to existing businesses (1984); and Virginia created a Center for Innovative Technology to foster the cooperative development of technology between industry and public institutions of higher education (1984).

Other areas of organizational activity in the states were quite varied.

Administration: Illinois, by executive order, created the Office of Inspector General "to investigate and/or coordinate the investigation, regulation, licensing, and inspection of all persons, matters, and entities subject to regulation, licensing, and inspection under the laws" of the state (1984); New Hampshire restructured its Department of Revenue Administration (1985); New Jersey established a General Services Administration in the Department of Treasury (1984); Texas created a real property asset management and inventory program under a new Asset Management Division to review state holdings every four years and make recommendations subject to comment by the state's Purchasing and General Services Commission; and Virginia revamped its cabinet form of administrative structure, by creating separate secretaries for administration and finance, and combining the transportation and public safety secretaries (1984).

Education: Indiana created a single 11-member State Board of Education by merging the Commission on General Education, the Commission on Teacher Training and Licensing, and the Commission of Textbook Adoptions (1984); Iowa set up a foundation to research educational issues and distribute results to schools and policy makers (1985); North Dakota voters rejected a 1984 statutory initiative to require the state Board of Higher Education to give up control over the state's three junior colleges; and South Dakota dropped a controversial plan to convert a branch of the state university into a prison (1984).

Energy: Kansas granted new powers to the entity that regulates the Wolf Creek nuclear power plant (1984); and West Virginia created a Department of Energy to oversee coal, oil, gas exploration, production, and conservation, and a Public Energy Development Authority to issue bonds for building energy-related facilities (1985).

Environment: Arizona established the Commission on Arizona Environment (1985); California created the Coastal Conservancy to assist in providing public access to beaches in the public domain, and the Tahoe Conservancy to acquire environmentally-sensitive lands in that basin (1985); Indiana set up a Natural Heritage Protection Fund (1984); Nebraska established a Water Management Board and a management fund (1984); and New Mexico created a Rangeland Protection Advisory Committee within the Department of Agriculture (1985).

Hazardous waste: Idaho set up a special planning committee for a statewide survey to identify areas best suited for hazardous waste facilities (1985); Kansas granted the Department of Health and Environment additional power to ban the burial of hazardous waste, and created a "superfund" to help finance cleanup efforts (1984); and in California, a controversial gubernatorial reorganization plan to create a Department of Waste Management by consolidating toxic waste control programs in 12 agencies was pending before the legislature at this writing.

Health: Florida established a statewide databank containing information on medical incidents and claims (1985); Iowa (1985) extended the life of its Health Data Commission; and Wyoming created a health care data authority to collect and report financial and other data (1985). Several reorganization measures were related to cost containment in the health area: Florida authorized the state Hospital Cost Containment Board to approve each of the state's hospitals' budgets annually and to assess fines when the approved budget rates are exceeded (1984); Hawaii declared the Health Planning and Development Agency's principal function to be health care cost containment (1984); Washington legislation continued the Hospital Commission in order to assist the legislature in enacting positive cost containment legislation, although much of importance in the act was vetoed by the governor (1984); and West Virginia created the state Hospital Authority to sell bonds and notes to provide financing for hospital improvements and equipment purchases (1984).

Human services: Arkansas reorganized the Department of Human Services, and shifted the powers of three boards to its director (1985); Hawaii established a Human Services Citizen Advisory Board to help revise provider roles and responsibilities, and a State Council on Mental Illness (1984); and New Mexico created a state agency on aging (1984). Some states directed their attention to children: Arkansas combined children's services from several divisions into the Children and Family Services Division, and established a Missing Children Information Clearinghouse; Wisconsin created a Child Abuse and Neglect Prevention Board (1984); and Wyoming set up a state commission on child support (1985).

Transportation: Florida once again reorganized its Department of Transportation (1985); Minnesota set up a Regional Transit Board for the greater Minneapolis-St. Paul metropolitan area (1984); and New Hampshire created a new Department of Transportation incorporating the Department of Public Works and Highways, the Aeronautics Commission, the transportation function of the Public Utilities Commission, and the mass and urban transit planning function of the Office of State Planning.

Miscellaneous: Connecticut voters approved a 1984 constitutional amendment to move the Criminal Justice Division to the executive branch; Illinois, by executive order, set up a new Department of Employment Security to administer the unemployment insurance program (1984); Missouri established a Public Telecommunications Authority to expand public programming to rural areas of the state; New Hampshire consolidated individual agencies to create a new Department of Libraries, Arts, and Historical Resources, and created a new Department of Justice, by combining the attorney general's office with some others (1985); Oregon consolidated the state Banking Division and Office of Savings and Loan Supervisor into a new Division of Financial Institutions in the Department of Commerce (1985); and West Virginia created a new authority to sell bonds to set up jails by region, instead of by county (1985).

Some entities were dismantled during the biennium: Alaska voters adopted a 1985 initiative repealing the Alaska Transportation Commission; Rhode Island eliminated the Department of Community Affairs, along with several boards and commissions (1985); and in Texas, the Health Facilities Commission was abolished, making it the first major state agency to close under the Sunset Act (1985). In 1984, the New Hampshire Sunset Committee recommended abolishing 16 of the 64 state programs under review, and making major changes in 21 others. The 1978 law calls for the review of one-third of the state's agencies every two years; since 1981, the state has reviewed 180 programs, terminated 35, and altered 65.

Executive Branch Issues
Selection of officials
Another state may join the list of those conducting their state and local elections in non-presidential election years in an effort to insulate those races from national election trends and impacts. In 1985, the North Carolina General Assembly took action to place on the 1986 first primary ballot a referendum on the question of shifting state and county elections from even- to odd-numbered years, beginning in 1989. If adopted, the statewide officials elected in 1988 would serve an extra year—through 1993—thus placing the state's elections in the same cycle as New Jersey and Virginia.

That would leave only 12 states remaining on the presidential-year cycle.[2] In 1964, 29 states held their elections in the same year as national races; by 1972, the number had dropped to 19. As in North Carolina, many of the election year shifts have been state Democratic Party responses to the electoral problems posed by national party candidates for president and vice-president.

In 1985, Alabama took a step in reaction to increasing Republican strength in the state, by moving the state's primary elections (first primary and runoff) from September to June, beginning in 1986. The move is expected to allow party nominees more time to heal any political wounds suffered in a bruising runoff before the general election—from less than a month and a half to four and a half months between the primaries and general election.[3]

During the biennium, some states changed the method used to select particular executive branch officials. In 1985, Louisiana abolished the unique tradition of electing the state Board of Education and the superintendent, in favor of having the Board appoint the superintendent. In 1984, Colorado voters adopted a constitutional amendment making the insurance commissioner a gubernatorial appointee rather than a civil servant.

One state changed the specifics involved in recalling its officials. In 1984, Oregon voters agreed to a constitutional proposal changing the necessary number of signatures on recall petitions from 25 percent of the votes cast in the last election for Supreme Court justice to 15 percent of the votes cast for governor.

Other proposed changes, however, were not successful. In 1984, Georgia voters rejected a constitutional amendment providing for the appointment of the state superintendent. In the same year, South Dakota voters defeated a constitutional amendment to eliminate the elective office of state treasurer.

In 1984, four states redefined eligibility for service in particular offices. California now permits its state constitutional officers to reside anywhere in the state. Georgia voters, in approving a constitutional amendment, banned dual office holding by state and local government officials. Maryland voters adopted a constitutional amendment requiring all constitutional elected officials to be registered voters. And North Carolina voters agreed to an amendment requiring attorneys general and district attorneys to be authorized to practice law.

Policy management

During the biennium, there appeared to be little change in how state governments are managed on a day-to-day basis. No new management systems—such as MBO, Zero-Base Budgeting, or strategic planning—were being pushed through the states, and activities tended to focus on data management systems for the budget process.[4] Instead, it appears that the states are incorporating a range of sophisticated tools into their management and budgeting processes, and in doing so are finding varying degrees of effectiveness in the use of these tools.

A 1984 study reported that Forward-Year Projection of Expenditures and Revenues was in use in 42 states (26 reported it effective); Program Analysis prior to program approval, in 40 states (24 reported it effective); Program Budgeting, in 37 states (only 14 re-

ported it effective); Program Evaluation, in 34 states (13 reported it effective); Performance Measurement, Reporting and Monitoring, in 31 states (only four reported it effective); a computerized Management Information System, in 30 states (only 16 reported it effective); Zero-Base Budgeting, in 10 states (only seven found it effective); Management by Objective, in 10 states (only four found it effective); and Quality Circles, in nine states (four found it effective). States in the northeast and north central parts of the country reported greater use of these tools, as did states with larger budgets.[5]

There was, however, growing concern over the central management capabilities of the states. Two surveys conducted during the biennium revealed that less than half of the states had discernable central management improvement units. Those that had such units located them in the governor's office (New York), in a management and budget office reporting directly to the governor (Alaska, Maryland, Michigan, Tennessee), in a budget and planning office (Florida, Georgia, Texas, Wisconsin), or in departments of administration (Colorado, Minnesota, North Carolina, Ohio, Pennsylvania).[6]

Some reports have called for the governors to give management improvement a stronger emphasis in their administrations. In addition to the effort noted above, the National Governors' Association also provided an analysis of the management capabilities of the states.[7]

On the policy side, some of the states have undertaken a process known as "issue scanning." A variety of officials scan relevant periodicals, papers, and other materials for information and events that may be indicative of trends, and then funnel the items into a central coordinating location. Periodically, officials with a variety of perspectives review these bits of information, note trends that could affect the state, and determine their policy implications.

Eight states (Colorado, Florida, Minnesota, Missouri, Nebraska, New Jersey, Oklahoma, and Pennsylvania) are reported to conduct issue scanning, while several other states are attempting to develop similar processes. Some regional organizations have conducted issue scanning projects for their regional constituents, and the Council of State Policy and Planning Agencies coordinates an 11-member "State Scanning Network," which reports bi-monthly to the governors of all states.[8]

In other policy developments during the biennium: Delaware created an Office of State Planning and Coordination, designed to work through four new cabinet councils in providing a three-year policy agenda for the state; Florida now requires the governor's office to submit a plan for orderly growth management; and futures projects were undertaken in Connecticut, Idaho, Iowa, Kentucky, Maryland, Minnesota, Ohio, South Carolina, and Virginia.

Patronage

States continued to address the question of how far down the bureaucracy a governor's power should extend. North Carolina increased the job security of state employees in 1985 by reducing the seniority necessary to qualify for protection against arbitrary or political firings, and by setting caps on the number of employees who serve at the pleasure of the governor.[9]

That same year, however, Virginia removed 500 top state policy makers from coverage under the commonwealth's grievance procedures in order to give the governor more control over policy.[10]

Whistleblower protection

Two more states took steps to protect state employees from retaliation for reporting wrongdoing in government. In Iowa, legislation enacted in 1984 protects state employees from reprisals for disclosing waste or mismanagement, and in Rhode Island, 1984 legislation stipulates the employees no longer can be threatened, fired, or discriminated against for reporting violations of law or for participating in investigations.

Ethics

With legislation enacted in 1984, three states took steps to more clearly define ethical behavior for public officials: an Illinois law requires state officials to file annual economic disclosure statements or face new penalties; Nebraska legislation prohibits the attorney general and all assistant attorneys general from engaging in the private practice of law; and the conflict of interest law in Rhode Island now covers all state employees.

For two other states, however, efforts in the area were not as successful. In 1984, Mississippi voters rejected a constitutional amendment that would have banned public officials or employees from misusing their office for profit. The amendment would have prohibited a public official from doing business with (or having an interest in) a business that contracts with the level of government in which he or she serves. In July 1985, the Massachusetts Supreme Judicial Court ruled that the State Ethics Commission lacks the authority

Table A
Sunshine Laws In The States: Major Provisions

Provision	Number of states
Injunctive relief or other remedial action is provided if law violated	47
Committee meetings must be open	46
Meetings of local entities must be open	46
Discussions, in addition to actual decision making, must be held in open meeting	42
No exemptions to open-meeting provisions are allowed unless specified in the law	40
A policy statement says the sunshine law should be liberally construed	37
Where closed (executive) sessions are allowed, all final actions must be taken in open meetings	37
Quasi-judicial meetings must be open	34
When the law permits closed meetings, the parties involved may request that they be opened	29
There is no provision for discussing investments, donations, or other financial matters in executive session	25
Labor negotiations must be open	25

Source: Harlan Cleveland and Sandra Braman, "Report to the Association of Governing Boards of Universities and Colleges," (Minneapolis: Hubert H. Humphrey Institute of Public Affairs, 1984) as reported in *The Chronicle of Higher Education*, (October 10, 1984), p. 18.

to fine a public official for violation of the commonwealth's conflict of interest law.[11]

Open government

During the biennium, sunshine laws and provisions continued to be of interest in the states. A 1984 Virginia law amended the state's Freedom of Information Act in response to a court ruling—public bodies will no longer be able to conduct meetings through telephonic, video, electronic, or other communications means. In 1985, Hawaii amended its sunshine law—establishing the right of private citizens to sue if a meeting subject to the law is closed (in violation of the law), and restricting the holding of executive sessions by bodies covered under the law. Moreover, the amendment provides an affirmative right to the public to speak on any agenda item at any meeting held by those bodies covered under sunshine requirements.[12]

A 1984 study of the sunshine laws across the states identified 23 separate provisions that can be contained in these laws, and found that the states varied considerably in their definition of sunshine (as measured by the combinations of these provisions). Tennessee and Florida led the states by containing 21 and 20 of these provisions, respectively, while Pennsylvania, Wisconsin, and Wyoming contained only eight each. Table A presents the 11 most common provisions of these laws, and indicates how many states' laws contain these provisions.

Nearly all of the states' sunshine laws provide for remedial action if the law is violated, for open committee and local government meetings, and for no exemptions to open-meeting provisions unless specified in the law. The remaining provisions pertain to a variety of procedural and substantive points and vary considerably across the states.

Notes

1. James Conant, "Reorganization and the Bottom Line," *Public Administration Review* 46:1 (January/February 1986): 55.

2. Three of the 12 remaining states—New Hampshire, Rhode Island, and Vermont—hold their elections every two years, so they swing back and forth from a presidential to a non-presidential election year. As such, only nine of the remaining states elect their officials in conjunction with the presidential election.

3. David L. Martin, "Alabama Legislative Developments," *Comparative State Politics Newsletter* 6:3 (June 1985): 2.

4. "State Government Management," *State Policy Reports* 3:23 (December 1985): 9.

5. Stanley B. Botner, "The Use of Budgeting/Management Tools by State Governments," *Public Administration Review* 45:5 (September/October, 1985): 616-20.

6. Coalition to Improve Management in State and Local Government, *The Governor's Management Improvement Program: How to Do It* (Washington, D.C.: National Academy of Public Administration, 1985): 14-16.

7. Office of State Services, *Reorganization and Management Improvement Initiatives: An Essay of State Experience* (Washington, D.C.: National Governor's Association, 1986).

8. National Scanning Board, *Report to the Governors* (Washington, D.C.: Council of State Policy and Planning Agencies, bi-monthly), and Committee on Southern Trends, *Looking Forward: Visions of the Future of the South* (Research Triangle Park, N.C.: Southern Growth Policies Board, December 1985).

9. Joel Thompson, "The 1985 Session of the North Carolina General Assembly," *Comparative State Politics Newsletter* 6:4 (August 1985): 11.

10. John McClennon, "The 1985 General Assembly Session," *Comparative State Politics Newsletter* 6:4 (August 1985): 17.

11. Joseph F. Zimmerman, "Mass. Ethics Board Can't Fine Officials," *National Civic Review* 74:9 (October 1985): 428.

12. Anne F. Little, "Hawaii Legislative Report: 1985 Session," *Comparative State Politics Newsletter* 6:5 (October 1985): 16.

Table 2.9
CONSTITUTIONAL AND STATUTORY PROVISIONS FOR LENGTH AND NUMBER OF TERMS OF ELECTED STATE OFFICIALS

State or other jurisdiction	Governor	Lt. governor	Secretary of state	Attorney general	Treasurer	Auditor	Comptroller	Education	Agriculture	Labor	Insurance	Other
Alabama	4/2	4/2	4/2	4/2	4/2	4/2	...	...	4/2(a)	...	...	Bd. of Education—4/-; Public Service Commn.—4/-
Alaska	4/2(b)	4/2	(c)	...	...	...	...	...	...	...	...	
Arizona	4/-	(d)	4/-	4/-	4/2	...	...	4/-	...	...	...	Corporation Commn.—6/-; Mine inspector—2/-
Arkansas	4/-	4/-	4/-	4/-	4/-	4/-	(e)	...	...	...	...	Land Commr.—4/-
California	4/-	4/-	4/-	4/-	4/-	...	4/-	4/-	...	...	...	Bd. of Equalization—4/-
Colorado	4/-	4/-	4/-	4/-	4/-	...	...	...	...	...	...	Regents of Univ. of Colo.—6/-; Bd. of Education—6/-
Connecticut	4/-	4/-	4/-	4/-	4/-	...	4/-	...	...	...	...	
Delaware	4/2(f)	4/-	...	4/-	4/-	4/-	...	...	...	...	4/-	
Florida	4/2	4/-	4/-	4/-	4/-	...	4/-	4/-	4/-	...	(g)	
Georgia	4/2	4/-	4/-	4/-	...	...	4/-	4/-	4/-	4/-	(h)	Public Service Commn.—6/-
Hawaii	4/2	4/2	(c)	...	...	...	...	...	...	...	...	Bd. of Education—4/U
Idaho	4/-	4/-	4/-	4/-	4/-	4/-	(i)	4/-	...	...	...	
Illinois	4/-	4/-	4/-	4/-	4/-	...	4/-	...	...	...	...	Bd. of Trustees, Univ. of Ill.—6/-
Indiana	4/2(j)	4/-	4/2(j)	4/-	4/2(j)	4/2(j)	(i)	4/-	(c)	...	...	
Iowa	4/U	4/U	4/U	4/U	4/U	4/U	...	...	4/U	...	...	
Kansas	4/2	4/2	4/-	4/-	4/-	...	...	...	...	...	4/-	Bd. of Education—4/-
Kentucky	4/0	4/0	4/0	4/0	4/0	4/0	(e)	4/0	4/0	...	...	Railroad Commn.—4/-
Louisiana	4/2	4/-	4/-	4/-	4/-	...	(k)	...	4/-	...	4/-	Bd. of Education—4/-; Public Service Commn.—6/-; Elections Commr.—4/-
Maine	4/2	(l)	...	...	...	...	...	...	...	...	...	
Maryland	4/2(b)	4/-	...	4/U	...	...	4/-	...	...	...	...	
Massachusetts	4/-	4/-	4/-	4/-	4/-	4/-	...	...	...	...	...	Exec. Council—2/-
Michigan	4/-	4/-	4/-	4/-	...	...	(m)	...	...	...	...	Univ. Regents—8/-; Bd. of Education—8/-
Minnesota	4/-	4/-	4/-	4/-	4/-	4/-	...	...	...	...	...	
Mississippi	4/0	4/-	4/-	4/0	4/-	4/-	(i)	...	4/-	...	4/-	Public Service Commn.—4/-; Highway Commn.—4/-
Missouri	4/2(f)	4/-	4/-	4/-	4/2(f)	4/U	...	...	...	...	...	
Montana	4/-	4/-	4/-	4/-	...	4/-	...	4/-	...	...	(i)	Public Service Commn.—4/-
Nebraska	4/2(b)	4/-	4/-	4/-	4/2(n)	4/-	...	...	...	...	...	Regents of Univ. of Neb.—6/-; Bd. of Education—4/-; Public Service Commn.—6/-
Nevada	4/2	4/-	4/-	4/-	4/-	...	4/-	...	...	...	...	Bd. of Regents—6/-; Bd. of Education—4/3
New Hampshire	2/-	(l)	...	...	...	...	...	...	...	...	...	Exec. Council—2/-
New Jersey	4/2	(l)	...	...	...	...	...	...	...	...	...	

State or other jurisdiction	Governor	Lt. governor	Secretary of state	Attorney general	Treasurer	Auditor	Comptroller	Education	Agriculture	Labor	Insurance	Other
New Mexico	4/0(o)	4/0(o)	4/0(o)	4/0(o)	4/0(o)	4/0(o)	...	...	...	...	...	Commr. of Public Lands—4/0(o); Bd. of Education—6/-; Corporation Commn.—6/-
New York	4/-	4/-	...	4/-	...	(p)	4/-	...	...	...	...	
North Carolina	4/2(f)	4/2(f)	4/-	4/-	4/-	4/-	(q)	4/-	4/-	4/-	4/-	
North Dakota	4/-	4/-	4/-	4/-	4/2	4/-	...	4/-	4/-(r)	4/-(r)	4/-	Public Service Commn.—6/-; Tax Commr.—4/-
Ohio	4/2	4/-	4/-	4/-	4/-	4/-	(m)	...	...	...	...	Bd. of Education—6/-
Oklahoma	4/2	4/U	...	4/U	4/U	4/U	...	4/U	...	...	4/-	Corporation Commn.—6/-
Oregon	4/2(j)	(d)	4/2(j)	4/-	4/2(j)	(s)	...	4/-	...	4/-	...	
Pennsylvania	4/2	4/2	...	4/2	4/2(t)	4/2	...	...	...	...	...	
Rhode Island	2/-	2/-	2/-	2/-	2/-	...	...	...	...	...	...	
South Carolina	4/2	4/-	4/-	4/-	4/-	...	4/-	4/-	4/-	...	...	Adjutant General—4/-
South Dakota	4/2	4/2	4/-	4/-	4/-	4/-	(i)	...	...	...	...	Commr. of School & Public Lands—4/-; Public Utilities Commn.—6/-
Tennessee	4/2	(l)	...	...	...	(p)	...	...	...	...	...	Public Service Commn.—6/-
Texas	4/-	4/-	...	4/-	4/-	...	4/-	...	4/-	...	...	Commr. of General Land Off.—6/-; Railroad Commn.—6/-
Utah	4/-	4/-	(c)	4/-	4/-	4/-	...	...	...	...	...	Bd. of Education—4/-
Vermont	2/-	2/-	2/-	2/-	2/-	2/-	...	...	...	...	...	
Virginia	4/0	4/U	...	4/U	...	...	...	...	...	...	...	
Washington	4/-	4/-	4/-	4/-	4/-	4/-	(m)	4/-	...	...	4/-	Commr. of Public Lands—4/-
West Virginia	4/2	(l)	4/-	4/-	4/-	4/-	(i)	...	4/-	...	...	
Wisconsin	4/-	4/-	4/-	4/-	4/-	...	(e)	4/-	...	...	...	
Wyoming	4/-	(d)	4/-	...	4/-	4/-	...	4/-	...	...	...	
Dist. of Col.	4/U(u)	...	...	...	...	...	...	...	...	...	...	Chmn. of Council of Dist. of Col.—4/U
American Samoa	4/2	4/2	(c)	...	...	...	(m)	...	...	...	...	
Guam	4/2(b)	4/-	(c)	...	...	...	...	...	...	...	(v)	Bd. of Education—4/-; Village Commr.—4/U
No. Mariana Is.	4/3	4/-	...	...	...	...	(e)	...	(w)	...	...	
Puerto Rico	4/-	(d)	...	...	...	...	...	...	...	...	...	
Virgin Islands	4/2(b)	4/-	(c)	...	(e)	...	...	...	...	...	(c)	

Note: First entry in a column refers to number of years per term. Entry following the slash refers to the maximum number of consecutive terms allowed. This table reflects a literal reading of the state constitutions and statutes. Blank cells indicate no specific administrative official performs function.

Key:

- —No provision specifying number of terms allowed.

0—Provision specifying officeholder may not succeed self.

U—Provision specifying individual may hold office for an unlimited number of terms.

. . .—Position is appointed or elected by governmental entity (not chosen by electorate).

(a) Commissioner of agriculture and industries.

(b) After two consecutive terms, must wait four years before being eligible again.

(c) Lieutenant governor performs function.

(d) Secretary of state is next in line of succession to the governorship.

(e) Finance administrator performs function.

(f) Absolute two-term limitation, but not necessarily consecutive.

(g) State treasurer also serves as insurance commissioner.

(h) Comptroller general is ex-officio insurance commissioner.

(i) State auditor performs function.

(j) Eligible for eight out of 12 years.

(k) Head of administration performs function.

(l) President of the senate is next in line of succession to the governorship. In Tennessee, speaker of the senate has the statutory title "lieutenant governor."

(m) State treasurer performs function.

(n) After two consecutive terms, must wait two years before being eligible again.

(o) Must wait four years before being eligible to any office, with the exception of the lieutenant governor who is immediately eligible for the office of the governor.

(p) Comptroller performs function.

(q) Budget administrator performs function.

(r) Constitution provides for a secretary of agriculture and labor. However, the legislature was given constitutional authority to provide for (and has provided for) a department of labor distinct from agriculture, and a commissioner of labor distinct from the commissioner of agriculture.

(s) Secretary of state's office performs function.

(t) Treasurer must wait four years before being eligible to the office of auditor general.

(u) Mayor.

(v) Taxation administrator performs function.

(w) Natural resources administrator performs function.

Table 2.10
SELECTED STATE ADMINISTRATIVE OFFICIALS: METHODS OF SELECTION

State	Governor	Lieutenant governor	Secretary of state	Attorney general	Treasurer	Adjutant general	Administration	Agriculture	Banking	Budget
Alabama	CE	CE	CE	CE	CE	G	...	CE	G	CS
Alaska	CE	CE	...	GB	GB	GB	A	A	A	A
Arizona	CE	...	CE	CE	CE	G	GS	B	GS	G
Arkansas	CE	CE	CE	CE	CE	G	G	(f)	AG	AG
California	CE	CE	CE	CE	CE	GS	...	GS	GS	(a-20)
Colorado	CE	CE	CE	CE	CE	G	GS	GS	A	GS
Connecticut	CE	CE	CE	CE	CE	G	GE	GE	GE	A
Delaware	CE	CE	GS	CE	CE	GS	GS	GS	GS	GS
Florida	CE	CE	CE	CE	CE	GS	GS	CE	(a-12)	A
Georgia	CE	CE	CE	CE	(a-20)	G	GS	CE	GS	G
Hawaii	CE	CE	...	GS	(a-9)	GS	...	GS	AG	GS
Idaho	CE	CE	CE	CE	CE	G	GS	GS	GS	G
Illinois	CE	CE	CE	CE	CE	G	GS	GS	GS	G
Indiana	CE	CE	CE	SE	CE	G	G	A	G	G
Iowa	CE	CE	CE	CE	CE	GS	A	SE	GS	(a-12)
Kansas	CE	CE	CE	CE	SE	GS	GS	B	GS	CS
Kentucky	CE	CE	CE	CE	CE	G	G	CE	G	(a-20)
Louisiana	CE	CE	CE	CE	CE	GS	G	CE	GS	GS
Maine	CE	...	CL	CL	CL	G	...	GLS	GLS	AG
Maryland	CE	CE	GS	CE	CL	GS	(a-31)	GS	AGS	GS
Massachusetts	CE	CE	CE	CE	CE	G	G	G	G	AG
Michigan	CE	CE	CE	CE	GS	GS	GS	B	GS	GS
Minnesota	CE	CE	CE	CE	CE	G	GS	GS	BS	(a-20)
Mississippi	CE	CE	CE	CE	CE	GS	...	SE	GS	B
Missouri	CE	CE	CE	CE	CE	GS	GS	GS	AS	A
Montana	CE	CE	CE	CE	A	G	GS	GS	A	G
Nebraska	CE	CE	CE	CE	CE	G	GS	GS	GS	A
Nevada	CE	CE	CE	CE	CE	G	G	BG	A	(a-6)
New Hampshire	CE	...	CL	GC	CL	GC	GC	GC	GC	(a-6)
New Jersey	CE	...	GS	GS	GS	GS	A	BG	GS	A
New Mexico	CE	CE	CE	CE	CE	GS	(a-22)	BG	GS	GS
New York	CE	CE	GS	CE	GS	G	(a-22)	GS	G	G
North Carolina	CE	CE	CE	CE	CE	G	G	CE	GS	AG
North Dakota	CE	CE	CE	CE	CE	G	(a-31)	CE	GS	(hh)
Ohio	CE	CE	CE	CE	CE	G	GS	GS	A	GS
Oklahoma	CE	CE	GS	CE	CE	GS	...	GS	GS	(a-20)
Oregon	CE	...	CE	SE	CE	G	GS	GS	AG	A
Pennsylvania	CE	CE	GS	CE	CE	GS	G	GS	GS	G
Rhode Island	CE	CE	CE	CE	CE	G	GS	A	G	CS
South Carolina	CE	CE	CE	CE	CE	CE	(a-9)	CE	(a-4)	B
South Dakota	CE	CE	CE	CE	CE	GS	G	GS	A	(a-20)
Tennessee	CE	(tt)	CL	CT	CL	G	G	G	G	A
Texas	CE	CE	GS	CE	CE	GS	...	SE	BS	G
Utah	CE	CE	...	CE	CE	G	GS	GS	GS	G
Vermont	CE	CE	CE	SE	CE	SL	GS	GS	GS	GS
Virginia	CE	CE	GB	CE	GB	GB	GB	GB	B	GB
Washington	CE	CE	CE	CE	CE	GS	GS	GS	A	(a-20)
West Virginia	CE	...	CE	CE	CE	GS	(a-31)	CE	GS	(yy)
Wisconsin	CE	CE	CE	CE	CE	G	GS	B	GS	A
Wyoming	CE	...	CE	GS	CE	G	G	B	G	G

Note: The chief administrative officials responsible for each function were determined from information given by the states for the same function as listed in *State Administrative Officials Classified by Function 1985-86*, published by The Council of State Governments.

Key:

... —No specific chief administrative official or agency in charge of function.
CE —Constitutional, elected by public
CL —Constitutional, elected by legislature
SE —Statutory, elected by public
SL —Statutory, elected by legislature
L —Selected by legislature or one of its organs
CT —Constitutional, elected by state Supreme Court

Appointed by:
G —Governor
GS —Governor
GB —Governor
GE —Governor
GC —Governor
GD —Governor
GLS —Governor
GOC —Governor & Council or cabinet

Approved by:
Senate
Both houses
Either house
Council
Departmental board
Appropriate legislative committee & Senate

LG —Lieutenant governor
AT —Attorney general
SS —Secretary of state

Appointed by:
A —Agency head
AB —Agency head
AG —Agency head
AGC —Agency head
AS —Agency head
AGS —Agency head
ASH —Agency head

B —Board or commission
BG —Board
BGC —Board
BGS —Board
BS —Board or commission
BA —Board or commission
CS —Civil Service
ACB —Nominated by audit committee

Approved by:
Board
Governor
Governor & Council
Senate
Governor & Senate
Senate president & House speaker

Governor
Governor & Council
Governor & Senate
Senate
Agency head

Both houses

SELECTED OFFICIALS: METHODS OF SELECTION—Continued

State	Civil rights	Commerce	Community affairs	Comptroller	Computer services	Consumer affairs	Corrections	Economic development	Education	Elections administration
Alabama	...	G	G	AG	CS	AT	G	G	B	(a-2)
Alaska	G	GB	GB	GB	A	AT	GB	A	BG	LG
Arizona	A	(d)	(a-32)	(a-20)	AG	AT	GS	(d)	CE	(a-2)
Arkansas	...	G	G	(a-6)	GS	AT	GS	(a-10)	BG	(a-2)
California	G	GS	GS	CE	G	GS	GS	(a-10)	CE	(a-2)
Colorado	A	A	A	A	A	AT	GS	A	B	SS
Connecticut	B	(a-15)	A	CE	A	GE	GE	G	B	GE
Delaware	...	(a-2)	AG	L	A	(a-11)	GS	AG	B	GS
Florida	A	(a-1)	GS	CE	GS	A	GS	A	CE	SS
Georgia	...	B	G	CE	A	G	GD	(a-10)	CE	SS
Hawaii	...	GS	(a-15)	GS	A	G	A	GS	B	LG
Idaho	BGS	G	...	(o)	(a-6)	(a-3)	BGS	(a-10)	CE	(a-2)
Illinois	GS	GS	(a-10)	CE	(a-6)	(a-3)	GS	(a-10)	B	GS
Indiana	G	(a-1)	A	(o)	A	AT	G	LG	SE	B
Iowa	GS	GS	A	GS	CS	AT	GS	GS	B	SS
Kansas	B	GS	A	A	A	(a-3)	GS	(a-10)	B	(a-2)
Kentucky	B	G	G	(a-20)	(a-20)	(a-3)	AG	AG	CE	(a-2)
Louisiana	(a-3)	GS	GS	(a-6)	A	GS	GS	(a-10)	B	CE
Maine	B	GS	...	AG	CS	GLS	AG	(a-10)	GLS	(a-2)
Maryland	GS	A	AG	CE	A	AT	AGS	AG	B	G
Massachusetts	AT	G	G	G	A	G	G	G	B	SS
Michigan	B	GS	A	(a-4)	A	A	B	CS	B	A
Minnesota	GS	GS	A	(a-20)	A	GS	GS	A	BG	(a-2)
Mississippi	...	(a-15)	(a-32)	(a-33)	B	AT	B	G	BS	SS
Missouri	B	(a-15)	(a-15)	A	A	GS	GS	A	B	SS
Montana	G	G	A	(a-6)	A	G	A	A	CE	SS
Nebraska	B	GS	A	(a-6)	A	AT	GS	...	B	(a-2)
Nevada	G	G	G	CE	A	A	G	A	B	(a-2)
New Hampshire	B	(a-15)	(a-32)	GOC	B	(a-3)	GOC	GC	B	(a-2)
New Jersey	A	GS	GS	(a-9)	A	GS	GS	A	GS	(cc)
New Mexico	GS	GS	GS	(a-4)	A	AT	A	A	B	SS
New York	G	GS	(a-2)	CE	(a-22)	GS	GS	(a-10)	B	G
North Carolina	A	G	A	A	AG	AT	G	A	CE	G
North Dakota	(a-27)	(a-15)	A	(hh)	A	AT	GS	G	CE	(a-2)
Ohio	GS	G	A	(a-4)	A	B	GS	A	B	(a-2)
Oklahoma	B	(a-15)	G	AG	A	B	B	G	CE	L
Oregon	CS	GS	A	A	A	A	AG	A	CE	SS
Pennsylvania	GS	GS	GS	AG	AG	A	AG	(a-10)	GS	G
Rhode Island	B	(a-15)	...	A	A	BS	GS	G	B	B
South Carolina	B	G	A	CE	(a-22)	B	B	(a-10)	CE	B
South Dakota	A	GS	(a-15)	CE	(a-6)	AT	AG	GS	B	(a-2)
Tennessee	B	(a-15)	(a-15)	CL	A	A	G	G	G	SS
Texas	B	G	GS	CE	B	AT	B	B	BS	SS
Utah	B	GS	(uu)	(a-20)	AG	AG	BA	A	B	(a-1)
Vermont	AT	(a-15)	GS	(a-20)	CS	AT	GS	A	BG	(a-2)
Virginia	...	GB	A	GB	GB	A	GB	GB	GB	GB
Washington	B	GS	GS	(a-4)	B	AT	GS	A	CE	SS
West Virginia	GS	GS	(zz)	CE	A	AT	GS	(aaa)	B	(a-2)
Wisconsin	A	(a-1)	A	A	A	(bbb)	A	A	CE	BA
Wyoming	A	(a-15)	(a-15)	(a-33)	A	AT	BG	G	CE	(a-2)

(a) Chief administrative official or agency in charge of function:
(a-1) Lieutenant governor
(a-2) Secretary of state
(a-3) Attorney general
(a-4) Treasurer
(a-5) Adjutant general
(a-6) Administration
(a-7) Agriculture
(a-8) Banking
(a-9) Budget
(a-10) Commerce
(a-11) Community affairs
(a-12) Comptroller
(a-13) Computer services
(a-14) Consumer affairs
(a-15) Economic development
(a-16) Education (chief state school officer)
(a-17) Employment services
(a-18) Energy resources
(a-19) Environmental protection
(a-20) Finance
(a-21) Fish and wildlife
(a-22) General services
(a-23) Health
(a-24) Highways
(a-25) Historic preservation
(a-26) Insurance
(a-27) Labor
(a-28) Mental health and retardation
(a-29) Natural resources
(a-30) Parks and recreation
(a-31) Personnel
(a-32) Planning
(a-33) Post audit
(a-34) Public utility regulation
(a-35) Public welfare
(a-36) Purchasing
(a-37) Revenue
(a-38) Social services
(a-39) Solid waste management
(a-40) Transportation

(b) Responsibilities shared by Receiver of the Department of Mental Health and Associate Commissioner of the Mental Retardation Division of the same department.

(c) Responsibilities shared by Director and Program Administrator of the Mental Health and Development Disabilities Division of the Health and Social Services Department.

(d) Responsibilities shared by Director of Department of Commerce and Director of Development Division.

(e) Responsibilities shared by Assistant Director of Community Behavioral Health Services, Department of Health Services and Director, Disabilities Division, Department of Economic Security.

State	Emergency management	Employment services	Energy resources	Environmental protection	Finance	Fish & wildlife	General services	Health	Higher education	Highways
Alabama	CS	A	CS	G	G	(a-29)	A	B	B	G
Alaska	A	A	A	GB	GB	GB	A	A	BG	(a-40)
Arizona	G	GS	GS	GS	AG	B	GS	GS	B	(a-40)
Arkansas	AG	G	GS	G	(a-6)	B	(a-6)	GS	BG	G
California	GS	GS	B	GS	GS	GS	GS	GS	B	(a-40)
Colorado	A	A	G	A	(a-12)	BA	(a-6)	GS	B	GS
Connecticut	GE	AG	A	GE	GE	GE	(a-6)	GE	B	A
Delaware	AG	(a-31)	G	A	GS	A	(a-6)	AG	B	(a-40)
Florida	A	A	A	GS	A	GS	GOC	A	B	(a-40)
Georgia	(a-5)	A	G	A	A	A	(a-6)	BG	B	(a-40)
Hawaii	(a-5)	A	A	AG	(a-9)	AB	(a-12)	GS	B	AG
Idaho	A	GS	G	GS	(a-9)	GS	A	A	BGS	(a-40)
Illinois	GS	A	(a-29)	GS	GS	A	(a-6)	GS	B	(a-40)
Indiana	GC	G	G	B	(a-9)	A	(a-6)	G	B	G
Iowa	A	GS	GS	GS	(a-12)	A	GS	GS	GS	A
Kansas	A	GS	GS	A	(a-6)	B	(a-6)	GS	B	(a-40)
Kentucky	G	A	G	G	G	B	(a-20)	AG	B	G
Louisiana	GS	GS	GS	GS	(a-6)	GS	(a-6)	GS	B	G
Maine	AG	GLS	G	GLS	GLS	GLS	(a-20)	A	GLS	(a-40)
Maryland	G	AG	A	AG	(a-12)	G	GS	GS	B	AG
Massachusetts	G	G	G	G	(a-6)	G	(a-36)	G	B	(v)
Michigan	A	B	G	A	(a-9)	(a-29)	(a-9)	GS	CS	(a-40)
Minnesota	G	GS	GS	(w)	GS	A	(a-6)	GS	GS	A
Mississippi	G	G	G	B	(a-9)	B	B	B	B	SE
Missouri	GS	A	A	A	(a-6)	B	(a-6)	A	B	B
Montana	A	A	G	A	. . .	GS	(a-6)	GS	GS	GS
Nebraska	(a-5)	A	GS	GS	(z)	B	(a-6)	GS	GS	GS
Nevada	G	G	. . .	A	(a-12)	G	A	A	B	(a-40)
New Hampshire	G	GC	G	. . .	(a-6)	B	(a-6)	GC	A	GC
New Jersey	A	A	GS	GS	(a-4)	AGC	(a-6)	GS	BG	(a-40)
New Mexico	A	GS	GS	A	GS	A	GS	GS	B	GS
New York	(a-5)	(a-27)	GS	G	. . .	(a-19)	GS	GS	(a-16)	(a-40)
North Carolina	G	G	AG	(a-29)	(a-9)	A	A	G	BG	AG
North Dakota	A	G	(a-11)	A	(hh)	G	(ii)	G	B	G
Ohio	AG	GS	GS	GS	(a-6)	A	(a-6)	GS	BG	(a-40)
Oklahoma	GS	B	B	B	G	AB	A	B	B	(a-40)
Oregon	CS	AG	GS	B	(a-6)	B	GS	AG	B	AB
Pennsylvania	B	CS	GS	GS	GS	(nn)	GS	GS	AG	(a-40)
Rhode Island	(a-5)	G	(a-34)	GS	G	B	A	GB	B	(a-40)
South Carolina	A	B	G	AG	(a-9)	B	AG	B	B	B
South Dakota	A	A	A	A	A	G	(a-6)	GS	B	A
Tennessee	A	G	BG	A	(a-6)	B	G	G	B	(a-40)
Texas	G	B	B	. . .	. . .	B	B	B	B	B
Utah	BG	AG	A	B	AG	BA	(a-6)	GS	B	(a-40)
Vermont	G	GS	G	GS	AGS	AS	(a-6)	GS	B	(a-40)
Virginia	GB	GB	A	GB	GB	B	GB	GB	GB	GB
Washington	GS	GS	GS	GS	GS	B	(a-6)	A	B	(a-40)
West Virginia	G	GS	B	(a-29)	GS	A	A	CS	B	GS
Wisconsin	GS	A	A	A	A	A	A	GS	BG	A
Wyoming	G	G	G	G	(a-33)	G	(a-6)	G	G	B

(f) Responsibilities shared by Director, Veterinarian, Livestock and Poultry Commission and Director, Plant Board, and International Marketing Representative, Marketing Division, Industrial Development Commission.

(g) Responsibilities shared by Director, Department of Industrial Relations and Supervisor, Conciliation Service of the same department.

(h) Responsibilities shared by Director, Department of Mental Health, and Director, Developmental Services Department.

(i) Responsibilities shared by Director, Division of Mental Health and Director, Division of Developmental Disabilities.

(j) Responsibilities shared by Commissioner, Department of Mental Health and Commissioner, Department of Mental Retardation.

(k) Responsibilities shared by Director, Division of Alcoholism, Drug Abuse & Mental Health and Director, Division of Mental Retardation.

(l) Responsibilities shared by Secretary, Department of Services for Children, Youth, & Their Families and Secretary, Department of Health & Social Services.

(m) Not a state employee.

(n) Responsibilities shared by Chief of the Mental Health Division in the Department of Health and Chief of the Waimano Training School & Hospital.

(o) State auditor, CE.

(p) Responsibilities shared by Chief, Bureau of Mental Health and Executive Director, Developmental Disabilities both in the Department of Health and Welfare.

(q) Responsibilities shared by Commissioner and Assistant Commissioner, Developmental Disabilities Division, both in Department of Mental Health.

(r) Responsibilities shared by Director, Merit Employment Department and Head of Personnel, Office of State Comptroller.

(s) Responsibilities shared by Deputy Assistant Secretary, Office of Mental Health and Assistant Secretary, Office of Mental Retardation.

(t) Responsibilities shared by Director, Bureau of Mental Health and Director, Bureau of Mental Retardation.

(u) Responsibilities shared by Director, Mental Retardation & Developmental Disabilities and Director, Mental Hygiene Administration.

(v) Responsibilities shared by Secretary and Commissioner of the Department of Public Works.

(w) Responsibilities shared by Executive Director, Pollution Control Agency and Executive Director, Environmental Quality Board.

(x) Responsibilities shared by Director, Department of Mental Health and Director, Mental Retardation Division.

(y) Responsibilities shared by Administrator, Mental Health Division and Administrator, Developmental Disabilities Division.

(z) Responsibilities shared by the following administrative officials: Director of Department of Administrative Services; State Budget Administrator of the Budget Division within the same department; Auditor of Public Accounts; and State Tax Commissioner of the Department of Revenue.

SELECTED OFFICIALS: METHODS OF SELECTION—Continued

State	Historic preservation	Insurance	Labor	Licensing	Mental health & retardation	Natural resources	Parks & recreation	Personnel	Planning	Post audit
Alabama	B	G	G	...	(b)	G	G	B	...	L
Alaska	A	A	GB	A	(c)	GB	A	G	G	L
Arizona	B	GS	B	...	(e)	GS	B	AG	A	L
Arkansas	GS	AG	GS	...	(a-38)	GS	GS	AG	...	L
California	G	GS	(g)	(a-14)	(h)	GS	GS	G	G	(a-20)
Colorado	GD	A	A	GS	(i)	GS	BA	GS	(a-9)	ACB
Connecticut	G	GE	GE	G	(j)	(a-19)	CS	G	A	L
Delaware	AG	CE	GS	AG	(k)	(a-19)	AG	GS	...	CE
Florida	A	(a-4)	A	GS	A	GOC	A	GS	(a-9)	L
Georgia	A	(a-12)	CE	SS	BG	(a-19)	A	G	(a-9)	SL
Hawaii	(a-29)	AG	GS	(a-10)	(n)	GS	AB	GS	GS	A
Idaho	B	GS	GS	G	(p)	...	GS	BGS	(a-10)	L
Illinois	GS	GS	GS	GS	GS	GS	(a-21)	(a-6)	GS	L
Indiana	B	G	G	G	(q)	G	A	G	LG	G
Iowa	B	GS	GS	...	A	G	GD	(r)	G	CE
Kansas	B	SE	(a-17)	...	AS	(a-19)	BG	G	(a-9)	L
Kentucky	BG	G	G	G	G	(a-19)	G	G	(a-6)	CE
Louisiana	GS	CE	GS	...	(s)	GS	GS	B	GS	(a-9)
Maine	B	GLS	A	A	(t)	(a-19)	B	GLS	G	SL
Maryland	A	GS	GS	GS	(u)	GS	A	GS	GS	ASH
Massachusetts	G	G	G	G	G	G	A	AG	(a-11)	CE
Michigan	CS	GS	GS	GS	GS	B	CS	B	...	CL
Minnesota	B	BS	GS	GS	GS	GS	A	GS	G	CE
Mississippi	B	SE	...	...	(x)	B	AB	B	G	CE
Missouri	A	AS	GS	A	B	GS	A	G	(a-9)	CE
Montana	B	A	GS	A	(y)	GS	A	AG	(a-11)	L
Nebraska	B	GS	(aa)	A	(bb)	B	(a-21)	GS	G	CE
Nevada	A	A	G	...	A	G	A	G	...	L
New Hampshire	(a-29)	GC	GC	...	GC	GC	GC	AGC	GC	L
New Jersey	A	GS	GS	(a-14)	(dd)	GS	A	G	G	L
New Mexico	A	B	GS	G	(ee)	GS	A	G	...	CE
New York	(a-30)	GS	GS	(a-2)	(ff)	(a-19)	GS	GS	(gg)	(a-12)
North Carolina	G	CE	CE	...	G	G	G	G	G	CE
North Dakota	B	CE	SE	...	A	...	G	AB	(a-11)	(jj)
Ohio	(m)	GS	GS	...	(kk)	G	A	GS	A	CE
Oklahoma	B	CE	GS	...	(ll)	G	G	GS	...	CE
Oregon	A	AG	SE	(a-10)	(mm)	G	AB	A	G	A
Pennsylvania	BG	GS	GS	G	A	(a-19)	CS	AG	G	CE
Rhode Island	B	G	G	G	(pp)	(a-19)	A	CS	CS	(qq)
South Carolina	B	B	GS	...	(rr)	(a-18)	B	B	B	B
South Dakota	GS	A	GS	A	(ss)	GS	GS	GS	...	L
Tennessee	AB	G	G	A	G	G	A	G	G	(a-12)
Texas	B	B	G	...	B	...	(a-21)	...	G	L
Utah	AB	GS	GS	AG	(vv)	GS	BA	A	(a-9)	CE
Vermont	A	(a-8)	GS	(a-2)	GS	(a-19)	A	GS	G	CE
Virginia	(a-29)	(a-8)	GB	GB	GB	GB	A	GB	(a-9)	GB
Washington	GS	SE	GS	GS	(ww)	CE	B	G	(a-20)	CE
West Virginia	A	GS	GS	...	(a-23)	GS	A	GS	GS	CE
Wisconsin	G	GS	GS	GS	A	B	A	GS	(a-9)	L
Wyoming	(a-30)	B	G	...	A	...	G	G	G	CE

(aa) Responsibilities shared by Commissioner, Labor Department and Clerk, Commission of Industrial Relations.

(bb) Responsibilities shared by Director, Medical Services and Director, Office of Mental Retardation.

(cc) Responsibilities shared by Director, Elections Division, Department of State and Executive Director, Election Law Enforcement Commission.

(dd) Responsibilities shared by Director, Mental Health & Hospitals Divison and Director, Mental Retardation Division, both in the Department of Human Services.

(ee) Responsibilities shared by Chief, Mental Health Bureau and Chief, Developmental Disabilities Bureau.

(ff) Responsibilities shared by Commissioner, Office of Mental Health and Commissioner, Mental Retardation & Developmental Disabilities.

(gg) No central planning agency. Responsibilities shared among the Departments of Commerce, State, and Transportation and the State Energy Office.

(hh) Responsibilities shared by Director of the Office of Management and Budget and Executive Budget Analyst of the same office. The Director of Management and Budget is also responsible for the function Pre-Audit.

(ii) Responsibilities shared by Director, Office of Budget & Management and Director of Institutions.

(jj) Responsibilities shared by the Legislative Budget Analyst and Auditor and the State Auditor.

(kk) Responsibilities shared by Director, Department of Mental Health and Director, Department of Mental Retardation.

(ll) Responsibilities shared by Director, Mental Health Department and Director, Developmental Disabilities Services.

(mm) Responsibilities shared by Administrator, Mental Health Division and Assistant Administrator, Mental Retardation & Developmental Disabilities Section.

(nn) Responsibilities shared by Executive Director, Fish Commission and Executive Director, Game Commission.

(oo) Responsibilities shared by Deputy Secretary for Children, Youth, & Their Families and Director, Office of Medical Assistance.

(pp) Responsibilities shared by Director, Mental Health, Retardation & Hospitals Department and Associate Director, Retardation Services.

(qq) Responsibilities shared by Auditor General and Director, Bureau of Audits.

(rr) Responsibilities shared by Commissioners of Department of Mental Health and Department of Mental Retardation.

(ss) Responsibilities shared by Executive Director of Department of Charities & Corrections and Administrator of Developmental Disabilities.

(tt) Speaker of the Senate has the statutory title of Lieutenant Governor, and is elected by the Senate from among its membership.

(uu) Responsibilities shared by Director, Division of Community Development and Deputy Director, Economic and Industrial Development Division.

SELECTED OFFICIALS: METHODS OF SELECTION—Continued

State	Pre-audit	Public library	Public utility regula-tion	Public welfare	Pur-chasing	Revenue	Social services	Solid waste manage-ment	State police	Tourism	Transpor-tation
Alabama	(a-12)	B	SE	G	CS	G	(a-35)	A	G	G	G
Alaska	A	A	GB	AG	(a-22)	AG	(a-23)	GB	A	A	GB
Arizona	AG	B	CE	(a-6)	AG	GS	GS	(a-19)	A	GS	GS
Arkansas	A	B	GS	(a-38)	AG	AG	AG	(a-19)	AG	(a-30)	(a-24)
California	(a-12)	GS	GS	(a-38)	GS	BS	GS	B	GS	G	GS
Colorado	(a-12)	A	GS	(a-38)	A	GS	GS	A	A	B	...
Connecticut	(a-12)	B	GB	GE	A	GE	GE	CS	GE	CS	GE
Delaware	(a-33)	AG	GS	GS	AG	AG	(l)	(m)	A	AG	GS
Florida	A	A	GS	A	A	GOC	A	GS	G	A	GS
Georgia	(a-33)	A	CE	A	A	GS	(a-35)	A	BG	A	B
Hawaii	A	B	GS	A	A	GS	GS	(a-19)	...	(a-15)	GS
Idaho	(a-12)	B	GS	GB	A	GS	GS	A	A	(a-10)	BGS
Illinois	(a-12)	A	G	GS	(a-6)	GS	A	(a-29)	GS	(a-10)	GS
Indiana	(a-12)	B	G	G	(a-6)	G	(a-35)	A	G	A	G
Iowa	(a-33)	...	(a-10)	A	CS	GS	GB	(a-19)	GS	GS	GD
Kansas	(a-12)	GS	GS	GS	A	GS	GS	(a-19)	GS	A	GS
Kentucky	(a-20)	G	G	AG	A	G	AG	AG	AG	G	G
Louisiana	(a-9)	B	CE	GS	(a-6)	GS	(a-35)	A	GS	GS	GS
Maine	(a-12)	BG	GS	A	AGS	AG	(a-35)	(a-19)	AG	(a-10)	GLS
Maryland	A	A	GS	(a-38)	CS	(a-12)	AG	A	GS	G	GS
Massachusetts	(a-12)	A	G	G	A	G	G	A	G	A	G
Michigan	(a-33)	...	GS	(a-38)	CS	AG	GS	(a-19)	GS	GS	GS
Minnesota	GS	A	GS	GS	A	GS	GS	A	A	A	GS
Mississippi	(a-33)	B	SE	G	A	GS	(a-35)	A	GS	A	(a-18)
Missouri	(a-12)	B	GS	A	A	GS	GS	A	GS	B	(a-24)
Montana	...	B	SE	(a-38)	A	GS	GS	A	AT	A	B
Nebraska	(a-6)	B	CE	(a-38)	A	GS	A	(a-19)	G	A	(a-24)
Nevada	(a-6)	G	G	A	(a-22)	G	G	(a-19)	A	G	B
New Hampshire	(a-6)	B	GC	A	AGC	GC	GC	A	GC	A	(a-24)
New Jersey	...	A	GS	AB	A	GS	GS	A	GS	A	GS
New Mexico	A	A	GS	A	GS	G	G	(a-19)	GD	A	GS
New York	(a-12)	(a-16)	GS	(a-38)	(a-22)	(a-4)	GS	(a-19)	GS	(a-10)	GS
North Carolina	(a-12)	G	GB	G	AG	G	G	G	G	A	G
North Dakota	(hh)	A	CE	G	A	CE	G	A	G	B	A
Ohio	(a-12)	B	GS	(a-38)	A	GS	GS	GS	AG	A	GS
Oklahoma	(a-20)	B	CE	(a-38)	A	GS	GS	A	GS	(a-30)	B
Oregon	...	B	G	AG	A	GS	GS	A	GS	A	BS
Pennsylvania	(a-4)	A	GS	A	(a-22)	(a-20)	(oo)	CS	GS	(a-10)	GS
Rhode Island	A	GS	GS	A	CS	CS	GS	B	G	A	GS
South Carolina	(a-12)	B	GS	(a-38)	B	GS	B	B	B	A	(a-24)
South Dakota	...	B	SE	AG	A	GS	GS	(a-19)	AG	A	GS
Tennessee	A	A	SE	G	A	G	A	A	A	G	G
Texas	(a-12)	B	GS	(a-38)	(a-22)	(a-12)	BS	A	B	B	(a-24)
Utah	(a-20)	AB	GS	GS	AG	GS	GS	A	AG	AB	GS
Vermont	(a-20)	G	GS	GS	G	GS	GS	A	A	A	GS
Virginia	(a-12)	GB	(a-8)	(a-38)	A	GB	GB	A	GB	A	GB
Washington	...	B	GS	(xx)	A	GS	(a-23)	A	GS	A	B
West Virginia	(a-20)	B	GS	GS	A	GS	A	B	GS	A	A
Wisconsin	A	A	GS	(a-38)	A	GS	GS	A	GS	A	GS
Wyoming	(a-33)	B	GS	A	A	G	(a-35)	G	AB	G	...

(vv) Responsibilities shared by Director, Mental Health Division and Director, Services to the Handicapped.

(ww) Responsibilities shared by Directors of Division of Mental Health and Division of Developmental Disabilities.

(xx) Responsibilities shared by Secretary of Department of Social and Health Services and Director, Division of Income Assistance in same department.

(yy) Responsibilities shared by Commissioner, Department of Finance & Administration and Director, Budget Division, Department of Finance & Administration.

(zz) Responsibilities shared by Director, Office of Community and Industrial Development and Director of Community Affairs in the same office.

(aaa) Responsibilities shared by Director, Office of Community and Industrial Development and Director of Economic Development in the same department.

(bbb) Responsibilities shared by Administrator, Trade & Consumer Protection Division and Assistant Attorney General, Office of Consumer Protection.

Table 2.11
SELECTED STATE ADMINISTRATIVE OFFICIALS: ANNUAL SALARIES

State or other jurisdiction	Governor	Lieutenant governor	Secretary of state	Attorney general	Treasurer	Adjutant general(a)	Administration	Agriculture	Banking	Budget
Alabama	$63,839	$27,975 (b)	$32,928	$58,000	$45,000	$52,848	...	$49,152	$52,848	$40,118
Alaska	85,728	79,992	...	66,816	64,620	66,816	$66,816	62,508	62,508	66,816
Arizona	62,500	...	35,000	56,250	37,500	40,456	58,411	40,456	40,456	44,365
Arkansas	35,000	14,000	22,500	26,500	22,500	45,895	64,880	(h)	58,000	27,066
California	49,100	42,500	42,500	47,500	42,500	68,699	...	83,383	78,207	(c-20)
Colorado	60,000	32,000	32,000	40,000	32,000	78,996	64,710	66,530	55,680	64,525
Connecticut	65,000	40,000	35,000	50,000	35,000	49,379	64,958	49,379	52,268	46,469
Delaware	70,000	30,000	50,000	52,330	34,000	45,000	49,900	42,200	50,900	59,200
Florida	78,757	68,458	67,246	67,246	67,246	68,011	54,500	67,246	(c-12)	58,,850
Georgia	79,356	48,150	60,500	62,000	(c-20)	68,011	58,500	60,500	58,500	64,542
Hawaii	59,400	53,460	...	50,490	(c-9)	78,472	...	50,490	44,124	50,490
Idaho	50,000	14,000	37,500	42,000	37,500	61,900	48,484	49,690	45,925	49,545
Illinois	58,000	45,500	50,500	50,500	48,000	37,000	62,500	60,000	60,000	67,104
Indiana	65,988	50,986	45,994	51,012	34,008	39,520	47,554	32,604	43,316	47,554
Iowa	64,000	21,900	41,000	54,000	41,000	54,550	44,000	41,000	43,100	(c-12)
Kansas	65,000	18,216	50,000	57,500	50,000	46,116	60,984	56,052	40,863	57,456
Kentucky	61,200	52,028	52,028	52,028	52,028	60,700	60,700	52,000	52,000	(c-20)
Louisiana	73,400	63,366	60,169	66,561	60,168	70,000	66,492	60,168	50,000	52,908
Maine	35,000	...	32,531	47,091	32,531	36,483	...	41,246	38,875	36,483
Maryland	75,000	62,500	45,000	62,500	62,500	50,196	(c-31)	66,500	51,400	66,500
Massachusetts	75,000	60,000	60,000	65,000	60,000	68,011	73,549	39,064	42,467	54,557
Michigan	85,800	58,850	75,000	75,000	65,700	56,000	66,000	60,000	55,100	65,700
Minnesota	84,560	46,510	46,510	66,060	44,000	54,935	60,000	59,774	51,386	(c-20)
Mississippi	63,000	34,000	45,000	51,000	45,000	42,000	...	45,000	41,000	53,493
Missouri	81,000	48,600	64,800	70,200	64,800	39,290	70,200	62,100	62,100	47,759
Montana	50,452	36,141	33,342	46,016	25,263	50,500	50,500	50,500	27,578	50,500
Nebraska	40,000	32,000	32,000	39,500	32,000	43,692	49,500	38,352	50,393	45,809
Nevada	65,000	10,500	42,250	52,500	41,000	36,381	48,537	39,608	38,333	(c-6)
New Hampshire	62,880	...	34,437	56,133	34,437	44,167	56,133	40,122	44,167	(c-6)
New Jersey	85,000	...	68,640	70,000	70,000	67,500	65,000	68,640	70,000	67,500
New Mexico	60,000	38,500	38,500	44,000	38,500	48,720	(c-22)	43,128	43,128	47,400
New York	100,000	85,000	75,445	85,000	79,435	75,445	(c-22)	75,445	75,445	83,500
North Carolina	98,196	58,140	58,140	58,140	58,140	55,656	58,140	58,140	55,920	67,572
North Dakota	60,862	49,992	43,380	52,000	46,000	69,280	(c-31)	45,996	42,996	(jj)
Ohio	65,000	35,000	50,000	50,000	50,000	55,910	66,684	48,214	41,350	59,196
Oklahoma	70,128	43,944	37,500	54,996	50,004	68,016	...	48,300	57,000	(c-20)
Oregon	72,000	...	52,826	60,000	52,826	50,304	61,152	55,416	50,304	55,416
Pennsylvania	75,000	57,500	58,000	65,000	58,000	48,000	59,000	58,000	58,000	59,000
Rhode Island	49,500	35,500	35,500	41,875	35,500	34,872	55,626	27,103	34,872	49,584
South Carolina	60,000	35,000	55,000	55,000	55,000	55,000	(c-9)	55,000	(c-4)	66,939
South Dakota	55,120	7,670	37,440	46,800	37,440	50,003	44,990	46,800	38,147	(c-20)
Tennessee	68,200	(vv)	62,500	57,403	62,500	55,000	62,500	53,000	55,000	32,640
Texas	94,350	7,200	64,890	73,235	73,270	55,825	...	73,230	79,300	58,900
Utah	60,009	50,007	...	49,005	44,996	56,418	53,850	50,342	48,108	49,152
Vermont	60,000	25,002	35,006	44,990	35,006	36,712	51,314	37,336	37,336	42,952
Virginia	75,000	20,000	45,959	56,000	66,089	46,481	73,751	60,902	65,285	67,580
Washington	63,000	28,600	31,000	47,100	37,200	68,012	63,800	63,800	42,672	(c-20)
West Virginia	72,000	...	43,200	50,400	50,400	34,000	(c-31)	46,800	36,500	(aaa)
Wisconsin	75,337	41,390	37,334	58,139	37,334	44,424	69,347	61,736	53,000	58,884
Wyoming	70,000	...	52,500	48,900	52,500	51,955	50,127	40,143	38,209	43,222
Dist. of Col.	81,380 (eee)	...	65,930	65,930	65,930	(fff)	72,300	...	...	65,930
American Samoa	50,000	45,000	...	35,000	35,000	...	33,000	33,000	38,000	35,000
Guam	50,000	45,000	...	40,838	18,798	45,000	36,838	34,838	(c-37)	36,838
No. Mariana Is.(jjj)	20,000	18,000	...	36,000	21,095	...	36,000	(c-29)	(c-10)	35,000
Puerto Rico	35,000	...	49,500	40,000	40,000	39,500	(c-31)	40,000	65,000	40,000
Virgin Islands	52,400	47,000	...	43,500	38,646	38,640	38,640	34,865	33,000	38,640

Source: The Council of State Governments' survey of state personnel agencies, 1985.

Note: The chief administrative officials responsible for each function were determined from information given by the states for the same functions as listed in State Administrative Officials Classified by Function 1985-86, published by The Council of State Governments. Salary figures (as of January 1986) are presented as submitted by the states for these same officials except when ranges were given. In those instances, the minimum figure was chosen. When necessary, figures have been rounded to the nearest dollar.

Key:
N.A.—Not available
. . .—No specific chief administrative official or agency in charge of function.
(a) Salary listed may be of military grade.
(b) $10/day for 105 days (compensation while legislature is in regular session); $85/day for 105 days (expense compensation while legislature

is in regular session); $1,500/month (annual office expenses).
(c) Chief administrative official or agency in charge of function:
(c-1) Lieutenant governor
(c-2) Secretary of state
(c-3) Attorney general
(c-4) Treasurer
(c-5) Adjutant general
(c-6) Administration
(c-7) Agriculture
(c-8) Banking
(c-9) Budget
(c-10) Commerce
(c-11) Community affairs
(c-12) Comptroller
(c-13) Computer services
(c-14) Consumer affairs
(c-15) Economic development

State or other jurisdiction	Civil rights	Commerce	Community affairs	Comptroller	Computer services	Consumer affairs	Corrections	Economic development	Education	Elections administration
Alabama	...	$52,848	$56,602	$40,118	$40,118	$42,189	$63,792	$52,848	$74,749	(c-2)
Alaska	$62,508	66,816	66,816	56,244	62,508	60,252	66,816	66,816	66,816	$62,508
Arizona	48,618	(f)	(c-32)	(c-20)	44,365	48,618	58,411	(f)	45,000	(c-2)
Arkansas	...	54,894	35,430	(c-6)	58,691	42,215	58,648	(c-10)	63,953	(c-2)
California	69,006	48,768	53,652	42,500	64,596	69,006	78,207	(c-10)	42,500	(c-2)
Colorado	53,028	55,680	58,464	58,464	58,464	53,028	66,870	43,632	81,000	47,064
Connecticut	52,268	(c-15)	42,971	35,000	49,379	55,786	60,057	55,786	60,057	41,310
Delaware	...	(c-2)	50,000	55,000	53,700	(c-11)	60,000	60,000	80,100	32,300
Florida	33,531	(c-1)	65,000	67,246	53,500	43,395	66,500	46,000	67,246	46,512
Georgia	...	64,542	64,542	60,500	56,344	49,182	58,500	(c-10)	65,646	50,356
Hawaii	...	50,490	(c-15)	50,490	36,588	44,550	44,550	50,490	50,490	33,300
Idaho	27,643	39,870	...	37,500	(c-6)	(c-3)	46,175	(c-10)	37,500	(c-2)
Illinois	52,000	60,000	(c-10)	48,000	(c-6)	(c-3)	60,000	(c-10)	90,000	35,820
Indiana	32,604	(c-1)	35,932	34,008	39,520	32,604	47,554	35,932	47,554	28,678
Iowa	21,800	47,400	39,395	54,600	48,651	45,700	54,600	40,500	54,600	26,000
Kansas	36,132	53,496	43,920	58,860	51,710	(c-3)	57,708	(c-10)	67,572	(c-2)
Kentucky	50,100	60,700	45,800	(c-20)	(c-20)	(c-3)	60,700	49,800	52,000	(c-2)
Louisiana	(c-3)	53,353	52,366	(c-6)	51,156	32,445	55,000	(c-10)	60,168	60,169
Maine	27,310	41,246	...	36,483	32,510	38,875	41,246	(c-10)	41,246	(c-2)
Maryland	54,100	49,300	46,700	62,500	51,400	51,400	56,300	45,200	68,500	49,300
Massachusetts	39,064	46,170	60,178	46,170	50,191	57,935	54,557	63,492	54,557	45,000
Michigan	56,600	64,100	25,000	(c-4)	40,319	47,210	64,100	25,000	70,900	36,248
Minnesota	52,000	60,000	59,654	(c-20)	57,858	48,500	59,774	59,654	68,640	(c-2)
Mississippi	...	(c-15)	(c-32)	(c-33)	44,936	40,052	40,000	57,083	60,005	N.A.
Missouri	42,634	(c-15)	(c-15)	46,105	46,105	62,100	62,100	39,290	70,200	36,000
Montana	27,578	50,500	30,123	(c-6)	35,957	27,578	50,500	30,123	39,672	30,472
Nebraska	51,660	41,165	32,508	(c-6)	46,344	N.A.	54,612	...	64,896	(c-2)
Nevada	31,344	46,391	36,761	41,000	43,875	29,085	55,456	47,238	51,980	(c-2)
New Hampshire	28,567	(c-15)	(c-32)	44,167	50,143	(c-3)	47,898	41,917	56,133	(c-2)
New Jersey	50,888	70,000	68,640	(c-9)	43,960	53,433	70,000	53,000	70,000	(ee)
New Mexico	N.A.	52,260	52,260	(c-4)	50,088	43,128	52,260	43,128	57,456	34,440
New York	68,620	75,445	(c-2)	85,000	(c-22)	63,475	85,000	(c-10)	85,000	68,620
North Carolina	43,848	58,140	36,144	N.A.	69,756	41,808	58,140	48,972	58,140	61,332
North Dakota	(c-27)	(c-15)	32,004	(jj)	49,584	26,700	43,968	42,000	47,000	(c-2)
Ohio	36,316	56,188	51,500	(c-4)	47,424	51,792	N.A.	50,960	78,748	(c-2)
Oklahoma	37,704	(c-15)	45,648	48,792	49,380	40,356	60,000	51,600	54,996	52,500
Oregon	41,352	55,416	50,304	50,304	50,304	50,304	55,416	39,396	52,826	50,304
Pennsylvania	40,959	61,500	48,000	52,000	37,575	39,218	61,500	(c-10)	65,000	30,240
Rhode Island	27,103	(c-15)	...	41,530	39,517	26,077	55,626	51,599	70,000	(dd)
South Carolina	49,574	67,699	45,000	55,000	(c-22)	53,291	59,849	(c-10)	55,000	48,210
South Dakota	30,222	46,800	(c-15)	37,440	(c-6)	29,600	45,219	33,280	48,755	(c-2)
Tennessee	27,372	(c-15)	(c-15)	62,500	32,640	26,196	55,000	62,000	62,000	34,116
Texas	48,200	58,900	52,220	73,230	56,820	55,475	68,290	55,930	67,360	49,230
Utah	40,841	56,418	(ww)	(c-20)	63,934	29,462	59,675	43,347	49,465	(c-1)
Vermont	44,990	(c-15)	34,299	(c-20)	40,747	44,900	40,851	37,336	50,190	(c-2)
Virginia	...	73,571	55,365	65,130	67,502	29,897	67,580	71,700	77,903	47,260
Washington	53,800	71,000	55,700	(c-4)	60,400	29,460	66,564	39,624	42,800	28,752
West Virginia	36,564	65,000	(bbb)	46,800	45,360	38,850	36,500	(ccc)	70,000	(c-2)
Wisconsin	49,730	(c-1)	44,032	45,884	51,178	(ddd)	61,510	44,032	66,536	43,616
Wyoming	43,222	(c-15)	(c-15)	(c-33)	43,222	33,737	43,222	40,143	52,500	(c-2)
Dist. of Col.	61,978	65,930	44,928	61,978	52,847	(ggg)	65,930	61,928	81,380	65,930
American Samoa	...	(c-15)	(c-15)	(c-4)	31,621	33,300	15,098	33,000	35,000	(c-3)
Guam	(c-3)	34,838	(c-15)	(c-6)	(c-6)	(c-3)	34,838	34,838	36,000	31,000
No. Mariana Is.(jjj)	...	36,000	30,000	(c-20)	30,000	(c-3)	16,530	(c-10)	30,000	17,800
Puerto Rico	32,000	40,000	35,000	42,000	(c-22)	40,000	38,000	N.A.	40,000	42,500
Virgin Islands	18,500	43,500	29,019	34,570	36,810	34,778	34,779	38,000	38,640	35,000

(c-16) Education (chief state school officer)
(c-17) Employment services
(c-18) Energy resources
(c-19) Environmental protection
(c-20) Finance
(c-21) Fish and wildlife
(c-22) General services
(c-23) Health
(c-24) Highways
(c-25) Historic preservation
(c-26) Insurance
(c-27) Labor
(c-28) Mental health and retardation
(c-29) Natural resources
(c-30) Parks and recreation
(c-31) Personnel
(c-32) Planning
(c-33) Post audit

(c-34) Public utility regulation
(c-35) Public welfare
(c-36) Purchasing
(c-37) Revenue
(c-38) Social services
(c-39) Solid waste management
(c-40) Transportation
(d) Responsibilities shared by Receiver of the Department of Mental Health, $52,848, and Associate Commissioner of the Mental Retardation Division of the same department, $54,002.
(e) Responsibilities shared by Director, $62,508, and Program Administrator, $52,584, of the Mental Health and Development Disabilities Division of the Health and Social Services Department.
(f) Responsibilities shared by Director of Department of Commerce, $48,618, and Director of Development Division, $40,456.
(g) Responsibilities shared by Assistant Director of Community Behavioral Health Services, Department of Health Services, $48,618, and Director, Disabilities Division, Department of Economic Security, $48,618.

State or other jurisdiction	Emergency management	Employment services	Energy resources	Environmental protection	Finance	Fish & wildlife	General services	Health	Higher education	Highways
Alabama	$52,848	$37,232	$46,776	$52,848	$52,848	(c-29)	$32,136	$96,168	$74,749	$52,848
Alaska	62,508	58,296	62,508	66,816	56,244	$66,816	62,508	66,816	66,816	(c-40)
Arizona	33,684	48,618	36,922	48,618	48,618	44,365	58,411	63,992	48,500	(c-40)
Arkansas	35,310	61,262	46,044	44,938	(c-6)	52,412	(c-6)	65,777	65,747	70,935
California	63,256	78,207	74,757	83,383	83,383	69,006	78,207	78,207	79,500	(c-40)
Colorado	55,680	58,464	21,400	58,464	(c-12)	N.A.	(c-6)	78,450	80,000	65,695
Connecticut	36,723	52,268	49,379	60,057	64,958	33,950	(c-6)	66,431	83,850	52,268
Delaware	31,000	(c-31)	43,400	55,000	65,000	37,900	(c-6)	60,000	42,800	(c-40)
Florida	40,425	49,609	47,236	59,302	39,576	55,562	59,404	37,000	97,000	(c-40)
Georgia	(c-5)	47,550	49,182	65,000	50,100	54,469	(c-6)	80,250	105,000	(c-40)
Hawaii	(c-5)	34,884	34,884	44,500	(c-9)	33,300	(c-12)	50,490	95,000	44,550
Idaho	39,875	54,787	66,622	49,545	(c-9)	56,140	41,870	57,033	58,240	(c-40)
Illinois	37,000	65,000	(c-29)	60,000	50,000	60,000	(c-6)	65,000	90,000	(c-40)
Indiana	28,678	43,316	35,932	47,554	(c-9)	28,678	(c-6)	47,554	79,976	47,554
Iowa	32,400	46,000	30,400	44,800	(c-12)	31,800	43,200	36,400	54,600	53,865
Kansas	37,944	59,280	37,944	55,000	(c-6)	43,920	(c-6)	N.A.	N.A.	(c-40)
Kentucky	44,100	44,500	60,700	60,700	60,700	47,500	(c-20)	75,300	73,200	56,600
Louisiana	35,954	43,841	53,584	54,000	(c-6)	52,366	(c-6)	63,327	78,479	49,931
Maine	29,370	32,510	36,483	41,246	41,246	41,246	(c-20)	41,240	(t)	(c-40)
Maryland	39,800	54,500	49,300	58,500	(c-12)	51,400	66,500	68,500	68,500	59,100
Massachusetts	36,254	33,569	55,692	63,492	(c-6)	42,467	(c-36)	54,557	65,000	(w)
Michigan	35,976	43,681	25,000	25,000	(c-9)	(c-29)	(c-9)	70,000	40,319	(c-40)
Minnesota	43,639	43,869	59,654	(x)	70,000	51,323	(c-6)	59,774	57,483	61,471
Mississippi	28,000	43,000	40,000	29,700	(c-9)	29,116	41,075	67,290	N.A.	45,000
Missouri	39,290	46,104	39,290	39,290	(c-6)	64,800	(c-6)	62,100	62,100	65,004
Montana	27,578	32,901	30,123	35,957	. . .	50,500	(c-6)	35,957	68,000	50,500
Nebraska	(c-5)	39,643	36,012	42,324	(aa)	65,652	(c-6)	59,712	N.A.	55,140
Nevada	33,247	43,700	. . .	40,564	(c-12)	40,564	45,046	43,533	87,000	(c-40)
New Hampshire	(dd)	50,143	30,401	. . .	(c-6)	41,917	(c-6)	54,640	32,939	56,133
New Jersey	65,124	48,465	68,640	70,000	(c-4)	48,465	(c-6)	70,000	70,000	(c-40)
New Mexico	28,324	52,260	52,260	52,260	52,260	46,368	52,260	52,260	40,128	52,260
New York	(c-5)	(c-27)	75,445	79,435	. . .	(c-19)	79,435	85,000	(c-16)	(c-40)
North Carolina	37,956	55,920	38,904	(c-29)	(c-9)	48,216	49,380	94,380	131,000	67,572
North Dakota	35,676	49,920	(c-11)	54,000	(jj)	41,304	(kk)	68,000	76,908	52,000
Ohio	34,403	53,456	44,990	61,006	(c-6)	39,915	(c-6)	68,515	87,588	(c-40)
Oklahoma	35,052	53,724	39,816	37,704	58,896	56,244	56,784	80,752	86,580	(c-40)
Oregon	37,524	55,416	55,416	55,416	(c-6)	52,776	55,416	50,304	85,020	58,236
Pennsylvania	37,575	51,700	40,959	55,000	51,500	(pp)	51,500	51,500	54,000	(c-40)
Rhode Island	(c-5)	51,599	(c-34)	51,599	47,570	30,353	37,500	72,347	78,865	(c-40)
South Carolina	43,303	65,223	33,753	63,229	(c-9)	62,971	58,797	77,028	65,899	70,286
South Dakota	31,034	31,450	32,178	37,814	60,008	46,800	(c-6)	43,596	59,529	44,949
Tennessee	29,892	29,892	32,640	32,640	(c-6)	55,000	53,000	58,500	80,000	(c-40)
Texas	41,328	57,630	60,975	. . .	. . .	48,720	56,860	66,640	65,920	68,700
Utah	56,418	43,242	37,458	54,476	53,850	41,948	(c-6)	77,298	85,000	(c-40)
Vermont	31,366	40,747	45,635	45,635	40,747	38,500	(c-6)	56,992	N.A.	(c-40)
Virginia	49,878	56,562	68,459	51,420	73,751	48,881	59,730	74,194	76,376	73,594
Washington	42,600	33,336	47,600	71,000	98,000	63,800	(c-6)	78,900	63,528	(c-40)
West Virginia	35,000	34,000	65,000	(c-29)	45,500	38,392	30,000	54,500	70,000	47,500
Wisconsin	38,891	51,000	44,978	51,235	56,468	38,802	45,410	61,195	81,120	60,594
Wyoming	29,785	39,165	26,998	42,161	(c-33)	48,900	(c-6)	55,327	60,000	51,375
Dist. of Col.	65,930	65,930	44,928	N.A.	(c-4)	. . .	65,930	65,930	(hhh)	61,978
American Samoa	20,009	. . .	30,000	27,361	(c-4)	30,000	30,000	35,504	(iii)	40,000
Guam	34,838	34,838	34,838	34,838	(c-6)	(c-7)	(c-6)	36,838	45,838	36,838
No. Mariana Is.(jjj)	26,500	(c-31)	36,000	36,000	30,000	27,000	(c-6)	44,000	30,000	30,000
Puerto Rico	33,000	18,210	40,000	38,000	(c-9)	(c-29)	38,000	40,000	44,000	38,000
Virgin Islands	27,674	33,171	36,005	36,000	(c-4)	26,447	36,000	43,058	0	31,000

(h) Responsibilities shared by Director, Veterinarian, Livestock and Poultry Commission, $41,739, and Director, Plant Board, $43,682, and International Marketing Representative, Marketing Division, Industrial Development Commission, $46,044.

(i) Responsibilities shared by Director, Department of Industrial Relations, $83,383, and Supervisor, Conciliation Service of the same department, $45,588.

(j) Responsibilities shared by Director, Department of Mental Health, $78,207, and Director, Developmental Services Department, $78,207.

(k) Responsibilities shared by Director, Division of Mental Health, $58,464, and Director, Division of Developmental Disabilities, $55,680.

(l) Responsibilities shared by Commissioner, Department of Mental Health, $66,431, and Commissioner, Department of Mental Retardation, $60,057.

(m) Responsibilities shared by Director, Division of Alcoholism, Drug Abuse & Mental Health, $55,100, and Director, Division of Mental Retardation, $56,900.

(n) Responsibilities shared by Secretary, Department of Services for Children, Youth, & Their Families, $55,000, and Secretary, Department of Health & Social Services, $60,000.

(o) Responsibilities shared by Chief of the Mental Health Division in the Department of Health, $57,816, and Chief of the Waimano Training School & Hospital, $34,884.

(p) Responsibilities shared by Chief, Bureau of Mental Health, $37,980, and Executive Director, Developmental Disabilities, $38,940, both in the Department of Health and Welfare.

(q) Responsibilities shared by Commissioner, $47,554, and Assistant Commissioner, Developmental Disabilities Division, $39,520, both in Department of Mental Health.

(r) Responsibilities shared by Director, Merit Employment Department, $42,600, and Head of Personnel, Office of State Comptroller, $35,000.

(s) Responsibilities shared by Deputy Assistant Secretary, Office of Mental Health, $74,196, and Assistant Secretary, Office of Mental Retardation, $48,960.

SELECTED OFFICIALS: ANNUAL SALARIES—Continued

State or other jurisdiction	Historic preservation	Insurance	Labor	Licensing	Mental health & retardation	Natural resources	Parks & recreation	Personnel	Planning	Post audit
Alabama	$45,000	$52,848	$52,848	...	(d)	$52,848	$34,554	$67,152	...	$65,904
Alaska	62,508	62,508	66,816	$62,508	(e)	66,816	62,508	62,508	$62,508	62,508
Arizona	28,128	40,456	44,365	...	(g)	53,297	36,922	48,618	40,456	44,365
Arkansas	22,282	50,080	53,399	...	(c-38)	39,496	49,482	27,066	...	58,226
California	51,168	78,207	(i)	(c-14)	(j)	69,006	69,006	68,460	59,844	(c-20)
Colorado	52,550	N.A.	69,040	64,525	(k)	71,725	55,680	64,525	(c-9)	57,128
Connecticut	33,950	52,268	55,786	44,680	(l)	(c-19)	36,723	52,268	42,971	54,364
Delaware	42,600	34,000	50,000	29,500	(m)	(c-19)	38,500	44,000	...	34,000
Florida	44,820	(c-4)	56,341	35,436	$53,500	59,402	44,966	49,600	(c-9)	37,000
Georgia	40,278	(c-12)	60,500	47,669	80,460	(c-19)	47,500	64,542	(c-9)	58,000
Hawaii	(c-29)	44,880	50,490	(c-10)	(o)	50,490	34,884	50,490	34,884	34,884
Idaho	42,910	38,000	45,000	38,940	(p)	...	45,070	50,920	(c-10)	42,910
Illinois	55,000	55,000	55,000	55,000	65,000	52,000	(c-21)	(c-6)	67,095	60,000
Indiana	21,502	43,316	35,932	35,932	(q)	47,554	32,604	47,554	35,932	47,554
Iowa	46,000	37,800	39,700	...	53,800	44,900	33,945	(r)	48,000	41,000
Kansas	25,680	50,000	(c-17)	...	56,052	(c-19)	47,268	54,720	(c-9)	N.A.
Kentucky	44,100	53,500	60,700	31,400	56,300	(c-19)	53,000	53,000	(c-6)	52,000
Louisiana	43,841	60,168	56,020	...	(s)	58,451	43,841	50,760	40,067	(c-9)
Maine	29,370	38,875	41,246	18,616	(u)	(c-19)	34,091	41,246	36,483	34,091
Maryland	39,600	57,700	54,500	66,500	(v)	66,500	51,400	66,500	66,500	60,000
Massachusetts	33,925	42,467	39,064	36,254	54,557	46,170	54,557	50,191	(c-11)	60,000
Michigan	25,000	55,100	55,100	60,000	70,700	43,681	43,681	25,000	...	69,500
Minnesota	75,000	59,774	59,774	33,721	56,961	59,774	54,246	59,774	60,000	50,740
Mississippi	37,000	45,000	...	...	(y)	42,536	38,299	44,268	37,172	45,000
Missouri	28,080	39,290	62,100	44,452	76,500	62,100	39,290	44,452	(c-9)	64,800
Montana	21,231	32,000	50,500	25,263	(z)	50,500	30,123	32,901	(c-11)	48,000
Nebraska	39,240	40,080	(bb)	32,876	(cc)	44,436	(c-21)	39,312	38,076	32,000
Nevada	30,679	38,333	32,594	...	51,088	45,167	34,506	42,797	...	43,000
New Hampshire	(c-29)	56,133	38,327	...	45,660	56,133	41,917	45,653	35,080	41,920
New Jersey	31,241	70,000	70,000	(c-14)	(ff)	63,780	50,000	39,873	70,000	63,000
New Mexico	34,440	39,876	37,980	52,260	(gg)	52,260	39,876	44,856	...	38,500
New York	(c-30)	75,445	79,435	(c-2)	(hh)	(c-19)	75,445	75,445	(ii)	(c-12)
North Carolina	25,980	58,140	58,140	...	94,884	58,140	41,760	58,140	N.A.	58,140
North Dakota	35,688	46,000	46,000	...	45,516	...	38,184	27,696	(c-11)	(ll)
Ohio	N.A.	55,140	53,456	...	(mm)	66,684	38,209	46,176	27,497	50,000
Oklahoma	35,052	50,004	37,500	...	(nn)	46,176	48,300	50,004	...	50,004
Oregon	33,996	50,304	52,826	(c-10)	(oo)	52,776	52,776	50,304	55,416	50,304
Pennsylvania	39,218	58,000	65,000	32,998	51,500	(c-19)	37,575	39,218	49,000	58,000
Rhode Island	28,174	34,872	45,556	25,093	(rr)	(c-19)	31,463	39,517	37,500	(ss)
South Carolina	44,666	63,766	52,312	...	(tt)	(c-18)	52,312	56,275	60,695	61,765
South Dakota	32,947	33,092	46,800	46,800	(uu)	54,995	28,995	43,680	...	38,563
Tennessee	22,968	55,000	53,000	22,968	55,000	55,000	29,892	55,000	50,688	(c-12)
Texas	46,970	60,875	55,000	...	72,610	...	(c-21)	...	58,900	68,965
Utah	44,495	48,630	50,342	43,034	(xx)	52,638	44,892	48,588	(c-9)	37,646
Vermont	28,517	(c-8)	37,336	(c-2)	50,960	(c-19)	37,336	40,747	42,640	35,006
Virginia	(c-29)	(c-8)	52,434	45,764	74,818	52,934	35,730	63,220	(c-9)	43,930
Washington	42,600	37,200	63,800	35,028	(yy)	42,800	60,400	63,800	(c-20)	37,200
West Virginia	25,800	35,000	34,000	...	(c-23)	45,500	45,000	36,500	63,000	30,400
Wisconsin	36,187	47,250	70,483	53,002	58,274	71,875	49,484	66,079	(c-9)	59,825
Wyoming	(c-30)	35,464	33,737	...	38,209	...	40,143	43,222	36,358	52,520
Dist. of Col.	38,018	52,847	(c-17)	52,847	52,847	...	61,978	65,930	65,930	65,930
American Samoa	18,155	24,000	...	...	17,986	...	33,000	35,000	(c-15)	33,000
Guam	(c-30)	(c-37)	34,838	(c-37)	34,838	(c-7)	34,838	(c-6)	34,838	(c-9)
No. Mariana Is.(jjj)	25,000	...	(c-10)	(c-10)	(c-23)	30,000	18,223	36,000	(c-9)	36,000
Puerto Rico	35,000	38,000	...	13,224	30,324	40,000	40,000	39,500	40,000	(c-12)
Virgin Islands	31,631	(c-8)	34,776	22,002	35,000	35,178	23,525	34,776	36,000	34,783

(t) Expenses only.

(u) Responsibilities shared by Director, Bureau of Mental Health, $31,096, and Director, Bureau of Mental Retardation, $31,096.

(v) Responsibilities shared by Director, Mental Retardation & Developmental Disabilities, $51,400, and Director, Mental Hygiene Administration, $67,808.

(w) Responsibilities shared by Secretary, $28,844, and Commissioner, $54,557, of the Department of Public Works.

(x) Responsibilities shared by Executive Director, Pollution Control Agency, $59,774, and Executive Director, Environmental Quality Board, $44,454.

(y) Responsibilities shared by Director, Department of Mental Health, $54,000, and Director, Mental Retardation Division, $37,140.

(z) Responsibilities shared by Administrator, Mental Health Division, $39,310, and Administrator, Developmental Disabilities Division, $30,123.

(aa) Responsibilities shared by the following administrative officials: Director of Department of Administrative Services, listed under Administration; State Budget Administrator of the Budget Division within the same department, listed under Budget; Auditor of Public Accounts, listed under Post Audit; and State Tax Commissioner of the Department of Revenue, listed under Taxation.

(bb) Responsibilities shared by Commissioner, Labor Department, $40,080, and Clerk, Commission of Industrial Relations, per diem.

(cc) Responsibilities shared by Director, Medical Services, $74,470, and Director, Office of Mental Retardation, $63,120.

(dd) Per diem rate. In New Hampshire, Director of State Civil Defense, $131.25/day. In Rhode Island, Chairman of Board of Elections, $50/day.

(ee) Responsibilities shared by Director, Elections Division, Department of State, $36,166, and Executive Director, Election Law Enforcement Commission.

(ff) Responsibilities shared by Director, Mental Health & Hospitals Divison, $61,855, and Director, Mental Retardation Division, $58,910, both in the Department of Human Services.

(gg) Responsibilities shared by Chief, Mental Health Bureau, $39,000,

State or other jurisdiction	Pre-audit	Public library	Public utility regula-tion	Public welfare	Pur-chasing	Revenue	Social services	Solid waste manage-ment	State police	Tourism	Transpor-tation
Alabama	(c-12)	$50,688	$44,550	$52,848	$40,118	$52,848	(c-35)	$37,323	$29,094	$52,848	$37,232
Alaska	$43,080	62,508	62,508	62,508	(c-22)	62,508	(c-23)	58,296	62,508	62,508	66,816
Arizona	40,456	36,922	48,618	(c-6)	40,456	58,411	$48,618	(c-19)	53,297	36,922	63,992
Arkansas	23,764	45,237	49,482	(c-38)	27,066	50,140	64,880	(c-19)	44,370	(c-30)	(c-24)
California	(c-12)	61,908	74,757	(c-38)	58,980	78,207	78,207	74,757	83,383	53,652	78,207
Colorado	(c-12)	51,428	48,400	(c-38)	58,464	67,785	69,040	50,508	58,464	35,124	. . .
Connecticut	(c-12)	39,721	56,839	55,786	49,379	52,268	55,786	39,721	55,786	35,309	64,958
Delaware	(c-33)	33,500	36,800	55,500	38,500	54,300	(n)	N.A.	47,300	N.A.	60,000
Florida	43,500	43,600	56,123	33,373	44,828	63,089	53,500	36,480	59,403	46,200	66,929
Georgia	(c-33)	57,318	58,000	61,200	53,310	58,500	(c-35)	49,950	64,542	42,084	86,625
Hawaii	34,884	44,550	47,520	34,884	30,288	50,490	50,490	(c-19)	. . .	(c-15)	50,490
Idaho	(c-12)	41,185	36,500	47,050	18,260	34,500	42,910	36,170	51,230	(c-10)	61,900
Illinois	(c-12)	47,004	65,000	65,000	(c-6)	65,000	60,000	(c-29)	60,000	(c-10)	65,000
Indiana	(c-12)	32,604	47,554	47,554	(c-6)	47,554	(c-35)	26,546	47,554	32,604	43,316
Iowa	(c-33)	. . .	(c-10)	46,488	40,019	54,600	54,600	(c-19)	42,200	32,048	54,600
Kansas	(c-12)	47,268	N.A.	42,876	46,116	59,820	63,732	(c-19)	47,268	37,944	59,820
Kentucky	(c-20)	45,800	52,100	54,600	53,300	60,700	55,700	42,200	55,600	60,700	60,700
Louisiana	(c-9)	48,712	61,536	42,624	(c-6)	52,366	(c-35)	49,000	52,000	43,841	58,454
Maine	(c-12)	34,091	48,400	28,309	34,091	38,875	(c-35)	(c-19)	36,483	(c-10)	41,246
Maryland	51,400	52,097	57,500	(c-38)	41,741	(c-12)	54,500	48,800	53,000	43,600	68,500
Massachusetts	(c-12)	37,470	39,064	54,557	42,467	54,557	73,549	36,254	46,170	33,569	63,492
Michigan	(c-33)	. . .	58,700	(c-38)	25,000	51,000	64,100	(c-19)	64,100	25,000	64,100
Minnesota	57,858	45,017	47,000	47,084	46,583	60,000	56,961	54,246	50,363	58,777	70,000
Mississippi	(c-33)	37,000	40,000	45,000	36,984	50,000	(c-35)	41,910	40,000	27,008	(c-18)
Missouri	(c-12)	36,000	62,100	47,759	44,452	70,200	64,800	33,705	59,443	39,290	(c-24)
Montana	. . .	30,123	37,363	(c-38)	27,578	50,500	50,500	27,578	43,807	27,578	30,123
Nebraska	(c-6)	42,024	25,740	(c-38)	36,051	48,540	51,180	(c-19)	41,228	29,871	(c-24)
Nevada	(c-6)	38,451	47,601	45,980	(c-22)	43,098	53,453	(c-19)	39,381	44,356	53,360
New Hampshire	(c-6)	41,917	56,133	44,167	42,221	56,133	56,133	29,913	41,917	41,917	(c-24)
New Jersey	. . .	. . .	54,843	68,640	58,910	58,910	61,855	70,000	56,104	65,124	52,310	70,000
New Mexico	41,472	36,168	50,088	33,720	41,472	52,260	40,128	(c-19)	52,260	43,128	52,260
New York	(c-12)	(c-16)	79,435	(c-38)	(c-22)	(c-4)	79,435	(c-19)	79,435	(c-10)	85,000
North Carolina	(c-12)	53,076	59,140	58,140	57,024	58,140	61,332	32,220	58,392	41,808	58,140
North Dakota	(jj)	37,500	46,000	64,248	N.A.	46,000	35,352	42,600	45,960	32,520	40,356
Ohio	(c-12)	48,526	61,006	(c-38)	47,840	52,312	58,593	33,155	42,993	33,508	65,769
Oklahoma	(c-20)	39,996	47,340	(c-38)	48,300	52,332	69,504	40,548	49,356	(c-30)	60,000
Oregon	. . .	45,600	61,152	55,416	45,600	55,416	61,152	39,396	55,416	39,396	61,152
Pennsylvania	(c-4)	31,609	42,500	55,000	(c-22)	(c-20)	(qq)	36,088	61,500	(c-10)	55,000
Rhode Island	24,148	41,530	41,530	37,500	45,556	47,750	55,626	28,174	69,404	29,241	55,626
South Carolina	(c-12)	42,124	50,510	(c-38)	58,294	55,566	67,090	53,349	54,438	51,265	(c-24)
South Dakota	. . .	31,491	29,182	43,555	30,000	46,800	57,200	(c-19)	46,134	36,005	50,003
Tennessee	32,640	50,688	54,696	53,000	29,892	53,000	32,640	28,608	53,000	53,000	58,500
Texas	(c-12)	48,400	55,620	(c-38)	(c-22)	(c-12)	68,300	47,790	66,640	45,730	(c-24)
Utah	(c-20)	47,627	50,342	46,437	41,530	63,141	59,675	54,476	34,494	44,495	58,965
Vermont	(c-20)	31,346	49,150	43,992	34,986	41,163	30,534	40,248	46,509	42,931	45,635
Virginia	(c-12)	53,869	(c-8)	(c-38)	29,897	67,434	62,716	38,150	53,869	39,058	73,571
Washington	. . .	60,400	60,400	(zz)	37,716	63,800	(c-23)	38,664	63,800	39,624	78,900
West Virginia	(c-20)	56,158	42,732	45,500	39,000	47,500	37,535	34,928	42,500	45,000	28,312
Wisconsin	42,552	54,889	58,000	(c-38)	41,880	63,843	71,328	50,434	59,830	44,032	66,041
Wyoming	(c-33)	34,590	44,303	42,161	41,142	46,550	(c-35)	31,303	38,229	34,590	. . .
Dist. of Col.	(c-4)	65,930	61,978	65,930	52,847	65,930	65,930	61,978	65,930	N.A.	65,930
American Samoa	. . .	19,806	. . .	. . .	(c-22)	31,503	. . .	18,000	35,000	30,000	33,000
Guam	(c-9)	34,838	27,000	(c-23)	(c-6)	36,838	(c-23)	(c-24)	36,838	34,000	30,000
No. Mariana Is.(jjj)	(c-33)	13,601	N.A.	30,000	23,256	20,093	. . .	(c-24)	5,700	36,000	(c-24)
Puerto Rico	(c-4)	16,368	38,000	(c-38)	. . .	23,556	40,000	. . .	21,048	52,000	13,896
Virgin Islands	(c-12)	36,810	27,250	23,061	24,170	38,640	36,000	25,226	38,640	37,906	34,783

and Chief, Developmental Disabilities Bureau, $35,400.

(hh) Responsibilities shared by Commissioner, Office of Mental Health, $85,000, and Commissioner, Mental Retardation & Developmental Disabilities, $85,000.

(ii) No central planning agency. Responsibilities shared among the Departments of Commerce, State, and Transportation, and the State Energy Office, whose department heads' salaries range from the mid-$70,000s to the mid-$80,000s.

(jj) Responsibilities shared by Director of the Office of Management and Budget, $57,204, and Executive Budget Analyst of the same office, $48.876, the Director of Management and Budget is also responsible for the function Pre-Audit.

(kk) Responsibilities shared by Director, Office of Budget & Management, $57,204, and Director of Institutions, salary not available.

(ll) Responsibilities shared by the Legislative Budget Analyst and Auditor, $52,536, and the State Auditor, $46,000.

(mm) Responsibilities shared by Director, Department of Mental Health, $54,017, and Director, Department of Mental Retardation, $65,769.

(nn) Responsibilities shared by Director, Mental Health Department, $86,736, and Director, Developmental Disabilities Services, $55,200.

(oo) Responsibilities shared by Administrator, Mental Health Division, $55,416, and Assistant Administrator, Mental Retardation & Developmental Disabilities Section, $45,600.

(pp) Responsibilities shared by Executive Director, Fish Commission, $39,218, and Executive Director, Game Commission, $32,998.

(qq) Responsibilities shared by Deputy Secretary for Children, Youth, & Their Families, $48,500, and Director, Office of Medical Assistance, $52,400.

(rr) Responsibilities shared by Director, Mental Health, Retardation & Hospitals Department, $57,639, and Associate Director, Retardation Services, $43,544.

(ss) Responsibilities shared by Auditor General, $55,850, and Director, Bureau of Audits, $37,500.

SELECTED OFFICIALS: ANNUAL SALARIES—Continued

(tt) Responsibilities shared by Commissioners of Department of Mental Health, $74,818, and Department of Mental Retardation, $65,629.

(uu) Responsibilities shared by Executive Director of Department of Charities & Corrections, listed under Corrections, and Administrator of Developmental Disabilities, $34,715.

(vv) Speaker of the Senate has the statutory title of Lieutenant Governor.

(ww) Responsibilities shared by Director, Division of Community Development, $51,511, and Deputy Director, Economic and Industrial Development Division, $43,347.

(xx) Responsibilities shared by Director, Mental Health Division, $56,418, and Director, Services to the Handicapped, $39,108.

(yy) Responsibilities shared by Directors of Division of Mental Health, $44,832 ($69,924, if psychiatrist), and Division of Developmental Disabilities, $44,832.

(zz) Responsibilities shared by Secretary of Department of Social and Health Services, listed under Health, and Director, Division of Income Assistance, $42,672, in same department.

(aaa) Responsibilities shared by Commissioner, Department of Finance & Administration, listed under Finance, and Director, Budget Division, Department of Finance & Administration, $39,500.

(bbb) Responsibilities shared by Director, Office of Community and Industrial Development, listed under Planning, and Director of Community Affairs, $38,382, in the same office.

(ccc) Responsibilities shared by Director, Office of Community and Industrial Development, listed under Planning, and Director of Economic Development, $54,600, in the same department.

(ddd) Responsibilities shared by Administrator, Trade & Consumer Protection Division, $48,304, and Assistant Attorney General, Office of Consumer Protection, $49,032.

(eee) Mayor.

(fff) Military employee, salary not paid by the District government.

(ggg) Responsibilities shared by Chief, Office of Compliance, $52,847, and Chief, Office of Consumer Education & Information, Consumer & Regulatory Affairs Department, $44,928.

(hhh) Responsibilities shared by Chairman, Board of Trustees (compensation for expenses only to a maximum of $4,000/year), and Acting President, University of District of Columbia, $67,285.

(iii) Responsibilities shared by President of the Community College, $33,000, and Chairman of the Board of Higher Education, no salary.

(jjj) Current data not available. Salary information is as of February 1984.

Table 2.12
LIEUTENANT GOVERNORS: QUALIFICATIONS AND TERMS

State or other jurisdiction	Minimum age	State citizen (years)	U.S. citizen (years)	State resident (years)	Qualified voter (years)	Length of term (years)	Maximum consecutive terms allowed
Alabama	30	7	10	7	...	4	2
Alaska	30	...	7	7	★	4	2
Arizona				----(a)----			
Arkansas	30	...	★	7	★	2	...
California	18	...	5	5	★	4	...
Colorado	30	...	★	2	...	4	...
Connecticut	30	...	...	...	★	4	...
Delaware	30	...	12	6	...	4	...
Florida	30	...	...	7	★	4	...
Georgia	30	6	15	6	...	4	...
Hawaii	30	...	★	5	★	4	2
Idaho	30	...	★	2	...	4	...
Illinois	25	...	★	3	...	4	...
Indiana	30	...	5	5	...	4	...
Iowa	30	...	★	2	...	4	...
Kansas	...	...	...	...	...	4	2
Kentucky	30	6	★	6	...	4	(b)
Louisiana	25	5	5	...	★	4	...
Maine				----(a)----			
Maryland	30	...	(c)	5	5	4	...
Massachusetts	...	...	...	7	...	4	...
Michigan(d)	30	...	...	...	4	4	...
Minnesota	25	...	★	1	...	4	...
Mississippi	30	...	20	5	...	4	...
Missouri	30	...	15	10	...	4	...
Montana	25	...	★	2	...	4	...
Nebraska	30	5	5	5	...	4	...
Nevada	25	2	...	2	★	4	...
New Hampshire				----(a)----			
New Jersey				----(a)----			
New Mexico	30	...	★	5	★	4	(b)
New York	30	...	★	5	...	4	...
North Carolina	30	...	5	2	...	4	2
North Dakota	30	...	★	5	★	4	...
Ohio	...	...	...	...	★	4	...
Oklahoma	31	...	★	...	10	4	...
Oregon				----(a)----			
Pennsylvania	30	...	★	7	...	4	2
Rhode Island	...	...	...	...	★	2	...
South Carolina	30	5	★	5	★	4	...
South Dakota	...	...	2	2	...	4	2
Tennessee				----(a)----			
Texas	30	...	★	5	...	4	...
Utah	30	5	...	5	★	4	...
Vermont	...	...	...	4	...	2	...
Virginia	30	...	★	5	5	4	...
Washington	...	...	★	...	★	4	...
West Virginia				----(a)----			
Wisconsin	...	...	★	...	★	4	...
Wyoming				----(a)----			
American Samoa	35	...	★	5	...	4	2
Guam	30	...	5	★	★	4	...
No. Mariana Is.	30	...	...	7	★	4	...
Puerto Rico				----(a)----			
Virgin Islands	30	...	5	★	★	4	...

Note: This table includes constitutional and statutory qualifications.
Key:
★—Formal provision; number of years not specified.
. . .—No formal provision.
(a) No lieutenant governor. In Tennessee, the speaker of the senate, elected from senate membership, has statutory title of "lieutenant governor."

(b) Successive terms forbidden.
(c) *Crosse v. Board of Supervisors of Elections* 243 Md. 555, 221 A.2d431 (1966)—opinion rendered indicated that U.S. citizenship was, by necessity, a requirement for office.
(d) A person who has been convicted of felony or breach of public trust is not eligible to the office for a period of 20 years after conviction.

Table 2.13
LIEUTENANT GOVERNORS: POWERS AND DUTIES

State or other jurisdiction	Presides over Senate	Appoints committees	Breaks roll-call ties	Assigns bills	Authority for governor to assign duties	Member of governor's cabinet or advisory body	Serves as acting governor when governor out of state
Alabama	★	★	★	★	. . .	. . .	★(a)
Alaska	. . .	. . .	. . .	. . .	★	★	★(b)
Arizona	--------------------------------(c)--------------------------------						
Arkansas	★	. . .	★	. . .	. . .	. . .	★
California	★	. . .	★	. . .	★	. . .	★
Colorado	. . .	. . .	. . .	. . .	★	★	★
Connecticut	★	. . .	★	★	★	★	★
Delaware	★	. . .	★	★	★	. . .	. . .
Florida	. . .	. . .	. . .	. . .	★	. . .	. . .
Georgia	★	★	. . .	★	★	. . .	. . .
Hawaii	. . .	. . .	. . .	. . .	★	★	★
Idaho	★	★(d)	★	★	★	. . .	★
Illinois	. . .	. . .	. . .	. . .	★	. . .	. . .
Indiana	★	. . .	★	. . .	★	★	. . .
Iowa	★	★	(e)	★	. . .	. . .	(f)
Kansas	. . .	. . .	. . .	. . .	★	(g)	(f)
Kentucky	★	(h)	★	(h)	★	★	★
Louisiana	. . .	. . .	. . .	. . .	★	. . .	★
Maine	--------------------------------(c)--------------------------------						
Maryland	. . .	. . .	. . .	. . .	★	★	★
Massachusetts	. . .	. . .	. . .	. . .	★	★	★
Michigan	★	. . .	★	. . .	★	★	★
Minnesota	. . .	. . .	. . .	. . .	★	. . .	. . .
Mississippi	★	★	★	★	. . .	. . .	★
Missouri	★	. . .	★	. . .	★	. . .	★
Montana	. . .	. . .	. . .	. . .	★	★	★(a)
Nebraska	★(i)	. . .	★(j)	. . .	★	. . .	★
Nevada	★	(k)	(l)	. . .	. . .	. . .	★
New Hampshire	--------------------------------(c)--------------------------------						
New Jersey	--------------------------------(c)--------------------------------						
New Mexico	★	(m)	★	. . .	★	★	★
New York	★	. . .	★	. . .	★	★	★
North Carolina	★	★	★	★	★	★	★
North Dakota	★	. . .	★	★	★	. . .	★
Ohio	. . .	. . .	. . .	. . .	(n)	★	(o)
Oklahoma	★	. . .	★	. . .	★	★	★
Oregon	--------------------------------(c)--------------------------------						
Pennsylvania	★	. . .	★(j)	★	★	★	. . .
Rhode Island	★	. . .	★	★	★	. . .	★
South Carolina	★	. . .	★	. . .	. . .	. . .	(f)
South Dakota	★	(p)	★	★	★	. . .	(q)
Tennessee	--------------------------------(c)--------------------------------						
Texas	★	★	★	★	. . .	. . .	★
Utah	. . .	. . .	. . .	. . .	★	. . .	★
Vermont	★	★	★	★	. . .	★	★
Virginia	★	. . .	★	. . .	★	★	. . .
Washington	★	(r)	★(j)	. . .	★	. . .	★
West Virginia	--------------------------------(c)--------------------------------						
Wisconsin	. . .	. . .	. . .	. . .	★	. . .	(s)
Wyoming	--------------------------------(c)--------------------------------						
American Samoa	. . .	. . .	. . .	. . .	★	. . .	★
Guam	. . .	. . .	. . .	. . .	. . .	★	★
No. Mariana Is.	. . .	. . .	. . .	. . .	★	★	★
Puerto Rico	--------------------------------(c)--------------------------------						
Virgin Islands	. . .	. . .	. . .	. . .	★	★	★

Key:

★—Provision for responsibility.

. . .—No provision for responsibility.

(a) After 20 days absence. In Montana, after 45 days.

(b) Alaska constitution identifies two types of absence from state: (1) temporary absence during which the lieutenant serves as acting governor; and (2) continuous absence for a period of six months, after which the governor's office is declared vacant and lieutenant governor succeeds to the office.

(c) No lieutenant governor; secretary of state is next in line of succession to governorship. In Tennessee, speaker of the Senate bears the additional statutory title of "lieutenant governor."

(d) Select and special purpose committees in consultation with majority/minority leadership.

(e) Only on amendments.

(f) Only in emergency situations.

(g) Governor's cabinet is made up of heads of the state departments; since the state's statutes provide that the lieutenant governor may be assigned to serve as head of a department, the officeholder could become part of the official cabinet at some point during the tenure.

(h) As a member of Senate committee responsible for activity.

(i) Unicameral legislative body.

(j) Except on final enactments.

(k) Temporary committees to carry out duties in formal legislative ceremonies.

(l) Constitution provides that lieutenant governor ". . .shall be President of the Senate, but shall only have a casting vote therein." However, interpretation of clause regarding casting vote is in dispute.

(m) Special committees only for joint sessions to inform the House and the governor.

(n) Presides over cabinet meetings in absence of governor.

(o) Only if governor asks the lieutenant to serve in that capacity, in the former's absence.

(p) Conference committees.

(q) Only in event of governor's continuous absence from state.

(r) In theory, lieutenant governor is responsible; in practice, appointments are made by majority caucus.

(s) Only in situations of an absence which prevents governor from discharging duties which need to be undertaken prior to his return.

Table 2.14
SECRETARIES OF STATE: QUALIFICATIONS FOR OFFICE

State or other jurisdiction	Minimum age	U.S. citizen (years)	State resident (years)	Qualified voter (years)	Method of selection to office
Alabama	25	7	5	★	E
Alaska	(a)				
Arizona	25	10	5	★	E
Arkansas	18	★	★	★	E
California	18	★	★	★	E
Colorado	25	★	★	. . .	E
Connecticut	18	★	★	★	E
Delaware	. . .	. . .	. . .	. . .	A
Florida	30	. . .	7	★	E
Georgia	25	10	4	. . .	E
Hawaii	(a)				
Idaho	25	★	2	. . .	E
Illinois	25	★	3	. . .	E
Indiana	. . .	. . .	. . .	. . .	E
Iowa	. . .	. . .	★	. . .	E
Kansas	. . .	. . .	. . .	. . .	E
Kentucky	30	2	2(b)	. . .	E
Louisiana	25	5	(b)	★	E
Maine	. . .	. . .	. . .	. . .	(c)
Maryland	. . .	. . .	. . .	★	A
Massachusetts	. . .	. . .	5	. . .	E
Michigan(d)	. . .	. . .	. . .	★	E
Minnesota	21	★	★	. . .	E
Mississippi	25	★	5(b)	★	E
Missouri	18	★	★	★	E
Montana(e)	25	★	2	. . .	E
Nebraska(f)	18	★	. . .	. . .	E
Nevada	25	★	2	★	E
New Hampshire	18	★	★	★	(c)
New Jersey	. . .	. . .	. . .	. . .	A
New Mexico	30	★	★	★	E
New York	18	★	★	. . .	A
North Carolina	21	. . .	. . .	★	E
North Dakota	25	★	. . .	★	E
Ohio	18	★	★	★	E
Oklahoma	31	★	10	10	A
Oregon	18	★	. . .	★	E
Pennsylvania	. . .	. . .	. . .	. . .	A
Rhode Island	18	★	★	★	E
South Carolina	21	. . .	★	★	E
South Dakota	18	★	★	. . .	E
Tennessee	21	★	★	★	(c)
Texas	. . .	. . .	. . .	. . .	A
Utah	(a)				
Vermont	. . .	. . .	. . .	. . .	E
Virginia	. . .	. . .	. . .	. . .	A
Washington	18	★	30 da.	★	E
West Virginia	18	★	★	★	E
Wisconsin	18	. . .	10 da.	. . .	E
Wyoming	25	★	★	★	E
American Samoa	(a)				
Guam	(a)				
No. Mariana Is.	(a)				
Puerto Rico	35	★	★	★	A
Virgin Islands	(a)				

Note: This table contains constitutional and statutory provisions. "Qualified voter" provision may infer additional residency and citizenship requirements.

Key:
★—Formal provision; number of years not specified.
. . .—No formal provision.
A—Appointed by governor.
E—Elected by voters.
(a) No secretary of state.
(b) Additional state citizenship requirement. Kentucky-two years. Loui-

siana, Mississippi-five years.
(c) Chosen by joint ballot of state senators and representatives. In Maine and New Hampshire, every two years. In Tennessee, every four years.
(d) A person convicted of a felony or breach of public trust is not eligible to the office for a period of 20 years after conviction.
(e) No person convicted of a felony is eligible to hold public office until final discharge from state supervision.
(f) No person in default as a collector and custodian of public money or property shall be eligible to public office; no person convicted of a felony shall be eligible unless restored to civil rights.

Table 2.15
SECRETARIES OF STATE: ELECTION AND REGISTRATION DUTIES

State or other jurisdiction	Chief election officer	Determines ballot eligibility of political parties	Receives initiative and/or referendum petition	Files certificate of nomination or election	Supplies election ballots or materials to local officials	Files candidates' expense papers	Files other campaign reports	Conducts voter education programs	Prepares extradition papers or warrants of arrest	Registers corporations (a)	Processes and/or commissions notaries public	Registers securities	Registers trade names/marks
	Election								Registration				
Alabama	★	★	★	★	★	★	★	★	★	★	★	★	★
Alaska(b)	★	...	★	★	...	...	...	...	...	★	★	...	...
Arizona	★	★	★	★	★	★	★	★	(c)	...	★	...	★
Arkansas	★	★	★	★	★	★	★	★	(c)	★	★	...	★
California	★	★	★	★	★	★	★	★	(c)	★	★	...	★
Colorado	★	★	★	★	★	★	★	★	...	...	★	...	★
Connecticut	★	★	...	★	★	★	★	★	★	★	★	★	★
Delaware	...	...	...	★	★	★	★	...	...	★	★	...	★
Florida	★	★	★	★	★	★	★	★	...	★	★	...	★
Georgia	★	★	★	★	★	★	★	★	...	★	★	★	★
Hawaii(b)	★	★	...	★	★	★	★	★	...	★	★	...	★
Idaho	★	★	★	★	★	★	★	★	...	★	★	...	★
Illinois	...	...	★	★	...	★	...	...	★	★	★	★	★
Indiana	...	★	...	★	★	...	...	...	...	★	★	★	★
Iowa	★	★	...	★	★	...	...	...	...	★	★	...	★
Kansas	★	★	...	★	★	★	★	...	...	★	★	...	★
Kentucky	★	...	★	★	★	★	...	★	★	★	★	...	★
Louisiana	★	★	★	★	★	★	...	★	★	★	★	...	★
Maine	★	★	★	★	★	★	★	★	...	★	★	...	★
Maryland	...	...	★	...	...	...	...	...	★	★(d)	★	...	...
Massachusetts	★	★	★	★	★	★	★	...	...	★	★	★	★
Michigan	★	★	★	★	★	★	★	★	★	★	★	★	★
Minnesota	★	★	★	★	★	★	★	...	...	★	★	...	★
Mississippi	(e)	★	...	★	★	★	★	...	...	★	★	★	★
Missouri	★	★	★	★	★	★	★	★	...	★	★	★	★
Montana	★	★	★	★	★	...	...	★	★	★	★	...	★
Nebraska	★	★	★	★	★	★	...	★	(c)	★	★	...	★
Nevada	★	★	★	★	★	★	★	★	...	★	★	★	★
New Hampshire	★	★	★	★	★	★	...	★	★	★	★	...	★
New Jersey	★	★	...	★	★	★	★	★	(c)	★	★	...	★
New Mexico	★	★	★	★	★	★	★	...	(c)	...	★	...	★
New York	...	...	...	...	...	...	...	...	...	★	★	...	★
North Carolina	...	...	...	★	...	...	...	...	...	★	★	★	★
North Dakota	★	★	★	★	★	★	★	...	...	★	★	...	★
Ohio	★	★	★	★	★	★	★	★	(c)	★	...	★	★
Oklahoma	...	...	★	★	...	★	★	...	...	★	★	...	★
Oregon	★	★	★	★	★	★	★	★	...	★	★	...	...
Pennsylvania	★	★	★	★	★	★	...	★	★	★	★	...	★
Rhode Island	★	★	★	★	★	...	...	★	...	★	★	...	★
South Carolina	...	...	...	...	...	...	...	...	...	★	★	★	★
South Dakota	★	★	★	★	★	★	★	★	★	★	★	...	★
Tennessee	(f)	★	...	★	★	★	★	...	...	★	★	...	★
Texas	★	★	...	★	★	★	★	★	...	★	★	...	★
Utah(b)	★	★	★	★	...	★	★	★	★	★	★	...	★
Vermont	★	★	...	★	★	★	★	★	...	★	★	...	★
Virginia	...	...	...	(g)	...	...	...	...	★	...	★	...	★
Washington	★	...	★	★	★	★	★	★	...	★	★	...	...
West Virginia	★	★	★	★	★	...	...	★	★	★	★	...	★
Wisconsin	...	...	...	...	...	...	...	...	(c)	★	★	...	★
Wyoming	★	★	★	(h)	★	★	★	★	(c)	★	★	★	★
Puerto Rico	...	...	...	...	...	...	...	...	...	...	★	...	...

Key:
★—Responsible for activity.
. . .—Not responsible for activity.
(a) Unless otherwise indicated, office registers domestic, foreign and non-profit corporations.
(b) No secretary of state. Duties indicated are performed by lieutenant governor.
(c) Attests to governor's signature on extradition papers or warrants of arrest. In Arizona and Nebraska, signs and places state seal on document; New Jersey, commissions prepared by governor's counsel's office, but signed by secretary: Ohio, certifies papers; Wisconsin, retains copies after affixing seal.
(d) Non-profit only.
(e) State Election Commission composed of governor, secretary of state and attorney general.
(f) Secretary appoints state coordinator of elections.
(g) Certificates of election for U.S. House and Senate; writs of election for special state legislative races.
(h) Files applications for nomination and issues certificates of nomination; governor issues certificates of election.

Table 2.16
SECRETARIES OF STATE: CUSTODIAL, PUBLICATION AND LEGISLATIVE DUTIES

State or other jurisdiction	Custodial				Publication					Legislative			
	Archives state records and documents	Files state agency rules and regulations	Administers uniform commercial code provisions	Files other corporate documents	State manual or directory	Session laws	State constitution	Statutes	Administrative rules and regulations	Opens legislative sessions(a)	Enrolls and engrosses bills	Retains copies of acts	Registers lobbyists
Alabama	...	...	★	★	...	★	★	★	...	...	★	★	★
Alaska(b)	...	★	...	...	...	...	★	...	★	★	...	★	★
Arizona	...	★	★	...	★	...	★	★	★	...	...	★	★
Arkansas	...	★	★	...	★	★	★	...	★	...	...	★	...
California	★	★	★	★	★	...	...	...	...	...	...	...	★
Colorado	...	★	★	★	...	...	★	...	...	...	...	★	★
Connecticut	★	★	★	★	★	...	★	...	...	(c)	...	★	...
Delaware	★	★	★	★	...	...	...	...	...	...	...	...	★
Florida	★	★	★	★	★	★	★	★	★	...	...	★	...
Georgia	★	★	...	★	★	★	★	★	★	...	...	★	★
Hawaii(b)	(d)	★	...	...	★	(e)	...	(e)	(e)	...	...	...	...
Idaho	...	★	★	★	...	★	★	★	...	...	...	★	...
Illinois	★	★	★	★	★	★	★	★	...	H	...	★	★
Indiana	★	★	★	★	★	...	...	...	...	★	...	★	★
Iowa	(f)	...	★	★	★	...	...	...	...	...	★	...	...
Kansas	★	...	★	★	★	★	★	...	...	★	★	★	★
Kentucky	★	★	★	★	...	...	...	...	...	...	...	★	...
Louisiana	★	...	...	★	★	★	★	...	...	...	...	★	...
Maine	★	★	★	★	...	...	...	★	...	...	★	★	★
Maryland	★(g)	★	...	...	...	...	...	...	★	...	...	★	...
Massachusetts	★	★	★	★	★	★	★	★	...	...	...	...	★
Michigan	★	★	★	...	★	...	...	...	...	...	★	...	...
Minnesota	★	★	★	★	...	...	...	...	...	H	...	★	...
Mississippi	...	★	★	★	★	★	★	...	...	H	...	★	★
Missouri	★	...	★	★	...	★	★	★	...	H	...	...	...
Montana	★(g)	★	★	★	★	...	★	...	★	H	...	★	...
Nebraska	★	★	★	★	★	★	★	...	★	(h)	...	★	...
Nevada	...	★	★	★	★	...	★	...	...	H	★	★	...
New Hampshire	★	★	★	★	★	...	★	...	...	(i)	★	...	★
New Jersey	★	...	★	★	★	...	...	...	...	...	★	...	...
New Mexico	★	★	★	...	★	★	★	★	★	H	...	★	...
New York	...	★	★	★	★	...	★	...	★	...	...	★	...
North Carolina	★	...	★	★	★	...	★	...	...	H(j)	...	★	...
North Dakota	...	...	★	★	★	★	...	...	...	...	...	...	★
Ohio	★	★	★	★	★	★	★	★	★	...	★	...	...
Oklahoma	...	★	...	★	...	...	...	...	...	...	...	★	...
Oregon	★	★	★	...	★	...	...	...	★	...	...	★	...
Pennsylvania	...	...	★	★	...	...	...	...	...	...	...	★	(k)
Rhode Island	★	★	★	★	★	★	★	★	★	...	★	★	★
South Carolina	★	...	★	★	...	...	...	...	...	...	...	...	★
South Dakota	★	★	★	★	★	...	★	...	...	(l)	H	★	★
Tennessee	★	★	★	★	★	...	★	★	...	H	...	★	★
Texas	★	★	★	★	★	★	...	★	★	H	...	★	★
Utah(b)	(d)	...	★	★	...	...	...	...	...	S	★	★	★
Vermont	★	★	★	★	★	★	★	★	...	H(j)	★	★	★
Virginia	...	...	...	...	★	...	...	...	...	...	...	...	★
Washington	★	...	...	★	...	...	...	...	...	...	...	(m)	...
West Virginia	★	★	★	★	...	...	...	...	...	...	...	★	...
Wisconsin	★	★	★	...	★	★	...	...	...	...	...	★	★
Wyoming	...	★	★	★	★	...	★	...	...	H	...	★	...
Puerto Rico	★	★	...	★	...	★	★	★	...	...	...	...	...

Key:
★—Responsible for activity.
. . .—Not responsible for activity.
(a) In this column only: ★ Both houses; H—House; S—Senate.
(b) No secretary of state. Duties indicated are performed by lieutenant governor.
(c) Both houses during trailer sessions (to act on vetoed bills only).
(d) Limited responsibility.
(e) Distributes and sells session laws, statutes and administrative rules and regulations.

(f) Serves as chair of State Records Commission.
(g) As specified by law. In Maryland, Hall of Records is the archivist.
(h) Certifies and seats members of unicameral legislature.
(i) Convenes both houses during special sessions of the legislature.
(j) Until speaker is elected.
(k) Only those making political contributions to candidates or their committees.
(l) Board of Elections and Finance only.
(m) Files session laws.

Table 2.17
ATTORNEYS GENERAL:
QUALIFICATIONS FOR OFFICE

State or other jurisdiction	Minimum age	U.S. citizen (years)	State resident (years)	Qualified voter (years)	Licensed attorney (years)	Membership in the state bar (years)	Method of selection to office
Alabama	25	7	5	...	...	...	E
Alaska	...	★	...	...	...	...	A
Arizona	25	10	5	...	...	...	E
Arkansas	...	★	★	★	...	...	E
California	18	...	...	...	(a)	(a)	E
Colorado	25	★	2	...	★	...	E
Connecticut	18	★	★	★	10	10	E
Delaware	...	...	...	...	...	...	E
Florida	30	...	7	★	5	5	E
Georgia	25	10	4	...	7	7	E
Hawaii	...	★	1	...	...	...	A
Idaho	30	★	2	...	★	★	E
Illinois	25	★	3	...	...	...	E
Indiana	...	...	(b)	...	★	...	E
Iowa	...	...	...	...	...	...	E
Kansas	...	★	...	...	★	★	E
Kentucky	30	2	2(b)	...	8	2	E
Louisiana	25	5	(b)	★	5	5	E
Maine	...	...	...	...	...	...	(c)
Maryland	...	★(d)	10(b)	...	10	10(e)	E
Massachusetts	...	...	5	...	...	★	E
Michigan(f)	...	...	...	★	...	...	E
Minnesota	21	...	30 da.	★	...	...	E
Mississippi	26	...	5(b)	...	5	5	E
Missouri	...	...	...	...	...	...	E
Montana(g)	25	★	2	...	5	★	E
Nebraska(h)	21(e)	...	(e)	...	(e)	...	E
Nevada	25	★	2(b)	★	...	...	E
New Hampshire	...	...	...	...	★	★	A
New Jersey	18(e)	...	★	...	★	★	A
New Mexico	30	★	5	...	★	★	E
New York	30	★	5	...	(e)	...	E
North Carolina	21	...	...	★	★	(e)	E
North Dakota	25	★	★	★	...	...	E
Ohio	18	★	★	★	...	...	E
Oklahoma	31	★	10	10	...	...	E
Oregon	...	...	...	★	...	...	E
Pennsylvania	30	★	7	...	★	★	E
Rhode Island	18	★	★	★	...	...	A
South Carolina	...	...	★	★	...	...	E
South Dakota	...	★	★	...	★	★	E
Tennessee	...	...	...	...	...	...	A(i)
Texas	...	...	...	...	★	★	E
Utah	25	...	5(b)	★	★	★	E
Vermont	...	...	...	...	...	...	E
Virginia	30	★	5(j)	...	...	5(j)	E
Washington	...	★	30 da.	★	★	★	E
West Virginia	25	★	(b)	★	★	...	E
Wisconsin	...	...	...	...	...	...	E
Wyoming	...	...	★	★	4	4	A
American Samoa	...	★	...	...	...	...	A
Guam	...	...	...	...	...	...	A
No. Mariana Is.	...	...	...	...	5	...	A
Puerto Rico	21(e)	★	...	...	(e)	(e)	A
Virgin Islands	...	★	...	...	(k)	...	A

Note: This table contains constitutional and statutory provisions. "Qualified voter" provision may infer additional residency and citizenship requirements.

Key:
★—Formal provision; number of years not specified.
. . .—No formal provision.
A—Appointed by governor.
E—Elected by voters.
(a) No statute specifically requires this, but the State Bar act can be interpreted as making this a qualification.
(b) Additional state citizenship requirement. Kentucky, Nevada—two years. Louisiana, Mississippi, Utah, West Virginia—five years.
(c) Chosen biennially by joint ballot of state senators and representatives.

(d) *Crosse v. Board of Supervisors of Elections* 243 Md. 555, 2221A.2d431 (1966)—opinion rendered indicated that U.S. citizenship was, by necessity, a requirement for office.
(e) Implied.
(f) A person convicted of a felony or breach of public trust is not eligible to the office for a period of 20 years after conviction.
(g) No person convicted of felony is eligible to hold public office until final discharge from state supervision.
(h) No person in default as a collector and custodian of public money or property shall be eligible to public office; no person convicted of a felony shall be eligible unless restored to civil rights.
(i) Appointed by judges of state Supreme Court.
(j) Same as qualifications of a judge of a court of records.
(k) Must be admitted to practice before highest court.

Table 2.18
ATTORNEYS GENERAL: PROSECUTORIAL AND ADVISORY DUTIES

State or other jurisdiction	Authority to initiate local prosecutions	May intervene in local prosecutions	May assist local prosecutor	May supersede local prosecutor	To state executive officials	To legislators	To local prosecutors	On the interpretation of statutes	On the constitutionality of bills or ordinances	Prior to passage	Before signing
	Authority in local prosecutions:				Issues advisory opinions:					Reviews legislation:	
Alabama	A	A,D	A,D	A	★	★	★	★	★	★	...
Alaska	(a)	(a)	(a)	(a)	★	★	...	★	★	★	★
Arizona	A,B,C,D,F	B,D	B,D	B	★	★	★	★	★	★	...
Arkansas	...	D	D	...	★	★	★	★	★	...	★
California	A,E	A,D,E	A,B,D	A	★	★	★	★	★	★	★
Colorado	B,F	B	D,F(b)	B	★	★	★	★	★	★	★
Connecticut	...	...	...	...	★	...	...	★	★	★	★
Delaware	...	...	...	...	★	★	...	★	★	★	★
Florida	F	D	D	...	★	★	★	★	★	★	★
Georgia	A,B,F	A,B,D,G	A,B,D,F	B	★	★	★	★	★	★	★
Hawaii	E	A,D,G	A,D	A,G	★	★	★	★	★	★	★
Idaho	A,D,F	A	A,D	A	★	★	★	★	...	★	★
Illinois	A,D,E,F,G	A,D,E	A,D,E,F	F	★	★	★	★	★	(c)	(c)
Indiana	F(b)	...	A,D,E,F	G	★	★	★	★	★	...	★
Iowa	D,F	D	D	...	★	★	★	★	★	★	★
Kansas	B,C,D,F	D	D	A,F	★	★	★	★	★	★	★
Kentucky	A,B	B,D	B,D,F	G	★	★	★	★	★	★	...
Louisiana	G	G	D	G	★	★	★	★	★	★	★
Maine	A	A	A	A	★	★	...	★	★	★	★
Maryland	B,C,F	B,C,D	B,C,D	B,C	★	★	★	★	★	★	★
Massachusetts	A,B,C,D,E,F,G	A,B,C,D,E,G	A,B,C,D,E	A,B,C,E	★	★	...	★	★	★	★
Michigan	A	A	D	A	★	★	★	★	★	★	★
Minnesota	B	B,D,G	A,B,D	B	★	★	...	★	★	...	(c)
Mississippi	B,E,F	...	B,F	...	★	★	★	★	★	(c)	(c)
Missouri	F	...	B	...	★	★	★	★	...	★	...
Montana	C,F	A,B,C,D	A,B,C,D,F	A,C	★	★(d)	★	★	★	...	...
Nebraska	A	A	A,D	A	★	★	★	★	★	...	...
Nevada	D,F,G(e)	D(e)	(e,f)	G,F	★	...	★	★	...	...	...
New Hampshire	A	A	A	A	★	...	...	★	★	...	...
New Jersey	A	A,B,D,G	A,D	A,B,D,G	★	★	★	★	★	★	★
New Mexico	A,B,E,F,G	B,D,G	D	B	★	★	★	★	★	★	★
New York	B,F	B	D	B	★	...	★	★	★	...	★
North Carolina	...	D	D	...	★	★	★	★	★	★	...
North Dakota	A,G	A,D	A,D	A	★	★	★	...	...	...	(c)
Ohio	B,C,F	B,F	F	B,C	★	★(g)	★	★	...	...	...
Oklahoma	B,C	B,C	B,C	B,C	★	★	★	★	★	★	★
Oregon	B,F	B,D	B,D	B	★	★	★	★	★	(c)	(c)
Pennsylvania	A,D,G	D,G	D	G	★	...	...	★	...	★	★
Rhode Island	A	D	D	...	★	★	...	★	...	★	★
South Carolina	A	A,D	A,D	A	★	★	★	★	★	★	★
South Dakota	A(h)	A	A	A	★	★	★	★	★	★	★
Tennessee	D,F,G(b)	D,G(b)	D	F	★	★	★	★	★	(c)	(c)
Texas	F	...	D	...	★	★	★	★	★	★	★
Utah	A,B,D,E,F,G	E,G	D,E	E	★	...	★	★	★	(c)	(c)
Vermont	A	A	A	A	★	★	★	★	★	★	★
Virginia	B,F	A,B,D,F	B,D,F	B	★	★	★	★	★	★	★
Washington	B,D,G	B,D,G	D	B	★	★	★	★	★	★	★
West Virginia	...	...	D	...	★	★	★	★	★	(i)	(i)
Wisconsin	B,C,F	B,C,D	D	B,C(j)	★	★	★	★	★	(i)	(i)
Wyoming	B,D(e)	B,D	B,D	...	★	★	★	★	...	★	★
American Samoa	A,E	A,E	A,E	A,E	★	★	...	★	★	★	★
No. Mariana Is.	A	...	...	...	★	★	...	★	★	★	★
Puerto Rico	A,B,E	A,B,E	A,E	A,B,E	★	★	...	★	★	★	★
Virgin Islands	A	...	...	...	★	★	...	★	★	★	★

Key:
A—On own initiative.
B—On request of governor.
C—On request of legislature.
D—On request of local prosecutor.
E—When in state's interest.
F—Under certain statutes for specific crimes.
G—On authorization of court or other body.
★—Has authority in area.
. . .—Does not have authority in area.
(a) Local prosecutors serve at pleasure of attorney general.

(b) Certain statutes provide for concurrent jurisdiction with local prosecutors.
(c) Only when requested by governor or legislature.
(d) To legislative leadership.
(e) In connection with grand jury cases.
(f) Will prosecute as a matter of practice when requested.
(g) To legislature as a whole not individual legislators.
(h) Has concurrent jurisdiction with states' attorneys.
(i) No legal authority, but sometimes informally reviews laws at request of legislature.
(j) If the governor removes the district attorney for cause.

Table 2.19
ATTORNEYS GENERAL: CONSUMER PROTECTION ACTIVITIES, SUBPOENA POWERS, AND ANTITRUST DUTIES

State or other jurisdiction	May commence civil proceedings	May commence criminal proceedings	Represents the state before regulatory agencies	Administers consumer protection programs	Handles consumer complaints	Subpoena powers (a)	Antitrust duties
Alabama	★	★	...	★	★	•	A, B
Alaska	★	★	★	★	★	★	B, C
Arizona	★	...	...	★	★	★	A, B, D
Arkansas	★	...	★	★	★	★	B, C, D
California	★	...	...	...	★	★	B, C, D
Colorado	★	★	★	★	★	•	B, C, D(b)
Connecticut	★	...	★	★	...	•	A, B, D
Delaware	★	★	★	★	...	★	A, B, C
Florida	★	★	...	★	★	★	A, B, C, D
Georgia	★	★	★	...	...	★	B, C, D
Hawaii	★	★	★	★	★	★	A, B, C, D
Idaho	★	...	★	★	★	•	D
Illinois	★	★	★	★	★	•	A, B, D
Indiana	★	...	★	★	★	...	B, C, D
Iowa	★	★	★	★	★	•	A, B, C, D
Kansas	★	★	★	★	★	★	B, C, D
Kentucky	★	★	★	★	★	(c)	A, B, D
Louisiana	★	...	★	...	★	★	B, C
Maine	★	★	★	★	★	•	B, C
Maryland	★	★	★	★	★	★	B, C, D
Massachusetts	★	★	★	★	★	•	A, B, C, D
Michigan	★	★	★	★	★	•	A, B, C, D
Minnesota	★	...	★	★	★	•	B, D
Mississippi	★	...	★	★	★	•	B, C
Missouri	★	...	...	...	★	•	A, B, C, D
Montana	★	★	★	...	...	•	B, C, D
Nebraska	★	...	★	★	★	•	A, B, C(d), D
Nevada	★	★	...	...	★	★	A, B, C, D
New Hampshire	★	★	★	★	★	•	B, C, D
New Jersey	★	★	★	★	★	★	A, B, C, D
New Mexico	★	★	★	★	★	•	A, C
New York	★	★	...	★	★	★	A, B, C, D
North Carolina	★	...	★	★	★	★	A, B, C, D
North Dakota	★	★	...	★	★	★	C, D
Ohio	★	★	★	★	★	•	B, C, D
Oklahoma	★	...	(e)	★	★	•	B, D
Oregon	★	★	(c)	★	★	•	A, B, C, D
Pennsylvania	★	...	★	★	★	•	D
Rhode Island	★	★	★	★	★	•	A, B, C, D
South Carolina	★	★	★	...	★	•	A, B, C, D
South Dakota	★	★	...	★	★	•	A, B, C, D
Tennessee	★	★	★(c)	★	★	•	A, B, C, D
Texas	★	...	★	★	★	•	B, D
Utah	★(d)	...	★(d,f)	...	★(f)	★	A(g), B, C, D(g)
Vermont	★	★	★	★	★	•	A, B, C, D
Virginia	★	(e)	★	★(f)	★(f)	•	A, B, C, D
Washington	★	...	★	★	★	•	A, B, D
West Virginia	★	...	★	★	★	★	A, B, D
Wisconsin	★	...	★	★	★	•	A, B, C, D
Wyoming	★	...	★	★	★	...	...
American Samoa	★	★	★	...	...	★	
No. Mariana Is.	★	★	★	★	★	★	B, C, D
Puerto Rico	★	★	★	★(e)	★(e)	★	A, B, C
Virgin Islands	★	★(h)	★	...	...	★	A, B(i), C, D

Key:
A—Has *parens patriae* authority to commence suits on behalf of consumers in state antitrust damage actions in state courts.
B—May initiate damage actions on behalf of state in state courts.
C—May commence criminal proceedings.
D—May represent cities, counties and other governmental entities in recovering civil damages under federal or state law.
★—Has authority in area.
...—Does not have authority in area.
(a) In this column only: ★ broad powers and • limited powers.

(b) Only under Rule 23 of the Rules of Civil Procedure.
(c) When permitted to intervene.
(d) Attorney general has exclusive authority.
(e) To a limited extent.
(f) Attorney general handles legal matters only with no administrative handling of complaints.
(g) Opinion only, since there are no controlling precedents.
(h) May prosecute in inferior courts. May prosecute in district court only by request or consent of U.S. Attorney General.
(i) May initiate damage actions on behalf of jurisdiction in district court.

Table 2.20
ATTORNEYS GENERAL: DUTIES TO ADMINISTRATIVE AGENCIES AND OTHER RESPONSIBILITIES

State or other jurisdiction	Serves as counsel for state	Appears for state in criminal appeals	Issues official advice	Interprets statutes or regulations	Conducts litigation: In behalf of agency	Conducts litigation: Against agency	Prepares or reviews legal documents	Represents the public before the agency	Involved in rule-making	Reviews rules for legality
Alabama	A, B, C	★(a)	★	★	★	★	★	(b)	...	★
Alaska	A, B, C	★	★	★	★	★	★	...	★	★
Arizona	A, B, C	(c,d)	★	★	★	★	★	★	★	★
Arkansas	A, B, C	★(a)	★	★	★	...	★	★	★	★
California	A, B, C	★(a)	★	★	★	★	★	...	...	...
Colorado	A, B, C	★(a)	★	★	★	★	★	...	★	★
Connecticut	A, B, C	...	★	★	★	...	★	...	★	★
Delaware	A, B, C	★(a)	★	★	★	★	★	★	★	★
Florida	A, B, C	★(a)	★	★	★	★	★	★	★	★
Georgia	A, B, C	(b,c)	★	★	★	★	★	...	★	★
Hawaii	A, B	(b,c)	★	★	★	★	★	★	★	★
Idaho	A, B, C	★(a)	★	★	★	★	★	...	★	★
Illinois	A, B*, C	(b,c,e)	★	★	★	★	★	★	...	...
Indiana	A, B, C	★(a)	★	★	★	...	★	...	★	★
Iowa	A, B, C	★(a)	★	★	★	★	★	...	★	★
Kansas	A, B, C	★(a)	★	★	★	★	★	...	...	★
Kentucky	A, B*, C	★	★	★	★	★	★	...	★	★
Louisiana	A, B, C	(c)	★	★	★	★	★	...	★	★
Maine	A, B, C	(b,d)	★	★	★	...	★	...	★	★
Maryland	A, B, C	★	★	★	★	(b)	★	★	★	★
Massachusetts	A, B, C	(b,c,d)	★	★	★	★	★	★	★	★
Michigan	A, B, C	(b,c,d)	★	★	★	...	★	★	...	★
Minnesota	A, B, C	(c)	★	★	★	★	★	★	...	★
Mississippi	A, B, C	★	★	★	★	...	★	...	...	★
Missouri	A, B, C	★	★	★	★	...	★	...	★	★
Montana	A, B, C	★	★	★	★	...	★	...	★	★
Nebraska	A, B, C	★	★	★	★	★	★	...	...	★
Nevada	A, B, C	★(d)	★	★	★	★	★	★	★	★
New Hampshire	A, B, C	★(a)	★	★	★	★	★	★	★	★
New Jersey	A, B, C	★(d)	★	★	★	★	★	...	★	★
New Mexico	A, B, C	★(a)	★	★	★	★	★	★	★	★
New York	A, B, C	(b)	★	★	★	★	...	★	...	...
North Carolina	A, B, C	★	★	★	★	★	★	(b)	★	★
North Dakota	A, B, C	(b)	★	★	★	...	★	...	★	★
Ohio	A, B, C	...	★	★	★	★	★	★	★	...
Oklahoma	A, B, C	(b)	★	★	★	★	★	★	★	★
Oregon	A, B, C	★	★	★	★	...	★	...	★	★
Pennsylvania	A, B, C	(c)	★	★	★	★	★	...	★	★
Rhode Island	A, B, C	★(a)	★	★	★	...	★	...	★	★
South Carolina	A, B, C	★(d)	★	★	★	...	★	...	★	★
South Dakota	A, B, C	★(a)	★	★	★	★	★	...	★	★
Tennessee	A, B, C	★(a)	★	★	★	...	★	(b)	★	★
Texas	A, B, C	(c)	★	★	★	★	★	...	★	★
Utah	A, B, C	★(a)	★	★	★	★	★	★	★	★
Vermont	A, B, C	(b)	★	★	★	★	★	(b)	...	★
Virginia	A, B, C	★(a)	★	★	★	★	★	★	★	★
Washington	A, B, C	(c,f)	★	★	★	★	★	★	★	★
West Virginia	A, B, C	★(a)	★	★	★	(f)	★	★	★	...
Wisconsin	A, B, C	(b)	★	★	★	★	★	(b)	★	...
Wyoming	A, B, C	★(a)	★	★	★	...	★	...	★	★
American Samoa	A, B, C	★(a)	★	★	★	...	★	...	★	★
No. Mariana Is.	A, B, C	★	★	★	★	...	★	...	★	★
Puerto Rico	A, B, C	★	★	★	★	...	★	...	★	★
Virgin Islands	A, B, C(g)	★	★	★	★	...	★	...	★	★

Key: A—Defend state law when challenged on federal constitutional grounds.
B—Conduct litigation on behalf of state in federal and other states' courts.
C—Prosecute actions against another state in U.S. Supreme Court.
*Only in federal courts.
★—Has authority in area.
. . .—Does not have authority in area.

(a) Attorney general has exclusive jurisdiction.
(b) In certain cases only.
(c) When assisting local prosecutor in the appeal.
(d) Can appear on own discretion.
(e) In certain courts only.
(f) If authorized by the governor.
(g) Except in cases in which the U.S. Attorney is representing the Government of the Virgin Islands.

CHAPTER THREE

STATE LEGISLATIVE BRANCH

THE STATE LEGISLATURES

By William T. Pound

The growth in the capacity and responsibilities of American state legislatures which has been taking place over the past 30 years continues unabated during the 1980s. The state legislature, which can be appropriately characterized as "the first branch of government," went through a period of revitalization between the late 1950s and the mid-1970s. During that time, the legislative reform movement affected virtually every state legislative body. This movement was stimulated not only by judicial decisions, active and effective citizen groups, and the changing nature of governmental responsibilities, but also by the state legislators themselves. The increase in legislative capacity and function has paralleled the overall growth in state governments' responsibilities and functions, but the state legislatures have been more affected by change than any other governmental institution.

The Modernization of the State Legislature

Legislative development during the past decade can best be characterized as a consolidation of previous reforms. The external relationships of the legislatures—with governors and the executive branch, with the federal government, and with interest groups—have undergone considerable change. Trends toward decentralization within legislatures and greater autonomy for individual legislators are apparent. There is greater emphasis on the constituent service role of legislators, and computers and modern information systems are having a dramatic effect on the legislatures.

The "New Federalism" proposals put forth by President Ronald Reagan have had a major impact on state government and the state legislatures. While Congress has not enacted "New Federalism" in any systematic statutory form, it has had a significant effect on state legislative responsibilities and the environment in which state legislatures function. Increasingly, the state legislatures are becoming the primary arena for policymaking and for financing governmental functions hitherto dominated by the federal and local governments.

The legislative modernization movement had several components. Legislatures had begun to build their capacity in the postwar period. The Legislative Council movement, which had originated 20 years earlier, spread to many states. Specialized legislative staffs, particularly in the fiscal area, were established in states such as California and Texas. Legislatures began to move from biennial to annual sessions. At the beginning of World War II, only four states held annual legislative sessions. By 1962, the number of legislatures meeting annually had increased to 19; by 1972, to 35; and by 1986, to 43.

Many of the changes in state legislatures required constitutional amendment. Constitutional restrictions on both regular and special sessions, on legislator salaries, and on legislative authority in the budget and oversight area were diluted or removed. Modifications were made to the restrictions on interim activity, the review of gubernatorial vetoes, and the legislature's ability to call itself into session or to determine matters that could be considered in certain sessions.

A critical stimulus to the legislative modernization movement was the series of state and federal judicial decisions that followed the U.S. Supreme Court rulings on legislative districting in *Baker v. Carr* (1963) and *Reynolds v. Sims* (1965)—decisions requiring equality of representation based on population in both houses of the state legislature. The result was a shift of power in many state legislatures from rural to urban, and especially suburban, interests, and inevitably, a change in the composition of legislatures. The number of farmers and lawyers has declined, while the number of educators, urban professionals, women and racial minorities, has grown.

Legislative Operations, Organization, and Procedures

The increase in the capacity and willingness of legislatures to deal with modern societal problems has involved more than

William T. Pound is Director of State Services for the National Conference of State Legislatures, Denver, Colorado.

changes in patterns of representation. Legislative organization and procedures are constantly evolving. Many legislatures regularly review their structures and procedures, often through a Rules Committee or an interim study. Many procedural changes in recent years have had the objective either of opening and formalizing the process and providing more information to both the public and members of the legislative body, or of more effectively using legislative time.

Concern about legislative use of time has been motivated by at least two issues: How much time should a legislature spend in session, and should it be considered "full-time" or "part-time" in nature?; and, how can the legislature most effectively use the time available and avoid the end-of-session logjam that occurs in many states?

Length of legislative sessions

Twelve states place no limit on session length, while 32 operate with constitutional limits (two of these, Colorado and Kansas, limit only the second year), and six states (Arizona, Iowa, Nevada, Rhode Island, Tennessee, and Vermont) have statutory or indirect limitations based on cutoffs in legislator's salaries or per diem expense payments.

The argument about session limitations often is couched in terms of preserving the "citizen" nature of state legislatures, as opposed to developing "professional" or full-time legislatures on the congressional model. There is no question that the amount of time spent in session and the level of compensation affect the composition of the membership of legislative bodies. Many argue it is desirable that the predominant occupation of members of the legislature not be that of "legislator," but that legislative bodies represent a broad spectrum of vocations. However, the growing demands on state legislatures and the greater legislative role in policy initiation, budgeting, and program oversight have increased the pressure on legislative time.

The 1960s and 1970s were a time of elimination or relaxation of the limits on legislative sessions. More recently, however, there has been a mixed response to the question of session length. In 1984, Alaska adopted a 120-day limit, replacing its previously unlimited sessions. In 1982, Colorado adopted a limit of 140 days for the second year of the

session, and in 1981, Washington included session limitations when it moved from biennial to annual sessions. In 1984, Utah lengthened its sessions by 10 days per biennium when it changed from a 60-day (first year)/20-day (second year) system to 45 days per session. New Hampshire adopted annual sessions, effective in 1985. Several legislatures, notably Arizona and Iowa, have limited their sessions by legislative rule or statute. Movements to adopt more restrictive session limits surface periodically, particularly in those states that hold the longest sessions.

"Full-time" legislatures and legislators

Whether a legislature is full-time in nature generally can be measured by factors such as time spent in session, level of compensation, and occupational self-definition of members. Moreover, full-time legislatures are likely to have a pattern of considerable legislator time spent in district offices and a high priority placed on constituent service functions.

The legislatures of California, Illinois, Massachusetts, Michigan, New Jersey, New York, Ohio, Pennsylvania, and Wisconsin have lengthy sessions, relatively high legislator salaries and many members whose primary occupation is "legislator." None of these states have constitutionally-imposed session limitations, although both California and Wisconsin adopt a systematic schedule of committee and floor activity, as well as recess periods, at the beginning of each biennium. Many of the legislatures which have longer sessions meet only two or three days per week, while in other states with more restricted sessions, five- and six-day workweeks are common. Several of the medium-sized states spend as many actual days in session as do the full-time legislatures.

The number of legislators who define their occupation as "legislator" is increasing. A recent occupational survey of state legislators conducted by the National Conference of State Legislatures found that more than half of the legislators in New York and Pennsylvania define their occupation as "legislator." The study also indicated that in larger states the number of "business owners" who are members of the legislature is much smaller than it is in the states with more limited session lengths. Lawyer legislators exist in greatest numbers in the South. In a number of states, members engaged in "education" outnumber those coming from any other professional background. Individuals engaged in "agriculture" still are found in every legislature, but are in greatest number in the rural midwestern and mountain states. The number of women and minorities in the legislatures continues to increase each biennium—there are now more than 1,100 women and nearly 400 minorities among the 7,461 state legislators.

Legislative scheduling

The effective use of time during legislative sessions is a continuing preoccupation of legislatures. A majority of the legislatures have experimented with committee and floor scheduling systems and the use of deadlines. There is increasing interest in deadline systems which establish specific dates for the introduction of bills, periods for committee consideration in each house, and cutoff dates for floor consideration in the chambers. Such systems provide a more even flow of work during a legislative session and can avoid the end-of-session logjam. The logjam is not entirely eliminated, but instead, is spread over several deadline periods during a session. Another effect of such deadlines is to kill bills at various stages of the legislative process—often providing a convenient excuse for inaction, rather than having all of the bills that have been introduced remain alive throughout a session. Most legislatures using deadlines have found them to be effective in managing sessions.

Bill introductions

Another procedural tool for more effective use of legislative time is the limit on bill introductions. Colorado is the most restrictive, limiting legislators to six (in the first year) and four (in the second year) bill introductions. Other states are experimenting with limiting requests for bill drafts or with concept or committee bills (by which a number of bill ideas or requests may be combined into a single draft). The sheer number of bills introduced and considered each session has necessitated the implementation of such procedures.

More than 200,000 bills are introduced in the state legislatures each biennium—in recent years ranging from lows of approximately 1,000 to 1,400 in states such as Kentucky, Montana, Nebraska, North Dakota, South Dakota, Utah, Vermont, and Wyoming, to a high of more than 30,000 in New York. States also vary widely in the number of bills which are enacted—from a low of approximately 250 per biennium to more than 5,000 per biennium in New York. Twenty-five legislatures permit bills introduced in the first session to carry over to the second year; approximately 50,000 bills carry over each biennium.

Committee work - sessions and interim periods

The modernization of the legislatures has resulted in stronger committee systems in many states. Committee strength varies across the state legislatures, but in the most effective bodies, the primary shaping of legislation occurs in committee, not on the floor. Many legislatures now make committee assignments and arrange committee and floor schedules to eliminate meeting conflicts and maximize the time available to committees early in the session.

Legislatures also have become more active during the interim period—the period between sessions. Florida and Washington use committee weeks or weekends as a means of effectively performing interim work. By concentrating all interim committee meetings within a three- or four-day period each month, the time demands on legislators are minimized.

The effectiveness of interim committees varies widely. There is a growing trend to utilize standing committees during the interim. In states with strong interim or Legislative Council traditions, interim committees' bills often have a high rate of passage. Even where no direct legislation results from interim work, the interim period may have a substantial educational effect on subsequent legislative action.

Special sessions

Other reflections of the reduction in constitutional restrictions and the changing operating environment of state legislatures can be found in the ability of the legislatures to call themselves into special session (nearly 60 percent can do so), the increased frequency with which special sessions have been held, and the emerging practice in some of the states which do not have constitutionally-limited sessions of not adjourning *sine die*, but instead recessing subject to the call of the leadership. The latter practice allows the legislature to act at any time, and to react immediately to changing situations, instead of reposing interim authority entirely in the executive branch.

Special sessions were numerous in the 1981-83 period as a result of the legislatures' grappling with fiscal problems and reapportionment, but have been less frequent in the mid-1980s. Veto sessions and the legislative override of gubernatorial vetoes have occurred more frequently in the 1980s.

Legislative compensation

An important element of the legislative reform movement was the payment of adequate compensation to legislators. In recent years, legislators' salaries have been adjusted more frequently than in earlier periods. The removal of constitutional restrictions on legislator salaries has been accomplished in 41 states; in nine states, salaries still are set in the constitution. In at least 20 states, some form of compensation commission or advisory group has been established to make recommendations on legislative compensation. Most of these groups are advisory, but in four states (Hawaii, Idaho, Maryland, and Michigan), compensation commission recommendations take effect unless specifically negated by the legislature.

The states that have retained constitutional salary limitations tend to be the ones that provide the lowest levels of compensation. As of early 1986, legislator salaries range from $100 per year in New Hampshire to $46,800 annually in Alaska. The average legislative salary in 1986 was just over $17,000. Salaries are paid on an annual basis in 38 states, and on a daily or weekly rate (tied to time spent in session) in the remainder. Biennial salaries now total more than $40,000 in 15 states, while 14 pay salaries less than $10,000 per biennium. Legislators in all but six states receive a per diem allowance when the legislature is in session or during the interim when on legislative business. In some cases, these payments reflect actual expenses, and in others, a specific unvouchered sum.

Forty-two states provide some additional compensation for legislative leaders, and 11 provide extra compensation to some committee chairmen. In New York, nearly all members receive additional compensation. The variation in legislative practices makes it difficult to accurately determine the total amount of legislator compensation.

Legislative staffing

The expansion of institutional resources which accompanied legislative modernization is continuing. This expansion of resources to support the legislative process can be seen in increased legislative staff and greater staff specialization, improved and expanded facilities, and greater informational resources. The development of permanent legislative research and library reference staff began early in the 20th century. Legislative staff in the early years were part-time, few in number, and dedicated to the recording and administration of the legislative process. The offices of legislative clerk and secretary can be traced to our English parliamentary heritage. Permanent research staff grew out of the Legislative Council movement, which was initiated to enable the legislature to function during the interim and to provide independent research capability. Permanent staff for bill drafting and legal services also appeared in the early years of this century.

By the 1950s, several states had begun to develop their own fiscal and budget staffs, rather than relying solely on executive budget assistance. This trend toward independent budget analysis and information had reached all 50 states by 1975. Post audit and program evaluation also had become important legislative functions in a majority of the states by the late 1970s—agencies often characterized by large professional staff units. By the 1980s, the state legislatures had more than 16,000 full-time employees, with an additional part-time complement of approximately 9,000 persons.

The development of legislative staff has reduced the dependence of the legislatures on the executive branch, lobbyists, and other external sources of information. Many legislatures once relied on the attorney general or private lawyers for bill drafting, and on the executive for budget and fiscal data. The legislative branch has become more independent each biennium, particularly in areas such as fiscal analysis, revenue estimation, program evaluation, and the development and operation of information systems. A byproduct of this legislative independence has been the number of constitutional confrontations between the legislative and executive branches—often in challenges of legislative assertions of authority. The budget power and review of administrative regulations are two key areas of conflict. Colorado, South Carolina, and Wisconsin recently have experienced challenges to legislative direction to the executive, or assertions of authority contained in the budget bill. Conflict over legislative assertions of authority is likely to increase in the future.

Legislative staff organization originally was characterized by a high degree of centralization. This remains true in many states where staff is organized in one or a few central staff agencies performing all legislative support functions. Increasingly, the trend in recent years has been to decentralization and more specialization. This is exemplified by the growth of staff who work for individual legislators, or one house or a committee of the legislature, rather than the institution as a whole. Separate committee staffing now exists to some extent in many legislatures, although it is most highly developed in California, Florida, Pennsylvania, and New York. Illinois, which had a highly diverse staff structure, recently has moved to a somewhat more centralized system with stronger leadership control.

In recent years, there also has been a growth in partisan staff. Until the 1960s, nearly all permanent legislative staff were hired on a non-partisan basis. But with the increase in leadership staff, caucus staff, and the partisan staffing of committees, there are now several states (including California, Hawaii, Illinois, Indiana, Michigan, Minnesota, New Jersey, New York, and Pennsylvania) that are characterized by sizeable partisan staffs.

In the past few years, there have been no major structural changes in legislative staff. Personal staff for legislators continues to be the area of greatest staff growth. Staff who provide direct constituent services and aid in election campaigns also are becoming increasingly prominent in state legislatures.

Legislative facilities

Accompanying this staff expansion has been an improvement in legislative facilities in most states. In a majority of states, legislators now are provided office space and no longer have to depend solely on their desks on the floor of the legislature. In a number of states, legislative office buildings have been constructed to house legislators and the expanded staff component. Most recently, legislative facilities in Alabama, Connecticut, Mississippi, and North Carolina have been improved or expanded. Modern, functional space for committees frequently is found in these facilities or in the many state capitol buildings which have been modernized and restored in the past decade. These improved facilities affect the legislature in several ways: the public has better access to legislators and the legislative process; and the legislature works under much better conditions. However, many observers feel that the interaction among legislators is affected in a negative way.

The institutional sense which accompanied the centralized, more confined working conditions of earlier years is no longer as strong in today's more decentralized working environment—one where legislators no longer spend as much time with each other. Instead, there is greater emphasis on the individual legislator, and the individual legislator has greater resources at his command. The addition of resources and their dispersal among the membership has made the legislator more independent, and in some cases, has weakened legislative leadership.

Information systems

Legislatures are continuing to install modern information systems and to utilize computer technology. The advent of small computer technology has had a significant impact on state legislatures. Many have developed new computer applications and sophisticated word processing systems, and have moved away from the large mainframe state systems which had been used primarily for bill drafting and bill status. Detailed fiscal analysis and tracking or modeling packages are now in use in many states. These newer systems allow more efficient and less expensive production of legislative journals and session laws, as well as improve bill drafting and make bill status information more quickly and widely available. Alabama, Kentucky, Nevada, New Jersey, North Carolina recently have made major improvements in their legislative information systems.

These legislative information systems bring much more information to the legislature, and in most cases, make it more widely available within the legislature. Now, individual legislators and legislative committees are able to demand and analyze much greater information about government programs and activities. Where word processing is available in the individual legislator's office, it alters the ability to communicate with constituents, and changes the way in which (and the frequency with which) such communication takes place. Several legislatures now provide computer terminals in the office of every legislator. Such developments contribute to the independence of the individual legislator and the decentralization of the legislative process. Even with this modernization and institutional reform of state legislatures, and the consequent expansion of legislative activity in many areas, legislatures still spend no more than one half of one percent of state general fund expenditures on their own operations.

Party Control

In 1985, the number of state legislators increased from 7,438 to 7,461 as a result of reapportionment-related increases in the size of the Idaho Legislature (total increase of 21 seats) and the Maine Senate (increase of 2 seats). The large increase in the size of the Idaho Legislature was the result of a judicial decision in a reapportionment lawsuit. Republicans gained strength in the state legislatures, but these gains returned the two-party balance to approximately the same position it had been in prior to the 1982 elections. As a result of the 1984 and 1985 elections, party control changed in 12 chambers, with the Republicans taking control of both houses in Connecticut, the Delaware House, the Minnesota House, the Nevada Assembly, the New Jersey General Assembly, the North Dakota House, and the Ohio Senate. Control switched to the Democrats in the Alaska House and the Vermont Senate. In two legislative bodies, the Montana House and the New Mexico Senate, the parties tied.

Coalition control—crossing party lines—has occurred in several legislative bodies in recent years. Currently, coalitions exist in the Alaska Senate and both houses of the New Mexico Legislature. The Montana House functions as a "shared power" situation in its current partisan tie. The Montana constitution anticipated such a situation, and provides that the party controlling the governor's office shall elect the speaker in a tie situation. The Vermont House, although majority Republican, elected a Democratic speaker for the second time in the past decade.

The Evolving Legislature

During the past biennium, state legislatures continued the trend toward increased capacity and a co-equal, policymaking role with the executive branch. Legislatures today are more capable and aggressive in budgeting and program oversight, including programs involving federal funds, than they were a decade or two ago.

State legislatures are dynamic institutions. The environment in which they function is changing considerably, as the responsibility for most domestic programs becomes centered in the states. This is reflected in the increased lobbying pressure on legislatures and the rapidly rising costs of legislative election campaigns. The number of registered lobbyists in many states has more than doubled in the last two years. And the costs of some state legislative election campaigns have risen to hundreds of thousands of dollars in the larger states, with proportionate increases in the smaller states.

There is evidence that legislatures are examining their internal operations and procedures to a greater extent than was the case after the earlier period of modernization and reform. This is the result of a changing environment, of experience with more staff, of new procedures and activities, and of a new wave of legislators in the 1980s. Legislatures are developing new constituent and information services, realizing that they must develop more formal management and evaluation procedures for legislative staff, and are continuing to seek new procedures to effectively use time and deal with the many current demands on state government and the legislatures.

Table 3.1
NAMES OF STATE LEGISLATIVE BODIES AND CONVENING PLACES

State or other jurisdiction	Both bodies	Upper house	Lower house	Convening place
Alabama	Legislature	Senate	House of Representatives	State Capitol
Alaska	Legislature	Senate	House of Representatives	State Capitol
Arizona	Legislature	Senate	House of Representatives	State Capitol
Arkansas	General Assembly	Senate	House of Representatives	State Capitol
California	Legislature	Senate	Assembly	State Capitol
Colorado	General Assembly	Senate	House of Representatives	State Capitol
Connecticut	General Assembly	Senate	House of Representatives	State Capitol
Delaware	General Assembly	Senate	House of Representatives	Legislative Hall
Florida	Legislature	Senate	House of Representatives	The Capitol
Georgia	General Assembly	Senate	House of Representatives	State Capitol
Hawaii	Legislature	Senate	House of Representatives	State Capitol
Idaho	Legislature	Senate	House of Representatives	State Capitol
Illinois	General Assembly	Senate	House of Representatives	State House
Indiana	General Assembly	Senate	House of Representatives	State House
Iowa	General Assembly	Senate	House of Representatives	State Capitol
Kansas	Legislature	Senate	House of Representatives	State House
Kentucky	General Assembly	Senate	House of Representatives	State Capitol
Louisiana	Legislature	Senate	House of Representatives	State Capitol
Maine	Legislature	Senate	House of Representatives	State House
Maryland	General Assembly	Senate	House of Delegates	State House
Massachusetts	General Court	Senate	House of Representatives	State House
Michigan	Legislature	Senate	House of Representatives	State Capitol
Minnesota	Legislature	Senate	House of Representatives	State Capitol
Mississippi	Legislature	Senate	House of Representatives	New Capitol
Missouri	General Assembly	Senate	House of Representatives	State Capitol
Montana	Legislature	Senate	House of Representatives	State Capitol
Nebraska	Legislature	(a)		State Capitol
Nevada	Legislature	Senate	Assembly	Legislative Building
New Hampshire	General Court	Senate	House of Representatives	State House
New Jersey	Legislature	Senate	General Assembly	State House
New Mexico	Legislature	Senate	House of Representatives	State Capitol
New York	Legislature	Senate	Assembly	State Capitol
North Carolina	General Assembly	Senate	House of Representatives	State Legislative Building
North Dakota	Legislative Assembly	Senate	House of Representatives	State Capitol
Ohio	General Assembly	Senate	House of Representatives	State House
Oklahoma	Legislature	Senate	House of Representatives	State Capitol
Oregon	Legislative Assembly	Senate	House of Representatives	State Capitol
Pennsylvania	General Assembly	Senate	House of Representatives	Main Capitol Building
Rhode Island	General Assembly	Senate	House of Representatives	State House
South Carolina	General Assembly	Senate	House of Representatives	State House
South Dakota	Legislature	Senate	House of Representatives	State Capitol
Tennessee	General Assembly	Senate	House of Representatives	State Capitol
Texas	Legislature	Senate	House of Representatives	State Capitol
Utah	Legislature	Senate	House of Representatives	State Capitol
Vermont	General Assembly	Senate	House of Representatives	State House
Virginia	General Assembly	Senate	House of Delegates	State Capitol
Washington	Legislature	Senate	House of Representatives	Legislative Building
West Virginia	Legislature	Senate	House of Delegates	State Capitol
Wisconsin	Legislature	Senate	Assembly(b)	State Capitol
Wyoming	Legislature	Senate	House of Representatives	State Capitol
Dist. of Col.	Council of the District of Columbia	(a)		District Building
American Samoa	Legislature	Senate	House of Representatives	Maota Fono
Guam	Legislature	(a)		Congress Building
No. Mariana Is.	Legislature	Senate	House of Representatives	Civic Center
Puerto Rico	Legislative Assembly	Senate	House of Representatives	The Capitol
Federated States of Micronesia	Congress	(a)		Congress Office Building
Virgin Islands	Legislature	(a)		Capitol Building

(a) Unicameral legislature. Except in District of Columbia, members go by the title Senator.
(b) Members of the lower house go by the title Representatiave.

Table 3.2
LEGISLATIVE SESSIONS: LEGAL PROVISIONS

State or other jurisdiction	Regular sessions				Special sessions		
	Year	Month	Day	Limitation on length of session(a)	Legislature may call	Legislature may determine subject of session	Limitation on length of session
Alabama	Annual	Jan. Apr. Feb.	2nd Tues.(b) 3rd Tues.(c,d) 1st Tues.(e)	30 L in 105 C	No	Yes(f)	12 L in 30 C
Alaska	Annual	Jan. Jan.	3rd Mon.(c) 2nd Mon.(e)	120 C(g)	By 2/3 vote of members	Yes(h)	30 C
Arizona	Annual	Jan.	2nd Mon.	(i)	By petition, 2/3 members, each house	Yes(h)	None
Arkansas	Biennial-odd year	Jan.	2nd Mon.	60 C(g)	No	Yes(f,j)	(j)
California	(k)	Jan.	1st Mon.(d)	None	No	No	None
Colorado	Annual	Jan.	Wed. after 1st Tues.	(l)	By request, 2/3 members, each house	Yes(h)	None
Connecticut	Annual(m)	Jan. Feb.	Wed. after 1st Mon.(n) Wed. after 1st Mon.(o)	(p)	Yes(q)	(q)	None(r)
Delaware	Annual	Jan.	2nd Tues.	June 30	Joint call, presiding officers, both houses	Yes	None
Florida	Annual	Apr.	Tues. after 1st Mon.(d)	60 C(g)	Joint call, presiding officers, both houses	Yes	20 C(g)
Georgia	Annual	Jan.	2nd Mon.(d)	40 L	By petition, 3/5 members, each house	Yes(h)	(s)
Hawaii	Annual	Jan.	3rd Wed.	60 L(g)	By petition, 2/3 members, each house	Yes	30 L(g)
Idaho	Annual	Jan.	Mon. on or nearest 9th day	None	No	No	20 C
Illinois	Annual	Jan.	2nd Wed.	None	Joint call, presiding officers, both houses	Yes	None
Indiana	Annual	Jan.	2nd Mon.(d,t)	odd-61 L or Apr. 30; even-30 L or Mar. 15	No	Yes	30 L in 40 C
Iowa	Annual	Jan.	2nd Mon.	(u)	By petition, 2/3 members, both houses	Yes	None
Kansas	Annual	Jan.	2nd Mon.	odd-None; even-90 C(g)	Petition to governor of 2/3 members, each house	Yes	None
Kentucky	Biennial-even yr.	Jan.	Tues. after 1st Mon.(d)	60 L(v)	No	No	None
Louisiana	Annual	Apr.	3rd Mon.	60 L in 85 C	By petition, majority, each house	Yes(h)	30 C
Maine	(k,m)	Dec. Jan.	1st Wed.(b) Wed. after 1st Tues.(o)	100 L(g) 50 L(g)	Joint call, presiding officers, with consent of majority of members of each political party, each house	Yes(h)	None
Maryland	Annual	Jan.	2nd Wed.	90 C(g)	By petition, majority, each house	Yes	30 C

LEGISLATIVE SESSIONS: LEGAL PROVISIONS—Continued

State or other jurisdiction	Regular sessions Year	Legislature convenes Month	Day	Limitation on length of session(a)	Special sessions Legislature may call	Legislature may determine subject	Limitation on length of session
Massachusetts	Annual	Jan.	1st Wed.	None	By petition(w)	Yes	None
Michigan	Annual	Jan.	2nd Wed.(d)	None	No	No	None
Minnesota	(x)	Jan.	Tues. after 1st Mon.(n)	120 L or 1st Mon. after 3rd Sat. in May(x)	No	Yes	None
Mississippi	Annual	Jan.	Tues. after 1st Mon.	125 C(g,y); 90 C(g,y)	No	No	None
Missouri	Annual	Jan.	Wed. after 1st Mon.	odd-June 30; even-May 15	No	No	60 C
Montana	Biennial-odd yr.	Jan.	1st Mon.	90 L(g)	By petition, majority, both houses	Yes	None
Nebraska	Annual	Jan.	Wed. after 1st Mon.	odd-90 L(g); even-60 L(g)	By petition, 2/3 members, each house	Yes	None
Nevada	Biennial-odd yr.	Jan.	3rd Mon.	60 C(u)	No	No	20 C(u)
New Hampshire	Annual	Jan.	Wed. after 1st Tues.	45 L	By 2/3 vote of members	Yes	(u)
New Jersey	Annual	Jan.	2nd Tues.	None	By petition, majority, each house	Yes	None
New Mexico	Annual(m)	Jan.	3rd Tues.	odd-60 C; even-30 C	By petition, 3/5 members, each house	Yes(h)	30 C
New York	Annual	Jan.	Wed. after 1st Mon.	None(x)	By petition, 2/3 members, each house	Yes(h)	None
North Carolina	(x)	Jan.	Wed. after 2nd Mon.(n)	None(x)	By petition, 3/5 members, each house	Yes	None
North Dakota	Biennial-odd yr.	Jan.	Tues. after Jan. 3, but not later than Jan. 11(d)	80 L(z)	No	Yes	None
Ohio	Annual	Jan.	1st Mon.	None	Joint call, presiding officers, both houses	Yes	None
Oklahoma	Annual	Jan.	Tues. after 1st Mon.	90 L	By 2/3 vote of members	Yes	None
Oregon	Biennial-odd yr.	Jan.	2nd Mon.	None	By petition, majority, each house	Yes	None
Pennsylvania	Annual	Jan.	1st Tues.	None	By petition, majority, each house	No	None
Rhode Island	Annual	Jan.	1st Tues.	60 L(u)	No	No	None
South Carolina	Annual	Jan.	2nd Tues.(d)	1st Thurs. in June(g)	No	Yes	None
South Dakota	Annual	Jan.	Tues. after 1st Mon.	odd-40 L; even-35 L	No	No	None
Tennessee	(x)	Jan.	(aa)	90 L(u)	By petition, 2/3 members, each house	Yes	30 L(u)

84

LEGISLATIVE SESSIONS: LEGAL PROVISIONS—Continued

State or other jurisdiction	Regular sessions				Special sessions		
	Legislature convenes			Limitation on length of session(a)	Legislature may call	Legislature may determine on length subject of session	Limitation on length of session
	Year	Month	Day				
Texas..................	Biennial-odd yr.	Jan.	2nd Tues.	140 C	No	No	30 C
Utah..................	Annual	Jan.	2nd Mon.	45 C	No	No	30 C
Vermont...............	(x)	Jan.	Wed. after 1st Mon.(n)	(u)	No	Yes	None
Virginia...............	Annual	Jan.	2nd Wed.	odd-30 C(g); even-60 C(g)	By petition, 2/3 members, each house	Yes	None
Washington...........	Annual	Jan.	2nd Mon.	odd-105 C; even-60 C	By petition, 2/3 members, each house	Yes	30 C
West Virginia.........	Annual	Feb. / Jan.	2nd Wed.(c,d) / 2nd Wed.(e)	60 C(g)	By petition, 3/5 members, each house	Yes(bb)	None
Wisconsin.............	Annual(cc)	Jan.	1st Tues. after Jan. 8(d,n)	None	No	No	None
Wyoming..............	Annual(m)	Jan. / Feb.	2nd Tues.(n) / 2nd Tues.(o)	odd-40 L; even-20 L	No	Yes	None
Dist. of Col..........	(dd)	Jan.	2nd day	None			
American Samoa	Annual	Jan. / July	2nd Mon. / 2nd Mon.	45 L / 45 L	No	No	None
Guam.................	Annual	Jan.	1st Mon.(ee)	None	No	No	None
Puerto Rico...........	Annual	Jan.	2nd Mon.	Apr. 30(g)	No	No	20 C
Virgin Islands	Annual	Jan.	2nd Mon.	75 L	No	No	15 C

Note: Some legislatures will also reconvene after normal session to consider bills vetoed by governor. Connecticut—if governor vetoes any bill, secretary of state must reconvene General Assembly on second Monday after the last day on which governor is either authorized to transmit or has transmitted every bill with his objections, whichever occurs first; General Assembly must adjourn *sine die* not later than three days after its reconvening. Hawaii—legislature may reconvene on 45th day after adjournment *sine die*, in special session, without call. Louisiana—legislature meets in a maximum five-day veto session on the 40th day after final adjournment. Missouri—if governor returns any bill on or after the fifth day before the last day on which legislature may consider bills (in even-numbered years), legislature automatically reconvenes on first Monday in September for a maximum 10 C session. New Jersey—legislature meets in special session (without call or petition) to act on bills returned by governor on 45th day after *sine die* adjournment of the first year of a two-year legislature; a special session may not be convened if the 45th day falls on or after the last day of the legislative year in which the second session occurs. Virginia—legislature reconvenes on sixth Wednesday after adjournment for a maximum three-day session (may be extended to seven days upon vote of majority of members elected to each house). Utah—if 2/3 of the members of each house favor reconvening to consider vetoed bills, a maximum five-day session is set by the presiding officers. Washington—upon petition of 2/3 of the members of each house, legislature meets 45 days after adjournment for a maximum five-day session.

Key:
C—Calendar day
L—Legislative day (in some states, called a session day or workday; definition may vary slightly, however, generally refers to any day on which either house of the legislature is in session)

(a) Applies to each year unless otherwise indicated.
(b) General election year (quadrennial election).
(c) Year after quadrennial election.
(d) Legal provision for organizational session prior to stated convening date. Alabama—in the year after quadrennial election, on the second Tuesday in January for 10 C. California—in the even-numbered, general election year, on first Monday in December for an organizational session, recess until the first Monday in January of the odd-numbered year. Florida—in general election year, 14th day after election. Georgia—in odd-numbered year. Indiana—third Tuesday after first Monday in November. Kentucky—in odd-numbered year, Tuesday after first Monday in January for 10 L. Michigan—held in odd-numbered year. New Hampshire—in even-numbered year, first Wednesday in December. North Dakota—in even-numbered year, Tuesday after first Monday in December of three-day session. South Carolina—in even-numbered year, Tuesday after certification of election of its members for a maximum three-day session. West Virginia—in year after general election, on second Wednesday in January.
(e) Other years.
(f) By 2/3 vote each house.
(g) Session may be extended by vote of members in both houses. Alaska: 2/3 vote for 10-day extension. Arkansas: 2/3 vote. Florida: 3/5 vote. Hawaii: petition of 2/3 membership for maximum 15-day extension. Kansas: 2/3 vote. Maryland: 3/5 vote for maximum 30 C. Mississippi: 2/3 vote for 30-day extension, no limit on number of extensions. Nebraska: 4/5 vote. South Carolina: 2/3 vote. Virginia: 2/3 vote for 30-day extension. West Virginia: 2/3 vote (or if budget bill has not been acted upon three days before session ends, governor issues proclamation extending session). Puerto Rico: joint resolution.
(h) Only if legislature convenes itself. Special sessions called by the legislature are unlimited in scope in Arizona, Georgia, Maine, and New Mexico.
(i) No constitutional or statutory provision; however, legislative rules require that regular sessions

LEGISLATIVE SESSIONS: LEGAL PROVISIONS—Continued

adjourn no later than Saturday of the week during which the 100th day of the session falls.

(j) After governor's business has been disposed of, members may remain in session up to 15 C by a 2/3 vote of both houses.

(k) Regular sessions begin after general election, in December of even-numbered year. In California, legislature meets in December for an organizational session, recesses until the first Monday in January of the odd-numbered year and continues in session until Nov. 30 of next even-numbered year. In Maine, session which begins in December of general election year runs into the following year (odd-numbered); second session begins in next even-numbered year.

(l) A 1982 constitutional amendment imposed a time limit of 140 C on regular sessions convening in even-numbered years.

(m) Second session limited to consideration of specific types of legislation. Connecticut—individual legislators may only introduce bills of a fiscal nature. Maine—budgetary matters; legislation in the governor's call; emergency legislation; legislation referred to committees for study. New Mexico—budgets, appropriations and revenue bills; bills drawn pursuant to governor's message; vetoed bills. Wyoming—budget bills.

(n) Odd-numbered years.

(o) Even-numbered years.

(p) Odd-numbered years—not later than Wednesday after first Monday in June; even-numbered years—not later than Wednesday after first Monday in May.

(q) Constitution provides for regular session convening dates and allows that sessions may also be held "...at such other times as the General Assembly shall judge necessary." Call by majority of legislators is implied.

(r) Upon completion of business.

(s) Limited to 40 days if called by governor and 30 days if called by petition of the legislature, except in cases of impeachment proceedings.

(t) Legislators may reconvene at any time after organizational meeting; however, second Monday in January is the final date by which regular session must be in process.

(u) Indirect limitation; usually restrictions on legislator's pay, per diem, or daily allowance.

(v) May not extend beyond April 15.

(w) Joint rules provide for the submission of a written statement requesting special session by a specified number of members of each chamber.

(x) Legal provision for session in odd-numbered year; however, legislature may divide, and in practice has divided, to meet in even-numbered years as well.

(y) A 1968 constitutional amendment calls for 90 C sessions every year, except the first year of a gubernatorial administration during which the legislative session runs for 125 C.

(z) No legislative day is shorter than a natural day.

(aa) Commencement of regular session depends on concluding date of organizational session. Legislature meets, in odd-numbered year, on second Tuesday in January for a maximum 15 C organizational session, then returns on the Tuesday following the conclusion of the organizational session.

(bb) According to a 1955 attorney general's opinion, when the legislature has petitioned to the governor to be called into session, it may then act on any matter.

(cc) The legislature, by joint resolution, establishes the session schedule of activity for the remainder of the biennium at the beginning of the odd-numbered year.

(dd) Each Council period begins on January 2 of each odd-numbered year and ends on January 1 of the following odd-numbered year.

(ee) Legislature meets on the first Monday of each month following its initial session in January.

Table 3.3
THE LEGISLATORS
Numbers, Terms, and Party Affiliations

State or other jurisdiction	Senate						House						Senate and House totals
	Demo-crats	Repub-licans	Other	Vacan-cies	Total	Term	Demo-crats	Repub-licans	Other	Vacan-cies	Total	Term	
All States	1,188	753	3	2	1,995		3,136	2,317	8	5	5,466		7,461
Alabama............	28	4	3(a)	...	35	4	87	12	5(a)	1	105	4	140
Alaska.............	9	11	...	...	20	4	21	18	1(b)	...	40	2	60
Arizona............	12	18	...	...	30	2	22	38	...	...	60	2	90
Arkansas	31	4	...	...	35	4	91	9	...	...	100	2	135
California..........	25	15	...	...	40	4	47	33	...	...	80	2	120
Colorado	11	24	...	...	35	4	18	47	...	...	65	2	100
Connecticut	12	24	...	...	36	2	66	85	...	...	151	2	187
Delaware	13	8	...	...	21	4	19	22	...	...	41	2	62
Florida	32	8	...	...	40	4	77	43	...	...	120	2	160
Georgia	47	9	...	...	56	2	154	26	...	...	180	2	236
Hawaii	21	4	...	...	25	4	40	11	...	...	51	2	76
Idaho	14	28	...	...	42	2	17	67	...	...	84	2	126
Illinois............	31	28	...	...	59	4(c)	67	51	...	...	118	2	177
Indiana	20	30	...	...	50	4	39	61	...	...	100	2	150
Iowa	29	21	...	...	50	4	60	40	...	...	100	2	150
Kansas	16	24	...	...	40	4	49	76	...	...	125	2	165
Kentucky	28	10	...	...	38	4	74	26	...	...	100	2	138
Louisiana	38	1	...	...	39	4	91	14	...	...	105	4	144
Maine	24	11	...	...	35	2	85	66	...	...	151	2	186
Maryland	41	6	...	...	47	4	124	17	...	...	141	4	188
Massachusetts	32	8	...	...	40	2	126	34	...	...	160	2	200
Michigan	18	19	...	1	38	4	57	53	...	...	110	2	148
Minnesota	42(d)	24(e)	...	1	67	4	65(d)	69(e)	...	...	134	2	201
Mississippi	49	3	...	...	52	4	116	6	...	...	122	4	174
Missouri	21	13	...	...	34	4	108	55	...	...	163	2	197
Montana...........	28	22	...	...	50	4(f)	50	50	...	...	100	2	150
Nebraska	----------Nonpartisan election----------				49	4	----------------------Unicameral----------------------						49
Nevada	13	8	...	...	21	4	17	25	...	...	42	2	63
New Hampshire	6	18	...	...	24	2	102	297	...	1	400	2	424
New Jersey.........	23	17	...	...	40	4(g)	30	50	...	1	80	2	120
New Mexico........	21	21	...	...	42	4	42	28	...	...	70	2	112
New York..........	26	35	...	...	61	2	94	56	...	...	150	2	211
North Carolina	38	12	...	...	50	2	82	38	...	...	120	2	170
North Dakota	24	29	...	...	53	4	42	64	...	...	106	2	159
Ohio	15	18	...	...	33	4	58	40	...	1	99	2	132
Oklahoma	34	14	...	...	48	4	69	32	...	...	101	2	149
Oregon	18	12	...	...	30	4	34	26	...	...	60	2	90
Pennsylvania	23	27	...	...	50	4	103	100	...	...	203	2	253
Rhode Island	38	12	...	...	50	2	77	21	1(a)	1	100	2	150
South Carolina	36	10	...	...	46	4	96	27	...	1	124	2	170
South Dakota	10	25	...	...	35	2	13	57	...	...	70	2	105
Tennessee	23	10	...	...	33	4	62	37	...	...	99	2	132
Texas..............	25	6	...	...	31	4	98	52	...	...	150	2	181
Utah	6	23	...	...	29	4	14	61	...	...	75	2	104
Vermont	18	12	...	...	30	2	72	78	...	...	150	2	180
Virginia............	31	8	...	1	40	4	65	33	2(a)	...	100	2	140
Washington	27	22	...	...	49	4	53	45	...	...	98	2	147
West Virginia	30	4	...	...	34	4	73	27	...	...	100	2	134
Wisconsin..........	19	14	...	...	33	4	52	47	...	...	99	2	132
Wyoming	11	19	...	...	30	4	18	46	...	...	64	2	94
Dist. of Col.(h)......	11	1	1(i)	...	13	4	----------------------Unicameral----------------------						13
American Samoa	---Nonpartisan selection---			2	18	4	--------Nonpartisan election--------				21	2	39
Guam	11	10	...	...	21	2	----------------------Unicameral----------------------						21
No. Mariana Is.	2	7	...	...	9	4	6	8	...	1	15	2	24
Puerto Rico	18(j)	8(k)	1(l)	...	27	4	34(j)	15(k)	1(l)	1	51	4	78
Virgin Islands	8	1	6(m)	...	15	2	----------------------Unicameral----------------------						15

Note: Table reflects the legislatures as of January 1985, except for New Jersey, Virginia, and the Northern Mariana Islands; information for those jurisdictions is as of January 1986.
  (a) Independent.
  (b) Libertarian.
  (c) The entire Senate is up for election every 10 years, beginning in 1972. Senate districts are divided into three groups. One group elects senators for terms of 4-years, 4-years, and 2-years, the second group for terms of 4-years, 2-years, and 4-years, the third group for terms of 2-years, 4-years, and 4-years.
  (d) Democratic-Farmer-Labor.
  (e) Independent-Republican.

  (f) After each decennial reapportionment, lots are drawn for half of the senators to serve an initial 2-year term. Subsequent elections are for 4-year terms.
  (g) Senate terms beginning in January of second year following the U.S. decennial census are for 2 years only.
  (h) Council of the District of Columbia.
  (i) Statehood Party.
  (j) Popular Democratic Party.
  (k) New Progressive Party.
  (l) Independent Puerto Rican Party.
  (m) Five Independents and one Independent Citizens Movement.

Table 3.4
MEMBERSHIP TURNOVER IN THE LEGISLATURES: 1984

State	Senate Total number of members	Number of membership changes	Percentage change of total	House Total number of members	Number of membership changes	Percentage change of total
Alabama	35 (a)			105 (a)		
Alaska	20 (b)	4	20	40	20	50
Arizona	30	2	6	60	9	15
Arkansas	35 (b)	5	14	100	20	20
California	40 (b)	2	5	80	3	4
Colorado	35 (b)	8	23	65	21	32
Connecticut	36	15	42	151	40	26
Delaware	21 (b)	1	5	41	7	17
Florida	40 (b)	3	8	120	13	11
Georgia	56	6	11	180	22	12
Hawaii	25 (b)	3	12	51	12	24
Idaho	42 (c)			84 (c)		
Illinois	59 (b)	7	12	118	24	20
Indiana	50 (b)	6	12	100	15	15
Iowa	50 (b)	7	14	100	12	12
Kansas	40	10	25	125	25	20
Kentucky	38 (a)			100	23	23
Louisiana	39 (a)			105 (a)		
Maine	35 (c)			151	47	31
Maryland	47 (a)			141 (a)		
Massachusetts	40	8	20	160	30	19
Michigan	38 (a)			110	16	14
Minnesota	67 (a)			134	29	22
Mississippi	52 (a)			122 (a)		
Missouri	34 (b)	5	15	163	26	16
Montana	50 (b)	12	24	100	34	34
Nebraska	49 (b)	14	28	Unicameral		
Nevada	21 (b)	6	28	42	13	31
New Hampshire	24	8	33	400	165	41
New Jersey	40 (a)			80 (a)		
New Mexico	42	18	43	70	18	26
New York	61	10	16	150	19	13
North Carolina	50	20	40	120	41	34
North Dakota	53 (b)	8	15	106	32	30
Ohio	33 (b)	7	21	99	13	13
Oklahoma	48 (b)	4	8	101	25	25
Oregon	30 (b)	6	20	60	19	32
Pennsylvania	50 (b)	5	10	203	23	11
Rhode Island	50 (d)	16 (d)	32 (d)	100	25	25
South Carolina	46	18	39	124	31	25
South Dakota	35	8	23	70	20	28
Tennessee	33 (b)	6	18	99	20	20
Texas	31 (b)	2	6	150	37	25
Utah	29 (b)	3	10	75	18	24
Vermont	30	7	23	150	39	26
Virginia	40 (a)			100 (a)		
Washington	49 (b)	10	20	98	27	28
West Virginia	34 (b)	7	20	100	38	38
Wisconsin	33 (b)	8	24	99	29	29
Wyoming	30 (b)	9	30	64	16	25

Note: Turnover calculated after 1984 legislative elections. Data was obtained by comparing the 1983-84 (and 1984 update) and 1985-86 editions of *State Elective Officials and the Legislatures,* published by The Council of State Governments.
(a) No election held in 1984.
(b) Entire Senate membership not up for reelection in 1984.

(c) Total number of seats changed. Turnover cannot be determined using method employed here.
(d) Senate elections were held in 1983 instead of 1982 as a result of court-ordered redistricting. Data reported for Senate were obtained by comparing 1983 post-election roster of members against 1985 roster.

Table 3.5
THE LEGISLATORS: QUALIFICATIONS FOR ELECTION

State or other jurisdiction	House — Minimum age	U.S. Citizen (years)	State resident (years)	District resident (years)	Qualified Voter (years)	Senate — Minimum age	U.S. Citizen (years)	State resident (years)	District resident (years)	Qualified Voter (years)
Alabama	21		3(a)	1		25		3(a)	1	★
Alaska	21		3	1	★	25		3	1	★
Arizona	25	★	3	1	★	25	★	3	1	★
Arkansas	21	★	2	1	★	25	★	2	1	
California	18	3	3	1	★	18	3	3	1	★
Colorado	25	★		1		25	★		1	
Connecticut	18				★	18				★
Delaware	24		3(a)	1	★	27		3(a)	1	★
Florida	21		2			21		2		
Georgia	21	★	(a)	1		25	★	(a)	1	★
Hawaii	18		3	(b)	★	18		3	(b)	★
Idaho	18	★		1	★	18	★		1	★
Illinois	21	★		2(c)		21	★		2(c)	
Indiana	21	★	2		★	25	★	2	1	
Iowa	21		1	60 da.	★	25		1	60 da.	★
Kansas	18		2(a)	1	★	18		6(a)	1	★
Kentucky	24		2	1	★	30		2	1	
Louisiana	18	5	1	3 mo.		18	5	2	3 mo.	★
Maine	21		1(a)	6 mo.(d)	★	25		1(a)	6 mo.(d)	
Maryland	21	★	1(a)			25	★			★
Massachusetts	18			1	★	18		5	(b)	★
Michigan(e)	21			(b)	★	21	★	1	6 mo.	★
Minnesota	21		1	6 mo.	★	21		4	2	4
Mississippi	21		4(a)	2	★	25			1(f)	3
Missouri	24			1(f)	2	30				
Montana(g)	18		1(a)	6 mo.(h)	★	18		1(a)	6 mo.(h)	★
Nebraska	U	U	U	U	U	21		1(a)	1	★
Nevada	21		1(a)	(b)	U	21		1(a)	(b)	★
New Hampshire	18		2	★		30		7(a)	★	
New Jersey	21		2(a)	1	★	30		4(a)	1	★
New Mexico	21	★		★		25		5	★	★
New York	18	★	5	1(i)	★	18	★	2(a)	1(i)	★
North Carolina	21(j)		1	1	★	25	★	1	1	4
North Dakota	18		1	(b)	★	18		1	(b)	★
Ohio(k)	18			1	★	18			1	★

THE LEGISLATORS: QUALIFICATIONS FOR ELECTION—Continued

State or other jurisdiction	House					Senate				
	Minimum age	U.S. Citizen (years)	State resident (years)	District resident (years)	Qualified Voter (years)	Minimum age	U.S. Citizen (years)	State resident (years)	District resident (years)	Qualified Voter (years)
Oklahoma	21	★	. . .	(b)	. . .	25	. . .	. . .	(b)	★
Oregon	21	★	. . .	. . .	. . .	21	★	. . .	1	. . .
Pennsylvania	21	. . .	4(a)	1	. . .	25	. . .	4(a)	—	. . .
Rhode Island(l)	18	. . .	. . .	. . .	★	18	. . .	. . .	. . .	★
South Carolina	21	. . .	. . .	(b)	★	25	. . .	. . .	(b)	★
South Dakota(k,l)	25	★	2	(b)	★	25	★	2	(b)	★
Tennessee	21	★	(a)	1(b)	★	30	★	3	1(b)	★
Texas	21	★	2	1	★	26	★	5	1	★
Utah	25	. . .	3	6 mo.(b)	★	25	★	3	6 mo.(b)	★
Vermont	18	. . .	2	1	. . .	18	. . .	2	1	. . .
Virginia	21	. . .	. . .	★	★	21	. . .	. . .	★	★
Washington	18	★	. . .	(b)	★	18	★	. . .	(b)	★
West Virginia(l)	18	. . .	(a)	1	★	25	. . .	(a)	1	★
Wisconsin	18	. . .	1	(b)	★	18	. . .	1	(b)	★
Wyoming	21	★	(a)	1	. . .	25	★	(a)	1	. . .
Dist. of Col.	U	U	U	U	U	18	. . .	1	★	★
American Samoa(l)	25	★(m)	5	1	. . .	30(n)	★(m)	5	1	. . .
Guam(c)	U	U	U	U	U	25	★	5	. . .	. . .
No. Mariana Is.	21	. . .	3	. . .	★	25	. . .	. . .	. . .	★
Puerto Rico(p)	25	★	2(a)	1(q)	. . .	30	. . .	2(a)	1(q)	. . .
Virgin Islands(o)	U	U	U	U	U	21	★	3	. . .	★

Note: This table includes constitutional and statutory provisions.

Key:

U—Unicameral legislature; members are called senators, except in District of Columbia.

★—Formal provision; number of years not specified.

. . .—No formal provision.

(a) Additional state citizenship requirement. Alabama, Delaware—three years. Georgia, New Jersey-House, two years; Senate, four years. Mississippi—four years. New Hampshire—seven years. North Carolina—two years. Pennsylvania—four years. West Virginia—five years.

(b) Must be a qualified voter of the district; number of years not specified.

(c) Following redistricting, a candidate may be elected from any district that contains a part of the district in which he resided at the time of redistricting, and reelected if a resident of the new district he represents for 18 months prior to reelection.

(d) If the district was established for less than six months, residency is length of establishment of district.

(e) No person convicted of a felony or breach of public trust within preceding 20 years or convicted of subversion shall be eligible.

(f) Only if the district has been in existence for one year; if not, then legislator must have been a one year resident of the district(s) from which the new district was created.

(g) No person convicted of a felony is eligible to hold office until final discharge from state supervision.

(h) Shall be a resident of the county if it contains one or more districts or of the district if it contains all or parts of more than one county.

(i) After redistricting, must have been a resident of the county in which the district is contained for one year immediately preceding election.

(j) A conflict exists between two articles of the constitution, one specifying age for House members (i.e., "qualified voter of the state") and the other related to general eligibility for elective office (i.e., "every qualified voter . . . who is 21 years of age . . . shall be eligible for election").

(k) No person convicted of embezzlement of public funds shall hold any office.

(l) Disqualification for bribery. In South Dakota and West Virginia, disqualification also for perjury or other infamous crimes. In American Samoa, also for felony.

(m) Or U.S. national.

(n) Must be registered matai.

(o) Disqualification for felony or crime involving moral turpitude unless person received pardon restoring civil rights.

(p) Read and write the Spanish or English language.

(q) When there is more than one representative district in a municipality, residence in the municipality shall satisfy this requirement.

Table 3.6
SENATE LEADERSHIP POSITIONS—METHODS OF SELECTION*

State or other jurisdiction	President	President pro tem	Majority leader	Assistant majority leader	Majority floor leader	Assistant majority floor leader	Majority whip	Majority caucus chairman	Minority leader	Assistant minority leader	Minority floor leader	Assistant minority floor leader	Minority whip	Minority caucus chairman
Alabama	(a)	ES	EC						EC					
Alaska	ES	(b)	EC	EC					EC				EC	
Arizona	ES	ES												
Arkansas	ES												EC	EC
California	(a)	ES		EC	EC		EC	EC	EC	EC	EC		EC	EC
Colorado	ES	ES	EC	EC		EC		EC	EC	EC	EC		EC	EC
Connecticut	(a)	ES	AT	AT/6(c)			AT/2	EC	EC	AL/8(c)	EC		EC	EC
Delaware	ES	ES	EC				EC	AP	EC	EC(d)	EC		EC	
Florida	ES	ES	EC	EC(d)			EC	EC	EC		EC		EC	EC
Georgia	(a)	ES	EC				EC	EC	EC		EC			
Hawaii	ES	ES(e)	EC	EC	EC	EC	(f)	EC	EC	EC	EC		(f)	EC
Idaho	(a)	ES	EC	EC			AP/2	AP	EC	AL/3	EC			AL
Illinois	ES(g)	ES	(g)	AP/3	AT	AT	AT	EC	AL	AL/3	AL	AL	AL	EC
Indiana	(a)	ES	EC						EC					
Iowa	(a)	ES	EC	EC/2		EC	EC	EC	EC	EC/3	EC			
Kansas	ES	ES(e)	EC	EC	EC		EC	EC	EC	EC	EC		EC	EC
Kentucky	(a)	ES						EC	EC	EC			EC	EC
Louisiana	ES	ES												
Maine	ES				EC	EC			EC		EC	EC	EC	
Maryland	ES	ES	AP	AP(h)	EC	EC	AP(h)		EC		EC			
Massachusetts	ES(i)	ES	EC	EC	AP	AP/2	AP	(i)	EC(i)	EC	EC	AL/3	AL	(i)
Michigan	(a)	ES	EC	EC	EC	EC	EC	EC	EC	EC	EC	EC	EC	EC
Minnesota	ES	ES	EC				EC/3		EC		EC	EC/4	EC	
Mississippi	(a)	ES				EC								
Missouri	(a)	ES		EC	EC				EC	EC	EC	EC		
Montana	ES	ES					EC	EC	EC	EC	EC		EC	
Nebraska(U)	(a)	ES(j)						AT						
Nevada	ES	ES	AP	AP			AP		AP					
New Hampshire	ES	AP(e)	AP	AP			AP		AP	AL			AL	
New Jersey	ES	ES	EC	EC/3	EC		EC/3	EC	EC	EC/2	EC	EC	EC	
New Mexico	(a)	ES	(k)		EC		EC/2	EC	EC	AL	EC		EC	EC
New York	(a)	ES(k)	EC	AT	AT		AT	AT	EC	AL	EC	EC	AL/2	AL
North Carolina	(a)	ES	EC					EC	EC	AL	EC		EC	
North Dakota	(a)	ES	EC	EC					EC	EC	EC			
Ohio	ES(i)	ES			ES		ES	(i)	ES(i)	ES			ES	(i)

91

SENATE LEADERSHIP POSITIONS—METHODS OF SELECTION—Continued

State or other jurisdiction	President	President pro tem	Majority leader	Assistant majority leader	Majority floor leader	Assistant majority floor leader	Majority whip	Majority caucus chairman	Minority leader	Assistant minority leader	Minority floor leader	Assistant minority floor leader	Minority whip	Minority caucus chairman
Oklahoma	(a)	ES	...	EC/2	EC	EC	EC/2	EC	...	EC	EC	EC	EC	EC
Oregon	(a)	ES	EC	...	...	...	EC	...	EC	EC	EC	EC	EC	EC
Pennsylvania	(a)	ES	EC	EC/7	...	...	EC	...	EC	EC/2	EC	EC	EC	EC
Rhode Island	(a)	ES	EC	...	...	...	EC	...	EC	...	...	...	...	...
South Carolina	(a)	ES	...	...	...	...	...	...	...	...	...	...	...	...
South Dakota	(a)	ES	EC	EC	EC	...	EC/4	EC	EC	...	EC	...	...	EC
Tennessee	ES(j)	EC	...	...	...	...	...	...	...	...	...	...	...	...
Utah	(a)	ES	EC	EC	EC	...	EC	...	EC	...	EC	...	EC	...
Vermont	(a)	ES	EC	...	...	...	...	...	EC	...	EC	...	...	...
Virginia	(a)	ES	EC	EC	...	...	EC	EC	EC	EC	EC	EC	EC	EC
Washington	(a)	ES	EC	EC	...	...	EC	EC	EC	EC	EC	...	...	EC
West Virginia	ES	AP	AP	...	...	...	AP	EC	EC	...	EC	...	...	...
Wisconsin	ES	ES	EC	EC	EC	...	...	EC	EC	EC	EC	...	EC	EC
Wyoming	ES	ES(e)	...	...	EC	...	...	...	EC	...	EC	...	EC(l)	(l)
Dist. of Col.(U)	(m)	(n)	...	...	...	...	...	...	...	...	...	...	...	...
American Samoa	ES	ES	...	...	...	...	...	...	EC	...	EC	...	...	...
Guam(U)	ES(j)	ES(e)	EC	...	EC	...	...	(i)	EC	EC	EC	...	...	(i)
Puerto Rico	ES(i)	EC(i)	...	...	...	...	...	...	EC(i)	EC	...	...	EC(i)	(i)
Virgin Islands(U)	ES	ES(e)	ES(o)	...	...	...	...	...	(p)	...	EC	...	...	...

Note: In some states, the leadership positions in the Senate are not empowered by the law or by the rules of the chamber, but rather by the party members themselves. Entry following slash indicates number of individuals holding specified position.

Key:
ES—Elected or confirmed by all members of the Senate.
EC—Elected by party caucus.
AP—Appointed by president.
AT—Appointed by president pro tempore.
AL—Appointed by party leader.
(U)—Unicameral legislative body.
. . .—Position does not exist or is not selected on a regular basis.

(a) Lieutenant governor is president of the Senate by virtue of the office.
(b) President *may* name any member as president pro tempore to serve during the former's absence. The appointment may extend throughout the session unless terminated by the Senate.
(c) Assistant majority leader: three deputy majority leaders and three assistant majority leaders. Assis-

tant minority leader: deputy minority leader and seven assistant minority leaders.
(d) Official titles are majority leader pro tempore and minority leader pro tempore.
(e) Official title is vice president. In Guam, vice speaker.
(f) Majority policy leader; minority policy leader.
(g) President is also majority leader.
(h) Joint appointment by president and the majority leader.
(i) President and minority floor leader are also caucus chairmen. In Ohio and Puerto Rico, president and minority leader.
(j) Official title is speaker of the Senate. In Tennessee, officer has the statutory title of "lieutenant governor."
(k) President pro tempore is also majority leader.
(l) Minority whip is also caucus chairman.
(m) Chairman of the Council.
(n) Appointed by the chairman.
(o) Officer designated by a majority of the members.
(p) Any three or more senators may meet in order to select the minority leader.

Table 3.7
HOUSE LEADERSHIP POSITIONS—METHODS OF SELECTION

State or other jurisdiction	Speaker	Speaker pro tem	Majority leader	Assistant majority leader	Majority floor leader	Assistant majority floor leader	Majority whip	Majority caucus chairman	Minority leader	Assistant minority leader	Minority floor leader	Assistant minority floor leader	Minority whip	Minority caucus chairman
Alabama	EH	EH	EC				EC		EC				EC	
Alaska	EH	EH	EC				EC		EC	EC			EC	
Arizona	EH	AS	(a)				EC		EC	EC			EC	
Arkansas	EH	EH											EC	
California	EH	EH		EC	AS(b)		EC	EC	EC		EC		EC/2	EC
Colorado	EH	AS(c)	EC	EC				EC	EC					EC
Connecticut	EH		EC	AL/11(d)			EC		EC	AL/13(d)			AL/2	
Delaware	EH	EH	AS	AS/3			EC		EC	EC(e)			EC	
Florida	EH	EH	AS				AS		EC				AL/2	AL
Georgia	EH	EH	EC				EC	EC	EC				EC	EC
Hawaii	EH	EH(f)	EC	EC	EC	EC/6		EC	EC		EC	EC/2		
Idaho	EH		EC	AS/4			AS/2		EC	EC				EC
Illinois	EH	AS	AS		EC		AS	AS	EC	AL/4	EC		AL/2	AL
Indiana	EH	EH						EC			EC		EC	EC
Iowa	EH	EH	EC	EC/4	EC				EC	EC/4				
Kansas	EH	EH	EC	EC	EC		EC	EC	EC	EC			EC	EC
Kentucky	EH	EH	EC										EC	EC
Louisiana	EH	EH		EC		AS								
Maine	EH		EC	EC			EC		EC	EC			EC	
Maryland	EH	EH	EC		EC	EC	EC	EC	EC					
Massachusetts	EH(g)	EH	AS	AS/2			EC/16	(g)	EC(g)	AL/2			EC	(g)
Michigan	EH(g)	EH	EC	EC/5	EC	EC/4		(g)	EC(g)	EC			EC	(g)
Minnesota	EH							(g)	EC(g)	EC/4				(g)
Mississippi	EH	EH												
Missouri	EH	EH					EC	EC	EC				EC	EC
Montana	EH	EH			EC		EC	EC	EC		EC		EC	
Nebraska(h)														
Nevada	EH	AS	AS	AS	EC	EC	AS		AS	AL	EC			
New Hampshire	EH	EH							EC	AL			AL	
New Jersey	EH	EH	EC	EC/4			EC/2		EC	EC/3			EC	

HOUSE LEADERSHIP POSITIONS—METHODS OF SELECTION—Continued

State or other jurisdiction	Speaker	Speaker pro tem	Majority leader	Assistant majority leader	Majority floor leader	Assistant majority floor leader	Majority whip	Majority caucus chairman	Minority leader	Assistant minority leader	Minority floor leader	Assistant minority floor leader	Minority whip	Minority caucus chairman
New Mexico	EH	AS	AS	...	EC	...	EC	EC/2	EC	...	EC	...	EC/2	EC
New York	EH	EH(i)	(i)	...	...	...	AS	...	EC	...	...	...	AL	EC
North Carolina	EH	EH	EC	EC	...	...	...	...	EC	...	...	...	EC	EC
North Dakota	EH	EH	...	...	...	...	...	...	EH	...	...	...	...	...
Ohio	EH	EH	...	...	EH	EH	EH	EC	EH	EH	EC	...	EH	EC
Oklahoma	EH	EH	EC	...	AS	AS/6(j)	AS	EC	EC	...	...	EC/3	EC	EC
Oregon	EH	EC	EC	EC	...	...	EC	EC	EC	EC/3	...	...	EC	EC
Pennsylvania	EH	AS	EC	...	...	...	EC	...	EC	...	...	...	EC	...
Rhode Island	EH	EH	EC	EC/9	...	...	EC	...	EC	EC/5	...	...	...	...
South Carolina	EH	EH	...	...	...	...	...	...	EC	...	EC	...	EC	EC
South Dakota	EH	EH	EC	...	EC	...	EC	EC	EC	EC	...	...	EC	EC
Tennessee	EH	EH	EC	...	...	...	EC/6	EC	EC	...	...	...	...	EC
Texas	EH	AS	...	...	...	...	...	...	EC	EC	...	...	...	...
Utah	EH	EH	EC	...	...	...	EC	...	EC	EC	...	...	EC	...
Vermont	EH	EH	EC	...	...	...	EC	EC	EC	...	...	...	EC	...
Virginia	EH	EH	EC	...	...	...	EC	EC	EC	...	EC	...	EC	EC
Washington	EH	EH	EC	...	...	...	EC	EC	EC	...	...	...	AL	EC
West Virginia	EH	AS	AS	AS/2(k)	...	...	(k)	(k)	EC	...	...	...	AL	...
Wisconsin	EH	EH	EC	EC	EC	...	EC	EC	EC	...	EC	...	EC(l)	EC
Wyoming	EH	EH	EC	...	...	...	...	EC	EC	...	EC	...	...	EC(l)
Dist. of Col.(h)	EH	EH(f)	...	...	EC	...	...	...	...	...	EC	...	...	...
American Samoa	EH	...	...	...	...	...	...	...	...	...	...	...	...	...
Guam(h)	...	...	...	...	...	...	...	...	...	...	...	...	...	...
Puerto Rico	EC(f)	...	EC	...	EC	...	...	(m)	EC(m)	...	...	EC	...	(m)
Virgin Islands(h)	EH(m)	...	...	...	...	...	...	...	...	...	...	...	...	...

Note: In some states, the leadership positions in the House are not empowered by the law or by the rules of the chamber, but rather by the party members themselves. Entry following slash indicates number of individuals holding specified position.

Key:
EH—Elected or confirmed by all members of the House.
EC—Elected by party caucus.
AS—Appointed by speaker.
AL—Appointed by party leader.
. . .—Position does not exist or is not selected on a regular basis.

(a) Outgoing speaker, by agreement of the House.
(b) Appointed by speaker, after consultation with members of supporting majority.
(c) Official title is deputy speaker.
(d) Assistant majority leader: two deputy majority leaders (appointed by majority leader), and nine assistant majority floor leaders. Assistant minority leader: deputy minority leader (appointed by minority leader) and 12 assistant minority leaders.
(e) Minority leader pro tempore.
(f) Official title is vice speaker.
(g) Speaker and minority leader are also caucus chairmen.
(h) Unicameral legislature; see entries in table on Senate leadership positions.
(i) Speaker pro tempore is also majority leader.
(j) Assistant majority floor leader: first assistant floor leader, five assistant floor leaders.
(k) One also serves as majority whip; the other also serves as majority caucus chairman.
(l) Minority whip is also caucus chairman.
(m) Also serves as caucus chairman.

Table 3.8

LEGISLATIVE COMPENSATION: REGULAR AND SPECIAL SESSIONS

State	Regular sessions Per diem salary	Regular sessions Limit on days	Salaries Annual salaries	Special sessions Per diem salary	Special sessions Limit on days	Travel allowance Cents per mile	Travel allowance Round trips home to capital during session	Per diem living expenses
Alabama	$10	105C		$10	30C	10	One	$85 (U)
Alaska	...	...	$46,800	...	...	0	One(a)	None
Arizona	...	...	$15,000	...	...	21	Unlimited	$65 ($30 for those living inside Maricopa County, location of capital) (U)
Arkansas	$20	(b)	$ 7,500	$20	(b)	20.5	Weekly	Up to $350/w (V)
California	...	...	$33,732	...	...	15(c)	One	$75 (U)
Colorado	...	...	$17,500	...	...	20 (24/4-wheel drive)	Weekly(d)	$35 for first 140C ($20 thereafter) for those living in Denver metro area; $70 for first 140C ($40 thereafter) for those living outside of Denver metro area (U)
Connecticut	...	...	$13,000	...	...	20	Unlimited	(e)
Delaware	...	...	$20,000	...	...	20	Unlimited	(f)
Florida	...	...	$18,000	...	...	20	Weekly	$50 (U)
Georgia	...	...	$ 7,200(g)	...	...	20	Weekly	$59
Hawaii	$30	None	$15,600	...	...	(h)	Unlimited	$45 for neighbor island legislators (U)
Idaho	...	...	...	$30	20C	20.5	Five during regular session; one during special session	$60 if maintaining second home in capital; otherwise, $35 (U)
Illinois	...	...	$32,500	...	...	20.5	Weekly	$65 (U)
Indiana	...	...	$11,600	$40(i)	(i)	25	Weekly	$75 (U)
Iowa	...	...	$14,600	...	...	24	Weekly	$40 (U)
Kansas	$52	None	...	$52	None	20.5	Weekly	$50 (U)
Kentucky	$100	(j)	$16,800 (odd yr)	$100	(j)	20.5	Weekly	$75 (U)
Louisiana	$75	85C		$75	30C	20.5	Weekly	None
Maine	...	...	$ 7,500 (odd yr) $ 4,000 (even yr)	$50	None	22	Weekly(k)	$26 for meals and $24 for lodging(k) (U)
Maryland	...	...	$21,000	...	...	19	One per diem if no lodging expense was incurred that day	$72 for lodging and meals (V)
Massachusetts	...	...	$30,000	...	...	Included in living expense allowance	See living expense allowance	Amount covering mileage, meals, and lodging ranges from $5 to $50, depending on distance legislator's district is from capital (U)
Michigan	...	...	$36,520	...	...	24	Weekly	(l)
Minnesota	...	...	$22,350	...	...	26	Weekly	$36 outstate; $23 metro (U)
Mississippi	...	...	$10,000	$50	None	20	Weekly	$74 (U)
Missouri	...	...	$19,524	...	...	20.5	Weekly	$35 (U)
Montana	$52.13	None	$ 4,800	$52.13	(m)	21	Four	$45 (U)
Nebraska	(m)	(m)		(m)	(m)	21(m)	One(m)	None
Nevada	$104(n)	60C		$140	20C	27(o)	Unlimited(o)	$56 (U)
New Hampshire	...	...	$ 200/b	$3(p)	15L(p)	38/first 45 mi., 19 thereafter	Unlimited	None

95

LEGISLATIVE COMPENSATION: REGULAR AND SPECIAL SESSIONS—Continued

State	Regular sessions			Special sessions		Travel allowance		Per diem living expenses
	Per diem salary	Limit on days	Annual salaries	Per diem salary	Limit on days	Cents per mile	Round trips home to capital during session	
New Jersey	$75		$25,000			0		None
New Mexico		6C (odd yr) 30C (even yr)	...	$75	30C	25	One	None
New York	...	...	$43,000	...	...	0	Weekly	$75 for legislators who remain in capital; otherwise, $45 (V)
North Carolina ...	...	...	$ 8,400	...	None	25	Weekly	$60 (U)
North Dakota	$90	(q)	$31,659	$90		20	Weekly	$35 for lodging, not to exceed $600/m (U)
Ohio(r)	...	...				20.5		(s)
Oklahoma	...	...	$20,000	...	...	20.5	(t)	$35, up to 4L/w
Oregon	...	...	$ 9,300(u)	...	...	0	Weekly	$50 (U)
Pennsylvania	$5	60L	$35,000	...	...	20(v)	Unlimited	$75 or actual expenses. (V)
Rhode Island			$10,000	...	...	8	Weekly	None
South Carolina ..				...	...	20.5		$68 (V)
South Dakota			$ 3,200 (odd yr) $ 2,800 (even yr)			21	Each weekend legislature is in session	$75 (U)
Tennessee........	$30	140C	$12,500	$30	30C	20(w)	Weekly(w)	$71 (U)
Texas	$65	45C	$ 7,200	$65	30L	23(x)	(y)	None
Utah						20.5	One	$25 subsistence allowance and $50 lodging allowance for legislators residing outside Salt Lake or Davis counties (U)
Vermont.........	$300/w	None		$60	None	20.5	Weekly if room rented in capital or vicinity; otherwise daily	$32.50 for room and $22.50 for meals if renting room in capital or vicinity; $23.75 for meals, if commuting. (U)
Virginia.........	...	...	$11,000	...	...	20.5	Weekly	$71 (U)
Washington......	...	...	$13,700	$50	30C	20.5	One	None
West Virginia....	...	...	$ 6,500	$50	None	20	Weekly	$30 for meals (U); $40 for lodging (V)
Wisconsin.......	...	...	$27,202(z)	...		21.5	Weekly	$45 for legislators who establish temporary residence in state capital; otherwise, $22.50 (U)(aa)
Wyoming........	$75	None		$75	None	35	One	$60 (U)

LEGISLATIVE COMPENSATION: REGULAR AND SPECIAL SESSIONS—Continued

Note: Compensation as of January 1986. In many states, legislators who receive an annual salary or per diem salary also receive an additional per diem amount for living expenses. Consult appropriate columns for a more complete picture of legislative compensation during sessions. For information on interim compensation and other direct payments and services to legislators, see Table 3.9, "Legislative Compensation: Interim Payments and Other Direct Payments."

Key:
C—Calendar day
L—Legislative day
U—Unvouchered
(V)—Vouchered
d—day
w—week
m—month
y—year
b—biennium
. . .—Not applicable

(a) Legislators are reimbursed for whatever expenses are incurred in coming to and from the capital one time; this includes any moving expenses (V).

(b) Legislators receive per diem salary for each day of actual attendance at regular and special sessions.

(c) Or actual expenses incurred when traveling by common carrier.

(d) Paid only to those who do not live in the Denver metro area.

(e) Legislators receive $3,500/y expense allowance (U).

(f) Legislators receive $5,000/y expense allowance (U).

(g) Beginning January 1987, $10,000.

(h) Travel allowance to neighbor islands during a session on official legislative business, (excluding attendance at a legislative session for neighbor island legislators) to be equal to the maximum allowance for such expenses payable to any public officer or employee. Presently, this equals $45/d inter-island, $60/d out-of-state (U).

(i) Legislators receive $40/L ($25/L for Polk County legislators) during special sessions.

(j) While regular sessions are limited to 60L every other year, per diem amount is paid for every calendar day of the session. Per diem amount is also paid for every calendar day of the special session (no limitation on length).

(k) Plus one round-trip (in lieu of lodging) for each session day.

(l) Legislators receive $6,700/y expense allowance (V).

(m) Legislators who live over 50 miles from capital receive $55 and mileage allowance for one round-trip per week; legislators who live less than 50 miles from capital receive $25, plus allowance for daily mileage.

(n) Beginning in 1987, all legislators elected in 1986 will receive $130/d for 60C.

(o) To a maximum of $5,000 per regular session, beginning in 1987.

(p) In addition to the biennial salary of $200, a legislator receives $3/d for up to 15L of the special session.

(q) There is a constitutional limit on legislative sessions of 80 natural days during a biennium. The per diem is payable each calendar day during a session.

(r) All amounts are for 1986 only. Compensation for all positions will increase by 5 percent on Jan. 1, 1987 and increase again by 5 percent on Jan. 1, 1988.

(s) Legislators may be reimbursed for actual and necessary traveling and other expenses incurred while traveling within the state on official business authorized by law or required in the performance of duties required by law.

(t) Four round-trips per week, if not claiming per diem reimbursement; otherwise one trip per week.

(u) $775/m from July 1, 1985 to June 30, 1986 and $850/m from July 1, 1986 to Jan. 1, 1987.

(v) One-half of the Senate membership is limited to 17 cents per mile.

(w) Legislators may be reimbursed the actual cost of commercial travel if residing more than 100 miles from the state capital.

(x) For travel in personally-owned automobiles. For travel in personally-owned or leased aircraft: 40 cents per highway mile in a single-engine aircraft, 65 cents per highway mile in a twin-engine aircraft, $1.15 per highway mile in a turbine-powered aircraft.

(y) Senators are reimbursed for weekly round trips home to capital during session. Representatives are reimbursed for their first four trips per month.

(z) $22,631 for senators elected prior to July 1984.

(aa) Legislators must sign statement listing days for which per diem is claimed.

Table 3.9

LEGISLATIVE COMPENSATION: INTERIM PAYMENTS AND OTHER DIRECT PAYMENTS

State	Compensation for committee or official business during interim			Other direct payments or services to legislators
	Per diem compensation for committee or official business	Travel allowance (cents per mile)	Per diem living expenses	
Alabama	...	10(a)	$85 per meeting day	$600/m for district expenses (U)
Alaska	...	25		$4,000 annual allowance during session (U)
Arizona	...	21	$65 ($30 for those living inside Maricopa County, location of capital) (U)	...
Arkansas	$60	20.5	...	$462/m for home office expenses (V) (b)
California	...	(c)	$75	...
Colorado	$75	20 (24 for 4-wheel drive)	Actual and necessary (U)	...
Connecticut	...	20	...	(d)
Delaware	...	20	...	(d)
Florida	...	20	...	$1,500/m for district office expenses (U)
Georgia	...	20	$59	$4,800/y expense allowance (V)
Hawaii	...	...	$45 inter-island travel; $60 out-of-state.	...
Idaho	$30(e)	20.5	Actual expenses (V)	...
Illinois	...	20.5	(f)	Senators receive $37,000/y, representatives receive $27,000/y as district office allowance (g)
Indiana	$75(h)	25	$90/w (U)	...
Iowa	$40	24	Actual expenses (V)	...
Kansas	$52	20.5	$50 (U)	$600/m April through December to defray expenses (U)
Kentucky	$75	20.5	Actual (V)	$950/m interim expense allowance; $50/session stationery allowance

LEGISLATIVE COMPENSATION: INTERIM PAYMENTS AND OTHER DIRECT PAYMENTS—Continued

Compensation for committee or official business during interim

State	Per diem compensation for committee or official business	Travel allowance (cents per mile)	Per diem living expenses	Other direct payments or services to legislators
Louisiana	$75	21	...	$350/m allowance to cover rent, utilities and/or expenses for a district office (U); $1,000 initial furniture and equipment allowance, plus $250 (major equipment repair) for legislators who have served one or more four-year terms (U); $1,047/m (average) salary for legislative assistants (U)
Maine	$50	22	$26 for meals (V); actual expenses for lodging (V)	$330 constituent service allowance provided at beginning of session (U)
Maryland	...	19	$72 for lodging and meals (i)	
Massachusetts ...	...	Included in living expense allowance	Amount for mileage, meals and lodging, ranges from $5 to $50 depending on distance legislator's district is from state capital	$2,400/y general expense allowance
Michigan	...	...	...	
Minnesota	$48	26	$45 for lodging (House) (V)	Senators receive $75 for telephone (V); representatives receive $600/y for telephone credit card (V) and postage allotment of 30 rolls/first year and 14 rolls/second year of session (U); senators receive $400 apartment allowance (V)
Mississippi	$40	20	$74 (U)	$500/m for months when legislature is not in session over 15 days
Missouri	...	20.5	Lodging and meals (V)	Representatives receive $600/m for office expenses (V), and $2,000/y mailing account (V). Senators receive $3,410/m for staff allowance
Montana	$52.13	21	(i)	...
Nebraska	...	21	Actual and necessary expenses (V)	...
Nevada	$104(k)	24	$47.50 for three meals and lodging in-state (V)	$1,800 telephone allowance/regular session, $300/special session (U); postage allowance of $60/regular session (U)
New Hampshire..	...	38 for first 45 mi.; 19 thereafter	...	...
New Jersey......	...	...	...	District office rent, office supplies, and telephone, postage allowances established at beginning of session

99

LEGISLATIVE COMPENSATION: INTERIM PAYMENTS AND OTHER DIRECT PAYMENTS—Continued

State	Compensation for committee or official business during interim			Other direct payments or services to legislators
	Per diem compensation for committee or official business	Travel allowance (cents per mile)	Per diem living expenses	
New Mexico	...	25	...	Stationery, postage, telephone, and telegraph (U)
New York	...	...	$75 for legislators who remain in capital; otherwise, $45 (U)	...
North Carolina	...	25	$60 (U)	$209/m for expenses (U)
North Dakota	$62.50	20	$35 lodging (U); $17 meals (U)	(l)
Ohio	...	(l)	...	(l)
Oklahoma	$35	20.5	...	...
Oregon	...	20	$50 (U)	$400/m for interim expenses (U); actual telephone expenses during interim; $14,065/b for staffing allowance
Pennsylvania	...	21 (Senate); 20 (House)	$75 or actual expenses (V)	$10,000/y for accountable expenses (V). Senators receive $15,000/y, representatives $10,000/y for home office expenses (V); representatives also receive $1,000/y postage allowance (V)
Rhode Island	...	...	...	...
South Carolina	$35	20.5	$68 (V)	...
South Dakota	$75	21	$18 for lodging (V); $16 for meals (V)	...
Tennessee	...	20(m)	$71 (U)	$325/m home office expense allowance (U)
Texas	...	23(n)	Actual expenses (V)	...
Utah	$65	20.5	$25 subsistence allowance on committee days; $50 lodging allowance if meeting is held in Salt Lake or Davis counties (for legislators residing outside counties) (U)	(o)
Vermont	$60	20.5	$32.50 for lodging (V) and $27.50 for meals if renting room in state capital or vicinity; $23.75 for meals otherwise (U)	...
Virginia	$100	20.5	Actual expenses (V)	$250/m for office expenses (U)

LEGISLATIVE COMPENSATION: INTERIM PAYMENTS AND OTHER DIRECT PAYMENTS

| | Compensation for committee or official business during interim | | | |
State	Per diem compensation for committee or official business	Travel allowance (cents per mile)	Per diem living expenses	Other direct payments or services to legislators
Washington	$50	20.5	...	$200/m for office expenses (U)
West Virginia ...	$50(p)	17	$30 for meals (U); $40 for lodging (V)	$50/d for extended sessions (U)
Wisconsin	...	21.5	$45 for legislator who must establish temporary residence in state capital; otherwise $22.50 (U)	Senators receive $75/m, representatives $25/m for interim expenses for full calendar months in which legislature is in actual session 3 days or less
Wyoming	$75	35	$60 or actual expenses for out-of-state travel (V)	Telephone credit card, stationery, and postage during session (U); postage allotment limited during interim

Note: Compensation as of January 1986. For more information on legislative compensation, see Table 3.8, "Legislative Compensation: Regular and Special Sessions."

Key:
(U)—Unvouchered
(V)—Vouchered
d—day
b—biennium
m—month
y—year

(a) For one round trip per week for interim committees. For other legislative business outside state capital, 22 cents per mile.
(b) For 1985-86. For 1986-87, $485/m. Standing, select, and joint committee chairmen and co-chairmen may draw an additional $110/m.
(c) Legislators are provided a leased vehicle gasoline credit card. Actual expenses or 15 cents per mile.
(d) See Table 3.8, "Legislative Compensation: Regular and Special Sessions" for information.
(e) For each day of authorized meetings. Plus $7/d for each day not in session.
(f) When not in session, legislators are permitted two round trips per month at $65/d (V).
(g) Allowance may be expended for additional staff, clerical help, office rent, printing, postage, etc.
(h) For interim committee meetings, caucuses, and approved constituent work at state capitol.

(i) Of total amount, maximum $28/d for meals. Legislators may claim lodging only if meetings are scheduled on consecutive days.
(j) For travel within state: $24/d for lodging (V) and $14.50 for meals (U). For travel outside state: $50/d for lodging (V) and $22.50/d for meals (U).
(k) Beginning in 1987, all legislators elected in 1986 will receive $130/d.
(l) Legislators may be reimbursed for actual and necessary traveling and other expenses incurred while traveling within the state on official business authorized by law or required in the performance of duties required by law. Approval of presiding officer is required. Receipts must be presented to verify expenses. Rules governing reimbursement rates for various expenses and situations are adopted by the Office of Budget and Management and apply to reimbursement for legislators. Conference registration fees and course fees will be reimbursed or they may be paid in advance by the state.
(m) Legislators may be reimbursed the actual cost of commercial travel if residing more than 100 miles from the state capital.
(n) For travel in personally-owned automobiles. For travel in personally-owned or leased aircraft: 40 cents per highway mile in a single-engine aircraft, 65 cents per highway mile in a twin-engine aircraft, $1.15 per highway mile in a turbine-powered aircraft.
(o) In emergency situations, the presiding officer and the majority and minority leaders of each chamber may authorize a $50/d lodging allowance for legislators residing in Salt Lake or Davis counties.
(p) Not to exceed $1,500 per member or a total of $65,000.

101

Table 3.10
ADDITIONAL COMPENSATION FOR SENATE LEADERS

State	President	President pro tem	Majority leader	Minority leader	Other
Alabama	$2/d(a)	0	...	...	
Alaska	$500/y	...	0	0	
Arizona	0	0	0	0	
Arkansas	(a)	$2,500/y(b)	...	...	
California	(a)	0	0	0	
Colorado	$75/d to max. $7,500/y	$75/d to max. $7,500/y	$75/d to max. $7,500/y	$75/d to max. $7,500/y	
Connecticut	(a)	$5,000/y	$4,000/y	$4,000/y	Dep. Maj. Ldrs., Dep. Min. Ldr.: $3,000/y; Asst. Maj. Ldrs., Asst. Min. Ldrs.: $2,000/y; Cmte. Chmn.: $2,000/y; Ranking Min. Mbrs.: $1,000/y
Delaware	(a)	$7,500/y	$5,500/y	$5,500/y	Maj. Whip, Min. Whip: $3,000/y; Joint Finance Cmte. Mbrs.: $3,000/y
Florida	$7,000/y	0	0	0	
Georgia	(a)	$2,800/y	0	0	
Hawaii	(a)	0(c)	0	0	
Idaho	(a)	0	0	0	
Illinois	$10,000/y(d)	...	(d)	$10,000/y	Asst. Maj. Ldrs., Asst. Min. Ldrs., Maj. Caucus Chmn., Min. Caucus Chmn., Maj. Whips, Min. Whip: $6,000/y
Indiana	(a)	$5,000/y	$3,500/y	$4,000/y	Maj. Caucus Chmn., Min. Caucus Chmn., Min. Asst. Fl. Ldr., Finance Cmte. Chmn.: $3,500/y; Budget Cmte. Chmn.: $1,500/y
Iowa	(a)	0	$2,500/y	$2,500/y	
Kansas	$8,285/y	$4,228/y(c)	$7,474/y	$7,474/y	Asst. Maj. Ldrs., Asst. Min. Ldrs., Ways & Means Cmte. Chmn.: $4,228/y
Kentucky	$25/d(a)	$25/d	$20/d	$20/d	Asst. Pres. Pro Tem, Maj. Whip, Min. Whip, Maj. Caucus Chmn., Min. Caucus Chmn.: $15/d; Standing and Interim Cmte. Chmn.: $10/meeting chaired
Louisiana	(e)	0	...	...	
Maine	(f)	...	(f)	(f)	Asst. Maj. Ldr., Asst. Min. Ldr.: (f)
Maryland	$5,000/y	0	0	0	
Massachusetts	$35,000/y	...	$22,500/y	$22,500/y	Asst. Maj. Fl. Ldr., Asst. Min. Fl. Ldr., 2nd Asst. Maj. Fl. Ldr., 2nd & 3rd Asst. Min. Fl. Ldrs., Post Audit & Oversight and Taxation Cmte. Chmn., Ways & Means Cmte. V-Chmn.: $15,000/y; Ways & Means Cmte. Chmn.: $25,000/y; Other Cmte. Chmn.: $7,500/y
Michigan	(a)	0	$16,000/y	$14,000/y	Maj. Fl. Ldr.: $7,500/y; Min. Fl. Ldr.: $6,000/y; Appropriations Cmte. Chmn.: $3,000/y
Minnesota	0	...	$8,456/y	$8,456/y	Tax and Finance Cmte. Chmn.: $4,228/y
Mississippi	(a)	0	...	...	
Missouri	(a)	$2,500/y	$1,500/y	$1,500/y	
Montana	$5/d	0	0	0	
Nebraska	(a)	0(g)	...	...	
Nevada	$2/d(a)	(h)	(h)	(h)	(h)
New Hampshire	$50/b	0(c)	0	0	
New Jersey	$8,333/y(i)	0	0	0	
New Mexico	(a)	0	0	0	
New York	(a)	$30,000/y(d)	(d)	$25,000/y	Dep. Maj. Ldr.: $24,500/y; Dep. Min. Ldr.: $15,000/y; Maj. Whip: $16,000/y; Min. Whip: $10,500/y; Maj. Conf. Chmn.: $18,000/y; Min. Conf. Chmn.: $12,000/y; Maj. Conf. Secy.: $16,000/y; Min. Conf. Secy.: $10,500/y; Cmte. Chmn. & Ranking Min. Mbrs.: Finance: $24,500/y & $15,000/y; Education, Judiciary, Codes: $13,000/y & $8,000/y; Banks, Health, Cities, Corporations: $11,000/y & $7,000/y; Other Cmtes., generally: $9,000/y & $6,500/y
North Carolina	(a)	$6,600/y	$2,100/y	$2,100/y	
North Dakota	(a)	0	$10/d	$10/d	Standing and Interim Cmte. and Legislative Council Chmn.: $5/d
Ohio	$17,690/y	$13,367/y	...	$13,367/y	Asst. Pres. Pro Tem: $10,754/y; Asst. Min. Ldr.: $9,450/y; Maj. Whip: $8,144/y; Min. Whip: $5,534/y; Asst. Min. Whip: $1,461/y; Finance Cmte. Chmn.: $5,250/y; Other Standing Cmte. Chmn.: $2,922/y; Standing Sub-Cmte. Chmn.: $1,462/y

ADDITIONAL COMPENSATION FOR SENATE LEADERS—Continued

State	President	President pro tem	Majority leader	Minority leader	Other
Oklahoma	(a)	$9,330/y	$6,440/y	$6,440/y	
Oregon	$9,300/y(j)	0	0	0	
Pennsylvania	(a)	$19,600/y	$15,680/y	$15,680/y	Maj. Whip, Min. Whip: $11,900/y; Maj. Caucus Chmn., Min. Caucus Chmn.: $7,420/y; Maj. Appropriations Cmte. Chmn., Min. Appropriations Cmte. Chmn.: $7,420/y; Maj. Caucus Secy., Min. Caucus Secy., Maj. Policy Chmn., Min. Policy Chmn., Maj. Caucus Administr., Min. Caucus Administr.: $4,900/y
Rhode Island	(a)	0	0	0	Standing Cmte. Chmn.: $400 during interim
South Carolina	$1,575/y(a)	$3,600/y	. . .	. . .	
South Dakota	(a)	0	0	0	
Tennessee.........	$12,450/y(a)	0	0	0	
Texas	(a)	0	. . .	. . .	
Utah	$1,000/y	. . .	$500/y	$500/y	
Vermont..........	(a)	0	0	0	
Virginia	(a)	0	0	0	
Washington	(a)	0	0	0	
West Virginia	$50/d(k)	0	$25/d	$25/d	
Wisconsin	0	. . .	0	0	
Wyoming	$3/d	0(c)	0	0	

Note: This table reflects the amount paid the leadership in addition to their regular legislative compensation.

Key:
d—day
m—month
y—year
b—biennium
. . .—Position does not exist or is not selected on a regular basis.

(a) Lieutenant governor is president of the Senate. Additional compensation noted is that which the lieutenant governor receives for services as president of the Senate. In Mississippi, constitution states that the salary of the lieutenant governor must be the same as that of the speaker of the House ($34,000), and that the lieutenant governor also receive the same per diem and expenses as members while in session. In Tennessee, lieutenant governor is a statutory title.

(b) Receives a special public relations expense allowance of $10,000/y.

(c) Official title is vice-president.

(d) President also serves as majority leader. In New York, president pro tempore also serves as majority leader.

(e) Receives $32,000/y in lieu of compensation paid to other legislators.

(f) Additional compensation for Senate leaders is calculated according to the following percentages of the base salaries during sessions: president, 50 percent; majority and minority leaders, 25 percent; and assistant majority and minority leaders, 12.5 percent.

(g) Official title is speaker of the Senate.

(h) Beginning in 1987, supplemental allowance for postage and telephone not to exceed $500 during regular session or $64 for special session. Chairmen of standing committees also eligible to receive allowance.

(i) Equal to one-third of regular annual salary.

(j) $775/m for period from July 1, 1985 to June 30, 1986, and $850/m for period from July 1, 1986 to Jan. 1, 1987.

(k) President also receives $100/d for up to 80 days for attending to legislative business in the capitol office when the legislature is not in formal session.

Table 3.11
ADDITIONAL COMPENSATION FOR HOUSE LEADERS

State	Speaker	Speaker pro tem	Majority leader	Minority leader	Other
Alabama	$2/d	0	...	...	
Alaska	$500/y	...	0	0	
Arizona	0	0	0	0	
Arkansas	$2,500/y(a)	0	0	0	
California	0	0	0	0	
Colorado	$75/d to max. $7,500/y	$75/d to max. $7,500/y	$75/d to max. $7,500/y	$75/d to max. $7,500/y	
Connecticut	$5,000/y	$3,000/y(b)	$4,000/y	$4,000/y	Dep. Maj. Ldrs., Dep. Min. Ldr.: $3,000/y; Asst. Maj. Ldrs., Asst. Min. Ldrs.: $2,000/y; Cmte. Chmn.: $2,000/y; Ranking Min. Mbrs.: $1,000/y
Delaware	$7,500/y	...	$5,500/y	$5,500/y	Maj. Whip, Min. Whip: $3,000/y; Joint Finance Cmte. Mbrs.: $3,000/y
Florida	$7,000/y	0	0	0	
Georgia	(c)	$2,800/y	0	0	
Hawaii	0	0(d)	0	0	
Idaho	0	...	0	0	
Illinois	$10,000/y	...	$7,500/y	$10,000/y	Asst. Maj. Ldrs., Asst. Min. Ldrs.: $6,000/y; Maj. Whips, Min. Whips, Maj. Conf. Chmn., Min. Conf. Chmn.: $6,000/y
Indiana	$5,000/y	$3,500/y	$3,500/y	$4,000/y	Maj. Whip, Maj. Caucus Chmn., Min. Caucus Chmn., Asst. Min. Fl. Ldr., Ways & Means Cmte. Chmn.: $3,500/y
Iowa	$7,300/y	0	$2,500/y	$2,500/y	
Kansas	$8,285/y	$4,228/y	$7,474/y	$7,474/y	Asst. Maj. Ldrs., Asst. Min. Ldrs.: $4,228/y; Ways & Means Cmte. Chmn.: $6,663/y
Kentucky	$25/d	$25/d	$20/d	$20/d	Maj. Whip, Min. Whip, Maj. Caucus Chmn., Min. Caucus Chmn.: $15/d; Standing and Interim Cmte. Chmn.: $10/meeting chaired
Louisiana	(e)	0	...	...	
Maine	(f)	...	(f)	(f)	Asst. Maj. Ldr., Asst. Min. Ldr.: (f)
Maryland	$5,000/y	0	0	0	
Massachusetts	$35,000/y	...	$22,500/y	$22,500/y	Asst. Maj. Fl. Ldrs., Asst. Min. Fl. Ldrs., 2nd Asst. Maj. Fl. Ldrs., 2nd & 3rd Asst. Min. Fl. Ldrs., Post Audit & Oversight and Taxation Cmte. Chmn., Ways & Means Cmte. V-Chmn.: $15,000/y; Ways & Means Cmte. Chmn.: $25,000/y; Post Audit & Oversight Cmte. V-Chmn., Ways & Means Cmte. Asst. V-Chmn., Other Cmte. Chmn.: $7,500/y
Michigan	$18,000/y	0	$7,500/y	$14,000/y	Min. Fl. Ldr.: $6,000/y; Appropriations Cmte. Chmn.: $3,000/y
Minnesota	(g)	...	(g)	(g)	
Mississippi	$24,000/y	...	...	...	
Missouri	$2,500/y	$1,500/y	$1,500/y	$1,500/y	
Montana	$5/d	0	0	0	
Nebraska	--Unicameral Legislature--				
Nevada	$2/d(h)	(h)	(h)	(h)	(h)
New Hampshire	$50/b	...	0	0	
New Jersey	$8,333/y(i)	0	0	0	
New Mexico	0	...	0	0	
New York	$30,000/y	$18,000/y	$25,000/y	$25,000/y	Dep. Spkr.: $18,000/y; Min. Ldr. Pro Tem: $15,000/y; Cmte. on Cmtes. Chmn.: $18,000/y; Dep. Maj. Ldr., Asst. Maj. Ldr.: $14,000/y; Maj. Whip, Asst. Min. Ldr., Dep. Min. Ldr., Cmte. on Cmtes. Ranking Min. Mbrs.: $13,000/y; Min. Whip, Maj. Conf. Chmn.: $12,000/y; Min. Conf. Chmn.: $11,000/y; Maj. Conf. V-Chmn.: $9,000/y; Min. Conf. V-Chmn.: $8,000/y; Cmte. Chmn. & Ranking Min. Mbrs.: Ways & Means: $24,500/y & $15,000/y; Education, Judiciary, Codes: $13,000/y & $8,000/y; Banks, Cities, Health, Local Govts., Corporations: $11,000/y & $7,000/y; Labor: $10,000/y & $6,500/y; Other Cmte. Chmn., generally: $9,000/y & $6,500/y
North Carolina	$16,644/y	$4,104/y(j)	(j)	$2,100/y	
North Dakota	$10/d	...	$10/d	$10/d	Standing and Interim Cmte. and Legislative Council Chmn.: $5/d
Ohio	$17,690/y	$13,368/y	$10,754/y	$13,368/y	Asst. Maj. Fl. Ldr.: $8,144/y; Maj. Whip, Min. Whip: $5,534/y; Asst. Min. Ldr.: $9,450/y; Asst. Maj. Whip: $2,922/y; Asst. Min. Whip: $1,462/y; Finance/Appropriations Cmte. Chmn.: $5,250/y; Other Standing Cmte. Chmn.: $2,922/y; Standing Sub-Cmte. Chmn.: $1,462/y

104

ADDITIONAL COMPENSATION FOR HOUSE LEADERS—Continued

State	Speaker	Speaker pro tem	Majority leader	Minority leader	Other
Oklahoma	$9,330/y	0	$6,440/y	$6,440/y	
Oregon	$9,300/y(k)	0	0	0	
Pennsylvania	$19,600/y	. . .	$15,680/y	$15,680/y	Maj. Whip, Min. Whip: $11,900/y; Maj. Caucus Chmn., Min. Caucus Chmn.; Maj. Appropriations Cmte. Chmn., Min. Appropriations Cmte. Chmn.: $7,420/y; Maj. Caucus Secy., Min. Caucus Secy., Maj. Policy Chmn., Min. Policy Chmn., Maj. Caucus Administr., Min. Caucus Administr.: $4,900/y
Rhode Island	$5/d	0	0	0	
South Carolina	$11,000/y	$3,600/y	0	0	
South Dakota	0	0	0	0	
Tennessee........	$12,450/y	0	0	0	
Texas	0	0	. . .	. . .	
Utah	$1,000/y	. . .	$500/y	$500/y	
Vermont..........	$6,300/y	. . .	0	0	
Virginia	$7,500/y	. . .	0	0	
Washington	0	0	0	0	
West Virginia	$50/d(l)	0	$25/d	$25/d	
Wisconsin	$25/m	0	0	0	
Wyoming.........	$3/d	0	0	0	

Note: This table reflects the amount paid the leadership in addition to their regular legislative compensation.

Key:
d—day
m—month
y—year
b—biennium
. . .—Position does not exist or is not selected on a regular basis.
(a) Receives a special public relations expense allowance of $10,000/y.
(b) Official title is deputy speaker.
(c) Receives an annual salary of $22,800 plus a sum equal to the amount of salary over $30,000/y which is received by the lieutenant governor.
(d) Official title is vice speaker.
(e) Receives $32,000 in lieu of compensation paid to other legislators.
(f) Additional compensation for House leaders is calculated according to the following percentage of the base salaries during sessions: speaker,

50 percent; majority and minority leaders, 25 percent; and assistant majority and minority leaders, 12.5 percent.
(g) Additional compensation for House leaders is calculated according to the following percentages of base salaries during sessions: speaker, majority and minority leaders: 40 percent.
(h) Beginning in 1987, supplemental allowance for postage and telephone, not to exceed $500 during a regular session or $64 during a special session. Chairmen of standing committees also eligible to receive allowance.
(i) Equal to one-third of regular annual salary.
(j) Speaker pro tempore is also majority leader.
(k) $775/m for period from July 1, 1985 to June 30, 1986, and $850/m for period from July 1, 1986 to Jan. 1, 1987.
(l) Speaker also receives $100/d for up to 80 days for attending to legislative business in the capitol office when the legislature is not in formal session.

105

Table 3.12
TIME LIMITS ON BILL INTRODUCTION

State or other jurisdiction	Time limit on introduction of bills	Procedure for granting exception to time limits
Alabama	24th L day of regular session(a).	House: 4/5 vote of quorum present and voting. Senate: majority vote after consideration by Rules Committee.
Alaska	35th C day of 2nd regular session(b).	2/3 vote of membership (concurrent resolution).
Arizona	29th day of regular session; 10th day of special session.	Permission of Rules Committee.
Arkansas	55th day of regular session (50th day for appropriations bills).	2/3 vote of membership.
California	March 8 of 1st year of regular session; Feb. 21 of 2nd year of regular session(c).	(c)
Colorado	45th L day in odd-year session; 25th L day in even-year session(d).	House, Senate Committees on Delayed Bills may extend deadline.
Connecticut	Depends on schedule set out by joint rules adopted for biennium(e).	
Delaware	House: no introductions during last 30 C days of 2nd session.	
Florida	House: noon 1st day of regular session(b); Senate: 4th L day of regular session(d,f).	House, Senate committees on Rules and Calendar determine whether existence of emergency compels bill's consideration.
Georgia	House: 30th L day of regular session; Senate: 33rd L day of regular session.	House: 3/5 of members present (provided quorum exists); Senate: 2/3 vote of membership.
Hawaii	Actual dates established during session.	2/3 vote of membership.
Idaho	House: 20th day of session(b); 45th day of session(g). Senate: 12th day of session(b); 35th day of session(g).	
Illinois	April 12 of odd year of session(h).	House: rules governing limitations may not be suspended. Senate: rules may be suspended by affirmative vote of majority of members; suspensions approved by Rules Committee, adopted by majority of members present.
Indiana	House: 16th day of odd year of session; 4th day of even year. Senate: 10th day of odd year of session; 4th day of even year.	House: 2/3 vote of membership; Senate: consent of Rules and Legislative Procedures Committee.
Iowa	House: Friday of 7th week of 1st regular session; Friday of 3rd week of 2nd regular session(i). Senate: Friday of 7th week of 1st regular session(i,j); Friday of 2nd week of 2nd regular session(b,i).	
Kansas	31st C day of regular session for individuals(k); 45th day of regular session for committees(l).	Resolution adopted by majority of members of either house may make specific exceptions to deadlines.
Kentucky	House: 38th L day of regular session; Senate: no introductions during last 20 days of session.	Majority vote of membership each house.
Louisiana	15th C day of regular session(m).	2/3 vote of elected members of each house.
Maine	Last Friday in January of 1st regular session; deadlines for 2nd regular session established by Legislative Council(b,n).	Approval of majority of members of Legislative Council.
Maryland	No introductions during last 35 C days of regular session.	2/3 vote of elected members of each house.
Massachusetts	1st Wednesday in December(o).	4/5 vote of members of each house.
Michigan	No limit.	
Minnesota	No limit.	
Mississippi	16th C day of 90-day session; 51st C day of 125-day session(d,p).	2/3 vote of members present and voting.
Missouri	60th L day of odd year of session; 30th L day of even year of session(d).	Majority vote of elected members each house; governor's request for consideration of bill by special message.
Montana	Individual introductions: 14th L day; revenue bills: 21st L day; committee bills: 40th L day; committee revenue bills: 66th L day(d,q).	2/3 vote of members.

State or other jurisdiction	Time limit on introduction of bills	Procedure for granting exception to time limits
Nebraska	10th L day of any session(d,r).	3/5 vote of elected membership (s).
Nevada	20th C day of regular session(t).	2/3 vote of members present; also standing committee of a house if request is approved by 2/3 members of committee. Consent to suspend rule may be given only by affirmative vote of majority members elected.
New Hampshire ...	House: money bills/resolutions, Feb. 26; other bills: March 18. Senate: no requests for bill drafting after March 1.	2/3 vote of members present or approval of majority of Rules Committee.
New Jersey.......	No limit.	
New Mexico.......	House: 30th L day of regular session(d,u); appropriations bills: 50th L day of regular session. Senate: time limit established by law.	
New York	Assembly: for unlimited introduction of bills, 1st Tuesday in March; for introduction of 10 or fewer bills, last Tuesday in March(v). Senate: temporary president may designate final date which is not prior to the 1st Tuesday of March(w).	Assembly only: unanimous vote(x).
North Carolina	House: April 15 for local bills or bills prepared to be introduced for departments, agencies or state institutions; Senate: same as House plus resolutions(y).	House: 2/3 of members present and voting; Senate: 2/3 vote of membership, except in case of deadline for local bills which may be suspended by 4/5 of senators present and voting.
North Dakota	15th L day(z); resolutions: 18th L day(aa); bills requested by executive agency or Supreme Court: Dec. 15 prior to regular session.	2/3 vote or approval of majority of Committee on Delayed Bills.
Ohio	After March 15 of 2nd regular session, either house by majority vote of its members may end bill introductions.	Majority vote on recommendation of bill by Reference Committee.
Oklahoma	27th L day for house of origin in 1st session(bb); 19th L day of 2nd session(cc).	2/3 vote of membership.
Oregon	House: 29th C day of session(dd); Senate: 36th C day following election of Senate president(ee).	
Pennsylvania	No limit(ff).	
Rhode Island	March 1(gg).	House: 2/3 vote of members present; Senate: majority vote of members present and voting.
South Carolina	House: April 15 of regular session; May 1 for bills first introduced in Senate(d,hh). Senate: May 1 of regular session for bills originating in House.	House: 2/3 vote of members present and voting; Senate: 2/3 vote of membership.
South Dakota	40-day session: 14th L day; committee bills and joint resolutions, 15th L day. 35-day session: 10th L day; committee bills and joint resolutions, 11th L day; bills introduced at request of department, board, commission, or state agency: 4th L day(ii).	2/3 of membership.
Tennessee	House: general bills, 10th L day of regular session(jj). Senate: general bills, 10th L day of regular session; resolutions, 30th L day.	House: 2/3 vote of members; Senate: 2/3 vote of members or unanimous consent of Committee on Delayed Bills.
Texas............	60th C day of regular session(kk).	4/5 vote of members present and voting.
Utah	30th C day of session.	House: 2/3 vote of members present; Senate: majority of membership.
Vermont	House, Individual introductions: 1st session, March 1; 2nd session, Feb. 1. Committees: 10 days after 1st Tuesday in March(ll). Senate, Individual and committee: 1st session, 53rd C day; 2nd session, sponsor requests bill drafting 25 days before session and all bills are introduced on 1st day(mm).	Approval by Rules Committee.
Virginia..........	Deadlines may be set during session.	
Washington	(Constitutional limit) No introductions during final 10 days of regular session(d,nn).	2/3 vote of elected members of each house.
West Virginia	House: 50th day of regular session(b,d); Senate: 41st day of regular session(d).	2/3 vote of members present.

TIME LIMITS ON BILL INTRODUCTION—Continued

State or other jurisdiction	Time limit on introduction of bills	Procedure for granting exception to time limits
Wisconsin	No limit.	
Wyoming	15th L day of odd year of session(d).	2/3 of elected members of either house.
American Samoa	15th L day.	2/3 of elected members.
Guam	No limit.	
Puerto Rico	60th day.	Majority vote of membership.
Virgin Islands	No limit.	

Key:
C—Calendar
L—Legislative

(a) Not applicable to local bills that have been advertised or general bills of local application.

(b) Not applicable to bills sponsored by standing committees. In Florida, also does not apply to short-form bills.

(c) Not applicable to constitutional amendments, committee bills introduced pursuant to Assembly Rule 47 or Senate Rule 23, bills introduced in Assembly with permission of speaker or bills introduced in Senate with permission of Senate Rules Committee. Subject to these deadlines, bills may be introduced at any time, except when the houses are in joint summer, interim, or final recess.

(d) Not applicable to appropriations bills. In West Virginia, supplementary appropriations bills.

(e) Not applicable to (1) bills providing for current government expenditures; (2) bills the presiding officers certify are of an emergency nature; (3) bills the governor requests because of emergency or necessity; and (4) the legislative commissioners' revisor's bills and omnibus validating act.

(f) Not applicable to local bills and joint resolutions.

(g) Not applicable to House State Affairs, Appropriations, Revenue and Taxation, or Ways and Means committees, nor to Senate State Affairs, Finance, or Judiciary and Rules committees.

(h) Not applicable to Senate bills, which must be introduced in the House by June 1; appropriations bills (introduced between 2nd Wednesday in January and 1st Friday in April of even year); certain standing committee bills (dependent on introduction date in house of origin); bills determined by Rules Committee to be an emergency; a bill carried over from the odd-numbered year on the interim study calendar of a standing committee on which public hearings have been conducted (during spring session of even-numbered year); a bill transferred from daily calendar of spring session of odd-numbered year by motion adopted by affirmative vote of 60 members prior to the applicable deadline for consideration on final passage (during spring session of even-numbered year).

(i) Unless written request for drafting bill had been filed before deadline.

(j) Not applicable to bills co-sponsored by majority and minority floor leaders.

(k) Deadline for introduction by individual members may be changed to an earlier date in either house by resolution adopted by majority of members.

(l) Not applicable to Ways and Means and Federal and State Affairs committees, the select committees of either house or the House Committee on Calendar and Printing.

(m) Not applicable to concurrent resolutions proposing suspension of law and bills reported by substitute.

(n) Not applicable to bills intended to facilitate legislative business.

(o) Not applicable to messages from governor, reports required or authorized to be made to legislature, petitions filed or approved by voters of cities or towns (or by mayors and city councils) for enactment of special legislation and which do not affect the powers and duties of state departments, boards, or commissions.

(p) Not applicable to revenue, local, and private bills.

(q) Not applicable to interim study resolutions or joint resolutions concerning administration.

(r) Not applicable to "A" bills and those introduced at the request of the governor.

(s) For standing or special committee to introduce bill after 10th L day.

(t) Requests submitted to legislative counsel for bill drafting. Does not apply to standing committees or to member who had requested bill drafting before 21st C day.

(u) Not applicable to bills to provide for current government expenses; bills referred to legislature by governor by special message setting forth emergency necessitating legislation.

(v) Does not apply to bills introduced by Rules Committee, by message from the Senate, with consent of the speaker or by members elected at special election who take office on or after the first Tuesday of March.

(w) Bills recommended by state department or agency must be submitted to office of temporary president not later than March 1. Bills proposed by governor, attorney general, comptroller, department of education or office of court administration must be submitted to office of temporary president no later than first Tuesday in April.

(x) In no case may a bill be introduced on Fridays, unless submitted by governor or introduced by Rules Committee or by message from Senate.

(y) Not applicable to those honoring memory of the deceased.

(z) No member may introduce more than three bills as prime sponsor after 10th L day.

(aa) Not applicable to resolutions proposing amendments to U.S. Constitution or directing Legislative Council to carry out a study (deadline, 33rd L day).

(bb) Final date for consideration on floor in house of origin during first session. Bills introduced after date are not placed on calendar for consideration until second session.

(cc) Not applicable to reapportionment bills.

(dd) Not applicable to measures approved by Committee on Legislative Rules and Operations or by speaker; appropriation or fiscal measures sponsored by Joint Committee on Ways and Means; true substitute measures sponsored by standing, special or joint committees, or measures drafted by legislative counsel.

(ee) Not applicable to measures approved by Rules Committee, appropriation or fiscal measures sponsored by Joint Committee on Ways and Means; measures requested for drafting by legislative counsel.

(ff) Resolutions fixing the last day for introduction of bills in the House are referred to the Rules Committee before consideration by the full House.

(gg) Not applicable to resolutions of condolence or congratulations, corporate charter renewals, claims bills or city and town bills.

(hh) Not applicable to joint resolutions approving or disapproving agency regulations.

(ii) Not applicable to governor's bills.

(jj) Not applicable to certain local bills or a bill correcting a typographical error or an earlier enactment of the Committee on Delayed Bills.

(kk) Not applicable to local bills, resolutions, emergency appropriations, all emergency matters submitted by governor in special messages to the legislature.

(ll) Not applicable to Appropriations or Ways and Means committees.

(mm) Not applicable to Appropriations or Finance committees.

(nn) Not applicable to substitute bills reported by standing committees for bills pending before such committees.

Table 3.13
BILL PRE-FILING, REFERENCE, AND CARRYOVER

State or other jurisdiction	Pre-filing of bills allowed(a)	Bills referred to committee by: Senate	Bills referred to committee by: House	Bill referral restricted by rule Senate	Bill referral restricted by rule House	Bill carryover allowed(b)
Alabama	★(c)	President(d)	Speaker			...
Alaska	★(e)	President	Speaker	★	★	★
Arizona	★	President	Speaker			...
Arkansas	★	Rules Cmte.	Speaker	★	★	
California	(f)	Rules Cmte.	Rules Cmte.	★		★(g)
Colorado	★	President	Speaker			...
Connecticut	★	President(d)	Speaker	★	★	
Delaware	★	President(d)	Speaker		★	★
Florida	★	President	Speaker	★	★	
Georgia	...	President(d)	Speaker			★
Hawaii	(h)	President	Speaker	★	★	★
Idaho	...	President(d)	Speaker			
Illinois	★	Cmte. on Assignment	Cmte. on Assignment			★
Indiana	★	Pres. Pro Tempore	Speaker			...
Iowa	★	President(d)	Speaker	★		★
Kansas	★	President	Speaker	★	★	★
Kentucky	★	Cmte. on Cmtes.(i)	Cmte. on Cmtes.	★	★	
Louisiana	★	President(j)	Speaker(j)	★	★	...
Maine	★(k)	-------Secy. of Senate and Clerk of House(l)-------				...
Maryland	★	President	Speaker	(m)	(m)	...
Massachusetts	★	Clerk(j)	Clerk(j)	★	★	...
Michigan	...	Majority Ldr.	Speaker			★
Minnesota	★(n)	President	Speaker	(m)	(m)	★
Mississippi	★	President(d)	Speaker			...
Missouri	★	Pres. Pro Tempore	Speaker	★	★	★
Montana	★	President	Speaker			
Nebraska(U)	★	Reference Cmte.		★		★
Nevada	★	Majority Ldr.	Speaker	★		
New Hampshire	★	President	Speaker	★	★	
New Jersey	★(k)	President	Speaker			★
New Mexico	...	Pres. Pro Tempore	Speaker	(m)	(m)	...
New York	★	Pres. Pro Tempore(o)	Speaker			★
North Carolina	...	President(d)	Speaker	(m)	(m)	★
North Dakota	★	President(d)	Speaker	★	★	
Ohio	★	Reference Cmte.	Reference Cmte.			★
Oklahoma	★	Pres. Pro Tempore	Speaker			★
Oregon	★	President	Speaker		★	
Pennsylvania	★	President(d)	Speaker			★
Rhode Island	★	President(d)	Speaker			★
South Carolina	★	Pres. Pro Tempore	Speaker			★
South Dakota	★	President(d)	Speaker			...
Tennessee	★	Speaker	Speaker	★		★
Texas	★	President(d)	Speaker		★	
Utah	★	President	Speaker			...
Vermont	★	President(d)	Speaker	★	★	★
Virginia	★	Clerk	Speaker	★	★	★
Washington	★	President	Speaker			★
West Virginia	★	President	Speaker			...
Wisconsin	★	Presiding Officer	Presiding Officer			★
Wyoming	★(k)	President	Speaker			...
American Samoa	★	President	Speaker	★	★	★
Guam(U)	★	Rules Cmte.		★		★
Puerto Rico	★	President	President	★	★	★
Virgin Islands(U)	★	President				★

BILL PRE-FILING, REFERENCE, AND CARRYOVER—Continued

Key:

. . .—Procedure not allowed.

(U)—Unicameral legislature.

(a) Unless otherwise indicated by footnote, bills may be introduced prior to convening each session of the legislature. In this column only: ★—pre-filing is allowed in both chambers (or in the case of Nebraska, Guam, and the Virgin Islands, in the unicameral legislature); . . .—pre-filing is not allowed in either chamber.

(b) Bills carry over from the first year of a legislature to the second (does not apply to legislatures meeting in session once every two years). Bills generally do not carry over after an intervening legislative election.

(c) Except between the end of the last regular session of the legislature in any quadrennium and the organizational session following the general election.

(d) Lieutenant governor is the president of the Senate.

(e) Maximum 10 bills.

(f) California has a continuous legislature. Members may introduce bills at any time during the biennium.

(g) Bills introduced in the first year of the regular session and passed by the house of origin on or before January 30 of the second year are "carryover bills."

(h) House only in even-numbered years.

(i) Lieutenant governor as president of the Senate is a member of committee.

(j) Subject to approval or disapproval. Louisiana—majority of members present. Massachusetts—by presiding officer.

(k) Prior to convening of first regular session only.

(l) For the joint standing committee system. Secretary of Senate and clerk of House, after conferring, suggest an appropriate committee reference for every bill, resolve and petition offered in either house. If they are unable to agree, the question of reference is referred to a conference of the president of the Senate and speaker of the House. If the presiding officers cannot agree, the question is resolved by the Legislative Council.

(m) Not restricted, except: Maryland—in House, local bills; in Senate, local bills and bills creating judgeships. Minnesota—bills on government structure and bills appropriating funds which are referred to Finance Committee. New Mexico—in House, bills referred to Appropriations and Finance Committee; in Senate, bills referred to Finance Committee. North Carolina—bills referred to Appropriations, Finance, and Ways and Means committees.

(n) Prior to convening of second regular session only.

(o) Also serves as majority leader.

Table 3.14
ENACTING LEGISLATION: VETO, VETO OVERRIDE, AND EFFECTIVE DATE

State or other jurisdiction	Governor may item veto appropriation bills — Amount	Governor may item veto appropriation bills — Other(b)	Days allowed governor to consider bill(a) — During session: Bill becomes law unless vetoed	After session: Bill becomes law unless vetoed	After session: Bill dies unless signed	Votes required in each house to pass bills or items over veto(c)	Effective date of enacted legislation(d)
Alabama	★	*	6	20P	10A	Majority elected	Immediately(e)
Alaska	★(f)	:	15	10A		2/3 elected(g)	90 days after enactment
Arizona	★	:	5	20A(h)		2/3 elected	90 days after adjournment
Arkansas	★	:	5			Majority elected	90 days after adjournment
California	★(f)	:	12(h,i)	(i)		2/3 elected	(i)
Colorado	★	*	10(h)	30A(h)		2/3 elected	Immediately(k)
Connecticut	★	:	5	15P(h)		2/3 elected	Oct. 1
Delaware	★	:	10		30A(h)	3/5 elected	Immediately
Florida	★	*	7(h)	15P(h)		2/3 elected	60 days after adjournment
Georgia(l)	★	:	6	40A(m)		2/3 elected	July 1(n)
Hawaii(l)	★(f)	:	10(o,p)	45A(o,p)	(p)	2/3 elected	Immediately
Idaho	★	*	5	10A		2/3 elected(g)	July 1(n)
Illinois	★(f)	:	60(h)	60P(h)		3/5 elected(g)	Jan. 1(n)
Indiana	:	*	7	7A		Majority elected	(q)
Iowa	(s)	:	3	(r)	(r)	2/3 elected	July 1(n)
Kansas	★	:	10	10P		2/3 elected	Upon publication
Kentucky	★	*	10	10A		Majority elected	90 days after adjournment
Louisiana(l)	★	*	10(h)	20P(h)		2/3 elected	60 days after adjournment
Maine	:	*	10	(m)		2/3 present	90 days after adjournment
Maryland(l)	(s)	*	6	30P(m)		3/5 elected	June 1(t)
Massachusetts	★(f)	*	10(o)	10P	10P	2/3 present	90 days after enactment
Michigan	★	*	14(h)	14P(h)	14P(h)	2/3 elected and serving	90 days after adjournment
Minnesota	★	*	3		14P	2/3 elected	Aug. 1(u)
Mississippi	★	*	5	15P(m,r)		2/3 elected	60 days after enactment
Missouri	★(f)	*	15(r)	45P(m,r)		2/3 elected	90 days after adjournment(u,v)
Montana	★(f)	*	5(h)	25A(h)		2/3 present	Oct. 1(u)
Nebraska	★(w)	:	5	5A		3/5 elected	3 months after adjournment
Nevada	:	:	5	10A		2/3 elected	July 1
New Hampshire	★(f)	:	5		5P	2/3 elected	60 days after enactment
New Jersey	:	:	(x)	(x)	(x)	2/3 elected	July 4
New Mexico	★	:	3		20A	2/3 present	90 days after adjournment(u)
New York	★	*	10		30A	2/3 elected	20 days after enactment
North Carolina	:	:	----(y)----				30 days after adjournment
North Dakota	★(f)	*	3	15A		2/3 elected	July 1
Ohio	★	*	10	10A		3/5 elected	90 days after filed with secretary of state
Oklahoma	★	:	5	20A	15A	2/3 elected(g)	90 days after adjournment
Oregon	★(f)	*	5	30A(h)		2/3 present	90 days after adjournment
Pennsylvania	★(f)	:	10(h)	10A(h)		2/3 elected	60 days after enactment
Rhode Island	:	*	6	(m)		3/5 present	10 days after adjournment
South Carolina	★	*	5	(m)		2/3 present	20 days after enactment

VETO, VETO OVERRIDE, AND EFFECTIVE DATE—Continued

State or other jurisdiction	Governor may item veto appropriation bills		Days allowed governor to consider bill(a)			Votes required in each house to pass bills or items over veto(c)	Effective date of enacted legislation(d)
	Amount	Other(b)	During session: Bill becomes law unless vetoed	After session: Bill becomes law unless vetoed	After session: Bill dies unless signed		
South Dakota	★	★	5	15A		2/3 elected	July 1(n)
Tennessee	★(f)	...	10	10A		Majority elected	40 days after enactment
Texas	★	...	10	20A		2/3 present	90 days after adjournment
Utah	★	...	10(h)	20A(h)	3A	2/3 elected	60 days after adjournment
Vermont	...	...	5			2/3 present	July 1
Virginia	★	★	7(h)	20A	30A(h)	2/3 present(z)	July 1(u,aa)
Washington	★	★	5			2/3 present	90 days after adjournment
West Virginia	★(f)	★	5	15A(bb)		Majority elected(g)	90 days after enactment
Wisconsin	★	★	6		6P	2/3 present	Day after publication
Wyoming	★		3	15A(h)		2/3 elected	Immediately
American Samoa	★		10		30P	2/3 elected	60 days after adjournment(cc)
Guam	★(f)		10		30P	14 members	Immediately(dd)
No. Marianas	★(f)		40(ee)		30P(h)	2/3 elected	Immediately
Puerto Rico	★(f)	★	10		30P(h)	2/3 elected	Specified in act
Virgin Islands	★	★	10		30P(h)	2/3 elected	Immediately

Note: Some legislatures reconvene after normal session to consider bills vetoed by governor. Connecticut—if governor vetoes any bill, secretary of state must reconvene General Assembly on second Monday after the last day on which governor is either authorized to transmit or has transmitted every bill with his objections, whichever occurs first; General Assembly must adjourn *sine die* not later than three days after its reconvening. Hawaii—legislature may reconvene on 45th day after adjournment *sine die*, in special session, without call. Louisiana—legislature meets in a maximum five-day veto session on the 40th day after final adjournment. Missouri—if governor returns any bill on or after the fifth day before the last day on which legislature may consider bills (in even-numbered years), legislature automatically reconvenes on first Monday in September for a maximum 10C session. New Jersey—legislature meets in special session (without call or petition) to act on bills returned by governor on 45th day after *sine die* adjournment of the first year of a two-year legislature; a special session may not be convened if the 45th day falls on or after the last day of the legislative year in which the second session occurs. Virginia—legislature reconvenes on sixth Wednesday after adjournment for a maximum three-day session (may be extended to seven days upon vote of majority of members elected to each house). Utah—if 2/3 of the members of each house favor reconvening to consider vetoed bills, a maximum five-day session is set by the presiding officers. Washington—upon petition of 2/3 of the members of each house, legislature meets 45 days after adjournment for a maximum five-day session.

Key:
★—Yes
...—No
A—days after adjournment of legislature
P—days after presentation to governor
(a) Sundays excluded, unless otherwise indicated.
(b) Includes language in appropriations bill.
(c) Bill returned to house of origin with governor's objections.
(d) Effective date may be established by the law itself or may be otherwise changed by vote of the legislature. Special or emergency acts are usually effective immediately.

(e) Penal acts, 60 days.
(f) Governor can also reduce amounts in appropriations bills. In Hawaii, governor can reduce items in executive appropriations measures, but cannot reduce nor item veto amounts appropriated for the judicial or legislative branches.
(g) Different number of votes required for revenue and appropriations bills. Alaska—3/4 elected. Illinois—appropriations reductions, majority elected. Oklahoma—emergency bills, 3/4 vote. West Virginia—budget and supplemental appropriations, 2/3 elected.
(h) Sundays included.
(i) A bill presented to the governor that is not returned within 12 days becomes a law; provided that any bill passed before Sept. 1 of the second calendar year of the biennium of the legislative session and in the possession of the governor on or after Sept. 1 that is not returned by the governor on or before Sept. 30 of that year becomes law. The legislature may not present to the governor any bill after Nov. 15 of the second calendar year of the biennium of the session. If the legislature, by adjournment of a special session prevents the return of a bill with the veto message, the bill becomes law unless the governor vetoes within 12 days by depositing it and the veto message in the office of the secretary of state.
(j) For legislation enacted in regular sessions: 91 days after adjournment. For legislation enacted in special sessions: Jan. 1 next following 90-day period from date of enactment. Does not apply to statutes calling elections, statutes providing for tax levies or appropriations for the usual current state expenses or urgency statutes, all of which take effect immediately.
(k) An act takes effect on the date stated in the act, or if no date is stated in the act, then on its passage.
(l) Constitution withholds right to veto constitutional amendments.
(m) Bills vetoed after adjournment are returned to the legislature for reconsideration. Georgia: bills vetoed during last three days of session and not considered for overriding, and all bills vetoed after *sine die* adjournment may be considered at next session. Maine: returned within three days after the next meeting of the same legislature which enacted the bill or resolution. Maryland: reconsidered at the next meeting of the same legislature. Mississippi: returned within three days after the beginning of the next meeting of the same General Assembly.

ning of the next session. Missouri: bills returned within four days of adjournment or later in first session are considered at beginning of second session; bills returned in second session are considered in automatic veto session. South Carolina: within two days after the next meeting.

(n) Effective date for bills which become law on or after July 1. Georgia—Jan. 1, unless a specific date has been provided for in legislation. Idaho—special sessions, 60 days after adjournment. Illinois—a bill passed after June 30 does not become effective prior to July 1 of the next calendar year unless legislature, by a 3/5 vote provided for an earlier effective date. Iowa—if governor signs bill after July 1, bill becomes law on Aug. 15; for special sessions, 90 days after adjournment. South Dakota—91 days after adjournment.

(o) Except Sundays and legal holidays. In Hawaii, except Saturdays, Sundays, holidays and any days in which the legislature is in recess prior to its adjournment.

(p) The governor must notify the legislature 10 days before the 45th day of his intent to veto a measure on that day. The legislature may convene on the 45th day after adjournment to consider the vetoed measures. If the legislature fails to reconvene, the bill does not become law. If the legislature reconvenes, it may pass the measure over the governor's veto or it may amend the law to meet the governor's objections. If the law is amended, the governor must sign the bill within 10 days after it is presented to him in order for it to become law.

(q) No act takes effect until it has been published and circulated in the counties, by authority, except in cases of emergency.

(r) Governor must sign or veto all bills presented to him. Iowa—any bill submitted to the governor for his approval during the last three days of a session must be deposited by him in the secretary of state's office within 30 days after adjournment with his approval or objections. Missouri—otherwise, legislature, by joint resolution, reciting fact of such failure, may direct the secretary of state to enroll the bill as an authentic act and it becomes law.

(s) Item veto on supplementary appropriations bills and capital construction bills only.

(t) Bills passed over governor's veto are effective in 30 days or on date specified in bill, whichever is later.

(u) Different date for fiscal legislation. Minnesota, Montana, New Mexico—immediately.

(v) In event of a recess of 30 days or more, legislature may prescribe, by joint resolution, that laws previously passed and not effective shall take effect 90 days from beginning of recess.

(w) No appropriation can be made in excess of the recommendations contained in the governor's budget except by a 2/3 vote. The excess is not subject to veto by the governor.

(x) If a bill is not returned by the governor within 10 days after it is presented to him (excluding Sundays), it becomes law, unless the house of origin is in temporary adjournment. In that case, the bill becomes law on the day the house of origin reconvenes. If on the 10th day, the legislature is in adjournment sine die, the bill becomes law if the governor signs it within 45 days (excluding Sundays) after the adjournment. On the 45th day, the bill becomes law unless he returns it with his objections (1) on the 45th day if the house of origin has convened in regular or special session of the same two-year legislature; (2) on the day upon which the house reconvenes, if it is in temporary adjournment on the 45th day; or (3) on the 45th day (if the house is in adjournment sine die) at the special session which convenes on that day (without petition or call) for the sole purpose of acting on returned bills.

(y) Governor has no approval or veto power.

(z) Must include majority of elected members.

(aa) Special sessions—first day of fourth month after adjournment.

(bb) Five days for appropriations bills.

(cc) Laws required to be approved only by the governor. An act required to be approved by the U.S. Secretary of the Interior only after it is vetoed by the governor and so approved takes effect 40 days after it is returned to the governor by the secretary.

(dd) U.S. Congress may annul.

(ee) Twenty days for appropriations bills.

Table 3.15
BILL AND RESOLUTION INTRODUCTIONS AND ENACTMENTS:
1983, 1984, 1985 REGULAR SESSIONS

State	Duration of session*	Introductions Bills	Introductions Resolutions	Enactments Bills	Enactments Resolutions	Measures vetoed by governor	Length of session
Alabama...............	April 19-Aug. 1, 1983	1,489	N.A.	190	393	N.A.	105C
	Feb. 7-May 21, 1984	N.A.	N.A.	398	270	N.A.	105C
	Feb. 5-May 20, 1985	1,803	787	343	696	4	105C
Alaska...............	Jan. 17-June 27, 1983	767	(a)	109	(a)	9(b)	162C
	Jan. 9-June 8, 1984	509	(a)	171	(a)	10(b)	152C
	Jan. 14-May 14, 1985	770	161	107	37	1	120C
Arizona...............	Jan. 10-April 27, 1983	872	38	329	8	9	108C
	Jan. 9-May 4, 1984	971	31	398	20	12	117C
	Jan. 14-May 8, 1985	972	50	368	26	12	115C
Arkansas	Jan. 10-April 4, 1983	1,583	221	937	184	23	68C
	No regular session in 1984						
	Jan. 14-March 29, 1985	1,774	224	1,097	N.A.	37(b,c)	75C
California..............	Dec. 6, 1982-Nov. 30, 1984(d)	6,394	569	3,068	376	465	(e)
	Dec. 3, 1984-Sept. 13, 1985(f)	4,264	307	1,024	127	100	(e)
Colorado	Jan. 5-Oct. 1, 1983	1,046	73(g)	547	50	21	290C
	Jan. 4-May 22, 1984	659	73(g)	337	53	13(c)	140C
	Jan. 2-Aug. 21, 1985	643	87	347	65	18(c)	181C
Connecticut	Jan. 5-June 8, 1983	3,459	316	655	N.A.	10	111L
	Feb. 8-May 9, 1984	1,609	164	622	N.A.	9	58L
	Jan. 9-June 5, 1985	3,879	81	725	N.A.	9	103L
Delaware	Jan. 11-June 30, 1983	717	467	218	N.A.	16	51L
	Jan. 10-June 30, 1984	558	409	262	N.A.	15	51L
	Jan. 8-June 30, 1985	707	392	220	N.A.	22	(e)
Florida	April 5-June 13, 1983	2,490	91	580	82	10	70C
	April 3-June 1, 1984	2,385	113	684	105	16(c)	60C
	April 2-May 31, 1985	2,511	236	517	133	12	60C
Georgia...............	Jan. 10-March 4, 1983	1,199	695	571	628	12	40L
	Jan. 9-Feb. 29, 1984	1,085(h)	751(h)	783	683	11	40L
	Jan. 14-March 8, 1985	1,492	727	770	51	4	40L
Hawaii	Jan. 19-April 22, 1983	3,119	1,073	301	411	10(b)	60L
	Jan. 18-April 19, 1984	1,747	918	291	329	17	60L
	Jan. 16-April 22, 1985	3,147	912	332	310	24	61L
Idaho	Jan. 10-April 14, 1983	589	71	305	40	23	95C
	Jan. 9-March 31, 1984	586	81	303	31	14	83C
	Jan. 7-March 13, 1985	566	67	274	29	4(c)	66C
Illinois................	Jan. 12-Nov. 4, 1983	3,708	1,195	1,269	1,091	311(c)	(e)
	Jan. 11, 1984-Jan. 9, 1985	1,441	1,421	425	1,350	30(c)	(e)
	Jan. 9-Nov. 14, 1985	4,065	1,742	1,221(i)	1,600	135(c,j)	(e)
Indiana	Nov. 16, 1982-April 15, 1983	954	223(k)	209	2(l)	1	61L
	Nov. 22, 1983-March 1, 1984	1,587	242(k)	386	2(l)	4	30L
	Nov. 20, 1984-April 15, 1985	1,564	241(k)	376	3(l)	4	61L
Iowa	Jan. 10-May 14, 1983	1,215	20	215	3	2(b)	125C
	Jan. 9-April 20, 1984	898(h)	11(h)	330	3	9(b)	103C
	Jan. 14-May 5, 1985	1,374	14	274	1	6	111C
Kansas	Jan. 10-June 3, 1983	1,049	88(m)	345	32(m)	7(b)	70L
	Jan. 9-June 1, 1984	972(h)	91(m)	383	36(m)	13(b)	69L
	Jan. 14-June 7, 1985	1,025	54(m)	346	20(m)	14(b)	69L
Kentucky	No regular session in 1983						
	Jan. 3-April 13, 1984	1,438	302	391	30	6(c)	60L
	No regular session in 1985						
Louisiana	April 18-July 1, 1983	2,043	396	760	285	30	49L
	April 16-July 5, 1984	3,025	473	980	297	17	54L
	April 15-July 8, 1985	3,097	435(m)	1,020	316(m)	13	(e)
Maine	Dec. 1, 1982-June 24, 1983	1,792	14	692	3	3	100L
	Jan. 4-April 25, 1984	702	6	353	3	3	51L
	Dec. 5, 1984-June 20, 1985	1,660	2	642(n)	N.A.	5	96L
Maryland	Jan. 12-April 11, 1983	2,456	93	752	29	64	90C
	Jan. 11-April 9, 1984	2,813	120	882	31	84	90C
	Jan. 9-April 8, 1985	2,601	117	882	31	95(c)	90C

1983, 1984, 1985 REGULAR SESSIONS—Continued

State	Duration of session*	Introductions Bills	Introductions Resolutions	Enactments Bills	Enactments Resolutions	Measures vetoed by governor	Length of session
Massachusetts	Jan. 5, 1983-Jan. 3, 1984	9,222 (o)	(o)	723	11	0	(e)
	Jan. 4, 1984-Jan. 1, 1985	8,631 (o)	(o)	493	14	5	(e)
	Jan. 2, 1985-Dec. 31, 1985	9,494	N.A. (p)	812	14 (p)	2	169L
Michigan	Jan. 12-Dec. 29, 1983	1,820	1,941	261	N.A.	2	352C
	Jan. 11-Dec. 28, 1984	943	1,761	436	N.A.	4	353C
	Jan. 9-Dec. 30, 1985	1,903	N.A.	230	N.A.	3	355C
Minnesota	Jan. 4-May 23, 1983	2,690	94	387	11	1	60L
	March 6-April 24, 1984	1,803	91	298	11	5	24L
	Jan. 8-May 20, 1985	3,259	69	310	5	1	65L
Mississippi	Jan. 4-April 21, 1983	2,217	397	607	230	7	108C
	Jan. 3-May 15, 1984	2,326	336	587	191	7	134C
	Jan. 8-April 11, 1985	2,340	333 (m)	576	156 (m)	6	68C
Missouri	Jan. 5-June 15, 1983	1,260	55 (l)	206	2 (l)	4	(e)
	Jan. 4-April 30, 1984	1,097	61 (l)	178	4 (l)	5	(e)
	Jan. 9-June 30, 1985	1,272	68 (l)	221	4 (l)	12	(e)
Montana	Jan. 3-April 21, 1983	1,392	82	748	57	0	90L
	No regular session in 1984						
	Jan. 7-April 25, 1985	1,428	115	761	75	1	90L
Nebraska	Jan. 5-May 25, 1983	632	219	295	72	10 (b,c)	90L
	Jan. 4-April 9, 1984	499 (h)	252	291	72	30 (b,c)	60L
	Jan. 9-June 25, 1985	728	303	248	N.A.	8 (c)	90L
Nevada	Jan. 17-May 22, 1983	1,164	214 (h,q)	626	164 (q)	2 (r)	90L
	No regular session in 1984						
	Jan. 21-June 4, 1985	1,252	228	683	142	6	135C
New Hampshire	Jan. 1, 1983-Dec. 31, 1984	1,063	5 (l)	471	3 (l)	11	36L
	Jan. 2-June 28, 1985	1,042	112	417	65	14 (c)	30L
New Jersey	Jan. 11, 1983-Jan. 10, 1984	1,931	318	579	46	203	(e)
	Jan. 10, 1984-Jan. 8, 1985	5,598	593	248	59	67	(e)
	Jan. 8, 1985-Jan. 14, 1986(s)	1,974	219	329	31	54	(e)
New Mexico	Jan. 18-March 19, 1983	923	13 (l)	384	0 (l)	50	60C
	Jan. 17-Feb. 16, 1984	609	29 (l)	134	1 (l)	3	30C
	Jan. 15-March 16, 1985	1,177	33 (l)	272	4 (l)	30	60C
New York	Jan. 5, 1983-Jan. 4, 1984	15,225	3,390	1,021	3,305	92	(t)
	Jan. 4-Dec. 31, 1984	18,410	3,700	1,018	3,656	113	(t)
	Jan. 9, 1985-Jan. 8, 1986(u)	15,059	3,797	1,026	N.A.	92	(t)
North Carolina	Jan. 12-July 22, 1983	2,010	167	929	55	(v)	138L
	June 7-July 7, 1984	451	76	187	51	(v)	23L
	Feb. 5-July 18, 1985	2,278 (o)	(o)	839	46	(v)	118L
North Dakota	Jan. 4-April 20, 1983	1,239	169	713	136	12	75L
	No regular session in 1984						
	Jan. 8-April 5, 1985	1,175	201	701	164	12	62L
Ohio	Jan. 3-Dec. 1, 1983	905	39 (l)	273	14 (l)	0	(e)
	Jan. 3-Dec. 31, 1984	416	44 (l)	70	11 (l)	0	(e)
	Jan. 7-Dec. 31, 1985	1,042	72 (l)	123	16 (l)	2	(e)
Oklahoma	Jan. 4-June 23, 1983	764	164 (q)	334	88 (q)	2	90L
	Jan. 3-May 31, 1984	723 (h)	197 (h,q)	299	122 (q)	6 (c)	(e)
	Jan. 7-July 19, 1985	925	69 (l)	357	14 (l)	10 (b)	90L
Oregon	Jan. 10-July 16, 1983	1,946	129	871	54	40 (c)	188C
	No regular session in 1984						
	Jan. 14-June 21, 1985	2,070	131	825	53	32	159C
Pennsylvania	Jan. 4, 1983-Jan. 3, 1984	3,042	262	147	104	1	(e)
	Jan. 3-Nov. 30, 1984	1,142	182	317	110	10	(e)
	Jan. 1, 1985-Jan. 7, 1986(w)	3,281 (x)	337	177 (y)	217	0	(e)
Rhode Island	Jan. 3-May 13, 1983	2,321	466	1,007	466	23	66L
	Jan. 2-May 10, 1984	2,421	427	1,014	427	18	63L
	Jan. 1-June 21, 1985	2,795	N.A.	1,025	339	54 (c)	(e)
South Carolina	Jan. 11-July 27, 1983	1,376	N.A.	262	N.A.	12 (c)	(e)
	Jan. 10-Aug. 31, 1984	792	N.A.	367	N.A.	12 (c)	(e)
	Jan. 15-June 26, 1985	1,797 (o)	(o)	303	N.A.	9 (c)	163C

115

State	Duration of session*	Introductions Bills	Introductions Resolutions	Enactments Bills	Enactments Resolutions	Measures vetoed by governor	Length of session
South Dakota	Jan. 11-March 23, 1983	625	92 (m)	387	83 (m)	16 (c)	40L
	Jan. 10-March 13, 1984	581	98 (k)	338	90 (k)	15 (c)	35L
	Jan. 8-March 14, 1985	684	69	393	59	9	39L
Tennessee	Jan. 11-May 12, 1983	2,625	502	635 (z)	436	10 (b)	(aa)
	Feb. 23-May 24, 1984	1,967	588	625 (z)	511	11 (b,c)	(e)
	Jan. 8-June 19, 1985	2,254	765	586 (z)	693	9 (c)	55L
Texas	Jan. 11-May 30, 1983	3,891	2,006	1,134	1,684	40 (b)	82C
	No regular session in 1984						
	Jan. 8-May 27, 1985	4,021	1,793	1,024	1,487	44	140C
Utah	Jan. 10-March 10, 1983	788	91	362	52	12 (c)	60C
	Jan. 9-Jan. 28, 1984	33	19	23	15	0	20C
	Jan. 14-Feb. 27, 1985	706	88	267	48	5	45C
Vermont	Jan. 5-April 23, 1983	621 (bb)	74 (l,bb)	95 (bb)	N.A.	1	66L
	Jan. 4-April 17, 1984	368	94 (l)	180	N.A.	1	63L
	Jan. 9-May 11, 1985	573	96	107	77	0	75L
Virginia	Jan. 12-April 6, 1983	1,234	245	622	222	25	45L
	Jan. 11-April 18, 1984	1,471 (h)	319	779	229	28	90L
	Jan. 9-Feb. 23, 1985	1,357	114	617	114	23	36L
Washington	Jan. 10-April 24, 1983	2,378	189	315	35	11 (b)	105C
	Jan. 9-March 8, 1984	1,271	83	289	21	8 (b)	60C
	Jan. 14-April 28, 1985	2,267	170	378	29	7 (b)	105C
West Virginia	Jan. 12-March 16, 1983	1,798	193 (q)	203	77 (q)	8 (cc)	64C
	Jan. 11-March 14, 1984	1,827	174 (q)	190	52 (q)	3 (cc)	64C
	Feb. 13-April 16, 1985	1,846	229	192	73	16 (c,cc)	60C (dd)
Wisconsin	Jan. 3, 1983-Jan. 7, 1985	1,902	223 (ee)	521	93 (ee)	3 (b)	(e)
	Jan. 7, 1985-Jan. 5, 1987(ff)	1,026	137	34 (gg)	48	(b)	(e)
Wyoming	Jan. 11-March 2, 1983	646	24	203	2	11 (hh)	40L
	Feb. 14-March 9, 1984	157	9	73	5	3	20L
	Jan. 8-Feb. 23, 1985	771	25	235	9	4	40L

*Actual adjournment dates are listed regardless of constitutional or statutory limitations. For more information on provisions, see Table 3.2, "Legislative Sessions: Legal Provisions."

Key:

C—Calendar day.

L—Legislative day (in some states, called a session or workday; definition may vary slightly, however, generally refers to any day on which either chamber of the legislature is in session).

N.A.—Not available.

(a) The total number of resolutions introduced in 1983 and 1984 was 271, while the total number enacted was 40. Separate totals for each year were not available.

(b) Plus line item vetoes. Alaska: 1983—8, 1984—10; Arkansas: 1985—5; Hawaii: 1983—2; Iowa: 1983—8, 1984—10; Kansas: 1983—1, 1984—1, 1985—7; Nebraska: 1983—3, 1984—5; Oklahoma: 1985—3; Tennessee: 1983—1, 1984—2; Texas: 1983—2; Washington: 1983—12, 1984—25, 1985—52; Wisconsin: 1983-85—8 (of which 2 were overriden), 1985-87—1 partial veto (2 vetoed items overriden).

(c) Number of vetoes overriden: Arkansas: 1985—1; Colorado: 1984—2, 1985—3; Florida: 1984—2; Idaho: 1985—1; Illinois: 1983—46, 1984—4, 1985—23 (includes override of amendatory vetoes); Kentucky: 1984—1; Maine: 1985—2; Nebraska: 1983—2, 1984—12, 1985—1; New Hampshire: 1985—1; Oklahoma: 1984—1; Oregon: 1983—1; Rhode Island: 1985—2; South Carolina: 1983—6, 1984—6, 1985—8; South Dakota: 1983—2, 1984—2; Tennessee: 1984—2, 1985—6; Utah: 1983—6; West Virginia: 1985—1.

(d) During this period, the Assembly met Dec. 6, 1982-Sept. 15, 1983 (144C) and Jan. 3-Aug. 31, 1984 (118C).

(e) California: 1982-84 Senate = 266L, Assembly = 262C; 1984-85 (portion of session) Senate = 129L, Assembly = 128L. Delaware: 1985 Senate = 51L, House = 50L. Illinois: 1983 Senate = 77L, House = 88L; 1984 Senate = 62L, House = 64L; 1985 Senate = 78L, House = 87L. Louisiana: 1985 Senate = 47L, House 57L. Massachusetts: 1983 Senate = 133L, House = 107L; 1984 Senate = 119L, House = 153L. Missouri: 1983 Senate = 93L, House = 89L; 1984 Senate = 69L, House = 67L; 1985 Senate = 91L, House = 90L. New Jersey: 1983 Senate = 27L, Assembly = 29L; 1984 Senate = 24L, Assembly = 28L; 1985 Senate = 22L, Assembly = 24L. Ohio: 1983 Senate = 115L, House = 111L; 1984 Senate = 89L, House = 90L; 1985 Senate = 91L, House = 100L. Oklahoma: 1984 Senate = 87L, House = 88L. Pennsylvania: 1983 Senate = 93L, House = 99L; 1984 Senate = 65L, House = 70L; 1985 Senate = 78L, House = 80L. Rhode Island: 1985 Senate = 84L, House = 83L. South Carolina: 1983 Senate = 109L, House = 107L; 1984 Senate = 103L, House = 99L. Tennessee: 1984 Senate = 79L, House = 81L. Wisconsin: 1983-85 Senate = 72L, Assembly = 80L; 1985-87 Senate = 45L, Assembly = 45L (as of Oct. 26, 1985).

(f) September 1985 date is recess date. After organizational session in December, legislature recesses until the first Monday in January of the odd-numbered year and continues in session until Nov. 30 of next even-numbered year.

(g) Excludes simple resolutions.

(h) Plus carryover legislation from the previous session. Georgia—599 bills and 62 resolutions; Iowa—number not available; Kansas—575 bills; Nebraska—224 bills; Nevada—8 joint resolutions; Oklahoma—385 bills and 39 joint resolutions; and Virginia—244 bills.

(i) Includes amendatory vetoes accepted.

(j) Does not include item and reduction vetoes; does include amendatory vetoes not overriden or accepted.

(k) Joint and concurrent resolutions.

(l) Joint resolutions.

(m) Concurrent resolutions.

(n) Plus 15 held by the governor.

(o) Figures given under bill introductions includes resolution introductions.

(p) Resolves.

(q) Includes joint, concurrent and single-house resolutions.

(r) Twelve vetoed bills from the 1981 session were returned to the 1983 session for reconsideration. The legislature overrode three of those bills in 1983. The two vetoed bills of the 1983 session were returned to the 1985 session.

(s) Through Nov. 1, 1985.

(t) Session is divided into "workdays" during which the legislature is actually meeting in session, and "legislative days" in which only one or two legislators perfunctorily open and adjourn for the day in order to speed up the bill consideration process. In 1983, the Senate and Assembly met for 71 workdays. In 1984, the Senate met for 65 workdays and the Assembly for 71. In 1985, the Senate met for 70 workdays and the Assembly for 71.

(u) During this period, the Assembly met Jan. 9-Dec. 31, 1985.

(v) Governor has no veto power.

(w) During this period, the House met from Jan. 1, 1985-Dec. 12, 1985.

(x) Includes joint resolutions (in bill form) proposing constitutional amendments.

(y) Includes bills enacted, as well as two joint resolutions (in bill form) proposing constitutional amendments which were approved by the General Assembly and by the electorate in 1985.

(z) Public and private acts.

(aa) Five organizational days and 41 legislative days.

(bb) Includes bills and resolutions from the 1983 special session.

(cc) In 1983, one was amended, re-passed and approved by the governor, while one other veto was overriden notwithstanding objections of the governor. In 1984, one was amended, re-passed and approved by the governor. In 1985, three measures were amended, re-passed and approved by the governor.

(dd) Extended three days for budget work.

(ee) Includes joint and single-house resolutions.

(ff) Scheduled end of regular session. All information as of Oct. 26, 1985.

(gg) Fifty-five bills pending action.

(hh) One bill was voided (not signed by the speaker).

Table 3.16
Table 3.16
BILL AND RESOLUTION INTRODUCTIONS AND ENACTMENTS:
1983, 1984, 1985 SPECIAL SESSIONS

State	Duration of session*	Introductions Bills	Introductions Resolutions	Enactments Bills	Enactments Resolutions	Measures vetoed by governor	Length of session
Alabama	Jan.11-Jan.18, 1983(a)	0	N.A.	0	38	N.A.	8C
	Jan. 25-Jan.29, 1983	79	N.A.	15(b)	47	N.A.	5C
	Feb. 1-Feb. 24, 1983	76	N.A.	30(b)	77	N.A.	24C
	May 22-June 9,1984	N.A.	N.A.	75(c)	90	N.A.	19C
	Dec. 17, 1984-Jan. 9, 1985	N.A.	N.A.	18(c)	59	N.A.	24C
	Aug. 28-Sept. 20, 1985	475	326	134	296	0	12L
Alaska	No special sessions in 1983/1984						
	July 15-Aug. 5, 1985	0	0	2	2	0	21C
Arizona	Oct. 3, 1983-Jan. 19, 1984	48	1	17	0	4	109C
	June 21-July 5, 1984	20	6	6	4	2	15C
	July 20-July 20, 1984	2	0	1	0	0	1C
	No special sessions in 1985						
Arkansas	Oct. 4- Nov. 10, 1983	208	33	121	29	1	37C
	No special sessions in 1984						
	June 17-June 21, 1985	56	12	43	N.A.	0	5C
California	Dec. 6, 1982-July 19, 1983	65	6	16	2	0	(d)
	Jan. 19-Feb. 17, 1984	1	2	1	1	0	(d)
	No special sessions in 1985						
Colorado	No special sessions in 1983/1984						
	Sept. 23-Sept. 25, 1985	1	4	1	4	0	2C
Connecticut	June 10-June 29,1983	60	9	57	0	0	8L
	Oct. 11-Oct. 13, 1983	4	13	4	0	0	3L
	Dec. 9-Dec. 9, 1983	1	4	1	0	0	1L
	June 25-June 25, 1984	0	32	0	32	0	1L
	No special sessions in 1985						
Delaware	(e)	0	0	0	0	0	(e)
Florida	March 1-March 3, 1983	14	2	6	2	0	3C
	June 15-June 24, 1983	95	2	45	2	1	10C
	July 12-July 13, 1983	19	2	11	2	0	1L(f)
	Dec. 6-Dec. 7, 1984(a)	37	4	14	3	0	2L
	No special sessions in 1985						
Georgia	No special sessions in 1983/1984/ 1985						
Hawaii	No special sessions in 1983						
	July 9-July 13, 1984	2	2	1	2	0	5L
	No special sessions in 1985						
Idaho	May 9-May 11, 1983	8	0	5	0	0(g)	3C
	No special sessions in 1984/1985						
Illinois	No special sessions in 1983/1984						
	July 8-July 8, 1985	0	14	1	14	0	1L
	Oct. 2-Nov. 14, 1985	2	15	0	15	0	4L
Indiana	No special sessions in 1983/1984/ 1985						
Iowa	No special sessions in 1983/1984/ 1985						
Kansas	No special sessions in 1983/1984/ 1985						
Kentucky	No special sessions in 1983/1984						
	July 8-July 19, 1985	21	74	6	4	0	10L
Louisiana	Jan. 4-Jan. 17, 1983	134	32	62	23	1	10L
	Dec. 3-Dec. 14, 1983	51	59	7	38	1	6L
	March 19-March 26, 1984	28	25	16	24	1	6L
	No special sessions in 1985						
Maine	Sept. 6-Sept. 7, 1983	13	0	8	0	0	2L
	Nov. 18-Nov. 18, 1983	3	0	2	0	0	1L
	Sept. 4-Sept. 11, 1984	20	0	17	0	0	5L
	Nov. 13-Nov. 13, 1985	9	0	8	0	0	1L
Maryland	June 12-June 12, 1983	3	0	1	0	0	1C
	No special sessions in 1984						
	May 1-May 28, 1985	31	2	14	0	2(h)	3L
	Oct. 17-Nov. 15, 1985	45	1	6	0	0(h)	8L

State	Duration of session*	Introductions		Enactments		Measures vetoed by governor	Length of session
		Bills	Resolutions	Bills	Resolutions		
Massachusetts	No special sessions in 1983/1984/ 1985						
Michigan	No special sessions in 1983/1984/ 1985						
Minnesota	No special sessions in 1983/1984						
	June 19-June 21, 1985	49	2	18	2	0	3C
Mississippi	June 24-June 24, 1983	6	6	5	6	0	1C
	Nov. 16-Nov. 19, 1983	23	5(i)	5	4(i)	0	4C
	June 25-June 27, 1984	22	6(i)	22	6(i)	0	3C
	No special sessions in 1985						
Missouri	Oct. 19-Dec. 17, 1983	39	0	11	0	0	(a)
	No special sessions in 1984/1985						
Montana...............	Dec. 12-Dec. 17, 1983	14	3	3	0	0	5L
	No special sessions in 1984						
	June 28-June 28, 1985	4	0	2	0	0	1L
Nebraska	Aug. 16-Aug. 30, 1984	3	7	0	1	0	6L
	Sept. 19-Sept. 25, 1985	5	0	1	0	0	7L
	Oct. 17-Nov. 15, 1985	35	0	8	0	1(j)	16L
Nevada	No special sessions in 1983						
	March 29-March 30, 1984	2	7(k)	2	7(k)	0	2L
	No special sessions in 1985						
New Hampshire..........	No special sessions in 1983/1984/ 1985						
New Jersey..............	No special sessions in 1983/1984/ 1985						
New Mexico.............	No special sessions in 1983						
	March 9-March 22, 1984	38	0	10	0	0	14C
	May 11-May 18, 1985	174	1	15	0	0	7C
	June 8-June 9, 1985	10	0	0	0	0	2C
New York	(l)						
North Carolina	Aug. 26-Aug. 26, 1983	6	1	6	1	0	1L
	March 7-March 8, 1984	9	1	7	1	0	2L
	No special sessions in 1985						
North Dakota	No special sessions in 1983/1984/ 1985						
Ohio	No special sessions in 1983/1984/ 1985						
Oklahoma	Sept. 19-Sept. 23, 1983	10	12(k)	1	9(k)	0	5L
	Nov. 28-Nov. 30, 1983	5	3(m)	0	2(m)	0	3L
	No special sessions in 1984/1985						
Oregon	Sept. 14-Oct. 4, 1983	13	5(o)	6	3(o)	0	21C
	July 30-July 30, 1984	2	1	2	1	0	1C
	No special sessions in 1985						
Pennsylvania	No special sessions in 1983/1984/ 1985						
Rhode Island	No special sessions in 1983						
	June 27-June 27, 1984	57	6	41	6	0	1L
	No special sessions in 1985						
South Carolina	Nov. 8-Nov. 9, 1983	1	0	1	0	0	2L
	Dec. 4-Dec. 5, 1984(a)	0	0	0	0	0	2L
	No special sessions in 1985						
South Dakota	No special sessions in 1983						
	May 2-May 3, 1984	2	0	1	0	0	2L
	No special sessions in 1985						
Tennessee	No special sessions in 1983						
	Jan. 10-Feb. 23, 1984	83	143	14	141	0	27L
	Nov. 5-Jan. 14, 1986	95	75(p)	12	73(p)	0	16L
Texas..................	June 22-June 25, 1983	58	80	8	66	0	4C
	June 4-July 3, 1984	193	564	34	517	0	30C
	May 28-May 30, 1985	17	25	3	18	0	3C

State	Duration of session*	Introductions		Enactments		Measures vetoed by governor	Length of session
		Bills	Resolutions	Bills	Resolutions		
Utah	June 23-July 21, 1983	N.A.	26	N.A.	9	N.A.	29C
	No special session in 1984						
	June 26-June 28, 1985	20	14	14	14	1	3C
Vermont	July 19-July 27, 1983	----------------------------------(q)--------------------------------					7L
	No special sessions in 1984/1985						
Virginia................	No special sessions in 1983/1984						
	April 3-April 3, 1985	0	0	0	4 (r)	0	1L
Washington	April 25-May 24, 1983	N.A.	N.A.	76	N.A.	3 (g)	30C
	May 25-May 25, 1983	N.A.	N.A.	3	N.A.	0 (g)	1C
	No special sessions in 1984						
	June 10-June 11, 1985	5	4	6	4	0	2C
West Virginia	May 17-Aug. 17, 1983	47	31 (s)	18	21 (k)	0 (j)	12L
	May 19-May 19, 1984	6	7 (k)	6	7 (k)	2	1L
	No special sessions in 1985						
Wisconsin...............	Jan. 4-Jan. 6, 1983	----------------------------------(t)--------------------------------					3C
	April 12-April 14, 1983	----------------------------------(t)--------------------------------					3C
	July 11-July 14, 1983	----------------------------------(t)--------------------------------					4C
	Oct. 18-Oct. 28, 1983	----------------------------------(t)--------------------------------					10C
	Feb. 2-March 22, 1984	----------------------------------(t)--------------------------------					54C
	May 22-May 24, 1984	----------------------------------(t)--------------------------------					3C
	March 19-March 21, 1985	6	1	3	1	0	3C
	Sept. 24-Oct. 29, 1985	22	1	(u)	1	0	26C
	Oct. 31-Oct. 31, 1985	1	3	1	3	0	1C
Wyoming	Aug. 4-Aug. 5, 1983	2	0	2	0	0	2L
	No special sessions in 1984/1985						

*Actual adjournment dates are listed regardless of constitutional or statutory limitations. For more information on provisions, see Table 3.2, "Legislative Sessions: Legal Provisions."

Note: Information on the 1985 special sessions was collected in a November survey of legislative agencies. If, at that time, a state indicated a special session was likely to occur prior to the end of the year, or was in progress, then a follow-up survey was undertaken and the session information is presented here.

Key:
C—Calendar day.
L—Legislative day (in some states, called a session or workday; definition may vary slightly, however, generally refers to any day on which either chamber of the legislature is in session).
N.A.—Not available.

(a) Organizational session.
(b) Local and general acts.
(c) Local acts, general acts, and constitutional amendments.
(d) California: 1983 Senate = 72L, Assembly = 68C; 1984 Senate = 3L, Assembly = 5C. Missouri: Senate = 32L, House = 24L. Wisconsin: Senate = 39L, Assembly = 30L.
(e) In 1983 the Senate met on July 1, July 6, Sept. 28 and Oct. 20 to confirm gubernatorial appointments. In 1984, the Senate met on July 1, Aug. 2 and Sept. 13 (and in 1985, on Sept. 30) for the same purpose.

(f) From 10 a.m., July 12, until 1:30 a.m., July 13.
(g) Plus line item vetoes: Idaho—1; Washington, 1st special session—9, 2nd special session—1; Wisconsin—3.
(h) No action until next session.
(i) Concurrent resolutions.
(j) One veto overriden by the legislature.
(k) Concurrent and single-house resolutions.
(l) Extraordinary session was held Dec. 10, 1985-Jan. 6, 1986 (one workday); information not available.
(m) Joint and single-house resolutions.
(n) Single-house resolutions.
(o) Includes memorials.
(p) Joint resolutions.
(q) Included in numbers given in Table 3.15, "Bill and Resolution Introductions and Enactments: 1983, 1984, 1985 Regular Sessions." Separate figures not available.
(r) Joint resolutions that were introduced in 1985 regular session.
(s) Concurrent, joint and simple resolutions.
(t) The following are totals for action taken during the six special sessions held in 1983-84 (separate figures not available): bills introduced-34; resolutions introduced-16; bills enacted-24; resolutions enacted-14; vetoes-0.
(u) Seventeen bills pending.

Table 3.17
STAFF FOR INDIVIDUAL LEGISLATORS

	Senate			House		
	Capitol			Capitol		
State	*Personal*	*Shared*	*District*	*Personal*	*Shared*	*District*
Alabama	. . .	YR	. . .	. . .	YR	. . .
Alaska	YR	. . .	. . .	YR	. . .	. . .
Arizona	YR	. . .	. . .	YR	. . .	. . .
Arkansas	. . .	YR	. . .	. . .	YR	. . .
California	YR	. . .	YR	YR	YR/3	YR
Colorado	(a)	YR/5(b)	. . .	(a)	YR/1.4(b)	. . .
Connecticut	(a)	YR/1.5	. . .	(a)	YR/5	. . .
Delaware	SO	YR/3(c)	. . .	SO	YR/5(c)	. . .
Florida	YR(d)	. . .	(d)	YR(d)	. . .	(d)
Georgia	(e)	YR/3	. . .	(e)	YR/6	. . .
Hawaii	YR	(f)	. . .	YR	(f)	. . .
Idaho	. . .	YR	. . .	. . .	YR	. . .
Illinois	YR	YR	(g)	. . .	YR	(g)
Indiana	. . .	YR/2(h)	. . .	. . .	YR(h)	. . .
Iowa	SO	. . .	. . .	SO	. . .	. . .
Kansas	SO	. . .	. . .	. . .	SO/3	. . .
Kentucky	. . .	. . .	. . .	. . .	. . .	. . .
Louisiana	SO	YR	YR	. . .	. . .	YR
Maine	(a)	SO/10	. . .	(a)	SO/30	. . .
Maryland	YR	. . .	(g)	(g)	YR/3	(g)
Massachusetts	YR	. . .	. . .	YR	YR	. . .
Michigan	YR	. . .	. . .	YR	. . .	. . .
Minnesota	YR	. . .	. . .	(i)	YR/3	. . .
Mississippi	. . .	YR	. . .	. . .	YR/15	. . .
Missouri	YR(g)	. . .	YR(g)	SO	IO/5	YR
Montana	. . .	SO	. . .	. . .	SO	. . .
Nebraska	YR	. . .	. . .	---------Unicameral---------		
Nevada	. . .	YR/2	. . .	. . .	YR/4	. . .
New Hampshire	. . .	SO/2	. . .	. . .	YR/8(b)	. . .
New Jersey	YR(d)	. . .	(d)	YR(d)	. . .	(d)
New Mexico	(a)	SO/2-10	. . .	(a)	SO/2-10	. . .
New York	YR	. . .	YR	YR	. . .	YR
North Carolina	SO	. . .	. . .	SO	. . .	. . .
North Dakota	. . .	SO/11	. . .	. . .	SO/13	. . .
Ohio	YR	YR	. . .	(a)	YR/2(j)	(k)
Oklahoma	SO	. . .	. . .	SO	YR/2(l)	. . .
Oregon	(g)	. . .	(g)	(g)	. . .	(g)
Pennsylvania	YR	. . .	YR	YR	. . .	YR
Rhode Island	. . .	YR	. . .	. . .	YR	. . .
South Carolina	YR	YR/2	. . .	YR	YR/10	. . .
South Dakota	. . .	. . .	. . .	. . .	. . .	. . .
Tennessee	YR	. . .	. . .	YR	. . .	. . .
Texas	YR	. . .	YR	YR	. . .	YR
Utah	. . .	SO/4	. . .	. . .	SO/4	. . .
Vermont	. . .	YR	. . .	. . .	YR	. . .
Virginia	YR	SO/2	. . .	YR	SO/2	. . .
Washington	YR(m)	. . .	(m)	SO	YR	. . .
West Virginia	SO	. . .	. . .	SO	SO/3	. . .
Wisconsin	YR(m)	. . .	(m)	YR	. . .	. . .
Wyoming	. . .	SO(n)	. . .	. . .	SO(n)	. . .

Note: For entries under column heading "Shared," figure after slash indicates approximate number of legislators per staff person, where available.

Key:
. . .—Staff not provided for individual legislators.
YR—Year-round.
SO—Session only.
IO—Interim only.
(a) Personal staff provided to leadership only (may include specific committee chairmen).
(b) Staff sizes are reduced during interim.
(c) Upon member's request to, and subsequent approval by, chamber leadership, staff may be provided to legislator at any time.
(d) Personal and district staff are the same.
(e) Permanent year-round staff and additional staff during sessions. Number of legislators for whom a single staff member will work varies from one staff member to another.
(f) Majority and minority offices provide staff year-round. Number increases during session.

(g) Expense allowance may be used for staffing. Illinois—legislators may employ staff from district office allowance. Maryland—legislators may employ staff from discretionary funds in expense account. Oregon—biennial allowance may be used for session and/or interim staffing, depending on legislator's needs.
(h) Varies depending on workload and time of year (interim versus session).
(i) Each committee chairman has a committee secretary and committee administrator. The secretary also serves as the primary administrative support person for the chairman on non-committee business.
(j) Secretarial staff shared; caucus staff shares aide duties.
(k) District staff not provided; however, some representatives establish district offices at their own expense.
(l) Secretarial staffing.
(m) Senators may choose to have some or all personal staff in a district office. In Wisconsin, the total of all employees' salaries for each senator must be within the limits established by the Senate.
(n) During sessions, legislators are served by temporary sessional staff; during interim period, by Legislative Service Office.

Table 3.18
STAFF FOR LEGISLATIVE STANDING COMMITTEES

| State or other jurisdiction | Committee staff assistance | | | | Source of staff services* | | | | | | | |
| | Senate | | House | | Joint central agency(a) | | Chamber agency(b) | | Caucus or leadership | | Committee or committee chairman | |
	Prof.	Cler.	Prof.	Cler.	Prof.	Cler.	Prof.	Cler.	Prof.	Cler.	Prof.	Cler.
Alabama	(c)	★	(c)	★	B						B	B
Alaska	★	★	★	★	B			B	B	B	B	B
Arizona	★	★	★	★	(d)		B	B	B		B	
Arkansas	★	★	★	★	B	B		B				
California	★	★	★	★			B	B				
Colorado	★	...	★	...	B							
Connecticut	★(e)	★(e)	★(e)	★(e)	(e)	(e)						
Delaware	(c)	★(f)	(c)	★(f)	B	B		B	B			
Florida	★	★	★	★							B	B
Georgia	★	★(f)	★	★(f)	B		S			B	H	
Hawaii	(g)	★	(g)	★	B	B	B	B	B	B	B	B
Idaho	(c)	★	(c)	★	B							B
Illinois	★	★	★	★					B	B		
Indiana	★	★	★	...	B					S		
Iowa	★	★	★	★	B			B(h)	B			B(h)
Kansas	★	★	★	★	B	B		B		B		B
Kentucky	★	★	★	★	B	B						
Louisiana	★	★	★	★				B			B	B
Maine	★(e)	★(e)	★(e)	★(e)	(e)							(e)
Maryland	★	★	★	★	B							B
Massachusetts	★	★	★	★	B		B		B	B	B	
Michigan	★	★	★	★				H	B		B	B
Minnesota	★	★	★	★							B	
Mississippi	•	★	•	★	B	B						
Missouri	(c,f)	★	(c,f)	★					B	B	B	B
Montana	★	★	★	★	B	B						B
Nebraska	★	★					U	U			U	U
Nevada	(c)	★	(c)	★	B			B				
New Hampshire	•	★(f)	•	★(f)	B	B			H			
New Jersey	★	★	★	★	B							
New Mexico	•	★	•	★	B			B				
New York	★	★	★	★	B	B	B	B	B	B	B	B
North Carolina	•	★	•	★	B		B	B	B			
North Dakota	(c)	★	(c)	★	B			B				
Ohio	★	★	★	★	B				B	B		
Oklahoma	•	★	•	★			B	B				
Oregon	★	★	★	★							B	B
Pennsylvania	★	★	★	★			B	B				
Rhode Island	★	★	★	★							B	B
South Carolina	•	★	•	★	B	B	B	B		B	B	B
South Dakota	★	★	★	★	B					B		
Tennessee	★	★	★	★	B				B	B	S	B
Texas	★	★	★	★	B	B		B(f)			B	B
Utah	★	★	★	★	B	B				B		
Vermont	★	★	★	★	B	B						
Virginia	★	★	★	★	B			B				B(h)
Washington	★	★	★	★			B	B	B	B	B	
West Virginia	★	★	★	★	B	B	B	B			B	B
Wisconsin	★	★	★	★	B		B	B			B	B
Wyoming	★(f)	★	★(f)	★	B			B				
American Samoa	★(f)	...	★(f)	...	B							
Guam	★	★			U	U			U	U	U	U
Puerto Rico	★	★	★	★							B	B
Virgin Islands	★	★			U	U						U

*Multiple entries reflect a combination of organizational location of services.

Key:
★—All committees
•—Some committees
...—No committees
B—Both chambers
H—House
S—Senate
U—Unicameral
(a) Includes legislative council or service agency or central management agency.
(b) Includes chamber management agency, office of clerk or secretary and House or Senate research office.
(c) Money committees only.
(d) Joint Legislative Budget Committee provides staff assistance to the fiscal committees of both houses.
(e) Standing committees are joint House and Senate committees.
(f) Provided on a pool basis.
(g) All professional committee staff (except Finance committees) during session only. During interim, assistance provided by year-round majority and minority research offices.
(h) The Senate secretary and House clerk maintain supervision of committee clerks. Iowa: during the session each committee selects its own clerk.

Table 3.19
STANDING COMMITTEES: APPOINTMENT AND NUMBER

State or other jurisdiction	Committee members appointed by:		Committee chairpersons appointed by:		Number of standing committees during regular 1985 session(a)	
	Senate	House	Senate	House	Senate	House
Alabama	P(b)	S	P(b)	S	22	23
Alaska	CC(c)	CC(c)	CC(c)	CC(c)	9(d)	9(d)
Arizona	P	S	P	S	11(d)	16(d)
Arkansas	CC	S	CC	S	10(d)	10(d)
California	CR	S	CR	S	22(d)	30(d)
Colorado	MjL,MnL(e)	S,MnL(e)	MjL	S	11	12
Connecticut	PT	S	PT	S	(f)	(f)
Delaware	PT	S	PT	S	18(d)	14(d)
Florida	P	S	P	S	16(d)	23(d)
Georgia	P(b)	S	P(b)	S	24	28
Hawaii	P(g)	(h)	P(g)	(h)	16	19
Idaho	PT(i)	S	PT	S	10	14
Illinois	CC	S,MnL	P	S	18	25
Indiana	PT	S	PT	S	18	25
Iowa	P(b)	S	P(b)	S	15(d)	15(d)
Kansas	CC	S	CC	S	18(d)	21(d)
Kentucky	CC	CC	CC	CC	15	15
Louisiana	P	S	P	S	15	15
Maine	P	S	P	S	(f)	(f)
Maryland	P	S	P	S	6(d)	7(d)
Massachusetts	P	S	P	S	6(d)	7(d)
Michigan	MjL	S	MjL	S	15	30
Minnesota	(j)	S	(j)	S	16	18
Mississippi	P(b)	S	P(b)	S	28(d)	30(d)
Missouri	PT	S	PT	S	22(d)	54(d)
Montana	CC	S	CC	S	17	14
Nebraska(U)	CC		(k)		14	
Nevada	(l)	S(m)	MjL	S	9	13
New Hampshire	P	S	P	S	17(d)	23(d)
New Jersey	P	S	P	S	14(d)	19(d)
New Mexico	CC	S	CC	S	8	16
New York	PT(n)	S	PT(n)	S	31(d)	35(d)
North Carolina	P(b)	S	P(b)	S	29	58
North Dakota	CC	S	CC	S	20(d)	19(d)
Ohio	CC	S	CC	S	12	26
Oklahoma	PT(o)	S	PT	S	18(d)	30(d)
Oregon	P	S	P	S	11(d)	13(d)
Pennsylvania	PT	CC(p)	PT	S	21	24
Rhode Island	MjL	S	MjL	S	6(d)	7(d)
South Carolina	E(q)	S	E	E	15	11
South Dakota	(r)	S	(r)	S	11(d)	11(d)
Tennessee	S	S	S	S	12(d)	12(d)
Texas	P(b)	S(s)	P(b)	S	11	34
Utah	P	S	P	S	10(d)	10(d)
Vermont	P(b)	S	P(b)	S	12(d)	15(d)
Virginia	E	S	(t)	S	11	20
Washington	P(b,u)	S(u)	(u)	S(u)	12	16
West Virginia	P	S	P	S	15(d)	13(d)
Wisconsin	(v)	S	(v)	S	11(d)	26(d)
Wyoming	P(w)	S(w)	P(w)	S(w)	11(d)	12(d)
Dist. of Col.(U)	(x)		(x)		11	
American Samoa	P,E	S,E	P	S	16	11
Guam(U)	(y)		E		10	
Puerto Rico	P	S	P	S	19(d)	22(d)
Virgin Islands(U)	P		P		11	

STANDING COMMITTEES: APPOINTMENT AND NUMBER—Continued

Note: Standing committees are those which regularly consider legislation during the legislative session.

Key:
CC—Committee on Committees
CR—Committee on Rules
E—Election
MjL—Majority leader
MnL—Minority leader
P—President
PT—President pro tempore
S—Speaker
(U)—Unicameral legislature

(a) If legislature had no regular session in 1985, then number of standing committees is for 1984.

(b) Lieutenant governor is president of the Senate.

(c) Report of Committee on Committees is subject to approval by majority vote of chamber's membership.

(d) Also, joint standing committees. Alaska, 2; Arizona, 1; Arkansas, 4; California, 2; Delaware, 2; Florida, 1; Iowa, 1; Kansas, 5; Maryland, 8; Massachusetts, 21; Mississippi, 6; Missouri, 5; New Hampshire, 4; New Jersey, 3; New York, 11; North Dakota, 1; Oklahoma, 3; Oregon, 4; Rhode Island, 8; South Dakota, 2; Tennessee, 1; Utah, 10; Vermont, 4; West Virginia, 2; Wisconsin, 7; Wyoming, 1; Puerto Rico, 2.

(e) Minority leader appoints committee members from minority party.

(f) Substantive standing committees are joint committees. Connecticut, 20; Maine, 19.

(g) President appoints committee members and chairpersons; minority members on committees are nominated by minority party caucus.

(h) By resolution, with members of majority party designating the chairmen, vice-chairmen and majority party members of committees, and members of minority party designating minority party members.

(i) Committee members appointed by the Senate leadership under the direction of the president pro tempore, by and with the Senate's advice.

(j) Subcommittee on Committees of the Committee on Rules and Administration.

(k) Secret ballot by legislature as a whole.

(l) Committee composition and leadership usually determined by party caucus.

(m) For Committee on Ethics, minority leader appoints one member of minority party.

(n) President pro tempore is also majority leader.

(o) Minority floor leader appoints minority members of committees (subject to Senate approval).

(p) Committee on Committees recommends to House for approval the names of committee members.

(q) Seniority system is retained in process.

(r) Presiding officer announces committee membership after selection by president pro tempore, majority and minority leaders.

(s) A maximum of one-half of the membership on each standing committee, exclusive of the chair and vice chair, is determined by seniority; the remaining membership is appointed by the speaker.

(t) Senior member of the majority party on the committee is the chair.

(u) With majority caucus.

(v) Committee on Senate Organization.

(w) With the advice and consent of the Rules and Procedures Committee.

(x) Chairman of the Council.

(y) Chairman of each committee.

Table 3.20
STANDING COMMITTEES: PROCEDURE

State or other jurisdiction	Uniform rules of committee procedure			Public access to committee meetings				Recorded roll call on vote to report bill to floor	
				Open to public		Advance notice required (number of days)			
	Senate	House	Joint	Senate	House	Senate	House	Senate	House
Alabama	...	★		★	★	...	...	Al	Nv
Alaska	...	...		★	★	...	...	Sm	Sm
Arizona	...	★		★	★	5	(a)	Nv	Nv
Arkansas	★	★	★	★	★	2	2	Sm	Sm
California	★	★	★	★	★	4	4	Al	Al
Colorado	★	★		★	★	...	...	Al	Al
Connecticut			★	★(b)	★(b)	1	1	Al	Al
Delaware	★	★	...	★	★	(c)	(c)	Al	Al
Florida	★	★		★	★	7	2(d)	Al	Al
Georgia	...	...		★	★	...	...	Nv	Nv
Hawaii	★	★		★	★	2	2	Al	Al
Idaho	★	★		★	★	...	...	Us	Us
Illinois	★	★	...	★	★	6	6.5	Al	Al
Indiana	...	...		★	★	3	1	Al	Al
Iowa	★	★		★	★	...	...	Al	Al
Kansas	★	★		★	★	...	(c)	Sm	Sm
Kentucky	...	...		★	★	...	3	Al	Al
Louisiana	★	★		★	★	1(e)	1(e)	Sm	Al
Maine			★	★	★	(c)	(c)	Sm	Sm
Maryland	★	★		★	★	(c)	(c)	Al	Al
Massachusetts	...	...	...	★	★	...	...	Nv	Nv
Michigan	★	★		★	★	(f)	(f)	Al	Al
Minnesota	★	★	★	★	★	3	3	Sm	Sm
Mississippi	...	...		★	★	...	...	Sm	Sm
Missouri	★	★	★	★	★	1	1	Al	Al
Montana	...	...		★	★	(g)	(g)	Al	Al
Nebraska(U)	★			★		5-7		Al	
Nevada	★	★		★	★	(c)	5(h)	Al	Al
New Hampshire	...	★		★	★	3	3	Al	Al
New Jersey	★	★		★	★	5	5	Al	Al
New Mexico	...	...		★	★	...	...	Sm	Al
New York	★	★		★	★	7	7	Al	Al
North Carolina	...	...	...	★(b)	★(b)	(c)	(c)	Sm	Sm
North Dakota	...	...		★	★	(i)	(i)	Al	Al
Ohio	★	★		★	★	5	(c)	Al	Al
Oklahoma	★	★		★	★	(c)	(c)	Sm	Sm
Oregon	★	★		★	★	1(j)	1(k)	Al	Al
Pennsylvania	...	...		★	★	3	3	Al	Al
Rhode Island	★	★	★	★	★	...	...	Sm	Sm
South Carolina	★	★	★	★	★	1	1	Sm	Sm
South Dakota	★	★		★	★	2	2	Al	Al
Tennessee	★	★		★	★	(l)	(l)	Al	Sm
Texas	...	★		★	★	1	5	Sm	Al
Utah	★	★	★	★	★	1	1	Al	Al
Vermont	★	★	★	★	★	...	...	Sm	Sm
Virginia	★	★		★	★(m)	(c)	(c)	Al	Al
Washington	★	★		★	★	5	5	Sm	Sm
West Virginia	...	...		★	★	...	...	Sm	Sm
Wisconsin	★	★	★	★	★	7	7	Al	Al
Wyoming	...	...	...	★	★	...	...	Sm	Sm
American Samoa	...	...	...	★	★	(d)	1.5	Nv	Nv
Guam(U)	★			★(b)		7		Al	
Puerto Rico	★	★		★	★	...	...	Nv	Nv
Virgin Islands(U)	★			★		7(n)		Us	

STANDING COMMITTEES: PROCEDURE—Continued

(a) Rules: Thursday of previous week. Statute: 24 hours.

(b) Certain matters specified by statute can be discussed in executive session. Connecticut—upon a 2/3 vote of committee members present and voting and stating the reason for such executive session. North Carolina—appropriations committees are required to sit jointly in open session. Guam—hearings are open to the public, but meetings may be closed.

(c) No specified time. Kansas—"due notice" required by House rules. Maine—usually seven days notice given. Maryland—"from time to time," usually seven days. Nevada—"adequate notice." North Carolina—notice must be given in the House or Senate; two methods to waive notice in the Senate. Ohio—"due notice," usually seven days. Virginia—notice published in the daily calendar.

(d) During session—two days notice for first 45 days, two hours thereafter.

(e) One day during session, five days during interim.

(f) Committees meet on regular schedule during sessions. For rescheduled or special meetings 18 hours notice, unless legislature is adjourned or recessed for less than 18 hours.

(g) There is an informal agreement to give three days notice.

(h) Public hearings on bills or resolutions of "high public importance" must receive five calendar days notice. All other committee meetings must have 24 hours notice.

(i) Rules require posting of bills and resolutions to be considered at each meeting and provide deadlines for such posting depending upon the schedules for particular committees.

(j) Except in case of meeting to resolve conflicts or inconsistencies among two or more measures, in which case posting and notice to the public shall be given immediately upon call of the meeting, and notice of the meeting shall be announced on the floor if the Senate is in session.

(k) In case of actual emergency, a meeting may be held upon such notice as is appropriate to the circumstances.

(l) Committees meet on a fixed schedule during sessions. Five days notice required during interim.

(m) Committee meetings are required to be open for final vote on bill.

(n) Advance notice may be waived if the committee determines there is cause to conduct a meeting sooner. In that case, notice must be given at least 48 hours in advance. Items on the agenda may be considered by unanimous consent.

Table 3.21
LEGISLATIVE APPROPRIATIONS PROCESS: BUDGET DOCUMENTS AND BILLS

State or other jurisdiction	Legal source of deadline		Budget document submission — Submission date relative to convening					Budget bill introduction		
	Constitutional	Statutory	Prior to session	Within one week	Within two weeks	Within one month	Over one month	Same time as budget document	Another time	Not until committee review of budget document
Alabama........	...	★	...	2nd day	...	...	...	★	...	...
Alaska.........	...	★	...	★	...	...	...	★	...	...
Arizona........	...	★	...	★	...	...	...	...	...	(a)
Arkansas	..	...	...	...	(b)	...	...	...	...	★
California......	★	...	...	...	...	...	(c)	★	...	...
Colorado	...	★	...	...	★(d)	...	...	...	...	★
Connecticut	...	★	...	...	...	★(e)	...	★	...	...
Delaware	...	★	...	...	...	Feb. 1	...	★(f)	...	...
Florida	..	★	30 days	...	...	...	...	...	...	★(g)
Georgia........	★	...	...	★	...	...	...	★	...	...
Hawaii	...	★	20 days	...	...	...	...	...	★	...
Idaho	...	★	...	★	...	...	..	...	..	★
Illinois........	...	★	...	...	...	...	★	...	★	...
Indiana	...	★	7 days(h)	...	...	...	...	★	...	...
Iowa	...	★	...	...	...	★	...	...	...	★(g)
Kansas	...	★	...	...	...	★(e)	...	...	★(i)	...
Kentucky	...	...	...	...	...	...	(j)	★	...	...
Louisiana	...	★	...	1st day	...	...	...	...	(k)	...
Maine	...	★	...	...	★(l)	...	...	★	...	...
Maryland	★	...	...	★(l)	...	...	...	★(m)	...	...
Massachusetts ...	★	...	...	...	...	★(l)	...	★(a)	...	...
Michigan	...	★	...	...	★(n)	...	...	★	...	...
Minnesota	...	★	...	...	...	★	...	...	...	★
Mississippi	...	★	Dec. 15	...	...	...	...	★	...	★
Missouri	★	...	...	...	...	★	...	★	...	...
Montana........	...	★	...	1st day	...	...	...	...	★	...
Nebraska	...	★	...	...	★	...	...	...	...	★(f)
Nevada	...	★	...	...	★	...	...	...	...	★
New Hampshire .	...	★	...	...	...	...	★	...	...	★
New Jersey.....	...	★	...	...	...	★(l)	...	...	...	★
New Mexico....	...	★	...	(o)	...	...	...	★	...	...
New York	★	...	...	...	★(l)	...	...	★(p)	...	...
North Carolina ..	...	...	...	(b)	...	...	...	★	...	...
North Dakota ...	...	★	...	3rd day(q)	...	...	...	★	...	...
Ohio	...	★	...	...	...	★(l)	...	★	...	...
Oklahoma	...	★	...	★	...	...	...	★	...	...
Oregon	...	★	Dec. 1(l)	...	...	...	...	★	...	...
Pennsylvania	...	★	...	...	...	...	★(l,r)	...	...	★
Rhode Island	...	★	...	...	...	...	(s)	★	...	...
South Carolina ..	...	★	1st Tues. in Jan.	...	...	...	...	...	...	★
South Dakota ...	...	★	Dec. 1	...	...	...	...	...	...	★
Tennessee	...	★	...	...	★(l)	...	...	★	...	...
Texas..........	...	★	...	★	...	...	...	★	...	...
Utah	...	★	(t)	...	★(e)	...	...	...	...	★
Vermont	...	★	...	...	...	★	...	...	...	★
Virginia........	...	★	Dec. 20	★	...	...	...	★	...	...
Washington	...	★	Dec. 1	...	...	...	...	★	★	...
West Virginia ...	★	...	...	1st day(l)	...	...	...	★	...	...
Wisconsin	...	★	...	...	...	★(u)	...	★	...	...
Wyoming	...	★	Jan. 1	...	...	...	...	...	...	★
American Samoa	...	...	(b)	...	...	...	...	...	★	...
Guam	...	★	...	...	...	★	...	★	...	...
Puerto Rico	★	...	...	...	...	★	...	...	...	★
Virgin Islands ...	...	★	...	...	★(v)	...	...	★	...	...

LEGISLATIVE APPROPRIATIONS PROCESS—Continued

(a) General appropriations bill only.

(b) By custom only. No statutory or constitutional provisions.

(c) Session begins in December. Within the first 10 days of each calendar year.

(d) Copies of agency budgets to be presented to the legislature by November 1. Governor's budget usually is presented in January.

(e) Even year. Connecticut—first day; Kansas—second day; Utah—first day.

(f) Later for first session of a new governor. Executive budget bill is introduced and used as working tool for committee. Delaware: after hearings on executive bill, a new bill is then introduced. The committee bill is considered by the legislature.

(g) Executive submits bill, but it is not introduced; used as a working tool by committee.

(h) Budget document submitted prior to session does not necessarily reflect budget message which is given sometime during the first three weeks of session.

(i) Within one month for most bills; however, some are introduced later.

(j) No set time.

(k) Subject to same 15-day limit as other bills.

(l) Later for first session of a new governor. Maine—six weeks; Maryland—10 days; Massachusetts—two months; New Jersey—February 15; New York—February 1; Ohio—March 16; Oregon—February 1; Pennsyl-vania—first full week in March; Tennessee—March 1; West Virginia—one month.

(m) Appropriations bills other than the budget bill (supplementary) may be introduced at any time. They must provide their own tax source and may not be enacted until the budget bill is enacted.

(n) Long-range capital budget: 30 days.

(o) Statutes provide for submission by 25th legislative day; however, the executive budget is usually presented by the first day of the session. The legislative budget is usually presented on the first day or at the pre-legislative session conference of the standing finance committees.

(p) Governor has 30 days to amend or complete submission bills which enact the recommendations contained in this executive budget, computed from the designated submission date for the budget.

(q) For whole legislature. The Legislative Council only receives budget on December 1.

(r) Submitted by governor as soon as possible after General Assembly organizes, but not later than the first full week in February.

(s) Twenty-fourth legislative day.

(t) Must submit to fiscal analyst 30 days prior to session.

(u) Last Tuesday in January. A later submission date may be requested by the governor.

(v) Organic Act specifies at opening of each regular session; statute specifies on or before May 30.

Table 3.22
FISCAL NOTES: CONTENT AND DISTRIBUTION

State or other jurisdiction	Content — Intent or purpose of bill	Cost involved	Projected future cost	Proposed source of revenue	Fiscal impact on local government	Other	Distribution — Legislators — All	Available on request	Bill sponsor	Appropriations committee — Members	Appropriations committee — Chairman only	Fiscal staff	Executive budget staff
Alabama	...	★	...	★	★(a)		★(b)	...	...	...	...	...	...
Alaska	...	★	★	★(c)	...		★(d)	...	...	...	...	...	...
Arizona	...	★	★	★	★		★	...	...	...	...	★	★
Arkansas	(e)	(e)	(e)	...	(e)		(e)	...	...	...	...	...	...
California	★	★	★	★	★		★	...	...	...	...	★	★
Colorado	★	★	★	★	★		★	...	...	...	...	★	...
Connecticut	...	★	★	...	★		★	...	...	...	...	★	...
Delaware	...	★	★	...	...	★(f)	...	★	...	★	...	★	★
Florida	★	★	★	★	★	★(g)	★	...	...	...	...	★	★
Georgia	...	★	★	★	★		...	★	...	...	...	...	...
Hawaii	...	...	...	...	...		...	...	...	...	...	...	...
Idaho	★	★	★	★(h)	★		★	...	...	...	...	...	...
Illinois	...	★	★	★	★	(i)	...	★(j)	★(j)	...	...	...	...
Indiana	★	★	★	★	★		★	...	...	...	...	★	...
Iowa	...	★	★	★	★		★	...	...	...	...	...	...
Kansas	★	★	★	★	★		...	★	...	...	★(k)	★	★
Kentucky	★	★	★	★	...		...	★	★	★	...	★	...
Louisiana	...	★	★	...	★		...	★	★	...	...	★(l)	...
Maine	...	★	★	...	...		★	...	...	...	...	★	...
Maryland	★	★	★	★	★		...	★	★	★(k)	...	★	★
Massachusetts	...	★(m)	...	...	...		★	...	...	...	...	★	...
Michigan	★	★	★	★	★	★(n)	★(o)	★	...	★	...	★	...
Minnesota	★	★	★	★	...		★	★	★	...	...	...	...
Mississippi	★	★	★	...	★		...	★	...	...	★	...	...
Missouri	...	★	★	...	★		★	...	...	...	...	...	...
Montana	★(p)	★	★	★	★	★(g)	★	...	...	...	...	...	...
Nebraska	...	★	★	★	★		★	...	...	...	...	★	★
Nevada	★	★	★	★	★		★	...	...	...	...	...	★
New Hampshire	★	★	★	★	★		★	...	...	...	...	★	★
New Jersey	★	★	★	...	★	★	★(q)	...	...	...	...	★	★
New Mexico	★	★	★	...	(h)	★(r)	...	(s)	...	...	★(s)	★	...
New York	★	★(t)	...	...	★		...	★	★	★	...	★	...
North Carolina	★	★	★	...	★	★(u)	...	★	★	...	★	★	...
North Dakota	★	★	★(v)	★	...		...	★	★	...	★	★	...
Ohio	★	★	★	★	★		★(w)	★	★	★	...	★	...
Oklahoma	...	...	...	...	...		...	...	...	...	...	...	...
Oregon	...	★	★	★	★		★	...	...	...	...	...	...
Pennsylvania	...	★	★	★	★	★(i)	★	...	...	...	...	★	★
Rhode Island	...	★	★	...	★	★(x)	...	★	...	...	★	★	★
South Carolina	...	★	★	...	...		...	★	★	...	...	...	...
South Dakota	...	★	★	★	★		...	★	...	...	...	...	...
Tennessee	★	★	★	★	★	★(y)	★	...	...	...	...	★	★
Texas	...	★	★	★	★		...	★	★	★(k)	...	...	★
Utah	...	★	★	★	★		★	...	...	...	...	...	...
Vermont	★	★	★	★	...		...	★	...	...	★	...	...
Virginia	★	★	★	★(z)	...	★	...	★	★	★	...	...	...
Washington	★	★	★	★	★		...	★	...	...	...	★	★
West Virginia	★	★	★	...	★(aa)		★	...	...	...	...	...	...
Wisconsin	...	★	★	★	★		★	...	...	...	...	...	...
Wyoming	...	★	★	★	★		★	...	...	...	...	...	...
American Samoa	...	...	...	...	...		...	...	...	...	...	...	...
Guam	★	★	★	★	★		★	...	...	...	...	★	★
Puerto Rico	...	★	...	...	★		★	...	...	...	...	...	...
Virgin Islands	★	★	...	★	...		★	...	...	...	...	...	...

FISCAL NOTES: CONTENT AND DISTRIBUTION—Continued

Key:

★—Yes

. . .—No

(a) Senate only.

(b) Fiscal notes are included in bills for final passage calendar.

(c) Contained in the bill, not in the fiscal note.

(d) Fiscal notes are attached to the bill before it is reported to the Rules Committee. Governor's bills must have fiscal note before introduction.

(e) Required on retirement and local government bills and distributed to all legislators.

(f) Relevant data and prior fiscal year cost information.

(g) Mechanical defects in bill and effective date.

(h) Occasionally.

(i) Bill proposing changes in retirement system of state or local government must have an actuarial note.

(j) A summary of the fiscal note is attached to the summary of the relevant bill in the Legislative Synopsis and Digest. Fiscal notes are prepared for the sponsor of the bill and are attached to the bill on file in either the office of the clerk of the House or the secretary of the Senate.

(k) Or to committee to which referred.

(l) Prepared by Legislative Fiscal Office; copies sent to House and Senate staff offices respectively.

(m) Fiscal notes are prepared only if cost exceeds $100,000 or matter has not been acted upon by the Joint Committee on Ways and Means.

(n) Other revelant data.

(o) Analyses prepared by Senate Fiscal Agency, distributed to Senate members only; analyses prepared by House Fiscal Agency, distributed to House members only.

(p) Comment or opinion on the merits of the bills is prohibited.

(q) Sponsor may disapprove fiscal note; if disapproved, fiscal note is not printed or distributed.

(r) Impact of revenue bills reviewed by Legislative Council Service and executive agencies.

(s) Legislative Finance Committee staff prepared fiscal notes for Appropriations Committee chairman; other fiscal impact statements prepared by Legislative Council Service and executive agencies are available to anyone upon request.

(t) Rules of the Assembly require sponsors' memoranda to include estimate of cost to state and/or local government. Fiscal note required by law to be included on all pension bills.

(u) Fiscal note required in Senate. In House, staff prepares a summary.

(v) A two-year projection.

(w) If a bill comes up for floor consideration.

(x) Technical or mechanical defects may be noted.

(y) Effects of revenue bills.

(z) The Department of Taxation prepares revenue impact notes including the intent and revenue impact.

(aa) House of Delegates only.

Table 3.23
LEGISLATIVE REVIEW OF ADMINISTRATIVE REGULATIONS: STRUCTURES AND PROCEDURES

State	Type of reviewing committee	All rules reviewed	Time limits for submission of rules for review
Alabama	Joint	★	35 days before adoption
Alaska	Joint	★	45 days
Arizona	(a)	(b)	Immediately after adoption
Arkansas	Joint	★	10 days before agency hearing
California	--(a)--		
Colorado	Joint	(c)	20 days after approval by attorney general
Connecticut	Joint bipartisan	★	After approval by attorney general
Delaware	--(a)--		
Florida	Joint	★	21 days
Georgia	Standing cmtes.	★	30 days
Hawaii	(d)	(c)	None
Idaho	Standing cmtes. & germane jt. sub-cmtes.	★	Beginning of each session or upon adoption
Illinois	Joint bipartisan	★	45 days
Indiana	Joint bipartisan	(e)	
Iowa	Joint	★	35 days(f)
Kansas	Joint	★	By Dec. 15 of each year
Kentucky	Joint subcmte.	★	None(g)
Louisiana	Standing cmtes.	★	15 days before adoption(h)
Maine	Joint standing cmtes.	. . .	None
Maryland	Joint	★	60 days before adoption
Massachusetts	Joint standing cmtes.(i)	. . .	None(j)
Michigan	Joint	★	None
Minnesota	Joint bipartisan	★(k)	None
Mississippi	--(a)--		
Missouri	Joint	★	None
Montana	Joint	★	None
Nebraska	Standing cmtes.	★	None
Nevada	Joint	★	After adoption
New Hampshire	Joint	★	30 days
New Jersey	--(a)--		
New Mexico	--(a)--		
New York	Joint	★	21 days before effective date
North Carolina	--(a)--		
North Dakota	Joint interim	★	None
Ohio	Joint	(l)	60 days before adoption
Oklahoma	Standing cmtes.	★	10 days after adoption
Oregon	Joint	(m)	Within 10 days after filing with secretary of state
Pennsylvania	Standing cmtes.	. . .	None
Rhode Island	--(a)--		
South Carolina	Standing cmtes.	★	None(n)
South Dakota	Joint interim	★	10 days before regular rules become effective; 3 days before emergency rules become effective
Tennessee	Standing cmtes.(o)	★	45 days before effective date
Texas	Standing cmtes.	★	30 days before adoption
Utah	Joint bipartisan	★	30 days before effective date
Vermont	Joint	★	2 weeks before adoption
Virginia	Standing cmtes.	★	60 days before public hearing
Washington	Joint	★	Immediately upon filing with code revisor
West Virginia	Joint	★	None
Wisconsin	Joint(p)	★	None
Wyoming	Joint	★	Before the rules can be filed

STRUCTURES AND PROCEDURES—Continued

Note: Even though a state legislature may not have a formal mechanism in place to take action on administrative rules and regulations, rules could be submitted and standing committees could review on an informal basis. In some states, the courts' determinations that statutes providing for formal legislative review of administrative rules were unconstitutional led the legislatures to reenact or revise those procedures. Consult annotated state statutes and court actions for more details.

Key:
★—Yes
. . .—No

(a) No formal mechanism for legislative review of administrative rules.

(b) Provides only for legislative review of those rules promulgated by State Parks Board.

(c) Reviews rules when adopted, amended, or repealed.

(d) Review is by office of legislative auditor which submits reports to the legislature for appropriate action.

(e) Rules are not routinely submitted for review.

(f) Published in Iowa Administrative Code 35 days prior to adoption.

(g) Legislation passed in 1986 states that all regulations shall expire 90 days after the adjournment of the next General Assembly. Those regulations that an administrative body wishes to remain in effect must be enacted into the statutes.

(h) Thirty days before the regular session, agencies must submit an annual report to the legislature on all rules adopted over the previous year.

(i) Joint standing committees have the power but are not exercising it as a practical matter.

(j) Except in selected statutory provisions for particular rules.

(k) Commission reviews only those rules brought to its attention by specific complaints.

(l) Certain rules exempt from review.

(m) Committee may review or may direct the legislative counsel to review a rule. Review is not automatic.

(n) But rule cannot go into effect until 90 days after submission. During interim, emergency regulations can be issued with an immediate effective date.

(o) House and Senate Government Operations committees.

(p) All standing committees review proposed rules. If there is an objection, it is referred to the Joint Committee for Review of Administrative Rules. The joint committee reviews all existing rules.

Table 3.24
LEGISLATIVE REVIEW OF ADMINISTRATIVE REGULATIONS: POWERS

State	Reviewing committee's powers: Review of proposed rules	Review of existing rules	No objection constitutes approval of proposed rule	Committee may suspend rule	Legislative powers: Legislature must sustain committee action	Time limit for legislative action	Legislature can amend or modify rule
Alabama	★	★	★	★	★	End of regular session	...
Alaska	★	★	★	★	★	30 days after convening of regular session	...
Arizona				(a)			
Arkansas	★	★	...	...	...		
California				(a)			
Colorado	...	★	...		★	Next regular session	★
Connecticut	★	★	★	★	(b)	(b)	★(c)
Delaware				(a)			
Florida	★	★	★	...			...
Georgia	★	...	★	...	★	30 days after convening of regular session	★
Hawaii	(d)	...	...	...			...
Idaho	★	★	★	...	★	End of regular session	★
Illinois	★	★	★	★	★	150 days	★
Indiana	(e)	★	...	...			...
Iowa	★	★	★	★	★	45 session days	...
Kansas	★	★	...	...	★	End of regular session	...
Kentucky	★	★	★	...	(f)		...
Louisiana	★	★	★	★(g)	...		★
Maine	...	★	...	...			...
Maryland	★	★	★	...			...
Massachusetts	★(h)	★	★(h)	...	★	Practices vary	...
Michigan	★	...	...	(i)	★		...
Minnesota	(j)	★	...	★(a)	(k)	End of next regular session	...
Mississippi				(a)			
Missouri	...	★	...	★	...		
Montana	★	★	...	...	★	None	★
Nebraska	...	★	...	★	★	Next regular session	...
Nevada	★	...	★	★	★	30 session days	...
New Hampshire	★	★	★	(l)	...		...
New Jersey				(a)			
New Mexico				(a)			
New York	★	★	...	...	...		
North Carolina				(a,m)			
North Dakota	★	★	★	...	★		...
Ohio	★	...	★	★	★	60 days	...
Oklahoma	...	★	...	...	★	30 days	...
Oregon	★	★	★	...	...		...
Pennsylvania	(j)	...	...	...	...		
Rhode Island				(a)			
South Carolina	★	...	★	...	★	Next regular session	...
South Dakota	★	★	★	★	★	30 days after convening of regular session	★
Tennessee	★	★	★	★	...		...
Texas	★	★	★	★	...		...
Utah	★	★	...	...	...		...
Vermont	★	★	★	...	...		...
Virginia	★	...	★	...	...	End of regular session	...
Washington	★	★	★	...	...		...
West Virginia	★	★	...	...	★	End of session	★
Wisconsin	★	★	★	★	★	End of next regular session	...
Wyoming	★	★	...	...	★		

Note: Even though a state legislature may not have a formal mechanism in place to take action on administrative rules and regulations, rules could be submitted and standing committees could review on an informal basis. In some states, the courts' determinations that statutes providing for formal legislative review of administrative rules were unconstitutional led the legislatures to reenact or revise those procedures. Consult annotated state statutes and court actions for more details.

Key:
★—Yes
...—No

(a) No formal mechanism for legislative review of administrative rules.
(b) It is not mandatory for legislature to approve or disapprove committee action. However, disapproval of a rule implementing a federally subsidized program must be sustained by legislature before end of the regular session or committee's action is reversed.
(c) Committee may disapprove a part of a rule.
(d) Reviews rules when adopted, amended, or repealed.
(e) Committee may receive and review complaints regarding an agency rule or practice. Committee may also review an agency rule or practice on its own motion, and may recommend that a rule be modified, repealed, or adopted.
(f) Legislation passed in 1986 states that all regulations shall expire 90 days after the adjournment of the next General Assembly. Those regulations that an administrative body wishes to remain in effect must be enacted into the statutes.
(g) If committee determines that rule is unacceptable, it submits a report to the governor. The governor has five days to accept or reject the report.
(h) Provided in statute for certain rules but not others.
(i) Committee may suspend rules during interim only, if granted authorization to do so by legislature.
(j) Some rules may be submitted for "review and comment."
(k) Yes, if the commission action is to suspend a rule; otherwise its recommendations are self-executing.
(l) Committee may object to rule. Rule may be adopted over committee objection, but committee can shift burden of proof to agency.
(m) Committee abolished.

Table 3.25
SUMMARY OF SUNSET LEGISLATION

State or other jurisdiction	Scope	Preliminary evaluation conducted by	Other legislative review	Other oversight mechanisms in bill	Phase-out period	Life of each agency (in years)	Other provisions
Alabama	C	Select Jt. Cmte.	Dept. of Examiners of Public Accounts	Zero-base budgeting	180/d	4	1-hour time limit on floor debate on each bill.
Alaska	R	Standing cmtes.	...	Perf. audit	1/y	Varies	Specific programs authorized for termination by Legis. Budget & Audit Cmte.
Arizona	C	Off. of the Auditor General	Jt. Legis. Oversight Cmte.	Perf. audit	(a)	10	1984 legislation allows Jt. Legis. Oversight Cmte. to establish priorities for and reschedule sunset audits. Cmte. may also request special performance audits not required by sunset schedule.
Arkansas	(b)	...	...	...	...	...	...
California	(c)	...	...	...	...	...	...
Colorado	R	Dept. of Admin. reports to Legis. Council by July 1, preceding year of termination	Standing cmtes.	Perf. audit	1/y	10	There also is legislation requiring a study of 20 principal depts. of state government on a schedule concluding in 1994.
Connecticut	R(d)	Legis. Prog. Review & Investigations Cmte.	Govt. Admin. & Elections Cmte.	Perf. audit	1/y	5	...
Delaware	C	Agencies under review submit report to Del. Sunset Comm. based on criteria for review and set forth in statute. Comm. staff conducts separate review	...	Perf. audit	Dec. 31 of next succeeding calendar year	4	Yearly Sunset Review schedules must include at least 9 agencies. If the number automatically scheduled for review or added by the General Assembly is less than a full schedule, additional agencies shall be added in order of their appearance in the Del. Code to complete the review schedule.
Florida	R	Appropriate substantive cmte. shall begin review 15 months prior to repeal date	...	...	1/y	10	Provides for periodic review of limitations on the initial entry into a profession, occupation, business, industry, or other endeavor.

Key:
C—Comprehensive
R—Regulatory
S—Selective
D—Discretionary
d—day
m—month
y—year

SUNSET LEGISLATION—Continued

State or other jurisdiction	Scope	Preliminary evaluation conducted by	Other legislative review	Other oversight mechanisms in bill	Phase-out period	Life of each agency (in years)	Other provisions
Georgia	R	Standing cmtes.	Dept. of Audits	Perf. audit	1/y	1-6	A performance audit of each regulatory agency must be conducted at least once every 6 years.
Hawaii	R	Legis. Auditor	Consumer Protection Cmte. of each house	...	None	6	Proposed new regulatory measures must be referred to the Auditor for sunrise analysis.
Idaho				——No program——			
Illinois.........	(e)	...	Off. of Auditor General; standing cmtes. of each house	...	...	...	...
Indiana	C	Legis. Services Agency; Off. of Fiscal & Mgt. Analysis	Jt. Interim Sunset Evaluation Cmte.	Governor submits recommendations	None(f)		Each newly-established agency subject to termination with 10-year life span. Agencies established by exec. order, terminate when a Governor leaves office. Agencies established by concurrent resolution by General Assembly terminate after adjournment of the 2nd session.
Iowa	(c)	...	...	...	...	...	...
Kansas	R(d)	Standing cmtes. of each house	Legis. Post Audit, if directed by legislative cmte., or Legis. Post Audit Cmte.	Perf. audit	1/y	Subject to legislative discretion	Act terminates in July 1992 unless reenacted.
Kentucky				——No program——			
Louisiana	C	Standing cmtes. of the two houses which have usual jurisdiction over the affairs of the entity. Process begins 2 years prior to the termination date	Bill authorizing re-creation referred to cmte. performing initial review	Zero budget review	July 1 of year before end of legislative authority	9	Standing cmtes. may conduct a more extensive evaluation of selected statutory entities under their jurisdiction or of particular programs of such entities.
Maine	R	Off. of Fiscal & Prog. Review	...	Perf. eval.	1/y	10	Performance reviews also scheduled for executive departments (no terminations).
Maryland	R	Dept. of Fiscal Services	Standing cmtes.	...	None	6	Sunset cycle was completed in 1983 and will resume again in 1989.
Massachusetts				——No program——			

Key:
C—Comprehensive
R—Regulatory
S—Selective
D—Discretionary
d—day
m—month
y—year

SUNSET LEGISLATION—Continued

State or other jurisdiction	Scope	Preliminary evaluation conducted by	Other legislative review	Other oversight mechanisms in bill	Phase-out period	Life of each agency (in years)	Other provisions
Michigan	(c)	...	...	...	...	...	...
Minnesota	(c)	...	...	...	...	...	...
Mississippi	S	...	Jt. Cmte. on Performance Evaluation and Expenditure Review	...	...	...	Sunset Act terminated Dec. 31, 1984.
Missouri				——No program——			
Montana	D	Legis. Audit Cmte.	Standing cmtes.	...	1/y	...	Sunset audits can be performed on any agency.
Nebraska	(g)	...	...	...	...	...	...
Nevada	(h)	...	...	...	...	...	...
New Hampshire	D/C	Jt. Legis. Cmte. on Review of Agencies & Progs.	Standing cmtes.	...	9/m	6	...
New Jersey	(c)			——No program——			
New Mexico	R	Legis. Finance Cmte.	...	...	(a)	6	Legis. Finance Cmte. is responsible for introducing legislation to continue any agency reviewed.
New York				——No program——			
North Carolina	(i)	...	...	...	...	...	...
North Dakota				——No program——			
Ohio	(c)	...	...	...	...	...	...
Oklahoma	R	Jt. Cmte. on Sunset Review(j)	Standing cmtes.	...	1/y	6	Rules & regulations of terminated agencies continue in effect unless terminated by law; includes agencies established by exec. order.
Oregon	R	Interim cmte.	Standing cmtes.	...	None	8	...
Pennsylvania	S	Legis. Budget and Finance Cmte.	Standing cmtes.	Perf. eval.	6/m	10	...
Rhode Island	C	Oversight Comm.	Auditor General	Zero-base budgeting	1/y	(k)	Oversight Comm. established to conduct sunset reviews.
South Carolina	R	Legis. Audit Council	Reorganization Comm.; standing cmtes.	Perf. audit	1/y	6	...

Key:
C—Comprehensive
R—Regulatory
S—Selective
D—Discretionary
d—day
m—month
y—year

SUNSET LEGISLATION—Continued

State or other jurisdiction	Scope	Preliminary evaluation conducted by	Other legislative review	Other oversight mechanisms in bill	Phase-out period	Life of each agency (in years)	Other provisions
South Dakota	S	Special interim cmte.	Legis. Research Council	Perf. audit	180/d	10	The sunset review cycle pertains only to an agency's administrative rules. Only through legislation can an agency be terminated.
Tennessee	C	Special evaluation cmte. in each house	State Auditor	Perf. audit	1/y	8	Establishment of new agencies subject to review by Govt. Operations cmtes. of each house.
Texas	C	Sunset Advisory Comm.	...	Perf. eval.	1/y	12	Initial review conducted by agencies themselves.
Utah	R	Interim study cmte.	Off. of Legis. Research	Interim cmte.'s discretion	1/y	10	...
Vermont	R	Legis. Council staff	Standing cmtes.	...	1/y	13	...
Virginia	(l)	...	...	...	...	...	...
Washington	C	Legis. Budget Cmte.	Standing cmtes.	Prog. review	1/y	(k)	Select jt. cmte. prepares termination legislation.
West Virginia	S	Jt. Cmte. on Govt. Operations	Legis. Post Audit Div.	Perf. audit	1/y	6	Jt. Cmte. on Govt. Operations composed of 5 House members, 5 Senate members & 5 citizens appointed by Governor. Agencies may be reviewed more frequently.
Wisconsin	(c)	...	...	...	...		...
Wyoming	S	Legis. Service Office	11-mbr. cmte. appt'd. by Mgt. Council	...	1/y	Subject to legislative discretion	Every 2 years, the legislature selects a group of agencies to undergo sunset review.

Key:
C—Comprehensive
R—Regulatory
S—Selective
D—Discretionary
d—day
m—month
y—year

(a) Agency termination is scheduled on July 1 of the year prior to the scheduled termination of statutory authority for that agency.
(b) Arkansas' sunset law terminated on June 30, 1983.
(c) While they have not enacted sunset legislation in the same sense as the other states with detailed information in this table, the legislatures in California, Iowa, Michigan, Minnesota, New Jersey, Ohio, and Wisconsin have included sunset clauses in selected programs.
(d) Primarily.

(e) Illinois sunset law remains on the books but without any staff support since summer 1985.
(f) Through an executive order, the governor may provide a terminated agency with one year to wind up its affairs.
(g) Nebraska's Sunset Act terminated in 1985.
(h) Nevada law provided for a one-cycle pilot program under which three agencies were reviewed in 1980. No further expansion of the law has been enacted.
(i) North Carolina's sunset law terminated on June 30, 1983.
(j) Joint Committee on Sunset Review makes a recommendation by drafting legislation to either recreate or sunset an agency. Sunset bills are then assigned to standing committees of the two houses which have usual jurisdiction over the affairs of the agency.
(k) Subject to legislative discretion.
(l) By joint resolution, Senate and House of Delegates establish a schedule for review of "functional areas" of state government. Program evaluation is carried out by Joint Legislative Audit and Review Commission. Agencies are not scheduled for automatic termination. Commission reports are made to standing committees which conduct public hearings.

Table 3.26
LEGISLATIVE ACTIVITIES PERFORMED WITH THE USE OF COMPUTERS

State	Statutory retrieval	Bill drafting	Bill status report	Statutory revision	Case law retrieval	Redistricting	Other	Revenue forecasting	Revenue analysis	Budget comparison	Budget effects of legislation	Fiscal notes	Local fiscal notes	Economic impact note	Impact of salary and fringe changes	State aid formulas	Tracking federal dollars	Other	Computer printing	Legislative accounting	Mailing lists	Other
	Statutory, bill systems, legal applications							**Fiscal, budget, economic applications**											**Legislative management**			
Alabama	★★★	★★★★★	★★★★★	★★		★						★★							★★	★	★	
Alaska	★(a)	★★														★★★★	★				★★	
Arizona		★★																				
Arkansas	★(a)	★★	★★★★	★(a)	★(a)			★	★	★	★	★(a)		★(a)		★★★★	★				★★	(b)
California	★★	★★★★★	★★★★★	★★	★	★	(c)	★★	★	★	★	★★	★★			★★★★	★		★	★	★★★★	(f)
Colorado	★	★★(g)	★★★★	★★(g)		★★★★★	(e)	★★★★★	★★★★★	★★★★★	★★★★★	★★	★★	★	★★★★	★★★★	★★	(d)	★	★★	★★★★★	
Connecticut				★		★★★★	(h,i)										★					
Delaware	★★(g)	★★(g)	★★★★	★(g)	★	★★★★	(e,j)										★★					(l)
Florida	★★	★★	★★★★	★★		★★★★		★	★	★	★★	★★	★	★	★★★★	★★★★	★★(p)		★	★★	★★★★★	(m,n,o)
Georgia				★																	★	(q)
Hawaii																						
Idaho							(p)															
Illinois	★★★★★	★★★★★	★★★★★	★★★★★	★	★		★★★★★(r)	★★(r)	★★★★★(r)	★★★★★	★★(r)	★★(r)	★★(r)	★★(r)	★★(r)	★★		★	★★★	★★	(b,w)
Indiana	★★★★★	★★★★★	★★★★★	★★★★★	★	★★★★		★	★	★★★★★	★★★★★	★★	★	★	★	★	★		★	★★	★	
Iowa	★★★★★	★★★★★	★★★★★	★★★★★	★★	★★★★	(s)	★	★	★★★★★	★★★★★	★★	★★	★★	★★★★★	★★★★	★★		★★★★★	★★★★★	★★★★★	
Kansas	★★★★★	★★★★★	★★★★★	★★★★★	★	★★★★	(t,u,v)	★★	★	★★★★★	★★★★★	★★	★	★	★(a)	★(a)	★(a)		★★★★★	★★★★★	★★★★	(b,z,aa) (v,bb)
Kentucky	★★★★★	★★★★★	★★★★★	★★★★★	★★	★★★★		★★	★	★★★★★	★★★★★	★★	★★	★	★(a)	★★★★	★(a)		★★	★★★	★★	
Louisiana	★★★★★	★★★★★	★★★★★	★★★★★	★	★★★★		★	★	★★★★★	★★★★★	★★	★★	★	★(a)	★(a)	★(a)		★★★★★	★★★★★	★★★★	
Maine	★★★★★	★★★★★	★★★★★	★★★★★	★	★★★★															★★(a)	
Maryland	★★★★★	★★★★★	★★★★★	★★★★★	★	★★★★	(h,x,y)	★★	★★(a)	★★★★★	★★(a)			★		★(a)	★(a)	(z)	★★★★★	★★★★★	★★★★★(a)	
Massachusetts	★(a)	★(a)	★★★★★	★(a)	★(a)	★★(a)		★	★	★★★★★	★★(a)	★(a)										
Michigan		★(a)	★★★★★			★★(a)																
Minnesota	★★★	★★	★★★★★	★★★	★★	★★★	(e,u)	★★	★★	★★★★★	★★★★★	★★	★★	★★	★★	★★★★	★★		★★★★	★★★★	★★★	
Mississippi				★(g)		★★																
Missouri	(g)																				★	
Montana	★	★★★★	★★★★	★★★	★★	★★		★★	★	★★★★★	★★★★★	★★	★★	★★	★★★	★★★	★★		★★★★	★★★	★★★	
Nebraska												★(cc)	★(cc)									
Nevada	★	★	★			★						★★(cc)	★(cc)				★★	(ff)			★	
New Hampshire																			★(g)	★(g)		
New Jersey																					★	
New Mexico							(e,x, dd,ee)															
New York																						
North Carolina																						
North Dakota							(s)						★(cc)									
Ohio	★	★★★★	★★★★	★		★		★	★	★★★★★	★★★★★	★★	★★	★★	★★	★★	★		★	★	★	

LEGISLATIVE ACTIVITIES PERFORMED WITH THE USE OF COMPUTERS—Continued

State	Statutory retrieval	Bill drafting	Bill status report	Statutory revision	Case law retrieval	Redistricting	Other	Revenue forecasting	Revenue analysis	Budget comparison	Budget effects of legislation	Fiscal notes	Local fiscal notes	Economic impact note	Impact of salary and fringe changes	State aid formulas	Tracking federal dollars	Other	Computer printing	Legislative accounting	Mailing lists	Other
Oklahoma	★	★	★(a)	★(a)	★(a)	★		★(a)	(g)	★	★(a)		★		★(a)	★	★		★	★(a)	★	(n)
Oregon	★	★	★	★		★	(ee)		★	★	★	★	★			★			★	★	★	
Pennsylvania	★	★	★	★		★	(e,s,y, gg)	★	★	★	★	★	★			★			★	★	★	
Rhode Island	★	★	★	★		★	(e)	★	★	★	★	★	★			★	★		★	★	★	
South Carolina	★	★	★	★		★		★	★	★	★	★	★			★	★		★	★	★	
South Dakota	★	★	★	★		★		★	★	★	★	★	★			★			★	★	★	
Tennessee	★	★	★	★		★		★	★	★	★	★	★	★	★	★	★		★	★	★	
Texas	★	★	★	★		★		★	★	★	★	★	★	★	★	★	★		★	★	★	
Utah	★	★	★	★		★	(e,j,vy)		★	★	★	★		★	★	★			★	★	★	(w,aa)
Vermont	★	★	★	★					★	★	★	★							★		★	
Virginia	★	★	★	★	★	★				★	★	★	★	★		★	★		★	★	★	
Washington	★	★	★	★	★	★		★(hh)	★	★	★	★	★	★		★	★	(ii)	★	★	★	
West Virginia	★	★	★	★						★	★	★				★	★		★	★	★	
Wisconsin	★	★	★	★	★	★		★	★	★	★	★	★	★	★	★	★		★	★	★	
Wyoming	★	★	★	★				(g)	(g)	(g)	(g)	(g)	(g)	(g)	(g)	(g)	(g)		★	★	★	

Key:

★ —Existing application.
· —Not an existing application.
(a) Reported use in one chamber or agency.
(b) Payroll.
(c) State legislative redistricting only.
(d) Public school finance.
(e) Preparation/printing of journals, calendars, public laws and/or supplements/annotations.
(f) Budget.
(g) In development or currently being implemented.
(h) Engrossment of bills.
(i) Session laws.
(j) Committee activities. In Florida: committee bill reference, proposed committee bills. In Texas: committee bill status and hearing schedules.
(k) Preparation/publication of Administrative Rules, Regulations.
(l) Specific fiscal applications, including: hospital cost containment, public utility rate analysis, fiscal and management audit, AFDC, Medicaid, Medicare, FRAMD.
(m) Supply/inventory.
(n) Listing of registered lobbyists.
(o) Telephone call tracking.
(p) Performed by an outside contractor.
(q) Preparation of budget bill.
(r) Performed by auxiliary or executive agency.
(s) Roll call votes.
(t) Publications.
(u) Bill-statute conflict.
(v) Indexing of bills, journals.
(w) Correspondence.
(x) Bill tracking and/or registry.
(y) Word searching of bills and/or existing statutes.
(z) For general budget development and analyses, and for internal comparison between executive and legislative budgets.
(aa) Word processing.
(bb) Electronic mail.
(cc) Tracking only.
(dd) General bill analyses.
(ee) Retrieval/access to Administrative Codes/Rules and/or Attorney General's opinions.
(ff) Expenditure information for executive agencies and for legislative staff; accounting.
(gg) Photo composition.
(hh) Executive branch.
(ii) Engrossment and enrollment of budget bill, preparing budget amendment, statistical data analysis.

Table 3.27
LOBBYISTS: AS DEFINED IN STATE STATUTES*

State	"Lobbyist" includes:				"Lobbyist" does not include:						
	Anyone receiving compensation to influence legislative action	Anyone spending money to influence legislation	Anyone representing someone else's interests	Anyone attempting to influence legislation(a)	Public officials acting in an official capacity	Anyone who speaks only before committees or boards	Anyone with professional knowledge acting as a professional witness	Members of the media	Representatives of religious organizations(b)	Anyone performing professional bill drafting services(c)	Others
Alabama	★	...	...	...	(d)	★	★	...	...	...	...
Alaska(e)	★	★	...	...	★	★	...	★	...	★	...
Arizona	★	...	★	★	★	★	...	...	...	★	(f,g)
Arkansas	★	...	★	...	(d)	...	...	...	...	...	...
California	★	...	...	...	★(h)	...	...	★	★	...	...
Colorado	★	...(k)	...	...	★	★(i)	...	...	...	...	(f,j)
Connecticut	★(k)	★(k)	...	...	★	★	...	...	...	...	(l)
Delaware	★	★	★	...	★	★	★	★	★	★	...
Florida	...	...	...	★(m)	(d)	★	...	...	...	...	...
Georgia	★	...	...	★	★	★	...	...	...	★	...
Hawaii	★(k)	★(k)	★	...	★	★	★	★	★	...	...
Idaho	★	...	...	...	★	★	★	★	★	...	...
Illinois	★	...	★	...	(d)	★	★	★	★	★	(n)
Indiana	★(k)	★(k)	...	...	★	★	...	★	...	...	(o)
Iowa	★	★	★	...	★	...	★	★	...	...	(o)
Kansas	★	★(k)	★	...	★	...	...	...	...	...	(p)
Kentucky	★	★	...	★(q)	...	...	...	...	...	...	...
Louisiana	★	...	...	...	★	★	...	★	...	...	...
Maine	★(k)	★	★	...	★	★	...	★	...	...	(j)
Maryland	★(k)	★(k)	...	...	★	★	★	★	★	★	(r)
Massachusetts	★	...	...	...	...	...	...	...	...	...	...
Michigan	★(k)	★(k)	...	...	★(s)	...	★	★	...	...	...
Minnesota	★(k)	★(k)	...	...	★	...	★	★	...	★	(t)
Mississippi	★	...	...	...	...	★	...	★	★	...	...
Missouri	★	...	...	...	(d)	...	...	...	...	...	...
Montana	★	★(k)	...	...	★	...	...	...	...	...	...
Nebraska	...	...	★	...	★(u)	★	★	★	...	...	...
Nevada	...	...	★	★	★	★	★	★	...	...	(n,v)
New Hampshire	★	...	...	...	...	...	...	...	...	...	...
New Jersey	★(k)	...	...	...	★	...	...	★	★	...	(o,v)
New Mexico	★	...	...	...	★	★	★	...	...	...	(n)
New York	★	...	...	...	★(u)	...	★	★	...	★	(f,j)
North Carolina	★	...	...	...	★(d)	★	★	★	...	★	(j,v)
North Dakota	...	...	...	★	★(d)	★	...	★	...	...	(v)
Ohio	★	...	★	★	★	...	...	★	...	★	...
Oklahoma	★(k)	★(k)	★	...	★	★	★	...	...	...	(f,v)
Oregon	★(k)	★(k)	★	★(m)	(d,w)	★	★	...	★	...	...
Pennsylvania	★	★(k)	★	...	★	★	★	★	...	...	...
Rhode Island	★(k)	★(k)	★	...	★	...	...	...	...	...	...
South Carolina	★	...	★	★(q)	★	★	...	★	★	★	(v)
South Dakota	★	...	...	★(q,m)	...	★	★	...	★	...	(x)
Tennessee	...	★(k)	...	★(m)	★	★	...	★	...	...	(f,j)
Texas	★(k)	★(k)	...	...	★	...	...	★	...	...	(y)
Utah	★	★	...	...	★	★	...	★	★	★	(f,o)
Vermont	★	...	...	...	★	★	...	...	...	...	...
Virginia	...	...	★	...	★	★	...	...	...	...	...
Washington	...	★(k)	...	★	★	★	...	...	...	...	...
West Virginia	★	...	★	★	★	...	...	★	...	...	(o)
Wisconsin	★	★(k)	...	...	★	★	★	...	...	...	(j)
Wyoming	★	...	★	...	★	...	...	...	...	...	...

*Definitions used to determine who is required to register and, in most cases, report as lobbyist.

Note: Entries reflect a literal reading of statutes. Consult lobbyist regulation provisions in each state for more details.

Key:

★—Specifically included or excluded in statute wording.

...—Not specifically included or excluded in statute wording.

LOBBYISTS: AS DEFINED IN STATE STATUTES—Continued

(a) Does not link activity to compensation or expenditures.

(b) Persons representing a bona fide church or religious society for the purpose of protecting the public right to practice the doctrines of such church.

(c) Or advising clients as to the construction or effects of proposed legislation.

(d) Specifically excludes members of the state legislature. In Missouri, stipulates only elected officials.

(e) An individual who lobbies without compensation or who limits lobbying activities to appearances before the legislature, its committees or other public hearings may elect to register with and report to the secretary of state.

(f) Attorneys representing clients before any court or quasi-judicial body or proceedings.

(g) Anyone contacting an official for the sole purpose of acquiring information.

(h) Also does not apply to any state employee acting within the scope of employment, provided that an employee (other than a legislative official) who attempts to influence legislative action and who would otherwise be required to register as a lobbyist is not allowed to make gifts of more than $10/month to an elected state officer or legislative official.

(i) Unless person makes more than three such appearances in a calendar year.

(j) Communications by person in response to an inquiry or request for information. Lobbying as an activity in Colorado does not include communications made by a person in response to a statute, rule, regulation or order requiring such a communication.

(k) Compensation and/or expenditures or time spent lobbying must exceed a specific amount before individual is required to register as a lobbyist. Connecticut—compensation, reimbursement or expenditures (or combined total) of $500 or more/year. Hawaii—anyone who spends more than five hours/month or $275/six months for lobbying activities. Indiana—compensation or expenditures of $500 or more/year. Kansas—expenditures of $100 or more/year. Maine—anyone who spends more than eight hours/month on lobbying activities. Maryland—compensation of $500 or more/reporting period; expenditures of $2,000/reporting period. Michigan—"lobbyist agent" is an individual who receives at least $250/year in compensation; "lobbyist" is an individual who spends more than $1,000/year on activities (more than $250/year, if amount is spent on a single public official). Minnesota—anyone who spends more than five hours/month or more than $250/year. Montana—anyone who spends more than $1,000/year. New Jersey—anyone who is reimbursed over $100/three months. Oklahoma—compensation or expenditures over $250/quarter. Oregon—anyone who spends over 16 hours/quarter or over $50/quarter. Pennsylvania—anyone who spends over $300/month. Rhode Island—compensation or expenditures over $100/year. Tennessee—anyone who spends more than $200/report period. Texas—compensation or expenditures over $200/quarter. Washington—anyone who spends more than four days/three months and over $25. Wisconsin—anyone who spends over $250/year.

(l) Lobbying as an activity does not include communications by or on behalf of a public service company in connection with public utilities control authority's rate hearings.

(m) Any public official who lobbies. In Florida, includes state executive and judicial or quasi-judicial department employees. In South Dakota, executive employees register as "public employee lobbyists."

(n) Legislative employees.

(o) Officers, employees, or representatives of state political parties.

(p) Non-profit organizations that are interstate in their operations.

(q) Specifies legislation affecting private pecuniary interests.

(r) Appearances (as part of official duties) by an officer, director, member, or employee of an association engaged exclusively in lobbying for counties and municipalities.

(s) Although all elected and appointed officials of state or local government are excluded, the categorization itself does not refer to the employees of colleges and universities, townships and other local governments, the state executive departments, the judicial branch, or appointed members of state-local boards and commissions.

(t) Individuals engaged in selling goods or services to be paid for by public funds; stockholders of family farm corporations not spending over $250/year in communication with public officials.

(u) College officials and employees are not excluded from lobbyist definition. In Nebraska, the University of Nebraska is specified.

(v) Persons who express a personal opinion to their legislators.

(w) Governor, secretary of state, treasurer, attorney general (and attendant deputies for the latter three officers), superintendent of public instruction, and the commissioner of the Bureau of Labor and Industries.

(x) Public corporations.

(y) Persons whose only activity is to encourage or solicit members, employees, or stockholders of an entity by which individual is employed to communicate with legislative members to influence legislation; persons whose only activity is to compensate another to act on their behalf; persons whose only activity is to attend meetings or entertainment events attended by executive or legislative branch members.

Table 3.28
LOBBYISTS: REGISTRATION AND REPORTING

State	Lobbyist registers with	Activity reports(a) Frequency	Information required(b) Total expenditures	Expenditures by category	Sources of income	Monies or gifts to individual officials	Legislation supported/ opposed by lobbyist	Other	Penalties:
Alabama	Ethics Comm.	Monthly(c)	★	★	★	★	★	(d)	Fine of not more than $10,000 or imprisonment for not more than 10 years, or both.
Alaska	Public Offices Comm.	Monthly(e)	★	★	…	★	…	(d)	For failure to register or file report on time: $10/day until filed; for violation of provisions: fine of not more than $1,000 or imprisonment for not more than 1 year, or both.
Arizona	Secy. of State	Annually(f)	★	…	…	★	★	…	Prosecuted as a Class 1 misdemeanor.
Arkansas	Clerk of House; Secy. of Senate	+++	…	…	…	…	★	…	None specified.
California	Secy. of State	Quarterly	★	★	★	★	★	(d)	Prosecuted as misdemeanor, subject to civil fines.
Colorado	Secy. of State	Monthly(g)	★	…	…	★	★	(h)	Fine of not more than $5,000 or imprisonment in county jail for 1 year, or both; revocation of registration at discretion of secretary of state.
Connecticut	Ethics Comm.	Quarterly(i)	★★	…	…	★★	…	(j)	Fine of not more than $1,000 or imprisonment for 1 year, or both.
Delaware	Legislative Council	Quarterly	★	…	…	★★	…	…	For failure to register or for furnishing false information: prosecuted as a Class C misdemeanor; for failure to file report: deemed voluntary cancellation of registration.
Florida	Clerk of House; Secy. of Senate(k)	Semi-annually	★	…	★	…	★	…	For violation of provisions: reprimand, censure, prohibition from lobbying for or part of the legislative biennium during which violation occurred (l); for false swearing to material fact: prosecuted as 2nd degree misdemeanor.
Georgia	Secy. of State	+++	★	…	…	★	…	…	For violation of provisions or non-compliance: prosecuted as a misdemeanor.
Hawaii	Ethics Comm.	Semi-annually	★	★	★	★	★	…	For failure to file statement or for falsifying statement: prosecuted as a misdemeanor.
Idaho	Secy. of State	Annually(i)	★	…	…	★	★	…	For registration and reporting violations: prosecuted as a misdemeanor and liable to max. civil fine of $250 or max. 6 months imprisonment, or both; for late filing of report: $10/day at discretion of secretary of state; for violation of statutory duties of lobbyists: possible revocation of registration.
Illinois	Secy. of State	Jan., Apr., July(m)	★	…	…	★	…	…	Prosecuted as a Class 3 felony(n).
Indiana	Secy. of State	Semi-annually	★	★	…	★	★	(o)	For failure to file report: $10/day (to max. of $100) until filed; for violation of provisions or false reporting: prosecuted as a Class D felony.
Iowa	Clerk of House; Secy. of Senate	Monthly	★	…	…	★	…	…	For failure to file report: cancellation of registration.
Kansas	Secy. of State	Monthly(p)	★	★	★	★	…	…	Prosecuted as a Class B misdemeanor.
Kentucky	Attorney General	After session	★	★	★	★★	…	…	Fine of not more than $5,000 or imprisonment for not more than 5 years, or both.
Louisiana	Clerk of House; Secy. of Senate	+++	…	…	…	…	★	…	Prosecuted as a misdemeanor, punishable by fine of not more than $500 or imprisonment for not more than 6 months, or both.
Maine	Secy. of State	Monthly(c)	★	…	…	★★	★	…	For failure to register or report: fine of $50.
Maryland	Ethics Comm.	Semi-annually	…	…	…	…	…	(o)	Prosecuted as a misdemeanor.

Note: Entries reflect a literal reading of statutes. Consult lobbyist regulation provisions in each state for more details.

Key:
★—Not required in report.
… —Not required in report.
+ + +—Report not required.

142

LOBBYISTS: REGISTRATION AND REPORTING—Continued

State	Lobbyist registers with	Frequency	Total expenditures	Expenditures by category	Sources of income	Monies or gifts to individual officials	Legislation supported/opposed by lobbyist	Other	Penalties:
Massachusetts	Secy. of State	Semi-annually	★			★			For failure to register or report: fine of not less than $100 nor more than $5,000; additionally, for legislative agent, disqualification until end of 3rd regular session of legislature after conviction.
Michigan	Secy. of State	Annually(q)		★		★		(o)	For failure to register or file report: $10/day (to max. $300); for failure to register over 30 days: prosecuted as a misdemeanor, with fine of not more than $1,000.
Minnesota	Ethical Practices Bd.	Quarterly	★	★	★	★		(o)	For late registration or failure to report after first notice: $5/day (to max. $100); for failure to report after second notice: prosecuted as a misdemeanor.
Mississippi	Secy. of State	Annually	★	★	★	★			For first violation: fine of $1,000 or imprisonment for not more than 6 months, or both; for second offense: $5,000, imprisonment for not more than 3 years, or both.
Missouri	Clerk of House; Secy. of Senate	3 times during session	★	★		★	★		Prosecuted as a misdemeanor; may not register for 2 years.
Montana	Commr. of Political Practices	(r)			★	★	★		For violation of licensing provision: revocation. Prosecuted as a misdemeanor; subject to civil penalties of not less than $250 nor more than $7,500.
Nebraska	Clerk of Legislature	Monthly(c,s)	★	★	★	★	★	(o)	For violation of gifting provision: prosecuted as Class III misdemeanor.
Nevada	Dir., Legislative Counsel Bureau	After session(t)	★	★		★	★		For late reports: $5/day for first 30 days; $100 after period at discretion of Director. Prosecuted as a misdemeanor.
New Hampshire	Secy. of State	(u)		★	★	★	★	(o)	Prosecuted as a misdemeanor. For filing false statement: punished as perjury.
New Jersey	Attorney General	Quarterly(g)		★	★	★	★		Prosecuted as a misdemeanor.
New Mexico	Secy. of State	(v)		★	★	★	★		Prosecuted as a misdemeanor; fine of not more than $1,000.
New York	Temporary State Comm. on Lobbying	(w)	★	★	★	★	★		Prosecuted as a Class A misdemeanor.
North Carolina	Secy. of State	Annually				★			Prosecuted as a misdemeanor: fine of not less than $50 nor more than $1,000 or imprisonment for not more than 2 years, or both; upon conviction, may not lobby for 2 years.
North Dakota	Secy. of State	Annually	★			★			Prosecuted as a Class B misdemeanor.
Ohio	Jt. Cmte. on Agency Rule Review	Semi-annually		★		★	★		Prosecuted as a misdemeanor of the 4th degree.
Oklahoma	Jt. Legislative Ethics Cmte.	Semi-annually	★			★			For violation of provisions: prosecuted as a misdemeanor; for failure to register or report, liable for amount equal to 3 times the expenditure; for third violation: prohibited from lobbying for 5 years. Either house of legislature may prescribe penalty.
Oregon	Govt. Ethics Comm.	Quarterly		★		★	★		Prosecuted as a 3rd degree misdemeanor.
Pennsylvania	Clerk of House; Secy. of Senate	Semi-annually		★	★	★	★		For person, corporation, or association engaging lobbyist: fine of not less than $200 nor more than $5,000; for legislative counsel or agent: fine of not less than $100 nor more than $1,000 and disqualification for 3 years.
Rhode Island	Secy. of State	3 times during session	★		★			(x)	
South Carolina	Secy. of State	Annually		★		★			Prosecuted as a misdemeanor; upon conviction, disqualification for 2 years.

Activity reports(a) — Information required(b)

Key:
... —Not required in report.
+ + + —Report not required.

143

LOBBYISTS: REGISTRATION AND REPORTING—Continued

State	Lobbyist registers with	Frequency	Total expenditures	Expenditures by category	Sources of income	Monies or gifts to individual officials	Legislation supported/opposed by lobbyist	Other	Penalties:
South Dakota	Secy. of State	Annually	...	★	...	★	...	(d)	Disqualification from lobbying for 3 years.
Tennessee	State Librarian & Archivist	Annually	...	...	...	★★	...	...	For late filing: suspension of registration; for violation of registration or reporting provisions: prosecuted as a misdemeanor.
Texas	Secy. of State	Monthly(s)	...	★	...	...	★	(h)	For late filing: civil liability of $100; for failure to register or report: amount equal to 3 times the compensation or expenditure; for violation of provisions: prosecuted as a Class A misdemeanor.
Utah	Lieutenant Governor	+ + +	...	...	...	...	...	...	For violation of provisions: prosecuted as a Class C misdemeanor.
Vermont	Secy. of State	Annually(y)	★	...	...	...	...	...	Fine of not more than $500.
Virginia	Secy. of Commonwealth	After session	★	...	★	...	★	...	For failure to report: $50/day until filed; for violation of provisions: prosecuted as a misdemeanor.
Washington	Public Disclosure Comm.	Monthly	...	★	...	★	★	...	Determined by Comm. No individual penalty may exceed $250; for multiple violations: max. aggregate penalty of $5,000.
West Virginia	Clerk of Senate(z)	After session	★	...	...	★	★	...	None specified.
Wisconsin	Secy. of State	Semi-annually (aa)	★	...	★	★	★	...	Fine of not more than $5,000 depending on offense.
Wyoming	Dir., Legislative Service Office	+ + +	...	...	...	...	...	...	For failure to register: prosecuted as a misdemeanor, subject to $200 fine.

Key:
. . .—Not required in report.
+ + +—Report not required.

(a) When activity or financial reports are required, they are filed with the official or entity responsible for registering lobbyist.
(b) Reports must contain the stated information; however, additional information may be volunteered by the lobbyist or principal responsible for reporting.
(c) During legislative session.
(d) Statement of business association or partnership with any official; may include entities with which lobbyist has engaged in exchange.
(e) As long as individual continues to engage in lobbying activities.
(f) Supplemental reports filed monthly to show any single expenditure over $25 occurring during month.
(g) Also, annual cumulative disclosure statement.
(h) Media expenditures.
(i) Also, interim monthly reports of lobbying activities during legislative session.
(j) Terms of any contracts, agreements, or promises.
(k) As defined by statute, a central office designated jointly by the president of the Senate and the speaker of the House and under the immediate responsibility of the secretary of the Senate and the clerk of the House.
(l) If a legislative committee finds there has been a violation of the lobbying provisions, it reports its findings to the presiding officer along with a recommended penalty. The presiding officer brings committee report and recommendations to entire chamber for determination by a majority of members.
(m) April and July of the year during which legislature is in regular session; within 20 days after adjournment of special session; and January each year for the preceding year during which the legislature was not in session.
(n) Corporations violating provisions are guilty of a business offense and receive a maximum fine of $10,000. Any individual convicted of violation is prohibited from lobbying (for compensation) for three years.
(o) Update of information required at registration.
(p) Only required for months during which expenditures are made, or gifts, payments, or honoraria given.
(q) On Jan. 31, covering the calendar year ending Dec. 31, and on Aug. 31 covering immediately preceding Dec. 31 to July 31.
(r) Before Feb. 15, when legislature is in session; before the 16th day of the calendar month when principal spent $5,000 or more in the previous month; 60 days after adjournment.
(s) Also, during the interim. In Nebraska, once during interim. In Texas, quarterly during interim.
(t) Monthly during session if lobbyist is attempting to influence legislative action.
(u) If registered for regular session—file April and Aug. 15 of each odd year; if regular session days are held after Aug. 1 of odd year, must file 30 days after each calendar day in which legislative business is conducted. If registered for special session—15 days after conclusion.
(v) Upon filing registration statement for all pre-session expenditures and 60th day after regular or special session.
(w) Any lobbyist who receives, spends, or incurs over $2,000/year files by the 15th day following reporting period in which cumulative total equalled amount (reporting periods—Jan. 1-May 31; April 1-May 31; June 1-Aug. 31) and files an annual cumulative report.
(x) Monthly expenses incurred on behalf of each person in whose interest individual engaged in lobbying.
(y) Also after two months of legislative session.
(z) Copies of registration and report sent to clerk of House.
(aa) By principal.

CHAPTER FOUR

STATE JUDICIAL BRANCH

STATE OF THE JUDICIARY

By Marcia J. Lim

The current picture of the state court systems reveals a judiciary that is wrestling with familiar concerns—such as court system financing, caseload backlog, and maintenance of the quality of the judiciary—as well as emergent ones. The state court systems are employing both established and innovative techniques to reduce delay, and are continuing to discover new applications for technology.

The recent swing in the philosophical mood of the country has had an impact on the entire criminal justice system. Judges are being confronted with the public's increasing concern for the needs and interests of crime victims, as well as the demands for mandatory or longer sentences for offenders, particularly in cases of driving while intoxicated (DWI).

Moreover, the judiciary has been compelled to accommodate demands placed on the state courts as a result of recently enacted federal laws, demographic shifts, and the growing presence of women and minorities in the court systems. The following discussion focuses on the familiar concerns and new challenges that face the court community, and examines some of the judiciary's responses.

State Court System Financing

Court systems in over half of the states are funded primarily by the state treasury, or are committed to attaining this status.[1] The move toward state assumption of court system costs often is attributed to the need for a more reliable and stable funding base. While this movement has gained support in recent years, it has not been welcomed by certain groups. Local government officials, in particular, commonly resist state funding of court systems out of a fear of loss of political control over local judges and the loss of court-generated revenues.[2] Typically, state-funded court systems return local court-generated revenues to state treasuries. For many lower-level courts— particularly municipal and traffic courts—filing fees, surcharges, and fines represent a significant percentage of their total revenues. The potential loss of this additional income, as a result of state assumption of court system costs, would appear to strengthen opposition to this movement.

In fact, there is evidence that state funding of court systems will not necessarily yield more reliable and increased support for trial courts.[3] Some believe that jurisdictions would do well to develop a financing strategy that involves court budgetary control at both the state and local levels—the rationale being that it would allow for the establishment of a diversified funding base, which in turn would provide more adequate funding for varied court operations at all levels. For those deciding the best method of court system financing, however, there is no simple answer. The unique characteristics and needs of each jurisdiction and court system must be considered in determining whether state funding or an alternative funding system will be the most appropriate.

The Judges

The history of unpredictable and inadequate funding for the judiciary has contributed to the inability of state judicial salaries to keep pace with those of private attorneys. While this has long been an issue of concern to the judiciary, in recent years, the gap in compensation levels between these two groups has widened dramatically. Results of a 1985 study indicate that in the period from 1974 to 1984, salaries of veteran attorneys grew in real terms by 9 percent, while those of state Supreme Court justices declined by 15 percent.[4] Aside from the judges' claims that salary increases are deserved, there is concern for the future of the judiciary itself as more and more highly qualified attorneys dismiss judgeships as unworthy or unattractive career options, and experienced judges leave the bench, either by choice or out of economic necessity.

Marcia J. Lim is Staff Associate with the Research and Information Service of the National Center for State Courts, Williamsburg, Virginia. This essay is based on the "Report on Trends in the State Courts," prepared by the staff of the Research and Information Service in July 1985.

Recognizing this looming crisis, The American Bar Association's Judicial Administration Division Committee on Judicial Salaries recently investigated methods by which states can obtain (or have obtained) judicial salary increases. The Committee found that some states have judicial compensation committees or commissions for the purpose of submitting recommendations to the legislature.[5] In other states, bar committees have been formed to handle the matter of judicial salary increases. State bar associations often have been advocates of increased judicial compensation, frequently acting as legislative lobbyists. Although some states have been successful in obtaining significant increases in their judges' salaries,[6] the long history and inherent nature of inadequate judicial compensation will continue to demand the attention of the judiciary in coming years.

Along with the lack of financial rewards, judges often must manage excessive court caseloads. Moreover, the specialized nature of their job demands that they remain in peak form and abreast of the current law. Recognizing the unique stress and hazards to which judges are susceptible, three jurisdictions have established provisions for judicial sabbaticals. A recent national survey on judicial leave policies revealed that Alaska, Oregon, and Puerto Rico statutorily authorize sabbatical leave for the purposes of a respite or educational improvement. Nine other states have expressed an interest in this area.[7] While most states lack formal provisions for sabbatical leave, some have granted judges special permission on an ad hoc basis.

Concern for the future composition and quality of the judiciary may explain some states' recent activity in the area of judicial performance evaluation. Although this is not a new concept, past efforts at evaluating judges have been primarily for retention purposes (as in the cases of Alaska and the District of Columbia). Typically, evaluations have been undertaken by state bar associations in the form of member polling, or by the media through editorials and public endorsements. These activities often have been criticized for their lack of objectivity.

In recent years, however, judicial evaluation has been viewed as a means of providing judges with constructive feedback for the purpose of improving their job performance. Judges understandably have been wary of any form of judicial performance evaluation; past attempts in this area often furnished unreliable information to both the judges and the public. A major concern of the judiciary is the potential threat to judges' independence in deciding cases based upon their merit, as opposed to popular sentiment.

Judicial performance evaluation programs operating in Nebraska and the U.S. Ninth Circuit have developed credible methods of collecting information for the improvement of judicial performance.[8] The evaluative information used by these programs is obtained (typically by mail questionnaire) from attorneys, lay persons, the media, jurors, court personnel, and judges. Pilot programs testing judicial performance evaluation procedures for the purpose of performance improvement have been instituted in Connecticut, New Jersey, and more recently, in Vermont.[9] Louisiana and the Navajo Nation have developed extensive plans for future programs, and at least five other states have expressed an interest in the area. To date, operational and pilot programs have been well received; but it appears the key to continued program acceptance is preserving judges' independence and providing for their involvement in the performance evaluation process.

Technological Innovations

In recent years, practitioners in the fields of judicial administration and law have found varied applications for such technological innovations as word processors, computerized case and financial management systems, and the computerized legal research services of Westlaw® , Lexis® , and Dialog® . One of the latest innovations in this field is the electronic database which can be accessed by remote computer terminals. Montgomery County, Pennsylvania and Atlanta, Georgia are reported to use this electronic system to transmit case information and court records between courts and law offices.

In Montgomery County, Pennsylvania, the publicly-administered database is made available free of charge to its users. Operation of the system is financed through the fees of losing clients and defendants. Efforts are being made to enter all public records—including court dockets, case histories, real estate deeds, and tax liens—onto the system.[10] The system also lists the status of lawyers' cases, and has the capability of automatically scheduling cases, thus minimizing scheduling conflicts for lawyers and their parties.

Information America, Inc., a private, for-profit corporation, offers this database to lawyers in Atlanta for a monthly fee of $100.[11] Court calendars, notices, filings, lawsuits, and judgments are available to clients. In addition to court files and documents, clients of this service also have access to records maintained by the Georgia secretary of state's office. Thus far, the electronic database appears to be an expeditious method of providing the legal community with necessary and comprehensive information, and will surely emerge as an important technological tool in future years.

Videotape technology has far-reaching applications for the judicial system, and has been used extensively for recording depositions, demonstrative evidence, juror orientation, and the execution of wills. It also has been used, although not as commonly, to advise defendants of their rights in court before arraignment and to record evidence of intoxication in drunk driving arrests. In recent years, use of this technology, along with closed circuit television (CCTV), has become more widespread for preliminary hearings and arraignments. Electronic arraignment procedures are favored by many court and justice system officials for saving time and eliminating security problems associated with transporting defendants from jail to court. Selected jurisdictions in eight states are reported to have used or experimented with videophones or CCTV in arraignment hearings.[12]

Recently, these same technologies have been used to record and transmit the testimony of child witnesses in order to eliminate the trauma of appearing in court. At least 14 states have enacted legislation permitting the admission of videotaped testimony of children, and four states (Kentucky, Louisiana, Oklahoma, and Texas) statutorily authorize the use of CCTV to transmit a child's testimony from an adjacent room to the courthouse.[13] The increasing concern for child witnesses, along with the need to conserve resources and staff time, may give rise to further activity in this area by the state courts.

Court Delay: A Continuing Dilemma

Persistent caseload backlog and delay in the courts have forced the judiciary to explore various methods to combat these problems. One tactic has been to resolve disputes through alternative methods to formal litigation. Common techniques include mediation, arbitration, mini-trials, summary jury trials, and the use of retired judges and referees. In addition to these alternative measures, the court community has sought ways to facilitate the trial process itself. One procedure employed by the courts to manage the high volume of litigation is the multi-track calendar system. Although use of this case management technique has been common among appellate courts, it has been adopted by numerous trial courts in recent years. As a result of a surge of cases involving discovery and extended trials, the District of Columbia Superior Court instituted a two-track caseload management system for civil cases; the system provides for routine master calendaring of cases requiring minimal or no discovery, and placement of more complex cases on an individual calendar.[14] This differentiation of cases was viewed as a means of preventing complex cases from disrupting the court's ability to schedule motion hearings, pretrials, and trials. Routine cases assigned to the master calendar would adhere to rule-prescribed time standards for discovery completion. On the other hand, judges assigned to individual calendar cases would have the discretion to determine limits on discovery and motion, as well as pretrial and trial dates. The placement of cases on separate calendars, according to their level of complexity, was seen as a way of ensuring that each case was adequately addressed in a timely fashion, and that judicial resources were used efficiently.

Four counties in Maine have instituted an experimental caseflow management program that provides for expedited processing of routine cases.[15] More complex actions are conducted according to existing rules of civil procedure. In addition, a fast-tracking system employing part-time judges has been adopted in Phoenix, Arizona,[16] and the New Jersey Supreme Court Committee on Civil Case Management and Procedures recently recommended trial court provisions for the differentiation of civil cases into categories of expedited, standard, and complex.[17] Trial court managers who have used or experimented with this procedure have observed the value of tracking systems in reducing delay in case scheduling and disposition.

Growing concern with delay in litigation proceedings also has prompted the imposition of monetary sanctions to discourage improper delaying tactics on the part of attorneys and litigants. Delay tactics in discovery, for example, may take the form of evasive, inadequate, or late responses to discovery requests, and use of excessively lengthy interrogatories and depositions. Most state courts have rules that provide for monetary sanctions for delaying tactics in discovery, which are modeled after Rule 37 of the Federal Rules of Civil Procedure. In addition, 40 states have adopted Rule 56(g) of the Federal Rules (or a similar one), which provides that if affidavits are presented in bad faith or with the intent to delay proceedings, the court is authorized to order the litigant employing them to pay the opposing party incurred expenses associated with the filing of affidavits (including reasonable attorney's fees).[18]

Furthermore, a 1983 amendment to Rule 11 of the Federal Rules of Civil Procedure provides for the imposition of monetary sanctions with regard to certifications made by attorneys by signing a pleading, motion, or other paper. To date, 10 states have adopted the amended Rule 11 or a comparable one. Growing recognition of delay tactics in discovery and other parts of the litigation process may encourage other states to adopt rules providing for monetary sanctions in order to arrest these abuses.

Court-annexed arbitration is used by a number of state trial courts. Recently, however, it has found application at the appellate court level. In October 1984, the South Carolina Supreme Court entered an order establishing the first voluntary binding arbitration program involving an appellate court. According to the terms of the program, all civil cases under appeal that do not involve a government agency are eligible for the arbitration procedure. Litigants' appeals are arbitrated by a three-member panel comprised of retired judges or lawyers. Moreover, parties in a case are authorized to participate in the panel selection process.

The program was instituted at the initiative of state Supreme Court Justice C. Bruce Littlejohn in an attempt to manage the state's overwhelming backlog of appeals awaiting review. Chief Justice Littlejohn observed that litigants often had waited an average of two years before their appeals could be heard. He estimated that under the new program an appeal could be disposed of in less than two months, and that the total volume of cases presented before the Supreme Court could be reduced by one-third.[19]

In New Jersey, similar concerns about appellate court caseload delay prompted that state's Administrative Office of the Courts to propose the use of retired appellate judges to arbitrate certain civil appeals. The proposal, which is to be studied by the state bar association, specifies that arbitration of appeals would be voluntary. Furthermore, once appeals are disposed of, additional review would not be permitted.[20]

While arbitration may not be an appropriate technique for resolving all disputes, it does offer an expeditious alternative to formal litigation. Based on the experiences of South Carolina's program thus far, arbitration appears to have potential for reducing caseload delay at the appellate level.

Relieving Prison Overcrowding

Controlling prison population levels and maintaining safe conditions for both inmates and correctional staff generally are not viewed as the responsibility of the judiciary. Yet judges' decisions in sentencing have an obvious impact on these variables. Efforts by the judiciary to alleviate prison overcrowding typically have been in the form of sentencing alternatives to incarceration. Community service sentencing is one alternative that has been favored by judges in recent years. In New Jersey, this sentencing option has been available to judges since 1979. The state's criminal code authorizes courts to order offenders to perform community service work, either as an alternative to incarceration or in addition to other penalties. Assigned tasks may range from street cleaning and painting to more specialized jobs, such as computer programming. The program is administered by the county probation departments, and more than tripled in size over a two-year period—the number of participants jumped from 5,000 in 1982 to over 15,000 in 1984.[21] Similar community service sentencing programs have been established in other jurisdictions including Georgia, Hawaii, Massachusetts, New York, Oklahoma, Utah, Virginia, and the District of Columbia.

Aside from relieving prison overcrowding and the related financial strain, this alternative provides for offender restitution and the performance of necessary public service tasks. In some instances, offenders may continue in community work after their term expires, in the capacity of a volunteer or permanent employee.

Prevailing Public Sentiment

In recent years, there has been growing national concern for the needs and interests of crime victims. Many Americans have recognized the indignities victims may experience in dealing with the criminal justice system, particularly during the processing of a case. The creation of the President's Task Force on Crime Victims in April 1982 served as formal recognition of the neglect of victims by the criminal justice system, and prompted over 100 judges from the 50 states, the District of Columbia, and Puerto Rico to convene the following year to examine the issue. While the National Organization for Victim Assistance has noted that there are thousands of programs and services designed to assist victims—ranging in nature from rape-crisis and child abuse programs to special procedures for notifying victims of court appearances or postponements—the majority of these services are provided by organizations other than the courts.[22] Some courts, however, have established procedures or programs to assist victims. Comprehensive court-sponsored programs exist in Florida and Minnesota.

Services provided by the Victim/Witness Liaison Office of the 17th Judicial Circuit Court in Broward County, Florida, include telephone standby assistance, notification of case disposition, assistance with compensation claims, referrals to community social service agencies, assistance in securing employment leave, and provision of escort services to court for sexual assault victims.

While many courts do not sponsor programs of their own, some establish cooperative working relations with agencies that serve victims.[23] With the recent enactment of the federal Victims of Crime Act of 1984 (P.L. 98-473, Title II, Chapter 14), grant funds are now available to states that have victim assistance and compensation programs already in place.

Americans' recent and growing concern for the crime victim has been accompanied by an increasingly punitive attitude toward the criminal defendant. This has been exemplified by the national movement to address the problem of drunk driving through legislation and stiffer penalties for the offender.

Recognizing the need and demand for drunk driving control measures, some states, including Minnesota, Ohio, Tennessee, and Washington, have enacted legislation requiring mandatory incarceration for drunk driving violations. Among the obvious ramifications of this move are increased caseloads in the courts and additional strains on jail facilities. One study revealed that the introduction of mandatory jail terms for drunk driving in Seattle required additional judges to hear these cases, and significantly increased the number of jury trials held, as defendants frequently contested court decisions. The new provision resulted in a 97 percent incarceration rate for convicted drunk driving offenders in Seattle, as opposed to only 9 percent before mandatory confinement was introduced.[24] Although there is evidence that mandatory confinement can be instituted without necessarily incurring serious consequences for courts and jails,[25] the potential impact of this provision on the entire criminal justice system requires careful consideration.

Federal Action Affecting State Courts

Recently-enacted federal laws and case decisions in at least three areas carry significant implications for state court personnel policies and procedures.

At issue in the case of *American Federation of State, County and Municipal Employees, et al. v. State of Washington* (578 F. Supp. 846 [1983]) was the claim that compensation levels for state jobs held predominantly by females were significantly lower than those for jobs held predominantly by males. This case, involving the matter of pay equity—more recently referred to as "comparable worth"—received national attention largely because it was one of the first to address gender-based discrimination in pay. The U.S. District Court for the Western District of Washington found for the more than

15,000 female plaintiffs, noting that the state was in violation of Title VII of the Civil Rights Act of 1964. A plan to begin redressing the pay inequity problem in 1984 was thwarted by state budgetary problems, and in September 1985, the case decision was reversed. However, a settlement in favor of the female state employees was reached in December 1985. The case has given rise to similar activity in other states.

Although the issue of comparable worth has greater application to the executive branch, state judicial branch employees also could be affected. To date, Alaska, Hawaii, Minnesota, New York, and West Virginia have studied this issue as it relates to their judicial branch employees.[26] With the growing presence of women in the work force, more state court systems may be forced to examine their compensation and job evaluation policies.

Another federal case also holds important implications for the state court community. In *Garcia v. San Antonio Metropolitan Transit Authority* (53 U.S.L.W. 4135), the U.S. Supreme Court overturned the findings of a 1976 case, *National League of Cities v. Usery* (426 U.S. 833), thus providing some formerly-exempted state and local government employees coverage under the Fair Labor Standards Act (FLSA). The act requires that hourly overtime compensation must not be less than one and one-half times the worker's normal hourly pay rate. Recent amendments to the act, signed by President Ronald Reagan on November 13, 1985, now permit state and local governments to provide time-and-a-half compensatory time off in lieu of overtime payments. Coverage for state and local employees was scheduled to take effect on April 15, 1986.

Application of these provisions, as broadly defined under the terms of the FLSA, appears to extend to court employees, with some exceptions (such as volunteers, trainees, independent contractors, elected officials and their appointees serving as personal staff or policy advisors, and certain administrative, executive, and professional employees). As a result of this ruling, court administrators will be required to amend court personnel policies to allow for these new overtime provisions.

Passage of the federal Child Support Enforcement Amendments of 1984 (P.L. 98-378) calls for more rigorous enforcement and monitoring of child support collection procedures in the states. The amendments include the institution of expedited procedures for obtaining and enforcing support orders, and optionally, for establishing paternity.[27] The federal law grants the states the option of conducting expedited proceedings under the judicial system or through administrative channels. In issuing guidelines for the implementation of these amendments, however, the U.S. Secretary of Health and Human Services (HHS) specified that while states have the discretion to determine whether the expedited procedures will be handled through administrative or judicial processes, the presiding officer is not to be a judge of the court.[28] This stipulation already has generated concern among some court officials. They assert that in order to comply with the HHS regulations, a new set of employees will need to be hired if the court system is to conduct expedited judicial proceedings. Unless exemptions are granted to allow judges to be used, additional personnel will be required; otherwise, the entire process will need to be turned over to an administrative agency.

Minorities and the Judicial System

Demographic changes in the country, resulting from an influx of immigrants—primarily from Latin America and Asia—may present new challenges for the judicial system, particularly in ensuring accessibility to the courts. The recent dramatic increase in the Asian-American population,[29] for example, may affect the need for court interpreter services. States with large urban areas are the more likely residences of immigrant groups, and presumably the sites where extensive interpreter programs have been established. The Los Angeles County Court system maintains a roster of over 400 court interpreters proficient in Spanish and 80 other languages.[30] The Judicial Language Center of Massachusetts' Superior Court Department maintains a staff of 125 court interpreters who are knowledgeable in 20 languages, including Spanish, Vietnamese, Taiwanese, and various Chinese dialects.[31] Less urbanized states—such as Iowa, Louisiana, and Oregon—however, also have become residences for a growing number of Southeast Asian immigrants. The recent influx of this immigrant group to Iowa, combined with the state's considerable Hispanic population, has placed greater demands for court interpreters on the court system.

As jurisdictions in California, Iowa, Massachusetts, and various other states[32] have established provisions for language interpreters, there is concern for the uniformity in testing and certification of interpreters. Aside from the federal government, California is the only state known to have a certification program.

Although a formal statewide program has not been instituted, Arizona's Superior Court does provide testing and certification for interpreters hired by the court on a permanent or contractual basis. Noting the often inconsistent and substandard interpreter services offered to linguistic minorities in the state, the New Jersey Supreme Court Task Force on Interpreter and Translation Services issued a set of recommendations in the fall of 1985 to remedy these deficiencies. The recommendations included the adoption of minimum qualifications for court interpreters, promotion of training programs, creation of a statewide court interpreter service to which all state and municipal trial courts may have access, and establishment of compensation policies and a code of ethics.[33] Similarly, in Texas, the State Bar Committee on Court Interpreters has drafted a legislative proposal recommending the establishment of testing and certification procedures for court interpreters.[34] With the arrival of increasing numbers of immigrants, further development of qualified court interpreters and testing and certification programs by state court systems appears imminent.

In Arizona, New Jersey, New York, and Rhode Island, an increasing awareness of pervasive discrimination against female judges, attorneys, court personnel, litigants, and offenders has precipitated the formation of task forces and committees to study gender bias in the court system.

The New Jersey Supreme Court Task Force on Women, created in 1982, was charged with the tasks of examining the extent to which gender bias exists in the state's courts, designing educational programs to eliminate any bias, and developing recommendations for remedial action. The task force's first year report, issued in June 1984, included findings and recommendations based on data compiled from attorneys' responses to a survey questionnaire and other communications on their perceptions of the treatment of women within the state judiciary. The task force identified areas that are susceptible to gender bias, including damage awards, marital law (the distribution of assets and property, and child support enforcement), counsel fee awards, sentencing, and employment opportunity.[35]

In 1984, New York and Rhode Island, and in 1985, Arizona established similar study committees to examine the prevalence of gender bias in the judiciary.

Superior Court Judge Marilyn Loftus, who chairs the New Jersey Task Force and the National Association of Women Judges' National Task Force on Gender Bias, has noted that 14 percent of the state's attorneys are female, and that in recent years, women have constitued half of the graduating class at one of the state's major law schools. Moreover, one-third of all graduating law students nationwide are women.[36] This evidence of the potential for growth in the number of women in the judicial system—not only as litigants and jurors, but also as attorneys, judges, and court officials—points to a need for greater efforts to eradicate any presence of gender bias in the court system.

Conclusion

Heightened awareness of limited court resources, together with new federal rulings, changes in demography and the composition of the work force, and the public's changing attitudes toward crime victims and offenders have compelled the state court community to develop innovative ways of dealing with emerging issues. These combined forces will require even greater creativity and resourcefulness on the part of the judiciary—not only in addressing the traditional concerns and new challenges that face the state courts, but also in reconciling the concerns of the public with those of the court community.

Notes

1. Alabama, Alaska, Colorado, Connecticut, Delaware, Hawaii, Iowa, Kansas, Kentucky, Maine, Maryland, Massachusetts, Michigan, Missouri, Nebraska, New Hampshire, New Mexico, New York, North Carolina, North Dakota, Oklahoma, Oregon, Rhode Island, South Dakota, Vermont,

Virginia, West Virginia, and Wyoming.

2. Sue Dosal, "Strategic Considerations in State Assumption of Trial Court Operating Costs," *State Funding of the Trial Courts* (Calif. Legislature, Assembly Committee on the Judiciary, Hearing as of November 18, 1981): 86-121.

3. Thomas A. Henderson, *The Significance of Judicial Structure: The Effect of Unification on Trial Court Operations* (March 1984): 175.

4. Thomas B. Marvell, "Judicial Salaries: Doing More Work for Less Pay," *The Judges Journal* 24 (Winter 1985): 34-37; 46-47.

5. The following 17 states are reported to have such commissions: Alabama, Arizona, Colorado, Connecticut, Florida, Georgia, Illinois, Iowa, Kentucky, Louisiana, Maryland, Michigan, Montana, Rhode Island, South Dakota, Utah, and Washington.

6. Upon the recommendations of the Maine State Compensation Commission in 1984, legislation was enacted providing for compensation of Maine's state judges at a rate comparable to that of federal court judges. See "Maine State Compensation Commission: Final Report," (March 27, 1984): 1-16.

7. Arizona, Colorado, Florida, Louisiana, Massachusetts, Minnesota, New Jersey, North Dakota, and Utah. See "Examination of Judicial Leave Policy in the Fifty States" (National Center for State Courts' Research and Information Service staff memorandum, February 23, 1984). See also, *Alaska Rules of Court Procedure and Administration* (Administrative Rule 28(e), 1983 Supplement); Oregon Revised Statutes §1.290; and Laws of Puerto Rico Annotated §§251-252.

8. Daina Farthing-Capowich, "Developing Court-Sponsored Programs," *State Court Journal* 8 (Summer 1984): 27-37.

9. Daina Farthing-Capowich, "Recent Activities and Developments in Judicial Performance Evaluation," prepared for the Conference of Chief Justices Committee on Judicial Performance Evaluation, July 22, 1985.

10. Cheryl Frank, "Fee or Free? Split Views on Public Records," *ABA Journal* 71 (February 1985): 33.

11. Ibid.

12. Arizona, California, Florida, Idaho, Louisiana, Nevada, Pennsylvania, and Virginia.

13. The 14 states permitting the use of videotaped testimony for child witnesses include: Alaska, Arizona, Arkansas, California, Colorado, Florida, Kentucky, Maine, New Mexico, New York, Oklahoma, South Dakota, Texas, and Wisconsin. See National Institute of Justice, "Prosecution of Child Sexual Abuse: Innovations in Practice," *Research in Brief* (November 1985): 1-7.

14. Michael D. Planet, et al., "Screening and Tracking Civil Cases; Managing Diverse Caseloads in the District of Columbia," *Justice System Journal* 8 (1983): 338-353.

15. "Advisory Committee's Explanatory Memorandum Concerning Administrative Order in Regard to Civil Case Flow Expedition," *Maine Bar Bulletin* (November 1984): 267-68; 270; 272.

16. Roger W. Kaufman, "Fast-Track Courts with Part-Time Judges," *Litigation* (Fall 1982).

17. "Civil Case Management and Procedures Report: Report of the Supreme Court Committee," *New Jersey Law Journal* (March 28, 1985, Special Supplement).

18. The 40 states that have adopted Rule 56(g) of the Federal Rules of Civil Procedure, or a similar one, include: Alabama, Alaska, Arizona, Arkansas, Colorado, Connecticut, Delaware, Florida, Georgia, Hawaii, Idaho, Illinois, Indiana, Iowa, Kansas, Kentucky, Maine, Michigan, Minnesota, Mississippi, Missouri, Montana, Nevada, New Jersey, New Mexico, North Carolina, North Dakota, Ohio, Oregon, Pennsylvania, Rhode Island, South Carolina, South Dakota, Tennessee, Texas, Vermont, Washington, West Virginia, Wisconsin, and Wyoming.

19. Jef Feeley, "Appellate Arbitration Set in S.C.," *The National Law Journal* (January 14, 1985): 11, 38.

20. "Association to Study Use of Retired Appellate Division Judges to Arbitrate Civil Appeals," *Advocate* (October 1984).

21. "Community Service Hours Reach a Million," *Courtworks* 4 (Spring 1985): 7.

22. A national evaluative study of the roughly 200 victim/witness programs known to exist in 1979 were discovered to be largely sponsored and administered by prosecutors, police, or sheriffs' departments. See Roberta C. Cronin and Blair B. Bourque, *National Evaluation Program, Phase I Assessment of Victim/Witness Assistance Projects: Final Report* (May 1980).

23. Relationships established between courts and victim assistance programs are known to exist in Georgia, New York, Pennsylvania, Virginia, and Wisconsin.

24. National Institute of Justice, "Jailing Drunk Drivers: Impact on the Criminal Justice System," *Research in Brief* (November 1984): 1-4.

25. Ibid.

26. Dixie K. Knoebel, "The Issue of Comparable Worth," *State Court Journal* 9 (Summer 1985): 4-11.

27. "The Child Support Enforcement Amendments of 1984: Public Law 98-378," *American Bar Association Child Support Project*, August 20, 1984.

28. U.S. Department of Health and Human Services, *Federal Register*, Child Support Enforcement Program; Implementation of Amendments of 1984; Final Rule (May 9, 1985).

29. Leon F. Bouvier and Anthony J. Agresta, "The Fastest Growing Minority," *American Demographics* (May 1985): 31-33; 46.

30. "Problems Cited in Greater Use of Court In-

terpreters," *Criminal Justice Newsletter* 16 (July 1, 1985).

31. "In Court Language Is No Barrier" and "Court Interpreters: Accuracy Under Pressure," *Bay State Briefs* 2 (September 1984): 1-2.

32. Arizona, Arkansas, Florida, Hawaii, Kansas, New Jersey, New York, and Washington.

33. "Supreme Court Task Force Studies Interpreter and Translation Services," *New Jersey Law Journal* (September 19, 1985): 1; 18.

34. J. Manuel Banales, "Court Interpreters," *Texas Bar Journal* (July 1984): 796-97.

35. "Women in the Courts," *New Jersey Law Journal* (December 8, 1983): 1; 8; 12-13.

36. "Judge Marilyn Loftus on Gender Bias," *Chronicle* (May/June 1985): 3.

Table 4.1
STATE COURTS OF LAST RESORT

State or other jurisdiction	Name of court	Justices chosen(a) At large	Justices chosen(a) By district	No. of judges(b)	Term (in years)(c)	Chief justice Method of selection	Chief justice Term of service as chief justice
Alabama	S.C.	★		9	6	Popular election	6 years
Alaska	S.C.	★		5	10	By court	3 years(d)
Arizona	S.C.	★		5	6	By court	5 years
Arkansas	S.C.	★		7	8	Popular election	8 years
California	S.C.	★		7	12	Appointed by governor(e)	12 years
Colorado	S.C.	★		7	10	By court	At pleasure of court
Connecticut	S.C.	★		6	8	Nominated by governor, appointed by General Assembly	8 years
Delaware	S.C.		★	5	12	Appointed by governor with consent of Senate	12 years
Florida	S.C.			7	6	By court	6 years
Georgia	S.C.	★		7	6	By court	6 years
Hawaii	S.C.	★		5	10	Appointed by governor, with consent of Senate	10 years
Idaho	S.C.	★		5	6	Justice with shortest remaining term(f)	Remainder of term
Illinois	S.C.		★	7	10	By court	3 years
Indiana	S.C.	★		5	10	Selected by judicial nominating commission from S.C. members	5 years
Iowa	S.C.	★		9	8	By court	Remainder of term
Kansas	S.C.	★		7	6	By seniority of service(g)	Remainder of term
Kentucky	S.C.		★	7	8	By court	4 years
Louisiana	S.C.		★	7	10	By seniority of service	Remainder of term
Maine	S.J.C.	★		7	7	Appointed by governor, with consent of Senate	7 years
Maryland	C.A.		★	7	10	Designated by governor	Remainder of term
Massachusetts	S.J.C.	★		7	To age 70	Appointed by governor	To age 70
Michigan	S.C.	★		7	8	By court	2 years
Minnesota	S.C.	★		9	6	Popular election	6 years
Mississippi	S.C.		★	9	8	By seniority of service	Remainder of term
Missouri	S.C.	★		7	12	By court	Fixed by court
Montana	S.C.	★		7	8	Popular election	8 years
Nebraska	S.C.		★	7	6	Appointed by governor	6 years
Nevada	S.C.	★		5	6	By seniority of service(h)	Remainder of term
New Hampshire	S.C.	★		5	To age 70	Appointed by governor and Council	To age 70
New Jersey	S.C.	★		7	7(i)	Appointed by governor, with consent of Senate	7 years(i)

STATE COURTS OF LAST RESORT—Continued

State or other jurisdiction	Name of court	Justices chosen(a) At large	Justices chosen(a) By district	No. of judges(b)	Term (in years)(c)	Chief justice Method of selection	Chief justice Term of service as chief justice
New Mexico	S.C.	*		5	8	By court	2 years
New York	C.A.	*		7	14(i)	Appointed by governor, with consent of Senate	14 years(i)
North Carolina	S.C.	*		7	8	Popular election	8 years
North Dakota	S.C.	*		5	10	By Supreme and district court judges	5 years(j)
Ohio	S.C.	*		7	6	Popular election	6 years
Oklahoma	S.C.		**	9	6	By court	2 years
	C.C.A.		**	3	6		
Oregon	S.C.			7	6	By seniority of service	6 years
Pennsylvania	S.C.	**		7	10	By seniority of service	Remainder of term
Rhode Island	S.C.	**		5	Life	By legislature	Life
South Carolina	S.C.			5	10	Joint public vote of General Assembly	10 years
South Dakota	S.C.		*	5	8	By court	4 years
Tennessee	S.C.	*		5	8	By court	18 months
Texas	S.C.	*		9	6	Popular election	6 years
	C.C.A.	*		9	6	Popular election(k)	6 years(k)
Utah	S.C.	*		5	10	Justice with shortest term(f)	Remainder of term
Vermont	S.C.	*		5	6	Appointed by governor, with consent of Senate	6 years
Virginia	S.C.	*		7	12	By seniority of service	Remainder of term
Washington	S.C.	*		9	6	Justice with shortest term(f)	Remainder of term
West Virginia	S.C.A.	*		5	12	By court	Pleasure of court
Wisconsin	S.C.	*		7	10	By seniority of service(l)	Remainder of term
Wyoming	S.C.	*		5	8	By court	Pleasure of court
Dist. of Col.	C.A.	*		9	15	Designated by President(m)	4 years
American Samoa	H.C.	*		8 years(n)	(o)	Appointed by Secretary of the Interior	(o)
Puerto Rico	S.C.	*		8	To age 70	Appointed by President with consent of U.S. Senate	To age 70

Sources: State constitutions, statutes and court administration offices.

Key:
S.C.—Supreme Court
S.C.A.—Supreme Court of Appeals
S.J.C.—Supreme Judicial Court
C.A.—Court of Appeals
C.C.A.—Court of Criminal Appeals
H.C.—High Court

(a) See Table 4.4, "Selection and Retention of Judges," for details.
(b) Number includes chief justice.
(c) The initial term may be shorter. See Table 4.4, "Selection and Retention of Judges," for details.
(d) A justice may serve more than one term as chief justice, but may not serve consecutive terms

in that position.
(e) Subsequently, must run on record for retention.
(f) Not holding office by selection to fill a vacancy.
(g) If two or more qualify, then senior in age.
(h) If two or more qualify, then determined by lot.
(i) May be reappointed to age 70.
(j) Or expiration of term, whichever is first.
(k) Presiding judge of Court of Criminal Appeals.
(l) If two or more qualify, then justice with least number of years remaining in term.
(m) From list of nominees submitted by Judicial Nominating Commission.
(n) Chief justice and associate judges sit on appellate and trial divisions.
(o) For good behavior.

Table 4.2
STATE INTERMEDIATE APPELLATE COURTS AND GENERAL TRIAL COURTS: NUMBER OF JUDGES AND TERMS

State or other jurisdiction	Intermediate appellate court — Name of court	No. of judges	Term (years)	General trial court — Name of court	No. of judges	Term (years)
Alabama	Court of Criminal Appeals	5	6	Circuit courts	124	6
	Court of Civil Appeals	3	6			
Alaska	Court of Appeals	3	6	Superior courts	29	6
Arizona	Court of Appeals	12	6	Superior courts	97	4
Arkansas	Court of Appeals	6	8	Chancery courts	30	4
				Circuit courts	32	6
California	Courts of Appeal	73	12	Superior courts	679	6
Colorado	Court of Appeals	10	8	District Court	110	6
Connecticut	Appellate Court	6	8	Superior courts	137(a)	8
Delaware				Superior courts	13(b)	12
Florida	District Court of Appeals	45	6	Circuit courts	347	6
Georgia	Court of Appeals	9	6	Superior courts	127	4(c)
Hawaii	Intermediate Court of Appeals	3	10	Circuit courts	17	10
Idaho	Court of Appeals	3	6	District courts	33	4
Illinois	Appellate Court	34	10	Circuit courts	386(d)	6
Indiana	Court of Appeals	12	10	Circuit courts	90	6
Iowa	Court of Appeals	6	6	District courts	99(e)	6
Kansas	Court of Appeals	7	4	District courts	71(f)	4
Kentucky	Court of Appeals	14	8	Circuit courts	91	8
Louisiana	Court of Appeals	48	10	Circuit courts	179	6
Maine				Superior Court	17	7
Maryland	Court of Special Appeals	13	10	Circuit courts	109(g)	15
Massachusetts	Appeals Court	10	To age 70	Trial Court	281	To age 70
Michigan	Court of Appeals	18	6	Circuit courts	167	6
Minnesota	Court of Appeals	12	6	District courts	144	6
Mississippi	. . .			Chancery courts	40	4
				Circuit courts	39	4
Missouri	Court of Appeals	32	12	Circuit courts	133(h)	6
Montana	. . .			District courts	36	6
Nebraska	. . .			District courts	48	6
Nevada	. . .			District courts	35	6
New Hampshire				Superior Court	21	To age 70
New Jersey	Appellate Division of Superior Court	28	7	Superior Court	329	7

STATE INTERMEDIATE APPELLATE COURTS AND GENERAL TRIAL COURTS—Continued

	Intermediate appellate court			General trial court		
State or other jurisdiction	Name of court	No. of judges	Term (years)	Name of court	No. of judges	Term (years)
New Mexico	Court of Appeals	7	8	District courts	56	6
New York	Appellate Division of Supreme Court	46	5(i)	Supreme Court	323(j)	14(i)
North Carolina	Court of Appeals	12	8	Superior Court	72	8
North Dakota				District courts	26	6
Ohio	Court of Appeals	53	6	Courts of common pleas	211	6
Oklahoma	Court of Appeals	12	6	District Court	72(k)	4
Oregon	Court of Appeals	10	6	Circuit courts	85	6
	Tax Court	1	6			
Pennsylvania	Superior Court	15	10	Courts of common pleas	309	10
	Commonwealth Court	9	10			
Rhode Island				Superior Court	18	Life
South Carolina	Court of Appeals	6	6	Circuit Court	31	6
South Dakota				Circuit courts	33	8
Tennessee	Court of Appeals	12	8	Chancery courts	30	8
	Court of Criminal Appeals	9	8	Circuit courts	92(l)	8
Texas	Courts of Appeals	80	6	District courts	374	4
Utah				District courts	29	6
Vermont				Superior courts	10	6
				District courts	14	6
Virginia	Court of Appeals	10	8	Circuit courts	120	8
Washington	Court of Appeals	16	6	Superior courts	129	4
West Virginia				Circuit courts	60	8
Wisconsin	Court of Appeals	12	6	Circuit courts	197	6
Wyoming				District courts	17	6
Dist. of Col.				Superior Court	44	15
American Samoa				High Court: trial level	8(m)	(n)
Guam				Superior Court	5	7
Puerto Rico				Superior Court	92	12

Sources: State statutes and court administration offices.

Key:

. . .—Court does not exist in jurisdiction.

(a) Includes the judges of the Supreme and appellate courts.
(b) President judge, three resident judges and nine associate judges.
(c) For judges of the Superior Court of the Atlanta Judicial Court, term of office is eight years.
(d) Plus 339 associate judges.
(e) Plus 39 district associate judges and 14 senior judges.
(f) Plus 69 district associate judges and 71 district magistrates.

(g) Includes judges of Circuit Court for Baltimore City.
(h) Plus 170 associate circuit judges.
(i) To age 70.
(j) Trial divisions, 272 justices; certified retired justices, 51.
(k) Plus 72 associate judges and 56 special judges.
(l) With civil jurisdiction, 66 judges; with criminal jurisdiction, 26.
(m) Chief Justice and associate judges sit on appellate and trial divisions.
(n) For good behavior.

Table 4.3
QUALIFICATIONS OF JUDGES OF STATE APPELLATE COURTS AND GENERAL TRIAL COURTS

State or other jurisdiction	U.S. citizenship (years)		Years of minimum residence — In state		In district		Minimum age		Member of state bar (years)		Other	
	A	T	A	T	A	T	A	T	A	T	A	T
Alabama	5	5	(a)	(a)	...	1	25	25	★	★	...	...
Alaska	★	★	5(a)	5(a)	...	...	...	...	★(b)	★(b)	...	...
Arizona	...	...	10(c)	5	3(d,e)	...	30(d)	30	10(c)	5	(f,g)	(f,g)
Arkansas	★	★	2	2	...	...	30	28	(h,i)	(h,i)	(f)	(f)
California	...	...	...	...	...	...	...	...	10(i)	10(i)	...	...
Colorado	...	...	(e)	...	...	(e)	...	...	5	5	(g)	(g)
Connecticut	...	...	...	...	...	...	...	...	★	★	...	...
Delaware	...	...	(a)	(a)	...	...	...	...	(h)	(h)	...	...
Florida	...	...	(e)	(e)	★	★	...	...	10	5	(g)	(g)
Georgia	3	3	(a)	(a)	...	...	30	30	7	7	...	...
Hawaii	★	★	★(a)	★(a)	...	...	...	...	10	10	...	...
Idaho	★	★	2	2	...	(e)	30	30	★	(h)	...	...
Illinois	★	★	...	...	★	★	...	...	★	★	...	...
Indiana	★	★	...	...	★	★	...	...	10(i)	★	...	...
Iowa	...	...	...	...	...	...	...	...	★	★	...	...
Kansas	...	...	...	...	...	★	30	30	★(i)	★(i)	...	...
Kentucky	★	★	2	2	2	2	...	...	8	8	...	...
Louisiana	...	...	...	...	2	2	...	...	5	5	...	...
Maine	...	...	...	...	...	...	...	...	(h)	(h)	(f)	(f)
Maryland	...	...	5(a,e)	5(a,e)	6 mo.	6 mo.	30	30	★	★	(f)	(f)
Massachusetts	...	...	...	...	...	...	...	...	...	...	...	...
Michigan	...	...	(e)	...	(e)	(e)	...	...	★	★	(g,j)	(g,j)
Minnesota	...	...	...	...	...	...	...	...	(h)	(h)	...	...
Mississippi	...	...	(a)	(a)	...	...	30	26	5	5	...	...
Missouri	15	10	(e)	(e)	★	1	30	30	★	★	...	...
Montana	★	★	2	2	...	...	...	...	5	5	...	...
Nebraska	★	★	3	...	★(e)	★	30	30	5(i)	5(i)	...	...
Nevada	...	...	2(e)	2(e)	...	...	25	25	★	★	(k)	(k)
New Hampshire	...	...	...	...	...	...	...	...	10	10	(l)	(l)
New Jersey	...	...	...	...	...	...	...	...	10	10	...	...
New Mexico	...	...	3	3	...	★	30	30	3(h,i)	3(h,i)	...	...
New York	...	...	...	...	...	...	...	...	10	10	...	...
North Carolina	...	...	...	...	...	...	...	...	★	★	...	...
North Dakota	★	★	★	★	...	...	...	...	★(h)	★(h)	...	...
Ohio	...	...	...	...	...	★	...	...	6(i)	6(i)	(g)	(g)
Oklahoma	...	...	(e)	...	(e)	(e)	30	...	5(i)	4(i)	...	...
Oregon	...	...	3	★	(e)	★	...	...	★	★	...	...
Pennsylvania	★	★	1(a)	(a)	...	1	...	...	★	★	...	...
Rhode Island	...	...	...	...	...	...	...	...	...	...	...	...
South Carolina	★	★	5(a)	5(a)	...	★(e)	26	26	5	5	...	...
South Dakota	★	★	★	★	★(e)	★(e)	...	...	★	★	...	...
Tennessee	...	...	5(a)	5	...	1	35(m)	30	★	★	...	...
Texas	★	★	(a)	(a)	(d)	2	35	25	★(i)	★(i)	...	...
Utah	...	...	5	3	...	★	30	25	★	★	...	...
Vermont	...	...	★	★	...	...	...	...	★(i)	★(i)	...	...
Virginia	...	...	★	★	...	...	...	...	5	5	...	...
Washington	...	...	...	...	1	1	...	...	★(n)	★	...	...
West Virginia	...	...	5	5	...	...	30	30	★(i)	★(i)	...	...
Wisconsin	...	...	(e)	...	...	(e)	...	...	5	5	...	...
Wyoming	★	★	3	2	...	...	30	28	1(h,i)	1(h)	...	...
Dist. of Col.	★	★	...	...	...	...	...	...	5(i)	5(i)	...	...
American Samoa	★	★	...	...	...	...	...	...	★	★	...	...
Guam	...	★	...	...	...	...	...	...	...	(h)	...	...
No. Mariana Is.	...	★	...	...	...	...	...	30	...	(h)	...	...
Puerto Rico	★	★	...	...	...	...	...	25	★(i)	★(i)	...	...

QUALIFICATIONS OF JUDGES—Continued

Note: The information in this table is based on a literal reading of the state constitutions and statutes. Requirements that an individual be a member of the state bar or a qualified elector may imply additional requirements.

Key:

A—Judges of courts of last resort and intermediate appellate courts.

T—Judges of general trial courts.

★—Provision; length of time not specified.

. . .—No specific provision.

(a) Citizen of the state. In Alabama, Mississippi and Tennessee (court of criminal appeals), five years; in Georgia, three years.

(b) Must have been engaged in active practice of law for specific number of years. Alaska: appellate—eight years; trial—five years.

(c) For court of appeals, five years.

(d) For court of appeals judges only.

(e) Qualified elector. For Arizona court of appeals, must be elector of county of residence. For Michigan Supreme Court, elector in state; court of appeals, elector of appellate circuit. For Missouri Supreme and appellate courts, electors for nine years; for circuit courts, electors for three years. For Oklahoma Supreme Court and Court of Criminal Appeals, elector for one year; court of appeals and district courts, elector for six months. For Oregon court of appeals, qualified elector in county.

(f) Specific personal characteristics. Arizona, Arkansas—good moral character. Maine—sobriety of manners. Maryland—integrity, wisdom and sound legal knowledge.

(g) Nominee must be under certain age to be eligible. Arizona—under 65. Colorado—under 72, except when name is submitted for vacancy. Florida—under 70, except upon temporary assignment or to complete a term. Michigan, Ohio—under 70.

(h) Learned in law.

(i) Years as a practicing lawyer and/or service on bench of court of record in state may satisfy requirement. Arkansas—appellate: eight years; trial: six years. Indiana—10 years admitted to practice or must have served as a circuit, superior or criminal court judge in the state for at least five years. Kansas—appellate: 10 years; trial: five years (must have served as an associate district judge in state for two years). Texas—appellate: 10 years; trial: four years. Vermont—five of 10 years preceding appointment. West Virginia—appellate: 10 years; trial: five years. Puerto Rico—appellate: 10 years; trial: five years.

(j) A person convicted of a felony or breach of public trust is not eligible to the office for a period of 20 years after conviction.

(k) May not have been previously removed from judicial office.

(l) Except that record of birth is required.

(m) Thirty years for judges of court of appeals and court of criminal appeals.

(n) For court of appeals, admitted to practice for five years.

Table 4.4
SELECTION AND RETENTION OF JUDGES

Alabama.........	Appellate, circuit, district and probate judges elected on partisan ballots. Municipal court judges appointed by the governing body of the municipality (majority vote of its members).
Alaska...........	Supreme Court, court of appeals, superior court and district court judges appointed by governor from nominations submitted by Judicial Council. Supreme Court, court of appeals and superior court judges approved or rejected at first general election held more than three years after appointment. Reconfirmation every 10 and six years, respectively. District court judges approved or rejected at first general election held more than one year after appointment. Reconfirmation every four years. District court magistrates appointed by and serve at pleasure of presiding judge of superior court in each judicial district.
Arizona..........	Supreme Court justices and court of appeals judges appointed by governor from a list of not less than three nominees submitted by a nine-member Commission on Appellate Court Appointments. Superior court judges (in counties with population of at least 150,000) appointed by governor from a list of not less than three nominees submitted by a nine-member commission on trial court appointments. Judges initially hold office for term ending 60 days following next regular general election after expiration of two-year term. Judges who file declaration of intention to be retained in office run at next regular general election on non-partisan ballot. Superior court judges in counties having population less than 150,000 elected on non-partisan ballot; justices of the peace elected on partisan ballot; police judges and magistrates selected as provided by charter or ordinance; Tucson city magistrates appointed by mayor and council from nominees submitted by non-partisan Merit Selection Commission on magistrate appointments.
Arkansas	All elected on partisan ballot.
California........	Supreme Court and courts of appeal judges appointed by governor, confirmed by Commission on Judicial Appointments. Judges run unopposed on non-partisan ballot at next general election after appointment. Superior court judges elected on non-partisan ballot or selected by method described above; judges elected to full term at next general election on non-partisan ballot. Municipal court and justice court judges initially appointed by governor and county board of supervisors, respectively, retain office by election on non-partisan ballot.
Colorado	Supreme Court and court of appeals judges appointed by governor from nominees submitted by Supreme Court Nominating Commission. Other judges appointed by governor from nominees submitted by Judicial District Nominating Commission. After initial appointive term of two years, judges run on record for retention. Municipal judges appointed by municipal governing body. Denver County judges appointed by mayor from list submitted by nominating commission; judges run on record for retention.
Connecticut	Supreme and superior court judges appointed by legislature from nominations submitted by governor. Judicial Review Council makes recommendations on nominations for reappointment. Probate judges elected on partisan ballots.
Delaware	All appointed by governor with consent of majority of senate.
Florida	Supreme Court and district court of appeals judges appointed by governor from nominees submitted by appropriate judicial nominating commission. Judges run for retention at next general election preceding expiration of term. Circuit and county court judges elected on non-partisan ballots.
Georgia..........	Supreme Court, court of appeals and superior court judges elected on non-partisan ballots. Probate judges and justices of peace elected on partisan ballots. Other county and city court judges appointed.
Hawaii	Supreme Court and intermediate court of appeals justices and circuit court judges nominated by Judicial Selection Commission (on list of at least six names) and appointed by governor with consent of senate. District court judges nominated by Commission (on list of at least six names) and appointed by chief justice.
Idaho	Supreme Court and court of appeals justices and district court judges elected on non-partisan ballot. Magistrates appointed on non-partisan merit basis by District Magistrates Commission and run for retention in first general election next succeeding the 18-month period following initial appointment; thereafter, run every four years.
Illinois...........	Supreme Court, appellate court and circuit court judges nominated at primary elections or by petition and elected at general or judicial elections on partisan ballot. Circuit court associate judges appointed by circuit judges for four-year terms.
Indiana	Supreme Court justices and court of appeals judges appointed by governor from list of three nominees submitted by seven-member Judicial Nominating Commission. Judges serve until next general election after two years from appointment date; thereafter, run for retention on record. Circuit, superior and county judges in most counties run on partisan ballot. Marion County municipal judges appointed by governor from nominations submitted by county nominating commission.
Iowa	Supreme Court, court of appeals and district court judges appointed by governor from lists submitted by nominating commissions. Judges serve initial one-year term and until January 1 following next general election, then run on records for retention. Full-time judicial magistrates appointed by district judges in judicial election district from nominations submitted by county judicial magistrate appointing commission. Part-time magistrates appointed by county judicial magistrate appointing commission.
Kansas	Supreme Court and court of appeals judges appointed by governor from nominations submitted by Supreme Court Nominating Commission. Judges serve until second Monday in January following first general election after one year in office; thereafter run on record for retention every six (Supreme Court) and four (court of appeals) years. District judges in most judicial districts selected by non-partisan commission plan.
Kentucky	All judges elected on non-partisan ballot.
Louisiana	All justices and judges (except Orleans Parish District and Family Court judges) elected on non-partisan ballot.
Maine	All appointed by governor with confirmation of the senate, except probate judges who are elected on partisan ballot.
Maryland	Court of Appeals and special appeals judges nominated by Judicial Nominating Commission, and appointed by governor with advice and consent of senate. Judges run on record for retention after one year of service. Judges of circuit courts and Supreme Bench of Baltimore City nominated by Commission and appointed by governor. Judges run in first general election after year of service (may be challenged by other candidates). District court judges nominated by Commission and appointed by governor, subject to senate confirmation.

Massachusetts ..... All nominated and appointed by governor with advice and consent of Governor's Council. Judicial Nominating Commission, established by executive order, submits names on non-partisan basis to governor.

Michigan .... All elected on non-partisan ballot, except remaining municipal judges who are selected in accordance with local procedures for selecting public officials.

Minnesota .... All elected on non-partisan ballot.

Mississippi .... All elected on partisan ballot, except municipal court judges who are appointed by governing authority of each municipality.

Missouri .... Judges of Supreme Court, court of appeals and several circuit courts appointed initially by governor from nominations submitted by judicial selection commissions. Judges run for retention after one year in office. All other judges elected on partisan ballot.

Montana .... All elected on non-partisan ballot. Judges unopposed in reelection effort, run for retention.

Nebraska .... All judges appointed initially by governor from nominees submitted by judicial nominating commissions. Judges run for retention on non-partisan ballot in general election following initial three-year term; subsequent terms are six years.

Nevada .... All elected on non-partisan ballot.

New Hampshire ... All appointed by governor and confirmed by majority vote of five-member Executive Council.

New Jersey .... All appointed by governor with advice and consent of senate, except judges of municipal courts serving a single municipality who are appointed by the governing body.

New Mexico ...... All elected on partisan ballot.

New York .... All elected on partisan ballot, except judges of Court of Appeals who are appointed by governor with advice and consent of senate. Governor also appoints judges of court of claims and designates members of appellate division of supreme court. Mayor of New York City appoints judges of criminal and family courts in the city.

North Carolina .... All elected on partisan ballot, except special judges of superior court who are appointed by governor.

North Dakota ..... All elected on non-partisan ballot.

Ohio .... All elected on non-partisan ballot, except court of claims judges who may be appointed by chief justice of Supreme Court from ranks of Supreme Court, court of appeals, court of common pleas or retired judges.

Oklahoma .... Supreme Court justices and Court of Criminal Appeals judges appointed by governor from lists of three submitted by Judicial Nominating Commission. Judges run for retention on non-partisan ballot at first general election following completion of one year's service. Judges of court of appeals, and district and associate district judges elected on non-partisan ballot. Special judges appointed by district judges within judicial administrative districts. Municipal judges appointed by governing body of municipality.

Oregon .... All judges elected on non-partisan ballot for six-year terms, except municipal judges who are generally appointed and serve as prescribed by city council.

Pennsylvania ...... All initially elected on partisan ballot and thereafter on non-partisan retention ballot, except judges of traffic court and magistrates (Pittsburgh) who are appointed by mayor.

Rhode Island ...... Supreme Court justices elected by legislature. Superior, district and family court judges appointed by governor with advice and consent of senate. By executive order, governor selects appointees from names submitted by a judicial nominating commission. Probate and municipal court judges appointed by city or town councils.

South Carolina .... Supreme Court, court of appeals, circuit court and family court judges elected by legislature from names submitted on a non-partisan basis by judiciary committee of legislature. Probate judges elected on partisan ballot. Magistrates appointed by governor with advice and consent of senate. Municipal judges appointed by mayor and alderman of city.

South Dakota ..... Supreme Court justices appointed by governor from nominees submitted by Judicial Qualifications Commission. Justices run for retention at first general election after three years in office. Circuit court judges elected on non-partisan ballot. Magistrates appointed by presiding judge of judicial court.

Tennessee .... Judges of intermediate appellate courts appointed initially by governor from list of three nominees submitted by Appellate Court Nominating Commission. Judges run for election to full term at biennial general election held more than 30 days after occurrence of vacancy. Supreme Court judges and all other judges elected on partisan ballot, except some municipal judges who are appointed by governing body of city.

Texas .... All elected on partisan ballot (method of selection for municipal judges determined by city charter or local ordinance).

Utah .... Supreme Court, district court, circuit court and juvenile court judges appointed by governor from list of at least three nominees submitted by Judicial Nominating Commission. Judges run unopposed for retention in general election following initial three-year term; thereafter run on record for retention every 10 (Supreme Court) and six (other courts of record) years.

Vermont .... Supreme Court justices, superior court and district court judges nominated by Judicial Nominating Board and appointed by governor with advice and consent of senate. Judges retained in office unless legislature votes for removal.

Virginia .... All full-time judges elected by majority vote of legislature.

Washington .... All elected on non-partisan ballot (method of selection for some municipal judges locally determined).

West Virginia ..... Supreme Court of Appeals judges, circuit court judges and magistrates elected on partisan ballot.

Wisconsin .... Supreme Court, court of appeals and circuit court judges elected on non-partisan ballot. Method of selection for municipal judges determined locally.

Wyoming .... Supreme Court justices, district and county court judges appointed by governor from list of three nominees submitted by judicial nominating commission. Judges run for retention on non-partisan ballot at first general election occurring more than one year after appointment. Justices of the peace elected on non-partisan ballot. Municipal (police) judges appointed by mayor with consent of council.

Dist. of Col. ...... Court of appeals and superior court judges nominated by president of the United States from a list of persons recommended by District of Columbia Judicial Nominating Commission; appointed upon advice and consent of U.S. Senate.

American Samoa .. Chief justice and associate justice(s) appointed by the U.S. Secretary of the Interior pursuant to presidential delegation of authority. Associate judges appointed by governor of American Samoa on recommendation of the chief justice, and subsequently confirmed by the senate of American Samoa.

Guam .... All appointed by governor with consent of legislature from list of nominees submitted by Judicial Council; thereafter, run on record for retention every seven years.

No. Mariana Is. ... All appointed by governor with advice and consent of senate.

Puerto Rico .... All appointed by governor with advice and consent of senate.

Virgin Islands ..... All appointed by governor with advice and consent of legislature.

Sources: Larry Berkson, Scott Beller and Michele Grimaldi, *Judicial Selection in the United States: A Compendium of Provisions* (Chicago: American Judicature Society) and update; Donna Vandenberg, "Judicial Merit Selection: Current Status," American Judicature Society; and state constitutions and statutes.

Table 4.5
METHODS FOR REMOVAL OF JUDGES AND FILLING OF VACANCIES

State or other jurisdiction	How removed	Vacancies: how filled
Alabama	Judicial Inquiry Commission investigates, receives or initiates complaints concerning any judge. Complaints are filed with the Court of the Judiciary which is empowered to remove, suspend, censure or otherwise discipline judges in the state.	By gubernatorial appointment. At next general election held after appointee has been in office one year, office is filled for a full term. In some counties, vacancies in circuit and district courts are filled by gubernatorial appointment on nominations made by judicial commission.
Alaska	Justices and judges subject to impeachment for malfeasance or misfeasance in performance of official duties. On recommendation of Judicial Qualifications Commission or on its own motion, Supreme Court may suspend judge without salary when judge pleads guilty or no contest or is found guilty of a crime punishable under state or federal law or of any other crime involving moral turpitude under that law. If conviction is reversed, suspension terminates and judge is paid salary for period of suspension. If conviction becomes final, judge is removed from office by Supreme Court. On recommendation of Judicial Qualifications Commission, Supreme Court may censure or remove a judge for action (occurring not more than six years before commencement of current term) which constitutes willful misconduct in office, willful and persistent failure to perform duties, habitual intemperance or conduct prejudicial to the administration of justice that brings the judicial office into disrepute. The Court may also retire a judge for a disability that seriously interferes with the performance of duties and is (or is likely to become) permanent.	By gubernatorial appointment, from nominations submitted by Judicial Council.
Arizona	Judges subject to recall election. Electors, equal in number to 25% of votes cast in last election for judge, may petition for judge's recall. All Supreme Court, court of appeals and superior court judges (judges of courts of record) are subject to impeachment. On recommendation of Commission on Judicial Qualifications or on its own motion, Supreme Court may suspend without salary, a judge who pleads guilty or no contest or is found guilty of a crime punishable as felony or involving moral turpitude under state or federal law. If conviction is reversed, suspension terminates and judge is paid salary for period of suspension. If conviction becomes final, judge is removed from office by Supreme Court. Upon recommendation of Commission on Judicial Qualifications, Supreme Court may remove a judge for willful misconduct in office, willful and persistent failure to perform duties, habitual intemperance or conduct prejudicial to the administration of justice that brings the office into disrepute. The Court may also retire a judge for a disability that seriously interferes with performance of duties and is (or is likely to become) permanent.	Vacancies on Supreme Court, court of appeals and superior courts (in counties with population over 150,000) are filled as in initial selection. Vacancies on superior courts in counties of less than 150,000 may be filled by gubernatorial appointment until next general election when judge is elected to fill remainder of unexpired term. Vacancies on justice courts are filled by appointment by county board of supervisors.
Arkansas	Supreme, appellate, circuit and chancery court judges are subject to removal by impeachment or by the governor upon the joint address of 2/3 of the members elected to each house of General Assembly.	By gubernatorial appointment. Appointee serves remainder of unexpired term if it expires at next general election.
California	All judges subject to impeachment for misconduct. All judges subject to recall election. On recommendation of the Commission on Judicial Performance or on its own motion, the Supreme Court may suspend a judge without salary when the judge pleads guilty or no contest or is found guilty of a crime punishable as a felony or any other crime that involves moral turpitude under that law. If conviction is reversed, suspension terminates and judge is paid salary for period of suspension. If conviction becomes final, judge is removed from office by Supreme Court. Upon recommendation of Commission on Judicial Performance, Supreme Court may remove judge for willful misconduct in office, persistent failure or inability to perform duties, habitual intemperance or conduct prejudicial to the administration of justice that brings the office into disrepute. The Court may also retire a judge for disability that seriously interferes with performance of duties and is (or is likely to become) permanent.	Vacancies on appellate courts are filled by gubernatorial appointment with approval of Commission on Judicial Appointments until next general election at which appointee has the right to become a candidate. Vacancies on superior courts are filled by gubernatorial appointment until next election. Vacancies on municipal courts are filled by gubernatorial appointment for remainder of unexpired term; on justice courts by appointment of county board of supervisors or by nonpartisan special election.
Colorado	Supreme, appeals and district court judges are subject to impeachment for high crimes and misdemeanors or malfeasance in office by 2/3 vote of senate. Supreme Court, on its own motion or upon petition, may remove a judge from office upon final conviction for a crime punishable as felony under state or federal law or of any other crime involving moral turpitude under that law. Upon recommendation of Commission on Judicial Discipline, Supreme Court may remove or discipline a judge for willful misconduct in office, willful or persistent failure to perform the duties of office, intemperance or violation of judicial conduct, or for disability that seriously interferes with performance and is (or is likely to become) permanent. Denver county judges are removed in accordance with charter and ordinance provisions.	By gubernatorial appointment (or mayoral appointment in case of Denver county court) from names submitted by appropriate judicial nominating commission.

METHODS FOR REMOVAL OF JUDGES—Continued

State or other jurisdiction	How removed	Vacancies: how filled
Connecticut	Supreme and superior court judges are subject to removal by impeachment or by the governor on the address of 2/3 of each house of the General Assembly. On recommendation of Judicial Review Council or on its own motion, the Supreme Court may remove or suspend a judge of the Supreme or superior court after an investigation and hearing. If the investigation involves a Supreme Court justice, such judge is disqualified from participating in the proceedings. If a judge becomes permanently incapacitated and cannot adequately fulfill the duties of office, the judge may be retired for disability by the Judicial Review Council on its own motion or on application of the judge.	If General Assembly is in session, vacancies are filled by gubernatorial nomination and legislative appointment. Otherwise vacancies are filled temporarily by gubernatorial appointment.
Delaware	Judges are subject to impeachment for treason, bribery or any high crime or misdemeanor. The Court on the Judiciary may (after investigation and hearing) censure or remove a judge for willful misconduct in office, willful and persistent failure to perform the duties of office or an offense involving moral turpitude or other persistent misconduct in violation of judicial ethics. The Court may also retire a judge for permanent mental or physical disability interfering with the performance of duties.	Vacancies are filled as in initial selection.
Florida	Supreme Court, district courts of appeal and circuit court judges are subject to impeachment for misdemeanors in office. On recommendation of Judicial Qualifications Commission, Supreme Court may discipline or remove a judge for willful or persistent failure to perform duties or for conduct unbecoming to a member of the judiciary, or retire a judge for a disability that seriously interferes with the performance of duties and is (or is likely to become) permanent.	By gubernatorial appointment, from nominees recommended by appropriate judicial nominating commission.
Georgia...........	Judges are subject to impeachment for cause. Upon recommendation of the Judicial Qualifications Commission (after investigation of alleged misconduct), the Supreme Court may retire, remove or censure any judge.	By gubernatorial appointment (by executive order) on nonpartisan basis from names submitted by Judicial Nominating Commission.
Hawaii	Upon recommendation of the Commission on Judicial Discipline (after investigation and hearings), the Supreme Court may reprimand, discipline, suspend (with or without salary), retire or remove any judge as a result of misconduct or disability.	Vacancies on Supreme, intermediate court of appeals and circuit courts are filled by gubernatorial appointment (subject to consent of senate) from names submitted by Judicial Selection Committee. Vacancies on district courts are filled by appointment by chief justice from names submitted by Committee.
Idaho	Judges are subject to impeachment for cause. Upon recommendation by Judicial Council, Supreme Court (after investigation) may remove judges of Supreme Court, court of appeals and district court judges. District court judges (or judicial district sitting en banc), by majority vote in accordance with Supreme Court rules, may remove magistrates for cause. District Magistrate's Commission may remove magistrates without cause during first 18 months of service.	Vacancies on Supreme Court, court of appeals and district courts are filled by gubernatorial appointment from names submitted by Judicial Council for unexpired term. Vacancies in magistrates' division of district court are filled by District Magistrate's Commission for remainder of unexpired term.
Illinois...........	Judges are subject to impeachment for cause. The Judicial Inquiry Board receives (or initiates) and investigates complaints, and files complaints with the Courts Commission which may remove, suspend without pay, censure or reprimand a judge for willful misconduct in office, persistent failure to perform duties or other conduct prejudicial to the administration of justice or that brings the judicial office into disrepute. The Commission may also suspend (with or without pay) or retire a judge for mental or physical disability.	Vacancies on Supreme, appellate and circuit courts are filled by appointment by Supreme Court until general election. Associate judge vacancies on circuit courts are filled as in initial selection.
Indiana	Upon the recommendation of the Judicial Qualifications Commission or on its own motion, the Supreme Court may suspend or remove an appellate judge for pleading guilty or no contest to a felony or crime involving moral turpitude. The Supreme Court may also retire, censure or remove a judge for other matters. The Supreme Court may also discipline or suspend without pay a non-appellate judge.	Appellate vacancies are filled as in initial selection. Vacancies on circuit courts are filled by gubernatorial appointment until general election. Vacancies on most superior courts are filled by gubernatorial appointment.
Iowa	Supreme and district court judges are subject to impeachment for misdemeanor or malfeasance in office. Upon recommendation of Commission on Judicial Qualifications, the Supreme Court may retire a Supreme, district or associate district judge for permanent disability, or remove such judge for failure to perform duties, habitual intemperance, willful misconduct, conduct which brings the office into disrepute or substantial violations of the canons of judicial ethics. Judicial magistrates may be removed by a tribunal in the judicial election district of the magistrate's residence.	Vacancies are filled as in initial selection.

State or other jurisdiction	How removed	Vacancies: how filled
Kansas	All judges are subject to impeachment for treason, bribery or other high crimes and misdemeanors. Supreme Court justices are subject to retirement upon certification to the governor (after a hearing by the Supreme Court nominating commission) that such justice is so incapacitated as to be unable to perform adequately the duties of office. Upon recommendation of the Judicial Qualifications Commission, the Supreme Court may retire for incapacity, discipline, suspend or remove for cause any judge below the Supreme Court level.	Vacancies on Supreme Court and court of appeals are filled as in initial selection. Vacancies on district courts (in areas where commission plan has not been adopted) are filled by gubernatorial appointment until next general election, when vacancy is filled for remainder of unexpired term; in areas where commission plan has been adopted, vacancies are filled by gubernatorial appointment from names submitted by judicial nominating commission.
Kentucky	Judges are subject to impeachment for misdemeanors in office. Retirement and Removal Commission, subject to rules of procedure established by Supreme Court, may retire for disability, suspend without pay or remove for good cause any judge. The Commission's actions are subject to review by Supreme Court.	By gubernatorial appointment (from names submitted by appropriate judicial nominating commission) or by chief justice if governor fails to act within 60 days. Appointees serve until next general election after their appointment at which time vacancy is filled.
Louisiana	Judges are subject to impeachment for commission or conviction of felony or malfeasance or gross misconduct. Upon investigation and recommendation by Judiciary Commission, Supreme Court may censure, suspend (with or without salary), remove from office or retire involuntarily a judge for misconduct relating to official duties, willful and persistent failure to perform duties, persistent and public conduct prejudicial to the administration of justice that brings the office into disrepute, or conduct while in office which would constitute a felony or conviction of felony. The Court may also retire a judge for disability which is (or is likely to become) permanent.	Vacancies are filled by Supreme Court appointment if remainder of unexpired term is six months or less; if longer than six months, vacancies are filled in special election.
Maine	Judges are subject to removal by impeachment or by governor upon the joint address of the legislature. Upon recommendation of the Committee on Judicial Responsibility and Disability, the Supreme Judicial Court may remove, retire or discipline any judge.	Vacancies are filled as in initial selection.
Maryland	Judges are subject to impeachment. Judges of Court of Appeals, court of special appeals, trial courts of general jurisdiction and district courts are subject to removal by governor on judge's conviction in court of law, impeachment, or physical or mental disability. Judges are also subject to removal upon joint address of the legislature. Upon recommendation of the Commission on Judicial Disabilities (after hearing), the Court of Appeals may remove or retire a judge for misconduct in office, persistent failure to perform duties, conduct prejudicial to the proper administration of justice, or disability that seriously interferes with the performance of duties and is (or is likely to become) permanent. Elected judges convicted of felony or misdemeanor relating to public duties and involving moral turpitude may be removed from office by operation of law when conviction becomes final.	Vacancies are filled as in initial selection.
Massachusetts	Judges are subject to impeachment. The governor, with the consent of the Executive Council, may remove judges upon joint address of the legislature, and may also (after a hearing and with consent of the Council) retire a judge because of advanced age or mental or physical disability. The Commission on Judicial Conduct, using rules of procedure approved by the Supreme Judicial Court, may investigate the action of any judge that may, by consequence of willful misconduct in office, willful or persistent failure to perform his duties, habitual intemperance or other conduct prejudicial to the administration of justice, bring the office into disrepute.	Vacancies are filled as in initial selection.
Michigan	Judges are subject to impeachment. With the concurrence of 2/3 of the members of the legislature, the governor may remove a judge for reasonable cause insufficient for impeachment. Upon recommendation of Judicial Tenure Commission, Supreme Court may censure, suspend (with or without salary), retire or remove a judge for conviction of a felony, a physical or mental disability, or a persistent failure to perform duties, misconduct in office, habitual intemperance or conduct clearly prejudicial to the administration of justice.	Vacancies in all courts of record are filled by gubernatorial appointment from nominees recommended by a bar committee. Appointee serves until next general election at which successor is selected for remainder of unexpired term. Vacancies on municipal courts are filled by appointment by city councils.

METHODS FOR REMOVAL OF JUDGES—Continued

State or other jurisdiction	How removed	Vacancies: how filled
Minnesota	Supreme and district court judges are subject to impeachment. Upon recommendation of Board of Judicial Standards, Supreme Court may censure, suspend (with or without salary), retire or remove a judge for conviction of a felony, physical or mental disability, or persistent failure to perform duties, misconduct in office, habitual intemperance or conduct prejudicial to the administration of justice.	As a result of executive order, by gubernatorial appointment from names submitted by appropriate committee on judicial nominations. Appointee serves until general election occurring more than one year after appointment at which time a successor is elected to serve a full term.
Mississippi	Judges are subject to impeachment. For reasonable cause which is not sufficient for impeachment, the governor may, on joint address of legislature, remove judges of Supreme and inferior courts. Upon recommendation of Commission on Judicial Performance, Supreme Court may remove, suspend, fine, publicly censure or reprimand a judge for conviction of a felony (in a court outside the state), willful misconduct, willful and persistent failure to perform duties, habitual intemperance or conduct prejudicial to the administration of justice which brings the office into disrepute. The Commission may also retire any judge for physical or mental disability that seriously interferes with performance of duties and is (or is likely to become) permanent.	By gubernatorial appointment, from names submitted by a nominating commission. The office is filled for remainder of unexpired term at next state or congressional election held more than seven months after vacancy.
Missouri	Upon recommendation of Commission on Retirement, Removal and Discipline, Supreme Court may retire, remove or discipline any judge.	Vacancies on Supreme Court, court of appeals and circuit courts which have adopted commission plan are filled as in initial selection. Vacancies on other circuit courts and municipal courts are filled, respectively, by special election and mayoral appointment.
Montana..........	All judges are subject to impeachment. Upon recommendation of Judicial Standards Commission, Supreme Court may suspend a judge and remove same upon conviction of a felony or other crime involving moral turpitude. The Supreme Court may retire any judge for a disability that seriously interferes with the performance of duties, and that is (or may become) permanent. The Court may also censure, suspend, or remove any judge for willful misconduct in office, willful and persistent failure to perform duties, violation of canons of judicial ethics adopted by the Supreme Court, or habitual intemperance.	Vacancies on Supreme and district courts are filled by gubernatorial appointment (with confirmation by senate) from names submitted by judicial nominating commission. Vacancies on municipal and city courts are filled by appointment by city councils for remainder of unexpired term.
Nebraska	Judges are subject to impeachment. In case of impeachment of Supreme Court justice, judges of district court sit as court of impeachment with 2/3 concurrence required for conviction. In case of other judicial impeachments, Supreme Court sits as court of impeachment. Upon recommendation of the Commission on Judicial Qualifications, the Supreme Court may reprimand, discipline, censure, suspend or remove a judge for willful misconduct in office, willful failure to perform duties, habitual intemperance, conviction of crime involving moral turpitude, disbarment or conduct prejudicial to the administration of justice that brings the office into disrepute. The Supreme Court also may retire a judge for physical or mental disability that seriously interferes with performance of duties and is (or is likely to become) permanent.	Vacancies are filled as in initial selection.
Nevada	All judges, except justices of peace, are subject to impeachment. Judges are also subject to removal by legislative resolution and by recall election. The Commission on Judicial Discipline may censure, retire or remove a Supreme Court justice or district judge for willful misconduct, willful or persistent failure to perform duties or habitual intemperance, or retire a judge for advanced age which interferes with performance of duties or for mental or physical disability that is (or is likely to become) permanent.	Vacancies on Supreme or district courts are filled by gubernatorial appointment from among three nominees submitted by Commission on Judicial Selection. Vacancies on justice courts are filled by appointment by board of county commissioners or by special election.
New Hampshire....	Judges are subject to impeachment. Governor, with consent of Executive Council, may remove judges upon address of both houses of legislature.	Vacancies are filled as in initial selection.

167

METHODS FOR REMOVAL OF JUDGES—Continued

State or other jurisdiction	How removed	Vacancies: how filled
New Jersey........	Supreme and superior court judges are subject to impeachment by the legislature. Except for Supreme Court justices, judges are subject to a statutory removal proceeding that is initiated by the filing of a complaint by the Supreme Court on its own motion or the governor or either house of the legislature acting by a majority of its total membership. Prior to institution of the formal proceedings, complaints are usually referred to the Supreme Court's Advisory Committee on Judicial Conduct, which conducts a preliminary investigation, makes findings of fact and either dismisses the charges or recommends that formal proceedings be instituted. The Supreme Court's determination is based on a plenary hearing procedure, although the Court is supplied with a record created by the Committee. The formal statutory removal hearing may be either before the Supreme Court sitting en banc or before three justices or judges (or combination thereof) specifically designated by chief justice. If Supreme Court certifies to governor that it appears a Supreme Court or superior court judge is so incapacitated as to substantially prevent the judge from performing the duties of office, the governor appoints a commission of three persons to inquire into the circumstances. On their recommendation, the governor may retire the justice or judge from office, on pension, as may be provided by law.	Vacancies on Supreme, superior, appellate division of superior, county, district, tax and municipal courts are filled as in initial selection.
New Mexico.......	Judges are subject to impeachment. The Judicial Standards Commission may discipline or remove a judge for willful misconduct in office, willful and persistent failure to perform duties or habitual intemperance, or retire a judge for disability that seriously interferes with performance of duties and is (or is likely to become) permanent.	Vacancies on Supreme and district courts are filled by gubernatorial appointment (may use nominating commission). Appointee serves until next general election when a successor is elected for remainder of unexpired term. Vacancies on court of appeals are filled by gubernatorial appointment (may use nominating commission), with appointee serving until Dec. 31 following general election or the remainder of the unexpired term, whichever is longer.
New York	All judges are subject to impeachment. Court of Appeals and supreme court judges may be removed by 2/3 concurrence of both houses of legislature. Court of claims, county court, surrogate's court, family court, civil and criminal court (NYC) and district court judges may be removed by 2/3 vote of the senate on recommendation of governor. Commission on Judicial Conduct may determine that a judge be admonished, censured or removed from office for cause, or retired for disability, subject to appeal to the Court of Appeals.	Vacancies on Court of Appeals and appellate division of supreme court are filled as in initial selection. Vacancies in elective judgeships (outside NYC) are filled at the next general election for full term; until election, governor makes appointment (with consent of senate if in session).
North Carolina	Upon recommendation of Judicial Standards Commission, Supreme Court may censure or remove a court of appeals or trial court judge for willful misconduct in office, willful and persistent failure to perform duties, habitual intemperance, conviction of a crime involving moral turpitude, conduct prejudicial to the administration of justice that brings the office into disrepute, or mental or physical incapacity that interferes with the performance of duties and is (or is likely to become) permanent. Upon recommendation of Judicial Standards Commission, a seven-member panel of the court of appeals may censure or remove (for the above reasons) any Supreme Court judge.	Vacancies on Supreme, appeals and superior courts are filled by gubernatorial appointment until next general election. Superior court judges are selected from names submitted by judicial nominating commission.
North Dakota	Supreme and district court judges are subject to impeachment for habitual intemperance, crimes, corrupt conduct, malfeasance or misdemeanor in office. Governor may remove county judges after hearing. All judges are subject to recall election. On recommendation of Commission on Judicial Qualifications or on its own motion, Supreme Court may suspend a judge without salary when judge pleads guilty or no contest or is found guilty of a crime punishable as a felony under state or federal law or any other crime involving moral turpitude under that law. If conviction is reversed, suspension terminates and judge is paid salary for period of suspension. If conviction becomes final, judge is removed by Supreme Court. Upon recommendation of Commission on Judicial Qualifications, Supreme Court may censure or remove a judge for willful misconduct, willful failure to perform duties, willful violation of the code of judicial conduct or habitual intemperance. The Court may also retire a judge for disability that seriously interferes with the performance of duties and is (or is likely to become) permanent.	Vacancies on Supreme and district courts are filled by gubernatorial appointment from nominees submitted by Judicial Nominating Committee until next general election, unless governor calls for a special election to fill vacancy for remainder of term. Vacancies on county courts are filled by appointment by board of county commissioners from names submitted by nominating commission.

State or other jurisdiction	How removed	Vacancies: how filled
Ohio	Judges are subject to impeachment. Judges may be removed by concurrent resolution of 2/3 members of both houses of legislature or removed for cause upon filing of a petition signed by 15% of electors in preceding gubernatorial election. The Board of Commissioners on Grievances and Discipline of the Judiciary may disqualify a judge from office when judge has been indicted for a crime punishable as felony under state or federal law. Board may also remove or suspend a judge for willful and persistent failure to perform duties, habitual intemperance, conduct prejudicial to the administration of justice or which would bring the office into disrepute, or suspension from practice of law, or retire a judge for physical or mental disability that prevents discharge of duties. Judge may appeal action to Supreme Court.	Vacancies are filled by gubernatorial appointment until next general election when successor is elected to fill unexpired term. If unexpired term ends within one year following such election, appointment is made for unexpired term.
Oklahoma	Judges are subject to impeachment for willful neglect of duty, corruption in office, habitual intemperance, incompetency or any offense involving moral turpitude. Upon recommendation of Council on Judicial Complaints, chief justice of Supreme Court may bring charges against any judge in the Court on the Judiciary. Court on the Judiciary may order removal of judge for gross neglect of duty, corruption in office, habitual intemperance, an offense involving moral turpitude, gross partiality in office, oppression in office, or any other ground specified by law. Judge may also be retired (with or without salary) for mental or physical disability that prevents performance of duties, or for incompetence to perform duties.	Vacancies on Supreme Court and Court of Criminal Appeals are filled as in initial selection. Vacancies on court of appeals and district courts are filled by gubernatorial appointment from nominees submitted by Judicial Nominating Commission. For court of appeals vacancies, judge is elected to fill unexpired term at next general election.
Oregon	On recommendation of Commission on Judicial Fitness, Supreme Court may remove a judge for conviction of a felony or crime involving moral turpitude, willful misconduct in office, willful or persistent failure to perform judicial duties, habitual intemperance, illegal use of narcotic drugs, willful violation of rules of conduct prescribed by Supreme Court or general incompetence. A judge may also be retired for mental or physical disability after certification by Commission. Judge may appeal action to Supreme Court.	Vacancies on Supreme Court, court of appeals and circuit courts are filled by gubernatorial appointment, until next general election when judge is selected to fill unexpired term.
Pennsylvania	All judges are subject to impeachment for misdemeanor in office. Upon recommendation of Judicial Inquiry and Review Board, a judge may be suspended, removed or otherwise disciplined by Supreme Court for specific forms of misconduct, neglect of duty or disability.	By gubernatorial appointment (with advice and consent of senate), from names submitted by appropriate nominating commission. Appointee serves until next election if the election is more than 10 months after vacancy occurred.
Rhode Island	All judges are subject to impeachment. The Supreme Court on its own motion may suspend a judge who pleaded guilty or no contest or was found guilty of a crime punishable as felony under state or federal law or any other crime involving moral turpitude. Upon recommendation of the Commission on Judicial Tenure and Discipline, the Supreme Court may censure, suspend, reprimand or remove from office a judge guilty of a serious violation of the canons of judicial ethics or for willful or persistent failure to perform duties, a disabling addiction to alcohol, drugs or narcotics, or conduct that brings the office into disrepute. The Supreme Court may also retire a judge for physical or mental disability that seriously interferes with performance of duties and is (or is likely to become) permanent. Whenever the Commission recommends removal of a Supreme Court justice, the Supreme Court transmits the findings to the speaker of the house of representatives, recommending the initiation of proceedings for the removal of the justice by resolution of the legislature.	Vacancies on Supreme Court are filled by the two houses of the legislature in grand committee until the next election. In case of a judge's temporary inability, governor may appoint a person to fill vacancy. Vacancies on superior, family and district courts are filled by gubernatorial appointment (with advice and consent of senate) from names submitted by nominating commission.
South Carolina	Judges are subject to removal by impeachment or by governor on address of 2/3 of each house of legislature. Supreme Court may retire judges for mental and/or physical disability. Judicial Standards Commission enforces code of judicial conduct.	Vacancies are filled as in initial selection for remainder of unexpired term; if remainder is less than one year, vacancy is filled by gubernatorial appointment. Vacancies on probate courts are filled by gubernatorial appointment until next general election.
South Dakota	Supreme Court justices and circuit court judges are subject to removal by impeachment. Upon recommendation of Judicial Qualifications Commission, Supreme Court may remove a judge from office.	Vacancies on Supreme and circuit courts are filled by gubernatorial appointment from names submitted by Judicial Qualifications Commission for balance of unexpired term.

METHODS FOR REMOVAL OF JUDGES—Continued

State or other jurisdiction	How removed	Vacancies: how filled
Tennessee	Judges are subject to impeachment for misfeasance or malfeasance in office. Upon recommendation of the Court on the Judiciary, the legislature (by concurrent resolution) may remove a judge for willful misconduct in office or physical or mental disability.	Vacancies on Supreme, circuit, criminal and chancery courts are filled by gubernatorial appointment until next biennial election held more than 30 days after vacancy occurred. At election, successor is chosen as in initial selection. Vacancies on court of appeals and court of criminal appeals are filled as in initial selection.
Texas............	Supreme Court, court of appeals and district court judges are subject to removal by impeachment or by joint address of both houses. Supreme Court may remove district judges from office. District judges may remove county judges and justices of the peace. Upon charges filed by the State Commission on Judicial Conduct, the Supreme Court may remove a judge for willful or persistent violation of the code of judicial conduct, and willful or persistent conduct that is clearly inconsistent with the proper performance of duties, or casts public discredit upon the judiciary or administration of justice. The Court may also retire a judge for disability.	Vacancies on appellate and district courts are filled by gubernatorial appointment until next general election, at which time a successor is chosen. Vacancies on county courts are filled by appointment by county commissioner's court until next election when successor is chosen. Vacancies on municipal courts are filled by governing body of municipality for remainder of unexpired term.
Utah	All judges, except justices of the peace, are subject to impeachment. Following investigations and hearings, the Judicial Conduct Commission may order the reprimand, censure, suspension, removal, or involuntary retirement of any judge for willful misconduct, final conviction of a crime punishable as a felony under state or federal law, willful or persistent failure to perform judicial duties, disability that seriously interferes with performance, or conduct prejudicial to the administration of justice that bring the judicial office into disrepute. Prior to implementation, the Supreme Court reviews the order. Lay justices of the peace may be removed for willful failure to participate in judicial education program.	Vacancies on Supreme, district and circuit courts are filled by gubernatorial appointment from candidates submitted by appropriate nominating commission.
Vermont	All judges are subject to impeachment. Supreme Court may discipline, impose sanctions on, or suspend from duties any judge in the state.	Vacancies on Supreme, superior and district courts are filled as in initial selection if senate is in session. Otherwise, by gubernatorial appointment from nominees submitted by judicial nominating board.
Virginia..........	All judges are subject to impeachment. Upon certification of charges against judge by Judicial Inquiry and Review Commission, Supreme Court may remove a judge.	Vacancies are filled as in initial selection if General Assembly is in session. Otherwise, by gubernatorial appointment, with appointee serving until 30 days after commencement of next legislative session.
Washington	A judge of any court of record is subject to impeachment. After notice, hearing and recommendation of Judicial Qualifications Commission, Supreme Court may censure, suspend or remove a judge for violating a rule of judicial conduct. The Supreme Court may also retire a judge for disability that seriously interferes with the performance of duties and is (or is likely to become) permanent.	Vacancies on appellate and general trial courts are filled by gubernatorial appointment until next general election when successor is elected to fill remainder of term.
West Virginia......	Judges are subject to impeachment for maladministration, corruption, incompetency, gross immorality, neglect of duty or any crime or misdemeanor. The Supreme Court of Appeals may censure or suspend a judge for any violation of the judicial code of ethics or retire a judge who is incapable of performing duties because of advancing age, disease or physical or mental infirmity.	Vacancies on appellate and general trial courts are filled by gubernatorial appointment (from names submitted by nominating commission). If unexpired term is less than two years (or such additional period not exceeding three years), appointee serves for remainder of term. If unexpired term is more than three years, appointee serves until next general election, at which time successor is chosen to fill remainder of term.

METHODS FOR REMOVAL OF JUDGES—Continued

State or other jurisdiction	How removed	Vacancies: how filled
Wisconsin	All judges are subject to impeachment. Supreme Court, court of appeals and circuit court judges are subject to removal by address of both houses of legislature with 2/3 of members concurring, and by recall election. As judges of courts of record must be licensed to practice law in state, removal of judge may also be by disbarment. Upon petition of Judicial Commission or on its own motion, Supreme Court may declare a judgeship vacant for judge's misconduct or disability. In case of disability, judge receives salary and benefits for balance of term or until temporary vacancy terminates, whichever comes first.	Vacancies on Supreme Court, court of appeals and circuit courts are filled by gubernatorial appointment from nominees submitted by nominating commission.
Wyoming	All judges, except justices of peace, are subject to impeachment. Upon recommendation of Judicial Supervisory Commission, the Supreme Court may retire or remove a judge. After a hearing before a panel of three district judges, the Supreme Court may remove justices of the peace.	Vacancies are filled as in initial selection. Vacancies on justice of the peace courts are filled by appointment by county commissioners until next general election.
Dist. of Col.	Commission on Judicial Disabilities and Tenure may remove a judge upon conviction of a felony (including a federal crime), for willful misconduct in office, willful and persistent failure to perform judicial duties or for other conduct prejudicial to the administration of justice which brings the office into disrepute.	Vacancies are filled as in initial selection, unless president of the United States fails to nominate candidate within 60 days of receipt of list of nominees from D.C. Judicial Nominating Commission; then Commission nominates and appoints, wth advice and consent of U.S. Senate.
American Samoa ...	U.S. Secretary of the Interior may remove chief and associate justices for cause. Upon recommendation of governor, chief justice may remove associate judges for cause.	Vacancies are filled as in initial selection.
Guam	On recommendation of Judicial Qualifications Commission, a special court of three judges may remove a judge for misconduct or incapacity.	By gubernatorial appointment.
No. Mariana Is.	Judges are subject to impeachment for treason, commission of a felony, corruption or neglect of duty. Upon recommendation of an advisory commission on the judiciary, the governor may remove, suspend or otherwise sanction a judge for illegal or improper conduct.	By gubernatorial appointment.
Puerto Rico	Supreme Court justices are subject to impeachment for treason, bribery, other felonies and misdemeanors involving moral turpitude. Supreme Court may remove other judges for cause (as provided by judiciary act) after a hearing on charges brought by order of chief justice, who disqualifies self from final proceedings.	Vacancies are filled as in initial selection.

Sources: American Judicature Society, 1984 (used with permission); and update by The Council of State Governments.

Table 4.6
COMPENSATION OF JUDGES OF APPELLATE COURTS
AND GENERAL TRIAL COURTS

State or other jurisdiction	Appellate courts				General trial courts	Salary
	Court of last resort	Salary	Intermediate appellate court	Salary		
Alabama	Supreme Court	$77,420(a)	Court of Criminal Appeals	$76,420(b)	Circuit courts	$52,800(c)
			Court of Civil Appeals	76,420(b)		
Alaska	Supreme Court	85,728(d)	Court of Appeals	79,992	Superior courts	77,304(d)
Arizona	Supreme Court	67,500	Court of Appeals	65,500	Superior courts	62,500
Arkansas	Supreme Court	66,010(a)	Court of Appeals	63,463(b)	Chancery court	61,513
					Circuit courts	61,513
California	Supreme Court	94,147(a)	Courts of Appeal	88,264	Superior courts	77,129
Colorado	Supreme Court	63,000(a)	Court of Appeals	58,500(b)	District Court	54,000
Connecticut	Supreme Court	69,103(a,b)	Appellate Court	65,938(b)	Superior courts	62,878
Delaware	Supreme Court	74,640(a)	---	---	Superior courts	70,320(b)
Florida	Supreme Court	78,064	District Court of Appeals	70,448	Circuit courts	67,276
Georgia	Supreme Court	70,885	Court of Appeals	70,340	Superior courts	58,320(c)
Hawaii	Supreme Court	53,460(a)	Intermediate Court of Appeals	51,975(b)	Circuit courts	50,490
Idaho	Supreme Court	59,750(a)	Court of Appeals	58,750	District courts	56,000
Illinois	Supreme Court	85,000	Appellate Court	80,000	Circuit courts	68,000(b)
Indiana	Supreme Court	60,000(e)	Court of Appeals	55,000(e)	Circuit courts	47,000(f)
					Superior courts	47,000(f)
Iowa	Supreme Court	60,900(a)	Court of Appeals	57,800(b)	District courts	54,000(b)
Kansas	Supreme Court	62,396(a)	Court of Appeals	60,169(b)	District courts	(g)
Kentucky	Supreme Court	59,531(a)	Court of Appeals	57,101(b)	Circuit courts	54,671
Louisiana	Supreme Court	66,566	Court of Appeals	63,367	District courts	60,169(h)
Maine	Supreme Judicial Court	65,244(a)	---	---	Superior Court	63,625(a)
Maryland	Court of Appeals	71,000(a)	Court of Special Appeals	68,100(b)	Circuit courts	65,900
Massachusetts	Supreme Judicial Court	80,500(a)	Appeals Court	74,500(b)	Trial Court(i)	71,520(b)
Michigan	Supreme Court	77,000	Court of Appeals	74,592	Circuit courts	42,735(c)
					Recorder's Court (Detroit)	71,484
Minnesota	Supreme Court	68,400(a)	Court of Appeals	63,100(b)	District courts	60,500
Mississippi	Supreme Court	58,000(a)	---	---	Chancery courts	51,000
					Circuit courts	51,000
Missouri	Supreme Court	78,300(a)	Court of Appeals	72,900	Circuit courts	67,500(j)
Montana	Supreme Court	50,452(a)	---	---	District courts	49,178
Nebraska	Supreme Court	61,662	---	---	District courts	57,038
Nevada	Supreme Court	73,500	---	---	District courts	67,000
New Hampshire	Supreme Court	57,641(a)	---	---	Superior Court	56,133(b)
New Jersey	Supreme Court	78,000(a)	Appellate division of Superior Court	75,000	Superior Court	70,000(k)
New Mexico	Supreme Court	57,500(a)	Court of Appeals	54,600(b)	District courts	51,765
New York	Court of Appeals	92,500(a)	Appellate divisions of Supreme Court	87,500(b)	Supreme Court	82,000
North Carolina	Supreme Court	69,144(a,l)	Court of Appeals	65,472(b,l)	Superior Court	58,140(b,l)
North Dakota	Supreme Court	56,856(a)	---	---	District courts	53,383(b)
Ohio	Supreme Court	73,000(a)	Court of Appeals	68,000	Courts of common pleas	57,500(m)
Oklahoma	Supreme Court	68,006(a)	Court of Appeals	63,756	District Court	(n)
	Court of Criminal Appeals	68,006(a)				
Oregon	Supreme Court	69,552(a)	Court of Appeals	67,896(b)	Circuit courts	63,096
			Tax Court	65,172		
Pennsylvania	Supreme Court	76,500(a)	Superior Court	74,500(b)	Courts of common pleas	65,000(b)
			Commonwealth Court	74,500(b)		
Rhode Island	Supreme Court	(a,o)	---	---	Superior Court	(b,o)
South Carolina	Supreme Court	76,773(a)	Court of Appeals	72,935(b)	Circuit Court	72,935
South Dakota	Supreme Court	54,784(a)	---	---	Circuit courts	51,106(b)
Tennessee	Supreme Court	65,650(a)	Court of Appeals	63,125(b)	Chancery courts	60,600
			Court of Criminal Appeals	63,125(b)	Circuit courts	60,600
					Criminal courts	60,600
Texas	Supreme Court	78,795(a)	Courts of Appeals	70,916(b,c)	District courts	56,135(c)
	Court of Criminal Appeals	78,795(a)				
Utah	Supreme Court	58,000(a)	---	---	District courts	54,000
Vermont	Supreme Court	51,700(a)	---	---	Superior courts	49,150(b)
					District courts	49,150(b)
Virginia	Supreme Court	73,619(a)	Court of Appeals	69,938(b)	Circuit courts	68,343
Washington	Supreme Court	66,000	Court of Appeals	63,000	Superior courts	60,000
West Virginia	Supreme Court of Appeals	55,000	---	---	Circuit courts	50,000
Wisconsin	Supreme Court	73,903(a)	Court of Appeals	69,556	Circuit courts	65,208
Wyoming	Supreme Court	63,500	---	---	District courts	61,000
Dist. of Col.	Court of Appeals	74,880(a)	---	---	Superior Court	70,830(b)
American Samoa	High Court	70,026(a)	---	---	(p)	(p)
Guam	---	---	---	---	Superior Court	60,000(b)
Puerto Rico	Supreme Court	60,000(a)	---	---	Superior Court	38,000
					District Court	32,000
Virgin Islands	---	---	---	---	Territorial Court	57,200(b)

COMPENSATION OF JUDGES—Continued

Source: National Center for State Courts, "Survey of Judicial Salaries."
Note: Compensation is shown according to most recent legislation, even though laws may not yet have taken effect.

(a) These jurisdictions pay the following additional amounts to the chief justice or presiding judge of court of last resort:
Alabama, New Mexico, Utah—$1,000.
Arkansas—$5,860.
California—$4,581
Colorado, Missouri, New York, Pennsylvania—$2,500.
Connecticut—$6,857.
Delaware—$4,360.
Hawaii—$2,970.
Idaho—$1,500.
Iowa, Minnesota—$5,300.
Kansas—$1,729.
Kentucky—$1,215.
Maine—$3,241.
Maryland—$1,600.
Massachusetts—$3,000.
Mississippi—chief justice, $2,000; presiding judge, $1,000.
Montana—$1,270.
New Hampshire—$2,235.
New Jersey, South Dakota—$2,000.
North Carolina—$1,464.
North Dakota—$1,591.
Ohio—$5,000.
Oklahoma—$3,036.
Oregon—$1,740.
Rhode Island—see note (o).
South Carolina—$4,041.
Tennessee—$2,525.
Texas—$515.
Vermont—$2,475.
Virginia—$4,868 (plus $4,000 in lieu of travel expenses).
Wisconsin—$8,617.
District of Columbia—$500.
American Samoa—$2,980.
Puerto Rico—$2,600.

(b) Additional amounts paid to various judges:
Alabama—presiding judge, $500.
Arkansas—chief judge, $1,424.
Colorado—chief judge, $2,500.
Connecticut—state court administrator who is also a judge of superior court, $3,270; chief presiding judge of appellate court, $4,225.
Delaware—presiding judge, $4,680.
Hawaii—chief judge, $1,485.
Illinois—chief judge, $5,000.
Iowa—chief judge of court of appeals, $1,300; chief judge of district court, $2,500.
Kansas—chief judge, $1,641.
Kentucky—chief judge, $608.
Maine—chief justice, $3,181.
Maryland—chief judge of court of special appeals, $1,700.

Massachusetts—chief justice of appeals court, $3,000; chief administrative justice, $3,180.
Minnesota—chief judge, $2,700.
New Hampshire—chief judge of superior court, $1,508.
New Mexico—chief judge, $1,050.
New York—presiding judge of appellate division of supreme court, $2,500.
North Carolina—chief judge of court of appeals, $1,464; senior judge of superior court, $1,908.
North Dakota—presiding judge, $1,266.
Oregon—chief judge, $1,656.
Pennsylvania—presiding judges of superior court and commonwealth court, $1,500; president judges of courts of common pleas, additional amounts to $2,000, depending on number of judges and population.
Rhode Island—presiding judge of superior court, see note (o).
South Carolina—chief judge, $3,070.
South Dakota—presiding circuit judge, $1,000.
Tennessee—presiding judge of intermediate appeals court, $1,010.
Texas—chief judge, $463.
Vermont—administrative judges of superior and district courts, $2,550.
Virginia—chief judge, $1,000.
District of Columbia—chief judge of superior court, $500.
Guam—presiding judge, $2,500.
Virgin Islands—presiding judge of territorial court, $2,750.

(c) Plus local supplements, if any. In Texas, for court of appeals, supplements to salary $1,000 less than salary for Supreme Court justice; for district court, supplements to salary $1,000 less than salary of court of appeals judge.

(d) Salaries range from $85,728 to $97,728 for Supreme Court justices and $77,304 to $90,828 for superior court judges, depending on location and cost-of-living differentials.

(e) Plus $3,000 subsistence allowance.

(f) Salaries range from $47,000 to $50,000.

(g) Salary varies according to designation: district judge designated administrative judge, $54,862; district judge, $54,245; associate district judge, $51,779; district magistrate judge, $26,000; associate district judge designated as administrative judge, $52,397.

(h) Base figure.

(i) Superior court department of the trial court.

(j) Circuit court associate judges receive $59,400.

(k) Assignment judges receive $73,000.

(l) Plus 4.8 percent after five years, 9.6 percent after 10 years, 14.4 percent after 15 years, and 19.2 percent after 20 years.

(m) Salaries range from $57,500 to $64,500.

(n) District judges, $56,672. Associate district judges paid on basis of population ranges: over 30,000—$51,005; 10,000 to 30,000—$45,338; under 10,000—$42,504.

(o) Salary varies depending on longevity: associate judges of Supreme Court—$65,660 to $78,237; chief judge of Supreme Court—$68,735 to $81,927; associate judges of superior court—$57,877 to $69,452; presiding judge of superior court—$64,076 to $76,891.

(p) General trial court responsibilities handled by the chief justice or associate judges of the High Court.

173

Table 4.7
SELECTED DATA ON COURT ADMINISTRATIVE OFFICES

State or other jurisdiction	Title	Established	Appointed by(a)	Salary
Alabama	Administrative Director of Courts	1971	CJ	$62,712
Alaska	Administrative Director	1959	CJ (b)	83,728
Arizona	Court Administrator	1960	SC	62,500
Arkansas	Executive Secretary, Judicial Department	1965	CJ (c)	48,117
California	Administrative Director of the Courts	1960	JC	88,264
Colorado	State Court Administrator	1959	SC	58,500
Connecticut	Chief Court Administrator(d)	1965	CJ	72,373
Delaware	Director, Delaware Court System	1971	CJ	50,600
Florida	State Courts Administrator	1972	SC	50,400
Georgia	Director, Administrative Office of the Courts	1973	JC	54,245
Hawaii	Administrative Director of the Courts	1959	CJ (b)	50,490
Idaho	Administrative Director of the Courts	1967	SC	50,000
Illinois	Administrative Director of the Courts	1959	SC	80,000
Indiana	Executive Director, Division of State Court Administration	1975	SC	50,284
Iowa	Court Administrator	1971	SC	48,600
Kansas	Judicial Administrator	1965	CJ	54,245
Kentucky	Administrative Director of the Courts	1976	CJ	46,748
Louisiana	Judicial Administrator	1954	SC	60,169
Maine	Court Administrator	1975	CJ	52,395
Maryland	State Court Administrator	1955	CJ	63,300
Massachusetts	Administrator of Courts for the Trial Court	1978	SC	73,000
Michigan	State Court Administrator	1952	SC	74,592
Minnesota	State Court Administrator	1963	SC	45,500-54,000
Mississippi	Executive Assistant to the Supreme Court	1974	SC	51,000
Missouri	State Court Administrator	1970	SC	62,100
Montana	State Court Administrator	1975	SC	34,099
Nebraska	State Court Administrator	1972	CJ	47,586
Nevada	Director, Office of Court Administration	1971	SC	40,000
New Hampshire	Director of Administrative Services	1980	SC	56,249
New Jersey	Administrative Director of the Courts	1948	CJ	75,000
New Mexico	Director, Administrative Office of the Courts	1959	SC	50,400
New York	Chief Administrator of the Courts(e)	1978	CJ (f)	91,250
North Carolina	Director, Administrative Office of the Courts	1965	CJ	60,048
North Dakota	Court Administrator(g)	1971	CJ	51,504
Ohio	Administrative Director of the Courts	1955	SC	68,200
Oklahoma	Administrative Director of the Courts	1967	SC	63,756
Oregon	Court Administrator	1971	CJ	55,416
Pennsylvania	Court Administrator	1968	SC	60,000
Rhode Island	Court Administrator	1969	CJ	47,570-65,020
South Carolina	Director of Court Administration	1973	CJ	55,767
South Dakota	State Court Administrator	1974	SC	50,065
Tennessee	Executive Secretary of the Supreme Court	1963	SC	63,125
Texas	Administrative Director of the Courts(h)	1977	SC	56,135
Utah	Court Administrator	1973	SC	54,000
Vermont	Court Administrator(i)	1967	SC	49,150
Virginia	Executive Secretary to the Supreme Court	1952	SC	68,343
Washington	Administrator for the Courts	1957	SC (j)	57,000
West Virginia	Administrative Director of the Supreme Court of Appeals	1975	SC	51,000
Wisconsin	Director of State Courts	1978	SC	69,556
Wyoming	Court Coordinator	1974	SC	38,577
Dist. of Col.	Executive Officer of D.C. Courts	1971	(k)	70,830
American Samoa	Court Administrator	1977	CJ	20,177
Guam	Administrative Director of Superior Court	N.A.	CJ (l)	36,838
Puerto Rico	Administrative Director of Court Administration	1952	CJ	40,000

Source: Salary information derived from "Survey of Judicial Salaries," National Center for State Courts.

Key:
SC—State court of last resort.
CJ—Chief justice or chief judge of court of last resort.
JC—Judicial council.
(a) Term of office for all court administrators is at pleasure of appointing authority.
(b) With approval of Supreme Court.
(c) With approval of Judicial Council.
(d) Administrator is a judge of the superior court.
(e) If incumbent is a judge, the title is Chief Administrative Judge of the Courts.
(f) With advice and consent of Administrative Board of the Courts.
(g) Serves as executive secretary to Judicial Council.
(h) Serves as executive director of Judicial Council.
(i) Also clerk of the Supreme Court.
(j) Appointed from list of five submitted by governor.
(k) Joint Committee on Judicial Administration.
(l) Presiding judge of Superior Court (general trial court).

CHAPTER FIVE

STATE ELECTIONS

ELECTION LEGISLATION: 1984-85

By Richard G. Smolka

Although little in the way of major election legislation was initiated by the states during the 1984-85 biennium, federal court decisions continued to affect existing state election laws. Two important decisions, if upheld by the U.S. Supreme Court, could substantially limit state authority over legislative districting and primary elections. At issue are state laws affecting the methods by which state legislatures draw district lines and the way political parties conduct nominations.

A federal court ruled legislative district lines drawn by the Indiana state legislature for the purpose of enhancing the political strength of one party were unconstitutional "political gerrymanders." Indiana appealed the ruling to the U.S. Supreme Court whose forthcoming decision in *Bandemer v. Davis* (No. 85-766) will ultimately affect how all legislative districts may be drawn, not only for the state legislature, but for Congress and local governments as well.

A second major federal court decision affects the relationship between state law and party organization. For many states, the law prescribes a closed party system in which only voters registered in a political party may vote in that party's primary. However, the Connecticut Republican Party recently changed its rules to allow independents to vote in its party primary for candidates for certain offices.

After failing to get the state law changed, the party filed suit in federal court and won. A three-judge panel for the Second Circuit Court of Appeals in Manhattan upheld the lower court ruling that the state cannot prohibit a party from determining who may vote in its primary elections (*Republican Party of Connecticut v. Tashjian*, No. 85-7011). The U.S. Supreme Court agreed to hear argument on the case during its fall 1986 term.

If the Supreme Court upholds the lower court ruling, state legislatures would no longer be able to mandate closed primary elections against party wishes. Depending upon how much authority the court is willing to allow the political parties, other laws regarding the method of nomination or even the date of the primary election could be affected.

A series of federal court decisions is also having an impact on state election calendars. At issue is the period of time that is necessary to ensure that military and overseas citizens are able to obtain and return an absentee ballot. Testimony in these cases indicates that thousands of persons who made a timely application for a ballot were unable to obtain it, and hence, were disfranchised.

The federal courts have consistently ruled that states must count absentee ballots voted by election day even though they were not returned by the legal deadline—unless the absentee ballots were made available approximately 45 days before an election. Florida, Minnesota, New York, and Wisconsin are among the states that have been affected by the court rulings. Election calendars are being changed to allow greater time between the first day absentee ballots may be sent and the deadline for their return.

Voting Procedures for Handicapped Persons

For more than 20 years, state laws have been changing to make voter registration more accessible and voting more convenient—for most citizens. More recently, however, state legislatures, as well as the Congress, have begun to recognize the special needs of physically handicapped persons. During 1984-85, new federal and state laws required that every polling place be accessible to handicapped persons and that certain notices be printed in large type to aid the visually-impaired. Many states, whether required to or not, also initiated services to aid the hearing-impaired with registration and voting.

The federal government enacted the Voting Accessibility for the Elderly and Handicapped Act (P. L. 98-435) on September 29, 1984. This legislation required the chief election officers of each state to ensure that all polling places used in federal elections would be accessible to the elderly and the handicapped. (The law allows each state to define "ac-

Richard G. Smolka is Professor of Government at the American University in Washington, D.C., and Editor of *Election Administration Reports*.

cessibility.") Recognizing that accessibility would not be immediate for each of the approximately 175,000 polling places across the nation, Congress allowed the chief election officer in each state to permit exceptions. Before an exemption can be granted, however, the local government must survey and determine that none are accessible (or can be made temporarily accessible), and that handicapped or elderly voters may be assigned to an accessible polling place or be provided with an alternative means of casting a ballot in a federal election.

The chief election officer also must determine the number of accessible and inaccessible polling places around the state on election day (along with the reasons for any cases of inaccessibility), and report this information to the Federal Election Commission not later than December 31 of each even-numbered year.

Prior to passage of the federal law, several states had required all polling places to be accessible to the handicapped in the same manner as other public buildings, although most allowed exceptions under certain conditions. Others made provisions for "curbside voting" or other means to accommodate persons who could not get to the polls. Following passage of the federal law, many states enacted legislation either requiring accessibility or specifically authorizing procedures that would allow handicapped persons to vote at other polling places or in a way not possible under existing law.

The federal law also required that instructions—printed in large type—be conspicuously displayed at each permanent registration facility and each polling place, and mandated states to provide voter information by telecommunications devices for the deaf. State legislatures incorporated some of these provisions into the appropriate sections of their state election codes.

State Administrative Responsibility

During 1984-85, several states moved to concentrate authority over various aspects of elections in a single agency. The role of the office of the secretary of state or the state board of elections was expanded to allow the agencies to prescribe details of administration. This centralization of authority was furthered by the requirements of the federal law on voting accessibility, but included other matters ranging from standard voter registration forms to statewide absentee ballot application forms and other administrative procedures.

States also moved to exercise more authority over certification and decertification of vote counting devices. Developments in punchcard vote counting, electronic voting, and voting systems standards were considered in several states. State boards of elections or chief election officers were given greater authority in certifying and monitoring new voting machines and vote counting devices, and several states attempted to specify with greater precision exactly what such devices must do. New York, Illinois, and Texas were among the states that expanded state authority over the technology of counting votes. The Federal Election Commission's National Clearinghouse on Election Administration convened an advisory panel of state and local officials to help states develop standards for the use of voting equipment.

States also expanded responsibility over multicounty elections and experimental developments in elections. Following the lengthy congressional recount of the 8th Congressional District race in 1984, Indiana provided for a single recount board for multicounty offices rather than allowing separate recount boards in each county. Kansas, Montana, and Oregon provided extensive state monitoring of mail ballot elections. Secretaries of state in California and Oregon each appointed for the first time a state investigator to work with local election officials to identify possible violations of the law and to protect the integrity of the election system.

Voter Registration

The trend of easing voter registration continued during 1984-85. No state made registration more difficult; in fact, many states eased the process through greater involvement by state officials and/or private citizens. Executive orders by governors in Idaho, New York, Ohio, and Texas, allowed state employees to provide certain registration services, including making registration forms available through a variety of state offices. Although the gubernatorial initiatives were questioned by the federal Office of Personnel Management as a potential misuse of state employees in violation of the Intergovernmental Personnel Act, possible objections were withdrawn when the states reacted strongly and emphasized that the registration process was being conducted in a non-partisan manner.

Several states introduced or liberalized deputy registrar programs that allowed almost anyone to register voters. Illinois law provided that deputies be named by civic groups, but allowed such groups to name any number of deputy registrars. In Chicago, some of the deputy registrars failed to return completed registration forms by the deadline prior to the election. The Chicago Board of Election Commissioners ultimately obtained a court order compelling the delinquent deputies to submit the completed registrations so that no one who registered with these deputies would be denied the vote.

Exit Polls

Since the 1980 presidential election, several states have attempted to eliminate or reduce potential adverse effects on voter turnout created by media projections of presidential election results while polls are still open in some states. State legislation took the form of prohibiting certain kinds of activity within specified distances of polling places. A federal court, however, ruled that the State of Washington could not enforce a blanket prohibition against exit poll activity, although any specific activity deemed to be disruptive at the polls could be regulated. As a result, state law has become more specific as to what types of exit poll activity can take place near the polling places.

Elections by All-Mail Ballot

Montana and Kansas became the latest states to permit local jurisdictions to use an all-mail ballot option in lieu of an election at the polls. The use of all-mail ballots proved as popular in those states as in California and Oregon where the procedure has been used for special district and small jurisdiction elections because it costs much less to administer and produces higher voter participation. All-mail ballots, however, rarely have been used in contested candidate elections. Although opponents of the procedure have cited possible fraud as a major argument, there has been no evidence of vote fraud in the states where the procedure has been used.

Presidential Primaries

The number of states holding presidential primaries had been increasing over several elections, but declined in 1984. Following that election, several states—primarily southern states determined to have a greater impact on the choice of presidential nominees—attempted to establish primary election days that would fall early in the year. The concept of a southern regional primary election (to be conducted around the second week of March) took hold, and legislatures in the region began to pass laws with the hope that up to 11 southern and border states would join in a single important primary election day.

At least some of the momentum for the southern regional primary has been attributed to the fact that states have been subjected against their will to national party rules for conducting the primary election; and setting the election date seems to many to be about the most important action a legislature can take. Some legislators in states outside the South reacted to the idea of the regional primary by introducing legislation that would move their own state primary elections to the same week. Although this flurry of activity was not intended to create a national primary election, the prospect of such an event is no longer as remote as it once was.

Selected References

Alexander, Herbert E. *Financing Politics*. 3rd ed. Washington, D.C.: CQ Press, 1984.
_____. "Before Nomination: Our Primary Problems." Washington, D.C.: American Enterprise Institute, 1985.
Moore, Jonathan, ed. *Campaign for President: The Managers Look at '84*. Dover, Mass.: Auburn House, 1986.
Palmer, James A. and Edward D. Feigenbaum. *Campaign Finance Law 1986*. Washington, D.C.: Federal Election Commission, 1986.
Smolka, Richard G. *Election Administration Reports*. A biweekly newsletter for election officials. Washington, D.C.
_____. "Symposium: Gerrymandering and the Courts." *UCLA Law Review* 33, 1 (October 1985): 1-282.

Table 5.1

STATE OFFICIALS TO BE ELECTED: 1986 AND 1987

State or other jurisdiction	Date of general elections in 1986(a)	Governor	Lieutenant governor	Secretary of state	Attorney general	Treasurer	Auditor	Judges of court of last resort(b)	Judges of intermediate appellate court(b)	Board of education members	Public utilities commissioners	Superintendent of public instruction	Other	Senate	House
Alabama	Nov. 4	★	★	★	★	★	★	3	1(c)	4	2		Commr. of agriculture and industries	All	All
Alaska	Nov. 4	★	★					1	2					1/2	All
Arizona	Nov. 4	★		★	★	★	★	1	2				State mine inspector; corporation commr.	All	All
Arkansas	Nov. 4	★	★	★	★	★	★	1	2				Land commr.	1/2(d)	All
California	Nov. 4	★	★	★	★	★	★			1		★	Comptroller; 4 mbrs. bd. of equalization	1/2	All
Colorado	Nov. 4	★	★	★	★	★				1			3 Univ. of Colorado regents	1/2	All
Connecticut	Nov. 4	★	★	★	★	★							Comptroller	All	All
Delaware	Nov. 4				★	★	★	5	19				Comptroller; commr. of agriculture	1/2(d)	All
Florida	Nov. 4	★		★	★	★		2	5		2	★	Comptroller general; commr. of agriculture; commr. of labor	1/2	All
Georgia	Nov. 4	★	★	★	★						2	★		All	All
Hawaii	Nov. 4	★	★							6				1/2(d)	All
Idaho	Nov. 4	★	★	★	★	★	★	2	1			★	Comptroller; 3 Univ. of Illinois trustees	All	All
Illinois	Nov. 4	★	★	★	★	★			8				Secy. of agriculture	2/3(d)	All
Indiana	Nov. 4			★		★	★							1/2	All
Iowa	Nov. 4	★	★	★	★	★	★	2	3					1/2	All
Kansas	Nov. 4	★	★	★	★	★		2	3	5			Insurance commr.		All
Kentucky (1987)	Nov. 3	★	★	★	★	★	★	1					Commr. of agriculture	1/2	All
Louisiana (1987)	(e)	★	★	★	★	★		2	3		2	★	Commr. of agriculture; commr. of elections; commr. of insurance	All	All
Maine	Nov. 4	★						1						All	All
Maryland	Nov. 4	★	★		★			1	1				Comptroller	All	All
Massachusetts	Nov. 4	★	★	★	★	★	★	2	6				9 executive councillors	All	All
Michigan	Nov. 4	★	★	★	★			2	6	2			2 university regents	All	All
Minnesota	Nov. 4	★	★	★	★	★	★	2						All	All
Mississippi (1987)	Nov. 3	★	★	★	★	★	★				3		Commr. of agriculture and commerce; commr. of insurance		All
Missouri	Nov. 4			★	★	★	★	1	7				Comptroller	1/2	All
Montana	Nov. 4						★	1		4	2			1/2(d)	All
Nebraska	Nov. 4	★	★	★	★	★	★	2	6	5	2		Controller; 3 university regents	1/2(d)	U
Nevada	Nov. 4	★	★	★	★	★	★	2					5 executive councillors	1/2(d)	All
New Hampshire (1987)	Nov. 3	★												All	All
New Mexico	Nov. 4	★	★	★	★	★	★	2	2	3			Corporation commr.; commr. of public lands	All	All
New York	Nov. 4	★	★		★			2	2				Comptroller	All	All
North Carolina	Nov. 4			★	★	★	★	3	2					All	All
North Dakota	Nov. 4					★		2			1		Labor commr.	1/2	All
Ohio	Nov. 4	★		★	★	★	★	3	53	21				1/2	All

STATE OFFICIALS TO BE ELECTED: 1986 AND 1987—Continued

State or other jurisdiction	Date of general elections in 1986(a)	Governor	Lieutenant governor	Secretary of state	Attorney general	Treasurer	Auditor	Judges of court of last resort(b)	Judges of intermediate appellate court(b)	Board of education members	Public utilities commissioners	Superintendent of public instruction	Other	State legislatures: members to be elected — Senate	State legislatures: members to be elected — House
Oklahoma	Nov. 4	★	★		★	★	★	6(f)	6			★	Corporation commr.; insurance commr.	1/2	All
Oregon	Nov. 4	★			★	★	★		2			★	Labor commr.	1/2	All
Pennsylvania	Nov. 4	★	★		★	★							...	1/2	All
Rhode Island	Nov. 4	★	★	★	★	★							...	All	All
South Carolina	Nov. 4	★	★	★	★	★						★	Comptroller; commr. of agriculture; adjutant general	...	All
South Dakota	Nov. 4	★	★	★	★	★	★	2			1		Commr. of school and public lands	All	All
Tennessee	Nov. 4	★		★		★							...	1/2(d)	All
Texas	Nov. 4	★			★			7(g)					Comptroller; commr. of agriculture; commr. of general land office	1/2(d)	All
Utah	Nov. 4							1		5			...	1/2(d)	All
Vermont	Nov. 4	★	★	★	★	★	★						...	All	All
Virginia ......(1987)	Nov. 3												...	All	All
Washington	Nov. 4							3	3				...	1/2(d)	All
West Virginia	Nov. 4							1	4				...	1/2	All
Wisconsin	Apr. 1							1	1				...	...	All
Wisconsin (1987)	Apr. 7							1	1				...	1/2(d)	All
Wyoming	Nov. 4	★		★		★	★					★	...	1/2	All
Dist. of Col.	Nov. 4	★(h)											...	(i)	U
American Samoa	Nov. 4												...	All	All
Guam	Nov. 4	★								3			Village commrs.	All	U
No. Mariana Is.(1987)	Nov. 3									3			...	...	All
Puerto Rico	Nov. 4												...	All	...
Virgin Islands	Nov. 4												...	All	U

Source: State election administration offices.

Note: In several states, elections for some state offices do not occur in 1986 or 1987. When a number appears in a column instead of a star, the figure indicates the number of individuals on the state court or other government body up for election in 1986 or 1987. The information in this table is current as of February 1986.

Key:
★—Office up for election.
...—Office not up for election.
U—Unicameral legislative body.

(a) Elections for 1987 are indicated by (1987) before date for general election.
(b) For some states, information on number of judges facing election in 1986 or 1987 is tentative given the nature of the selection and retention processes.

(c) Court of Civil Appeals.
(d) Actual number of seats up for election: Arkansas (17); Delaware (11); Hawaii (12); Illinois (39); Nebraska (24); Nevada (11); Tennessee (17); Texas (16); Utah (14); Washington (24); Wisconsin (17).
(e) Under Louisiana's election law, candidates of all parties run together on a single ballot in September; if no candidate for an office wins a majority of the vote, the top two finishers oppose each other in a November runoff. In 1986, the elections will be held on Sept. 27, 1986 and Nov. 4, 1986. In 1987, the elections will be held on Oct. 24, 1987 and Nov. 21, 1987.
(f) Supreme Court (5); Court of Criminal Appeals (1).
(g) Supreme Court (4); Court of Criminal Appeals (3).
(h) Mayor.
(i) Chairman and four members of the Council of the District of Columbia.

Table 5.2
METHODS OF NOMINATING CANDIDATES FOR STATE OFFICES

State or other jurisdiction	Method(s) of nominating candidates
Alabama...................	Primary election; however, the state executive committee or other governing body of any political party may choose instead to hold a state convention for the purpose of nominating candidates (meetings must be held at least 60 days prior to the date on which primaries are conducted).
Alaska....................	Primary election.
Arizona...................	Primary election.
Arkansas	Primary election.
California................	Primary election.
Colorado	Primary election; however, a political party may hold a pre-primary convention (at least 55 days before the primary) for the designation of candidates. Each candidate who receives at least 20 percent of the convention delegates' votes is listed on the primary ballot, with the candidate receiving the most votes listed first.
Connecticut	Convention/primary election. Political parties hold state conventions (convening not earlier than the 61st day and closing not later than the 43rd day before the date of the primary) for the purpose of endorsing candidates. If no one challenges the endorsed nominee (who received at least 20 percent of the delegate vote), no primary election is held. However, if anyone challenges the nominee by filing a candidacy of nomination (having also received at least 20 percent of the delegate vote), a primary election is held to determine the party candidate for the general election.
Delaware	Primary election.
Florida	Primary election.
Georgia...................	Primary election; however, the state executive committee or other governing body of any political party may choose instead to hold a state convention for the purpose of nominating candidates (meetings must be held at least 90 days before the date on which primaries are held).
Hawaii	Primary election.
Idaho	Primary election.
Illinois...................	Primary election; however, state conventions are held for the nomination of candidates for trustees of the University of Illinois.
Indiana	Primary election held for the nomination of candidates for governor and U.S. senator; state party conventions held for the nomination of candidates for other state offices.
Iowa	Primary election; however, if there are more than two candidates for any nomination and none receives at least 35 percent of the primary vote, the primary is deemed inconclusive and the nomination is made by party convention.
Kansas	Primary election; however, candidates of any political party whose secretary of state did not poll at least 5 percent of the total vote cast for all candidates for that office in the preceding general election are restricted to nomination by delegate or mass convention.
Kentucky	Primary election.
Louisiana	Primary election. Open primary system requires all candidates, regardless of party affiliation, to appear on a single ballot. Candidate who receives over 50 percent of the vote in the primary is elected to office; if no candidate receives a majority vote, a runoff election is held between the two candidates who received the most votes.
Maine	Primary election.
Maryland	Primary election.
Massachusetts	Primary election.
Michigan	Primary election held for the nomination of candidates for governor, U.S. congressional seats and state senators and representatives; state conventions held for the nomination of candidates for lieutenant governor, secretary of state and attorney general.
Minnesota	Primary election.
Mississippi	Primary election.
Missouri	Primary election.
Montana..................	Primary election.

State or other jurisdiction	Method(s) of nominating candidates
Nebraska	Primary election.
Nevada	Primary election.
New Hampshire	Primary election.
New Jersey	Primary election.
New Mexico	Primary election; however, minor parties (those receiving less than 15 percent of the total number of votes cast at the last general election for governor or U.S. president) may nominate candidates by political convention.
New York	Convention/primary election. The person who receives the majority vote at the state party committee meeting becomes the designated candidate for nomination; however, all other persons who received at least 25 percent of the convention vote may demand that their names appear on the primary ballot as candidates for nomination.
North Carolina	Primary election.
North Dakota	Primary election.
Ohio	Primary election.
Oklahoma	Primary election.
Oregon	Primary election.
Pennsylvania	Primary election.
Rhode Island	Primary election.
South Carolina	Primary election; however, the state executive committee or other governing body of any political party may choose instead to hold a state convention for the purpose of nominating candidates (nominations must be announced no later than poll closing time on the date of the primary election).
South Dakota	Primary election. Any candidate who receives a plurality of the primary vote becomes the nominee; however, if no individual receives at least 35 percent of the vote for the candidacy for the offices of governor or U.S. congressman, the nominee is selected by party convention.
Tennessee	Primary election.
Texas	Primary election.
Utah	Convention/primary election. Delegates from the county primary conventions are elected to the state primary convention for the purpose of selecting the political party nominees to run at the regular primary election.
Vermont	Primary election.
Virginia	Primary election; however, the state executive committee or other governing body of any political party may choose instead to hold a state convention for the purpose of nominating candidates (party opting for convention can only do so within 32 days prior to date on which primary elections are normally held).
Washington	Primary election.
West Virginia	Primary election.
Wisconsin	Primary election.
Wyoming	Primary election.
Dist. of Col.	Primary election.

Note: The nominating methods described here are for state offices; procedures may vary for local candidates. Also, independent candidates may have to petition for nomination. For more information on primaries, see Table 5.3, "Primary Election Information."

Table 5.3
PRIMARY ELECTION INFORMATION

State or other jurisdiction	Dates of 1986 primaries for state officials(a)		Party affiliation for primary voting		Voters receive ballot of:	
	Primary	Runoff primary(b)	Voters must declare/change affiliation prior to election day	Voters select party on election day	One party (c)	All parties partici- pating(d)
Alabama	June 3	June 24	...	★	★	...
Alaska	Aug. 26	...		(e)	...	★(e)
Arizona	Sept. 9	...	At least 50 days before	...	★	...
Arkansas	May 27	June 10	...	★	★	...
California	June 3	...	At least 29 days before	...	★	...
Colorado	Aug. 12	...	At least 32 days before	...	★	...
Connecticut	Sept. 9	...	At least 6 months before(f)	...	★	...
Delaware	Sept. 6	...	At least 21 days before	...	★	...
Florida	Sept. 2	Sept. 30	At least 30 days before	...	★	...
Georgia	Aug. 12	Sept. 2	...	★	★	...
Hawaii	Sept. 20	...	...	★	...	★
Idaho	May 27	...	...	★	...	★
Illinois	March 18	...	...	★	★	...
Indiana	May 6	...	...	★	★	...
Iowa	June 3	...	...	★	★	...
Kansas	Aug. 5	...	At least 20 days before(f)	(f)	★	...
Kentucky	May 27	...	At least 30 days before	...	★	...
Louisiana	Sept. 27(g)	Nov. 4(g)	...	(g)	...	(g)
Maine	June 10	...	At least 90 days before(f)	(f)	★	...
Maryland	Sept. 9	...	At least 4 months before(f)	...	★	...
Massachusetts	Sept. 16	...	At least 28 days before(f)	(f)	★	...
Michigan	Aug. 5	...	...	★	...	★
Minnesota	Sept. 9	...	...	★	...	★
Mississippi	June 3	June 24	...	★	★	...
Missouri	Aug. 5	...	...	★	★	...
Montana	June 3	...	...	★	...	★
Nebraska	May 13	...	At least 10 days before	...	★	...
Nevada	Sept. 2	...	At least 30 days before	...	★	...
New Hampshire	Sept. 9	...	At least 10 days before	...	★	...
New Jersey	June 3	...	At least 50 days before(f)	(f)	★	...
(1987)	June 2					
New Mexico	June 3	...	At least 42 days before(h)	...	★	...
New York	Sept. 9	...	At least 1 year before(f)	...	★	...
North Carolina	May 6	June 3	At least 21 days before(i)	...	★	...
North Dakota	June 10	...	...	★	...	★
Ohio	May 6	...	...	★	★	...
Oklahoma	Aug. 26	Sept. 16	(j)	(j)	★	...
Oregon	May 20	...	At least 20 days before(f)	...	★	...
Pennsylvania	May 20	...	At least 30 days before	...	★	...
Rhode Island	Sept. 9	...	At least 90 days before(f)	(f)	★	...
South Carolina	June 10	June 24	...	★	★	...
South Dakota	June 3	...	At least 15 days before	...	★	...
Tennessee	Aug. 7	...	...	★	★	...
Texas	May 3	June 7	...	★	★	...
Utah	Aug. 19	...	...	★	...	★
Vermont	Sept. 9	...	...	★	...	★
Virginia	June 10	...	...	★	★	...
(1987)	June 9					
Washington	Sept. 16	...	...	(e)	...	★(e)
West Virginia	May 13	...	At least 30 days before	...	★	...
Wisconsin	Sept. 9	...	...	★	...	★
Wyoming	Aug. 19	...	...	★	★	...
Dist. of Col.	Sept. 9	...	At least 30 days before	...	★	...
Guam	Sept. 2	...	...	★	...	★
Virgin Islands	Sept. 2	...	At least 30 days before	...	★	...

PRIMARY ELECTION INFORMATION—Continued

Sources: Federal Election Commission; League of Women Voters, *Easy Does It*; state election administration offices.

(a) Primaries for state offices in 1987 have (1987) before the date.

(b) A runoff election between the top two candidates is held if the leading candidate does not get a majority of the votes cast in the first primary.

(c) The type of primary in which voters receive only the ballot of their party choice in a primary (voters must declare their affiliation on, or prior to, election day) is generally referred to as a *closed* primary.

(d) The type of primary in which voters receive a ballot for all parties and select the party of their choice in the privacy of the voting booth is generally referred to as an *open* primary.

(e) Voters are not restricted to one party. In Alaska and Washington, voters participate in a *blanket* primary. As in regular open primaries, voters receive a ballot that contains the primary ballot for all parties. However, a voter in the blanket primary may pick and choose among the parties in moving through the lists of candidates for various offices. The only restriction is that the voter can indicate only one preference for each office.

(f) Applies to previously affiliated registered voters. In Connecticut, unaffiliated voters must declare at least 14 days before. In Kansas, Maine, Massachusetts, New Jersey (new voters), and Rhode Island, unaffiliated voters may declare party at the polls. In Maryland and Oregon, new registrants declare at time of registration. In New York, new voters declare affiliation at least 30 days before, while previously eligible voters declare at least 60 days before.

(g) Louisiana has an open primary which requires all candidates, regardless of party affiliation, to appear on a single ballot. If a candidate receives over 50 percent of the vote in the primary, he is elected to the office. If no candidate receives a majority vote, then a single election is held between the two candidates receiving the most votes.

(h) Previously affiliated voters may not change party affiliation after proclamation of primary.

(i) Business days.

(j) New registrants declare at time of registration; however, no changes in party affiliation are allowed between July 1 and Sept. 30 in an even-numbered year.

Table 5.4
CAMPAIGN FINANCE LAWS: GENERAL FILING REQUIREMENTS
(As of January 1986)

State or other jurisdiction	Statements required from	Statements filed with	Time for filing
Alabama	Political committees.	Secy. of state for statewide and judicial offices. Secy. of state and probate judge in county of residence for legislative office.	15 days after primary or runoff and 30 days after any other election.
Alaska	Candidates; groups and individuals who contribute $250 or more per year to any group or candidate; a business entity, labor organization or municipality making a contribution or expenditure; suppliers receiving more than $250 from a candidate or group.	Alaska Public Offices Commission, central office.	30 days and 1 week before and 10 days after election; annually on Dec. 31 for contributions and expenditures received but not reported that year.(a)
Arizona	Candidates, committees and continuing political organizations.	Secy. of state.	10-15 days before and 20 days after primary; 10-15 days before and 20 days after general or special election; supplemental reports annually by Apr. 1 for contributions and expenditures subsequent to post-election report.
Arkansas	Candidates and persons acting on their behalf receiving contributions in excess of $250/election from any person.	Secy. of state and county clerk in county of residence.	Contributions: 25 and 7 days before and 30 days after election. Expenditures: 30 days after election. Supplemental reports for expenditures subsequent to post-election report.
California	Candidates receiving or spending more than $500 in an election; certain committees; elected officers.	Secy. of state, registrar of Los Angeles and San Francisco and clerk of county of residence; legislative candidates also file with clerk of county with largest number of registered voters in district.	Semiannual: July and Jan. 31; periodic: March and Sept. 22 and 12 days before 1st Tues. after 1st Mon. in June and Nov.; 40 and 12 days before and 65 days after any election not held on the 1st Tues. after the 1st Mon. of June or Nov.(b)
Colorado	Candidates; certain political committees; persons making independent expenditures of more than $100.	Secy. of state.	11 days before and 30 days after election. Supplemental reports annually on the anniversary of the election until no unexpended balance or deficit.(c)
Connecticut	Candidates, political committees, and party committees receiving or spending over $500 in a single election.	Secy. of state.	2nd Thurs. of Jan., Apr., July, Oct.; 7 days before and 30 days after primary (45 days after general election). Supplemental reports for deficits: 90 days after election and within 30 days after any change and within 7 days after distribution of surplus funds.
Delaware	Candidates, committees.	State election commissioner.	20 days before election, Dec. 31 of election year, Dec. 31 of post-election year and annually by Dec. 31 until fund closes.
Florida	Candidates; political committees; committees of continuous existence; party executive committees; persons making independent expenditures of $100 or more.	Qualifying officer and supervisor of elections in county of residence for candidates. Division of elections and supervisor of elections in county where election is held for statewide committees.	Pre-election: 10th day of each calendar quarter from time treasurer is appointed through last day of qualifying for office; the 4th, 18th and 32nd days preceding the first and second primaries, and the 4th and 18th days preceding the general election for unopposed candidates. Post-election report 10 days after each quarter until no unexpended surplus.
Georgia	Candidates, committees, and certain other individuals or organizations.	Secy. of state and copy to probate judge in candidate's county of residence.	45 and 15 days before and 10 days after primary and 15 days before general or special election; Dec. 31 of election year; and annually on Dec. 31 for winning candidates with additional contributions or expenditures since filing post-election report.
Hawaii	Candidates, parties, committees.	Campaign Spending Commission.	10 working days before each election; 20 days after primary and 30 days after general or special election. Supplemental reports in event of surplus or deficit over $250 on 5th day after the last day of election year, and every 6 months thereafter.

GENERAL FILING REQUIREMENTS—Continued

State or other jurisdiction	Statements required from	Statements filed with	Time for filing
Idaho	Candidates; political committees; organizations which contribute more than $500 to a political committee; persons making independent expenditures of more than $50.	Secy. of state.	By 7 days before election and 30 days after.(d) Supplemental reports on 10th day of Jan., Apr., July and Oct. annually in the event of an unexpended balance or expenditure deficit.
Illinois..............	Political committees.	State Board of Elections.	Contributions: 15 days before election and 90 days after each general election. Annual reports of contributions and expenditures: July 31.
Indiana	Political committees and any person making an independent expenditure.	State Election Board; legislative candidate committees file duplicate with elections board of candidate's county of residence.	10 days (if postmarked) or 8 days (if hand-delivered) before election or convention; 20 days after convention, if no pre-convention report is filed; annually by Jan. 15.
Iowa	Candidates and committees receiving contributions of or spending more than $250.	Campaign Finance Disclosure Commission.	20th day of Jan., May, July, and Oct. annually. In years in which the candidate does not stand for election, the May and July reports are not required of a candidate committee.
Kansas	Candidates; political committees; party committees; persons making independent expenditures of more than $100.	Secy. of state.	6 days before election and Dec. 10 of election years.
Kentucky	Candidates, campaign committees, political party executive committees, permanent committees.	Kentucky Registry of Election Finance with duplicates to clerk of county where candidate resides. Campaign committees file with appropriate central campaign committees.	Candidates and campaign committees: 32 and 12 days before and 30 days after election. Political party executive committees: 30 days after election. Permanent committees: last day of each calendar quarter. Semiannual supplemental reports June 30 and Dec. 31 until fund shows a zero balance.
Louisiana	Candidates; political committees; any person (not a candidate) making independent expenditures or accepting contributions (other than to or from a candidate) of more than $500.	Supervisory Committee.	Candidates and committees: 180, 90, 30, and 10 days before primary; 10 days before and 40 days after general election; Jan. 15 annually until a deficit has been paid, or if the candidate or committee has received contributions or made expenditures during the year.(e)
Maine	Candidates; political committees; state party committees; political action committees; any person (not a candidate) making expenditures of more than $50.	Commission on Governmental Ethics and Election Practices.	7 days before and 42 days after election; gubernatorial candidates also file Jan. 15 after non-election years if they received or spent more than $1,000 in that year, and 42 days before election. Disposition of surplus or deficit in excess of $50 on 1st day of each quarter of fiscal year until eliminated.(f)
Maryland	Candidates receiving contributions of or spending $300 or more; political committtees; political clubs spending more than $50.	Board at which candidate filed certificate of candidacy. Central committees and political committees file with State Administrative Board of Election Laws.	4th Tues. before primary; 2nd Fri. before any election; 3rd Tues. after general election or before taking office, whichever is earlier. Disposition of surplus or deficit 6 months after general election and annually on anniversary of election until eliminated.
Massachusetts	Candidates and political committees.	Director of campaign and political finance.	8 days before election and Jan. 10 of year after general election for General Assembly candidates; 3rd business day after designating depository and Jan. 10 of year after general election for others.
Michigan	Candidates; political committees; party committees; persons making independent expenditures of $100 or more.	Secy. of state.	11 days before and 30 days after election; committees other than independent committees by Jan. 31 of each year.(g)

State or other jurisdiction	Statements required from	Statements filed with	Time for filing
Minnesota	Candidates; political committees; party committees; and individuals making independent expenditures over $100.	Ethical Practices Board. Legislative candidates file copies with auditor of each county in district.	10 days before election and Jan. 31 annually.(h)
Mississippi	Candidates and political committees.	Secy. of state.	Contributions: 5th day of each month of candidacy and Sat. before election. Expenditures: candidates report within 60 days after election; committees, within 30 days.
Missouri	Candidates who spend or receive more than $1,000 or who receive a single contribution in excess of $250; committees; and persons making independent expenditures of $500 or more.	Secy. of state for statewide candidates and committees, and candidates for Supreme Court or appellate court; candidates for legislature file with secy. of state and election authority of candidate's place of residence.	40 and 7 days before and 30 days after election. Supplemental reports each Jan. 15 if contributions or expenditures of $500 or more were made or received since last report. Quarterly reports if post-election report shows outstanding debts of more than $500, until deficit is below $500.(i)
Montana	Candidates and political committees.	Commissioner of political practices and county clerk or recorder where candidate resides or political committee has headquarters.	Statewide office: March 10 and Sept. 10 in election years. 15 and 25 days before and 20 days after election; supplemental reports March 10 and Sept. 10 until all debts and obligations are extinguished and no more contributions are accepted or expenditures made. Legislative office: 10 days before and 20 days after election.(j)
Nebraska	Candidate committees, political party committees, and certain other committees.	Nebraska Accountability and Disclosure Commission and election commissioner or clerk of candidate's county of residence.	30 and 10 days before and 40 days after election. June 1 annually for certain committees.(k)
Nevada	Candidates, party committees, and other committees spending over $500.	Officer with whom candidate filed declaration of candidacy.	15 days before primary and 15 days before and 30 days after general election.
New Hampshire	Candidates, and political committees spending over $500.	Secy. of state.	Wed. 3 weeks before and Wed. immediately before election; 2nd Fri. after election and every 6 months thereafter until outstanding debt or obligation is satisfied or surplus depleted.(l)
New Jersey	Candidates and political committees.	Election Law Enforcement Commission.	29 and 11 days before and 20 days after election; every 60 days after election (starting with the 19th day after election) until no balance remains.(m)
New Mexico	Candidates receiving or spending more than $500; political committees.	Secy. of state.	10 days before and 30 days after election; 6 months after if any contributions are unspent or debt remains unpaid, and 12 months after an election (and annually thereafter) if debt remains unpaid.
New York	Candidates and political committees spending or receiving more than $1,000 in a filing period.	State Board of Elections.	Primary election reports filed on the 32nd and 11th day before, and 10th day after; general election reports filed 32nd and 11th day before, and 27th day after. Additional statements on Jan. 15 and July 15 until satisfaction of all liabilities and disposition of all assets.(n)
North Carolina	Candidates, political committees, and individuals making independent expenditures over $100.	State Board of Elections for statewide and multicounty district offices. County board of elections for others.	10 days before and after election (losing candidates in primary file 10 days after election). Supplemental reports due Jan. 7 after general election and annually following years in which contributions are received or expenditures made. Independent expenditure reports are filed within 10 days after expenditure is made.
North Dakota	Candidates receiving more than $100 in contributions; political parties receiving contributions of more than $100 or contributing more than $100 to a candidate; political committees.	Secy. of state. Legislative candidates file with county auditor of candidate's county of residence.	Candidates: 10 days before election and 30 days after close of calendar year. Political committees: by Oct. 15, with supplemental report 30 days after close of calendar year. Political parties: 30 days after close of calendar year.(o)

State or other jurisdiction	Statements required from	Statements filed with	Time for filing
Ohio	Candidate campaign committees, political committees, political parties.	Secy. of state. Legislative candidates file with Board of Elections for county with largest population.	12 days before and 45 days after election and last business day of Nov. annually.
Oklahoma	Candidates, political parties, and organizations.	State Election Board.	10 days before election and 40 days after general election. Supplemental reports within 6 months and 10 days after general election if any contributions are received or expenditures made within 6 months after general election.
Oregon	Candidates, political committees.	Secy. of state.	29-39 and 4-7 days before and 30 days after election. If post-election statement shows an unexpended balance of contributions or a deficit, supplemental reports are required annually on Sept. 10 until there is no balance or deficit.(p)
Pennsylvania	Candidates and political committees receiving or spending over $250.	Secy. of the commonwealth.	6th Tues. and 2nd Fri. before and 30 days after election. Annual reports required on Jan. 31 until there is no balance or debt in the report.
Rhode Island	Candidates, political action committees, and political party committees spending more than $5,000 or receiving any contribution in excess of $200; and those making independent expenditures of $200 or more.	State Board of Elections; independent expenditures are to be reported to the appropriate candidate or party committee.	28 and 7 days before and 28 days after election. Party committees also file by March 1 annually. Supplemental reports are required at 90-day intervals commencing 120 days after election until dissolution.
South Carolina	Candidates and committees.	State Ethics Commission; Senate or House Ethics Committee for legislative office.	30 days after election and 10 days after end of each calendar quarter in which funds are received or spent.
South Dakota	Candidates and certain committees.	Secy. of state.	Last Tues. before election and Feb. 1 of each year (for statewide offices); July 1 and Dec. 31 of each year (for legislative office).(q)
Tennessee	Candidates and political campaign committees.	Secy. of state; copy filed with county election commission of residence for legislative office.	7 days before any election and 48 days after general election. Supplemental report one year after election (or sooner if no surplus or deficit).
Texas..............	Candidates and political committees.	Secy. of state.	30 and 7 days before and 30 days after election; annually on Jan. 15 if contributions are received or expenditures made.(r)
Utah	Personal campaign committees for gov., state auditor, state treasurer, atty. gen.; state senate or house of representatives candidates; party committees.	Lt. governor.	10th day of July, Oct., and Dec. of election year and 5th day before election for state office candidates and for political parties 30 days after election for legislative candidates.
Vermont	Candidates, political parties, and political committees.	Secy. of state for state office, political parties, and political committees. Senatorial or representative district clerk for legislative office.	State office, political parties, and political committees: 40 and 10 days before any election and 10 days after general election. Legislative office: within 10 days before any election and within 30 days after general election. Supplemental reports for all candidates annually on July 15 until all expenditures are accounted for and all deficits are eliminated.
Virginia.............	Candidates, political action committees, and political party committees meeting certain thresholds.	State Board of Elections and election board where candidate resides.	8 days before and 30 days after election. Statewide candidates and committees also report 30 days before election.(s)
Washington	Candidates and political committees.	Public Disclosure Commission and county auditor in county of candidate's residence. Continuing political committees: commission and auditor in county where committee maintains its office.	Initial report at time of appointment of treasurer; 21 and 7 days before election and 21 days after any election; 10th day of each month in which no other report is filed if total contributions or expenditures since last report exceed $200.(t)

GENERAL FILING REQUIREMENTS—Continued

State or other jurisdiction	Statements required from	Statements filed with	Time for filing
West Virginia	Candidates and their financial agents; party committees, persons, and treasurers supporting or opposing any candidate.	Secy. of state for multicounty office. Clerk of county commission for single-county office.	Last Sat. in March or 15 days after that day before a primary; 7-10 days before and 25-30 days after any election.
Wisconsin..........	Candidates; political party committees, political committees, and others receiving or spending over $25.	State Elections Board. Legislative candidates also file duplicate with county clerk of counties in district.	8-14 days before election; continuing reports by committees and individuals, Jan. 1-31 and July 1-10 annually.(u)
Wyoming	Candidates, political party committees, and political action committees.	Secy. of state. Legislative candidates also file with county clerk.	10 days after election. Non-party committees: 14 days after election; party committees: 7 days after election. Committees formed after election report July 1 and Dec. 31 of odd-numbered years until all debts are paid.
Dist. of Col.	Candidates spending more than $250; political committees; and individuals making independent expenditures of $50 or more.	Director of campaign finance.	Each year: Jan. 31. Election years: 10th day of March, June, Aug., Oct., and Dec. and 8 days before election. Non-election years: July 31.(v)

Source: James A. Palmer and Edward D. Feigenbaum, *Campaign Finance Law 1986* (Washington, D.C.: National Clearinghouse on Election Administration, Federal Election Commission, 1986).

Note: This table deals with filing requirements for statewide and legislative offices in general terms. For detailed legal requirements or requirements for county and local offices, state statutes should be consulted.

(a) Contributions exceeding $250 made within one week before the election must be reported within 24 hours.

(b) Contributions or independent expenditures of $1,000 or more received after the final pre-election report must be reported within 48 hours.

(c) Contributions exceeding $500 received within 16 days before the election must be reported within 48 hours.

(d) Winning candidates in a primary do not file a post-primary report.

(e) Special report is required within 48 hours after receipt of a contribution of more than $2,000, or a candidate's expenditure of more than $200 to any candidate, committee, or other person required to file disclosure reports who makes endorsements during the period from 20 days before any election through election day.

(f) Contributions to or expenditures by candidates of $1,000 or more made after the 11th day and more than 48 hours before any election must be reported within 48 hours.

(g) Contributions of $200 or more received after the closing date of a pre-election statement, but before the second day prior to the election, must be reported within 48 hours after receipt.

(h) Contributions of $2,000 or more ($200 or more for a legislative candidate) received between the closing date of the last pre-election report and the election must be reported within 48 hours after receipt.

(i) Contributions of more than $1,000 ($500 for a legislative candidate) received after the closing date of the last pre-election report but before election day must be reported within 48 hours after receipt.

(j) Contributions of $500 or more received by a statewide candidate between the 10th day before the election and election day must be reported within 24 hours. Contributions of $100 or more received by a legislative candidate between the 15th day before the election and election day must be reported within 24 hours.

(k) Contributions of $500 or more received after last pre-election statement must be reported within five days after receipt.

(l) Contributions exceeding $500 received after Wednesday before any election must be reported within 24 hours.

(m) Contributions of $250 or more received by a candidate or political committee between the 13th day before and the election day must be reported within 48 hours.

(n) Contributions of more than $1,000 received after the final pre-election statement must be reported within 24 hours after receipt.

(o) Contributions of $500 or more received by a candidate in the 15-day period before any election must be reported within 48 hours of receipt.

(p) Contributions of $500 or more received after the eighth day before the day preceding the election must be reported on the day before the election.

(q) Contributions of $500 or more received within the nine days immediately prior to the election must be reported within 48 hours after receipt.

(r) Aggregate contributions of more than $1,000 for a Senate candidate or more than $200 for a House candidate accepted between the ninth and second day before an election must be reported within 48 hours of acceptance.

(s) Contributions of $1,000 or more received between the 11th day before any nomination or election and the day of nomination or election must be reported within 72 hours, but no later than the day prior to the day of nomination or election.

(t) Contributions of $500 or more made or received after the last pre-election report and before any election must be reported within 24 hours after the contribution is made or received. Candidates and committees may also qualify for abbreviated reporting.

(u) Contributions of more than $500 received after the last pre-election report must be reported within 24 hours after receipt.

(v) Contributions of $200 or more received after last pre-election report must be reported within 24 hours.

Table 5.5
CAMPAIGN FINANCE LAWS: LIMITATIONS ON CONTRIBUTIONS BY ORGANIZATIONS
(As of January 1986)

State or other jurisdiction	Corporate	Labor union	Separate segregated fund— political action committee (PAC)	Regulated industry	Political party
Alabama	Limited to $500 to any one candidate, political committee, or political party per election.	Unlimited.	Unlimited.	Public utility regulated by public service commission may only contribute through a PAC.	Unlimited.
Alaska(a)	Limited to $1,000 per year for each elective office.	Same as corporate.	Same as corporate.	...	Unlimited.
Arizona	Prohibited.	Prohibited.	Unlimited.	Prohibited.	Unlimited.
Arkansas(a)	Limited to $1,500 per candidate, per election.	Same as corporate.	Same as corporate.	...	Limited to $2,500 per candidate, per election.
California(a)	Unlimited.	Unlimited.	Unlimited.	...	Unlimited.
Colorado(a)	Unlimited.	Unlimited.	Unlimited.	...	Unlimited.
Connecticut(a)	Prohibited.	Prohibited.	Labor organization PAC limited to an aggregate of $50,000 per election, and same limits per candidate as individuals. Corporate PAC limited to an aggregate of $100,000 per election, and twice the limits per candidate as individuals.	Prohibited.	Unlimited.
Delaware(a)	Limited to $1,000 per statewide candidate per election, $500 per non-statewide candidate, per election.	Same as corporate.	Same as corporate.	...	...
Florida(a)	Limited to $3,000 for statewide office candidate per election; $2,000 for candidate for retention as district court of appeal judge; $1,000 for any other candidate or committee, per election.	Same as corporate.	Same as corporate.	...	Unlimited, except that party may not contribute to a candidate for judicial office.
Georgia	Unlimited.	Unlimited.	Unlimited.	Public utility corporation regulated by public service commission may not contribute, directly or indirectly.	Unlimited.
Hawaii(a)	Limited to $2,000 in any election period.	Same as corporate.	Same as corporate.	...	Sliding scale percentage limit based upon candidate expenditure limits.
Idaho	Unlimited.	Unlimited.	Unlimited.	...	Unlimited.
Illinois	Unlimited.	Unlimited.	Unlimited.	...	Unlimited.

State or other jurisdiction	Corporate	Labor union	Separate segregated fund— political action committee (PAC)	Regulated industry	Political party
Indiana	Limited to an aggregate of $5,000 for statewide candidates; an aggregate of $5,000 for state party central committees; an aggregate of $2,000 for other offices; and an aggregate of $2,000 for other party committees.	Same as corporate.	Unlimited.	. . .	Unlimited.
Iowa	Prohibited.	Unlimited.	Unlimited.	Prohibited for insurance companies.	Unlimited.
Kansas	Limited to $3,000 per statewide candidate per election, and $750 per candidate, per election for other offices.	Same as corporate.	Same as corporate.	Same as corporate.	Unlimited.
Kentucky(a)	Prohibited.	Unlimited.	Unlimited.	Prohibited.	Unlimited.
Louisiana(a)	Unlimited.	Unlimited.	Unlimited.	. . .	Unlimited.
Maine	Limited to $5,000 per candidate per election.	Same as corporate.	Same as corporate.	Same as corporate.	Same as corporate.
Maryland(a)	Limited to an aggregate of $2,500 per election and $1,000 per candidate, per election.	Same as corporate.	Unlimited.	. . .	Unlimited.
Massachusetts(a)	Prohibited.	Unlimited.	Unlimited.	Prohibited.	Unlimited.
Michigan(a)	Prohibited for candidate elections. Corporations may contribute up to $40,000 to a ballot question committee.	Limited to $1,700 for a statewide office, $450 for state senator, $250 for state representative candidates per election.	Same as labor union.	Prohibited.	State central committee is limited to $34,000 for a statewide office, $4,500 for state senator, $2,500 for state representative candidates, per election. Local party is limited to $17,000 for a statewide office, $4,500 for a state senator, $2,500 for state representative candidates, per election.
Minnesota	Prohibited.	Limited to $60,000 per election year for governor/lt. governor ($12,000 in non-election years); $10,000 per election year for attorney general ($2,000 in non-election years); $5,000 per election year for other statewide offices ($1,000 in non-election years); $1,500 per election year for state senator ($300 in non-election years); $750 per election year for state representative ($150 in non-election years).	Same as labor union.	Prohibited for insurance companies.	Limited to $300,000 per election year for governor/lt. governor ($60,000 in non-election years); $50,000 per election year for attorney general ($10,000 in non-election years); $25,000 per election year for other statewide offices ($5,000 in non-election years); $7,500 per election year for state senator ($1,500 in non-election years); $3,750 per election year for state representative ($750 in non-election years).

State or other jurisdiction	Corporate	Labor union	Separate segregated fund—political action committee (PAC)	Regulated industry	Political party
Mississippi	Limited to $1,000 per candidate per year and $250 for judicial office primary candidates.	Unlimited, except in contributions to judicial office primary candidates ($250 limit).	Same as labor union.	Generally prohibited.	Same as labor union.
Missouri(a)	Unlimited.	Unlimited.	Unlimited.	. . .	Unlimited.
Montana	Prohibited.	Limited for all elections in a campaign to $1,500 for governor/lt. governor; $750 for other statewide candidates; $400 for public service commissioner or state senator; $250 for other candidates.	Limited for all elections in a campaign to $8,000 for governor/lt. governor; $2,000 for other statewide candidates; $1,000 for public service commissioner; $600 for state senator ($1,000 total from all nonparty political committees); $300 for other candidates ($600 total for house candidates from all nonparty political committees).	Prohibited.	Contributions to judicial candidates are prohibited; otherwise, same as PAC.
Nebraska(a)	Unlimited.	Unlimited.	Unlimited.	. . .	Unlimited.
Nevada	Unlimited.	Unlimited.	Unlimited.	. . .	Unlimited.
New Hampshire	Prohibited.	Prohibited.	Limited to $5,000.	Prohibited.	Unlimited.
New Jersey(a)	Unlimited, except in contributions to governor in any primary or general election ($800 limit).	Same as corporate.	Same as corporate.	Prohibited for insurance corporations or associations and certain other corporations.	Unlimited, except state committee contribution to governor in general election ($800 limit).
New Mexico	Unlimited.	Unlimited.	Unlimited.	. . .	Prohibited in primary elections, otherwise unlimited.
New York(a)	Limited to an aggregate of $5,000 per calendar year.	Unlimited.	Unlimited.	Public utilities may not contribute from public service revenues unless cost is charged to shareholders.	Unlimited.
North Carolina(a)....	Prohibited.	Prohibited.	Limited to $4,000 per committee or candidate, per election.	Prohibited.	Unlimited.
North Dakota	Prohibited.	Prohibited.	Unlimited.	Prohibited.	Unlimited.
Ohio(a)	Prohibited.	Unlimited.	Prohibited for corporate PAC; otherwise, unlimited.	Prohibited for public utilities.	Unlimited.
Oklahoma	Prohibited.	Limited to $5,000 to a political party or organization or a state office, and $1,000 for a local office candidate.	Same as labor union.	Prohibited.	Same as labor union.
Oregon	Unlimited.	Unlimited.	Unlimited.	Generally prohibited.	Unlimited.
Pennsylvania(a)	Prohibited.	Prohibited.	Unlimited.	Prohibited.	Unlimited.
Rhode Island	Unlimited.	Unlimited.	Unlimited.	. . .	Unlimited.

State or other jurisdiction	Corporate	Labor union	Separate segregated fund—political action committee (PAC)	Regulated industry	Political party
South Carolina	Unlimited.	Unlimited.	Unlimited.	. . .	Unlimited.
South Dakota	Prohibited.	Prohibited if union is a corporation; otherwise, unlimited.	Unlimited.	Prohibited.	Unlimited.
Tennessee	Prohibited.	Unlimited.	Unlimited.	Prohibited.	Unlimited.
Texas(a)	Prohibited.	Prohibited.	Unlimited.	Prohibited.	Unlimited.
Utah	Unlimited.	Unlimited.	Unlimited.	Unlimited.	Unlimited.
Vermont(a)..........	Limited to $1,000 per candidate or committee, per election.	Same as corporate.	Limited to $5,000 per candidate or committee per election.	Same as corporate.	Same as corporate.
Virginia............	Unlimited.	Unlimited.	Unlimited.	. . .	Unlimited.
Washington(a)	Unlimited, except aggregate contributions of more than $5,000 may not be made to a candidate or political committee within 21 days of a general election.	Same as corporate.	Same as corporate.	Same as corporate.	Same as corporate.
West Virginia(a)	Prohibited.	Limited to $1,000 per candidate, per election.	Same as labor union.	Prohibited.	Same as labor union.
Wisconsin(a)	Prohibited.	Limited according to formula for statewide candidates; and $1,000 for state senator; $500 for state representative; and $6,000 for political parties.	Same as labor union.	Public utilities may not offer special privileges to candidates.	Certain specified percentage limits per candidate.
Wyoming	Prohibited.	Prohibited.	Unlimited.	Prohibited.	Prohibited in primary elections.
Dist. of Col.(a)	Limited to an aggregate of $4,000 per election and $2,000 for mayor, $1,500 for council chairman, $1,000 for council member at-large, $400 for council member from a district and board of education member at-large, $200 for board of education member from a district or a party official, $25 for neighborhood advisory commission member.	Same as corporate.	Same as corporate.	. . .	. . .

Source: James A. Palmer and Edward D. Feigenbaum. *Campaign Finance Law 1986.* (Washington, D.C.: National Clearinghouse on Election Administration, Federal Election Commission, 1986).

Note: Consult state statutes for more details.

Key:

. . .—No reference to contribution in the law.

(a) Restriction on cash contributions. In Alaska, Arkansas, Florida, Kentucky, Maryland, Missouri, New York, North Carolina, Ohio, and Texas (no limit for general purpose committee): must be $100 or less. In California and Colorado: must be less than $100. In Connecticut, Delaware, Massachusetts, Nebraska, Vermont, Washington, West Virginia, and Wisconsin: must be $50 or less. In Hawaii: cash contribution of more than $100 requires a receipt to the donor and a record of the transaction. In Louisiana: cash contributions of more than $300 must be by written instrument; all cash contributions by corporations, labor organizations, and associations must be by check. In New Jersey: cash contributions are prohibited unless in response to public solicitation, or a written contributor statement is filed (cumulative maximum of $100). In Pennsylvania: must be $100 or less per candidate. In District of Columbia: must be less than $50.

Table 5.6
CAMPAIGN FINANCE LAWS: LIMITATIONS ON CONTRIBUTIONS
BY INDIVIDUALS
(As of January 1986)

State or other jurisdiction	Individual	Candidate	Candidate's family member	Government employees	Anonymous or in name of another
Alabama...........	Unlimited.	Unlimited.	Unlimited.	No solicitation of state employees for state political activities. City employees may contribute to coun-ty/state political activities; county employees may contribute to ci-ty/state political activities.	. . .
Alaska(a)	Limited to $1,000 per year for each elective office.	Unlimited.	Same as individual.	Contribution may not be required of state employees.	Prohibited.
Arizona............	Unlimited.	Unlimited.	Unlimited.	. . .	. . .
Arkansas(a)	Limited to $1,500 per candidate, per election.	Unlimited.	Same as individual.	Contribution may not be required of state employees. State division of so-cial services/county board of public wel-fare employees may not solicit, nor may certain judges so-licit for campaigns other than their own.	Anonymous contri-bution must be less than $50 per year. Contribution in the name of another prohibited.
California(a)	Unlimited.	Unlimited.	Unlimited.	Local agency em-ployees may not so-licit employees of their agency except incidentally through a large solicitation.	Anonymous contri-bution must be less than $100 per year. Contribution in the name of another prohibited.
Colorado(a)	Unlimited.	Unlimited.	Unlimited.	. . .	Contribution in the name of another prohibited.
Connecticut(a)	Limited to an ag-gregate of $15,000 per election and $2,000 for gover-nor; $1,500 for other statewide of-fice; $1,000 for sheriff; $500 for state senator or probate judge; $250 for state represen-tative, town, city or borough office; $5,000 per year to state party.	Unlimited.	Unlimited.	May not be re-quired. State de-partment heads and deputy department heads may not soli-cit.	Anonymous contri-bution must be less than $15. Contribu-tion in the name of another prohibited.
Delaware(a)	Limited to $1,000 per statewide candi-date, per election; $500 per non-state-wide candidate per election.	Limited to $5,000 per election.	Same as candidate.	. . .	Prohibited.
Florida(a)	Limited to $3,000 for statewide office candidate per elec-tion; $2,000 for candidate for reten-tion as district court of appeal judge; $1,000 for any other candidate or com-mittee per election.	Unlimited.	Same as individual.	Judges not elected in public elections between competing candidates may not make contributions. Solicitation general-ly prohibited for state employees. Judges may not so-licit contributions.	Contribution in the name of another prohibited.

LIMITATIONS ON CONTRIBUTIONS BY INDIVIDUALS—Continued

State or other jurisdiction	Individual	Candidate	Candidate's family member	Government employees	Anonymous or in name of another
Georgia............	Unlimited.	Unlimited.	Unlimited.	State employee may not coerce another state employee into contributing.	Anonymous contribution prohibited.
Hawaii(a)..........	Limited to $2,000 in any election period.	Limited to an aggregate of $50,000 in any election year.	Same as candidate.	Solicitation of contributions prohibited. Contribution to other employees is prohibited.	Prohibited.
Idaho	Unlimited.	Unlimited.	Unlimited.	Contributions permitted. State employee may not coerce another state employee into contributing.	Anonymous contribution must be $50 or less. Contribution in the name of another prohibited.
Illinois.............	Unlimited.	Unlimited.	Unlimited.	Generally prohibited.	Prohibited.
Indiana	Unlimited.	Unlimited.	Unlimited.	Contribution may not be required. Employees may not solicit or receive contributions.	Contribution in the name of another prohibited.
Iowa	Unlimited.	Unlimited.	Unlimited.	...	Prohibited.
Kansas	Limited to $3,000 per statewide candidate, per election; and $750 per candidate per election for other offices.	Unlimited.	Spouse is unlimited.	Contribution may not be required.	Anonymous contribution must be $10 or less. Contribution in the name of another prohibited.
Kentucky(a)........	Limited to $3,000 per candidate per election.	Unlimited.	Same as individual.	Contribution may not be required. Contribution may be prohibited, depending on who is recipient.	Anonymous contribution must be $50 or less. Contribution in the name of another prohibited.
Louisiana(a)........	Unlimited.	Unlimited.	Unlimited.	Contribution may not be solicited.	Anonymous contribution generally prohibited if more than $25. Contribution in the name of another prohibited.
Maine	Limited to an aggregate of $25,000 in a calendar year and $1,000 per candidate, per election.	Unlimited.	Spouse is unlimited.	State employee may not coerce another state employee into contributing.	Contribution in the name of another prohibited.
Maryland(a)........	Limited to an aggregate of $2,500 per election and $1,000 per candidate per election.	Unlimited.	Spouse is unlimited.	Contribution may not be required.	Prohibited.
Massachusetts(a).....	Limited to $1,000 per candidate, per year. Minors limited to $25 per year.	Unlimited.	Same as individual.	Contribution may not be required. Solicitation generally prohibited.	Contribution in the name of another prohibited.
Michigan(a)........	Limited to $1,700 for statewide office, $450 for state senator, $250 for state representative candidates per election.	Limited to $25,000 per gubernatorial campaign.	Same as candidate.	Contribution may not be required.	Prohibited.

LIMITATIONS ON CONTRIBUTIONS BY INDIVIDUALS—Continued

State or other jurisdiction	Individual	Candidate	Candidate's family member	Government employees	Anonymous or in name of another
Minnesota	Limited to $60,000 per election year for governor/lt. governor ($12,000 in non-election years); $10,000 per election year for attorney general ($2,000 in non-election years); $5,000 per election year for other statewide offices ($1,000 in non-election years); $1,500 per election year for state senate ($300 in non-election years); $750 per election year for state representative ($150 in non-election years).	Unlimited.	Same as individual.	Contribution may not be required. Solicitation prohibited during hours of employment.	Anonymous contribution must be less than $20. Contribution in the name of another prohibited.
Mississippi	Unlimited, except in contributions to judicial office primary candidates ($250 limit).	Same as individual.	Same as individual.	Contribution may not be required. Highway patrol or correctional system employees may not contribute. Solicitation prohibited for state correctional system employees.	. . .
Missouri(a)	Unlimited.	Unlimited.	Unlimited.	. . .	Anonymous contribution must be $10 or less. Contribution in the name of another prohibited.
Montana	Limited for all elections in a campaign to $1,500 for governor/lt. governor; $750 for other statewide candidates; $400 for public service commissioner, district court judge, or state senator; $250 for other candidates.	Unlimited.	Same as individual.	Contributions by municipal employees in city with municipal commission form of government prohibited. Solicitation by municipal government employees prohibited.	Prohibited.
Nebraska(a)	Unlimited.	Unlimited.	Unlimited.	Solicitation prohibited during hours of employment.	Prohibited.
Nevada	Unlimited.	Unlimited.	Unlimited.	Employees may not solicit from other employees.	. . .
New Hampshire	Limited to $5,000.	Unlimited.	Same as individual.	Contribution may not be solicited or required from classified state employees.	Prohibited.
New Jersey	Unlimited, except in contribution to governor in any primary or general election ($800 limit). Contributor's spouse may contribute up to $800 for governor in general election.	Unlimited, but if receiving public funds for governor, limited to $25,000 per election from own funds.	Unlimited, except in contribution to governor in any primary or general election ($800 limit).	Prohibited to demand from other public employees.	Prohibited.

State or other jurisdiction	Individual	Candidate	Candidate's family member	Government employees	Anonymous or in name of another
New Mexico........	Unlimited.	Unlimited.	Unlimited.	Solicitation prohibited while on duty.	Anonymous contribution in excess of $50 subject to special report.
New York(a)	Limited to an aggregate of $150,000 in a calendar year and a maximum aggregate per office. Statewide: $0.025 x voters (voters in party in primaries). Senate or assembly: $0.05 x voters in district (voters in party in primaries) with $2,500 min./ $50,000 max. for assembly member, and $4,000 min./ $50,000 max. for senator.	Unlimited.	Spouse is unlimited. Other family member contributions are aggregated and subject to a maximum aggregate per office. Statewide: $0.025 x voters (voters in party in primaries). Senate or assembly: $0.25 x voters in district (voters in party in primaries) with $20,000 min./ $100,000 max. for senator; $12,500 min./$100,000 max. for assembly member.	Contributions permitted, but may not be required. Judicial candidates may not solicit government employees or receive contributions from them. Police force members may not solicit for contributions from government employees. State employees may not coerce other state employees into contributing.	Prohibited.
North Carolina(a)....	Limited to $4,000 per committee or candidate, per election.	Unlimited.	Unlimited.	State employee may not coerce another state employee into contributing.	Prohibited.
North Dakota	Unlimited.	Unlimited.	Unlimited.	. . .	Prohibited.
Ohio(a)	Unlimited.	Unlimited.	Unlimited.	Classified service employees may not solicit or be solicited. Judge may not contribute to a political party in the year of candidacy. Court employees may not be solicited for a judicial candidate.	Anonymous contribution generally prohibited. Contribution in the name of another prohibited.
Oklahoma	Limited to $5,000 to a political party or organization or a state office, and $1,000 for a local office candidate, per person or family.	Unlimited.	Same as individual.	State employee may not solicit. Certain state employees may not receive contributions.	Prohibited.
Oregon	Unlimited.	Unlimited.	Unlimited.	Contribution may not be required. Solicitation prohibited during hours of employment.	Prohibited.
Pennsylvania(a)	Unlimited.	Unlimited.	Unlimited.	State employees may not be solicited, and may not solicit from other state employees.	Prohibited.
Rhode Island	Unlimited.	Unlimited.	Unlimited.	State classified employees may not be solicited, and may not solicit other state employees.	Prohibited.
South Carolina	Unlimited.	Unlimited.	Unlimited.	. . .	. . .
South Dakota	Limited to $1,000 for any statewide candidate; $250 for any other candidate; or $3,000 to a political party in any calendar year.	Unlimited.	Unlimited.	. . .	. . .

LIMITATIONS ON CONTRIBUTIONS BY INDIVIDUALS—Continued

State or other jurisdiction	Individual	Candidate	Candidate's family member	Government employees	Anonymous or in name of another
Tennessee	Unlimited.	Unlimited.	Unlimited.	Superiors may not solicit their employees. Certain government contractors may not be solicited.	. . .
Texas..............	Unlimited.	Unlimited.	Unlimited.	. . .	Contribution in the name of another prohibited unless there is disclosure.
Utah	Unlimited.	Unlimited.	Unlimited.	Solicitation prohibited during hours of employment.	. . .
Vermont(a).........	Limited to $1,000 per candidate or committee, per election.	Unlimited.	Unlimited.	Solicitation by employees prohibited.	. . .
Virginia............	Unlimited.	Unlimited.	Unlimited.	. . .	. . .
Washington	Unlimited, except aggregate contributions of more than $5,000 may not be made to a candidate or political committee within 21 days of a general election.	Same as individual.	Unlimited.	. . .	Prohibited.
West Virginia(a)	Limited to $1,000 per candidate, per election.	Same as individual.	Same as individual.	Contribution may not be solicited.	Anonymous contribution prohibited. Contributor disclosure required for contribution in the name of another.
Wisconsin..........	Limited to $10,000 for statewide candidates; $1,000 for state senator; $500 for state representative; other offices by formula, with an aggregate limit of $10,000.	Unlimited, unless candidate receives a grant from the election campaign fund, then limited to 200% of individual limit.	Unlimited as to funds or property owned jointly or as marital property by candidate and spouse.	Contribution and solicitation prohibited during hours of employment, or while engaged in official duties.	Anonymous contribution must be less than $10. Contribution in the name of another prohibited.
Wyoming	Limited to an aggregate of $25,000 and $1,000 per candidate in any general election and the year preceding.	Unlimited.	Unlimited.	. . .	. . .

LIMITATIONS ON CONTRIBUTIONS BY INDIVIDUALS—Continued

State or other jurisdiction	Individual	Candidate	Candidate's family member	Government employees	Anonymous or in name of another
Dist. of Col.(a)	Limited to an aggregate of $4,000 per election and $2,000 for mayor, $1,500 for council chairman, $1,000 for council member at-large, $400 for council member from a district or board of education member at-large, $200 for board of education member from a district or a party official, $25 for neighborhood advisory commission member.	Same as individual.	Same as individual.	Contributions permitted, but district employees may not solicit or collect political contributions.	Contribution in the name of another prohibited.

Source: James A. Palmer and Edward D. Feigenbaum. *Campaign Finance Law 1986.* (Washington, D.C.: National Clearinghouse on Election Administration, Federal Election Commission, 1986).
Note: Consult state statutes for more details.
Key:
. . .—No reference to contribution in the law.
(a) Restriction on cash contributions. In Alaska, Arkansas, Florida, Kentucky, Maryland, New York, North Carolina, and Ohio: must be $100 or less. In California and Colorado: must be less than $100. In Connecticut, Delaware, Massachusetts, Nebraska, Vermont, West Virginia: must be $50 or less. In Hawaii and Missouri: cash contribution of more than $100 requires a receipt to the donor and a record of the transaction. In Louisiana: cash contributions of more than $300 must be by written instrument. In Michigan: must be $20 or less. In Pennsylvania: must be $100 or less per candidate. In District of Columbia: must be less than $50.

Table 5.7

CAMPAIGN FINANCE LAWS: LIMITATIONS ON EXPENDITURES
(As of January 1986)

State or other jurisdiction	Who may make expenditures	Total expenditures allowed	Expenditures prior to first filing	For certain purposes	Use of surplus funds(a)
Alabama	Committee named and designated by candidate.	...	...	Candidate's travel, filing fees, stenographic work, clerks for mailings, communications and stationery, voter lists, office rent, broadcast, advertising, campaign literature, compensation to those distributing literature, rent for rally halls, bands.	...
Alaska(b)	Candidate, treasurer, deputy treasurer.	Gov./lt. gov.: $.40 x total population (with no more than 50% spent in any one primary or general election); senate/ house: $1 x district population divided by number of seats in district.	None permitted, except for personal travel expenses and public opinion surveys/polls.	...	May be given to charity, used to repay contributors, spent on a future campaign, used to repay candidate or used as income, contributed to another committee, or transferred to office allowance fund.
Arizona	...	...	None permitted until registration form is properly filed.	...	...
Arkansas(b)	...	...	...	...	...
California(b)	Must have authorization of treasurer or treasurer's designated agents.	...	...	Must be reasonably related to election, voter registration, or political education.	May be contributed to a non-profit or charitable organization or to the state or political subdivision, but not to candidate or party.
Colorado(b)	...	...	...	Polls, meeting halls and rally expenses, printing and advertising, professional services fee, travel, staff salaries, rent, supplies, voter transportation, communications, expenses incurred in circulating nominating petitions, and other necessary expenses.	May be donated to another committee(c) or distributed on a pro rata basis to contributors or used for transition expenses. Ballot question committees may distribute surplus to government agencies or tax exempt organizations.
Connecticut(b)	...	...	None permitted until treasurer and campaign depository have been properly designated.	Staff salaries, travel expenses, filing fees, communications and printing, food, office supplies, voter lists and canvasses, poll watchers, rent, advertising, rallies, state licensed counsel.	May be contributed to tax-exempt charitable or political organization with candidate's authorization.
Delaware	Those with candidate's written approval.	Primary: statewide candidates: $.25 x qualified voters; senate: greater of $.25 x qualified voters or $4,000; house: greater of $.25 x qualified voters or $2,000. General election: all figures doubled.	None permitted until registration form is properly filed.		

200

LIMITATIONS ON EXPENDITURES—Continued

State or other jurisdiction	Who may make expenditures	Total expenditures allowed	Expenditures prior to first filing	For certain purposes	Use of surplus funds(a)
Florida(b)	...	...	...	Expenditures only to influence results of election.	May be used to reimburse a candidate for his contributions; transferred to a public office account in amount up to $10,000 for statewide candidate, $5,000 for multi-county candidate, and $2,500 x number of years in term of office for which legislative candidate is elected; returned pro rata to contributors; donated to a non-profit or charitable organization; or given to state or political subdivision.
Georgia	...	...	...	...	...
Hawaii	Campaign treasurer and deputy treasurer.	Voluntary election year limits: gov.: $1.25 x qualified voters; lt. gov.: $.70 x qualified voters; mayor: $1 x qualified voters; house/senate/council/prosecutor: $.70 x qualified voters; others: $.10 x qualified voters.	...	Donations to community, youth, social, or recreational organizations; reports, surveys, or polls.	May be used for fundraising; candidate-sponsored politically-related activity; ordinary and necessary officeholder expenses; or donated to any community service, scientific, educational, youth, recreational, charitable, or literary organization.
Idaho(b)	...	...	...	...	...
Illinois	...	...	...	...	Must be returned to contributors or transferred to other political or charitable organizations.
Indiana	Treasurer.	...	...	...	May be transferred to one or more political party committees or to the state election board.(d)
Iowa	...	...	...	Only for legitimate campaign purposes in general elections, including salaries, rent, advertising, supplies, travel, campaign paraphernalia, contributions to other candidates, and the like.	(e)
Kansas	...	...	None permitted until registration form is properly filed.	...	...
Kentucky	Treasurer must make or authorize all expenditures on behalf of candidate.	...	None permitted until primary campaign depository is designated.	...	May be returned pro rata to all contributors, transferred to candidate's party committee, or retained for election to the same office.

201

LIMITATIONS ON EXPENDITURES—Continued

State or other jurisdiction	Who may make expenditures	Total expenditures allowed	Expenditures prior to first filing	For certain purposes	Use of surplus funds(a)
Louisiana(b)	...	...	None aggregating in excess of $500 until statement of organization is properly filed.	...	...
Maine	Candidate, treasurer.	Political action committee limited to $5,000 per candidate or political committee in any election.	...	...	...
Maryland(b)	Public funds may only be spent upon authority of candidate or treasurer; other expenditures must be made by or through treasurer.	Publicly-financed candidates limited per primary or general elections: gov./lt. gov./senate: $.10 x qualified voters; atty. gen./comptr.: $.025 x qualified voters; house: $.05 x qualified voters; state's atty.: greater of $2,500 or $.025 x qualified voters; other: greater of $1,000 or $.01 x qualified voters.(f)	None permitted until registration form is properly filed.	Public contributions may only be used to further candidate's nomination or election, for legal purposes, and for expenses not incurred later than 30 days after election.	Surplus public contributions must be paid not later than 60 days after the election for which the funds were granted. Other funds must be returned on a pro rata basis to contributors, paid to a party central committee, or donated to a local board of education, recognized nonprofit educational organization, or charitable organization.
Massachusetts(b)	...	...	...	Candidates: limited to reasonable and necessary expenses directly related to candidate's campaign. Other committees: for enhancement of political future of candidate or principle.	Pro rata portion of public funds revert to state. Other funds must be donated to local aid fund.
Michigan(b)	Expenditure may only be made with authorization of treasurer or treasurer's designee.	Publicly-financed candidates limited to $1 million per election.(g)	...	Public funds may be spent only on services, facilities, materials, or other things of value to further candidate's election during election year.	Surplus public funds must be promptly repaid and may not be used in subsequent election. Other funds may be transferred to another committee, party, tax-exempt charitable institution or returned to contributors.
Minnesota(b)	Authorized by treasurer or deputy treasurer of committee or fund.	Publicly-financed candidates limited in election year to greater of following amounts. Gov./lt. gov.: $.125 per capita or $600,000; atty. gen.: $.025 per capita or $100,000; secy. of state, treas., aud.: $.0125 per capita or $50,000; senate: $.20 per capita or $15,000; house: $.20 per capita or $7,500. In non-election year, to 20% of applicable limit.	...	Salaries, wages, fees, communications, mailing, transportation and travel, advertising and printing, office space and furnishings, supplies, and other expenses reasonably related to election.	...

LIMITATIONS ON EXPENDITURES—Continued

State or other jurisdiction	Who may make expenditures	Total expenditures allowed	Expenditures prior to first filing	For certain purposes	Use of surplus funds(a)
Mississippi	...	...	...	...	...
Missouri(b)	Expenditures must be made by or through treasurer; when treasurer's office is vacant candidate serves as treasurer.	...	...	...	...
Montana(b)	Campaign treasurers, authorized deputy campaign treasurers of candidates and political committees.	...	...	...	...
Nebraska(b)	Treasurers or treasurer's designees; however candidates and agents also permitted to make expenditures.	...	None may be made by committee until it files statement of organization and has treasurer.	Committee (other than political party committee) may use funds for goods, materials, services, or facilities to assist or oppose candidate or ballot question.(h)	...
Nevada	...	...	...	...	...
New Hampshire	Candidate or fiscal agent, treasurer of political committee.	...	None may be made by non-party political committee until registration statement is filed and (if organized to support a candidate) written consent of candidate or financial agent has been secured and filed.	...	...
New Jersey	Treasurer or deputy treasurer of candidate, political party committee, political committee, and continuing political committees.	Max. amount for gov. in primary: $.35 x number of voters in preceding presidential election; in general election: $.70 x number of voters in preceding presidential election.	...	...	...
New Mexico	Treasurer of candidate or political committee.	...	None permitted until treasurer appointed.	...	...
New York(b)	Treasurer of candidate or political committee.	...	None may be made by a political committee until designation of treasurer and depository have been filed.	Any lawful purpose.	Surplus campaign funds may be used for any lawful purpose, including transfer to political party committee, return to donor, or held for use in subsequent campaign.
North Carolina(b)	Treasurer or asst. treasurer of candidate or political committee.(i)	...	None permitted until treasurer appointed and certified.(i)	...	...
North Dakota	...	...	...	...	...

203

LIMITATIONS ON EXPENDITURES—Continued

State or other jurisdiction	Who may make expenditures	Total expenditures allowed	Expenditures prior to first filing	For certain purposes	Use of surplus funds(a)
Ohio	Campaign treasurer, authorized deputy campaign treasurers for a campaign committee.	...	None may be made by candidate's campaign committee until candidate designates treasurer.	...	...
Oklahoma	Agents and sub-agents in the case of candidates and political parties.	...	...	Only to defray campaign expenditures or ordinary and necessary expenses incurred in connection with duties of public officeholder.	...
Oregon(b)	...	...	...	...	...
Pennsylvania	...	...	No expenditures except as provided by law.	...	...
Rhode Island	Campaign treasurers, deputy campaign treasurers.	...	...	...	...
South Carolina	...	...	...	...	...
South Dakota	...	...	...	Necessary expenditure of money for ordinary or usual expense of conducting political campaign unless expressly forbidden.	...
Tennessee	Political treasurer of candidate and political campaign committee.	...	None permitted until candidate and political committee certify name and address of treasurer.	Clerical/office force, dissemination of literature, public speakers, newspaper announcement of candidacy and transportation of voters unable to go to polls.	...
Texas	Candidate and campaign treasurer or asst. campaign treasurer, and campaign treasurer or asst. campaign treasurer of political committee.	Independent expenditures by individuals limited to $100(j), unless contribution is made or individual reports as a political committee.	None permitted until name of campaign treasurer has been filed.	...	...
Utah	Candidate and secretary and members of personal campaign committee in case of candidate.	...	None permitted until state office candidate files statement of appointment of personal campaign committee.	Any expenditures may be made, except those prohibited by law.	...
Vermont(b)	Designated treasurer.	...	...	...	May be used by candidate to reduce personal campaign debts.
Virginia(b)	...	...	(k)	...	After filing of final report, surplus funds may be used for next election.

LIMITATIONS ON EXPENDITURES—Continued

State or other jurisdiction	Who may make expenditures	Total expenditures allowed	Expenditures prior to first filing	For certain purposes	Use of surplus funds(a)
Washington(b)	Campaign treasurer or candidate or person on authority of campaign treasurer or candidate.	...		...	...
West Virginia	Candidates, financial agents, political party committee treasurers.	...	None may be made by political party committee until treasurer appointed.	...	...
Wisconsin(b)	Treasurer of candidate, political committee, political group, or individual.	State office candidates who receive election campaign fund grant may not spend more for campaign than amount specified in authorized disbursement schedule.	None permitted until registration statement is filed.	For any lawful purpose.	
Wyoming	...	...	...	...	
Dist. of Columbia(b)	Chairman, treasurer, or designated agents.	...	...	...	May be contributed to a political party for political purposes; returned to donors; transferred to a scientific, technical, or literary or educational organization; or used for constituent services with certain limitations.

Source: James A. Palmer and Edward D. Feigenbaum, *Campaign Finance Law 1986*. (Washington, D.C.: National Clearinghouse on Election Administration, Federal Election Commission, 1986).

Note: Consult state statutes for more details.

Key:
... —No reference in the law.
(a) Post election.
(b) Restrictions on cash expenditures. In Alaska, California, Colorado, Connecticut, Louisiana, and New York: may not exceed $100. In Arkansas, Massachusetts, Michigan, Nebraska, Oregon, Washington, and the District of Columbia: may not exceed $50. In Florida: must be less than $30. In Idaho and Maryland: must be less than $25. In Minnesota: petty cash expenditures limited to $100 per week for statewide elections and $20 per week for legislative elections. In Missouri: single cash expenditures from petty cash fund may not exceed $50; aggregate calendar year expenditures may not exceed the lesser of $5,000 or 10 percent of the committee's total calendar year expenditures. In Montana: petty cash fund may be established to pay for office supplies, transportation expenses and other necessities of less than $10. In North Carolina: cash expenditures permitted for non-media expenses of $50 or less. In Vermont: expenditures by a candidate who has made expenditures or received contributions of $500 or more and by a political committee must be paid by the treasurer by check from a single checking account. In Virginia: petty cash expenditures of less than $25 are permitted; otherwise, only by check.

In Wisconsin: cash expenditures are prohibited.
(c) Except one established to further the candidate's future campaigns.
(d) Unless otherwise provided by the committee in its statement of organization.
(e) Public funds may not be used to lease or purchase any item whose benefits extend beyond the time within which the funds must be spent.
(f) In general election, parties are limited to expenditures for greater of $250 or $.0025 per qualified voter in addition to the candidate limits.
(g) Except up to $200,000 more can be spent to solicit contributions, and additional expenditures are authorized in response to editorials, endorsements, and the like.
(h) After an election, a committee may expend or transfer funds for: continued operation of campaign offices; social events for workers and volunteers; obtaining public input and opinion; repayment of campaign loans; newsletters and other political communications; gifts of acknowledgement; and candidate-related meals, lodging, and travel by officeholder and family.
(i) Except for independent expenditures.
(j) Plus donated services and personal traveling expenses.
(k) Candidate must appoint one campaign treasurer no later than upon acceptance of a contribution, expenditure of funds, or qualification as a candidate, whichever occurs first.

Table 5.8
FUNDING OF STATE ELECTIONS: TAX PROVISIONS AND PUBLIC FINANCING
(As of January 1986)

State or other jurisdiction	Tax provisions relating to individuals				Public financing	
	Credit	Deduction	Checkoff	Surcharge	Source of funds	Distribution of funds
Alabama	...	...	...	$1(a)	Surcharge	To political party designated by taxpayer
Alaska	$50	...	...	...	...	...
Arizona	...	$100(a)	...	...	...	...
Arkansas	...	$25	...	...	...	...
California	...	$100	...	$1, $5, $10, or $25(b)	Surcharge and an equal amount matched by state	To political parties for party activities and distribution to statewide general election candidates
Hawaii	...	$100 for contributions to central or county party committees or $500 for contributions to candidates who abide by expenditure limits, with max. of $100 of a total contribution to a single candidate deductible	$2(a)	...	Checkoff, appropriated funds, other moneys	To candidates for all non-federal elective offices
Idaho	50% of contribution to max. $5(a)	...	$1	...	Checkoff	To political party designated by taxpayer
Indiana	...	...	...	...	Revenue from personalized motor vehicle license plates	Percentage divided equally between the qualified political parties
Iowa	...	...	$1(a)	$2(a)	Checkoff/surcharge	To political party designated by taxpayer; if not specified, amount divided among qualifying parties for party activities and distribution to general election candidates
Kentucky	...	...	$2(a)	...	Checkoff	To political party designated by taxpayer for party activities and distribution to general election candidates
Maine	...	...	...	$1	Surcharge	To political party designated by taxpayer
Maryland	...	...	...	...	Direct appropriations	To candidates for state or county office; Baltimore city offices
Massachusetts	...	...	...	$1(a)	Surcharge	To candidates in statewide primary and general elections
Michigan	...	...	$2(a)	...	Checkoff and an equal amount matched by state	To candidates in gubernatorial primaries and candidates for governor and lt. governor in general election
Minnesota	50% of contribution to max. $50(a)	...	$2(a)	...	Checkoff and excess anonymous contributions	To candidates for governor, lt. governor, attorney general, secretary of state, state auditor, state treasurer, state senator and representative in primary and general elections

FUNDING OF STATE ELECTIONS—Continued

| State or other jurisdiction | Tax provisions relating to individuals | | | | | Public financing |
	Credit	Deduction	Checkoff	Surcharge	Source of funds	Distribution of funds
Montana	...	$100(a)	$1(a)	$1(a) for those with no tax liability	Checkoff/surcharge	To candidates opposed in elections for governor, lt. governor, Supreme Court chief justice and justices
New Jersey	...	...	$1(a)	...	Direct appropriations and checkoff	To gubernatorial candidates
North Carolina	...	$25	$1(a)	...	Checkoff	Divided among political parties according to registration; of amount—50% goes to party, 50% for other purposes
Oklahoma	...	$100	$1(a)	...	Checkoff	50% to political parties(c) and 50% to eligible general election candidates(d)
Oregon	Lesser of 50% of contribution to max. $25(a) or the taxpayer's tax liability	...	...	...	...	...
Rhode Island	(e)	...	$2(a)	...	Credit/checkoff	To political party designated by taxpayer; other funds allocated to parties based on number of elected state officials and of votes in most recent election
Utah	...	...	$1	...	Checkoff	To political party designated by taxpayer; allocated 50% to county central committees
Virginia	...	...	...	$2(a)	Surcharge	To political party designated by taxpayer
Wisconsin	...	...	$1(a)	...	Checkoff	According to formula, to general election candidates for state executive office, Supreme Court, and legislative offices(f)
Dist. of Col.	50% of contribution to max. $50(a)	...	...	...	...	...

Source: James A. Palmer and Edward D. Feigenbaum, *Campaign Finance Law 1986.* (Washington, D.C.: National Clearinghouse on Election Administration, Federal Election Commission, 1986).

Note: This table shows only those states that have a tax provision relating to individuals or a provision for public financing of state elections. Credits and deductions may be allowed only for certain types of candidates and/or political parties. Consult state laws for further details.

Key:

... —No provision.

(a) For joint returns, amount indicated above may be doubled.

(b) And a separate designation of $1, $5, $10, or $25.

(c) 10 percent to each party and remainder divided according to registration figures.

(d) 20 percent for governor, 15 percent for lieutenant governor, 15 percent for attorney general and 10 percent each for state treasurer, state auditor and inspector, commissioner of insurance, superintendent of public instruction, and corporation commissioner.

(e) See checkoff.

(f) Candidates must meet certain qualifications.

Table 5.9
VOTER REGISTRATION INFORMATION

State or other jurisdiction	Mail registration allowed for all voters	Minimum state residence requirement (days)	Closing date for registration before general election (days)	Persons eligible for absentee registration(a)	Automatic cancellation of registration for failure to vote after ____ years
Alabama		1	10	D,S,T	
Alaska	★	30	30	(b)	2
Arizona		50	50	S,T	2
Arkansas		. . .	20	D	4
California	★	29	29	(b)	4
Colorado		32	32	D,S,T	2
Connecticut		. . .	21(c)	D	
Delaware	★	. . .	3rd Sat. in Oct.(c)	(b)	4
Florida		. . .	30	(d)	2
Georgia		. . .	30	B,D,R,S,T	3
Hawaii		. . .	30	B,D,E,R,S,T	2
Idaho		30	17/10(e)	B,D,S,T	4
Illinois		30	28	(f)	4
Indiana		30	29(g)	B,D,S,T	2
Iowa	★	. . .	10	(b)	4
Kansas	★	20	20	(b)	4
Kentucky	★	30	30	(b)	4
Louisiana		. . .	24(c)	D,T	4
Maine	★	. . .	Election day	(b)	
Maryland	★	29	29	(b)	5
Massachusetts		. . .	28	D,T	
Michigan		30	30	D,S,T	10
Minnesota	★	20	Election day	(b)	4
Mississippi		30	10	(f)	4
Missouri	★	. . .	28	(b)	
Montana	★	30	30	(b)	4
Nebraska		. . .	10	D,S,T	
Nevada		30	30	S,T	2
New Hampshire		10	10	B,D,R,S	
New Jersey	★	30	29	(b)	4
New Mexico		. . .	42	T	2
New York	★	30	30	(b)	4
North Carolina		30	21(h)	D	8
North Dakota(i)		30			
Ohio	★	30	30	(b)	4
Oklahoma		. . .	10	D	4
Oregon	★	20	Election day	(b)	2
Pennsylvania	★	30	30	(b)	2
Rhode Island		30	30	D	5
South Carolina		. . .	30	D,S,T	4
South Dakota		. . .	15	S,T	4
Tennessee	★	50	30	(b)	4
Texas	★	. . .	30	(b)	
Utah	★	30	5	(b)	4
Vermont		. . .	17	(d)	4
Virginia		. . .	31	(f)	4
Washington		30	30	(f)	2
West Virginia	★	30	30	(b)	4
Wisconsin	★	10	Election day	(b)	2
Wyoming		. . .	30	B,D,E,S,T	2
Dist. of Col.	★	30	30	(b)	4
Puerto Rico		. . .	50	(f)	2
Virgin Islands		45	45	S	4

Source: Adapted from *Easy Does It.* League of Women Voters Education Fund, 1730 M St., N.W., Washington, D.C. (Copyright 1984).

Key:
. . .—No residence requirement.
(a) In this column: B—Absent on business; D—Disabled persons; E—Not absent, but prevented by employment from registering; R—Absent for religious reasons; S—Students; T—Temporarily out of jurisdiction.
(b) All voters. See column on mail registration.
(c) Closing date differs for primary election. In Connecticut, 14 days; Delaware, 21 days; Louisiana, 30 days.
(d) Anyone unable to register in person.
(e) With precinct registrar, 17 days before; with county clerk, 10 days.
(f) No one is eligible to register absentee.
(g) Before deputy registrar, 45 days.
(h) Business days.
(i) No voter registration.

Table 5.10
POLLING HOURS: GENERAL ELECTIONS

State or other jurisdiction	Polls open	Polls close	Notes on hours(a)
Alabama	No later than 8 a.m.	Between 6 and 8 p.m.	Polls must be open at least 10 consecutive hours; hours set by county commissioner.
Alaska	8 a.m.	8 p.m.	
Arizona	6 a.m.	7 p.m.	
Arkansas	Between 7 and 8 a.m.	7:30 p.m.	
California	7 a.m.	8 p.m.	
Colorado	7 a.m.	7 p.m.	
Connecticut	6 a.m.	8 p.m.	
Delaware	7 a.m.	8 p.m.	
Florida	7 a.m.	7 p.m.	
Georgia	7 a.m.	7 p.m.	
Hawaii	7 a.m.	6 p.m.	
Idaho	8 a.m.	8 p.m.	Polls may open earlier at option of county clerk. Polls may close earlier if all registered electors in a precinct have voted.
Illinois	6 a.m.	7 p.m.	
Indiana	6 a.m.	6 p.m.	
Iowa	7 a.m.	9 p.m.	
Kansas	Between 6 and 7 a.m.	Between 7 and 8 p.m.	Hours may be changed by county election officer, but polls must be open at least 12 consecutive hours between 6 a.m. and 8 p.m.
Kentucky	6 a.m.	6 p.m.	Persons in line may vote only until 7 p.m.
Louisiana	6 a.m.	8 p.m.	
Maine	Between 6 and 9 a.m.	8 p.m.	Opening hour is determined by municipal election officer. Towns with population less than 100 may open and close at any time.
Maryland	7 a.m.	8 p.m.	
Massachusetts	Between 7 and 8 a.m.	8 p.m.	
Michigan	7 a.m.	8 p.m.	
Minnesota	7 a.m.	8 p.m.	Municipalities of less than 1,000 may establish hours of no later than 9 a.m. to 8 p.m.
Mississippi	7 a.m.	6 p.m.	
Missouri	6 a.m.	7 p.m.	
Montana	7 a.m.	8 p.m.	In precincts of over 200 registered voters.
	noon	8 p.m.	In precincts of less than 200 registered voters, polls may close when all registered electors have voted.
Nebraska	7 a.m.	7 p.m.	Mountain Time Zone.
	8 a.m.	8 p.m.	Central Time Zone.
Nevada	7 a.m.	7 p.m.	
New Hampshire	Varies	Varies	Cities: Polls open not less than 8 hours and may be opened not earlier than 6 a.m. nor later than 8 p.m. Small towns: In towns of less than 700 population the polls must be open at least five consecutive hours. On written request of seven registered voters the polls shall be kept open until 6 p.m. In towns of less than 100 population, the polls close if all registered voters have appeared. Other towns: Polls may not open later than 10 a.m. and may not close earlier than 6 p.m. On written request of 10 registered voters the polls may close at 7 p.m.
New Jersey	7 a.m.	8 p.m.	
New Mexico	7 a.m.	8 p.m.	
New York	6 a.m.	9 p.m.	
North Carolina	6:30 a.m.	7:30 p.m.	In precincts where voting machines are used, county board of elections may permit closing at 8:30 p.m.
North Dakota	Between 7 and 9 a.m.	Between 7 and 9 p.m.	In precincts where less than 75 votes were cast in previous election, polls may open at noon.
Ohio	6:30 a.m.	7:30 p.m.	
Oklahoma	7 a.m.	7 p.m.	
Oregon	8 a.m.	8 p.m.	
Pennsylvania	7 a.m.	8 p.m.	
Rhode Island	Between 7 a.m. and noon	9 p.m.	Opening hours vary across cities and towns.

POLLING HOURS: GENERAL ELECTIONS—Continued

State or other jurisdiction	Polls open	Polls close	Notes on hours(a)
South Carolina	8 a.m.	7 p.m.	
South Dakota	7 a.m. 8 a.m.	7 p.m. 8 p.m.	Mountain Time Zone. Central Time Zone.
Tennessee	Varies.	7 p.m. (CST); 8 p.m. (EST)	Counties with population over 120,000 may not open later than 8 a.m.
Texas	7 a.m.	7 p.m.	Counties with population over one million may open polls at 6 a.m.
Utah	7 a.m.	8 p.m.	
Vermont	Between 6 and 10 a.m.	No later than 7 p.m.	
Virginia	6 a.m.	7 p.m.	
Washington	7 a.m.	8 p.m.	
West Virginia	6:30 a.m.	7:30 p.m.	
Wisconsin	7 a.m. Between 7 and 9 a.m.	8 p.m. 8 p.m.	1st, 2nd and 3rd class cities. 4th class cities, towns and villages.
Wyoming	7 a.m.	7 p.m.	
Dist. of Col.	7 a.m.	8 p.m.	
American Samoa	6 a.m.	6 p.m.	
Guam	8 a.m.	8 p.m.	
Puerto Rico	9 a.m.	3 p.m.	
Virgin Islands	8 a.m.	6 p.m.	

Sources: State statutes and state election administration offices.

Note: Hours for primary, municipal and special elections may differ from those noted.

(a) In all states, voters standing in line when the polls close are allowed to vote; however, provisions for handling those voters vary across jurisdictions.

Table 5.11
VOTING STATISTICS FOR GUBERNATORIAL ELECTIONS*

	Primary election			General election						
State	Republican	Democrat	Total votes	Republican	Per-cent	Democrat	Per-cent	Other	Per-cent	Total votes
Alabama.........	unopposed	1,000,295 (a)	1,000,295	440,815	39.1	650,538	57.6	37,372	3.3	1,128,725
Alaska...........	81,732	55,315	137,047	72,291	37.1	89,918	46.1	32,676	16.7	194,885
Arizona..........	176,245	166,051	342,296	235,877	32.5	453,795	62.5	36,692	5.0	726,364
Arkansas‡	19,040	492,686	511,726	331,987	37.4	554,561	62.6	0	0.0	886,548
California........	2,281,115	2,827,348	5,108,463	3,881,014	49.3	3,787,669	48.1	208,015	2.6	7,876,698
Colorado	unopposed	unopposed	0	302,740	31.7	627,960	65.7	25,321	2.6	956,021
Connecticut	(b)	(b)	(b)	497,773	45.9	578,264	53.4	8,119	0.7	1,084,156
Delaware‡	unopposed	34,658	34,658	135,250	55.5	108,315	44.5	0	0.0	243,565
Florida	376,448	993,534	1,369,982	949,013	35.3	1,739,553	64.7	0	0.0	2,688,566
Georgia..........	61,410	899,990 (a)	961,400	434,496	37.2	734,090	62.8	455	0.0	1,169,041
Hawaii	12,395	239,452	251,847	81,507	26.2	141,043	45.2	89,303	28.6	311,853
Idaho	99,554	unopposed	99,554	161,157	49.4	165,365	50.6	0	0.0	326,522
Illinois...........	606,446	unopposed	606,446	1,816,101	49.4	1,811,027	49.3	46,553	1.3	3,673,681
Indiana‡	446,667	611,261	1,057,928	1,146,497	52.2	1,036,922	47.2	14,569	0.6	2,197,988
Iowa	unopposed	196,071	196,071	548,313	52.8	483,291	46.5	6,625	0.6	1,038,229
Kansas	235,828	131,565	367,3933	39,356	44.4	405,772	53.2	18,135	2.4	763,263
Kentucky†	97,836	658,454	756,290	454,650	44.1	561,674	54.5	14,347	1.4	1,030,671
Louisiana†	(c)	(c)	1,615,905	(c)	(c)	(c)	(c)	(c)	(c)	(c)
Maine	84,794	74,2091	59,003	172,949	37.6	281,066	61.1	6,280	1.3	460,295
Maryland	134,590	590,648	725,238	432,826	38.0	705,910	62.0	413	0.0	1,139,149
Massachusetts	178,683	1,181,421	1,360,104	749,679	36.6	1,219,109	59.4	81,466	4.0	2,050,254
Michigan	641,377	810,184	1,451,561	1,369,582	45.1	1,561,291	51.4	109,135	3.5	3,040,008
Minnesota	309,292	538,603	847,895	715,796	40.0	1,049,104	58.6	24,639	1.4	1,789,539
Mississippi†	unopposed	828,211 (a)	828,211	288,764	38.9	409,209	55.1	44,764	6.0	742,737
Missouri‡	363,638	514,845	878,483	1,194,506	56.7	913,700	43.3	4	0.0	2,108,210
Montana‡.........	unopposed	99,056	99,056	100,070	26.4	266,578	70.3	12,322	3.3	378,970
Nebraska	184,819	123,853	308,672	270,203	49.3	277,436	50.7	263	0.0	547,902
Nevada	68,986	108,236	177,222	100,104	41.8	128,132	53.4	11,515	4.8	239,751
New Hampshire‡ ..	62,689	46,156	108,845	256,574	66.8	127,156	33.1	180	0.1	383,910
New Jersey§.......	unopposed	326,403	326,403	1,372,631	69.6	578,402	29.3	21,191	1.1	1,972,224
New Mexico.......	65,599	177,490	243,089	191,626	47.0	215,840	53.0	0	0.0	407,466
New York	576,045	1,297,256	1,873,301	2,494,827	47.5	2,675,213	50.9	84,851	1.6	5,254,891
North Carolina‡ ...	140,354	955,799 (a)	1,096,153	1,208,167	54.3	1,011,209	45.4	7,351	0.3	2,226,727
North Dakota‡	unopposed	41,641	41,641	140,460	44.7	173,922	55.3	0	0.0	314,382
Ohio	673,564	1,030,418	1,703,982	1,303,962	38.9	1,981,882	59.0	70,877	2.1	3,356,721
Oklahoma	113,846	459,036	572,882	332,207	37.6	548,159	62.1	2,764	0.3	883,130
Oregon	252,798	313,376	566,174	639,841	61.4	374,316	35.9	27,852	2.7	1,042,009
Pennsylvania	unopposed	756,818	756,818	1,872,784	50.8	1,772,353	48.1	38,848	1.1	3,683,985
Rhode Island‡	unopposed	126,131	126,131	245,059	60.0	163,311	40.0	5	0.0	408,375
South Carolina	20,944	unopposed	20,944	202,806	30.2	468,819	69.8	0	0.0	671,625
South Dakota	unopposed	41,017	41,017	197,426	70.9	81,136	29.1	0	0.0	278,562
Tennessee	unopposed	635,830	635,830	737,963	59.6	500,937	40.4	27	0.0	1,238,927
Texas............	265,851	1,317,814	1,583,665	1,465,937	45.9	1,697,870	53.2	27,284	0.9	3,191,091
Utah‡	167,287	82,723	250,010	351,792	55.9	275,669	43.8	2,158	0.3	629,619
Vermont‡	49,985	unopposed	49,985	113,264	48.5	116,938	50.0	3,551	1.5	233,753
Virginia§.........	(b)	(b)	(b)	601,652	46.2	700,438	53.8	153	0.0	1,302,243
Washington‡	250,656	654,221	904,877	881,994	46.7	1,006,993	53.5	0	0.0	1,888,987
West Virginia‡	128,337	371,609	499,946	394,937	53.3	346,565	46.7	0	0.0	741,502
Wisconsin.........	334,347	586,127	920,474	662,838	41.9	896,812	56.8	20,694	1.3	1,580,344
Wyoming.........	70,667	52,116	122,783	62,128	36.9	106,427	63.1	0	0.0	168,555

*Figures are for 1982, except where indicated: †1983; ‡1984; §1985.
Sources: America Votes and state election administration offices.

(a) Total shown is for first Democratic primary. Total votes for runoff election: Alabama, 1,000,647; Georgia, 911,024; Mississippi, 773,301; North Carolina, 678,629.
(b) Candidates nominated by convention.

(c) Louisiana has an open primary which requires all candidates, regardless of party affiliation, to appear on a single ballot. If a candidate receives over 50 percent of the vote in the primary, he is elected to the office. If no candidate receives a majority vote, then a single election is held between the two candidates receiving the most votes. In 1983, 62.3 percent of the votes in the open primary were cast for one candidate, a Democrat, who was therefore considered elected.

Table 5.12
VOTER TURNOUT IN NON-PRESIDENTIAL ELECTION YEARS:
1974, 1978 AND 1982
(In thousands)

State or other jurisdiction	1982 Voting age population (a)	Number registered	Number voting (b)	1978 Voting age population (a)	Number registered	Number voting (b)	1974 Voting age population (a)	Number registered	Number voting (b)
United States	169,339	110,477	67,592	158,373	104,829	61,038	145,031	97,303	57,357
Alabama	2,812	2,136	1,128 (c)	2,669	1,938	730 (d)	2,404	1,793	598 (c)
Alaska	287	266	195 (c)	269	238	130	213	169	99
Arizona	2,061	1,141	726 (c)	1,766	969	551	1,444	891	564
Arkansas	1,650	1,116	789 (c)	1,575	1,047	524 (c)	1,420	997	546 (c)
California	18,277	11,559	7,876 (c)	16,546	10,130	7,132	14,595	9,928	6,635
Colorado	2,225	1,456	956 (c)	1,974	1,345	848	1,710	1,227	829 (c)
Connecticut	2,378	1,647	1,084 (c)	2,254	1,626	1,061	2,149	1,562	1,125
Delaware	443	286	191 (d)	426	278	166	390	279	160 (e)
Florida	8,169	4,866	2,689 (c)	6,862	4,217	2,530	5,856	3,621	1,828 (c)
Georgia	4,040	2,316	1,169 (c)	3,667	2,183	663 (c)	3,251	2,090	936 (c)
Hawaii	716	405	312 (c)	657	395	293	574	343	273
Idaho	661	541	327 (c)	612	526	297	528	440	264
Illinois	8,346	5,965	3,691 (f)	8,132	5,809	3,343	7,612	5,906	3,085
Indiana	3,904	2,937	1,817 (d)	3,812	2,851	1,405	3,577	2,937	1,753 (d)
Iowa	2,094	1,586	1,038 (c)	2,075	1,588	843 (c)	1,958	1,013	920 (d)
Kansas	1,759	1,186	763 (c)	1,681	1,182	749 (d)	1,581	1,143	794 (d)
Kentucky	2,620	1,827	700 (e)	2,528	1,666	477 (d)	2,284	1,473	746 (d)
Louisiana	3,055	1,965	(g)	2,760	1,821	840	2,443	1,727	546 (e)
Maine	831	766	460 (c)	791	692	375 (d)	714	632	364 (c)
Maryland	3,190	1,968	1,139 (c)	3,014	1,888	1,012 (c)	2,783	1,738	949 (c)
Massachusetts	4,394	3,027	2,051 (d)	4,213	2,920	2,044	4,054	2,928	1,896
Michigan	6,554	5,625	3,040 (c)	6,406	5,230	2,985	6,077	4,786	2,657 (c)
Minnesota	2,988	2,668	1,805 (d)	2,823	2,511	1,625	2,631	1,922	1,296
Mississippi	1,745	1,508	645 (d)	1,672	1,150 (h)	584 (d)	1,505	1,152	306 (e)
Missouri	3,640	2,749	1,544 (d)	3,499	2,579	1,546 (i)	3,306	2,165	1,224 (d)
Montana	569	446	321 (d)	548	410	297	494	374	260
Nebraska	1,144	832	548 (c)	1,108	833	511	1,056	788	467
Nevada	661	322	240 (d)	520	268	195	390	237	172
New Hampshire ...	697	462	285 (c)	638	489	279	551	421	236
New Jersey	5,544	3,681	2,194 (d)	5,326	3,602	2,060	5,070	3,502	2,184
New Mexico	936	583	407 (c)	841	598	357	717	504	339
New York	13,153	7,635	5,222 (c)	12,912	7,801	4,929	12,701	8,341	5,544
North Carolina	4,417	2,675	1,321 (e)	4,088	2,430	1,136 (d)	3,677	2,280	1,020 (d)
North Dakota	473	(j)	262 (d)	455	(j)	235	425	(j)	242
Ohio	7,793	5,674	3,395 (d)	7,638	5,222	3,018	7,296	4,442	3,151
Oklahoma	2,299	1,614	883 (c)	2,081	1,366	801	1,872	1,341	822
Oregon	1,954	1,517	1,042 (c)	1,808	1,473	911 (c)	1,581	1,143	793
Pennsylvania	8,883	5,703	3,684 (c)	8,673	5,590	3,742 (c)	8,312	5,529	3,500 (c)
Rhode Island	726	534	343 (d)	707	534	332	654	514	322 (c)
South Carolina	2,291	1,229	672 (c)	2,104	1,098	633 (d)	1,842	998	523 (c)
South Dakota	482	426	279 (c)	480	421	260 (c)	459	402	279 (d)
Tennessee	3,375	2,273	1,260 (d)	3,179	2,138	1,190 (c)	2,859	1,960	1,064
Texas	10,793	6,415	3,191 (c)	9,350	5,682	2,370 (c)	8,075	5,348	1,655 (c)
Utah	986	749	531 (d)	858	667	385	741	620	423
Vermont	379	316	169 (c)	353	286	125	316	267	145
Virginia	4,078	2,234	1,415 (d)	3,794	2,027	1,251	3,375	2,051	924 (e)
Washington	3,154	2,106	1,368 (d)	2,792	1,961	1,029	2,419	1,896	1,044
West Virginia	1,408	948	565 (d)	1,363	1,021	493	1,240	1,025	416 (e)
Wisconsin	3,464	(j)	1,580 (c)	3,263	1,682	1,501 (c)	3,090	(j)	1,199
Wyoming	354	230	169 (c)	296	201	142	245	185	132
Dist. of Col.	487	361	111 (e)	515	250	103	515	273	108 (k)

Sources: U.S. Department of Commerce, Bureau of the Census, *Statistical Abstract of the United States* and unpublished data from the Republican National Committee.

(a) Estimated as of November 1 of the year indicated. Includes armed forces stationed in each state, aliens and institutional population.

(b) Number represents total voting in general election for all races for the year indicated, except where noted. Total persons voting restricted to number of ballots recorded by secretaries of state as having been cast.

(c) Total vote for largest race—governor.

(d) Total vote for largest race—senator.

(e) Total vote for largest race—congressional.

(f) Total vote for largest race—secretary of state.

(g) Under Louisiana's election law, candidates of all parties run together on a single non-partisan ballot in September. If no candidate wins a majority of the vote, the top two finishers, regardless of party, oppose each other in a November runoff. In 1982, the congressional incumbents were reelected in the September race.

(h) Estimated.

(i) Total vote for largest race—state auditor.

(j) No required statewide registration.

(k) Total vote for largest race—mayor.

Table 5.13
VOTER TURNOUT FOR PRESIDENTIAL ELECTIONS: 1976, 1980 AND 1984
(In thousands)

State or other jurisdiction	1984 Voting age population (a)	1984 Number registered	1984 Number voting (b)	1980 Voting age population (a)	1980 Number registered	1980 Number voting (b)	1976 Voting age population (a)	1976 Number registered	1976 Number voting (b)
United States	173,937	123,842	92,708	164,473	112,929	86,485	152,309	105,838	82,645
Alabama	2,875	2,343	1,442	2,755	2,132	1,342	2,554	1,865	1,183
Alaska............	345	305	207	276	259	158	257	207	128
Arizona...........	2,200	1,463	1,026	1,962	1,121	874	1,611	980	765
Arkansas	1,694	1,160	884	1,626	1,186	838	1,502	1,021	768
California........	19,063	13,074	9,559	17,525	11,362	8,586	15,598	9,982	8,137
Colorado	2,365	1,621	1,295	2,121	1,434	1,184	1,838	1,349	1,082
Connecticut	2,404	1,809	1,467	2,304	1,719	1,405	2,201	1,669	1,408
Delaware	457	314	255	431	301	236	412	301	236
Florida	8,529	5,574	4,180	7,566	4,810	3,686	6,408	4,094	3,151
Georgia...........	4,204	2,732	1,776	3,872	2,467	1,597	3,494	2,302	1,467
Hawaii	755	419	336	696	403	303	624	363	309
Idaho	681	582	411	645	581	437	567	520	355
Illinois...........	8,410	6,470	4,819	8,230	6,230	4,749	7,939	6,252	4,839
Indiana	3,969	3,050	2,233	3,890	2,944	2,242	3,692	3,010	2,279
Iowa	2,119	1,763	1,320	2,097	1,747	1,317	2,026	1,407	1,279
Kansas	1,794	1,113	1,022	1,728	1,159	980	1,628	1,113	958
Kentucky	2,700	2,023	1,369	2,594	1,821	1,296	2,434	1,713	1,167
Louisiana	3,147	2,244	1,707	2,916	2,015	1,549	2,623	1,866	1,278
Maine	848	811	553	810	760	523	759	696	486
Maryland	3,259	2,253	1,676	3,082	2,065	1,540	2,920	1,950	1,440
Massachusetts	4,422	3,254	2,559	4,277	3,157	2,520	4,132	2,912	2,594
Michigan	6,530	5,889	3,802	6,529	5,726	3,909	6,214	5,202	3,722
Minnesota	3,044	2,893	2,084	2,931	2,787	2,046	2,726	2,566	1,979
Mississippi	1,810	1,670	941	1,722	1,486	893	1,603	(c)	769
Missouri	3,682	2,969	2,123	3,576	2,845	2,099	3,408	2,553	1,954
Montana	591	527	384	560	496	364	519	455	339
Nebraska	1,163	903	652	1,130	856	640	1,081	841	624
Nevada	689	356	287	602	297	244	457	251	206
New Hampshire ...	722	544	389	671	551	384	593	478	359
New Jersey........	5,659	4,073	3,218	5,418	3,761	2,976	5,220	3,770	3,037
New Mexico.......	997	651	514	899	653	456	783	527	426
New York	13,326	9,044	6,807	12,929	7,898	6,201	12,892	8,199	6,668
North Carolina	4,559	3,271	2,176	4,272	2,775	1,856	3,907	2,554	1,679
North Dakota	491	(c)	309	466	(c)	302	442	(c)	309
Ohio	7,846	6,359	4,563	7,738	5,927	4,284	7,461	4,693	4,195
Oklahoma	2,452	1,929	1,256	2,202	1,469	1,150	1,990	1,401	1,108
Oregon	1,961	1,609	1,227	1,928	1,569	1,180	1,679	1,420	1,049
Pennsylvania	8,989	6,194	4,845	8,783	5,754	4,562	8,531	5,750	4,621
Rhode Island	733	542	409	709	547	416	689	545	411
South Carolina	2,386	1,396	969	2,213	1,236	890	1,993	1,113	803
South Dakota	498	443	318	487	448	328	469	426	301
Tennessee	3,476	2,580	1,712	3,320	2,359	1,617	3,033	1,912	1,476
Texas............	11,487	7,900	5,398	10,117	6,640	4,541	8,789	6,319	4,072
Utah	1,040	840	630	938	782	604	791	705	548
Vermont	391	334	235	370	312	213	337	284	194
Virginia...........	4,203	2,544	2,147	3,924	2,302	1,866	3,613	2,124	1,716
Washington	3,202	2,458	1,875	3,037	2,237	1,742	2,601	2,065	1,585
West Virginia	1,433	1,025	736	1,398	1,035	738	1,314	1,084	751
Wisconsin.........	3,490	(c)	2,212	3,375	(c)	2,272	3,163	2,566	2,104
Wyoming	365	240	184	332	219	177	267	195	160
Dist. of Col.	482	282	210	494	289	173	525	268	171

Sources: Republican National Committee, *1985 Republican Almanac*; U.S. Department of Commerce, Bureau of the Census, *Statistical Abstract of the United States, 1982-83*. (Compiled from U.S. Bureau of the Census, *Current Population Reports* and unpublished data from the National Republican Congressional Committee.)

(a) Estimated population as of November of year indicated. Includes armed forces in each state, aliens and institutional population.

(b) For 1980 and 1984, "number voting" is number of ballots cast in presidential race. For 1976, "number voting" is restricted to number of ballots recorded by secretaries of state as having been cast for any electoral office or referendum; or in those states which do not count total number of ballots, the largest number of votes cast for a particular office.

(c) No statewide registration required. Excluded from totals for persons registered.

Table 5.14
INITIATIVE PROVISIONS FOR STATE LEGISLATION

State or other jurisdiction	Type(a)	Basis for number of signatures required on petition(b)
Alaska...............	D	10% of votes cast in last general election and resident in at least 2/3 of election districts
Arizona...............	D	10% of qualified electors based on votes cast in last general election for governor
Arkansas	D	8% of legal voters based on votes cast in last general election for governor
California............	D	5% of votes cast in last general election for governor
Colorado	D	5% of votes cast in last general election for secretary of state
Idaho	D	10% of votes cast in last general election for governor
Maine	I	10% of votes cast in last general election for governor
Massachusetts	I	3% of votes cast in last general election for governor
Michigan	I	8% of votes cast in last general election for governor
Missouri	D	5% of voters in each of 2/3 of congressional districts
Montana..............	D	5% of qualified electors in each of at least 1/3 of legislative representative districts; total must be at least 5% of the total qualified electors in state
Nebraska	D	7% of votes cast in last general election for governor; petition must include 5% of electors of each of 2/5 of counties in state
Nevada	I	10% of votes cast in last general election in at least 75% of counties in state
North Dakota	D	2% of state's resident population at last federal decennial census
Ohio	B	3% of electors
Oklahoma	D	8% of legal voters based on total vote cast in last general election for state office receiving largest number of votes
Oregon	D	6% of total votes cast in last election for governor
South Dakota	I	5% of qualified voters based on votes cast in last general election for governor
Utah	B	10% (direct) or 5% (indirect) of total votes cast in last general election for governor with same percentage required from a majority of counties in state
Washington	B	8% of votes cast in last general election for governor
Wyoming	D	15% of qualified voters based on votes cast in last general election and resident in at least 2/3 of counties in state
Dist. of Col.	D	5% of registered qualified voters; total must include 5% of registered voters in each of five or more of the wards in the district
Guam	D	20% of voters in last general election for governor
No. Mariana Is.	D	20% of qualified voters

Note: This table refers only to those jurisdictions that allow proposed state laws to be placed on a state ballot by citizen petition and enacted or rejected by the electorate.

(a) The initiative may be direct or indirect. The direct type, designated D in this column, allows proposed measures to be placed on the ballot by securing a specific number of signatures on a petition—no legislative action is required. The indirect type, designated I, requires that the petition for a proposed measure first be submitted to the legislature allowing the legislators an opportunity to enact or alter the measure before it is placed on the ballot for consideration by the electorate. In some states, both types, designated B, are used.

(b) A majority of the popular vote is required to enact a measure in every jurisdiction except the Northern Mariana Islands where enactment requires approval by 2/3 of the votes cast. In Massachusetts and Nebraska, respectively, apart from satisfying the requisite majority vote, the measure must receive, 30 and 35 percent of the total votes cast in favor.

Table 5.15
PROVISIONS FOR REFERENDUM ON STATE LEGISLATION

State or other jurisdiction	Basis of referendum(a)	Basis for number of signatures on citizen petition(b)
Alaska...............	Citizen petition	10% of votes cast in last general election for governor and resident in at least 2/3 of election districts
Arizona..............	Citizen petition Submission by legislature	5% of qualified voters
Arkansas	Citizen petition	6% of legal voters based on votes cast in last general election for governor
California............	Citizen petition Constitutional requirement(c)	5% of votes cast in last general election for governor
Colorado	Citizen petition Submission by legislature	5% of votes cast in last general election for secretary of state
Connecticut	Submission by legislature	
Florida	Constitutional requirement(c)	
Georgia...............	Constitutional requirement(c)	
Idaho	Citizen petition	10% of votes cast in last general election for governor
Illinois................	Submission by legislature(c)	
Iowa	Constitutional requirement(c)	
Kansas	Constitutional requirement(c)	
Kentucky	Citizen petition(d) Submission by legislature(d) Constitutional requirement(d)	5% of legal voters based on votes cast in last general election for governor
Maine	Citizen petition Submission by legislature Constitutional requirement(c)	10% of votes cast in last general election for governor
Maryland	Citizen petition	3% of qualified voters based on votes cast in last general election for governor; not more than 1/2 can be residents of Baltimore or any one county
Massachusetts	Citizen petition	2% of votes cast in last general election for governor
Michigan	Citizen petition Submission by legislature Constitutional requirement(c)	5% of votes cast in last general election for governor
Missouri	Citizen petition Submission by legislature	5% of legal voters in each of 2/3 of congressional districts
Montana..............	Citizen petition Submission by legislature	5% of total qualified electors and 5% in at least 1/3 of legislative districts
Nebraska	Citizen petition	5% of votes cast in last general election for governor
Nevada	Citizen petition	10% of votes cast in last general election
New Jersey...........	Submission by legislature Constitutional requirement(c)	
New Mexico..........	Citizen petition Constitutional requirement(c)	10% of qualified electors of each of 3/4 of counties; total must be at least 10% of qualified electors in state
New York	Constitutional requirement(c)	
North Carolina	Constitutional requirement(c)	
North Dakota	Citizen petition	2% of state's resident population from last federal decennial census
Ohio	Citizen petition Constitutional requirement(c)	6% of electors

State or other jurisdiction	Basis of referendum(a)	Basis for number of signatures on citizen petition(b)
Oklahoma	Citizen petition	5% of votes cast for state office receiving largest number of votes in last general election
	Submission by legislature Constitutional requirement(c)	
Oregon	Citizen petition	4% of votes cast in last election for governor
Pennsylvania	Constitutional requirement(c)	
Rhode Island	Constitutional requirement(c)	
South Dakota	Citizen petition	5% of votes cast in last general election for governor
Utah	Citizen petition	10% of votes cast in last general election for governor and same percentage required from a majority of the counties
Virginia..............	Submission by legislature Constitutional requirement(c)	
Washington	Citizen petition	4% of voters registered and voting in last general election for governor
	Submission by legislature Constitutional requirement(c)	
Wisconsin............	Submission by legislature Constitutional requirement(c)	
Wyoming	Citizen petition	15% of voters in last general election and resident in at least 2/3 of counties
Dist. of Col.	Citizen petition	5% of registered qualified voters; total must include 5% of registered voters in each of five or more wards in district
Guam	Citizen petition	20% of persons voting in last general election for governor
	Submission by legislature	
No. Mariana Is.	Citizen petition	20% of qualified voters
Puerto Rico	Citizen petition	20% of persons voting in last general election for governor
	Submission by legislature	

Note: This table refers only to those jurisdictions which provide for a process whereby a state law passed by the legislature may be referred to the voters before it goes into effect.

(a) Three forms of referendum exist: (1) Citizen petition—the people may petition for a referendum, usually with the intention of rejecting an act passed by the legislature (in many states, the right to petition for referendum may not extend to specific types of legislation); (2) Submission by legislature—the legislature may voluntarily submit laws to the voters for their approval; (3) Constitutional requirement—the state constitution may require that certain questions, such as debt authorization, be submitted to the voters.

(b) A majority of the popular vote is required to enact a referendum measure in every jurisdiction. In Massachusetts, the measure must also receive at least 30 percent of the total ballots cast in the election.

(c) Applies to laws regarding state debt authorization: California, Il-linois (debt may be incurred by law passed by legislature or by submission of question to voters), Iowa, Kansas, New Jersey, New Mexico, New York, North Carolina, Oklahoma, Pennsylvania, Rhode Island, Virginia, Washington, Wisconsin; state bond issuance: Florida, Maine; taxation: Georgia (exemptions from ad valorem taxes), Michigan (taxing and spending over prescribed limits); and authorization of banking powers for associations: Iowa, Ohio.

(d) Applies only to referendum on legislation classifying property and providing for taxation on the same. The referendum, required by the state constitution, may be ordered by citizen petition or submitted by the legislature.

Table 5.16

PROVISIONS FOR RECALL OF STATE OFFICIALS

State or other jurisdiction	Officers to whom applicable	Basis for number of signatures on petition(a)
Alaska...........	All elective officials except judicial officers	25% of voters in last general election in jurisdiction of official sought to be recalled
Arizona..........	All elective officials	25% of votes cast in last election for office of official sought to be recalled
California........	All elective officials	Statewide officers: 12% of votes cast in last election for officer sought to be recalled; signatures must be obtained from at least five different counties equal in number to 1% of last vote for office in each of the five counties. State legislators, members of Board of Equalization and courts of appeals justices: 20% of last vote for office
Colorado	All elective officials	25% of votes cast in last election for office of official sought to be recalled
Georgia..........	All elective officials	Statewide officers: 15% of electors registered and qualified to vote at the last general election for office of official sought to be recalled. At least 1/15 of electors must reside in each of the U.S. congressional districts in state. Others: 30% of electors registered and qualified to vote in last general election for office of official sought to be recalled
Idaho	All elective officials except judicial officers	Statewide officers: 20% of number of electors registered to vote in last general election for governor. Others: 20% of electors registered to vote in last general election in jurisdiction of official sought to be recalled
Kansas	All elective officials except judicial officers	40% of votes cast at last general election for office of official sought to be recalled
Louisiana	All elective officials except judicial officers	25% of electors in jurisdiction of official sought to be recalled
Michigan	All elective officials except judges of courts of records and courts of like jurisdiction	25% of voters in last election for governor in district of official sought to be recalled
Montana..........	All public officials elected or appointed(b)	Statewide officers: 10% of registered voters at last general election. Others: 15% of number registered to vote in last election in jurisdiction of official sought to be recalled
Nevada	All elective officials	25% of voters in last election in jurisdiction of official sought to be recalled
North Dakota	All elective officials	25% of electors voting in last general election for governor in jurisdiction of official sought to be recalled
Oregon	All elective officials	15% of votes cast in last gubernatorial election
Washington	All elective officials except judges of courts of record	25% or 35% of qualified voters depending on office
Wisconsin.........	All elective officials	25% of votes cast in last general election for governor in jurisdiction of official sought to be recalled
Dist. of Col.	All elective officials except D.C. delegate to U.S. Congress	At-large officers: 10% of registered electors in each of five or more of the city's wards. Others: 10% of registered electors in ward of official sought to be recalled
Guam	Governor	50% of votes cast in last gubernatorial election(c)
No. Mariana Is. ...	All elective officials	40% of persons qualified to vote for official sought to be recalled
Virgin Islands	Governor	50% of votes cast in last gubernatorial election(c)

Note: This table refers only to those jurisdictions that allow the voters to remove state elective officials from office in a recall election.

(a) A majority of the popular vote is required to recall an official in every jurisdiction except the Northern Mariana Islands where recall requires approval by 2/3 of votes cast. In Guam and the Virgin Islands, apart from satisfying the requisite majority vote, the "yes" votes must total 2/3 of the votes cast in the last gubernatorial election.

(b) An elective official may be recalled by qualified voters entitled to vote for individual's successor. An appointed official may be recalled by qualified voters entitled to vote for the successor(s) of the elective officer(s) authorized to appoint an individual to the position.

(c) Referendum on governor (recall) may be initiated by petition described above or by 2/3 vote of members of legislature.

CHAPTER SIX

STATE FINANCES

Table 6.1
STATE BUDGETARY PRACTICES

State or other jurisdiction	Budget-making authority	Date estimates must be submitted by dept. or agencies	Power of legislature to change budget(a)	Fiscal year begins	Frequency of budget
Alabama............	Governor	Oct. 15 for Jan. session; Nov. 15 for Feb. session	Unlimited	Oct. 1	Annual
Alaska..............	Governor	Oct. 1	Unlimited	July 1	Annual
Arizona.............	Governor	Sept. 1	Unlimited	July 1	Annual
Arkansas	Governor	Sept. 1 in even years	Unlimited	July 1	Biennial, odd yr.(b)
California..........	Governor	Specific date for each agency set by Dept. of Finance	Unlimited	July 1	Annual
Colorado	Governor	Aug. 1-15	Unlimited	July 1	Annual
Connecticut	Governor	Sept. 1	Unlimited	July 1	Annual
Delaware	Governor	Sept. 15; schools, Oct. 15	Unlimited	July 1	Annual
Florida	Governor	Nov. 1 each year	Unlimited	July 1	Biennial, odd yr.(b)
Georgia............	Governor	Sept. 1	Unlimited	July 1	Annual
Hawaii	Governor(c)	Aug. 31	Unlimited	July 1	Biennial, odd yr.(b,d)
Idaho	Governor	Sept. 1 before Jan. session	Unlimited	July 1	Annual
Illinois.............	Governor	Specific date for each agency set by Bur. of the Budget	Unlimited	July 1	Annual
Indiana	Governor	Sept. 1 in even years, flexible policy	Unlimited	July 1	Biennial, odd yr.(b)
Iowa	Governor	Sept. 1	Unlimited	July 1	Biennial, odd yr.(b)
Kansas	Governor	Not later than Oct. 1	Unlimited	July 1	Annual
Kentucky	Governor	Specific date set by administrative action but may not be later than Nov. 15 of each odd year	Unlimited	July 1	Biennial, even yr.(b)
Louisiana	Governor	Dec. 15	Unlimited	July 1	Annual
Maine	Governor	Sept. 1 in even years	Unlimited	July 1	Biennial, odd yr.(b)
Maryland	Governor	Sept. 1	Limited: legislature may decrease but not increase, except appropriations for legislature and judiciary	July 1	Annual
Massachusetts	Governor	Set by administrative action	Unlimited	July 1	Annual
Michigan	Governor	Set by administrative action	Unlimited	Oct. 1	Annual
Minnesota	Governor	Oct. 1 preceding convening of legislature	Unlimited	July 1	Biennial, odd yr.(b)
Mississippi	Governor, Fiscal Mgt. Bd.	Aug. 1 preceding convening of legislature	Unlimited	July 1	Annual
Missouri	Governor	Oct. 1	Unlimited	July 1	Annual
Montana............	Governor	Sept. 1 of year before each session	Unlimited	July 1	Biennial, odd yr.(b)

STATE BUDGETARY PRACTICES—Continued

State or other jurisdiction	Budget-making authority	Date estimates must be submitted by dept. or agencies	Power of legislature to change budget(a)	Fiscal year begins	Frequency of budget
Nebraska	Governor	Not later than Sept. 15	Limited: 3/5 vote required to increase governor's recommendations; majority vote required to reject or decrease such items	July 1	Annual
Nevada	Governor	Sept. 1	Unlimited	July 1	Biennial, odd yr.(b)
New Hampshire	Governor	Oct. 1 in even years	Unlimited	July 1	Biennial, odd yr.(b)
New Jersey.........	Governor	Oct. 1	Unlimited	July 1	Annual
New Mexico........	Governor	Sept. 1	Unlimited	July 1	Annual
New York	Governor	Early in Sept.	Limited: may strike out items, reduce items, or add separate items of expenditure	April 1	Annual
North Carolina	Governor	Sept. 1 preceding session	Unlimited	July 1	Biennial, odd yr.(b)
North Dakota	Governor	July 15 in even years; may extend 45 days	Unlimited	July 1	Biennial, odd yr.(e)
Ohio	Governor	Nov. 1; Dec. 1 when new governor is elected	Unlimited	July 1	Biennial, odd yr.(b)
Oklahoma	Governor	Sept. 1	Unlimited	July 1	Annual
Oregon	Governor	Sept. 1 in even year preceding legislative year	Unlimited	July 1	Biennial, odd yr.(e)
Pennsylvania	Governor	Nov. 1 each year	Unlimited	July 1	Annual
Rhode Island	Governor	Oct. 1	Unlimited	July 1	Annual
South Carolina	State Budget & Control Bd.(f)	Sept. 15 or discretion of board	Unlimited	July 1	Annual
South Dakota	Governor	Sept. 1	Unlimited	July 1	Annual
Tennessee	Governor	Oct. 1	Unlimited	July 1	Annual
Texas..............	Governor, Legis. Budget Bd.	Date set by budget director and Legis. Budget Bd.	Unlimited	Sept. 1	Biennial, odd yr.(e)
Utah	Governor	Sept. 1-30(g)	Unlimited	July 1	Annual
Vermont	Governor	Sept. 1	Unlimited	July 1	(h)
Virginia............	Governor	Feb.-Sept. in odd years	Unlimited	July 1	Biennial, even yr.(b)
Washington	Governor	Date set by governor	Unlimited	July 1	Biennial, odd yr.(b)
West Virginia	Governor	Aug. 15	Limited: may not increase items of budget bill except appropriations for legislature and judiciary	July 1	Annual
Wisconsin..........	Governor	Dates are set by secretary, Dept. of Administration	Unlimited	July 1	Biennial, odd yr.(b)

State or other jurisdiction	Budget-making authority	Date estimates must be submitted by dept. or agencies	Power of legislature to change budget(a)	Fiscal year begins	Frequency of budget
Wyoming	Governor	Sept. 15 preceding session in Feb.	Unlimited	July 1	Biennial, even yr.(b)
Guam	Governor	Date set by director, Bur. of Budget & Mgt. Research	Unlimited	Oct. 1	Annual
Puerto Rico	Governor	Oct. 15	Unlimited	July 1	Annual
Virgin Islands	Governor	Dec. 30	Unlimited	Oct. 1	Annual

Note: For related information, see Table 6.2, "Officials or Agencies Responsible for Budget Preparation, Review, and Controls; Table 3.21, "Legislative Appropriations Process: Budget Documents and Bills; and Table 3.14, "Enacting Legislation: Veto, Veto Override, and Effective Date."

(a) Limitations listed in this column relate to legislative power to increase or decrease budget items generally. Specific limitations, such as constitutionally earmarked funds or requirements to enact revenue measures to cover new expenditure items, are not included.

(b) Budget is adopted biennially, but appropriations are made for each year of the biennium separately. Minnesota and Wisconsin—some appropriations are made for the biennium. North Carolina, Washington, and Wyoming—biennial appropriations with annual review. Virginia—amendments to current budget can be made in any year, but there is no formal provision for annual review of the entire biennial appropriation.

Wisconsin—statutes authorize an annual budget review, and the governor may recommend changes in even years.

(c) Governor has budget-making authority for executive branch. Judicial and legislative branch budgets are the responsibility of the respective branches, and the governor may only veto the budget bills as a whole, not by item.

(d) Increases or decreases may be made in even-year sessions.

(e) Appropriations made for the biennium.

(f) Composition of board: governor (chairman), treasurer, comptroller general, chairman Senate Finance Committee, chairman House Ways and Means Committee.

(g) Thirty days prior to each department or agency hearing before the governor.

(h) Legislation authorizes governor to submit annual or biennial budgets, at discretion of governor.

Table 6.2
OFFICIALS OR AGENCIES RESPONSIBLE FOR BUDGET PREPARATION, REVIEW AND CONTROLS

State or other jurisdiction	Official/agency responsible for preparing budget document	Special budget review agency in legislative branch	Agency(ies) responsible for budgetary and related accounting controls
Alabama	Budget Officer, Dept. of Finance	Legis. Fiscal Off., Joint Fiscal Cmte.	Dept. of Finance
Alaska	Director, Off. of Mgt. & Budget	Div. of Legis. Finance, Legis. Budget & Audit Cmte.	Div. of Treasury, Dept. of Revenue
Arizona	Exec. Budget Officer, Finance Div., Dept. of Admin.	Joint Legis. Budget Cmte.	Div. of Finance, Dept. of Admin.
Arkansas	Administrator, Off. of Budget, Dept. of Finance & Admin.	Budget & Fiscal Review Sect., Legis. Council	Dept. of Finance & Admin.
California	Director, Dept. of Finance	Legis. Budget Cmte.	Dept. of Finance, Off. of Controller
Colorado	Exec. Director, Off. of State Planning & Budgeting	Joint Budget Cmte.	Div. of Accounts & Control, Dept. of Admin.
Connecticut	Budget Director, Off. of Policy & Mgt.	Off. of Fiscal Analysis, Joint Cmte. on Legis. Mgt.	Off. of Policy & Mgt., Off. of the Comptroller
Delaware	Director, Off. of the Budget	Off. of Controller General	Dept. of Finance; Off. of Controller General
Florida	Director, Off. of Planning & Budgeting	Senate, House Appropriations cmtes.	Comptroller; Finance Div., Dept. of Banking & Finance
Georgia	Director, Off. of Planning & Budget	Legis. Budget Analyst, Legis. Budget Off.	Fiscal Div., Dept. of Administrative Services; Comptroller General
Hawaii	Director, Dept. of Budget & Finance	Senate Ways & Means, House Finance cmtes., Off. of the Legis. Auditor	Dept. of Budget & Finance; Comptroller, Dept. of Accounting & General Services
Idaho	Administrator, Div. of Financial Mgt., Off. of the Governor	Legis. Budget Off., Joint Finance-Appropriations Cmte.	Div. of Financial Mgt., Off. of the Governor; Off. of State Auditor
Illinois	Director, Bur. of the Budget	Economic & Fiscal Comm.; Senate, House Appropriations cmtes.	Off. of the Comptroller
Indiana	Director, Budget Agcy.	Off. of Fiscal & Mgt. Analysis, Legis. Services Agcy.	Budget Agcy.; Off. of State Auditor
Iowa	State Comptroller	Legis. Fiscal Bur.	Off. of the State Comptroller
Kansas	Director, Div. of the Budget, Dept. of Admin.	Fiscal Analyst, Legis. Research Dept.	Div. of Accounts & Reports, Dept. of Admin.
Kentucky	Secretary, Finance & Admin. Cabinet	Budget Review, Legis. Research Comm.	Finance & Admin. Cabinet
Louisiana	Budget Director, Div. of Admin., Off. of the Governor	Legis. Fiscal Off., Joint Legis. Cmte. on the Budget	Div. of Admin., Off. of the Governor
Maine	State Budget Officer, Bur. of the Budget, Dept. of Finance & Admin.	Legis. Finance Off., Joint Appropriations & Financial Affairs Cmte.	Bur. of Accounts & Control, Dept. of Finance & Admin.
Maryland	Secretary, Dept. of Budget & Fiscal Planning	Div. of Budget Review; Div. of Fiscal Research, Dept. of Fiscal Services	Comptroller of the Treasury
Massachusetts	Budget Director, Exec. Off. for Admin. & Finance	Senate, House Ways & Means cmtes.	Comptroller's Div., Exec. Off. for Admin. & Finance
Michigan	Director, Dept. of Mgt. & Budget	Senate, House Fiscal Agencies	Dept. of Mgt. & Budget
Minnesota	Commissioner, Dept. of Finance	Senate Fiscal Analyst; House Appropriations Cmte.	Dept. of Finance
Mississippi	State Fiscal Officer, Fiscal Mgt. Bd.	Joint Legis. Budget Off.	Fiscal Mgt. Bd.; Off. of State Auditor

State or other jurisdiction	Official/agency responsible for preparing budget document	Special budget review agency in legislative branch	Agency(ies) responsible for budgetary and related accounting controls
Missouri	Director, Div. of Budget & Planning, Off. of Admin.	Senate Appropriations Cmte.; House Budget Cmte.	Div. of Accounting, Off. of Admin.
Montana	Director, Budget & Program Planning Off.	Off. of Legis. Fiscal Analyst, Legis. Finance Cmte.	Dept. of Admin.
Nebraska	Budget Administrator, Budget Div., Administrative Services Dept.	Off. of Legis. Fiscal Analyst	Dept. of Administrative Services; State Auditor
Nevada	Director, Dept. of Admin.	Fiscal Analysis Div., Legis. Counsel Bur.	Off. of the Controller
New Hampshire	Commissioner, Dept. of Admin. Services	Off. of Legis. Budget Asst., Fiscal Cmte. of the General Court	Bur. of Accounting, Dept. of Admin. Services
New Jersey	Director, Off. of Mgt. & Budget, Dept. of Treasury	Div. of Budget & Program Review, Off. of Legis. Services	Dept. of Treasury
New Mexico	Director, Budget Div., Dept. of Finance & Admin.	Legis. Finance Cmte.	Dept. of Finance & Admin.; Off. of Treasurer
New York	Director, Div. of Budget, Exec. Dept.	Senate Finance Cmte.; Assembly Ways & Means Cmte.	Comptroller, Dept. of Audit & Control
North Carolina	Budget Officer, Off. of Budget & Mgt.	Fiscal Research Div., Legis. Services Off.	Off. of Budget & Mgt.
North Dakota	Director; Exec. Budget Analyst, Off. of Mgt. & Budget	Legis. Budget Analyst & Auditor, Legis. Council	Off. of Mgt. & Budget
Ohio	Director, Off. of Budget & Mgt.	Legis. Budget Off.	Dept. of Administrative Services; Off. of Treasurer
Oklahoma	Director, Off. of State Finance	Joint Fiscal Operations Cmte.; Legis. Fiscal Off.	Off. of State Finance; State Comptroller
Oregon	Administrator, Budget & Mgt. Div., Exec. Dept.	Legis. Fiscal Off.	Accounting Div., Exec. Dept; Off. of State Treasurer
Pennsylvania	Secretary, Off. of Budget, Off. of the Governor	Legis. Budget & Finance Cmte.	Comptroller Operations, Off. of the Governor
Rhode Island	Finance & Planning, Dept. of Admin.	Senate, House Finance cmtes.	Accounts & Control, Dept. of Admin.
South Carolina	Exec. Director, State Budget & Control Bd.	State Auditor; Joint Appropriations Review Cmte.	Off. of Comptroller General; State Budget & Control Bd.
South Dakota	Commissioner, Bur. of Finance & Mgt.	Off. of Fiscal Analysis, Legis. Research Council	Bur. of Finance & Mgt.; Off. of State Auditor
Tennessee	Commissioner, Budget Div., Dept. of Finance & Admin.	Fiscal Review Cmte.	Dept. of Finance & Admin.; Off. of Comptroller of the Treasury
Texas	Director, Governor's Off. of Mgt. & Budget	Legis. Budget Bd.	Comptroller, Public Accounts
Utah	Director, Off. of Planning & Budget	Legis. Fiscal Analyst, Legis. Mgt. Cmte.	Div. of Finance, Admin. Services Dept.
Vermont	Commissioner, Dept. of Budget & Mgt.	Joint Fiscal Cmte.	Finance & Information Support Dept., Agcy. of Admin.
Virginia	Director, Dept. of Planning & Budget	Senate Finance Cmte.; House Appropriations Cmte.	Comptroller, Dept. of Accounts
Washington	Director, Off. of Financial Mgt.	Legis. Auditor, Legis. Budget Cmte.; Legis. Evaluation & Accountability Prog. Cmte.	Off. of Financial Mgt.; State Treasurer
West Virginia	Director, Budget Div.; Commissioner, Dept. of Finance & Admin.	Off. of Legis. Auditor, Joint Cmte. on Government & Finance	Dept. of Finance & Admin.; Off. of State Auditor

BUDGET OFFICIALS OR AGENCIES—Continued

State or other jurisdiction	Official/agency responsible for preparing budget document	Special budget review agency in legislative branch	Agency(ies) responsible for budgetary and related accounting controls
Wisconsin	Administrator, State Exec. Budget & Planning, Dept. of Admin.	Legis. Fiscal Bur.	Bur. of Financial Operations; State Finance & Program Mgt., Dept. of Admin.
Wyoming	Administrator, Budget Div., Admin. & Fiscal Control Dept.	Budget Analysis Div., Legis. Service Off.	Off. of State Auditor
Dist. of Col.	Director, Off. of the Budget	. . .	Off. of Controller
American Samoa	Director, Program Planning & Budget Development	Fiscal Officer, Legis. Financial Off.	Dept. of Treasury
Guam	Director, Bur. of Budget & Mgt. Research	Ways & Means Cmte.	Dept. of Admin.
No. Mariana Is.	Planning & Budget, Off. of the Governor	Senate Fiscal Affairs Cmte.; House Appropriations Cmte.	Dept. of Finance
Puerto Rico	Director, Off. of Budget & Mgt.	Economics Div., Off. of Legis. Services	Off. of Budget & Mgt.; Off. of Comptroller
Virgin Islands	Budget Director, Off. of the Budget	Legis. Finance Cmte.	Accounting Div., Dept. of Finance

STATE GOVERNMENT FINANCES IN 1984

By Vance Kane

The states generally reflected more comfortable financial conditions at the end of fiscal year 1984. The spread between total expenditures and revenues was the highest in several years (see Table A).

This improved outlook came from increased revenue rates imposed during the earlier lean years, expenditure controls, and a sharp reduction in unemployment costs from $24.1 billion in fiscal year 1983 to $14 billion in 1984.[1]

Revenue Base of State Governments

Total revenues in 1984 came to $397 billion (see Table 6.5). Intergovernmental payments from the federal government provided 19 percent of these funds; taxes, 50 percent; charges and miscellaneous income, 13 percent; and insurance trust revenue, 15 percent.

The major share of federal aid was $35 billion for welfare (primarily in the Aid to Needy Children Program and Medicaid payments). Education grants to the states totaled $14 billion and highway grants, $10 billion. These programs continue to be the core of federal aid, both in terms of volume and consistency.

As shown in Table 6.7, the major tax resource of the states continued to be the sales tax—which provided 49 percent of the total tax revenue—followed by the individual income tax (30 percent), and the corporation net income tax (8 percent). License taxes also provided a significant share, with 6 percent of total taxes. The largest license tax—totaling $6.4 billion—was the motor vehicle license tax. Other taxes included the volatile severance tax at $7.3 billion (reflecting the continuing decline in oil prices), and the property tax (levied by 43 states) at $3.9 billion.

Charges and miscellaneous revenues comprised 13 percent of total revenues. Most significant were education charges ($14.6 billion) and interest earnings ($13.3 billion).

An important source of miscellaneous income for 17 states was the net income from lottery operations. In 1984, $2.7 billion was available for other purposes after the costs of lottery operation (including prizes) were deducted from the $6.2 billion in total ticket sales.

Utility revenues came primarily from electric charges totaling $1.9 billion and transit fees totaling $0.7 billion. Insurance trust revenues totaled $61 billion, with $39 billion for retirement systems and $17 billion for unemployment compensation. Liquor store revenues, generated from sales in the 17 states which own and operate liquor stores, totaled $2.8 billion.

Expenditure Activities

As shown in Table 6.5, total state expenditures in 1984 were $351 billion, an increase of 5 percent from the $334 billion in 1983. States spent more on education than any other function—$116 billion or 33 percent of the total. Intergovernmental expenditure for education comprised a major portion with $67.5 billion, primarily for elementary and secondary school support.

Welfare, the next highest expenditure function, amounted to $63 billion, of which vendor payments for medical assistance (primarily Medicaid) required $31 billion, and intergovernmental welfare aid took $13.6 billion.

Other expenditures in major functional areas included: highways, $29 billion; hospitals, $15 billion; corrections, $7.7 billion; and police protection, $3.1 billion.

State-operated utility expenditures were $4.8 billion, of which transit payments were $2.8 billion and electric utility costs were $2 billion. Insurance trust expenditures included employee retirement payments of $16.5 billion, unemployment compensation costs of $14 billion, and workers' compensation costs of $3.1 billion. Liquor store expenditures totaled $2.3 billion.

As shown in Table 6.9, current operations required $157 billion of the $243 billion spent on direct operations. Salaries and wages totaled $65 billion. Intergovernmen-

---

Vance Kane is Assistant Division Chief for Programs, and was assisted by Lisa McNelis, Social Science Analyst, both of the Governments Division, U.S. Bureau of the Census.

Table A
Revenue, Expenditure, and Excess for Fiscal Years 1975 to 1984[1]
(in billions of dollars)

Fiscal year	Total revenue	Total expenditure	Excess of revenue or expenditure(−)
1984	397.1	351.4	45.7
1983	357.7	334.0	23.7
1982	330.9	310.3	20.6
1981	310.8	291.5	19.3
1980	277.0	257.8	19.2
1979	247.0	224.7	22.3
1978	225.0	203.8	21.2
1977	204.4	191.2	13.2
1976	183.8	180.9	2.9
1975	157.0	158.9	−1.9

tal outlays accounted for 31 percent ($108 billion) of state expenditures. Construction costs totaled $20 billion—a $1 billion increase from 1983.

Debt
State debt increased to $186 billion in 1984 (see Tables 6.5 and 6.13). Non-guaranteed long-term debt increased from $110 billion to $126 billion, reflecting the heavy use of industrial development bonds (IDBs). Full-faith and credit debt totaled $57 billion, an increase of only 4 percent compared to the 15 percent rise in non-guaranteed obligations.

New York far outspent all other states in debt payments—$2.5 billion in 1984 interest payments alone (see Table 6.9). California ranked second in interest payments (nearly $1 billion), and New Jersey ranked third ($0.8 billion). Only seven states spent more than $500 million on interest payments.

Cash and Security Holdings
At the close of fiscal year 1984, states held $443 billion in cash and assets (see Table 6.5). Cash and security holdings increase sharply every year due to the influx of employee retirement system receipts. More volatile are the holdings in unemployment fund balances, which totaled $12 billion in 1980 and $6 billion in 1984. Cash and deposits totaled $45 billion, compared with $392 billion in securities. Insurance trusts held $274 billion of these investments, with debt offsets at $82 billion.

Note
1. The data, taken from the U.S. Bureau of the Census' annual report *State Government Finances in 1984*, should not be interpreted as surplus or deficit amounts. The classification system used by the Bureau is statistical in nature and may not be used to develop an accounting statement of financial condition. For example, out of the $443 billion reported as cash and asset holdings, $274 billion (62 percent) are held for various trust purposes, and thus are not available to meet general revenue shortfalls.

The classification system provides for four major sectors: general government, insurance trusts, state-operated liquor stores, and state-owned utilities. Therefore, total state revenue includes not only general taxes, fees, and charges, but also gross revenues of 17 state-run liquor stores, employee contributions to their retirement system, plus the interest earned and fees or charges collected from utility operations.

Table 6.3
SUMMARY FINANCIAL AGGREGATES, BY STATE: 1983
(In millions of dollars)

State	Revenue Total	General	Insur-ance trust	Liquor stores	Utilities	Bor-rowing	Expenditure Total	General	Insur-ance trust	Liquor stores	Utilities	Debt redemp-tion
All states	$357,637	$290,456	$61,971	$2,819	$2,390	$29,397	$334,019	$285,042	$42,180	$2,381	$4,417	$11,574
Alabama...........	5,250	4,405	711	134	0	425	5,220	4,638	458	125	0	142
Alaska.............	5,247	4,871	376	0	0	1,112	3,836	3,422	160	0	253	147
Arizona...........	3,969	3,104	857	0	8	330	3,589	3,215	366	0	8	11
Arkansas	2,739	2,355	384	0	0	157	2,488	2,254	234	0	0	45
California.........	43,768	34,972	8,755	0	41	2,378	42,493	36,488	6,001	0	4	640
Colorado	4,203	3,253	950	0	0	415	4,062	3,486	576	0	0	33
Connecticut	4,707	4,159	533	0	16	941	4,427	3,833	534	0	61	386
Delaware	1,315	1,166	146	0	4	339	1,072	989	74	0	9	95
Florida	10,569	9,057	1,506	0	7	486	9,874	9,145	703	0	26	122
Georgia...........	6,992	6,064	927	0	0	330	6,563	6,013	550	0	0	166
Hawaii	2,308	1,937	371	0	0	465	2,178	1,977	201	0	0	255
Idaho	1,349	1,083	225	41	0	37	1,245	1,038	176	32	0	16
Illinois............	15,120	12,037	3,082	0	0	1,067	15,004	12,269	2,735	0	0	864
Indiana	6,166	5,420	746	0	0	230	5,843	5,211	632	0	0	46
Iowa	4,106	3,324	649	133	0	150	4,157	3,624	440	93	0	17
Kansas	2,990	2,548	442	0	0	6	2,864	2,542	322	0	0	24
Kentucky	5,364	4,523	841	0	0	455	5,165	4,549	616	0	0	151
Louisiana	6,947	5,767	1,180	0	0	1,405	7,431	6,294	1,137	0	0	315
Maine	1,685	1,435	201	48	0	264	1,671	1,434	192	45	0	59
Maryland	6,598	6,003	554	0	42	819	6,921	5,969	727	0	226	370
Massachusetts	9,383	8,455	926	0	3	1,899	9,332	8,305	1,002	0	25	528
Michigan	16,097	12,479	3,211	407	0	1,149	14,789	12,150	2,302	338	0	351
Minnesota	8,074	6,841	1,234	0	0	427	6,496	5,826	670	0	0	1,041
Mississippi	3,346	2,783	452	111	0	61	3,132	2,746	291	96	0	50
Missouri	5,319	4,503	816	0	0	591	4,780	4,326	454	0	0	196
Montana...........	1,376	1,109	224	43	0	149	1,263	1,057	171	35	0	33
Nebraska	1,881	1,779	102	0	0	105	1,807	1,722	85	0	0	13
Nevada	1,696	1,166	492	0	39	128	1,570	1,191	282	0	97	18
New Hampshire	1,167	875	139	152	0	387	1,109	913	75	122	0	129
New Jersey.........	12,604	10,281	2,146	0	177	2,150	11,764	9,735	1,518	0	511	640
New Mexico........	3,343	2,915	427	0	0	316	2,692	2,524	168	0	0	105
New York	35,851	27,895	6,335	0	1,621	2,616	31,921	26,578	2,827	0	2,516	861
North Carolina	7,662	6,509	1,153	0	0	146	7,232	6,428	804	0	0	115
North Dakota	1,330	1,157	172	0	0	87	1,302	1,201	101	0	0	30
Ohio	17,682	11,294	6,056	332	0	1,475	15,901	11,933	3,667	300	0	421
Oklahoma	4,805	4,245	455	0	105	238	4,772	4,133	485	0	155	41
Oregon	4,696	3,601	945	150	0	562	4,356	3,536	731	89	0	197
Pennsylvania	17,776	13,719	3,466	592	0	680	16,733	12,874	3,306	552	0	382
Rhode Island	1,835	1,562	265	0	7	418	1,708	1,476	212	0	19	179
South Carolina	4,598	3,642	634	0	322	610	4,229	3,296	428	0	506	534
South Dakota	961	820	142	0	0	112	859	819	39	0	0	30
Tennessee	4,783	4,175	608	0	0	334	4,578	4,062	516	0	0	116
Texas.............	17,400	14,938	2,462	0	0	570	15,796	14,115	1,681	0	0	141
Utah	2,442	1,930	446	66	0	311	2,304	2,007	249	48	0	55
Vermont	900	788	83	29	0	143	890	803	60	28	0	52
Virginia...........	7,540	6,270	1,017	253	0	782	6,747	6,098	437	211	0	501
Washington	8,353	6,483	1,646	224	0	529	7,908	6,400	1,319	188	0	477
West Virginia	3,202	2,436	695	71	0	51	3,046	2,368	629	50	0	179
Wisconsin..........	8,545	6,925	1,619	0	0	471	7,633	6,957	676	0	0	215
Wyoming	1,597	1,396	168	33	0	91	1,263	1,074	159	30	0	43

Source: U.S. Bureau of the Census, *State Government Finances in 1983.*
Note: Detail may not add to totals due to rounding.

Table 6.4
SUMMARY FINANCIAL AGGREGATES, BY STATE: 1984
(In millions of dollars)

State	Revenue						Expenditure					Debt redemption
	Total	General	Insurance trust	Liquor stores	Utilities	Borrowing	Total	General	Insurance trust	Liquor stores	Utilities	
All states	$397,087	$330,740	$60,950	$2,759	$2,638	$27,611	$351,446	$309,684	$34,632	$2,313	$4,817	$10,364
Alabama............	6,195	5,319	741	135	0	516	5,191	4,713	356	123	0	−27
Alaska..............	5,463	5,025	437	0	1	1,192	3,969	3,633	176	0	160	328
Arizona............	4,552	3,762	782	0	8	125	4,046	3,724	313	0	8	22
Arkansas	2,967	2,627	340	0	0	180	2,636	2,455	181	0	0	126
California..........	50,634	40,432	10,059	0	143	2,501	44,716	39,380	5,331	0	5	1,209
Colorado	4,878	3,833	1,044	0	0	262	4,560	3,986	574	0	0	156
Connecticut	5,514	4,930	566	0	18	550	4,869	4,345	457	0	67	325
Delaware	1,494	1,328	161	0	4	210	1,211	1,124	69	0	18	129
Florida	11,896	10,322	1,567	0	7	392	10,320	9,681	623	0	17	214
Georgia............	7,458	6,469	990	0	0	189	6,699	6,236	464	0	0	200
Hawaii	2,541	2,090	451	0	0	302	2,244	2,040	204	0	0	127
Idaho	1,478	1,203	236	40	0	133	1,347	1,188	131	28	0	17
Illinois.............	16,470	14,160	2,310	0	0	1,506	15,050	13,423	1,626	0	0	579
Indiana	7,163	6,519	644	0	0	360	6,416	6,000	416	0	0	92
Iowa	4,351	3,712	512	127	0	89	4,277	3,906	280	91	0	32
Kansas	3,363	2,905	458	0	0	5	2,974	2,746	228	0	0	28
Kentucky	5,448	4,826	622	0	0	446	5,358	4,910	448	0	0	115
Louisiana	7,201	6,112	1,090	0	0	1,468	7,664	6,710	954	0	0	349
Maine	1,873	1,635	192	47	0	200	1,775	1,551	178	46	0	80
Maryland	7,296	6,548	700	0	48	481	6,880	6,033	681	0	166	379
Massachusetts	10,253	9,266	984	0	3	1,613	9,736	8,910	799	0	27	632
Michigan	17,071	14,636	2,027	409	0	813	15,368	13,396	1,643	330	0	237
Minnesota	8,826	7,824	1,002	0	0	783	7,536	6,984	553	0	0	195
Mississippi	3,641	3,095	438	109	0	170	3,351	3,034	225	93	0	54
Missouri	5,964	5,065	899	0	0	694	5,263	4,913	350	0	0	115
Montana............	1,538	1,224	272	42	0	199	1,385	1,177	174	35	0	13
Nebraska	2,047	1,922	125	0	0	297	1,884	1,817	67	0	0	13
Nevada	1,767	1,263	463	0	40	154	1,485	1,195	247	0	43	45
New Hampshire	1,276	1,015	104	157	0	351	1,128	941	60	127	0	230
New Jersey..........	14,677	11,942	2,481	0	254	1,906	12,635	10,642	1,417	0	576	676
New Mexico.........	3,338	2,944	394	0	0	226	2,833	2,671	162	0	0	141
New York	42,412	34,094	6,692	0	1,626	2,697	35,917	29,958	2,883	0	3,076	1,130
North Carolina	8,735	7,428	1,307	0	0	292	7,588	7,024	564	0	0	101
North Dakota	1,553	1,391	162	0	0	101	1,440	1,347	93	0	0	38
Ohio	18,682	13,370	4,996	316	0	1,052	16,348	13,188	2,887	274	0	362
Oklahoma	5,064	4,430	513	0	120	692	4,708	4,124	386	0	198	145
Oregon	4,981	3,817	1,018	147	0	238	4,443	3,712	640	91	0	282
Pennsylvania	18,985	15,328	3,072	586	0	561	16,601	13,788	2,271	542	0	423
Rhode Island	1,987	1,683	297	0	8	301	1,832	1,632	178	0	21	200
South Carolina	5,017	3,969	690	0	358	331	4,396	3,651	310	0	435	171
South Dakota	999	898	101	0	0	171	953	903	50	0	0	36
Tennessee	5,335	4,617	717	0	0	139	4,830	4,474	355	0	0	201
Texas..............	18,912	16,429	2,483	0	0	1,072	16,880	15,402	1,478	0	0	200
Utah	2,877	2,325	485	67	0	297	2,446	2,230	168	48	0	168
Vermont	992	886	77	29	0	106	941	861	51	28	0	61
Virginia............	8,171	7,035	896	240	0	359	7,096	6,528	368	200	0	124
Washington	8,833	6,800	1,816	216	0	688	8,139	6,633	1,324	183	0	116
West Virginia	3,547	2,785	698	64	0	54	3,136	2,571	518	47	0	96
Wisconsin..........	9,572	7,935	1,637	0	0	535	7,530	6,924	606	0	0	202
Wyoming	1,802	1,569	202	31	0	167	1,415	1,271	115	29	0	32

Source: U.S. Bureau of the Census, *State Governmental Finances in 1984.*
Note: Detail may not add to totals due to rounding.

Table 6.5

NATIONAL TOTALS OF STATE GOVERNMENT FINANCES FOR SELECTED YEARS: 1970-84

Item	Amount (in millions) 1984	1983	1982	1981	1980	1978	1976	1974	1972	1970	Percentage change 1983 to 1984	Percentage change 1982 to 1983	Per capita 1984	Per capita 1983
Revenue and borrowing	$424,698	$386,626	$350,688	$329,213	$293,696	$238,475	$199,626	$148,775	$120,931	$93,463	9.8	10.1	$1,803.12	$1,656.66
Borrowing	27,611	28,966	19,790	18,385	16,734	13,464	15,805	7,959	8,622	4,523	-4.7	42.9	117.23	124.10
Revenue total	397,087	357,660	330,898	310,828	276,962	225,011	183,821	140,816	112,309	88,939	11.0	8.1	1,685.89	1,532.56
General revenue	330,740	290,480	275,111	258,159	233,592	189,099	152,118	122,327	98,632	77,755	13.9	5.6	1,404.21	1,244.68
Taxes total	196,795	171,464	162,607	149,738	137,075	113,261	89,256	74,207	59,870	47,961	14.8	5.4	835.52	734.67
Intergovernmental revenue	81,450	72,704	69,166	70,786	64,326	53,461	44,717	33,170	27,981	20,248	12.0	5.1	345.81	311.56
From federal government	76,140	68,962	66,026	67,868	61,892	50,200	42,013	31,632	26,791	19,252	10.4	4.4	323.26	295.52
Public welfare	35,423	32,949	31,510	28,892	24,680	20,007	16,867	13,320	12,289	7,818	7.5	4.6	150.29	141.19
Education	13,975	13,185	13,149	14,100	12,765	9,819	8,661	6,720	5,984	4,554	6.0	0.3	59.33	56.50
Highways	10,380	8,927	8,304	9,369	8,860	6,301	6,262	4,503	4,871	4,431	16.3	7.5	44.07	38.25
General revenue sharing	(b)	(b)	(b)	1,118	2,278	2,255	2,102	2,045	—	—	0.0	0.0		
Employment security administration	2,606	2,531	2,352	2,362	2,050	1,887	1,658	1,295	1,148	769	3.0	7.6	11.06	10.85
Other	13,756	11,370	10,711	12,027	11,258	9,931	6,463	3,749	2,499	1,680	21.0	6.2	58.51	48.73
From local governments	5,310	3,742	3,139	2,918	2,434	3,261	2,704	1,538	1,191	995	41.9	19.2	22.55	16.04
Charges and miscellaneous revenue	52,495	46,312	43,338	37,636	32,190	22,377	18,145	14,950	10,780	9,545	13.4	6.9	222.88	198.45
Utility revenue(a)	2,638	2,390	2,085	1,823	1,304	962	0	0	0	0	10.4	14.6	11.20	10.24
Liquor stores revenue	2,759	2,819	2,854	2,805	2,765	2,388	2,196	2,049	1,904	1,748	-2.1	-1.2	11.71	12.08
Insurance trust revenue	60,950	61,971	50,848	48,401	39,301	32,562	29,508	16,439	11,773	9,437	-1.6	21.9	258.77	265.56
Unemployment compensation	16,671	21,480	16,854	18,443	13,468	13,083	15,057	5,711	3,588	3,090	-22.4	27.4	70.78	92.05
Employee retirement	38,564	35,236	29,035	25,122	21,146	16,026	12,171	8,919	6,827	5,205	9.4	21.4	163.73	151.00
Other	5,715	5,255	4,959	4,476	4,686	3,452	2,269	1,809	1,359	1,143	8.8	6.0	24.26	22.51
Debt outstanding at end of fiscal year, total	186,377	167,291	147,470	134,847	121,958	102,569	84,825	65,296	53,833	42,008	11.4	13.4	791.29	716.88
Long-term	183,208	164,696	143,702	132,521	119,821	99,671	78,814	61,697	50,379	38,903	11.2	14.6	777.84	705.76
Non-guaranteed	125,859	109,617	92,195	79,940	70,457	53,356	39,972	30,842	25,314	21,167	14.8	18.9	534.36	469.74
Full-faith and credit	57,349	55,079	51,507	52,582	49,364	46,316	38,842	30,855	25,065	17,736	4.1	6.9	243.48	236.02
Short-term	3,169	2,595	3,768	2,325	2,137	2,897	6,011	3,599	3,454	3,104	22.1	-31.1	13.45	11.12
Net long-term	101,681	94,779	87,047	81,538	79,810	72,089	62,488	53,847	45,082	34,479	7.3	8.9	431.70	406.15
Full-faith and credit only	46,976	41,442	39,766	41,429	39,357	39,147	33,708	26,967	21,932	14,832	13.4	4.2	199.44	177.59
Expenditure and debt redemption	361,810	345,162	317,482	297,466	263,494	208,533	184,511	134,948	111,933	87,152	4.8	8.7	1,536.12	1,478.84
Debt redemption	10,364	11,143	7,190	5,938	5,682	4,701	3,585	2,814	2,690	2,096	-7.0	55.0	44.00	47.74
Expenditure, total	351,446	334,019	310,292	291,527	257,812	203,832	180,926	132,134	109,243	85,055	5.2	7.6	1,492.12	1,431.10
General expenditure	309,684	285,042	269,490	253,654	228,223	179,802	153,690	119,891	98,810	77,642	8.6	5.8	1,314.81	1,221.26
Education	116,058	107,703	102,984	96,921	87,939	69,702	59,630	46,860	38,348	30,865	7.8	4.6	492.74	461.45
Intergovernmental expenditure	67,485	63,118	60,684	57,257	52,688	40,125	34,084	27,107	21,195	17,085	6.9	4.0	286.52	270.43
State institutions of higher education	40,016	36,496	34,296	31,488	27,927	23,259	19,707	14,358	13,381	11,011	9.6	6.4	169.89	156.37
Other	8,557	8,089	8,005	8,175	7,324	6,318	5,839	5,358	3,773	2,769	5.8	1.0	36.33	34.65
Public welfare	62,749	57,544	55,257	51,463	44,219	35,776	29,633	22,538	19,191	13,206	9.0	4.1	266.41	246.55
Intergovernmental expenditure	13,628	13,091	13,744	12,882	10,977	10,047	9,476	7,369	6,944	5,003	4.1	-4.8	57.86	56.09
Cash assistance, categorical programs	8,297	7,461	7,337	7,579	6,831	5,712	5,203	4,984	5,089	3,534	11.2	1.7	35.23	31.97
Cash assistance, other	1,154	1,200	875	801	686	624	353	212	192	145	-3.8	37.1	4.90	5.14
Other public welfare	39,670	35,792	33,301	30,201	25,725	19,393	14,601	9,973	6,966	4,523	10.8	7.5	168.42	153.35
Highways	28,937	26,431	25,131	25,439	25,044	18,479	18,100	15,887	15,380	13,483	9.5	5.2	122.86	113.24
Regular state highway facilities	21,971	19,961	19,078	19,659	19,652	13,970	14,223	11,887	12,089	10,482	10.1	4.6	93.28	85.52
State toll highway facilities	1,278	1,193	1,025	1,028	1,009	687	636	749	658	562	7.1	16.4	5.43	5.11
Intergovernmental expenditure	5,688	5,277	5,028	4,751	4,383	3,821	3,241	3,211	2,633	2,439	7.8	5.0	24.15	22.61

NATIONAL TOTALS OF STATE GOVERNMENT FINANCES—Continued

Item	Amount (in millions)										Percentage change 1983 to 1984	Percentage change 1982 to 1983	Per capita 1984	Per capita 1983
	1984	1983	1982	1981	1980	1978	1976	1974	1972	1970				
Health and hospitals	24,982	23,926	22,284	20,593	17,855	13,883	11,110	8,443	6,963	5,355	10.1	15.0	106.07	102.51
State hospitals and institutions for handicapped	15,068	14,663	13,681	12,360	11,015	8,979	7,572	5,957	4,825	3,941	2.8	7.2	63.97	62.83
Other	9,914	9,263	8,603	8,233	6,840	4,905	3,538	2,486	2,138	1,414	7.0	8.1	42.10	39.68
Natural resources	5,945	5,834	5,485	5,008	4,346	3,411	3,863	3,053	2,595	2,223	1.9	6.4	25.24	25.00
Corrections	7,732	6,743	5,889	5,093	4,449	3,275	2,480	1,812	1,389	1,104	14.7	14.5	32.85	28.89
Financial administration	4,517	4,206	3,735	3,331	3,031	2,482	1,955	1,594	1,235	1,032	7.4	12.6	19.18	18.02
General control	4,654	4,271	3,909	3,419	3,232	2,331	1,688	1,273	944	717	14.0	9.3	19.76	18.30
Employment security administration	2,546	2,464	2,278	2,269	2,001	1,757	1,570	1,304	1,133	767	3.3	8.2	10.81	10.56
Police	3,140	3,002	2,730	2,558	2,263	1,826	1,569	1,262	983	741	4.6	10.0	13.33	12.86
Miscellaneous and unallocable	48,424	42,918	39,808	37,560	33,843	26,879	22,091	15,906	10,647	8,149	12.8	7.8	205.56	183.88
State aid for unspecified purposes	10,745	10,364	10,044	9,570	8,501	6,819	5,674	4,804	3,752	2,958	4.0	4.0	45.62	44.40
Interest	13,137	11,252	9,015	7,844	6,763	5,268	4,140	2,863	2,135	1,499	16.8	24.8	55.78	48.21
Veteran's services	99	75	64	57	61	54	64	156	51	67	32.0	17.2	.42	.32
Other (includes intergovernmental aid for specified purposes not elsewhere classified)	24,443	21,227	20,685	20,089	18,518	14,738	12,213	8,083	4,709	3,626	15.2	2.6	103.74	90.95
Utility expenditure(a)	4,817	4,417	3,730	3,347	2,401	1,544	0	0	0	0	9.1	18.4	20.45	18.92
Liquor expenditure	2,313	2,380	2,408	2,305	2,206	1,991	1,781	1,653	1,495	1,404	−2.9	−1.1	9.82	10.20
Insurance trust expenditure	34,632	42,180	34,664	32,221	24,981	20,495	25,455	10,590	8,938	6,010	−17.9	21.7	147.04	180.72
Unemployment compensation	13,987	24,068	18,028	17,846	12,006	10,672	17,780	4,673	4,722	2,713	−41.9	33.5	59.38	103.12
Employee retirement	16,467	14,204	13,133	11,419	10,257	7,811	6,045	4,591	3,175	2,376	15.9	8.2	69.91	60.86
Other	4,178	3,908	3,503	2,955	2,718	2,011	1,629	1,326	1,041	921	12.1	19.8	17.75	16.74
Total expenditure by character and object	351,446	334,019	310,292	291,527	257,812	203,832	180,926	132,134	109,243	85,055	5.2	7.6	1,492.12	1,431.10
Direct expenditure	243,073	232,710	211,549	198,348	173,307	136,545	123,069	86,193	72,483	56,163	4.5	10.0	1,032.00	997.04
Current operation	156,734	144,018	133,152	122,794	108,131	86,153	68,175	50,803	39,790	30,971	8.8	8.2	665.44	617.04
Capital outlay	25,583	23,351	23,466	24,286	23,325	16,064	18,009	15,417	15,283	13,295	9.6	−0.5	108.62	100.05
Construction	19,671	18,616	19,560	20,632	19,736	13,260	15,285	12,655	13,022	11,185	5.7	−4.8	83.52	79.76
Purchase of land and existing structures	1,816	1,507	1,316	1,152	1,345	1,171	1,274	1,540	1,369	1,240	20.5	14.5	7.71	6.46
Equipment	4,096	3,228	2,590	2,502	2,243	1,633	1,450	1,222	892	870	26.9	24.6	17.39	13.83
Assistance and subsidies	12,386	11,452	10,867	10,889	9,818	8,341	7,290	6,521	6,337	4,387	8.2	5.4	52.59	49.07
Interest on debt	13,738	11,708	9,400	8,157	7,052	5,493	4,140	2,863	2,135	1,499	17.3	24.6	58.33	50.16
Insurance benefits and repayments	34,632	42,181	34,664	32,221	24,981	20,495	25,455	10,590	8,938	6,010	−17.9	21.7	147.02	180.72
Intergovernmental expenditure	108,373	101,309	98,743	93,180	84,504	67,287	57,858	45,941	36,759	28,892	7.0	2.6	460.12	434.06
Cash and security holdings at end of fiscal year	443,366	391,224	338,274	305,237	273,047	212,107	157,210	134,493	99,769	84,810	13.3	15.7	1,882.38	1,676.20
Unemployment fund balance in U.S. Treasury	5,707	4,811	6,789	11,634	11,945	7,450	4,425	10,773	8,942	12,236	18.7	−29.2	24.23	20.62
Cash and deposits	45,232	39,288	35,400	32,797	30,782	25,345	18,477	18,387	12,372	8,463	−3.2	−24.7	192.04	168.33
Securities	392,427	347,125	296,084	260,806	230,320	179,312	134,308	105,332	78,456	64,110	13.1	17.2	1,666.11	1,487.25
Total by purpose:														
Insurance trust	274,378	246,022	211,493	187,158	166,656	124,371	94,679	80,840	62,947	54,982	11.5	16.3	1,164.91	1,054.27
Debt offsets	81,527	69,915	56,655	50,983	40,011	27,582	15,880	7,849	5,309	4,424	16.6	23.4	346.14	299.61
Other	87,461	75,287	70,126	67,096	66,381	60,154	46,651	45,804	31,514	25,404	12.8	21.1	371.33	322.62

Sources: U.S. Bureau of the Census, annual reports on *State Government Finances* and *Historical Statistics on Governmental Finances and Employment* (vol. 6, no. 4, of the 1977 *Census of Governments*).

(a) Reported separately only since 1977, previously included with general revenue or general expenditure.

(b) State participation ended September 1980.

Table 6.6
STATE GENERAL REVENUE, BY SOURCE AND BY STATE: 1983
(In thousands of dollars)

State	Total general revenue(a)	Taxes Total(b)	Sales and gross receipts Total(b)	Sales and gross receipts General	Sales and gross receipts Motor fuels	Licenses Total(b)	Licenses Motor vehicle	Individual income	Corporation net income	Intergovernmental revenue	Charges and miscellaneous general revenue
All states	$290,455,865	$171,440,020	$83,894,609	$53,639,404	$10,793,330	$10,658,074	$5,784,050	$49,788,567	$13,152,503	$72,703,679	$46,312,166
Alabama	4,405,328	2,341,219	1,385,526	659,653	240,850	119,384	32,756	556,390	133,717	1,224,801	839,308
Alaska	4,870,752	2,046,086	74,614	0	36,675	56,316	15,820	1,540	266,302	385,342	2,439,324
Arizona	3,104,344	2,060,317	1,145,486	845,306	151,780	140,094	101,402	480,716	160,429	570,771	473,256
Arkansas	2,355,032	1,337,881	706,742	437,474	132,781	112,428	67,341	388,341	86,921	710,248	306,903
California	34,972,478	22,259,940	9,952,672	7,766,551	925,560	846,144	537,725	7,649,231	2,553,948	8,867,643	3,844,895
Colorado	3,253,266	1,752,071	885,909	622,548	143,016	99,359	54,354	655,491	56,184	805,841	695,354
Connecticut	4,158,575	2,537,725	1,798,600	1,104,136	159,014	128,045	75,290	178,535	357,364	860,595	760,255
Delaware	1,165,516	639,271	90,052	0	37,707	176,273	26,554	313,986	29,790	215,099	311,146
Florida	9,056,548	6,224,717	4,795,751	3,334,207	451,940	444,038	274,468	0	371,453	1,963,069	868,762
Georgia	6,064,488	3,504,220	1,784,280	1,173,027	353,429	107,037	55,792	1,342,092	238,834	1,920,181	640,087
Hawaii	1,936,636	1,150,503	755,861	601,127	33,761	17,687	8,777	347,016	22,026	395,676	390,457
Idaho	1,083,167	620,035	288,608	165,403	77,327	71,919	35,472	223,774	31,114	295,208	167,924
Illinois	12,037,448	7,420,382	3,869,061	2,394,075	361,416	438,628	308,329	2,200,670	603,900	3,066,541	1,550,525
Indiana	5,420,009	3,195,745	2,010,813	1,522,846	316,935	153,313	118,414	819,220	139,968	1,285,990	938,274
Iowa	3,324,371	2,014,289	889,277	571,087	188,271	195,156	146,728	724,127	138,483	813,401	496,681
Kansas	2,547,684	1,565,625	728,372	498,495	115,180	111,243	69,376	530,657	141,347	606,481	375,578
Kentucky	4,522,808	2,601,949	1,187,337	700,407	197,100	131,423	71,625	647,170	121,120	1,172,073	748,786
Louisiana	5,766,744	3,029,003	1,366,588	847,188	186,105	204,057	58,292	229,261	321,372	1,328,821	1,408,920
Maine	1,435,278	780,052	421,911	270,309	55,440	63,883	32,993	235,933	33,043	425,260	229,966
Maryland	6,002,631	3,468,190	1,546,315	865,087	233,404	134,438	85,194	1,458,654	148,423	1,428,920	1,105,521
Massachusetts	8,454,687	5,155,631	1,735,723	1,051,712	250,425	159,308	93,018	2,472,278	660,654	2,156,903	1,142,153
Michigan	12,478,885	7,022,658	2,773,197	1,969,377	456,490	366,545	258,794	2,567,038	1,004,269	3,449,141	2,007,086
Minnesota	6,840,559	4,319,483	1,698,291	992,259	262,101	262,331	183,823	1,977,991	253,970	1,508,741	1,012,335
Mississippi	2,783,449	1,537,795	1,023,288	761,391	135,226	121,005	47,328	201,114	68,794	849,242	396,412
Missouri	4,503,419	2,640,325	1,387,915	984,874	194,290	210,009	117,529	885,272	118,625	1,200,544	662,550
Montana	1,108,856	513,658	107,323	0	48,890	47,989	24,339	151,784	35,825	321,992	273,206
Nebraska	1,779,122	987,054	560,307	356,608	119,752	81,100	44,932	280,662	51,635	461,676	330,392
Nevada	1,165,598	779,338	669,071	368,332	66,871	86,152	30,789	0	0	252,452	133,808
New Hampshire	875,450	329,458	158,975	0	60,994	56,568	28,894	16,727	73,960	289,860	256,132
New Jersey	10,280,914	6,128,035	3,309,264	1,660,284	288,981	478,007	259,230	1,440,183	664,415	2,193,335	1,959,544

GENERAL REVENUE, BY SOURCE: 1983—Continued

State	Total general revenue(a)	Taxes Total(b)	Sales and gross receipts Total(b)	General	Motor fuels	Licenses Total(b)	Motor vehicle	Individual income	Corporation net income	Intergovernmental revenue	Charges and miscellaneous general revenue
New Mexico	2,915,290	1,165,975	659,789	479,618	93,509	62,548	38,994	16,626	61,742	750,605	998,710
New York	27,895,296	16,177,994	5,697,816	3,531,930	436,796	554,837	318,642	8,275,754	1,339,005	8,599,472	3,117,830
North Carolina	6,509,333	4,028,477	1,763,988	825,703	379,480	296,402	151,585	1,550,107	306,534	1,657,588	823,268
North Dakota	1,157,476	526,006	219,338	146,377	35,539	51,938	29,107	35,136	30,594	275,885	355,585
Ohio	11,294,337	6,734,008	3,685,835	2,004,589	588,531	469,132	293,080	1,972,089	415,017	2,622,373	1,937,956
Oklahoma	4,245,075	2,622,542	795,669	409,125	128,102	254,891	180,890	651,202	103,325	908,415	714,118
Oregon	3,601,212	1,783,680	211,859	0	97,118	182,146	111,638	1,181,731	125,110	905,831	911,701
Pennsylvania	13,718,646	8,430,271	4,175,875	2,365,061	558,402	927,887	362,293	2,044,544	830,108	3,513,153	1,775,222
Rhode Island	1,561,904	726,421	374,083	212,446	44,493	29,735	21,784	261,139	42,446	405,922	429,561
South Carolina	3,642,319	2,112,640	1,140,747	691,575	213,909	89,311	42,782	718,861	128,180	885,116	644,563
South Dakota	819,768	324,587	279,173	173,539	55,155	28,352	14,486	0	2,565	270,185	224,996
Tennessee	4,175,442	2,246,288	1,704,157	1,177,234	282,937	214,928	106,939	52,151	203,858	1,316,811	612,343
Texas	14,938,084	9,019,075	5,671,153	3,319,992	490,375	999,948	308,612	0	0	3,156,473	2,762,536
Utah	1,929,632	974,098	527,377	391,346	85,895	47,282	26,990	345,813	31,592	537,986	417,548
Vermont	788,292	358,097	175,176	66,711	28,134	38,134	26,962	113,775	25,400	259,457	170,738
Virginia	6,270,367	3,553,236	1,516,281	721,580	321,394	208,205	144,330	1,549,147	183,215	1,423,863	1,293,268
Washington	6,482,524	4,191,161	3,116,201	2,453,969	241,353	234,267	119,460	0	0	1,522,487	768,876
West Virginia	2,435,543	1,470,331	1,005,196	745,360	106,290	87,234	59,010	310,583	45,146	617,033	348,179
Wisconsin	6,925,295	4,296,576	1,825,864	1,209,440	287,576	205,079	124,935	1,734,056	339,781	1,685,648	943,071
Wyoming	1,395,988	735,902	241,903	190,046	36,631	55,939	36,153	0	0	363,529	296,557

Source: U.S. Bureau of the Census, State Government Finances in 1983.
Note: Detail may not add to totals due to rounding.
(a) Total general revenue equals total taxes plus intergovernmental revenue plus charges and miscellaneous revenue.
(b) Total includes other taxes not shown separately in this table.

Table 6.7
STATE GENERAL REVENUE, BY SOURCE AND BY STATE: 1984
(In thousands of dollars)

State	Total general revenue(a)	Taxes Total(b)	Sales and gross receipts Total(b)	General	Motor fuels	Licenses Total(b)	Motor vehicle	Individual income	Corporation net income	Intergovernmental revenue	Charges and miscellaneous general revenue
All states	$330,740,178	$196,795,248	$95,801,167	$62,563,602	$12,395,562	$11,921,805	$6,353,571	$58,942,227	$15,511,378	$81,449,805	$52,495,125
Alabama	5,318,865	2,704,250	1,512,535	735,318	253,053	150,679	29,183	623,173	223,816	1,313,988	1,300,627
Alaska	5,024,981	1,973,252	88,255	0	32,169	54,444	14,636	1,151	304,621	412,515	2,639,214
Arizona	3,761,516	2,525,812	1,498,229	1,140,734	193,299	161,653	115,580	528,275	197,363	681,504	554,200
Arkansas	2,626,742	1,541,361	847,161	562,686	139,756	110,043	66,890	434,021	106,241	756,096	329,285
California	40,432,273	25,617,718	11,077,270	8,787,026	1,212,892	908,311	559,720	9,238,455	3,218,856	10,116,893	4,697,662
Colorado	3,833,095	2,132,825	1,104,424	791,382	188,739	125,807	67,069	763,627	87,721	938,132	762,138
Connecticut	4,929,803	3,086,003	2,118,444	1,339,110	197,507	140,114	78,809	278,682	401,801	956,239	887,561
Delaware	1,328,390	712,596	93,247	0	37,394	200,478	31,085	343,451	44,857	235,580	380,214
Florida	10,322,378	7,329,368	5,731,434	3,980,949	617,252	453,504	274,885	0	365,446	2,101,642	891,368
Georgia	6,468,836	3,954,615	2,006,885	1,361,598	372,751	125,618	59,862	1,465,773	315,960	1,875,954	638,267
Hawaii	2,089,712	1,248,177	780,840	639,247	34,556	19,082	9,096	402,821	36,978	418,874	422,661
Idaho	1,202,762	687,244	361,273	241,819	79,821	68,547	30,681	227,763	25,374	321,481	194,037
Illinois	14,159,818	8,701,267	4,275,685	2,651,128	533,166	598,734	437,253	2,961,077	563,961	3,489,287	1,969,264
Indiana	6,519,441	4,043,446	2,481,455	1,969,547	331,636	152,983	112,222	1,214,975	129,939	1,440,861	1,035,134
Iowa	3,712,233	2,241,503	1,061,857	736,265	196,128	199,253	143,227	788,001	132,093	887,460	583,270
Kansas	2,905,100	1,789,628	798,488	518,907	143,362	115,828	71,929	567,469	136,665	670,272	445,200
Kentucky	4,825,781	2,798,662	1,259,443	754,320	200,722	146,467	84,937	710,474	198,261	1,283,680	743,439
Louisiana	6,111,788	3,131,667	1,407,667	885,447	195,904	219,939	62,480	407,101	262,100	1,467,947	1,512,174
Maine	1,634,575	920,273	504,578	315,373	85,190	72,226	39,558	261,956	52,004	463,289	251,013
Maryland	6,547,563	3,946,833	1,785,296	988,284	290,259	147,004	90,877	1,607,502	198,364	1,398,961	1,201,769
Massachusetts	9,265,978	5,839,414	1,992,605	1,248,045	274,916	174,354	103,434	2,790,067	729,634	2,223,490	1,203,074
Michigan	14,635,682	8,568,674	3,184,465	2,273,137	564,998	405,207	283,069	3,383,794	1,289,915	3,920,617	2,146,391
Minnesota	7,824,103	5,077,158	2,041,863	1,250,835	332,616	290,781	205,655	2,316,365	305,498	1,645,507	1,101,438
Mississippi	3,094,782	1,740,692	1,106,830	866,040	122,439	151,422	51,993	260,061	110,196	930,027	424,063
Missouri	5,065,318	3,053,002	1,722,056	1,328,464	197,044	230,194	129,155	903,604	165,652	1,280,565	731,751
Montana	1,223,718	583,341	134,730	0	79,230	52,477	25,963	170,346	35,396	377,775	262,602
Nebraska	1,922,251	1,068,742	596,517	374,541	129,981	85,031	48,543	304,318	66,909	497,214	356,295
Nevada	1,262,700	861,115	731,640	411,413	71,610	97,121	34,212	0	0	255,545	146,040
New Hampshire	1,014,585	423,465	195,994	0	64,500	60,065	34,239	22,244	95,664	303,267	287,853
New Jersey	11,942,024	7,137,452	3,789,820	2,054,059	301,160	505,702	288,768	1,767,684	830,106	2,462,517	2,342,055

GENERAL REVENUE, BY SOURCE: 1984—Continued

State	Total general revenue(a)	Taxes Total(b)	Sales and gross receipts Total(b)	General	Motor fuels	Licenses Total(b)	Motor vehicle	Individual income	Corporation net income	Intergovernmental revenue	Charges and miscellaneous general revenue
New Mexico	2,943,540	1,377,444	782,666	578,387	107,119	82,209	41,784	74,862	53,399	530,006	1,036,090
New York	34,093,878	18,817,736	6,679,462	3,900,395	422,232	740,689	424,557	9,373,945	1,524,619	11,594,813	3,681,329
North Carolina	7,427,611	4,636,021	1,998,866	1,002,119	398,634	338,671	176,713	1,784,987	368,047	1,828,544	963,046
North Dakota	1,391,049	684,399	304,658	204,342	53,754	58,133	33,013	73,951	43,712	329,241	377,409
Ohio	13,369,983	7,985,012	4,257,614	2,602,174	615,996	548,989	302,258	2,486,822	524,891	3,015,351	2,369,620
Oklahoma	4,430,405	2,661,981	899,093	456,679	145,453	260,720	181,536	657,831	97,223	901,373	867,051
Oregon	3,816,748	1,850,523	216,308	0	105,362	206,646	125,917	1,217,842	144,065	982,234	983,991
Pennsylvania	15,327,696	9,600,168	4,649,816	2,720,628	598,533	977,646	360,241	2,536,872	865,299	3,702,717	2,024,811
Rhode Island	1,682,698	809,986	416,437	247,786	45,410	30,642	22,264	285,141	59,274	419,753	452,959
South Carolina	3,969,209	2,384,926	1,278,177	798,896	237,422	111,672	45,705	795,481	159,334	937,082	647,201
South Dakota	898,380	358,773	290,524	179,179	57,567	30,823	14,583	0	17,881	296,078	243,529
Tennessee	4,617,315	2,511,631	1,899,363	1,356,733	290,029	250,843	114,721	54,723	226,242	1,494,589	611,095
Texas	16,429,012	9,829,191	6,382,568	3,803,548	515,494	1,130,297	348,877	0	0	3,470,499	3,129,322
Utah	2,325,441	1,196,687	670,440	529,091	87,947	53,250	29,511	386,052	45,035	663,109	465,645
Vermont	886,374	412,987	210,799	81,097	36,968	39,707	26,390	132,153	22,606	280,475	192,912
Virginia	7,034,907	4,064,368	1,696,025	832,982	324,973	247,017	177,597	1,760,732	242,706	1,529,943	1,440,596
Washington	6,800,483	4,542,268	3,461,177	2,725,534	338,610	234,985	121,052	0	0	1,423,968	834,247
West Virginia	2,784,730	1,713,819	1,113,659	786,689	159,612	89,606	62,349	394,690	92,173	685,033	385,878
Wisconsin	7,934,742	5,116,236	2,074,672	1,374,566	343,897	206,444	121,530	2,181,913	393,481	1,805,323	1,013,183
Wyoming	1,569,184	801,537	227,857	177,103	36,500	59,748	37,963	0	0	432,495	335,152

Source: U.S. Bureau of the Census, State Government Finances in 1984.
Note: Detail may not add to totals due to rounding.
(a) Total general revenue equals total taxes plus intergovernmental revenue plus charges and miscellaneous revenue.
(b) Total includes other taxes not shown separately in this table.

Table 6.8
STATE EXPENDITURE, BY CHARACTER AND OBJECT AND BY STATE: 1983
(In thousands of dollars)

State	Intergovernmental expenditure	Total	Direct expenditure Current operation	Capital outlay Total	Construction	Land and existing structures	Equipment	Assistance and subsidies	Interest on debt	Insurance benefits and repayments	Exhibit: Total salaries and wages
All states	$101,309,230	$232,709,906	$144,018,263	$23,351,301	$18,616,028	$1,507,758	$3,227,515	$11,452,417	$11,707,802	$42,180,123	$60,347,578
Alabama	1,285,260	3,935,236	2,585,213	585,586	496,740	20,543	68,303	152,301	154,114	458,022	1,065,947
Alaska	1,088,608	2,747,375	1,546,754	587,682	517,235	3,824	66,623	49,117	403,504	160,318	694,851
Arizona	1,384,609	2,204,877	1,526,416	197,321	148,537	21,134	27,650	92,862	22,286	365,992	873,601
Arkansas	688,475	1,799,361	1,274,826	175,054	145,898	5,561	23,595	62,447	53,483	233,551	570,106
California	17,950,512	24,542,698	15,980,628	1,513,938	1,100,794	194,699	218,445	230,868	816,125	6,001,139	6,164,775
Colorado	1,265,765	2,796,013	1,892,789	224,644	154,557	29,168	40,919	29,683	72,690	576,207	916,860
Connecticut	853,283	3,574,068	2,197,165	240,307	206,061	16,411	17,835	253,027	349,894	533,675	990,384
Delaware	213,817	858,360	502,788	137,663	113,411	5,993	18,259	37,610	106,377	73,922	293,816
Florida	3,654,944	6,218,774	4,098,383	909,054	695,233	119,920	93,901	297,673	210,936	702,728	2,144,221
Georgia	1,963,168	4,600,067	2,977,979	735,665	669,291	2,748	63,626	217,694	118,483	550,246	1,356,805
Hawaii	26,883	2,151,197	1,400,493	286,408	250,157	6,054	30,197	110,808	152,305	201,183	730,447
Idaho	320,197	925,191	529,984	155,323	137,688	5,160	12,475	28,802	35,414	175,668	239,648
Illinois	3,635,455	11,368,425	5,851,854	985,504	842,686	16,368	126,450	1,222,901	572,984	2,735,182	2,107,412
Indiana	1,956,529	3,886,803	2,698,826	382,736	272,365	29,276	81,095	92,094	81,101	632,046	1,108,955
Iowa	1,300,227	2,857,011	1,894,635	310,928	258,723	12,031	40,174	177,641	34,233	439,574	929,313
Kansas	736,372	2,127,988	1,438,500	208,675	168,262	8,132	32,281	137,622	20,927	322,264	693,795
Kentucky	1,257,071	3,908,051	2,376,531	521,482	452,094	32,316	37,072	162,586	231,378	616,074	1,087,984
Louisiana	1,602,450	5,828,869	3,224,026	959,527	808,865	72,294	78,368	190,498	317,483	1,137,335	1,372,506
Maine	332,567	1,338,628	880,532	108,447	71,031	12,167	25,249	85,856	71,731	192,062	304,987
Maryland	1,718,524	5,202,500	3,296,134	620,085	545,653	24,841	49,591	300,854	258,892	726,535	1,237,528
Massachusetts	2,441,427	6,890,597	4,288,863	541,042	431,934	72,228	36,880	533,072	525,466	1,002,154	1,658,668
Michigan	3,837,848	10,951,514	6,385,914	472,756	360,986	24,887	86,883	1,472,396	318,851	2,301,597	2,588,535
Minnesota	2,251,310	4,244,339	2,954,565	363,187	285,143	30,011	48,033	57,546	199,242	669,799	1,335,181
Mississippi	970,254	2,162,121	1,492,727	235,632	188,390	13,123	34,119	86,837	55,810	291,115	535,944
Missouri	1,281,189	3,499,025	2,261,458	381,148	313,297	27,299	40,552	244,165	158,268	453,986	1,001,495
Montana	267,419	995,886	606,713	151,244	126,720	6,719	17,805	33,865	33,279	170,785	301,039
Nebraska	507,138	1,299,562	929,858	179,475	145,765	10,756	22,954	67,761	37,638	84,830	465,621
Nevada	478,671	1,091,305	532,280	208,999	172,756	5,743	30,500	17,042	50,813	282,171	264,919
New Hampshire	136,529	972,501	665,033	88,827	73,622	5,963	9,242	37,614	106,454	74,573	229,341
New Jersey	4,145,247	7,619,209	4,599,493	719,247	432,342	84,948	201,957	109,510	672,646	1,518,313	1,864,078

EXPENDITURE, BY CHARACTER AND OBJECT: 1983—Continued

State	Intergovernmental expenditure	Total	Current operation	Direct expenditure — Capital outlay Total	Construction	Land and existing structures	Equipment	Assistance and subsidies	Interest on debt	Insurance benefits and repayments	Exhibit: Total salaries and wages
New Mexico	936,147	1,756,092	1,139,393	319,211	281,424	18,012	19,775	55,925	73,308	168,255	528,451
New York	10,783,637	21,137,635	13,429,538	2,036,129	1,381,583	146,926	507,620	612,502	2,232,188	2,827,278	4,909,268
North Carolina	2,578,834	4,652,972	3,067,104	409,877	328,180	1,988	79,709	215,651	156,050	804,290	1,514,611
North Dakota	375,508	926,471	665,833	113,260	102,075	1,597	9,588	21,252	25,622	100,504	259,905
Ohio	4,298,362	11,602,235	5,713,095	1,128,103	953,777	51,709	122,617	699,859	393,701	3,667,477	2,244,978
Oklahoma	1,302,079	3,470,112	2,318,883	450,009	358,444	26,136	65,429	152,100	64,537	484,583	1,075,313
Oregon	1,020,668	3,335,779	1,774,767	246,080	193,124	17,197	35,759	122,604	460,962	731,366	797,512
Pennsylvania	4,192,970	12,539,886	6,663,990	615,568	526,214	8,052	81,302	1,495,335	458,649	3,306,344	2,332,569
Rhode Island	264,434	1,443,077	906,106	89,319	73,313	4,057	11,949	86,146	149,131	212,375	368,749
South Carolina	1,060,351	3,168,967	2,161,985	248,572	197,452	6,763	44,357	97,380	233,367	427,663	1,028,077
South Dakota	167,898	690,629	471,384	107,199	90,839	2,534	13,826	22,689	50,146	39,211	199,199
Tennessee	1,065,758	3,512,583	2,332,791	427,009	349,371	32,966	44,672	106,988	129,315	516,480	1,037,860
Texas	4,598,193	11,198,298	7,410,130	1,568,957	1,213,453	143,337	212,167	370,124	168,082	1,681,005	3,215,707
Utah	580,592	1,723,315	1,111,316	234,704	191,677	9,729	33,298	66,270	61,984	249,041	501,885
Vermont	130,312	759,614	529,939	67,033	56,964	1,966	8,103	51,737	51,403	59,502	194,874
Virginia	1,790,792	4,955,782	3,509,454	585,381	478,764	37,260	69,357	226,436	197,053	437,458	1,711,125
Washington	2,245,150	5,662,452	3,087,979	749,327	644,531	29,461	75,335	316,621	189,098	1,319,427	1,300,148
West Virginia	665,589	2,380,744	1,312,794	274,268	225,525	21,382	27,361	66,814	97,754	629,114	534,765
Wisconsin	3,294,624	4,338,252	3,078,358	302,698	214,778	21,951	65,969	55,392	225,437	676,367	1,218,552
Wyoming	405,584	857,460	442,064	191,011	168,304	4,418	18,289	17,840	47,208	159,337	245,268

Source: U.S. Bureau of the Census, State Government Finances in 1983.
Note: Detail may not add to totals due to rounding.

237

Table 6.9
STATE EXPENDITURE, BY CHARACTER AND OBJECT AND BY STATE: 1984
(In thousands of dollars)

State	Intergovernmental expenditure	Direct expenditure						Assistance and subsidies	Interest on debt	Insurance benefits and repayments	Exhibit: Total salaries and wages
		Total	Current operation	Capital outlay							
				Total	Construction	Land and existing structures	Equipment				
All states	$108,373,188	$243,072,779	$156,733,973	$25,582,891	$19,670,539	$1,816,326	$4,096,026	$12,386,123	$13,737,605	$34,632,187	$65,196,325
Alabama	1,310,399	3,880,656	2,624,771	543,876	426,441	32,355	85,080	150,479	205,963	355,567	1,169,107
Alaska	1,183,094	2,785,481	1,520,460	506,968	402,143	16,464	88,361	53,839	528,514	175,700	747,814
Arizona	1,547,438	2,498,177	1,748,139	293,802	226,435	27,399	39,968	103,999	39,271	312,966	745,803
Arkansas	789,131	1,847,073	1,359,639	173,087	133,303	5,998	33,786	73,636	59,456	181,255	599,389
California	19,125,775	25,589,888	17,496,933	1,580,135	1,100,680	168,386	311,069	226,578	955,422	5,330,820	6,582,527
Colorado	1,522,105	3,038,226	2,033,722	297,745	214,984	40,244	42,517	30,596	102,186	573,977	1,004,426
Connecticut	967,483	3,901,270	2,509,161	275,089	218,958	26,604	29,527	263,345	396,506	457,169	1,110,413
Delaware	218,833	992,607	624,802	139,922	99,982	7,212	32,728	37,997	120,741	69,145	308,160
Florida	3,561,701	6,758,604	4,400,984	1,100,981	809,412	205,813	85,756	370,013	263,814	622,812	2,498,319
Georgia	1,947,978	4,751,480	3,283,830	615,267	508,413	3,770	103,084	251,581	137,089	463,713	1,509,655
Hawaii	25,231	2,218,647	1,437,107	295,649	245,943	18,019	31,687	106,418	175,237	204,236	730,480
Idaho	408,686	938,045	579,427	156,383	126,476	6,473	23,434	29,649	42,074	130,512	252,262
Illinois	3,910,634	11,139,237	6,364,757	1,243,450	1,080,709	24,987	137,754	1,305,833	598,765	1,626,432	2,141,779
Indiana	2,321,187	4,095,182	2,985,404	519,481	400,949	28,611	89,921	73,264	100,853	416,180	1,173,455
Iowa	1,321,682	2,955,325	1,993,519	431,955	350,917	11,456	69,582	206,742	43,529	279,580	936,596
Kansas	846,726	2,126,800	1,498,996	255,440	198,307	9,546	47,587	122,909	21,955	227,500	713,726
Kentucky	1,288,688	4,069,727	2,508,931	693,599	588,685	36,012	68,902	183,235	235,836	448,126	1,268,739
Louisiana	1,746,045	5,917,723	3,454,319	947,908	674,293	113,815	159,800	174,693	386,704	954,099	1,537,567
Maine	349,880	1,425,526	966,260	94,712	59,442	15,038	20,232	101,929	84,819	177,806	318,200
Maryland	1,635,537	5,244,621	3,305,796	657,106	534,862	46,753	75,491	320,550	279,727	681,442	1,259,738
Massachusetts	2,617,378	7,118,128	4,684,144	442,722	374,347	18,066	50,309	557,862	634,080	799,320	1,845,171
Michigan	4,037,673	11,330,770	7,064,421	674,816	544,622	33,142	97,052	1,581,155	367,604	1,642,774	2,720,288
Minnesota	2,880,437	4,655,999	3,324,980	457,352	367,495	36,065	53,792	85,274	235,760	552,633	1,423,190
Mississippi	1,065,912	2,285,279	1,629,708	267,737	210,723	17,855	39,159	88,984	74,238	224,612	616,482
Missouri	1,589,484	3,673,120	2,445,811	445,104	348,169	35,096	61,839	221,733	210,375	350,097	1,087,367
Montana	293,193	1,092,233	641,200	193,756	170,361	4,169	19,226	40,062	43,477	173,738	370,742
Nebraska	511,721	1,371,864	957,824	225,994	178,732	12,376	34,886	71,596	49,625	66,825	515,582
Nevada	487,427	997,754	558,365	120,827	107,248	2,658	10,921	13,813	57,432	247,317	296,045
New Hampshire	157,680	970,514	683,493	82,664	70,334	3,654	8,676	36,633	107,531	60,193	251,398
New Jersey	4,133,531	8,501,366	5,452,076	718,351	542,647	46,103	129,601	94,469	819,342	1,417,128	2,042,399

EXPENDITURE, BY CHARACTER AND OBJECT: 1984—Continued

State	Intergovernmental expenditure	Direct expenditure Total	Current operation	Capital outlay Total	Construction	Land and existing structures	Equipment	Assistance and subsidies	Interest on debt	Insurance benefits and repayments	Exhibit: Total salaries and wages
New Mexico	967,744	1,865,553	1,190,894	372,194	331,513	5,845	34,836	57,685	82,708	162,072	537,627
New York	12,262,857	23,654,489	15,230,661	2,508,101	1,688,111	34,387	785,603	563,750	2,468,478	2,883,499	5,853,899
North Carolina	2,722,596	4,865,041	3,396,552	447,481	343,053	2,514	101,914	251,400	205,756	563,852	1,583,628
North Dakota	412,386	1,027,639	728,828	144,038	122,442	263	21,333	24,660	37,319	92,794	271,928
Ohio	4,779,871	11,568,615	6,146,830	1,218,230	688,324	429,246	100,660	780,733	535,780	2,887,042	2,535,883
Oklahoma	1,284,809	3,423,590	2,319,832	382,100	311,470	17,197	53,433	150,497	184,722	386,439	1,055,998
Oregon	993,012	3,450,418	1,928,951	280,731	214,807	26,133	39,791	129,187	471,061	640,488	870,650
Pennsylvania	4,703,507	11,897,276	6,998,352	735,267	632,843	3,319	99,105	1,426,222	466,893	2,270,542	2,488,350
Rhode Island	275,000	1,556,771	985,529	123,612	102,822	6,315	14,475	82,357	186,945	178,328	392,831
South Carolina	1,095,298	3,301,022	2,355,269	294,233	217,307	14,564	62,362	97,881	243,752	309,887	1,111,187
South Dakota	165,296	787,630	514,498	129,265	102,160	4,352	22,753	22,007	71,557	50,303	206,807
Tennessee	1,105,881	3,723,847	2,597,012	516,950	426,597	33,532	56,821	110,456	143,932	355,497	1,040,967
Texas	4,965,245	11,914,745	8,152,291	1,601,816	1,266,361	79,180	256,275	418,841	263,635	1,478,162	3,407,603
Utah	610,987	1,834,752	1,229,651	281,589	227,179	7,607	46,803	68,769	87,160	167,583	522,700
Vermont	135,974	805,077	570,618	65,363	52,623	3,064	9,676	57,304	60,473	51,319	199,868
Virginia	1,928,473	5,167,183	3,790,446	567,049	457,964	33,425	75,660	219,879	221,954	367,855	1,774,133
Washington	2,290,339	5,848,690	3,317,458	611,844	489,838	35,000	87,006	355,604	240,061	1,323,723	1,485,540
West Virginia	702,912	2,432,846	1,458,437	272,708	230,728	8,992	32,988	85,838	97,425	518,438	559,085
Wisconsin	2,638,645	4,891,366	3,224,061	353,049	247,933	13,379	91,737	479,526	228,933	605,797	1,255,003
Wyoming	529,687	884,907	458,824	225,393	200,452	3,873	21,068	24,661	61,136	114,893	265,819

Source: U.S. Bureau of the Census, State Government Finances in 1984.
Note: Detail may not add to totals due to rounding.

239

Table 6.10
STATE GENERAL EXPENDITURE, BY FUNCTION AND BY STATE: 1983
(In thousands of dollars)

	Total general expenditure(a)	Education	Public welfare	Highways	Hospitals	Natural resources	Health	Corrections	Financial administration	Employment security administration	Police
All states	$285,041,605	$107,702,727	$57,544,499	$26,430,814	$14,914,997	$5,833,949	$9,010,726	$6,743,152	$4,206,315	$2,463,570	$3,002,168
Alabama	4,637,675	2,197,274	552,671	514,477	334,894	94,341	127,799	82,140	63,895	32,392	38,350
Alaska	3,422,267	924,391	173,014	361,269	25,234	222,228	91,022	74,231	58,342	12,360	49,989
Arizona	3,215,109	1,552,791	266,464	373,405	113,958	50,753	67,937	105,825	50,331	23,135	62,793
Arkansas	2,254,285	945,490	391,984	291,745	109,516	68,421	62,574	45,295	42,100	26,002	20,908
California	36,487,972	13,921,646	10,000,112	1,835,727	1,062,943	962,486	1,211,711	772,465	515,847	225,791	363,422
Colorado	3,485,571	1,573,381	586,879	323,094	203,366	78,791	95,187	72,083	60,811	23,926	38,500
Connecticut	3,832,501	1,075,092	842,247	267,621	306,400	36,660	87,807	101,769	54,618	48,851	43,507
Delaware	989,082	422,518	64,029	114,354	40,424	23,473	26,545	32,468	23,851	7,926	17,872
Florida	9,144,868	4,076,586	1,141,738	956,301	401,134	337,574	493,771	293,032	105,830	45,602	116,188
Georgia	6,012,989	2,561,427	1,011,453	778,092	289,575	135,242	230,672	197,688	71,949	56,825	58,699
Hawaii	1,976,897	709,289	288,550	107,365	113,980	56,640	66,713	27,823	25,212	14,015	1,887
Idaho	1,038,020	423,104	121,114	160,099	29,962	54,786	36,477	21,604	16,642	16,399	9,360
Illinois	12,268,698	4,262,278	3,193,161	1,254,911	469,811	139,134	320,005	282,062	235,292	134,280	112,171
Indiana	5,211,286	2,385,191	837,208	546,916	228,259	97,696	151,195	115,976	59,103	47,853	54,934
Iowa	3,624,310	1,575,272	629,561	496,572	258,473	77,762	42,183	69,650	45,153	36,144	26,203
Kansas	2,542,096	1,124,700	489,130	297,588	166,159	75,962	45,827	54,674	49,114	26,313	18,666
Kentucky	4,549,048	1,847,442	749,398	640,725	139,088	118,356	116,056	78,087	82,531	25,015	76,921
Louisiana	6,293,984	2,292,628	917,902	824,022	466,549	204,825	153,045	151,680	70,344	22,935	90,560
Maine	1,434,204	463,214	360,874	163,333	37,334	48,052	40,528	23,052	37,367	13,501	15,049
Maryland	5,968,601	1,797,089	1,024,227	759,845	492,707	103,177	197,869	215,997	91,048	32,026	143,288
Massachusetts	8,304,957	1,886,345	2,195,438	444,301	421,408	48,996	405,811	165,081	103,501	58,500	52,066
Michigan	12,149,659	3,815,789	3,535,777	878,963	754,746	146,762	577,166	245,137	115,509	158,911	116,964
Minnesota	5,825,850	2,058,177	1,196,838	600,412	310,947	163,989	90,145	72,531	69,214	54,651	46,827
Mississippi	2,745,531	1,139,530	425,212	356,451	145,442	93,724	74,239	44,384	21,664	36,701	29,939
Missouri	4,326,228	1,753,145	805,680	495,501	268,893	106,055	128,557	72,993	71,610	49,329	43,473
Montana	1,057,422	384,070	151,517	168,297	30,432	64,772	38,116	19,056	33,491	7,237	13,894
Nebraska	1,721,870	606,093	285,411	272,434	106,397	68,790	63,199	42,783	16,982	15,429	17,076
Nevada	1,190,828	460,268	109,045	164,115	24,048	20,451	28,567	41,863	30,766	18,366	9,749
New Hampshire	912,538	225,789	164,833	142,639	40,597	14,529	46,259	16,502	11,353	9,152	12,543
New Jersey	9,734,768	2,895,702	1,873,873	642,517	459,410	144,127	181,907	203,752	121,115	51,837	111,459

GENERAL EXPENDITURE, BY FUNCTION: 1983—Continued

	Total general expenditure(a)	Education	Public welfare	Highways	Hospitals	Natural resources	Health	Corrections	Financial adminis- tration	Employment security adminis- tration	Police
New Mexico	2,523,984	1,098,558	217,763	324,900	111,958	49,246	79,289	90,705	39,617	19,697	28,144
New York	26,577,965	7,944,286	6,929,476	1,403,574	1,918,924	164,145	777,906	744,933	466,774	255,416	171,349
North Carolina	6,427,516	3,124,452	851,486	625,123	367,935	152,350	210,600	205,397	54,478	39,688	82,244
North Dakota	1,201,475	498,395	116,580	148,887	58,032	44,170	32,569	15,814	14,005	5,133	5,227
Ohio	11,932,799	4,630,704	2,698,014	1,103,157	717,902	131,532	564,701	245,872	196,394	139,863	76,368
Oklahoma	4,132,856	1,955,546	719,937	489,582	268,897	80,813	106,527	107,744	65,383	34,911	44,884
Oregon	3,536,494	1,131,185	444,066	344,337	173,571	114,259	80,035	67,657	108,374	30,227	37,229
Pennsylvania	12,874,280	4,126,631	3,512,807	1,382,494	790,712	210,181	403,452	175,256	211,483	120,037	168,421
Rhode Island	1,476,208	440,728	377,333	58,578	101,294	10,442	56,803	38,119	25,327	16,544	13,005
South Carolina	3,296,100	1,545,457	452,665	270,852	225,686	79,669	133,174	84,193	48,901	36,953	37,250
South Dakota	819,316	242,338	114,906	128,203	23,900	43,669	24,326	9,573	18,618	11,968	8,283
Tennessee	4,061,861	1,650,903	695,339	519,657	223,932	70,349	148,223	115,428	46,386	48,699	26,145
Texas	14,115,486	7,441,919	1,924,401	1,564,518	904,559	246,329	295,865	345,306	179,478	137,682	136,480
Utah	2,006,815	1,029,287	252,971	196,225	93,515	54,094	56,600	55,581	28,659	27,326	22,419
Vermont	802,610	267,026	143,523	92,608	23,912	27,212	33,798	14,952	15,645	13,213	14,379
Virginia	6,098,226	2,435,962	863,513	779,217	552,939	63,959	184,440	246,445	107,150	27,228	196,479
Washington	6,400,028	2,993,309	935,740	717,071	207,507	191,916	199,441	271,680	76,403	69,318	51,096
West Virginia	2,367,676	981,368	297,543	367,045	92,988	61,992	66,951	16,474	42,560	23,792	21,802
Wisconsin	6,956,509	2,477,181	1,536,109	478,021	206,643	132,850	232,245	133,927	89,319	62,785	35,703
Wyoming	1,074,102	331,781	74,987	203,674	28,105	46,218	24,892	16,413	18,776	11,686	12,004

Source: U.S. Bureau of the Census, *State Government Finances in 1983*.
Note: Totals may not add due to rounding.
(a) Does not represent sum of state figures because total includes miscellaneous expenditure not shown separately.

Table 6.11

STATE GENERAL EXPENDITURE, BY FUNCTION AND BY STATE: 1984

(In thousands of dollars)

	Total general expenditure(a)	Education	Public welfare	Highways	Hospitals	Natural resources	Health	Corrections	Financial adminis- tration	Employment security adminis- tration	Police
All states	$309,683,589	$116,057,775	$62,749,207	$28,936,578	$15,278,077	$5,944,606	$9,703,771	$7,732,000	$4,516,508	$2,545,614	$3,139,737
Alabama	4,712,847	2,119,924	583,408	566,654	289,174	97,522	140,581	92,591	75,233	30,412	35,328
Alaska	3,633,012	1,061,878	219,652	377,690	39,145	178,374	75,984	71,253	67,066	9,259	55,237
Arizona	3,724,393	1,646,878	407,459	492,372	114,580	50,769	89,411	117,401	70,424	21,336	67,021
Arkansas	2,454,949	1,045,021	446,059	305,402	109,757	72,944	76,505	47,848	49,145	28,637	21,215
California	39,379,826	15,561,379	10,095,139	2,073,865	1,175,294	1,009,981	1,146,297	880,951	566,048	220,919	430,743
Colorado	3,986,354	1,747,886	641,607	473,514	211,131	87,436	104,721	72,291	65,094	25,384	32,933
Connecticut	4,344,526	1,175,535	937,914	337,161	343,694	41,635	97,528	108,999	61,594	51,612	49,021
Delaware	1,123,925	443,314	110,445	113,016	41,722	21,886	30,340	36,869	29,786	7,271	19,376
Florida	9,680,737	4,098,672	1,276,163	1,036,700	382,553	330,145	600,388	358,506	104,278	47,678	122,714
Georgia	6,235,745	2,729,395	1,022,316	612,533	318,866	148,064	278,873	213,483	83,868	59,610	62,547
Hawaii	2,039,642	707,626	289,853	123,095	105,637	44,990	72,568	35,202	34,119	14,012	2,380
Idaho	1,187,730	531,371	128,494	182,704	20,936	59,383	39,362	17,472	17,438	20,712	10,893
Illinois	13,423,439	4,492,938	3,291,239	1,560,408	471,179	150,005	372,190	378,776	226,347	143,578	115,151
Indiana	6,000,189	2,645,591	895,444	677,197	244,304	110,444	160,204	129,715	63,837	51,571	52,698
Iowa	3,905,979	1,682,778	695,883	600,996	246,568	66,903	49,382	75,013	47,278	42,161	26,959
Kansas	2,746,026	1,239,252	460,890	363,203	171,470	74,315	47,875	62,496	52,283	25,308	17,934
Kentucky	4,910,289	1,970,857	813,462	713,947	147,851	140,687	127,292	99,522	106,596	22,215	69,464
Louisiana	6,709,669	2,509,459	1,018,707	779,722	495,377	204,857	162,235	150,814	74,536	24,827	93,901
Maine	1,551,425	517,689	402,203	151,830	38,748	49,784	43,607	24,366	44,206	15,641	15,870
Maryland	6,032,883	1,860,340	1,085,295	793,821	346,042	88,301	212,133	238,497	94,141	27,264	142,792
Massachusetts	8,909,612	2,150,064	2,286,692	434,905	466,804	57,364	397,463	199,914	124,767	58,858	52,592
Michigan	13,395,803	3,926,090	4,042,806	1,071,234	722,497	161,685	812,801	279,519	111,070	152,061	125,387
Minnesota	6,983,803	2,636,488	1,354,283	676,970	325,351	165,569	107,397	90,111	77,691	57,643	47,634
Mississippi	3,033,762	1,232,192	478,691	365,453	158,094	99,988	95,614	53,010	24,023	37,693	34,506
Missouri	4,912,507	2,062,946	849,903	509,764	282,021	118,864	147,350	85,504	78,475	53,885	54,562
Montana	1,176,708	417,877	171,821	199,830	29,806	70,776	46,112	20,443	37,536	8,573	15,589
Nebraska	1,816,760	627,193	293,535	316,928	108,247	72,164	68,218	41,545	5,085	15,609	18,577
Nevada	1,194,567	440,011	108,090	156,571	25,245	21,280	30,607	42,415	31,516	19,422	10,036
New Hampshire	941,261	222,956	175,989	140,575	42,601	15,489	50,370	18,468	12,858	10,184	14,055
New Jersey	10,642,145	3,144,035	1,969,277	693,587	481,448	100,298	220,073	257,321	136,220	49,980	130,369

GENERAL EXPENDITURE, BY FUNCTION: 1984—Continued

	Total general expenditure(a)	Education	Public welfare	Highways	Hospitals	Natural resources	Health	Corrections	Financial administration	Employment security administration	Police
New Mexico	2,671,225	1,146,369	232,239	341,880	123,059	52,039	90,274	106,147	41,782	22,364	23,388
New York	29,957,629	8,549,857	8,813,770	1,289,787	2,010,403	134,980	919,958	912,157	462,596	282,905	227,477
North Carolina	7,023,785	3,349,923	938,061	692,917	376,543	161,742	242,917	224,607	58,665	32,346	87,351
North Dakota	1,347,231	548,819	142,762	190,551	55,234	45,844	28,216	10,516	13,960	5,192	7,442
Ohio	13,187,936	4,941,552	2,991,665	1,546,744	712,336	144,623	351,805	263,392	219,829	134,420	82,471
Oklahoma	4,124,295	1,853,938	712,012	477,565	266,488	75,539	107,923	114,573	74,177	37,615	37,389
Oregon	3,712,289	1,168,531	468,128	412,038	192,945	118,758	90,987	78,330	102,634	30,626	43,744
Pennsylvania	13,788,499	4,567,812	3,705,456	1,404,442	816,981	212,767	364,369	195,559	197,301	128,339	175,185
Rhode Island	1,632,270	461,310	406,847	79,625	103,971	12,238	56,125	32,532	29,206	17,051	15,087
South Carolina	3,651,435	1,678,910	440,833	319,983	242,490	90,904	188,118	107,792	53,733	42,798	40,760
South Dakota	902,623	251,620	127,543	153,354	30,678	47,380	22,123	12,781	24,096	11,815	9,647
Tennessee	4,474,231	1,689,736	839,379	628,782	225,373	74,676	172,442	127,451	53,953	46,528	30,504
Texas	15,401,828	8,065,079	2,047,817	1,494,831	974,458	280,950	344,960	407,931	197,498	169,366	142,732
Utah	2,229,744	1,067,713	278,841	290,922	98,458	56,581	65,537	51,895	31,993	27,803	20,408
Vermont	861,465	284,031	157,446	108,275	20,909	27,629	33,605	15,820	15,810	11,582	14,289
Virginia	6,527,895	2,746,864	904,923	816,954	512,270	68,518	199,640	345,690	116,101	34,392	117,581
Washington	6,632,645	3,109,918	1,040,979	637,805	226,820	183,236	195,471	247,964	92,019	69,854	50,096
West Virginia	2,570,649	1,068,418	325,230	361,341	96,002	63,467	80,507	19,669	55,747	19,005	21,318
Wisconsin	6,924,214	2,439,323	1,542,185	544,412	209,149	137,215	217,381	135,364	83,637	55,916	32,078
Wyoming	1,271,177	420,417	80,372	242,723	27,368	43,618	27,932	21,515	19,213	12,382	13,306

Source: U.S. Bureau of the Census, State Government Finances in 1984.
Note: Totals may not add due to rounding.
(a) Includes miscellaneous expenditures not shown separately in this table.

Table 6.12
STATE DEBT OUTSTANDING AT END OF FISCAL YEAR, BY STATE: 1983
(In thousands of dollars, except per capita amounts)

State	Total	Per capita	Long-term Total	Full-faith and credit	Non-guaranteed	Short-term	Net long-term(a) Total	Full-faith and credit
All states	$167,289,946	$ 716.88	$164,694,874	$55,078,060	$109,616,814	$2,595,072	$94,779,404	$41,442,488
Alabama...........	2,339,606	590.96	2,317,731	734,675	1,583,056	21,875	1,618,848	723,439
Alaska............	4,665,456	9,739.99	4,665,456	946,183	3,719,273	0	3,481,881	946,108
Arizona...........	558,627	188.53	550,669	0	550,669	7,958	530,960	0
Arkansas..........	650,995	279.64	630,995	0	630,995	20,000	128,381	0
California.........	12,071,209	479.51	12,049,859	4,292,711	7,757,148	21,350	7,320,040	575,353
Colorado	1,150,530	366.53	1,150,530	0	1,150,530	0	198,792	0
Connecticut	5,236,226	1,668.65	5,079,281	2,127,224	2,952,057	156,945	2,497,150	1,968,233
Delaware	1,562,169	2,577.84	1,541,850	490,078	1,051,772	20,319	1,237.451	490,078
Florida	3,566,782	333.97	3,566,782	1,151,936	2,414,846	0	2,167,977	502,454
Georgia...........	1,884,100	321.72	1,844,100	989,096	885,004	0	1,410,941	971,219
Hawaii	2,320,186	2,268.02	2,263,787	1,590,351	673,436	56,399	1,948,373	1,586,126
Idaho	448,342	453.33	448,342	465	447,877	0	81,145	463
Illinois...........	7,862,325	684.51	7,809,712	3,160,700	4,649,012	52,613	4,611,450	3,074,527
Indiana	1,208,419	220.55	1,061,593	0	1,061,593	146,826	618,404	0
Iowa	594,381	204.61	594,190	0	594,190	191	214,182	0
Kansas	379,435	156.47	379,435	27,800	351,635	0	321,844	27,800
Kentucky	3,030,863	816.06	3,030,863	226,425	2,804,438	0	1,878,098	217,385
Louisiana	5,244,181	1,181.65	5,227,562	2,344,116	2,883,446	16,619	3,659,048	2,315,767
Maine	1,073,016	936.31	1,072,986	300,452	772,534	30	384,466	300,452
Maryland	4,661,773	1,083.13	4,577,566	2,421,259	2,156,307	84,207	2,918,924	2,373,523
Massachusetts	7,888,009	1,367.78	7,439,182	3,321,820	4,117,362	448,827	4,038,303	3,310,942
Michigan	4,669,139	514.85	4,636,865	655,070	3,981,795	32,274	2,823,010	643,879
Minnesota	2,761,480	666.38	2,751,920	906,693	1,845,227	9,560	921,478	747,554
Mississippi	908,310	351.11	908,310	661,459	246,851	0	701,567	614,396
Missouri	2,250,613	452.84	2,240,613	134,970	2,105,643	10,000	871,541	124,405
Montana..........	511,569	626.16	511,546	57,940	453,606	23	127,157	44,066
Nebraska	387,355	242.55	387,201	0	387,201	154	16,663	0
Nevada	757,067	849.68	757,067	217,065	540,002	0	365,316	202,398
New Hampshire	1,531,667	1,597.15	1,528,403	332,226	1,196,177	3,264	778,556	322,819
New Jersey........	10,306,360	1,380.07	10,304,129	2,467,678	7,836,451	2,231	6,860,713	2,432,152
New Mexico........	1,076,327	769.35	1,074,170	18,782	1,055,388	2,157	284,853	10,503
New York	27,765,418	1,571.60	27,044,979	4,178,327	22,866,652	720,439	14,544,633	2,879,986
North Carolina	1,622,561	266.78	1,615,334	944,645	670,689	7,227	1,238,532	919,504
North Dakota	381,830	561.51	380,536	6,965	373,571	1,294	44,156	0
Ohio	6,094,837	567.17	5,959,594	2,508,685	3,450,909	135,243	5,568,333	2,504,138
Oklahoma	1,331,290	403.67	1,331,290	147,004	1,184,286	0	1,081,509	49,187
Oregon	6,589,036	2,475.22	6,499,036	5,803,090	695,946	90,000	341,926	244,040
Pennsylvania	6,496,934	546.19	6,366,196	3,926,815	2,439,381	130,738	5,219,550	3,879,141
Rhode Island	2,225,528	2,330.40	2,194,689	279,839	1,914,850	30,839	636,268	279,839
South Carolina	3,153,922	966.28	3,092,772	560,316	2,532,456	61,150	1,934,819	208,835
South Dakota	791,107	1,130.15	789,280	0	789,280	1,827	47,598	0
Tennessee	1,797,131	383.59	1,600,031	659,650	940,381	197,100	803,202	581,122
Texas	3,028,877	192.63	3,028,877	965,080	2,063,797	0	1,688,394	170,447
Utah	1,070,279	661.07	1,070,279	236,950	833,329	0	401,558	228,207
Vermont	764,745	1,456.66	764,624	297,744	466,880	121	365,438	297,744
Virginia...........	2,666,034	480.37	2,574,964	277,214	2,297,750	91,070	498,325	229,213
Washington	2,527,097	587.70	2,527,021	2,008,413	518,608	76	2,110,997	1,977,078
West Virginia	1,675,680	852.76	1,675,254	822,884	852,370	426	891,012	623,928
Wisconsin	3,210,023	675.65	3,196,323	1,877,265	1,319,058	13,700	2,277,718	1,844,038
Wyoming	581,100	1,130.54	581,100	0	581,100	0	67,924	0

Source: U.S Bureau of the Census, *State Government Finances in 1983.*
Note: Debt figures include revenue bonds and other special obligations
of state agencies as well as state general obligations.
(a) Long-term debt outstanding minus long-term debt offsets.

244

Table 6.13
STATE DEBT OUTSTANDING AT END OF FISCAL YEAR, BY STATE: 1984
(In thousands of dollars, except per capita amounts)

State	Total	Per capita	Long-term Total	Long-term Full-faith and credit	Long-term Non-guaranteed	Short-term	Net long-term(a) Total	Net long-term(a) Full-faith and credit
All states	$186,376,896	$ 791.29	$183,208,224	$57,349,274	$125,858,950	$3,168,672	$101,681,364	$46,976,314
Alabama...........	2,896,714	725.99	2,896,714	713,175	2,183,539	0	1,773,698	710,053
Alaska.............	5,529,672	11,059.34	5,529,672	1,648,823	3,880,849	0	1,847,231	948,914
Arizona............	607,720	199.06	607,720	0	607,720	0	236,729	0
Arkansas	703,344	299.42	683,344	0	683,344	20,000	122,244	0
California..........	13,553,823	528.99	13,512,623	4,355,073	9,157,550	41,200	8,539,818	4,224,752
Colorado	1,256,257	395.30	1,256,257	0	1,256,257	0	131,134	0
Connecticut	5,469,783	1,734.24	5,401,583	2,208,981	3,192,602	68,200	3,375,032	2,005,370
Delaware	1,809,003	2,951.07	1,792,904	563,515	1,229,389	16,099	1,330,201	563,515
Florida	3,909,566	356.19	3,909,566	1,095,934	2,813,632	0	2,944,286	481,547
Georgia............	1,842,122	315.59	1,842,122	999,556	842,566	0	1,360,067	970,462
Hawaii	2,512,093	2,417.80	2,448,957	1,641,695	807,262	63,136	2,026,110	1,637,070
Idaho	574,359	573.79	574,359	345	574,014	0	128,855	344
Illinois.............	8,636,544	750.29	8,356,132	3,329,500	5,026,632	280,412	4,748,525	3,227,154
Indiana	1,563,271	284.32	1,391,471	0	1,391,471	171,800	767,749	0
Iowa	651,311	223.82	651,311	0	651,311	0	263,336	0
Kansas	356,136	146.08	356,136	27,800	328,336	0	296,687	27,800
Kentucky	3,384,183	908.99	3,384,183	206,600	3,177,583	0	1,958,076	140,380
Louisiana	6,517,978	1,460.77	6,517,580	2,624,006	3,893,574	398	4,326,692	2,621,811
Maine	1,195,410	1,034.09	1,194,398	294,584	899,814	1,012	375,466	294,584
Maryland	4,761,182	1,094.78	4,691,104	2,325,688	2,365,416	70,078	2,814,085	2,284,853
Massachusetts	8,865,155	1,529.00	8,462,966	3,481,225	4,981,741	402,189	4,248,174	3,468,264
Michigan	5,222,480	575.48	5,220,913	691,315	4,529,598	1,567	3,282,580	685,400
Minnesota	3,388,868	814.24	3,140,473	1,072,643	2,067,830	248,395	1,099,596	915,460
Mississippi	1,025,222	394.62	1,025,222	617,845	407,377	0	664,073	563,809
Missouri	2,831,238	565.34	2,781,003	225,920	2,555,083	50,235	1,038,948	213,574
Montana...........	696,071	844.75	656,996	107,541	549,455	39,075	145,114	89,405
Nebraska	606,254	377.49	606,139	0	606,139	115	92,017	0
Nevada	864,520	948.98	864,499	275,440	589,059	21	478,710	260,224
New Hampshire	1,734,333	1,775.16	1,712,904	374,431	1,338,473	21,429	1,118,190	364,851
New Jersey	11,544,014	1,536.13	11,543,916	2,421,332	9,122,584	98	7,556,873	2,405,071
New Mexico.........	1,150,884	808.21	1,148,143	12,641	1,135,502	2,741	329,005	4,606
New York	29,390,713	1,657.22	28,783,037	4,154,255	24,628,782	607,676	15,659,562	2,745,637
North Carolina	1,885,929	305.91	1,878,829	886,042	992,787	7,100	1,307,420	864,284
North Dakota	444,756	648.33	443,881	5,807	438,074	875	42,445	0
Ohio	6,664,321	619.82	6,567,019	2,439,125	4,127,894	97,302	5,299,718	2,434,470
Oklahoma	3,041,744	922.30	3,030,230	135,964	2,894,266	11,514	1,467,462	60,588
Oregon	6,544,694	2,447.53	6,277,694	5,617,356	660,338	267,000	561,071	360,392
Pennsylvania	6,637,824	557.75	6,596,259	4,000,290	2,595,969	41,565	5,267,529	3,912,749
Rhode Island	2,291,705	2,382.23	2,236,186	241,150	1,995,036	55,519	621,196	241,150
South Carolina	3,241,814	982.37	3,106,767	624,544	2,482,223	135,047	2,054,069	453,627
South Dakota	917,562	1,299.66	917,295	0	917,295	267	35,429	0
Tennessee	1,735,309	367.88	1,568,509	604,750	963,759	166,800	741,242	523,557
Texas..............	4,009,048	250.74	4,009,048	1,290,661	2,718,387	0	2,053,260	427,145
Utah	1,200,096	726.45	1,200,096	271,940	928,156	0	398,215	221,672
Vermont	809,901	1,528.12	809,756	296,468	513,288	145	361,179	296,468
Virginia............	2,901,912	514.89	2,822,310	391,554	2,430,756	79,602	464,306	336,657
Washington	3,098,219	712.40	2,898,159	2,314,678	583,481	200,060	2,467,994	2,278,533
West Virginia	1,633,392	836.78	1,633,392	771,912	861,480	0	986,491	754,342
Wisconsin..........	3,552,127	745.31	3,552,127	1,987,170	1,564,957	0	2,423,325	1,955,770
Wyoming	716,320	1,401.80	716,320	0	716,320	0	50,150	0

Source: U.S Bureau of the Census, *State Government Finances in 1984.*
Note: Debt figures include revenue bonds and other special obligations
of state agencies, as well as state general obligations.
(a) Long-term debt outstanding minus long-term debt offsets.

Table 6.14
STATE BALANCED BUDGETS AND DEFICIT LIMITATIONS: CONSTITUTIONAL AND STATUTORY PROVISIONS

State	Balanced budget requirement	Deficit carried over must be corrected in next fiscal year	Deficit cannot be carried over into next biennium	Deficit cannot be carried over into next fiscal year	Passed constitutional convention petition for balanced budget amendment to U.S. Constitution(a)
Alabama(b)	C	...	...	C	★
Alaska	C,S	C	...	...	★
Arizona(b)	C	...	...	C	★
Arkansas	S	...	...	S	★
California(b)	C	C	...	...	...
Colorado(b)	C	...	...	C	★
Connecticut	S	S	...	...	...
Delaware(b)	C	...	...	C	★
Florida	C,S	...	...	C,S	★
Georgia(b)	C	...	...	C	★
Hawaii(b)	C,S	...	C	C	...
Idaho(b)	C	...	...	C	★
Illinois	C	...	...	...	...
Indiana	C	...	...	C	★
Iowa(b)	C	...	...	C	★
Kansas(b)	C	...	...	C	★
Kentucky(b)	C,S	...	C	S	★
Louisiana	C	...	...	...	★
Maine(b)	S	...	...	S	...
Maryland	C	C	...	...	★
Massachusetts	C	...	...	...	...
Michigan	C	C	...	...	...
Minnesota	C,S	...	C,S	...	...
Mississippi(b)	S	...	...	S	★
Missouri(b)	C	...	...	C	★
Montana	C	...	C	C	...
Nebraska(b)	C	...	...	C	★
Nevada(b)	C,S	...	...	...	★
New Hampshire	S	...	...	...	★
New Jersey(b)	C	...	...	C	...
New Mexico(b)	C	...	...	C	★
New York	C	...	...	...	...
North Carolina	C,S	...	...	C,S	★
North Dakota(b)	C	...	C	...	★
Ohio(b)	C,S	...	...	C,S	...
Oklahoma(b)	C	...	...	C	★
Oregon	C,S	...	C	...	★
Pennsylvania	C,S	C,S	...	...	★
Rhode Island(b)	C	...	...	C	...
South Carolina	C,S	C,S	...	C	★
South Dakota(b)	C,S	...	...	C,S	★
Tennessee	C	C	...	C	★
Texas(b)	C	...	C	...	★
Utah(b)	C,S	...	...	C,S	★
Vermont	...	...	...	...	...
Virginia	C,S	...	C,S	...	★
Washington	C,S	...	C,S	...	...
West Virginia	C	...	...	C	...
Wisconsin(b)	C	C	...	...	...
Wyoming(b)	C	...	C	...	★

Sources: U.S. Advisory Commission on Intergovernmental Relations, *Significant Features of Fiscal Federalism 1985-86 Edition*; The Council of State Governments; state constitutions and statutes.

Key:
C—Constitutional provision
S—Statutory provision
★—Yes
... —No provision
(a) As of early 1986.
(b) Constitutional debt limits. Alabama—$300,000; Arizona—$350,000; California—no debt in excess of $300,000 without popular vote; Colorado—$100,000; Delaware—2 percent fund and 5 percent budget reserve account to be used for unanticipated deficit; Georgia—total not to exceed 15 percent of total revenue receipts in the preceding fiscal year; Hawaii—total not to exceed 18.5 percent of general fund revenue average of state in the three preceding fiscal years; Idaho—$2,000,000; Iowa—$250,000; Kansas—$1,000,000; Kentucky—$500,000; Maine—$2,000,000; Mississippi—1.5 x sum of all revenue collected by state for all purposes during any one of the four preceding fiscal years; Missouri—$1,000,000; Nebraska—$100,000; Nevada—1 percent of assessed valuation of state; New Jersey—1 percent of appropriations; New Mexico—$200,000; North Dakota—not to exceed 5 percent of the full and true value of all taxable property in state; Ohio—$750,000; Oklahoma—$500,000; Rhode Island—$50,000; South Dakota—$100,000; Texas—$200,000; Utah—1.5 percent of taxable property value; Wisconsin—$100,000; Wyoming—1 percent of assessed value of taxable property in state.

TRENDS IN STATE TAXATION: 1984-85

By John Gambill

In 1984-85, a number of states increased their tax rates—particularly those for sales taxes and taxes on motor fuel, cigarettes, and alcoholic beverages. However, a sizeable number of states did reduce the rates for their individual income taxes during this period.

General Sales Taxes

1984 actions

Sales tax rates were increased in: Louisiana (3 to 4 percent), Missouri (4.125 to 4.225 percent, effective July 1, 1985); Oklahoma (2 to 3 percent); South Carolina (4 to 5 percent); Tennessee (4.5 to 5.5 percent); and Texas (4 to 4.125 percent).

Idaho's rate dropped from 4.5 to 4 percent on July 1, 1984; under 1983 legislation, the rate had been scheduled to drop to 3 percent on that date.

1985 actions

Sales tax rates were increased in: Nebraska (3.5 to 4.5 percent, effective January 1, 1987); and Oklahoma (3 to 3.25 percent).

As a result of 1985 actions, Utah is scheduled to reduce its rate from 4.625 to 4.594 on July 1, 1986, and to 4.5 percent on January 1, 1990.

In 1985, Tennessee repealed a food exemption (enacted in 1984) before it was scheduled to take effect.

Individual Income Taxes

1984 actions

Delaware lowered its rates from a range of 1.4—13.5 percent to 1.3—10.7 percent. Michigan reduced its rate from 6.1 to 5.35 percent. Nebraska reduced its tax from 20 to 19 percent of federal tax liability. Rhode Island reduced its rate from 26 to 24.9 percent of federal liability for 1984, and set the 1985 rate at 25.65 percent. Vermont increased its tax from 26 to 26.5 percent of federal tax liability. Minnesota and Wisconsin repealed temporary surtaxes, and Ohio provided for a refund of 2 percent of a taxpayer's 1983 individual income tax liability.

1985 actions

Colorado suspended a rate decrease that

had been enacted previously. Connecticut reduced the rates of its tax on dividends and interest from a range of 6—13 percent to a range of 1—13 percent. Delaware lowered its rates from a range of 1.3—10.7 percent to a range of 1.2—9.7 percent. Massachusetts repealed a long-standing surtax. Minnesota reduced its rates from a range of 1.6—16 percent to a range of 1.3—14 percent (for single taxpayers deducting federal taxes), and created a separate set of rates for taxpayers who do not deduct federal income taxes. New York reduced its top bracket rate and its maximum rate on personal service income. North Dakota raised its tax from 7.5 to 10.5 percent of federal tax liability. Ohio reduced its rates across the board. Pennsylvania reduced its tax rate from 2.35 to 2.2 percent. Rhode Island reduced its tax from 25.65 percent of federal liability to 23.15 percent. Wisconsin's tax rates changed from a range of 3.4—10 percent to a range of 5—7.9 percent.

Corporation Income Taxes

1984 actions

Nebraska reduced the rate on incomes under $50,000 from 5 to 4.75 percent, effective with 1984 tax years. Pennsylvania reduced its tax rate from 10.5 to 9.5 percent, effective with 1985 tax years. Utah raised its rate from 4.65 to 5 percent, effective with 1984 tax years. Vermont increased its bracket rates from a 5—7.5 percent range to a 6—9 percent range, effective with 1984 tax years. Wisconsin repealed a 10 percent corporate income surtax a year ahead of schedule. The District of Columbia raised its tax rate from 9.9 percent to 10 percent, effective October 1, 1984.

1985 actions

Kentucky increased its rate on incomes over $250,000 from 6 to 7.25 percent for tax years beginning after July 31, 1985. New Hampshire increased its business profits tax from 8 to 8.25 percent for a two-year period. Ohio reduced its 5.4 percent corporate sur-

John Gambill is Senior Research Associate and Director of Publications, The Federation of Tax Administrators.

tax to 2.7 percent for 1987, and eliminated it thereafter. Oklahoma raised its tax rate from 4 to 5 percent for tax years ending after December 31, 1984. West Virginia enacted legislation (effective July 1, 1987) that repeals the business and occupation (gross receipts) tax and raises the corporation income tax rate to a flat 9.75 percent (instead of the current 6 percent tax on incomes under $50,000 and 7 percent on incomes over $50,000).

Motor Fuel Taxes
1984 actions
Motor fuel tax rates were increased in: Connecticut (14 to 15 cents, with subsequent increases scheduled to bring the rate to 23 cents by 1993); Louisiana (8 to 16 cents); New Jersey (diesel fuel from 8 to 11 cents); Oklahoma (6.5 to 9 cents); Texas (gasoline from 5 to 10 cents, and diesel fuel from 6.5 to 10 cents); and Utah (11 to 14 cents).

1985 actions
Rates were increased in: Arizona (13 to 16 cents); Arkansas (gasoline from 9.5 to 13.5 cents, and diesel fuel from 10.5 to 12.5 cents); Hawaii (gasoline from 8.5 to 11 cents, and diesel fuel from 8.5 to 12 cents); Indiana (gasoline from 11.1 to 14 cents, and diesel fuel from 11.1 to 15 cents); Iowa (gasoline from 13 to 16 cents, and diesel fuel from 15.5 to 17.5 cents), Nebraska (11.5 to 12.5 cents in the basic tax rate); Nevada (12 to 13 cents, including a statewide local tax); Oklahoma (9 to 10 cents); Oregon (10 to 11 cents, effective January 1, 1986, and 12 cents, effective January 1, 1987); and Tennessee (9 to 12 cents).

Other changes
Indiana imposed an 8 cent per gallon surcharge on fuel used by motor carriers, making a total tax of 23 cents for motor carriers using diesel fuel.

Wyoming imposed an 8 cent per gallon tax on diesel fuel, the same as its rate for gasoline. Previously, diesel fuel was exempt and diesel-powered trucks were subject to higher weight and mileage taxes.

Rhode Island repealed its 1 percent gross earnings tax on petroleum companies and enacted a 2 percent excise tax on fuel distributors.

Tax rates in two states and the District of Columbia were affected by existing variable rate laws. In Nebraska, the tax rate was changed each quarter, sometimes increasing, other times decreasing. The rate on January 1, 1986 was 17.2 cents, compared to 15.4 cents at the beginning of 1984; this increase was due, in part, to the increase in the basic fuel tax rate noted above. Wisconsin's tax rate increased from 16 to 16.5 cents on April 1, 1985. And in the District of Columbia, the tax rate increased from 14.8 to 15.5 cents on June 1, 1984.

Cigarette Taxes
1984 actions
Tax rates were increased in: Alabama (16 to 16.5 cents per pack of 20 cigarettes); Arizona (13 to 15 cents); Louisiana (11 to 16 cents); Maine (20 to 28 cents); and Texas (18.5 to 20.5 cents). Texas also made snuff subject to its 25 percent tax on tobacco products.

1985 actions
Tax rates were increased in: Alaska (8 to 16 cents); Illinois (12 to 20 cents); Iowa (18 to 26 cents); Kansas (16 to 24 cents); Minnesota (18 to 23 cents); Mississippi (11 to 18 cents); Nebraska (18 to 23 cents, effective March 1, 1986); Oregon (19 to 27 cents); Rhode Island (23 to 23.4 cents); South Dakota (15 to 23 cents); and Tennessee (13 to 13.05 cents). Florida imposed a 25 percent tax on the wholesale price of certain tobacco products, and Oregon imposed a 35 percent tax.

Alcoholic Beverage Taxes
1984 actions
Oklahoma and Texas increased their tax rates on all alcoholic beverages.

1985 actions
Taxes were increased on one or more major categories of alcoholic beverages in: Arkansas (beer and wine); Iowa (wine); Michigan (distilled spirits); Mississippi (all alcoholic beverages); Montana (beer and wine); and Nebraska (all alcoholic beverages).

Louisiana imposed a 5 percent retail sales tax on alcoholic beverages in 1984, but repealed it by legislation enacted in 1985.

Table 6.15
AGENCIES ADMINISTERING MAJOR STATE TAXES
(As of January 1, 1986)

State or other jurisdiction	Income	Sales	Gasoline	Motor vehicle
Alabama	Dept. of Revenue	Dept. of Revenue	Dept. of Revenue	Dept. of Revenue
Alaska	Dept. of Revenue	. . .	Dept. of Revenue	Dept. of Public Safety
Arizona	Dept. of Revenue	Dept. of Revenue	Dept. of Transportation	Dept. of Transportation
Arkansas	Dept. of Fin. & Admin.	Dept. of Fin. & Admin.	Dept. of Fin. & Admin.	Dept. of Fin. & Admin.
California	Franchise Tax Bd.	Bd. of Equalization	Bd. of Equalization	Dept. of Motor Vehicles
Colorado	Dept. of Revenue	Dept. of Revenue	Dept. of Revenue	Dept. of Revenue
Connecticut	Dept. of Revenue Serv.	Dept. of Revenue Serv.	Dept. of Revenue Serv.	Dept. of Motor Vehicles
Delaware	Div. of Revenue	. . .	Dept. of Public Safety	Dept. of Public Safety
Florida	Dept. of Revenue	Dept. of Revenue	Dept. of Revenue	Div. of Motor Vehicles
Georgia	Dept. of Revenue	Dept. of Revenue	Dept. of Revenue	Dept. of Revenue
Hawaii	Dept. of Taxation	Dept. of Taxation	Dept. of Taxation	County Treasurer
Idaho	Dept. of Revenue & Tax.	Dept. of Revenue & Tax.	Dept. of Revenue & Tax.	Transportation Dept.
Illinois	Dept. of Revenue	Dept. of Revenue	Dept. of Revenue	Secretary of State
Indiana	Dept. of Revenue	Dept. of Revenue	Dept. of Revenue	Bur. of Motor Vehicles
Iowa	Dept. of Revenue	Dept. of Revenue	Dept. of Revenue	Dept. of Transportation
Kansas	Dept. of Revenue	Dept. of Revenue	Dept. of Revenue	Dept. of Revenue
Kentucky	Revenue Cabinet	Revenue Cabinet	Revenue Cabinet	Transportation Cabinet
Louisiana	Dept. of Revenue & Tax.	Dept. of Revenue & Tax.	Dept. of Revenue & Tax.	Dept. of Public Safety
Maine	Bur. of Taxation	Bur. of Taxation	Bur. of Taxation	Secretary of State
Maryland	Comptroller	Comptroller	Comptroller	Dept. of Transportation
Massachusetts	Dept. of Revenue	Dept. of Revenue	Dept. of Revenue	Reg. of Motor Vehicles
Michigan	Dept. of Treasury	Dept. of Treasury	Dept. of Treasury	Secretary of State
Minnesota	Dept. of Revenue	Dept. of Revenue	Dept. of Revenue	Dept. of Public Safety
Mississippi	Tax Comm.	Tax Comm.	Tax Comm.	Tax Comm.
Missouri	Dept. of Revenue	Dept. of Revenue	Dept. of Revenue	Dept. of Revenue
Montana	Dept. of Revenue	. . .	Dept. of Revenue	Div. of Motor Vehicles
Nebraska	Dept. of Revenue	Dept. of Revenue	Dept. of Revenue	Dept. of Motor Vehicles
Nevada	. . .	Dept. of Taxation	Dept. of Taxation	Dept. of Motor Vehicles
New Hampshire	Dept. of Revenue Admin.	. . .	Dept. of Safety	Dept. of Safety
New Jersey	Dept. of Treasury	Dept. of Treasury	Dept. of Treasury	Dept. of Law & Public Safety
New Mexico	Tax & Revenue Dept.	Tax & Revenue Dept.	Tax & Revenue Dept.	Transportation Dept.
New York	Dept. of Tax. & Finance	Dept. of Tax. & Finance	Dept. of Tax. & Finance	Dept. of Motor Vehicles
North Carolina	Dept. of Revenue	Dept. of Revenue	Dept. of Revenue	Dept. of Transportation
North Dakota	Tax Commr.	Tax Commr.	Tax Commr.	Dept. of Motor Vehicles
Ohio	Dept. of Taxation	Dept. of Taxation	Dept. of Taxation	Bur. of Motor Vehicles
Oklahoma	Tax Comm.	Tax Comm.	Tax Comm.	Tax Comm.
Oregon	Dept. of Revenue	. . .	Dept. of Transportation	Dept. of Transportation
Pennsylvania	Dept. of Revenue	Dept. of Revenue	Dept. of Revenue	Dept. of Transportation
Rhode Island	Dept. of Administration	Dept. of Administration	Dept. of Administration	Dept. of Transportation
South Carolina	Tax Comm.	Tax Comm.	Tax Comm.	Dept. of Hwys. & Pub. Transportation
South Dakota	. . .	Dept. of Revenue	Dept. of Revenue	Dept. of Revenue
Tennessee	Dept. of Revenue	Dept. of Revenue	Dept. of Revenue	Dept. of Revenue
Texas	. . .	Comptroller	Comptroller	Dept. of Hwys. & Pub. Transportation
Utah	Tax Comm.	Tax Comm.	Tax Comm.	Tax Comm.
Vermont	Commr. of Taxes	Commr. of Taxes	Dept. of Motor Vehicles	Dept. of Motor Vehicles
Virginia	Dept. of Taxation	Dept. of Taxation	Dept. of Motor Vehicles	Dept. of Motor Vehicles
Washington	. . .	Dept. of Revenue	Dept. of Licensing	Dept. of Licensing
West Virginia	Tax Dept.	Tax Dept.	Tax Dept.	Dept. of Motor Vehicles
Wisconsin	Dept. of Revenue	Dept. of Revenue	Dept. of Revenue	Dept. of Transportation
Wyoming	. . .	Dept. of Revenue & Tax.	Dept. of Revenue & Tax.	Dept. of Revenue & Tax.
Dist. of Col.	Dept. of Fin. & Revenue	Dept. of Fin. & Revenue	Dept. of Fin. & Revenue	Dept. of Fin. & Revenue

Source: The Federation of Tax Administrators

249

State or other jurisdiction	Tobacco	Death	Alcoholic beverage	Number of agencies administering taxes
Alabama	Dept. of Revenue	Dept. of Revenue	Alcoh. Bev. Control Bd.	2
Alaska	Dept. of Revenue	Dept. of Revenue	Dept. of Revenue	2
Arizona	Dept. of Revenue	Dept. of Revenue	Dept. of Revenue	2
Arkansas	Dept. of Fin. & Admin.	Dept. of Fin. & Admin.	Dept. of Fin. & Admin.	1
California	Bd. of Equalization	Controller	Bd. of Equalization	4
Colorado	Dept. of Revenue	Dept. of Revenue	Dept. of Revenue	1
Connecticut	Dept. of Revenue Serv.	Dept. of Revenue Serv.	Dept. of Revenue Serv.	2
Delaware	Div. of Revenue	Div. of Revenue	Div. of Revenue	2
Florida	Dept. of Business Reg.	Dept. of Revenue	Dept. of Business Reg.	3
Georgia	Dept. of Revenue	Dept. of Revenue	Dept. of Revenue	1
Hawaii	Dept. of Taxation	Dept. of Taxation	Dept. of Taxation	2
Idaho	Dept. of Revenue & Tax.	Dept. of Revenue & Tax.	Dept. of Revenue & Tax.	2
Illinois	Dept. of Revenue	Attorney General	Dept. of Revenue	3
Indiana	Dept. of Revenue	Dept. of Revenue	Dept. of Revenue	2
Iowa	Dept. of Revenue	Dept. of Revenue	Dept. of Revenue	2
Kansas	Dept. of Revenue	Dept. of Revenue	Dept. of Revenue	1
Kentucky	Revenue Cabinet	Revenue Cabinet	Revenue Cabinet	2
Louisiana	Dept. of Revenue & Tax.	Dept. of Revenue & Tax.	Dept. of Revenue & Tax.	2
Maine	Bur. of Taxation	Bur. of Taxation	Liquor Comm.	3
Maryland	Comptroller	Local	Comptroller	3
Massachusetts	Dept. of Revenue	Dept. of Revenue	Dept. of Revenue	2
Michigan	Dept. of Treasury	Dept. of Treasury	Liquor Control Comm.	3
Minnesota	Dept. of Revenue	Dept. of Revenue	Dept. of Revenue	2
Mississippi	Tax Comm.	Tax Comm.	Tax Comm.	1
Missouri	Dept. of Revenue	Dept. of Revenue	Dept. of Revenue	1
Montana	Dept. of Revenue	Dept. of Revenue	Dept. of Revenue	2
Nebraska	Dept. of Revenue	Dept. of Revenue	Liquor Control Comm.	3
Nevada	Dept. of Taxation	. . .	Dept. of Taxation	2
New Hampshire	Dept. of Revenue Admin.	Dept. of Revenue Admin.	Liquor Comm.	3
New Jersey	Dept. of Treasury	Dept. of Treasury	Dept. of Treasury	2
New Mexico	Tax & Revenue Dept.	Tax & Revenue Dept.	Tax & Revenue Dept.	2
New York	Dept. of Tax. & Finance	Dept. of Tax. & Finance	Dept. of Tax. & Finance	2
North Carolina	Dept. of Revenue	Dept. of Revenue	Dept. of Revenue	2
North Dakota	Tax Commr.	Tax Commr.	Treasurer	3
Ohio	Dept. of Taxation	Dept. of Taxation	Dept. of Taxation	2
Oklahoma	Tax Comm.	Tax Comm.	Tax Comm.	1
Oregon	Dept. of Revenue	Dept. of Revenue	Liquor Control Comm.	3
Pennsylvania	Dept. of Revenue	Dept. of Revenue	Dept. of Revenue	2
Rhode Island	Dept. of Administration	Dept. of Administration	Dept. of Administration	2
South Carolina	Tax Comm.	Tax Comm.	Tax Comm.	2
South Dakota	Dept. of Revenue	Dept. of Revenue	Dept. of Revenue	1
Tennessee	Dept. of Revenue	Dept. of Revenue	Dept. of Revenue	1
Texas	Comptroller	Comptroller	Alcoh. Bev. Comm.	3
Utah	Tax Comm.	Tax Comm.	Tax Comm.	1
Vermont	Commr. of Taxes	Commr. of Taxes	Commr. of Taxes	2
Virginia	Dept. of Taxation	Dept. of Taxation	Dept. of Taxation	2
Washington	Dept. of Revenue	Dept. of Revenue	Liquor Control Comm.	3
West Virginia	Tax Dept.	Tax Dept.	Alcoh. Bev. Control Commr.	3
Wisconsin	Dept. of Revenue	Dept. of Revenue	Dept. of Revenue	2
Wyoming	Dept. of Revenue & Tax.	Dept. of Revenue & Tax.	Liquor Comm.	2
Dist. of Col.	Dept. of Fin. & Revenue	Dept. of Fin. & Revenue	Dept. of Fin. & Revenue	1

Table 6.16
STATE EXCISE RATES
(As of January 1, 1986)

State or other jurisdiction	Sales and gross receipts (percent)	Cigarettes (cents per pack of 20)	Distilled spirits(a) (dollars per gallon)	Motor fuel(b) (cents per gallon) Gasoline	Motor fuel(b) (cents per gallon) Diesel
Alabama	4	16.5	. . .	13(c)	14(c)
Alaska	. . .	16	$5.60	8	8
Arizona	5(d)	15	3.00	16	16
Arkansas	4	21	2.50	13.5	12.5
California	4.75	10	2.00(e)	9	9
Colorado	3	15	2.28(f)	12	13
Connecticut	7.5	26	3.00	16	16
Delaware	. . .	14	2.25	11	11
Florida	5(g)	21	6.50(h)	9.7(i)	9.7(i)
Georgia	3	12	3.79(f)	7.5	7.5
Hawaii	4(j)	40% of wholesale price	20% of wholesale price	11	12
Idaho	4	9.1	. . .	14.5	14.5
Illinois	5	20	2.00	13	15.5
Indiana	5	10.5	2.68	14(k)	15(k)
Iowa	4	26	. . .	16	17.5
Kansas	3	24	2.50	11	13
Kentucky	5	3.1	1.92	10(l)	10(l)
Louisiana	4	16	2.50(f)	16	16
Maine	5	28	. . .	14	14
Maryland	5	13	1.50(f)	13.5	13.5
Massachusetts	5	26	4.05	11	11
Michigan	4	21	. . .	15	15
Minnesota	6(m)	23	4.39(f)	17	17
Mississippi	6(n)	18	. . .	9	10
Missouri	4.225	13	2.00	7	7
Montana	. . .	16	. . .	15	17
Nebraska	3.5	18	2.90	17.2	17.2
Nevada	5.75(o)	15	2.05	13	13
New Hampshire	. . .	17	. . .	14	14
New Jersey	6	25	2.80	8	11
New Mexico	3.75	12	3.94(f)	11	11
New York	4	21	4.09(f)	8	10
North Carolina	3(p)	2	. . .	12	12
North Dakota	4(q)	18	4.05	13	13
Ohio	5	14	. . .	12	12
Oklahoma	3.25	18	5.00	10	10
Oregon	. . .	27	. . .	11	11
Pennsylvania	6	18	. . .	12	12
Rhode Island	6	23.4	2.50	13	13
South Carolina	5	7	2.96(f,r)	13	13
South Dakota	4	23	3.80	13	13
Tennessee	5.5(s)	13.05(t)	4.00	12	12
Texas	4.125	20.5	2.40	10	10
Utah	4.625	12	. . .	14	14
Vermont	4	17	. . .	13	14
Virginia	3	2.5	. . .	11(u)	11(u)
Washington	6.5(v)	23	. . .	18	18
West Virginia	5(w)	17	. . .	15.35(i)	15.35(i)
Wisconsin	5	25	3.25(f)	16.5	16.5
Wyoming	3	8	. . .	8	8
Dist. of Col.	6(x)	13	1.50	15.5	15.5

STATE EXCISE RATES—Continued

Source: The Federation of Tax Administrators (based on legislation enacted at the 1985 sessions).

Key:

. . .—Not applicable.

(a) Seventeen states have liquor monopoly systems: Alabama, Idaho, Iowa, Maine, Michigan, Mississippi, Montana, New Hampshire, Ohio, Oregon, Pennsylvania, Utah, Vermont, Virginia, Washington, West Virginia, and Wyoming. North Carolina has county-operated stores on a local option basis. Some of the monopoly states impose taxes, generally expressed in terms of percentage of retail price. Only gallonage taxes imposed by states with license systems are reported in the table.

(b) In some states, different tax rates apply to liquefied petroleum gas, compressed natural gas, and gasohol. Several states have variable-rate motor fuel taxes, under which the motor fuel tax rate is changed periodically by administrative action according to a statutory formula. Connecticut, New York, Pennsylvania, and Virginia have gross receipts or franchise taxes on oil companies, which are not covered in this table.

(c) Includes a 2 cent per gallon inspection fee.

(d) This rate is for retailers. Selected other businesses are taxed at rates ranging from 0.46875 to 5 percent.

(e) If not over 50 percent alcohol by weight. If over 50 percent, $4.00 per gallon.

(f) Several states express the tax rate dollars per liter (one gallon = 3.7854 liters): Colorado, $0.6026; Georgia, $1.00; Louisiana, $0.66; Maryland, $0.3963; Minnesota, $1.16; New Mexico, $1.04; New York, $1.08; South Carolina, $0.7828925 (includes 9 percent surcharge, but excludes case charges); and Wisconsin, $0.8586.

(g) Self-propelled or power-driven farm equipment is taxed at 3 percent.

(h) On beverages containing 14 to 48 percent alcohol. The tax rate on beverages containing more than 48 percent alcohol is $9.53 per gallon. Lower (but variable) rates apply to beverages made from citrus products and sugarcane.

(i) The rates shown include a motor fuel sales tax, imposed on a cents-per-gallon basis and adjusted annually to reflect changes in motor fuel prices.

(j) Wholesalers and manufacturers, 0.5 percent; retailers, 4 percent.

(k) An additional tax of 8 cents per gallon is imposed on motor carriers on a use basis.

(l) Heavy equipment motor carriers pay a 12.2 cents per gallon tax on a use basis.

(m) Farm machinery is taxed at 2 percent, and special tooling and capital equipment is taxed at 4 percent.

(n) Among other rates imposed under the tax: aircraft, automobiles, trucks, and truck tractors—3 percent; manufacturing machinery—1.5 percent; farm tractors—1 percent; contractors (on compensation exceeding $10,000)—3.5 percent.

(o) Includes mandatory, statewide, state-collected 3.75 percent county and school sales tax.

(p) Motor vehicles, boats, railway cars and locomotives, and airplanes—2 percent (maximum tax is $300). A tax of 1 percent is imposed on various items used in agriculture and industry; on some items, this tax is limited to $80.

(q) The tax on farm machinery, agricultural irrigation equipment, and mobile homes is 3 percent. A 5 percent tax is imposed on alcoholic beverages.

(r) Includes a 9 percent surtax. In addition, there is a tax of $5.84 ($5.36 + 9 percent surtax) per case on wholesale sales.

(s) The tax on water sold to or used by manufacturers is 1 percent; the tax on various fuels is 1.5 percent.

(t) Includes a 0.05 cent per pack enforcement and administrative fee.

(u) A 13 cent per gallon tax is imposed on motor carriers of property on a use basis.

(v) Also has a gross income tax with rates varying from 0.011 percent to 1.5 percent (including surtax), according to type of business. Retailers are subject to a 0.471 percent business and occupation tax.

(w) Sales of mobile homes to be used by purchasers as their principal year-round residence and dwelling—3 percent. There is also a gross income tax at rates ranging from 0.27 to 8.63 percent, according to type of business. Retailers are subject to a 0.55 percent rate under this tax.

(x) Parking charges—12 percent; hotel accommodations—10 percent; food or drink for immediate consumption—8 percent; rental vehicles—8 percent.

Table 6.17
FOOD AND DRUG SALES TAX EXEMPTIONS
(As of January 1, 1986)

State or other jurisdiction	Tax rate	Exemptions Food	Exemptions Pre-scription drugs	Related income tax credit	State or other jurisdiction	Tax rate	Exemptions Food	Exemptions Pre-scription drugs	Related income tax credit
Alabama	4		★		New Jersey	6	★	★	
Arizona	5	★	★		New Mexico	3.75			★
Arkansas	4		★		New York	4	★	★	
California	4.75	★	★		North Carolina	3		★	
Colorado	3	★	★		North Dakota	4	★	★	
Connecticut	7.5	★	★		Ohio	5	★	★	
Florida	5	★	★		Oklahoma	3.25		★	
Georgia	3		★		Pennsylvania	6	★	★	
Hawaii	4			★	Rhode Island	6	★	★	
Idaho	4		★	★	South Carolina	5		★	
Illinois	5	★	★		South Dakota	4		★	
Indiana	5	★	★		Tennessee	5.5		★	
Iowa	4	★	★		Texas	4.125	★	★	
Kansas	3		★		Utah	4.625		★	
Kentucky	5	★	★		Vermont	4	★	★	★
Louisiana	4	★	★		Virginia	3		★	
Maine	5	★	★		Washington	6.5	★	★	
Maryland	5	★	★		West Virginia	5	★	★	
Massachusetts	5	★	★		Wisconsin	5	★	★	
Michigan	4	★	★		Wyoming	3		★	
Minnesota	6	★	★		Dist. of Col.	6	★	★	
Mississippi	6		★						
Missouri	4.225		★						
Nebraska	3.5	★	★						
Nevada	5.75	★	★						

Source: The Federation of Tax Administrators (based on legislation enacted at the 1985 sessions).

Table 6.18
STATE INDIVIDUAL INCOME TAXES
(As of January 1, 1986)

State or other jurisdiction	Rate range(a) (percent)	Income brackets		Personal exemptions			Federal income tax deductible
		Lowest (ends)	Highest (over)	Single	Married	Dependents	
Alabama	2.0 - 5.0(3)	$ 500(c)	$ 3,000(c)	$1,500	$ 3,000	$ 300	★
Arizona(b)	2.0 - 8.0(7)	1,122(c)	6,738(c)	1,941	3,882	1,165	★
Arkansas	1.0 - 7.0(6)	3,000	25,000	17.50(d)	35(d)	6(d)	. . .
California(b)	1.0 - 11.0(11)	5,030(e)	27,820(e)	42(d)	84(d)	13(d)	. . .
Colorado	3.0 - 8.0(11)(f)	1,420	14,150	1,200	2,400	1,200	★
Delaware	1.2 - 9.7(14)	1,000	40,000	1,000	2,000	1,000	★(g)
Georgia	1.0 - 6.0(6)	750(h)	7,000(h)	1,500	3,000	700	. . .
Hawaii	2.25 - 11.0(11)	1,300(e)	30,800(e)	1,040	2,080	1,040	. . .
Idaho	2.0 - 7.5(6)(i)	1,000	5,000	1,080(i,j)	2,160(i,j)	1,080(i,j)	. . .
Illinois	2.5	--------------Flat rate--------------		1,000	2,000	1,000	. . .
Indiana	3.0	--------------Flat rate--------------		1,000	2,000	1,000	. . .
Iowa(b)	0.5 - 13.0(13)(k)	1,023	76,725	20	40	15(d)	★
Kansas	2.0 - 9.0(8)	2,000(c)	25,000(c)	1,000	2,000	1,000	★(g)
Kentucky	2.0 - 6.0(5)	3,000	8,000	20	40	20(d)	★
Louisiana	2.0 - 6.0(3)	10,000	50,000	4,500(l)	9,000(l)	1,000	★
Maine(b)	1.0 - 10.0(8)	2,000(c)	25,000(c)	1,000	2,000	1,000	. . .
Maryland	2.0 - 5.0(4)	1,000	3,000	800	1,600	800	. . .
Massachusetts	5.1875(m)	--------------Flat rate--------------		2,200	4,400(n)	700	. . .
Michigan	5.1	--------------Flat rate--------------		1,500	3,000	1,500	. . .
Minnesota(b)	1.0 - 9.9(11)(o)	300	16,200	70(d)	140(d)	70(d)	(o)
Mississippi	3.0 - 5.0(3)	5,000	10,000	6,000	9,500	1,500	. . .
Missouri	1.5 - 6.0(10)	1,000	9,000	1,200	2,400	400	★
Montana(b)	2.0 - 11.0(10)	1,300	45,900	1,040	2,080	1,040	★
Nebraska	19% of U.S. tax	. . .	. . .	. . .	. . .	. . .	. . .
New Jersey	2.0 - 3.5(3)	20,000	50,000	1,000	2,000	1,000	. . .
New Mexico	1.8 - 8.5(7)	5,200(p)	41,600(p)	2,000	4,000	2,000	. . .
New York	2.0 - 13.5(13)(q)	1,000	26,000	850	1,700	850	. . .
North Carolina	3.0 - 7.0(5)	2,000	10,000	1,100	3,300	800	. . .
North Dakota	2.0 - 9.0(8)(r)	3,000	50,000	1,080(j)	2,160(j)	1,080(j)	★(r)
Ohio	0.855- 8.55(8)	5,000	100,000	1,000(s)	2,000(s)	1,000(s)	. . .
Oklahoma	0.5- 6.0(7)(t)	1,000	7,500	1,000	2,000	1,000	(t)
Oregon(b)	4.0 - 10.0(7)	500	5,000	85(d)	170(d)	85(d)	★(g)
Pennsylvania	2.2	--------------Flat rate--------------		. . .	. . .	. . .	. . .
Rhode Island	22.21% of U.S. tax	. . .	. . .	. . .	. . .	. . .	. . .
South Carolina(b)	2.0 - 7.0(6)	4,410	12,490	1,080(j)	2,160(j)	1,080(j)	. . .
Utah	2.75 - 7.75(6)	750(c)	7,500(c)	750(j)	1,500(j)	750(j)	★
Vermont	26% of U.S. tax(u)	. . .	. . .	. . .	. . .	. . .	. . .
Virginia	2.0 - 5.75(4)	3,000	12,000	600	1,200	600	. . .
West Virginia	2.1- 13.0(18)	2,000(v)	60,000(v)	800	1,600	800	. . .
Wisconsin(b)	5.0 - 7.9(4)	7,500	30,000	. . .	. . .	50(d)	. . .
Dist. of Col.	2.0 - 11.0(10)	1,000	25,000	750(j)	1,500(j)	750(j)	. . .

STATE INDIVIDUAL INCOME TAXES—Continued

Source: The Federation of Tax Administrators, on the basis of legislation enacted at the 1985 sessions.

Note: This table excludes the following state taxes: Connecticut taxes interest and dividends at 1 to 13 percent and capital gains at 7 percent. New Hampshire taxes interest and dividends at 5 percent. Tennessee taxes interest and dividends at 6 percent.

Key:

. . .—Not applicable.

(a) The figure in parentheses is the number of steps in the range. For California, Hawaii, and South Carolina, the amount shown for the lowest bracket includes zero bracket amount and lowest positive bracket.

(b) Ten states have statutory provisions for automatic adjustment of tax brackets or personal exemptions, as well as other features, to reflect changes in price levels. Adjustments to be made for 1986 tax years will generally not be known until the latter part of 1986. The 1985 amounts are shown.

(c) For joint returns, the tax is twice the tax imposed on half the income.

(d) Tax credits.

(e) The range reported is for single persons. For married persons, the tax is twice the tax imposed on half the income. For heads of households, different rates apply.

(f) Imposes a surtax of 2 percent on gross income from intangibles which exceed $15,000.

(g) The federal tax deduction is limited. Delaware, to $300 for an individual, $600 for a joint return; Kansas, $5,000 individual, $10,000 joint (or to 50 percent of federal tax liability, whichever is greater); Oregon, to $7,000.

(h) The range reported is for single persons. For joint returns and heads of households, the same rates are applied to income brackets ranging from $1,000 to $10,000. For married persons filing separately, the income brackets range from $500 to $5,000.

(i) In the case of joint returns, the tax is twice the tax imposed on half the income. A filing fee of $10 is imposed on each return. A credit of $15 is allowed for each personal exemption.

(j) These states by definition allow personal exemptions provided in the Internal Revenue Code. Under existing law, Idaho follows the federal code as of January 1, 1985; North Dakota as of December 31, 1984; South Carolina, as of December 31, 1984; Utah (for purposes of personal exemptions) as of December 31, 1974; and the District of Columbia, as of July 1, 1975.

(k) No tax is imposed on persons whose net income does not exceed $5,000.

(l) Combined personal exemption and standard deduction.

(m) A 10.375 percent rate applies to interest and dividends (other than from savings deposits) and on net capital gains. The 5.1875 percent rate applies to all other income, including earned income and income from savings deposits. These rates include a 3.75 percent surtax.

(n) Maximum allowance; spouse's exemption is $1,000 plus the amount of earnings, but the total exemption for taxpayer and spouse may not exceed $4,400.

(o) The rate range shown is for single persons not deducting federal income tax. Married persons filing jointly have a range of 1.7 to 9.9 percent. Taxpayers who deduct federal income taxes have a range of 1.3 to 14 percent if single and 1.5 to 14 percent if married.

(p) The rate range reported is for single persons. For joint returns and heads of households, tax rates range from 2.4 percent on income not over $8,000, to 8.5 percent on income over $64,000. For married persons filing separately, a separate set of rates and brackets applies.

(q) Maximum rate of 9.5 percent on personal service income.

(r) Taxpayers have the option of paying 10.5 percent of adjusted federal income tax liability.

(s) Or, at taxpayers option, $650 deduction plus $20 credit per exemption.

(t) The rate range is for single persons not deducting federal income tax. Married persons filing separately have the same rates and brackets that are twice as wide. Separate schedules, with rates ranging from 0.5 percent to 17 percent, apply to taxpayers deducting federal income taxes.

(u) If Vermont tax liability for any taxable year exceeds Vermont tax liability determinable under federal tax law in effect on January 1, 1980, the taxpayer will be entitled to a credit equal to the excess, plus 6 percent of that amount. A credit is allowed for taxpayers with an adjusted gross income of under $7,000.

(v) The range reported is for single persons. For joint returns, the same rates are applied to brackets ranging from $4,000 to $120,000. Separate brackets apply to heads of households.

Table 6.19
RANGE OF STATE CORPORATE INCOME TAX RATES
(As of January 1, 1986)

State or other jurisdiction	Tax rate(a) (percent)	Federal income tax deductible
Alabama		★
Business corporations	5	
Banks & financial corps.....	6	
Alaska....................		...
$0 to $10,000.............	1	
Over $90,000	9.4(10)	
Arizona...................		★
$0 to $1,000.............	2.5	
Over $6,000	10.5(7)	
Arkansas		...
$0 to $3,000.............	1	
Over $25,000	6(5)	
California.................		...
Business corporations	9.6(b)	
Banks & financial corps.....	10.930(b)	
Colorado	5	...
Connecticut	11.5(c)	...
Delaware	8.7	...
Florida	5.5(d)	...
Georgia...................	6	...
Hawaii		...
Business corporations		
$0 to $25,000.............	5.85(e)	
Over $25,000	6.435	
Banks & financial corps.....	11.7	
Idaho	7.7(f)	...
Illinois....................	6.5(g)	...
Indiana	7(h)	...
Iowa		(i)
Business corporations		
$0 to $25,000.............	6	
Over $250,000	12(4)	
Financial institutions	5	
Kansas		...
Business corporations	4.5(j)	
Banks	4.25(j)	
Trust companies & savings		
& loan associations	4.5(j)	
Kentucky		...
$0 to $25,000.............	3	
Over $250,000	7.25(5)	
Louisiana		★
$0 to $25,000.............	4	
Over $200,000	8(5)	
Maine		...
$0 to $25,000.............	3.5	
Over $250,000	8.93(4)	
Maryland	7	...
Massachusetts		...
Business corporations	9.4962(k)	
Banks & trust companies ...	12.54	
Utility corporations	6.5	
Minnesota		...
$0 to $25,000.............	6	
Over $25,000	12(2)	
Mississippi		...
$0 to $5,000..............	3	
Over $10,000	5(3)	
Missouri		★
Business corporations	5	
Banks & trust companies ...	7	
Montana..................	6.75(l)	...
Nebraska		...
$0 to $50,000.............	4.75	
Over $50,000	6.65(2)(m)	
New Hampshire	8.25(n)	...
New Jersey................	9(o)	...
New Mexico...............		...
$0 to $1 million	4.8	
Over $2 million............	7.2(3)	
New York		...
Business corporations	10(p)	
Banks & financial corps.....	9(p)	
North Carolina		...
Business corporations	6	
Banks	4.5(q)	
North Dakota		★
Business corporations		
$0 to $3,000..............	3	
Over $50,000	10.5(6)	
Banks & financial corps.....	7(r)	
Ohio		...
$0 to $25,000.............	5.1(s)	
Over $25,000	9.2(2)(s)	
Oklahoma		...
Business corporations	5	
Banks	4	
Oregon	7.5(q)	...
Pennsylvania	9.5	...
Rhode Island	8(t)	...
South Carolina		...
Business corporations	6	
Banks	4.5	
Financial associations	8	
South Dakota		★
Banks & financial corps.....	6(u)	
Tennessee.................	6	...
Utah	5(v)	...
Vermont		...
$0 to $10,000.............	6	
Over $250,000	9(4)(w)	
Virginia...................	6	...
West Virginia		...
$0 to $50,000.............	6	
Over $50,000	7	
Wisconsin.................	7.9	...
Dist. of Col.	10(x)	...

STATE CORPORATE INCOME TAX RATES—Continued

Source: The Federation of Tax Administrators (based on legislation enacted at 1985 sessions.)

Note: Michigan imposes a single business tax (sometimes described as a business activities tax or value added tax) or 2.35 percent on the sum of federal taxable income of the business, compensation paid to employees, dividends, interest, and royalties paid, and other items.

(a) Figure in parentheses is number of steps in range.

(b) Minimum tax is $200.

(c) Or 3.1 mills per dollar of capital stock and surplus (maximum tax $100,000), or $100, or 5 percent of 50 percent of net income of corporation plus salaries and other compensation paid to officers and certain shareholders, whichever is greater.

(d) An exemption of $5,000 is allowed.

(e) Taxes capital gains at 3.08 percent.

(f) Minimum tax is $20. An additional tax of $10 is imposed on each return.

(g) Includes 2.5 percent personal property replacement tax.

(h) Consists of 3 percent on income from sources within state plus a 4 percent supplemental income tax.

(i) 50 percent of federal income tax deductible.

(j) Plus a surtax of 2.25 percent of taxable income in excess of $25,000 (2.125 percent for banks).

(k) Rate includes a 14 percent surtax, as does the following: an additional tax of $2.60 per $1,000 on taxable tangible property (or net worth allocable to state, for intangible property corporations); minimum tax of $228. Corporations engaged exclusively in interstate or foreign commerce are taxed at 5 percent of net income, and are not subject to surtax.

(l) Minimum tax is $50; for small business corporations, $10.

(m) 25 and 35 percent of individual income tax rate, determined annually.

(n) Business profits tax imposed on both corporations and unincorporated associations.

(o) This is the business franchise tax rate; there also is a net worth tax at rates ranging from 0.2 mills to 2 mills; minimum tax is $25 for domestic corporations, $50 for foreign corporations. Corporations not subject to the franchise tax are subject to a 7.25 percent income tax. Savings institutions are subject to a 3 percent tax.

(p) Or $250; 1.78 mills per dollar of capital; or 10 percent of 30 percent of net income plus salaries and other compensation to officers and stockholders owning more than 5 percent of the issued capital stock less $30,000 and any net loss, if any of these is greater than the tax computed on net income.

(q) Minimum tax is $10.

(r) Minimum tax is $50; plus an additional 2 percent privilege tax.

(s) Plus a surtax of 5.4 percent. Or 5.82 mills times the value of the taxpayer's issued and outstanding shares of stock as determined according to the total value of capital surplus, undivided profits, and reserves; minimum tax $50. An additional litter tax is imposed equal to 0.11 percent on the first $25,000 of taxable income, 0.22 percent on income over $25,000, or 0.14 mills on net worth. Corporations manufacturing or selling litter stream products are subject to an additional 0.22 percent tax on income over $25,000 or 0.14 mills on net worth.

(t) Or, for business corporations, the tax is 40 cents per $100 of net worth, if greater than the tax computed on net income. For banks, if a greater tax results, the alternative tax is $2.50 per $10,000 of capital stock; minimum tax is $100.

(u) Minimum tax is $200 per authorized location.

(v) Minimum tax is $100. There is a graduated gross receipts tax on corporations not otherwise required to pay income or franchise taxes, ranging up to 1 percent on receipts in excess of $1 billion.

(w) Minimum tax is $75.

(x) A 5 percent surtax is also imposed. Minimum tax is $100.

Table 6.20
STATE SEVERANCE TAXES: 1985

State	Title and application of tax(a)	Rate
Alabama	Iron Ore Mining Tax	$.03 ton
	Forest Products Severance Tax	Varies by species and ultimate use
	Oil and Gas Conservation & Regulation of Production Tax	2% of gross value at point of production
	Oil and Gas Production Tax	8% of gross value at point of production; 4% if wells produces 25 bbl. or less oil per day or 200,000 cu. ft. or less gas per day; 6% of gross value at point of production for certain on-shore and off-shore wells; 2% of gross value of occluded natural gas from coal seams at point of production for well's first five years
	Coal Severance Tax(b)	$.135/ton
	Coal and Lignite Severance Tax	$.20/ton in addition to Coal Severance Tax
Alaska	Fisheries Business Tax	3% to 5% of fish value based on type of fish
	Oil and Gas Production Tax	The greater of $.60/bbl. for old crude oil ($.80 for all other) or 15% of gross value at production point (multiplied by economic limit factor); the greater of $.064/1,000 cu. ft. of gas or 10% of gross value at production point (multiplied by economic limit factor). Additional $.00125/bbl. of oil (regulation and conservation tax)
Arizona	Severance Tax(c)	2.5% of net severance base for mining; 1.5% of value for timbering
Arkansas	Natural Resources Severance Tax	Separate rate for each substance
	Oil and Gas Conservation Tax	Maximum 25 mills/bbl. of oil and 5 mills/1,000 cu. ft. of gas
California	Oil and Gas Production Tax	Rate determined annually by Department of Conservation(d)
Colorado	Severance Tax(e)	Separate rate for each substance
	Oil and Gas Conservation Tax	Maximum 1 mill/$1 of market value at wellhead(f)
Florida	Oil and Gas Production Tax	8% (oil) and 5% (gas) of gross value at point of production; additional 12.5% for escaped oil. Wells producing less than 100 bbls./day or oil produced by tertiary methods are taxed at 5% of gross value at point of production
	Solid Minerals Tax(g)	5% of market value at point of severance, except $2.28/ton phosphate rock and $1.15/ton heavy minerals
Georgia	Tax on Phosphates	$1/ton
Idaho	Ore Severance Tax	2% of net value
	Oil and Gas Production Tax	Maximum of 5 mills/bbl. of oil and 5 mills/50,000 cu. ft. of gas(h)
	Additional Oil and Gas Production Tax	2% of market value at site of production
Illinois	Timber Fee	4% of purchase price(i)
Indiana	Petroleum Production Tax(j)	1% of value
Kansas	Severance Tax(k)	8% of gross value of oil and gas; $1/ton of coal; $.04 ton of salt
	Oil and Gas Assessments	$.008/bbl. of oil and $.00024/1,000 cu. ft. of gas, in addition to $.0125/bbl. of oil or petroleum and $.0033/1,000 cu. ft. of gas produced, sold, marketed or used(l)
	Mined-Land Conservation & Reclamation Tax	$50, plus per ton fee of between $.03 and $.10
Kentucky	Oil Production Tax	4.5% of market value
	Coal Severance Tax	4.5% of gross value
	Natural Resource Severance Tax(m)	4.5% of gross value, less transportation expenses
Louisiana	Natural Resources Severance Tax	Rate varies according to substance
Maine	Mining Excise Tax	The greater of a tax on facilities and equipment or a tax on gross proceeds
Maryland	Mine Reclamation Surcharge	$.09/ton (as per state authority) and $.06/ton (as per county authority) of coal removed by open pit or strip method
	Coal and Gas Severance Taxes(n)	$.40/ton of surface-mined coal; greater of 7% of wholesale market value of gas or 11/150 of 1%/1,000 cu. ft. of gas
Michigan	Gas and Oil Severance Tax	5% (gas), 6.6% (oil), and 4% (oil from stripper wells and marginal properties) of gross cash market value of the total production. Maximum additional fee of 1% of gross cash market value on all oil and gas produced in state in previous year
Minnesota	Iron Severance Tax(o)	15% to 15.5% (depending on ore) of value (minus credits)
	Ore Royalty Tax	15% to 15.5% (depending on ore) of royalty received (minus credits)
	Taconite, Iron Sulphides and Agglomerate Taxes	$1.25/ton ($.05/ton for agglomerates)
	Semi-Taconite Tax	$.10/ton ($.05/ton if agglomerated or sintered in state), plus $.001/ton depending on percentage of iron content
	Copper-Nickel Taxes	1% of value of ores mined or produced (occupation tax); $.025/gross ton, plus 10% of base tax/ton depending on copper-nickel content(p)

State	Title and application of tax(a)	Rate
Mississippi	Oil and Gas Severance Tax	6% of value at point of production; also, maximum 20 mills/bbl. oil or 2 mills/1,000 cu ft. gas (Oil and Gas Board maintenance tax).
	Timber Severance Tax	Varies depending on type of wood and ultimate use
	Salt Severance Tax	3% of value of entire production in state
Missouri	Surface Coal Mining Permittee Assessment	$.30/ton for first 50,000 tons sold (shipped, or otherwise disposed of) in calendar year, and $.20/ton for next 50,000 tons
Montana	Coal Severance Tax	Varies by quality of coal and type of mine
	Metalliferous Mines License Tax(q)	Progressive gross value tax from 0.5% to 1.5%
	Oil or Gas Producers' Severance Tax	5% of total gross value of petroleum and other mineral or crude oil(r), and 2.65% of total gross value of natural gas (license tax); maximum 0.2% of market value/bbl. of oil and of each 10,000 cu. ft. of gas (conservation tax)(h)
	Micaceous Minerals License Tax	$.05/ton
	Cement License Tax(s)	$.22/ton of cement, $.05/ton of cement, plaster, gypsum or gypsum products
	Mineral Mining Tax	$25 plus 0.5% of gross value over $5,000
Nebraska	Oil and Gas Severance Tax	3% of value of nonstripper oil and natural gas; 2% of value of stripper oil
	Oil and Gas Conservation Tax	Maximum 4 mills $1 of value at wellhead(h)
	Uranium Tax	2% of gross value over $5 million
Nevada	Net Proceeds of Mine Tax	Total property tax rate of place where mine is located
	Oil and Gas Conservation Tax	50 mills/bbl. of oil and 50 mills/50,000 cu. ft. of gas
New Hampshire ...	Refined Petroleum Products Tax	0.1% of fair market value
New Mexico	Resources Excise Tax(t)	Varies according to substance
	Severance Tax(t)	Varies according to substance
	Oil and Gas Severance Tax	3.75% of value (less credits) of oil, other liquid hydrocarbons and carbon dioxide; $.157/1,000 cu. ft. of gas
	Oil and Gas Privilege Tax	3.15% of value
	Natural Gas Processor's Tax	0.45% of value of products
	Oil and Gas Ad Valorem Production Tax	Varies
	Oil and Gas Conservation Tax(u)	Percentage varies each year(v)
North Carolina	Oil and Gas Conservation Tax	Maximum 5 mills/bbl. of oil and 0.5 mill/1,000 cu. ft. of gas(h)
	Primary Forest Product Assessment Tax	$.40 or $.50/1,000 board ft. and $.12 or $.20/cord depending on type of wood and use
North Dakota	Oil and Gas Gross Production Tax	5% of gross value at well
	Coal Severance Tax	$.85/ton and $.01/ton for every four-point increase in wholesale price index(w)
	Oil Extraction Tax	6.5% of gross value at well
Ohio	Resource Severance Tax(x)	$.10/bbl. of oil; $.025/1,000 cu. ft. of gas; $.04/ton of salt; $.01/ton of sand, gravel, limestone and dolomite; $.07/ton of coal
Oklahoma	Oil, Gas, and Mineral Gross Production Tax(y)	Separate rate for each substance
	Natural Gas and Casinghead Gas Conservation Excise Tax	$.07/1,000 cu. ft., less 7% of gross value of each 1,000 cu. ft. of gas
Oregon	Forest Products Harvest Tax	$.21/1,000 board ft. (privilege tax); $.15/1,000 board ft. (harvest tax)(z)
	Oil and Gas Production Tax	6% of gross value at well
	Severance Tax on Eastern Oregon Timber	5% of immediate harvest value and additional severance tax on reforestation land
	Severance Tax on Western Oregon Timber	6.5% of value and additional severance tax on reforestation land
South Dakota	Precious Metals Severance Tax	2% of gross yield from sale of metals plus 8% on net profits or royalties from sale of precious metals
	Energy Minerals Severance Tax	4.5% of taxable value of any energy minerals
	Conservation Tax	2.4 mills of taxable value of any energy minerals
Tennessee	Oil and Gas Severance Tax	3% of sales price
	Coal Severance Tax	$.20/ton
Texas.............	Natural Gas Production Tax	7.5% of market value
	Oil Production Tax	The greater of 4.6% of market value or $.046/bbl.
	Sulphur Production Tax	$1.03/long ton or fraction thereof
	Cement Production Tax	$.0275/100 lbs. or fraction thereof
Utah	Mining Occupation Tax(aa)	1% of gross value for metals; 4% of value for oil, and gas and other hydrocarbons at wellhead
	Oil and Gas Conservation Tax	2 mills/$1 of market value at wellhead
Virginia..........	Forest Products Tax	Varies by species and ultimate use
	Coal Surface Mining Reclamation Tax	Varies depending on balance of Coal Surface Mining Reclamation Fund
	Oil Severance Tax(bb)	0.5% of gross receipts from sale

STATE SEVERANCE TAXES—Continued

State	Title and application of tax(a)	Rate
Washington	Uranium and Thorium Milling Tax Enhanced Food Fish Tax	$.05/lb. 0.07% to 5% of value (depending on species) at point of landing
West Virginia	(cc)	(cc)
Wisconsin	Metalliferous Minerals Occupation Tax	Progressive net proceeds tax from 3% to 15%
Wyoming	Oil and Gas Production Tax Mining Excise and Severance Taxes	Maximum 0.8 mill/$1 of value at wellhead(h,dd) Varies by substance from 1.5% to 7.25% of value; additional coal excise tax of 2%

Source: Commerce Clearing House, *State Tax Guide.*

(a) Application of tax is same as that of title unless otherwise indicated by a footnote.

(b) Tax scheduled to terminate upon the redemption of, and payment of all accrued interest on, bonds issued by the Alabama State Docks Department.

(c) Timber, metalliferous minerals.

(d) For 1985, $.01803/bbl. of oil or per 10,000 cu. ft. of gas.

(e) Metallic minerals, coal, oil shale, oil and gas.

(f) For 1985, .6 mill.

(g) Clay, gravel, phosphate rock, lime, shells, stone, sand, heavy minerals and rare earths.

(h) Actual rate set by administrative actions.

(i) Buyer deducts amount from payment to grower; amount forwarded to Department of Conservation.

(j) Petroleum, oil, gas and other hydrocarbons.

(k) Coal, salt, oil and gas.

(l) Figures are total parts of tax designed for pollution and conservation.

(m) Coal and oil excepted.

(n) Limited to certain counties. Coal tax expires June 30, 1987.

(o) All ores.

(p) Additional ore royalty tax of 1% of royalties plus 1% of amount of royalty paid on precious metals.

(q) Metals, precious and semi-precious stones and gems.

(r) Except 2.5% of gross value of incremental petroleum and other mineral or crude oil produced in tertiary recovery projects. Over $250,000 gross value to over $1 million.

(s) Cement and gypsum or allied products.

(t) Natural resources except oil, natural gas, liquid hydrocarbons or carbon dioxide.

(u) Oil, coal, gas, liquid hydrocarbons, geothermal energy, carbon dioxide and uranium.

(v) Currently, rate is .18%.

(w) Currently, rate is $1.04/ton.

(x) Oil, gas, coal, salt, limestone, dolomite, sand and gravel.

(y) Asphalt, oil, gas, uranium and metals.

(z) Additional $.10/1,000 board ft. on forest products harvested until July 1, 1987.

(aa) Metals, oil, gas, other hydrocarbons, and uranium.

(bb) May be levied by counties and cities, until July 1, 1992.

(cc) Severance tax on coal, limestone, sandstone, natural gas, sand, gravel and other mineral products to become effective July 1, 1987; tax rates on gross value of articles will vary each year, until 1992.

(dd) Currently, rate is .1 mill/$1.

STATE TAX COLLECTIONS IN 1985

By Vance Kane

State tax collections in 1984-85 increased 9 percent to a total of $215 billion. While this increase was less than the 15 percent growth from 1983 to 1984, it still reflected a continuation of the improved economic conditions seen in 1984. Unemployment in 1985 was lower (6.9 percent), the inflation rate was basically stationary (less than 4 percent), interest rates were falling, and both energy prices and demand continued to drop, thus improving the outlook for state financial operations. (See Tables 6.21 and 6.22.)

State governments relied heavily on sales taxes and income taxes, which together provided 87 percent of total state taxes in 1985, as shown in Table A. While the percentage share of sales taxes has declined since 1957, the drop has been offset by a rise in income taxes so that those two revenue sources remain the backbone of most state taxation systems.

Each state has a mix of taxation levies that reflects its individual sources of wealth and political decisions for taxation. In 1985, 44 states levied individual income taxes; 46 collected corporate net income taxes; and 49 received death and gift taxes (see Table 6.23). All states have some form of sales tax, although exemptions for food and medicine vary, and all have a license structure which is used to protect general health and welfare, as well as raise revenue.

Eight states accounted for nearly one-half of all state tax revenues in fiscal 1985 (see Table B). The two sunbelt states shown, Florida and Texas, have a comparatively low per capita ranking (despite their size) as a result of rapidly rising populations and a relatively conservative spending philosophy.

While the 3.2 percent rate of increase for alcoholic beverage taxes in the states was a decline from the 6.6 percent increase posted in 1984, a substantial portion of the drop was accounted for by alcoholic beverage license taxes. The 11 percent decline reflects a two-year cycle for license collection, however, and does not indicate a substantial decline in the number of locations dispensing alcoholic beverages.

The continued decline in severance taxes (-0.5 percent) indicates a leveling in the values of natural gas and oil. These data do not reflect the rapid drop in market prices which has occurred since late 1985, and subsequently, has created problems in the energy-producing states of Alaska, Louisiana, New Mexico, Oklahoma, and Texas.

Individual State Tax Collections

Although the 1985 national state average was a 9.1 percent increase in total tax collections, four states—Alaska (-4.4 percent); Nebraska (-2.7 percent); South Dakota (-0.9 percent); and Wisconsin (-1.0 percent)—showed decreases. In 1984, only Alaska showed a percentage drop (-3.6 percent) from the previous year when the national state average growth was 14.8 percent.

In 1985, five states recorded tax collection increases over 15 percent: Arizona (17 percent); Louisiana (23 percent); South Carolina (15 percent); Tennessee (19 percent); and Texas (17 percent). In each case, a variety of factors ranging from the improved economy to tax rate adjustments accounted for the substantial tax rise.

Individual states often adjust tax levies to meet changing economic conditions within their boundaries, as well as state political demands. For example, Colorado repealed a special sales and use tax on July 31, 1984, in response to improved economic conditions. Connecticut increased its gasoline tax rate from 14 to 15 cents per gallon to take advantage of the oil price decline.

There is also a natural desire by states blessed with tourist attractions to levy taxes which are borne by temporary guests from outside their borders. Nevada received substantial receipt from amusement taxes on gambling and casino entertainment—approximately $200 million, plus an additional $48 million from amusement licenses on slot

Vance Kane is Assistant Division Chief for Programs, and was assisted by Lisa McNelis, Social Science Analyst, both of the Governments Division, U.S. Bureau of the Census. All data are from *State Tax Collections in 1985*, U.S. Bureau of the Census.

Table A
Percentage Distribution of State Tax Collections
by Major Tax Category

Year	Sales and gross receipt taxes	Income taxes	License taxes	Other
1957	58.1	17.6	15.1	9.2
1967	58.2	22.4	11.4	8.0
1977	51.8	34.3	7.1	6.8
1982	48.4	36.7	6.2	8.6
1983	48.9	36.7	6.2	8.1
1984	48.7	37.9	6.1	7.4
1985	48.8	37.8	6.3	7.1

machines and related games. New Jersey, with the Atlantic City casinos, netted $41 million in amusement licenses. Sales taxes on casinos and slot machines netted $160 million.

Other states levy a variety of licenses (more often to maintain control than to raise revenue) on such activities or items as fishing, hunting, snowmobiles, and boats. Illinois received $60 million from pari-mutuels; New York, $101 million; Maryland, $14 million; and Connecticut, $64 million. Other state levies are used to protect and promote local products such as the fruits and vegetables inspection licenses in Florida, and the hunting and fishing license surcharge for wildlife acquisition in Minnesota.

Miscellaneous taxes, which do not fit the standard classifications, are collected by 14 states (see "Other" column in Table 6.23). The most significant amount is "excess fees of office" in Maryland. The state also has a telephone tax to support emergency service. Colorado, Tennessee, Virginia, and Wisconsin require tax payments on various forms of litigation or lawsuits. Delaware collects a per capita head tax on citizens over the age of 21. Arkansas has a timber acreage tax, and Vermont has a tax on "land capital gains." Few of these taxes raise large sums of revenue, but exist to meet particular situations within these states.

Many states have shared tax structures with their local governments. This is particularly true of personal income taxes and sales taxes. For example, Maryland allows its counties and the city of Baltimore to impose a local income tax up to 50 percent of the state levy.

Comparison of State Taxation

The tax burden of individual state governments is difficult to compare since each state has its own blend of tax policies often developed to shift the burden to non-residents. However, it is possible to rank each state based on per capita collection by major types of tax. While the national state average in 1985 was $902 per capita, only 20 states exceeded that amount. The highest per capita amount was $3,620 in Alaska, and the lowest, $435 in New Hampshire. Hawaii had the highest per capita sales tax ($649); Delaware had the highest per capita income tax ($588).

As mentioned previously, Nevada receives substantial sums from sales taxes on amusement establishments, ranking third in per capita general sales taxes ($490). However, it is one of six states without a personal income tax and the only one without death and gift taxes. Any valid comparison of individual state taxation levels, however, requires a thorough understanding of each state's economic base.

Table B
Selected States' Tax Collections: 1985

State	Amount of taxes (in millions)	Per capita Amount	Per capita State ranking
California	$28,952	$1,098	9
New York	20,702	1,164	6
Texas	11,541	705	43
Pennsylvania	10,162	857	24
Illinois	9,228	800	32
Michigan	8,684	956	18
Ohio	8,652	805	29
Florida	7,883	694	44

Table 6.21
NATIONAL SUMMARY OF STATE GOVERNMENT TAX REVENUE, BY TYPE OF TAX: 1983 TO 1985

| | Amount (in thousands of dollars) | | | Percent change year-to-year | | | |
Tax source	1985 (preliminary)	1984	1983	1984 to 1985	1983 to 1984	Percent distribution, 1985	Per capita, 1985 (in dollars)
Total collections	$214,874,198	$196,904,625	$171,464,295	9.1	14.8	100.0	$902.40
Sales and gross receipts	104,902,240	95,806,235	83,875,722	9.5	14.2	48.8	440.55
General	69,206,886	62,563,604	53,643,010	10.6	16.6	32.2	290.64
Selective	35,695,354	33,242,631	30,232,712	7.4	10.0	16.6	149.91
Motor fuels	13,351,590	12,406,189	10,793,333	7.6	14.9	6.2	56.07
Public utilities	6,202,564	5,883,412	5,650,815	5.4	4.1	2.9	26.05
Insurance	4,533,973	3,949,021	3,859,060	14.8	2.3	2.1	19.04
Tobacco products	4,247,303	4,149,028	4,001,392	2.4	3.7	2.0	17.84
Alcoholic beverages	3,031,224	2,899,986	2,743,092	4.5	5.7	1.4	12.73
Other..................	4,328,700	3,954,995	3,185,020	9.4	24.2	2.0	18.18
Licenses	13,522,828	11,966,520	10,700,508	13.0	11.8	6.3	56.79
Motor vehicles............	7,022,031	6,366,314	5,788,383	10.3	10.0	3.3	29.49
Corporations in general.....	2,766,560	2,103,358	1,848,127	31.5	13.8	1.3	11.62
Motor vehicle operators	613,588	567,131	503,157	8.2	12.7	0.3	2.58
Hunting and fishing	589,799	559,923	534,569	5.3	4.7	0.3	2.48
Alcoholic beverages	231,208	260,946	223,470	−11.4	16.8	0.1	.97
Other....................	2,299,642	2,108,848	1,802,802	9.0	17.0	1.1	9.66
Individual income...........	63,643,517	59,002,227	49,788,567	7.9	18.5	29.6	267.28
Corporation net income	17,636,987	15,511,378	13,152,503	13.7	17.9	8.2	74.07
Severance	7,211,177	7,248,943	7,405,589	−0.5	−2.1	3.4	30.28
Property	3,984,293	3,861,655	3,280,844	3.2	17.7	1.9	16.73
Death and gift..............	2,327,515	2,226,041	2,544,640	4.6	−12.5	1.1	9.77
Other......................	1,645,641	1,281,626	715,923	28.4	79.0	0.8	6.91

Source: U.S. Bureau of the Census, *State Government Tax Collections in 1985.*

Note: Because of rounding, detail may not add to totals. Population figures as of July 1, 1985 were used to calculate per capita amounts; see Table 6.26.

Table 6.22
SUMMARY OF STATE GOVERNMENT TAX REVENUE, BY STATE: 1983 TO 1985

State	Amount (in thousands of dollars)			Percent change year-to-year		Per capita, 1985 (in dollars)
	1985 (preliminary)	1984	1983	1984 to 1985	1983 to 1984	
All states	$214,874,198	$196,904,625	$171,464,295	9.1	14.8	$902.40
Alabama	2,924,048	2,721,463	2,341,229	7.4	16.2	727.19
Alaska	1,885,811	1,973,252	2,046,086	-4.4	-3.6	3,619.60
Arizona	2,945,422	2,525,812	2,069,063	16.6	22.1	924.20
Arkansas	1,744,945	1,541,361	1,337,881	13.2	15.2	739.70
California	28,952,494	25,625,261	22,259,879	13.0	15.1	1,098.14
Colorado	2,284,417	2,129,032	1,752,071	7.3	21.5	707.03
Connecticut	3,497,970	3,086,003	2,537,725	13.3	21.6	1,102.07
Delaware	816,328	712,596	640,057	14.6	11.3	1,312.42
Florida	7,883,166	7,352,440	6,224,717	7.2	18.1	693.57
Georgia	4,525,038	3,954,615	3,504,220	14.4	12.9	757.20
Hawaii	1,362,595	1,247,968	1,150,503	9.2	8.5	1,292.78
Idaho	733,575	687,244	620,035	6.7	10.8	729.93
Illinois	9,227,777	8,701,267	7,426,499	6.1	17.2	799.98
Indiana	4,336,068	4,043,446	3,194,741	7.2	26.6	788.52
Iowa	2,307,406	2,241,503	2,014,289	2.9	11.3	800.07
Kansas	1,915,199	1,792,999	1,565,625	6.8	14.5	781.71
Kentucky	3,012,713	2,798,662	2,601,949	7.6	7.6	808.56
Louisiana	3,855,780	3,131,667	3,029,003	23.1	3.4	860.47
Maine	1,005,216	920,273	780,052	9.2	18.0	863.59
Maryland	4,321,772	3,946,833	3,468,193	9.5	13.8	984.01
Massachusetts	6,620,595	5,839,414	5,155,631	13.4	13.3	1,137.17
Michigan	8,684,163	8,556,725	7,022,658	1.5	21.8	955.56
Minnesota	5,228,004	5,077,158	4,319,483	3.0	17.5	1,246.84
Mississippi	1,811,598	1,740,692	1,537,705	4.1	13.2	693.30
Missouri	3,352,482	3,053,002	2,640,325	9.8	15.6	666.63
Montana	640,750	583,341	513,658	9.8	13.6	775.73
Nebraska	1,040,064	1,068,742	987,454	-2.7	8.2	647.61
Nevada	940,622	861,115	779,338	9.2	10.5	1,004.94
New Hampshire	433,873	423,465	329,458	2.5	28.5	434.74
New Jersey	7,718,790	7,137,452	6,128,035	8.1	16.5	1,020.73
New Mexico	1,439,262	1,377,444	1,165,975	4.5	18.1	992.59
New York	20,702,069	18,817,736	16,207,994	10.0	16.1	1,164.15
North Carolina	5,198,024	4,637,155	4,028,477	12.1	15.1	831.02
North Dakota	692,213	684,399	526,006	1.1	30.1	1,010.53
Ohio	8,651,690	7,985,012	6,734,008	8.3	18.6	805.26
Oklahoma	2,982,106	2,661,981	2,627,487	12.0	1.3	903.39
Oregon	1,982,956	1,850,523	1,783,670	7.2	3.7	737.98
Pennsylvania	10,162,436	9,600,168	8,430,271	5.9	13.9	857.37
Rhode Island	862,070	809,986	726,421	6.4	11.5	890.57
South Carolina	2,732,346	2,371,138	2,130,731	15.2	11.3	816.36
South Dakota	355,452	358,773	324,587	-0.9	10.5	502.05
Tennessee	2,998,373	2,511,631	2,246,288	19.4	11.8	629.65
Texas	11,540,836	9,837,309	8,959,075	17.3	9.8	705.00
Utah	1,323,699	1,196,687	974,098	10.6	22.9	804.68
Vermont	458,654	412,987	358,097	11.1	15.3	857.30
Virginia	4,469,391	4,064,368	3,558,982	10.0	14.2	783.28
Washington	4,585,551	4,560,933	4,195,757	0.5	8.7	1,040.04
West Virginia	1,855,583	1,773,819	1,470,331	4.6	20.6	958.46
Wisconsin	5,066,390	5,116,236	4,302,576	-1.0	18.9	1,061.02
Wyoming	806,416	801,537	735,902	0.6	8.9	1,584.31

Source: U.S. Bureau of the Census, *State Government Tax Collections in 1985.*

Note: Because of rounding, detail may not add to totals. Population figures as of July 1, 1985 were used to calculate per capita amounts; see Table 6.26.

Table 6.23
STATE GOVERNMENT TAX REVENUE, BY TYPE OF TAX: 1985
(In thousands of dollars)

State	Total	Sales and gross receipts	Licenses	Individual income	Corporation net income	Severance	Property	Death and gift	Documentary and stock transfer	Other
Number of states using tax	50	50	50	44	46	33	42	49	29	14
All states	$214,874,198	$104,902,240	$13,522,828	$63,643,517	$17,636,987	$7,211,177	$3,984,293	$2,327,515	$1,589,972	$55,669
Alabama	2,924,048	1,611,284	220,338	710,195	212,261	89,633	61,479	9,683	9,175	…
Alaska	1,885,811	112,908	56,708	1,268	204,600	1,389,262	120,548	517	…	…
Arizona	2,945,422	1,809,637	197,122	608,611	202,301	26,019	112,993	14,758	…	…
Arkansas	1,744,945	989,532	114,061	471,448	130,231	19,081	4,055	5,242	3,672	685
California	28,952,494	12,105,062	974,342	10,762,213	3,658,093	…	1,330,250	103,453	…	…
Colorado	2,284,417	1,081,766	133,062	907,619	101,654	30,401	8,373	14,031	49,326	7,511
Connecticut	3,497,970	2,379,145	165,213	291,640	489,507	…	12	123,127	…	…
Delaware	816,328	98,240	238,796	365,589	77,060	…	…	13,619	21,640	1,384
Florida	7,883,166	6,079,042	511,836	…	454,088	173,178	162,155	101,307	401,560	…
Georgia	4,525,038	2,207,367	138,611	1,718,326	418,251	…	13,946	15,255	12,161	1,121
Hawaii	1,362,595	851,297	19,061	429,398	48,717	…	241	12,260	1,862	…
Idaho	733,575	361,870	67,968	258,230	42,682	682	…	1,902	…	…
Illinois	9,227,777	4,950,229	706,093	2,600,864	706,009	…	196,267	61,149	7,166	…
Indiana	4,336,068	2,632,614	153,135	1,287,050	178,346	1,518	39,028	44,377	…	…
Iowa	2,307,406	1,071,146	196,442	824,551	154,412	…	…	58,247	2,608	…
Kansas	1,915,199	862,879	121,159	603,459	159,670	111,886	26,314	29,832	…	…
Kentucky	3,012,713	1,352,422	156,477	776,569	211,284	227,995	234,713	50,977	2,276	…
Louisiana	3,855,780	1,946,644	306,436	526,684	293,598	745,216	3,067	34,135	…	…
Maine	1,005,216	550,555	76,859	297,233	53,537	…	12,655	11,614	2,763	…
Maryland	4,321,772	1,949,496	153,449	1,768,256	246,123	…	105,457	36,459	47,827	14,705
Massachusetts	6,620,595	2,225,515	195,733	3,158,971	851,283	…	5,617	153,602	29,874	…
Michigan	8,684,163	3,519,875	413,442	3,048,512	1,391,863	…	172,054	62,688	…	…
Minnesota	5,228,004	2,163,282	319,899	2,233,467	383,264	75,729	4,087	17,996	26,046	…
Mississippi	1,811,598	1,190,037	151,369	259,447	106,484	79,963	675	10,688	…	…
Missouri	3,352,482	1,831,397	277,578	1,053,598	160,564	92,898	6,162	21,354	…	1,788
Montana	640,750	139,683	56,232	181,057	62,671	150,673	41,944	7,657	1,828	833
Nebraska	1,040,064	566,078	90,669	318,848	48,959	4,607	4,094	4,981	…	…
Nevada	940,622	803,902	104,441	…	…	61	32,218	…	…	…
New Hampshire	433,873	200,416	62,686	24,480	95,421	104	10,259	11,891	28,616	…
New Jersey	7,718,790	4,056,410	534,006	1,937,007	923,166	…	37,744	194,425	36,032	…

265

TAX REVENUE, BY TYPE OF TAX: 1985—Continued

State	Total	Sales and gross receipts	Licenses	Individual income	Corporation net income	Severance	Property	Death and gift	Documentary and stock transfer	Other
New Mexico	1,439,262	819,410	69,783	84,980	64,006	390,817	6,356	3,910	...	...
New York	20,702,069	6,910,616	756,025	10,395,165	1,859,979	...	...	241,061	539,223	...
North Carolina	5,198,024	2,161,583	365,082	2,023,463	490,296	1,469	79,489	76,642	...	...
North Dakota	692,213	291,574	57,253	76,182	84,445	176,278	1,821	2,660	...	...
Ohio	8,651,690	4,625,294	749,816	2,781,658	437,129	8,192	15,144	34,457	...	...
Oklahoma	2,982,106	1,123,120	270,152	727,100	104,522	708,816	...	38,052	6,597	3,747
Oregon	1,982,956	237,419	218,744	1,310,731	153,822	31,774	179	29,072	1,215	...
Pennsylvania	10,162,436	5,056,989	1,037,136	2,588,913	942,971	...	136,884	277,588	121,955	...
Rhode Island	862,070	454,392	32,548	281,742	70,504	...	6,589	13,773	2,470	52
South Carolina	2,732,346	1,497,892	136,480	850,814	199,771	...	7,091	23,938	16,360	...
South Dakota	355,452	293,444	30,453	...	16,938	4,521	...	10,096	...	...
Tennessee	2,998,373	2,292,690	303,268	61,825	259,198	2,819	...	33,780	33,627	11,166
Texas	11,540,836	7,612,317	1,602,675	...	...	2,175,337	...	150,507	...	...
Utah	1,323,699	728,433	57,904	430,711	52,191	49,353	321	4,786	...	...
Vermont	458,654	231,055	39,173	145,149	34,958	...	512	1,696	5,611	500
Virginia	4,469,391	1,845,506	269,929	1,948,199	287,747	1,647	23,575	28,139	59,305	5,344
Washington	4,585,551	3,449,085	249,056	...	...	36,217	727,102	20,138	103,953	...
West Virginia	1,855,583	1,136,514	91,812	503,186	98,766	959	1,422	20,146	3,063	674
Wisconsin	5,006,390	2,203,026	211,117	2,009,109	413,645	...	129,774	80,440	12,161	6,159
Wyoming	806,416	230,151	61,199	...	...	404,031	101,627	9,408	...	...

Source: U.S. Bureau of the Census, State Government Tax Collections
in 1985.

Key:
...—Not applicable.

Table 6.24
STATE GOVERNMENT SALES AND GROSS RECEIPTS TAX REVENUE: 1985
(In thousands of dollars)

State	Total	General sales or gross receipts	Selective sales and gross receipts								
			Total	Motor fuels	Public utilities	Tobacco products	Insurance	Alcoholic beverages	Parimutuels	Amusements	Other
Number of states using tax	50	45	50	50	40	50	50	50	32	27	36
All states	$104,902,240	$69,206,886	$35,695,354	$13,351,590	$6,202,564	$4,247,303	$4,533,973	$3,031,224	$710,379	$411,610	$3,206,711
Alabama	1,611,284	81,927	792,357	252,339	233,191	71,110	90,046	92,178	...	65	53,428
Alaska	112,908	...	112,908	35,842	1,846	5,211	17,557	13,634	...	...	38,818
Arizona	1,809,637	1,359,395	450,242	224,408	71,100	49,524	55,436	37,937	11,440	397	...
Arkansas	989,532	690,561	298,971	151,260	...	62,682	40,181	24,200	20,648	...	...
California	12,105,062	9,682,886	2,422,176	1,157,881	34,432	260,655	654,557	134,753	122,812	...	57,086
Colorado	1,081,766	762,484	319,282	186,619	3,353	52,271	43,647	24,840	8,097	455	...
Connecticut	2,379,145	1,538,542	840,603	204,975	289,292	90,399	92,840	32,676	64,036	14,116	52,269
Delaware	98,240	...	98,240	39,647	20,787	12,251	17,378	5,137	279	...	2,761
Florida	6,079,042	4,249,950	1,829,092	595,602	165,158	286,299	187,634	421,764	119,554	2,500	50,581
Georgia	2,207,367	1,532,811	674,556	385,768	...	88,068	91,310	109,410	...	...	...
Hawaii	851,297	683,630	167,667	35,593	62,305	19,717	29,417	20,635	...	...	1,594
Idaho	361,870	238,550	123,320	79,051	2,275	10,205	20,546	9,237	412	...	...
Illinois	4,950,229	3,180,453	1,769,776	609,780	658,357	166,678	116,027	69,814	60,002	8,178	80,940
Indiana	2,632,614	2,112,932	519,682	335,237	...	76,784	70,558	37,006	...	97	...
Iowa	1,071,146	757,766	313,380	182,417	...	59,060	55,632	16,271	...	...	...
Kansas	862,879	546,933	315,946	148,825	949	44,878	73,666	43,120	...	810	3,698
Kentucky	1,352,422	820,482	531,940	196,170	...	18,748	107,457	48,758	11,417	283	149,107
Louisiana	1,946,644	1,192,214	754,430	361,822	42,085	87,299	124,311	73,505	25,177	196	40,035
Maine	550,555	353,976	196,579	88,872	27,046	29,158	19,023	31,300	1,180	...	...
Maryland	1,949,496	1,098,445	851,051	297,015	86,278	66,930	82,248	28,431	14,385	1,112	274,652
Massachusetts	2,225,515	1,438,003	787,512	280,759	...	177,086	163,684	83,547	36,033	11,067	35,336
Michigan	3,519,875	2,542,053	977,822	620,308	...	126,251	116,994	91,473	22,796	...	...
Minnesota	2,163,282	1,348,222	815,060	349,965	54,343	85,011	76,525	52,228	...	...	196,988
Mississippi	1,190,037	932,174	257,863	131,462	...	36,599	54,084	35,405	...	313	...
Missouri	1,831,397	1,418,212	413,185	205,701	1,272	82,339	99,088	24,785	...	...	...
Montana	139,683	...	139,683	81,483	7,446	13,635	20,798	13,855	160	...	2,306
Nebraska	566,078	341,429	224,649	127,565	1,688	28,781	29,540	13,143	12,552	4,788	6,592
Nevada	803,902	458,311	345,591	74,361	3,087	20,233	28,420	13,104	11	196,200	10,175
New Hampshire	200,416	...	200,416	64,087	6,739	33,013	19,080	10,602	10,328	...	56,567
New Jersey	4,056,410	2,260,827	1,795,583	303,395	937,459	216,626	102,004	58,410	6,945	160,569	10,175

SALES AND GROSS RECEIPTS TAX REVENUE: 1985—Continued

State	Total	General sales or gross receipts	Selective sales and gross receipts								
			Total	Motor fuels	Public utilities	Tobacco products	Insurance	Alcoholic beverages	Parimutuels	Amusements	Other
New Mexico	819,410	607,193	212,217	104,170	2,468	14,598	42,297	15,692	2,533	107	30,352
New York	6,910,616	4,229,025	2,681,591	408,761	1,012,854	434,762	292,962	171,407	100,738	1,115	258,992
North Carolina	2,161,583	1,159,614	1,001,969	407,561	315,718	16,635	115,030	122,418	...	...	24,607
North Dakota	293,574	187,457	106,117	53,727	13,936	12,389	12,635	5,951	11,644	...	7,479
Ohio	4,625,294	2,880,548	1,744,746	622,579	684,952	184,548	170,805	70,211	...	...	7
Oklahoma	1,123,120	630,522	492,598	190,754	13,776	75,043	97,681	41,631	2,100	12	71,601
Oregon	237,419	...	237,419	119,026	2,277	58,693	41,414	10,887	5,122	...	...
Pennsylvania	5,056,989	3,019,349	2,037,640	621,648	550,470	239,201	204,758	130,176	12,933	201	278,253
Rhode Island	454,392	274,239	180,153	45,864	70,049	29,065	17,308	7,609	6,119	106	4,033
South Carolina	1,497,892	1,010,796	487,096	247,004	25,944	29,842	42,438	101,983	...	8,536	31,349
South Dakota	293,444	184,559	108,885	55,240	904	10,466	16,279	8,757	2,189	...	15,050
Tennessee	2,292,690	1,738,375	554,315	288,486	23,897	80,808	90,994	61,457	...	12	8,661
Texas	7,612,317	4,244,826	3,367,491	986,869	321,750	373,951	378,649	332,744	...	264	973,234
Utah	728,433	555,415	173,018	112,322	4,158	13,182	26,554	16,802	...	...	...
Vermont	231,055	87,950	143,105	37,391	17,811	13,041	8,853	14,232	684	...	51,093
Virginia	1,845,506	927,908	917,598	327,830	137,165	17,003	108,633	92,754	7,042	65	234,148
Washington	3,449,085	2,680,599	768,486	348,992	142,039	97,256	61,396	103,047	...	26	8,688
West Virginia	1,136,514	795,025	341,489	158,911	...	35,085	44,092	6,963	10,964	...	85,474
Wisconsin	2,203,026	1,453,526	749,500	370,427	151,908	129,384	53,315	43,864	...	20	582
Wyoming	230,151	179,792	50,359	35,819	...	4,850	8,192	1,451	47	...	...

Source: U.S. Bureau of the Census, *State Government Tax Collections in 1985.*

Key:

... —Not applicable.

Table 6.25

STATE GOVERNMENT LICENSE TAX REVENUE: 1985

(In thousands of dollars)

State	Total	Motor vehicle	Motor vehicle operators	Corporations in general	Occupations and businesses, n.e.c.	Hunting and fishing	Alcoholic beverages	Public utilities	Amusements	Other
Number of states using tax	50	50	49	49	50	50	48	31	34	48
All states	$13,522,828	$7,022,031	$613,588	$2,766,560	$1,818,660	$589,799	$231,208	$227,017	$123,913	$130,052
Alabama	220,338	59,532	8,924	73,681	63,832	10,127	2,684	1,558	...	...
Alaska	56,708	15,229	598	981	27,709	10,217	1,702	...	226	46
Arizona	197,122	146,226	5,571	3,363	12,016	10,098	2,289	...	32	17,527
Arkansas	114,061	70,817	4,781	3,931	14,708	12,070	1,000	6,237	362	155
California	974,342	552,848	60,740	7,248	222,033	46,821	29,697	49,584	550	4,821
Colorado	133,062	68,868	6,219	2,436	19,869	29,593	2,377	...	55	3,645
Connecticut	165,213	102,561	17,544	6,405	28,929	2,459	6,419	...	58	838
Delaware	238,796	34,664	1,159	121,057	76,990	542	578	3,240	53	513
Florida	511,836	298,017	32,729	18,086	113,044	9,989	17,383	15,468	748	6,372
Georgia	138,611	64,986	11,616	15,443	23,920	11,285	1,699	...	...	9,662
Hawaii	19,061	9,413	...	1,051	5,836	134	...	2,543	...	84
Idaho	67,968	29,916	2,911	277	19,004	12,829	989	1,948	...	94
Illinois	706,093	548,504	34,008	55,896	49,659	13,599	1,899	...	1,054	1,474
Indiana	153,135	115,439	(a)	4,321	15,527	7,664	8,645	132	186	1,221
Iowa	196,442	136,058	11,251	17,541	14,437	5,963	4,424	4,424	...	2,559
Kansas	121,159	75,148	4,559	9,690	19,391	8,621	1,227	1,643	18	862
Kentucky	156,477	92,298	6,385	20,202	21,003	8,809	1,866	3,658	510	1,746
Louisiana	306,436	61,574	8,386	201,857	24,459	6,186	2,309	1,248	107	310
Maine	76,859	42,193	4,789	966	17,407	8,465	1,650	...	229	1,160
Maryland	153,449	93,255	7,796	4,043	39,823	6,511	338	...	321	1,362
Massachusetts	195,733	116,829	31,056	9,593	31,773	4,038	564	...	680	1,200
Michigan	413,442	297,687	15,978	6,984	33,382	23,882	20,017	12,028	67	3,417
Minnesota	319,899	230,623	9,397	2,064	50,605	21,858	494	...	...	4,858
Mississippi	151,369	54,180	8,131	59,358	17,843	6,851	2,544	2,252	...	210
Missouri	277,578	165,174	11,030	41,532	33,484	12,993	2,208	8,490	950	1,717
Montana	56,232	27,232	1,321	752	8,661	15,676	1,411	1,098	...	81
Nebraska	90,669	50,452	2,680	4,507	16,568	6,926	248	...	...	9,288
Nevada	104,441	36,608	2,391	3,768	8,003	3,430	23	...	48,401	1,817
New Hampshire	62,686	35,839	4,571	3,648	10,020	3,580	2,063	1,546	154	1,265
New Jersey	534,006	312,627	23,984	107,252	32,029	6,616	3,975	3,610	41,082	2,831

LICENSE TAX REVENUE: 1985—Continued

State	Total	Motor vehicle	Motor vehicle operators	Corporations in general	Occupations and businesses, n.e.c.	Hunting and fishing	Alcoholic beverages	Public utilities	Amusements	Other
New Mexico	69,783	39,482	3,082	6,979	10,517	8,693	807	82	141	1,481
New York	756,025	457,566	56,818	16,350	106,697	21,055	31,788	51,219	13,051	1,172
North Carolina	365,082	188,543	27,687	86,671	45,084	10,906	2,255	...	2,764	...
North Dakota	57,253	32,078	1,741	474	17,116	4,141	245	20	1,430	8
Ohio	749,816	320,613	10,780	300,161	80,210	15,338	15,817	3,603	...	3,294
Oklahoma	270,152	189,878	6,918	32,630	21,371	9,463	1,761	4	1,712	6,415
Oregon	218,744	139,387	11,191	3,913	38,262	16,749	1,303	5,449	767	1,723
Pennsylvania	1,037,136	376,959	42,609	435,114	112,448	28,776	11,468	24,713	29	5,020
Rhode Island	32,548	23,568	(a)	2,583	5,227	676	155	...	120	219
South Carolina	136,480	48,380	3,979	14,764	49,000	6,743	1,446	...	5,757	6,411
South Dakota	30,453	12,573	1,138	1,049	7,459	7,375	208	1,579	...	651
Tennessee	303,268	120,749	19,943	117,350	27,621	10,830	1,424	4,527	1,878	3,772
Texas	1,602,675	530,754	36,321	910,427	63,650	22,226	25,905	...	...	6,987
Utah	57,904	31,811	4,760	...	8,931	11,858	283	...	204	261
Vermont	39,173	27,997	1,706	509	4,535	3,392	526	...	...	304
Virginia	269,929	186,455	15,763	11,343	40,010	10,645	3,527	9,064	37	2,149
Washington	249,056	127,158	13,889	7,349	63,570	19,060	7,057	4,723	180	1,729
West Virginia	91,812	62,603	(a)	5,000	7,536	7,432	2,298	11	...	2,220
Wisconsin	211,117	122,890	14,265	3,378	35,977	29,480	213	1,511	...	4,903
Wyoming	61,199	37,790	493	2,583	1,475	17,129	...	...	...	218

Source: U.S. Bureau of the Census, State Government Tax Collections in 1985.

Key:

...—Not applicable.

(a) Included with motor vehicle licenses.

Table 6.26
FISCAL YEAR, POPULATION AND PERSONAL INCOME, BY STATE

State	Date of close of fiscal year in 1985	Total population (excluding armed forces overseas)(a) (in thousands)		Personal income, calendar year 1984(b)		State government portion of state-local tax revenue in fiscal 1983-84(c) (percent)
		July 1, 1985 (provisional)	July 1, 1984	Amount (in millions of dollars)	Per capita (in dollars)	
All states		238,115	235,870	$3,009,601	$12,778	61.5
Alabama....................	September 30	4,021	3,989	39,869	9,992	74.0
Alaska.....................	June 30	521	505	8,739	17,487	83.9
Arizona....................	June 30	3,187	3,072	36,151	11,841	66.4
Arkansas	June 30	2,359	2,346	23,033	9,805	75.8
California.................	June 30	26,365	25,795	371,202	14,487	66.5
Colorado	June 30	3,231	3,190	44,004	13,847	50.1
Connecticut	June 30	3,174	3,155	52,221	16,556	59.1
Delaware	June 30	622	614	8,383	13,685	83.1
Florida	June 30	11,366	11,050	140,082	12,763	62.3
Georgia....................	June 30	5,976	5,842	67,416	11,551	63.1
Hawaii	June 30	1,054	1,037	13,547	13,042	77.9
Idaho	June 30	1,005	999	10,099	10,092	72.0
Illinois...................	June 30	11,535	11,522	158,876	13,802	53.8
Indiana	June 30	5,499	5,492	64,418	11,717	67.3
Iowa	June 30	2,884	2,903	35,382	12,160	60.5
Kansas	June 30	2,450	2,440	32,300	13,248	58.3
Kentucky	June 30	3,726	3,720	38,347	10,300	78.8
Louisiana	June 30	4,481	4,461	48,233	10,808	63.0
Maine	June 30	1,164	1,156	12,505	10,813	64.7
Maryland	June 30	4,392	4,349	62,906	14,464	60.4
Massachusetts	June 30	5,822	5,798	85,709	14,784	65.0
Michigan	September 30	9,088	9,058	114,408	12,607	59.9
Minnesota	June 30	4,193	4,163	55,129	13,247	71.5
Mississippi	June 30	2,613	2,598	22,802	8,777	77.0
Missouri	June 30	5,029	5,001	60,847	12,151	60.2
Montana....................	June 30	826	823	8,690	10,546	55.5
Nebraska	June 30	1,606	1,605	19,962	12,430	54.0
Nevada	June 30	936	917	12,132	13,320	69.8
New Hampshire	June 30	998	978	12,885	13,192	39.6
New Jersey.................	June 30	7,562	7,517	116,029	15,440	58.0
New Mexico.................	June 30	1,450	1,426	14,610	10,262	81.0
New York	March 31	17,783	17,746	253,934	14,318	49.8
North Carolina	June 30	6,255	6,166	66,891	10,850	73.2
North Dakota	June 30	685	687	8,479	12,352	74.8
Ohio	June 30	10,744	10,740	132,842	12,355	59.6
Oklahoma	June 30	3,301	3,310	38,438	11,655	69.7
Oregon	June 30	2,687	2,676	31,052	11,611	52.4
Pennsylvania	June 30	11,853	11,887	146,545	12,314	61.6
Rhode Island	June 30	968	962	12,331	12,820	60.0
South Carolina	June 30	3,347	3,302	33,385	10,116	73.7
South Dakota	June 30	708	705	7,813	11,069	52.0
Tennessee	June 30	4,762	4,726	49,142	10,419	60.6
Texas	August 31	16,370	16,083	201,013	12,572	55.1
Utah	June 30	1,645	1,623	16,074	9,733	63.9
Vermont	June 30	535	530	5,723	10,802	61.3
Virginia...................	June 30	5,706	5,636	74,694	13,254	59.6
Washington	June 30	4,409	4,349	55,633	12,792	73.7
West Virginia	June 30	1,936	1,951	18,991	9,728	78.9
Wisconsin..................	June 30	4,775	4,762	59,453	12,474	69.0
Wyoming	June 30	509	513	6,252	12,224	62.7

Source: U.S. Bureau of the Census, *State Government Tax Collections in 1985.*
Note: Because of rounding, detail may not add to totals.
(a) U.S. Bureau of the Census, *Current Population Reports.* Series P-25, January 1986.
(b) U.S. Department of Commerce, *Survey of Current Business,* August 1985.
(c) U.S. Bureau of the Census, *Governmental Finances in 1983-84,* October 1985.

CHAPTER SEVEN

STATE MANAGEMENT AND ADMINISTRATION

DEVELOPMENTS IN STATE ADMINISTRATION AND MANAGEMENT

By R. Douglas Roederer

In recent years, the states have been pressured to improve administrative management and operate state government more efficiently. The following is an overview of several components of state administration, and some of the significant recent developments in each: state personnel administration and statewide productivity improvement, purchasing, fleet management, facilities management, risk management, telecommunications, surplus property, and records management.

State Personnel Management

On February 19, 1985, the U.S. Supreme Court, in *Garcia v. San Antonio Metropolitan Transit Authority*, ruled that the minimum wage and overtime pay provisions of the Fair Labor Standards Act (FLSA) apply to state and local government employees. This ruling was viewed by many government officials as a severe blow to states' rights, especially since the Court, in *National League of Cities v. Usery* (1976), had declared that traditional state and local government functions were constitutionally protected from FLSA requirements.

The most immediate impact of the decision would have been to place state employees under the act's minimum wage, overtime, and reporting requirements. Traditionally, states have awarded compensatory time (in lieu of overtime payments) to employees who work in excess of a 40-hour work week. Under FLSA, the option would have been virtually eliminated. The fiscal impact of the decision was estimated at between $321 million and $1.5 billion, if all governments were in compliance.

The perceived impact of FLSA on state government forced personnel administrators to carefully examine their personnel systems to determine compliance with the act. For several months, many states were involved in comprehensive reviews of their classification and compensation systems. Although no direct correlation can be made between the ruling and the states' actions, 22 states reported a review of their personnel systems during this period.

In November, 1985, President Ronald Reagan signed Public Law 99-150, which was designed to remedy some of the problems caused by the ruling. The new law was the product of extensive efforts by the National Governors' Association, the National Association of Attorneys General, the National Conference of State Legislatures, and the National Association of State Personnel Executives, as well as numerous organizations representing the municipal governments.

The new law applies to all employees of a state, a political subdivision, or an interstate governmental agency, with limited exceptions. The law allows states to give their employees compensatory time off at the rate of time and a half in lieu of time-and-a-half pay for overtime work. The legislation changed the effective date of FLSA to April 15, 1986 for all state and local government employees brought under the act by the Garcia ruling, and eliminated any state liability through April 14, 1986. States have been given the option of deferring payment of monetary overtime compensation until August 1, 1986.

Along with the streamlining of classification and compensation systems, the states recently have undertaken a number of other activities and improvements in personnel administration. Some states have enhanced their fringe benefit packages by adding services such as on-site day care for employees' children, as well as counseling for workers with stress-related problems. Moreover, states have reported an increased emphasis on the professionalization and recognition of the services performed by career state workers.

R. Douglas Roederer is Director of the Center for Management and Administration at The Council of State Governments. He was assisted by Center staff: Linda Carroll, Keon Chi, John Olive, Wayne Masterman, and Marysia Tobin. Edwin C. Bridges, Director, Alabama Department of Archives and History, and Joel LeBauve, Louisiana Division of Administration, Property Assistance Agency, also contributed material.

Productivity improvement

Productivity improvement efforts aim at maximizing outputs with minimum necessary inputs in order to achieve program goals. Effectiveness and efficiency are two dimensions of state government productivity. Such programs have taken different forms in state government. Some have been initiated by the legislative branch, while others have been undertaken by the executive branch alone. Joint legislative-executive approaches also have been used. Line agencies in many states have conducted their own productivity programs, while a number of states have initiated centralized productivity efforts. However, some of these have not survived gubernatorial changes and legislative budget cuts.

Recent productivity improvement efforts made on a statewide basis include: Georgia—Management Review Division's Management Analysis; Massachusetts—Performance Management System, administered by the Department of Personnel Administration; Michigan—Council on Productivity and Productivity Improvement Center; Minnesota—Productivity Improvement Program by the Department of Administration's Management Analysis Division; Missouri—Productivity Analysis Unit in the Office of Administration; New York—Office of Management and Productivity; North Carolina—Governor's Management Council and the Governor's Commission on Government Productivity; Oregon—Governor's Productivity Improvement Program, by the Office of Budget and Management; Pennsylvania—productivity improvement programs administered by the Office of Administration; South Carolina—Productivity Council; Utah—State Productivity Coordinator, by the Department of Administrative Services; and Washington—Productivity Board. In 1985, Ohio established within its Department of Administrative Services an Office of Administrative Management charged with strengthening management and containing costs throughout state government.

States have made productivity improvement efforts in technology and employee motivation. Such programs as office automation, management information systems, and expanded computer and telecommunications services have contributed to productivity improvement. A greater emphasis, however, has been placed on employee motivation.

Quality circles have been used in 19 states; management training programs in Massachusetts, Minnesota, Montana, Pennsylvania, Texas, and Virginia; productivity incentive programs in California, Florida, Louisiana, Missouri, New York, North Carolina, Texas, Virginia, and Washington; employee appreciation programs in Connecticut, Georgia, New York, and North Carolina; and employee suggestion and reward systems in a majority of the states. In addition, early retirement programs have been established in several states, including Michigan, Minnesota, Rhode Island, and Wisconsin.

Purchasing

The purchase of public goods and services is an important facet of state administration. In 1985, the total volume of state procurement represented approximately three-fourths of all public purchasing done by the three levels of government.

The procurement function requires state purchasing officials to perform a complex set of duties. Those basic duties include the purchase of equipment, supplies, materials, and services. In most states, however, their responsibilities have increased dramatically. Purchasing officials also provide the states with inventory management, and conduct vendor evaluations and value/cost analyses.

In light of the dollar volume of purchasing done by the states and the growing list of procurement responsibilities, the centralization or decentralization of the purchasing function is one of debate and concern in the states.

All states now have some form of central purchasing; however, the degree and manner of centralization differs substantially. In some states, the function is largely one of approving prices, not contracting or buying. In seven states, central purchasing departments have authority for all departments, institutions, and agencies—including the legislative and judicial branches. No state, however, has fully centralized the purchase of land, construction of buildings, highways, or other public works projects.

Centralization is not the only concern of state procurement officials. These executive branch employees are charged with the responsibility of fostering competition and competitiveness; yet at times, barriers to absolute competition have been enacted in the states. At the moment, those barriers are in the form of preferences for various companies, products, or services. Purchasing preferences prevent acceptance of the lowest and best monetary bid from a responsible bidder. State purchasing officials argue that this creates an added burden to the taxpaying public by increasing government expenditures without improving performance and service.

In the mid-1980s, the concept of "contracting out" or "privatization" has become yet another issue facing those who are responsible for state procurement. States are examining the decision-making process that determines whether a good or service is produced in state government or purchased from an outside source. The procurement manager can make a significant contribution to the evaluation of the private sector contractor.

Fleet Management

The number of state-owned and -leased vehicles runs from zero in Alabama and Texas to 29,691 in California. The average number of vehicles in state government is estimated at 6,800. These numbers explain why the administration of a state fleet is a key concern to state officials.

In fact, one of the most challenging problems facing those involved in central management of state government is an effective means of containing the costs associated with operating a fleet of cars, trucks, vans, buses, and bulldozers that can be made available to state employees for permanent or temporary purposes. Questions of energy-efficient vehicles, statewide maintenance contracts, centralization, and expanded use for employees have forced state officials to take a hard look at increased fleet management.

The existence of fleet management programs in 30 states is the direct result of either statutory mandate or executive order. Of those states with fleet management programs, 23 are reported to have statewide systems. The majority of those programs are operated in departments of administration; however, Maryland and Michigan have placed the responsibility for their statewide fleet management programs in their budget departments, while Kentucky and Virginia have based their programs in departments of transportation or highways. The number of personnel in centralized fleet management programs ranges from two in Delaware to over 200 in Maryland. Of the states with active fleet management programs, 15 purchase vehicles for the entire government.

By implementing a variety of cost containment measures, the Ohio Department of Administrative Services reported a savings of $2 million in two years. Purchasing smaller and more energy-efficient vehicles or downsizing alone saved $1.5 million. These actions were generated first by Governor Richard Celeste, and followed by the enactment of a comprehensive fleet management program by the Ohio General Assembly. In addition to downsizing, the program limits the personal assignment of state cars, expands the use of the state motor pool, and charges state employees for the commute use of vehicles.

Colorado established a statewide motor vehicle fleet maintenance program in July 1985. The program is designed to provide centralized control and reporting of vehicle usage and costs. The Department of Administration leases all vehicles to state users, collects usage and maintenance statistics, and rotates vehicles to ensure uniform utilization.

Purchasing vehicles for state government is a time-consuming and detailed process. Specifications for vehicles must be carefully written and monitored, especially in states such as Ohio where the emphasis is on energy efficiency. Ohio reported a savings of approximately $1,200 per vehicle by shifting away from vehicle options and toward four- and six-cylinder engine vehicles. Similarly, California has required that all new vehicles get 23 miles per gallon.

State motor pools are common in nearly all states with active fleet management programs. Motor pool vehicles are available to state agency employees for temporary purposes. States report that the motor pool system is an effective means of financing the fleet. Louisiana, for example, instituted a break-even mileage recommendation; that is, the fee charged the using agency should be equal to the actual per mile cost of operating the vehicle. When the vehicle becomes too expensive to operate, it is removed from the pool.

The personal assignment of vehicles to state employees is an area of frequent criticism by the public and the media. Ohio and Louisiana took action to limit the private use of state motor vehicles. However, many states allow for personal assignment of state vehicles to specified personnel, as well as home storage of the vehicles.

Facility Management

Efficient and effective facility management is central to any properly administered organization. When that organization is a state government, the operation becomes the subject of public scrutiny. Today, state facility managers are no longer followers in the development of innovative management techniques; out of necessity, they often lead the way.

Facility management typically is organized within administrative or general services departments. The arena often includes—but is not limited to—maintenance, construction, renovation, and delivery of basic services to the state physical plant, and the leasing of capital equipment and transportation needs. It has grown to include strategic long-range planning, the implementation of computer-generated aids, office automation, and ergonomic concerns.

Areas of critical concern in facility management vary from state to state and within the states as well. There are, however, some common themes that span the regions.

One issue of current interest is the availability of funds to properly operate plants. Scheduled and preventive maintenance are areas that often absorb budgetary cuts; as a result, they are often deferred.

Asbestos removal and acceptable applications continue to be of concern in the states. With U.S. Environmental Protection Agency (EPA) standards and court-ordered actions for its removal, the states have faced an additional burden for which they had not provided. Crisis management has become the norm.

The age of the physical plant itself is another major concern. Most state facilities are over 20 years old, and many fall into the 50- to 100-year-old category. Retrofitting these structures to satisfy the demands of the rapidly-advancing technologies that must be housed within them has become a pressing issue.

These concerns, and many others, are high on the priority lists of facilities managers. Funding and long-range capital planning are keys to solving many of them, but budgetary cuts will continue to be the norm for most states.

Risk Management

The crisis surrounding the affordability and availability of liability insurance has left many public entities, including two states (Colorado and Wyoming), without commercial liability coverage. States are functioning with liability coverage much reduced from what it was in previous years and not nearly enough to cover the liability they must accept. This dramatic decrease in the availability of liability insurance, coupled with an increase in the number of suits brought against public entities in recent years, has caused many states to consider alternative ways to accept reasonable limits of liability without the threat of unreasonable damage claims resulting from that liability.

Although the specifics of how a state insures against liability vary, the states may be divided into two broad categories. In the first are those states whose liability insurance issues constitute but one of a series of concerns within a centralized risk management program. In the second category are those states without centralized risk management programs. Centralized risk management has played an important part in helping some states respond to the problems caused by acute premium rate increases, midterm cancellations, and the withdrawal of many insurance companies from underwriting certain types of liability insurance. In most states, various agencies, divisions, and offices within state government maintain risk managers whose primary responsibility centers on the purchase and administration of insurance policies for that unit.

While the states, as well as their political subdivisions, currently face a crisis in the area of tort liability, there are other areas of risk with which they must deal—contractual liability, fidelity risk, and property risk. Contractual liability deals primarily with breaches of contract of any type that are held by the state for services being rendered for or by the state. Fidelity risk concerns the loss of money or property by theft or fraud by a government employee or official. Property risks are those that the states incur as a result of damage to property due to vandalism, fire, or natural disasters. Each of these risks must be addressed by all public entities.

As of this writing, only 24 states have risk management programs in place. Only a few of these programs are centralized to the extent that all risk management functions and responsibilities for the state are administered through that single agency. For some states, the centralization of risk management functions has come as a result of a crisis situation precipitated by the cancellation of the state's auto and general liability insurance policy. Other states, such as Missouri, Oregon, and Pennsylvania, have had centralized programs in place for some time.

Telecommunications

During the 1984-85 biennium, state governments continued to improve the facilities and operations of telecommunications to transmit voice, data, and video. Some of the developments included: teleconferencing systems designed to save money; centralized information processing resources for more effective operations of communications facilities; statewide communications networks connected with high-tech enterprises and universities; establishment of special warning telecommunications systems used in emergency situations, such as a natural disaster; and toll-free lines and satellite and cable television networks designed to carry coverage of state government meetings for public viewing.

Some states have experimented with a state-owned telecommunications system to achieve cost savings over continued use of common carriers' facilities. For example, Ohio purchased microwave facilities to transmit voice and data signals throughout the state on 31 towers owned by three state agencies (the Educational Broadcasting Network Commission, the Turnpike Commission, and the Department of Administrative Services). The microwave system will serve all state agencies, thus saving the state an estimated $440,000 per month during the 15-year life of the project.

The state telecommunications system in Colorado is totally under state control, thus facilitating all intrastate communications needs. State ownership and operation of the system was expected to save $3 million per year. South Carolina also built its own system at a cost of $28 million. The system, which includes radio, television, and other information transmission capabilities, is expected to save the state an estimated $250 million over the next 20 years.

The most debated telecommunications issues during the biennium came as a result of the breakup of American Telephone and Telegraph (AT&T) in 1984. The divestiture of the world's largest telecommunications company raised several policy issues including: how state agencies should encourage competition and handle applications for certificates of public convenience and necessity; how rate requests should be handled; what requirements telephone companies and phone equipment dealers should have; how state agencies should regulate new businesses in the industry; and how new service boundaries should be drawn—such as local access and transport areas (LATAs) and local measured services (LMS) for equitable rates. Moreover, the lifeline program, designed to provide basic services at reduced rates to needy subscribers, also became a major issue during the biennium.

Telecommunications legislation during 1984-85 included provisions covering the above issues as well as other areas. One California law requires telephone equipment retailers to provide the consumers with information on "pulse" and "tone" equipment. Connecticut put a ban on competitive intrastate long distance telephone service. Local and private pay phones were deregulated in many states, including Colorado, Florida, and North Carolina. Many states also were concerned with new telecommunications services provided by cellular radio and fiber optics.

In the next biennium, state telecommunications officials will continue to face tough issues including: the need for long-range planning; management improvement, particularly in inventory and cost accounting techniques; updated personnel classification and purchasing practices; streamlined systems of technical assistance to state agencies; and development of a statewide program to ensure security and public safety.

Surplus Property

Personal property that has been declared surplus to the needs of the federal government is made available to states and local organizations for public purposes. Public agencies—including states and their political subdivisions—involved in such activities as conservation, economic development, education, park programs and recreation, public safety, and public health, are eligible recipients of surplus personal property.

The program is administered by the federal General Services Administration, and distribution is accomplished through the state surplus property agencies established in each state, the District of Columbia, Guam, the Northern Mariana Islands, Puerto Rico, and the Virgin Islands. These state surplus property agencies advise organizations of eligibility requirements and procedures to be followed in acquiring federal surplus property and of the conditions and restrictions placed on the property. Most agencies operate on a self-sustaining basis by assessing recipients a service charge to cover handling, transportation, and administrative expenses.

In fiscal year 1985, surplus property donation approvals totaled $399.2 million—a $67.2 million decrease from fiscal year 1984. These dollar amounts are based on the original cost of record to the federal government. A total of 310,816 items were approved for donation in fiscal year 1985. Actual donations completed in that fiscal year totaled $268.3 million and were distributed among the states and territories. The benefits to states can be measured by the resulting savings of taxpayer dollars when agency and institutional needs are met with donated equipment rather than the purchase of new items.

The availability and quality of property in the program, however, has declined over the past several years due to the effects of federal spending cuts and an emphasis on reutilization of items on the federal level. However, the program is expected to continue at the present level of activity in the future.

Archives and Records Management

Current procedures for creating and maintaining state government records are the product of centuries of accumulated traditions and legal requirements. The basic elements of a modern state records program now include requirements for the creation of records, terms for the use of records, the preservation of those of enduring value, and the disposition of non-permanent records.

Most public officials are obligated (either by laws or regulations) to maintain records documenting their work. These records serve, in part, as a mechanism by which society holds the officials accountable for the authority granted them. The records are the

government's responsibility when the information they contain affects the rights, commitments, or interests of the government or its citizens. They are also a resource when their information improves or enriches our understanding of the past and the ability to work more effectively. Because of their importance and cost, governmental records require a systematic management program to ensure that long-term records are preserved and that those which do not need to be kept are disposed of efficiently. The savings from the timely disposition of non-permanent records usually exceed the total operating costs of a complete records management and archival program.

Public records programs are generally divided into two parts. The records management component concentrates on the processes of records creation, maintenance, and disposition. The archival component concentrates on making accessible and preserving records of long-term value. In some states, these programs are separated administratively; in others, they are combined. Regardless of their administrative placement, close coordination between these two elements is necessary for an effective total records program.

Today, state governments are overwhelmed by the increasing quantity of modern records. The impermanence and variety of new records formats and the complexity of modern information and administrative systems make the preservation of permanent records an increasingly difficult problem. These challenges have been detailed in a number of recent reports about state records programs. The National Historical Publications and Records Commission sponsored a series of "assessment projects" in which the historical records advisory boards of 43 states analyzed and reported on the conditions and needs of historical records efforts in their states. Each of the states has published a report of its findings and recommendations, and a summary of the first 20 state reports, *Documenting America*, was published in 1984 by the National Association of Government Archives and Records Administrators.

These studies show that historically-valuable records of state governments are in jeopardy, because most states do not have adequate programs for managing their records. The archivists cannot properly preserve all records in their possession, and the records managers have not been able to maintain adequate control over the records outside of archives. Professional associations representing both groups are now involved in an extensive array of projects to develop the new tools and strategies to meet these challenges. The assessments indicate that without these new approaches and without sustained efforts by each state to meet its responsibilities in records administration, much of our documentary heritage may be lost.

Table 7.1
THE OFFICE OF STATE PERSONNEL ADMINISTRATOR

State or other jurisdiction	Method of selection	Reports to governor	Reports to personnel board	Directs departmental employees	Administers policies of personnel board	Administers merit tests, establishes qualifications for classified state employees	Maintains roster of state employees, classification and compensation plans	Makes budget recommendations to legislature	Other(a)
Alabama	B		★		★	★	★	★	★
Alaska	G	★		★		★	★	★	★
Arizona	D								
Arkansas	D	★		★	★	★	★	★	
California State Personnel Bd.	B		★	★	★	★	★	★	★
California Dept. of Personnel Admin.	G	★					★	★	★
Colorado	G	★	★	★	★	★	★	★	★
Connecticut	G	★	★	★	★	★	★	★	★
Delaware	G	★		★		★	★	★	★
Florida	G	★		★	★	★	★	★	★
Georgia	G	★		★	★	★	★	★	★
Hawaii	G	★	★	★	★	★	★	★	★
Idaho	B		★	★	★	★	★		
Illinois	D	★		★		★	★		★
Indiana	G	★		★		★	★	★	★
Iowa	G(b)	★	★	★	★	★	★		
Kansas	G	★		★		★	★	★	
Kentucky	G	★	★	★	★	★	★	★	★
Louisiana	G(c)	★		★	★	★	★		★
Maine	G	★		★		★	★	★	★
Maryland	G	★	★	★	★	★	★	★	★
Massachusetts	G(d)	★		★	★	★	★	★	★
Michigan	B	★	★	★		★	★	★	★
Minnesota	G			★		★	★	★	★
Mississippi	B		★	★	★	★	★	★	★
Missouri	G(e)	★	★	★	★	★	★	★	
Montana	G(f)			★	★	★	★	★	★
Nebraska	G	★		★		★	★		★
Nevada	G	★	★	★	★	★	★	★	★
New Hampshire	D	★	★	★	★	★	★	★	
New Jersey	G	★	★	★	★	★	★		

THE OFFICE OF STATE PERSONNEL ADMINISTRATOR—Continued

State or other jurisdiction	Method of selection	Reports to governor	Reports to personnel board	Directs departmental employees	Administers policies of personnel board	Administers merit tests, establishes qualifications for classified state employees	Maintains roster of state employees, classification and compensation plans	Makes budget recommendations to legislature	Other(a)
					Primary responsibilities:				
New Mexico...........	G	★	★	★	★	★	★	★	★
New York...........	G	★★		★★	★★	★★	★★	★★	
North Carolina........	G	★★	★★	★★	★★	★★	★★	★★	★
North Dakota.........	D(g)	★★		★★	★★	★★	★★		
Ohio	G	★★	★★	★★	★★	★★	★★	★	★
Oklahoma	G	★★	★	★★	★	★★	★★	★★	★
Oregon	D	★★		★★		★★	★★	★★	★
Pennsylvania									
Civil Service Comm..	(h)		★	★★	★★	★★	★★		★★
Bur. of Personnel....	(h)	★		★★		★★	★★	★	★★
Rhode Island.........	(h)	★★		★★		★★	★★		★
South Carolina.......	(i)	★★		★	★	★	★	★	
South Dakota	G	★★	★	★★	(j)	★★	★★	★★	★
Tennessee...........	G	★★		★★		★★	★★	★★	★
Texas...............	G	★★		★★		★★	★★		
Utah................	G	★★		★★	★★	★★	★★	★★	★★
Vermont	G	★★	★★	★★	★★	★★	★★	★★	
Virginia.............	G	★	★★★	★★	★★	★★	★★	★★	
Washington	G(k)	★★	★★	★★	★★	★★	★★	★★	
West Virginia	G(l)	★★		★★	★★	★★	★★	★	
Wisconsin	G			★★		★★	★★		
Wyoming............	G								
Puerto Rico	G					(m)			

THE OFFICE OF STATE PERSONNEL ADMINISTRATOR—Continued

Source: Information derived from survey of state personnel offices conducted by The Council of State Governments (March 1986) for the National Association of State Personnel Executives.

Key:

B—Appointment by personnel board
D—Appointment by department head
G—Appointment by governor

(a) Other responsibilities specified:

Alabama—appoints employees of Personnel Board; serves as secretary to Board.

Arizona—administers personnel rules and policies.

California—(State Personnel Board)—(oversees all aspects of merit employment. (Department of Personnel Administration)—represents governor in bargaining with employee representatives; administers training, performance evaluation, benefit, labor relations, and staff reduction programs.

Connecticut—supervises affirmative action activities; conducts collective bargaining negotiations and labor management programs; administers management relations and personnel development programs, job analysis and evaluation, workers' compensation.

Delaware—administers affirmative action programs; development and training; coordinates labor reductions for the executive branch.

Florida—represents governor in collective bargaining negotiations; supports state agency employee training programs; administers group insurance, retirement benefit programs.

Georgia—administers health insurance plan; coordinates training programs, deferred compensation plan; serves as secretary to Personnel Board; central payroll.

Hawaii—conducts recruitment and examinations, training and safety programs, classification and compensation review, employee services, labor relations.

Illinois—negotiates collective bargaining agreements.

Indiana—administers affirmative action, rules, medical-dental plans for employees, training and continuing education; publishes newsletter; processes applications; performance appraisals; approves payroll; establishes new personnel programs and policies.

Maine—administers all aspects of employee relations and collective bargaining, workers' compensation program, and training and development programs.

Maryland—administers equal opportunity employment program; adjudicates employee grievances and appeal of disciplinary actions; administers state employee training and development program, and health benefits.

Michigan—administers employee benefits, rules of employment conditions, employee development and assistance, grievance and unfair labor practices charges, technical appeals (including selection and classification issues); regulates collective bargaining system; conducts representation elections for exclusive collective bargaining agents.

Minnesota—negotiates contracts with 16 bargaining units; represents state in labor disputes.

Missouri—recommends pay plan revisions for approval by the Board and governor; directs central training function for all state agencies; participates in central labor relations; develops standard perfor-

mance appraisal system for the state.

Montana—collective bargaining supervisor; administers health benefits, deferred compensation, training and award programs, affirmative action.

Nebraska—promulgates system rules and regulations; administers health and life insurance benefits; coordinates labor relations programs.

New York—oversees agency affirmative action programs under governor's order; administers health insurance programs.

North Dakota—administers statewide appeal mechanism.

Oregon—maintains personnel system statewide.

Pennsylvania—(Civil Service Commission)—appoints staff; attends Commission meetings; recommends rules and amendments; investigates impact of Civil Service Act; appoints deputy; makes biennial report. (Bureau of Personnel)—develops personnel policy for all agencies under governor's jurisdiction; reviews and evaluates personnel programs; develops and administers senior management executive programs; administers training programs; negotiates collective bargaining.

Tennessee—administers provisions of Civil Service Act, rules of the Department of Personnel, including employment practices, classification, compensation, job performance planning and evaluation, attendance and leave, affirmative action, appeals and grievance procedures; acts as secretary of Civil Service Commission.

Utah—establishes rules and regulations.

Vermont—negotiates collective bargaining agreements; administers employee benefits; handles employee grievances.

(b) Selected by Iowa Merit Employment Commission.
(c) Appointed by the Louisiana Civil Service Commission following a competitive examination.
(d) Massachusetts' Civil Service Commission submits three names to the secretary of administration and finance who appoints the personnel administrator with the governor's consent. The personnel administrator is limited to a four-year term.
(e) From candidates certified by the Personnel Advisory Board.
(f) Selected through procedures specified in the Montana recruitment and selection rules.
(g) Director of Office of Management and Budget makes final choice from among the candidates presented by the State Personnel Board.
(h) Selected by competitive examination.
(i) Selected by State Budget and Control Board, a five-member board chaired by the governor.
(j) Decentralized personnel system.
(k) From three candidates recommended by the Personnel Board.
(l) From list of eligible candidates following competitive examination.
(m) Information not available.

Table 7.2

STATE PERSONNEL ADMINISTRATION: STRUCTURE AND FUNCTIONS

State or other jurisdiction	Legal basis for personnel department	Organizational status — Separate agency	Organizational status — Part of a larger agency	Human resource planning	Classification	Recruitment	Selection	Performance evaluation	Promotion	Employee assistance and counseling	Human resource development and training	Affirmative action	Labor and employee relations	Grievance and appeals	Compensation	Retirement
Alabama	C,S	★			•	★		•	•	•		•	★	★	★	★	
Alaska	C,S		★			•	•		•	★		•	★	•		•	
Arizona	S		★			•	•	★	•			•				•	
Arkansas	S		★			•	•	•		•			•	•	•	•	•
California																	
State Personnel Bd.	C,S,E	★			★	★	★	★	★	★			★	★	★	★	★
Dept. of Personnel Admin.	S	★														★	
Colorado	C,S,E	★		★	★	★	★	★	★	★		★	★	★	★	★	•
Connecticut	S	•	★		•	★	★			★		★	★	•	★	•	★
Delaware	S	•	★		•	★	★		•	★		★	★	•	★	•	
Florida	S	•	★		•	•	★		•	•		★	•	★	★	•	
Georgia	C,S	•	★		•	★	★		•	★	★	★	★	•	★	•	★
Hawaii	C,S	★			•	•	★	★	★	★	•	★	★	★	★	★	★
Idaho	S	★			•	•	★		•				•	•	•	•	★
Illinois	S		•			•	★		•	•		★	•	•	★	•	
Indiana	S		★		•	•	★		•	•		•	•	•	•	•	
Iowa	S		★			•	•		•	•		•	★	•	•	•	
Kansas	S		•	★	★	•	★			•		•	★	•	★	•	
Kentucky	C		★			•	★		•	•		•	•	•	★	•	
Louisiana	C		★			•	★		★	★	★	•	★	•	★	•	
Maine	S		★			★	★		★	•	★	•	•	•	★	•	
Maryland	S		•	★		•	★			•		★	•	•	•	•	•
Massachusetts	S	★				•	★	★	★	★	★	★	★	•	★	★	
Michigan	C	★			•	•	★	★	★	★	★	★	★	★	★	•	•
Minnesota	S	★			•	•	★	★	★	★	•	★	★	★	★	•	
Mississippi	S	★				•	★	★	•	•		•	•	•	★	•	
Missouri	C,S	★			•	•	★	★	•	•		•	•	★	•	•	
Montana	S		•		★	•	•		•	•		•	•	•	•	•	
Nebraska	S	★				•	•		•	•		★	★	•	•	•	
Nevada	S	★				•	•		•	•		•	•	★	•	•	•
New Hampshire	S		★		★	•	★		•	•	•	•	•	★	•	•	
New Jersey	C,S		•			•	•		★	•		•	•	•	•	•	
New Mexico	S	★			★	•	•		•	★	★	★	•	•	★	•	
New York	C,S,E(b)	★		★	•	•	•		★	•	•	★	★	★	★	•	
North Carolina	S			★	★	•	•		•	★	★	★	•	•	•	•	
North Dakota	S		★			•	•		•	★	•	★	•	★	★	★	★
Ohio	C		★		★	•	•		★	★	★	★	★	★	•	★	★

STATE PERSONNEL ADMINISTRATION: STRUCTURE AND FUNCTIONS—Continued

State or other jurisdiction	Legal basis for personnel department	Organizational status — Separate agency	Organizational status — Part of a larger agency	Human resource planning	Classification	Recruitment	Selection	Performance evaluation	Promotion	Employee assistance and counseling	Human resource development and training	Affirmative action	Labor and employee relations	Grievance and appeals	Compensation	Retirement
Oklahoma	S	★		★ •	★ •	• ★	★ ★	★ ★	★	• ★	★ ★	★	★ ★	★	• ★	
Oregon	S															
Pennsylvania																
Civil Service Comm.	S	★		★ ★	• •	★ ★	★ ★		★	★ ★		• •	• •	• •	★	
Bur. of Personnel	E		★	★ ★	• •	★ ★	★ ★	•	• •	• •	• •	• •	• •	• •	• •	
Rhode Island	C		★	★ •	• •	★ ★	★ ★	•	• •	• •	• •	•	•	•	• ★	
South Carolina	S		★	•	• •	• •	•	•	•	•	•	•	•	• ★	• •	
South Dakota	S	★		★ •	• •	• •	★ ★	★ ★	• •	• •	• •	★ •	• •	★ ★	★ •	
Tennessee	S	★ ★		★ ★	• •	★ •	★ ★		• •	• •	• •	★ •	• •	•	★ ★	•
Texas	S															
Utah	S		★ ★	★ ★	• •	• ★	• ★	• ★	• •	★ ★	• ★	• ★	• ★	★ ★	• •	•
Vermont	S		★ ★	★	• •	• •	• •	•	• •	• •	• •	• ★	• •	★ ★	• •	
Virginia	S	★		★	• ★	• •	• •	• •	★ •	• •	★ ★	★ ★	• •	: :	• •	
Washington	S	★			• •	• •	• •	• •	• :	• •	★ •	★ ★	• ★	★ ★	★ •	
West Virginia	S	★ ★			• •	• •	• •	• •	: :	★ ★	• •	★ ★	• •	★ ★	• •	•
Wisconsin	S	★ ★			• •	• •	• •	• •	: :	• •	★ ★	★ ★	• •	: :	• •	
Wyoming			★	•	•	•	•	: :	★ •	: :	•	•	: :	•	•	
Puerto Rico	S				•										•	

Source: Information derived from survey of state personnel offices conducted by The Council of State Governments (March 1986) for the National Association of State Personnel Executives.

Key:
C—Constitution
S—Statute
E—Executive order
(a) In these columns: ★—function performed in personnel department;
•—function centralized in personnel department.
(b) Also, Civil Service Commission regulations.
(c) Decentralized system.

Table 7.3
CLASSIFICATION AND COMPENSATION PLANS

	Classification plan:				
State or other jurisdiction	*Legal basis for plan*	*Current number of classifications*	*Requirement for periodic comprehensive review of plan(a)*	*Date of most recent comprehensive review*	*Legal basis for compensation plan*
Alabama...............	(b)	1,340	★/5	1982	S,R
Alaska.................	S	1,000	. . .	1985	S
Arizona................	S,R	1,450	. . .	1986(c)	S,R
Arkansas	S	2,100	. . .	1980	S
California..............	C,S	4,400	★/2	. . .	S
Colorado	C,S	1,600	. . .	1975(d)	C,S
Connecticut	S	2,500	. . .	1986(c)	S,CB
Delaware	S	1,100	. . .	1986	S
Florida	S	1,839	. . .	1985	S
Georgia................	S	1,500	. . .	1978	S
Hawaii	S,R	1,583	. . .	1985	S,R
Idaho	S	1,100	★/2	. . .	S
Illinois................	S	1,600	. . .	1986(c)	S
Indiana	S	1,525	. . .	1986(c)	S
Iowa	S	810	. . .	1985	S
Kansas	S,R	1,200	. . .	1986(c)	S,R
Kentucky	S,R	1,442	. . .	1982	S,R
Louisiana	C	2,440	. . .	1986	C
Maine	S	1,497	★/10	1982	CB
Maryland	S	3,000	. . .	1982	S
Massachusetts	S	N.A.	. . .	1980	S,CB
Michigan	C	1,766	. . .	1980	C
Minnesota	S	1,600	. . .	1986(c)	S,CB
Mississippi	S	1,700	. . .	1986(c)	S
Missouri	S,R	1,080(e)	. . .	(f)	S
Montana...............	S,R	1,500	. . .	1985	S,R
Nebraska	S	1,300	. . .	1969	S
Nevada	S	1,200	★/5	1986(c)	S
New Hampshire	S	1,470	. . .	1950	S
New Jersey.............	S,R	6,500	. . .	1986(c)	S,R
New Mexico............	S	800	. . .	. . .	S
New York	S	7,300	. . .	1954	S
North Carolina	S	3,012	. . .	1949	S
North Dakota	S	960	. . .	1986(c)	S
Ohio	S	1,737	. . .	1976	S
Oklahoma	S	1,136	. . .	1981	S
Oregon	S	1,185	. . .	1986(c)	S
Pennsylvania	S,R,E	2,700	. . .	1970	S,R,E
Rhode Island	S	1,500	. . .	1957	S
South Carolina	S	2,400	. . .	1979	S
South Dakota	S,R	579	. . .	1986	S,R
Tennessee	S	1,409	. . .	1984	S
Texas..................	S	1,324(e)	★/1	(g)	S
Utah	S	2,100	★/(c)	1986(c)	S
Vermont	S	1,063	. . .	1986(c)	S
Virginia................	S	2,100	. . .	1980	S
Washington	S	2,400	. . .	1986(c)	S
West Virginia	S	950	. . .	1986	S
Wisconsin..............	S	2,011	. . .	1947	S
Wyoming	S	1,350	. . .	1976	S
Puerto Rico	S	1,131	. . .	1986(c)	S

Source: Information derived from survey of state personnel offices conducted by The Council of State Governments (March 1986) for the National Association of State Personnel Executives.
Key:
C—Constitution
S—Statute
R—Regulation
E—Executive order
CB—Collective bargaining
N.A.—Not available
(a) In this column, number after slash represents frequency (in years) of required review.
(b) Authorization from state personnel board rules.
(c) Ongoing review. In Illinois, ongoing since 1969.
(d) Incremental reviews have been conducted, based on 1975 comprehensive review.
(e) Legal limit on number of classifications. Missouri—1,100; Texas—1,324.
(f) No comprehensive reviews; only reviews of sections of plan.
(g) With budget review.

Table 7.4
SELECTED EMPLOYEE LEAVE POLICIES

State or other jurisdiction	Annual leave accrual (in days per year) first year	Annual leave accrual (in days per year) fifth year	Sick leave accrual (in days per year)	Maternity leave — Treated as sick leave and/or annual leave or leave without pay	Maternity leave — Other provision(a)	Paternity leave — Treated as sick leave and/or annual leave or leave without pay	Paternity leave — Other provision(b)
Alabama	13	16.25	13	★	...	...	* ...
Alaska	15	18	15	...	★	...	...
Arizona	12	15	12	★	...	...	...
Arkansas	12	18	12	★	...	...	...
California	10	15	12	...	★	...	...
Colorado	12	15	15	★	...	★	...
Connecticut	12	15	15	★	...	★(c)	...
Delaware	15	15	15	★	...	★	...
Florida	13	16	13	★	...	...	...
Georgia	15	15	15	★	...	...	...
Hawaii	21	21	21	...	★	...	★
Idaho	12	15	12	★	...	...	...
Illinois	10	10	12	★	...	...	...
Indiana	12	15	6(d)	★	...	...	...
Iowa	12	17	18	★	...	...	★
Kansas	12	15	12	★	...	...	★
Kentucky	11	11	12	★	...	...	★
Louisiana	12	18	12	...	...	...	...
Maine	12	15	12	...	★	...	...
Maryland	10	10	15	★	...	...	...
Massachusetts	10	15	15	★	...	...	...
Michigan	13	15	13	...	...	...	...
Minnesota	13(e)	13(e)	13	★	...	★	...
Mississippi	18	21	12	...	...	★	...
Missouri	15	15	15	★	...	...	...
Montana	15	15	12	...	...	...	...
Nebraska	12	15	12	★	...	...	★
Nevada	15	15	15	★	...	★	...
New Hampshire	12	15	15	★	...	...	...
New Jersey	12	15	15	★	...	★	...
New Mexico	15	15	12	...	...	...	...
New York	14	18	13	★	...	★	...
North Carolina	11.75	16.75	12	★	...	...	★
North Dakota	12	15	12	★	...	...	...
Ohio	10	10	7	★	...	★	...
Oklahoma	15	18	15	★	...	★	...
Oregon	12	15	12	★	...	★	...
Pennsylvania	10.4(f)	15.6(f)	13	★	...	★	...
Rhode Island	10	15	15	...	★	...	...
South Carolina	15	15	15	★	...	...	...
South Dakota	15	15	14	★	...	...	...
Tennessee	12	18	12	★	...	...	...
Texas	10.5	13.5	12	★	...	★	...
Utah	13	13	13	★	...	...	...
Vermont	12	15	12	...	★	★	...
Virginia	12	15	15	★	...	★	...
Washington	12	15	12	★	...	★	...
West Virginia	15	18	18	★	...	...	...
Wisconsin	10	15	13	★	...	★	...
Wyoming	12	15	12	...	...	...	...
Puerto Rico	30	30	18	...	★	...	...

Source: Information derived from survey of state personnel offices conducted by The Council of State Governments (March 1986) for the National Association of State Personnel Executives.

Note: For information on holidays, see Table 7.5, "State Employees: Paid Holidays."

(a) Formal provision for maternity leave—Alaska, California, Vermont, Puerto Rico. After using sick leave, employee can acquire "child care" leave—Hawaii. Determined by union contract—Maine, Rhode Island.

(b) After using sick leave, employee can acquire "child care" leave—Hawaii. Annual leave available for family needs—Iowa and Kansas (five days), Kentucky (varies). Contingent upon approval of agency head—Nebraska, North Carolina.

(c) Three days of sick leave as paternity leave.

(d) Full-time employees with over five years of service, who have used all annual and sick leave, may apply for sick leave at the rate of one week for each year of service.

(e) Managerial personnel receive 19 1/2 days.

(f) As part of a collective bargaining agreement, new state employees (those hired since July 1, 1985) receive only 5.2 annual leave days in their first year of employment, and 10.4 in their fifth year.

Table 7.5
STATE EMPLOYEES: PAID HOLIDAYS*

State or other jurisdiction	Major holidays(a)	Martin Luther King's Birthday(b)	Lincoln's Birthday	Washington's Birthday(c)	Good Friday	Memorial Day(d)	Columbus Day(e)	Veterans Day	Day after Thanksgiving	Day before or after Christmas	Day before or after New Year's	Election Day(f)	Other(g)
Alabama	★		★★	★★★★			★	★★★★					★★
Alaska	★		★	★		★	★	★					★
Arizona	★			★		★		★					
Arkansas	★	★(h)	★	★		★	★	★	★	Before			★
California	★			★		★		★					★
Colorado	★	★		★		★	★	★					
Connecticut	★	★	★	★	★	★	★	★				★	
Delaware	★	★	★	★	★	★	★	★	★(i)	After (i)		★	★
Florida	★			★(i)		★	★	★					★
Georgia	★	★		★(i)		★			★				
Hawaii	★	★(i)	★(i)	★(i)		★	★(j)	★					
Idaho	★	★		★	★	★	★	★				★	★
Illinois	★		★(i)	★(i)(l)	★	★	★	★		After (l)		★(k)	★
Indiana	★					★	★	★	★				★
Iowa	★												
Kansas	★	★	★	★		★		★	★★	After (n)		★	★★
Kentucky	★				★(m)	★		★	★	(n)	(n)	★(o)	
Louisiana	★				★	★		★				★	
Maine	★	★	★	★	★	★	★	★					
Maryland	★					★							
Massachusetts	★	★	★	★		★	★	★	★★				
Michigan	★					★		★					★(p)
Minnesota	★					★		★	★				★(p)
Mississippi	★					★		★					★
Missouri	★	★	★	★	★	★	★	★				★(q)	★
Montana	★					★	★	★	★				
Nebraska	★			★		★		★	★			★	★(r)
Nevada	★	★		★		★	★(s)	★		Before			★(s)
New Hampshire	★	★		★		★	★	★	★			★(s)	★(s)
New Jersey	★	★	★	★	★	★	★	★				★	
New Mexico	★								★(i)	(i)		★	★
New York	★	★★	★★	★(i)		★	★	★	★	(i)			★
North Carolina	★	★		★		★	★	★					★
North Dakota	★	★		★		★	★	★		(t)			★
Ohio	★	★				★		★					
Oklahoma	★					★			★	After		★	★
Oregon	★	★★★★	★	★★★		★★★★	★★	★★★★					
Pennsylvania	★	★★		★		★	★	★				★	
Rhode Island	★	★		★		★							
South Carolina	★★			★		★★	★★	★★★	★	After		★★	★

STATE EMPLOYEES: PAID HOLIDAYS—Continued

State or other jurisdiction	Major holidays(a)	Martin Luther King's Birthday(b)	Lincoln's Birthday	Washington's Birthday(c)	Good Friday	Memorial Day(d)	Columbus Day(e)	Veterans Day	Day after Thanksgiving	Day before or after Christmas	Day before or after New Year's	Election Day(f)	Other(g)
South Dakota	★			★		★		★					★
Tennessee	★	★		★	★	★	★	★					
Texas	★			★		★		★					★
Utah	★		★	★		★	★	★					★
Vermont	★		★	★		★	★	★					★
Virginia	★	(u)		★		★	★ (v)	★					★
Washington	★	★	★	★		★		★	★				
West Virginia	★	★		★		★	★	★		Before	Before	★	★
Wisconsin	★	★			(m)	★			(w)			(k)	
Wyoming	★			★		★		★				★	
Dist. of Col.	★	★		★		★	★	★					★
American Samoa	★			★	★	★	★	★					★
Guam	★			★	★	★	★	★		Before		★	★
No. Mariana Is.	★			★		★	★	★					★
Puerto Rico	★			★	★	★	★	★		(x)		★	★
Virgin Islands	★	★	★	★	★	★	★	★				★	★

*Holidays in addition to any other authorized paid personal leave granted state employees.

Note: In some states, the governor may proclaim additional holidays or select from a number of holidays for observance by state employees. In some states, the list of paid holidays is determined by the personnel department at the beginning of each year; as a result, the number of holidays may change from year to year. Number of paid holidays may also vary across some employee classifications.

Key:

. . .—Paid holiday not granted.

(a) New Year's Day, Independence Day, Labor Day, Thanksgiving Day, and Christmas Day.

(b) With the adoption of Martin Luther King's birthday as a federal holiday, other states may be in the process of adding the day to their list of paid holidays.

(c) Third Monday in February. In some states, the holiday is called President's Day or Washington-Lincoln Day.

(d) Last Monday in May in all states indicated, except Delaware, Maryland, New Hampshire, New Mexico, South Dakota and Vermont, where holiday is observed on May 30.

(e) Second Monday in October.

(f) General election day only, unless otherwise indicated.

(g) Additional holidays:

Alabama—Robert E. Lee's Birthday (Jan. 20), Mardi Gras Day (varies), Thomas Jefferson's Birthday (April 14), Confederate Memorial Day (April 28), Jefferson Davis' Birthday (June 2).

Alaska—Seward's Day (last Mon. in March), Alaska Day (Oct. 18).

Arkansas—Robert E. Lee's Birthday (and Martin Luther King's) (Jan. 20), employee's birthday.

Colorado—Colorado Day (Aug. 4).

Georgia—Robert E. Lee's Birthday (Jan. 20), Confederate Memorial Day (April 28).

Hawaii—Prince Jonah Kuhio Kalanianaole Day (March 26), King Kamehameha Day (June 11), Admission Day (Aug. 15).

Louisiana—Mardi Gras Day (varies), Inauguration Day (every four years, in Baton Rouge only).

Maine—Patriot's Day (April 21).

Maryland—Maryland Day (March 25).

Massachusetts—Evacuation Day (March 17) in Suffolk County only, Patriot's Day (April 21), Bunker Hill Day (June 17).

Mississippi—Robert E. Lee's Birthday (Jan. 20), Confederate Memorial Day (April 28), Jefferson Davis' Birthday (June 2).

Missouri—Harry Truman's Birthday (May 8).

Nebraska—Arbor Day (April 22).

Nevada—Admissions Day (Oct. 31).

New Hampshire—Fast Day (April 28).

North Carolina—Easter Monday.

Rhode Island—Victory Day (2nd Mon. in Aug.).

South Dakota—Pioneer Day (2nd Mon. in Oct.).

Texas—Confederate Heroes' Day (Jan. 19- not observed on another day if falls on weekend), Texas Independence Day (March 2-not observed on another day if falls on weekend), Lyndon Johnson's Birthday (Aug. 27), Sesquicentennial Day (April 21), Emancipation Day (June 19).

Utah—Pioneer Day (July 24).

Vermont—Town Meeting Day (1st Tues. in March), Battle of Bennington Day (Aug. 5).

Virginia—Lee/Jackson Day (3rd Mon. in Jan., same as Martin Luther King's Birthday).

West Virginia—West Virginia Day (June 20).

District of Columbia—Inauguration Day (every 4 years).

American Samoa—Flag Day (April 17).

Guam—Guam Discovery Day (1st Mon. in March), Liberation Day (July 21), Lady of Camarin Day (Dec. 8).

Northern Mariana Islands—Commonwealth Day (Jan. 9), Covenant Day (March 24), Constitution Day (Dec. 8).

Puerto Rico—Three Kings Day (Jan. 6), DeHostos' Birthday (Jan. 11), Jose de Diego's Birthday (April 16), Luis Munoz Rivera's Birthday (July 17), Commonwealth Constitution Day (July 25), Jose C. Barbosa's Birthday (July 27), Discovery of Puerto Rico Day (Nov. 19).

Virgin Islands—Three Kings Day (Jan. 6), Transfer Day (March 31), Holy Thursday (varies), Easter Monday, Traditional Market Fair (3rd Tues. after Easter), Carnival Children's Parade (3rd Fri. after Easter), Organic Act Day (3rd Mon. in June), Emancipation Day (July 3), Hurricane Supplication Day (4th Mon. in July), Local Thanksgiving (3rd Mon. in Oct.).

(h) On Robert E. Lee's Birthday.

(i) Because legislature was in session during their normal occurrences, the paid holidays of Robert E. Lee's and Washington's Birthdays in Georgia and Lincoln's and Washington's Birthdays in Indiana and New Mexico will be observed instead on Nov. 28 (day after Thanksgiving) and Dec. 26 (day after Christmas); also in Indiana, Martin Luther King's birthday will be observed on Dec. 31 (New Year's Eve).

(j) Discoverer's Day.

(k) Also, primary election day.

(l) Floating holidays.

(m) Half days.

(n) One extra day designated for each holiday.

(o) Presidential election day only.

(p) One floating holiday.

(q) One day for any general, primary or other state election.

(r) Governor has option to create two additional holidays.

(s) State offices remain open; employees receive three floating holidays in lieu of these statutory holidays.

(t) One or two days depending on whether days preceding or following Christmas are normally workdays.

(u) Martin Luther King's Birthday *and* Lee/Jackson Day.

(v) And Yorktown Victory Day.

(w) Before Thanksgiving.

(x) Half day before and full day after.

COMPARABLE WORTH IN STATE GOVERNMENT: 1984-85

By Keon S. Chi

Comparable worth—the doctrine of equal pay for work of comparable value—continued to be a controversial issue in state government during the 1984-85 biennium. The issue was considered by many states and adopted by a few as a new approach to internal pay equity, aiming not only at equal pay for equal work, but also equal pay for comparable work as well.

Comparable worth proponents hold that sex-based wage differentials can be closed if an employer pays women according to the value of their work to the employer. The value of work is assessed by objective criteria, using such factors as required knowledge, demands or problem-solving, accountability, and working conditions.

The controversy over comparable worth dates back to 1974 when a consultant conducted a study for Washington state government. The now-famous Willis study showed that employees working in female-dominated job classes were paid approximately 20 percent less than those in male-dominated job classes for work of comparable value. It was not until 1981, however, that comparable worth legislation was introduced in Washington and other states.

Legislation

Between 1981 and 1983, at least 15 states considered comparable worth-related bills at some level (see Table 7.6). In 1984, comparable worth legislation was filed in 26 state legislatures. Of those, seven states defeated bills, and one tabled a bill for further study. During the 1985 legislative sessions, comparable worth bills were introduced in 24 states—in some states for the second or third time.

In all, between 1981 and 1985, comparable worth bills were filed in 38 state legislatures. By the end of 1985, at least eight states had funded comparable worth legislation; 16 states had agreed to study the issue; 13 states had defeated or tabled comparable worth bills; and 10 states had undertaken studies of classification and compensation issues without comparable worth legislation.

Lawsuits

Between 1981 and 1985, sex-based discrimination complaints and lawsuits were filed against 10 states: California, Connecticut, Delaware, Hawaii, Illinois, Michigan, Missouri, Rhode Island, Washington, and Wisconsin.

The most publicized case involved the state of Washington. In December 1983, in *AFSCME v. State of Washington* (No. 84-3569), Judge Jack E. Tanner, U.S. District Court for the Western District of Washington, ruled that the state had discriminated against women employees on the basis of sex. The judge ordered the state to award back pay to 15,500 employees in the predominantly-female job classes.

In December 1985, Judge Anthony Kennedy of the U.S. Court of Appeals for the Ninth Circuit, reversed the Tanner decision, by stating that the 1964 Civil Rights Act did not require the state to eliminate a pay gap. Earlier, in July 1984, the same court had ruled in *Spaulding v. University of Washington* (No. 82-3038) that the state was not guilty of the sex-discrimination charge brought by the nursing faculty members.

The largest lawsuit over comparable worth was filed in November 1984 by a California state employees group on behalf of 38,000 workers—in jobs predominantly held by women—seeking back pay and salary adjustments. In September 1985, U.S. District Court Judge Marilyn H. Patel rejected the argument by the state of California to drop the lawsuit, *California State Employees Association v. State of California* (No. C-84-7275 MHP).

At the federal level, comparable worth was not received favorably. In April 1985, the U.S. Commission on Civil Rights voted 5-2 to reject the idea of comparable worth, and urged Congress and federal agencies to do the same. And in June 1985, the Equal Employment Opportunity Commission ruled

Keon S. Chi is a Research Associate for The Council of State Governments.

that it would not act on behalf of women who allege sex-based discrimination in pay on the basis of comparable worth.

Implementation

During 1984-85, a few states began implementing comparable worth for their employees. In 1983, the Washington Legislature appropriated $1.5 million for fiscal 1984-85 to give pay raises to employees whose salaries were eight pay ranges below the comparable worth line. The legislature also passed a bill aiming at full implementation of comparable worth by 1993.

Under the first-year plan in 1984, approximately 20,000 of 45,000 state workers received an extra $8.33 per month ($100 per year). In 1985, the legislature appropriated another $3.9 million for comparable worth for fiscal 1985-86, and set aside $41.5 million for distribution beginning in July 1987—contingent upon a negotiated settlement of the lawsuit brought against the state by the American Federation of State, County and Municipal Employees (AFSCME). The legislature also authorized the hire of a consultant to conduct a review of the civil service system to correct gender pay gaps.

In December 1985, settlement was reached between the state and AFSCME and the Washington Federation of State Employees to use the $41.5 million to provide increases for all classified employees eligible for comparable worth raises. Under this agreement, comparable worth will be achieved by July 1992, one year earlier than initially required by the state legislature. The parties also agreed to dismiss the litigation in *AFSCME v. State of Washington.*

Minnesota is expected to achieve pay equity by 1987. In fiscal 1983-84, the state provided 8,225 employees in 157 classes with $21.8 million—an average of $1,600 for each employee. For fiscal 1986-87, the state legislature appropriated $11.8 million for pay equity. Nearly 9,500 employees in 144 job classes are scheduled to receive pay equity raises through the collective bargaining process. In Minnesota, all local units of government are also required to implement pay equity for their employees.

The 1985 Iowa General Assembly appropriated $22.6 million to implement the state's comparable worth plan for the period March 1985 to June 1986. The legislature,

the governor, and the state employees union reached an agreement in August 1985 after months of negotiations and a stalemate that prevented the spending of a $10 million appropriation approved during the 1984 legislative session. Under the Iowa plan, employees in the executive branch, higher education, and the judicial branch are expected to receive comparable worth pay raises. The legislative branch also is expected to implement comparable worth based on its own job evaluations.

The 1985 Wisconsin Legislature appropriated $9.1 million for comparable worth in the 1986-87 budget. Payment was expected to start in July 1986, contingent upon the governor's and the legislature's acceptance of recommendations made by the state's Task Force on Comparable Worth.

In addition, several other states adopted alternative ways to achieve comparable worth. For example, Massachusetts began implementing pay equity through executive initiatives, supplementing budgets, and collective bargaining. Connecticut is implementing pay adjustments based on "objective job evaluations"; and New York is expected to spend $35 million in 1986 for pay equity, based on two consultants' studies.

In some states, however, comparable worth was not a priority during the biennium. In 1985, the New Mexico Legislature did not appropriate additional pay equity funds for fiscal 1986. In 1983, the state had elevated the salary ranges of 23 low-paid, female-dominated jobs, and appropriated $3.2 million for pay equity. In 1985, the North Carolina General Assembly terminated a comparable worth study authorized in 1984. The measure (HB 236) stated that "the very conceptual basis of the comparable worth method is flawed, invalid, and contradictory to sound economic principles, as economists, and business people on all sides of the political spectrum have pointed out."

The Issues

Comparable worth is a new concept, and involves a multitude of issues. Its proponents and opponents offer contrasting views on almost every question raised: Can dissimilar jobs be compared objectively? Should government set pay rates irrespective of market forces? Would comparable worth be a remedy for occupational sex segregation, which is regarded as being the main cause of wage disparities between male and female workers?

However, both proponents and opponents agree that comparable worth is different from the equal pay for equal work principle as defined in the federal Equal Pay Act of 1963. The question is whether comparable worth is legally applicable under the 1964 Civil Rights Act.

Comparable worth is a partisan issue. In 1984, comparable worth was an issue in the Democratic and Republican national party conventions. The Democrats adopted comparable worth in their platform, pledging "to take every step to close the wage gap," whereas the Republicans rejected the pay equity concept, stating that "the free market system can determine the value of jobs better than any government authority." The Democrats' dominance in state legislatures also is associated with the introduction of comparable worth bills.

One major administrative issue concerns the job evaluation method. Many states have used, or are considering using, a quantitative, job content evaluation approach. A job evaluation system usually involves four steps: completing job descriptions; selecting factors and subfactors; weighting factors and subfactors and assigning numerical values; and determining pay grades according to total scores. An alternative method is the "economic" approach, which would consider personal characteristics, such as training needed to acquire a necessary license or certificate, work experience, and seniority.

The cost of implementing comparable worth is a real concern to state policymakers. There seems to be no formula for calculating the cost, since it depends upon the number of employees eligible for comparable worth raises, the wage gap, and the method and timing of funding. The wage gaps reported by state studies range from 13 to 28 percent, with an average of about 20 percent. Minnesota reduced a sex-based wage gap from 20 to 10 percent in two years. And the state's cost of full pay equity implementation for state employees is expected to be 3.7 percent of the state payroll.

Comparable worth has emerged as a dynamic policy issue in the states. No matter which way a state is headed on this issue, policymakers will be monitoring its evolution during the next biennium.

Table 7.6
INTRODUCTION OF COMPARABLE WORTH BILLS
(As of July 1985)

State	Year comparable worth bills introduced in state legislature		
	1983 or earlier	1984	1985
Alabama	...	...	...
Alaska	...	...	★
Arizona	...	...	★
Arkansas	...	...	...
California	★	★	...
Colorado	...	★	★
Connecticut	★	★	★
Delaware	★	★	★
Florida	...	★	★
Georgia	...	...	...
Hawaii	...	★	...
Idaho	...	...	...
Illinois	★	★	★
Indiana	...	★	...
Iowa	★	★	★
Kansas	...	...	★
Kentucky		...	...
Louisiana	...	...	...
Maine	...	★	...
Maryland	...	★	...
Massachusetts	★	...	★
Michigan	...	★	...
Minnesota	★	★	★
Mississippi	...	...	...
Missouri	★	★	★
Montana	★	...	...
Nebraska	...	★	★
Nevada	★	★	...
New Hampshire	★	...	...
New Jersey	...	★	★
New Mexico	...	...	★
New York	★	...	...
North Carolina	...	★	★
North Dakota	...	...	★
Ohio	★	★	★
Oklahoma	...	...	...
Oregon	★	...	★
Pennsylvania	...	★	...
Rhode Island	...	★	★
South Carolina	...	...	...
South Dakota	...	...	...
Tennessee	...	...	...
Texas	...	...	★
Utah	...	...	...
Vermont	...	★	...
Virginia	...	★	...
Washington	★	★	★
West Virginia	...	★	...
Wisconsin	...	★	★
Wyoming	...	...	★

Key:
★—Bill introduced/filed.

Table 7.7
SUMMARY OF STATE GOVERNMENT EMPLOYMENT: 1952-1984

| | Employment (in thousands) | | | | | | Monthly payrolls (in millions of dollars) | | | Average monthly earnings of full-time employees | | |
| | Total, full-time and part-time | | | Full-time equivalent | | | | | | | | |
Year	All	Educa-tion	Other	All	Educa-tion	Other	All	Educa-tion	Other	All	Educa-tion	Other
October:												
1984.............	3,898	1,708	2,190	3,177	1,091	2,086	$5,814.9	$2,178.0	$3,637.0	$1,825	$1,991	$1,740
1983.............	3,816	1,666	2,150	3,116	1,072	2,044	5,345.5	1,989.0	3,357.0	1,711	1,850	1,640
1982.............	3,747	1,616	2,131	3,083	1,051	2,032	5,027.7	1,874.0	3,153.7	1,625	1,789	1,551
1981.............	3,726	1,603	2,123	3,087	1,063	2,024	4,667.5	1,768.0	2,899.5	1,507	1,671	1,432
1980.............	3,753	1,599	2,154	3,106	1,063	2,044	4,284.7	1,608.0	2,676.6	1,373	1,523	1,305
1979.............	3,699	1,577	2,122	3,072	1,046	2,026	3,869.3	1,451.4	2,417.9	1,257	1,399	1,193
1978.............	3,539	1,508	2,032	2,966	1,016	1,950	3,483.0	1,332.9	2,150.2	1,167	1,311	1,102
1977.............	3,491	1,484	2,007	2,903	1,005	1,898	3,194.6	1,234.4	1,960.1	1,096	1,237	1,031
1976.............	3,343	1,434	1,910	2,799	973	1,827	2,893.7	1,111.5	1,782.1	1,031	1,163	975
1975.............	3,271	1,400	1,870	2,744	952	1,792	2,652.7	1,021.7	1,631.1	964	1,080	909
1974.............	3,155	1,357	1,798	2,653	929	1,725	2,409.5	932.7	1,476.9	906	1,023	855
1973.............	3,013	1,280	1,733	2,547	887	1,660	2,158.2	822.2	1,336.0	843	952	805
1972.............	2,957	1,267	1,690	2,487	867	1,619	1,936.6	746.9	1,189.7	778	871	734
1971.............	2,832	1,223	1,609	2,384	841	1,544	1,741.7	681.5	1,060.2	731	826	686
1970.............	2,755	1,182	1,573	2,302	803	1,499	1,612.2	630.3	981.9	700	797	605
1969.............	2,614	1,112	1,501	2,179	746	1,433	1,430.5	554.5	876.1	655	743	597
1968.............	2,495	1,037	1,458	2,085	694	1,391	1,256.7	477.1	779.6	602	687	544
1967.............	2,335	940	1,395	1,946	620	1,326	1,105.5	406.3	699.3	567	666	526
1966.............	2,211	866	1,344	1,864	575	1,289	975.2	353.0	622.2	522	614	483
1965.............	2,028	739	1,289	1,751	508	1,243	849.2	290.1	559.1	484	571	450
1964.............	1,873	656	1,217	1,639	460	1,179	761.1	257.5	503.6	464	560	427
1963.............	1,775	602	1,173	1,558	422	1,136	696.4	230.1	466.3	447	545	410
1962.............	1,680	555	1,126	1,478	389	1,088	634.6	201.8	432.8	429	518	397
1961.............	1,625	518	1,107	1,435	367	1,068	586.2	192.4	393.8	409	482	383
1960.............	1,527	474	1,053	1,353	332	1,021	524.1	167.7	356.4	386	439	365
1959.............	1,454	443	1,011	1,302	318	984	485.4	136.0	349.4	373	427	352
1958.............	1,408	406	1,002	1,259	284	975	446.5	123.4	323.1	355	416	333
April 1957	1,300	375	925	1,153	257	896	372.5	106.1	266.4	320	355	309
1956.............	1,268	353	915	1,136	250	886	366.5	108.8	257.7	321	358	309
1955.............	1,199	333	866	1,081	244	837	325.9	88.5	237.4	302	334	290
1954.............	1,149	310	839	1,024	222	802	300.7	78.9	221.8	294	325	283
1953.............	1,082	294	788	966	211	755	278.6	73.5	205.1	289	320	278
1952.............	1,060	293	767	958	213	745	260.3	65.1	195.2	271	298	262

Source: U.S. Bureau of the Census, annual *Public Employment* reports.
Note: Because of rounding, detail may not add to totals.

Table 7.8
EMPLOYMENT AND PAYROLLS OF STATE AND LOCAL
GOVERNMENTS, BY FUNCTION: OCTOBER 1983

Function	All employees, full-time and part-time (in thousands)			October payrolls (in millions of dollars)			Average October earnings of full-time employees
	Total	State govern-ments	Local govern-ments	Total	State govern-ments	Local govern-ments	
All functions	13,159	3,816	9,344	$18,224	$5,346	$12,876	$1,678
Education:							
Higher education	1,908	1,548	360	2,193	1,807	386	1,901
Instructional personnel only	659	480	179	1,118	888	230	2,631
Elementary/secondary schools	4,789	24	4,765	6,667	35	6,633	1,683
Instructional personnel only	3,149	15	3,134	5,210	25	5,184	1,868
Local libraries	99	0	99	89	0	89	1,317
Other education	94	94	0	147	147	0	1,688
Selected functions:							
Highways	527	243	284	777	393	384	1,535
Public welfare	397	176	221	532	263	269	1,422
Hospitals	1,147	556	592	1,504	763	741	1,420
Health	252	114	138	378	190	188	1,645
Police protection.....................	671	76	595	1,145	145	1,000	1,900
Police officers only	499	51	449	965	108	857	2,031
Fire protection	310	0	310	477	0	477	2,079
Firefighters only	286	0	286	452	0	452	2,100
Natural resources	196	159	37	276	232	44	1,655
Correction	305	197	109	487	318	169	1,640
Social insurance administration	112	112	0	168	168	0	1,646
Financial administration	306	119	187	417	184	233	1,509
General control.......................	547	127	421	723	243	480	1,714
Local utilities........................	408	25	383	769	60	710	1,992

Source: U.S. Bureau of the Census, *Public Employment in 1983.*
Note: Statistics for local governments are estimates subject to sampling variation. Because of rounding, detail may not add to totals.

Table 7.9
EMPLOYMENT AND PAYROLLS OF STATE AND LOCAL
GOVERNMENTS, BY FUNCTION: OCTOBER 1984

Function	All employees, full-time and part-time (in thousands)			October payrolls (in millions of dollars)			Average October earnings of full-time employees
	Total	State govern-ments	Local govern-ments	Total	State govern-ments	Local govern-ments	
All functions	13,494	3,898	9,595	$19,767	$5,815	$13,952	$1,778
Education:							
Higher education	1,954	1,586	368	2,398	1,979	418	2,030
Instructional personnel only	684	498	186	1,218	967	251	2,795
Elementary/secondary schools	4,970	24	4,947	7,275	36	7,239	1,778
Instructional personnel only	3,217	15	3,202	5,646	27	5,620	1,971
Local libraries	107	0	107	100	0	100	1,365
Other education	98	98	0	163	163	0	1,794
Selected functions:							
Highways	540	248	293	850	431	419	1,638
Public welfare	407	179	228	568	278	290	1,489
Hospitals	1,126	556	570	1,583	815	768	1,515
Health	266	120	146	410	202	207	1,688
Police protection.....................	684	80	605	1,236	162	1,074	2,013
Police officers only	505	51	453	1,037	119	918	2,156
Fire protection	316	0	316	518	0	518	2,206
Firefighters only	291	0	291	491	0	491	2,229
Natural resources	195	158	37	288	242	46	1,739
Correction	332	215	117	557	364	193	1,722
Social insurance administration	105	105	0	174	174	0	1,768
Financial administration	314	126	187	454	208	246	1,600
General control.......................	567	134	433	790	270	520	1,812
Local utilities........................	410	25	384	819	64	755	2,083

Source: U.S. Bureau of the Census, *Public Employment in 1984.*
Note: Statistics for local governments are estimates subject to sampling variation. Because of rounding, detail may not add to totals.

Table 7.10
STATE AND LOCAL GOVERNMENT EMPLOYMENT, BY STATE: OCTOBER 1983

State or other jurisdiction	All employees (full-time and part-time)		Full-time equivalent employment					
			Number			Number per 10,000 population		
	State	Local	Total	State	Local	Total	State	Local
United States	3,815,618	9,343,812	10,884,547	3,115,944	7,768,603	465	133	332
Alabama	75,501	146,094	191,567	62,151	129,416	484	157	327
Alaska	23,082	20,822	39,011	21,498	17,513	814	449	366
Arizona	48,850	118,869	133,557	34,786	98,771	451	117	333
Arkansas	42,569	79,724	103,475	35,641	67,834	444	153	291
California	319,389	1,086,638	1,102,090	254,289	847,801	438	101	337
Colorado	59,007	132,045	149,685	42,245	107,440	477	135	342
Connecticut	54,364	105,112	135,196	46,098	89,098	431	147	284
Delaware	19,947	16,624	30,696	16,356	14,340	507	270	237
Florida	128,234	406,623	467,821	110,085	357,736	438	103	335
Georgia	96,367	255,817	310,436	83,717	226,719	542	146	396
Hawaii	46,466	12,495	49,054	37,364	11,690	480	365	114
Idaho	17,590	39,303	45,035	13,859	31,176	455	140	315
Illinois	144,835	459,490	483,723	114,485	369,238	421	100	321
Indiana	90,402	206,649	238,454	62,750	175,704	435	115	321
Iowa	55,400	127,815	142,037	43,466	98,571	489	150	339
Kansas	51,335	112,323	126,922	38,810	88,112	523	160	363
Kentucky	66,164	108,330	152,314	57,056	95,258	410	154	256
Louisiana	102,654	158,394	229,966	85,724	144,242	518	193	325
Maine	23,537	44,085	51,723	18,325	33,398	451	160	291
Maryland	86,825	163,486	214,359	77,262	137,097	498	180	319
Massachusetts	86,966	217,145	257,134	75,454	181,680	446	131	315
Michigan	150,566	363,186	391,341	113,855	277,486	432	126	306
Minnesota	72,348	181,364	194,079	53,817	140,262	468	130	338
Mississippi	47,124	102,871	129,319	40,704	88,615	500	157	343
Missouri	71,470	183,993	214,497	60,576	153,921	432	122	310
Montana	20,234	35,114	42,317	14,698	27,619	518	180	338
Nebraska	34,810	81,923	92,838	29,265	63,573	581	183	398
Nevada	13,352	34,764	42,181	11,819	30,362	473	133	341
New Hampshire	20,063	33,147	40,177	13,985	26,192	419	146	273
New Jersey	100,048	318,139	365,913	86,436	270,477	478	116	362
New Mexico	42,593	51,087	79,176	34,026	45,150	566	243	323
New York	272,497	860,513	974,119	250,278	723,841	551	142	410
North Carolina	103,494	249,141	289,229	87,832	201,397	476	144	331
North Dakota	17,887	34,785	34,005	13,039	20,966	500	192	308
Ohio	149,377	426,564	460,436	114,453	345,983	428	107	322
Oklahoma	73,939	121,908	169,852	61,449	108,403	515	186	329
Oregon	53,574	112,074	128,677	40,496	88,181	483	152	331
Pennsylvania	143,125	398,663	454,939	121,278	333,661	382	102	281
Rhode Island	27,075	26,642	44,374	20,834	23,540	465	218	246
South Carolina	64,766	113,786	157,068	58,318	98,750	481	179	303
South Dakota	16,198	31,066	33,783	11,843	21,940	483	169	313
Tennessee	76,408	168,341	212,781	63,731	149,050	454	136	318
Texas	216,583	625,781	744,177	180,681	563,496	473	115	358
Utah	35,186	55,150	69,757	27,818	41,939	431	172	259
Vermont	11,707	17,619	24,059	10,373	13,686	458	198	261
Virginia	115,644	200,720	267,005	94,029	172,976	481	169	312
Washington	91,874	145,836	193,847	67,305	126,542	451	157	294
West Virginia	41,175	65,783	94,713	34,034	60,679	482	173	309
Wisconsin	80,777	207,027	214,265	57,551	156,714	451	121	330
Wyoming	12,240	30,333	33,980	10,000	23,980	661	195	467
Dist. of Col.	0	48,609	46,388	0	46,388	735	0	735

Source: U.S. Bureau of the Census, *Public Employment in 1983.*
Note: Statistics for local governments are estimates subject to sampling variation. Because of rounding, detail may not add to totals.

Table 7.11
STATE AND LOCAL GOVERNMENT EMPLOYMENT, BY STATE: OCTOBER 1984

| State or other jurisdiction | All employees (full-time and part-time) | | Full-time equivalent employment | | | | | |
| | | | Number | | | Number per 10,000 population | | |
	State	Local	Total	State	Local	Total	State	Local
United States..........	3,898,307	9,595,340	11,143,230	3,177,199	7,966,031	472	135	337
Alabama................	76,219	145,362	191,676	64,007	127,669	480	160	320
Alaska.................	24,462	22,149	39,653	20,866	18,787	793	417	376
Arizona................	51,826	124,485	139,768	36,091	103,677	458	118	340
Arkansas	42,932	80,269	106,127	36,288	69,839	452	154	297
California..............	327,441	1,134,829	1,146,248	260,536	885,712	447	102	346
Colorado	59,154	136,123	153,254	42,122	111,132	482	133	350
Connecticut	57,112	105,982	139,014	48,461	90,553	441	154	287
Delaware	19,860	16,885	30,929	16,173	14,756	505	264	241
Florida	131,256	425,391	488,322	112,286	376,036	445	102	343
Georgia................	95,835	252,729	306,535	82,220	224,315	525	141	384
Hawaii	46,685	12,691	49,427	37,763	11,664	476	363	112
Idaho	18,556	39,715	45,711	14,636	31,075	457	146	310
Illinois.................	148,983	467,402	489,734	116,890	372,844	425	102	324
Indiana	91,942	214,494	241,760	65,661	176,099	440	119	320
Iowa	56,517	130,539	143,588	45,544	98,044	493	157	337
Kansas	52,182	116,111	127,777	38,848	88,929	524	159	365
Kentucky	69,608	113,620	158,292	59,247	99,045	425	159	266
Louisiana	100,656	166,374	235,454	86,193	149,261	528	193	335
Maine	24,149	43,975	52,355	18,718	33,637	453	162	291
Maryland	90,391	161,660	213,524	79,358	134,166	491	182	308
Massachusetts	87,439	215,212	256,464	75,340	181,124	442	130	312
Michigan	149,066	379,551	404,920	113,426	291,494	446	125	321
Minnesota	74,434	181,666	191,768	54,406	137,362	461	131	330
Mississippi	49,886	105,789	134,674	42,632	92,042	518	164	354
Missouri	72,778	187,132	219,336	61,497	157,839	438	123	315
Montana................	20,712	36,773	44,204	15,182	29,022	536	184	352
Nebraska	35,023	78,001	90,600	29,255	61,345	564	182	382
Nevada	14,605	35,497	43,837	12,559	31,278	481	138	343
New Hampshire	20,809	35,515	42,179	15,323	26,856	432	157	275
New Jersey.............	101,821	318,570	360,668	88,066	272,602	480	117	363
New Mexico............	41,131	52,893	79,789	32,254	47,535	560	227	334
New York	284,874	867,464	998,141	259,648	738,493	563	146	416
North Carolina	102,049	269,576	301,636	88,276	213,360	489	143	346
North Dakota	19,335	34,979	35,756	13,484	22,272	521	197	325
Ohio	151,328	430,665	463,314	113,314	350,000	431	105	326
Oklahoma	73,047	123,869	168,440	60,714	107,726	511	184	327
Oregon	54,465	114,094	129,816	41,292	88,524	485	154	331
Pennsylvania	143,718	395,286	452,958	121,881	331,077	381	102	278
Rhode Island	27,736	27,456	44,757	20,484	24,273	465	213	252
South Carolina	70,119	117,409	163,975	61,509	102,466	497	186	311
South Dakota	16,315	32,591	34,931	11,874	23,057	495	168	327
Tennessee	77,777	170,549	217,206	64,991	152,215	460	138	323
Texas..................	220,855	658,786	780,854	185,486	595,368	488	116	372
Utah	36,645	60,359	74,364	29,092	45,272	450	176	274
Vermont	12,100	18,438	24,602	10,496	14,106	464	198	266
Virginia................	117,155	213,343	277,242	94,849	182,393	492	168	324
Washington	96,788	157,231	204,784	71,702	133,082	471	165	306
West Virginia	42,531	65,373	95,383	34,798	60,585	489	178	310
Wisconsin	85,609	219,143	225,355	61,540	163,815	473	129	344
Wyoming	12,391	31,124	34,603	9,921	24,682	677	194	483
Dist. of Col.	0	50,221	47,526	0	47,526	763	0	763

Source: U.S. Bureau of the Census, *Public Employment in 1984*.
Note: Statistics for local governments are estimates subject to sampling variation. Because of rounding, detail may not add to totals.

Table 7.12
STATE AND LOCAL GOVERNMENT PAYROLLS AND
AVERAGE EARNINGS OF FULL-TIME EMPLOYEES,
BY STATE: OCTOBER 1983

State or other jurisdiction	Amount of payroll (in thousands of dollars)			Percentage of October payroll		Average earnings of full-time state and local government employees (dollars)		
	Total	State government	Local governments	State government	Local governments	All	Education employees	Other
United States	$18,223,631	$5,345,538	$12,878,094	29.3	70.7	$1,678	$1,727	$1,634
Alabama	254,052	97,851	156,200	38.5	61.5	1,326	1,361	1,296
Alaska	107,128	54,213	52,915	50.6	49.4	2,737	2,763	2,717
Arizona	242,480	63,538	178,943	26.2	73.8	1,820	1,838	1,800
Arkansas	126,299	50,775	75,524	40.2	59.8	1,218	1,243	1,191
California	2,314,977	532,615	1,782,362	23.0	77.0	2,106	2,151	2,074
Colorado	263,059	83,979	179,080	31.9	68.1	1,754	1,748	1,760
Connecticut	237,607	85,656	151,951	36.0	64.0	1,765	1,791	1,740
Delaware	48,147	25,360	22,787	52.7	47.3	1,558	1,693	1,442
Florida	734,360	199,246	535,114	27.1	72.9	1,579	1,571	1,585
Georgia	408,565	129,460	279,104	31.7	68.3	1,320	1,353	1,295
Hawaii	82,072	61,757	20,315	75.2	24.8	1,666	1,739	1,612
Idaho	63,850	22,022	41,827	34.5	65.5	1,422	1,408	1,436
Illinois	888,503	210,851	677,652	23.7	76.3	1,842	1,943	1,753
Indiana	356,867	111,293	245,574	31.2	68.8	1,483	1,654	1,290
Iowa	224,908	75,796	149,112	33.7	66.3	1.575	1,655	1,484
Kansas	180,411	57,320	123,091	31.8	68.2	1,423	1,461	1,382
Kentucky	213,316	85,733	127,583	40.2	59.8	1,410	1,484	1,325
Louisiana	316,266	125,677	190,589	39.7	60.3	1,377	1,468	1,295
Maine	70,701	27,736	42,964	39.2	60.8	1,368	1,331	1,413
Maryland	378,592	121,323	257,269	32.0	68.0	1,774	1,958	1,622
Massachusetts	436,696	121,446	315,250	27.8	72.2	1,706	1,784	1,645
Michigan	774,034	225,467	548,567	29.1	70.9	1,984	2,076	1,888
Minnesota	352,243	108,846	243,396	30.9	69.1	1,851	1,887	1,816
Mississippi	151,417	54,687	96,730	36.1	63.9	1,173	1,265	1,089
Missouri	307,245	83,664	223,582	27.2	72.8	1,432	1,501	1,372
Montana	68,593	24,851	43,743	36.2	63.8	1,630	1,784	1,480
Nebraska	134,275	38,839	95,436	28.9	71.1	1,453	1,429	1,474
Nevada	77,196	22,518	54,678	29.2	70.8	1,834	1,787	1,862
New Hampshire	57,016	21,075	35,940	37.0	63.0	1,419	1,429	1,407
New Jersey	629,111	156,530	472,582	24.9	75.1	1,767	1,980	1,571
New Mexico	116,092	50,358	65,734	43.4	56.6	1,463	1,531	1,395
New York	1,905,382	485,138	1,420,244	25.5	74.5	1,967	2,133	1,881
North Carolina	399,610	131,947	267,663	33.0	67.0	1,388	1,442	1,332
North Dakota	55,843	20,925	34,917	37.5	62.5	1,645	1,850	1,417
Ohio	722,297	175,639	546,658	24.3	75.7	1,579	1,677	1,488
Oklahoma	234,931	93,989	140,941	40.0	60.0	1,379	1,425	1,334
Oregon	224,845	74,452	150,392	33.1	66.9	1,744	1,711	1,774
Pennsylvania	739,483	200,271	539,212	27.1	72.9	1,632	1,698	1,574
Rhode Island	78,972	36,290	42,682	46.0	54.0	1,784	1,949	1,656
South Carolina	204,986	86,811	118,175	42.3	57.7	1,308	1,353	1,260
South Dakota	44,751	17,587	27,164	39.3	60.7	1,324	1,326	1,321
Tennessee	286,707	87,933	198,774	30.7	69.3	1,352	1,483	1,241
Texas	1,138,109	310,603	827,507	27.3	72.7	1,531	1,516	1,549
Utah	111,786	44,706	67,080	40.0	60.0	1,613	1,576	1,663
Vermont	34,973	16,895	18,078	48.3	51.7	1,451	1,426	1,481
Virginia	404,601	147,609	256,992	36.5	63.5	1,523	1,606	1,438
Washington	365,511	123,427	242,084	33.8	66.2	1,897	1,854	1,934
West Virginia	124,179	43,927	80,252	35.4	64.6	1,312	1,411	1,190
Wisconsin	367,183	98,262	268,921	26.8	73.2	1,724	1,765	1,682
Wyoming	58,446	18,641	39,805	31.9	68.1	1,723	1,837	1,615
Dist. of Col.	104,958	0	104,958	0.0	100.0	2,276	2,386	2,243

Source: U.S. Bureau of the Census, *Public Employment in 1983.*
Note: Statistics for local governments are estimates subject to sampling
variation. Because of rounding, detail may not add to totals.

Table 7.13
STATE AND LOCAL GOVERNMENT PAYROLLS AND AVERAGE EARNINGS OF FULL-TIME EMPLOYEES, BY STATE: OCTOBER 1984

State or other jurisdiction	Amount of payroll (in thousands of dollars)			Percentage of October payroll		Average earnings of full-time state and local government employees (dollars)		
	Total	State government	Local governments	State government	Local governments	All	Education employees	Other
United States.........	$19,766,832	$5,814,935	$13,951,898	29.4	70.6	$1,778	$1,830	$1,732
Alabama...............	282,025	111,648	170,377	39.6	60.4	1,478	1,522	1,438
Alaska................	117,236	57,832	59,404	49.3	50.7	2,958	3,106	2,859
Arizona...............	264,391	68,312	196,079	25.8	74.2	1,897	1,922	1,869
Arkansas	138,459	53,752	84,707	38.8	61.2	1,307	1,379	1,226
California.............	2,580,502	601,022	1,979,479	23.3	76.7	2,263	2,287	2,244
Colorado	284,969	92,234	192,735	32.4	67.6	1,865	1,810	1,919
Connecticut	264,788	100,016	164,772	37.8	62.2	1,915	1,888	1,941
Delaware	52,079	26,663	25,415	51.2	48.8	1,676	1,777	1,585
Florida	798,009	180,638	617,371	22.6	77.4	1,639	1,696	1,597
Georgia...............	430,956	134,058	296,898	31.1	68.9	1,411	1,450	1,379
Hawaii	87,197	66,223	20,974	75.9	24.1	1,758	1,815	1,717
Idaho	69,925	24,946	44,979	35.7	64.3	1,534	1,545	1,521
Illinois...............	923,241	229,342	693,898	24.8	75.2	1,890	1,980	1,812
Indiana	384,727	124,461	260,266	32.4	67.6	1,582	1,779	1,360
Iowa	241,469	85,501	155,968	35.4	64.6	1,656	1,725	1,578
Kansas	200,839	63,294	137,545	31.5	68.5	1,561	1,610	1,505
Kentucky	230,871	92,870	138,002	40.2	59.8	1,469	1,524	1,408
Louisiana	343,901	137,421	206,480	40.0	60.0	1,456	1,554	1,372
Maine	76,295	30,408	45,886	39.9	60.1	1,457	1,429	1,490
Maryland	396,467	130,969	265,498	33.0	67.0	1,868	2,034	1,726
Massachusetts	455,535	132,768	322,767	29.1	70.9	1,785	1,871	1,719
Michigan	835,321	237,428	597,894	28.4	71.6	2,074	2,155	1,984
Minnesota	380,111	119,447	260,664	31.4	68.6	1,995	2,076	1,920
Mississippi	160,632	56,780	103,852	35.3	64.7	1,187	1,251	1,126
Missouri	334,714	89,353	245,360	26.7	73.3	1,535	1,614	1,465
Montana..............	75,306	27,019	48,287	35.9	64.1	1,717	1,873	1,554
Nebraska	138,233	40,701	97,532	29.4	70.6	1,529	1,486	1,570
Nevada	81,323	23,431	57,892	28.8	71.2	1,869	1,800	1,911
New Hampshire	61,901	22,868	39,033	36.9	63.1	1,474	1,500	1,447
New Jersey............	674,337	170,870	503,467	25.3	74.7	1,875	2,071	1,694
New Mexico............	126,470	54,541	71,929	43.1	56.9	1,591	1,655	1,529
New York	2,048,443	548,325	1,500,118	26.8	73.2	2,062	2,214	1,981
North Carolina	448,494	144,015	304,479	32.1	67.9	1,505	1,593	1,418
North Dakota	61,200	22,159	39,041	36.2	63.8	1,713	1,925	1,459
Ohio	783,323	199,172	584,151	25.4	74.6	1,695	1,815	1,581
Oklahoma	242,115	94,720	147,395	39.1	60.9	1,437	1,472	1,403
Oregon	232,830	75,383	157,447	32.4	67.6	1,797	1,776	1,818
Pennsylvania	786,506	214,429	572,077	27.3	72.7	1,745	1,811	1,686
Rhode Island	84,066	36,965	47,101	44.0	56.0	1,881	2,097	1,694
South Carolina	229,377	97,566	131,811	42.5	57.5	1,403	1,458	1,344
South Dakota	48,759	18,766	29,993	38.5	61.5	1,402	1,454	1,341
Tennessee	315,402	100,078	215,323	31.7	68.3	1,458	1,590	1,346
Texas.................	1,271,591	332,262	939,329	26.1	73.9	1,631	1,623	1,640
Utah	122,977	49,591	73,386	40.3	59.7	1,668	1,595	1,772
Vermont	37,581	17,640	19,941	46.9	53.1	1,533	1,519	1,552
Virginia...............	443,970	158,616	285,354	35.7	64.3	1,614	1,678	1,547
Washington	396,258	132,970	263,288	33.6	66.4	1,950	1,895	1,996
West Virginia	135,217	49,181	86,036	36.4	63.6	1,417	1,540	1,264
Wisconsin	413,577	117,378	296,199	28.4	71.6	1,846	1,935	1,753
Wyoming	62,422	18,902	43,521	30.3	69.7	1,805	1,963	1,666
Dist. of Col.	110,496	0	110,496	0.0	100.0	2,338	2,400	2,318

Source: U.S. Bureau of the Census, *Public Employment in 1984.*
Note: Statistics for local governments are estimates subject to sampling variation. Because of rounding, detail may not add to totals.

Table 7.14
STATE GOVERNMENT EMPLOYMENT (FULL-TIME EQUIVALENT), FOR SELECTED FUNCTIONS, BY STATE: OCTOBER 1983

State	All functions	Education		Selected functions							
		Higher educa-tion(a)	Other educa-tion(b)	High-ways	Public welfare	Hospi-tals	Correc-tion	Police protection	Natural resources	Financial adminis-tration	General control
All states	3,115,944	965,661	106,481	239,458	172,515	528,161	193,523	75,871	138,015	115,125	115,168
Alabama........	62,151	21,207	3,888	4,014	4,152	11,158	2,636	946	2,781	2,229	1,969
Alaska.........	21,498	4,741	3,228	3,181	1,078	418	708	428	2,343	1,002	1,547
Arizona........	34,786	13,869	2,234	2,852	1,844	2,024	2,873	1,617	1,112	1,382	980
Arkansas	35,641	11,272	2,195	3,508	2,145	4,761	1,540	770	2,110	1,419	272
California	254,289	80,648	4,471	15,294	2,648	31,227	16,339	9,279	14,305	9,095	6,078
Colorado	42,245	18,413	834	3,019	1,156	6,160	2,104	744	1,753	1,721	2,571
Connecticut	46,098	10,264	2,359	4,127	2,687	10,023	3,330	1,338	480	2,294	3,536
Delaware	16,356	4,547	220	1,333	682	2,596	1,343	613	474	753	1,003
Florida	110,085	25,426	2,155	7,837	6,082	16,308	13,373	2,575	5,881	4,111	7,416
Georgia........	83,717	23,792	2,692	6,113	5,472	13,618	7,329	1,670	4,567	1,955	1,840
Hawaii	37,364	5,555	16,406	846	949	2,887	904	0	1,187	713	1,709
Idaho	13,859	5,199	312	1,575	1,146	1,125	499	268	1,248	697	225
Illinois........	114,485	38,273	2,442	7,215	10,370	16,252	7,855	3,190	3,484	6,445	5,016
Indiana........	62,750	29,497	3,710	5,057	1,216	8,359	3,623	1,642	2,099	1,868	732
Iowa	43,466	16,124	1,239	3,144	3,432	8,571	1,654	805	2,332	1,522	1,099
Kansas	38,810	14,589	783	3,447	2,771	5,516	1,654	687	2,205	2,092	1,849
Kentucky	57,056	16,938	3,692	5,250	3,731	7,164	2,845	1,662	3,089	1,938	2,858
Louisiana	85,724	23,748	4,236	7,523	4,381	19,503	5,690	1,420	4,715	3,003	1,712
Maine	18,325	4,667	1,146	2,629	1,585	1,843	828	528	1,374	783	752
Maryland	77,262	20,928	2,117	4,822	6,180	12,746	5,128	2,144	2,540	3,413	2,773
Massachusetts ...	75,454	15,119	1,659	4,325	8,267	19,227	5,347	1,682	1,527	3,585	5,917
Michigan	113,855	46,157	2,104	3,987	13,325	16,896	6,509	2,943	4,094	2,042	3,616
Minnesota	53,817	23,248	1,396	4,637	1,282	8,687	1,771	826	3,055	1,814	1,097
Mississippi	40,704	11,035	1,359	2,995	2,785	6,718	1,970	1,072	4,594	1,254	488
Missouri	60,576	15,223	1,964	5,814	5,119	12,208	2,967	1,707	2,886	2,027	3,099
Montana........	14,698	4,091	368	1,746	1,011	1,238	634	296	2,164	996	345
Nebraska	29,265	11,984	689	2,308	2,459	3,678	1,316	508	2,663	553	778
Nevada	11,819	3,114	213	1,265	685	647	1,117	285	668	615	474
New Hampshire .	13,985	4,968	337	1,727	1,092	1,874	455	286	515	196	349
New Jersey......	86,436	19,889	1,788	8,250	4,653	16,698	5,975	4,308	1,637	3,242	4,461
New Mexico.....	34,026	12,050	592	2,722	1,743	4,270	1,647	658	1,539	1,256	1,340
New York	250,278	41,758	5,188	13,833	6,790	68,147	20,561	5,140	3,245	10,284	18,840
North Carolina ..	87,832	26,795	3,074	10,225	976	15,323	8,344	2,488	4,962	2,498	4,188
North Dakota ...	13,039	4,952	367	961	440	2,274	293	257	1,123	369	351
Ohio	114,453	46,957	2,327	8,299	1,401	22,128	6,451	1,947	3,973	3,604	2,284
Oklahoma	61,449	20,023	2,140	3,602	7,782	10,554	3,953	1,591	2,381	1,531	1,500
Oregon	40,496	10,688	863	3,120	3,144	5,755	1,821	1,018	3,101	1,849	2,119
Pennsylvania	121,278	22,178	2,251	14,394	10,473	28,787	4,333	4,787	5,417	5,898	3,052
Rhode Island	20,834	4,680	926	894	1,623	1,705	951	232	489	852	998
South Carolina ..	58,318	17,798	2,788	4,534	3,894	9,792	3,545	1,268	1,925	1,917	1,295
South Dakota ...	11,843	3,944	367	1,159	921	1,446	337	292	776	351	536
Tennessee	63,731	22,495	2,480	5,023	4,794	9,428	4,428	1,059	2,444	2,257	1,253
Texas..........	180,681	71,001	3,120	14,175	11,439	34,425	9,468	2,956	8,282	6,439	2,694
Utah	27,818	13,390	778	1,716	1,464	3,398	952	466	1,064	777	808
Vermont	10,373	3,195	202	1,058	668	731	458	439	652	522	587
Virginia........	94,029	31,754	2,466	10,021	1,118	18,610	7,851	1,985	3,336	3,225	2,291
Washington	67,305	26,771	1,314	5,212	5,024	8,415	3,431	1,276	4,151	2,091	1,319
West Virginia ...	34,034	9,349	1,373	5,399	2,592	5,034	669	857	1,796	1,441	1,038
Wisconsin.......	57,551	28,790	1,425	1,597	1,340	6,704	3,294	664	2,668	2,490	1,753
Wyoming	10,000	2,568	204	1,674	504	1,105	420	252	809	715	361

Source: U.S. Bureau of the Census, *Public Employment in 1983*.
(a) Includes instructional and other personnel.
(b) Includes instructional and other personnel in elementary and secondary schools.

301

Table 7.15
STATE GOVERNMENT EMPLOYMENT (FULL-TIME EQUIVALENT), FOR SELECTED FUNCTIONS, BY STATE: OCTOBER 1984

		Education		Selected functions							
State	All functions	Higher education(a)	Other education(b)	Highways	Public welfare	Hospitals	Correction	Police protection	Natural resources	Financial administration	General control
All states	3,177,199	981,167	109,869	243,851	174,511	529,289	213,168	78,676	136,135	122,644	121,946
Alabama........	64,007	21,977	3,937	4,063	4,200	11,239	3,088	942	2,695	2,251	2,403
Alaska..........	20,866	3,513	3,416	3,217	1,117	427	892	455	2,359	1,080	1,571
Arizona.........	36,091	14,420	2,108	2,863	1,967	1,904	2,965	1,552	1,161	1,668	1,084
Arkansas	36,288	10,777	2,333	3,534	2,276	5,450	1,597	765	2,315	1,456	241
California	260,536	84,559	4,249	15,777	2,657	31,160	20,454	10,926	12,770	9,483	5,653
Colorado	42,122	19,088	861	2,905	948	6,054	1,767	863	1,700	1,729	2,625
Connecticut	48,461	10,251	2,536	4,446	2,215	10,138	3,638	1,444	585	2,854	4,864
Delaware	16,173	4,636	229	1,243	727	2,307	1,453	609	467	747	1,013
Florida	112,286	24,831	2,191	7,916	6,442	16,037	14,334	2,801	6,541	4,047	7,725
Georgia.........	82,220	24,098	2,969	6,091	5,453	13,296	7,317	1,699	4,639	1,953	1,215
Hawaii	37,763	5,635	16,061	821	976	2,803	955	0	1,210	720	1,941
Idaho	14,636	5,059	464	1,710	552	1,862	668	273	1,211	751	248
Illinois..........	116,890	37,180	2,528	7,348	10,718	16,579	9,217	3,343	3,758	6,462	5,211
Indiana	65,661	30,145	4,271	4,924	1,251	9,551	3,831	1,716	2,071	1,906	741
Iowa	45,544	17,553	1,234	3,199	3,485	9,003	1,589	815	2,390	1,538	1,201
Kansas	38,848	14,595	1,008	3,565	2,549	5,513	1,712	709	2,258	2,113	1,857
Kentucky	59,247	17,464	3,708	6,524	4,151	6,329	2,752	1,657	2,984	2,435	3,493
Louisiana	86,193	23,549	4,636	6,846	5,156	18,511	5,422	1,167	4,166	3,184	2,375
Maine	18,718	4,694	1,261	2,553	1,746	1,897	827	544	1,352	859	636
Maryland	79,358	20,913	2,162	4,824	5,634	12,777	6,893	2,154	2,471	3,402	2,802
Massachusetts ...	75,340	15,473	1,403	4,558	8,172	18,387	5,241	1,726	2,209	4,016	5,042
Michigan	113,426	46,507	2,106	3,683	13,084	16,982	6,669	2,865	4,123	2,182	3,597
Minnesota	54,406	22,846	1,398	4,723	1,369	8,661	1,805	831	3,249	2,158	1,235
Mississippi	42,632	13,007	1,400	2,983	2,838	7,429	2,049	1,017	3,723	1,174	454
Missouri	61,497	15,228	1,977	6,033	5,276	12,216	3,634	1,752	2,571	2,248	3,165
Montana	15,182	4,203	383	1,844	1,033	1,252	642	297	2,262	1,076	369
Nebraska	29,255	11,915	704	2,381	2,504	3,676	1,468	521	1,843	560	805
Nevada	12,559	3,878	199	1,311	586	642	1,120	293	690	677	450
New Hampshire .	15,323	5,612	273	1,727	1,106	1,813	463	286	671	192	784
New Jersey......	88,066	20,111	2,890	8,336	4,772	16,895	6,419	4,303	1,633	3,111	4,690
New Mexico.....	32,254	11,850	609	2,581	1,714	5,719	1,971	663	1,419	1,388	1,634
New York	259,648	41,158	5,211	14,454	6,816	72,274	22,392	5,295	3,251	12,813	19,303
North Carolina ..	88,276	24,889	2,984	11,031	1,076	15,299	8,520	2,548	5,370	2,655	4,383
North Dakota ...	13,484	5,151	352	1,004	439	2,296	304	305	1,020	362	371
Ohio	113,314	48,360	2,368	8,479	1,440	18,819	6,793	1,969	3,861	3,792	2,369
Oklahoma	60,714	19,387	2,002	3,601	8,663	9,304	4,042	1,614	2,182	1,695	1,593
Oregon	41,292	11,588	799	3,181	3,176	5,390	1,877	1,061	3,125	1,831	2,177
Pennsylvania ...	121,881	22,567	2,199	14,132	10,646	27,972	4,698	4,888	4,995	5,958	5,428
Rhode Island	20,484	5,447	871	1,058	1,462	1,667	1,200	228	599	883	1,001
South Carolina ..	61,509	18,910	3,013	4,578	3,828	10,286	3,886	1,478	1,984	1,927	1,315
South Dakota ...	11,874	3,825	462	1,159	959	1,451	383	293	815	364	481
Tennessee	64,991	22,780	2,112	4,997	4,976	9,278	4,777	1,089	2,391	2,481	1,293
Texas...........	185,486	71,436	3,269	14,233	11,592	34,098	12,478	2,854	8,454	6,633	2,794
Utah	29,092	13,773	1,063	1,774	1,541	3,313	1,193	494	1,092	838	826
Vermont	10,496	3,411	196	1,075	690	714	513	443	608	505	511
Virginia.........	94,849	32,322	2,753	10,060	865	18,420	8,071	1,999	3,347	3,400	2,363
Washington	71,702	27,137	1,546	5,509	5,082	9,031	4,697	1,331	4,198	2,162	1,378
West Virginia ...	34,798	9,395	1,468	5,516	2,670	5,028	726	845	1,870	1,654	1,040
Wisconsin.......	61,540	31,735	1,492	1,809	1,412	7,123	3,327	690	2,672	2,548	1,798
Wyoming	9,921	2,349	205	1,672	504	1,017	439	264	805	723	398

Source: U.S. Bureau of the Census, *Public Employment in 1984.*
(a) Includes instructional and other personnel.
(b) Includes instructional and other personnel in elementary and secondary schools.

Table 7.16
STATE GOVERNMENT PAYROLLS
FOR SELECTED FUNCTIONS, BY STATE: OCTOBER 1983
(In thousands of dollars)

State	All functions	Education		Selected functions							
		Higher education(a)	Other education(b)	Highways	Public welfare	Hospitals	Correction	Police protection	Natural resources	Financial administration	General control
All states	$5,345,538	$1,807,005	$181,916	$392,865	$263,179	$762,974	$317,550	$145,411	$232,296	$183,860	$243,309
Alabama........	97,851	35,778	6,382	5,812	5,887	15,030	3,857	1,759	4,397	3,264	4,680
Alaska.........	54,213	10,578	8,906	7,134	2,206	944	2,001	1,594	6,277	2,661	4,616
Arizona.........	63,538	28,635	3,390	4,858	2,665	3,879	4,639	3,310	1,812	2,182	1,701
Arkansas	50,775	17,913	3,119	5,087	2,623	6,068	1,848	1,173	2,804	1,801	540
California.......	532,615	179,256	9,829	30,249	4,785	56,885	30,818	19,304	31,075	17,315	16,867
Colorado	83,979	38,777	1,529	6,436	2,106	10,585	4,014	1,387	3,708	3,016	5,069
Connecticut	85,656	20,146	4,440	8,979	4,536	15,690	6,681	2,870	1,020	3,946	6,900
Delaware	25,360	9,031	409	1,809	894	2,856	1,970	1,156	706	991	1,586
Florida	199,246	48,116	3,880	10,418	11,436	31,443	24,924	4,132	9,692	6,122	15,241
Georgia.........	129,460	45,222	4,214	8,445	7,719	16,799	9,683	2,660	6,770	3,079	3,110
Hawaii	61,757	11,521	26,898	1,392	1,309	3,960	1,199	0	2,159	1,133	2,950
Idaho	22,022	8,104	519	2,549	1,634	1,568	763	471	2,159	1,070	478
Illinois.........	210,851	80,100	4,275	14,174	16,010	25,942	13,110	6,358	6,156	9,231	11,358
Indiana.........	111,293	61,464	4,608	6,933	1,522	14,220	4,898	2,729	3,063	2,659	2,159
Iowa	75,796	32,428	2,117	4,856	5,345	12,234	2,795	1,535	3,607	2,464	2,265
Kansas	57,320	22,479	1,165	5,323	4,288	6,716	2,239	1,133	3,392	2,791	2,876
Kentucky	85,733	28,888	6,292	8,725	5,124	7,767	3,890	2,907	4,112	3,140	4,562
Louisiana	125,677	42,331	6,558	11,276	5,352	20,261	8,227	2,303	7,626	4,822	3,072
Maine	27,736	7,230	1,714	3,947	2,264	2,471	1,308	869	2,364	1,071	1,124
Maryland	121,323	33,322	3,673	7,064	8,585	18,769	8,220	4,086	3,115	5,146	4,591
Massachusetts ...	121,446	26,681	2,913	8,123	12,702	25,358	8,338	3,072	2,297	5,167	11,366
Michigan	225,467	87,958	4,632	9,062	25,668	31,837	13,329	6,815	8,038	4,236	8,759
Minnesota	108,846	49,523	2,956	10,014	2,282	14,236	3,531	1,842	5,595	3,388	3,568
Mississippi	54,687	18,401	1,847	3,608	3,141	6,415	2,216	1,644	6,277	1,767	1,076
Missouri	83,664	24,867	2,405	8,356	5,925	13,383	4,131	3,255	3,879	2,290	5,000
Montana........	24,851	7,551	653	3,342	1,576	1,890	980	588	2,809	1,485	867
Nebraska	38,839	15,934	986	3,306	2,898	4,555	1,733	927	3,336	786	1,208
Nevada	22,518	6,009	438	2,463	1,230	1,224	2,064	538	1,251	1,066	1,103
New Hampshire .	21,075	8,346	525	2,144	1,480	2,388	669	501	848	337	654
New Jersey......	156,530	43,915	3,516	15,712	7,262	23,529	9,743	7,998	2,858	5,143	10,028
New Mexico.....	50,358	20,169	815	4,543	1,946	4,855	2,779	1,064	2,480	1,362	2,684
New York	485,138	89,331	9,933	23,085	14,041	115,329	38,518	11,120	6,580	17,368	42,415
North Carolina ..	131,947	43,274	4,491	13,467	1,538	20,174	11,122	5,013	7,452	3,922	7,843
North Dakota ...	20,925	8,842	541	1,478	704	2,653	421	432	2,000	543	706
Ohio	175,639	74,847	3,969	13,513	2,184	27,344	9,926	3,583	6,111	5,712	4,575
Oklahoma	93,989	34,036	3,439	5,226	10,872	12,587	5,439	2,659	4,110	2,436	3,275
Oregon	74,452	22,485	1,539	5,447	5,036	8,311	4,047	2,413	5,362	3,048	4,711
Pennsylvania	200,271	42,669	4,072	22,329	17,516	41,253	7,535	9,511	9,445	9,001	5,186
Rhode Island....	36,290	8,395	1,805	1,348	3,097	2,950	1,614	556	720	1,367	1,783
South Carolina ..	86,811	31,620	4,185	5,001	5,062	11,762	4,671	2,061	2,628	2,622	2,587
South Dakota ...	17,587	6,200	552	1,840	1,166	1,499	449	448	1,354	549	923
Tennessee	87,933	35,967	3,341	6,294	5,624	10,936	5,476	1,447	2,908	2,956	2,630
Texas...........	310,603	132,526	5,686	24,536	15,572	46,824	15,784	5,407	14,092	12,214	7,928
Utah	44,706	20,301	1,372	3,346	2,388	4,228	1,684	936	1,961	1,329	1,660
Vermont	16,895	5,746	341	1,633	973	1,013	681	890	1,044	761	990
Virginia.........	147,609	59,986	3,700	12,959	1,689	23,905	10,148	3,262	5,149	4,493	4,287
Washington	123,427	53,581	2,388	11,394	7,266	11,967	5,901	2,835	7,191	3,497	2,982
West Virginia ...	43,927	14,499	1,832	6,737	2,861	4,919	692	1,216	2,447	1,656	1,698
Wisconsin	98,262	46,938	2,723	3,662	2,345	10,023	6,002	1,155	4,463	4,239	4,195
Wyoming	18,641	5,089	406	3,434	850	1,538	645	488	1,597	1,213	873

Source: U.S. Bureau of the Census, *Public Employment in 1983.*
(a) Includes instructional and other personnel.
(b) Includes instructional and other personnel in elementary and secondary schools.

Table 7.17
STATE GOVERNMENT PAYROLLS
FOR SELECTED FUNCTIONS, BY STATE: OCTOBER 1984
(In thousands of dollars)

State	All functions	Education — Higher education(a)	Education — Other education(b)	Highways	Public welfare	Hospitals	Correction	Police protection	Natural resources	Financial administration	General control
All states	$5,814,935	$1,979,451	$198,493	$431,171	$278,446	$815,336	$363,971	$162,475	$241,712	$207,977	$269,940
Alabama	111,648	41,249	7,427	6,624	6,722	16,809	5,070	1,943	4,911	3,875	4,678
Alaska	57,832	11,403	9,452	7,640	2,317	990	2,602	1,736	6,470	3,056	4,752
Arizona	68,312	30,918	3,482	5,281	3,081	3,828	4,779	3,391	1,924	2,311	1,985
Arkansas	53,752	19,572	3,380	5,269	2,750	6,262	1,960	1,256	3,310	1,892	516
California	601,022	214,681	10,679	38,469	4,784	62,331	34,305	23,780	30,368	19,741	14,689
Colorado	92,234	42,935	1,728	6,762	2,038	11,377	4,177	2,058	4,005	3,482	5,866
Connecticut	100,016	21,167	5,235	8,676	3,902	19,010	8,039	4,389	1,584	5,013	11,565
Delaware	26,663	8,965	468	2,136	1,039	2,738	2,217	1,294	703	1,040	1,822
Florida	180,638	49,929	3,191	13,405	7,321	21,125	23,624	4,476	8,554	5,901	15,241
Georgia	134,058	46,603	4,702	8,931	8,120	17,516	10,249	3,089	7,139	3,309	2,952
Hawaii	66,223	11,973	27,605	1,550	1,536	4,362	1,388	0	2,368	1,281	3,579
Idaho	24,946	8,623	811	2,991	800	2,799	1,063	489	2,297	1,263	561
Illinois	229,342	83,868	4,707	15,164	17,188	27,664	16,026	8,467	7,664	9,789	12,156
Indiana	124,461	70,229	5,803	7,051	1,658	14,774	5,580	3,007	3,490	2,935	2,192
Iowa	85,501	37,970	2,228	5,378	5,720	13,863	2,817	1,809	3,942	2,627	2,667
Kansas	63,294	24,107	1,714	6,212	4,132	7,305	2,787	1,298	3,901	2,966	3,429
Kentucky	92,870	29,812	6,568	9,671	6,027	8,243	4,074	3,111	4,462	3,408	5,756
Louisiana	137,421	44,991	7,644	10,603	7,030	23,497	8,288	1,934	6,806	5,207	4,868
Maine	30,408	8,049	2,057	4,085	2,658	2,574	1,328	986	2,461	1,234	1,289
Maryland	130,969	34,470	3,970	7,640	8,637	19,566	12,165	4,309	3,881	5,744	5,144
Massachusetts ...	132,768	27,834	2,789	9,233	14,236	27,239	9,449	3,653	3,610	7,084	11,202
Michigan	237,428	92,679	4,819	8,895	26,610	34,317	14,913	7,426	8,344	4,738	9,249
Minnesota	119,447	54,962	3,113	10,568	2,576	15,034	3,887	1,904	6,653	4,175	3,945
Mississippi	56,780	20,882	1,880	3,582	3,159	6,962	2,340	1,626	4,898	1,637	1,214
Missouri	89,353	25,879	2,328	9,174	6,430	14,392	4,769	3,492	3,736	2,855	5,675
Montana	27,019	8,388	680	3,585	1,631	1,901	1,076	610	3,300	1,623	942
Nebraska	40,701	16,133	1,162	3,593	3,219	4,729	2,093	893	2,059	863	1,495
Nevada	23,431	6,588	406	2,604	1,116	1,212	2,154	583	1,278	1,156	1,105
New Hampshire .	22,868	9,014	454	2,144	1,613	2,357	673	501	789	318	1,467
New Jersey	170,870	47,231	6,152	17,134	8,152	25,139	11,605	8,505	3,086	5,419	11,132
New Mexico.....	54,541	22,098	986	4,405	2,666	8,072	3,043	1,098	2,519	2,283	2,899
New York	548,325	97,987	10,814	27,180	14,983	131,629	45,569	12,366	7,005	22,633	48,757
North Carolina ..	144,015	44,866	4,822	15,670	1,840	22,155	12,932	4,991	8,490	4,465	7,867
North Dakota ...	22,159	9,585	525	1,571	703	2,828	448	534	1,643	541	774
Ohio	199,172	91,754	4,237	14,939	2,450	28,448	11,076	3,969	6,569	6,195	4,168
Oklahoma	94,720	33,694	3,050	5,216	11,862	12,203	5,699	2,651	3,805	2,692	3,416
Oregon	75,383	23,149	1,455	5,637	5,065	8,348	4,326	2,504	5,345	3,095	4,239
Pennsylvania	214,429	46,187	4,161	23,261	18,552	42,286	8,498	10,164	9,092	9,483	11,203
Rhode Island	36,965	10,385	1,676	1,762	2,404	2,635	2,355	682	923	1,556	1,975
South Carolina ..	97,566	35,129	4,966	5,661	5,245	13,313	5,404	2,418	2,907	2,752	2,682
South Dakota ...	18,766	6,972	686	1,895	1,261	1,534	527	463	1,427	586	771
Tennessee	100,078	40,335	3,307	6,801	6,758	12,162	6,013	1,775	3,322	3,593	2,956
Texas..........	332,262	137,359	6,083	26,344	19,274	48,396	21,608	5,222	15,041	12,939	7,188
Utah	49,591	22,530	1,846	3,664	2,633	4,375	2,144	1,014	2,140	1,484	1,774
Vermont	17,640	6,240	331	1,735	995	1,003	806	927	1,075	753	899
Virginia	158,616	63,610	4,463	14,014	1,383	23,926	12,284	3,558	5,822	5,272	5,012
Washington	132,970	54,216	2,939	12,156	7,503	13,400	8,017	2,909	7,618	4,048	2,934
West Virginia ...	49,181	16,205	2,151	7,574	3,238	5,534	789	1,317	2,702	1,949	1,734
Wisconsin	117,378	60,944	2,962	4,131	2,584	11,771	6,264	1,388	4,657	4,493	4,694
Wyoming	18,902	5,105	400	3,504	843	1,400	672	512	1,614	1,222	863

Source: U.S. Bureau of the Census, Public Employment in 1984.
(a) Includes instructional and other personnel.
(b) Includes instructional and other personnel in elementary and secondary schools.

FINANCES OF STATE-ADMINISTERED PUBLIC EMPLOYEE RETIREMENT SYSTEMS

By Vance Kane

The number and membership of public employee retirement systems administered by state governments increased in fiscal year 1984 (see Table 7.18).[1] The growth in the number of state employee retirement systems—from 194 in fiscal 1983 to 202 in fiscal 1984—is attributed primarily to the establishment of state systems to cover local government employees. Membership in state retirement systems increased to 10 million during this period (a growth of 168,000 members), while local government retirement system membership actually declined by 24,000 persons to a total of 1.5 million members. Receipts of state-administered systems totaled $48.7 billion in fiscal 1984, as compared to payments of $16.5 billion (see Table 7.19). Assets at the end of fiscal year 1984 were $255.7 billion, representing an 11 percent growth over the $230 billion in assets from the previous year.

Membership Size

Of the 202 state-administered systems operating in 1984, 96 had a membership of 10,000 or more; 35 had a membership between 1,000 and 10,000; 51 had a membership between 100 and 999; and 20 systems had less than 100 members (see Table A). The 96 largest state systems had 9,868,871 members or 98.3 percent of the total members.

In 1984, there were 8.7 million active members and 1.4 million individuals in a nonactive status—i.e., individuals who are no longer employed in the system, but who have left their funds for a later or "deferred" retirement income when they reach the age qualification (see Table 7.18). There were 2.6 million persons receiving monthly benefits, of which 130,000 individuals were classified as disabled (see Table 7.20). Georgia and Louisiana had the largest number of state systems (10), followed by Michigan, Minnesota, and North Carolina with nine each, and Connecticut and Montana with eight systems. Twenty-seven states had three systems or less. California had the largest membership with 866,000 persons, followed

by Ohio (766,000), New York (746,000), Texas (656,000), Illinois (414,000), and Florida (410,000). All other states had less than 400,000 members; the Vermont retirement systems had the smallest number of members (18,000).

Benefit Payments

Benefits paid in fiscal 1984 totaled $14.6 billion, reflecting a $1.8 billion increase in payments since 1983 (see Table 7.19). Receipts over payments (which include benefits, withdrawals, and miscellaneous expenditures) were $32 billion, compared to $30.5 billion in 1983.

Recurrent benefit payments for the last month of fiscal year 1984 were $1.2 billion, with $1.1 billion for service retirement, $61 million for disability, and $37 million for survivors of deceased former members (see Table 7.20). The percentage distribution of benefit payments in 1984 was 91.6 percent for service or age retirement, 5.2 percent for disability, and 3.2 percent to survivors.

The average monthly service payment was $466 in 1984, $443 in 1983, and $421 in 1982 (see Table 7.18).

Compared to the $466 state average for service payments, local government retirement systems showed higher average monthly payments in 1984 ($634). Local retirement systems also spent more for both disability payments ($824 versus state average of $466) and payments to survivors of former members ($358 versus $252).

California had the largest number of beneficiaries for state public employee retirement systems. There were 326,000 persons receiving monthly benefit payments, of which 274,000 were age or service retirements, 31,000 were disability, and 21,000 were survivor benefits. California had over 10 percent of the national statewide total for each category of beneficiary. New York ranked second

Vance Kane is Assistant Division Chief for Programs, and was assisted by Lisa McNelis, Social Science Analyst, both in the Governments Division, U.S. Bureau of the Census.

Table A
Number and Membership of State Government
Employee Retirement Systems By Size-Group: 1983-84

Number of systems with membership of—

Total	10,000 or more	5,000 to 9,999	1,000 to 4,999	500 to 999	200 to 499	100 to 199	Less than 100
202	96	13	22	14	23	14	20

Number of members in systems with membership of—

Total	10,000 or more	5,000 to 9,999	1,000 to 4,999	500 to 999	200 to 499	100 to 199	Less than 100
10,044,368	9,868,871	97,395	57,460	10,523	7,324	2,112	683

in number of beneficiaries (249,000), followed by Ohio, Pennsylvania, Texas, and Illinois (each with over 100,000 beneficiaries). The average national state retirement system payment for service or age retirement was $466. The highest state average payment for service was Alaska ($892), followed by Louisiana ($640) and Maryland ($637); the lowest payments were in Nebraska ($157), Kansas ($190), and Wyoming ($200).

Some of the mitigating factors explaining different payment levels among the states include: varying length-of-service requirements, the general wage levels of the region, and whether or not the retirement system may be supplemented with other retirement programs (such as social security, deferred compensation, or investment programs). Moreover, some states operate a two-tier system whereby new employees might work longer to qualify for pension benefits than older employees whose system essentially is closed.

Revenues

In 1983-84, revenue of state-administered public employee retirement systems totaled $48.7 billion, an increase of 8 percent above the $45.1 billion for the previous fiscal year. Employee contributions were $7.3 billion or 15 percent of the total. Government contributions were $18.5 billion—of which $10.4 billion came from state governments, and $8.1 billion from local governments. Earnings on investments accounted for $22.9 billion (see Table 7.19).

The percentage share of employee and government payments has been declining as a portion of total revenue, while earnings on investments has grown rapidly. This increase in return on investments has resulted not only from higher yields in recent years, but also improved flexibility in legally-authorized investments. There has been a strong effort in some states to reduce the actuarial deficits through aggressive investments. Investment returns in 1983-84 totaled $22.9 billion, which exceeded all other single sources of revenue.

Since each state operates its retirement program independently, the distribution of employer/employee contributions of each system varies considerably from state to state (see Tables 7.21 and 7.22). Employees in New Hampshire provided the highest share of total revenue, with 39.7 percent. Moreover, there were 20 states in which employee contributions comprised over 20 percent of all revenue.

Investments and Assets

Cash and security holdings totaled $256 billion, of which $180 billion was invested in non-governmental securities, $67 billion in governmental securities, and $8 billion in cash and deposits (see Table 7.19). With the relaxation of investment regulations and the adoption of aggressive investment procedures, state retirement systems held $66 billion in corporate stocks, $60 billion in corporate bonds, and $22 billion in mortgages. Economic conditions in 1984 resulted in a sharp growth of corporate stock holdings. Investments in corporate bonds declined $2 billion, and was the lowest amount since 1978-79. Total holdings increased 11 percent from the previous year, down from the 19 percent rise between 1981-82 and 1982-83.

Note

1. The U.S. Bureau of the Census defines a publicly-administered retirement system as a system sponsored by a recognized unit of government whose membership is comprised of public employees compensated with public funds. There must be an identifiable retirement fund financed in whole or in part with public contributions. Direct payments to retired or disabled individuals by appropriation of general funds do not constitute a retirement system. Payments to a private trustee or insurance carrier also are excluded as a publicly-administered employee retirement system.

Table 7.18
NUMBER, MEMBERSHIP AND MONTHLY BENEFIT PAYMENTS OF STATE-ADMINISTERED EMPLOYEE RETIREMENT SYSTEMS: 1981-82 THROUGH 1983-84

Item	1983-84	1982-83	1981-82
Number of systems	202	194	190
Membership, last month of fiscal year:			
Total number	10,044,368	9,876,495	10,141,062
Active members	8,676,214	8,583,560	8,740,602
Other	1,368,154	1,292,935	1,400,460
Percent distribution	100.0	100.0	100.0
Active members	86.4	86.9	86.2
Other	13.6	13.1	13.8
Beneficiaries receiving periodic benefits:			
Total number	2,579,174	2,426,500	2,262,175
Persons retired on account of age or length of service	2,300,605	2,155,347	1,958,960
Persons retired on account of disability	130,280	137,535	149,092
Survivors of deceased former members	148,289	133,618	154,123
Percent distribution	100.0	100.0	100.0
Persons retired on account of age or length of service	89.1	88.8	86.0
Persons retired on account of disability	5.1	5.7	6.6
Survivors of deceased former members	5.8	5.5	6.8
Recurrent benefit payments for last month of fiscal year:			
Total amount (in thousands)	$1,169,579	$1,044,381	$927,217
To persons retired on account of age or length of service	$1,071,542	$953,819	$825,219
To persons retired on account of disability	$60,701	$56,727	$60,527
To survivors of deceased former members	$37,336	$33,835	$41,472
Percent distribution	100.0	100.0	100.0
For persons retired on account of age or length of service	91.6	91.3	89.0
For persons retired on account of disability	5.2	5.4	6.5
For survivors of deceased former members	3.2	3.2	4.5
Average monthly payment for beneficiaries:			
Average for all beneficiaries (in dollars)	$453	$430	$410
For persons retired on account of age or length of service	$466	$443	$421
For persons retired on account of disability	$466	$412	$406
For survivors of deceased former members	$252	$253	$269
Lump-sum survivors' benefits for the month:			
Amount (in thousands)	$20,077	$45,967	$43,443
Number of beneficiaries (payees)	5,128	11,741	20,276
Average amount of payments (in dollars)	$3,915	$3,915	$2,143

Source: U.S. Bureau of the Census, *Finances of Employee Retirement Systems of State and Local Governments in 1983-84.*
Note: Because of rounding, detail may not add to totals.

Table 7.19
NATIONAL SUMMARY OF FINANCES OF STATE-ADMINISTERED EMPLOYEE RETIREMENT SYSTEMS: SELECTED YEARS, 1978-1984

	Amount (in millions of dollars)							Percentage distribution			
	1983-84	1982-83	1981-82	1980-81	1979-80	1978-79	1977-78	1983-84	1982-83	1981-82	1980-81
Receipts	$48,724	$45,124	$37,944	$33,340	$28,603	$24,659	$21,488	100.0	100.0	100.0	100.0
Employee contributions	7,306	7,196	6,674	5,982	5,285	4,968	4,619	15.0	15.9	17.6	17.9
Government contributions	18,521	17,197	15,777	14,749	13,010	11,490	10,000	38.0	38.1	41.6	44.2
From state governments	10,458	9,611	8,898	8,353	7,399	6,318	5,736	21.5	21.3	23.5	25.1
From local governments	8,063	7,585	6,879	6,395	5,611	5,173	4,264	16.5	16.8	18.1	19.2
Earnings on investments	22,897	20,734	15,492	12,609	10,308	8,200	6,868	47.0	45.9	40.8	37.8
Benefits and withdrawal payments	16,492	14,204	13,134	11,393	10,257	8,937	7,811	100.0	100.0	100.0	100.0
Benefits	14,594	12,757	11,430	9,964	8,809	7,704	6,821	88.5	89.8	87.0	87.4
Withdrawals	1,898	1,447	1,704	1,429	1,448	1,233	990	11.5	10.2	13.0	12.5
Cash and security holdings at end of fiscal year, total	255,669	229,685	193,295	164,624	144,682	125,803	110,357	100.0	100.0	100.0	100.0
Cash and deposits	8,036	6,063	2,427	2,611	2,647	1,883	1,304	3.1	2.6	1.3	1.6
Governmental securities	67,405	55,826	44,216	34,292	26,724	20,872	14,743	26.4	24.3	22.9	20.8
Federal	66,723	55,066	43,368	33,716	26,213	20,510	14,425	26.1	24.0	22.4	20.5
U.S. Treasury	45,677	33,982	24,494	19,503	13,814	10,375	6,680	17.9	14.8	12.7	11.8
Federal agency	21,046	21,083	18,874	14,212	12,399	10,136	7,745	8.2	9.2	9.8	8.6
State and local	683	760	848	577	511	362	318	0.3	0.3	0.4	0.4
Nongovernmental securities	180,228	167,796	146,652	127,721	115,311	103,048	94,309	70.5	73.1	75.9	77.6
Corporate bonds	60,430	62,305	68,948	65,246	60,871	55,108	51,266	23.6	27.1	35.7	39.6
Corporate stocks	65,963	55,858	44,025	36,438	31,146	26,987	24,404	25.8	24.3	22.8	22.1
Mortgages	22,222	23,983	17,742	14,174	11,966	10,711	9,794	8.7	10.4	9.2	8.6
Other securities	23,339	15,202	12,525	9,684	10,677	8,944	7,637	9.1	6.6	6.5	5.9
Other investments	8,272	10,448	3,412	2,179	651	1,298	1,208	3.2	4.5	1.8	1.3

Sources: U.S. Bureau of the Census, Census of Governments reports for 1977 and 1982: *Employee Retirement Systems of State and Local Governments* (Volume 6, No. 1); annual reports for other years: *Finances of Employee Retirement Systems of State and Local Governments*.

Table 7.20
MEMBERSHIP AND BENEFIT OPERATIONS OF
STATE-ADMINISTERED EMPLOYEE RETIREMENT SYSTEMS:
LAST MONTH OF FISCAL YEAR 1983-84

Benefit Operations, last month of fiscal year

State	Membership, last month of the fiscal year	Beneficiaries receiving periodic benefit payments				Periodic benefit payment for the month (in thousands of dollars)				Lump-sum survivors benefit payments during the month (in thousands of dollars)
		Total(a)	Persons retired on account of age or length of service	Persons retired on account of disability	Survivors of deceased former members (no. of payees)	Total(a)	Persons retired on account of age or length of service	Persons retired on account of disability	To survivors of deceased former members	
All states	10,044,368	2,579,174	2,300,605	130,280	148,289	$1,169,579	$1,071,542	$60,701	$37,336	$20,077
Alabama	151,820	32,037	28,099	1,980	1,958	12,568	11,646	595	327	13
Alaska	48,076	5,790	5,318	175	297	5,143	4,743	249	151	38
Arizona	135,610	27,382	26,833	223	326	11,322	11,034	147	140	150
Arkansas	79,899	18,010	15,275	1,707	1,028	5,786	5,111	454	221	0
California	866,026	326,214	274,342	30,962	20,910	177,480	158,158	16,364	2,958	3,864
Colorado	102,956	25,462	20,934	2,972	1,556	12,542	10,517	1,523	501	0
Connecticut	98,164	30,925	27,716	2,070	1,139	20,553	18,941	1,192	420	141
Delaware	25,180	7,919	5,778	927	1,214	3,103	2,264	363	476	0
Florida	410,030	81,210	67,389	5,857	7,964	33,202	29,128	1,717	2,356	0
Georgia	236,176	39,827	33,365	2,633	3,829	19,586	16,977	1,403	1,206	27
Hawaii	56,767	14,136	13,392	684	60	6,636	6,406	212	18	275
Idaho	51,839	13,356	11,861	339	1,156	4,080	3,652	188	240	14
Illinois	413,608	114,272	91,703	4,598	17,971	47,946	42,009	2,277	3,660	2,190
Indiana	212,247	49,173	47,601	1,452	120	17,040	16,516	459	65	92
Iowa	182,835	39,633	39,525	29	79	8,445	8,385	30	30	546
Kansas	101,392	35,146	31,762	1,280	2,104	6,763	6,041	466	256	92
Kentucky	148,295	35,812	33,553	903	1,356	16,309	14,747	626	936	0
Louisiana	234,772	55,076	45,944	3,745	5,387	34,356	29,386	2,197	2,773	103
Maine	68,169	19,021	17,516	739	766	9,264	8,565	538	161	37
Maryland	164,726	37,495	37,495	0	0	23,895	23,895	0	0	760
Massachusetts	172,552	85,904	85,774	40	90	46,524	46,475	25	24	153
Michigan	358,941	86,027	81,443	2,287	2,297	42,188	40,060	1,215	914	0
Minnesota	225,997	45,406	39,688	1,658	4,060	16,265	14,850	926	489	102
Mississippi	182,286	24,528	20,786	1,417	2,325	6,786	5,731	397	658	19
Missouri	131,286	32,969	28,303	2,275	2,391	11,839	10,726	576	537	100
Montana	56,112	13,744	12,281	897	566	5,395	4,879	328	188	60
Nebraska	33,319	5,820	5,590	39	191	925	880	10	35	0
Nevada	58,573	8,005	6,882	476	647	3,855	3,515	214	126	0
New Hampshire	31,051	7,226	6,803	304	119	2,041	1,814	144	83	38
New Jersey	386,554	90,640	90,640	0	0	51,140	51,140	0	0	256

MEMBERSHIP AND BENEFIT OPERATIONS—Continued

State	Membership, last month of fiscal year	Beneficiaries receiving periodic benefit payments				Periodic benefit payment for the month (in thousands of dollars)				Lump-sum survivors benefit payments during the month (in thousands of dollars)
		Total(a)	Persons retired on account of age or length of service	Persons retired on account of disability	Survivors of deceased former members (no. of payees)	Total(a)	Persons retired on account of age or length of service	Persons retired on account of disability	To survivors of deceased former members	
New Mexico	73,770	14,791	14,356	397	38	6,346	6,162	157	28	0
New York	746,346	248,513	222,664	11,312	14,537	112,586	103,957	5,157	3,472	2,622
North Carolina	330,821	63,722	63,722		0	25,787	25,787	0	0	4
North Dakota	24,057	4,728	4,293	71	364	1,116	1,032	16	68	0
Ohio	766,379	192,017	156,413	14,477	21,127	87,061	72,329	8,575	6,157	1,588
Oklahoma	119,428	35,400	31,621	1,652	2,127	16,743	15,124	923	696	262
Oregon	124,807	41,103	38,205	2,875	23	12,806	11,827	965	14	88
Pennsylvania	350,360	143,496	128,599	6,772	8,125	68,047	63,187	2,671	2,189	3,910
Rhode Island	34,245	10,734	10,569	0	165	5,766	5,682	0	84	116
South Carolina	246,568	31,326	26,597	2,370	2,359	12,589	11,014	924	651	430
South Dakota	29,049	7,482	6,615	118	749	1,609	1,422	40	146	0
Tennessee	157,017	43,644	38,817	2,374	2,453	14,034	12,482	763	789	0
Texas	656,444	114,500	97,384	6,354	10,762	56,110	51,208	2,439	2,463	1,182
Utah	62,711	13,809	13,809	0	0	3,852	3,852	0	0	93
Vermont	17,881	4,544	4,387	0	157	1,598	1,573	0	25	0
Virginia	299,656	42,436	36,163	5,653	620	17,005	14,722	2,107	176	179
Washington	195,426	65,967	65,937	8	22	36,683	36,679	1	3	0
West Virginia	81,277	29,742	29,602	29	111	10,237	10,166	19	52	0
Wisconsin	249,180	56,860	51,738	3,059	2,063	15,357	14,041	1,069	247	492
Wyoming	47,270	6,195	5,523	91	581	1,270	1,107	37	126	44

Benefit Operations, last month of fiscal year

Source: U.S. Bureau of the Census, Finances of Employee Retirement Systems of State and Local Governments in 1983-84.
(a) Detail may not add to totals because of rounding.

311

Table 7.21
FINANCES OF STATE-ADMINISTERED EMPLOYEE RETIREMENT SYSTEMS, BY STATE: 1983-84
(In thousands of dollars)

State	Total	Employee contributions	From state	From local governments	Earnings on investments	Payments Total	Benefits	Withdrawals	Other
All states	$48,723,551	$7,306,180	$10,457,978	$8,062,695	$22,896,698	$16,748,297	$14,594,292	$1,897,797	$256,208
Alabama............	726,704	115,365	225,098	17,456	368,785	190,181	169,662	20,518	0
Alaska..............	420,372	69,180	108,106	65,432	177,653	85,591	71,058	12,928	1,605
Arizona.............	645,594	156,138	86,660	78,268	324,527	164,149	119,573	43,671	904
Arkansas	343,370	38,214	105,306	21,329	178,521	82,032	68,822	12,007	1,203
California..........	7,483,973	1,146,647	1,049,978	1,420,641	3,866,707	2,419,693	2,217,034	202,572	87
Colorado	792,981	156,705	100,927	163,417	371,932	215,049	180,411	34,638	0
Connecticut	639,924	89,968	319,372	10,385	220,198	266,230	244,351	21,844	35
Delaware	172,432	12,947	65,690	0	93,795	41,697	37,234	1,730	2,733
Florida	1,338,353	8,100	207,673	574,956	547,625	382,403	366,319	8,168	7,916
Georgia............	1,023,270	163,199	292,344	90,794	476,933	283,960	250,548	33,244	168
Hawaii	471,420	80,429	107,194	37,249	246,548	144,086	133,951	8,895	1,240
Idaho	149,930	36,133	21,910	41,177	50,709	61,881	51,792	10,078	11
Illinois.............	1,616,889	420,775	335,922	115,963	744,229	675,969	604,311	64,576	7,082
Indiana	543,984	89,690	191,861	57,209	205,224	220,368	201,037	19,150	181
Iowa	399,446	69,955	48,284	68,988	212,220	121,284	98,290	20,619	2,375
Kansas	331,254	68,649	71,633	30,854	160,118	93,888	78,794	15,094	0
Kentucky	585,376	124,477	170,829	29,866	260,204	205,752	191,357	14,396	0
Louisiana	935,210	229,168	362,115	34,747	309,179	444,274	404,777	37,379	2,118
Maine	205,430	40,115	97,367	17,551	50,398	119,575	110,305	7,993	1,277
Maryland	789,142	89,881	449,610	28,539	221,112	372,843	338,677	28,256	5,911
Massachusetts	840,906	178,226	434,412	0	228,268	439,138	398,065	39,517	1,557
Michigan	1,755,329	24,778	449,586	339,192	941,773	912,329	506,021	363,546	42,762
Minnesota	858,110	167,013	162,483	97,793	430,821	257,255	191,629	63,374	2,252
Mississippi	355,251	93,161	50,248	89,396	122,447	123,294	96,318	26,912	64
Missouri	723,055	111,732	120,868	122,216	368,239	167,782	144,098	20,466	3,218
Montana............	185,276	51,160	20,325	37,758	76,034	76,964	65,586	11,360	18
Nebraska	71,971	15,464	7,388	13,478	35,641	15,664	11,810	3,854	0
Nevada	215,182	21,198	21,449	70,187	102,348	70,571	51,219	7,839	11,513
New Hampshire	64,285	25,510	9,377	11,258	18,139	31,166	23,501	7,248	417
New Jersey.........	1,934,311	290,843	518,011	326,392	799,066	625,686	610,941	13,814	930
New Mexico........	366,881	94,062	41,973	53,340	177,505	96,147	74,276	21,863	7
New York	5,447,225	119,022	715,587	1,616,531	2,996,084	1,502,536	1,442,996	59,540	0
North Carolina	1,271,036	242,998	318,334	52,984	656,720	361,491	309,355	52,042	94
North Dakota	72,795	19,714	7,362	14,662	31,057	19,149	12,870	4,951	1,328
Ohio	3,668,950	740,809	307,056	948,708	1,672,376	1,480,988	1,368,641	95,208	17,138
Oklahoma	552,967	88,918	253,224	24,152	186,673	208,711	194,614	13,384	712
Oregon	605,362	126,617	90,847	167,103	220,795	185,506	156,552	26,234	2,719
Pennsylvania	2,545,153	382,745	845,607	310,695	1,006,106	985,000	905,982	79,018	0
Rhode Island	195,205	38,500	51,605	26,325	78,775	73,541	69,244	4,280	17
South Carolina	601,652	122,071	76,966	91,070	311,544	183,846	154,576	26,848	2,423
South Dakota	87,941	22,573	9,939	14,211	41,217	41,655	18,473	22,265	916
Tennessee	645,879	59,777	242,518	35,513	308,071	191,670	168,411	23,259	0
Texas..............	2,382,254	570,005	615,915	57,436	1,138,898	761,088	630,049	129,861	1,178
Utah	355,493	85,742	36,147	53,276	180,328	72,933	51,137	18,986	2,810
Vermont	66,605	2,379	24,948	881	38,396	21,683	18,939	733	2,012
Virginia............	784,403	71,604	156,996	255,758	300,045	244,649	203,396	41,253	0
Washington	1,145,847	216,740	386,930	93,335	448,842	489,341	442,269	39,432	7,640
West Virginia	242,304	63,661	76,701	15,748	86,194	135,874	122,771	13,103	0
Wisconsin...........	1,353,521	18,309	121,375	272,322	941,516	229,151	192,040	34,434	2,677
Wyoming	120,777	9,801	12,379	32,977	65,620	23,787	16,266	6,634	887

Source: U.S. Bureau of the Census, *Finances of Employee Retirement Systems of State and Local Governments in 1983-84.*
Note: Because of rounding, detail may not add to totals.

State	Total	Cash and deposits	Cash and security holdings at end of fiscal year				Non-governmental securities
			Governmental securities				
			Federal securities			State and local	
			Total	U.S. Treasury	Federal agency		
All states	$255,669,084	$8,035,898	$66,722,583	$45,676,870	$21,045,713	$682,777	$180,227,825
Alabama..............	3,523,247	5,791	5,134	0	5,134	0	3,512,322
Alaska................	1,584,167	112,085	723,222	270,626	452,597	0	748,860
Arizona..............	3,797,278	457,491	1,261,664	1,261,317	347	0	2,078,123
Arkansas	1,768,220	208,676	731,122	598,029	133,093	0	828,422
California.............	41,378,773	1,595,818	3,856,513	2,998,975	857,538	9,262	35,917,181
Colorado	3,987,112	42,416	731,904	234,737	497,167	55	3,212,736
Connecticut	2,749,628	31,789	619,452	457,992	161,460	19,847	2,078,540
Delaware	667,508	105,521	29,176	29,176	0	0	532,811
Florida	6,448,574	21,560	2,264,014	899,398	1,364,616	0	4,162,999
Georgia...............	4,971,965	196,762	1,809,456	1,725,957	83,499	0	2,965,748
Hawaii	2,198,768	38,894	575,160	28,303	546,857	0	1,584,713
Idaho	662,791	65,731	73,487	56,626	16,861	0	523,574
Illinois...............	8,665,157	218,874	2,412,191	1,663,951	748,240	779	6,033,313
Indiana	2,391,412	63,202	1,209,980	885,166	324,814	2,000	1,116,230
Iowa	2,277,531	594	889,775	556,024	333,750	0	1,387,163
Kansas	1,726,421	142,779	267,016	146,956	120,060	14,078	1,302,547
Kentucky	2,905,521	208,647	659,711	414,837	244,874	380	2,036,783
Louisiana	4,109,267	381,703	1,955,237	726,567	1,228,670	0	1,772,327
Maine	667,146	31,795	108,539	75,582	32,957	998	525,814
Maryland	3,813,773	379,828	523,785	376,156	147,629	0	2,910,160
Massachusetts	2,274,287	140,499	1,173,207	37,502	1,135,706	0	960,581
Michigan	10,099,948	505,001	2,139,075	2,105,052	34,023	0	7,455,873
Minnesota	5,160,420	406,338	501,770	374,310	127,461	425	4,251,887
Mississippi	2,002,153	240,688	1,244,213	979,734	264,480	0	517,252
Missouri	3,794,283	35,323	826,930	252,939	573,991	0	2,932,030
Montana..............	788,746	11,985	89,055	88,067	988	1,400	686,306
Nebraska	389,795	7	181,033	133,434	47,599	0	208,755
Nevada	1,374,776	1,206	344,363	163,099	181,265	0	1,029,206
New Hampshire	536,499	536,499	0	0	0	0	0
New Jersey.............	10,371,802	4,040	1,433,000	103,286	1,329,714	244	8,934,518
New Mexico............	1,667,771	39,480	889,676	828,815	60,861	0	738,614
New York	33,058,943	6,000	10,073,460	8,284,939	1,788,521	534,107	22,445,376
North Carolina	7,122,429	13,382	1,519,269	1,047,230	472,039	0	5,589,779
North Dakota	315,006	24,921	89,581	72,657	16,924	0	200,504
Ohio	20,269,330	215,377	5,719,831	3,985,728	1,734,103	1,795	14,332,328
Oklahoma	2,235,356	217,303	1,046,645	489,322	557,323	0	971,408
Oregon	3,036,486	24,999	474,032	363,538	110,494	0	2,537,455
Pennsylvania	11,209,019	324,527	4,910,592	3,749,810	1,160,782	38	5,973,862
Rhode Island	856,430	68,850	347,493	345,893	1,600	0	440,087
South Carolina	3,692,508	5,213	2,701,084	1,613,747	1,087,336	2,365	983,847
South Dakota	507,436	5,138	203,918	203,918	0	0	298,380
Tennessee	3,307,015	285,022	854,884	796,752	58,132	0	2,167,109
Texas.................	13,749,164	40,897	5,254,419	3,595,132	1,659,287	0	8,453,848
Utah	1,647,449	10	470,852	470,852	0	0	1,176,587
Vermont	313,871	5,079	8,329	7,794	535	0	300,463
Virginia...............	3,405,030	2,430	803,953	803,953	0	61	2,598,585
Washington	5,136,571	401,825	977,124	349,737	627,387	90,617	3,667,005
West Virginia	1,006,608	111,873	550,554	549,754	800	4,326	339,856
Wisconsin..............	6,426,724	442,803	1,104,111	0	1,104,111	0	4,879,810
Wyoming	579,255	10,701	328,213	143,589	184,624	0	240,340

Table 7.22
COMPARATIVE STATISTICS FOR STATE-ADMINISTERED PUBLIC EMPLOYEE RETIREMENT SYSTEMS: 1983-84

State	Percent of receipts paid by			Annual benefit payments as a percentage of		Average benefit payments(a)	Investment earnings as a percentage of cash and security holdings	Cash and deposits	Percentage distribution of cash and security holdings		
									Governmental securities		Nongovernmental securities
	Employee contribution	State government	Local government	Annual receipts	Cash and security holdings				Federal	State and local	
All states	15.0	21.5	16.5	29.9	5.7	$453	8.9	3.1	26.1	0.3	70.5
Alabama	15.9	30.9	2.4	23.3	4.8	392	10.4	0.2	0.1	0.0	99.7
Alaska	16.5	25.7	15.6	16.9	4.4	888	11.2	7.1	45.1	0.0	47.3
Arizona	24.2	13.4	12.1	18.5	3.1	413	8.5	12.0	33.2	0.0	54.7
Arkansas	11.1	30.6	6.2	20.0	3.9	321	10.1	11.8	41.3	0.0	46.9
California	15.3	14.0	18.9	29.6	5.3	544	9.3	3.9	9.3	0.0	86.8
Colorado	19.8	12.7	20.6	22.7	4.5	493	9.3	1.1	18.4	0.0	80.6
Connecticut	14.1	49.9	1.6	38.1	8.8	665	8.0	1.2	22.5	0.7	75.6
Delaware	7.5	38.1	0.0	21.6	8.5	392	14.0	15.8	4.4	0.0	79.8
Florida	0.6	15.5	42.9	27.3	5.6	409	8.5	0.3	35.1	0.0	64.6
Georgia	15.9	28.5	8.8	24.4	5.0	492	9.6	4.0	36.4	0.0	59.6
Hawaii	17.1	22.7	7.9	28.4	6.1	469	11.2	1.8	26.2	0.0	72.1
Idaho	24.1	14.6	27.4	34.5	7.8	305	7.6	9.9	11.1	0.0	79.0
Illinois	26.0	20.7	7.1	37.3	6.9	420	8.5	2.5	27.8	0.0	69.6
Indiana	16.5	35.2	10.5	36.9	8.4	347	8.5	2.6	50.6	0.1	46.7
Iowa	17.5	12.0	17.2	24.6	4.3	213	9.3	0.0	39.1	0.0	60.9
Kansas	20.7	21.6	9.3	23.7	4.5	192	9.2	8.3	15.5	0.8	75.4
Kentucky	21.3	29.1	5.1	32.6	6.5	455	8.9	7.2	22.7	0.0	70.1
Louisiana	24.5	38.7	3.7	43.2	9.8	624	7.5	9.3	47.6	0.0	43.1
Maine	19.5	47.3	8.5	53.7	16.5	487	7.5	4.8	16.3	0.1	78.8
Maryland	11.4	56.9	3.6	42.9	8.8	637	5.8	10.0	13.7	0.0	76.3
Massachusetts	21.2	51.6	0.0	47.3	17.5	542	10.0	6.2	51.6	0.0	42.2
Michigan	1.4	25.6	19.3	28.8	5.0	490	9.3	5.0	21.2	0.0	73.8
Minnesota	19.5	18.9	11.4	22.3	3.7	358	8.3	7.9	9.7	0.0	82.4
Mississippi	26.2	14.1	25.6	27.1	4.8	277	6.1	12.0	62.1	0.0	25.8
Missouri	15.5	16.7	16.9	19.9	3.8	359	9.7	0.9	21.8	0.0	77.3
Montana	27.6	10.9	20.3	35.4	8.3	393	9.6	1.5	11.3	0.2	87.0
Nebraska	21.5	10.2	18.7	16.4	3.0	159	9.1	0.1	46.4	0.0	53.6
Nevada	9.9	9.9	32.6	23.8	3.7	482	7.4	0.1	25.0	0.0	74.9
New Hampshire	39.7	14.5	17.5	36.5	4.3	282	3.3	100.0	0.0	0.0	0.0
New Jersey	15.0	26.7	16.8	31.5	5.9	564	7.7	0.0	13.8	0.0	86.1

COMPARATIVE STATISTICS: 1983-84—Continued

| State | Percent of receipts paid by | | | Annual benefit payments as a percentage of | | Average benefit payments(a) | Investment earnings as a percentage of cash and security holdings | Percentage distribution of cash and security holdings | | | |
| | Employee contribution | State government | Local government | Annual receipts | Cash and security holdings | | | Cash and deposits | Governmental securities | | Nongovernmental securities |
									Federal	State and local	
New Mexico	25.6	11.4	14.5	20.2	4.4	429	10.6	2.4	53.3	0.0	44.3
New York	2.2	13.1	29.6	26.5	4.3	453	9.0	0.0	30.5	1.6	67.9
North Carolina	19.1	25.0	4.1	24.3	4.3	405	9.2	0.2	21.3	0.0	78.5
North Dakota	27.1	10.1	20.1	17.6	4.1	236	9.8	7.9	28.4	0.0	63.7
Ohio	20.2	8.3	25.8	37.3	6.7	453	8.2	1.1	28.2	0.0	70.7
Oklahoma	16.1	45.7	4.3	35.2	8.7	473	8.3	9.7	46.8	0.0	43.5
Oregon	20.9	15.0	27.6	25.8	5.1	312	7.2	0.8	15.6	0.0	83.6
Pennsylvania	15.0	33.2	12.2	35.6	8.0	474	8.9	2.9	43.8	0.0	53.3
Rhode Island	19.7	26.4	13.4	35.4	8.0	537	9.2	8.0	40.6	0.0	51.4
South Carolina	20.3	12.8	15.1	25.7	4.1	402	8.4	0.1	73.2	0.1	26.6
South Dakota	25.7	11.3	16.1	21.0	3.6	215	8.1	1.0	40.2	0.0	58.8
Tennessee	9.3	37.5	5.5	26.0	5.1	322	9.3	8.6	25.9	0.0	65.5
Texas	23.9	25.8	2.4	26.4	4.6	490	8.2	0.3	38.2	0.0	61.5
Utah	24.1	10.1	14.9	14.3	3.1	279	10.9	0.0	28.6	0.0	71.4
Vermont	3.6	37.4	1.3	28.4	6.0	352	12.2	1.6	2.7	0.0	95.7
Virginia	9.1	20.1	32.6	25.9	5.9	401	8.8	0.1	23.6	0.0	76.3
Washington	18.9	33.7	8.1	38.6	8.6	556	8.7	7.8	19.0	1.7	71.4
West Virginia	26.3	31.6	6.4	50.6	12.2	344	8.5	11.1	54.7	0.4	33.8
Wisconsin	1.4	8.9	20.1	14.1	2.9	273	14.6	6.9	17.2	0.0	75.9
Wyoming	8.1	10.2	27.3	13.4	2.8	205	11.3	1.8	56.7	0.0	41.5

Source: U.S. Bureau of the Census, *Finances of Employee Retirement Systems of State and Local Governments in 1983-84.*

(a) Average benefit payment for last month of fiscal year.

315

STATE LIBRARY AGENCIES

By Sandra M. Cooper

Every state has an agency responsible for providing various statewide library services and carrying out library development activities. Most of these agencies provide library services to state officials and employees, as well as the public. Although their role, function, and structure vary from state to state, all of these agencies share common goals and responsibilities.

Library Standards and Functions

In 1985, the American Library Association (ALA) published the third edition of *Standards for Library Functions at the State Level*. Recognizing that the state library must work cooperatively with a variety of groups to develop the full range of library and information services and resources required in today's society, the ALA *Standards* emphasize the importance of leadership and coordination to state library success.

The principles for the organization and operation of these agencies, as outlined in the *Standards*, are based on the premise that a "strong library agency at the state level must have the legal authority and financial support to respond to the consumer's needs through a coordinated library system." The *Standards* acknowledge that the organization of these services will differ in each state; however, they stipulate that the agency providing state library services "shall rest upon clear statutory provisions which define the functions to be performed, provide authority for these activities, and ensure the legal basis for a flexible program to meet the needs of the state."

According to the *Standards*, the position of the state library agencies in the organizational structure of government should be such that they have the authority and status necessary to discharge their responsibilities; moreover, the agencies meeting the state's library services responsibilities should be "unified as one department or division of government to the extent possible and advisable under state law, policy, and tradition."

The location and organizational structure of the library agency in government differs across the states. A 1985 survey of state

library agencies indicates that 20 are independent agencies (12 function under a state library board or commission and eight report directly to the governor), 16 are part of the department of education, 12 are part of other departments in state government, and two are part of the state's legislative branch (see Table 7.23).

The *Standards* acknowledge the difficulty of establishing national standards for state libraries—given the diversity of state needs, economic resources, and organizational patterns. Rather than attempting to set quantitative measures of resources, they describe five functions of library agencies: statewide library development, financing library programs, development of resources, information networks, and services to state government (see Table 7.24).

Statewide library development

The broad function of statewide library development has been a priority in most state libraries in recent decades, and the 1970 amendments to the federal Library Services and Construction Act (LSCA) placed particular emphasis on strengthened planning and development activities. Activities in this category include: coordination of public libraries and library systems; the provision of consulting services; legislative review; statistical gathering and analysis; research; interlibrary loan, reference and bibliographic services; interstate library compacts and other cooperative efforts; public relations; specialized resource development; and activities related to recruitment, training, and certification of professional librarians and other library staff members.

State library agencies play an important leadership role in developing programs and policies that ensure the information and library needs of the state's citizens are met. In 1984, the California State Library joined with the UCLA Graduate School of Library

Sandra M. Cooper is Executive Director of the Association of Specialized and Cooperative Library Agencies, a division of the American Library Association.

and Information Science to co-sponsor a conference on "Libraries and the Information Economy of California," to discuss the public policy issues involved in the use of information, both as a public benefit and an economic resource.

State libraries also have joined with other statewide groups and organizations to sponsor and support efforts to combat illiteracy: the Illinois State Library is administering a $2 million literacy grant program and coordinating the state's adult literacy initiative; the Connecticut State Library awarded funds for literacy activities in 21 public libraries in 1984-85; and the State Library of Florida, a founding member of the Florida Literacy Coalition, awarded more than $1.5 million in LSCA funds for library literacy activities.

Forty-four state library agencies collect, analyze, and disseminate statistics on library activities. They also cooperate with national efforts to collect library statistics. In 1986-87, 10 state library agencies will be working with the ALA in a pilot project funded by the U.S. Department of Education to establish the groundwork for a national cooperative system of public library data collection; the goal is to develop a core of data elements and definitions to be reported nationally.

Financing library programs

All state library agencies distribute federal LSCA funds, and 42 agencies distribute state funds to libraries.

State aid programs for libraries are designed to ensure equal access to library services for all citizens, assist in organizing larger units of service for more effective use of resources, support cooperative efforts among all types of libraries, aid specific activities and services, and assist large libraries that serve as resource centers for the entire state. The figures in Table 7.23 indicate that the amount of money appropriated by the states for direct assistance to public libraries and networks increased by approximately 29.7 percent between fiscal years 1984 and 1986. Recent years have seen an increase in state funds distributed to support cooperative activities among libraries—a trend that has been reflected in both the amount of money allocated for cooperative activities and in changes in state legislation.

In 1984, the federal LSCA was extended for another five years and amended. The revised act, influenced significantly by the findings of the 1979 White House Conference on Libraries and Information Services, emphasizes the role of public libraries as community information and referral centers, serving persons whose first language is not English, supporting literacy programs, requiring new planning for resource sharing among all types of libraries, and providing a new program to support services to American Indians living on reservations.[1]

Development of resources

As a part of this third functional area, state libraries are involved in long-range planning; determination of the size and scope of collections in the state; mobilization of resources; subject and reference centers; resources of books, other printed materials, and multi-media; resources and materials for the blind and physically handicapped; coordination of resources; and the storage of little-used materials.

Thirty-seven state libraries provide services to blind and physically-handicapped citizens through a network of libraries organized by the Library of Congress to provide braille and talking books. The states are responsible for services that achieve the levels set forth in *Revised Standards and Guidelines for the Library of Congress Network of Libraries for the Blind and Physically Handicapped* (American Library Association, 1984).

Information networks

The state library agencies are active in planning and funding for local library participation in local, statewide, interstate, and national networks. The explosion of knowledge in a variety of formats has made it impossible for a single library to meet the needs of its patrons. This factor, combined with advances in communications and computer technology, has created a new range of options for the development of networks and resource sharing. Libraries have found that resource sharing means more effective use of the dollars available to support library services.

Network and resource-sharing development activities are operating in all 50 states. State library efforts are enabling the development of statewide databases available both on-line and off-line to give the local library patron access to all of the state's resources. The South Carolina State Library is implementing a network that first will include the state library and 46 county libraries to provide circulation, public access catalogs, and interlibrary loan. In late 1986, state agencies will be added to the network, and in 1987, dial access will be extended to academic and technical libraries. In 1984, the state legislature in New York appropriated $1.3 million for the development of a database with 57 million records from all types of libraries in the state.

Service to state government

Almost every state library provides some kind of information service to state government agencies. The ways in which state libraries fulfill this responsibility, the variety of services offered, the intensity of effort, and the degree of coordination with other agencies vary widely among the states. However, some of the more common activities include government documents, information and reference, legislative reference, law library, genealogy and state history, archives, and liaison with state institutional libraries.

Several trends are strengthening and expanding the traditional services provided to state government by state library agencies:

• *Cooperative projects among state libraries and state agency libraries.* State agencies frequently maintain internal libraries ranging in size from small office collections to significant resources. These agency libraries are working with their state libraries to improve access to information for state government. In some states, organizations have been formed to foster this cooperation—the State Agency Libraries of Texas (SALT), the New York State Interagency Information Group (NYSIIG), and the Michigan Council of State Agency Libraries are examples. The New Jersey State Library staff provides consulting services and training to state agency library staff members, as well as brokering the purchase of on-line database services to reduce costs for libraries in state government. In New York, state agency libraries are participating in a pilot project that gives them dial-up access to the state library's on-line catalog.

• *Outreach and marketing.* The California State Library is among those libraries that provide on-site service outlets for the legislature, and in 1986, the New York State Library's on-line catalog was ex-

tended to 26 state Senate offices, giving them instant access to the information resources of the state library.

• *Strengthening state document collections.* State libraries attempt to collect and maintain a comprehensive collection of publications generated by state government. Recently, several states have begun or have redesigned document depository systems to improve the collection and dissemination of documents through legislation, studies of current systems, and improved communications with publishing agencies to encourage deposit of their documents.

• *Cooperation with other information providers.* State library agencies also are cooperating with other organizations to improve service to state officials. One example is the U.S. Bureau of the Census' State Data Center Program, which was created to improve information in machine-readable, print, and microfiche formats, and has agencies working with state libraries to improve information for state agency personnel and library patrons in many states.

Note

1. The titles of the current LSCA are: Title I, Public Library Services; Title II, Public Library Construction; Title III, Interlibrary Cooperation; Title IV, Indian Library Services; and Title V, Library Literacy Programs.

Selected References

American Library Association. Association of Specialized and Cooperative Library Agencies. *Revised Standards and Guidelines for the Library of Congress Network of Libraries for the Blind and Physically Handicapped 1984.* Chicago, 1984.

American Library Association. Association of Specialized and Cooperative Library Agencies. *Standards for Library Functions at the State Level.* 3rd ed. Chicago, 1985.

American Library Association. Association of Specialized and Cooperative Library Agencies. *The State Library Agencies: A Survey Project Report.* 7th ed. Chicago, 1985.

Eberhart, W. Lyle. "State Library Agencies in the United States." *World Encyclopedia of Library and Information Services.* Chicago, 1980.

McClure, Charles R. *State Library Services and Issues: Facing Future Challenges.* Norwood, N.J., 1986.

McCrossan, John A., ed. "State Library Development Agencies." *Library Trends* 27, 2 (Fall 1978).

Table 7.23
STATE LIBRARY AGENCIES
Structure and Appropriations
Fiscal 1986

State	Organization structure(a)	Agency reports to:(b)	Appropriations State — Agency appropriation	State — Direct assistance to public libraries & networks	Federal — Library Services and Construction Act	Federal — Other	Other sources of income	Total
All states			$130,874,191	$282,570,411	$111,158,561	$2,208,521	$28,918,005	$555,729,689
Alabama............	I	B	2,052,060	3,621,316	1,552,674	0	0	7,226,050
Alaska.............	U	E	3,123,800	1,282,500	364,300	0	11,600	4,782,200
Arizona............	U	L	2,984,600	500,000	1,727,100	31,500	310,000	5,553,200
Arkansas	U	E	1,674,433	2,530,871 (c)	1,296,579	0	0	5,501,883
California..........	U	E	8,659,000	29,298,000	10,580,417	0	0	48,537,417
Colorado	U	E	820,777	2,229,347	1,613,367	0	0	4,663,491
Connecticut	U	B,E	5,321,668	1,800,300	1,320,453	0	92,076	8,534,497
Delaware	U	D	469,900	295,600	588,784	0	0	1,354,284
Florida	U	S	1,940,229	6,623,934	4,679,644	18,500	0	13,262,307
Georgia............	U	E	778,574	12,940,706	2,423,417	69,938	0	16,212,635
Hawaii	U	E	13,054,163	0 (d)	970,255	0	0	14,024,418
Idaho	U	E	1,338,200	0	745,200	0	25,000	2,108,400
Illinois............	U	S	4,509,154	31,173,466	6,620,807	0	13,000,000	55,303,427
Indiana............	I	G	1,958,694	1,858,095	2,440,665	0	0	6,257,454
Iowa	I	C	1,158,233	1,480,556	1,470,786	0	19,000	4,128,575
Kansas	I	G	890,965	1,394,545	1,443,982	0	136,050	3,865,542
Kentucky	I	G	7,778,800	1,958,100	1,870,859	0	530,200	12,137,959
Louisiana	U	R	846,702	922,231	1,830,780	310,274	124,555	4,034,542
Maine	U	E	1,965,359	423,500	811,034	0	0	3,199,893
Maryland	U	E	1,246,311	14,360,078	1,469,786	213,000	0	17,289,175
Massachusetts	I	C	1,387,113 (e)	13,129,820	2,724,192	0	0	17,241,125
Michigan	U	L	4,034,400	15,790,000	5,194,100	251,300	810,000	26,079,800
Minnesota	U	E	940,535	5,128,700	2,053,716	0	69,500	8,192,451
Mississippi	I	C	1,506,878	1,979,153	1,373,398	0	0	4,859,429
Missouri	U	E	859,628	1,765,500	2,389,089	0	40,000	5,054,217
Montana...........	U	C	631,223	371,541	457,752	0	225,000	1,685,516
Nebraska	I	C	1,326,227	563,198	1,034,857	0	84,795	3,009,077
Nevada	I	G	1,287,796	0	703,227	0	0	1,991,023
New Hampshire......	U	R	1,200,000	0	475,000	234,000	0	1,909,000
New Jersey..........	U	E	3,478,000	13,415,000	3,423,000	0	1,848,000	22,164,000
New Mexico(f)	U	R	1,972,700	241,800	836,300	38,100	50,000	3,138,900
New York	U	E	7,088,186	45,779,380	7,624,019	0	130,000	60,621,585
North Carolina	U	R	3,417,032	10,789,462	2,835,731	0	30,800	17,073,025
North Dakota	U	I	436,500	550,000	618,640	0	0	1,605,140
Ohio	I	B	3,920,547	1,150,968	4,335,048	0	485,288	9,891,851
Oklahoma	I	B	2,414,579	1,368,086	1,677,636	0	949,049	6,409,350
Oregon	I	G	1,828,896	320,000	1,837,419	0	51,582	4,037,897
Pennsylvania	U	E	2,721,000	18,350,000	5,265,534	705,060	2,163,789	29,205,383
Rhode Island	I	G	784,242	2,257,023	702,120	82,657	17,259	3,843,306
South Carolina	I	B	2,052,074	3,121,820	1,678,050	0	0	6,851,944
South Dakota	U	R	1,371,534	0	653,667	0	96,093	2,121,294
Tennessee	U	S	2,440,000	2,646,100	1,705,540	0	0	6,791,640
Texas..............	I	C	5,196,686	5,770,011	6,795,907	0	0	17,762,604
Utah	U	D	2,044,100	0	961,139	203,500	549,800	3,758,539
Vermont	I	G	1,289,113	0 (g)	420,000	0	378,500	2,087,613
Virginia............	I	G	3,435,490	9,863,300	2,365,000	0	100,000	15,763,790
Washington	I	C	4,262,000	0	1,188,000	0	5,649,269	11,099,269
West Virginia	I	C	1,759,157	5,636,804	1,153,113	0	0	8,549,074
Wisconsin	U	E	2,345,500	7,889,600	2,307,478	50,692	65,800	12,659,070
Wyoming	I	B	871,428	0	549,000	0	875,000	2,295,428

Source: Chief Officers of State Library Agencies; and Phillis M. Wilson and Mara Karduck, Association of Specialized and Cooperative Library Agencies.

Note: Appropriations vary depending on the state library's functions; therefore, the reader is advised to view appropriation figures in this table in tandem with information provided in Table 7.24, "Functions and Responsibilities of State Library Agencies." For further information, consult: The State Library Agencies: A Survey Project Report, 1985 (Chicago: American Library Association/ASCLA, 1986).

(a) For this column: I—Independent; U—Unit within larger unit.

(b) For this column: A—Department of Administration; B—Board; C—Commission; D—Department of Community Affairs and Economic Development; E—Department of Education; G—Governor or Governor's Board; I—Director of Institutions; L—Legislature; R—Department of Cultural Resources; S—Secretary of State.

(c) Of the $2,530,871 appropriated, $2,292,492 was allocated.

(d) Has a statewide public library system; all public and state library support is included in the previous column.

(e) This figure reflects the $740,000 appropriation for the Massachusetts State Library and $647,113 for the Board of Library Commissioners (state library development agency).

(f) FY85 appropriations; FY86 figures not available at time of compilation.

(g) Included in state appropriation for agency operation.

Table 7.24
FUNCTIONS AND RESPONSIBILITIES
OF STATE LIBRARY AGENCIES

State	Library services to state governments							Statewide library services development															
	Documents	Information and reference service	Legislative reference	Law library	Genealogy and state history	Archives	Liaison with institutional libraries	Coordination of academic libraries	Coordination of public libraries	Coordination of school libraries	Coordination of institutional libraries	Research	Coordination of library systems	Consulting services	Interlibrary loan, reference and bibliographic service	Statistical gathering and analysis	Library legislation review	Interstate library compacts and other cooperative efforts	Specialized resource centers	Direct service to the public	Annual reports	Public relations	Continuing education
Alabama	★	★	...	...	...	...	★	...	★	...	★	...	★	★	★	★	★	★	★	★	★	★	★
Alaska	★	★	†	†	★	...	★	†	★	†	★	†	★	★	★	★	★	★	★	★	†	★	★
Arizona	★	★	★	★	★	★	★	★	★	†	★	★	★	★	★	★	★	★	★	★	★	†	★
Arkansas	★	★	...	...	...	...	★	†	★	†	★	★	★	★	★	★	★	★	†	★	★	★	★
California	★	★	★	★	★	...	★	†	★	...	†	†	★	★	★	★	★	†	★	†	...	★	†	†
Colorado	★	...	...	...	...	...	★	†	★	★	★	★	★	★	†	★	★	★	...	†	★	†	†
Connecticut	★	★	†	★	★	†	★	...	★	★	★	†	★	★	★	★	★	★	★	★	★	★	★
Delaware	†	★	†	...	†	...	★	...	★	†	★	†	★	★	★	★	★	★	★	★	★	★	★
Florida	★	★	†	...	★	...	★	†	★	...	★	†	★	★	★	★	★	★	★	★	★	†	†
Georgia	†	★	...	...	...	...	★	...	★	...	★	†	★	★	★	★	★	★	...	†	★	†	†
Hawaii	★	★	...	...	★	...	★	...	★	...	★	†	†	†	†	†	†	†	...	★	★	†	†
Idaho	†	★	†	...	†	†	★	...	★	†	★	★	★	★	...	★	★	★	★	★	★	★	†
Illinois	★	★	†	...	...	...	†	†	★	†	†	†	★	†	†	†	†	†	★	†	★	★	†
Indiana	★	★	†	...	...	...	★	†	★	†	★	†	†	★	†	★	★	†	★	†	★	★	†
Iowa	★	★	†	★	†	...	★	...	★	†	†	†	★	★	★	★	★	★	★	★	★	★	†
Kansas	★	★	†	...	...	...	★	†	★	†	†	†	★	★	★	★	★	†	★	†	★	†	†
Kentucky	†	★	†	...	†	★	★	†	★	...	†	†	★	★	★	★	★	★	★	†	★	†	†
Louisiana	†	★	†	...	★	...	★	†	★	†	★	★	★	★	★	★	★	★	†	★	†	★	†
Maine	★	★	†	...	★	...	★	†	★	†	★	★	★	★	★	★	★	★	†	★	†	★	†
Maryland	†	†	...	...	...	...	★	†	★	★	★	★	★	★	★	★	★	★	★	★	†	★	★
Massachusetts	...	†	...	...	...	...	★	...	★	...	★	★	★	★	†	†	†	★	†	†	★	†	★
Michigan	★	★	†	★	★	★	★	...	★	†	★	★	†	★	★	★	†	†	★	†	★	†	★
Minnesota	...	†	...	...	...	...	†	†	★	†	†	★	★	★	★	★	★	†	★	★	★	★	†
Mississippi	★	†	†	...	...	...	★	†	★	†	★	†	★	★	★	★	★	★	†	†	★	★	†
Missouri	†	†	†	...	...	...	★	†	★	†	★	...	...	★	★	★	★	★	★	★	★	★	★
Montana	†	★	†	...	...	...	★	†	★	†	†	†	★	★	★	★	★	★	†	†	★	★	†
Nebraska	★	★	†	...	...	...	★	†	★	†	†	★	★	★	★	★	★	★	★	★	★	★	†
Nevada	★	★	†	...	†	★	★	†	★	†	★	★	★	★	★	★	★	★	†	★	★	★	★
New Hampshire	★	★	★	★	★	...	★	...	★	†	★	†	★	★	★	★	★	★	...	†	★	★	★
New Jersey	★	★	†	★	★	...	★	†	★	★	†	...	★	★	★	†	★	†	★	†	★	†	†
New Mexico	★	★	†	...	†	†	★	†	★	†	★	†	★	★	★	★	★	†	†	†	★	★	★
New York	★	★	★	†	★	†	★	★	★	†	★	†	★	★	★	★	★	†	★	★	★	†	★
North Carolina	★	★	†	†	†	...	★	†	★	†	†	†	★	★	★	★	★	★	†	†	★	★	★
North Dakota	★	★	†	...	†	...	★	★	★	†	★	★	★	★	★	★	★	★	★	†	★	★	★
Ohio	★	★	†	...	†	...	★	†	★	†	†	†	★	★	★	★	★	†	★	†	†	†	★
Oklahoma	★	★	★	★	...	★	★	†	★	†	★	★	★	★	★	★	★	★	†	...	★	★	★
Oregon	★	★	★	...	†	...	★	†	★	†	★	★	★	★	★	★	★	†	★	...	★	★	★
Pennsylvania	★	★	†	★	†	...	★	★	★	†	★	★	★	★	★	★	★	†	★	★	★	★	★
Rhode Island	...	†	...	...	...	...	★	★	★	...	★	★	★	★	★	★	†	★	★	†	†	†	†
South Carolina	†	★	★	...	†	...	★	...	★	...	★	†	★	★	★	★	★	★	...	...	★	★	†
South Dakota	★	★	★	...	†	★	★	†	★	†	†	†	★	★	★	★	★	★	★	★	★	★	★
Tennessee	★	†	†	†	★	★	†	...	★	★	★	†	★	★	★	★	†	†	†	†	★	★	†
Texas	★	★	†	★	★	★	★	†	★	†	†	†	★	★	★	★	†	†	†	†	★	★	★
Utah	★	★	...	...	...	...	★	†	★	†	★	...	★	★	★	★	★	†	★	★	★	★	★
Vermont	★	★	†	★	★	...	★	...	★	...	★	†	★	★	★	★	★	†	★	†	★	★	†
Virginia	★	†	†	...	†	★	★	...	★	...	★	★	★	★	★	★	†	★	†	...	★	†	†
Washington	★	★	★	...	†	†	★	†	★	...	†	★	★	★	★	★	★	†	†	★	★	★	★
West Virginia	†	†	†	...	...	...	★	†	★	★	★	★	★	★	★	★	★	★	★	...	★	★	★
Wisconsin	†	★	†	...	...	...	★	†	★	★	★	★	★	★	★	★	★	★	†	...	★	†	★
Wyoming	★	★	★	...	†	...	★	†	★	†	★	†	...	★	★	★	★	...	★	†	★	★	†

Note: For additional information, see *Standards for Library Functions at the State Level*, 3rd edition. (American Library Association, 1985).

Key:
★—Primary.
†—Shared.
. . . .—None.

State	Long-range planning	Determination of size and scope of collections in the state	Mobilization of resources	Subject and reference centers	Resources—books	Resources—other printed materials	Resources—multimedia	Resources—materials for the blind and handicapped	Coordination of resources	Little-used materials	Planning of information networks	Provision of centralized facilities	Exchange of information and materials	Interstate cooperation	Administration of federal aid	Administration of state aid	Financing of library systems and networks
	Statewide development of library resources										*Statewide development of information networks*				*Financing library programs*		
Alabama	★	★	★	★	★	★	★	★	★	...	★	†	★	★	★	★	★
Alaska	★	†	★	†	†	†	★	★	★	†	★	★	†	★	★	★	★
Arizona	★	★	★	★	★	★	★	★	★	...	★	★	★	★	★	★	★
Arkansas	★	★	★	★	★	★	★	★	★	★	★	★	★	★	★	★	★
California	★	†	†	†	†	†	†	†	★	†	★	†	†	†	★	★	★
Colorado	★	†	†	†	†	†	†	★	†	†	†	†	†	★	★	★	★
Connecticut	★	†	★	★	★	★	★	★	★	†	★	★	★	★	★	★	★
Delaware	★	†	★	★	★	★	★	★	†	★	★	★	★	★	★	★	★
Florida	★	†	†	★	†	†	†	★	★	★	★	★	★	★	★	★	★
Georgia	★	★	★	★	★	★	★	★	★	★	★	★	★	★	★	★	★
Hawaii	†	†	†	†	†	†	†	★	★	★	†	†	†	†	★	...	†
Idaho	★	†	★	†	★	★	★	★	★	★	†	†	★	★	★	★	†
Illinois	†	†	†	†	†	†	†	†	†	...	†	†	†	★	★	★	★
Indiana	★	...	†	†	†	†	†	★	†	†	†	†	†	★	★	★	★
Iowa	★	★	★	★	★	★	★	†	★	★	†	★	★	★	★	★	★
Kansas	★	★	†	†	†	†	†	†	†	†	★	★	★	★	★	★	★
Kentucky	★	†	†	†	†	†	†	★	★	†	★	†	★	★	★	★	★
Louisiana	†	†	†	†	†	†	†	★	†	...	†	★	★	★	★	★	★
Maine	★	★	★	★	★	★	★	★	†	★	†	★	†	★	★	★	★
Maryland	★	...	...	...	...	...	...	★	★	★	★	★	★	★	★	★	★
Massachusetts	†	...	†	...	†	†	†	†	†	†	†	†	†	★	★	★	★
Michigan	★	...	†	★	†	†	†	★	★	†	★	...	†	★	★	★	★
Minnesota	★	†	★	†	†	†	†	★	★	★	★	†	★	★	★	★	†
Mississippi	★	★	★	★	★	★	★	★	★	★	★	†	★	★	★	★	†
Missouri	★	†	★	★	★	★	†	†	★	★	★	†	†	†	★	★	†
Montana	★	★	★	★	★	★	★	★	†	†	★	†	★	★	★	★	★
Nebraska	★	...	★	★	★	★	★	★	★	...	★	...	†	★	★	★	★
Nevada	★	†	†	†	†	†	†	★	★	†	★	★	★	★	★	★	★
New Hampshire	★	★	†	†	†	★	★	★	★	★	★	★	★	★	★	★	★
New Jersey	★	†	★	†	†	†	†	★	†	†	★	★	★	★	★	★	★
New Mexico	★	†	★	...	†	†	†	★	★	...	★	★	★	★	†	★	★
New York	★	†	†	†	★	★	★	†	★	...	★	★	★	†	★	★	★
North Carolina	★	†	†	★	★	★	†	★	★	★	★	★	★	★	★	★	★
North Dakota	★	...	★	★	★	★	★	†	★	★	★	★	★	★	★	★	★
Ohio	★	†	†	†	†	†	†	†	★	†	★	★	★	★	★	★	★
Oklahoma	★	†	†	★	★	★	★	★	†	†	★	★	†	★	★	★	★
Oregon	★	★	★	...	†	★	†	†	†	†	★	...	†	★	★	★	†
Pennsylvania	★	†	★	†	★	†	†	★	★	†	★	...	★	...	★	★	★
Rhode Island	★	†	★	†	†	†	†	★	★	...	★	†	★	★	★	★	†
South Carolina	★	†	...	★	†	†	★	★	†	...	★	★	★	★	★	★	...
South Dakota	★	†	★	★	†	†	★	★	★	★	★	†	★	★	★	...	★
Tennessee	★	...	†	†	†	†	†	†	†	†	★	†	★	★	★	★	★
Texas	★	†	†	†	†	★	★	†	★	†	★	†	★	★	★	★	★
Utah	★	†	†	†	†	†	†	★	†	...	★	†	†	★	★	★	†
Vermont	★	†	†	†	†	†	†	★	★	†	†	†	★	★	†	★	†
Virginia	★	...	†	†	†	†	†	†	†	†	★	★	★	★	★	★	†
Washington	★	...	★	†	...	...	...	†	...	...	★	★	★	★	★	★	★
West Virginia	★	...	...	†	★	...	★	★	★	†	★	★	†	★	★	†	†
Wisconsin	★	...	...	†	†	†	†	†	★	†	†	★	†	★	★	★	★
Wyoming	★	†	†	†	†	†	†	†	★	★	†	★	★	★	★	...	...

Key:
★—Primary.
†—Shared.
... —None.

CHAPTER EIGHT

SELECTED STATE ACTIVITIES, ISSUES AND SERVICES

UNIFORM STATE LAWS: 1984-85

By John M. McCabe

In 1984 and 1985, the Uniform Law Commissioners substantially revised two older Uniform Acts, adopted amendments to two others, and promulgated five completely new acts. In addition, the financing provisions of the Uniform Land Transactions Act were extracted to create the Uniform Land Security Interest Act. Summaries of all of these activities follow.

Uniform Fraudulent Transfer Act

This act substantially revises the Uniform Fraudulent Conveyance Act of 1918. It creates a class of transfers of property by debtors that is fraudulent to creditors. This class of transfers generally would have the effect of depriving creditors of assets that would otherwise be available to satisfy debts when the debtor becomes insolvent or is about to become insolvent. Fraudulent transfers are those that are intended to defraud creditors, that are made "without receiving reasonably equivalent value" to make the debtor "judgment proof," or that are made "without receiving reasonably equivalent value" when the debtor is insolvent. Such transfers generally are voidable on behalf of creditors. Creditors also may have damages. This new act updates terminology that has become obsolete since 1918, is more specific on what constitutes fraud, and introduces new law on "insider" transactions and on the effect of fraudulent transfers on innocent transferees.

Uniform Health-Care Information Act

This act governs access to patient health-care records held by any person or entity providing health-care services. A patient must consent to the disclosure of his or her own health-care records to any other person, unless the disclosure fits one of a limited number of exceptions. Exceptions relate to specific instances when disclosure is essential to the patient's health or is absolutely essential to the functioning of the health-care provider. A patient also has a right to inspect and copy his or her own records and to demand correction of any errors. The only exceptions involve clearly-demonstrated cases in which such access to his or her own records would injure the patient. Remedies, including criminal penalties, are provided for violations of the act.

Uniform Law Commissioners' Model Insanity Defense and Post-Trial Disposition Act

This act provides a "cognitive" test for determining whether a criminal defendant lacks criminal responsibility. There is no criminal responsibility if the defendant "is substantially unable to appreciate the wrongfulness of the conduct." The burden of proof for establishing criminal responsibility remains with the prosecution. The act provides procedures for obtaining expert opinion on the defendant's mental condition and for the disposition of anyone found not criminally responsible into appropriate treatment for dangerous mental illness.

Uniform Land Security Interest Act

This act is derived from Article 3 of the Uniform Land Transactions Act. Its provisions govern the financing of real estate transactions, basic rules for establishing a valid security agreement, assignment of interests under such agreements, and default. It also provides for usury. An agreement generally is effective according to its terms. A security interest on the part of a creditor in real property "attaches" when a security agreement is signed, value has been given, and the debtor acquires his or her interest in the property. The act prohibits clogging the equity of redemption. Priorities between creditors with competing security interests generally are based on first in time to record or attach. Futures advances relate back to the time the security interest is effective, for advances initially agreed upon or made to protect collateral. Adopting jurisdictions may choose their approach to usury. The alternatives permit either agreement between parties to determine interest rates in all cases, or agreement between the parties excepting

John M. McCabe is Legislative Director of the National Conference of Commissioners on Uniform State Laws.

interest rates for residential real estate security interests. A ceiling would apply to such interest rates. Upon default, property may be foreclosed as agreed by the parties, by judicial foreclosure, or by "power of sale." When security interests attach to residential property, the debtor is known as a protected party and benefits from a number of special provisions in the act.

Uniform Limited Partnership Act Amendments

The 1985 amendments to the Uniform Limited Partnership Act provide for a notice certificate, which does not contain the kinds of information on partner identification and contributions that formerly were required. Much of the information that the certificate contained must be retained for the benefit of partners in the partnership agreement or the partnership records. A reliance test, based on the conduct of a limited partner, replaces the prior test for determining when a limited partner loses limited liability. The so-called "safe harbor" provisions are expanded so that certain actions available to limited partners do not result in liability as general partners. Less than unanimous consent for admission of new general partners may be provided for in the partnership agreement. These substantive amendments are accompanied by other clarifying and conforming amendments.

Uniform Personal Property Leasing Act

This act governs any lease of personal property (or goods), whether the transaction is a "true lease" or a "finance lease." The former occurs when the lessor gives possession and right to use the personal property to the lessee for a fixed period of time in return for rent. The title to the property remains with the lessor. A "finance lease" occurs when the lessor is not the fundamental supplier of the goods leased, but leases goods to lessees as a means of financing their sale. The act is largely derived from the sales article of the UCC, Article 2, and provides basic contract rules, including matters of offer and acceptance, statutes of frauds, warranties, assignment of interests, and remedies upon breach of contract. Appended to the act is an amendment to Article 9 of the UCC. The amendment establishes when a lease involves a security interest.

Uniform Rights Of The Terminally Ill Act

This act provides for a declaration (popularly known as a "living will") that instructs attending physicians to withhold life-sustaining treatment for any person who makes such a declaration in writing, in the event that person is in the last stages of a terminal illness and is unable to personally express his or her requirements. The declaration must be witnessed, is effective when communicated to an attending physician, and is a binding instruction. The act provides language that may be used to make a declaration, although a person may provide any instructions he or she wants to provide. "Life-sustaining treatment" and "terminal illness" are defined. Even though treatment may be "life-sustaining," it must be continued if the "comfort care" of the patient requires it.

Uniform Securities Act

This act updates the 1956 Uniform Securities Act. It provides for the licensing of those who sell securities and those who advise buyers. It provides for the registration of securities issues in one of three ways—"registration by filing," "registration by coordination," and "registration by qualification." The first two types of registration are available to issuers who have qualified to sell under applicable federal law. The last type of registration involves full merit review by the state administrator. Certain specified securities issues and transactions are exempted from registration. In general, exemptions apply if other law or institutional arrangements provide protection for buyers. The act has anti-fraud provisions, including new provisions prohibiting market manipulations. A person injured by these kinds of fraudulent activities may seek a remedy in a court of law. The administrator has substantial enforcement powers as well, including powers to investigate, to hear allegations of violation of the act, to issue cease and desist orders, and to exact monetary penalties.

Uniform Statutory Will Act

This act provides anyone who desires to leave most of an estate to a spouse with a simple, effective system of distribution that may be elected by incorporating the statute by reference in a will. The election offered in this act allows a person to avoid intestate succession, but at the same time, saves the expense of a fully-written will. The distribution under this act would go entirely to the spouse if there are no children. If there are children, the spouse gets the residential home of the testator, all tangible personal property, and either one-half the remaining estate or assets of value up to $300,000, whichever is greater. The remainder goes into trust for the surviving spouse's life. The surviving spouse receives the income from the trust, and the trust is divided equally among the children at the death of the surviving spouse. If there are children, but no surviving spouse, the children share equally. A trust is created to hold and manage the estate of minor children until they come of age. If there is no spouse, nor any children or issue of the testator, the estate goes by intestate succession.

Uniform Trade Secrets Act Amendments

This act was amended in 1985 to provide that: (1) contractual remedies are subject to contract law, even though a misappropriation may have occurred under the act; (2) a continuing misappropriation, beginning before the act becomes effective, is subject to prior law; (3) damages may be assessed in the form of a reasonable royalty, if other methods of measuring damages are inadequate; and (4) a reasonable royalty as an equitable remedy is available when "exceptional circumstances" require (exceptional circumstances being any situation in which a party has materially changed position so that injunctive relief would not be adequate to the situation).

The Uniform Law Commissioners continue to work on a large number of drafting projects. Among the acts scheduled for completion in 1986 and 1987—a Criminal History Records Act, a Franchise and Business Opportunities Act, a Rights of Putative Fathers Act, and a Status of Children of the New Biology Act. More details on the work of the Uniform Law Commissioners can be obtained from the National Conference of Commissioners on Uniform State Laws, 645 North Michigan Avenue, Suite 510, Chicago, Illinois 60611.

Table 8.1
RECORD OF PASSAGE OF UNIFORM ACTS
(As of September 1, 1985)

State or other jurisdiction	Adoption (1953) (1969) (1971)	Alcoholism and Intoxication Treatment (1971)	Anatomical Gift (1968)	Arbitration (1956)	Attendance of Out of State Witnesses (1931) (1936)	Audio-Visual Deposition (1978)	Certification of Questions of Law (1967)	Child Custody Jurisdiction (1968)	Class Actions (1976)	Commercial Code (1951) (1957) (1962) (1966)	Commercial Code—Article 8 (1977)	Commercial Code—Article 9 (1972)	Common Interest Ownership (1982)	Common Trust Fund (1938) (1952)	Comparative Fault (1977) (1979)	Condominium (1977) (1980)	Conflict of Laws—Limitations (1982)
Alabama	...	...	★	...	•	...	...	★	...	•	...	★	...	★	...	...	...
Alaska	...	★	★	★	•	...	...	★	...	•	...	★	★	★	...	...	...
Arizona	...	...	★	★	•	...	...	★	...	•	...	★	...	★	...	...	...
Arkansas	•	...	★	★	★	...	...	★	...	•	★	★	...	★	...	...	★
California	...	...	☆	☆	•	...	...	★	...	•	★	★	...	★	...	...	...
Colorado	★	★	★	...	•	...	★	★	...	•	★	★	...	★	...	...	...
Connecticut	☆	★	★	☆	•	...	★	★	...	•	★	★	★	★	...	...	★
Delaware	★	★	★	★	•	...	...	★	...	•	★	★	...	★	...	...	...
Florida	☆	★	★	★	•	...	☆	★	...	•	...	★	...	★	★	...	...
Georgia	★	★	...	...	•	...	...	★	...	•	...	★	...	★	...	...	...
Hawaii	...	...	★	☆	•	...	...	★	...	•	...	★	...	★	...	...	...
Idaho	...	★	★	★	★	...	...	★	...	•	★	★	...	★	...	...	...
Illinois	...	★	★	★	★	...	...	★	...	•	...	★	...	★	...	...	...
Indiana	...	...	★	★	★	...	...	★	...	•	...	★	...	...	...	...	...
Iowa	•	★	★	★	☆	...	★	★	★	•	★	★	...	•	...	...	...
Kansas	...	★	★	★	•	...	★	★	...	•	...	★	...	★	...	...	...
Kentucky	...	...	★	★	•	...	...	★	...	•	...	...	...	...	☆	...	...
Louisiana	...	☆	★	...	•	...	...	★	...	...	...	...	...	...	...	...	...
Maine	...	★	★	★	•	...	☆	★	...	•	...	★	...	★	...	•	...
Maryland	☆	★	★	★	•	...	★	★	...	•	...	★	...	★	...	...	...
Massachusetts	☆	...	★	★	•	...	☆	★	...	★	...	★	...	★	...	...	...
Michigan	☆	★	★	☆	☆	...	...	★	...	•	...	★	...	★	...	...	...
Minnesota	☆	★	★	★	•	...	...	★	...	•	...	★	...	★	...	★	...
Mississippi	...	...	★	...	•	...	...	★	...	•	...	★	...	★	•	...	...
Missouri	...	...	★	☆	•	...	...	★	...	•	...	★	...	★	★	•	...
Montana	★	★	★	★	•	...	...	★	...	•	★	★	...	★	...	...	...
Nebraska	...	★	★	...	•	...	...	★	...	•	...	...	...	★	...	•	...
Nevada	...	★	★	★	•	...	...	★	...	•	★	★	...	★	...	...	...
New Hampshire	...	★	★	☆	•	...	★	★	...	•	...	★	...	...	...	★	...
New Jersey	...	★	★	☆	•	...	...	★	...	•	...	★	...	...	...	...	...
New Mexico	☆	...	★	★	•	...	...	★	...	•	...	★	...	★	...	•	...
New York	...	...	★	☆	•	...	...	★	...	•	★	★	...	★	...	...	...
North Carolina	...	...	★	★	•	...	...	★	...	•	...	★	...	★	...	...	...
North Dakota	•	...	★	...	★	★	★	★	★	•	★	★	...	...	...	...	★
Ohio	...	...	★	☆	•	...	...	★	...	•	★	★	...	•	...	...	...
Oklahoma	★	★	★	★	•	...	★	★	...	•	★	★	...	•	...	...	...
Oregon	...	...	★	☆	•	...	★	★	...	•	★	★	...	•	...	...	...
Pennsylvania	...	...	★	★	•	...	...	★	...	•	...	★	...	★	...	...	★
Rhode Island	...	☆	★	☆	★	...	...	★	...	•	...	★	...	...	...	•	...
South Carolina	...	...	★	★	•	...	...	★	...	•	...	...	...	...	...	...	...
South Dakota	...	★	★	★	•	...	...	★	...	•	★	★	...	★	...	...	...
Tennessee	...	...	★	★	•	...	...	★	...	•	...	★	...	•	...	...	...
Texas	...	...	★	☆	•	...	...	★	...	•	★	★	...	★	...	...	...
Utah	...	...	★	☆	•	...	...	★	...	•	...	★	...	★	...	...	...
Vermont	...	...	★	...	•	...	...	★	...	•	...	...	...	...	...	...	...
Virginia	...	...	★	...	•	★	...	★	...	•	★	★	...	...	...	...	...
Washington	...	★	★	★	•	...	☆	★	...	•	...	★	...	★	...	☆	★
West Virginia	...	...	★	...	•	...	★	★	...	•	★	★	★	★	★	★	★
Wisconsin	...	★	★	☆	•	...	...	★	...	•	★	★	...	★	...	...	...
Wyoming	...	...	★	★	★	...	...	★	...	•	★	★	...	★	...	...	...
Dist. of Col.	...	☆	★	★	•	...	...	★	...	•	...	...	...	★	★	...	...
Puerto Rico	...	...	...	☆	★	...	...	...	...	...	...	...	...	...	...	...	...
Virgin Islands	...	...	...	☆	•	...	...	...	★	...	...	...	...	...	...	...	...

Source: National Conference of Commissioners on Uniform State Laws,
1985-86 Reference Book, and update.

Key:
★—Enacted
•—Amended version enacted
☆—Substantially similar version enacted
. . .—Not enacted

State or other jurisdiction	Conservation Easement (1981)	Consumer Credit Code (1968) (1974)	Consumer Sales Practices (1970) (1971)	Controlled Substances (1970) (1973)	Crime Victims Reparations (1973)	Deceptive Trade Practices (1964) (1966)	Declaratory Judgments (1922)	Determination of Death (1978) (1980)	Disclaimer of Property Interests (1973) (1978)	Disclaimer of Transfers by Will, Intestacy or Appt. (1973) (1978)	Disclaimer of Transfers under Nontestamentary Instruments (1973) (1978)	Disposition of Community Property Rights at Death (1971)	Division of Income for Tax Purposes (1957)	Durable Power of Attorney (1979)	Duties to Disabled Persons (1972)	Enforcement of Foreign Judgments (1948) (1964)	Evidence, Rules of (1953) (1974)
Alabama	...	...	...	★	...	...	★	•	•	...	•	...	★	★	...	•	...
Alaska	...	...	...	...	...	...	...	...	...	...	...	★	★	★	...	•	...
Arizona	★	...	...	★	...	...	★	★	...	...	...	★	★	★	...	•	•
Arkansas	★	...	...	☆	...	...	★	•	•	...	...	★	★	★	...	★	•
California	...	...	...	☆	...	...	...	...	...	...	...	★	★	★	...	...	★
Colorado	...	★	...	...	...	•	★	•	...	...	...	★	★	★	★	•	•
Connecticut	...	...	...	★	...	...	★	★	...	...	...	...	☆	☆	★	•	...
Delaware	...	...	...	★	...	★	★	★	...	...	...	...	☆	☆	...	•	•
Florida	...	...	...	☆	...	...	★	•	•	...	...	...	☆	☆	...	•	•
Georgia	...	...	...	☆	...	...	★	•	•	...	...	...	☆	...	☆	...	...
Hawaii	...	...	...	☆	...	...	...	★	...	...	...	★	★	★	...	•	•
Idaho	...	★	...	★	...	...	★	•	...	...	...	★	★	★	...	•	...
Illinois	...	...	...	☆	...	★	★	...	...	★	...	...	★	★	...	★	...
Indiana	★	★	...	★	...	...	★	•	...	...	...	...	★	★	...	•	...
Iowa	...	★	...	★	...	...	★	...	...	...	...	...	...	★	...	...	...
Kansas	...	★	★	★	☆	...	...	...	...	...	...	...	★	★	...	•	★
Kentucky	...	...	...	☆	★	...	★	...	...	★	...	★	★	☆	...	•	...
Louisiana	...	...	...	★	...	...	★	...	...	...	...	...	...	...	...	...	...
Maine	★	★	...	★	...	★	★	•	...	★	★	...	★	★	...	•	...
Maryland	...	...	...	★	...	...	★	☆	★	...	...	...	★	★	...	•	•
Massachusetts	...	...	...	★	...	...	★	...	...	...	...	...	★	★	...	...	...
Michigan	...	...	...	★	...	...	★	...	...	...	...	★	★	★	...	...	•
Minnesota	★	...	...	☆	☆	•	★	...	...	...	...	☆	★	★	★	•	•
Mississippi	...	...	...	★	...	...	★	•	...	...	...	...	...	☆	...	...	...
Missouri	...	...	...	★	...	...	★	...	...	...	...	...	★	★	...	★	...
Montana	...	...	...	☆	★	...	★	•	...	...	...	...	★	★	...	★	•
Nebraska	...	...	...	★	...	•	★	•	...	...	...	...	★	★	...	★	•
Nevada	★	...	...	★	...	...	★	•	...	...	...	...	★	★	...	•	•
New Hampshire	...	...	...	...	...	...	...	...	...	...	...	...	☆	☆	...	...	...
New Jersey	...	...	...	★	★	★	★	...	...	★	★	...	...	...	...	...	★
New Mexico	...	...	...	★	...	☆	★	...	...	...	...	...	★	★	...	...	...
New York	...	...	...	★	...	...	★	★	...	...	...	★	★	☆	...	•	...
North Carolina	...	...	...	☆	...	...	★	...	...	...	...	★	★	☆	...	•	•
North Dakota	...	...	...	★	★	...	★	...	...	★	...	★	★	★	★	•	•
Ohio	...	...	☆	...	...	•	★	☆	...	...	...	...	☆	★	...	•	...
Oklahoma	...	★	☆	★	...	★	★	...	...	...	...	...	...	...	★	•	...
Oregon	★	...	...	★	...	...	★	•	•	★	★	★	★	☆	...	•	...
Pennsylvania	...	...	...	★	...	...	★	•	...	...	...	...	★	★	☆	•	...
Rhode Island	...	...	...	☆	...	...	★	•	☆	...	...	...	...	☆	...	•	...
South Carolina	...	☆	...	★	...	...	★	•	...	...	...	...	☆	★	...	•	...
South Dakota	★	...	...	★	...	...	★	...	...	...	...	...	★	★	...	•	•
Tennessee	...	...	...	★	☆	...	★	...	...	...	...	...	☆	★	...	•	★
Texas	★	...	...	★	☆	...	★	...	...	...	...	...	☆	☆	...	•	•
Utah	...	★	•	★	...	...	★	...	...	...	...	...	☆	★	...	•	•
Vermont	...	...	...	★	...	...	★	•	...	...	...	...	★	★	...	•	•
Virginia	...	...	...	☆	★	...	★	...	...	...	...	★	★	☆	...	...	...
Washington	...	...	...	★	...	...	★	•	...	...	...	...	★	★	...	•	•
West Virginia	...	...	...	★	...	...	★	★	•	...	...	...	★	☆	...	•	•
Wisconsin	★	☆	...	★	...	...	★	•	...	...	...	...	☆	★	...	•	•
Wyoming	...	★	...	★	...	...	★	★	...	...	...	...	★	...	...	•	•
Dist. of Col.	...	...	...	☆	...	...	☆	•	...	...	...	...	...	...	...	...	...
Puerto Rico	...	...	...	★	...	...	★	...	...	...	...	...	...	...	...	★	•
Virgin Islands	...	...	...	★	...	...	★	...	...	...	...	...	...	...	...	...	★

Key:
★—Enacted
•—Amended version enacted
☆—Substantially similar version enacted
. . .—Not enacted

State or other jurisdiction	Facsimile Signatures of Public Officials (1958)	Federal Lien Registration (1978) (1982)	Fiduciaries (1922)	Foreign Money Judgments Recognition (1962)	Fraudulent Transfer (1984)	International Wills (1977)	Interstate Arbitration of Death Taxes (1943)	Interstate Compromise of Death Taxes (1943)	Jury Selection and Service (1970) (1971)	Limited Partnership (1976) (1983) (1985)	Management of Institutional Funds (1972)	Mandatory Disposition of Detainers (1958)	Marriage and Divorce (1970) (1973)	Notarial Acts (1982)	Parentage (1973)	Partnership (1914)
Alabama	...	...	★	...	...	...	...	...	...	★	...	...	...	...	★	☆
Alaska	...	...	...	★	...	...	...	...	...	...	...	...	...	...	...	★
Arizona	...	...	★	...	...	...	...	...	...	★	...	★	★	...	...	★
Arkansas	★	...	...	...	...	...	...	...	...	★	...	...	...	...	...	★
California	★	★	...	★	...	...	★	★	...	☆	☆	...	...	...	★	★
Colorado	★	...	★	★	...	...	★	★	★	★	★	★	★	...	★	★
Connecticut	...	...	...	...	...	...	★	★	...	★	★	...	...	...	★	★
Delaware	★	...	...	...	...	...	...	...	...	★	★	...	...	★	★	★
Florida	★	...	...	...	...	...	...	...	...	...	...	...	...	...	...	★
Georgia	...	...	...	★	...	...	...	...	...	...	...	...	☆	...	...	...
Hawaii	...	...	★	...	★	...	...	...	...	...	...	...	...	...	★	★
Idaho	★	★	★	...	...	...	...	...	★	★	...	★	...	...	...	★
Illinois	★	...	★	★	...	...	...	☆	...	...	★	...	...	...	•	★
Indiana	...	...	★	...	...	...	...	...	☆	...	...	...	...	...	...	★
Iowa	...	...	...	...	...	...	...	...	...	★	...	...	...	...	...	★
Kansas	★	...	...	...	...	...	...	...	...	★	☆	★	...	★	★	★
Kentucky	...	...	...	...	...	...	...	...	...	...	★	...	...	...	...	★
Louisiana	...	...	★	...	...	...	...	...	...	...	★	...	...	...	...	...
Maine	...	...	...	...	...	...	★	★	★	...	★	...	...	...	...	★
Maryland	★	★	★	★	...	...	★	★	...	★	★	...	...	...	...	★
Massachusetts	...	...	★	...	...	...	★	★	...	★	★	☆	...	...	...	★
Michigan	...	...	★	...	...	...	★	★	★	★	★	...	...	...	...	★
Minnesota	★	★	★	★	...	★	☆	★	•	★	★	★	☆	...	★	★
Mississippi	...	...	...	...	...	...	...	☆	...	★	★	★	...	...	...	★
Missouri	★	...	★	★	...	...	...	...	...	★	★	★	...	...	...	★
Montana	★	•	...	...	...	...	...	...	...	★	★	...	•	...	★	★
Nebraska	...	...	...	...	...	...	★	★	...	★	...	...	...	...	...	☆
Nevada	★	★	★	...	...	...	...	...	...	★	★	...	...	...	★	★
New Hampshire	★	...	...	...	...	...	...	★	...	★	★	...	...	...	★	★
New Jersey	...	...	★	...	...	...	...	★	...	★	★	...	...	...	★	★
New Mexico	★	...	★	...	...	...	...	...	...	...	...	...	...	...	...	★
New York	...	...	☆	★	...	...	★	...	...	...	☆	...	...	...	...	★
North Carolina	...	...	★	...	...	...	...	...	...	...	★	...	...	...	...	★
North Dakota	...	★	...	...	★	★	...	...	★	★	★	★	...	...	★	★
Ohio	...	...	★	...	...	...	...	...	...	★	☆	...	...	...	...	☆
Oklahoma	★	...	...	★	★	...	...	...	...	★	...	...	...	★	...	★
Oregon	...	...	...	★	★	...	...	...	...	★	★	...	...	★	...	★
Pennsylvania	★	...	★	...	...	...	★	★	...	...	...	...	...	...	...	★
Rhode Island	★	...	☆	...	...	...	...	...	...	★	★	★	...	...	★	★
South Carolina	...	...	...	...	...	...	...	...	...	★	★	★	...	...	...	★
South Dakota	...	...	★	...	...	...	...	...	...	★	...	...	...	...	...	★
Tennessee	...	...	★	...	...	...	☆	☆	...	...	★	...	...	...	...	★
Texas	★	...	★	...	...	...	...	...	...	...	...	...	...	...	...	★
Utah	...	...	★	...	...	...	...	...	...	...	...	...	★	...	...	★
Vermont	...	...	...	...	...	...	★	★	...	...	★	...	...	...	...	★
Virginia	...	...	...	...	...	...	★	★	...	★	★	...	...	...	...	★
Washington	★	...	...	★	...	...	★	★	...	★	★	...	☆	...	★	★
West Virginia	★	...	...	...	★	...	★	★	...	★	★	...	...	...	★	★
Wisconsin	...	★	★	...	...	...	★	...	...	★	★	...	...	★	...	★
Wyoming	★	...	★	...	...	...	...	...	...	★	...	...	...	...	★	★
Dist. of Col.	...	...	★	...	...	...	...	...	...	...	...	...	...	...	...	★
Puerto Rico	...	...	★	...	...	...	...	...	...	...	...	...	...	...	...	...
Virgin Islands	...	...	★	...	...	...	...	...	...	...	...	...	...	...	...	★

Key:
★—Enacted
•—Amended version enacted
☆—Substantially similar version enacted
...—Not enacted

PASSAGE OF UNIFORM ACTS—Continued

State or other jurisdiction	Photographic Copies as Evidence (1949)	Post-Conviction Procedure (1980)	Premarital Agreement (1983)	Principal and Income (1931)(1962)	Probate Court (1969)(1975)(1982)	Public Assembly (1972)	Reciprocal Enforcement of Support (1950)(1958)(1968)	Residential Landlord and Tenant (1972)	Securities (1956)(1958)(1985)	Simplification of Fiduciary Security Transfers (1958)	State Antitrust (1973)(1979)	Status of Convicted Persons (1964)	Supervision of Trustees for Charitable Purposes (1954)	Testamentary Additions to Trusts (1960)	Trade Secrets (1979)(1985)	Transboundary Pollution Reciprocal Access (1982)	Transfers to Minors (1983)	Trustees' Powers (1964)	Unclaimed Property (1981)
Alabama	★	...	...	★	...	...	•	...	•	★	...	...	...	☆	...	...	...	...	...
Alaska	★	...	...	...	★	...	•	★	...	•	...	...	...	★	...	...	...	...	...
Arizona	...	...	...	•	★	...	•	★	...	★	★	★	...	★	...	...	★	★	★
Arkansas	★	...	...	...	...	...	•	...	•	•	...	...	...	★	★	...	★	★	★
California	★	...	★	•	...	...	•	...	...	★	...	...	★	★	★	...	...	...	...
Colorado	★	...	...	★	•	...	•	...	•	★	★	...	...	☆	...	...	★	★	...
Connecticut	★	...	...	★	...	...	•	...	...	★	...	...	...	★	★	...	...	...	...
Delaware	...	...	...	...	...	...	•	...	...	★	...	...	...	...	...	...	...	...	...
Florida	★	...	...	...	...	...	•	★	•	★	...	...	...	☆	...	...	★	★	...
Georgia	★	...	...	...	...	...	•	...	...	★	...	...	...	★	...	...	...	...	...
Hawaii	★	...	...	•	...	...	•	★	•	★	...	★	...	★	...	...	★	★	★
Idaho	★	...	...	•	★	...	•	...	•	★	...	...	...	★	...	...	★	★	★
Illinois	★	...	...	•	...	...	•	...	•	★	...	...	★	☆	...	...	★	...	...
Indiana	...	...	...	•	...	...	•	...	☆	★	...	...	...	☆	★	...	...	...	...
Iowa	★	...	...	...	...	...	•	★	☆	★	★	...	...	★	...	...	...	...	...
Kansas	★	...	...	...	...	...	•	☆	•	★	★	...	...	★	★	...	★	★	...
Kentucky	★	...	...	★	...	...	•	★	☆	★	...	...	...	★	...	...	...	...	...
Louisiana	...	...	...	★	...	...	•	...	...	★	...	...	...	...	...	...	...	...	...
Maine	★	...	...	...	...	...	•	...	★	★	...	...	...	...	...	...	...	...	...
Maryland	★	...	...	•	...	...	•	...	•	★	...	...	...	☆	...	...	...	...	...
Massachusetts	★	...	...	...	...	...	•	...	•	...	...	...	...	★	...	...	...	...	...
Michigan	...	...	...	•	☆	...	•	...	•	★	★	...	...	★	★	...	★	...	...
Minnesota	★	...	...	•	★	...	•	...	•	★	...	...	...	★	★	...	★	☆	...
Mississippi	...	...	...	•	...	...	•	...	•	★	...	...	...	☆	...	...	★	★	...
Missouri	...	...	...	...	...	...	•	...	•	★	...	...	...	...	...	...	...	...	...
Montana	★	...	...	★	...	...	★	★	•	★	...	...	☆	☆	★	★	★	★	☆
Nebraska	★	...	...	★	...	...	★	☆	•	★	...	...	...	...	...	...	...	...	...
Nevada	...	...	...	...	...	...	•	...	•	•	...	...	...	★	...	...	★	...	★
New Hampshire	★	...	...	...	...	...	•	...	•	...	...	★	...	★	...	...	★	★	...
New Jersey	★	...	...	...	☆	...	•	...	•	★	...	...	...	☆	...	★	★	...	...
New Mexico	★	...	...	•	★	...	★	...	•	★	...	...	...	★	...	...	...	...	...
New York	★	...	...	...	...	...	•	...	...	★	...	...	...	☆	...	...	...	...	...
North Carolina	★	...	...	...	...	...	•	...	...	★	...	...	...	☆	...	...	...	...	...
North Dakota	★	★	★	•	•	...	•	...	...	★	...	...	...	★	...	...	...	...	★
Ohio	...	...	...	...	...	...	•	...	...	...	...	...	...	☆	...	...	...	...	...
Oklahoma	★	...	...	★	...	★	•	...	•	★	...	...	...	★	★	...	...	...	...
Oregon	★	...	...	•	...	...	★	...	•	★	...	...	★	★	...	...	★	★	★
Pennsylvania	★	...	...	★	☆	...	•	...	☆	★	...	...	...	☆	...	...	...	...	...
Rhode Island	★	...	...	•	...	...	•	...	...	★	...	...	...	★	...	...	★	...	...
South Carolina	...	...	...	•	...	...	•	...	•	★	...	...	...	★	...	...	...	...	...
South Dakota	★	...	...	•	...	...	•	...	...	★	...	...	...	★	...	...	★	...	...
Tennessee	★	...	...	★	...	...	•	★	•	★	...	...	...	★	...	...	...	...	...
Texas	...	...	...	★	...	...	•	...	★	★	...	...	...	☆	...	...	...	★	★
Utah	★	...	...	★	★	...	•	...	•	★	...	...	...	☆	...	...	...	★	★
Vermont	★	...	...	★	...	☆	•	...	...	★	...	...	...	★	...	...	...	...	...
Virginia	★	...	★	★	...	...	•	★	...	★	...	...	...	...	...	...	...	...	★
Washington	★	...	...	•	...	...	•	...	☆	★	...	...	...	☆	★	★	★	...	★
West Virginia	★	...	...	★	...	...	•	...	...	★	...	...	...	...	★	★	★	...	★
Wisconsin	★	...	...	★	...	...	•	...	...	★	...	...	...	...	...	...	...	...	...
Wyoming	★	...	...	...	...	...	•	...	...	★	...	...	...	☆	...	...	...	★	...
Dist. of Col.	...	...	...	...	...	...	•	...	•	★	...	...	...	☆	...	...	★	...	...
Puerto Rico	...	...	...	...	...	...	•	...	•	...	...	...	...	...	...	...	...	...	...
Virgin Islands	★	...	...	...	...	...	...	...	...	...	...	...	...	...	...	...	...	...	...

Key:
★—Enacted
•—Amended version enacted
☆—Substantially similar version enacted
...—Not enacted

Table 8.2

RECORD OF PASSAGE OF MODEL ACTS
(As of September 1, 1985)

State or other jurisdiction	Act to Provide for the Appointment of Commissioners (1944)	Anti-Discrimination (1966)	Eminent Domain Code (1974)	Insanity Defense and Post-Trial Disposition (1984)	Juvenile Court (1968)	Land Sales Practices (1966)	Minor Student Capacity to Borrow (1969)	Periodic Payment of Judgments (1980)	Post-Mortem Examinations (1954)	Public Defender (1970) (1974)	Real Estate Cooperative (1981)	Real Estate Time-Share (1980) (1982)	Statutory Construction (1965)
Alabama	★	...	★	...	...	...	...	...	...	...	...	...	...
Alaska	...	...	...	...	...	★	...	...	...	...	...	...	...
Arizona	★	...	...	...	...	...	★	...	...	...	...	...	...
Arkansas	★	...	...	...	...	...	...	...	...	...	...	...	...
California	...	...	...	...	...	...	...	...	...	...	...	...	...
Colorado	...	...	...	...	...	...	...	...	...	...	...	...	★
Connecticut	...	...	...	...	...	★	★	...	...	...	...	...	...
Delaware	...	...	...	...	...	...	...	...	...	...	...	...	...
Florida	...	...	...	...	...	★	...	...	...	...	...	...	...
Georgia	...	...	...	...	☆	☆	...	...	...	...	...	...	...
Hawaii	...	★	...	...	...	★	...	...	...	...	...	...	...
Idaho	...	...	...	...	...	...	...	...	...	...	...	...	...
Illinois	...	...	...	...	...	...	...	...	...	...	...	...	...
Indiana	...	...	...	...	...	...	...	...	...	...	...	...	...
Iowa	★	...	...	...	...	...	...	...	☆	...	...	...	★
Kansas	★	...	...	...	...	★	...	...	...	...	...	...	...
Kentucky	★	...	...	...	...	...	...	...	...	...	...	...	...
Louisiana	...	...	...	...	...	...	...	...	...	...	...	☆	...
Maine	★	...	...	...	...	...	...	...	...	...	...	...	...
Maryland	...	...	...	...	...	...	...	...	☆	...	...	☆	...
Massachusetts	...	...	...	...	...	...	...	...	...	...	...	...	...
Michigan	...	...	...	...	...	...	...	...	...	...	...	...	...
Minnesota	...	...	...	...	...	...	...	...	...	...	...	...	...
Mississippi	★	...	...	...	...	...	...	...	...	...	...	...	...
Missouri	...	...	...	...	...	...	...	...	...	...	...	...	...
Montana	★	...	...	...	...	★	☆	...	...	...	...	...	...
Nebraska	★	...	...	...	...	...	...	...	...	...	...	...	...
Nevada	...	...	...	...	...	...	...	...	...	...	...	...	...
New Hampshire	★	...	...	...	...	...	...	...	...	...	...	...	...
New Jersey	...	...	...	...	...	...	...	...	...	...	...	...	...
New Mexico	...	...	...	...	...	...	...	...	...	...	...	...	...
New York	...	...	...	...	...	...	...	...	...	...	...	...	...
North Carolina	...	...	...	...	...	...	...	...	...	...	...	...	...
North Dakota	★	...	...	☆	★	...	★	...	...	...	...	...	...
Ohio	...	...	...	...	...	...	...	...	...	...	...	...	...
Oklahoma	★	★	...	...	...	...	★	...	★	...	...	...	...
Oregon	★	...	...	...	...	...	...	...	★	...	...	...	...
Pennsylvania	...	...	...	...	...	...	...	...	...	...	...	...	...
Rhode Island	...	...	...	...	...	...	...	...	...	...	...	★	...
South Carolina	...	...	...	...	...	...	...	...	...	...	...	...	...
South Dakota	...	...	...	...	...	...	...	...	★	...	...	...	...
Tennessee	...	...	...	...	...	...	...	...	...	...	...	...	...
Texas	★	...	...	...	...	...	...	...	★	...	...	...	...
Utah	...	...	...	...	...	...	...	...	...	...	...	...	...
Vermont	...	...	...	...	...	...	...	...	...	...	...	...	...
Virginia	...	...	...	...	...	...	...	...	...	...	★	...	...
Washington	...	...	...	...	...	...	★	...	...	...	...	...	...
West Virginia	...	...	...	...	...	...	...	...	☆	...	...	...	...
Wisconsin	★	...	...	...	...	...	...	...	...	...	...	...	★
Wyoming	...	...	...	...	...	...	...	...	...	...	...	...	...
Dist. of Col.	...	...	...	...	...	...	...	...	...	...	...	...	...
Puerto Rico	...	...	...	...	...	...	...	...	...	...	...	...	...
Virgin Islands	...	...	...	...	...	...	...	...	...	...	...	...	...

Source: National Conference of Commissioners on Uniform State Laws, *1985-86 Reference Book*, and update.

Key:
★—Enacted
☆—Substantially similar version enacted
...—Not enacted

Table 8.3
MINIMUM AGE FOR SPECIFIED ACTIVITIES

State or other jurisdiction	Age of majority (a)	Minimum age for marriage with consent(b)		Minimum age for making a will	Minimum age for buying(c)		Minimum age for serving on a jury	Minimum age for leaving school(d)
		male	female		liquor	beer or wine		
Alabama	19	14(e)	14(e)	19	21	21	19	16
Alaska	18	16(f)	16(f)	18	21	21	18	16
Arizona	18	16(f)	16(f)	18	21	21	18	(g)
Arkansas	18	17(f)	16(f)	18	21	21	18	15
California	18	(h)	(h)	18(i)	21	21	18	18
Colorado	18	16(f)	16(f)	18	21	18(j)	18	16
Connecticut	18	16(f)	16(f)	18	21	21	18	16(k,l)
Delaware	18	18(f,m)	16(f,m)	18	21	21	18	16
Florida	18	16(f)	16(f)	18	21	21	18	16
Georgia	18	16(f,m)	16(f,m)	18	21	21	18	16
Hawaii	18	16	16(f)	18	18	18	18	18(l)
Idaho	18	16(f)	16(f)	18(i)	19	19	18	16
Illinois	18	16(f)	16(f)	18	21	21	18	16
Indiana	18	17(f)	17(f)	18	21	21	18	16
Iowa	18	16	16	18	19	19	18	16(k,l)
Kansas	18	(h)	(h)	18	21	21	18	16
Kentucky	18	(h)	(h)	18	21	21	18	16
Louisiana	18	18(f)	16(f)	16(i)	18	18	18	16
Maine	18	16(f)	16(f)	18	21	21	18	17(n)
Maryland	18	16(f)	16(f)	18	21	21	18	16
Massachusetts	18	(h)	(h)	18	21	21	18	16
Michigan	18	16	16	18	21	21	18	16
Minnesota	18	16(o)	16(o)	18	19	19	18	16
Mississippi	18	17(f)	15(f)	18	21	21	21	14(p)
Missouri	18	15(f)	15(f)	18	21	21	21	16
Montana	18	18(f)	18(f)	18	19	19	18	16(q)
Nebraska	19	17	17	18	21	21	19	16
Nevada	18	16(f)	16(f)	18	21	21	18	17
New Hampshire	18	14(o)	13(o)	18	21	21	18	16
New Jersey	18	16(r)	16(r)	18	21	21	18	16
New Mexico	18	16(f)	16(f)	18	21	21	18	18(s)
New York	(t)	16	14(o)	18	21	21	18	17(u)
North Carolina	18	16	16(f)	18	21	21	18	16
North Dakota	18	16	16	18	21	21	18	16
Ohio	18	18(f)	16(f)	18	21	19	18	18
Oklahoma	18	16(f)	16(f)	18	21	21	18	16
Oregon	18	17	17	18	21	21	18	16(v)
Pennsylvania	21	16(f)	16(f)	18	21	21	18	16(v)
Rhode Island	18	18(f)	16(f)	18	21	21	18	16
South Carolina	18	18(f)	14(f)	18	21	21	18	16
South Dakota	18	16(f)	16(f)	18	21	19(j)	18	16
Tennessee	18	16(f)	16(f)	18	21	21	18	16
Texas	18	14(o)	14(o)	18(i)	21	21	18	17
Utah	18	(h)	(h)	18	21	21	18	18
Vermont	18	16(f)	16(f)	18	21	21	18	18
Virginia	18	16(f)	16(f)	18	21	21	18	17
Washington	18	17(f)	17(f)	18	21	21	18	18(v)
West Virginia	18	(w)	(w)	18	20	20	18	16
Wisconsin	18	16	16	18	19	19	18	16(v)
Wyoming	19	16(f)	16(f)	19	19	19	19	16
Dist. of Col.	18	16	16	18	21	18	18	16(l)

(a) Generally, the age at which an individual has legal control over own actions and business (e.g. ability to contract) except as otherwise provided by statute. In many states, age of majority is arrived at upon marriage if minimum legal marrying age is lower than prescribed age of majority.

(b) With parental consent. Minimum age for marrying without consent is 18 years in all states, except Mississippi (21 years) and Wyoming (19 years).

(c) As of early 1986. Legislation enacted; may not yet be effective.

(d) Without graduating.

(e) Bond is required if under 18.

(f) Legal procedure for younger persons to obtain license.

(g) To 10th grade, effective with 1986-87 school year.

(h) Statute provides that any unmarried male or female under 18 may marry with consent (usually with order of court granting permission).

(i) Age may be lower for a minor who is living apart from parents or legal guardians and managing own financial affairs, or who has contracted a lawful marriage.

(j) In Colorado and South Dakota, 3.2 beer only.

(k) Unless parent or guardian is able to show child is receiving equivalent instruction.

(l) Younger, if lawfully employed. Connecticut, Iowa, District of Columbia, 14 years; Hawaii, 15 years.

(m) Parental consent not required when female is pregnant or applicants are parents of a living child.

(n) Does not apply to those who have reached age 15 or completed ninth grade, or who otherwise have permission to leave.

(o) Parental consent and judicial consent required.

(p) Mississippi's compulsory attendance statute is being implemented in a staggered fashion (began with 1982-83 school year) until every child who is six years old and has not reached the age of 14 years is covered by the mandatory attendance provision.

(q) Or completion of eighth grade, whichever is earlier.

(r) Parental consent required for ages 16 to 18; judicial approval for individuals under 16.

(s) Does not apply to those who have completed 10th grade and have consent of parents and school officials.

(t) As defined in general obligations (for purposes of contracting) and civil rights codes, 18 years.

(u) In cities having over 4,500 population and union-free school districts.

(v) With certain exceptions.

(w) Under 16, must have parental consent and approval of circuit judge.

Table 8.4
GENERAL REVENUE OF PUBLIC SCHOOL SYSTEMS BY SOURCE: 1983-84
(In thousands of dollars)

State or other jurisdiction	Total(a)	Intergovernmental(a): Total	Directly from federal government	From state: Federal aid distributed by state	From state: Other	From other local governments	From own sources: Total	Taxes	Parent government contributions	Current charges: School lunch	Current charges: Other	Other
United States	$133,449,502	$70,995,457	$1,291,368	$7,384,204	$60,525,977	$1,793,908	$62,454,045	$41,633,040	$10,688,194	$2,497,117	$3,505,153	$4,130,541
Alabama	1,376,562	1,088,989	17,771	169,255	810,003	91,960	287,573	169,243	0	60,105	5,512	52,713
Alaska	819,367	610,710	36,539	12,082	562,089	0	208,657	0	172,617	7,054	8,108	20,878
Arizona	1,737,781	1,041,565	68,645	96,928	822,116	53,876	696,216	528,101	42	31,294	69,287	67,492
Arkansas	968,478	593,174	3,957	100,285	485,506	3,426	375,304	293,334	0	20,950	36,005	25,015
California	14,698,595	10,433,470	144,312	937,504	9,283,753	67,901	4,265,125	3,132,158	139,739	202,584	239,261	551,383
Colorado	1,920,586	839,011	11,021	68,655	757,964	1,371	1,081,575	880,276	0	34,255	53,649	113,395
Connecticut	1,744,040	679,056	7,831	71,009	530,712	69,504	1,064,984	0	1,012,504	37,868	8,337	6,275
Delaware	332,273	248,662	3,238	22,615	222,809	0	83,611	68,422	0	6,982	326	7,881
Florida	5,689,933	3,456,777	48,422	370,659	3,037,144	552	2,233,156	1,631,474	0	112,152	285,225	204,305
Georgia	2,625,270	1,564,788	20,850	129,875	1,410,063	4,000	1,060,482	863,781	0	47,515	34,882	114,304
Hawaii	464,979	445,322	50,681	0	394,641	0	19,657	0	0	9,362	9,373	922
Idaho	468,224	318,412	6,975	29,307	282,111	19	149,812	120,408	0	10,599	6,008	12,797
Illinois	6,631,831	2,707,605	71,722	278,638	2,345,313	11,932	3,924,226	3,272,439	0	102,276	242,404	307,107
Indiana	2,717,541	1,560,467	6,016	120,540	1,391,194	42,717	1,157,074	977,651	0	89,071	22,006	68,346
Iowa	1,768,886	901,869	9,473	56,394	835,519	483	867,017	716,276	15	41,620	67,373	41,733
Kansas	1,488,932	729,859	14,207	31,972	606,469	77,211	759,073	593,373	0	35,777	55,758	74,165
Kentucky	1,428,307	1,042,678	6,795	145,647	889,209	1,027	385,629	287,095	0	42,095	12,311	44,128
Louisiana	2,141,290	1,316,198	11,315	193,058	1,106,169	5,656	825,092	670,824	0	37,594	17,638	99,036
Maine	551,109	276,498	3,999	31,041	241,458		274,611	93,706	155,079	13,583	5,971	6,272
Maryland	2,483,010	926,014	25,587	120,613	779,713	101	1,556,996	0	1,369,040	49,377	102,034	36,545
Massachusetts	3,247,398	1,469,052	6,229	155,590	1,127,460	179,773	1,778,346		1,684,198	62,232	15,987	15,929
Michigan	6,215,459	2,005,558	46,133	287,106	1,552,786	119,533	4,209,901	3,622,358	0	107,840	260,680	219,023
Minnesota	2,690,522	1,508,288	18,300	119,965	1,362,229	7,794	1,182,234	913,316	0	61,405	86,348	121,165
Mississippi	1,110,103	796,789	14,368	160,411	619,959	2,051	313,314	203,764	1,018	23,446	50,912	34,174
Missouri	2,401,933	1,431,780	11,634	136,406	879,643	404,097	970,153	736,374	0	53,315	94,847	85,617
Montana	580,571	396,120	21,996	14,688	208,792	150,644	184,451	141,193	0	8,935	3,680	30,643
Nebraska	983,557	350,363	11,831	40,424	235,308	62,800	633,194	512,149	0	21,198	62,106	37,741
Nevada	447,579	301,669	3,841	14,879	282,949	0	145,910	122,372	0	9,180	2,231	12,127
New Hampshire	448,658	45,251	1,393	14,904	28,222	732	403,407	291,772	90,094	11,396	4,304	5,841
New Jersey	5,108,527	1,978,619	17,263	224,860	1,724,990	11,506	3,129,908	2,390,751	452,735	73,373	97,305	115,744
New Mexico	879,862	759,694	40,420	58,415	660,844	15	120,168	71,182	0	11,892	3,680	33,414
New York	12,586,047	5,598,495	28,696	452,299	5,112,445	5,055	6,987,552	3,960,988	2,330,749	137,922	316,165	241,728
North Carolina	2,899,686	2,060,159	26,151	239,652	1,793,282	1,074	839,527		624,067	95,180	60,070	60,010
North Dakota	415,230	256,443	11,448	18,297	215,938	10,760	158,787	115,542	0	8,756	16,051	18,438
Ohio	5,882,847	2,809,741	21,975	272,545	2,505,638	9,583	3,073,106	2,631,945	0	147,045	112,318	181,798

GENERAL REVENUE OF PUBLIC SCHOOL SYSTEMS: 1983-84—Continued

State or other jurisdiction	Total(a)	Intergovernmental(a)					From own sources					
		Total	Directly from federal government	From state		From other local governments	Total	Taxes	Parent government contributions	Current charges		Other
				Federal aid distributed by state	Other					School lunch	Other	
Oklahoma	1,658,954	1,128,001	34,768	99,003	956,030	38,200	530,953	464,306	0	35,874	9,194	21,579
Oregon	2,005,676	807,033	35,763	82,716	653,702	34,852	1,198,643	1,018,032	0	26,719	93,033	60,859
Pennsylvania ...	6,701,508	3,010,371	90,454	291,970	2,627,947	0	3,691,137	3,091,056	0	131,511	201,381	267,189
Rhode Island ...	493,369	210,990	3,698	23,352	174,214	9,726	282,379	0	277,768	1,561	882	2,168
South Carolina ..	1,360,633	762,628	9,885	142,094	610,388	261	598,005	464,421	0	33,588	48,923	51,073
South Dakota ...	368,844	151,608	21,566	21,351	101,631	7,060	217,236	181,878	0	9,505	2,867	22,986
Tennessee	1,646,925	957,754	8,022	169,248	598,328	182,156	689,171	0	592,875	48,192	22,560	25,544
Texas	9,593,101	5,055,920	112,592	825,557	4,086,870	30,901	4,537,181	3,689,616	0	167,610	359,031	320,924
Utah	916,799	539,327	9,161	43,232	486,934	0	377,472	290,737	0	22,527	7,451	56,757
Vermont	273,202	88,067	317	9,350	78,361	39	185,135	169,801	0	6,059	975	8,300
Virginia	2,922,783	1,402,952	25,294	162,513	1,213,440	1,705	1,519,831	0	1,397,195	77,536	14,933	30,167
Washington	2,449,080	1,903,142	19,674	124,647	1,757,263	1,558	545,938	358,793	0	39,169	85,697	62,279
West Virginia ...	972,251	659,342	2,153	77,363	579,826	0	312,909	258,456	0	15,412	3,353	35,688
Wisconsin	3,023,750	1,394,037	17,283	102,804	1,239,043	34,907	1,629,713	1,359,266	0	46,357	152,056	72,034
Wyoming	660,863	329,621	4,185	12,486	257,560	55,390	331,242	274,411	0	7,654	25,136	24,041
Dist. of Col.	446,791	45,519	45,519	0	0	0	401,272	0	388,459	2,615	9,329	869

Source: U.S. Bureau of the Census, *Finances of Public School Systems in 1983-84.*

Note: Because of rounding, detail may not add to totals. Revenue from state sources for state dependent school systems is included as intergovernmental revenue from state rather than as parent government contributions.

(a) To avoid duplication, interschool system transactions are excluded.

Table 8.5
GENERAL EXPENDITURES OF PUBLIC SCHOOL SYSTEMS: 1983-84
(In thousands of dollars)

State or other jurisdiction	Total(a)	Elementary and secondary Total	E&S Current operation Salaries and wages	E&S Current operation Other	E&S Capital outlay Construction	E&S Capital outlay Other	Higher education Total	HE Current operation Salaries and wages	HE Current operation Other	HE Capital outlay Construction	HE Capital outlay Other	Interest on debt	Inter-governmental(a)
United States	$130,375,146	$119,926,508	$76,832,776	$36,272,430	$3,971,654	$2,849,648	$7,583,106	$4,501,320	$2,621,846	$235,670	$224,270	$2,441,989	$423,543
Alabama	1,428,318	1,415,534	976,440	313,974	82,732	42,388	0	0	0	0	0	8,909	3,875
Alaska	865,904	816,489	436,396	224,502	141,285	14,306	0	0	0	0	0	46,726	2,689
Arizona	1,771,311	1,498,123	897,834	382,334	139,879	78,076	215,104	121,100	77,251	7,535	9,218	58,084	0
Arkansas	958,413	935,622	613,599	283,253	36,902	1,868	0	0	0	0	0	22,791	0
California	14,412,270	12,489,867	8,410,552	3,652,322	173,058	253,935	1,850,192	1,189,029	592,242	32,991	35,930	64,458	7,753
Colorado	1,893,396	1,798,392	1,119,472	480,592	88,096	110,232	34,423	12,171	20,234	1,131	887	60,581	0
Connecticut	1,661,551	1,627,703	1,105,302	475,006	15,191	32,204	0	0	0	0	0	33,848	0
Delaware	337,342	336,715	196,643	128,883	5,187	6,002	0	0	0	0	0	627	0
Florida	5,478,887	4,877,945	2,840,303	1,622,137	217,001	198,504	543,998	314,081	171,728	38,396	19,793	56,944	0
Georgia	2,448,630	2,393,752	1,642,729	598,814	116,620	35,589	20,591	14,340	6,251	0	0	29,741	4,546
Hawaii	464,978	464,978	328,186	90,585	38,073	8,134	0	0	0	0	0	0	0
Idaho	433,715	404,183	284,505	89,964	12,996	16,718	20,448	11,109	8,474	64	801	9,084	0
Illinois	6,106,672	5,392,547	3,636,133	1,552,578	66,399	137,437	583,719	347,351	202,152	11,137	23,079	120,197	10,209
Indiana	2,683,352	2,502,402	1,723,038	599,971	130,739	48,654	0	0	0	0	0	23,949	157,001
Iowa	1,715,764	1,518,788	930,432	520,149	26,652	41,555	174,501	87,655	74,424	8,012	4,410	22,475	0
Kansas	1,448,285	1,287,552	812,699	377,476	54,316	43,061	139,398	67,839	55,648	11,599	4,312	21,335	0
Kentucky	1,411,878	1,374,848	895,155	393,067	48,359	38,267	0	0	0	0	0	37,030	0
Louisiana	2,085,911	2,017,925	1,303,634	557,512	105,263	51,516	2,858	1,776	1,007	36	39	65,128	0
Maine	547,907	534,623	346,906	159,984	11,427	16,306	0	0	0	0	0	13,284	0
Maryland	2,577,137	2,320,547	1,523,691	705,746	60,924	30,186	235,185	141,892	85,085	4,193	4,015	21,405	0
Massachusetts	2,951,136	2,880,516	1,883,617	936,153	35,312	25,434	5,135	3,601	1,534	0	0	65,485	0
Michigan	5,948,192	5,370,636	3,598,216	1,615,383	49,589	77,448	438,441	254,925	158,179	10,061	15,276	139,115	0
Minnesota	2,595,588	2,531,913	1,693,382	687,458	73,233	77,840	0	0	0	0	0	63,675	0
Mississippi	1,084,902	936,533	585,312	307,571	24,361	19,289	138,789	74,450	52,699	7,501	4,139	9,580	0
Missouri	2,316,498	2,166,417	1,426,855	638,714	38,554	62,294	116,632	71,528	39,737	936	4,431	33,449	0
Montana	566,294	547,288	321,910	189,772	16,946	18,660	9,168	4,010	3,020	1,472	666	9,838	0
Nebraska	967,670	882,037	524,744	303,082	31,536	22,675	69,281	36,596	28,056	2,450	2,179	16,352	0
Nevada	414,516	400,406	276,331	108,062	4,865	11,148	0	0	0	0	0	14,110	0
New Hampshire	432,688	425,637	252,029	160,335	3,955	9,318	0	0	0	0	0	7,051	0
New Jersey	4,924,604	4,559,589	2,897,731	1,468,863	98,929	94,066	259,152	152,838	89,209	10,934	6,171	90,531	15,332
New Mexico	899,179	884,186	481,715	276,348	116,479	9,644	0	0	0	0	0	14,993	0
New York	12,729,940	11,782,803	6,908,631	4,396,760	311,831	165,581	706,531	456,299	237,003	4,473	8,756	240,606	0
North Carolina	2,905,004	2,567,699	1,655,037	823,449	59,296	29,917	313,463	177,845	116,160	5,063	14,395	23,842	0
North Dakota	397,457	382,901	222,588	134,301	14,114	11,898	9,301	5,380	3,411	73	437	3,015	2,240
Ohio	5,665,922	5,464,873	3,668,738	1,670,092	52,706	73,337	128,515	63,461	55,589	5,866	3,599	72,534	0

GENERAL EXPENDITURES OF PUBLIC SCHOOL SYSTEMS: 1983-84—Continued

State or other jurisdiction	Total(a)	Elementary and secondary						Higher education						Interest on debt	Inter-governmental(a)
		Total	Current operation		Capital outlay			Total	Current operation		Capital outlay				
			Salaries and wages	Other	Construction	Other			Salaries and wages	Other	Construction	Other			
Oklahoma	1,728,391	1,703,867	1,068,962	423,661	135,806	75,438		0	0	0	0	0		24,524	0
Oregon	1,893,057	1,666,099	974,085	637,148	22,777	32,089		197,531	112,625	77,847	2,226	4,833		29,427	0
Pennsylvania	6,172,220	5,612,105	3,622,299	1,795,888	77,672	116,246		209,569	120,179	79,310	2,772	7,308		139,515	211,031
Rhode Island	476,315	470,619	320,065	145,309	0	5,245		0	0	0	0	0		5,696	0
South Carolina	1,380,518	1,322,847	824,689	377,479	91,093	29,586		0	0	0	0	0		57,671	0
South Dakota	351,659	349,491	203,277	121,170	15,110	9,934		0	0	0	0	0		2,168	0
Tennessee	1,670,012	1,612,155	1,054,940	433,507	89,549	34,159		0	0	0	0	0		57,815	0
Texas	9,592,034	8,515,363	5,583,586	1,941,982	687,508	302,287		703,997	392,388	238,327	38,299	34,983		372,674	0
Utah	930,547	893,385	503,712	288,458	64,889	36,326		0	0	0	0	0		37,162	0
Vermont	275,809	269,327	157,431	104,017	2,464	5,415		0	0	0	0	0		6,379	103
Virginia	2,812,172	2,760,476	1,769,108	883,179	69,671	38,518		0	0	0	0	0		51,688	8
Washington	2,399,575	2,346,434	1,506,439	675,121	84,130	80,744		0	0	0	0	0		53,141	0
West Virginia	973,076	964,346	653,729	255,952	27,131	27,534		0	0	0	0	0		8,730	0
Wisconsin	3,056,152	2,698,431	1,590,410	1,019,678	24,301	64,042		299,407	180,396	104,942	4,469	9,600		49,600	8,714
Wyoming	666,003	564,145	278,870	185,672	61,382	38,221		76,831	30,102	21,220	21,494	4,015		25,027	0
Dist. of Col.	466,395	385,449	300,689	59,017	15,366	10,377		80,946	56,354	21,107	2,487	998		0	0

Source: U.S. Bureau of the Census, Finances of Public School Systems in 1983-84.
Note: Because of rounding, detail may not add to totals.
(a) To avoid duplication, interschool system transactions are excluded.

Table 8.6

FEDERAL FUNDS OBLIGATED FOR CHILD NUTRITION PROGRAMS, BY STATE: FISCAL YEARS 1983-84

(In thousands of dollars)

State or other jurisdiction	Total, fiscal year 1983	Fiscal year 1984									
		Total	Special milk	School lunch	Special meal assistance	School breakfast	State administrative expense	Commodities and cash in lieu of commodities	Child care	Summer food service	Nutrition education and training
United States	$3,906,153	$4,183,309	$18,626	$447,583	$1,985,744	$347,599	$40,787	$862,137	$376,695	$101,719	$4,726
Alabama	104,271	114,007	70	11,032	54,965	10,486	1,114	23,860	7,971	4,434	75
Alaska	8,303	10,499	30	1,299	4,595	517	305	1,934	1,767	2	50
Arizona	44,197	50,806	430	4,999	23,148	4,408	533	9,826	6,581	831	50
Arkansas	49,882	51,507	55	5,188	26,549	4,944	621	11,072	2,752	276	50
California	385,554	451,975	1,662	37,837	222,904	45,405	3,832	87,953	41,067	10,891	424
Colorado	31,969	44,802	99	5,560	17,920	2,060	358	8,672	9,323	761	49
Connecticut	34,856	37,403	568	4,480	17,141	1,004	490	7,206	5,120	1,338	56
Delaware	10,058	10,454	46	900	4,051	909	266	2,206	1,349	677	50
Florida	181,495	195,906	135	20,650	96,326	19,242	1,743	40,891	12,603	4,157	159
Georgia	142,125	149,540	56	17,443	70,105	14,110	1,485	31,534	12,434	2,269	104
Hawaii	21,666	22,669	18	3,101	10,894	2,056	211	4,686	1,325	328	50
Idaho	13,322	15,570	93	2,471	8,246	288	271	2,949	1,140	62	50
Illinois	169,774	179,021	2,908	19,855	87,214	11,712	1,717	37,042	14,657	3,703	213
Indiana	69,086	64,703	245	10,833	30,130	2,980	686	13,994	4,394	1,337	104
Iowa	43,126	37,935	145	7,099	17,386	1,061	509	7,994	3,347	342	52
Kansas	33,257	32,676	88	5,328	14,624	623	426	6,764	4,575	197	51
Kentucky	85,571	89,463	113	9,998	44,098	11,082	839	18,768	3,142	1,356	67
Louisiana	118,439	128,625	246	11,788	63,277	11,007	1,040	26,302	12,957	1,921	87
Maine	18,978	21,483	80	2,365	11,051	914	332	4,136	2,282	273	50
Maryland	56,768	57,712	353	5,969	26,894	4,111	656	12,157	5,757	1,738	77
Massachusetts	76,991	85,800	472	9,128	34,896	4,803	997	16,688	16,902	1,808	106
Michigan	122,612	127,793	1,050	13,973	62,534	4,723	911	26,178	14,732	3,507	185
Minnesota	62,319	68,684	214	9,715	27,285	1,841	865	12,826	14,771	1,092	75
Mississippi	83,812	104,775	13	8,307	49,479	12,041	1,059	21,580	10,112	2,134	50
Missouri	80,088	76,734	271	9,991	36,734	5,279	614	16,390	6,293	1,075	87
Montana	12,387	12,068	64	1,629	4,957	544	344	2,508	1,838	134	50
Nebraska	21,730	21,958	117	3,391	9,191	634	217	4,404	3,722	232	50
Nevada	8,189	8,563	31	1,198	3,782	1,044	253	1,642	469	94	50
New Hampshire	10,070	11,258	242	1,546	5,310	461	274	2,094	1,012	269	50
New Jersey	99,447	96,351	1,075	10,208	43,183	5,323	1,103	21,700	9,065	4,562	132

FEDERAL FUNDS OBLIGATED FOR CHILD NUTRITION PROGRAMS—Continued

State or other jurisdiction	Total, fiscal year 1983	Fiscal year 1984						Commodities and cash in lieu of commodities			Nutrition education and training
		Total	Special milk	School lunch	Special meal assistance	School breakfast	State administrative expense		Child care	Summer food service	
New Mexico	32,395	37,927	98	2,988	19,405	2,627	476	7,582	3,937	764	50
New York	311,203	353,886	2,356	28,661	165,677	26,222	2,340	71,631	32,930	23,760	309
North Carolina	142,948	148,958	91	16,438	69,496	20,173	1,383	31,602	7,730	1,934	111
North Dakota	10,925	11,677	13	1,708	4,003	292	317	2,213	2,934	147	50
Ohio	153,569	159,311	1,388	19,854	77,797	11,718	1,471	32,698	11,408	2,777	200
Oklahoma	53,811	53,462	57	6,032	26,156	4,791	630	11,337	4,008	396	55
Oregon	33,220	35,364	217	4,764	17,243	1,841	293	6,963	3,648	345	50
Pennsylvania	156,247	148,044	745	17,757	71,455	5,743	1,527	31,933	11,444	7,234	206
Rhode Island	12,461	14,539	90	1,168	6,566	830	303	2,786	1,156	1,590	50
South Carolina	84,337	91,437	37	9,543	46,635	8,139	674	19,346	4,111	2,890	62
South Dakota	13,227	14,373	31	1,691	6,578	1,097	302	2,817	1,404	403	50
Tennessee	95,978	100,185	45	11,482	48,118	10,847	735	20,992	6,577	1,305	84
Texas	311,250	332,128	245	31,552	157,831	47,672	3,024	69,132	19,732	2,650	290
Utah	27,329	25,962	47	4,202	11,304	545	253	5,256	4,165	140	50
Vermont	5,910	7,041	177	849	3,799	67	258	1,312	478	51	50
Virginia	84,516	83,310	154	10,215	40,850	5,783	664	18,786	5,413	1,350	95
Washington	56,191	59,166	329	6,624	25,738	2,267	368	11,741	11,454	570	75
West Virginia	44,236	46,859	37	4,010	21,941	7,501	471	10,102	2,106	641	50
Wisconsin	56,364	56,870	1,430	8,645	26,025	2,146	639	11,201	5,958	740	86
Wyoming	5,983	5,957	22	1,044	2,248	101	266	1,164	1,104	8	0
Dist. of Col.	13,711	16,113	28	1,075	8,010	1,572	322	3,293	1,539	224	50

Source: U.S. Department of Agriculture, Food and Nutrition Service, Budget Division, unpublished data.

Table 8.7
AVERAGE ANNUAL SALARY OF INSTRUCTIONAL STAFF
IN PUBLIC ELEMENTARY AND SECONDARY SCHOOLS: 1939-40 to 1983-84

State or other jurisdiction	Average annual salary for: (in unadjusted dollars)					
	1939-40	1949-50	1959-60	1969-70	1979-80 (a)	1983-84 (a)
Alabama................	$ 744	$2,111	$4,002	$ 6,954	$13,338	$18,229
Alaska.................	N.A.	N.A.	6,859	10,993	27,697	38,400
Arizona................	1,544	3,556	5,590	8,975	16,180	23,662
Arkansas	584	1,801	3,295	6,445	12,704	17,503
California.............	2,351	N.A.	6,600	9,980	18,626	26,022
Colorado	1,393	2,821	4,997	7,900	16,840	24,191
Connecticut	1,861	3,558	6,008	9,400	17,062	23,699
Delaware	1,684	3,273	5,800	9,300	16,873	21,684
Florida	1,012	2,958	5,080	8,600	14,875	20,710
Georgia...............	770	1,963	3,904	7,372	14,547	19,518
Hawaii	N.A.	N.A.	5,390	9,829	20,436	25,069
Idaho	1,057	2,481	4,216	7,257	14,110	18,687
Illinois...............	1,700	3,458	5,814	9,950	18,271	25,003
Indiana	1,433	3,401	5,542	9,574	16,256	22,320
Iowa	1,017	2,420	4,030	8,200	15,600	20,884
Kansas	1,014	2,628	4,450	7,811	14,513	20,607
Kentucky	826	1,936	3,327	7,624	15,350	20,500
Louisiana	1,006	2,983	4,978	7,220	14,020	18,790
Maine	894	2,115	3,694	8,059	13,743	17,880
Maryland	1,642	3,594	5,557	9,885	18,308	25,091
Massachusetts	2,037	3,338	5,545	9,175	22,500	26,650
Michigan	1,576	3,420	5,654	10,125	19,277	28,200
Minnesota	1,276	3,013	5,275	9,957	16,654	25,080
Mississippi	559	1,416	3,314	6,012	12,274	16,355
Missouri	1,159	2,581	4,536	8,091	14,543	20,073
Montana...............	1,184	2,962	4,425	8,100	15,080	21,387
Nebraska	829	2,292	3,876	7,855	14,236	20,013
Nevada	1,557	3,209	5,693	9,689	17,290	23,380
New Hampshire	1,258	2,712	4,455	8,018	12,930	18,030
New Jersey............	2,093	3,511	5,871	9,500	18,851	24,362
New Mexico...........	1,144	3,215	5,382	8,125	15,406	21,650
New York	2,604	3,706	6,537	10,200	20,400	28,000
North Carolina	946	2,688	4,178	7,744	14,445	18,990
North Dakota	745	2,324	3,695	6,900	13,839	19,830
Ohio	1,587	3,088	5,124	8,594	16,100	22,142
Oklahoma	1,014	2,736	4,659	7,139	13,500	19,220
Oregon	1,333	3,323	5,535	9,200	16,996	24,847
Pennsylvania	1,640	3,006	5,308	9,000	17,060	23,333
Rhode Island	1,809	3,294	5,499	8,900	18,425	26,214
South Carolina	743	1,891	3,450	7,000	13,670	18,209
South Dakota	807	2,064	3,725	6,700	13,010	17,125
Tennessee	862	2,302	3,929	7,290	14,193	18,240
Texas.................	1,079	3,122	4,708	7,503	14,729	20,993
Utah	1,394	3,103	5,096	8,049	17,403	22,981
Vermont...............	981	2,348	4,466	8,225	13,300	18,186
Virginia...............	899	2,328	4,312	8,200	14,655	20,457
Washington	1,706	3,487	5,643	9,500	19,735	25,428
West Virginia	1,170	2,425	3,952	7,850	14,395	18,201
Wisconsin..............	1,379	3,007	4,870	9,150	16,335	23,300
Wyoming	1,169	2,798	4,937	8,532	16,830	25,439
Dist. of Col.	2,350	3,920	6,280	11,075	23,027	28,725

Sources: U.S. Department of Education, National Center for Education Statistics, *Statistics of State School Systems*; National Education Association, *Estimates of School Statistics, 1984-85* (Copyright 1985).
Note: Includes supervisors, principals, classroom teachers, and other instructional staff.
Key:
N.A.—Not available.
(a) Estimated.

Table 8.8
MEMBERSHIP AND ATTENDANCE IN PUBLIC ELEMENTARY AND SECONDARY SCHOOLS, BY STATE: 1980-81 AND 1983-84

State or other jurisdiction	1980-81			1983-84(a)		
	Estimated average daily membership (ADM)	Average daily attendance (ADA)	ADA as a percent of ADM	Estimated average daily membership (ADM)	Estimated average daily attendance (ADA)	ADA as a percent of ADM
United States.........	40,256,675	37,703,744	93.7	38,794,000 (b)	36,399,867	93.8
Alabama...............	741,534	701,925	94.7	715,396	679,494	95.0
Alaska................	86,604	83,745	96.7	91,631	86,240	94.1
Arizona...............	491,812	476,149	96.8	482,828	461,431	95.6
Arkansas	441,432	417,080	94.5	426,376	403,285	94.6
California(c)	4,097,000 (d)	4,014,917	98.0	N.A.	4,086,512	
Colorado	527,721	508,750	96.4	524,300	503,732	96.1
Connecticut	534,400	501,085	93.8	476,813	453,665	95.1
Delaware	97,713	89,609	91.7	90,227	83,897	93.0
Florida	1,510,225	1,389,487 (e)	92.0	1,495,880	1,375,013	91.9
Georgia...............	1,046,400	988,612	94.5	1,035,000	978,500	94.5
Hawaii	162,666	151,713	93.3	160,534	150,143	93.5
Idaho	203,250	190,144	93.6	N.A.	196,934	
Illinois...............	1,876,356	1,765,357	94.1	1,730,278	1,616,711	93.4
Indiana	994,492	944,424	95.0	966,802	917,753	94.9
Iowa	524,800	501,403	95.5	488,912	465,784	95.3
Kansas	384,870	374,451	97.3	384,879	363,557	94.5
Kentucky	659,950	614,676	93.1	621,920	565,861	91.0
Louisiana	773,000	715,844	92.6	761,300	716,800	94.2
Maine	220,000	207,554	94.3	208,096	196,169	94.3
Maryland	725,818	664,866	91.6	677,860	611,361	90.2
Massachusetts	1,020,382	950,675	93.2	885,301	796,711	90.0
Michigan	1,832,631 (d)	1,711,139	93.4	N.A.	1,597,011	
Minnesota	750,073	710,836	94.8	699,465	661,463	94.6
Mississippi	471,100	446,515	94.8	458,062	437,790	95.6
Missouri	831,448	756,536	91.0	N.A.	715,155	
Montana..............	148,300	141,641	95.5	145,600	138,100	94.8
Nebraska	274,830	263,797	96.0	263,765	252,289	95.6
Nevada	141,825	138,481	97.6	147,400	139,000	94.3
New Hampshire.........	162,656	150,316	92.4	154,087	144,915	94.0
New Jersey.............	1,265,089	1,121,272	88.6	1,143,365	1,060,166	92.7
New Mexico...........	271,198	240,496	88.7	269,949	256,452	95.0
New York	2,808,160	2,475,055	88.1	2,610,770	2,363,010	90.5
North Carolina	1,123,506	1,055,651	94.0	1,084,728	1,022,138	94.2
North Dakota	116,416	111,759 (e)	96.0	117,241	112,509	96.0
Ohio	1,948,600	1,801,914	92.5	1,811,607	1,693,851	93.5
Oklahoma	574,000	542,800	94.6	585,962	553,236	94.4
Oregon	449,925	417,009	92.7	441,645	414,055	93.8
Pennsylvania	1,897,000	1,754,782	92.5	1,720,000	1,584,600	92.1
Rhode Island	142,457	135,096	94.8	135,102	123,501	91.4
South Carolina	601,708	580,132	96.4	585,091	552,791	94.5
South Dakota	127,068	121,663	95.7	122,598	117,101	95.5
Tennessee	857,373	797,237	93.0	816,666	774,346	94.8
Texas.................	2,794,671	2,647,288	94.7	2,923,362	2,745,338	93.9
Utah	340,827	323,048	94.8	376,312	356,072	94.6
Vermont	95,940	90,884	94.7	89,150	83,355	93.5
Virginia...............	1,000,378	938,794	93.8	958,087	900,378	94.0
Washington	751,287	704,655	93.8	730,739	685,068	93.8
West Virginia	389,428 (d)	351,823	90.3	N.A.	343,320	
Wisconsin.............	771,485	743,505	96.4	735,503	691,845	94.1
Wyoming	98,000 (d)	91,381	93.2	99,000	93,600	94.5
Dist. of Col.	98,871	85,773	86.8	88,293	77,859	88.2

Source: U.S. Department of Education, National Center for Education Statistics, survey of "Common Core of Data"; and National Education Association, *Estimates of School Statistics, 1984-85* (Copyright 1985).
Key:
N.A.—Not available.
(a) Data compiled by the National Education Association.

(b) Total includes National Center for Education Statistics estimates for non-reporting states.
(c) Data for California are not strictly comparable with those for other states because state's attendance figures include excused absences.
(d) Data estimated by the National Center for Education Statistics.
(e) Data estimated by state education agencies.

Table 8.9
ENROLLMENT, AVERAGE DAILY ATTENDANCE,
AND CLASSROOM TEACHERS IN PUBLIC ELEMENTARY
AND SECONDARY SCHOOLS, BY STATE: 1983-84

State or other jurisdiction	Enrollment(a)	Estimated average daily attendance(b)	Classroom teachers	Pupils per teacher based on enrollment	Pupils per teacher based on average daily attendance
United States..	39,327,797	36,399,867	2,125,756	18.5	17.1
Alabama.......	721,901	679,494	35,619	20.3	19.1
Alaska.........	92,918	86,240	5,747	16.2	15.0
Arizona........	503,228	461,431	26,268	19.2	17.6
Arkansas	432,120	403,285	23,696	18.2	17.0
California......	4,089,017	4,086,512	174,290	23.5	23.4
Colorado	542,196	503,732	28,421	19.1	17.7
Connecticut	477,585	453,665	32,317	14.8	14.0
Delaware	91,406	83,897	5,429	16.8	15.5
Florida	1,495,543	1,375,013	85,028	17.6	16.2
Georgia.........	1,050,859	978,500	56,491	18.6	17.3
Hawaii	162,241	150,143	7,007	23.2	21.4
Idaho	206,352	196,934	9,847	21.0	20.0
Illinois.........	1,853,316	1,616,711	102,130	18.1	15.8
Indiana	984,384	917,753	50,509	19.5	18.2
Iowa	497,287	465,784	31,779	15.6	14.7
Kansas	405,222	363,557	26,096	15.5	13.9
Kentucky	647,414	565,861	32,458	19.9	17.4
Louisiana	782,434	716,800	42,179	18.6	17.0
Maine	209,753	196,169	13,492	15.5	14.5
Maryland	683,491	611,361	37,275	18.3	16.4
Massachusetts ...	878,844	796,711	56,873	15.5	14.0
Michigan	1,735,881	1,597,011	79,982	21.7	20.0
Minnesota	705,242	661,463	39,392	17.9	16.8
Mississippi	467,744	437,790	24,955	18.7	17.5
Missouri	795,453	715,155	46,761	17.0	15.3
Montana.......	153,646	138,100	9,479	16.2	14.6
Nebraska	266,998	252,289	17,548	15.2	14.4
Nevada	150,442	139,000	7,366	20.4	18.9
New Hampshire..	159,030	144,915	9,821	16.2	14.8
New Jersey......	1,147,571	1,060,166	73,593	15.6	14.4
New Mexico.....	269,711	256,452	14,532	18.6	17.6
New York	2,674,818	2,363,010	145,647	18.4	16.2
North Carolina ..	1,089,606	1,022,138	55,126	19.8	18.5
North Dakota ...	117,213	112,509	7,067	16.6	15.9
Ohio	1,827,300	1,693,851	96,927	18.9	17.5
Oklahoma	591,389	553,236	34,999	16.9	15.8
Oregon	447,109	414,055	24,409	18.3	17.0
Pennsylvania	1,737,952	1,584,600	102,207	17.0	15.5
Rhode Island	136,180	123,501	8,848	15.4	14.0
South Carolina ..	604,553	552,791	32,323	18.7	17.1
South Dakota ...	123,060	117,101	8,355	14.7	14.0
Tennessee	822,057	774,346	39,409	20.9	19.6
Texas..........	2,989,796	2,745,338	170,629	17.5	16.1
Utah	379,065	356,072	15,650	24.2	22.8
Vermont	90,416	83,355	6,242	14.5	13.4
Virginia.........	966,110	900,378	56,388	17.1	16.0
Washington	736,239	685,068	34,757	21.2	19.7
West Virginia ...	371,251	343,320	22,503	16.5	15.3
Wisconsin	774,646	691,845	45,311	17.1	15.3
Wyoming	100,965	93,600	7,010	14.4	13.4
Dist. of Col.	88,843	77,859	5,569	16.0	14.0

Source: U.S. Department of Education, National Center for Education Statistics, survey of "Common Core of Data"; and National Education Association, *Estimates of School Statistics, 1984-85* (Copyright 1985).
(a) Data are for fall 1983.
(b) Data collected by the National Education Association.

Table 8.10
STATE COURSE REQUIREMENTS FOR HIGH SCHOOL GRADUATION

State or other jurisdiction	All courses	English/ language arts	Social studies	Mathe-matics	Science	Physical education /health	Electives	Other courses	First graduating class to which requirements apply
Alabama	20	4	3	2	1	3½	6½	...	1985
Alaska	21	4	3	2	2	1	9	...	1985
Arizona	20	4	2	2	2	...	9½	½-essentials of free enterprise system	1987
Arkansas	20	4	3	------------5------------		1	6½	½-fine arts	1988
California	13	3	3	2	2	2	...	1-fine arts or foreign language	1987
Colorado(a)		...	...	...	...	...	...		
Connecticut	20	4	3	3	2	1	6	1-arts or vocational education	1988
Delaware	19	4	3	2	2	1½	6½	...	1987
Florida	24	4	3	3	3	1	9	½-practical or exploratory vocational education, ½-performing fine arts	1987
Georgia	21	4	3	2	2	1	8	1-fine arts, vocational education, or computer technology	1988
Hawaii	20	4	4	2	2	1½	6	½-guidance	1983
Idaho	20	4	2	2	2	1½	6	½-reading; ½-speech, ½-consumer education,1-humanities	1988
Illinois	16	3	2	2	1	4½	2¼	¼-consumer education,1-art, foreign language, music or vocational education	1988
Indiana	19½	4	2	2	2	1½	8	...	1989
Iowa	...		1½	...	...	1	...		(a,b)
Kansas	20	4	3	2	2	1	8	...	1988
Kentucky	20	4	2	3	2	1	7	1-additional mathematics, science, social studies, or vocational education	1987
Louisiana	23	4	3	3	3	2	7½	½-computer literacy	1989
Maine	16	4	2	2	2	1½	3½	1-fine arts	1989
Maryland	20	4	3	2	2	1	8	...	(c)
Massachusetts		...	1	...	...	4	...	...	(a,b)
Michigan		...	½	...	...	...	...	...	(a,b)
Minnesota	20	4	3	1	1	1½	9½	...	1982
Mississippi	16	3	2½	1	1	...	8½	...	1970(d)
Missouri									
Standard diploma	22	3	2	2	2	1	10	1-practical arts, 1-fine arts	1988
College preparatory studies certificate	24	4	3	3	3	1	8	1-practical arts, 1-fine arts	
Montana	20	4	1½ or 2	2	1	1	10½ or 10	...	1986
Nebraska		...	...	...	...	...	...		1991(e)
Nevada	20	3	2	2	1	2½	9½	...	1986
New Hampshire	18¾	4	2½	2	2	¼	4	½-arts; ½-computer science; 3 from 2 of the following: arts, foreign language, practical arts, and vocational education	1989
New Jersey	18½	4	2	2	1	4	4	1-fine, practical or performing arts; ½-career exploration	(f)
New Mexico	21	4	2	2	2	1	9	1-practical arts or fine arts	1987
New York									
Local diploma	18½	4	4	2	3	½	varies	1-arts and/or music(g)	1989
Regent's diploma	18½	4	4	2	2	½	varies	(g)	
North Carolina	20	4	2	2	2	1	9	...	1987
North Dakota	17	4	3	2	2	1	5	...	1984
Ohio	18	3	2	2	1	1	9	...	1988

Years of instruction in . . .

State or other jurisdiction	All courses	English/ language arts	Social studies	Mathe-matics	Science	Physical education /health	Electives	Other courses	First gradua-ting class to which require-ments apply
Oklahoma									
High school graduation requirement	20	4	2	2	2	...	10	...	1987
College preparatory	15	4	2	3	2	...	...	4-from: foreign language, computer science, economics, English, geography, government, math, history, sociology, science, speech, psychology	1988
Oregon	22	3	3½	2	2	2	8	½-career development, 1-applied arts, fine arts, or foreign language	1988
Pennsylvania	21(a)	4	3	3	3	1	...	2-arts and humanities	1989
Rhode Island									
Career bound	16	4	2	2	2	...	6	...	1989
College bound	18	4	2	3	2	...	4	2-foreign languages; ½-arts; ½-computer literacy	
South Carolina	20	4	3	3	2	1	7	...	1987
South Dakota	20	4	3	2	2	...	8	½-computer studies, ½-fine arts	1989
Tennessee	20	4	1½	2	2	1½	9	...	1987
Texas									
High school graduation requirements	21	4	2½	3	2	2	7	½-economics/free enterprise	1988
Additional requirements	22	4	2½	3	3	2	3	½-economics/free enterprise; 2-foreign languages; 1-computer science, 1-fine arts	1988
Utah	24	3	3	2	2	2	9	1½-arts; 1-vocational education; ½-computer science	1988
Vermont	15½	4	3	3	3	1½	...	1-arts	1989
Virginia									
Standard diploma	20	4	3	2	2	2	6	1-additional science or mathematics	1988
Advanced studies diploma	22	4	3	3	3	2	4	3-foreign languages	(h)
Washington	18	3	2½	2	2	2	5½	1-occupational education	1989
West Virginia	20	4	3	2	1	2	7	1-applied arts, fine or performing arts or second language	1985
Wisconsin	13½	4	3	2	2	2	(i)	½-computer science	1989
Wyoming	18(a)	1	...	...	...	...	...	...	(f)
Dist. of Col.									
Comprehensive	20½	4	2	2	2	1½	8	1-foreign language	1985
Career/vocational	23	4	2	2	2	1½	1½	1-foreign language; 9-specialized preparation	

Source: Chris Pipho, ECS Clearinghouse, and Patricia Flakus-Mosqueda, ECS Governance Center, Education Commission of the States, Denver, Colorado.

Note: Requirements as of November 1984; information for some states as of August 1985.

Key:

. . .—No requirement.

(a) Local school boards determine remaining requirements. In Colorado, state has constitutional prohibition against state requirements. In Pennsylvania, local boards determine remaining five units.

(b) Legislative requirements in effect for many years.

(c) Possible changes (late 1984).

(d) In July 1984, new requirements were approved and scheduled to be field-tested for two years.

(e) At least 80 percent of credit hours must be in core curriculum courses, state is defining core courses.

(f) In effect for many years.

(g) Plus, three to five units of a sequence of specific courses chosen by the student; choices vary for the different diplomas.

(h) Available for 1985 graduates.

(i) Option of the local school district.

Table 8.11
NUMBER OF INSTITUTIONS OF HIGHER EDUCATION AND BRANCHES, BY TYPE, CONTROL OF INSTITUTION, AND STATE: 1984-85

State or other jurisdiction	All institutions			Universities		All other 4-year institutions		2-year institutions	
	Total	Public	Private	Public	Private	Public	Private	Public	Private
United States	3,331	1,501	1,830	93	62	473	1,397	935	371
Alabama...............	77	53	24	2	0	14	17	37	7
Alaska................	15	12	3	1	0	2	3	9	0
Arizona...............	31	19	12	2	0	1	9	16	3
Arkansas	36	20	16	1	0	9	11	10	5
California.............	289	137	152	2	4	29	123	106	25
Colorado	47	28	19	2	1	11	11	15	7
Connecticut	48	24	24	1	1	6	20	17	3
Delaware	8	5	3	1	0	1	3	3	0
Florida	88	37	51	2	1	7	37	28	13
Georgia...............	80	34	46	1	1	17	30	16	15
Hawaii	12	9	3	1	0	2	3	6	0
Idaho	10	6	4	1	0	3	3	2	1
Illinois...............	163	62	101	3	4	9	82	50	15
Indiana	74	28	46	4	1	9	36	15	9
Iowa	59	19	40	2	1	1	33	16	6
Kansas	52	29	23	3	0	5	20	21	3
Kentucky	45	9	36	2	0	6	21	1	15
Louisiana	31	20	11	1	2	13	8	6	1
Maine	30	13	17	1	0	7	12	5	5
Maryland	56	32	24	1	1	12	21	19	2
Massachusetts	121	31	90	1	7	13	64	17	19
Michigan	92	44	48	3	1	12	42	29	5
Minnesota	69	29	40	1	0	9	32	19	8
Mississippi	42	25	17	2	0	7	12	16	5
Missouri	93	28	65	1	2	12	53	15	10
Montana..............	16	9	7	2	0	4	3	3	4
Nebraska	28	13	15	1	1	6	12	6	2
Nevada	8	6	2	1	0	1	2	4	0
New Hampshire	28	12	16	1	0	3	12	8	4
New Jersey............	60	31	29	1	2	13	24	17	3
New Mexico...........	20	17	3	2	0	4	3	11	0
New York	300	86	214	2	12	39	157	45	45
North Carolina	128	74	54	2	2	14	34	58	18
North Dakota	19	11	8	2	0	4	4	5	4
Ohio	141	59	82	8	1	14	63	37	18
Oklahoma	46	29	17	2	1	12	12	15	4
Oregon	47	21	26	2	0	6	25	13	1
Pennsylvania	204	62	142	3	4	22	102	37	36
Rhode Island	13	3	10	1	0	1	10	1	0
South Carolina	63	33	30	2	0	10	20	21	10
South Dakota	18	7	11	1	0	6	8	0	3
Tennessee	80	24	56	1	1	9	39	14	16
Texas.................	157	98	59	6	4	33	49	59	6
Utah	14	9	5	2	1	2	2	5	2
Vermont	22	6	16	1	0	3	14	2	2
Virginia...............	71	39	32	3	0	12	30	24	2
Washington	52	33	19	2	0	4	18	27	1
West Virginia	29	16	13	1	0	11	9	4	4
Wisconsin.............	62	30	32	1	1	12	27	17	4
Wyoming	8	8	0	1	0	0	0	7	0
Dist. of Col.	19	2	17	0	5	2	12	0	0
U.S. Service Schools	10	10	0	0	0	9	0	1	0

Source: U.S. Department of Education, National Center for Education Statistics.

Table 8.12
ESTIMATED UNDERGRADUATE TUITION AND FEES AND ROOM AND BOARD RATES IN INSTITUTIONS OF HIGHER EDUCATION, BY CONTROL OF INSTITUTION AND BY STATE: 1984-85*

State or other jurisdiction	Public institutions				Private institutions			
	Total	Tuition (in state)	Room	Board	Total	Tuition	Room	Board
Alabama	$2,955	$914	$894	$1,147	$5,646	$3,359	$961	$1,326
Alaska	3,121	759	912	1,450	6,545	3,228	1,492	1,825
Arizona	3,556	661	1,474	1,421	5,898	3,647	922	1,329
Arkansas	2,695	839	862	994	4,866	3,017	726	1,123
California	3,440	389	1,550	1,501	9,806	6,511	1,533	1,762
Colorado	3,718	1,147	1,106	1,465	9,402	5,727	2,148	1,527
Connecticut	3,759	1,029	1,356	1,374	10,718	7,213	1,869	1,636
Delaware	3,791	1,405	1,366	1,020	6,539	3,587	1,662	1,290
Florida	3,402	746	1,164	1,492	7,222	4,502	1,418	1,302
Georgia	3,188	1,076	865	1,247	6,556	4,004	1,177	1,375
Hawaii	2,755	596	1,183	976	6,744	3,365	1,745	1,634
Idaho	3,313	886	1,013	1,414	4,097	1,983	753	1,361
Illinois	3,500	1,044	1,223	1,233	8,514	5,456	1,705	1,353
Indiana	3,597	1,367	1,028	1,202	7,940	5,387	1,220	1,333
Iowa	3,049	1,076	912	1,061	7,395	5,231	957	1,207
Kansas	3,101	946	1,064	1,091	5,988	3,621	1,088	1,279
Kentucky	3,317	878	1,184	1,255	6,000	3,904	911	1,185
Louisiana	3,113	817	971	1,325	8,354	5,346	1,459	1,549
Maine	4,068	1,426	1,281	1,361	9,389	6,238	1,506	1,645
Maryland	4,293	1,168	1,745	1,380	9,147	5,881	1,699	1,567
Massachusetts	3,504	1,123	1,240	1,141	10,943	7,143	2,086	1,714
Michigan	3,794	1,336	1,076	1,382	6,566	4,165	1,078	1,323
Minnesota	3,644	1,503	1,038	1,103	7,939	5,635	1,137	1,167
Mississippi	2,677	890	731	1,056	4,597	2,861	669	1,067
Missouri	2,794	943	952	899	7,147	4,630	1,191	1,326
Montana	3,209	834	876	1,499	4,843	2,809	648	1,386
Nebraska	2,286	1,069	815	402	5,805	4,031	1,011	763
Nevada	3,222	909	1,171	1,142	7,228	2,528	2,700	2,000
New Hampshire	3,977	1,800	1,304	873	9,681	6,505	1,588	1,588
New Jersey	4,077	1,208	1,687	1,182	8,843	5,916	1,614	1,313
New Mexico	2,895	722	893	1,280	4,941	3,033	929	979
New York	4,163	1,352	1,548	1,263	9,068	5,851	1,694	1,523
North Carolina	2,556	488	971	1,097	6,542	4,297	939	1,306
North Dakota	2,724	983	583	1,158	4,753	2,982	727	1,044
Ohio	4,077	1,570	1,368	1,139	7,300	4,705	1,223	1,372
Oklahoma	2,572	635	837	1,100	5,946	3,648	1,019	1,279
Oregon	3,232	1,010	905	1,317	8,320	5,673	1,211	1,436
Pennsylvania	4,157	1,854	1,237	1,066	8,369	5,485	1,452	1,432
Rhode Island	4,664	1,306	1,678	1,680	9,733	6,395	1,660	1,678
South Carolina	3,250	1,072	1,101	1,077	5,970	3,671	1,041	1,258
South Dakota	2,986	1,272	746	968	6,702	4,336	1,154	1,212
Tennessee	2,790	808	964	1,018	6,171	3,845	1,067	1,259
Texas	2,979	389	1,229	1,361	6,441	3,882	1,187	1,372
Utah	3,626	977	1,019	1,630	3,739	1,531	678	1,530
Vermont	5,324	2,424	1,781	1,119	10,400	7,642	1,337	1,421
Virginia	3,808	1,307	1,330	1,171	7,424	4,861	1,220	1,343
Washington	3,481	848	1,461	1,172	8,627	5,433	1,552	1,642
West Virginia	3,549	888	1,237	1,424	6,612	4,164	1,083	1,365
Wisconsin	3,247	1,076	1,109	1,062	7,694	5,164	1,143	1,387
Wyoming	2,861	564	923	1,374	. . .	. . .	. . .	. .
Dist. of Col.	. . .	496	. . .	. . .	9,275	5,835	1,834	1,606

*Preliminary

Source: U.S. Department of Education, National Center for Education Statistics.

Note: Data are for the entire academic year.

Table 8.13
TOTAL ROAD AND STREET MILEAGE: 1984
(Classified by jurisdiction)

State or other jurisdiction	Rural mileage Under state control	Rural mileage Under local control(a)	Rural mileage Under federal control(b)	Rural mileage Total rural roads	Urban mileage Under state control	Urban mileage Under local control(a)	Urban mileage Total urban mileage	Total rural and urban mileage
United States	817,813	2,133,888	266,395	3,218,096	102,968	569,792	673,685	3,891,781
Alabama	10,177	62,747	307	73,231	1,511	12,818	14,329	87,560
Alaska	9,930	0	0	9,930	1,496	125	1,621	11,551
Arizona	5,352	26,288	35,673	67,313	434	8,390	8,824	76,137
Arkansas	14,931	53,096	1,440	69,467	1,180	6,398	7,578	77,045
California	14,946	62,542	30,618	108,106	3,267	61,621	64,899	173,005
Colorado	8,452	49,529	7,219	65,200	849	9,677	10,526	75,726
Connecticut	2,203	6,686	0	8,889	1,693	8,997	10,690	19,579
Delaware	3,546	228	3	3,777	1,160	365	1,525	5,302
Florida	7,702	59,816	0	67,518	3,834	27,632	31,466	98,984
Georgia...................	86,236	378	0	86,614	419	18,500	18,919	105,533
Hawaii	864	1,693	76	2,633	195	1,194	1,424	4,057
Idaho	4,834	26,672	35,159	66,665	251	1,690	1,951	68,616
Illinois...................	13,180	90,231	290	103,701	4,429	26,341	30,781	134,482
Indiana	9,734	64,164	0	73,898	1,610	16,059	17,669	91,567
Iowa	9,259	94,482	115	103,856	901	7,638	8,543	112,399
Kansas	10,085	113,689	0	123,774	607	7,826	8,433	132,207
Kentucky	23,270	38,290	301	61,861	1,850	5,442	7,478	69,339
Louisiana	14,851	30,395	653	45,899	1,568	10,656	12,224	58,123
Maine	7,713	11,695	173	19,581	286	2,061	2,357	21,839
Maryland(c)	4,070	12,917	337	17,324	1,169	8,865	10,101	27,425
Massachusetts	1,750	11,369	87	13,206	1,863	18,696	20,588	33,794
Michigan	7,736	84,577	0	92,313	1,774	23,456	25,230	117,543
Minnesota	12,398	104,380	1,652	118,430	1,045	12,080	13,125	131,555
Mississippi	9,598	54,426	303	64,327	726	6,191	6,953	71,280
Missouri	30,774	72,577	709	104,060	1,543	13,284	14,827	118,887
Montana..................	7,665	53,698	7,850	69,213	165	2,105	2,273	71,486
Nebraska	10,052	76,908	132	87,092	333	4,539	4,872	91,964
Nevada	4,908	22,688	13,215	40,811	275	2,737	3,014	43,825
New Hampshire	3,836	8,131	142	12,109	562	1,846	2,408	14,517
New Jersey................	1,591	9,906	21	11,518	1,576	20,767	22,361	33,879
New Mexico(c)	11,553	31,797	6,326	49,676	853	3,598	4,451	54,127
New York	12,335	60,714	0	73,049	4,059	32,772	36,831	109,880
North Carolina	69,331	3,333	2,438	75,102	7,589	9,780	17,618	92,720
North Dakota	7,111	76,538	704	84,353	193	1,421	1,614	85,967
Ohio	16,477	65,134	29	81,640	3,744	26,405	30,149	111,789
Oklahoma	12,033	85,877	0	97,910	1,023	11,278	12,301	110,211
Oregon	10,071	33,901	82,502	126,474	785	7,626	8,448	134,922
Pennsylvania	86,662	397	0	87,059	20,666	8,154	28,820	115,879
Rhode Island(c)............	217	1,519	0	1,736	1,735	2,804	4,539	6,275
South Carolina	34,496	19,478	598	54,572	5,842	2,925	8,767	63,339
South Dakota	7,726	61,946	1,950	71,622	170	1,605	1,775	73,397
Tennessee(c)...............	9,698	61,119	1,308	72,125	1,473	10,511	11,984	84,109
Texas.....................	65,649	146,311	978	212,938	5,799	60,066	65,865	278,803
Utah	4,949	22,015	16,326	43,290	635	4,439	5,074	48,364
Vermont	2,680	10,324	71	13,075	107	817	933	14,008
Virginia..................	50,022	801	1,519	52,342	4,760	8,025	12,993	65,335
Washington	17,486	38,135	10,060	65,681	1,039	13,999	15,038	80,719
West Virginia	30,154	644	1,213	32,011	1,202	1,773	2,975	34,986
Wisconsin.................	11,185	83,059	184	94,428	1,334	12,588	13,922	108,350
Wyoming	6,335	26,648	3,714	36,697	287	1,210	1,497	38,194
Dist. of Col.	0	0	0	0	1,102	0	1,102	1,102

Source: Federal Highway Administration, U.S. Department of Transportation. Compiled for calendar year ending Dec. 31, 1984 from reports of state authorities.

Note: This table does not include mileage of non-public roads.

(a) Includes mileage not identified by administrative authority.

(b) Mileage in federal parks, forests and reservations that are not a part of the state and local highway systems.

(c) Incomplete 1984 data submitted for these states; 1983 data used. 1982 data used for Tennessee and factored to 1984 levels.

Table 8.14

STATE RECEIPTS FOR HIGHWAYS: 1984
(In thousands of dollars)

State or other jurisdiction	State highway user tax revenues	Roads and crossing tolls(a)	Other state imposts, general fund revenues	Miscellaneous income	Federal funds — Federal Highway Administration	Federal funds — Other agencies	Transfers from local governments	Bond proceeds (b)	Total receipts
United States	$19,426,238	$1,825,219	$1,756,887	$1,287,124	$10,649,885	$322,810	$365,894	$1,638,720	$37,272,777
Alabama.........	321,388		150,196	18,465	236,052	3,404	12,358		741,863
Alaska...........	38,886	15,570	125,534	6,585	115,656	942		39,181	342,354
Arizona.........	405,759		2,350	32,606	178,938	4,114	4,683		628,450
Arkansas	240,512		4,409	489	99,372	5,841	2,483		353,106
California........	1,756,868	69,705		126,883	607,512	34,929	77,324		2,673,221
Colorado	256,055		87,041	8,043	193,355	3,018	20,321		567,833
Connecticut	242,643	68,031		16,983	140,691	1,180		158,359	627,887
Delaware	56,215	37,390		13,018	45,898	582		39,020	192,123
Florida	764,347	108,015	24,729	88,122	337,054	6,487	14,071	206,884	1,549,709
Georgia..........	323,948		81,025	57,180	346,580	3,519		41,607	853,859
Hawaii	56,721		15,781	1,027	59,349	469	550	18,800	152,697
Idaho	119,339			397	71,402	5,289	1,975		198,402
Illinois..........	1,029,839	157,357	105,225	24,933	555,991	5,747	20,529	45,000	1,944,621
Indiana..........	426,286	39,791	14,227	24,264	234,167	2,582	11,512		752,829
Iowa	319,428	223	93,189	37,141	187,346	1,853	2,749		641,929
Kansas	209,233	26,910	13,656	42,955	154,940	2,540	14,592	64,903	529,729
Kentucky	432,452	21,170	29,282	46,632	245,958	3,077	3,992	296,724	1,079,287
Louisiana	358,584		32,904	2,184	216,134	4,553		163,185	777,544
Maine	127,471	22,563	4,854	5,535	61,936	362	4,770	12,300	239,791
Maryland	485,536	70,826		84,082	292,520	1,823	91	24,122	959,000
Massachusetts	339,592	90,636	52,266	21,592	116,402	3,160	632		624,280
Michigan	777,314	8,340	116,718	37,205	322,814	6,397	4,306	49,179	1,322,273
Minnesota	534,111		24,926	36,493	239,332	3,297	15,226	73,764	927,149
Mississippi	177,376		134,925	49,376	123,907	10,218	7,983		503,785
Missouri	318,056		102,728	15,611	267,336	3,498	4,843		712,072
Montana.........	112,621		1,830	2,017	128,015	12,995		38,762	296,240
Nebraska	165,685	53,158		5,373	127,244	2,994	9,863		364,317
Nevada	97,124			3,151	93,920	764	2,388		197,347
New Hampshire ...	107,782	18,374		6,157	58,951	529	3,223		195,016
New Jersey.......	341,810	270,053		48,847	226,373	3,016		168,007	1,058,106
New Mexico......	171,558		50,225	14,777	124,167	1,989	625	23,046	386,387
New York	797,686	350,881	42,503	91,367	528,220	9,670		38,425	1,858,752
North Carolina	576,742	890	15,863	50,045	238,387	3,226	4,279		889,432
North Dakota	96,224		6,662	1,938	95,035	1,450	10,015		211,324
Ohio	999,372	68,376		44,569	429,917	6,559	28,689		1,577,482
Oklahoma	317,738	42,063	51,364	18,921	124,410	2,601	6,138		563,235
Oregon	224,306	1,450	35,236	13,604	141,744	44,746	4,073		465,159
Pennsylvania	1,341,882	178,887	500	60,321	533,810	8,291	7,723		2,131,414
Rhode Island	58,665	6,865	500	1,498	64,692	652			132,872
South Carolina	280,024			2,350	135,116	2,991	731		421,212
South Dakota	80,918		19,733	4,015	86,290	1,384	2,060		194,400
Tennessee	377,534		34,240	1,337	261,972	6,541	6,703		688,327
Texas.............	1,069,914	18,125	23,229	56,691	545,086	8,565	16,841		1,738,451
Utah	120,182		15,415	6,528	150,200	4,973	3,150	43,115	343,563
Vermont	82,383			831	49,495	1,314		5,228	139,251
Virginia..........	636,789	57,612	53,709	14,585	228,552	3,954	13,012		1,008,213
Washington	476,667	52,508		19,542	315,742	13,745	1,936	66,669	946,809
West Virginia	218,693	22,608	73,302	11,679	193,806	1,233	793		522,114
Wisconsin.........	440,098			248	211,199	3,242	16,170	8,023	678,980
Wyoming	61,946		63,453	8,618	77,410	55,993	2,492		269,912
Dist. of Col.	53,936			314	29,490	512		14,417	98,669

Source: Federal Highway Administration, U.S. Department of Transportation. Compiled for calendar year ending Dec. 31, 1984, from reports of state authorities.

(a) Toll receipts allocated for non-highway purposes are excluded.
(b) Par value of bonds issued and redeemed by refunding is excluded.

Table 8.15
STATE DISBURSEMENTS FOR HIGHWAYS: 1984
(In thousands of dollars)

State or other jurisdiction	Capital outlay — Federal-aid Systems — Interstate	Other federal aid systems	Other roads & streets	Total	Mainte-nance & traffic services	Adminis-tration & highway police	Bond interest	Grants-in-aid to local governments	Bond retire-ment(a)	Total dis-burse-ments
United States	$5,237,303	$8,128,555	$1,568,102	$16,991,835	$5,884,505	$4,600,169	$1,245,956	$5,742,036	$1,158,714	$35,623,215
Alabama	157,383	185,806	21,061	364,250	72,609	55,291	6,167	131,618	20,900	650,835
Alaska				172,264 (b)	100,733	43,591	17,699	10,233	2,003	346,523
Arizona	143,133	97,458	70,336	310,927	38,628	81,805	17,858	199,779	7,585	656,582
Arkansas	39,989	100,935	21,257	162,181	51,431	54,603		42,845		311,060
California				899,622 (b)	382,864	539,896	9,414	694,363	9,081	2,535,240
Colorado	95,299	137,611	3,847	236,757	100,460	43,352		146,052		526,621
Connecticut	115,050	95,351	12,073	222,474	63,733	60,778	60,559	22,754	98,861	529,159
Delaware	13,841	61,498	25,030	100,369	24,109	34,500	24,794	2,000	23,058	208,830
Florida	309,706	249,278	88,419	647,403	128,302	109,130	42,979	234,628	79,772	1,242,214
Georgia	231,933	265,189	24,036	521,158	135,144	77,189	36,710	9,759	31,608	811,568
Hawaii	45,867	23,733	12,791	82,391	13,957	14,522	10,064	21,982	10,496	153,412
Idaho	30,333	59,224	1,586	91,143	41,552	25,306		42,920		200,921
Illinois	253,647	740,290	48,964	1,042,901	233,714	183,759	84,635	315,556	104,720	1,965,285
Indiana...........	100,042	210,213	27,666	337,921	126,334	71,776	25,570	186,816	6,487	754,904
Iowa	85,825	197,276		283,101	72,029	57,855	127	236,785	195	650,092
Kansas	82,480	123,834	66,500	272,814	67,239	44,278	13,890	65,326	9,812	473,359
Kentucky	151,744	244,699	40,610	437,053	121,469	80,699	73,688	58,588	35,176	806,673
Louisiana				505,408 (b)	59,178	94,259	87,478	52,236	60,957	859,516
Maine	26,934	51,496	4,935	83,365	69,322	22,673	7,222	16,246	8,050	206,878
Maryland				399,591 (b)	120,697	116,004	48,200	188,708	5,925	879,125
Massachusetts	75,197	56,907	121,058	253,162	115,602	139,488	65,078	86,882	59,129	719,341
Michigan	155,349	208,949		364,298	133,164	216,128	14,169	542,589	28,320	1,298,668
Minnesota	169,984	216,002	68,886	454,872	101,382	76,559	14,390	193,292	16,429	856,924
Mississippi	40,281	183,957	22,259	246,497	51,200	53,014	49,981	57,625	5,072	463,389
Missouri...........	121,334	191,239	10,336	322,909	159,587	115,395		96,678		694,569
Montana	94,738	76,822	127	171,687	39,511	22,431	8,858	25,206		267,693
Nebraska	16,116	139,522	11,696	167,334	44,036	28,564	348	119,749	1,000	361,031
Nevada	48,334	66,727	2,492	117,553	23,114	35,386	2,554	14,392	5,000	197,999
New Hampshire	20,230	43,346	429	64,005	61,793	36,645	9,217	505	8,350	180,515
New Jersey	170,836	131,088	128,634	430,558	190,587	200,807	80,615			902,567
New Mexico	92,629	130,116		222,745	61,834	58,143	9,850	13,656	20,159	386,387
New York	157,821	582,940	168,586	909,347	311,660	240,497	55,917	185,188	136,896	1,839,505
North Carolina.....	90,431	215,503	35,228	341,162	278,616	142,383	21,198	45,443	16,500	845,302
North Dakota	20,247	94,642	8,162	123,051	26,622	16,112		39,028		204,833
Ohio	228,590	360,204	12,054	600,848	178,605	214,898	23,715	449,660	60,201	1,527,927
Oklahoma	56,308	162,923	29,500	248,731	72,401	99,418	10,313	147,566	6,956	585,385
Oregon...........	81,346	113,255	18,752	213,353	54,901	66,241	3,289	112,736	18,300	468,820
Pennsylvania	339,304	422,298	17,302	778,904	536,393	233,680	119,971	216,091	103,556	1,988,595
Rhode Island				80,990 (b)	17,938	13,439	7,859	390	10,300	130,916
South Carolina.....	83,903	83,488	49,424	216,815	105,898	51,945	2,209	17,107	9,930	403,904
South Dakota	13,341	103,472	8,198	125,011	32,280	25,050		18,630		200,971
Tennessee..........	143,281	198,316	71,753	413,350	109,025	49,892	4,492	119,774	13,220	709,753
Texas	359,859	578,838	109,010	1,047,707	363,565	213,862	29,345	76,644	170	1,731,293
Utah	127,000	78,050	4,050	209,100	41,452	33,293	3,351	25,879	14,000	327,075
Vermont...........	7,625	38,305	5,677	51,607	33,483	19,028	3,822	14,402	8,150	130,492
Virginia	135,008	183,039	86,567	404,614	304,614	126,847	22,913	88,818	4,581	952,387
Washington	224,518	193,779	1,513	419,810	141,311	115,014	50,250	182,544	23,030	931,959
West Virginia	131,281	117,468	21,998	270,747	101,468	43,749	43,819		55,723	515,506
Wisconsin	88,771	153,973	66,722	309,466	95,884	65,592	6,010	164,161	14,304	655,417
Wyoming..........	51,026	134,809	10,667	196,502	48,363	23,555		8,207		276,627
Dist. of Col.	9,409	24,687	7,911	42,007	24,712	11,828	15,369		4,752	98,668

Source: Federal Highway Administration, U.S. Department of Transportation. Compiled for calendar year ending Dec. 31, 1984 from reports of state authorities.

(a) Par value of bonds issued and redeemed by refunding is excluded.
(b) Segregation by federal-aid systems not identified by state.

348

Table 8.16
APPORTIONMENT OF FEDERAL-AID HIGHWAY FUNDS: FISCAL 1985
(In thousands of dollars)

State or other jurisdiction	Consolidated primary(a)	Rural secondary (a)	Urban system (a)	Interstate (b)	Interstate resurfacing (c)	Total highway systems funds	Highway safety programs(d)	Total highway safety funds(a,d)	Total(e)
	Highway systems funds								
United States	$2,305,382(f)	$640,281	$788,038	$3,640,202	$2,758,141	$11,871,618	$117,762	$2,036,362	$13,960,200
Alabama	42,209	13,638	10,200	111,272	48,111	225,430	2,098	43,018	269,073
Alaska	74,581	35,307	3,940	18,201	23,543	155,572	592	8,335	164,168
Arizona	30,611	10,444	10,179	60,767	58,863	171,371	1,577	9,897	181,945
Arkansas	28,297	11,566	4,811	18,201	31,600	107,484	1,421	35,620	143,365
California	166,899	24,617	99,786	327,693	261,912	1,002,615	10,149	85,150	1,094,763
Colorado	32,770	11,321	10,561	65,007	53,398	188,384	1,641	24,983	214,081
Connecticut	25,211	4,095	11,308	68,607	35,636	283,147	1,308	37,360	321,326
Delaware	11,328	3,201	3,940	18,201	13,791	50,461	592	6,002	56,724
Florida	75,158	14,881	37,593	246,165	93,662	467,459	4,336	43,179	513,267
Georgia	55,340	17,206	14,993	144,449	95,365	343,429	2,816	43,587	387,937
Hawaii	11,328	3,201	3,940	96,333	13,791	128,593	592	5,886	134,740
Idaho	18,465	8,003	3,940	27,288	25,896	83,592	854	9,065	92,918
Illinois	89,642	18,628	43,243	18,201	100,986	438,610	5,270	74,686	516,232
Indiana	52,473	15,104	15,661	18,201	62,711	268,216	2,730	53,686	322,823
Iowa	36,364	14,455	7,168	18,201	38,392	158,535	1,914	47,462	206,327
Kansas	33,529	13,291	6,700	18,201	32,448	104,169	1,854	52,093	156,564
Kentucky	39,925	13,579	8,014	73,318	51,591	186,427	1,878	31,448	218,311
Louisiana	38,763	10,928	12,779	170,559	48,328	281,357	2,000	48,777	330,913
Maine	14,449	5,671	3,940	18,201	13,791	56,052	592	9,337	65,650
Maryland	33,920	5,983	15,503	94,617	41,222	310,652	1,781	34,565	346,329
Massachusetts	44,528	6,353	21,972	165,377	34,981	289,341	2,399	47,450	338,364
Michigan	82,472	19,590	29,713	65,041	91,200	348,344	4,332	40,901	391,291
Minnesota	44,646	16,452	11,915	75,303	52,003	207,577	2,453	35,218	243,522
Mississippi	31,775	11,848	5,025	18,201	35,548	102,397	1,465	42,672	145,330
Missouri	51,686	17,339	14,749	18,201	77,221	216,628	2,712	82,347	299,902
Montana	26,824	12,147	3,940	18,201	44,025	105,137	818	18,201	123,599
Nebraska	25,936	10,632	4,337	18,201	24,619	87,031	1,261	34,399	121,691
Nevada	18,758	7,722	3,940	18,201	24,738	73,359	620	6,464	80,084
New Hampshire ...	11,328	3,201	3,940	18,201	13,791	50,461	592	12,789	63,511
New Jersey	53,376	5,613	30,267	109,590	35,030	288,083	3,010	95,842	386,152
New Mexico	25,039	10,282	4,144	18,201	45,340	103,006	885	9,662	112,929
New York	134,533	19,547	68,194	263,460	99,324	602,514	7,388	180,550	787,946
North Carolina ...	64,612	19,997	12,209	38,796	47,010	272,906	2,881	58,295	331,910
North Dakota	18,158	8,113	3,940	18,201	23,190	71,602	873	13,651	85,514
Ohio	93,666	19,707	35,988	67,295	114,261	463,612	4,871	72,405	538,331
Oklahoma	34,671	12,978	8,769	26,783	41,499	178,898	1,939	43,127	222,473
Oregon	29,768	11,015	7,836	26,985	42,192	137,770	1,965	23,302	161,521
Pennsylvania	107,624	24,341	36,980	237,417	77,544	502,204	5,295	118,814	623,555
Rhode Island	11,328	3,201	3,940	18,201	13,791	141,872	592	7,996	150,148
South Carolina	32,900	10,124	7,238	49,832	43,292	144,775	1,634	20,198	165,394
South Dakota	19,369	8,754	3,940	18,201	27,694	77,958	796	12,340	90,559
Tennessee	47,536	15,013	12,318	18,201	73,290	229,868	2,334	62,196	292,802
Texas.............	132,499	40,189	50,897	188,796	213,331	877,894	7,352	95,558	976,683
Utah	19,222	6,913	5,540	72,342	42,132	146,149	885	7,671	154,192
Vermont	11,328	3,201	3,940	18,201	14,228	50,898	592	10,563	61,722
Virginia...........	49,791	14,021	15,966	136,306	74,229	294,235	2,481	32,279	327,592
Washington	39,386	11,006	13,651	156,259	61,975	282,277	2,177	37,926	321,131
West Virginia	23,669	8,467	3,940	55,922	20,946	112,944	984	33,292	146,497
Wisconsin.........	48,880	15,187	13,269	18,201	39,839	189,106	2,556	47,097	237,030
Wyoming	17,565	7,890	3,940	18,201	37,259	84,855	592	6,508	91,624
Dist. of Col.	11,328		3,940	18,201	13,791	68,871	592	11,244	80,376
American Samoa ..							296	791	791
Guam							296	791	791
No. Mariana Is. ...							296	791	791
Puerto Rico	29,919	4,319	9,462		13,791	57,491	1,257	8,105	66,205
Virgin Islands							296	791	791

Source: Federal Highway Administration, U.S. Department of Transportation.

Note: This table does not include funds from the mass transit account of the Highway Trust Fund.

(a) Apportioned Oct. 1, 1984.

(b) Apportioned March 13, 1985. Interstate funds are made available one year earlier than other federal-aid highway funds.

(c) Apportioned Oct. 1, 1984. Interstate funds are made available one year earlier than other federal-aid highway funds.

(d) Apportionment of funds authorized by Public Law 98-363. Includes $9.9 million administered by the Federal Highway Administration.

(e) Does not include funds from the following programs: Emergency relief, forest highways, public lands highways, parkways and park highways, Indian reservation roads, interstate discretionary, bridge discretionary, truck and bus safety grants, or allocated interstate highway substitute funds. These funds are allocated from the Highway Trust Fund.

(f) Does not include $11,328,075 apportioned to the territories.

Table 8.17
STATE MOTOR VEHICLE REGISTRATIONS: 1984

State or other jurisdiction	Automobiles(a)	Motorcycles(a)	Buses(a,b)	Trucks(a)	Comparison of total motor vehicle registrations 1983	1984	Percentage change
United States	127,866,900	5,479,822	583,671	38,047,099	169,394,780	171,977,492	15.2
Alabama....................	2,266,571	69,637	8,375	927,109	3,217,275	3,271,692	1.7
Alaska.....................	227,375	9,925	1,794	138,439	361,067	377,-33	4.6
Arizona....................	1,504,204	82,511	4,044	602,631	2,378,905	2,193,390	-7.8
Arkansas	981,174	28,161	4,734	517,154	1,469,275	1,531,223	4.2
California..................	14,095,912	704,986	33,804	3,835,287	18,471,865	18,669,989	1.1
Colorado	2,007,519	114,957	5,648	741,140	2,767,362	2,869,264	3.7
Connecticut	2,207,317	76,015	9,309	148,875(c)	2,381,507	2,441,516	2.5
Delaware	366,024	11,421	1,609	91,763	437,460	470,817	7.6
Florida....................	7,552,367	240,879	34,406	1,807,402	9,040,974	9,635,054	6.6
Georgia....................	2,890,291	113,988	13,578	1,556,530	4,313,425	4,574,387	6.0
Hawaii	555,299	15,762	3,834	78,889	618,419	653,784	5.7
Idaho	546,519	50,780	3,127	390,460	929,634	990,886	6.6
Illinois....................	6,069,551	222,644	20,451	1,508,236	7,745,936	7,820,882	1.0
Indiana	2,933,754	137,193	17,959	998,605	3,992,234	4,087,511	2.4
Iowa	1,734,951	250,515	7,791	691,294	2,717,825	2,693,551	0.9
Kansas	1,456,286	100,794	3,902	661,605	2,147,852	2,222,587	3.5
Kentucky	1,772,287	52,644	8,904	808,863	2,679,460	2,642,698	-1.4
Louisiana	2,048,123	60,160	19,737	890,307	2,941,970	3,018,327	2.6
Maine	584,018	47,756	2,465	213,271	813,957	847,510	4.1
Maryland	2,668,985	72,113	10,669	513,717	3,085,605	3,265,484	5.8
Massachusetts	3,321,357	100,640	10,689	456,150	3,952,304	3,888,836	-1.6
Michigan	5,071,361	227,651	21,587	1,275,569	6,527,915	6,596,168	1.0
Minnesota	2,276,192	167,982	16,657	674,801	3,411,161	3,135,632	-8.1
Mississippi	1,060,940	26,390	7,913	374,782	1,589,352	1,470,025	-7.5
Missouri	2,595,214	89,180	9,835	916,115	3,527,411	3,610,344	2.4
Montana...................	405,716	30,112	1,745	277,401	862,524	714,974	-17.1
Nebraska	829,583	45,687	4,110	423,804	1,281,153	1,303,184	1.7
Nevada	534,912	21,210	1,662	208,108	752,411	765,892	1.8
New Hampshire	742,456	56,950	1,506	126,102(c)	855,511	927,014	8.4
New Jersey.................	4,402,243	125,727	15,419	478,741(c)	5,042,113	5,022,130	-0.4
New Mexico................	771,96	50,245	3,829	444,339	1,291,318	1,269,889	-1.6
New York	7,563,584	209,264	32,817	1,048,049(c)	8,617,052	8,853,714	2.7
North Carolina	3,183,688	67,735	31,249	1,153,868	4,719,541	4,436,540	-6.0
North Dakota	414,510	31,530	1,911	274,857	697,873	722,808	3.6
Ohio	6,524,410	271,611	31,138	1,338,229	8,054,635	8,165,388	1.4
Oklahoma	1,758,481	108,147	11,748	1,010,682	2,899,573	2,889,058	-0.4
Oregon	1,554,913	83,574	9,100	618,512	2,204,233	2,266,099	2.8
Pennsylvania	5,805,361	226,865	27,206	1,248,704(c)	7,071,977	7,308,136	3.3
Rhode Island	538,307	25,873	1,540	82,528(c)	625,207	648,248	3.7
South Carolina	1,626,800	37,264	12,587	488,959	2,094,079	2,165,610	3.4
South Dakota	405,626	39,040	2,044	235,467	668,793	682,177	2.0
Tennessee	2,822,315	101,029	11,555	734,791	3,616,977	3,669,690	1.4
Texas......................	8,417,227	312,393	51,822	3,702,644	12,019,140	12,484,086	3.9
Utah	748,483	60,178	1,147	340,785	1,141,711	1,150,593	0.8
Vermont	287,838	21,927	1,319	88,105	389,729	399,189	2.4
Virginia....................	3,450,039	81,248	13,388	583,628	3,975,369	4,128,303	3.8
Washington	2,420,225	138,541	11,013	999,114	3,477,841	3,568,893	2.6
West Virginia	966,099	34,213	3,429	408,284	1,327,244	1,412,025	6.4
Wisconsin..................	2,386,500	197,194	12,422	695,534	3,424,668	3,291,650	3.9
Wyoming	290,972	22,298	2,311	200,996	525,026	516,577	-1.6
Dist. of Col.	212,545	5,283	2,833	15,874	238,932	236,535	-1.0

Source: Federal Highway Administration, U.S. Department of Transportation. Compiled for the calendar year ending Dec. 31, 1984, from reports of state authorities.

Note: Where the registration year is not more than one month removed from the calendar year, registration-year data are given. Where the registration year is more than one month removed, registrations are given for the calendar year.

(a) Includes federal, state, county and municipal vehicles. Vehicles owned by the military services are not included.

(b) The numbers of private and commercial buses included in the figures are estimates by the Federal Highway Administration of the numbers in operation, rather than the registration counts of the states.

(c) The following farm trucks, registered at a nominal fee and restricted to use in the vicinity of the owner's farm, are not included in this table: Connecticut, 7,050; New Hampshire, 4,744; New Jersey, 6,796; New York, 19,475; Pennsylvania, 22,554; and Rhode Island, 992.

Table 8.18
MOTOR VEHICLE LAWS
(As of September 1984*)

State or other jurisdiction	Minimum Age for driver's license(a)			Liability laws(b)	Vehicle inspection (c)	Transfer of plates to new owner	Child restraints mandatory for passengers under ___ years(d)	Mandatory seat belt law(e)
	Regular	Learner's	Restrictive					
Alabama	16	15(f)	14(g)	S	(h)	★	4	...
Alaska	18		14(i)	S	spot	★	7	...
Arizona	18	15+7mo.(f,i)	16(i)	C	(j)	★	5	...
Arkansas	18	(f)	14(i,k)	S,NF	★	...	6	...
California	18	15(k,l)	16(l)	(m)	...	★	4(n)	★(o)
Colorado	21	15+6mo.(f,p)	16(i)	S,NF	(j)	...	4(n)	...
Connecticut	18		16(l)	S,NF	★	...	4	★
Delaware	18	15+10mo.(f,k,l)	16(l)	S,NF	★	★	5	...
Florida	18	(f)	15(i)	(q)	...	...	6	...
Georgia	18	15	16(i)	C,NF	(j)	★	4	...
Hawaii	18	(f)	15(i)	S,NF	★	★	4	★
Idaho	16	(f)	14(l)	S,C	...	...	4	...
Illinois	18	(f)	16(i,l)	S	(r)	...	6	★
Indiana	18	15(p)	16+1mo.(i,l)	S,C	...	...	5	★
Iowa	18	14	16(l)	S	spot	...	6	...
Kansas	16		14(k)	NF	spot	...	4	...
Kentucky	18	(f)	16(i)	C,NF	...	★	(n)	...
Louisiana	17		15(s)	C	★	★	5	★
Maine	17	(f,k)	15(l)	S	★	...	4	...
Maryland	18	15+9mo.(f,k)	16(i,l)	NF	(t)	...	5	...
Massachusetts	18	16(f)	16+6mo.(i,l,s)	C,NF	★	...	5	...
Michigan	18	(f)	16(i,l,u)	C,NF	spot	...	4	★
Minnesota	18	(f)	16(l)	NF	spot(h)	★	4	...
Mississippi	15	(f)		S,F	★	★	2	...
Missouri	16		15(p)	S	★	...	4	★
Montana	18	(f)	15(i,l)	C	...	...	4(n)	...
Nebraska	16	15(f,k)	(u)	F	...	...	4	★
Nevada	18	15+6mo.	16(i)	F,C	(t)	...	5	...
New Hampshire	18	(v)	16(l)	S,F	★	...	5	...
New Jersey	17	(k)	(u)	S,NF,UJ	★	...	5	★(o)
New Mexico	16	15(k)	15(i,l)	S,UM	...	...	11	★
New York	18	(f,k)	16(i,s)	S,C,NF,UM	★	...	5	★(o)
North Carolina	18	15(k,l)		S,C	★	...	6	★
North Dakota	16	(f)	14(l)	S,C,NF, UM,UJ	spot	★	4	...
Ohio	18(w)	(k)	(u)	S,C	spot	...	5(n)	...
Oklahoma	16	(p)	15+6mo.(l)	S,C	★	★	5	★
Oregon	16	15(f)	(u)	F,C,NF	spot(j)	★	5	★
Pennsylvania	18	(f)	16(i,s)	(x)	★	...	4	...
Rhode Island	18	(f)	16(l)	S	★	...	4	...
South Carolina	16	15(k)	15	C,NF,UM	★	★	4	...
South Dakota	16	14(k)	14(s)	F,NF	...	★	5	...
Tennessee	16	15(f)		S,F	(h)	...	4	...
Texas	18	15(k,p)	16(l,u)	S,F,C,NF, UM	★	★	4	★
Utah	16(l)	(f)		S,NF	★	...	6	...
Vermont	18	15(k)	16(k)	S	★	...	4	...
Virginia	18	15+8mo.(f,i,k)	16(i,l)	S,NF	★	...	5	...
Washington	18	15(f,p)	16(l)	S,F	spot	★	5	...
West Virginia	18	(f)	16(i)	S,C	★	...	5	...
Wisconsin	18	(f)	16(l)	S	spot	...	4	...
Wyoming	18	15(k)	16(i)	S,C	...	...	3	...
Dist. of Col.	18	(f)	16(i)	NF	★	...	7	...
American Samoa	18	(f,k)	16(i,l)	C	★	★	...	...
Guam	18	15(i,k)	16(i)	S	★	...	...	...
Puerto Rico	18	(f)	16(i)	(x)	★	★	...	★
Virgin Islands	18		16(l)	C	★	★	...	...

MOTOR VEHICLE LAWS—Continued

*Except information on enactment of mandatory seat belt provisions, which is current as of October 1985.

Sources: American Automobile Association, *Digest of Motor Laws,* (1985); "State Health Legislation Report," August 1985; and state motor vehicle departments.

Note: All jurisdictions except Guam have chemical test laws for intoxication. All except the District of Columbia have an implied consent provision. (Colorado has expressed consent law).

Key:

★—Provision.

. . .—No provision.

(a) See Table 8.20, "Motor Vehicle Operators and Chauffeurs Licenses 1984" for additional information on driver licenses.

(b) All jurisdictions except Colorado, Hawaii, American Samoa, Guam, Puerto Rico, and the Virgin Islands have a non-resident service of process law. Alabama, Arkansas, California, Georgia, Hawaii, Illinois (applicable to hitchhikers only), New Mexico, Oregon, Texas, Virginia, Wyoming, and the Virgin Islands each have a guest suit law. In this column only: S—"Security-type" financial responsibility law (following accident report, each driver/owner of the vehicles involved must show ability to pay damages which may be charged in subsequent legal actions arising from accident); F—"Future-proof type" financial responsibility law (persons who have been convicted of certain serious traffic offenses or who have failed to pay a judgment against them for damages arising from an accident must make a similar showing of financial responsibility); C—"Compulsory insurance" law (motorists must show proof of financial responsibility—liability insurance—usually as a condition of vehicle registration); NF—"No-fault insurance" law (vehicle owner looks to own insurance company for reimbursement for accident damages, rather than having to prove in court that the other party was responsible); UJ—"Unsatisfied judgment funds" law (financed with fees from motorists unable to provide evidence of insurance or from assessments levied on auto insurance companies to cover pedestrians and others who do not have no-fault insurance); UM—"Uninsured motorist" law (insurance companies must offer coverage against potential damage by uninsured motorists).

(c) "Spot" indicates spot check, usually for reasonable cause, or random roadside inspection for defective equipment.

(d) The type of child restraint (safety seat or seat belt) required may differ depending upon the age of the child.

(e) These states have enacted mandatory seat belt legislation; effective dates of legislation range from 1985 to 1987. Unless otherwise specified, legislation covers driver and front-seat passengers.

(f) Permit required. In Arkansas, for 30 days prior to taking driving test. In Delaware, for up to two months prior to 16th birthday. In Michigan, for 30 days prior to application for first license. In Minnesota, not required if driver can pass road test. In Oregon, not required if applicant can already drive.

(g) Restricted to mopeds.

(h) Cities have authority to maintain inspection stations. In Alabama, state troopers also authorized to inspect at their discretion.

(i) Guardian or parental consent required.

(j) Emission inspections. In Arizona and Colorado, mandatory annual emission inspections in certain counties. In Oregon, biennial inspections in Portland metro area.

(k) Driver must be accompanied by licensed operator. In California and Vermont (learner's permit), a licensed operator 25 years or older. In Maine, New York, Texas, Vermont (restrictive license), Virginia and Wyoming, a licensed operator 18 years or older. In Maryland, individual, 21 years or older, licensed to drive vehicle of that class, and licensed for 3 or more years. In Nebraska, a licensed operator 19 years or older. In New Jersey, an individual licensed for same classification as the learner's permit. In South Carolina, a licensed operator 21 years or older. In American Samoa and Guam, must be accompanied by parent or legal guardian.

(l) Must have successfully completed approved driver education course.

(m) Financial responsibility required of every driver/owner of motor vehicle at all times.

(n) Other restrictions. In California, Colorado, Montana, and Ohio, age restriction or child under 40 pounds. In Kentucky, 40 inches in height or under.

(o) Covers other passengers in vehicle. California, all passengers. New Jersey, all passengers between 5 and 18 years, as well as driver and all front-seat passengers over 18 years. New York, all back seat occupants under 10 years and under 3 years, as well as all front-seat occupants.

(p) Must be enrolled in driver education course.

(q) Proof of personal injury protection is required. In event of an accident in which operator is charged with a moving violation, the operator must prove liability insurance in force on date of accident.

(r) Trucks, buses, and trailers only.

(s) Driving hours restricted. In Louisiana, drivers under 17 not permitted to operate vehicles between hours of 11 p.m. and 5 a.m. Monday through Thursday; between midnight and 5 a.m. Friday through Sunday. In Massachusetts, drivers prohibited from driving between 1 a.m. and 4 a.m., unless accompanied by parent or legal guardian. In New York, drivers may operate certain classes of vehicles alone during the daylight hours and with a parent or guardian at night; may drive alone during darkness if on direct route between home and school or to place of business. In Pennsylvania, drivers prohibited from driving between midnight and 5 a.m., unless accompanied by parent or spouse 18 years or older or in possession of employer's affidavit. In South Dakota, driver not permitted to operate vehicle between 8 p.m. and 6 a.m., unless accompanied by licensed driver in front seat.

(t) Mandatory inspection only under certain circumstances. In Maryland, all used cars upon resale or transfer. In Nevada, used cars registered to new owner and emissions test for first-time registration in Clark and Washoe counties.

(u) License will be granted at lower age under special conditions. In Michigan (extenuating circumstances), 14. In New Jersey (school permit), 14. In New Jersey (agriculture pursuit), 16. In Ohio (proof of hardship), 14. In Oregon, (special conditions), 14. In Texas (proof of hardship), 15.

(v) Required for motorcyclists only. Otherwise, unlicensed persons who are being taught to drive must be accompanied by licensed operator 21 years or older.

(w) Probationary license issued to persons 16-18 upon completion of approved driver education course.

(x) Has financial responsibility law; details not available.

Table 8.19
STATE NO-FAULT MOTOR VEHICLE INSURANCE LAWS

State or other jurisdiction	Purchase of first-party benefits	Minimum tort liability threshold(a)	Maximum first-party (no-fault) benefits			
			Medical	Income loss	Replacement services	Survivors/funeral benefits
Arkansas	O	None	$5,000 if incurred within 2 yrs. of accident	70% of lost income up to $140/wk. beginning 8 days after accident, for up to 52 wks.	Up to $70/wk. beginning 8 days after accident, for up to 52 wks.	$5,000
Colorado	M	$2,500	$50,000 if incurred within 5 yrs. (additional $50,000 for rehabilitation expenses incurred within 5 yrs. of accident)	100% of first $125/wk., 70% of next $125/wk., 60% of remainder up to $400, for up to 52 wks.	Up to $25/day for up to 52 wks.	$1,000
Connecticut	M	$400	—————$5,000 overall max. on first-party benefits—————			
			Limited only by total benefits limit	85% of lost income up to $200/wk.	85% of replacement services up to $200/wk.	85% of actual loss for income and replacement services up to $200/wk. Funeral benefit: $2,000
Delaware	M	None, but amt. of no-fault benefits received cannot be used as evidence in suits for general damage	————$15,000 per person, $30,000 per accident overall max. on first-party benefits————			
			Limited only by total benefits limit, but must be incurred within 2 yrs. of accident	Limited only by total benefits limit, but must be incurred within 2 yrs. of accident	Limited only by total benefits limit, but must be incurred within 2 yrs. of accident	Funeral benefit: $3,000 (must be incurred within 2 yrs. of accident)
Florida	M	No dollar threshold(b)	—————————$10,000 overall max. on first-party benefits—————			
			80% of all costs	60% of lost income	Limited only by total benefits limit	Funeral benefit: $1,750
Georgia	M	$500	—————$5,000 overall max. on first-party benefits—————			
			$2,500	85% of lost income up to $200/wk.	$20/day	Max. wage loss and replacement services amounts. Funeral benefit: $1,500
Hawaii	M	$5,000 modified annually by percentage change in CPI for Honolulu metro area	—————————$15,000 overall max. on first-party benefits—————			
			Limited only by total benefits limit	Up to $900/mo. for income loss and replacement services		Up to $900/mo. Funeral benefit: $1,500
Kansas	M	$500	$2,000 (additional $2,000 for rehabilitation)	85% of lost income up to $650/mo. for 1 yr.	$12/day for 365 days	Up to $650/mo. for lost income and $12/day for replacement services for up to 1 yr., less disability payments received before death. Funeral benefit: $1,000
Kentucky	(c)	$1,000	—————————$10,000 overall max. on first-party benefits—————————			
			Limited only by total benefits limit	85% of lost income (more if tax advantage is less than 15%) up to $200/wk.	Up to $200/wk.	Up to $200/wk. each for survivors' economic loss and survivors' replacement services loss. Funeral benefit: $1,000
Maryland	M	None	—————————$2,500 overall max. on first-party benefits—————————			
			—————————for expenses incurred within 3 yrs. of accident—————			
			Limited only by total benefits limit	Limited only by total benefits limit	Limited only by total benefits limit; payable only to non-wage earners	Funeral benefit: limited only by total benefits limit

State or other jurisdiction	Pur-chase of first-party benefits	Minimum tort liability threshold(a)	Maximum first-party (no-fault) benefits			
			Medical	Income loss	Replacement services	Survivors/funeral benefits
Massachusetts ...	M	$500	—————————$2,000 overall max. on first-party benefits—————————			
			Limited only by total benefits limit, if incurred within 2 yrs.	Up to 75% of lost income	Limited only by total benefits limit; payments made to nonfamily members for services that would have been performed by victim	Funeral benefit: limited only by total benefits limit
Michigan(d)	M	No dollar thres-hold(e)	Unlimited	85% of lost income up to $1,475/30-day period for up to 3 yrs.; max. amt. adjusted annually for cost of living	$20/day for up to 3 yrs.	Up to $1,475/30-day period for lost income for up to 3 yrs. and $20/day for replacement services. Funeral benefits: $1,000
Minnesota	M	$4,000	—————————$20,000 max. for first-party benefits other than medical—————————			
			$20,000	85% of lost income up to $250/wk.	$200/wk., beginning 8 days after accident	Up to $200/wk. ea. for survivors' economic loss and survivors' replacement services loss. Funeral benefit: $2,000
New Jersey......	M	$200 or $1,500 (f)	Unlimited	Up to $100/wk. for one yr.	Up to $12/day for a max. of $4,380/person	Max. amount of benefits victim would have received. Funeral benefit: $1,000
New York	M	No dollar thres-hold(g)	—————————$50,000 overall max. on first-party benefits—————————			
			Limited only by total benefits limit	80% of lost income up to $1,000/mo. for 3 yrs.	$25/day for 1 yr.	$2,000 in addition to other benefits
North Dakota ...	M	$2,500	—————————$30,000 overall max. on first-party benefits—————————			
			Limited only by total benefits limit	85% of lost income up to $150/wk.	Up to $15/day	Up to $150/wk. for survivors income loss and $15/day for replacement services. Funeral benefit: $1,000
Oregon	M	None	$5,000 if incurred within 1 yr. of accident	If victim is disabled at least 14 days, 70% of lost income up to $750/mo. for up to 52 wks.	If victim is disabled at least 14 days, up to $18/day for up to 52 wks.	Funeral benefit: $1,000
Pennsylvania(h)..	M	None	$10,000	After 5 workdays, up to $5,000, limited to $1,000/mo. and 80% of actual lost income(i)	None	Funeral benefit: $1,500
South Carolina ..	O	None	—————————$1,000 overall max. on first-party benefits—————————			
			Limited only by total benefits limit if incurred within 3 yrs. of accident	Limited only by total benefits limit	Limited only by total benefits limit	Funeral benefit: limited only by total benefits limit
South Dakota ...	O	None	$2,000 if incurred within 2 yrs. of accident	$60/wk. for up to 52 wks. for disability extending beyond 14 days of date of accident	None	$10,000 if death occurs within 90 days of accident

NO-FAULT INSURANCE LAWS—Continued

State or other jurisdiction	Purchase of first-party benefits	Minimum tort liability threshold(a)	Maximum first-party (no-fault) benefits			
			Medical	Income loss	Replacement services	Survivors/funeral benefits
Texas..........	O	None	—————————$2,500 overall max. on first-party benefits—————————			
			Limited only by total benefits limit if incurred within 3 yrs. of accident	Limited only by total benefits limit if incurred within 3 yrs. of accident	Limited only by total benefits limit if incurred within 3 yrs. of accident. Payable only to non-wage earners	Limited only by total benefits limit if incurred within 3 yrs. of accident
Utah	M	$500	$2,000	85% of lost income up to $150/wk. for up to 52 wks. subject to 3-day waiting period which does not apply if disability lasts longer than 2 wks.	$12/day for up to 365 days subject to 3-day waiting period which does not apply if disability lasts longer than 2 wks.	$2,000 survivors benefit. Funeral benefit: $1,000
Virginia.........	O	None	$2,000 if incurred within 1 yr. of accident	100% of lost income up to $100/wk. for up to 52 wks.	None	Funeral benefit: included in medical benefit
Dist. of Col.	M	$5,000 (to be adjusted annually to reflect cost-of-living changes)	$100,000 (medical and rehabilitation)	80% of lost income up to $2,000/mo. (max. of $24,000)	Up to $50/day up to 3 yrs. (max. of $24,000)	Funeral benefit: $2,000

Source: *No Fault Press Reference Manual*, State Farm Insurance Companies.

Key: O—Optional; M—Mandatory.

(a) Refers to minimum amount of medical expenses necessary before victim can sue for general damages ("pain and suffering"). Lawsuits allowed in all states for injuries resulting in death and permanent disability. Some states allow lawsuits for one or more of the following: serious and permanent disfigurement, certain temporary disabilities, loss of body member, loss of certain bodily functions, certain fractures, or economic losses (other than medical) which exceed stated limits.

(b) Victim cannot sue for general damages unless injury results in significant and permanent loss of important body function, permanent injury, significant and permanent scarring or disfigurement, or death.

(c) Accident victim is not bound by tort restriction if (1) he has rejected the tort limitation in writing or (2) he is injured by a driver who has rejected the tort limitation in writing. Rejection bars recovery of first-party benefits.

(d) Liability for property damage for all states with no-fault insurance is under the state tort system. Michigan has no tort liability for vehicle damage.

(e) Victim cannot sue for general damages unless injuries result in death, serious impairment of bodily function, or serious permanent disfigurement.

(f) Motorist chooses one of two optional limitations.

(g) Victim cannot recover general damages unless injury results in inability to perform usual daily activities for at least 90 days during the 180 days following the accident; dismemberment; significant disfigurement; fracture; permanent loss of use of a body organ, member, function, or system; permanent consequential limitation of use of a body organ or member; significant limitation of use of a body function or system; or death.

(h) Pennsylvania repealed its no-fault act on February 12, 1984 and replaced it with a law that requires motorists to carry certain first-party coverages but places no restriction on the right to sue for general damages.

(i) May be waived by policyholder who has no expectation of actual income loss because of age, disability, or lack of employment history. Amount includes benefits for hiring substitute to perform self-employment services and hiring special help to enable victim to work.

Table 8.20
MOTOR VEHICLE OPERATORS AND CHAUFFEURS LICENSES: 1984

State or other jurisdiction	Operators licenses			Chauffeurs licenses			Estimated total licenses in force during 1984 (in thousands) (a)
	Years for which issued	Renewal date	Amount of fee	Years for which issued	Renewal date	Amount of fee	
Alabama..........	4	Issuance	$15.00(b)				2,473
Alaska............	5	Birthday	5.00				305
Arizona..........	3 and 4(c)	Birthday	5.25 or 7.00	3 or 4(c)	Birthday	$ 7.50 or 10.00	2,257
Arkansas	2 or 4	Birth month	7.00 or 13.00	2 or 4	Birth month	11.00 or 21.00	1,674
California*.......	4	Birthday	10.00				16,947
Colorado*	4	Birthday	5.50				2,269
Connecticut*	4	Birthday	21.00(b)				2,337
Delaware*	4(d)	Birthday	10.00(d)				440
Florida	4	Birthday	9.50	4	Birthday	13.50	8,186
Georgia*.........	4(e)	Birthday	4.50				3,901
Hawaii*	2 or 4(f)	Birthday	5.50 or 8.50(f)				583
Idaho	3	Birthday	10.00	3	Birthday	12.00	669
Illinois*..........	3 and 4(g)	Birthday	8.00 or 10.00(h)				6,685
Indiana	4	Birth month	6.00(h)	2	Birth month	8.00	3,574
Iowa*	2 or 4(i)	Birthday	5.00 or 10.00(i)	2 or 4(i)	Birthday	10.00 or 20.00(i)	1,927
Kansas*	4	Birthday	7.00				1,692
Kentucky	4	Birth month	8.00	4	Birth month	8.00(j)	2,249
Louisiana*	4	Birthday	10.00				2,830
Maine*	2 or 4(k)	Birthday	8.00 or 18.00(k)				790
Maryland*	4	Birthday	6.00(l)				2,861
Massachusetts*	4	Birthday	25.00(b)				3,832
Michigan*	4(m)	Birthday	6.00(l)	4(l)	Birthday	14.50(l)	6,392
Minnesota*	4	Birthday	10.00(n)				2,397
Mississippi	4	Birth month	13.00				1,786
Missouri	3	Issuance	3.00	3	Issuance	10.00	3,354
Montana..........	4	Birthday	8.00	4	Birthday	8.00	474
Nebraska*	4(o)	Birthday	10.00(o)				1,108
Nevada*	4	Birthday	10.00(h)				681
New Hampshire* ..	4	Birthday	20.00				715
New Jersey*......	2(p)	Issuance	8.00(p)				5,680
New Mexico*......	4	30 days after Birthday	8.00				810
New York*	4	Birthday	16.00(b)				9,716
North Carolina* ...	4	Birthday	10.00				4,049
North Dakota*	4	Birthday	8.00				434
Ohio	4	Birthday	5.00	4	Birthday	5.00	7,389
Oklahoma	2	Birth month	7.00(b)	2	Birth month	11.00	2,206
Oregon	4	Birthday	13.00(l)	4	Birthday	5.00(l)	2,079
Pennsylvania*	4	Birth month	21.50				7,470
Rhode Island*.....	2	Birthday	8.00(b)				611
South Carolina* ...	4	Birthday	4.00				2,100
South Dakota	4	Birthday	6.00				487
Tennessee	2	Birthday	6.00(b)	2	Birthday	8.00(b)	2,978
Texas.............	4	Birthday	7.00				10,856
Utah*	4	Birthday	10.00				928
Vermont	2 or 4	Birthday	10 or 16.00(b)				371
Virginia*.........	4	Birth month	9.00	2	Birth month	12.00	3,773
Washington*	4	Birthday	14.00(b)				2,973
West Virginia	4	Issuance	10.00	4	Issuance	15.00	1,208
Wisconsin*........	2	Birthday	9.00(l)	1	Birthday	9.00(l)	3,148
Wyoming	4	Birthday	2.50(q)				360
Dist. of Col.	4	Issuance	15.00				374

MOTOR VEHICLE LICENSES—Continued

Source: Federal Highway Administration, U.S. Department of Transportation. Compiled from reports of state authorities and other sources. Status of requirements as of Jan. 1, 1984.

Key:

*—Classified drivers licenses are issued; permit qualified persons to operate specified vehicles on the public highways.

(a) Compiled for calendar year ending Dec. 31, 1984 from reports of state authorities and other sources. For Alabama, Arizona, Arkansas, and Michigan, data were estimated by (and for Louisiana, data were adjusted by) the Federal Highway Administration.

(b) The following examination fees are in addition to the fee shown for an original license: Alabama, Massachusetts, Rhode Island and Wisconsin—$5; Connecticut—$10, plus $.45 per month, maximum $2.50 for six months, plus $2.00 photo fee; New York and Oklahoma—$9 and $2, respectively, for license application fee; Tennessee—$2; Vermont—$10; Washington—$3.

(c) Beginning in 1984, a portion of all applicants were issued new four-year licenses. Replacement of three-year licenses will be complete by Jan. 1, 1987.

(d) An indefinite term license ($25 fee) is issued for drivers meeting specified requirements, but a reexamination (with a $1 photo fee) is required every four years.

(e) A permanent free drivers license is issued to veterans who entered the Armed Forces as a resident of the state.

(f) Licenses issued for two years to persons 15-24 years and 65 years and over. Cost varies depending on place of issuance; fees shown are for Honolulu.

(g) Beginning in 1984, licenses were issued for both three- and four-year terms to phase-in use of four-year term.

(h) Illinois—$4 for persons 69 years and over; Indiana—$3 for two-year renewal license for persons 75 years and over; Nevada—$5 for original or renewal license for persons over 70 years.

(i) Two-year operators and chauffeurs licenses at $5 and $10, respectively, issued to persons under 18 and over 70 years old.

(j) Graduated fee for chauffeurs license, issued to expire with the holder's operator's license.

(k) Two-year license for persons 65 years and over at $8.

(l) Maryland—$20 for original operators license; Michigan—$7.50 for original operators, $16 for original chauffeurs (expires first birthday after issue date); Oregon—$21 for original operators and $10 for original chauffeurs; Wisconsin—$11 for original chauffeurs.

(m) Persons with unsatisfactory driving records renew for two-year term.

(n) For persons under 19 years old, $6.

(o) Original license expires on licensee's birthday in the first year after issuance that licensee's age is divisible by four. Fees are: $3.50 for one year; $5.50 for two years; $8 for three years.

(p) Persons under 21 years are issued three-year basic driver permits for $12 (plus $1.50 photo fee).

(q) $5 renewed by mail.

Table 8.21
STATE PUBLIC UTILITY COMMISSIONS

State or other jurisdiction	Regulatory authority	Members		Selection of chair	Length of commissioners' terms (in years)	Number of full-time employees
		Number	Selection			
Alabama	Public Service Commission	3	E	E	4	90
Alaska	Public Utilities Commission	5	GL	G(a)	6	49
Arizona	Corporation Commission	3	E	C	6	167
Arkansas	Public Service Commission	3	GS	G	6	101
California	Public Utilities Commission	5	GS	G	6	987
Colorado	Public Utilities Commission	3	GS	G	6	96
Connecticut	Public Utilities Control Authority	5	GL	C	4	107
Delaware	Public Service Commission	5	GS	G	5	17
Florida	Public Service Commission	5	GS	C	4	336
Georgia	Public Service Commission	5	E	C	6	119
Hawaii	Public Utilities Commission	3	GS	G	6	17
Idaho	Public Utilities Commission	3	GS	G	6	55
Illinois	Commerce Commission	7	G	G	5	348
Indiana	Public Service Commission	5	G(b)	G	4	91
Iowa	State Commerce Commission	3	GS	G	6	175
Kansas	State Corporation Commission	3	GS	C	4	254
Kentucky	Public Service Commission	3	G	G	3	90
Louisiana	Public Service Commission	5	E	C	6	74
Maine	Public Utilities Commission	3	GS	G	6	54
Maryland	Public Service Commission	5	GS	G	5	123
Massachusetts	Dept. of Public Utilities	3	G	G	4(c)	134
Michigan	Public Service Commission	3	GS	G	6	215
Minnesota	Public Utilities Commission	5	GS	G	6	24
Mississippi	Public Service Commission	3	E	C	4	115
Missouri	Public Service Commission	5	GS	G	6	261
Montana	Public Service Commission	5	E	C	4	44
Nebraska	Public Service Commission	5	E	C	6	54
Nevada	Public Service Commission	3	G	G	4	82
New Hampshire	Public Utilities Commission	3	G	G	6	51
New Jersey	Board of Public Utilities	3	GS	G	6	323
New Mexico	Public Service Commission	3	GS	G	6	40
New York	Public Service Commission	6	GS	G	6	605
North Carolina	Utilities Commission	7	GL	G	8	164
North Dakota	Public Service Commission	3	E	C	6	60
Ohio	Public Utilities Commission	5	GS	G	5	375
Oklahoma	Corporation Commission	3	E	C	6	433
Oregon	Public Utility Commissioner	1	G		4	349
Pennsylvania	Public Utility Commission	5	GS	G	10	575
Rhode Island	Public Utilities Commission	3	GS	G	6	41
South Carolina	Public Service Commission	7	GS	(d)	4	145 (e)
South Dakota	Public Utilities Commission	3	E	C	6	24
Tennessee	Public Service Commission	3	E	C	6	155
Texas	Public Utility Commission	3	GS	C	6	204
Utah	Public Service Commission	3	GS	G	6	48
Vermont	Public Service Board	3	GS	G	6	26 (e)
Virginia	State Corporation Commission	3	L	C	6	468
Washington	Utilities and Transportation Commission	3	GS	G	6	199
West Virginia	Public Service Commission	3	GS	G	6	177
Wisconsin	Public Service Commission	3	GS	G(f)	6	158
Wyoming	Public Service Commission	3	GS	C	6	41
Dist. of Col.	Public Service Commission	3	M	C	3	31
Puerto Rico	Public Service Commission	5	GS	GS	4	243

Source: National Association of Regulatory Utility Commissioners, *Annual Report on Utility and Carrier Regulation*, 1984. (Washington, D.C.: 1985).

Key:
G—Appointed by Governor.
GS—Appointed by Governor, with consent of Senate.
GL—Appointed by Governor, with consent of entire Legislature.
E—Elected by the Public.
C—Elected by the Commission.
L—Appointed by the Legislature.
M—Appointed by the Mayor.

(a) Chairman serves in that position for four years.
(b) Legislation enacted in 1983 created a nominating commission, members of which submit a panel of three candidates to the governor for consideration.
(c) Co-terminous with governor's.
(d) Chairmanship rotates every two years.
(e) Updated information not available. No response to survey.
(f) Chairman serves in that position for two years.

Table 8.22
SELECTED REGULATORY FUNCTIONS OF STATE PUBLIC UTILITIES COMMISSIONS*

State or other jurisdiction	Controls rates of privately owned utilities on sales to ultimate consumers of — Electric	Gas	Telephone	CATV	Prescribe temporary rates, pending investigation — Electric	Gas	Telephone	Require prior authorization of rate changes — Electric	Gas	Telephone	Suspend proposed rate changes — Electric	Gas	Telephone	Initiate rate investigation on its own motion — Electric	Gas	Telephone
Alabama	★	★	★	...	★	★	...	★	★	...	★	★	★	★	★	★
Alaska	★	★	★	...	★	★	★	★	★	★	★	★	★	★	★	★
Arizona	★	★	★	...	★	★	★	★	★	★	(a)	(a)	(a)	★	★	★
Arkansas	★	★	★	...	★	★	★	★	★	★	★	★	★	★	★	★
California	★	★	★	...	★	★(b)	★(b)	★	★	★	★	★	★	★	★	★
Colorado	★	★	★	...	★(c)	★(c)	★(c)	★	★	★	★	★	★	★	★	★
Connecticut	★	★	★	★	★	★	★	★	★	★	★	★	★	★	★	★
Delaware	★	★	★	★	★	★	★	★	★	★	★	★	★	★	★	★
Florida	★	★	★	...	★	★	★	★	★	★	★	★	★	★	★	★
Georgia	★	★	★	...	★	★	★	★	★	★	★	★	★	★	★	★
Hawaii	★	★	★	(d)	★	★	★	★	★	★	...	...	...	★	★	★
Idaho	★	★	★	...	★	★	★	★(e)	★(e)	★(e)	★	★	★	★	★	★
Illinois	★	★	★	...	★	★	★	★	★	★	★	★	★	★	★	★
Indiana	★	★	...	...	...	...	...	★	★	★	★	★	★	★	★	★
Iowa	★	★	★(f)	...	★(g)	★(g)	★(g)	★	★	★(f)	★	★	★(f)	★	★	★(f)
Kansas	★	★	★	...	★	★	★	★	★	★	★	★	★	★	★	★
Kentucky	★	★	★	...	★	★	★	★	★	★	★	★	★	★	★	★
Louisiana	★	★(h)	★	...	★	★	★	★	★	★	★	★	★	★	★	★
Maine	★	★	★	...	★	★	...	★	★	★	★	★	★	★	★	★
Maryland	★	★	★	...	...	...	★	★	★	★	★	★	★	★	★	★
Massachusetts	★	★	★	...	...	...	...	★	★	★	★	★	★	★	★	★
Michigan	★	★	★	...	★(i)	★(i)	★(i)	★	★	★	(j)	(j)	(j)	★	★	★
Minnesota	★	★(k)	★(l)	...	★	★	★(l)	★	★	★(l)	★	★	★(l)	★	★	★(l)
Mississippi	★	★	★	...	★	★	★	★	★	★	★	★	★	★	★	★
Missouri	★	★	★	...	★	★	★	★	★	★	★	★	★	★	★	★
Montana	★	★	★	...	★	★	★	★	★	★	★	★	★	★	★	★
Nebraska(m)	...	...	★	...	...	...	★	...	...	...	...	...	★	...	...	★
Nevada	★	★	★	★	...	...	...	★	★	★	★	★	★	★	★	★
New Hampshire	★	★	★	...	★	★	★	★	★	★	★	★	★	★	★	★
New Jersey	★	★	★	★	★	★	★	★	★	★	★	★	★	★	★	★
New Mexico	★	★	...	...	★	★	★	★	★	★	★	★	...	★	★	...
New York	★	★	★	...	★	★	★	★	★	★	★	★	★	★	★	★
North Carolina	★	★	★	...	★	★	★	★	★	★	★	★	★	★	★	★
North Dakota	★	★	★	...	★	★	★	★	★	★	★	★	★	★	★	★
Ohio	★	★	★	...	★	★	★	★	★	★	★	★	★	★	★	★
Oklahoma	★	★	★	...	★	★	★	★	★	★	★	★	★	★	★	★
Oregon	★	★	★	...	★	★	★	★	★	★	★	★	★	★	★	★
Pennsylvania	★	★	★	...	★	★	★	★	★	★	★	★	★	★	★	★
Rhode Island	★	★	★	...	★	★	★	★	★	★	★	★	★	★	★	★
South Carolina	★	★	★	...	★	★	★	★	★	★	★	★	★	★	★	★
South Dakota	★	★	★(n)	...	★	★	★	★	★	★	★	★	★	★	★	★
Tennessee	★	★	★	...	★(o)	★(o)	★	★	★	★	★	★	★	★	★	★
Texas Pub. Utilities Comm.	★	...	★	...	★	...	...	★	...	...	★	...	★	★	...	★
Texas Railroad Comm.	...	★	...	...	...	★	...	...	★	...	...	★	...	...	★	...
Utah	★	★	★	...	★	★	★	★	★	★	★	★	★	★	★	★
Vermont	★	★	★	★	★	★	★	★	★	★	★	★	★	★	★	★
Virginia	★	★	★	...	★	★	★	★	★	★	★	★	★	★	★	★
Washington	★	★	★	...	★	★	★	★	★	★	★	★	★	★	★	★
West Virginia	★	★	★	...	★	★	★	★	★	★	★	★	★	★	★	★
Wisconsin	★	★	★	...	★	★	★	★	★	★	(j)	(j)	(j)	★	★	★
Wyoming	★	★	★	...	★	★	★	★	★	★	★	★	★	★	★	★
Dist. of Col.	★	★	★	...	...	...	...	★	★	★	★	★	...	★	★	★
Puerto Rico	...	★	(p)	★	...	...	(p)	...	...	(p)	...	...	(p)	...	★	(p)

*Full names of commissions are shown on Table 8.21.
Source: National Association of Regulatory Utility Commissioners, *Annual Report on Utility and Carrier Regulation*, 1984 (Washington, D.C.: 1985).
Key:
★—Yes
...—No

(a) Rates cannot be increased without hearings and a subsequent order of the Commission; consequently no suspension is required.

(b) May fix temporary rates, but practice is not followed.

(c) No specific statutory authority.

(d) Regulated by the Cable Television Division of the Department of Regulatory Agencies.

(e) Rates become effective after seven months if Commission does not take action.

(f) Not for companies with less than 15,000 customers and less than 15,000 access lines.

(g) Interim rates must be approved and are collected under bond, subject to refund.

(h) Except no authority over rates charged to industrial customers by any gas company.

(i) Commission has authority to grant partial and immediate rate relief during pendency of final order, after statutory requirements are met.

(j) Specific authority required to change rates. Rates do not become effective after a specified period; consequently, no suspension is required.

(k) Rates not regulated for gas utilities serving fewer than 650 customers.

(l) Has authority only at the election of the cooperative.

(m) Telephone is the only regulated utility.

(n) PUC does not regulate rates of rural telephone cooperatives.

(o) Emergency only.

(p) The Puerto Rico Telephone Authority, a state public corporation, purchased the Puerto Rico Telephone Company.

LABOR LEGISLATION: 1984-85

By Richard R. Nelson

A significant amount of employment standards legislation—covering a variety of subjects—was enacted in the states during the biennium. Laws were enacted in many traditional labor fields, including minimum wage protection, garnishment and assignment of wages for child support, employment discrimination, and restrictions on the use of polygraph examinations. But there was also a good deal of interest in subjects of more recent concern, including the rights of employees to receive information and training on toxic substances found in the workplace, pay equity for jobs of comparable worth, and the impact of plant closings or relocations on employees and communities. Other emerging issues led to legislation or regulations restricting door-to-door sales by children and requiring background checks of child daycare personnel. Major court decisions also had an impact in a number of areas.

Wages and Hours
Minimum wages
In 1984-85, a cluster of New England states enacted increases in their hourly minimum wage rates to levels in excess of the $3.35 per hour federal standard that became effective in 1981: Maine—increased its rate from $3.35 to $3.45 on January 1, 1985, and to $3.55 on January 1, 1986, with a scheduled increase to $3.65 effective January 1987; Massachusetts—will increase its rate to $3.55 in 1986, $3.65 in 1987, and $3.75 in 1988; Vermont—will increase its rate to $3.45 effective July 1, 1986, with further increases to $3.55 and $3.65 scheduled for 1987 and 1988, respectively.

The federal standard previously had been exceeded in Alaska, Connecticut, and the District of Columbia.

As of January 1, 1986, 24 jurisdictions had minimum wage rates equal to or higher than the federal standard for some or all occupations; one other state, Montana, will reach the federal level on October 1, 1986.

If the federal rate is increased before July 1, 1987, a North Carolina amendment requires matching increases of up to $3.60 per hour in the state minimum.

During the biennium, there were other minimum wage developments in the states. Legislation increased minimum hourly rates to $3.25 in Georgia, to $3.05 in Montana, and to $3.35 in Oregon. Revised mandatory decrees in Puerto Rico raised minimum rates to varying levels for workers in several industries,[1] and wage order revisions in the District of Columbia raised the minimum hourly wage rates for private household workers to $3.90, and to $3.95 for manufacturing, printing, publishing, and wholesale trade occupations. Rate increases in Arkansas, Colorado, and Illinois, and for some workers in the District of Columbia, resulted from increases provided for in previous enactments.

The New Hampshire provision permitting a youth rate of 75 percent of the applicable minimum wage rate was limited to those age 16 or under, rather than those 17 or under as before.

Minnesota provided for a phased elimination of its tip credit allowance—a 5 percent annual reduction with total elimination achieved by 1988—and in Illinois, the tip credit allowance declined to 40 percent of the minimum wage for a required cash wage of not less than $2.01 per hour. Indiana repealed sections of its law providing for tip and meal credits, thereby requiring employers to pay the full minimum wage rate of $2.00 per hour.

New exemptions from minimum wage or

Richard R. Nelson is a State Standards Adviser in the Division of State Employment Standards Programs, Office of State Liaison and Legislative Analysis, Employment Standards Administration, U.S. Department of Labor. The portion of the Occupational Safety and Health section reporting on federal developments was prepared by Arlene Perkins, Project Officer, Directorate of Federal-State Operations, Office of State Programs, Occupational Safety and Health Administration, U.S. Department of Labor. The Workers' Compensation section was prepared by LaVerne C. Tinsley, State Standards Adviser, Division of State Workers' Compensation Programs, Office of State Liaison and Legislative Analysis, Employment Standards Administration, U.S. Department of Labor.

overtime requirements for limited groups of employees were enacted in Connecticut, Maine, Minnesota, New Jersey, and Wisconsin. Coverage was extended in Maryland, Oregon, and Rhode Island.

On February 19, 1985, the U.S. Supreme Court ruled in *Garcia v. San Antonio Metropolitan Transit Authority et al.*, that the minimum wage and overtime pay provisions of the Fair Labor Standards Act (FLSA) apply to employees of state and local governments. Subsequently, the Fair Labor Standards Amendments of 1985 were enacted on November 13, 1985. These amendments changed certain provisions of the FLSA as they relate to state and local government employees, and were scheduled to become effective on April 15, 1986. Among other things, the amendments will permit state and local governments to give their employees compensatory time off with pay in lieu of overtime pay in cash—at a rate of not less than one and one-half hours for each hour of overtime worked, pursuant to certain conditions. The amendments also exclude from the FLSA definition of "employee" most legislative employees and individuals who volunteer their services to state or local governments under certain conditions and within certain restrictions. The legislation also generally eliminates liability for unpaid back wages accrued before the effective date of the amendments. The U.S. Department of Labor intends to issue regulations to implement the legislation.

Wage garnishment and assignment

During 1984-85, most states enacted legislation designed to strengthen enforcement of court-ordered child support, in total or partial compliance with new federal requirements under the Child Support Enforcement Amendments of 1984. These amendments include requirements that state laws provide for automatic wage withholding to cover overdue and current child support, limit the total wages withheld according to the federal wage garnishment law, and provide a fine against an employer for retaliating against an employee or job applicant because of such withholding.

Prevailing wage

In 1985, three states—Colorado, Idaho, and New Hampshire—repealed their prevailing wage laws; 34 states still have laws of this kind.[2] During the biennium, many other measures were introduced to repeal, enact, or modify these laws, which specify that wage rates paid on publicly-funded construction contracts may not be less than those prevailing in the locality for similar work. Among several amendments to the Oklahoma law, the threshold amount for coverage was raised to $600,000, use of rates determined under the federal Davis-Bacon Act was required, debarment of contractors in violation of the law was added, and the public awarding agency was made liable for underpayment of wages in certain situations. Amendments in Nevada increased the threshold amount, provided for debarment, and required setting prevailing rates in each county through the use of an annual survey. Dollar threshold amounts also were increased in Connecticut and Wisconsin.

In 1984, Arizona voters approved a proposition forbidding state agencies and political subdivisions from requiring that prevailing wages be paid to workers on public construction projects. In Iowa, a prevailing wage bill passed the state legislature, but was vetoed by the governor.

The Illinois Supreme Court upheld the constitutionality of that state's prevailing wage law, including its exclusive use of rates paid on public construction projects in determining prevailing rates. In a separate case, an Illinois circuit court judgment, affirmed by a state appellate court, and currently on appeal to the state Supreme Court, upheld the right of certain cities and counties with home-rule status under the state constitution to continue to exempt themselves from coverage of the prevailing wage law.

At the federal level, on December 21, 1984, the U.S. District Court for the District of Columbia issued an order lifting the injunction on several key provisions of revised regulations under the Davis-Bacon Act issued by the U.S. Secretary of Labor in May 1982, and largely upheld on appeal. On January 31, 1985, the U.S. Department of Labor implemented those provisions. The District Court injunction remains in effect for certain provisions pertaining to the expanded use of "helpers" on Davis-Bacon projects.

Wage payment and collection

A number of states enacted measures designed to help in collecting wages owed—but not paid—employees. Labor departments in Arizona, Delaware, and Maine were given increased authority to collect these unpaid wages on behalf of employees. In other actions, the Oregon wage payment and collection law was amended to extend coverage to public sector employees, and in Illinois and Iowa, coverage was extended to additional categories of employees. Also in Oregon, an employer-financed wage security fund was established to pay the wage claims of employees whose employers have ceased doing business and do not have sufficient assets to pay the claims.

In Illinois, wages collected by the Department of Labor that cannot be paid to affected employees will be deposited into the state's general revenue fund, rather than returned to the employer. On September 6, 1985, a U.S. Court of Appeals reversed and remanded a District Court decision which held that the Federal Employee Retirement Income Security Act of 1974 preempted a California statute barring forfeiture of vacation pay and requiring payment of a pro rata share of such pay on the employee's termination.

Comparable worth

The concept of equal pay for jobs of comparable value in state government continued to be an area of interest and controversy. Among the more notable actions taken, the state legislatures in Iowa, Washington, and Wisconsin appropriated money for comparable worth implementation. In Minnesota, where the pay equity principle previously had been incorporated into the state pay system, legislation enacted in 1984 requires every political subdivision to establish equitable compensation relationships among its employees by August 1, 1987. In New Jersey, an interim task force report recommending pay increases for certain low-paid state employees was submitted in 1985, and implementing legislation was adopted. Legislatures in several other states commissioned studies of pay equity in the public sector, with most requiring reports on recommendations and legislative proposals.

In an important court action, a 1983 U.S. District Court decision ordering comparable pay for Washington state employees was overturned on appeal in 1985. Implementa-

tion in Washington will continue, however, according to the terms of an agreement reached between the state and the Washington Federation of State Employees. The agreement provides for pay raises through 1992 for state employees in female-dominated job classifications. As part of the agreement, the union will withdraw its petition for a rehearing by the U.S. Court of Appeals.

[For additional information on comparable worth activities in the states, see "Comparable Worth in State Government: 1984-85," in Chapter Seven.]

Equal Employment Opportunity

During the biennium, legislation in a number of states addressed the issue of compulsory retirement based solely on age. Hawaii and New York banned such forced retirement in both the public and private sectors, as did New Jersey (excepting state police officers). Massachusetts and Wisconsin[3] lifted the upper age limit on protection from age discrimination, thus prohibiting the mandatory retirement of public and private sector employees over the age of 40. Georgia and North Carolina eliminated mandatory retirement under public employees' retirement systems. Age discrimination in employment for those 40 to 70 years old was prohibited in Oklahoma and Wyoming, and coverage of Louisiana's law against age discrimination was expanded to include employers subject to the Federal Age Discrimination in Employment Act. Other provisions applicable only to police and fire personnel were enacted in Montana, Pennsylvania, and Rhode Island.

Legislation in 32 jurisdictions addressed other forms of employment discrimination. New laws were enacted—or coverage of existing fair employment practice laws was amended—to provide handicapped persons protection from employment discrimination in six states (Arizona, Florida, Massachusetts, Nevada, North Carolina, and Wyoming), and discrimination because of blindness was barred in South Dakota. Mississippi legislation, applicable to state employees, expressed a policy of non-discrimination on the basis of race, color, religion, sex, national origin, age, or handicap. Delaware added discrimination on the basis of marital status to the list of unlawful employment practices in both the public and private sectors. Legislation in New York, South Carolina, and the Virgin Islands addressed the rights of pregnant employees. In California, a new law required employers of 25 persons or more to provide reasonable accommodation to those enrolled in alcoholic rehabilitation programs. In Nevada, legislation banning discrimination in the public sector was amended to prohibit discrimination because of political affiliation.

Industrial Relations

Although only a small number of industrial relations laws were enacted during 1984-85, some of the legislation was significant. North Dakota adopted the State and Political Subdivision Employees Relations Act, which gives public employees the right to join employee organizations. Legislation in Mississippi made strikes by public employees, generally, and by public school teachers, specifically, unlawful. In 1985, a right-to-work law was enacted in Idaho, although enforcement was delayed by court action until the state Supreme Court ruled in January 1986 that the law could be enforced. The measure is scheduled to be voted on as a referendum item at the November 1986 general election.

The Michigan Strikebreaker Law was held unconstitutional by a state circuit court because of preemption by the National Labor Relations Act.

Occupational Safety and Health

"Right-to-know" laws requiring employees to be informed of and given training on toxic substances found in the workplace were adopted by 15 more states during 1984-85.[4] A majority of the states now have legislation of this kind. Many of these laws, all of recent origin, specify that the information must be provided not only to workers, but also to the communities in which companies using the toxic substances are located. Separate legislation providing for community access to toxic substance information was enacted in Maine, Oregon, and West Virginia, where prior laws gave protection to the employees.

The issuance of a federal regulation on "Chemical Hazard Communication" in 1983 raised the issue of federal preemption. Section 18 of the Occupational Safety and Health Act of 1970 provided that federal standards issued under the act preempt competing state laws or standards, unless those laws or standards are part of a federally-approved state occupational safety and health program, or "State Plan," operated in accordance with the requirements set forth in the section.

The Occupational Safety and Health Administration's (OSHA's) Hazard Communication Standard reflects the principle of preemption in its language. In March 1985, the U.S. Third Circuit Court of Appeals, ruling in a suit brought by the United Steelworkers of America and others, upheld this preemption explicitly with regard to the manufacturing sector of employment. Among other things, the court's decision also required OSHA to reconsider expanding the scope of the federal standard beyond manufacturing employment. In November 1985, OSHA published an advance notice of proposed rulemaking requesting information and comment on expansion of the Hazard Communication Standard to non-manufacturing employment. In another suit brought by the New Jersey Chamber of Commerce and others challenging the state's right-to-know law, the Third Circuit Court of Appeals ruled on the extent of preemption of the state law by the federal standard, providing an example of the results a court might reach in separating community-related (non-preempted) from employee-related (preempted) provisions of a state right-to-know law.

Of the 25 "State Plan" jurisdictions (see Table 8.25), 23 operate complete state plans—covering both private and public sector employees—and two states (Connecticut and New York) cover public employees only. Of these 25 states, 11 were granted "final approval" status under Section 18(e) of the Occupational Safety and Health Act during the biennium.[5]

Other significant worker safety measures included: a comprehensive new Occupational Safety and Health Act in New Jersey, applicable to public employees; amendments in New Hampshire and Oklahoma limiting the application of the laws in those states to public sector employment; legislation authorizing the commissioner of labor and industry in Maryland to bring suit to enforce payment of overdue civil penalties imposed by the state's Occupational Safety and Health Administration; an Oregon field sanitation law that requires employers of certain specified farm workers to provide convenient toilet and handwashing facilities and clean drinking water; and an executive order issued in New Mexico regulating the use of video display terminals by state employees. Several other jurisdictions enacted legislation regulating various aspects of asbestos, elevator, mine, boiler, and amusement ride safety.

Workers' Compensation

Many legislative proposals designed to improve or modify state workers' compensation programs were introduced during the biennium; of these, 331 became law.

Most of the changes affecting injured workers and their families related to benefits and coverage. Forty-eight states, the District of Columbia, and the Virgin Islands increased the maximum weekly benefit levels for temporary total disability (see Table 8.23). Laws in Mississippi and Tennessee were modified to include an escalation (in steps) of maximum weekly compensation levels for disability and death. Alabama, Alaska, and Illinois raised the percentage of the state average weekly wage used in computing maximum weekly compensation in most cases of disability and death. Laws in Georgia and North Dakota extended the compensable period for death benefits for dependent children beyond age 18 (until age 22, if they are full-time students). Burial allowances were increased in nine states.[6] Hawaii established a competitive state fund for insurance.

Maryland enacted legislation that allows coverage of all farmworkers, except those who work within 25 miles of their home for less than 13 weeks per year. In Virginia, the numerical exemption for agricultural or horticultural employment was reduced from four to two full-time regularly employed workers; and North Carolina made coverage mandatory for agricultural employees when there are 10 or more full-time non-seasonal employees regularly employed by the same employer.

Private Employment Agencies

During 1984-85, 13 states enacted legislation relating to the regulation of private employment agencies. Of particular importance was a comprehensive new law enacted in the District of Columbia. Among other provisions, the legislation: requires the licensing of employment agencies, counseling services, job-listing firms and others; requires posting of a surety bond by applicant-paid fee agencies and employment counseling services; and provides that contracts with job-seekers contain a three-day "cooling-off period" during which the contract may be cancelled.

Tennessee adopted a revised law to be administered by a personnel recruiting services board, and South Carolina made several amendments to its legislation to specifically extend coverage to executive search firms and related activities and to prohibit charging a fee unless services result in the applicant's acceptance of employment. Private employment agency laws are in effect in 42 states, the District of Columbia, Puerto Rico, and the Virgin Islands.

Child Labor/School Attendance

In 1985, the employment of minors in door-to-door sales emerged as an issue. Such work was prohibited administratively for children under age 15 in Oklahoma, and for minors under 16 in Oregon. Oregon also issued special rules for the employment of 16- and 17-year-olds in door-to-door sales. Arizona amended its restrictions on nightwork hours for children under age 16 to prohibit such solicitation after 7 p.m.

Among the other significant measures enacted during the biennium: Kentucky eliminated employment certificate requirements for minors under age 18; Pennsylvania permitted the use of transferable work permits by minors age 16 and older; and New York made employers who violate the child labor law subject to a civil penalty (in addition to any other penalties imposed). Iowa enacted legislation regulating the employment of children under age 16 as models, and Illinois adopted new certificate requirements for those under the age of 16 who are employed in motion picture, radio, or television productions.

Plant Closings

As in previous years, legislative efforts were aimed at assisting workers and communities facing mass layoffs or plant closings. Michigan, New Jersey, and Pennsylvania initiated programs to assist eligible employee groups in purchasing plants that are

365

about to be closed or have already closed, and operating them as employee-owned enterprises. Washington directed its Department of Community Development to study and develop a similar program. Procedures to aid failing businesses, and, in case of failure, to assist displaced workers in finding alternative employment or retraining opportunities were established by legislation in Massachusetts, and by executive order in New Jersey.

The New Jersey order also provides for voluntary advance notice of any transfer or termination of business operations. Maryland provided for at least six months advance notice to state employees adversely affected by the closing of a facility employing 50 or more workers, and in separate legislation, directed that voluntary guidelines, including appropriate advance notice and continuation of employee benefits, be developed for private-sector employees faced with a closing, relocation, or reduction in operations. Wisconsin expanded existing advance notice requirements to include affected employees, their collective bargaining representatives, and the community in which the business is located.

Legislation in California, Iowa, and Kentucky provides for the continuation of various health care benefits at employee expense for those who would otherwise be ineligible due to causes such as layoff or reduction in working hours; an amended provision in Connecticut requires employers of 100 or more, who close or relocate their establishments, to pay for the continuation of existing group health insurance for each affected employee and dependent for up to 120 days.

Federal legislation that would have required employers to give 90 days advance notice of plant closings or permanent layoffs affecting at least 100 employees or 30 percent of an employer's work force was defeated in 1985.

Other Legislation

A number of other laws, covering an array of labor standards, were enacted during the biennium. Several states adopted legislation requiring criminal history checks of prospective child care operators or workers. In 1984-85, a number of laws were enacted or revised to give preference to state contrac-tors or state residents on public works projects. In the same period, however, the Illinois Preference Act was held unconstitutional by a federal appeals court, the Alaska Supreme Court declared the state's resident preference law unconstitutional, and Oklahoma's resident bidder preference law was repealed. Nine states (Arizona, California, Connecticut, Iowa, Kansas, Maine, New York, Rhode Island, and Utah) enacted or expanded coverage of "whistleblower" laws to protect employees from retaliation for reporting violations of law to a public body, or for participating in an investigation, hearing, or court action.

Florida, Oregon, and Tennessee passed legislation to provide employment opportunities to persons in economically-depressed areas, designated as enterprise zones. A study of the feasibility of establishing such zones will be conducted in West Virginia.

In other actions during the biennium: Maine and Rhode Island prohibited employers from charging applicants a fee for filing employment applications; comprehensive new laws enacted in Hawaii and Vermont prohibit employers from requiring employees to take a polygraph test as a condition of employment or continued employment; and Tennessee adopted legislation making it unlawful to knowingly employ or refer for employment any illegal alien. Stiff employer penalties include license revocation and being permanently barred from doing business in the state.

Notes
1. In Puerto Rico, revised mandatory decrees issued by the Commonwealth Minimum Wage Board raised minimum rates in late 1983, 1984, and 1985 for: the transportation industry; bread, cracker, bakery products, and alimentary pastes industry; dairy industry; transportation vehicle manufacturing and assembly industry; metal, machinery, electrical products, instruments, and related products industry; and for the personal services and communications industries.
2. Alaska, Arkansas, California, Connecticut, Delaware, Hawaii, Illinois, Indiana, Kansas, Kentucky, Louisiana, Maine, Maryland, Massachusetts, Michigan, Minnesota, Missouri, Montana, Nebraska, Nevada, New Jersey, New Mexico, New York, Ohio, Oklahoma, Oregon, Pennsylvania, Rhode Island, Tennessee, Texas, Washington, West Virginia, Wisconsin, and Wyoming. Guam and the Virgin Islands also have prevailing wage laws.

3. A federal court in Wisconsin subsequently ruled that changes enacted in that state are preempted by the federal Employee Retirement Income Security Act (ERISA) to the extent that the state law applies to an employee benefit plan covered by ERISA.

4. Alabama, Delaware, Florida, Iowa, Louisiana, Maryland, Missouri, Montana, North Carolina, Pennsylvania, Tennessee, Texas, Vermont, Virginia, and Washington.

5. Alaska, Arizona, Hawaii, Iowa, Kentucky, Maryland, Minnesota, Tennessee, Utah, Virgin Islands, and Wyoming.

6. Alaska, Arkansas, California, Connecticut, Georgia, Mississippi, South Dakota, Utah, and Virginia.

Table 8.23
MAXIMUM BENEFITS FOR TEMPORARY TOTAL DISABILITY
PROVIDED BY WORKERS' COMPENSATION STATUTES
(As of November 1985)

State or other jurisdiction	Maximum percentage of wages	Maximum payment per week		Maximum period		Total maximum stated in law
		Amount	Based on*	Duration of disability	Number of weeks	
Federal (FECA)(a) ..	66-2/3-75(b)	$ 979.90	66-2/3% of the pay of specific grade level in federal civil service(b)	★	...	...
(LHWCA)(a)	66-2/3	579.66	200% of NAWW	★	...	...
Alabama	66-2/3	303.00	100% of SAWW	...	300	...
Alaska	80 of worker's spendable earnings	1,114.00(c)	200% of SAWW	★	...	...
Arizona	66-2/3	203.86(d)	...	★	...	...
Arkansas	66-2/3	154.00	...	...	450	$69,300
California	66-2/3	224.00	...	★	...	...
Colorado	66-2/3	336.00(e)	80% of SAWW	★	...	...
Connecticut	66-2/3	397.00(f)	100% of SAWW	★	...	...
Delaware	66-2/3	235.69	66-2/3% of SAWW	★	...	...
Florida	66-2/3	307.00(c)	100% of SAWW	...	350	...
Georgia	66-2/3	155.00(g)	...	★	...	...
Hawaii	66-2/3	291.00	100% of SAWW	★	...	...
Idaho	60-90	260.00 – 361.23(h)	90% of SAWW	...	52(i)	...
Illinois	66-2/3	502.36	133-1/3% of SAWW	★	...	...
Indiana	66-2/3	178.00(j)	...	...	500	89,000(k)
Iowa	80 of worker's spendable earnings	598.00	200% of SAWW	★	...	...
Kansas	66-2/3	239.00	75% of SAWW	★	...	75,000
Kentucky	66-2/3	304.80	100% of SAWW	★	...	...
Louisiana	66-2/3	254.00(l)	75% of SAWW	★	...	...
Maine	66-2/3	447.92(l,m)	166-2/3% of SAWW	★	...	...
Maryland	66-2/3	327.00	100% of SAWW	★	...	...
Massachusetts	66-2/3	360.50(n)	100% of SAWW	★	...	(o)
Michigan	80 of worker's spendable earnings	358.00(p)	90% of SAWW	★	...	...
Minnesota	66-2/3	342.00	100% of SAWW	★	...	...
Mississippi	66-2/3	133.00(q)	...	...	450	59,850(r)
Missouri	66-2/3	233.84	75% of SAWW		400	...
Montana	66-2/3	292.00(e)	100% of SAWW	★	...	...
Nebraska	66-2/3	225.00	...	★	...	...
Nevada	66-2/3	332.46	100% of SAWW	★	...	...
New Hampshire	66-2/3(s)	462.00	150% of SAWW	★	...	...
New Jersey	70	269.00	75% of SAWW	...	400	...
New Mexico	66-2/3	298.63	100% of SAWW	...	600	(t)
New York	66-2/3	300.00	...	★	...	...
North Carolina	66-2/3	280.00	100% of SAWW	★	...	...
North Dakota	66-2/3	291.00(u,v)	100% of SAWW	★	...	...
Ohio	72 for first 12 weeks; 66-2/3 thereafter	354.00(w)	100% of SAWW	★	...	...
Oklahoma	66-2/3	217.00	66-2/3% of SAWW	...	300	...
Oregon	66-2/3	334.58	100% of SAWW	★	...	...
Pennsylvania	66-2/3	336.00	100% of SAWW	★	...	...
Rhode Island	66-2/3	307.00(x)	100% of SAWW	★	...	...
South Carolina	66-2/3	287.02	100% of SAWW	...	500	...
South Dakota	66-2/3	254.00	100% of SAWW	★	...	...
Tennessee	66-2/3	168.00(y)	...	★	...	67,200
Texas	66-2/3	217.00(z)	...	...	401	...
Utah	66-2/3	323.00(aa)	100% of SAWW	...	312	...
Vermont	66-2/3	293.00(bb)	100% of SAWW	★	...	...
Virginia	66-2/3	311.00	100% of SAWW	...	500	...
Washington	60-75	260.94(e)	75% of SAMW	★	...	...
West Virginia	70	332.83	100% of SAWW	...	208	...
Wisconsin	66-2/3	321.00(e)	100% of SAWW	★	...	...
Wyoming	66-2/3	359.86(z)	100% of SAMW	★	...	...
Dist. of Col.	66-2/3 or 80 of worker's spend-able earnings	413.26	100% of SAWW	★	...	...
Puerto Rico	66-2/3	45.00	...	...	312	...
Virgin Islands	66-2/3	183.00	66-2/3% of SAWW	★	...	...

MAXIMUM BENEFITS—Continued

Source: Division of State Workers' Compensation Programs, Office of State Liaison and Legislative Analysis, Employment Standards Administration, U.S. Department of Labor.

*SAWW—State's average weekly wage; SAMW—State's average monthly wage; NAWW—National average weekly wage; AWW—Average weekly wage.

(a) Federal Employees' Compensation Act (FECA) and the Longshoremen's and Harbor Workers' Compensation Act (LHWCA). LHWCA benefits are for private-sector maritime employees (not seamen) who work on navigable waters of the U.S., including dry docks.

(b) Benefits under FECA are computed at a maximum of 75 percent of the pay of a specific grade level in the federal civil service.

(c) Payments subject to Social Security and Unemployment Insurance benefits offsets.

(d) Additional $10 monthly added to benefits of dependents residing in the U.S.

(e) Payments subject to Social Security benefit offsets.

(f) Additional $10 weekly for each dependent child under 18 years of age, up to 50 percent of basic benefit, not to exceed 75 percent of worker's wage.

(g) Effective July 1, 1986, maximum weekly benefit will be $175.

(h) Additional 7 percent ($20.23) of SAWW is payable for each dependent child up to five children.

(i) After 52 weeks, payments are 60 percent of SAWW for duration of disability.

(j) Effective July 1, 1986, maximum weekly benefit will be $190.

(k) Effective July 1, 1986, total maximum amount payable will be $95,000.

(l) Payments subject to Unemployment Insurance benefit offsets.

(m) Benefit payments are frozen at $447.92 until June 30, 1988.

(n) Additional $6 will be added per dependent if weekly benefits are below $150.

(o) Total maximum payable not to exceed 250 times the SAWW in effect at time of injury.

(p) Payments subject to reduction by Unemployment Insurance and Social Security benefits, in addition to benefits paid by an employer disability, retirement or pension plan.

(q) Effective July 1, 1986, maximum weekly benefit will be $140.

(r) Effective July 1, 1986, total maximum payable will be $63,000.

(s) If the employee's AWW exceeds 40 percent of the SAWW, compensation will increase to 66-2/3 percent of the employee's AWW (not to exceed 150 percent of the SAWW).

(t) Total maximum equals the sum of 600 multiplied by the maximum weekly benefit payable at time of injury.

(u) Additional $5 per week for each dependent child, not to exceed worker's net wage.

(v) Payments are reduced by 50 percent of Social Security benefits.

(w) Payments are subject to offset if concurrent and/or duplicate with those under employer non-occupational benefits plan.

(x) Additional $9 for each dependent; including a non-working wife; aggregate not to exceed 80 percent of worker's AWW.

(y) Effective July 1, 1986, maximum weekly benefit will be $189.

(z) Each cumulative $10 increase in the AWW for manufacturing production workers will increase the maximum weekly benefit by $7 per week.

(aa) Additional $5 for dependent spouse and each dependent child up to four, but not to exceed 100 percent of SAWW.

(bb) Additional $10 will be paid for each dependent under age 21.

Table 8.24

ESTIMATES OF WORKERS' COMPENSATION PAYMENTS, BY STATE AND TYPE OF INSURANCE: 1982-83*

(In thousands of dollars)

State or other jurisdiction	1982				1983				Percentage change in total payment from 1982 to 1983
	Total	Insurance losses paid by private insurance(a)	State and federal fund disbursements(b)	Self insurance payments(c)	Total	Insurance losses paid by private insurance(a)	State and federal fund disbursements(b)	Self insurance payments(c)	
Total	$16,263,318	$8,646,734	$4,737,906	$2,878,678	$17,533,341	$9,263,797	$5,037,750	$3,231,794	7.8
Alabama........	132,422	94,422	....	38,000	146,626	104,726	....	41,900	10.7
Alaska.........	63,876	51,576	....	12,300	76,774	63,174	....	13,600	20.2
Arizona........	137,513	74,310	49,858	13,345	170,936	79,295	76,284	15,357	24.3
Arkansas.......	103,163	72,163	....	31,000	118,199	78,799	....	39,400	14.6
California.....	2,032,558	1,192,510	259,317	580,731	2,240,567	1,290,575	273,063	676,929	10.2
Colorado	180,498	65,210	90,888	24,400	209,655	80,842	103,413	25,400	16.2
Connecticut	209,165	166,121	....	43,044	230,097	180,597	....	49,500	10.0
Delaware	27,066	20,916	....	6,150	30,276	23,326	....	6,950	11.9
Florida	519,747	360,947	....	158,800	645,119	424,419	....	220,700	24.1
Georgia	235,355	202,855	....	32,500	255,903	220,603	....	35,300	8.7
Hawaii	95,628	66,578	....	29,050	105,136	75,436	....	29,700	9.9
Idaho..........	44,280	30,389	8,191	5,700	46,061	32,561	8,100	5,400	4.0
Illinois........	673,032	565,032	....	108,000	655,705	551,705	....	104,000	-2.6
Indiana........	118,163	100,163	....	18,000	128,764	103,564	....	25,200	9.0
Iowa	106,468	93,568	....	12,900	109,600	97,600	....	12,000	2.9
Kansas	105,148	88,348	....	16,800	114,597	96,297	....	18,300	9.0
Kentucky	167,752	125,752	....	42,000	168,062	125,962	....	42,100	0.2
Louisiana	384,419	320,319	....	64,100	408,642	340,542	....	68,100	6.3
Maine	123,724	90,824	....	32,900	145,317	109,517	....	35,800	17.5
Maryland	241,767	159,805	29,062	52,900	254,782	167,269	31,813	55,700	5.4
Massachusetts ...	368,982	338,565	....	30,417	407,554	373,954	....	33,600	10.5
Michigan	672,881	372,319	31,562	269,000	665,397	368,197	31,200	266,000	-1.1
Minnesota	335,750	282,150	....	53,600	377,735	292,835	....	84,900	12.5
Mississippi	70,671	63,471	....	7,200	74,485	66,485	....	8,000	5.4
Missouri	151,640	125,240	....	26,400	172,352	139,452	....	32,900	13.7
Montana	55,880	20,957	28,189 (d)	6,734	65,667	24,878	32,857 (d)	7,932	17.5
Nebraska	52,648	46,548	....	6,100	56,482	49,382	....	7,100	7.3
Nevada	91,755	724	83,638	7,393	95,704	1,824	84,000	9,880	4.3
New Hampshire .	60,129	53,679	....	6,450	63,482	56,682	....	6,800	5.6
New Jersey......	350,042	311,492	....	38,550	394,527	333,677	....	60,850	12.7
New Mexico.....	80,794	76,194	....	4,600	92,296	87,096	....	5,200	14.2
New York.......	760,225	412,008	214,217	134,000	758,142	413,172	211,470	133,500	-0.3
North Carolina ..	159,873	126,473	....	33,400	172,472	130,472	....	42,000	7.9
North Dakota ...	22,128	86	22,042	....	23,091	30	23,061	....	4.4
Ohio	924,263	2,887	600,376	321,000	1,079,842	3,634	715,708	360,500	16.8

ESTIMATES OF WORKERS' COMPENSATION PAYMENTS—Continued

State or other jurisdiction	1982				1983				Percentage change in total payment from 1982 to 1983
	Total	Insurance losses paid by private insurance(a)	State and federal fund disbursements(b)	Self insurance payments(c)	Total	Insurance losses paid by private insurance(a)	State and federal fund disbursements(b)	Self insurance payments(c)	
Oklahoma	210,981	150,267	27,814	32,900	227,881	160,351	31,930	35,600	8.0
Oregon	306,455	92,114	150,141	64,200	311,807	97,709	154,498	59,600	1.7
Pennsylvania	722,948	496,198	62,250 (d)	164,500	780,738	540,149	62,689 (d)	177,900	8.0
Rhode Island	70,565	63,565	...	7,000	81,283	73,183	...	8,100	15.2
South Carolina	98,902	82,618	...	16,284	106,960	89,295	...	17,665	8.1
South Dakota	16,706	14,506	...	2,200	17,706	15,406	...	2,300	6.0
Tennessee	149,098	133,098	...	16,000	148,660	135,160	...	13,500	-0.3
Texas	981,735	981,735	...	...	1,083,994	1,083,994	...	...	10.4
Utah	51,377	16,905	26,472	8,000	50,814	20,137	22,777	7,900	-1.1
Vermont	19,297	17,747	...	1,550	23,598	21,698	...	1,900	22.3
Virginia	249,362	171,962	...	77,400	264,859	182,659	...	82,200	6.2
Washington	419,178	15,578	310,000	93,600	510,529	16,529	380,000	114,000	21.8
West Virginia	211,655	725	134,880	76,050	222,246	1,159	142,356	78,731	5.0
Wisconsin	205,811	169,011	...	36,800	211,797	173,897	...	37,900	2.9
Wyoming	37,234	366	36,868	...	36,653	341	36,312	...	-1.6
Dist. of Col.	80,468	65,738	...	14,730	77,551	63,551	...	14,000	-3.6
Federal:									
Civilian Employee Program(e)	899,080	...	899,080	...	918,925	...	918,925	...	2.2
Black Lung Benefits Program(f)	1,666,908	...	1,666,908	...	1,691,049	...	1,691,049	...	1.4
Other(g)	6,153	...	6,153	...	6,245	...	6,245	...	1.5

*Data for 1983 are preliminary. Calendar year figures, except that data for Montana, Nevada, and West Virginia, for federal civilian employees and "other" federal workers' compensation, and for state fund disbursements in Maryland, North Dakota, and Wyoming represent fiscal years ended in 1982 and 1983. Includes benefit payments under the Longshoremen's and Harbor Workers' Compensation Act and extensions for the states in which such payments are made.

Source: Daniel N. Price, Division of Retirement and Survivors Studies, Office of Retirement and Survivors Insurance, Social Security Administration, *Social Security Bulletin*, February 1986.

Note: The above figures are the most recent ones available for workers' compensation payment estimates.

(a) Net cash and medical benefits paid during the calendar year by private insurance carriers under standard workers' compensation policies. Data primarily from A.M. Best Company, a national data-collecting agency for private insurance.

(b) Net cash and medical benefits paid by state funds compiled from state reports (published and unpublished); estimated for some states.

(c) Cash and medical benefits paid by self-insurers, plus the value of medical benefits paid by employers carrying worker's compensation policies that do not include the standard medical coverage. Estimated from available state data.

(d) Includes payment of supplemental pensions from general funds.

(e) Payments to civilian federal employees (including emergency relief workers) and their dependents under the Federal Employees' Compensation Act.

(f) Includes $590,871,000 in 1982 and $628,349,000 in 1983 paid by the Department of Labor.

(g) Primarily payments made to dependents of reservists who died while on duty in the Armed Forces, to individuals under the War Hazards Act, War Claims Acts, and Civilian War Benefits Act, and to Civil Air Patrol and Reserve Officers Training Corps personnel, persons involved in maritime war risks, and law enforcement officers under Public Law 90-921.

Table 8.25
STATUS OF APPROVED STATE PLANS DEVELOPED IN ACCORDANCE WITH THE FEDERAL OCCUPATIONAL SAFETY AND HEALTH ACT
(As of March 1986)

State or other jurisdiction	Operational status agreement(a)	Different standards(b)	7(c)(l)On-site consultation agreements(c)	On-shore maritime coverage	Date of initial approval	Date certified(d)	Date of 18(e) final approval(e)
Alaska	...	★	★	...	7/31/73	9/09/77	9/26/84
Arizona	...	...	...	...	10/29/74	9/18/81	6/20/85
California	★	★	★	★	4/24/73	8/12/77	
Connecticut(f)	...	...	★	...	10/02/78		
Hawaii	...	★	★	...	12/28/73	4/26/78	4/30/84
Indiana	★	...	...	...	2/25/74	9/24/81	
Iowa	...	...	★	...	7/20/73	9/14/76	7/02/85
Kentucky	...	...	...	...	7/23/73	2/08/80	6/13/85
Maryland	...	...	★	...	6/28/73	2/15/80	7/18/85
Michigan	★	★	★	...	9/24/73	1/16/81	
Minnesota	...	...	★	★	5/29/73	9/28/76	7/30/85
Nevada	★	...	...	...	12/28/73	8/13/81	
New Mexico	★	...	...	...	12/04/75	12/04/84	
New York(f)	...	...	★	...	6/01/84		
North Carolina	★	...	★	...	1/26/73	9/29/76	
Oregon	★	★	★	★	12/22/72	9/15/82	
South Carolina	★	...	★	...	11/30/72	7/28/76	
Tennessee	...	...	★	...	6/28/73	5/03/78	7/22/85
Utah	...	...	★	...	1/04/73	11/11/76	7/16/85
Vermont	★	...	★	★	10/01/73	3/04/77	
Virginia	★	...	★	...	9/23/76	8/15/84	
Washington	★	★	...	★	1/19/73	1/26/82	
Wyoming	...	...	★	...	4/25/74	12/18/80	6/27/85
Puerto Rico	★	...	...	...	8/30/77	9/07/82	
Virgin Islands	...	...	...	...	9/11/73	9/22/81	4/17/84

Source: Directorate of Federal-State Operations, Office of State Programs, Occupational Safety and Health Administration, U.S. Department of Labor.

Key:
★—Yes
...—No
(a) Concurrent federal jurisdiction suspended.

(b) Standards frequently not identical to the federal.
(c) On-site consultation is available in all states either through a 7(c)(l) Agreement or under a State Plan.
(d) Developmental steps satisfactorily completed.
(e) Concurrent federal jurisdiction relinquished (supersedes Operational Status Agreement).
(f) Plan covers only state and local government employees.

Table 8.26
SELECTED STATE CHILD LABOR STANDARDS AFFECTING MINORS UNDER 18
(As of December 1985)

(Occupational coverage, exemptions and deviations usually omitted)

State or other jurisdiction	Documentary proof of age required up to age indicated(a)	Maximum daily and weekly hours and days per week for minors under 16 unless other age indicated(b)	Nightwork prohibited for minors under 16 unless other age indicated(b)
Federal (FLSA)..	(c)	8-40, non-school period. Schoolday/week: 3-18(d)	7 p.m. (9 p.m. June 1 through Labor Day) to 7 a.m.
Alabama..........	17; 19 in mines and quarries.	8-40-6. Schoolday/week: 4-28.	8 p.m. to 7 a.m.
Alaska............	18	6-day week, under 18. Schoolday/week: 9(e)-23.	9 p.m. to 5 a.m.
Arizona..........	(f)	8-40. Schoolday/week: 3-18.	9:30 p.m. (7 p.m. in door-to-door sales or deliveries) to 6 a.m.
Arkansas.........	16	8-48-6. 10-54-6, 16 and 17.	7 p.m. (9 p.m. before non-schoolday) to 6 a.m. 11 p.m. before schoolday to 6 a.m., 16 and 17.
California........	18	8-48-6, under 18. Schoolday/week: 4-28(g) under 18, except 8 before non-schoolday, 16 and 17.	10 p.m. (12:30 a.m. before non-schoolday) to 5 a.m., under 18.
Colorado.........	16	8-40, under 18. Schoolday: 6.	9:30 p.m. to 5 a.m., before schoolday.
Connecticut......	18	9-48, under 18. 8-48-6, under 18 in stores, and under 16 in agriculture. (Overtime permitted in certain industries.)	10 p.m. (midnight before non-schoolday in supermarkets) to 6 a.m., under 18. 11 p.m. (midnight before non-schoolday or if not attending school) to 6 a.m., 16 and 17 in restaurants or as usher in non-profit theater.
Delaware	18	8-48-6.	7 p.m. (9 p.m. in stores on Friday, Saturday and vacation) to 6 a.m.
Florida	18	10-40-6. Schoolday: 4 when followed by schoolday, except if enrolled in vocational program.	9 p.m. (11 p.m before non-schoolday) to 6:30 a.m. 1 a.m. to 5 a.m., 16 and 17.
Georgia..........	18	8-40. Schoolday: 4.	9 p.m. to 6 a.m.
Hawaii	18	8-40-6. Schoolday: 10(e).	7 p.m. to 7 a.m. (9 p.m. to 6 a.m. June 1 through day before Labor Day).
Idaho	(f)	9-54.	9 p.m. to 6 a.m.
Illinois..........	16	8-48-6. Schoolday/week: 3 [8(e)]-23(g).	7 p.m. (9 p.m. June 1 through Labor Day) to 7 a.m.

SELECTED STATE CHILD LABOR STANDARDS—Continued

State or other jurisdiction	Documentary proof of age required up to age indicated(a)	Maximum daily and weekly hours and days per week for minors under 16 unless other age indicated(b)	Nightwork prohibited for minors under 16 unless other age indicated(b)
Indiana	17	8-40-6, under 17, except minors of 16 not enrolled in school. 9-48 during summer vacation, minors of 16 enrolled in school. Schoolday/week: 3-23.	7 p.m. (9 p.m. before non-schoolday) to 6 a.m.
Iowa	18	8-40. Schoolday/week: 4-28.	10 p.m. (midnight before non-schoolday) to 6 a.m., minors of 16 enrolled in school.
Kansas	16(f)	8-40.	7 p.m. (9 p.m. June 1 through Labor Day) to 7 a.m.
Kentucky	18	8-40 Schoolday/week: 3-18, under 16. 6 (8 Saturday and Sunday)-40, 16 and 17 if attending school.	10 p.m. before schoolday to 7 a.m. 7 p.m. (9 p.m. June 1 through Labor Day) to 7 a.m. 11:30 p.m. (1 a.m. Friday and Saturday) to 6 a.m. when school in session, 16 and 17.
Louisiana	18	8-40-6. Schoolday: 3.	10 p.m. to 7 a.m.
Maine	16	8-48-6. Schoolday/week: 4-28.	9 p.m. to 7 a.m., under 15. 10 p.m. to 7 a.m., 15.
Maryland	18	8-40. Schoolday/week:4-23(g), under 16. 12(e), under 18.	8 p.m. (9 p.m. Memorial Day through Labor Day) to 7 a.m. 8 hours of non-work, non-school time required in each 24-hour day, 16 and 17.
Massachusetts	18	8-48-6. 4-24 in farmwork, under 14. 9-48-6, 16 and 17.	6 p.m. to 6:30 a.m. 10 p.m. (midnight in restaurants on Friday, Saturday and vacation) to 6 a.m., 16 and 17.
Michigan	18	10-48-6, under 18. Schoolweek: 48(e), under 18.	9 p.m. to 7 a.m. 10:30 p.m. to 6 a.m., 16 and 17 if attending school. 11:30 p.m. to 6 a.m., 16 and 17 if not attending school.
Minnesota	18	8-40.	9 p.m. to 7 a.m.
Mississippi	(f)	8-44 in factory, mill, cannery or workshop.	7 p.m. to 6 a.m. in factory, mill, cannery or workshop.
Missouri	16	8-40-6.	7 p.m. (10 p.m. before non-schoolday and for minors not enrolled in school) to 7 a.m.
Montana	18	. . .	. . .
Nebraska	16	8-48.	8 p.m. to 6 a.m. under 14. 10 p.m. (beyond 10 p.m. before non-schoolday with special permit) to 6 a.m., 14 and 15.
Nevada	17(f)	8-48.	. . .

SELECTED STATE CHILD LABOR STANDARDS—Continued

State or other jurisdiction	Documentary proof of age required up to age indicated(a)	Maximum daily and weekly hours and days per week for minors under 16 unless other age indicated(b)	Nightwork prohibited for minors under 16 unless other age indicated(b)
New Hampshire ...	18	8 on non-schoolday, 48-hour week during vacation, if enrolled in school. 10-48 at manual or mechanical labor in manufacturing, 10¼-54 at such labor in other employment, under 16 if not enrolled in school, and 16 and 17. Schoolday/week: 3-23 if enrolled in school.	9 p.m. to 7 a.m. if enrolled in school.
New Jersey.........	18	8-40-6, under 18. 10-hour day, 6-day week in agriculture. Schoolday: 8(e).	6 p.m. to 7 a.m. 11 p.m. to 6 a.m., 16 and 17 during school term, with specified variations.
New Mexico........	16	8-44 (48 in special cases), under 14.	9 p.m. to 7 a.m., under 14.
New York	18	8-40-6. 8-48-6, 16 and 17. Schoolday/week: 3-23, under 16. 4-28, 16 if attending school.	7 p.m. to 7 a.m. Midnight to 6 a.m., 16 and 17.
North Carolina	18	8-40. Schoolday/week: 3-18(g).	7 p.m. (9 p.m. before non-schoolday) to 7 a.m.
North Dakota	16	8-48-6, under 18. Schoolday/week: 3-24 if not exempted from school attendance.	7 p.m. (9 p.m. June 1 through Labor Day) to 7 a.m.
Ohio	18	8-40. Schoolday/week: 3-18.	7 p.m. (9 p.m. June 1 through September 1 or during school holidays of 5 days or more) to 7 a.m.
Oklahoma	16	8-48.	6 p.m. to 7 a.m. in factories, factory workshops, pool halls or steam laundries.
Oregon	18	10-44 (emergency overtime with permit)-6. 44-hour week (emergency overtime with permit), 16 and 17.	6 p.m. to 7 a.m., except with special permit.
Pennsylvania	18	8-44-6, under 18. Schoolday/week: 4-26(g), under 16. 28 in schoolweek, 16 and 17 if enrolled in regular day school.	7 p.m. (10 p.m. during vacation from June to Labor Day) to 7 a.m. 11 p.m. (midnight before non-schoolday) to 6 a.m., 16 and 17 if enrolled in regular day school.
Rhode Island	18	8-40. 9-48, 16 and 17.	7 p.m. to 6 a.m. 11:30 p.m. (1:30 a.m. before non-schoolday) to 6 a.m., 16 and 17 if regularly attending school.
South Carolina	(f)	8-40. Schoolday/week: 3-18.	7 p.m. (9 p.m. June 1 through Labor Day) to 7 a.m.
South Dakota	16	8-40.	After 7 p.m. in mercantile establishments, under 14.
Tennessee.........	18	8-40. Schoolday/week: 3-18.	7 p.m. to 7 a.m. (9 p.m. to 6 a.m. before non-schooldays).
Texas.............	(f)	8-48.	10 p.m. (midnight before non-school day or in summer if not enrolled in summer school) to 5 a.m.

SELECTED STATE CHILD LABOR STANDARDS—Continued

State or other jurisdiction	Documentary proof of age required up to age indicated(a)	Maximum daily and weekly hours and days per week for minors under 16 unless other age indicated(b)	Nightwork prohibited for minors under 16 unless other age indicated(b)
Utah	(f)	8-40 Schoolday: 4.	9:30 p.m. to 5 a.m. before schoolday.
Vermont	16(f)	8-48-6. 9-50, 16 and 17.	7 p.m. to 6 a.m.
Virginia	16	8-40-6.	7 p.m. (9 p.m. before non-schoolday and June 1 to Labor Day or with special permit) to 7 a.m.
Washington	18	8-hour day, 5-day week, under 18. Schoolday/week: 3-18.	7 p.m. (9 p.m. during summer vacation) to 7 a.m. After 9 p.m. on consecutive nights preceding schoolday, 16 and 17.
West Virginia	18	8-40-6.	8 p.m. to 5 a.m.
Wisconsin	18	8-24-6 when school in session and 8-40-6 in non-schoolweek. 8-40-6 when school in session and 8-48-6 in non-schoolweek (voluntary overtime per day and week permitted in non-schoolweek up to 50-hour week), 16 and 17 if required to attend school.	8 p.m. (9:30 p.m. before non-schoolday) to 7 a.m. 12:30 a.m. to 6 a.m., except where under direct adult supervision, and with 8 hours rest between end of work and schoolday, 16 and 17 if required to attend school.
Wyoming	16	8-56.	10 p.m. (midnight before non-schoolday and for minors not enrolled in school) to 5 a.m. Midnight to 5 a.m., females 16 and 17.
Dist. of Col.	18	8-48-6, under 18.	7 p.m. (9 p.m. June 1 through Labor Day) to 7 a.m. 10 p.m. to 6 a.m., 16 and 17.
Guam	16	8-40-6, under 18. Schoolday: 9(e), under 18.	After 10 p.m. on schoolday, under 18.
Puerto Rico	18	8-40-6, under 18. Schoolday: 8(e).	6 p.m. to 8 a.m. 10 p.m. to 6 a.m., 16 and 17.

Source: Division of State Employment Standards Programs, Office of State Liaison and Legislative Analysis, Employment Standards Administration, U.S. Department of Labor.

(a) Many states require an employment certificate for minors under 16 and an age certificate for 16 and 17 year olds; in a few states other types of evidence are acceptable as proof of age. In most states the law provides that age certificates may be issued upon request for persons above the age indicated, or although not specified in the law, such certificates are issued in practice.

(b) State hours limitations on a schoolday and in a schoolweek usually apply only to those enrolled in school. Several states exempt high school graduates from the hours and/or nightwork or other provisions, or have less restrictive provisions for minors participating in various school-work programs. Separate nightwork standards in messenger service and street trades are common, but are not displayed in table.

(c) Not required. State age or employment certificates which show that the minor has attained the minimum age for the job are accepted under the Fair Labor Standards Act.

(d) Students of 14 and 15 enrolled in approved Work Experience and Career Ex-

ploration programs may work during school hours up to three hours on a schoolday and 23 hours in a schoolweek.

(e) Combined hours of work and school.

(f) Proof of age is not mandatory under state law in Arizona, Idaho, Mississippi, South Carolina, Texas and Utah; or in Kansas for minors enrolled in secondary schools, and in Nevada and Vermont for employment outside school hours. For purposes of the Fair Labor Standards Act (FLSA), federal age certificates are issued upon request by the State Department of Labor in South Carolina and by Federal Wage and Hour Offices in Mississippi and Texas. In Utah, state law directs schools to issue age certificates upon request.

Wage and Hour Offices will also issue federal age certificates upon request in Florida, Georgia, Kentucky, and Tennessee, where the states' required proof-of-age documents do not conform to those of Federal Child Labor Regulation No. 1. Also, for FLSA purposes, birth or baptismal certificates are accepted in lieu of age certificates in Alaska and Guam.

(g) More hours are permitted when school is in session less than five days.

Table 8.27
CHANGES IN BASIC MINIMUM WAGES IN NON-FARM EMPLOYMENT UNDER STATE LAW: SELECTED YEARS
1965 TO 1986

State or other jurisdiction	1965(a)	1968(a)	1970(a)	1972	1976(a)	1979	1980	1981	1983	1984	1985	1986
Federal (FLSA)	$1.15 & $1.25	$1.15 & $1.60	$1.30 & $1.60	$1.60	$2.20 & $2.30	$2.30	$3.10	$3.35	$3.35	$3.35	$3.35	$3.35
Alabama	...	...	...	...	...	...	...	...	...	...	...	...
Alaska	1.75	2.10	2.10	2.10	2.80	3.40	3.60	3.85	3.85	3.85	3.85	3.85
Arizona	18.72-26.40/wk.(b)	18.72-26.40/wk.(b)	18.72-26.40/wk.(b)	18.72-26.40/wk.(b)	...	...	...	...	...	...	...	...
Arkansas	1.25/day(b)	1.25/day(b)	1.10	1.20	1.90	2.30	2.55	2.70	2.95	3.05	3.15	3.15
California	1.30(b)	1.65(b)	1.65(b)	1.65(b)	2.00	2.90	2.90	3.35	3.35	3.35	3.35	3.35
Colorado	.60-1.00(b)	1.00-1.25(b)	1.00-1.25(b)	1.00-1.25(b)	1.00-1.25(b)	1.90	1.90	1.90	1.90	2.50	3.00	3.00
Connecticut	1.25	1.40	1.60	1.85	2.21 & 2.31	2.91	3.12	3.37	3.37	3.37	3.37	3.37
Delaware	...	1.25	1.25	1.60	2.00	2.00	2.00	2.00	2.00	3.00	3.00	3.00
Florida	...	...	...	...	...	...	...	...	...	...	...	...
Georgia	...	...	...	1.25	1.25	1.25	1.25	1.25	1.25	1.25	3.25	3.25
Hawaii	1.25	1.25	1.60	1.60	2.40	2.65	2.90	3.10	3.35	3.35	3.35	3.35
Idaho	1.00	1.15	1.25	1.40	1.60	2.30	2.30	2.30	2.30	2.30	2.30	2.30
Illinois	...	...	...	1.40	2.10	2.30	2.30	2.30	2.30	2.65	3.00	3.35
Indiana	...	1.15	1.25	1.25	1.25	2.00	2.00	2.00	2.00	2.00	2.00	2.00
Iowa	...	...	...	...	...	...	...	...	...	...	...	...
Kansas	.65-.75(b)	.65-.75(b)	.65-.75(b)	.65-.75(b)	1.60	1.60	1.60	1.60	1.60	1.60	1.60	1.60
Kentucky	...	...	...	...	1.60	2.00	2.15	2.15	2.60	2.60	2.60	2.60
Louisiana	...	...	...	...	...	...	...	...	...	...	...	...
Maine	1.00	1.40	1.60	1.40-1.80	2.30	2.90	3.10	3.35	3.35	3.35	3.45	3.55(c)
Maryland	...	1.00 & 1.15	1.30	1.60	2.20 & 2.30	2.90	3.10	3.35	3.35	3.35	3.35	3.35
Massachusetts	1.25	1.60	1.60	1.75	2.10	2.90	3.10	3.35	3.35	3.35	3.35	3.35(c)
Michigan	1.00	1.25	1.25	1.60	2.20	2.90	3.10	3.35	3.35	3.35	3.35	3.35
Minnesota	.70-1.15(b)	.70-1.15(b)	.70-1.15(b)	.75-1.60	1.80	2.30	2.90	3.10	3.35	3.35	3.35	3.35
Mississippi	...	...	...	...	...	...	...	...	...	...	...	...
Missouri	...	...	...	...	...	...	...	...	...	...	...	...
Montana	...	1.00	1.00	1.00	1.80	2.00	2.00	2.00	2.75	2.75	2.75	3.05(c)
Nebraska	1.15(b)	1.25	1.30	1.00	1.60	1.60	1.60	1.60	1.60	1.60	1.60	1.60
Nevada	1.25	1.25	1.45-1.60	1.60	2.20 & 2.30	2.75	2.75	2.75	2.75	2.75	2.75	2.75
New Hampshire	1.25	1.40	1.45-1.60	1.60	2.20-2.30	2.90	3.10	3.35	3.35	3.35	3.35	3.35
New Jersey	1.00-1.50(b)	1.40	1.50	1.50	2.20	2.50	3.10	3.35	3.35	3.35	3.35	3.35

CHANGES IN BASIC MINIMUM WAGE—Continued

State or other jurisdiction	1965(a)	1968(a)	1970(a)	1972	1976(a)	1979	1980	1981	1983	1984	1985	1986
New Mexico	.70-.80	1.15-1.40	1.30-1.60	1.30-1.60	2.00	2.30	2.65	2.90	3.35	3.35	3.35	3.35
New York	1.25	1.60	1.60	1.85	2.30	2.90	3.10	3.35	3.35	3.35	3.35	3.35
North Carolina	.85	1.00	1.25	1.45	2.00	2.50	2.75	2.90	3.35	3.35	3.35	3.35
North Dakota	.75-.85(b)	1.00-1.25	1.00-1.45	1.00-1.45	2.00-2.20	2.10-2.30	2.60-3.10	2.80-3.10	2.80-3.10	2.80-3.10	2.80-3.10	2.80-3.10
Ohio	.70-1.00(b)	.75-1.25(b)	.75-1.25(b)	.75-1.25(b)	1.60	2.30	2.30	2.30	2.30	2.30	2.30	2.30
Oklahoma	...	1.00	1.00	1.40	1.80	2.00	2.00	3.10	3.10	3.10	3.10	3.35
Oregon	.75-1.00	1.25	1.25	1.25	2.30	2.30	2.90	3.10	3.10	3.35	3.35	3.35
Pennsylvania	1.00	1.15	1.30	1.60	2.20	2.90	3.10	3.35	3.35	3.35	3.35	3.35
Rhode Island	1.25	1.40	1.60	1.60	2.30	2.30	2.65	2.90	3.35	3.35	3.35	3.35
South Carolina	...	...	...	...	...	...	...	...	...	...	...	...
South Dakota	17.00-20.00/wk.(b)	17.00-20.00/wk.	1.00	1.00	2.00	2.30	2.30	2.30	2.80	2.80	2.80	2.80
Tennessee	...	...	...	1.40	1.40	1.40	1.40	1.40	1.40	1.40	1.40	1.40
Utah	.95-1.10(b)	1.00-1.15(b)	1.00-1.15(b)	1.20-1.35(b)	1.55-1.70(b)	2.20-2.45(b)	2.35-2.60(b)	2.50-2.75(b)	2.50-2.75(b)	2.50-2.75(b)	2.50-2.75(b)	2.50-2.75(b)
Vermont	1.00	1.40	1.60	1.60	2.30	2.90	3.10	3.35	3.35	3.35	3.35	3.35(c)
Virginia	...	...	...	...	2.00	2.35	2.35	2.65	2.65	2.65	2.65	2.65
Washington	1.25	1.60	1.60	1.60	2.20-2.30	2.30	2.30	2.30	2.30	2.30	2.30	2.30
West Virginia	1.00	1.00	1.00	1.20	2.00	2.20	2.20	2.75	3.05	3.05	3.05	3.05
Wisconsin	1.00-1.10(b)	1.25(b)	1.30(b)	1.45(b)	2.10	2.80	3.00	3.25	3.25	3.25	3.25	3.25
Wyoming	.75	1.20	1.30	1.50	1.60	1.60	1.60	1.60	1.60	1.60	1.60	1.60
Dist. of Col.	40.00-46.00/wk.(b)	1.25-1.40	1.60-2.00	1.60-2.25	2.25-2.75	2.46-3.00	2.50-3.50	2.50-3.75	2.90-3.90	3.50-3.90	3.50-3.90	3.50-3.95
Puerto Rico	.35-1.25	.43-1.60	.43-1.60	.65-1.60	.76-2.50	1.20-2.50	1.20-2.50	1.20-3.10	1.20-3.35	1.20-3.35	1.20-3.35	1.20-3.35

Source: Prepared by the Division of State Employment Standards Programs, Office of State Liaison and Legislative Analysis, Employment Standards Administration, U.S. Department of Labor.

Note: Rates are for January 1 of each year, except in 1968 and 1972 which show rates as of February. The rates are per hour unless otherwise indicated. A range of rates, as in North Dakota and a few other states, reflects rates which differ by industry, occupation, geographic zone or other factors, as established under wage-board type laws or by statute.

(a) Under the federal Fair Labor Standards Act (FLSA), the two rates shown in 1965, 1968, 1970, and 1976 reflect the former multiple-track minimum wage system in effect from 1961 to 1978. The lower rate applied to newly-covered persons brought under the act by amendments, whose rates were gradually phased in. A similar dual-track system was also in effect in certain years under the laws in Connecticut, Maryland and Nevada.

(b) The law applies only to women and minors.

(c) Scheduled future increases have been enacted in Maine, Massachusetts, Montana, and Vermont. The rate in Maine is scheduled to increase to $3.65 per hour January 1, 1987; the rate in Massachusetts is scheduled to rise to $3.55 on July 1, 1986, to $3.65 on July 1, 1987, and to $3.75 on July 1, 1988; the rate in Montana will increase to $3.35 on October 1, 1986; and the rate in Vermont will increase to $3.45 on July 1, 1986, to $3.55 on July 1, 1987, and to $3.65 on July 1, 1988. Legislation enacted in early 1986 will raise the rates to $3.35 per hour in Kentucky (effective July 15, 1986) and in West Virginia (effective January 1, 1987).

STATE REGULATION OF OCCUPATIONS AND PROFESSIONS

By Frances Stokes Berry

Deciding When To Regulate

Over 800 occupations and professions are licensed in the states today. Only about 60, however, are licensed in common by the majority of states. (See Table 8.28 for information on the principal health professions regulated by the states.)

Occupational licensure is an exercise of the state's inherent police power to protect the health, safety, and welfare of its citizens. Five generally-accepted criteria indicate when licensure is appropriate: (1) unregulated practice of the occupation poses a serious risk to a consumer's life, health, safety, or economic well-being, and the potential for harm is recognizable and likely to occur; (2) the practice of the occupation requires a high degree of skill, knowledge, and training; (3) the functions and responsibilities of the practitioner require independent judgment and the members of the occupational group practice independently; (4) the scope-of-practice of the occupation is distinguishable from other licensed and unlicensed occupations; (5) the economic impact on the public of regulating this occupational group is justified. Generally, failure to meet these criteria indicates that licensure is not justified, or that some less restrictive type of regulation—such as registration or certification—may be appropriate.[1]

Occupational and professional groups seek licensure for many reasons. Licensure offers an opportunity for increased status for the practitioners, is sometimes a prerequisite for third-party reimbursement, and offers mechanisms for keeping unqualified or unscrupulous practitioners from engaging in the occupations or professions. Professional groups usually draft legislation providing for regulation of the profession, and then attempt to convince legislators of the utility of that regulation.

The benefits of protecting the public from incompetent practitioners are not without some negative side effects, however. Licensure laws frequently place restrictions on advertising and on various business structures and practices. By restricting the number of people entering a profession and the ability of new professions to work independently, licensure may increase the cost of some professional services for consumers. The mobility of practitioners has been hampered, and in many fields auxiliaries have been underused. Licensure often focuses on testing applicants for the initial license, and is less concerned about the competence and performance of practitioners after the license is granted.

As a result of the growth in the number of allied health professions over the past two decades, each year state legislatures are approached by numerous occupations requesting state regulation. In the last five years, seven states have instituted formal "sunrise" processes. Under sunrise programs, a legislative or legislatively-created body reviews applications for requests for state regulation from representatives of unregulated occupations. Generally, the process includes a series of questions designed to measure the costs and benefits of, and the need for, regulation. The reviewing body then recommends to the legislature whether regulation (and what type of regulation) is appropriate.[2]

Sunset

First proposed by Colorado in 1976 and later enacted in 38 states, sunset's unique feature is an automatic termination provision for boards and agencies—unless the legislature takes positive measures to reenact them. Without exception, state sunset laws have included occupational and professional licensing boards in their review cycles.

Many people believed sunset would lead to the wholesale deregulation of the professions, but that did not occur. Only a few occupational and professional licensing boards have been terminated under sunset, and in almost every case, state regulation has been reinstated within a few years.

Frances Stokes Berry is Director of the Center for Health and Regulation at The Council of State Governments.

While administrative and structural reforms were more common outcomes of sunset performance reviews, sunset laws themselves have come under fire by state legislatures as being unnecessary or ineffective. Mississippi, Nebraska, and North Carolina repealed their sunset laws. Other states, such as Kansas and Illinois, essentially have inactivated the sunset reviews while leaving the laws on the books. Still other states (for example, Connecticut and New Hampshire) have completed the initial review of occupational and professional licensing boards and will not resume another cycle of reviews until the late 1980s. (See Table 3.25, for a summary of sunset legislation in the states.)

Strengthening Enforcement

At the state and federal level, the issue of incompetent practitioners—how to find them and how to deal with them—has emerged as a number one priority for state legislators and regulators. Legislatures are providing increased funding for enforcement functions.

Practice acts are being amended to expand disciplinary sanctions (beyond suspension and revocation) available to regulators. The most common additional sanctions include administrative fines, reprimand, and probation.

State licensing boards increasingly are developing policies on dealing with practitioners who abuse drugs or alchohol—referring abusers to treatment programs for rehabilitation when possible, and tracking practitioners' successes and failures after treatment.

In 1984, investigative reporting series in leading national newspapers across the country drew attention to state licensing responsibilities. *The New York Times*, for instance, gave extensive coverage to the cases involving individuals who purchased phony medical degrees from Caribbean medical schools. It is estimated that there may be as many as 10,000 persons practicing medicine as hospital residents or licensed physicians with these fraudulently-obtained medical degrees. State medical boards and central licensing agencies (especially in high-problem states such as California, Florida, and New York) have developed detailed procedures for checking individual credentials and the legitimacy of non-American medical schools.

Examinations

State regulators are aware that there are well-documented professional and legal standards which a licensing exam must meet. For example, one set of legal standards is contained in the equal employment opportunity guidelines. The licensing exam must be job-related, and preferably, based on an empirically-conducted job analysis. The exam must be reliable, according to statistical procedures, and the exam's cutoff scores (which determine whether a person passes or fails the exam) must be established using accepted criteria.

Since licensing board members may not have the expertise to independently develop and administer licensing examinations, more and more states are establishing a central testing office staffed by exam specialists to assist board members. These specialists are using nationally-developed licensing exams to provide some assurance that the exam is developed properly.

A recent U.S. Supreme Court case involved an examination issue. In *Hoover v. Ronwin* (1984), an unsuccessful candidate for admission to the Arizona Bar sued members of the Committee on Examinations and Admissions, charging that the bar examiners established a cutoff score at an artificially high level in order to exclude competitors of current Arizona lawyers, rather than to protect the public against incompetent practitioners.

The Court ruled that the particular bar examiners were immune from suit under federal antitrust law, but said its finding was limited to the bar examiners and would not necessarily apply to health and other regulatory boards.

Organization of Licensure Boards

Historically, most licensure boards have been autonomous.[3] Over 35 states have established a central agency for some or all licensure boards. Often, the health boards are organized in an agency separate from the non-health boards.

However, central agencies differ widely in their statutorily-mandated responsibilities, and the extent of the authority exercised over board decisions.[4] In a majority of states, the central agency is responsible for administrative functions—such as processing applications, issuing licenses, record keeping, fee collection, and routine correspondence—while the boards continue to exercise primary policymaking powers—such as conducting examinations, exercising disciplinary authority, and drafting administrative regulations. In other states, such as Connecticut, Florida, Illinois, and New York, the central agency's powers extend to authority over board personnel, budget, investigations, and examinations.

The trend since the late 1970s to centralize administrative services for licensing boards continues, although at a reduced pace since 1983. In 1984, Indiana and New Mexico established central agencies; other states, such as Maine, are bringing additional boards into already-established agencies.

The composition of licensure boards is changing as well. Traditionally, boards have been comprised exclusively of members of the regulated profession. Most states now place one or more public members on licensure boards. The California Public Members Act requires that boards be made up of a majority of lay members; health and accountancy boards are to have one-third lay members. A related trend is the addition of practitioners who are specialists or auxiliaries to the profession regulated by the board—for example, the addition of a dental hygienist to a board of dentistry.

While states continue to add public members to licensing boards, the debate continues as to whether public members are effective. A Michigan study found public members had limited impact on licensing policies and procedures.[5]

Opponents of the trend toward centralization of licensure contend that it adds to bureaucracy and red tape, and reduces the responsiveness of the licensure authority to both licensee needs and citizen complaints. Further, they argue that individual licensure boards with professional members best understand the issues of examinations, professional practice, and discipline.

Exchanging Information

Responding to the expressed need for a forum to share information and discuss common problems, state licensing officials formed the National Clearinghouse on Licensure, Enforcement and Regulation (CLEAR) in 1980.

CLEAR, with staff support from The Council of State Governments, maintains an information library on state licensing practices and procedures. Sixteen publications provide comparative state information on model investigative practices, licensing structures, sunset audits, public membership, and financing patterns. An annual national conference, regional meetings, and a newsletter provide forums for information exchange on mutual problems and innovative solutions.

In response to the states' need for enforcement information, CLEAR has established the National Disciplinary Information System, which provides information to states on disciplinary actions taken by states against licensed practitioners.

Notes

1. "Licensure" is the most restrictive form of state regulation. Under licensure laws, it is illegal for a person to practice a profession without first meeting the standards imposed by the state. Under "certification," the state grants title protection to persons meeting predetermined standards. Those without the title may perform the services of the occupation, but may not use the title. "Registration," the least restrictive form of regulation, usually takes the form of requiring a person to file his name, address, and qualifications with a government agency before practicing the occupation. For further information on the types of regulation and the questions to answer in deciding among them, see *Occupational Licensing: Questions a Legislator Should Ask* (Lexington, Ky.: The Council of State Governments, 1978).

2. For detailed information on state sunrise programs, see *State Sunrise Programs: Deciding When to Regulate Occupations* (Lexington, Ky.: The Council of State Governments, 1986).

3. For a brief description of the regulatory system and a cogent discussion of key occupational licensing issues, see Benjamin Shimberg, *Occupational Licensing, A Public Perspective* (Princeton, N.J.: Educational Testing Service, 1982).

4. See *Centralizing State Licensing Functions* (Lexington, Ky.: The Council of State Governments, 1980).

5. See "A Report on the Role and Effectiveness of Public Members on Licensing Boards," Michigan Department of Licensing and Regulation, 1980.

Table 8.28
STATE REGULATION OF HEALTH OCCUPATIONS AND PROFESSIONS

State or other jurisdiction	Acupuncturist	Audiologist/speech pathologist	Chiropractor	Counselor (pastoral, guidance) family & marriage	Dentist	Denturist	Dietician	Emergency medical technician	Hearing aid dealer/fitter	Licensed practical nurse (LPN)	Registered nurse (RN)	Nurse midwife	Nurse practitioner	Medical lab technologist/technician	Nuclear medicine technologist
Alabama	...	L	L	L	L	...	C	L	L	L	L	C	C	...	...
Alaska	L	...	L	...	L	...	...	L	...	L	L	...	C	...	...
Arizona	C	...	L	...	L	C	...	L	L	L	L	C	C	...	...
Arkansas	...	L	L	L	L	...	...	L	L	L	L	C	C	...	...
California	L	L	L	L	L	...	C	L	L	L	L	C	C	L	...
Colorado	...	...	L	...	L	R	...	L	L	L	L	C	C	...	...
Connecticut	...	L	L	C	L	...	...	L	L	L	L	C	...	...	...
Delaware	...	L	L	...	L	...	...	L	L	L	L	C	C	...	...
Florida	L	L	L	L	L	...	...	L	L	L	L	C	C	L	...
Georgia	...	L	L	L	L	...	L	L	L	L	L	C	C	L	...
Hawaii	L	L	L	...	L	...	...	L	L	L	L	C	...	...	...
Idaho	...	...	L	L	L	L	...	L	L	L	L	C	C	...	...
Illinois	...	...	L	...	L	...	...	L	L	L	L	...	...	...	...
Indiana	...	L	L	...	L	...	...	L	L	L	L	C	...	...	...
Iowa	...	L	L	...	L	...	L	L	L	L	L	C	C	...	...
Kansas	...	...	L	...	L	...	...	L	L	L	L	C	C	...	...
Kentucky	..	L	L	...	L	...	...	L	L	L	L	C	C	...	...
Louisiana	C	L	L	...	L	...	C	L	L	L	L	C	C	...	...
Maine	...	L	L	R	L	L	...	L	L	L	L	C	C	...	L
Maryland	R	L	L	C	L	...	L	L	L	L	L	C	C	...	...
Massachusetts	...	L	L	...	L	...	...	L	...	L	L	C	C	...	...
Michigan	...	...	L	R	L	...	...	L	L	L	L	C	C	...	...
Minnesota	...	...	L	...	L	...	...	L	L	L	L	...	...	...	...
Mississippi	...	L	L	...	L	...	...	L	L	L	L	C	C	...	...
Missouri	...	L	L	...	L	...	...	L	L	L	L	...	...	...	...
Montana	L	L	L	L	L	L	C	L	L	L	L	C	C	...	...
Nebraska	...	L	L	...	L	...	...	L	L	L	L	C	C	...	...
Nevada	L	L	L	C	L	...	...	L	L	L	L	C	C	...	...
New Hampshire	..	...	L	C	L	...	...	L	L	L	L	C	C	...	...
New Jersey	L	L	L	L	L	...	...	L	L	L	L	C	C	...	L
New Mexico	L	L	L	...	L	...	...	L	L	L	L	C	C	...	...
New York	L	L	L	...	L	...	...	L	R	L	L	C	...	...	...
North Carolina	...	L	L	C	L	...	...	L	L	L	L	C	C	...	...
North Dakota	...	L	L	...	L	...	L	L	L	L	L	...	C	...	...
Ohio	...	L	L	L	L	...	...	L	L	L	L	C	...	...	...
Oklahoma	...	L	L	...	L	...	L	L	L	L	L	C	C	...	...
Oregon	L	L	L	...	L	C	...	L	L	L	L	C	C	...	...
Pennsylvania	...	L	L	...	L	...	...	L	L	L	L	C	C	...	...
Rhode Island	L	L	L	...	L	...	...	L	L	L	L	C	...	...	...
South Carolina	...	L	L	L	L	...	...	L	L	L	L	C	C	...	...
South Dakota	R	...	L	...	L	...	...	L	L	L	L	C	C	...	...
Tennessee	...	L	L	C	L	...	...	L	L	L	L	C	C	L	...
Texas	...	L	L	L	L	...	L	L	L	L	L	C	C	...	...
Utah	L	L	L	L	L	...	...	L	L	L	L	C	C	...	...
Vermont	...	...	L	...	L	...	...	L	...	L	L	C	C	...	...
Virginia	L	L	L	L/C	L	...	...	L	L	L	L	C	C	...	...
Washington	L	...	L	...	L	...	...	L	L	L	L	C	C	...	...
West Virginia	R	...	L	...	L	...	...	L	L	L	L	C	...	...	...
Wisconsin	...	...	L	...	L	...	...	L	L	L	L	C	...	...	...
Wyoming	...	L	L	...	L	...	...	L	L	L	L	C	C	...	...
Dist. of Col.	...	...	L	...	L	...	...	L	...	L	L	...	...	...	...
Guam	...	...	...	...	...	...	...	...	L	...	...	...	...	...	...
Puerto Rico	...	...	L	...	L	...	L	...	...	L	L	...	...	...	...
Virgin Islands	...	...	...	...	L	...	...	...	...	L	...	...	...	...	...

Source: Health Professions Licensure Information System, December 1984.

Note: In cases of dual designation (e.g., L/R), state has both types of regulation.

Key:
L—Licensure
C—Certification
R—Registration
. . .—State does not regulate.

State or other jurisdiction	Nursing home administrator	Occupational therapist	Physical therapist	Optician	Optometrist	Pharmacist	Physician (MD, DO)	Physician's assistant	Podiatrist	Psychologist	Radiologic technologist/technician	Respiratory therapist	Sanitarian	Social worker	Veterinarian
Alabama	L	...	L	...	L	L	L	C	L	L	...	...	...	L	L
Alaska	L	...	L	L	L	L	L	C	L	L	...	...	R	...	L
Arizona	L	...	L	L	L	L	L	C	L	C	L	...	R	L	L
Arkansas	L	L	L	L	L	L	L	C	L	L	...	L	R	L	L
California	L	C	L	L	L	L	L	L	L	L	L	R/C	R	L	L
Colorado	L	...	L	...	L	L	L	C	L	L	...	...	...	L/R	L
Connecticut	L	L	L	L	L	L	L	C	L	L	...	...	R	...	L
Delaware	L	...	L	...	L	L	...	...	L	L	(a)	...	...	L	L
Florida	L	L	L	L	L	L	L	C	L	L	L	L	R	L	L
Georgia	L	L	L	L	L	L	L	C	L	L	...	...	R	L	L
Hawaii	L	C	L	L	L	L	L	C	L	L	L	...	R	...	L
Idaho	L	...	L	...	L	L	L	C	L	L	...	...	R	L	L
Illinois	L	L	L	...	L	L	L	C	L	C	L	...	...	R	L
Indiana	L	...	L	...	L	L	L	C	L	C	L	...	R	...	L
Iowa	L	L	L	C	L	L	L	C	L	L	(a)	C	...	L	L
Kansas	L	...	R	...	L	L	L	C	L	C	...	...	R	L	L
Kentucky	L	...	L	L	L	L	L	...	L	L	L	...	R	L	L
Louisiana	L	...	L	...	L	L	L	C	L	C	...	L	R	L	L
Maine	L	L	L	...	L	L	L	C	L	L	(a)	L	...	R	L
Maryland	L	L	L	...	L	L	L	C	L	L	...	...	R	L	L
Massachusetts	L	L	L	L	L	L	L	C	L	L	...	...	R	L	L
Michigan	L	...	L	...	L	L	L	L	L	L	...	...	R	R	L
Minnesota	L	...	R	...	L	L	L	...	L	L	(a)	...	R	...	L
Mississippi	L	...	L	...	L	L	L	...	L	L	...	...	R	...	L
Missouri	L	...	L	...	L	L	L	...	L	L	...	...	R	...	L
Montana	L	L	L	...	L	L	L	...	L	L	L	...	R	L	L
Nebraska	L	L	L	...	L	L	L	C	L	L	...	...	R	...	L
Nevada	L	...	L	L	L	L	L	C	L	L	...	...	R	...	L
New Hampshire	L	L	L	...	L	L	L	C	L	C	...	...	...	C	L
New Jersey	L	...	L	L	L	L	L	...	L	L	L	...	...	...	L
New Mexico	L	L	L	...	L	L	L	C	L	C	(a)	L	...	...	L
New York	L	L	L	L	L	L	L	R	L	L	L	...	R	L	L
North Carolina	L	L	L	L	L	L	L	(b)	L	L	...	...	R	C	L
North Dakota	L	L	L	L	L	L	L	C	L	L	...	L	...	L	L
Ohio	L	L	L	L	L	L	L	C	L	L	...	...	R	L/R	L
Oklahoma	L	L	L	...	L	L	L	C	L	L	...	...	R	L	L
Oregon	L	L	L	...	L	L	L	C	L	L	L	...	R	R	L
Pennsylvania	L	L	L	...	L	L	L	C	L	L	...	...	...	R	L
Rhode Island	L	L	L	L	L	L	L	C	L	C	...	...	R	R	L
South Carolina	L	L	L	L	L	L	L	C	L	L	...	...	R	R	L
South Dakota	L	L	L	...	L	L	L	C	L	L	...	...	R	L	L
Tennessee	L	L	L	L	L	L	L	...	L	L	(a)	...	R	L	L
Texas	L	L	L	...	L	L	L	...	L	L	...	L	R	L/C	L
Utah	L	L	L	...	L	L	L	C	L	L	...	...	R	L	L
Vermont	L	...	L	L	L	L	L	C	L	L	L	...	...	...	L
Virginia	L	...	L	L	L	L	L	(b)	L	L	...	(c)	...	L	L
Washington	L	L	L	L	L	L	L	C	L	L	...	...	R	L	L
West Virginia	L	L	L	...	L	L	L	C	L	L	L	...	R	L	L
Wisconsin	L	...	L	...	L	L	L	C	L	L	...	...	R	...	L
Wyoming	L	...	L	...	L	L	L	(b)	L	L	...	...	...	...	L
Dist. of Col.	L	L	L	...	L	L	L	...	L	L	...	...	...	...	L
Guam	...	...	...	...	L	...	L	...	...	...	...	...	...	...	...
Puerto Rico	...	L	L	L	L	L	...	...	L	L	...	...	...	...	L
Virgin Islands	...	...	...	...	L	...	L	...	...	...	...	...	...	...	L

Key:
L—Licensure
C—Certification
R—Registration
. . .—State does not regulate.

(a) Enabling legislation.
(b) Board approval submitted by physicians.
(c) Voluntary certification.

STATE HEALTH AGENCY PROGRAMS

By Michael Barry and Sue Madden

The American public health system is a partnership of federal, state, and local agencies; together, these agencies provide a wide range of preventive and curative health services aimed at protecting and improving the health and well-being of the entire U.S. population.

Within each state, the District of Columbia, and the U.S. territories, the primary responsibility for ensuring public health has been vested in a single state-level agency. Generally, these state health agencies (SHAs) are responsible for setting statewide priorities, carrying out national and state mandates, responding to disease outbreaks and other health hazards, controlling the spread of infectious diseases, and assuring access to health care for underserved residents. As advocates and providers of preventive health services, and as providers of care to the medically indigent, SHAs play a unique and important role in the American health care system.

The following is an overview of the organization, responsibilities, services, expenditures, funding sources, and staffs of 50 of the nation's SHAs during fiscal year 1983.[1]

State Health Agency Organization and Responsibilities

Each state health agency is headed by a health commissioner or director, who is appointed by the governor, state legislature, or state board of health. The organization of public health services in a state affects how services are delivered, and to an extent, which services are provided. While some generalizations about public health organizations are possible, there is considerable variation from state to state.

The organizational structure of SHAs may be characterized by two models: (1) a free-standing, independent agency responsible directly to the governor or a board of health; or (2) one component of a superagency structure. Of the 50 reporting SHAs, 30 follow the first model, while 20 agencies follow the second (see Table 8.29).

Variations in the SHAs' organizational structure are reflected in the range of their designated responsibilities. Of the SHAs reporting for fiscal year 1983:

- 38 SHAs were the designated State Crippled Children's Agency (Title V, SSA);
- 10 SHAs were the designated State Mental Health Authority (PL 94-63);
- Nine SHAs were the designated Medicaid Single State Agency (Title XIX, SSA);
- 28 SHAs were the designated State Health Planning and Development Agency (PL 93-641);
- 13 SHAs acted as the lead environmental agency in their states; and
- 20 SHAs operated hospitals or other health care institutions.

State Health Agency Services

Despite differences in their structures and responsibilities, many SHAs share common features. Nearly all offer services related to maternal and child health, communicable disease control (including sexually-transmitted diseases, tuberculosis, and vaccine-preventable diseases), chronic diseases (such as cancer and hypertension), dental health, public health nursing (including home visits), nutrition, health education, consumer protection and sanitation, water quality, health statistics, and diagnostic laboratory tests.

In fiscal year 1983, the 50 reporting SHAs provided direct personal health services to 71 million people—nearly three in every 10 in the U.S. Table 8.30 displays the number of persons receiving direct services from SHAs. During the year, the agencies demonstrated their strong commitment to health promotion and disease prevention by:

- Preventing communicable diseases among preschool and school age children and influenza among the elderly and other high risk populations through the immunization of nearly 10 million people;

Michael Barry is Statistical Assistant and Sue Madden is Program Director, ASTHO Reporting System, Public Health Foundation.

- Using quick, effective, and low-cost screening techniques for the detection and prevention of disease among nearly 45 million people, including the screening of 15 million for sexually-transmitted diseases, 11 million for visual accuity, 8 million for hearing acuity, 7 million for nutritional status, 3 million for dental disease, and 3 million for tuberculosis;
- Making 1.4 million inspections of restaurants and other food-related facilities to ensure the availability of wholesome, unadulterated food and milk products;
- Reviewing over 75,500 design specifications for water supply facilities and issuing 152,900 licenses, registrations, and permits for treatment facilities, water supply sources, storage tanks, and line extensions;
- Preventing human exposure to toxic chemicals through 13,000 field inspections of solid and hazardous waste disposal sites;
- Collecting vital records and health statistics to provide essential population-based information on the health and demographic characteristics of communities and states;
- Fluoridating community water supplies to prevent tooth decay;
- Preventing and responding to disease outbreaks using epidemiologic methods, including disease surveillance;
- Training nearly 2,400 persons to respond to environmental emergencies caused by hazardous chemicals, radiation exposure, and contaminated air, water, and food;
- Analyzing 23 million laboratory samples and specimens to prevent and detect disease and identify environmental contaminants; and,
- Detecting and promoting control of hypertension by screening nearly 7 million people for high blood pressure (and for those SHAs able to provide the data), diagnosing nearly 5 percent as hypertensive. Public health agencies often provided follow-up services to those requiring treatment, including nutritional counseling.

Expenditures

In fiscal year 1983, the nation's state health agencies spent $5.4 billion[2] for their public health programs. SHA expenditures ranged from $7.6 million in American Samoa

to $591.5 million in California. A number of factors—including variation in state populations and differences in the responsibilities of these agencies—account for the tremendous range in SHA public health expenditures. Some SHAs are responsible only for such traditional public health services as communicable disease control, general sanitation, maternal and child health, and vital statistics; others have additional responsibilities, such as the provision of mental health services and the operation of hospitals. Moreover, the balance of responsibility for public health services between state and local governments varies greatly among the states.

Of the $5.4 billion in SHA expenditures, $3.99 billion (73 percent) was spent for personal health programs, including $936 million for the SHA-operated institutions in 20 states. Expenditures for health resources programs were $530 million (10 percent of the total); for environmental health programs, $350 million (6 percent); for laboratory programs, $585 million (11 percent); and for general administration, $318 million (6 percent). The remaining $76 million was reported as "funds to local health departments not allocated to program areas" (see Table 8.31 for state-by-state detail).

The Public Health Foundation estimates that SHAs spent $1.1 billion for hospital and other institutional inpatient services. This amount included $899 million spent for inpatient care in SHA-operated institutions, as well as $203 million for inpatient care services purchased from institutions other than those operated by the SHA. The $1.1 billion in purchased and SHA-provided inpatient care accounted for 24 percent of all personal health expenditures.

Sources of Funds

State health agencies are funded primarily by state, federal, and local governments. Additional funding is collected from fees and reimbursements for services and other sources such as foundation grants. Typically, state funds include both the required match for federal grants and general revenue support of state programs. State funding provides the core of support for public health programs. Of the $5.4 billion spent by the 50 reporting SHAs in fiscal year 1983, $3.03 billion (56 percent of the total) came from state funds. Federal grants and contracts, excluding direct federal assistance provided in lieu of cash, accounted for $1.95 billion (36 percent) of the total. Funds from local sources, fees, reimbursements, and other sources made up the remaining 8 percent (see Table A below and Table 8.32).

Of the $1.95 billion in federal grant and contract funds spent by the SHAs, over half came from the U.S. Department of Agriculture's Special Supplemental Food Program for Women, Infants, and Children (USDA-WIC). Although administered by the SHAs, WIC is primarily a food distribution program. Grants and contracts from the Department of Health and Human Services (DHHS) accounted for 42 percent of the federal funds spent by SHAs, with the remaining 6 percent from the Environmental Protection Agency, the Departments of Labor and Transportation, and other federal agencies. As shown in Table B, when USDA-WIC funds are excluded from total SHA expenditures, the proportion of 1983 SHA expenditures represented by federal grant and contract funds drops from 36 to 21 percent.

Among the federal grants for public health administered by DHHS, the Maternal and Child Health Services (MCH) and Preventive Health and Health Services (PHHS) block grants (created by the Omnibus Budget Reconciliation Act of 1981) are of special in-

terest. These two newly-created block grants encompassed 15 previously categorical grant programs. The 50 reporting SHAs spent a total of $338 million from block grant funds in 1983—$267 million from the MCH Block Grant and $71 million from the PHHS Block Grant.[3]

Nearly all of the MCH Block Grant funds were spent for personal health programs. The remaining 5 percent was distributed among health resources, environmental health, and laboratory programs and general administration. Of the SHAs' PHHS Block Grant Expenditures, 57 percent ($40.4 million) went for personal health programs; 21 percent ($15 million) for health resources programs; 12 percent for environmental health programs; 5 percent for laboratory programs; and 2 percent for general administration. The remaining 2 percent was reported as "funds provided to local health departments, but not allocable to program areas."

Variations in SHA Funding and Expenditures

The 48 SHAs reporting complete data for fiscal years 1982 and 1983 showed expenditures of $4.4 billion (excluding USDA-WIC funds) in 1983—an increase of 7.8 percent over 1982 expenditures for the same agencies.[4] The increase, however, was not re-

Table A
Expenditures of State Health Agencies By Source of Funds: Fiscal Year 1983

Source of funds	Expenditures	
	Amount (millions of dollars)	Percentage of total
Total	$5,446.7	100.0
State funds	3,027.1	55.6
Federal grant and contract funds	1,947.5	35.8
Local funds	124.3	2.3
Fees and reimbursements	249.7	4.6
Other sources	98.0	1.8

Table B
Expenditures of State Health Agencies (Excluding USDA-WIC Funds), By Source of Funds: Fiscal Year 1983

Source of funds	Expenditures	
	Amount, excluding USDA-WIC funds (millions of dollars)	Percentage of total
Total	$4,427.1	100.0
State funds	3,027.1	68.4
Federal grant and contract funds	927.9	21.0
Local funds	124.3	2.8
Fees and reimbursements	249.7	5.6
Other sources	98.0	2.2

flected evenly among the SHAs. Thirty-three reported overall expenditure increases and 15 reported decreases, ranging from a 32 percent increase in Iowa to an 11.1 percent decrease in Washington.

Among individual SHAs, there was great variation in the significance of federal grants and contracts as a source of funds for public health expenditures. For 11 SHAs (Colorado, Idaho, Kansas, Nebraska, New Jersey, New Hampshire, North Dakota, Ohio, Utah, Vermont, and Washington), federal funds were the source of more than 40 percent of total public health expenditures. For 10 (Alaska, Delaware, Hawaii, Kentucky, Maryland, Massachusetts, Virginia, West Virginia, Puerto Rico, and the Virgin Islands), these funds accounted for less than 15 percent of the total.

The $916 million in federal grant and contract funds spent by SHAs represents a 9.8 percent increase from 1982—again, an increase not reflected evenly among the SHAs. Between 1982 and 1983, changes in the amount of federal funds spent by SHAs ranged from an increase of 107.6 percent in Massachusetts to a decrease of 37.4 percent in the Virgin Islands.

State funding represented 68.4 percent of the total spent by all SHAs, with a range of 29.9 percent in Oregon to 95.6 percent in the Virgin Islands. For 10 SHAs, state funding represented more than 77 percent of total expenditures; for six agencies, less than 45.7 percent.

The $3 billion in state funds spent by the SHAs during 1983 represented a 6.2 percent increase from 1982. Like the increase in total expenditures and the increase in expenditures of federal funds, however, the aggregate increase in state funding was not evenly reflected among the individual SHAs. The change between 1982 and 1983 ranged from an increase of 58.5 percent in Iowa to a decrease of 23.7 percent in Washington.

Staffs of State Health Agencies

Forty-seven SHAs employed 108,100 full-time equivalent staff persons, as of the end of 1982.[5] The agencies varied greatly in total staff size—from a high of 15,100 in Puerto Rico to a low of 140 in Idaho. SHA staff per 10,000 population ranged from less than one in Illinois, Iowa, and Washington to 216 in the Virgin Islands.

As in the case of expenditures, variations in staff size reflect differences in SHA responsibilities, in division of responsibilities with local health departments, and in SHA organizational structure. The SHAs that operate institutions and those designated as mental health authorities generally had a higher ratio of total staff to population.

The five SHAs with the highest ratio of staff to population—in order of magnitude—were the Virgin Islands, American Samoa, Hawaii, Puerto Rico, and the District of Columbia.[6]

Trends and Projections in SHA Expenditures

Traditionally, SHAs have protected the public health through programs designed to control infectious diseases and to ensure the purity of food and water supplies. During the 1960s and 1970s, the SHAs experienced considerable expansion—nationwide disease prevention and health promotion initiatives were undertaken in such areas as hypertension and cancer control, genetic disease screening, air quality control, and hazardous waste management. The changing economic conditions of the early 1980s, however, have caused many SHAs to critically examine their public health priorities. A number of factors, including inflation, state and local tax and expenditure limitations, and cuts in federal aid have affected the SHAs' abilities to provide public health services.

Since 1979, total SHA expenditures have increased at an average rate of 11 percent

Table C
Expenditures of State Health Agencies: Fiscal Years 1979-1983
(in millions of dollars)

Fiscal year	Total expenditures	Adjusted for inflation	
		Total	Total (excluding USDA-WIC)
1979	$3,615	$3,615	$3,141
1980	4,378	3,832	3,256
1981	4,770	3,812	3,122
1982	5,004	3,741	3,089
1983	5,462	3,986	3,237

Table D
Inflation-Adjusted Expenditures of State Health Agencies
(Excluding USDA-WIC Funds), By Source of Funds, Fiscal Years 1979-1983*
(in millions of dollars)

Fiscal year	Total	State funds		Federal grant and contract funds		Local funds		Fees, reimbursements and other funds	
		Amount	Percent of total	Amount	Percent of total	Amount	Percent of total	Amount	Percent of total
1979	$3,141	$1,960	62.4	$805	25.6	$110	3.5	$266	8.5
1980	3,256	2,181	67.0	758	23.3	100	3.1	217	6.7
1981	3,123	2,093	67.0	692	22.2	96	3.1	241	7.8
1982	3,089	2,147	69.5	619	20.0	92	3.0	231	7.5
1983	3,251	2,223	68.4	669	20.6	94	2.8	274	8.2

*Expenditures are deflated to the equivalent of 1979 dollars. The rate of inflation is based on the "Consumer Price Index for Urban Wage Earners and Clerical Workers (CPI-W)," August 1984.

per year—from $3.6 billion in 1979 to $5.5 billion in 1983.[7] When adjusted for inflation using the overall Consumer Price Index, SHA expenditures (in constant dollars) increased at an average annual rate of approximately 2.5 percent from 1979 to 1983.[8]

Among the federal grant and contract funds spent by the SHAs, the single largest source of funding was the USDA-WIC. Large increases in this special categorical funding source masked some of the decline in resources available to the SHAs for broader public health purposes. If USDA-WIC funds are excluded, the remaining SHA expenditures, adjusted for inflation, increased at an average rate of less than 1 percent per year (see Table C).

As a percentage of total SHA expenditures, state funds represented the largest source during the period, accounting for at least 62 percent of the total in each of the five years (see Table D). State funds steadily increased as a percentage of total expenditures from 1979 to 1982, but then slightly decreased in 1983 for an overall net gain of 6 percentage points. Federal grant and contract funds accounted for the next largest portion of SHA expenditures, representing over 20 percent in each year. However, as a percentage of total expenditures, federal grant and contract funds declined from 25.6 percent in 1979 to 20.6 percent in 1983—nearly offsetting the 6 percentage point gain made by state funds. Local funds accounted for approximately 3 percent of all SHA expenditures in each of the five years, while fees, reimbursements, and other sources comprised the remaining 8 percent each year.

Based on the preceding analysis of the five-year period 1979-83, some projections can be made regarding future SHA spending and funding.

Total SHA expenditures for fiscal year 1984 are expected to run just under $6 billion, and by 1986, total expenditures should reach $8.5 billion. At this rate of increase, total SHA expenditures should reach $10 billion by 1993. Projected spending of USDA-WIC funds is expected to approximate $1.2 billion in 1984, $1.4 billion in 1986, and $2 billion by 1990. At the current pace, SHA spending of state funds should approximate $3.4 billion in 1984, $3.9 billion in 1986, and $4.9 billion by 1990. Agency spending of local funds is estimated to be $130 million in 1984, $138 million in 1986, and $154 million by 1990.

Notes

1. There are 57 state health agencies. The public health agencies in four states (Maine, Montana, New Mexico, and South Dakota) and three other jurisdictions (Guam, the Northern Mariana Islands, and the Trust Territory) did not provide complete data for fiscal year 1983. The data presented in this essay and accompanying tables were voluntarily submitted to the Public Health Foundation (formerly the ASTHO Foundation) by the SHAs.

For more complete information on specific programs, including state-by-state detail on services, expenditures, and sources of funds, see *Public Health Agencies* 1983, Vol. 1-4 (Kensington, Maryland: Association of State and Territorial Health Officials Foundation, 1985).

2. Including direct SHA expenditures and intergovernmental transfers to local health departments, but excluding SHA Medicaid expenditures.

3. The amount of block grant funds spent by the SHAs during their 1983 fiscal year was somewhat

less than the amount appropriated by Congress. One explanation for this is that the additional 1983 MCH Block Grant funds appropriated through the Emergency Job Appropriations Act were not available until late in the states' fiscal year. As a result, most of these funds were carried over for use in fiscal year 1984. Another reason is overlap between the budget periods of the block grants and the budget periods of many of the categorical programs that were included in the block grants. Because of this overlap, significant sums of federal fiscal year 1981 categorical funds were spent by the SHAs during their 1982 and 1983 fiscal periods. This enabled them to conserve a portion of their 1983 block grant allotments for expenditure the following year since, under PL 97-35, the states have two years in which to spend block grant funds.

4. The state health agencies in Wisconsin and American Samoa provided data for fiscal year 1983 only. These SHAs were excluded from the discussion.

USDA-WIC funds were excluded from this discussion of variations in SHA funding and expenditures for several reasons: (1) WIC is primarily a food distribution program; (2) expenditures of these grants totaled $1.02 billion in fiscal year 1983, an increase of 17.5 percent over 1982 expenditures; and (3) several SHAs did not expend any of these funds.

5. The public health agencies in four states (Maine, Montana, New Mexico, and South Dakota) and three other jurisdictions (Guam, the Northern Mariana Islands, and the Trust Territory) did not provide complete data for fiscal year 1983. The SHAs in three states (California, Ohio, and Oregon) did not report staffing data.

All counts of personnel include employees on the payroll of the SHA and contract workers as of December 31, 1982. The counts are based on full-time equivalents (40 hours per week or 2,080 hours per year).

6. The District of Columbia, the Virgin Islands, and American Samoa reported that no local health departments (LHDs) existed within their jurisdictions, and Hawaii and Puerto Rico reported the existence of only one LHD in each.

7. All expenditures contained in this analysis were obtained from data reported by the SHAs to the ASTHO Reporting System for each of the fiscal years 1979-83. The public health agencies in two states (Maine and Montana) and three other jurisdictions (American Samoa, Guam, and the Northern Mariana Islands) did not provide complete data for fiscal year 1983. For comparability, the expenditures of these five SHAs have been deleted from all analyses. Other minor adjustments have been made for comparability where necessary—e.g., change in program responsibilities during the reporting period. Complete documentation is available from the Public Health Foundation.

8. The adjustment for inflation was made by deflating 1983 expenditures to be equivalent in purchase power to 1979 dollars. The deflator used was based on June to June figures from the Consumer Price Index for Urban Wage Earners and Clerical Workers (CPI-W), U.S. Department of Labor, Bureau of Labor Statistics, August 1984.

Table 8.29
STATE HEALTH AGENCIES: ORGANIZATIONAL CHARACTERISTICS AND SELECTED PUBLIC HEALTH RESPONSIBILITIES—FISCAL 1983

State or other jurisdiction	Organizational structure		Responsibilities:					
	Freestanding independent agency	Component of superagency	State crippled children's agency (Title V, SSA)	Mental health authority (PL 94-63)	Medicaid single state agency (Title XIX, SSA)	State health planning & development agency (PL 93-641)	Lead environmental agency	Operates institutions
Total	30	20	38	10	8	28	13	20
Alabama	★	...	...	...	...	...	...	...
Alaska	...	★	★	...	...	...	...	...
Arizona	★	...	★	★	...	★	★	★
Arkansas	★	...	...	...	...	...	...	...
California	...	★	★	...	★	...	...	...
Colorado	★	...	★	...	...	★	★	...
Connecticut	★	...	★	...	...	★	...	★
Delaware	...	★	★	...	...	...	...	★
Florida	...	★	...	...	...	...	...	★
Georgia	...	★	★	...	...	...	...	...
Hawaii	★	...	★	★	...	★	★	★
Idaho	...	★	★	...	...	...	...	...
Illinois	★	...	...	...	...	★	...	...
Indiana	★	...	...	...	...	★	★	...
Iowa	★	...	...	...	...	★	...	...
Kansas	★	...	★	...	...	★	★	...
Kentucky	...	★	★	★	...	★	...	★
Louisiana	...	★	★	...	...	...	...	★
Maine(a)								
Maryland	★	...	★	★	...	★	★	★
Massachusetts	...	★	★	...	...	...	...	★
Michigan	★	...	★	...	...	...	...	★
Minnesota	★	...	★	...	...	...	...	...
Mississippi	★	...	★	...	...	...	...	...
Missouri	★	...	★	...	...	★	...	★
Montana(a)								
Nebraska	★	...	...	★	...	★	...	...
Nevada	...	★	★	...	...	...	...	...
New Hampshire	...	★	★	...	...	...	...	...
New Jersey	★	...	★	...	...	★	...	...
New Mexico(a)								
New York	★	...	★	...	...	★	...	★
North Carolina	...	★	★	...	...	...	...	★
North Dakota	★	...	...	...	...	★	★	...
Ohio	★	...	★	...	...	★	...	...
Oklahoma	★	...	...	...	...	...	★	...
Oregon	...	★	...	...	...	...	...	...
Pennsylvania	★	...	★	...	...	★	...	★
Rhode Island	★	...	★	...	...	★	...	...
South Carolina	★	...	★	...	...	★	★	★
South Dakota(a)								
Tennessee	★	...	★	...	★	...	★	...
Texas	★	...	★	...	...	★	...	★
Utah	★	...	★	...	★	★	★	...
Vermont	...	★	★	...	...	...	...	...
Virginia	★	...	★	...	★	★	...	...
Washington	...	★	★	...	...	★	...	...
West Virginia	★	...	...	★	...	★	★	★
Wisconsin	...	★	...	...	...	★	...	★
Wyoming	...	★	...	...	★	★	...	...
Dist. of Col.	...	★	★	★	★	...	...	★
American Samoa	★	...	★	★	★	★	...	★
Guam(a)								
No. Mariana Is.(a)								
Puerto Rico	★	...	★	★	★	...	...	★
Trust Territory(a)								
Virgin Islands	...	★	★	★	★	★	★	★

Source: Public Health Foundation, Washington, D.C.
Key:
★—Yes
...—No
(a) Not reporting.

Table 8.30
PERSONS RECEIVING SELECTED PERSONAL HEALTH SERVICES FROM STATE HEALTH AGENCIES: FISCAL 1983
(In thousands)

State or other jurisdiction	Receiving any service(a)	Health screening	Immuni-zation	Maternity services	Infant and child health ambulatory services	WIC food assistance	Family planning services	Genetic counseling	Dental services	Handi-capped children's ambulatory services
United States	70,901	45,118	9,721	628	1,871	4,894	3,794	39	1,984	466
Alabama............	1,045C	788E	242C	19C	51C	128C	83C	C	7	C
Alaska..............	384E	306E	134E	2	32	29	11	1	3	9
Arizona............	1,241E	922E	150E	22	24	78	21	U	5E	14
Arkansas	604E	415E	150	7C	44	39	41	0	1E	0
California..........	2,069	1,293	317	18	8	377	591	22	29	47
Colorado	260E	289E	–	2E	U	38	30	3	4E	7
Connecticut	679	369	221	2	7	70	1	1	–	3
Delaware	162E	110E	29	2	14	U	17	–	9	6
Florida............	3,227	3,022E	1,071	48	0	138	375	0	48	0
Georgia............	1,652E	1,530E	522E	43E	333	88	147	U	45	U
Hawaii	558E	291E	22	2	30	28	29	U	71	5
Idaho	257E	174	100	–	U	25	21	–	1E	3
Illinois	13,973	3,936	221	9	44	227	19	1	44	0
Indiana	532	444E	96	2	16	84	24	5E	4E	0
Iowa	384E	298E	54	6	9	59	25	2	5	0
Kansas	1,605E	1,176E	130	2E	64	38E	44	3E	138E	2
Kentucky	1,366E	991E	140	18	22	93	96	1	8	16
Louisiana	1,504E	1,120E	331E	30	85	128	81	U	8	16
Maine(b)...........										
Maryland	313E	197E	110	8	13	U	85	5	34	35
Massachusetts	2,062E	1,175E	741E	6	37E	48	8	1E	21E	7E
Michigan	1,710E	989E	564	U	U	130	97	1	–	8
Minnesota	1,588E	804E	13	26	49	107E	15	1	36	10
Mississippi	900E	853E	C	30	30	72	89C	0	3E	6C
Missouri	963E	643E	221	4	28	79	10	5	24	6
Montana(b)										
Nebraska	194E	136	–	4	3	20	27	2	–	0
Nevada	227E	181	46	1	1	23	5	U	3	2
New Hampshire	199E	105E	102	1	18	U	21	–	20	1
New Jersey.........	1,669E	1,371E	91	16	71	95	71	8	–	17
New Mexico(b)										
New York	1,448E	975C	453	U	1	200E	261	–	U	42
North Carolina	2,948E	1,332E	195	27	160E	901	141	9	44	4
North Dakota	219E	177E	32	0	0	13	24E	–	6	0
Ohio	2,795	2,199	467	12	62	162	103	U	2E	26
Oklahoma	993E	650E	123C	24E	85E	69	83E	–	5	0
Oregon	327E	171E	1	2	24	60	38C	U	26	0
Pennsylvania	4,353E	3,232E	650	45	38	196	20	9	595	73E
Rhode Island	303	296E	23E	2	5	2	12	2	1	3
South Carolina	778	561	255	10	82	197	99	0	4	6
South Dakota(b).....										
Tennessee..........	952E	726E	7E	27E	16E	80	159E	39E	7E	12
Texas..............	9,100	7,711	1,090	72	186	313	400	8	76	23
Utah	303E	339	4	1	9	20	9	1	1	6
Vermont	181E	143	4	1	3	22	15	–	26	5
Virginia............	1,133	686	114	U	6	135	84	1	55	16
Washington	730	592	U	34	69	68	88	4	5	5
West Virginia	1,055E	403E	325	5	25	32	78	2	6	11
Wisconsin..........	440E	377	47E	U	U	54	27	2E	26	0
Wyoming	404	44C	55	5	14	12	1	–	3E	2
Dist. of Col.	489E	238	18E	5E	50C	14	9E	–	20	10E
American Samoa	5	4	5	0	U	0	2	0	U	0
Guam(b)............										
No. Mariana Is.(b)...										
Puerto Rico	605E	319E	U	25	4	90	51	U	4	U
Trust Territory(b)										
Virgin Islands	13	16	32	2	U	11	6	0	U	3

Source: Public Health Foundation, Washington, D.C.
Key:
– —Less than 0.05 percent or less than 500.
E—Estimated.
C—Data combined with reporting of another service or program.
U—Data reported as unobtainable.

(a) Represents sum of estimated unduplicated counts for each reported program for each state health agency.
(b) Not reporting.

PERSONS RECEIVING SELECTED PERSONAL HEALTH SERVICES—Continued

State or other jurisdiction	Communicable disease ambulatory services			Chronic disease ambulatory services						
	Sexually transmitted diseases	Tuberculosis	Other	Cancer	Diabetes	Hypertension	Cardiovascular disease	Mental retardation	Renal dialysis	Other
United States	3,779	734	191	181	44	321	111	34	24	112
Alabama	77C	10C	C	C	C	2C	0	2	0	0
Alaska	72	15	1	1	2	U	0	1	0	–
Arizona	40	4	0	–	–	2	4	0	–	0
Arkansas	20E	U	3	1E	0	5E	0	0	0	0
California	820	–	U	U	U	U	U	0	U	U
Colorado	5	1	U	U	–	U	U	1	0	0
Connecticut	30	3	0	U	0	0	0	1	0	0
Delaware	6	1	0	–	U	U	U	0	–	6
Florida	150	77	0	0	6	3	–	0	–	9
Georgia	–	16	0	1	2	50	1E	0	–	0
Hawaii	6	18	2	–	–	U	1	5	–	1
Idaho	5	2	4	0	0	0	0	0	0	0
Illinois............	53	U	0	0	–	U	U	1	3	1
Indiana	24	6E	0	0	0	15	0	0	–	–
Iowa	7E	2	1	0	0	0	0	0	–	0
Kansas	–	5	4	U	U	–	–	U	–	–
Kentucky	18	54	86	–	5	22E	–	9E	0	1E
Louisiana	30	5	3E	0	0	0	0	U	0	–
Maine(b)										
Maryland	31	6	8	2	0	–	0	5E	2	2
Massachusetts	43	8E	0	–E	0	–	–C	0	–E	–E
Michigan	115	24	0	U	2E	0	0	U	0	0
Minnesota	26	19	74	5	5	0	69	1	0	28
Mississippi	13	8	0	1	4	12	2	0	0	0
Missouri	56	6	0	0	–	17	U	U	0	–
Montana(b)										
Nebraska	3	U	0	0	0	0	0	0	–	0
Nevada	25	10	U	–	–	–	–	U	0	–
New Hampshire	2	–	0	–	U	U	–	0	–	–
New Jersey..........	50	5	0	U	0	0	0	0	3	–
New Mexico(b)										
New York	890	7	0	1	–	U	3	0	U	–
North Carolina	58	260	U	2	–	22	–	U	–	2
North Dakota	2	0	–	0	0	0	0	0	0	0
Ohio	81	0	0	–E	–E	5	U	0	U	1E
Oklahoma	49C	9C	1	C	–C	–C	U	–	0	11E
Oregon	20	1	1	0	0	U	0	0	0	0
Pennsylvania	49E	16	–	6	8	–	12	–	5	8
Rhode Island	7	2E	–	–	–	U	1	1	–C	–
South Carolina	19	10	0	5	0	0	–	0	–	U
South Dakota(b)										
Tennessee	94E	U	0	U	U	U	U	–	1	4
Texas..............	192	57	0	2	3	–	11	1	6	29
Utah	10	2	–	U	–	–	U	–	0	–
Vermont	–	2	–	–	–	0	–	–	0	–
Virginia............	46	11	1	0	0	7	2	0	0	–
Washington	54	7	0	0	–	U	0	0	–	2
West Virginia	10	35	U	0	3	4	1	7	–	5
Wisconsin	15	U	0	0	0	144	0	0	1	–
Wyoming	6	1	U	–	0	0	1	–	–	0
Dist. of Col.	–E	2E	0	0	0	0	0	–	0	0
American Samoa	–	0	–	–	0	–	0	–	–	0
Guam(b)										
No. Mariana Is.(b) ...										
Puerto Rico	50	–	–	154	–	–	–	U	U	U
Trust Territory(b)										
Virgin Islands	1	7	0	–	2	10	–	U	0	U

Key:
– —Less than 0.05 percent or less than 500.
E—Estimated.
C—Data combined with reporting of another service or program.
U—Data reported as unobtainable.

State or other jurisdiction	Mental health, alcohol and drug abuse services			General ambulatory care	Home health care	Inpatient care	Other
	Mental health	Alcohol abuse	Drug abuse				
United States	302	185	74	1,395	314	564	303
Alabama	C	C	0	C	8C	–	0
Alaska	1	1	U	39	2	–	8
Arizona	23	13	5	9	0	17	–
Arkansas	1E	0	0	0	6	–	1
California	U	U	U	U	U	14	2
Colorado	U	11	3E	11	U	32	0
Connecticut	0	0	0	3	–	–	0
Delaware	–	0	0	3	2	1	0
Florida	0	0	0	89	4	–E	4
Georgia	0	0	0	17	–	9E	–
Hawaii	10	–	–	9	1	23E	4
Idaho	0	4	1	1	–E	4	0
Illinois	U	0	0	53	0	1	7
Indiana	1E	U	U	0	23	0	30
Iowa	0	0	0	0	16	0	0
Kansas	U	U	U	216E	4E	–E	0
Kentucky	50E	21E	4E	3E	16	18E	1
Louisiana	U	0	0	2	1	1	U
Maine(b)							
Maryland	45	24	17	1	73	29E	6
Massachusetts	1E	37E	6	16E	–	55E	6E
Michigan	U	18	12	U	–	19	0
Minnesota	13	1	–	226	23	–	107
Mississippi	0	0	0	2E	6	2	0
Missouri	U	0	0	4	0	25	–
Montana(b)							
Nebraska	0	0	0	10	–	–	0
Nevada	U	U	U	U	0	1	0
New Hampshire	U	0	0	21	0	–	0
New Jersey	U	4	10	0	22	17E	2
New Mexico(b)							
New York	U	–	0	U	U	8	0
North Carolina	0	0	0	53	31	5	2
North Dakota	0	0	0	4	5	0	0
Ohio	0	8	0	2	0	8E	0
Oklahoma	68	–	–	57	3	–	3E
Oregon	2	0	0	0	0	0	0
Pennsylvania	1	34	11	4	–	27	0
Rhode Island	–	0	0	7	U	–	11
South Carolina	0	0	0	–	17	2	0
South Dakota(b)							
Tennessee	1E	0	0	99E	6	18	12
Texas	0	0	0	4	10	9	3
Utah	1	U	U	–	0	1	1
Vermont	–	1	0	10	1	–	4
Virginia	0	0	0	252	10	1	3
Washington	0	0	0	–	U	1	0
West Virginia	–	5	–	6	7	11	77
Wisconsin	0	0	0	4	0	–	0
Wyoming	0	0	0	21E	1	–	8
Dist. of Col.	12	1	5E	72E	11	5	3
American Samoa	1	–	–	15	–	6	–
Guam(b)							
No. Mariana Is.(b) ...							
Puerto Rico	67	U	U	8	U	93	0
Trust Territory(b)							
Virgin Islands	2	–	–	41	–	–	0

Key:
– —Less than 0.05 percent or less than 500.
E—Estimated.
C—Data combined with reporting of another service or program.
U—Data reported as unobtainable.

Table 8.31
PUBLIC HEALTH PROGRAM EXPENDITURES
OF STATE HEALTH AGENCIES, BY PROGRAM: FISCAL 1983
(In thousands of dollars)

State or other jurisdiction	Total	Personal health	Environmental health	Health resources	Laboratory	General administration	Funds to LHDs not allocated to program areas
United States.............	$5,446,661	$3,988,005	$350,387	$529,949	$584,548	$317,641	$76,130
Alabama..................	61,383	41,529	1,592	2,983	4,152	4,353	6,773
Alaska...................	25,794	19,232	131	3,491	1,981	960	0
Arizona..................	104,470	83,562	11,737	1,991	1,760	5,420	0
Arkansas	43,927	31,598	4,709	1,662	1,833	4,124	0
California................	591,512	293,957	34,172	196,710	21,632	44,493	549
Colorado	64,420	41,777	9,005	2,823	2,183	4,690	3,942
Connecticut	50,452	33,091	1,995	6,992	4,766	2,595	1,013
Delaware	28,797	25,547	1,474	462	593	722	0
Florida	190,698	130,742	27,073	13,056	6,967	12,860	0
Georgia..................	114,847	77,548	717	3,621	3,588	1,089	28,284
Hawaii	163,688	137,564	6,911	14,237	1,494	3,483	0
Idaho	21,855	13,713	3,173	2,027	1,741	1,203	0
Illinois..................	90,290	60,159	5,484	7,493	3,243	8,262	5,649
Indiana	48,741	20,737	13,968	1,882	2,237	9,830	88
Iowa	31,031	25,713	423	3,434	0	1,461	0
Kansas	30,173	15,611	6,574	3,501	1,832	2,655	0
Kentucky	181,189	156,855	3,665	5,797	1,807	4,896	8,169
Louisiana	104,686	84,076	11,405	3,726	4,134	1,344	0
Maine(a)..................							
Maryland	440,161	374,803	27,822	10,279	6,220	21,037	0
Massachusetts	158,536	138,770	3,445	6,856	5,391	4,074	0
Michigan	200,317	155,622	15,880	10,472	12,181	6,162	0
Minnesota	56,644	28,075	2,916	6,815	2,905	4,818	11,115
Mississippi	71,012	61,351	3,048	2,134	947	3,533	0
Missouri	64,594	55,018	2,247	4,307	1,743	1,279	0
Montana(a)							
Nebraska	18,174	11,492	1,424	4,007	709	542	0
Nevada	15,411	11,095	1,116	1,232	888	401	678
New Hampshire	14,458	9,940	1,189	2,022	513	793	0
New Jersey...............	98,621	68,765	4,487	12,671	5,069	7,629	0
New Mexico(a)							
New York	440,972	283,319	11,926	77,142	35,982	32,602	0
North Carolina	125,462	109,458	6,134	1,659	5,296	2,914	0
North Dakota	13,598	6,809	2,815	1,399	913	1,163	500
Ohio	115,645	91,297	4,096	7,954	3,540	8,757	0
Oklahoma	70,490	47,637	12,885	3,949	1,404	4,615	0
Oregon	30,344	19,056	1,850	4,306	2,280	2,065	787
Pennsylvania	199,970	165,401	3,273	23,532	3,213	4,552	0
Rhode Island	26,666	14,267	3,412	4,129	3,496	1,363	0
South Carolina	119,283	81,483	22,144	3,422	3,487	8,747	0
South Dakota(a)							
Tennessee	110,442	82,910	14,952	6,112	2,372	4,095	0
Texas....................	242,594	182,128	19,487	20,712	5,609	14,659	0
Utah	31,410	19,069	5,063	2,768	2,636	1,874	0
Vermont	16,515	12,869	1,022	1,363	1,027	235	0
Virginia..................	146,189	95,932	21,708	6,135	1,459	16,291	4,664
Washington	43,267	33,491	3,323	3,448	2,220	806	0
West Virginia	112,208	95,105	1,388	4,155	1,848	5,792	3,920
Wisconsin	46,236	34,164	3,350	7,106	378	1,239	0
Wyoming	12,778	10,209	518	1,461	402	188	0
Dist. of Col.	88,572	71,288	0	1,019	2,142	14,123	0
American Samoa	7,602	7,055	145	232	0	170	
Guam(a)							
No. Mariana Is.(a)							
Puerto Rico	302,297	274,828	2,339	9,638	545	14,947	0
Trust Territory(a)							
Virgin Islands	58,240	42,291	777	1,623	1,812	11,737	0

Source: Public Health Foundation, Washington, D.C.
Note: The data in this table relate only to expenditures of official state health agencies. The public health expenditures of other agencies, such as separate mental health authorities, environmental agencies, and hospital authorities are not reflected.
(a) Not reporting.

Table 8.32

PUBLIC HEALTH EXPENDITURES OF STATE HEALTH AGENCIES, BY SOURCE OF FUNDS: FISCAL 1983
(In millions of dollars)

Source of funds	Total	Personal health		Environmental health	Health resources	Laboratory	General administration	Funds to LHDs not allocated to program areas
		Noninstitutional	SHA-operated institutions					
Total	$5,446.7	$3,051.9	$936.2	$350.4	$529.9	$184.5	$317.6	$76.1
Subtotal, excluding federal grant and contract funds	3,499.2	1,403.2	898.6	253.3	424.3	168.1	279.8	71.9
State funds	3,027.1	1,194.2	770.6	202.7	385.8	152.9	251.7	69.3
Local funds	124.3	78.1	—	27.5	1.8	2.0	13.3	1.7
Fees	249.7	90.1	115.3	18.9	16.7	3.2	4.5	0.9
Patient fees & reimbursements from Medicaid	80.6	35.2	45.1	...	0.1	0.2	...	...
Patient fees & reimbursements from other sources	121.6	44.3	70.2	3.1	1.0	—	2.1	0.9
Other fees	47.5	10.6	...	15.9	15.7	3.0	2.4	...
Other	98.0	40.9	12.6	4.2	20.1	9.9	10.3	...
Subtotal, federal grant and contract funds(a)	1,947.5	1,648.6	37.6	97.1	105.6	16.5	37.9	4.2
Department of Health and Human Services	810.6	629.2	33.6	13.6	101.8	11.8	16.3	4.2
Public Health Service	643.9	549.4	13.8	13.5	41.7	11.2	10.2	4.2
Alcohol, Drug Abuse & Mental Health Administration	87.9	86.3	...	...	1.3	—	0.2	...
ADAMHA Block Grant (PL 97-35)	82.2	81.1	...	...	0.8	...	0.2	...
Other ADAMHA	5.7	5.2	...	...	0.5	...	...	...
Centers for Disease Control	128.9	89.3	...	10.4	20.8	4.5	2.0	2.2
Preventive Health & Health Services Block Grant (PL 97-35)	70.7	40.4	...	8.7	15.0	3.6	1.5	1.6
Immunization (PHSA Sec. 317)	12.5	12.3	...	...	...	...	0.1	...
Refugee Assistance Act of 1980 (Sec. 412C3)	6.8	4.8	...	...	1.8	0.1	0.1	...
Venereal Disease (PHSA Sec. 318)	19.8	19.1	...	...	...	0.7	0.1	...
Diabetes Control (PHSA Sec. 301)	2.7	2.5	...	...	0.2	...	...	...
Tuberculosis (PHSA, Sec. 317)	0.1	0.1	...	...	...	...	...	...
Fluoridation (PHSA Sec. 317)	1.7	1.7	...	...	...	...	...	...
Health Education/Risk Reduction (PHSA Sec. 1703(a) & PL 95-626)	4.3	4.2	...	...	...	...	0.1	...
Emergency Medical Services (PHSA Title XII)	3.5	0.1	...	...	3.4	...	...	...
Hypertension (PHSA Sec. 317)	3.6	3.6	...	...	—	...	—	...
Rat Control (PHSA Sec. 317)	0.8	...	...	0.8	...	...	...	...
Health Incentive Grant (PHSA Sec. 314(d))	0.7	0.1	...	...	...	...	0.1	0.5
Other CDC	1.6	0.5	...	0.8	0.1	0.1	0.1	...
Food & Drug Administration	1.4	...	...	1.4	...	...	...	...

PUBLIC HEALTH EXPENDITURES—Continued

Source of funds	Total	Personal health		Environmental health	Health resources	Laboratory	General administration	Funds to LHDs not allocated to program areas
		Noninstitutional	SHA-operated institutions					
Health Resources and Services Administration	398.2	367.8	0.9	1.5	15.6	2.9	7.5	2.1
Maternal and Child Health Services Block Grant (PL 97-35)	267.3	254.8	0.8	1.0	0.8	2.5	5.4	2.1
Community Health Centers (PHSA Sec. 330)	6.8	6.1			0.6		0.1	
Family Planning (PHSA Title X)	68.2	67.9			0.1		0.2	
Migrant Health (PHSA Sec. 319)	3.7	3.3		0.4			—	
Crippled Children (SSA Title V)	7.9	7.3	—			0.1		
Genetic Disease (PHSA Sec. 1101)	5.5	5.2		0.1	0.1	—	0.3	
SIDS (PHSA Sec. 1121)	0.4	0.4					0.2	
Maternal and Child Health (SSA Title V)	16.1	15.2		0.1		0.2	0.6	
Services for Blind/Disabled Children (SSI, Sec. 1615 SSA)	1.0	1.0	—					
Lead-Based Paint Poisoning Prevention (PHSA Sec. 316)	0.4	0.4				—		
National Health Planning & Resources Development Act (PL 93-641)	14.0	—			13.5		0.5	
Other HRSA	6.9	6.1			0.5	—	0.3	
National Institutes of Health	24.9	6.0	12.9	0.2	1.7	3.7	0.3	
National Center for Health Statistics	2.6				2.5		0.1	
Health Care Financing Administration	121.3	38.6	19.0	—	57.7	0.7	5.3	
Medicaid grants and contracts (SSA Title XIX)	84.4	32.8	7.1	—	39.9		4.5	
Medicare grants and contracts (SSA Title XVIII)	34.8	4.8	11.9	—	16.7	0.6	0.8	
Other HCFA	2.1	0.9			1.1		0.1	
Social Security Administration	12.8	11.3			1.5			
Office of Human Development Services	30.6	29.4	—		0.9		0.2	
Developmental Disabilities (PL 91-517, PL 94-103)	3.9	3.0			0.8	—	0.1	
Grants for Services (SSA Title XX)	23.5	23.5	—		—			
Other OHDS	3.1	2.9						
Other DHHS	2.0	0.4	0.7	0.1	0.1		0.1	
Other Federal Agencies	1,126.0	1,019.1	3.7	83.3	3.3	4.5	12.1	
Department of Agriculture	1,025.9	1,012.3	0.5	4.3	1.0	0.1	7.7	
WIC	1,019.6	1,010.8		0.1	1.0		7.6	
Other	6.3	1.5	0.5	4.2				
Department of Labor	5.9	1.0	—	4.5	0.1	0.1		
Department of Transportation	2.4	0.3			1.7	0.2	0.1	
Consumer Product Safety Commission	—					0.2		
Environmental Protection Agency	75.2	0.1		71.4	0.1	2.7	1.0	
Nuclear Regulatory Commission	0.2			0.2				
Regional Commissions	0.3				0.3		—	
Other	16.1	5.4	3.2	2.8	0.1	1.3	3.3	
Unidentified federal	10.9	0.3	0.3	0.2	0.5	0.2	9.5	

Source: Public Health Foundation, Washington, D.C.
Note: The public health agencies in Maine, Montana, New Mexico, South Dakota, Guam, the Northern Mariana Islands, and the Trust Territory did not report in 1983.
Key:
— —Dollar amounts less than $50,000

(a) Four of the predecessor categorical grants were transferred from one federal agency to another when the block grants were created. In the table above, these four grants are reported under the agency that administered them as part of the block grants. Thus, expenditures from Emergency Medical Services, Hypertension, and Home Health Services grant funds are included in the Centers for Disease Control. Expenditures from lead-based paint poisoning prevention grant funds are included in Health Resources and Services Administration.

CRIMINAL JUSTICE AND LEGAL ISSUES

By Edward D. Feigenbaum

Prison Overcrowding

Overcrowding in state prisons continues to be an acute problem in the mid-1980s. As states have cracked down on plea bargain arrangements and imposed mandatory, fixed-length sentences for select transgressions, prison populations have grown at an alarming rate. (See Table 8.34 for more information on trends in state prison populations.) Moreover, the inmate population now consists of a higher proportion of individuals convicted of infamous crimes.

As prison populations have grown, additional judicial sanctions have compelled the states to enact early release programs, often sending inmates back into society well in advance of the time initially fixed by the courts for integration back into society. Each invocation of early release provisions leads to a greater likelihood that those who have served a minimal amount of time for more serious crimes will be set free.

Profiting From Crime

In 1985, the recantation of an Illinois woman resulted in the release of a man who already had served several years in prison for her alleged rape. The outcome has raised even more questions outside of the courtroom, however. In the late 1970s, several states enacted "Son of Sam" laws aimed at preventing convicted criminals from profiting from the marketing of their stories. Gary Dotson, the exonerated rapist, wants to sell his story now, and is finding the law in Illinois to be a roadblock. Actions against similar laws in New Jersey and New York are currently in progress.

Gun Control

In the 1980s, the focus on gun control issues has moved from sentence enhancement—use of a mandatory term for the commission of a crime while using specified weapons—to the local option for handgun prohibition in entire communities, an initiative ruled permissible in Illinois. Courts in Maryland have gone so far as to find that handgun manufacturers may be liable for certain abuses of their products, a ruling certain to spark a new wave of uproar, if not legislation.

Manufacturers' Liability

Gun manufacturers are not the only ones finding that they are being held to stricter standards of liability than they have been accustomed. Manufacturers of all types of products have become alarmed at the willingness of state courts to hold them liable for incidents involving their products, actions that would not have been credible a decade ago. The patchwork quilt of state laws and standards imposed by case law has led to an effort at the federal level—over the vehement protests of the states—to establish federal product liability standards that could have the effect of creating a level playing field for manufacturers.

Technology And The Law

As rapid technological changes have affected liability issues, so too has technology carved out its own niche in the law. State proscription of computer crime, unheard of until the waning days of the 1970s, has become a popular item on the legislative agenda of the 1980s. As technology (and its attendant abuse) has advanced, some of the states that rushed to regulate computer crime early in the process have come to realize that while their laws might be adequate enough to protect against the traditional notions of theft of property, they fail miserably when tested against the resources and scheming minds of young computer hackers, such as the Wisconsin "414s," who were able to gain entry into sensitive national computer databases and scan and manipulate important data. Amendments to the legislation have been necessary.

From The Courtroom To Arbitration

"The People's Court" has become more than just a Hollywood illusion for many seeking relief in the 1980s. As technology has

Edward D. Feigenbaum is Director of the Center for Legal Affairs at The Council of State Governments.

grown increasingly complex, methods of resolving legal disputes often have been simplified. In reaction to the litigation logjam, many states have established arbitration tribunals to ease the court workload. Some of these programs use retired judges to conduct proceedings voluntarily entered into by parties to a dispute.

Nowhere has the shift from the courtroom to arbitration or quasi-judicial tribunals created more discontent than in the area of medical malpractice. States, faced with spiraling damage awards in medical malpractice cases and medical professionals unable to afford exponentially-increasing malpractice insurance premiums, recently have taken steps to restrict malpractice claims. Many states have moved malpractice cases from the courts to special tribunals, and have limited damage awards, imposed restrictions on the nature of payment for prospective damages, and clamped down on contingency fees for legal representation. Whether all of these provisions will continue to be upheld as constitutional is questionable. Nevertheless, courts in California, Indiana, Nebraska, and Wisconsin have upheld components of such reform plans.

Health-Related Issues
Other health-related legal issues have become major concerns of the states in the mid-1980s. As drunk driving injuries continue to plague the nation, the states have been revising their DUI legislation to lower the presumptive levels necessary for convictions. This, along with raising the minimum drinking age in the states and the increase in legislation permitting administrative revocation of driver licenses for drunk driving offenses, is beginning to have a positive impact on lowering the death toll. As states make more progress on this front, the means for further regulating driving while under the influence of controlled substances and boating while intoxicated have come under scrutiny in the state legislatures.

AIDS (Acquired Immune Deficiency Syndrome) dominated the headlines in 1985, and has emerged as a major political and social issue for the states. Now, public health and education agencies are grappling with regulations governing AIDS victims, and the states are altering privacy laws and insurance laws to ease the availability of appropriate health insurance to individuals in light of recent insurance industry fears. AIDS discrimination likely will be a major public policy question as the decade continues.

The Future
As with Caesar, the beneficial effects of the administrative reforms of the 1970s are not as readily recognized as the evils that live on. The mid-1980s have become a time for addressing the issues that went by the wayside in the search for structural reform, and a period for correcting or fine-tuning many of the deficiencies in laws caused by a lack of sophistication in the 1970s.

Table 8.33
STATE DEATH PENALTY
(As of October 1985)

State or other jurisdiction	Method of execution	No. of women on death row	Persons on death row	State or other jurisdiction	Method of execution	No. of women on death row	Persons on death row
Alabama	Electrocution	2	81	Montana	Lethal injection or hanging	0	5
Alaska	...						
Arizona	Gas chamber	0	63	Nebraska	Electrocution	0	13
Arkansas	Lethal injection (or choice of electrocution for those sentenced before March 4, 1983)	0	27	Nevada	Lethal injection	2	29
				New Hampshire	+++	0	0
				New Jersey	Lethal injection	1	16
California	Gas chamber	0	176	New Mexico	Lethal injection	0	5
				New York	...		
Colorado	Gas chamber	0	1	North Carolina	Gas chamber or lethal injection	1	50
Connecticut	+++	0	0	North Dakota	...		
Delaware	Hanging	0	5	Ohio	Electrocution	3	50
Florida	Electrocution	1	221				
Georgia	Electrocution	2	108	Oklahoma	Lethal injection, firing squad, or hanging	1	50
Hawaii	...						
Idaho	Lethal injection or firing squad	1	14	Oregon	+++	0	0
				Pennsylvania	Electrocution	0	75
Illinois	Lethal injection	0	79	Rhode Island	...		
Indiana	Electrocution	1	33	South Carolina	Electrocution	0	38
Iowa	...						
				South Dakota	+++	0	0
				Tennessee	Electrocution	0	50
Kansas	...			Texas	Lethal injection	2	203
Kentucky	Electrocution	0	24	Utah	Firing squad or lethal injection	0	5
Louisiana	Electrocution	0	43				
Maine	...			Vermont(a)	+++	0	0
Maryland	Gas chamber	2	21				
Massachusetts	...			Virginia	Electrocution	0	28
Michigan	...			Washington	Lethal injection or hanging	0	6
Minnesota	...			West Virginia	...		
Mississippi	Gas chamber or lethal injection	1	43	Wisconsin	...		
				Wyoming	Lethal injection	0	3
Missouri	Gas chamber	0	37	Dist. of Col.	...		

Source: NAACP Legal Defense and Educational Fund, Inc.
Key:
. . .—State has no capital punishment statute.
+ + +—State has capital punishment statute, but no sentences imposed.

(a) The Vermont statute predates *Furman vs. Georgia*, 408 U.S. 238 (1972), but there has been no state action since 1971 to revalidate it.

399

Table 8.34
TRENDS IN STATE PRISON POPULATION

State or other jurisdiction	Total population			Population by maximum length of sentence					
				More than a year			Year or less and unsentenced		
	1984	1983	Percentage change	1984	1983	Percentage change	1984	1983	Percentage change
United States	429,603	405,322	6.0	417,779	393,400	6.2	11,824	11,922	−0.8
Alabama	10,482	9,856	6.4	10,246	9,641	6.3	236	215	9.8
Alaska(a)	1,995	1,634	22.1	1,290	1,075	20.0	705	559	26.1
Arizona	7,845	7,251	8.2	7,638	7,115	7.4	207	136	52.2
Arkansas	4,454	4,244	4.9	4,427	4,226	4.8	27	18	50.0
California(b)	43,314	39,373	10.0	41,780	38,025	9.9	1,534	1,348	13.8
Colorado(c)	3,364	3,244	3.7	3,347	3,244	3.2	17	0	ND
Connecticut(a)	5,718	5,474	4.5	3,748	3,577	4.8	1,970	1,897	3.8
Delaware(a)	2,200	2,198	0.1	1,615	1,579	2.3	585	619	−5.5
Florida	27,106	26,334	2.9	26,933	25,393	6.1	173	941	−81.6
Georgia	15,731	15,358	2.4	14,944	14,935	0.1	787	423	86.0
Hawaii(a)	1,934	1,700	13.8	1,299	1,065	22.0	635	635	0.0
Idaho	1,282	1,192	7.6	1,282	1,192	7.6	0	0	ND
Illinois(d)	17,187	15,595	10.2	17,187	15,522	10.7	0	73	−100.0
Indiana	9,328	9,296	0.3	9,063	8,973	1.0	265	323	−18.0
Iowa(b)	2,836	2,814	0.8	2,836	2,814	0.8	0	0	ND
Kansas	4,238	3,705	14.4	4,238	3,705	14.4	0	0	ND
Kentucky(c)	4,793	4,752	0.9	4,793	4,752	0.9	0	0	ND
Louisiana	13,919	12,812	8.6	13,919	12,812	8.6	0	0	ND
Maine	1,025	1,082	−5.3	840	861	−2.4	185	221	−16.3
Maryland	13,124	12,617	4.0	12,442	11,979	3.9	682	638	6.9
Massachusetts	4,890	4,482	9.1	4,890(e)	4,372(e)	11.8	(e)	110(e)	−100.0
Michigan	14,604	14,382	1.5	14,604	14,382	1.5	0	0	ND
Minnesota	2,167	2,113	2.6	2,167	2,113	2.6	0	0	ND
Mississippi	6,115	5,586	9.5	5,974	5,481	9.0	141	105	34.3
Missouri	8,808	8,275	6.4	8,808	8,275	6.4	0	0	ND
Montana	1,005	903	11.3	1,005	901	11.5	0	2	−100.0
Nebraska	1,623	1,629	−0.4	1,535	1,551	−1.0	88	78	12.8
Nevada	3,510	3,188	10.1	3,510	3,188	10.1	0	0	ND
New Hampshire	561	479	17.1	561	479	17.1	0	0	ND
New Jersey(c)	10,363	9,192	12.7	10,363	9,192	12.7	0	0	ND
New Mexico	2,129	1,977	7.7	1,908	1,708	11.7	221	269	−17.8
New York	33,155	30,541	8.6	33,155	30,541	8.6	0	0	ND
North Carolina	16,371	15,395	6.3	15,219	14,257	6.7	1,152	1,138	1.2
North Dakota	434	410	5.9	374	350	6.9	60	60	0.0
Ohio	18,694	18,007	3.8	18,694(e)	18,007(e)	3.8	(e)	(e)	ND
Oklahoma	7,872	7,428	6.0	7,872(e)	7,428(e)	6.0	(e)	(e)	ND
Oregon	4,563	3,941	15.8	4,563	3,941	15.8	0	0	ND
Pennsylvania	13,090	11,767	11.2	12,998	11,699	11.1	92	68	35.3
Rhode Island(a)	1,220	1,157	5.4	888	878	1.1	332	279	19.0
South Carolina	10,035	9,576	4.8	9,434	9,076	3.9	601	500	20.2
South Dakota	917	826	11.0	900	808	11.4	17	18	−5.6
Tennessee(c)	7,302	8,201	−11.0	7,302	8,201	−11.0	0	0	ND
Texas	36,682	35,259	4.0	36,682	35,259	4.0	0	0	ND
Utah	1,419	1,274	11.4	1,407	1,261	11.6	12	13	−7.7
Vermont(a)	515	497	3.6	392	378	3.7	123	119	3.4
Virginia	10,667	10,093	5.7	10,493	9,855	6.5	174	238	−26.9
Washington	6,821	6,659	2.4	6,821	6,659	2.4	0	0	ND
West Virginia	1,599	1,624	−1.5	1,599(e)	1,624(e)	−1.5	(e)	(e)	ND
Wisconsin	5,023	4,865	3.2	5,023(e)	4,865(e)	3.2	(e)	(e)	ND
Wyoming	740	721	2.6	740	721	2.6	0	0	ND
Dist. of Col.(a)	4,834	4,344	11.3	4,031	3,465	16.3	803	879	−8.6

Sources: Bureau of Justice Statistics, U.S. Department of Justice.
Note: This table reports all prisoners subject to confinement under the jurisdiction of a given correctional system whether or not they are in its physical custody.
Key:
ND—Not definable
(a) Figures include both jail and prison inmates; jails and prisons form an integrated system.

(b) All data are custody figures; jurisdiction counts are not available.
(c) Official prison population count excludes state prisoners held in local jails to ease overcrowding.
(d) Due to a legislative change, the Department of Corrections no longer has jurisdiction over inmates with a sentence of 1 year or less.
(e) Population counts for inmates with over 1 year maximum sentence include an undetermined number of inmates with a sentence of 1 year or less.

ENVIRONMENTAL AND NATURAL RESOURCE PROBLEMS: THE ROLE OF THE STATES

By R. Steven Brown

American public awareness of protection of natural resources began with Theodore Roosevelt's conservation efforts in the early 1900s. It was not until Aldo Leopold's *Sand County Almanac* of 1949 and especially Rachel Carson's *Silent Spring* in 1962, however, that the public's awareness of threats to the general environment began. Culminating in "Earth Day" in 1970, this public awareness resulted in the passage of 12 major federal environmental acts between 1969 and 1977. These acts created or strengthened rules governing the quality of air, water and coastal zones, the disposal of solid waste, the use of pesticides and other toxic materials, and the effects of coal mining.

Although amended on several occasions, each act has survived the pressures of economic doldrums and changing public interests. Today, each act not only is intact, but also, in many cases, is stronger. Even the acts which were not reauthorized have continued to receive funding, and recent polls have shown that public interest in environmental issues is again on the rise.

The state role in these acts was always to take the lead in program implementation, permitting, and enforcement. The federal government's role was to provide technical assistance, program review, enforcement backup, and the bulk of the funding. As public interest in environmental issues began to wane in the early 1980s, new federalism appeared and the federal dollars, which had provided generous financial support for program start-up and operation, waned as well. The federal mandates did not relax, however, and states found themselves shouldering more of the financial burden, while performing the same duties.

While Congress was busy with laws governing environmental management, it did not ignore the more traditional area of natural resources. The federal government has been interested in rules affecting the management of the nation's natural resources at least since 1849, when the U.S. Department of the Interior was founded. The origins of such well-known activities as forestry, soil conservation, fish and wildlife, and parks are all in the 1930s or earlier, but during the period 1965-77, eight major pieces of legislation passed, affecting natural resources such as wildlife, oceans, soil, water, rivers, forests, air, and lands. Unlike the environmental laws, the federal laws on natural resources require the federal government to be the primary force behind even routine events. State participation is significant, particularly in water resource management and forestry, but areas such as soil conservation and offshore ocean resources are largely the responsibility of the federal government. Even though state participation in water resources is significant, the federal role in construction projects such as dams and waterways remains large. The same situation occurs for forest resource management, as nearly 81 percent of all forest lands in government hands are controlled by the federal government.[1]

Like the environmental programs, natural resources programs also experienced change due to the new federalism. The contribution of state funds for soil conservation district programs, for example, rose from $65 million in 1979 to $96 million in 1983.[2] The state burden in managing water resources also has increased, with the 46 states which have dam safety laws shouldering all of the financial burden since the end of the National Dam Inspection program in 1981. State matches for coastal zone management programs changed from 20 to 50 percent in 1985.

Environmental Quality

The three main components of environmental quality are water, air, and lands. The state role in these areas has grown during the past few years and this trend is expected to continue. Many states have taken the initiative on environmental topics such as abandoned hazardous waste dumps, leaking underground storage tanks, indoor air pollu-

R. Steven Brown is Director of the Center for the Environment and Natural Resources at The Council of State Governments.

tion, groundwater protection, and toxic air emissions because the federal lead was either slow in coming, inadequate, or nonexistent. As the states continue to administer their environmental programs, their expertise grows and their ability to point out inadequacies in federal legislation increases.

The states are grappling with several significant problems related to the running of their environmental control programs. Some of these problems are not new, but others only recently have emerged.

One of these problems is financing. The federal government has made it clear that it will continue to reduce the amount of money available for the construction of pollution control facilities. The most obvious example of this trend is in the EPA Construction Grants program, which may be phased out completely. States also are concerned, however, about the withdrawal or reduction of federal financial support for the programs mandated by federal law. Thus, states are exploring financing options which may have been overlooked in the past.

A second problem facing the states is the manner in which future environmental impairment may be avoided. To some extent, liability may be defined by federal acts (for example, the Resource Conservation and Recovery Act [RCRA] or the Comprehensive Environmental Response, Compensation, and Liability Act [CERCLA]). However, there are many other areas in which liability for environmental damage is not so well defined. Some states have begun limitations or prohibitions on title transfers unless environmental or health standards can be demonstrated.

A continuing problem is that of determining the balance between economic development and environmental control. The use of risk management and conflict resolution techniques has helped to quantify and to clarify the manner in which this balance is defined. States will continue to improve their skills in these areas in order to help resolve this problem.

One of the most often cited problems is the permitting process. Almost all manufacturing industries are required to obtain permits for air emissions, water discharges, and solid or hazardous waste disposal. Few states have vigorously attempted to consolidate the permitting process or to commit themselves to the timely review of applications.

Another problem that needs attention is organizational overlap. Most states periodically review their organizations, but some states have ignored the effects of emerging issues on their organizations. Groundwater, for example, is regulated by at least seven major federal environmental acts, but is administered by an average of five divisions in a typical state. Even worse, in many states these divisions are in separate agencies. While this may assure that the pertinent component of the federal act is addressed, it does not necessarily assure the state's groundwater is adequately protected. Because of the overlap in duties, it may also not be the most efficient allocation of limited state staff resources.

Water quality problems

The quality of the nation's water is a concern of each federal act. Even the Clean Air Act is affected by water quality issues such as acid rain. The major causes of stream pollution are nonpoint sources (source of over 50 percent of stream pollution), municipal sources (about 25 percent), industrial sources (about 17 percent) and other sources (about 8 percent).[3] Obviously, the area of greatest concern should be nonpoint sources. Unfortunately, nonpoint sources, as the name implies, are not easy to pinpoint. The U.S. Environmental Protection Agency (EPA) has begun requiring industries to submit applications for storm water nonpoint source discharges, but even EPA acknowledges that "a combined effort of federal, state, and local governments is needed to help restore and protect surface and ground waters. . ."[4] The problem is exacerbated by agriculture, which creates increases in pollution, but which is a politically and economically sensitive area many are not willing to regulate.

Municipalities are the source of a large portion of stream pollution. Some of that pollution originates from nonpoint sources such as street runoff, but most of it comes from sewage treatment plants. In the last few years, most states have implemented "pretreatment discharge limitations" which reduce the loads of many pollutants, particulary heavy metals. These pretreatment programs are usually administered on a local level with the state providing an oversight role. A more important challenge for the states to face is the declining role of the federal government in financing sewage treatment plants ("construction grants"). The federal dollars spent in the post-1972 era for the Construction Grants Programs (CGP) are to be replaced with maintenance dollars for the next five to 15 years. States with high growth areas or states with municipalities which missed the CGP money will be responsible for providing their own funding for future construction. Fortunately, there will be fewer state regulatory requirements for this future construction, and the states can also consider the new trend of privatization. The federal discharge limitations will still have to be achieved, of course. During 1985, 12 states had revolving funds in operation, with 14 other states considering that method. Eleven states had loan/bond programs in operation.[5]

Industry, it has been noted, accounts for most of the remainder of stream pollution. With most conventional pollutants under control, the states must deal with the problem of organic pollutants. As many states have noted, determining limitations for these pollutants, without relying totally on partially-completed federal standards, is a difficult task.

In a 1985 survey of the states conducted by The Council of State Governments, all of the respondents identified groundwater as a threatened resource in the state; in fact, 65 percent stated that it was the most threatened resource. (See Table A for more information on the states' priority ranking of natural resource concerns.) Across the country, states have turned their attention to groundwater problems. Many have recently completed or are beginning work on a State Groundwater Policy. The U.S. EPA published its Groundwater Policy in 1984, in which primary responsibility for groundwater protection is placed with the states. In a 1984 report, the federal government contacted 15 states, all of which favored a federal role of funding and research, but opposed strong federal regulatory controls.[6] During 1985, members of the U.S. Senate pushed for a national groundwater policy requiring a lead agency in the state, a contamination source inventory, and designation of replacement water supplies. The administration, however, is opposed to any new groundwater bill.

Air quality problems

Although the states have made excellent progress on the quality of air during the last 15 years since passage of the Clean Air Act of 1970, a few tough problems remain. One is acid rain, which originally was a major concern in the northeast, but has more recently become a concern with several western and southern states. Congress can reach no agreement on what is to be done about acid rain, other than to encourage continued research, the results of which have been inconclusive thus far. The issue is further complicated by regional and even international considerations. States which are the supposed sources of the pollutants causing acid rain are for the most part unaffected by it, and thus have little incentive to pass legislation. States receiving the acid rain are unable to enforce legislation that might be enacted. As a result, an impasse can be expected until conclusive evidence on the exact sources, transport, and effects of acid rain are available. In early 1986, however, the president committed $5 billion over the next five years for the development of new technology to reduce sulfur emissions.

The second air quality problem is air toxics. These "air toxics" usually are organic chemicals or heavy metals, such as the organic chemicals released in Bhopal, India, and in Institute, West Virginia. It has been noted that toxic air leaks occur daily across the country, but that these emissions are tolerated until acute health problem occurs. The problem is also complicated by the fact that thousands of toxic chemicals are produced from thousands of sources. Furthermore, understanding characteristics of these chemicals is much more difficult than the air pollutants dealt with to date. At least one

Table A
Priority Ranking of
Natural Resource Concerns*

Number of states identifying resource	Name and priority rank of resource
40	1. Groundwater resources
36	2. Surface Water resources
34	3. Fish and Wildlife
28	4. Wetlands
17	5. Drinking Water
20	6. Soils

*The most often mentioned and highest-ranked resources.

Source: A survey of state natural resource trustees conducted by The Council of State Governments in the summer of 1985. Respondents were asked to indicate (and rank in order of priority) which natural resources were most threatened by spills/releases of oil and/or hazardous substances. Forty states responded to the survey.

state established a task force for the sole purpose of determining whether methyl isocyanate (the Bhopal chemical) was in the state. A state can spend a great deal of work determining facts about a thousand organic chemicals only to find a crisis occuring involving a chemical on which it has no data. Most states are in the process of completing amendments to their air pollution laws or regulations to deal with at least some of these chemicals, but many more chemicals will have to be ruled on during the upcoming years.

Another emerging pollution problem is that of indoor air pollution. The solution to this problem must address exposure to radon gas, "sick building" syndrome, aero-pathogens, asbestos, and other toxics. With better-sealed, energy-efficient homes, the problem of exposure to radioactive radon gas (which accumulates in these homes) has become serious in certain parts of the country.

Lands problems
(hazardous waste and mining)
Recently, states have been dealing with a massive flood of paperwork related to the Resource Conservation and Recovery Act of 1976 (RCRA). The 1984 RCRA Amendments required all hazardous waste disposal/storage facilities to submit comprehensive applications by November 1985, or cease operation. These amendments have caused some major changes in hazardous waste handling because of restrictions on materials which can be disposed of via burial. The emphasis for disposal now is either recycling or incineration. While states are grappling with reams of permit material for major sources, they also must continue to observe the 130,000 or so small businesses that generate wastes. In addition, many states are now in the process of creating their Underground Storage Tank regulatory units, which will oversee the underground storage of petroleum and other chemicals.

The "Superfund" hazardous waste clean-up process continues, with Congress working out details on a reauthorization bill that could expand the Superfund by as much as $10.1 billion over the next five years. With at least some action taken on 7,300 sites, an estimated 14,700 uncontrolled sites remain to be investigated. Some states have created their own Superfunds, but legal challenges have delayed the process.

The disposal of radioactive wastes continues to be a problem which the states must face. The Nuclear Waste Policy Act of 1982 is the federal act under which actions are being taken. For the most part, the western states have been dealing with matters such as site selection, transportation problems, public safety, and environmental protection. Part of the problem, however, lies with the separation of civilian radioactive waste disposal from that of defense. This can present a dual set of standards and procedures and cause numerous difficulties. The potential sites for the first repository have been identified, and considerable controversy is developing over the identification of the second repository site, which is to be in the East.

States with coal mining have settled into an administrative routine, for the most part, although a few major states regulated by the Surface Mining Control and Reclamation Act (SMCRA) of 1977 have lost or nearly lost primacy (authority for the state to administer SMCRA). In addition to the problems with mining activities under two acres (which are not regulated by SMCRA), many states are trying to improve their controls on the effects of mining on groundwater quality and quantity.

Natural Resources
The states continue to face a series of decisions in the field of natural resources, particularly as related to development, safety, and protection. The federal lead in these areas is very different from that in the environmental arena. In some areas, such as offshore oil development, the federal government has an almost adversary role with the states, while in other areas, such as dam safety, the federal government has been able to provide only limited support to the states.

Water resources
Three areas require state attention: dam safety, drought management, and emergency water planning.

A 1984 study funded by the Federal Emergency Management Agency, found that only 10 states had legislation that surpassed the U.S. Committee on Large Dam's model laws.[7] Another 16 states had adequate laws, 20 had marginal laws, and four states had no effective legislation. Only 24 states had both an adequate law and adequate funding. Unfortunately, it may take a major dam disaster, such as the one in Italy in 1985 that killed over 200 people, to assure adequate programs.

Nationwide, water resources are being recognized as a significant factor in economic development. It has been reported that the first question asked by major industries as they look for new plant sites is, "Is there enough water?" The water rich East has treated drought management with less respect than the West, but low water supply effects were minimized in the Delaware Valley in 1984-85 because advance drought planning had occurred. In the West, the federal government has begun to yield to state water claims. The most important piece of federal water resource legislation is the 1985 Water Resources Omnibus Bill, which provides authorization and funding for a wide range of water resource activities.

The Corps of Engineers is undertaking a program of Emergency Water Planning during 1985-86. The states will be asked to provide major contributions to planning regional, national and international emergencies which will require a predetermined mechanism for water management.

Coastal zone management

The biggest problem continues to be offshore oil development—a classic struggle between environmental protection and economic development. The states agree that their share of revenues for developed federal tracts is too small (currently negotiated at 27 percent), but disagree on how development should occur. Some states have issued or pressed for a moratorium on all or most offshore development. At issue is the question of whether offshore lease sales "directly affect" the state's coastal zones. In spite of the fact that no major oil spill related to development in the U.S. has occurred since 1969, the industry can still give no assurances to the states regarding the protection or rehabilitation of coasts which might be affected by a spill.

Forest resources

Like many other sectors of the ecomony, the forest industry is complaining about unfair foreign competition, mostly from Canada. In northern states, which have suffered in recent years because of the relocation of heavy industry, the problem is acute and

may jeopardize the comprehensive management programs developed under the Forest Resource Planning Act.

Forest lands still are threatened by development, even when the land use is temporary, such as mining. A 1985 estimate indicated that as many as 100,000 forested acres per year are mined for coal in the eastern part of the country, but are not reclaimed to forest. Several states have expressed concern over this trend and are seeking ways to reverse it.

Advances in integrated forest pest management continue, but the increased public awareness of pesticide threats to health has jeopardized this pest management component—even though the use of pesticides on forest lands is less than one percent of total pesticide use.[8] Improvements are needed not only in public awareness of pesticide use, but also in coordination of the monitoring of pesticide contamination in the environment.

Notes

1. *An Analysis of the Timber Situation in the United States 1952-2030*. U.S. Department of Agriculture, Forest Service, 1982.

2. National Association of Conservation Districts, and U.S. Department of Agriculture Soil Conservation Service, 1983.

3. *America's Clean Water*, Association of State and Interstate Water Pollution Control Administrators, 1984.

4. *Environmental Progress and Challenge: An EPA Perspective*, U.S. Environmental Protection Agency, 1984.

5. *State Alternative Financing Programs for Wastewater Treatment*, U.S. Environmental Protection Agency, 1986.

6. *Federal and State Efforts to Protect Groundwater*, U.S. General Accounting Office, 1984.

7. "Updated Review Summary of State Non-Federal Dam Safety Programs," Dr. Bruce Tschantz, University of Tennessee, 1984.

8. U.S. Forest Service, 1984.

Table 8.35
STATUS OF GROUNDWATER POLICY DEVELOPMENT

State or other jurisdiction	Specific state statutes for groundwater	Existing policy for protecting groundwater quality	Policy under development
Alabama	...	...	★
Alaska	...	...	...
Arizona	★	★	...
Arkansas	...	...	★
California	...	★	★
Colorado	...	...	★
Connecticut	...	★	...
Delaware	...	★	★
Florida	★	★	...
Georgia	★	★	...
Hawaii	...	★	★
Idaho	...	★	...
Illinois	...	...	★
Indiana	...	...	★
Iowa	...	...	★
Kansas	★	★	...
Kentucky	...	...	★
Louisiana	...	...	...
Maine	★	★	★
Maryland	...	...	...
Massachusetts	...	★	...
Michigan	...	★	★
Minnesota	...	★	★
Mississippi	...	...	★
Missouri	...	...	★
Montana	...	★	...
Nebraska	...	...	★
Nevada	...	★	...
New Hampshire	...	★	...
New Jersey	★	★	★
New Mexico	★	★	...
New York	★	★	...
North Carolina	...	★	...
North Dakota	...	...	★
Ohio	...	...	★
Oklahoma	★	★	...
Oregon	...	★	...
Pennsylvania	...	...	★
Rhode Island	...	...	★
South Carolina	...	...	★
South Dakota	...	...	★
Tennessee	...	...	★
Texas	...	...	...
Utah	...	★	★
Vermont	...	★	...
Virginia	★	...	...
Washington	...	★	★
West Virginia	...	...	★
Wisconsin	★	★	...
Wyoming	★	★	...
Puerto Rico	...	...	...
Virgin Islands	...	...	★

Source: Adapted from *Overview of State Groundwater Program Summaries*, U.S. Environmental Protection Agency, Office of Groundwater Protection (March 1985).

Table 8.36
MAJOR SOURCES OF GROUNDWATER CONTAMINATION

State or other jurisdiction	Septic tanks	Municipal landfills	On-site industrial landfills(a)	Other landfills	Surface impoundments(b)	Oil and gas brine pits	Underground storage tanks	Injection wells	Abandoned hazardous waste sites	Regulated hazardous waste sites	Saltwater intrusion	Agricultural
Alabama	...	★	★	★	★	★	★	★	★	★	★	★
Alaska	★	★	...	★	...	...	★	...	...	...	...	★
Arizona	...	★	...	★	★	...	★	...	★	...	★	...
Arkansas	...	...	...	★	...	★	...	...	...	...	★	...
California	...	★	★	...	★	...	★	...	★	★	★	★
Colorado	★	...	★	★	★	★	★	...	★	...	...	★
Connecticut	...	★	★	...	★	...	★	...	...	...	...	★
Delaware	...	★	★	★	...	...	★	...	...	...	★	★
Florida	★	★	★	★	★	...	★	★	★	...	...	★
Georgia	★	...	...	...	★	...	...	...	★	...	★	★
Hawaii	★	...	...	...	...	...	...	★	...	...	...	★
Idaho	★	...	...	...	★	...	★	★	...	...	...	★
Illinois	★	...	★	...	...	...	★	★	...	★	...	★
Indiana	★	...	★	...	...	...	★	★	★	...	...	...
Iowa	★	★	...	...	★	...	★	★	...	...	...	★
Kansas	...	...	...	...	...	★	...	...	...	★	...	...
Kentucky	...	★	★	★	★	...	...	★	★	...	...	...
Louisiana	...	...	...	★	★	★	★	...	...	...	...	★
Maine	★	★	★	...	★	...	★	...	★	...	★	★
Maryland	★	★	★	★	★	★	★	...	★	★	★	★
Massachusetts	★	★	★	...	★	...	★	...	★	...	...	★
Michigan	★	★	★	★	★	★	★	...	★	...	...	★
Minnesota	★	★	★	★	★	...	★	★	...	★	...	★
Mississippi	★	★	★	...	★	★	★	★	...	...	★	...
Missouri	★	...	...	...	★	...	...	...	...	★	...	★
Montana	★	★	...	★	...	★	★	★	...	...	★	...
Nebraska	★	★	...	...	★	★	★	...	★	...	...	★
Nevada	★	...	...	...	★	...	★	...	...	...	...	...
New Hampshire	★	★	★	...	★	...	★	...	...	...	...	...
New Jersey	★	★	★	★	★	★	★	★	...	★	★	...
New Mexico	★	...	...	...	★	★	★	...	★	...	...	★
New York	★	★	★	★	...	...	★	...	★	...	...	★
North Carolina	...	★	★	...	★	...	★	...	...	...	★	...
North Dakota	★	★	★	★	★	★	★	★	★	...	...	...
Ohio	★	...	★	★	★	★	...	...	...	★	...	...
Oklahoma	...	...	...	...	...	...	★	...	...	...	★	...
Oregon	★	★	★	...	...	...	★	★	★	★	...	...
Pennsylvania	★	★	★	★	★	★	...	★	...	...	...	★
Rhode Island	★	★	★	...	★	...	★	...	★	...	...	★
South Carolina	...	★	★	★	★	...	★	...	★	★	★	★
South Dakota	★	★	★	★	★	★	★	...	...	...	...	★
Tennessee	★	...	★	...	★	★	...	★	★	★	...	★
Texas	★	★	★	...	★	...	...	...	★	...	★	★
Utah	...	...	...	★	...	★	★	...	...	...	...	...
Vermont	★	★	★	...	★	...	★	...	★	...	...	...
Virginia	★	...	...	...	★	...	★	...	...	...	...	...
Washington	★	★	...	...	★	...	★	★	★	...	★	...
West Virginia	...	...	★	...	★	★	...	...	...	...	...	...
Wisconsin	★	...	...	...	...	...	★	...	...	★	...	★
Wyoming	★	...	...	...	...	★	★	...	...	...	...	...
Puerto Rico	★	★	...	...	...	...	★	...	...	★	★	★
Virgin Islands	★	...	...	...	...	...	...	...	...	...	★	...

Source: Adapted from *Overview of State Groundwater Program Summaries*, U.S. Environmental Protection Agency, Office of Groundwater Protection (March 1985).
(a) Excluding surface pits, lagoons, and surface impoundments.
(b) Excluding oil and gas brine pits.

Table 8.37
MAJOR TYPES OF GROUNDWATER CONTAMINANTS

State or other jurisdiction	Organic chemicals		Inorganic chemicals				Metals	Radio-active materials	Pesti-cides
	Volatile	Synthetic	Nitrates	Fluorides	Arsenic	Brine/salt			
Alabama	★	★	★	★(a)	...	★	★	★	★
Alaska	★	...	...	...	★(a)	...	...	...	...
Arizona	...	★	★(a)	★(a)	...	...	...	★(a)	...
Arkansas	...	★	★	★	★	★	★	★(a)	...
California	★	★	★(b)	★	★	★	★	...	★
Colorado	...	...	★	...	...	★	★	...	...
Connecticut	★	★	...	...	...	...	...	...	★
Delaware	...	...	★	...	...	...	...	...	...
Florida	★	★	★	...	...	★	★	...	★
Georgia	★	★	...	...	...	...	★	...	★
Hawaii	...	★	...	...	...	...	...	...	★
Idaho	★	...	★	★	...	★	★	...	...
Illinois	★	...	★	★	...	...	...	★(a)	...
Indiana	...	★	★	...	...	★	...	...	★
Iowa	...	★	★(b)	★(a)	...	...	...	★(a)	★
Kansas	...	...	...	...	...	★	...	...	...
Kentucky	★	★	...	...	...	★	★	★	...
Louisiana	...	★	...	★(a)	...	...	★	...	★
Maine	★	...	★	...	...	...	...	...	...
Maryland	★	...	★	...	...	...	...	...	...
Massachusetts	★	★	★	★	★	...	★	...	★
Michigan	★	★	★	...	...	★	★	...	★
Minnesota	★	★	★	...	★	...	★	...	★
Mississippi	★	★	...	...	...	★	★	...	...
Missouri	...	★	...	...	...	...	...	...	...
Montana	★	...	★	...	★	★	★	...	★
Nebraska	★	...	★(b)	...	...	★	★	...	★(b)
Nevada	...	★	★(a)	★(a)	★(a)	★(a)	★	★	...
New Hampshire	...	...	...	...	...	...	...	...	...
New Jersey	★	★	★	★	★	★	★	★	★
New Mexico	★	★	★	★(c)	...	★	★	...	...
New York	...	★	★	...	...	...	...	...	★
North Carolina	★	★	...	...	...	★	★	...	★
North Dakota	★	...	★	...	★	★	★	...	...
Ohio	★	★	...	...	...	★	★	...	...
Oklahoma	★	...	★	...	...	★	★	...	...
Oregon	★	★	★	★	★	...	...	...	...
Pennsylvania	...	...	...	...	...	...	...	...	...
Rhode Island	★	...	★	...	...	...	★	...	★
South Carolina	★	★	★	★	...	...	★	★	★
South Dakota	...	...	★	...	★	★	★	★	★
Tennessee	★	★	★	...	...	★	★	...	★
Texas	★	★	...	...	...	★	...	...	★
Utah	...	...	★	...	★	★	★	...	★
Vermont	★	★	★	...	★	★	★	★	★
Virginia	...	...	...	...	...	...	...	...	...
Washington	★	★	★	★	★	★	★	★	★
West Virginia	★	★	...	...	...	★	...	...	★
Wisconsin	★	...	★	...	...	★	...	★	★
Wyoming	...	...	...	...	...	★	...	...	...
Puerto Rico	...	...	★	...	...	...	...	...	...
Virgin Islands	★	...	...	...	...	...	★	...	...

Source: Adapted from *Overview of State Groundwater Program Summaries*, U.S. Environmental Protection Agency, Office of Groundwater Protection (March 1985).
(a) Natural mineral deposits.
(b) Agricultural activities.
(c) Sulfates.

Table 8.38
SUPERFUND SITES NATIONAL PRIORITY LIST

State or other jurisdiction	Number of sites(a)	State or other jurisdiction	Number of sites(a)
Alabama	9	Montana	8
Alaska	0	Nebraska	4
Arizona	6	Nevada	0
Arkansas	7	New Hampshire	13
California	60	New Jersey	97
Colorado	14	New Mexico	4
Connecticut	6	New York	58
Delaware	11	North Carolina	8
Florida	37	North Dakota	1
Georgia	5	Ohio	28
Hawaii	6	Oklahoma	4
Idaho	4	Oregon	5
Illinois	22	Pennsylvania	54
Indiana	22	Rhode Island	8
Iowa	7	South Carolina	10
Kansas	7	South Dakota	1
Kentucky	9	Tennessee	8
Louisiana	6	Texas	26
Maine	7	Utah	9
Maryland	6	Vermont	2
Massachusetts	21	Virginia	12
Michigan	61	Washington	23
Minnesota	34	West Virginia	6
Mississippi	2	Wisconsin	24
Missouri	17	Wyoming	1
		Outlying U.S. jurisdictions	12

(a) Actual and proposed sites on the U.S. Environmental Protection Agency's National Priority List (September 1985).

Table 8.39
LOW-LEVEL RADIOACTIVE WASTE DISTRIBUTION, BY STATE: 1984*

State or other jurisdiction	Volume (M3)	Activity (Curies)	State or other jurisdiction	Volume (M3)	Activity (Curies)
Total	75,429	600,909	Montana	27	0
			Nebraska	871	727
Alabama	4,282	6,241	Nevada	1,272	0
Alaska	0		New Hampshire	43	4
Arizona	16	38	New Jersey	3,286	44,378
Arkansas	947	1,375			
California	4,489	13,677	New Mexico	41	0
			New York	4,156	30,008
Colorado	243	60	North Carolina	2,825	5,527
Connecticut	1,631	186,298	North Dakota	0	
Delaware	33	1	Ohio	525	764
Florida	2,506	71,299			
Georgia	2,471	2,453	Oklahoma	140	1
			Oregon	1,698	32
Hawaii	97	1	Pennsylvania	6,190	97,401
Idaho	158	28,255	Rhode Island	42	1
Illinois	6,436	48,937	South Carolina	7,211	7,898
Indiana	81	13			
Iowa	348	917	South Dakota	0	
			Tennessee	6,787	3,005
Kansas	39	0	Texas	364	263
Kentucky	47	4	Utah	135	0
Louisiana	14	0	Vermont	363	286
Maine	343	359			
Maryland	1,180	39,171	Virginia	2,781	2,250
			Washington	1,276	537
Massachusetts	5,464	3,701	West Virginia	6	0
Michigan	1,089	947	Wisconsin	826	3,190
Minnesota	1,970	730	Wyoming	0	
Mississippi	432	9			
Missouri	186	134	Dist. of Col.	63	15

*As reported by disposal site operators.
  Source: Conference of Radiation Control Program Directors.

Table 8.40
LOW-LEVEL RADIOACTIVE WASTE COMPACTS

State	Appalachian States Compact	Central Compact	Central Midwest Compact	Midwest Compact	Northeast Compact	Northwest Compact	Rocky Mountain Compact	Southeast Compact	Western Compact
Alabama	...	...	...	...	...	...	...	★	...
Alaska	...	...	...	...	...	★	...	...	...
Arizona	...	...	...	...	...	...	...	...	★
Arkansas	...	★	...	...	...	...	...	...	...
California	...	...	...	...	...	...	...	...	(a)
Colorado	...	...	...	...	...	...	★	...	...
Connecticut	...	...	...	...	★	...	...	...	...
Delaware	...	...	...	...	★	...	...	...	...
Florida	...	...	...	...	...	...	...	★	...
Georgia	...	...	...	...	...	...	...	★	...
Hawaii	...	...	...	...	...	★	...	...	...
Idaho	...	...	...	...	...	★	...	...	...
Illinois	...	...	★	...	...	...	...	...	...
Indiana	...	...	...	★	...	...	...	...	...
Iowa	...	...	...	★	...	...	...	...	...
Kansas	...	★	...	...	...	...	...	...	...
Kentucky	...	...	★	...	...	...	...	...	...
Louisiana	...	★	...	...	...	...	...	...	...
Maine	----------------------------------(b)----------------------------------								
Maryland	...	...	...	...	★	...	...	...	...
Massachusetts	----------------------------------(b)----------------------------------								
Michigan	...	...	...	★	...	...	...	...	...
Minnesota	...	...	...	★	...	...	...	...	...
Mississippi	...	...	...	...	...	...	...	★	...
Missouri	...	...	...	★	...	...	...	...	...
Montana	...	...	...	...	...	★	...	...	...
Nebraska	...	★	...	...	...	...	...	...	...
Nevada	...	...	...	...	...	...	★	...	...
New Hampshire	----------------------------------(b)----------------------------------								
New Jersey	...	...	...	...	★	...	...	...	...
New Mexico	...	...	...	...	...	...	★	...	...
New York	----------------------------------(b)----------------------------------								
North Carolina	...	...	...	...	...	...	...	★	...
North Dakota	...	...	...	...	...	...	★(c)	...	...
Ohio	...	...	...	★	...	...	...	...	...
Oklahoma	...	★	...	...	...	...	...	...	...
Oregon	...	...	...	...	...	★	...	...	...
Pennsylvania	(a)	...	...	...	...	...	...	...	...
Rhode Island	----------------------------------(b)----------------------------------								
South Carolina	...	...	...	...	...	...	...	★	...
South Dakota	----------------------------------(b)----------------------------------								
Tennessee	...	...	...	...	...	...	...	★	...
Texas	----------------------------------(d)----------------------------------								
Utah	...	...	...	...	...	★	...	...	...
Vermont	----------------------------------(b)----------------------------------								
Virginia	...	...	...	...	...	...	...	★	...
Washington	...	...	...	...	...	★	...	...	...
West Virginia	★	...	...	...	...	...	...	...	...
Wisconsin	...	...	...	★	...	...	...	...	...
Wyoming	...	...	...	...	...	...	★	...	...

Source: U.S. Department of Energy.
Key:
★—Party state
(a) State designated in Compact, but has not yet ratified Compact.
(b) Undeclared.
(c) Effective July 1, 1987.
(d) Independent.

411

Table 8.41
LEAKING UNDERGROUND STORAGE TANKS
PRIMARY OVERSIGHT AGENCIES*

State or other jurisdiction	Agency
Alabama	Groundwater Sect./Water Div., Dept. of Environmental Mgt.
Alaska	Dept. of Environmental Conservation
Arizona	Environmental Health Services, Dept. of Health Services
Arkansas	Dept. of Pollution Control & Ecology
California	Water Resources Control Bd.
Colorado	Water Mgt. Div., Dept. of Health
Connecticut	Hazardous Materials Mgt. Unit, Dept. of Environmental Protection
Delaware	Div. of Air & Waste Mgt., Dept. of Natural Resources & Environmental Control
Florida	Solid Waste Sect., Dept. of Environmental Regulation
Georgia	Environmental Protection Div., Dept. of Natural Resources
Hawaii	Noise & Radiation Branch, Dept. of Health
Idaho	Div. of Environment, Dept. of Health & Welfare
Illinois	Div. of Fire Prevention, Off. of State Fire Marshal
Indiana	Div. of Land Pollution Control, State Bd. of Health
Iowa	Dept. of Water, Air & Waste Mgt.
Kansas	Off. of Environmental Geology, Dept. of Health & Environment
Kentucky	Div. of Waste Mgt., Natural Resources & Environmental Protection Cabinet
Louisiana	Dept. of Environmental Quality
Maine	Bur. of Oil & Hazardous Material Control, Dept. of Environmental Protection
Maryland	Science & Health Advisory Group, Off. of Environmental Prog.
Massachusetts	Dept. of Public Safety
Michigan	Groundwater Quality Div., Dept. of Natural Resources
Minnesota	Div. of Solid & Hazardous Wastes, Pollution Control Agency
Mississippi	Bur. of Pollution Control, Dept. of Natural Resources
Missouri	Dept. of Natural Resources
Montana	Solid & Hazardous Waste Bur., Dept. of Health & Environmental Science
Nebraska	State Fire Marshal
Nevada	Div. of Environmental Protection, Dept. of Conservation & Natural Resources
New Hampshire	Water Supply & Pollution Control Comm.
New Jersey	Div. of Water Resources, Dept. of Environmental Protection
New Mexico	Groundwater/Hazardous Waste Bur., Environmental Improvement Div.
New York	Div. of Water, Dept. of Environmental Conservation
North Carolina	Div. of Environmental Mgt./Groundwater Sect., Dept. of Natural Resources & Community Development
North Dakota	Div. of Hazardous Waste Mgt. & Special Studies, Dept. of Health
Ohio	State Fire Marshal's Off.
Oklahoma	Underground Storage Tank Prog., Corporation Comm.
Oregon	Hazardous & Solid Waste Div., Dept. of Environmental Quality
Pennsylvania	Bur. of Water Quality Mgt./Groundwater Unit, Dept. of Environmental Resources
Rhode Island	Dept. of Environmental Mgt.
South Carolina	Groundwater Protection Div., Dept. of Health & Environmental Control
South Dakota	Off. of Water Quality, Dept. of Water & Natural Resources
Tennessee	Div. of Groundwater Protection, Dept. of Health & Environment
Texas	Underground Storage Tank Prog., Water Comm.
Utah	Div. of Environmental Health
Vermont	Waste Mgt. Div., Agency of Environmental Conservation
Virginia	Water Control Bd.
Washington	Solid & Hazardous Waste Mgt. Div., Dept. of Ecology
West Virginia	Solid & Hazardous Waste/Groundwater Branch, Dept. of Natural Resources
Wisconsin	Bur. of Petroleum Inspection, Dept. of Industry, Labor & Human Relations
Wyoming	Water Quality Div., Dept. of Environmental Quality
Dist. of Col.	Pesticides & Hazardous Waste Mgt. Branch, Dept. of Consumer & Regulatory Affairs
American Samoa	Environmental Quality Comm.
Guam	Environmental Protection Agency
No. Mariana Is.	Div. of Environmental Quality
Puerto Rico	Environmental Quality Bd.
Virgin Islands	Div. of Natural Resources Mgt.

*Designated as the lead agency in the state or territory for development and/or administration of the Leaking Underground Storage Tank regulations arising from the 1984 Resource Conservation and Recovery Act (RCRA) amendments.

Table 8.42
STATE RIGHT-TO-KNOW LAWS

State	Worker(a)	Community(b)	Emergency response(c)	State	Worker(a)	Community(b)	Emergency response(c)
Alabama	★	...	★	Montana	★	★	★
Alaska	★	...	...	Nebraska	...	...	...
Arizona	...	...	...	Nevada	...	...	...
Arkansas	...	...	...	New Hampshire	★	★	...
California	★	...	...	New Jersey	★	★	...
Colorado	...	...	...	New Mexico	...	...	...
Connecticut	★	...	★	New York	★	...	...
Delaware	★	★	★	North Carolina	★	★	...
Florida	★	...	★	North Dakota	...	...	★
Georgia	...	...	...	Ohio	...	...	...
Hawaii	★	...	...	Oklahoma	...	...	...
Idaho	...	...	...	Oregon	★	★	★
Illinois	★	★	★	Pennsylvania	★	★	...
Indiana	...	...	...	Rhode Island	★	★	...
Iowa	★	★	★	South Carolina	...	...	...
Kansas	...	...	...	South Dakota	...	...	...
Kentucky	...	...	...	Tennessee	★	★	...
Louisiana	★	★	★	Texas	★	★	★
Maine	★	★	★	Utah	...	...	...
Maryland	★	★	★	Vermont	★	★	★
Massachusetts	★	★	...	Virginia	...	...	...
Michigan	★	...	...	Washington	★	★	...
Minnesota	★	...	...	West Virginia	★	★	★
Mississippi	...	...	...	Wisconsin	★	...	...
Missouri	★	★	...	Wyoming	...	...	...

Source: Chemical Manufacturers Association.

(a) Requires that workers have access to written summaries of chemicals' health effects, advice on protection, written hazard warnings in work areas, and labeling on chemicals leaving the workplace.

(b) Requires public access to information about transportation, storage, discharge, and handling of toxic materials.

(c) Requires firms handling toxic materials to create emergency response plans in cooperation with state and local officials.

Table 8.43
ALTERNATIVE STATE ASSISTANCE PROGRAMS FOR PUBLICLY-OWNED WASTEWATER TREATMENT WORKS

State	Revolving funds Operational	Under study/ legislation proposed	Loan/bond programs	State	Revolving funds Operational	Under study/ legislation proposed	Loan/bond programs
Alabama	...	★	...	Montana	★	...	...
Alaska	...	...	★	Nebraska	...	★	...
Arizona	...	★	...	Nevada	...	...	★
Arkansas	...	★	...	New Hampshire	...	...	★
California	★	...	...	New Jersey	★	...	...
Colorado	...	...	★	New Mexico	...	★	...
Connecticut	...	★	...	New York	...	★	...
Delaware	...	★	...	North Carolina	...	★	...
Florida	...	...	★	North Dakota	...	...	★
Georgia	★	...	...	Ohio	★	...	...
Hawaii	...	★	...	Oklahoma	★	...	...
Idaho	...	★	...	Oregon	...	...	★
Illinois	...	★	...	Pennsylvania	...	★	...
Indiana	...	★	...	Rhode Island	...	★	...
Iowa	...	★	...	South Carolina	...	★	...
Kansas	...	★	...	South Dakota	...	★	...
Kentucky	...	...	★	Tennessee	...	...	★
Louisiana	...	★	...	Texas	★	...	...
Maine	...	...	★	Utah	★	...	...
Maryland	...	★	...	Vermont	...	...	★
Massachusetts	...	★	...	Virginia	★	...	...
Michigan	...	★	...	Washington	★	...	...
Minnesota	...	★	...	West Virginia	★	...	...
Mississippi	...	★	...	Wisconsin	...	★	...
Missouri	...	★	...	Wyoming	★	...	...

Source: U.S. Environmental Protection Agency.

Table 8.44
STATE ACTIONS ON ASBESTOS IN BUILDINGS*

State or other jurisdiction	Legislation adopted	State funding	State assistance	Local funding option	Contractor certification and training	Air monitoring
Alabama	...	...	★(a)	...	...	...
Alaska	★	...	★	...	★	...
Arizona	...	...	...	...	...	...
Arkansas	★	...	...	...	★	...
California	★	★	...	...	★	★
Colorado	★(b)	...	...	...	...	★(c)
Connecticut	★	★	★	...	...	★
Delaware	★(b)	...	...	...	...	...
Florida	...	...	...	...	...	...
Georgia	...	★	★	...	...	...
Hawaii	...	...	...	...	...	...
Idaho	...	...	...	★	...	...
Illinois	★	★	★	★	★	...
Indiana	★	...	...	...	★	...
Iowa	★	...	...	★	★	...
Kansas	★	...	★	...	★	...
Kentucky	★(b)	...	★	...	...	...
Louisiana	★(b,d)	★	★	...	★	★(c)
Maine	...	...	★	...	...	...
Maryland	★	...	★	...	★	...
Massachusetts	★	★	★	★	...	...
Michigan	★	...	...	★	...	...
Minnesota	★	★	...	★	...	...
Mississippi	...	...	★	...	...	...
Missouri	...	...	...	...	...	...
Montana	...	...	...	...	...	...
Nebraska	★	...	...	★	...	...
Nevada	...	...	...	...	...	...
New Hampshire	...	...	...	...	...	...
New Jersey	★	★(e,f)	★	...	★	★
New Mexico	...	...	★	...	...	...
New York	★	★	★	...	(g)	...
North Carolina	...	★(e)	...	★	...	...
North Dakota	★	...	...	...	...	...
Ohio	★(b)	...	★	...	★	...
Oklahoma	★	...	★	...	★	...
Oregon	...	...	...	...	...	...
Pennsylvania	★(b)	★	...	...	...	...
Rhode Island	★	★	★	...	★	★
South Carolina	★(h)	...	★	...	★(i)	...
South Dakota	...	...	...	...	...	...
Tennessee	★(b)	...	★	...	...	...
Texas	...	...	...	...	...	...
Utah	...	...	...	...	...	...
Vermont	(b)	...	...	...	...	...
Virginia	★(b)	...	★	...	...	...
Washington	★	...	...	...	...	...
West Virginia	...	...	...	...	★	...
Wisconsin	(b)	...	★	...	★	...
Wyoming	...	...	...	...	...	...
Dist. of Col.	★(b)	...	...	...	...	...

*1984-85 actions

Source: Safe Building Alliance.

(a) Removal of asbestos in state schools is being done under court order obtained in a suit by state attorney general against the state school boards.

(b) Special task force or committee created to study problem.

(c) Commission recommendations for standard due January 1986.

(d) Attorney general to assist local schools in civil suits against manufacturers, suppliers, and installers of asbestos materials.

(e) Funding for control in state buildings.

(f) Available through foundation aid program or local funding mandatory.

(g) Training.

(h) Mandatory state inspection program.

(i) Inspector certification required.

Table 8.45
NATIONAL WILDLIFE REFUGE SYSTEM AND RELATED AREAS
OF U.S. FISH AND WILDLIFE SERVICE, BY STATE: 1984

State	Number of areas	Acres	State	Number of areas	Acres
Alabama	9	50,934	Montana	52	1,154,556
Alaska	33	77,053,592	Nebraska	13	157,097
Arizona	12	1,593,080	Nevada	13	2,372,097
Arkansas	10	204,942	New Hampshire	3	2,229
California	34	293,447	New Jersey	4	40,005
Colorado	8	59,925	New Mexico	11	382,167
Connecticut	1	183	New York	11	23,522
Delaware	3	25,403	North Carolina	12	256,748
Florida	28	473,394	North Dakota	109	1,273,545
Georgia	11	468,439	Ohio	5	8,685
Hawaii	7	255,825	Oklahoma	7	140,927
Idaho	16	85,072	Oregon	24	544,546
Illinois	7	118,063	Pennsylvania	5	9,173
Indiana	1	7,724	Rhode Island	4	1,244
Iowa	7	73,694	South Carolina	10	189,506
Kansas	3	51,443	South Dakota	53	499,495
Kentucky	3	2,174	Tennessee	7	84,709
Louisiana	10	291,221	Texas	19	303,037
Maine	10	31,565	Utah	8	101,855
Maryland	6	26,077	Vermont	3	5,943
Massachusetts	11	12,183	Virginia	11	104,971
Michigan	17	110,001	Washington	38	184,609
Minnesota	33	444,844	West Virginia	3	456
Mississippi	9	115,584	Wisconsin	20	221,079
Missouri	10	55,602	Wyoming	15	75,556

Source: Adapted from *Annual Report of Lands Under Control of the U.S. Fish and Wildlife Service as of September 30, 1984*, U.S. Department of the Interior (1985).

Table 8.46
STATE ENVIRONMENTAL QUALITY COMMISSIONS: NAMES AND FUNCTIONS

State or other jurisdiction	Name of body	Investigative	Sets standards	Decision making	Policy making	Appeals board	Advisory	Makes/adopts rules/regs.	Review board	Reporting	Other
Alabama(a)	...	...	...	...	(b)	...	...	...	...	...	...
Alaska	...	...	...	...	...	...	...	...	...	...	...
Arizona	(c)	...	...	...	...	...	...	...	...	...	...
Arkansas	Commission on Pollution Control and Ecology	...	...	★	★	...	...	...	...	...	...
California	...	...	...	...	(b)	...	...	...	...	...	...
Colorado	(c)	...	...	...	...	...	...	...	...	...	...
Connecticut	Council on Environmental Quality	★	...	...	...	...	...	...	★	★	...
Delaware	Council on Environmental Control	...	...	...	...	...	★	...	...	...	...
Florida	Environmental Regulation Commission	...	★	...	...	...	...	...	...	...	...
Georgia(a)	...	...	...	...	...	(d)	...	...	...	...	...
Hawaii	Environmental Council	...	...	...	...	...	...	...	...	...	...
Idaho	Board of Health & Welfare	...	...	...	...	★	...	★	...	...	...
Illinois	Pollution Control Board	...	...	...	...	...	...	★	★	...	(e)
Indiana	Environmental Management Board	...	...	...	★	...	...	★	...	...	...
Iowa	Water, Air, and Waste Management Commission	...	...	...	...	...	...	★	...	...	...
Kansas	Advisory Commission on Environment	...	...	...	...	...	★	...	...	...	...
Kentucky	Environmental Quality Commission	...	...	...	...	★	★	...	...	...	...
Louisiana	...	...	...	...	(b)	...	...	...	...	...	...
Maine	Board of Environmental Protection	...	...	...	...	★	...	★	...	...	(f)

Source: Survey of state environmental quality commissions conducted by The Council of State Governments in spring 1985.

Key:
★—Performs function.

417

STATE ENVIRONMENTAL QUALITY COMMISSIONS—Continued

State or other jurisdiction	Name of body	Investigative	Sets standards	Decision making	Policy making	Appeals board	Advisory	Makes/adopts rules/regs.	Review board	Reporting	Other
Maryland	Advisory Board to Secretary of Dept. of Natural Resources	…	…	…	…	…	…	…	…	…	(g)
Massachusetts(a)											
Michigan(a)						(b)					
Minnesota											
Mississippi	Natural Resource Commission; Natural Resources Permit Board	…	…	…	★	…	…	…	…	…	(h)
Missouri	Air Conservation Commission; Clean Water Commission	…	…	…	…	…	…	…	…	…	(i)
Montana	Board of Health and Environmental Sciences; Environmental Quality Control	★	…	…	…	…	…	★	★	…	…
Nebraska	Environmental Control Council	…	★	…	…	…	…	★	…	…	…
Nevada	State Environmental Commission	…	…	…	…	★	…	★	…	…	…
New Hampshire(a)											
New Jersey	(c)										
New Mexico						(b)					
New York	Environmental Board	…	…	…	…	…	★	…	…	…	(j)
North Carolina	Environmental Management Commission(k)	…	★	…	…	…	…	★	…	…	…
North Dakota	Air Pollution Control Advisory Council; Pollution Control Board	…	…	…	…	…	★	…	…	…	…
Ohio(a)											
Oklahoma	Pollution Control Coordinating Board	…	…	…	…	…	…	…	…	…	…
Oregon	Environmental Quality Commission	…	…	…	★	…	…	★	…	…	(l)
Pennsylvania	Environmental Quality Board	…	…	…	…	…	…	★	★	…	…

Roles and functions:

Key:
★—Performs function.

STATE ENVIRONMENTAL QUALITY COMMISSIONS—Continued

State or other jurisdiction	Name of body	\~Investi-gative	Sets standards	Decision making	Policy making	Appeals board	Advisory	Makes/adopts rules/regs.	Review board	Reporting	Other
Rhode Island	Advisory Council on Environmental Affairs						(d)				
South Carolina(a)											
South Dakota(a)											
Tennessee					(b)						
Texas(a)											
Utah	(m)	…	…	…	…	…	★	…	…	…	…
Vermont	(c)										
Virginia(a)											
Washington	Ecological Commission	…	…	…	…	…	★	…	…	…	…
West Virginia(a)											
Wisconsin	Natural Resources Board	…	…	…	★	…	…	…	…	…	…
Wyoming	Land, Air, Water(o)	…	…	…	…	…	★	…	…	…	(n)
Puerto Rico	Environmental Quality Board	…	…	…	★	…	…	★	…	…	…

Roles and functions:

Key:
★—Performs function.
(a) No response.
(b) No environmental quality commission.
(c) No single commission. In Arizona, Solid Waste Management Advisory Board, State Air Pollution Control Hearing Board, Statewide Health Coordinating Council Environmental Subcommittee, Water Quality Control Council. In Colorado, individual water and air quality commissions. In New Jersey, individual program committees. In Vermont, separate boards for each department; some advisory and some with rule-making and quasi-judicial authority.
(d) Information not available.
(e) Also serves as a court for enforcement cases.
(f) Also takes action on some categories of permits; final enforcement actions.
(g) Early citizen input in the formulation of policies, programs, and plans.

(h) Also enforces pollution control laws; Permit Board issues, modifies, and revokes permits.
(i) Holds hearings on regulations; refers litigation to attorney general's office.
(j) Votes on changes to numerical standards and criteria.
(k) Also separate commissions for mining, sediment control, soil and water, hazardous waste, drinking water, marine fisheries, wildlife, and wastewater treatment.
(l) Coordinates pollution control activities of all state agencies.
(m) Safe Drinking Water Commission, Solid and Hazardous Waste Commission, Water Pollution Control Commission, Radiation Control, General Sanitation Advisory Commission.
(n) Also selection of secretary.
(o) Separate advisory boards.

INTERSTATE WATER AGENCIES

By Larry Feazell

The concept of formal cooperation between states to resolve regional water problems is not a new one. The first effort, in fact, pre-dates the U.S. Constitution—in 1785, Maryland and Virginia formed a compact to discuss their concerns regarding the future of the Potomac River. It was not until the 1930s and later, however, that interstate agreements began to flourish.

In response to increasing water pollution, the initial agreements began in the East—the Interstate Commission on the Potomac River Basin in 1940; the New England Interstate Water Pollution Control Commission in 1947; and the Ohio River Valley Water Sanitation Commission in 1948. With the exception of the Potomac, each has enforcement powers.

To allocate water from the Colorado River, the first formal effort in the West brought together the states of Colorado, New Mexico, Utah, and Wyoming in the formation of the Upper Colorado River Commission (1948).

The 1950s saw the formation of the Interstate Commission on the Delaware River Basin to deal with water supply issues; it proved inadequate to do so. In 1961, Congress approved the present state/federal compact—the Delaware River Basin Commission—which has the authority to enforce regulations for water resources planning and management in the basin.

The Great Lakes Commission, formed in 1955 to deal primarily with navigation issues on the Great Lakes, now deals with a broad range of issues affecting water resources in the area. Some of these responsibilities were assumed as a result of the demise of the Great Lakes Basin Commission in 1981. The present Commission is advisory in nature.

In 1957, California and Oregon established the Klamath River Compact Commission (which has no enforcement authority) to resolve water allocation disputes.

While reluctantly involving itself in compacts with the states, the federal government, through the Water Resources Planning Act of 1965, sought a mechanism for national coordination of river basin planning. Title II of the act authorized the formation of interstate river basin commissions and mandated them to prepare comprehensive coordinated plans for managing the basins' water and related land resources. Commissions formed in 1967 were the Pacific Northwest, Great Lakes, and New England. The Ohio followed in 1970, the Upper Mississippi in 1971, and the Missouri in 1972. Funding was provided by the states and the federal government.

However, the law that gave rise to the basin commissions also limited their effectiveness. With no power to implement the plans mandated by law and the unwillingness of federal participating agencies to relinquish any of their planning authority, the commissions were only marginally successful. Their demise as state/federal commissions in September 1981 was brought about by then-Secretary of the Interior James Watt's decision to withdraw federal participation. With the exception of the Pacific Northwest Commission, the remaining commissions used unspent funds to continue operations as purely states' organizations. The New England became part of the New England Governors Conference, Inc., the Great Lakes was absorbed by the Great Lakes Commission, and the Missouri and the Upper Mississippi made name changes (becoming associations). The Ohio retained its name. These commissions exist today primarily as forums for members to discuss and conduct research on issues of common concern, and to see that those concerns are represented in Washington, D.C.

With 13 members and two associate members, the Western States Water Council is the largest of the interstate water agencies. Established in 1965, the Council is advisory and represents the states' governors on water policy issues.

Also in the West is the Tahoe Regional Planning Agency, organized in 1969 by California and Nevada to deal with Lake Tahoe water pollution and other issues.

Larry Feazell is Executive Director of the Ohio River Basin Commission.

The Susquehanna River Basin Commission, similar to the Delaware Commission, was approved by Congress in 1971. It, too, has enforcement powers for water resources planning and management.

Although many of the interstate water agencies are funded entirely by the states, there seems to be support for their continuance, at least in the short-term. Their long-term existence, however, is uncertain.

In order to remain viable, they will have to provide services which justify their support. If state water programs are enhanced through regional cooperation, and members' concerns are being heard in Washington, then the agencies are likely to remain in business even in this present period of fiscal austerity.

For additional information on interstate water agencies, see Table 8.47.

Table 8.47
INTERSTATE WATER AGENCIES

State or other jurisdiction	Delaware River Basin Comm. (1961)	Great Lakes Comm. (1955)	Interstate Comm. on the Potomac River Basin (1940)	Interstate Sanitation Comm. (1936)	Klamath River Compact Comm. (1957)	Missouri Basin States Assn. (1981)	New England Governors' Conf., Inc. (1936)	New England Interstate Water Pollution Control Comm. (1947)	Ohio River Basin Comm. (1981)	Ohio River Valley Water Sanitation Comm. (1948)	Susquehanna River Basin Comm. (1971)	Tahoe Regional Planning Agency (1969)	Upper Colorado River Comm. (1948)	Upper Mississippi River Basin Assn. (1981)	Western States Water Council (1965)
Alabama															
Alaska															★
Arizona															★
Arkansas															
California					★							★			★
Colorado						★							★		★
Connecticut				★			★	★							
Delaware	★														
Florida															
Georgia															
Hawaii															
Idaho															★
Illinois		★							★	★				★	
Indiana		★							★	★					
Iowa						★								★	
Kansas						★									★
Kentucky									★	★					
Louisiana															
Maine							★	★							
Maryland			★								★				
Massachusetts							★	★							
Michigan		★													
Minnesota		★												★	
Mississippi															
Missouri						★								★	
Montana						★									★
Nebraska						★									★
Nevada												★			★
New Hampshire							★	★							
New Jersey	★			★											
New Mexico													★		★
New York	★	★		★				★ (a)	★	★	★				
North Carolina															
North Dakota						★									★
Ohio		★							★	★					★ (b)

INTERSTATE WATER AGENCIES—Continued

State or other jurisdiction	Delaware River Basin Comm. (1961)	Great Lakes Comm. (1955)	Interstate Comm. on the Potomac River Basin (1940)	Interstate Sanitation Comm. (1936)	Klamath River Compact Comm. (1957)	Missouri Basin States Assn. (1981)	New England Governors' Conf., Inc. (1936)	New England Interstate Water Pollution Control Comm. (1947)	Ohio River Basin Comm. (1981)	Ohio River Valley Water Sanitation Comm. (1948)	Susquehanna River Basin Comm. (1971)	Tahoe Regional Planning Agency (1969)	Upper Colorado River Comm. (1948)	Upper Mississippi River Basin Assn. (1981)	Western States Water Council (1965)
Oklahoma															★
Oregon					★										★
Pennsylvania	★	★	★						★	★	★				
Rhode Island							★	★							
South Carolina															
South Dakota						★									★(b)
Tennessee															
Texas															★
Utah													★		★
Vermont							★	★							
Virginia			★						★	★					
Washington															★
West Virginia			★						★	★					
Wisconsin		★												★	
Wyoming						★							★		★
Dist. of Col.			★												
Other information about agency:															
Federal membership	•								•		•		•		
Advisory only						•	•		•					•	•
Enforcement powers	•			•				•(c)		•	•	•			
Funding state		•	•		•	•	•	•		•		•	•(d)	•	•
Funding federal/ state	•								•		•				

Key:
★ —Membership in agency
.. —Not applicable
• —Yes

(a) Not a formal member; cooperates on water issues through the New England/New York Water Council which is part of this conference.
(b) Associate member.
(c) Primarily advisory; has the power to enforce water quality regulations on interstate rivers.
(d) Allocates water from Colorado River.

CHAPTER NINE

INTER-GOVERNMENTAL AFFAIRS

DEVELOPMENTS IN FEDERAL-STATE RELATIONS: 1984-85

By Norman Beckman

Changes in the federal government's relationship with the states during the biennium may best be explained as part of a longer-term, grand design of devolution. This federal domestic strategy involves shifting authority for programs down to the states, while reducing federal financing for those programs. Deregulation, block grants, tax cuts, and reduced spending in domestic programs that assist state governments have contributed to the decentralization process in recent years. But the new tax reform and deficit reduction proposals dominating national debate early in 1986 could significantly accelerate the change in the relationship between the federal and state governments.

Federal Funding

Pervading all debate on federal-state issues is the size of the federal debt, an amount which in absolute terms has reached an all-time high. The budget deficit for fiscal year 1985 totaled $212 billion—an amount that approximated the combined tax collections for the 50 state governments. The total debt of the national government was reaching $2 trillion at the end of 1985, and is expected to top 50 percent of the Gross National Product (GNP) sometime in 1986.

Spending of all kinds would have had to decrease by over 22 percent or federal tax revenues to increase by almost 29 percent in order to bring the fiscal year 1985 budget into balance. The latter action, though, likely would have been an unpopular choice. A May 1985 public opinion survey conducted by the U.S. Advisory Commission on Intergovernmental Relations found that Americans identified the federal income tax as the "worst" tax.[1]

Federal assistance to states and localities now represents 11 percent of the federal budget. The federal government distributed about $107 billion in grants to states and localities in 1985, and an additional $44 billion in less direct forms of aid. Most of this assistance, however, has been devoted to programs where the national, state, and local governments have shared interests, as in poverty and health programs, the interstate highway system, and education.

In fiscal year 1985, these federal funds accounted for approximately 24 percent of the total state and local receipts, and 21 percent of state and local expenditures by the end of 1985. In 1980, federal grants comprised over 26 percent of the state and local government expenditures. The downward trend in grants has been partially offset by increased federal tax expenditures, but the latter also are being targeted for future reductions.

While federal funding for grants for individuals increased from $31.9 billion in 1980 to $50.6 billion in 1985 (a 20.4 percent increase in constant dollars), grants for state and local programs remained virtually unchanged in current dollars—from $59.5 billion in 1980 to $59.9 billion in 1985, representing an inflation-adjusted decrease of 23.5 percent.[2]

In 1980, state and local governments provided approximately 37 cents of matching funds for every dollar of federal aid; in 1985, the state and local share was about 50 cents for every dollar—an increase due in large part to the significant growth in programs such as Medicaid that require a larger than average matching share.

Federal aid on a per capita basis also varied across the regions of the country (see Table A). The highest per capita aid in 1984-85 went to the eastern states, which generally provide higher benefits for Medicaid and other income support programs. The lowest per capita aid in 1985 went to the southern, plains, and southwestern states.[3]

A major study issued in January 1986 by the Congressional Research Service on the effect of federal tax and budget policies in the

Norman Beckman is Director of the Washington, D.C. Office of The Council of State Governments. This essay was prepared with the assistance of Karin Kassabian, University of Indiana.

Table A
Distribution of Grants by Region, Selected Fiscal Years

Federal region	1985 total grants(a)	Dollars (per capita)			Average annual percent increase, 1975-85
		1975	1984	1985	
United States	105.9	227	413	437	6.6
I. Maine, Vermont, New Hampshire, Massachusetts, Connecticut, Rhode Island	6.3	247	456	501	7.1
II. New York, New Jersey, Puerto Rico, Virgin Islands ...	16.9	283	619	588	7.4
III. Virginia, Pennsylvania, Delaware, Maryland, West Virginia, District of Columbia	11.6	251	422	460	6.1
IV. Kentucky, Tennessee, North Carolina, South Carolina, Georgia, Alabama, Mississippi, Florida	16.0	205	349	381	6.2
V. Illinois, Indiana, Michigan, Ohio, Wisconsin, Minnesota..	19.1	195	393	417	7.7
VI. Arkansas, Louisiana, Oklahoma, New Mexico, Texas ...	9.6	210	326	344	4.9
VII. Iowa, Kansas, Missouri, Nebraska	4.7	196	363	395	7.1
VIII. Colorado, Montana, North Dakota, South Dakota, Utah, Wyoming..	4.0	263	515	530	7.1
IX. Arizona, California, Nevada, Hawaii, other territories ..	13.1	232	389	412	5.8
X. Idaho, Oregon, Washington, Alaska	4.5	263	470	517	6.8

Source: Special Analyses, Budget of the United States Government Fiscal Year 1986 and Fiscal Year 1987.

states drew a harsh conclusion from these statistics:

> ...Federal intergovernmental policy in the 1980s reflects a serious reevaluation of the federal responsibility to provide financial assistance to the state-local sector. All forms of federal financial assistance have either been reduced or have been threatened with reduction.... And federal tax subsidies to the state-local sector have been coveted as a primary revenue source to pay for reduction of federal income tax rates....

> These reductions have occurred at a time when federal spending increased by 23 percent in real terms. The conclusion seems clear that these accumulated policies reflect, at the least, a willingness by Congress and the administration to question the desirability or usefulness of the goods or services the state-local sector provides with federal funds.[4]

The Implications of Federal Legislation and Regulation

The 1984-85 biennium was not a smooth one for most congressional proposals of significance to the states; the bills were marked by controversy, and many of those that did survive the congressional end-of-session chaos preempted state powers. Congress tightened its regulatory grip on state govern-ment by imposing new penalties for non-compliance, adding conditions for receiving grants, and mandating new state expenditures. Overall, the outcome for states was mixed.[5]

In 1984, Congress passed legislation aimed at compelling the states to raise the minimum drinking age. In order to accomplish its objective, however, the legislation uses a "crossover sanction": any state that does not act quickly to adopt a minimum drinking age of 21 will face a 5 percent reduction in its federal highway construction money in 1986, and a 10 percent reduction in 1987. The legislation was enacted in response to strong grassroots lobbying efforts led by Mothers Against Drunk Driving (MADD), but a number of state government officials resented the use of the sanction and the federal intrusion into an area they previously had regulated.

On the plus side for state and local governments during the biennium, initiatives were taken to simplify the management of federal grant programs through the Single Audit Act of 1984. The new law eliminates audit requirements imposed on recipients of small amounts of federal assistance, and clarifies requirements for organization-wide audits of grant recipients. State and local governments that receive more than $100,000 in federal aid are allowed to conduct their own financial audits to ensure that the aid received was spent for the intended purposes, and that the recipients complied with accounting and administrative controls, and federal laws and regulations.

In mid-1984, Congress responded to public outcry over the national debt by approving a package of tax increases and spending cuts that is expected to result in a $63 billion "downpayment" on the deficit by fiscal year 1988. The Deficit Reduction Act imposed restrictions on tax-exempt private purpose bonds and changed the tax treatment of municipal sale-leasebacks and contracts. The act set a $150 per capita or $200 million per state annual volume cap (whichever is greater) on issuing tax exempt industrial development bonds (IDBs). The restriction applies to bonds for student loans, pollution control, private health care facilities, agriculture, and small-issue IDBs (including those for projects in economically-distressed areas).[6]

But the reduction act did not limit itself to spending cuts and tax increases. It amended the AFDC and Medicaid programs, creating increased expenditures by both national and state governments.

Legislation setting national policy for regulation of the cable television industry was enacted in 1984. The Cable Communications Policy Act recognized at least limited authority of states and municipalities to grant and renew cable franchises, but established national standards for renewal. After two years, state and local governments are preempted from setting rates for basic services.

In the Motor Carrier Safety Act of 1984, Congress preempted state commercial motor vehicle safety laws and regulations. Existing and future state laws, standards, and regulations in the area must be submitted to the U.S. Secretary of Transportation for review to determine whether they can co-exist with federal law.

The Child Support Enforcement Amendments were designed to strengthen state efforts to collect child support payments from delinquent parents, and require states to extend collection assistance to non-welfare families. However, several of its provisions—such as mandatory wage withholding from parents whose children are receiving child enforcement support services, the imposition

of liens against property for the amount overdue, and the withholding of state tax refunds due if the parent is delinquent in support payments—will mean more work for state administrators.

In 1984, Congress enacted several new grant programs, including a formula grant for state and local education agencies to train mathematics and science teachers, and a program to assist magnet schools in carrying out desegregation plans. An "anti-crime" package included a grant program to states for criminal justice projects, and created a new grant initiative that will allow up to $100 million per year in federal criminal fines and penalties to be distributed to existing state victim assistance and compensation programs.

And during the biennium, Congress reauthorized the following block grants, all at increased authorized funding levels: Alcohol, Drug Abuse and Mental Health; Preventive Health and Health Services; Maternal and Child Health; and Community Services.

In response to the U.S. Supreme Court's decision in *Garcia v. San Antonio Metropolitan Transit Authority*, Congress amended the Fair Labor Standards Act (FLSA) in 1985, thus permitting state and local governments to provide time-and-a-half compensatory time off for their employees in lieu of overtime payments.

Congress reorganized the farm credit system, and passed a new five-year farm act reducing price supports. The portion reauthorizing food stamps places a two-year delay on penalties to be assessed states for error rates, and moves to end state sales taxes on food stamp purchases.

In the area of environmental protection, Congress reauthorized and toughened the Resource Conservation and Recovery Act (RCRA), and designated 8.6 million acres as wilderness areas in 21 states (eight western and 13 eastern and southern states).

During 1984-85, executive branch agencies also revised several regulations affecting state and local governments.[7] For example, the U.S. Department of the Interior issued a rule authorizing the states to conduct inspections, audits, and investigations related to oil and gas royalties paid and collected on federal and Indian lands—a rule that could increase states' revenues as they receive half of all royalties collected. Interior also issued rules giving state and local governments a larger role in reviewing and approving applications for historic preservation programs.

In October 1985, the Office of Management and Budget (OMB) published an updated catalog identifying the 68 "crosscutting" requirements that affect federal financial assistance. To simplify one of these—the Uniform Relocation Assistance policies—the president signed a memorandum calling upon 20 agencies to issue common regulations.

A joint state and federal cash management task force signed a memorandum of understanding regarding proposed amendments to the Intergovernmental Cooperation Act and related administrative regulations. These amendments were designed to provide a mutually-agreeable means for transferring funds between the federal government and the states.

OMB and the U.S. Bureau of the Census, working with other federal agencies and the state governments, improved the reporting of federal grant and other expenditure statistics to local areas.

At the end of the biennium, however, a federal action was undertaken that is likely to affect the relationship between the national and state governments for the next several years. The Balanced Budget and Emergency Deficit Control Act—commonly referred to as "Gramm-Rudman-Hollings," after its congressional sponsors—or simply abbreviated as "Gramm-Rudman"—was enacted on December 12, 1985. The act establishes a new budget process designed to lower the federal deficit to zero over the next five years.

Under Gramm-Rudman, 50 percent of the cuts will come from domestic programs, and 50 percent from defense. Certain domestic programs are exempt from the across-the-board cuts (including Social Security, Medicaid, Aid to Families with Dependent Children, Supplemental Security Income, Child Nutrition, Food Stamps, Veterans' Pensions, and the Women, Infants and Children Program); however, for other non-defense spending, the act requires uniform percentage cuts in budget authority and outlays. These sequestrations would have to be uniform down to the level of individual programs.

From the perspective of state budgets and revenues, the Gramm-Rudman sequestration process may be a "least worst" solution to the federal budget dilemma. Right off the top, cuts must be shared on a 50-50 basis between defense and a number of vulnerable domestic programs of prime interest to the states. Moreover, most of the programs receiving protection or special treatment under the sequestering order are of major budgetary and program significance to the states. These "exempt" programs are saved from the automatic reduction provisions, but not necessarily from reductions made if the normal budget process achieves the annual targeted deficit reductions.

Federal Court Decisions

The U.S. Supreme Court plays a unique role in sorting out the balance required by federalism. Its decisions can affect the allocation of power to, the fiscal impact on, and the regulatory authority of the states.

In 1984-85, the Court sent out mixed signals in the realm of federal-state relations.[8] In the *Garcia* case, involving perhaps the most significant federalism decision of the last two terms, the Court—in holding that federal wage and hour standards apply to municipal and state workers—dashed state hopes that the Tenth Amendment could effectively shield states from federal regulation. Although the long-term effects of the ruling are not clear, the Court made clear that protection of state sovereign interests should be sought in the non-judicial branches of government.

For the most part, the Court took a broad view of the federal commerce power and a correspondingly narrow view of state authority. In *Armco v. Hardesty*, West Virginia's wholesale gross receipts tax was found to discriminate against interstate commerce. Moreover, despite the states' special status under the Twenty-first Amendment regarding commerce in liquor, in *Bacchus Imports, Ltd. v. Dias*, Hawaii's sales tax exemption for certain indigenous liquors was held to favor local products in violation of the Commerce Clause.

A notable exception among state preemption losses was the much publicized case of *Silkwood v. Kerr-McGee*. At issue before the Court was an Oklahoma statute allowing the recovery of punitive damages for contamination injuries. Kerr-McGee contended that the statute conflicted with the federal Atomic Energy Act and the Price-Anderson Act, which established an indemnification scheme for operators of nuclear facilities. The Court, however, found no such conflict with national objectives, and ruled that the state statute was not preempted by federal law.

In a number of other cases, however, the Supreme Court struck down state statutes on the ground that they were preempted by federal legislation governing interstate commerce. In *Aloha Airlines v. Director of Taxation of Hawaii*, the Court unanimously ruled that the state's tax on airlines' gross income was invalid as it was inconsistent with a provision of the Federal Airport Development Acceleration Act of 1973. *In State of Connecticut v. United States*, the Court affirmed a decision enjoining enforcement of the state's law banning tandem trailers from its highways, because of its preemption by the Surface Transportation Assistance Act of 1983. And in *Southland Corp. v. Keating*, a divided Court sustained a challenge to a provision of the California Franchise Investment Law that had the effect of invalidating compulsory arbitration provisions in franchise agreements. The Court ruled that the state law was preempted by the Federal Arbitration Act which made arbitration agreements enforceable.

In *Secretary of State of Maryland v. Joseph H. Munson Company*, the Court, in a 5-4 decision, struck down a state law prohibiting charitable organizations from paying fundraising expenses in excess of 25 percent of the amount raised.

In *Atascadero State Hospital v. Scanlon*, the Court, in a 5-4 decision, found that the Eleventh Amendment protected the state from suit by a handicapped individual under section 504 of the Rehabilitation Act. The majority concluded that the federal legislation did not abrogate the state's immunity from suit, and that the immunity was not waived by accepting federal funds under the act.

In *Roberts v. United States Jaycees*, the Court sustained the right of the state of Minnesota to require the Jaycees to admit women as full voting members under its Human Rights Act, thus rejecting a challenge based on the First Amendment freedom of association. The Court ruled that the right to associate for purposes of expression was not absolute, and in this case, was outweighed by the state's "compelling interest in eradicating discrimination against its female citizens."

In *Wallace v. Jaffree*, the Court, in a 6-3 decision, struck down an Alabama law authorizing a moment of silence for "meditation or voluntary prayer" in the public schools, and in *Estate of Thornton v. Caldor* struck down a Connecticut law that prohibited employers from requiring employees to work on the day they regard as their Sabbath. Emphasizing the absolute nature of the requirement, the Court found that it had a "primary effect" of "advanc(ing) a particular religious practice."

What Will This Mean For The States?

During the biennium, federal mandates continued to be imposed as the courts continued to protect federal sovereignty, usually at the expense of the states. But while the pace of federal withdrawal was being debated, other related uncertainties faced the states at the end of 1985. Many of the federal appropriations have been bound up in multiple continuing resolutions, so that states do not know their grant-in-aid levels for the current year. The president has promised and undertaken additional actions to use his rescission and deferral authorities over appropriations already made. Budget reconciliation legislation runs far behind schedule, and tax reform proposals have stopped the tax exempt bond market (both for revenue and general obligations) in its tracks.

All of this comes at a time when 18 states, in an effort to avert deficits, have been forced to cut back on their enacted 1986 budgets after the beginning of the fiscal year—a relatively large number of states for a non-recession period.[9]

While short-term uncertainties will be resolved, the federal budget and tax policies being debated in early 1986 indicate a continuing desire at the federal level to get on with the sorting-out, cutting-back process, with or without meaningful participation by the states.

John Shannon, Executive Director of the U.S. Advisory Commission on Intergovernmental Relations has described 1985 as "Year Seven for De Facto New Federalism." According to Shannon:

> . . .Federalism is becoming increasingly extrusive in character—the federal government is pulling aid funds and tax resources

from state and local governments to strengthen the financing of its own national programs.

New Federalism calls on the states to help themselves by setting up "rainy day" funds to cushion their finances from the shock of economic downturns. . .

De Facto New Federalism operates in a political climate that resolves [social equity concerns] in favor of economic development, defense expansion, and domestic public sector containment. . . .[10]

The prospect of continued federal withdrawal from the intergovernmental arena raises some classic intergovernmental issues:

Will the states with the weakest economic bases be at least partially shielded from federal budget cuts?

Will the federal aid programs that help states assist the poor continue to receive some protection?

Will federal withdrawal and new tax policies stimulate undesirable interstate competition?

Will states and localities be protected from new federal statutory and regulatory requirements that come without federal reimbursement?

Will the federal courts defer to Congress, or will the states retain some semblance of independence under the Tenth Amendment and various other clauses of the Constitution?

Notes

1. See *Significant Features of Fiscal Federalism: 1985-86* (Washington, D.C.: U.S. Advisory Commission on Intergovernmental Relations, 1986): 1-3.

2. Lillian Rymarowicz and Dennis Zimmerman, *The Effect of Federal Tax and Budget Policies in the 1980s on the State-Local Sector* (Washington, D.C.: Congressional Research Service, Report No. 86-2E, January 2, 1986), 5-8.

An inventory of federal grant-in-aid programs for fiscal year 1984 listed 392 categorical grant programs, a decrease of 27 percent from fiscal year 1981. The number of block grants increased from four to 12 over this period.

3. See Special Analysis H of the *Special Analyses, Budget of the United States Government Fiscal Year 1986*, and *Fiscal Year 1987* (Washington, D.C.: Government Printing Office, February 1985 and February 1986), H-19 (in both documents).

4. Rymarowicz and Zimmerman, *The Effect of Federal Tax and Budget Policies in the 1980s on the State-Local Sector*, p. 45.

5. For more information on 1984-85 legislation, see Susan Golonka, "Whatever Happened to Federalism?" *Intergovernmental Perspective* 2, 1 (Winter 1985): 8-9. See also, "Cuts Coming for States Under Federal Budget Balancing" (January 1986), "Congress' Record: Lots to Fix in '86" (January 1986), and "Congressional Action Disappointingly Mixed for States" (November 1984), all in *State Government News* (The Council of State Governments).

6. The act exempts IDBs used to finance multi-family housing, publicly-owned convention and transportation facilities, public and non-profit health facilities, and low- and moderate-income housing.

7. See Special Analysis H of *Special Analyses, Budget of the United States Government Fiscal Year 1986* and *Fiscal Year 1987*, p. H-24-25. See also *Management of the United States Government Fiscal Year 1987* (Washington, D.C.: Government Printing Office, February 1986), 16-19.

8. See "Supreme Court Helps, Hurts Federalism" (September 1985) and "States Win, Lose Federalism Battles in Supreme Court" (October 1984), both in *State Government News* (The Council of State Governments), and *Court Report* (State and Local Legal Center (September 1985). See also Douglas Ross, "Safeguarding our Federalism: Lessons for the States from the Supreme Court," *Public Administration Review* 45 (November 1985), special issue): 723-31.

9. See *Fiscal Survey of the States 1986* (Washington, D.C.: National Governors' Association and National Association of State Budget Officers, March 1986), 19-25.

10. John Shannon, "De Facto New Federalism— Phase II?" (Remarks made at the University of Massachusetts at Boston, November 18, 1985 and revised December 17, 1985): 1-3.

Table 9.1
TOTAL FEDERAL AID TO STATES: FISCAL 1979-1984
(In thousands of dollars)

State or other jurisdiction	1984	1983	1982	1981	1980	1979
Total.............	$97,208,644	$92,711,726	$88,221,369	$94,806,164	$91,365,284	$82,853,441
Alabama...........	1,532,194	1,469,539	1,429,024	1,493,313	1,583,543	1,367,631
Alaska.............	615,698	540,720	421,922	447,917	451,170	388,580
Arizona............	989,925	844,994	799,223	864,322	837,882	809,479
Arkansas	946,183	901,417	843,779	886,840	940,352	846,856
California..........	9,798,986	9,205,482	9,015,844	10,007,616	8,804,443	8,251,050
Colorado	1,176,127	1,058,269	966,730	1,021,503	995,230	942,865
Connecticut	1,221,429	1,190,471	1,120,139	1,180,030	1,156,824	1,074,780
Delaware	298,517	306,816	279,369	313,613	275,358	232,500
Florida	2,783,803	2,819,394	2,859,149	2,867,706	2,854,439	2,397,511
Georgia...........	2,213,733	2,110,175	2,185,305	2,169,244	2,373,419	2,181,048
Hawaii	458,783	456,678	407,598	442,955	463,258	407,881
Idaho	413,181	375,421	349,847	361,130	393,079	337,183
Illinois............	4,303,812	4,191,166	4,102,545	4,610,352	4,476,964	3,782,934
Indiana	1,759,904	1,610,777	1,558,397	1,728,750	1,608,494	1,391,558
Iowa	1,091,051	980,568	893,175	961,018	994,733	877,823
Kansas	804,770	762,936	706,359	773,800	818,463	722,878
Kentucky	1,589,665	1,488,891	1,424,407	1,433,417	1,471,228	1,349,703
Louisiana	1,776,119	1,709,614	1,591,449	1,729,516	1,567,591	1,513,376
Maine	590,372	575,000	526,788	535,999	522,546	508,122
Maryland	1,697,453	1,790,362	1,792,714	1,889,555	1,843,192	1,577,979
Massachusetts	2,634,160	2,897,635	2,745,416	2,888,996	2,886,740	2,726,189
Michigan	3,775,972	3,614,250	3,634,110	4,107,594	3,928,527	3,568,596
Minnesota	1,864,551	1,764,801	1,769,271	1,773,557	1,667,347	1,515,431
Mississippi	1,175,894	1,101,157	1,090,755	1,098,354	1,190,010	1,045,969
Missouri	1,774,670	1,674,905	1,651,796	1,662,812	1,702,897	1,514,482
Montana..........	531,604	476,667	381,641	448,779	486,363	434,433
Nebraska	636,981	574,797	523,785	517,337	546,513	474,570
Nevada	340,350	356,360	346,200	350,592	335,469	276,828
New Hampshire	367,567	351,751	317,026	306,355	345,912	292,753
New Jersey.........	2,871,056	2,811,523	2,718,474	2,891,042	2,833,075	2,716,267
New Mexico........	862,668	675,756	727,234	715,855	668,500	617,016
New York	10,268,490	10,006,891	9,287,674	10,374,341	9,569,624	8,872,407
North Carolina	1,929,252	1,877,549	1,852,428	1,908,847	1,929,241	1,788,832
North Dakota	453,685	371,668	301,489	317,578	347,200	295,243
Ohio	4,044,258	3,641,767	3,611,567	3,725,226	3,433,736	3,071,195
Oklahoma	1,166,536	1,075,391	991,209	1,043,326	1,061,483	949,388
Oregon	1,246,130	1,162,916	1,167,622	1,174,601	1,237,294	1,070,598
Pennsylvania	4,667,346	4,817,080	4,629,305	4,886,585	4,515,615	4,099,060
Rhode Island	547,622	486,162	470,960	481,978	477,446	412,418
South Carolina	1,168,961	1,112,715	1,042,943	1,009,353	1,067,706	987,215
South Dakota	435,909	360,952	324,773	355,544	443,253	316,487
Tennessee	1,885,172	1,686,750	1,607,375	1,909,665	1,695,667	1,506,920
Texas..............	4,136,482	3,805,616	3,725,332	4,146,183	3,964,357	3,592,345
Utah	708,143	621,539	604,617	593,277	571,693	455,561
Vermont	331,008	312,181	270,662	279,382	355,597	241,813
Virginia............	1,628,438	1,665,881	1,623,108	1,861,670	1,775,472	1,700,559
Washington	1,697,921	1,536,779	1,579,965	1,771,273	1,674,116	1,417,104
West Virginia	819,209	840,398	771,613	940,997	950,423	771,522
Wisconsin..........	2,063,878	1,903,748	1,894,379	2,298,782	2,024,519	1,725,467
Wyoming	556,326	425,629	348,521	320,876	294,386	242,518
Dist. of Col.	1,381,886	1,355,941	1,295,321	1,417,140	1,336,361	1,138,639
Puerto Rico	2,231,139	2,110,626	1,397,295	1,351,763	1,430,471	1,308,739
Virgin Islands	136,803	91,390	116,427	153,557	295,798	228,784
Other..............	341,672 (a)	347,784 (a)	270,008 (b)	277,515 (b)	215,163 (b)	281,269 (b)
Adjustments or undistributed to states...	465,200	406,081	-142,695	-273,164	-324,898	235,087

Sources: Figures for 1979 through 1982 from U.S. Department of the Treasury, *Federal Aid to States, Fiscal Year 1982* (rev. ed.); figures for 1983 and 1984 from U.S. Department of Commerce, Bureau of the Census, *Federal Expenditures by State for Fiscal Year 1983* and *Federal Expenditures by State for Fiscal Year 1984.*

(a) Includes American Samoa, Guam, Northern Mariana Islands, and Trust Territory.
(b) Includes American Samoa, Guam, Northern Mariana Islands, Tokelau Islands, Trust Territory of the Pacific, and Saipan.

DEVELOPMENTS IN STATE-LOCAL RELATIONS: 1984-85

By Joseph F. Zimmerman

State restraints and state mandates, the principal determinants of the discretionary authority of local governments, continued to be prominent features of developments affecting state-local relations in 1984-85. The former prevent local governments from initiating certain types of actions, and the latter—based upon a constitutional provision, statutory provision, or administrative regulation—require political subdivisions to undertake a specified activity and/or provide a service meeting minimum state standards.

Other actions taken by the states included the transfer of functional responsibility, state supervision of local government, and state financial assistance to political subdivisions.

State Mandates

Mandates can be placed in numerous categories, including entitlement, equal treatment, ethical behavior, good neighbor, personnel, procedural, structural, and tax base. Although surveys have shown that most local officials view any mandate as an irritant, the principal objection to mandates is the cost burden placed upon local governments.

Until 1984, only the constitutions of California and Massachusetts required the state to reimburse local governments for the costs associated with state mandates; both requirements were added by means of the initiative and referendum. In Tennessee, the constitution forbids the General Assembly to impose mandates upon cities and counties unless the state assumes responsibility for part of the resulting costs.

In 1984, however, voters in two states approved constitutional amendments related to state mandates and associated costs to local governments. New Hampshire voters ratified a proposed constitutional amendment requiring state reimbursement of mandated costs. In the same year, New Mexico voters approved a constitutional amendment stipulating the state must reimburse political subdivisions for new mandated costs or provide "a means of new funding to the county or city to pay the cost of performing the mandated

activity or service for the period of time during which the activity or service is required to be performed."

Also in 1984, the New York Legislature established guidelines to be employed in preparing "fiscal notes" to accompany bills (beginning with the 1985 legislative session). By way of contrast, the 1984 Connecticut General Assembly approved legislation eliminating, effective January 1, 1985, the requirement for fiscal notes on local bills, and requiring the committee of cognizance of the bills to specify whether the state should reimburse local governments for costs resulting from a law creating or enlarging a state mandate.

In 1984, Mississippi enacted legislation directing all local governments to use a new election form designed to eliminate dual voter registration. In other action, the secretary of state required all school boards to examine their land holdings and submit current lease information, classify unclassified land, reexamine post-1978 leases, and renegotiate leases, if necessary.

The Florida Local Government Comprehensive Planning and Land Development Regulation Act of 1985 stipulates that failure of a local government to revise its comprehensive plan to meet requirements of the act would result in the regional planning agency being directed to prepare and adopt the required revisions.

In 1985, Connecticut required municipalities to make "proper provision. . .for soil erosion and sediment control," and in other legislation, increased the property tax exemption of farm machinery from $10,000 to $100,000.

The 1985 Georgia General Assembly, employing powers authorized by its new state constitution, enacted the Zoning Procedures Law for the purpose of ensuring "that due process is afforded to the general public when local governments regulate the uses of prop-

Joseph F. Zimmerman is Professor of Political Science, Graduate School of Public Affairs, State University of New York at Albany.

erty through the exercise of the zoning power."

The Arkansas Solid Waste Management Code, promulgated by the Department of Pollution Control and Ecology in 1985, requires city, town, and county governments to maintain an adequate solid waste management system for all areas within their respective jursidictions. Each unit must submit a detailed plan to the department within 180 days of receipt of a request for a plan. Upon departmental approval, the local government must administer the plan.

In what may be construed as a "reverse" mandate, the Connecticut General Assembly approved legislation stipulating that "the Connecticut Resources Recovery Authority shall accept for disposal in any landfill owned by the Authority the residue from any municipal or private waste-to-energy plant the operation of which has been approved by the Commissioner of Environmental Protection. . .provided an engineer from the Authority certifies that such landfill has the capacity for disposal of such residue. . ."

Functional Transfers

The 1984 Kentucky General Assembly transferred the administration of most city pension systems to the commonwealth, although the cities and their employees will continue to pay the cost of the pension system. First-class cities and the merged Lexington-Fayette urban county government were exempted from the transfer.

In the same year, New York began a three-year partial takeover of the Medicaid costs of long-term medical care and care for a specific category of mentally-disabled patients. The local share dropped from approximately 25 to 10 percent.

Under provisions added to a 1981 New York law, a city, town, or village can decline responsibility for enforcement of the uniform Fire Prevention and Building Code subsequent to January 1, 1985, and responsibility will be tranferred automatically to the county. Should the county refuse enforcement, the Department of State will assume responsibility. New York City, however, was exempted from the legislation.

In 1984, the Rhode Island Family Day Care Home Act transferred responsibility for regulating family day care homes to the Department of Children and Their Families.

A type of "partial" transfer of responsibility was authorized by 1985 Connecticut legislation: the commissioner of environmental protection may designate as his agent any municipality for the purpose of conducting inspections relative to enforcement of any section of the act or any regulation, permit, or order issued by the commissioner.

Local Discretionary Authority

In 1984, Colorado voters ratified a constitutional amendment that allows citizens—by petitions signed by at least 5 percent of the registered voters in the state—to place the question of adopting a "home rule" charter on the ballot.

Although North Dakota's constitution was amended in 1982 to authorize "home rule" for counties, no implementing legislation was enacted until the 1985 Legislative Assembly approved a provision allowing the Board of County Commissioners to authorize the drafting of a "home rule" charter; otherwise, the process may be initiated by petition. The law stipulates that "the charter and the ordinances made pursuant to the charter in county matters must be liberally construed to supersede. . .any conflicting state law except for any state law as it applies to cities or any power of a city to govern its own affairs, without the consent of the governing body of the city."

In 1985, the Alaska Legislature provided for the following types of jurisdictions to adopt a "home rule" charter: first class city; first or second class borough; third class borough; an area in an unorganized borough that is voting to incorporate as a borough; and a second class city with at least 3,500 permanent residents and an area exceeding 35 square miles.

Two 1984 Oregon court decisions related to the powers of local units. The Court of Appeals, in *Oregon v. Klamath Falls* [682 P2d 779], upheld the validity of an initiated city ordinance relative to geothermal resource conservation against the contention that the state had preempted the regulation of groundwater. Reversing a decision of the Court of Appeals, the Supreme Court in *Michael Caffey v. Lane County* [691 P2d 94] ruled that a "home rule" county possesses authority to establish a civil infractions process for enforcement of its ordinances and no state statute requires a state judicial process instead of the county's administrative adjudicatory process.

In 1984, the Illinois Supreme Court in *Chicago Bar Association v. Cook County* [102 Ill.2d 438] ruled that a county cannot supersede state law by adding a third member to the county Board of Appeals absent authority under its "home rule" powers.

Connecticut legislation increased from 20 to 30 years the period during which the state or any municipal or regional authority may contract for the collection, transportation, volume reduction, and disposal of solid waste. In Rhode Island, the Solid Waste Management Corporation was given exclusive authority to regulate solid waste, thereby invalidating city and town ordinances on the subject.

A 1984 Illinois law allowed municipalities to sign cooperative agreements with any governmental or nonprofit community service unit relative to the expenditure of funds for senior centers, transportation, and social services for the aged and poor. Another piece of legislation authorized local units to issue notes and warrants in anticipation of revenue from any source. In New Jersey, the formation of local government insurance pools was authorized in 1983.

In 1984, New York authorized political subdivisions to create local authorities to construct and operate water supply and sewer facilities by issuing revenue bonds. In that same year, the South Carolina General Assembly enacted a law allowing municipal and county water companies to form regional water authorities.

Washington State, in 1984, authorized the formation of combined city and county municipal corporations, but mandated that school districts had to be retained as separate units.

Connecticut Public Act 85-143 exempted the Connecticut Resources Authority from local zoning and land use regulations.

In 1985, Pennsylvania authorized commissioners of a second class county to fix the salaries of specified elected officers, empowered commissioners of counties of the third through the eighth class to fix the services of the district attorney at full time (the services may be changed only by referendum), and exempted second class counties from the advertising and bidding requirements for congregate meals, home-delivered meals, transportation, and chore services provided through area agencies on aging.

The powers of local governments in various states were broadened or restricted by opinions of the attorneys general. Florida's attorney general held a municipal ordinance could not designate parking spaces for handicapped drivers on private property because a state statute preempted the regulatory authority (opinion no. 84-1). In another opinion (no. 84-100), he held that "a municipality has home rule power to contract with a private corporation for the purpose of providing fire protection and emergency medical services. . ."

Although Virginia's Attorney General Gerald L. Baliles informed the Carolina County Attorney on May 25, 1984 that the State Board of Health and Water Control Board were responsible for regulating sewage disposal, he did not "conclude that the state has occupied the entire field of regulation. . .to the exclusion of local legislation."

In an informal opinion (no. 85-1), the New York attorney general advised that a local government may not provide for the recall unless authorized expressly by statute. In another (no. 85-2), however, he advised that proposed Rochester regulations prohibiting glass beverage containers in city parks are not preempted by the State Returnable Container Act. Later, he advised that a county may enact a local law superseding the county law to establish a four-year term of office for coroner (no. 85-39).

Local discretionary authority also was affected by court decisions during the biennium. The New Hampshire Supreme Court in *Applied Chemical Technology, Incorporated v. Town of Merrimack, et al.* (1985) ruled that state law preempted the authority of a town to deny a site permit for construction of a hazardous waste treatment facility. On July 23, 1985, Merrimack County Superior Court Judge Philip Hollman, ruled the New Hampshire Air Resources Commission's ban on open burning did not unconstitutionally restrict the fundamental rights of cities and towns.

In *Consolidated Edison Company v. Town of Red Hook* [60 N.Y.2d 99], the New York Court of Appeals (the court of last resort), struck down a town ordinance requiring a license prior to a site study for a steam electric generating plant on the ground the ordinance was inconsistent with state law. In *Ames v. Smoot* [98 AD2d 216], the Appellate Division of the Supreme Court held the state evidenced an intention to preempt the regulation of pesticides, thereby excluding village laws on the subject. And in *Associated Builders v. City of Rochester* [491 NYS2d 871 (AD 4 Dept. 1985)], the Appellate Division upheld a Rochester ordinance granting competitive bidding preference to contractors with apprenticeship training programs, by ruling the ordinance did not contravene the public bidding requirements of state law.

State Supervision

In 1984, the New York Legislature established a State Financial Control Board for the City of Yonkers and required the city to develop a four-year financial plan to ensure that it has a balanced budget. New York City continues to operate under a similar board created in 1975.

During fiscal 1984-85, Kentucky's state-local finance officer closely monitored three counties, and in one county, temporarily suspended new hirings, pay increases, and borrowing.

In 1985, the Alaska Legislature granted the state assessor the authority to investigate municipal assessment and taxation practices, and to direct municipalities to correct "major errors" found in their procedures.

In 1984, Kentucky created the Local Correctional Facilities Authority "to construct, reconstruct, improve, or repair any jail and appurtenant facilities in any local government. . . ."

In 1984, Connecticut authorized the commissioner of environmental protection to grant up to six requests annually for the burning of brush in a municipal landfill. Chapter 820 of the New York Laws of 1985 directed the commissioner of environmental conservation to issue standards and criteria for emissions of air contaminants from municipal solid waste facilities.

State Aid

The 1984 Kentucky General Assembly increased the legal process tax from $1 to $3 and dedicated the additional revenue generated to a program to preserve vital records stored in county courthouses. Maine increased the state-local revenue sharing formula from 4 to 5.1 percent of state sales and income tax revenues.

A 1985 Virginia law, effective January 1, 1987, will transfer from the commonwealth to local units the proceeds of the tax levied on the rolling stock of railroads, freight car companies, and motor vehicle carriers operating under certificates issued by the Virginia Corporation Commission.

In 1984, New York legislation increased the state share of sewage treatment project costs from 12.5 to 30 percent. Chapter 699 of the Virginia Laws of 1984 created the Virginia Water and Sewer Assistance Authority to assist subdivisions in obtaining funds for the construction of sewerage and water systems. In 1985, the General Assembly changed the name to the Virginia Resources Authority and extended its responsibilities to include assistance with the funding of drainage facilities. Similarly, the 1984 Rhode Island Legislature established the Sewage and Water Supply Failure Fund to provide funds to remedy failed septic or water supply systems, solve the problem of private wells contamination, or failure of an individual sewage disposal system.

In response to decreased federal assistance, the 1985 Georgia Legislature established the Environmental Facilities Program and appropriated $20 million for low interest loans to local governments. The Connecticut General Assembly, in its July special session, established a Municipal Infrastructure Trust Fund and a Municipal Infrastructure Trust Fund Committee. Grants are to be provided to towns for: road construction, renovation, repair, or resurfacing; sewage treatment plants and sanitary or storm sewer lines; public building construction, other than schools; repair of bridges or dams; water treatment or filtration systems; and construction, renovation, or enlargement of solid waste facilities. In 1985, Virginia increased funds for road projects within municipalities.

Summary And Conclusions

In 1984-85, several states took significant actions affecting state-local relations. State mandates continued to be issued during the biennium, but New Hampshire voters approved a constitutional amendment requiring state reimbursement of costs resulting from new mandates, and New Mexico voters approved a similar amendment directing the legislature either to reimburse local governments for mandated costs or provide a new source of revenue. While the New York

Legislature adopted a joint rule requiring fiscal notes to accompany bills affecting political subdivisions, the Connecticut General Assembly repealed its fiscal note requirement and directed a committee to specify whether a mandate bill should require state reimbursement of mandated costs.

A constitutional amendment in Colorado and a statute in North Dakota granted "home rule" to counties. Most statutory enactments, except in the environmental area, increased local discretionary authority. Such authority also was broadened or restricted by opinions of attorneys general and the courts.

Recent evidence indicates states generally will continue to broaden local discretionary authority on a gradual basis and will provide additional financial assistance to cushion the effects of the declining amount of federal financial aid.

STATE AID TO LOCAL GOVERNMENTS

By Vance Kane

State payments to local governments increased from $99 billion to $107 billion between fiscal years 1983 and 1984. This 8 percent growth reflects a marked improvement in the fiscal health of many states and an effort to offset the lack of growth in direct federal aid to local governments. While state aid to other governments (including the federal government) increased $7 billion (or 7 percent) from 1983, as a percentage of local government general revenue it remained at 33 percent for both years. In contrast, direct federal aid to local governments held steady at close to $21 billion for both years, but declined as a percentage of local general revenue during the same period—from 7 to 6.5 percent.[1]

State Aid By Purpose

State intergovernmental aid by function varies widely across the states, particularly for the education and welfare functions. Some states treat these programs organizationally as "state" responsibilities; in others, these functions are operated by local governments and augmented by state government assistance.

In any case, education received the largest share of state intergovernmental expenditures, totaling $67.5 billion in 1984, an increase of $4.4 billion. This function also received the largest major increase in total intergovernmental dollars expended by state governments (see Table 9.2). In this same period, federal intergovernmental aid to state governments for education showed an increase of $791 million—from $13.2 billion to $14 billion.

In the welfare sector, states spent $11.9 billion in aid to local governments, as well as $1.7 billion to the federal government (mostly for supplemental welfare payments, a program that began in 1973-74 when the federal government assumed direct payment responsibility for aid programs to the elderly, disabled, and blind). These payments to the federal government peaked in fiscal year 1981, when $1.9 billion in state funds were transferred.

Other major state aid to local governments

was for general local government support ($10.7 billion) and highways ($5.7 billion).

The percentage distribution of state aid to other governments in the last decade reflects the increasing support of education, coupled with reduced shares for public welfare and highways. Payments to the federal government for categorical aid supplements declined in percentage shares; in part, this reflects a reduced inflationary pressure on these programs (see Table A).

Individual State Aid Payments

California spent substantially more in aid to local governments than any other state (see Table 9.3). In 1984, the $19.1 billion it paid to other units far exceeded the $12.3 billion paid by New York, the second largest state.

In California, Proposition 13 encouraged the state to increase aid programs to offset the loss in property taxes experienced by local governments. On a per capita basis, in 1984, California spent $746 as compared to the $691 per capita by New York. Hawaii spent the least, both in dollars ($25 million) and in per capita amounts ($24), as the state administers several programs (such as education) which are generally the responsibility of local governments in other states.

In per capita aid expenditures, Wyoming ranked only behind Alaska ($1,037 and $2,366, respectively), a factor attributed to substantial per capita aid for education ($551 and $1,188, respectively) and general local government support ($311 and $281). Seven states spent more than $600 per capita in intergovernmental aid programs, while only New Hampshire ($161) and Hawaii ($24) spent less than $200 per capita. The average per capita payment for all states was $460. The distribution for all states is shown in Table B.

Vance Kane is Assistant Division Chief for Programs, and was assisted by Lisa McNelis, Social Science Analyst, both of the Governments Division, U.S. Bureau of the Census.

Table A
Percent Distribution of State Aid, Selected Years 1974-1984

Fiscal year	Total	To federal government	General local government support	Education	Public welfare	Highways	Other
			To local government, by function				
1974	100.0	0.7	10.5	59.0	15.3	7.0	7.5
1978	100.0	2.2	10.1	59.6	12.8	5.7	9.6
1982	100.0	1.8	10.2	61.5	12.1	5.1	9.4
1984	100.0	1.6	9.9	62.3	11.0	5.2	10.0

Table B
State Per Capita Expenditure Distribution

Per capita amount	Number of states
Over $750	2
$500—$750	10
$400—$500	9
$350—$400	9
$300—$350	14
$250—$300	2
Less than $250	4

Miscellaneous State Aid Programs

Unique financial aid programs have been developed by state governments to deal with specific problems or needs faced by their subdivisions. For example, Florida sends funds to its cities and counties for mosquito control. Maine shares the proceeds of motor fuel taxes for snowmobile trail acquisition, construction, and maintenance. Minnesota appropriates funds to cities and counties for shade tree disease control.

In addition to these special programs, there are several state assistance programs that occur in various forms as aid to the elderly or the poor, though not necessarily as a direct state aid to local governments. In 1984, property tax relief programs were in effect in 32 states, according to the U.S. Advisory Commission on Intergovernmental Relations. Most of these programs result in direct reimbursement to the taxpayer, either in cash or a state income tax credit; several states, such as Kansas and Minnesota, provide funds to their local governments to offset or reduce the loss of local government revenues from property tax limits ("circuit breakers"). There are also widespread reimbursements of local taxing units for loss of property tax revenue from homestead exemptions.

In addition to property tax losses that are offset or reduced by state payments, some states provide local government assistance programs which do not require direct monetary aid, such as investment services for their local governments. Such investment aid offers economy-of-scale expert advice not affordable by local governments, greater diversification, and lower administrative costs. Currently, 17 states are providing investment pool services, according to Fidelity Management and Research Company of Boston.

Debt service assistance and regulation is another state assistance program that is becoming more commonplace. Perhaps one of the more influential state agencies of this type is the California Debt Advisory Commission, which must pass on the wisdom and timing of proposed local government debt sales. Similarly, the North Carolina Local Government Commission sells bonds or notes for its local governments, while Hawaii sells state general obligation bonds, which in turn are made available to local units with repayment costs withheld from state-administered real property taxes.

Another debt assistance vehicle, the "municipal bond bank," exists in several states to coordinate local government bond sales and secure lower rates. Since state governments generally have superior credit ratings, local funds secured through these banks achieve reduced overall borrowing costs.

State aid also is made available through a variety of state-imposed, but locally-collected, government taxes, such as income or sales taxes. The distribution formula varies in each state, but generally relies on such factors as population, site of tax payment, or taxpayer income levels.

In summary, with the reduction in federal

aid programs for local government units, state aid payments to local governments are expected to increase sharply in an attempt to fill the revenue vacuum created at the local level.

Note

1. Direct federal aid excludes all federal funds given to the state and later paid to local governments by the state. These funds, called "pass-through" aid, are included in state intergovernmental aid under the U.S. Bureau of the Census' classification which was the basis used for compiling these data.

Table 9.2
SUMMARY OF STATE INTERGOVERNMENTAL PAYMENTS: 1942 to 1984
(In millions, except per capita)

Fiscal year	Total Amount	Total Per capita	To federal government (a)	For general local government support	To local governments — For specified purposes Total	Education	Public welfare	Highways	All other
1942	$ 1,780	$ 13.37	. . .	$ 224	$ 1,546	$ 790	$ 390	$ 334	$ 32
1944	1,842	13.95	. . .	274	1,568	861	368	298	41
1946	2,092	15.05	. . .	357	1,735	953	376	339	67
1948	3,283	22.64	. . .	428	2,855	1,554	648	507	146
1950	4,217	28.11	. . .	482	3,735	2,054	792	610	279
1951	4,678	30.78	. . .	513	4,165	2,248	974	667	276
1952	5,044	32.55	. . .	549	4,497	2,525	976	728	268
1953	5,384	34.19	. . .	592	4,791	2,740	981	803	267
1954	5,679	35.42	. . .	600	5,078	2,934	1,004	871	269
1955	5,986	36.62	. . .	591	5,395	3,154	1,046	911	284
1956	6,538	39.28	. . .	631	5,907	3,541	1,069	984	313
1957	7,439	43.86	. . .	668	6,771	4,212	1,136	1,083	340
1958	8,089	46.76	. . .	687	7,402	4,598	1,247	1,167	390
1959	8,689	49.37	. . .	725	7,964	4,957	1,409	1,207	391
1960	9,443	52.75	. . .	806	8,637	5,461	1,483	1,247	446
1961	10,114	55.51	. . .	821	9,293	5,963	1,602	1,266	462
1962	10,906	58.94	. . .	844	10,062	6,474	1,777	1,326	485
1963	11,885	63.31	. . .	1,012	10,873	6,993	1,919	1,416	545
1964	12,968	68.06	. . .	1,053	11,915	7,664	2,104	1,524	623
1965	14,174	73.43	. . .	1,102	13,072	8,351	2,436	1,630	655
1966	16,928	86.79	. . .	1,361	15,567	10,177	2,882	1,725	783
1967	19,056	96.70	. . .	1,585	17,471	11,845	2,897	1,861	868
1968	21,950	110.27	. . .	1,993	19,956	13,321	3,527	2,029	1,079
1969	24,779	123.20	. . .	2,135	22,644	14,858	4,402	2,109	1,275
1970	28,892	142.73	. . .	2,958	25,934	17,085	5,003	2,439	1,407
1971	32,640	158.82	. . .	3,258	29,382	19,292	5,760	2,507	1,823
1972	36,759	177.16	. . .	3,752	33,007	21,195	6,944	2,633	2,235
1973	40,822	195.22	. . .	4,280	36,542	23,316	7,532	2,953	2,741
1974	45,941	218.07	$ 341	4,804	40,796	27,107	7,028	3,211	3,450
1975	51,978	244.71	975	5,129	45,874	31,110	7,127	3,225	4,412
1976	57,858	270.42	1,180	5,674	51,004	34,084	8,296	3,241	5,383
1977	62,460	288.65	1,386	6,373	54,701	36,964	8,756	3,631	5,350
1978	67,287	309.52	1,472	6,819	58,995	40,125	8,586	3,821	6,463
1979	75,975	346.18	1,493	8,224	66,258	46,206	8,667	4,149	7,236
1980	84,504	374.13	1,746	8,644	74,114	52,688	9,242	4,383	7,801
1981	93,180	412.47	1,873	9,570	81,735	57,257	11,009	4,751	8,718
1982	98,743	435.86	1,793	10,044	86,906	60,684	11,951	5,028	9,243
1983	100,887 (b)	434.14	1,765	10,364	88,758	63,118	10,920 (b)	5,277	9,443
1984	108,373	460.11	1,722	10,745	95,906	67,485	11,923 (b)	5,687	10,811

Sources: U.S. Bureau of the Census, *State Payments to Local Governments (Census of Governments: 1982*, vol. 6, no. 3) and *State Government Finances.*

(a) Represents primarily state reimbursements for the supplemental security income program.
(b) Revised.

Table 9.3
STATE INTERGOVERNMENTAL EXPENDITURE, BY STATE: 1978 TO 1984

State	Amount (in thousands)				Per capita amounts				Percentage change in per capita amounts		
	1984	1982	1980	1978	1984	1982	1980	1978	1982 to 1984	1980 to 1982	1978 to 1980
All states	$108,373,188	$98,742,976	$84,504,451	$67,287,260	$ 460.11	$ 435.86	$374.13	$309.52	5.6	16.5	20.9
Alabama	1,310,399	1,136,158	1,036,721	856,355	328.42	291.77	266.51	228.85	12.6	9.5	16.5
Alaska	1,183,094	992,519	340,319	265,975	2,366.19	2,468.95	850.80	659.99	-4.2	190.2	28.9
Arizona	1,547,438	1,192,237	1,040,614	814,662	506.86	438.64	382.86	346.08	15.6	14.6	10.6
Arkansas	789,131	667,184	624,261	505,103	335.94	291.86	273.20	231.06	15.1	6.8	18.2
California	19,125,775	17,625,121	15,360,365	9,905,969	746.46	744.68	648.97	444.33	0.2	14.7	46.1
Colorado	1,522,105	1,200,839	947,692	746,746	478.95	415.52	328.03	279.68	15.3	26.7	17.3
Connecticut	967,483	760,415	671,287	593,857	306.75	244.66	215.99	191.63	25.4	13.3	12.7
Delaware	218,833	214,619	189,577	183,973	356.99	361.31	318.62	315.56	-1.2	13.4	1.0
Florida	3,561,701	3,512,218	2,925,889	2,235,987	324.50	360.38	300.40	260.18	-10.1	20.0	15.5
Georgia	1,947,978	1,781,763	1,613,179	1,177,775	333.73	326.15	295.24	231.66	2.3	10.5	27.4
Hawaii	25,231	27,875	35,530	49,711	24.28	28.89	36.82	55.42	-16.1	-27.5	-33.6
Idaho	408,686	353,787	309,341	225,063	408.28	374.77	327.69	256.34	8.9	14.4	27.8
Illinois	3,910,634	3,725,170	3,817,128	2,869,480	339.73	326.00	334.31	255.22	4.2	-2.5	31.0
Indiana	2,321,187	2,045,228	1,805,564	1,481,065	422.19	372.54	328.88	275.60	13.3	13.3	19.3
Iowa	1,321,682	1,262,391	1,148,360	949,801	454.19	433.22	394.22	334.88	4.8	9.9	17.7
Kansas	846,726	711,548	601,939	474,426	347.30	300.99	254.74	202.06	15.4	18.2	26.1
Kentucky	1,288,688	1,107,357	1,006,756	774,679	346.14	302.56	274.99	221.46	14.4	10.0	24.2
Louisiana	1,746,045	1,599,993	1,315,201	1,116,896	391.31	380.41	321.62	281.62	2.9	21.6	11.1
Maine	349,880	297,274	303,746	274,718	302.66	264.24	270.00	251.80	14.5	-2.1	7.2
Maryland	1,635,537	1,708,142	1,431,805	1,199,885	376.07	405.06	339.61	289.62	-7.2	19.3	17.3
Massachusetts......	2,617,378	2,315,564	2,116,477	1,577,703	451.43	403.62	368.92	273.24	11.8	9.4	35.0
Michigan	4,037,673	3,824,824	3,578,343	3,071,384	444.92	412.96	386.51	334.25	7.7	6.8	15.6
Minnesota	2,880,437	3,016,693	2,237,164	1,960,373	692.08	740.11	548.73	489.12	-6.5	34.9	12.2
Mississippi	1,065,912	948,128	856,350	691,567	410.28	376.09	339.69	287.67	9.1	10.7	18.1
Missouri	1,589,484	1,167,399	1,088,886	812,678	317.39	237.42	221.45	167.22	33.7	7.2	32.4
Montana	293,193	243,384	230,463	215,838	355.82	309.26	292.84	274.95	15.1	5.6	6.5
Nebraska	511,721	482,635	412,081	10,075,469	318.63	307.41	262.47	222.22	3.6	17.1	18.1
Nevada	487,427	456,728	265,956	1,960,984	535.05	570.91	332.86	298.79	-6.3	71.5	11.4
New Hampshire....	157,680	139,824	137,723	177,804	161.39	151.82	149.54	120.69	6.3	1.5	23.9
New Jersey	4,133,531	4,030,065	3,056,970	2,610,757	550.04	547.19	415.12	295.19	0.5	31.8	40.6
New Mexico	967,744	829,899	595,464	631,479	679.60	636.91	458.05	380.44	6.7	39.0	20.4
New York	12,262,857	11,849,950	10,252,802	608,505	691.45	674.90	583.97	567.70	2.5	15.6	2.9
North Carolina	2,722,596	2,440,069	2,028,170	3,054,225	441.62	414.84	345.28	351.62	6.5	20.1	-1.8
North Dakota	412,386	355,610	216,844	170,414	601.15	544.58	332.07	272.71	10.4	64.0	21.8
Ohio.............	4,779,871	3,561,699	3,249,696	650,372	444.56	329.85	300.98	242.88	34.8	9.6	23.9
Oklahoma	1,284,809	1,160,761	800,260	631,479	389.57	383.72	264.55	219.26	1.5	20.7	23.4
Oregon	993,012	1,014,603	879,899	608,505	371.36	385.34	334.18	248.98	-3.6	34.2	37.7
Pennsylvania	4,703,507	4,014,697	3,541,237	3,054,225	395.22	338.39	298.41	259.93	16.8	14.8	11.6
Rhode Island	275,000	235,816	217,255	170,414	285.86	249.01	229.41	182.26	14.8	25.9	13.7
South Carolina	1,095,298	1,024,500	781,643	650,372	331.91	328.16	250.61	222.88	1.1	12.5	20.0
South Dakota......	165,296	160,201	121,758	85,935	234.13	231.84	176.46	124.54	0.9	41.7	25.1
Tennessee	1,105,881	1,067,709	974,485	798,272	234.45	232.57	212.26	183.22	0.8	15.8	17.4
Texas	4,965,245	4,252,176	3,458,969	2,724,758	310.54	298.84	243.11	209.37	3.9	16.1	21.0
Utah	610,987	525,165	459,404	369,324	369.85	359.46	314.44	282.57	3.8	11.3	20.4
Vermont	135,974	110,722	110,786	97,068	256.55	216.68	216.80	199.32	18.4	8.8	15.8
Virginia	1,928,473	1,658,077	1,268,683	1,045,710	342.17	310.09	237.31	203.13	10.3	16.8	1.2
Washington	2,290,339	2,128,066	1,601,814	1,138,795	526.64	515.02	387.85	301.75	2.3	28.5	15.0
West Virginia	702,912	674,956	533,286	461,282	360.10	346.13	273.48	248.00	4.0	10.3	26.6
Wisconsin	2,638,645	2,761,315	2,643,133	2,149,735	553.64	586.76	561.77	459.44	-5.2	22.3	13.4
Wyoming	529,887	369,903	263,176	150,624	1,036.57	787.03	558.76	355.25	31.7	57.1	28.0

Source: U.S. Bureau of the Census, *State Government Finances in 1984*, and previous annual reports.

Note: Includes payments to the federal government, primarily state reimbursements for the supplemental security income program.

442

Table 9.4
PER CAPITA STATE INTERGOVERNMENTAL EXPENDITURE, BY FUNCTION AND BY STATE: 1983

State	Total	General local government support	Specified functions:			
			Education	Public welfare	Highways	Miscellaneous and unallocable
All states	$ 434.14	$ 44.41	$ 270.48	$ 56.10	$ 22.62	$ 40.53
Alabama	324.64	16.95	257.79	1.26	28.24	20.40
Alaska	2,272.67	283.70	1,070.70	9.96	147.35	760.96
Arizona	467.30	102.46	293.54	0.33	57.95	13.02
Arkansas	295.74	18.60	219.20	0.21	27.48	30.25
California	713.06	50.39	372.67	206.78	26.55	56.67
Colorado	403.24	5.66	248.83	81.90	7.89	58.96
Connecticut	271.92	31.75	187.44	17.03	6.63	29.07
Delaware	352.83	. . .	315.78	0.69	6.40	29.96
Florida	342.22	27.72	284.49	. . .	12.01	18.00
Georgia	342.49	2.81	280.80	0.68	13.38	44.82
Hawaii	26.28	17.76	. . .	4.14	0.76	3.62
Idaho	323.76	24.23	244.79	. . .	37.42	17.32
Illinois	316.51	34.28	226.14	11.40	22.72	21.97
Indiana	357.10	65.09	206.41	36.81	34.15	14.64
Iowa	447.58	46.14	310.25	8.20	55.25	27.74
Kansas	303.66	11.52	259.73	0.21	18.44	46.17
Kentucky	338.47	. . .	283.96	. . .	15.31	39.20
Louisiana	361.07	48.27	274.24	0.01	10.92	27.63
Maine	290.20	26.12	225.49	8.96	13.63	16.00
Maryland	399.29	35.39	206.61	4.93	78.76	73.60
Massachusetts	423.34	107.33	202.14	21.08	11.11	81.68
Michigan	423.18	66.94	211.71	19.62	51.45	73.46
Minnesota	543.27	120.93	261.38	85.96	41.14	33.86
Mississippi	375.05	58.26	271.76	0.24	32.47	12.32
Missouri	257.78	0.84	214.25	1.46	16.70	24.53
Montana	327.32	24.98	257.83	8.51	8.16	27.84
Nebraska	317.56	46.98	170.53	14.55	47.59	37.91
Nevada	537.23	178.77	325.14	7.61	15.64	10.07
New Hampshire	142.37	36.85	73.50	. . .	12.86	19.16
New Jersey	555.07	158.77	257.52	99.90	8.67	30.21
New Mexico	669.15	154.71	490.02	. . .	8.60	15.82
New York	610.38	49.83	277.26	208.45	11.56	63.28
North Carolina	424.01	24.02	328.37	20.81	8.89	41.92
North Dakota	552.22	51.66	411.25	13.19	60.64	15.48
Ohio	400.00	40.22	246.94	50.68	36.17	25.99
Oklahoma	394.81	3.03	322.91	3.43	41.41	24.03
Oregon	383.42	59.01	235.52	0.99	34.69	53.21
Pennsylvania	352.50	5.24	217.36	43.90	17.06	68.94
Rhode Island	276.89	18.75	206.37	41.00	0.41	10.36
South Carolina	324.86	28.13	255.10	3.61	25.40	12.62
South Dakota	239.85	65.59	150.88	0.06	9.24	14.08
Tennessee	227.48	26.90	158.88	1.49	26.74	13.47
Texas	292.43	2.66	283.40	. . .	0.61	5.76
Utah	358.61	0.60	320.45	1.78	15.46	20.32
Vermont	248.21	0.37	196.94	11.59	23.90	15.41
Virginia	322.67	4.07	228.06	28.74	14.02	47.78
Washington	522.13	15.78	421.20	4.03	21.39	59.73
West Virginia	338.72	9.38	319.49	. . .	. . .	9.85
Wisconsin	693.46	193.33	279.23	121.44	33.91	65.55
Wyoming	789.07	224.90	402.09	0.23	35.54	126.31

Source: U.S. Bureau of the Census, *State Government Finances in 1983.*

Note: Includes payments to the federal government, primarily state reimbursements for the supplemental security income program (under public welfare).

Table 9.5
PER CAPITA STATE INTERGOVERNMENTAL EXPENDITURE, BY FUNCTION AND BY STATE: 1984

State	Total	General local government support	Specified functions			
			Education	Public welfare	Highways	Miscellaneous and unallocable
All states	$ 460.11	$ 45.62	$ 286.51	$ 57.86	$ 24.14	$ 45.98
Alabama..................	328.42	24.69	235.92	1.20	29.42	37.19
Alaska.....................	2,366.19	281.12	1,188.07	1.56	159.55	735.89
Arizona...................	506.86	121.13	299.63	0.39	66.49	19.21
Arkansas	335.94	18.16	251.68	0.22	34.42	31.46
California................	746.46	42.42	409.32	209.72	30.47	54.53
Colorado	478.95	5.55	285.25	90.65	31.37	66.12
Connecticut	306.75	37.16	204.69	22.12	6.57	36.21
Delaware	356.99	. . .	320.91	0.68	7.04	28.35
Florida	324.50	26.96	250.69	0.13	18.44	28.27
Georgia..................	333.73	2.47	270.90	. . .	11.59	48.77
Hawaii	24.28	17.49	. . .	3.37	. . .	3.43
Idaho	408.28	26.16	318.94	0.06	43.07	20.06
Illinois...................	339.73	39.04	231.97	11.65	27.25	29.82
Indiana	422.19	105.78	235.64	37.29	33.13	10.35
Iowa	454.19	47.25	316.67	9.15	59.53	21.58
Kansas	347.30	18.89	279.00	0.20	32.25	16.96
Kentucky	346.14	. . .	289.94	. . .	14.24	41.96
Louisiana	391.31	45.89	300.50	0.01	8.42	36.49
Maine	302.66	24.47	240.69	9.69	10.89	16.92
Maryland	376.07	35.25	204.52	3.70	55.73	76.87
Massachusetts	451.43	106.56	224.14	20.01	11.80	88.93
Michigan	444.92	75.68	214.61	14.82	57.77	82.04
Minnesota	692.08	143.12	348.71	106.29	46.86	47.10
Mississippi	410.28	63.30	294.91	0.24	27.65	24.17
Missouri	317.39	1.10	267.93	1.48	18.45	28.43
Montana..................	355.82	26.26	269.72	8.29	17.32	34.23
Nebraska	318.63	43.63	171.53	7.30	47.67	48.50
Nevada	535.05	186.49	312.77	3.95	15.74	16.10
New Hampshire	161.39	39.42	62.74	28.39	13.99	16.85
New Jersey...............	550.04	128.78	285.14	89.54	8.51	38.07
New Mexico..............	679.60	162.27	486.88	. . .	8.56	21.89
New York	691.45	55.81	308.10	240.75	8.19	78.60
North Carolina	441.62	27.40	329.06	24.09	11.49	49.59
North Dakota	601.15	55.32	444.02	15.90	61.35	24.56
Ohio	444.56	44.60	270.99	53.88	38.87	36.22
Oklahoma	389.57	3.31	312.86	3.95	42.76	26.68
Oregon	371.36	54.58	234.37	0.90	42.77	38.75
Pennsylvania	395.22	6.48	242.78	53.24	18.45	74.27
Rhode Island	285.26	27.79	218.79	30.31	0.40	8.57
South Carolina	331.91	31.71	268.24	3.85	11.24	16.87
South Dakota	234.13	64.37	147.99	0.05	9.46	12.26
Tennessee	234.45	29.64	160.42	2.13	25.91	16.34
Texas.....................	310.54	2.82	295.64	. . .	0.69	11.39
Utah.....................	369.85	1.31	321.78	1.94	15.43	29.39
Vermont	256.55	3.35	201.51	12.10	25.50	14.11
Virginia..................	342.17	3.97	247.47	29.24	14.65	46.86
Washington	526.64	12.98	418.32	6.33	25.73	63.27
West Virginia	360.10	6.58	343.41	. . .	. . .	10.10
Wisconsin.................	553.64	172.10	244.64	32.44	35.18	69.28
Wyoming	1,036.57	311.42	550.73	0.27	34.29	139.86

Source: U.S. Bureau of the Census, State Government Finances in 1984.
Note: Includes payments to the federal government, primarily state reimbursements for the supplemental security income program (under public welfare).

Table 9.6
STATE INTERGOVERNMENTAL EXPENDITURE,
BY FUNCTION AND BY STATE: 1983
(In thousands of dollars)

State	Total	General local govern-ment support	Education	Public welfare	Highways	Miscellaneous and combined
				Functions		
All states	$101,309,230	$10,364,144	$63,118,351	$13,090,707	$5,277,447	$9,458,581
Alabama....................	1,285,260	67,117	1,020,573	4,990	111,802	80,778
Alaska.....................	1,088,608	135,890	512,864	4,771	70,580	364,503
Arizona....................	1,384,609	303,605	869,753	981	171,716	38,554
Arkansas	688,475	43,305	510,290	491	63,985	70,404
California..................	17,950,512	1,268,611 (a)	9,381,479 (b)	5,205,518 (c)	668,460	1,426,444 (d)
Colorado	1,265,765	17,757	784,219	257,077	24,752	181,960
Connecticut	853,283	99,642	588,182	53,450	20,794	91,215
Delaware	213,817	0	191,363	419	3,877	18,158
Florida	3,654,944	296,005	3,038,315	0	128,319	192,305
Georgia....................	1,963,168	16,117	1,609,545	3,901	76,698	256,907
Hawaii	26,883	18,173	0	4,235	774	3,701
Idaho	320,197	23,965	242,097	0	37,010	17,125
Illinois....................	3,635,455	393,795	2,597,432	130,926	261,002	252,300
Indiana	1,956,529	356,612	1,130,933	201,659	187,094	80,231
Iowa	1,300,227	134,032	901,273	23,832	160,489	80,601
Kansas	736,372	27,950	629,855	520	44,727	33,320
Kentucky	1,257,071	0	1,054,610	0	56,857	145,604
Louisiana	1,602,450	214,232	1,217,060	56	48,446	122,656
Maine	332,567	29,932	258,413	10,263	15,624	18,335
Maryland	1,718,524	152,307	889,260	21,208	338,974	316,775
Massachusetts	2,441,427	618,990	1,165,755	121,542	64,094	471,046 (e)
Michigan	3,837,848	607,088	1,920,018	177,897	466,600	666,245 (f)
Minnesota	2,251,310	501,152	1,083,140	356,224	170,500	140,294
Mississippi	970,254	150,725	703,056	611	84,007	31,885
Missouri	1,281,189	4,186	1,064,822	7,261	82,992	121,928
Montana...................	267,419	20,408	210,649	6,956	6,668	22,738
Nebraska	507,138	75,029	272,343	23,234	76,000	60,532
Nevada	478,671	159,281	289,703	6,780	13,935	8,972
New Hampshire	136,529	35,338	70,482	0	12,333	18,376
New Jersey.................	4,145,247	1,185,701	1,923,184	746,025	64,769	225,568
New Mexico................	936,147	216,444	685,536	0	12,033	22,134
New York	10,783,637	880,280 (g)	4,898,284 (h)	3,682,706 (i)	204,316	1,118,051 (j)
North Carolina	2,578,834	146,065	1,997,172	126,557	54,078	254,962
North Dakota	375,508	35,129	279,652	8,970	41,235	10,522
Ohio	4,298,362	432,215	2,653,641	544,580	388,665	279,261
Oklahoma	1,302,079	10,002	1,064,956	11,312	136,574	79,235
Oregon	1,020,668	157,094	626,942	2,636	92,333	141,663
Pennsylvania	4,192,970	62,284	2,585,527	522,230	202,918	820,011
Rhode Island	264,434	17,907	197,085	39,153	390	9,899
South Carolina	1,060,351	91,813	832,636	11,796	82,916	41,190
South Dakota	167,898	45,916	105,613	40	6,466	9,863
Tennessee	1,065,758	126,035	744,360	6,987	125,288	63,088
Texas......................	4,598,193	41,850	4,456,127 (k)	0	9,631	90,585
Utah	580,592	965	518,804	2,888	25,022	32,913
Vermont	130,312	195	103,391	6,083	12,545	8,098
Virginia....................	1,790,792	22,577	1,265,707	159,513	77,832	265,163
Washington	2,245,150	67,873	1,811,143	17,349	91,959	256,826
West Virginia	665,589	18,438	627,803	0	0	19,348
Wisconsin..................	3,294,624	918,520	1,326,631	576,962	161,098	311,413
Wyoming	405,584	115,597	206,673	118	18,270	64,926

Source: U.S. Bureau of the Census, *State Government Finances in 1983.*
Note: Totals may not add due to rounding.

(a) Includes $491,229,000 business investment tax relief and $442,325,000 shared motor vehicle license taxes.

(b) Includes $1,494,138,000 redistribution of federal funds to school districts and $1,074,562,000 community college grants.

(c) Includes $2,675,823,000 aid to local governments for families with dependent children and $1,157,974 reimbursement to federal government for supplemental security income program.

(d) Includes $851,500,000 health aid.

(e) Includes $243,091,000 transit subsidies.

(f) Includes $340,863,000 mental health aid.

(g) Includes $880,280,000 state revenue sharing distribution.

(h) Includes $4,657,723,000 general school support and $206,668,000 community college support.

(i) Includes $1,194,877,000 aid to families with dependent children, $659,355,000 vendor payment to New York City Hospital Corp., and $354,481,000 for welfare medical assistance.

(j) Includes $168,694,000 health aid, $161,800,000 transit subsidies, and $99,178,000 municipal overburden aid.

(k) Includes $3,469,355,000 available and school foundation funds distribution to school districts and $376,402,000 to community colleges.

Table 9.7
STATE INTERGOVERNMENTAL EXPENDITURE, BY FUNCTION AND BY STATE: 1984
(In thousands of dollars)

State	Total	General local government support	Education	Public welfare	Highways	Miscellaneous and combined
All states	$108,373,188	$10,744,740	$67,484,926	$13,627,522	$5,686,834	$10,829,166
Alabama....................	1,310,399	98,500	941,335	4,798	117,366	148,400
Alaska.....................	1,183,094	140,558	594,033	780	79,776	367,947
Arizona....................	1,547,438	369,815	914,784	1,197	202,988	58,654
Arkansas	789,131	42,665	591,195	524	80,851	73,896
California.................	19,125,775	1,086,815 (a)	10,487,685 (b)	5,373,489 (c)	780,702	1,397,084
Colorado	1,522,105	17,648	906,534	288,096	99,702	210,105
Connecticut	967,483	117,202	645,592	69,767	20,722	114,200
Delaware	218,833	0	196,719	418	4,315	17,381
Florida	3,561,701	295,947	2,751,539	1,436	202,449	310,330
Georgia....................	1,947,978	14,417	1,581,237	0	67,663	284,661
Hawaii	25,231	18,173	0	3,497	0	3,561
Idaho	408,686	26,182	319,254	56	43,113	20,081
Illinois...................	3,910,634	449,332	2,670,188	134,111	313,692	343,311
Indiana....................	2,321,187	581,567	1,295,572	205,006	182,139	56,903
Iowa	1,321,682	137,499	921,520	26,622	173,230	62,811
Kansas	846,726	46,045	680,214	478	78,636	41,353
Kentucky	1,288,688	0	1,079,458	0	53,020	156,210
Louisiana	1,746,045	204,760	1,340,830	64	37,561	162,830
Maine	349,880	28,283	278,241	11,201	12,591	19,564
Maryland	1,635,537	153,301	889,466	16,082	242,383	334,305
Massachusetts	2,617,378	617,846	1,299,540	116,001	68,401	805,174
Michigan	4,037,673	686,825	1,947,624	134,481	524,237	744,506
Minnesota	2,880,437	595,661	1,451,338	442,380	195,011	196,047
Mississippi	1,065,912	164,466	766,187	628	71,832	62,799
Missouri	1,589,484	5,496	1,341,789	7,426	92,375	142,396
Montana....................	293,193	21,635	222,249	6,832	14,268	28,209
Nebraska	511,721	70,062	275,482	11,721	76,558	77,898
Nevada	487,427	169,889	284,933	3,600	14,342	14,663
New Hampshire	157,680	38,513	61,294	27,735	13,673	16,465
New Jersey.................	4,133,531	967,754	2,142,790	672,929	63,927	286,131
New Mexico.................	967,744	231,078	693,311	0	12,184	31,171
New York	12,262,857	989,779	5,464,220 (d)	4,269,742 (e)	145,224	1,393,892
North Carolina	2,722,596	168,892	2,028,634	148,538	70,818	305,714
North Dakota	412,386	37,948	304,595	10,909	42,088	16,846
Ohio	4,779,871	479,556	2,913,696	579,336	417,890	389,393
Oklahoma	1,284,809	10,907	1,031,826	13,039	141,038	87,999
Oregon	993,012	145,948	626,704	2,394	114,355	103,611
Pennsylvania	4,703,507	77,091	2,889,344	633,551	219,587	883,934
Rhode Island	275,000	26,735	210,478	29,159	380	8,248
South Carolina	1,095,298	104,656	885,191	12,703	37,092	55,656
South Dakota	165,296	45,443	104,483	35	6,678	8,657
Tennessee	1,105,881	139,819	756,704	10,037	122,224	77,097
Texas......................	4,965,245	45,073	4,726,991 (f)	0	11,110	182,071
Utah	610,987	2,171	531,574	3,205	25,485	48,552
Vermont	135,974	1,773	106,798	6,414	13,513	7,476
Virginia...................	1,928,473	22,381	1,394,752	164,795	82,560	263,985
Washington	2,290,339	56,433	1,819,290	27,541	111,914	275,161
West Virginia	702,912	12,852	670,345	0	167,649	19,715
Wisconsin..................	2,638,645	820,213	1,165,945	154,629	167,649	330,209
Wyoming	529,687	159,136	281,423	140	17,522	71,466

Source: U.S. Bureau of the Census, *State Government Finances in 1984*.
Note: Totals may not add due to rounding.
(a) Includes $465,798,000 shared motor vehicle license taxes and $287,052,000 business investment tax relief.
(b) Includes $8,429,670,000 redistribution of federal funds to school districts and $1,083,081,000 community college grants.
(c) Includes $2,887,926,000 aid to local governments for families with dependent children and $1,114,654,000 reimbursement to federal government for supplemental security income program.
(d) Includes $5,117,392,000 general school support and $326,666,000 community college support.
(e) Includes $1,544,180,000 aid to local governments for families with dependent children, $816,641,000 vendor payment to New York City Hospital Corp. and $272,040,000 for welfare medical assistance.
(f) Includes $4,286,596,000 available and school foundation funds distribution to school districts and $439,763,000 to community colleges.

Table 9.8
STATE INTERGOVERNMENTAL EXPENDITURE, BY TYPE OF RECEIVING GOVERNMENT AND BY STATE: 1983
(In thousands of dollars)

State	Total intergovernmental expenditure	Federal	School districts	Counties	Municipalities	Townships and New England "towns"	Special districts	Combined and unallocable
All states	$101,309,230	$1,764,821 (a)	$51,384,237	$22,492,788	$14,738,376	$1,133,514	$1,279,759	$8,515,735
Alabama................	1,285,260	0	1,020,573	193,614	69,235	0	0	1,838
Alaska.................	1,088,608	0	0	359,511	623,827	0	0	105,270
Arizona................	1,384,609	981	869,753	225,965	286,702	0	1,208	0
Arkansas	688,475	47	509,324	87,127	58,489	0	3,362	30,126
California..............	17,950,512	1,159,018	8,839,820	6,417,294	1,006,503	0	453,524	74,353
Colorado	1,265,765	117	783,057	334,463	127,821	0	13,843	6,464
Connecticut	853,283	458	11,396	0	423,243	344,568	1,799	71,819
Delaware	213,817	419	191,363	11,514	6,433	0	0	4,088
Florida	3,654,944	4,211	3,038,315	297,735	263,931	0	1,271	49,481
Georgia...............	1,963,168	57	1,609,545	243,435	70,588	0	4,917	34,626
Hawaii	26,883	4,235	0	13,260	9,388	0	0	0
Idaho	320,197	5,091	242,097	32,891	18,593	0	6,484	15,041
Illinois................	3,635,455	14,584	2,597,432	279,502	486,423	47,217	137,794	72,503
Indiana	1,956,529	4,549	1,130,933	333,188	163,869	0	7,141	316,849 (b)
Iowa	1,300,227	12,319	901,273	187,171	139,470	0	6,258	53,736
Kansas	736,372	1,976	629,848	53,974	33,854	793	1,916	14,011
Kentucky	1,257,071	0	1,054,610	166,134	25,074	0	467	10,786
Louisiana	1,602,450	556	1,217,060	190,503	60,676	0	7,372	126,283
Maine	332,567	6,433	0	2,651	25	3,852	0	319,606 (c)
Maryland	1,718,524	112	0	999,400	597,747	0	637	120,628
Massachusetts	2,441,427	110,095	45,950	279	1,262	0	230,504	2,053,337 (d)
Michigan	3,837,848	57,003	1,920,018	828,737	576,522	115,835	559	339,174 (e)
Minnesota	2,251,310	0	1,069,684	691,180	412,823	24,302	3,993	49,328
Mississippi	970,254	28	702,658	139,607	127,981	0	0	0
Missouri	1,281,189	0	1,064,822	71,805	64,549	0	3,162	76,851
Montana...............	267,419	897	209,604	42,049	14,515	0	354	0
Nebraska	507,138	1,074	272,343	80,345	48,747	0	10,344	94,285
Nevada	478,671	2,619	289,703	163,531	18,166	0	400	4,252
New Hampshire	136,529	0	18,939	2,081	32,065	21,957	470	61,017
New Jersey.............	4,145,247	23,421	1,486	786,267	123,997	207	1,860	3,208,009 (f)
New Mexico............	936,147	0	685,536	28,114	221,794	0	57	646
New York	10,783,637	220,801	3,276,369	1,741,128	5,383,336	155,535	5,741	727
North Carolina	2,578,834	0	0	2,354,832	207,495	0	14,510	1,997
North Dakota	375,508	36	279,652	44,330	27,258	8,268	834	15,130
Ohio	4,298,362	0	2,601,636	1,045,864	138,640	31,247	5,099	475,876 (g)
Oklahoma	1,302,079	0	1,064,956	156,275	19,715	0	2,625	58,508
Oregon	1,020,668	0	626,942	177,595	119,989	0	14,274	81,868
Pennsylvania	4,192,970	56,950	2,585,527	830,200	312,995	110,203	261,958	35,137
Rhode Island	264,434	7,376	19,940	0	133,406	89,095	0	14,617
South Carolina	1,060,351	18	832,581	200,212	21,421	0	632	5,487
South Dakota	167,898	40	105,613	50,669	3,561	283	193	7,539
Tennessee	1,065,758	86	14,759	609,700	435,776	0	0	5,437
Texas..................	4,598,193	0	4,456,127	46,590	57,727	0	5,651	32,098
Utah	580,592	463	518,804	40,934	15,129	0	84	5,178
Vermont	130,312	6,083	103,391	0	2,561	15,226	304	2,747
Virginia................	1,790,792	0	0	958,402	676,289	0	5,707	150,394
Washington	2,245,150	16,994	1,811,143	190,623	146,300	0	60,898	19,192
West Virginia	665,589	0	626,371	19,554	1,681	0	0	17,983
Wisconsin..............	3,294,624	45,556	1,326,631	705,196	790,963	164,926	0	261,352
Wyoming	405,584	118	206,673	57,357	129,822	0	1,553	10,061

Source: U.S. Bureau of the Census, *State Government Finances in 1983.*

Note: Totals may not add due to rounding.

(a) Includes $1,748,512,000 supplemental security income payments (additional transfers not separately identified by other states may not be included).

(b) Includes $313,188,000 property tax replacement distribution to local governments.

(c) Includes $257,254,000 for local schools.

(d) Includes $1,119,805,000 education subsidies, $491,416,000 assistance to cities and towns, and $97,051,000 lottery distribution.

(e) Includes $111,721,000 highway and $64,482,000 transit subsidies.

(f) Includes $1,853,435,000 education subsidies and $1,185,701,000 property tax relief and shared revenues.

(g) Includes $419,742,000 tax relief payments.

Table 9.9
STATE INTERGOVERNMENTAL EXPENDITURE, BY TYPE OF RECEIVING GOVERNMENT AND BY STATE: 1984
(In thousands of dollars)

State	Total intergovern- mental expenditure	Type of receiving government						
		Federal	School districts	Counties	Municipali- ties	Townships and New England "towns"	Special districts	Combined and un- allocable
All states	$108,373,188	$1,722,115(a)	$55,939,470	$23,853,417	$17,339,630	$1,201,480	$1,321,635	$6,995,441
Alabama...............	1,310,399	0	941,335	261,712	104,560	0	0	2,792
Alaska................	1,183,094	2,381	0	425,416	650,774	0	950	103,573
Arizona...............	1,547,438	1,197	914,784	273,125	339,528	0	1,358	17,446
Arkansas	789,131	4,079	590,234	98,059	64,239	0	2,888	29,632
California.............	19,125,775	1,117,440	9,868,507	6,676,599	1,030,704	0	354,420	78,105
Colorado	1,522,105	226	906,200	416,029	172,361	0	13,738	13,551
Connecticut	967,483	566	11,031	0	486,209	364,292	917	104,468
Delaware	218,833	418	196,719	9,029	6,507	0	0	6,160
Florida	3,561,701	5,177	2,751,384	350,206	310,800	0	14,820	129,314
Georgia...............	1,947,978	164	1,581,237	253,370	74,483	0	4,919	33,805
Hawaii	25,231	3,497	0	10,985	9,392	0	0	1,357
Idaho	408,686	434	319,064	41,198	26,514	0	5,126	16,350
Illinois...............	3,910,634	15,050	2,670,188	380,983	566,235	59,263	169,454	49,461
Indiana	2,321,187	6,363	1,295,572	312,139	160,613	0	3,735	542,765 (b)
Iowa	1,321,682	13,490	921,520	195,772	145,710	0	0	45,190
Kansas	846,726	77	680,214	83,054	55,746	1,566	2,079	23,990
Kentucky	1,288,688	0	1,079,458	162,627	34,894	0	390	11,319
Louisiana	1,746,045	64	1,340,830	211,715	67,723	0	1,175	124,538
Maine	349,880	6,533	0	2,696	0	4,812	0	335,839(c)
Maryland	1,635,537	84	0	998,891	508,371	0	137	128,054
Massachusetts..........	2,617,378	106,149	47,650	300	2,742	0	248,286	2,212,251 (d)
Michigan	4,037,673	59,274	1,947,624	1,028,082	615,024	130,896	498	256,275 (e)
Minnesota	2,880,437	0	1,443,464	881,351	465,150	27,679	4,032	58,761
Mississippi	1,065,912	20	765,585	140,122	160,185	0	0	0
Missouri	1,589,484	0	1,341,789	74,804	68,897	0	3,503	100,491
Montana..............	293,193	334	221,070	49,055	22,158	0	0	576
Nebraska	511,721	1,133	275,482	68,114	56,665	0	16,417	93,910
Nevada	487,427	2,360	284,933	177,832	17,139	0	424	4,739
New Hampshire	157,680	0	13,840	30,360	30,763	28,438	413	53,866
New Jersey	4,133,531	24,964	1,548,923	907,614	539,218	23,160	1,397	1,088,255 (f)
New Mexico............	967,744	0	693,311	24,951	247,607	0	582	1,293
New York	12,262,857	208,675	3,265,800	1,757,047	6,862,562	144,673	20,113	3,987
North Carolina	2,722,596	0	0	2,469,472	233,227	0	16,615	3,282
North Dakota	412,386	7	304,592	47,303	33,187	7,752	1,653	17,892
Ohio	4,779,871	0	2,855,130	1,166,878	150,105	32,513	5,719	569,526 (g)
Oklahoma	1,284,809	0	1,031,826	159,550	21,832	0	2,833	68,768
Oregon	993,012	0	626,704	204,746	71,540	0	13,287	76,735
Pennsylvania	4,703,507	62,250	2,889,344	907,212	339,677	116,537	323,757	64,730
Rhode Island	275,000	7,953	20,687	0	146,467	97,686	0	2,207
South Carolina	1,095,298	0	884,786	172,615	33,868	0	632	3,397
South Dakota	165,296	35	104,483	50,857	3,159	279	100	6,383
Tennessee	1,105,881	0	3,948	611,224	484,636	0	0	6,073
Texas.................	4,965,245	0	4,726,359	70,836	109,170	0	3,677	55,203
Utah	610,987	429	531,574	47,887	27,882	0	2,976	239
Vermont	135,974	6,414	106,798	0	2,602	17,452	295	2,413
Virginia..............	1,928,473	0	0	1,051,773	737,180	0	6,118	133,402
Washington	2,290,339	19,182	1,819,290	195,682	168,528	0	65,875	21,782
West Virginia	702,912	0	668,833	16,954	252	0	0	16,873
Wisconsin.............	2,638,645	45,556	1,165,945	305,707	714,679	144,482	0	262,276
Wyoming	529,687	140	281,423	71,484	158,166	0	6,327	12,147

Source: U.S. Bureau of the Census, *State Government Finances in 1984.*
Note: Totals may not add due to rounding.
(a) Includes $1,704,092,000 supplemental security income payments (additional transfers not separately identified by other states may not be included).
(b) Includes $540,209,000 property tax replacement distribution to local governments.
(c) Includes $276,690,000 for local schools.
(d) Includes $1,251,890,000 education subsidies, $520,285,000 assistance to cities and towns, and $96,803,000 lottery distribution.
(e) Includes $119,341,000 highway and $64,446,000 transit subsidies.
(f) Includes $967,754,000 property tax relief and shared revenues.
(g) Includes $467,150,000 tax relief payments.

Table 9.10
STATE INTERGOVERNMENTAL REVENUE FROM FEDERAL AND LOCAL GOVERNMENTS: 1983
(In thousands of dollars)

State	Total intergovernmental revenue	From federal government					From local government				
		Total(a)	Education	Public welfare	Health & hospitals	Highways	Total(a)	Education	Public welfare	Health & hospitals	Highways
All states	$72,703,679	$68,961,627	$13,184,565	$32,948,545	2,868,880	$8,926,706	$3,742,052	$374,775	$660,416	$651,351	$330,822
Alabama	1,224,801	1,200,725	318,352	427,546	44,708	195,646	24,076	2,873	64	5,801	6,220
Alaska	385,342	385,275	82,465	62,072	4,519	131,522	67	29	0	0	0
Arizona	570,771	492,349	178,269	91,143	31,257	95,654	78,422	2,304	50,588	522	14,257
Arkansas	710,248	706,299	146,239	315,140	31,631	101,695	3,949	900	0	0	2,064
California	8,867,643	8,686,053	1,465,761	4,609,654	187,337	598,673	181,590	27,680	3	20,138	48,319
Colorado	805,841	796,953	211,866	301,283	47,755	141,962	8,888	2,346	0	0	5,241
Connecticut	860,595	857,229	130,211	417,965	64,594	97,461	3,366	80	0	18	1,380
Delaware	215,099	212,347	47,008	58,791	7,785	38,207	2,752	1,708	0	0	0
Florida	1,963,069	1,884,745	460,622	660,805	231,085	290,531	78,324	2,040	4,703	50,609	326
Georgia	1,920,181	1,903,172	385,237	719,221	122,673	456,505	17,009	6,082	489	0	9,075
Hawaii	395,676	394,129	95,923	168,527	19,580	52,942	1,547	147	0	0	0
Idaho	295,208	291,988	49,602	92,306	13,364	60,954	3,220	765	254	534	539
Illinois	3,066,541	2,990,643	593,434	1,492,284	88,560	441,921	75,898	17,787	10,852	0	39,036
Indiana	1,285,990	1,271,554	285,641	577,633	68,128	155,868	14,436	3,311	0	202	6,216
Iowa	813,401	776,392	172,431	312,060	23,049	124,901	37,009	5	687	30,730	3,012
Kansas	606,481	595,694	119,454	258,794	24,926	114,965	10,787	1,789	0	0	8,998
Kentucky	1,172,073	1,159,200	248,358	479,489	46,798	172,572	12,873	3,634	0	0	4,620
Louisiana	1,328,821	1,318,674	274,208	640,200	70,289	168,513	10,147	114	0	0	0
Maine	425,260	407,361	75,886	196,518	9,655	52,556	17,899	0	590	0	2,878
Maryland	1,428,920	1,394,305	239,473	533,316	34,431	370,199	34,615	363	20	5,625	10,138
Massachusetts	2,156,903	1,942,688	276,937	1,199,148	53,646	134,725	214,215	4,556	0	2,556	362
Michigan	3,449,141	3,091,481	560,891	1,721,878	113,642	272,688	357,660	6,987	55,897	242,533	16,440
Minnesota	1,508,741	1,421,393	247,914	695,268	38,249	200,013	87,348	1,542	45,660	24,147	12,572
Mississippi	849,242	838,238	223,402	306,365	45,607	100,153	11,004	8,134	0	0	0
Missouri	1,200,544	1,175,984	220,772	522,957	52,468	177,789	24,560	4,161	0	311	13,062
Montana	321,992	313,502	18,885	98,602	16,387	106,103	8,490	491	7,708	0	0
Nebraska	461,676	429,719	71,458	183,608	32,189	81,915	31,957	3,370	17,024	2,525	7,829
Nevada	252,452	240,301	45,726	64,579	14,084	68,285	12,151	93	1,000	563	8,611
New Hampshire	289,860	266,757	45,421	89,197	15,289	49,357	23,103	789	17,911	65	2,249
New Jersey	2,193,335	1,993,714	297,891	1,018,267	42,559	175,374	199,621	18,279	13,862	73,729	1,855

STATE INTERGOVERNMENTAL REVENUE: 1983—Continued

State	Total intergovernmental revenue	From federal government					From local government				
		Total(a)	Education	Public welfare	Health & hospitals	Highways	Total(a)	Education	Public welfare	Health & hospitals	Highways
New Mexico	750,605	722,751	144,837	150,141	26,239	82,941	27,854	16,686	0	9,022	1,417
New York	8,599,472	7,147,747	846,592	4,825,550	214,995	448,073	1,451,725	98,282	319,001	30,285	0
North Carolina	1,657,588	1,560,284	361,967	632,969	75,565	275,541	97,304	4,860	84,577	46	2,890
North Dakota	275,885	261,491	56,469	82,535	15,807	54,037	14,394	448	4,958	680	6,710
Ohio	2,622,373	2,484,272	472,968	1,285,766	134,552	248,247	138,101	15,489	0	26,204	11,590
Oklahoma	908,415	888,886	173,477	474,824	41,603	87,329	19,529	4,894	837	1,722	4,855
Oregon	905,831	864,191	183,373	306,364	53,738	161,074	41,640	6,194	17,091	0	18,355
Pennsylvania	3,513,153	3,458,535	492,734	1,993,851	96,575	459,915	54,618	48,210	114	0	4,668
Rhode Island	405,922	393,067	82,449	196,936	14,831	32,404	12,855	291	0	0	0
South Carolina	885,116	863,020	220,359	336,236	48,531	98,341	22,096	8,917	3,435	4,414	278
South Dakota	270,185	260,993	49,088	90,711	17,660	56,799	9,192	0	306	2,656	0
Tennessee	1,316,811	1,287,327	274,438	495,982	59,761	182,782	29,484	4,686	1,264	11,022	10,366
Texas	3,156,473	3,148,493	915,346	1,279,467	177,357	475,937	7,980	7,674	0	0	0
Utah	537,986	526,255	136,379	177,053	23,796	79,372	11,731	3,503	1,203	695	0
Vermont	259,457	255,660	40,519	118,626	11,551	44,549	3,797	3,623	0	38	0
Virginia	1,423,863	1,350,368	335,534	554,968	63,201	218,218	73,495	8,488	0	33,191	23,864
Washington	1,522,487	1,419,930	336,679	446,383	92,322	314,535	102,557	18,817	0	70,702	3,393
West Virginia	617,033	612,199	125,287	191,087	26,732	176,141	4,834	887	0	0	0
Wisconsin	1,685,648	1,657,010	313,226	954,720	73,419	143,710	28,638	467	0	9	14,853
Wyoming	363,529	360,284	38,107	39,760	4,401	57,112	3,245	0	294	57	2,284

(a) Total includes revenue for other activities not shown separately in this table.

Source: U.S. Bureau of the Census, *State Government Finances in 1983*.
Note: Totals may not add due to rounding.

Table 9.11
STATE INTERGOVERNMENTAL REVENUE
FROM FEDERAL AND LOCAL GOVERNMENTS: 1984
(In thousands of dollars)

State	Total intergovernmental revenue	From federal government					From local government				
		Total(a)	Education	Public welfare	Health & hospitals	Highways	Total(a)	Education	Public welfare	Health & hospitals	Highways
All states	$81,449,805	$76,140,229	$13,975,321	$35,422,677	$3,243,382	$10,379,827	$5,309,576	$362,752	$1,877,486	$665,790	$387,745
Alabama	1,313,988	1,270,346	325,762	439,881	53,335	214,884	43,642	5,578	90	5,821	8,443
Alaska	412,515	409,986	88,947	82,743	2,763	148,013	2,529	1,717	0	0	0
Arizona	681,504	599,684	187,416	139,641	33,973	138,929	81,820	1,706	62,863	3,409	7,749
Arkansas	756,096	751,610	157,135	365,013	32,911	93,449	4,486	941	0	0	2,138
California	10,116,893	9,934,508	1,862,639	4,730,803	209,690	835,031	182,385	34,072	0	26,346	50,530
Colorado	938,132	927,584	228,088	304,073	43,481	201,833	10,548	2,463	0	0	6,858
Connecticut	956,239	950,920	146,678	459,739	74,176	119,395	5,319	138	0	0	2,042
Delaware	235,580	232,946	51,337	62,131	8,441	45,832	2,634	1,673	0	12	0
Florida	2,101,642	2,052,950	481,487	735,744	222,592	311,563	48,692	1,281	3,861	32,070	0
Georgia	1,875,954	1,867,584	303,293	745,952	149,171	387,474	8,370	839	0	0	5,799
Hawaii	418,874	415,768	93,059	174,151	14,312	65,391	3,106	128	0	0	0
Idaho	321,481	310,951	50,952	97,390	14,294	67,575	10,530	954	235	7,433	373
Illinois	3,489,287	3,416,139	612,640	1,560,914	111,645	620,997	73,148	17,110	11,930	0	39,980
Indiana	1,440,861	1,420,634	283,315	619,053	79,680	232,504	20,227	2,101	0	215	11,512
Iowa	887,460	848,966	171,252	359,005	25,445	189,892	38,494	0	294	32,088	3,713
Kansas	670,272	652,360	137,116	239,239	31,634	153,302	17,912	1,686	0	0	16,226
Kentucky	1,283,680	1,274,115	248,036	522,492	60,586	200,088	9,565	4,116	0	0	528
Louisiana	1,467,947	1,462,884	289,632	650,834	83,160	245,679	5,063	1,795	0	248	0
Maine	463,289	444,106	80,289	214,367	11,465	53,818	19,183	62	0	0	3,059
Maryland	1,398,961	1,366,518	274,879	569,760	44,829	267,757	32,443	1,819	244	6,097	4,948
Massachusetts	2,223,490	2,012,085	273,956	1,129,532	60,596	221,633	211,405	4,957	0	2,449	303
Michigan	3,920,617	3,521,635	595,965	1,855,998	116,704	354,523	398,982	7,082	58,836	286,386	23,506
Minnesota	1,645,507	1,566,999	258,326	758,567	44,288	218,256	78,508	1,530	43,065	12,367	17,734
Mississippi	930,027	918,800	216,490	339,088	54,974	123,992	11,227	7,855	0	0	0
Missouri	1,280,565	1,258,531	221,361	537,411	59,182	218,112	22,034	3,772	0	261	11,278
Montana	377,775	367,464	44,280	107,431	17,863	104,492	10,311	271	9,713	3,277	0
Nebraska	497,214	463,465	75,202	181,992	20,076	111,959	33,749	2,146	17,076	0	10,006
Nevada	255,545	248,364	41,245	62,229	13,832	65,984	7,181	227	1,067	568	2,808
New Hampshire	303,267	277,016	42,471	100,229	16,384	53,988	26,251	922	18,454	339	4,056
New Jersey	2,462,517	2,323,222	315,865	1,132,570	108,834	235,793	139,295	14,881	15,372	66,241	3,741

STATE INTERGOVERNMENTAL REVENUE: 1984—Continued

State	Total intergovernmental revenue	From federal government Total(a)	Education	Public welfare	Health & hospitals	Highways	From local government Total(a)	Education	Public welfare	Health & hospitals	Highways
New Mexico	530,006	496,963	141,648	175,821	21,105	110,965	33,043	17,662	2,464	10,152	887
New York	11,594,813	8,662,707	909,501	5,981,106	273,114	433,917	2,932,106	51,791	1,512,241	8,482	0
North Carolina	1,828,544	1,719,680	427,097	706,118	82,967	237,812	108,864	4,583	92,118	143	6,374
North Dakota	329,241	315,533	55,228	92,713	12,806	91,937	13,708	568	5,022	212	6,703
Ohio	3,015,351	2,874,065	516,920	1,435,538	154,181	316,957	141,286	15,161	0	28,704	25,588
Oklahoma	901,373	882,400	167,620	413,953	42,073	113,824	18,973	3,591	745	1,590	4,230
Oregon	982,234	914,233	186,234	323,684	22,750	161,036	68,001	7,189	17,091	0	41,936
Pennsylvania	3,702,717	3,628,817	564,461	1,946,493	157,306	406,848	73,900	67,510	1	0	4,827
Rhode Island	419,753	403,199	64,066	216,078	17,477	40,611	16,554	184	0	0	0
South Carolina	937,082	917,323	216,504	351,192	55,227	122,116	19,759	9,380	145	4,519	177
South Dakota	296,078	289,061	49,234	96,508	20,453	74,453	7,017	4,498	1,112	2,938	0
Tennessee	1,494,589	1,462,876	285,676	553,208	71,534	263,483	31,713	9,551	1,250	12,042	11,820
Texas	3,470,499	3,459,892	905,831	1,307,183	179,684	595,709	10,607	4,879	0	0	957
Utah	663,109	646,323	143,391	193,700	28,907	136,534	16,786	3,645	1,992	425	0
Vermont	280,475	276,646	42,350	124,988	20,668	43,103	3,829			40	0
Virginia	1,529,943	1,450,996	355,535	590,638	74,084	240,718	78,947	7,274	0	33,850	22,988
Washington	1,423,968	1,304,937	321,165	411,071	97,454	238,974	119,031	27,017	0	76,929	1,050
West Virginia	685,033	680,774	138,134	219,158	31,585	185,848	4,259	1,060	0	0	0
Wisconsin	1,805,323	1,759,970	296,016	953,554	55,771	183,346	45,353	3,387	0	127	16,875
Wyoming	432,495	425,694	29,597	52,001	3,920	79,498	6,801	0	205	10	6,003

(a) Total includes revenue for other activities not shown separately in this table.

Source: U.S. Bureau of the Census, State Government Finances in 1984.
Note: Totals may not add due to rounding.

INTERSTATE COMPACTS AND AGREEMENTS

By Edward D. Feigenbaum

Interstate compacts and agreements—two vehicles used to promote cooperation among the various state governments—were officially sanctioned in the Constitution of the United States. As we move toward the bicentennial of the Constitution in 1987, it is especially appropriate to review the major role that interstate compacts and agreements have played over the years.

The framers of the Constitution recognized that situations would arise, independent of federal authority, under which the states would need to work among themselves to promote certain ends. To facilitate this, the document provided for states to enter into compacts and agreements with each other, subject only to congressional consent. In the 1800s, several interpretations of the U.S. Supreme Court set forth guidelines that limited the need for congressional approval to those instances that would enhance state power at the expense of federal supremacy. "Congressional consent" also was interpreted by the Court to include situations in which years of congressional acquiescence to compact-created boundaries implied approval, and to circumstances in which Congress previously had opened an area of regulation to the states, disclaiming any federal role.

In spite of the flexibility and other advantages of the form of interstate compacts and agreements, only 36 compacts were entered into between 1783 and 1920. Since that time, however, approximately 150 new compacts have been entered into, with more than 100 of these having been set into motion since World War II. After 1970, however, the growth rate in compact formation slowed considerably; the emphasis shifted from the development of new interstate compacts and agreements to the fine-tuning of existing efforts, and additional states and territories joining existing compacts and agreements as signatories.

Several landmarks may be noted in the history of interstate compacts and agreements. In 1921, the first intergovernmental agency under a compact was formed; it continues to exist as the Port Authority of New York and New Jersey. That year also marked the first use of an interstate compact for regional purposes, as the Colorado River Compact—also still in existence—came into being. In 1934, the Interstate Compact for the Supervision of Parolees and Probationers was approved by Congress, and states began to enter into the compact in 1937. The Parole and Probation Compact Administrators' Association is planning several educational efforts to mark 1987 as the 50th anniversary of the first compact that was truly national in scope. All 50 states, the District of Columbia, Puerto Rico, and the Virgin Islands are signatories, and the Commonwealth of the Northern Mariana Islands may well join in the compact's 50th year.

Certain trends in compacts and agreements have become evident in recent years. States once relied upon interstate compacts and agreements to resolve matters of local, yet bilateral concern; today, the emphasis is on multistate compacts tackling tough national issues, creating interstate agencies with powers delegated to the entities by the states. Through these interstate agencies, states have been able to take the lead in a number of areas ranging from banking and taxation to radioactive waste management. Now, interstate compacts and agreements are likely to be more than mere promises on paper. They have become active forces for change.

In recent years, interstate compacts and agreements have been marked as potential answers to the hazardous and radioactive waste disposal dilemma. In 1980, Congress passed legislation that encouraged regional action as a means of disposing of low-level radioactive wastes. Four areas of the country—the Northeast, Rocky Mountains, Central Plains, and the Southeast—have established compacts. However, several states have entered into bilateral agreements with other states outside of these compacts, and others have refused to undertake any effort.

Edward D. Feigenbaum is Director of the Center for Legal Affairs at The Council of State Governments.

One recent U.S. Supreme Court action deserves attention. In 1985, the Court was called upon to declare unconstitutional reciprocal statutes enacted by Connecticut and Massachusetts; these statutes permitted an out-of-state bank holding company to acquire a local bank only if the holding company's principal place of business was within New England. Noting that there had been an express renunciation of federal interest in regulating interstate acquisitions of banks by bank holding companies when Congress passed the Douglas Amendment to the Bank Holding Company Act, the Court held that the state statutes were valid.

The Court then turned to the Compact Clause and found that the reciprocal legislation in this case did not amount to a compact. Although noting that the statutes were similar in requiring reciprocity and imposing a regional limitation, and that there was evidence of cooperation between the two states in studying the problem and implementing the laws, the Court concluded that several of the classic indicia of a compact were missing. The Court cited the absence of a joint regulatory body, noted that neither statute was conditioned on action by the other state and that each state was free to unilaterally modify or repeal its law; most importantly, neither statute required a reciprocation of the regional limitation.

Ultimately, the Court harkened back to the 1977 decision in *United States Steel v. Multistate Tax Commission*, and decided that the political power of the New England states would not be enhanced at the expense of other states nor have an impact upon federal supremacy—thus strengthening the holding in the 1977 action that permitted certain interstate compacts to escape the constitutional requirement for congressional ratification.

In coming years, it is likely that we will continue to see the applications of interstate compacts and agreements to national problems that may be best alleviated at a regional level. We also can expect that compacts will undergo fine-tuning in the future. Given the immense institutional changes in the balance of power between the states and the federal government since the Compact Clause to the Constitution was drafted in the 18th century, it is remarkable how venerable the interstate compacts and agreements have proven to be. Interstate compacts and agreements should continue to be of equal, if not greater, importance as we enter the third century of operation under the U.S. Constitution—a century that will likely see many of the burdens of government thrust upon the states.

THE COUNCIL OF STATE GOVERNMENTS

The Council of State Governments (CSG) is committed to excellence in all facets of state government. Founded on the premise that the states themselves are the best sources of innovations, ideas, insights, and information, CSG provides resources, discerns trends, supplies answers, and creates a network for state policymakers.

The Council has been operating as an information broker for the states for more than 50 years. A non-profit state-supported and -directed service organization, CSG is the only national association that serves the executive, legislative, and judicial branches of state government.

Through its national headquarters in Lexington, Kentucky, and regional offices in Atlanta, Chicago, New York City, and San Francisco, CSG works to synthesize the complex political, cultural, geographical, and philosophical differences inherent in our federal system into cohesive and constructive regional and national approaches. As the 1990s approach, the responsibilities and challenges confronting the nation will dictate the role CSG will play in interacting with the states' decision makers.

Governing Structure

Each state has an equal voice in directing CSG activities through representation on the governing board and an executive committee. The governing board includes all of the nation's governors and two legislators from each state and jurisdiction. Members of the governing board include representatives from the national organizations of lieutenant governors, attorneys general, chief justices, secretaries of state, and state auditors, comptrollers and treasurers. An annual governing board meeting provides an opportunity for the diverse members of the CSG family to interact in sessions on current and emerging state issues.

From this governing board of approximately 175 state officials, an executive committee is selected to manage CSG's day-to-day activities. State officials also serve on several CSG standing committees that advise the executive committee.

The states and U.S. territories and jurisdictions contribute to CSG's financial base. In addition, CSG administers federal and private foundation grants which support research and information projects that benefit the states. CSG also generates revenue from the sale of its publications.

Headquarters Office Structure and Activities

The headquarters office in Lexington, Kentucky, houses CSG's national program efforts, and is organized around four offices that report to the executive director: Finance and Administration; Communication Services; Research and State Services; and Information Services. Also reporting to the executive director is CSG's Intergovernmental Affairs Office, located in Washington, D.C. This office serves as CSG's eyes and ears in the nation's capital, monitoring federal regulations, legislation, policies, and programs that affect the states.

During 1985, CSG reorganized its research activities to emphasize the production of timely information that relates to the current and immediate concerns of state executive and legislative decision makers. As part of this reorganization, CSG established the State Government Research Institute, which consists of independent centers as focal points for expanded research and development efforts. Centers have been established for agriculture and rural development; management, administration, and productivity; transportation; financial management; and environment and natural resources. These units enhance CSG's capacity to provide information, insights, and assistance to state officials.

The Office of Information Services operates the States Information Center (SIC), a personal, direct-access inquiry and referral service that fields more than 7,000 questions each year from state officials. The SIC locates statistical information, provides in-depth information through documents available for loan, and identifies appropriate experts on a given issue. The SIC library maintains 20,000 documents, including CSG and other organizational studies and an extensive collection of state legislative and agency reports. The information needs of state officials will be further served as CSG develops an online, automated information database, dubbed "ISIS" (Integrated State Information

System).

Other CSG activities include:

• The Innovations Transfer Program, which reports on innovative solutions to specific state problems. Since 1975, more than 70 programs have been selected for study.

• The Committee on Suggested State Legislation, which collects, analyzes, and reviews draft legislation for publication in an annual volume.

• The Legal Affairs staff work on interstate compacts and legislation affecting such state programs as emergency management and election procedures.

• The Licensure and Regulation staff work providing information on licensure examinations, administration, disciplinary processes, member training, and sunset activities.

• The State Auditor Training program, which offers on-site training seminars for state employees and prepares auditor training materials for use by individual states.

Regional Office Structure and Activities

CSG's regional structure distinguishes it among state service agencies. Offices in Atlanta, Chicago, New York City, and San Francisco serve regional conferences of state officials. Regions are the backbone of CSG, providing elected and appointed state officials the opportunity to address issues pertinent to specific areas of the country. Regional task forces and committees are actively addressing their states' needs in agriculture and rural development, energy, environment and natural resources, fiscal affairs, and other priority areas.

The issues and activities of each regional office are selected by a regional executive committee of state officials. Regional offices of CSG produce newsletters and substantive issue reports for state officials in their region. In addition, annual conferences of regional organizations of state officials are staffed by CSG's regional offices.

Publications

CSG publishes a variety of materials about state government, including reference works, directories, periodicals, research reports, information briefs, and newsletters. Major CSG publications are:

• *The Book of the States*, a biennial reference guide to all major aspects of state government. This volume contains quantitative and comparative data, and essays written by experts in state operations.

• *State Elective Officials and the Legislatures; State Legislative Leadership, Committees and Staff; and State Administrative Officials Classified by Function*, supplemental directories that include names, addresses, and telephone numbers of state officials.

• *Suggested State Legislation*, an annual volume of draft legislation and legislative ideas selected by a committee of state officials.

• *State Government News*, CSG's monthly magazine on state developments, innovations, and issues. It is distributed to more than 14,000 state officials, including all elected state officials.

• *The Journal of State Government*, a quarterly publication that provides a forum for the discussion of state issues from political, academic, and practitioner viewpoints.

• *State Government Research Checklist*, a bimonthly inventory of state government reports and current information sources.

• *Conference Calendar*, a monthly listing of meetings involving CSG and its interacting organizations.

• *Backgrounder Series*, brief, special issue reports covering current state actions and trends.

• Research reports, in-depth topical information on state programs and policies.

Affiliated and Cooperating Organizations

CSG is an umbrella organization that allows the different branches of state government to come together on a regular basis and consider issues and challenges of mutual concern. CSG has a relationship with a wide range of state officials' groups. The more than 35 affiliated and cooperating organizations of CSG include nearly all state constitutional offices and many functional areas. Ties have been developed or expanded with state treasurers, general services officers, purchasing officials, surplus property administrators, personnel executives, archivists and records administrators, boating law administrators, emergency medical services directors, and controlled substances administrators.

A list of CSG affiliated, cooperating, and adjunct groups follows.

AFFILIATED ORGANIZATIONS

Conference of Chief Justices
Conference of State Court Administrators
National Association of Attorneys General
National Association of Secretaries of State
National Association of State Auditors, Comptrollers and Treasurers
National Association of State Purchasing Officials
National Conference of Lieutenant Governors
National Conference of State General Services Officers
National Conference of State Legislatures

COOPERATING ORGANIZATIONS

Adjutants General Association of the United States
Association of Juvenile Compact Administrators
Association of State and Interstate Water Pollution Control Administrators
Association of State Correctional Administrators
Coastal States Organization
Conference of State Sanitary Engineers
Council of State Administrators of Vocational Rehabilitation
Federation of Tax Administrators
Interstate Conference on Water Problems
National Association for State Information Systems
National Association of Extradition Officials
National Association of Regulatory Utility Commissioners
National Association of State Boating Law Administrators
National Association of State Comptrollers
National Association of State Departments of Agriculture
National Association of State Foresters
National Association of State Juvenile Delinquency Program Administrators
National Association of State Land Reclamationists
National Association of State Mental Health Program Directors
National Association of State Personnel Executives
National Association of State Treasurers
National Association of State Units on Aging
National Association of Tax Administrators
National Clearinghouse on Licensure, Enforcement and Regulation
National Conference of Commissioners on Uniform State Laws
National Conference of States on Building Codes and Standards
National Criminal Justice Association
National Emergency Management Association
National Reciprocal and Family Support Association
National State Auditors Association
Ohio River Basin Commission
Parole and Probation Compact Administrators' Association

ADJUNCT ORGANIZATIONS

Association of State Dam Safety Officials
Council on Governmental Ethics Laws
National Association of Government Archives and Records Administrators
National Association of State Agencies for Surplus Property
National Association of State Controlled Substances Authorities
National Association of State Emergency Medical Services Directors
National Association of State Telecommunications Directors
National Association of State Training and Development Directors

RELATED COMMITTEES

Committee on Intergovernmental Affairs
Committee on State Innovations
Committee on Suggested State Legislation

The Council of State Governments
Officers and Executive Committee
1985-86

Chairman	Vice Chairman
Representative John E. Miller, Arkansas	Senator Hugh T. Farley, New York
President	**Vice President**
Governor Robert D. Orr, Indiana	Governor Richard H. Bryan, Nevada

Governor Norman H. Bangerter, Utah
Attorney General Paul Bardacke, New Mexico
Speaker Carl B. Bledsoe, Colorado
Deputy Speaker John T. Bragg, Tennessee
Governor Terry Branstad, Iowa
Lieutenant Governor Winston Bryant, Arkansas
Comptroller Roland W. Burris, Illinois
Senator Thomas A. Casey, Louisiana
Governor Michael N. Castle, Delaware
Treasurer Bill Cole, Mississippi
Governor Martha Layne Collins, Kentucky
Senator Ross O. Doyen, Kansas
Secretary of State Jeannette Edmondson, Oklahoma
Treasurer Joan Finney, Kansas
Senate President Pro Tem Robert D. Garton, Indiana
Senator James I. Gibson, Nevada
Senator Barbara A. Gill, Maine
Speaker Bob F. Griffin, Missouri
Speaker Roy Hausauer, North Dakota
Chief Justice Edward F. Hennessey, Massachusetts
Senator Lawrence E. Jacobsen, Nevada
Senator Ted D. Little, Alabama
Senator John J. Marchi, New York
Governor James G. Martin, North Carolina
Attorney General Stephen E. Merrill, New Hampshire
Representative Timothy J. Moynihan, Connecticut
Chief Judge Robert C. Murphy, Maryland
Lieutenant Governor John M. Mutz, Indiana
Senator David E. Nething, North Dakota
Senator Oliver Ocasek, Ohio
Governor William A. O'Neill, Connecticut
Auditor General Anthony Piccirilli, Rhode Island
Representative George F. Pott Jr., Pennsylvania
Senate President Fred A. Risser, Wisconsin
Senate President Pro Tem David A. Roberti, California
Senator Kenneth C. Royall Jr., North Carolina
Secretary of State Edwin J. Simcox, Indiana
Representative Irving J. Stolberg, Connecticut
Senate President Ted L. Strickland, Colorado
Senator George Stuart Jr., Florida
Representative John J. Thomas, Indiana
Governor James R. Thompson, Illinois
Senator John Traeger, Texas
Senator Sue Wagner, Nevada
Wellington Webb, Executive Director, Department of
Regulatory Agencies, Colorado
Assemblyman Robert C. Wertz, New York
Representative W. Paul White, Massachusetts

The Council of State Governments
Regional Conferences
1985-86

EAST
Eastern Regional Conference
Senator Barbara A. Gill, Maine, Chairman

Eastern Association of Attorneys General
Attorney General Joseph Lieberman, Connecticut, Chairman

MIDWEST
Midwestern Governors' Conference
Governor Robert Kerrey, Nebraska, Chairman

Midwestern Legislative Conference
Speaker Bob F. Griffin, Missouri, Chairman

Midwestern Conference of Attorneys General
Attorney General Anthony J. Celebreeze Jr., Ohio, Chairman

SOUTH
Southern Governors' Association
Governor James G. Martin, North Carolina, Chairman

Southern Legislative Conference
Senator John Traeger, Texas, Chairman

Southern Conference of Attorneys General
Attorney General David Armstrong, Kentucky, Chairman

Southern Regional Conference,
National Association of State Budget Officers
William Putnam, Executive Director,
State Budget and Control Board, South Carolina, Chairman

Southern Council of State Planning Agencies
Beverly Hogan, Executive Director,
Office of the Governor, Mississippi, Chairman

Southern Environmental Resources Conference
Dr. Michael Bruner, Assistant Commissioner,
Bureau of Environment, Tennessee, Chairman

WEST
Western Legislative Conference
Speaker Carl B. Bledsoe, Colorado, Chairman

Conference of Western Attorneys General
Attorney General Dave Frohnmayer, Oregon, Chairman

The Council of State Governments
Offices and Directors

Headquarters Office

Carl W. Stenberg, Executive Director
Darrell D. Perry, Director
Finance and Administration
Frank Hersman, Director
Research and State Services
E. Norman Sims, Director
Information Services
Kirstin Thompson, Director
Communications

Iron Works Pike
P.O. Box 11910
Lexington, Kentucky 40578
(606) 252-2291

Eastern Office
Alan V. Sokolow, Director
270 Broadway, Suite 513
New York, New York 10007
(212) 693-0400

Midwestern Office
Virginia Thrall, Director
203 North Wabash Avenue
Chicago, Illinois 60601
(312) 236-4011

Southern Office
Charles J. Williams Jr., Director
3384 Peachtree Road, N.E.
Atlanta, Georgia 30326
(404) 266-1271

Western Office
Daniel M. Sprague, Director
720 Sacramento Street
San Francisco, California 94108
(415) 986-3760

Washington Office
Norman Beckman, Director
Hall of the States
444 North Capitol Street
Washington, D.C. 20001
(202) 624-5460

CHAPTER TEN

STATE PAGES

Table 10.1
OFFICIAL NAMES OF STATES AND JURISDICTIONS, CAPITALS, ZIP CODES AND CENTRAL SWITCHBOARDS

State or other jurisdiction	Name of state capitol(a)	Capital	Zip code	Area code	Central switchboard
Alabama, State of	State Capitol	Montgomery	36130	205	261-2500
Alaska, State of	State Capitol	Juneau	99811	907	465-2111
Arizona, State of	State Capitol	Phoenix	85007	602	255-4900
Arkansas, State of	State Capitol	Little Rock	72201	501	371-3000
California, State of	State Capitol	Sacramento	95814	916	322-9900
Colorado, State of	State Capitol	Denver	80203	303	866-5000
Connecticut, State of	State Capitol	Hartford	06106	203	566-2211
Delaware, State of.....................	Legislative Hall	Dover	19901	302	736-4000
Florida, State of.......................	The Capitol	Tallahassee	32301	904	488-1234
Georgia, State of	State Capitol	Atlanta	30334	404	656-2000
Hawaii, State of.......................	State Capitol	Hcnolulu	96813	808	548-2211
Idaho, State of........................	State Capitol	Boise	83720	208	334-2411
Illinois, State of	State House	Springfield	62706	217	782-2000
Indiana, State of	State House	Indianapolis	46204	317	232-3140
Iowa, State of.........................	State Capitol	Des Moines	50319	515	281-5011
Kansas, State of	State House	Topeka	66612	913	296-0111
Kentucky, Commonwealth of	State Capitol	Frankfort	40601	502	564-2500
Louisiana, State of.....................	State Capitol	Baton Rouge	70804	504	342-6600
Maine, State of........................	State House	Augusta	04333	207	289-1110
Maryland, State of.....................	State House	Annapolis	21401	301	269-6200
Massachusetts, Commonwealth of	State House	Boston	02133	617	727-2121
Michigan, State of	State Capitol	Lansing	48909	517	373-1837
Minnesota, State of	State Capitol	St. Paul	55515	612	296-6013
Mississippi, State of	New Capitol	Jackson	39201	601	359-1000
Missouri, State of......................	State Capitol	Jefferson City	65101	314	751-2151
Montana, State of	State Capitol	Helena	59620	406	444-2511
Nebraska, State of.....................	State Capitol	Lincoln	68509	402	471-2311
Nevada, State of	Legislative Hall	Carson City	89710	702	885-5000
New Hampshire, State of	State House	Concord	03301	603	271-1110
New Jersey, State of	State House	Trenton	08625	609	292-2121
New Mexico, State of	State Capitol	Santa Fe	87503	505	827-4011
New York, State of	State Capitol	Albany	12224	518	474-2121
North Carolina, State of................	State Legislative Building	Raleigh	27611	919	733-1110
North Dakota, State of	State Capitol	Bismarck	58505	701	224-2000
Ohio, State of.........................	State House	Columbus	43215	614	466-2000
Oklahoma, State of	State Capitol	Oklahoma City	73105	405	521-2011
Oregon, State of	State Capitol	Salem	97310	503	378-3131
Pennsylvania, Commonwealth of	Main Capitol Building	Harrisburg	17120	717	787-2121
Rhode Island and Providence Plantations, State of	State House	Providence	02903	401	277-2000
South Carolina, State of................	State House	Columbia	29211	803	758-0221
South Dakota, State of	State Capitol	Pierre	57501	605	773-3011
Tennessee, State of	State Capitol	Nashville	37219	615	741-3011
Texas, State of	State Capitol	Austin	78711	512	475-2323
Utah, State of.........................	State Capitol	Salt Lake City	84114	801	533-4000
Vermont, State of	State House	Montpelier	05602	802	828-1110
Virginia, Commonwealth of..............	State Capitol	Richmond	23219	804	786-0000
Washington, State of	Legislative Building	Olympia	98504	206	753-5000
West Virginia, State of	State Capitol	Charleston	25305	304	348-3456
Wisconsin, State of	State Capitol	Madison	53702	608	266-2211
Wyoming, State of	State Capitol	Cheyenne	82002	307	777-7220
District of Columbia	District Building	Washington	20004	202	727-1000
American Samoa, Territory of............	Maota Fono	Pago Pago	96799	684	633-4116
Federated States of Micronesia	. . .	Kolonia	96941	. . .	NCS
Guam, Territory of	Congress Building	Agana	96910	671	472-8931
Marshall Islands	. . .	Majuro	96960	. . .	NCS
No. Mariana Is., Commonwealth of	Civic Center	Saipan	96950	. . .	NCS
Puerto Rico, Commonwealth of	The Capitol	San Juan	00904	809	721-6040
Republic of Belau........................	. . .	Koror	96940	. . .	NCS
Virgin Islands, Territory of	Capitol Building	Charlotte Amalie	00801	809	774-0080

NCS—No central switchboard.
(a) In some instances the name is not official.

Table 10.2
HISTORICAL DATA ON THE STATES

State or other jurisdiction	Source of state lands	Date organized as territory	Date admitted to Union	Chronological order of admission to Union
Alabama	Mississippi Territory, 1798(a)	March 3, 1817	Dec. 14, 1819	22
Alaska	Purchased from Russia, 1867	Aug. 24, 1912	Jan. 3, 1959	49
Arizona	Ceded by Mexico, 1848(b)	Feb. 24, 1863	Feb. 14, 1912	48
Arkansas	Louisiana Purchase, 1803	March 2, 1819	June 15, 1836	25
California	Ceded by Mexico, 1848	(c)	Sept. 9, 1850	31
Colorado	Louisiana Purchase, 1803(d)	Feb. 28, 1861	Aug. 1, 1876	38
Connecticut	Fundamental Orders, Jan. 14, 1638; Royal charter, April 23, 1662(e)	. . .	Jan. 9, 1788(f)	5
Delaware	Swedish charter, 1638; English charter, 1683(e)	. . .	Dec. 7, 1787(f)	1
Florida	Ceded by Spain, 1819	March 30, 1822	March 3, 1845	27
Georgia	Charter, 1732, from George II to Trustees for Establishing the Colony of Georgia(e)	. . .	Jan. 2, 1788(f)	4
Hawaii	Annexed, 1898	June 14, 1900	Aug. 21, 1959	50
Idaho	Treaty with Britain, 1846	March 4, 1863	July 3, 1890	43
Illinois	Northwest Territory, 1787	Feb. 3, 1809	Dec. 3, 1818	21
Indiana	Northwest Territory, 1787	May 7, 1800	Dec. 11, 1816	19
Iowa	Louisiana Purchase, 1803	June 12, 1838	Dec. 28, 1846	29
Kansas	Louisiana Purchase, 1803(d)	May 30, 1854	Jan. 29, 1861	34
Kentucky	Part of Virginia until admitted as state	(c)	June 1, 1792	15
Louisiana	Louisiana Purchase, 1803(g)	March 26, 1804	April 30, 1812	18
Maine	Part of Massachusetts until admitted as state	(c)	March 15, 1820	23
Maryland	Charter, 1632, from Charles I to Calvert(e)	. . .	April 28, 1788(f)	7
Massachusetts	Charter to Massachusetts Bay Company, 1629(e)	. . .	Feb. 6, 1788(f)	6
Michigan	Northwest Territory, 1787	Jan. 11, 1805	Jan. 26, 1837	26
Minnesota	Northwest Territory, 1787(h)	March 3, 1849	May 11, 1858	32
Mississippi	Mississippi Territory(i)	April 7, 1798	Dec. 10, 1817	20
Missouri	Louisiana Purchase, 1803	June 4, 1812	Aug. 10, 1821	24
Montana	Louisiana Purchase, 1803(j)	May 26, 1864	Nov. 8, 1889	41
Nebraska	Louisiana Purchase, 1803	May 30, 1854	March 1, 1867	37
Nevada	Ceded by Mexico, 1848	March 2, 1861	Oct. 31, 1864	36
New Hampshire	Grants from Council for New England, 1622 and 1629; made Royal province, 1679(e)	. . .	June 21, 1788(f)	9
New Jersey	Dutch settlement, 1618; English charter, 1664(e)	. . .	Dec. 18, 1787(f)	3
New Mexico	Ceded by Mexico, 1848(b)	Sept. 9, 1850	Jan. 6, 1912	47
New York	Dutch settlement, 1623; English control, 1664(e)	. . .	July 26, 1788(f)	11
North Carolina	Charter, 1663, from Charles II(e)	. . .	Nov. 21, 1789(f)	12
North Dakota	Louisiana Purchase, 1803(k)	March 2, 1861	Nov. 2, 1889	39
Ohio	Northwest Territory, 1787	May 7, 1800	March 1, 1803	17
Oklahoma	Louisiana Purchase, 1803	May 2, 1890	Nov. 16, 1907	46
Oregon	Settlement and treaty with Britain, 1846	Aug. 14, 1848	Feb. 14, 1859	33
Pennsylvania	Grant from Charles II to William Penn, 1681(e)	. . .	Dec. 12, 1787(f)	2
Rhode Island	Charter, 1663, from Charles II(e)	. . .	May 29, 1790(f)	13
South Carolina	Charter, 1663, from Charles II(e)	. . .	May 23, 1788(f)	8
South Dakota	Louisiana Purchase, 1803	March 2, 1861	Nov. 2, 1889	40
Tennessee	Part of North Carolina until land ceded to U.S. in 1789	June 8, 1790(l)	June 1, 1796	16
Texas	Republic of Texas, 1845	(c)	Dec. 29, 1845	28
Utah	Ceded by Mexico, 1848	Sept. 9, 1850	Jan. 4, 1896	45
Vermont	From lands of New Hampshire and New York	(c)	March 4, 1791	14
Virginia	Charter, 1609, from James I to London Company(e)	. . .	June 25, 1788(f)	10
Washington	Oregon Territory, 1848	March 2, 1853	Nov. 11, 1889	42
West Virginia	Part of Virginia until admitted as state	(c)	June 20, 1863	35
Wisconsin	Northwest Territory, 1787	April 20, 1836	May 29, 1848	30
Wyoming	Louisiana Purchase, 1803(d,j)	July 25, 1868	July 10, 1890	44
Dist. of Col.	Maryland(m)	. . .	. . .	. . .
American Samoa	--Became a territory, 1900--			
Federated States of Micronesia	. . .	May 10, 1979	. . .	. . .
Guam	Ceded by Spain, 1898	Aug. 1, 1950	. . .	. . .
Marshall Islands	. . .	May 1, 1979	. . .	. . .
No. Mariana Is.	. . .	March 24, 1976	. . .	. . .
Puerto Rico	Ceded by Spain, 1898	. . .	July 25, 1952(n)	. . .
Republic of Belau	. . .	Jan. 1, 1981	. . .	. . .
Virgin Islands	--Purchased from Denmark, March 31, 1917--			

(a) By the Treaty of Paris, 1783, England gave up claim to the 13 original Colonies, and to all land within an area extending along the present Canadian border to the Lake of the Woods, down the Mississippi River to the 31st parallel, east to the Chattahoochie, down that river to the mouth of the Flint, east to the source of the St. Mary's, down that river to the ocean. The major part of Alabama was acquired by the Treaty of Paris, and the lower portion from Spain in 1813.

(b) Portion of land obtained by Gadsden Purchase, 1853.

(c) No territorial status before admission to Union.

(d) Portion of land ceded by Mexico, 1848.

(e) One of the original 13 Colonies.

(f) Date of ratification of U.S. Constitution.

(g) West Feliciana District (Baton Rouge) acquired from Spain, 1810; added to Louisiana, 1812.

(h) Portion of land obtained by Louisiana Purchase, 1803.

(i) See footnote (a). The lower portion of Mississippi also was acquired from Spain in 1813.

(j) Portion of land obtained from Oregon Territory, 1848.

(k) The northern portion of the Red River Valley was acquired by treaty with Great Britain in 1818.

(l) Date Southwest Territory (identical boundary as Tennessee's) was created.

(m) Area was originally 100 square miles, taken from Virginia and Maryland. Virginia's portion south of the Potomac was given back to that state in 1846. Site chosen in 1790, city incorporated 1802.

(n) On this date, Puerto Rico became a self-governing commonwealth by compact approved by the U.S. Congress and the voters of Puerto Rico as provided in U.S. Public Law 600 of 1950.

Table 10.3
STATE STATISTICS

State or other jurisdiction	Land area — In square miles	Land area — Rank in nation	Population — Size	Population — Rank in nation	Percentage change 1970 to 1980	Density per square mile	No. of representatives in Congress	Capital	Population	Rank in state	Largest city	Population
Alabama	50,767	28	3,893,888	22	13.1	76.7	7	Montgomery	177,857	3	Birmingham	284,413
Alaska	570,833	1	401,851	50	32.8	0.7	1	Juneau	19,528	3	Anchorage	174,431
Arizona	113,508	6	2,718,215	29	53.1	23.9	5	Phoenix	789,704	1	Phoenix	789,704
Arkansas	52,078	27	2,286,435	33	18.9	43.9	4	Little Rock	158,461	1	Little Rock	158,461
California	156,299	3	23,667,902	1	18.5	151.4	45	Sacramento	275,741	7	Los Angeles	2,966,850
Colorado	103,595	8	2,889,964	28	30.8	27.9	6	Denver	492,365	1	Denver	492,365
Connecticut	4,872	48	3,107,576	25	2.5	637.8	6	Hartford	136,392	2	Bridgeport	142,546
Delaware	1,932	49	594,338	47	8.4	307.6	1	Dover	23,512	3	Wilmington	70,195
Florida	54,153	26	9,746,324	7	43.5	180.0	19	Tallahassee	81,548	11	Jacksonville	540,920
Georgia	58,056	21	5,463,105	13	19.1	94.1	10	Atlanta	425,022	1	Atlanta	425,022
Hawaii	6,425	47	964,691	39	25.3	150.1	2	Honolulu(a)	762,874	1	Honolulu(a)	762,874
Idaho	82,412	11	943,935	41	32.4	11.5	2	Boise	102,451	1	Boise	102,451
Illinois	55,645	24	11,426,518	5	2.8	205.3	22	Springfield	99,637	4	Chicago	3,005,072
Indiana	35,932	38	5,490,224	12	5.7	152.8	10	Indianapolis	700,807	1	Indianapolis	700,807
Iowa	55,965	23	2,913,808	27	3.1	52.1	6	Des Moines	191,003	1	Des Moines	191,003
Kansas	81,778	13	2,363,679	32	5.1	28.9	5	Topeka	115,266	3	Wichita	279,272
Kentucky	39,669	37	3,660,777	23	13.7	92.3	7	Frankfort	25,973	9	Louisville	298,451
Louisiana	44,521	33	4,205,900	19	15.4	94.5	8	Baton Rouge	219,419	2	New Orleans	557,515
Maine	30,995	39	1,124,660	38	13.2	36.3	2	Augusta	21,819	6	Portland	61,572
Maryland	9,837	42	4,216,975	18	7.5	428.7	8	Annapolis	31,740	5	Baltimore	786,775
Massachusetts	7,824	45	5,737,037	11	0.8	733.3	11	Boston	562,994	1	Boston	562,994
Michigan	56,954	22	9,262,078	8	4.3	162.6	18	Lansing	130,414	5	Detroit	1,203,339
Minnesota	79,548	14	4,075,970	21	7.1	51.2	8	St. Paul	270,230	2	Minneapolis	370,951
Mississippi	47,233	31	2,520,638	31	13.7	53.4	5	Jackson	202,895	1	Jackson	202,895
Missouri	68,945	18	4,916,686	15	5.1	71.3	9	Jefferson City	33,619	12	St. Louis	453,085
Montana	145,388	4	786,690	44	13.3	5.4	2	Helena	23,938	5	Billings	66,798
Nebraska	76,644	15	1,569,825	35	5.7	20.5	3	Lincoln	171,932	2	Omaha	314,255
Nevada	109,894	7	800,493	43	63.8	7.3	2	Carson City	32,022	5	Las Vegas	164,674
New Hampshire	8,993	44	920,610	42	24.8	102.4	2	Concord	30,400	3	Manchester	90,936
New Jersey	7,468	46	7,364,823	9	2.7	986.2	14	Trenton	92,124	5	Newark	329,248
New Mexico	121,335	5	1,302,894	37	28.1	10.7	3	Santa Fe	48,953	5	Albuquerque	331,767
New York	47,377	30	17,558,072	2	-3.7	370.6	34	Albany	101,727	6	New York	7,071,639
North Carolina	48,843	29	5,881,766	10	15.7	120.4	11	Raleigh	150,255	2	Charlotte	314,447
North Dakota	69,300	17	652,717	46	5.7	9.4	1	Bismarck	44,485	3	Fargo	61,383
Ohio	41,004	35	10,797,630	6	1.3	263.3	21	Columbus	564,871	2	Cleveland	573,822

STATE STATISTICS—Continued

State or other jurisdiction	Land area		Population		Percentage change 1970 to 1980	Density per square mile	No. of representatives in Congress	Capital	Population	Rank in state	Largest city	Population
	In square miles	Rank in nation	Size	Rank in nation								
Oklahoma	68,655	19	3,025,290	26	18.2	44.1	6	Oklahoma City	403,213	1	Oklahoma City	403,213
Oregon	96,184	10	2,632,105	30	25.9	27.4	5	Salem	89,233	3	Portland	366,383
Pennsylvania	44,888	32	11,863,895	4	0.5	264.3	23	Harrisburg	53,264	10	Philadelphia	1,688,210
Rhode Island	1,055	50	947,154	40	-0.3	897.8	2	Providence	156,804	1	Providence	156,804
South Carolina	30,203	40	3,121,820	24	20.5	103.4	6	Columbia	101,208	1	Columbia	101,208
South Dakota	75,952	16	690,768	45	3.7	9.1	1	Pierre	11,973	9	Sioux Falls	81,343
Tennessee	41,155	34	4,591,120	17	16.9	111.6	9	Nashville	455,651	2	Memphis	646,356
Texas	262,017	2	14,229,191	3	27.1	54.3	27	Austin	345,496	6	Houston	1,595,138
Utah	82,073	12	1,461,037	37	37.9	17.8	3	Salt Lake City	163,033	1	Salt Lake City	163,033
Vermont	9,273	43	511,456	48	15.0	55.2	1	Montpelier	8,241	5	Burlington	37,712
Virginia	39,704	36	5,346,818	14	14.9	134.7	10	Richmond	219,214	3	Norfolk	266,979
Washington	66,511	20	4,132,156	20	21.1	62.1	8	Olympia	27,447	15	Seattle	493,846
West Virginia	24,119	41	1,949,644	34	11.8	80.8	4	Charleston	63,968	1	Charleston	63,968
Wisconsin	54,426	25	4,705,767	16	6.5	86.5	9	Madison	170,616	2	Milwaukee	636,212
Wyoming	96,989	9	469,557	49	41.3	4.8	1	Cheyenne	47,283	2	Casper	51,016
Dist. of Col.	63		638,333		-15.6	10,132.3	1(b)					
American Samoa	76		32,395		18.9	419.0		Pago Pago	3,075		Pago Pago	3,075
Federated States of Micronesia	271		73,160		24.7	506.3	1(b)	Kolonia, Ponape	5,549		Moen, Truk	10,351
Guam	209		105,816		34.9	443.5		Agana	896		Tamuning	8,862
Marshall Islands	70		31,042			91.1		Majuro	8,667		Majuro	8,667
No. Mariana Is.	184		16,780		74.1			Saipan	14,549		Saipan	14,549
Puerto Rico	3,421		3,187,570		17.9	931.8	1(b)	San Juan	424,600		San Juan	424,600
Republic of Belau	192		12,177		8.1	63.4		Koror	6,222		Koror	6,222
Virgin Islands	132		95,591		54.6	724.2	1(b)	Charlotte Amalie, St. Thomas	11,842		Charlotte Amalie, St. Thomas	11,842

Source: 1980 Bureau of the Census PC 80-1A final reports.
(a) Honolulu County.
(b) Delegate with committee voting privileges only.

Alabama

Nickname .... The Heart of Dixie
Motto .... *We Dare Defend Our Rights*
Flower .... Camellia
Gamebird .... Wild Turkey
Bird .... Yellowhammer
Tree .... Southern (Longleaf) Pine
Song .... *Alabama*
Dance .... Square Dance
Stone .... Marble
Mineral .... Hematite
Fish .... Tarpon
Nut .... Pecan
Fossil .... Species Basilosaurus Cetoides
Entered the Union .... December 14, 1819
Capital .... Montgomery

ELECTED EXECUTIVE BRANCH OFFICIALS

Governor .... George C. Wallace
Lieutenant Governor .... Bill Baxley
Secretary of State .... Don Siegelman
Attorney General .... Charlie Graddick
Treasurer .... Annie Laurie Gunter
Auditor .... Jan Cook
Commr. of Agriculture
& Industries .... Albert McDonald

SUPREME COURT

C. C. Torbert Jr., Chief Justice
Oscar W. Adams Jr.
Reneau P. Almon
Samuel A. Beatty
Gorman Houston
Richard L. Jones
Hugh Maddox
Janie L. Shores
(Vacancy)

LEGISLATURE

President of the Senate ... Lt. Gov. Bill Baxley
President Pro Tem
of the Senate .... John A. Teague
Secretary of the Senate .... McDowell Lee

Speaker of the House .... Tom Drake
Speaker Pro Tem of the House ... Roy Johnson
Clerk of the House .... John W. Pemberton

STATISTICS

Land Area (square miles) 50,767
  Rank in Nation 28th
Population 3,893,888
  Rank in Nation 22nd
  Density per square mile 76.7
Number of Representatives in Congress 7
Capital City .... Montgomery
  Population 177,857
  Rank in State 3rd
Largest City .... Birmingham
  Population 284,413
Number of Cities over 10,000 Population ... 40

Alaska

Motto .... *North to the Future*
Flower .... Forget-me-not
Bird .... Willow Ptarmigan
Tree .... Sitka Spruce
Song .... *Alaska's Flag*
Sport .... Dog Mushing
Gem .... Jade
Mineral .... Gold
Marine Mammal .... Bowhead Whale
Fish .... King Salmon
Purchased from Russia by the
  United States .... March 30, 1867
Entered the Union .... January 3, 1959
Capital .... Juneau

ELECTED EXECUTIVE BRANCH OFFICIALS

Governor .... Bill Sheffield
Lieutenant Governor .... Stephen McAlpine

SUPREME COURT

Jay A. Rabinowitz, Chief Justice
Edmond W. Burke
Allen Compton
Warren Matthews
Daniel Moore

LEGISLATURE

President of the Senate .... Don Bennett
Secretary of the Senate ...... Peggy Mulligan

Speaker of the House .... Ben Grussendorf
Chief Clerk of the House .... Irene Cashen

STATISTICS

Land Area (square miles) 570,833
  Rank in Nation 1st
Population 401,851
  Rank in Nation 50th
  Density per square mile 0.7
Number of Representatives in Congress 1
Capital City .... Juneau
  Population 19,528
  Rank in State 3rd
Largest City .... Anchorage
  Population 174,431
Number of Cities over 10,000 Population 3

Arizona

Nickname . . . . The Grand Canyon State
Motto . . . . *Ditat Deus* (God Enriches)
Flower . . . . Blossom of the Saguaro Cactus
Bird . . . . Cactus Wren
Tree . . . . Palo Verde
Song . . . . *Arizona March Song* and *Arizona*
Gemstone . . . . Turquoise
Official Neckwear . . . . Bola Tie
Entered the Union . . . . February 14, 1912
Capital . . . . Phoenix

ELECTED EXECUTIVE BRANCH OFFICIALS

Governor . . . . Bruce Babbitt
Secretary of State . . . . Rose Mofford
Attorney General . . . . Bob K. Corbin
Treasurer . . . . Ray Rottas
Supt. of Public Instruction . . . . Carolyn Warner
Mine Inspector . . . . James H. McCutchan

SUPREME COURT

William A. Holohan, Chief Justice
Frank X. Gordon Jr., Vice Chief Justice
James Duke Cameron
Stanley G. Feldman
Jack D. H. Hays

LEGISLATURE

President of the Senate . . . . Stan Turley
President Pro Tem of the Senate . . Jack Taylor
Secretary of the Senate . . . . . Shirley Wheaton

Speaker of the House . . . . . James J. Sossaman
Speaker Pro Tem
   of the House . . . . Sam A. McConnell Jr.
Chief Clerk of the House . . . . . . Jane Richards

STATISTICS

Land Area (square miles) 113,508
   Rank in Nation 6th
Population 2,718,215
   Rank in Nation 29th
   Density per square mile 23.9
Number of Representatives in Congress 5
Capital City . . . . Phoenix
   Population 789,704
   Rank in State 1st
Largest City . . . . Phoenix
Number of Places over 10,000 Population . . . 17

Arkansas

Nickname . . . . The Land of Opportunity
Motto . . . . . . *Regnat Populus* (The People Rule)
Flower . . . . Apple Blossom
Bird . . . . Mockingbird
Tree . . . . Pine
Song . . . . *Arkansas*
Gem . . . . Diamond
Entered the Union . . . . June 15, 1836
Capital . . . . Little Rock

ELECTED EXECUTIVE BRANCH OFFICIALS

Governor . . . . Bill Clinton
Lieutenant Governor . . . . Winston Bryant
Secretary of State . . . . W.J. "Bill" McCuen
Attorney General . . . . Steve Clark
Treasurer . . . . Jimmie Lou Fisher
Auditor . . . . Julia Hughs Jones
Land Commr. . . . . Charlie Daniels

SUPREME COURT

Jack Holt, Jr., Chief Justice
Robert H. Dudley
Steele Hays
Darrell Hickman
David Newbern
John I. Purtle
George Rose Smith

GENERAL ASSEMBLY

President
   of the Senate . . . ⹁ . . Lt. Gov. Winston Bryant
President Pro Tem
   of the Senate . . . . Paul B. Benham Jr.
Secretary of the Senate . . . . Hal Moody

Speaker of the House . . . . Lacy Landers
Speaker Pro Tem
   of the House . . . . Bobby Newman
Chief Clerk of the House . . . . Sue Smith

STATISTICS

Land Area (square miles) 52,078
   Rank in Nation 27th
Population 2,286,435
   Rank in Nation 33rd
   Density per square mile 43.9
Number of Representatives in Congress 4
Capital City . . . . Little Rock
   Population 158,461
   Rank in State 1st
Largest City . . . . Little Rock
Number of Places over 10,000 Population . . . 29

California

Nickname	The Golden State
Motto	*Eureka* (I Have Found It)
Flower	Golden Poppy
Bird	California Valley Quail
Tree	California Redwood
Reptile	California Desert Tortoise
Song	*I Love You, California*
Stone	Serpentine
Mineral	Native Gold
Animal	California Grizzly Bear
Fish	California Golden Trout
Insect	California Dog-Face Butterfly
Marine Mammal	California Gray Whale
Fossil	Saber-Toothed Cat
Gemstone	Benitoite
Entered the Union	September 9, 1850
Capital	Sacramento

ELECTED EXECUTIVE BRANCH OFFICIALS

Governor	George Deukmejian
Lieutenant Governor	Leo T. McCarthy
Secretary of State	March Fong Eu
Attorney General	John Van de Kamp
Treasurer	Jesse M. Unruh
Controller	Kenneth Cory
Supt. of Public Instruction	Bill Honig

SUPREME COURT

Rose Elizabeth Bird, Chief Justice
Allen E. Broussard
Joseph R. Grodin
Malcolm M. Lucas
Stanley Mosk
Edward Panelli
Cruz Reynoso

LEGISLATURE

President of the Senate	Lt. Gov. Leo T. McCarthy
President Pro Tem of the Senate	David A. Roberti
Secretary of the Senate	Darryl R. White
Speaker of the Assembly	Willie L. Brown Jr.
Speaker Pro Tem of the Assembly	Frank Vicencia
Chief Clerk of the Assembly	James D. Driscoll

STATISTICS

Land Area (square miles)	156,299
Rank in Nation	3rd
Population	23,667,902
Rank in Nation	1st
Density per square mile	151.4
Number of Representatives in Congress	45
Capital City	Sacramento
Population	275,741
Rank in State	7th
Largest City	Los Angeles
Population	2,966,850
Number of Places over 10,000 Population	256

Colorado

Nickname	The Centennial State
Motto	*Nil Sine Numine* (Nothing Without Providence)
Flower	Rocky Mountain Columbine
Bird	Lark Bunting
Tree	Colorado Blue Spruce
Song	*Where the Columbines Grow*
Stone	Aquamarine
Animal	Rocky Mountain Bighorn Sheep
Entered the Union	August 1, 1876
Capital	Denver

ELECTED EXECUTIVE BRANCH OFFICIALS

Governor	Richard D. Lamm
Lieutenant Governor	Nancy Dick
Secretary of State	Natalie Meyer
Attorney General	Duane Woodard
Treasurer	Roy R. Romer

SUPREME COURT

Joseph R. Quinn, Chief Justice
Jean Dubofsky
William H. Erickson
Howard M. Kirshbaum
George E. Lohr
Luis D. Rovira
Anthony Vollack

GENERAL ASSEMBLY

President of the Senate	Ted L. Strickland
President Pro Tem of the Senate	Harold McCormick
Secretary of the Senate	Marjorie L. Nielson
Speaker of the House	Carl "Bev" Bledsoe
Chief Clerk of the House	Lee Bahrych

STATISTICS

Land Area (square miles)	103,595
Rank in Nation	8th
Population	2,889,964
Rank in Nation	28th
Density per square mile	27.9
Number of Representatives in Congress	6
Capital City	Denver
Population	492,365
Rank in State	1st
Largest City	Denver
Number of Places over 10,000 Population	25

Connecticut

Nickname .... The Constitution State
Motto .... *Qui Transtulit Sustinet*
     (He Who Transplanted Still Sustains)
Animal .... Sperm Whale
Flower .... Mountain Laurel
Bird .... American Robin
Tree .... White Oak
Song .... *Yankee Doodle*
Mineral .... Garnet
Insect .... Praying Mantis
State Ship .... U.S.S. Nautilus
Entered the Union .... January 9, 1788
Capital .... Hartford

ELECTED EXECUTIVE BRANCH OFFICIALS

Governor .... William A. O'Neill
Lieutenant Governor .... Joseph J. Fauliso
Secretary of State .... Julia H. Tashjian
Attorney General .... Joseph Lieberman
Treasurer .... Joan R. Kemler
Comptroller .... J. Edward Caldwell

SUPREME COURT

Ellen Ash Peters, Chief Justice
Robert J. Callahan
Joseph F. Dannehy
Arthur H. Healey
Angelo G. Santaniello
David M. Shea

GENERAL ASSEMBLY

President
   of the Senate ..... Lt. Gov. Joseph J. Fauliso
President Pro Tem
   of the Senate .... Philip S. Robertson
Clerk of the Senate .... Alden B. Ives

Speaker of the House ..... R.E. Van Norstrand
Deputy Speaker
   of the House .... Richard O. Belden
Clerk of the House .... John T. Nugent

STATISTICS

Land Area (square miles) 4,872
   Rank in Nation 48th
Population 3,107,576
   Rank in Nation 25th
   Density per square mile 637.8
Number of Representatives in Congress 6
Capital City .... Hartford
   Population 136,392
   Rank in State 2nd
Largest City .... Bridgeport
   Population 142,546
Number of Places over 10,000 Population ... 22

Delaware

Nickname .... The First State
Motto .... *Liberty and Independence*
Flower .... Peach Blossom
Bird .... Blue Hen Chicken
Insect .... Ladybug
Tree .... American Holly
Song .... *Our Delaware*
Mineral .... Stillimanite
Fish .... Weakfish
Entered the Union .... December 7, 1787
Capital .... Dover

ELECTED EXECUTIVE BRANCH OFFICIALS

Governor .... Michael N. Castle
Lieutenant Governor .... S.B. Woo
Attorney General .... Charles M. Oberly III
Treasurer .... Janet C. Rzewnicki
Auditor .... Dennis E. Greenhouse
Insurance Commr. .... David Levinson

SUPREME COURT

Andrew D. Christie, Chief Justice
Henry R. Horsey
John J. McNeilly
Andrew G.T. Moore II
Joseph Walsh

GENERAL ASSEMBLY

President of the Senate ..... Lt. Gov. S.B. Woo
President Pro Tem
   of the Senate .... Richard S. Cordrey
Secretary of the Senate ... Betty Jean Caniford

Speaker of the House .... Charles Hebner
Chief Clerk of the House ...... JoAnn Hedrick

STATISTICS

Land Area (square miles) 1,932
   Rank in Nation 49th
Population 594,338
   Rank in Nation 47th
   Density per square mile 307.6
Number of Representatives in Congress 1
Capital City .... Dover
   Population 23,512
   Rank in State 3rd
Largest City .... Wilmington
   Population 70,195
Number of Places over 10,000 Population 3

Florida

Nickname	The Sunshine State
Motto	*In God We Trust*
Flower	Orange Blossom
Bird	Mockingbird
Tree	Sabal Palmetto Palm
Song	*Old Folks at Home*
Stone	Agatized Coral
Gem	Moonstone
Saltwater Mammal	Dolphin
Marine Mammal	Porpoise
Saltwater Fish	Atlantic Sailfish
Freshwater Fish	Florida Large Mouth Bass
Shell	Horse Conch
Animal	Florida Panther
Beverage	Orange Juice
Entered the Union	March 3, 1845
Capital	Tallahassee

ELECTED EXECUTIVE BRANCH OFFICIALS

Governor	Bob Graham
Lieutenant Governor	Wayne Mixson
Secretary of State	George Firestone
Attorney General	Jim Smith
Treasurer/Insurance Commr.	Bill Gunter
Comptroller	Gerald A. Lewis
Commr. of Education	Ralph D. Turlington
Commr. of Agriculture	Doyle Conner

SUPREME COURT

Joseph A. Boyd Jr., Chief Justice
James C. Adkins
Rosemary Barkett
Raymond Ehrlich
Parker Lee McDonald
Ben F. Overton
Leander J. Shaw Jr.

LEGISLATURE

President of the Senate	Harry A. Johnston II
President Pro Tem of the Senate	Betty Castor
Secretary of the Senate	Joe Brown
Speaker of the House	James Harold Thompson
Speaker Pro Tem of the House	Elaine Gordon
Clerk of the House	Allen Morris

STATISTICS

Land Area (square miles)	54,153
Rank in Nation	26th
Population	9,746,324
Rank in Nation	7th
Density per square mile	180
Number of Representatives in Congress	19
Capital City	Tallahassee
Population	81,548
Rank in State	11th
Largest City	Jacksonville
Population	540,920
Number of Places over 10,000 Population	96

Georgia

Nickname	The Empire State of the South*
Motto	*Wisdom, Justice and Moderation*
Flower	Cherokee Rose
Bird	Brown Thrasher
Tree	Live Oak
Song	*Georgia on My Mind*
Fish	Largemouth Bass
Entered the Union	January 2, 1788
Capital	Atlanta

*Unofficial

ELECTED EXECUTIVE BRANCH OFFICIALS

Governor	Joe Frank Harris
Lieutenant Governor	Zell Miller
Secretary of State	Max Cleland
Attorney General	Michael J. Bowers
Comptroller General	Warren Evans
Superintendent of Schools	Charles McDaniel
Commr. of Agriculture	Thomas T. Irvin
Commr. of Labor	Joe Tanner

SUPREME COURT

Harold N. Hill Jr., Chief Justice
Thomas O. Marshall, Presiding Justice
Richard Bell
Harold G. Clarke
Hardy Gregory Jr.
George T. Smith
Charles L. Weltner

GENERAL ASSEMBLY

President of the Senate	Lt. Gov. Zell B. Miller
President Pro Tem of the Senate	Joe Kennedy
Secretary of the Senate	Hamilton McWhorter Jr.
Speaker of the House	Thomas B. Murphy
Speaker Pro Tem of the House	Jack Connell
Clerk of the House	Glenn W. Ellard

STATISTICS

Land Area (square miles)	58,056
Rank in Nation	21st
Population	5,463,105
Rank in Nation	13th
Density per square mile	94.1
Number of Representatives in Congress	10
Capital City	Atlanta
Population	425,022
Rank in State	1st
Largest City	Atlanta
Number of Places over 10,000 Population	39

Hawaii

Nickname . . . . The Aloha State
Motto . . . *Ua Mau Ke Ea O Ka Aina I Ka Pono*
  (The Life of the Land Is Perpetuated
  in Righteousness)
Flower . . . . Hibiscus
Bird . . . . Hawaiian Goose
Tree . . . . Candlenut
Fish . . . . Humuhumunukunukuapuaa
Song . . . . *Hawaii Ponoi*
Entered the Union . . . . August 21, 1959
Capital . . . . Honolulu

ELECTED EXECUTIVE BRANCH OFFICIALS

Governor . . . . George R. Ariyoshi
Lieutenant Governor . . . . John Waihee

SUPREME COURT

Herman T.F. Lum, Chief Justice
Yoshimi Hayashi
Edward Nakamura
Frank Padgett
James H. Wakatsuki

LEGISLATURE

President of the Senate . . . . Richard S.H. Wong
Vice President
  of the Senate . . . . Duke T. Kawasaki
Clerk of the Senate . . . . T. David Woo Jr.

Speaker of the House . . . Henry Haalilio Peters
Vice Speaker of the House . . . . Marshall Ige
Clerk of the House . . . . George M. Takane

STATISTICS

Land Area (square miles) 6,425
  Rank in Nation 47th
Population 964,691
  Rank in Nation 39th
  Density per square mile 150.1
Number of Representatives in Congress 2
Capital City . . . . Honolulu
  Population (county & city) 762,874
  Rank in State 1st
Largest City . . . . Honolulu
Number of Places over 10,000 Population . . . 12

Idaho

Nickname . . . . The Gem State
Motto . . . . . *Esto Perpetua* (Let It Be Perpetual)
Flower . . . . Syringa
Bird . . . . Mountain Bluebird
Tree . . . . Western White Pine
Song . . . . *Here We Have Idaho*
Gemstone . . . . Idaho Star Garnet
Horse . . . . Appaloosa
Entered the Union . . . . July 3, 1890
Capital . . . . Boise

ELECTED EXECUTIVE BRANCH OFFICIALS

Governor . . . . John V. Evans
Lieutenant Governor . . . . David H. Leroy
Secretary of State . . . . Pete T. Cenarrusa
Attorney General . . . . Jim Jones
Treasurer . . . . Marjorie Ruth Moon
Auditor . . . . Joe R. Williams
Supt. of Public Instruction . . . . . Jerry L. Evans

SUPREME COURT

Charles R. Donaldson, Chief Justice
Robert E. Bakes
Stephen Bistline
Robert C. Huntley Jr.
Allan G. Shepard

LEGISLATURE

President
  of the Senate . . . . Lt. Gov. David H. Leroy
President Pro Tem
  of the Senate . . . . James Risch
Secretary of the Senate . . . . Dorthea Baxter

Speaker of the House . . . . Tom W. Stivers
Chief Clerk of the House . . . . . . Phyllis Watson

STATISTICS

Land Area (square miles) 82,412
  Rank in Nation 11th
Population 943,935
  Rank in Nation 41st
  Density per square mile 11.5
Number of Representatives in Congress 2
Capital City . . . . Boise
  Population 102,451
  Rank in State 1st
Largest City . . . . Boise
Number of Places over 10,000 Population . . . 11

Illinois

Nickname . . . . The Prairie State
Motto . . . . *State Sovereignty-National Union*
Flower . . . . Native Violet
Bird . . . . Cardinal
Tree . . . . White Oak
Song . . . . *Illinois*
Mineral . . . . Fluorite
Animal . . . . White-tailed Deer
Insect . . . . Monarch Butterfly
Entered the Union . . . . December 3, 1818
Capital . . . . Springfield

ELECTED EXECUTIVE BRANCH OFFICIALS

Governor . . . . James R. Thompson
Lieutenant Governor . . . . George H. Ryan
Secretary of State . . . . Jim Edgar
Attorney General . . . . Neil F. Hartigan
Treasurer . . . . James H. Donnewald
Comptroller . . . . Roland W. Burris

SUPREME COURT

William G. Clark, Chief Justice
Joseph H. Goldenhersh
Ben Miller
Thomas J. Moran
Howard C. Ryan
Seymour Simon
Daniel P. Ward

GENERAL ASSEMBLY

President of the Senate . . . . Philip J. Rock
Secretary of the Senate . . . . Kenneth A. Wright

Speaker of the House . . . . . Michael J. Madigan
Chief Clerk of the House . . . . . John F. O'Brien

STATISTICS

Land Area (square miles) 55,645
   Rank in Nation 24th
Population 11,426,518
   Rank in Nation 5th
   Density per square mile 205.3
Number of Representatives in Congress 22
Capital City . . . . Springfield
   Population 99,637
   Rank in State 4th
Largest City . . . . Chicago
   Population 3,005,072
Number of Places over 10,000 Population . . 177

Indiana

Nickname . . . . The Hoosier State
Motto . . . . *Crossroads of America*
Flower . . . . Peony
Bird . . . . Cardinal
Tree . . . . Tulip Poplar
Song . . *On the Banks of the Wabash, Far Away*
Stone . . . . Limestone
Entered the Union . . . . December 11, 1816
Capital . . . . Indianapolis

ELECTED EXECUTIVE BRANCH OFFICIALS

Governor . . . . Robert D. Orr
Lieutenant Governor . . . . John M. Mutz
Secretary of State . . . . Edwin J. Simcox
Attorney General . . . . Linley E. Pearson
Treasurer . . . . Julian L. Ridlen
Auditor . . . . Otis E. Cox
Supt. of Public Instruction . . . . . H. Dean Evans

SUPREME COURT

Richard M. Givan, Chief Justice
Roger O. DeBruler
Brent E. Dickson
Alfred J. Pivarnik
Randall Shepard

GENERAL ASSEMBLY

President
   of the Senate . . . . Lt. Gov. John M. Mutz
President Pro Tem
   of the Senate . . . . Robert Garton
Secretary of the Senate . . . . Carolyn Tinkle

Speaker of the House . . . . J. Roberts Dailey
Speaker Pro Tem
   of the House . . . . Jeffrey K. Espich
Principal Clerk
   of the House . . . . . . Sharon Cummins Thuma

STATISTICS

Land Area (square miles) 35,932
   Rank in Nation 38th
Population 5,490,224
   Rank in Nation 12th
   Density per square mile 152.8
Number of Representatives in Congress 10
Capital City . . . . Indianapolis
   Population 700,807
   Rank in State 1st
Largest City . . . . Indianapolis
Number of Places over 10,000 Population . . . 61

Iowa

Nickname . . . . The Hawkeye State
Motto . . . . *Our Liberties We Prize and
Our Rights We Will Maintain*
Flower . . . . Wild Rose
Bird . . . . Eastern Goldfinch
Tree . . . . Oak
Song . . . . *The Song of Iowa*
Stone . . . . Geode
Entered the Union . . . . December 28, 1846
Capital . . . . Des Moines

ELECTED EXECUTIVE BRANCH
OFFICIALS

Governor . . . . Terry E. Branstad
Lieutenant Governor . . . . . . Robert T. Anderson
Secretary of State . . . . Mary Jane Odell
Attorney General . . . . Thomas J. Miller
Treasurer . . . . Michael L. Fitzgerald
Auditor . . . . Richard D. Johnson
Secy. of Agriculture . . . . . Robert H. Lounsberry

SUPREME COURT

W. Ward Reynoldson, Chief Justice
James H. Carter
K. David Harris
Jerry L. Larson
Louis A. Lavorato
A. A. McGiverin
Louis W. Schultz
Harvey Uhlenhopp
Charles R. Wolle

GENERAL ASSEMBLY

President
of the Senate . . . Lt. Gov. Robert T. Anderson
President Pro Tem
of the Senate . . . . James Wells
Secretary of the Senate . . . . . . K. Marie Thayer

Speaker of the House . . . . Don Avenson
Speaker Pro Tem of the House . . John Connors
Chief Clerk of the House . . . . . . Joseph O'Hern

STATISTICS

Land Area (square miles) 55,965
  Rank in Nation 23rd
Population 2,913,808
  Rank in Nation 27th
  Density per square mile 52.1
Number of Representatives in Congress 6
Capital City . . . . Des Moines
  Population 191,003
  Rank in State 1st
Largest City . . . . Des Moines
Number of Places over 10,000 Population . . . 29

Kansas

Nickname . . . . The Sunflower State
Motto . . . . *Ad Astra per Aspera*
(To the Stars through Difficulties)
Flower . . . . Native Sunflower
Bird . . . . Western Meadowlark
Tree . . . . Cottonwood
Song . . . . *Home on the Range*
Animal . . . . American Buffalo
Insect . . . . Honeybee
Entered the Union . . . . January 29, 1861
Capital . . . . Topeka

ELECTED EXECUTIVE BRANCH
OFFICIALS

Governor . . . . John Carlin
Lieutenant Governor . . . . Tom Docking
Secretary of State . . . . Jack H. Brier
Attorney General . . . . Robert T. Stephan
Treasurer . . . . Joan Finney
Commr. of Insurance . . . . Fletcher Bell

SUPREME COURT

Alfred G. Schroeder, Chief Justice
Harold S. Herd
Richard W. Holmes
Tyler C. Lockett
Kay McFarland
Robert H. Miller
David Prager

LEGISLATURE

President
of the Senate . . . . Robert V. Talkington
Vice President
of the Senate . . . . Joseph C. Harder
Secretary of the Senate . . . . Lu Kenney

Speaker of the House . . . . Mike Hayden
Speaker Pro Tem of the House . . . . Jim Braden
Chief Clerk of the House . . . . . . Geneva Seward

STATISTICS

Land Area (square miles) 81,778
  Rank in Nation 13th
Population 2,363,679
  Rank in Nation 32nd
  Density per square mile 28.9
Number of Representatives in Congress 5
Capital City . . . . Topeka
  Population 115,266
  Rank in State 3rd
Largest City . . . . Wichita
  Population 279,272
Number of Places over 10,000 Population . . . 34

Kentucky

Nickname . . . . The Bluegrass State
Motto . . . . . . *United We Stand, Divided We Fall*
Flower . . . . Goldenrod
Bird . . . . Cardinal
Wild Animal . . . . Gray Squirrel
Tree . . . . Coffee Tree
Song . . . . *My Old Kentucky Home*
Entered the Union . . . . June 1, 1792
Capital . . . . Frankfort

ELECTED EXECUTIVE BRANCH OFFICIALS

Governor . . . . Martha Layne Collins
Lieutenant Governor . . . . . . Steven L. Beshear
Secretary of State . . . . Drexell Davis
Attorney General . . . . David Armstrong
Treasurer . . . . Frances Jones Mills
Auditor of Public Accounts . . . Mary Ann Tobin
Supt. of Public Instruction . . . . Alice McDonald
Commr. of Agriculture . . . . David Boswell

SUPREME COURT

Robert F. Stephens, Chief Justice
William Gant
Charles Leibson
James B. Stephenson
Roy Vance
John D. White
Donald Wintersheimer

GENERAL ASSEMBLY

President
 of the Senate . . . . Lt. Gov. Steven L. Beshear
President Pro Tem
 of the Senate . . . . Joseph W. Prather
Chief Clerk of the Senate . . . Marjorie Wagoner

Speaker of the House . . . . . Donald J. Blandford
Speaker Pro Tem
 of the House . . . . Pete Worthington
Chief Clerk of the House . . . . . Evelyn Marston

STATISTICS

Land Area (square miles) 39,669
 Rank in Nation 37th
Population 3,660,777
 Rank in Nation 23rd
 Density per square mile 92.3
Number of Representatives in Congress 7
Capital City . . . . Frankfort
 Population 25,973
 Rank in State 9th
Largest City . . . . Louisville
 Population 298,451
Number of Places over 10,000 Population . . . 30

Louisiana

Nickname . . . . The Pelican State
Motto . . . . *Union, Justice and Confidence*
Flower . . . . Magnolia
Bird . . . . Eastern Brown Pelican
Tree . . . . Bald Cypress
Songs . . . . *Give Me Louisiana* and
 You Are My Sunshine
Fossil . . . . Petrified Palmwood
Gemstone . . . . Agate
Dog . . . . Catahoula Leopard
Reptile . . . . Alligator
Crustacean . . . . Crawfish
Insect . . . . Honeybee
Beverage . . . . Milk
Entered the Union . . . . April 30, 1812
Capital . . . . Baton Rouge

ELECTED EXECUTIVE BRANCH OFFICIALS

Governor . . . . Edwin W. Edwards
Lieutenant Governor . . . . . . Robert L. Freeman
Secretary of State . . . . James H. Brown
Attorney General . . . . William J. Guste Jr.
Treasurer . . . . Mary Evelyn Parker
Supt. of Education . . . . Thomas G. Clausen
Commr. of Agriculture . . . . Bob Odom
Commr. of Insurance . . . . Sherman A. Bernard
Commr. of Elections . . . . Jerry M. Fowler

SUPREME COURT

John A. Dixon Jr., Chief Justice
Fred A. Blanche Jr.
Pascal F. Calogero Jr.
James L. Dennis
Harry T. Lemmon
Walter F. Marcus Jr.
Jack Crozier Watson

LEGISLATURE

President of the Senate . . . . . Samuel B. Nunez
President Pro Tem
 of the Senate . . . . Thomas Hudson
Secretary of the Senate . . . . Michael S. Baer III

Speaker of the House . . . . John Alario
Speaker Pro Tem of the House . . . . . Joe Delpit
Clerk of the House . . . . Alfred Speer

STATISTICS

Land Area (square miles) 44,521
 Rank in Nation 33rd
Population 4,205,900
 Rank in Nation 19th
 Density per square mile 94.5
Number of Representatives in Congress 8
Capital City . . . . Baton Rouge
 Population 219,419
 Rank in State 2nd
Largest City . . . . New Orleans
 Population 557,515
Number of Places over 10,000 Population . . . 34

Maine

Nickname . . . . The Pine Tree State
Motto . . . . *Dirigo* (I Direct)
Flower . . . . White Pine Cone and Tassel
Bird . . . . Chickadee
Tree . . . . Eastern White Pine
Song . . . . *State of Maine Song*
Mineral . . . . Tourmaline
Fish . . . . Landlocked Salmon
Insect . . . . Honeybee
Animal . . . . Moose
Entered the Union . . . . March 15, 1820
Capital . . . . Augusta

ELECTED EXECUTIVE BRANCH OFFICIALS

Governor . . . . Joseph E. Brennan

SUPREME JUDICIAL COURT

Vincent L. McKusick, Chief Justice
Caroline D. Glassman
David A. Nichols
David G. Roberts
Louis Scolnik
Elmer H. Violette
Daniel E. Wathen

LEGISLATURE

President of the Senate . . . . Charles P. Pray
Secretary of the Senate . . . . Joy J. O'Brien

Speaker of the House . . . . John L. Martin
Clerk of the House . . . . Edwin H. Pert

STATISTICS

Land Area (square miles) 30,995
   Rank in Nation 39th
Population 1,124,660
   Rank in Nation 38th
   Density per square mile 36.3
Number of Representatives in Congress 2
Capital City . . . . Augusta
   Population 21,819
   Rank in State 6th
Largest City . . . . Portland
   Population 61,572
Number of Places over 10,000 Population . . . 12

Maryland

Nickname . . . . The Old Line State
Motto . . . . *Fatti Maschii, Parole Femine*
     (Manly Deeds, Womanly Words)
Flower . . . . Black-eyed Susan
Bird . . . . Baltimore Oriole
Tree . . . . White Oak
Song . . . . *Maryland, My Maryland*
Dog . . . . Chesapeake Bay Retriever
Fish . . . . Striped Bass
Insect . . . . Baltimore Checkerspot Butterfly
Fossil . . . Ecphora Quadricostata (Extinct Snail)
Sport . . . . Jousting
Entered the Union . . . . April 28, 1788
Capital . . . . Annapolis

ELECTED EXECUTIVE BRANCH OFFICIALS

Governor . . . . Harry R. Hughes
Lieutenant Governor . . . . . J. Joseph Curran Jr.
Attorney General . . . . Stephen H. Sachs
Comptroller of Treasury . . . . Louis L. Goldstein

COURT OF APPEALS

Robert C. Murphy, Chief Judge
Harry A. Cole
James F. Couch Jr.
John C. Eldridge
Lawrence F. Rodowsky
Marvin H. Smith

GENERAL ASSEMBLY

President of the Senate . . . Melvin A. Steinberg
President Pro Tem
  of the Senate . . . . Frederick C. Malkus Jr.
Secretary of the Senate . . . . Oden Bowie

Speaker of the House . . . . . Benjamin L. Cardin
Speaker Pro Tem
  of the House . . . . Thomas B. Kernan
Chief Clerk of the House . . Jacqueline M. Spell

STATISTICS

Land Area (square miles) 9,837
   Rank in Nation 42nd
Population 4,216,975
   Rank in Nation 18th
   Density per square mile 428.7
Number of Representatives in Congress 8
Capital City . . . . Annapolis
   Population 31,740
   Rank in State 5th
Largest City . . . . Baltimore
   Population 786,775
Number of Places over 10,000 Population . . . 17

Massachusetts

Nickname . . . . The Bay State
Motto . . . . *Ense Petit Placidam Sub*
Libertate Quietem
(By the Sword We Seek Peace,
but Peace Only under Liberty)
Flower . . . . Mayflower
Bird . . . . Chickadee
Tree . . . . American Elm
Song . . . . *All Hail to Massachusetts*
Fish . . . . Cod
Insect . . . . Ladybug
Horse . . . . Morgan
Dog . . . . Boston Terrier
Beverage . . . . Cranberry Juice
Mineral . . . . Babingtonite
Entered the Union . . . . February 6, 1788
Capital City . . . . Boston

ELECTED EXECUTIVE BRANCH OFFICIALS

Governor . . . . Michael S. Dukakis
Lieutenant Governor . . . . (Vacancy)
Secretary of the
Commonwealth . . . . Michael J. Connolly
Attorney General . . . . Francis X. Bellotti
Treasurer . . . . Robert Q. Crane
Auditor of the
Commonwealth . . . . John J. Finnegan

SUPREME JUDICIAL COURT

Edward F. Hennessey, Chief Justice
Ruth I. Abrams
Paul J. Liacos
Neil L. Lynch
Joseph R. Nolan
Francis P. O'Connor
Herbert P. Wilkins

GENERAL COURT

President of the Senate . . . . William M. Bulger
Clerk of the Senate . . . . Edward B. O'Neill

Speaker of the House . . . . George Keverian
Clerk of the House . . . . Robert MacQueen

STATISTICS

Land Area (square miles) 7,824
Rank in Nation 45th
Population 5,737,037
Rank in Nation 11th
Density per square mile 733.3
Number of Representatives in Congress 11
Capital City . . . . Boston
Population 562,994
Rank in State 1st
Largest City . . . . Boston
Number of Places over 10,000 Population . . 149

Michigan

Nickname . . . . The Wolverine State
Motto . . . . *Si Quaeris Peninsulam Amoenam*
Circumspice (If You Seek a Pleasant
Peninsula, Look About You)
Flower . . . . Apple Blossom
Bird . . . . Robin
Tree . . . . White Pine
Insect . . . . Dragonfly
Song . . . . *Michigan, My Michigan*
Stone . . . . Petoskey Stone
Gem . . . . Chlorastrolite
Fish . . . . Trout
Entered the Union . . . . January 26, 1837
Capital . . . . Lansing

ELECTED EXECUTIVE BRANCH OFFICIALS

Governor . . . . James Blanchard
Lieutenant Governor . . . . Martha Griffiths
Secretary of State . . . . Richard H. Austin
Attorney General . . . . Frank J. Kelley

SUPREME COURT

G. Mennen Williams, Chief Justice
Patricia J. Boyle
James H. Brickley
Michael F. Cavanagh
Charles L. Levin
Dorothy Comstock Riley

LEGISLATURE

President
of the Senate . . . . . . Lt. Gov. Martha Griffiths
President Pro Tem
of the Senate . . . . Harry A. DeMaso
Secretary of the Senate . . . William C. Kandler

Speaker of the House . . . . Gary M. Owen
Speaker Pro Tem
of the House . . . . Matthew McNeely
Clerk of the House . . . . David H. Evans

STATISTICS

Land Area (square miles) 56,954
Rank in Nation 22nd
Population 9,262,078
Rank in Nation 8th
Density per square mile 162.6
Number of Representatives in Congress 18
Capital City . . . . Lansing
Population 130,414
Rank in State 5th
Largest City . . . . Detroit
Population 1,203,339
Number of Places over 10,000 Population . . . 88

Minnesota

Nickname .... The North Star State
Motto .... *L'Etoile du Nord*
    (The Star of the North)
Flower .... Pink and White Lady's-Slipper
Bird .... Common Loon
Tree .... Red Pine
Song .... *Hail! Minnesota*
Gemstone .... Lake Superior Agate
Fish .... Walleye
Grain .... Wild Rice
Mushroom .... Morel
Beverage .... Milk
Entered the Union .... May 11, 1858
Capital .... St. Paul

ELECTED EXECUTIVE BRANCH OFFICIALS

Governor .... Rudy Perpich
Lieutenant Governor .... Marlene Johnson
Secretary of State ...... Joan Anderson Growe
Attorney General .... Hubert H. Humphrey III
Treasurer .... Robert W. Mattson
Auditor .... Arne Carlson

SUPREME COURT

Douglas K. Amdahl, Chief Justice
M. Jeanne Coyne
Glenn E. Kelley
C. Donald Peterson
George M. Scott
John E. Simonett
John J. Todd
Rosalie E. Wahl
Lawrence R. Yetka

LEGISLATURE

President of the Senate .... Jerome M. Hughes
Secretary of the Senate ... Patrick E. Flahaven

Speaker of the House ...... David M. Jennings
Chief Clerk of the House .. Edward A. Burdick

STATISTICS

Land Area (square miles) 79,548
    Rank in Nation 14th
Population 4,075,970
    Rank in Nation 21st
    Density per square mile 51.2
Number of Representatives in Congress 8
Capital City .... St. Paul
    Population 270,230
    Rank in State 2nd
Largest City .... Minneapolis
    Population 370,951
Number of Places over 10,000 Population ... 65

Mississippi

Nickname .... The Magnolia State
Motto ... *Virtute et Armis* (By Valor and Arms)
Flower .... Magnolia
Bird .... Mockingbird
Water Mammal .... Bottlenosed Dolphin
Tree .... Magnolia
Song .... *Go, Mississippi*
Insect .... Honeybee
Fossil .... Prehistoric Whale
Beverage .... Milk
Entered the Union .... December 10, 1817
Capital .... Jackson

ELECTED EXECUTIVE BRANCH OFFICIALS

Governor .... William A. Allain
Lieutenant Governor .... Brad Dye
Secretary of State .... Dick Molpus
Attorney General .... Edwin Lloyd Pittman
Treasurer .... William J. Cole III
Auditor of Public Accounts .... Ray Mabus
Commr. of Agriculture
    and Commerce .... Jim Buck Ross
Commr. of Insurance .... George Dale

SUPREME COURT

Neville Patterson, Chief Justice
Roy Noble Lee, Presiding Justice
Harry Walker, Presiding Justice
Reuben V. Anderson
Armis E. Hawkins
Dan M. Lee
Lenore L. Prather
James Robertson
Michael Sullivan

LEGISLATURE

President of the Senate ..... Lt. Gov. Brad Dye
President Pro Tem
    of the Senate .... Glen DeWeese
Secretary of the Senate ..... Charles H. Griffin

Speaker of the House .... C.B. Newman
Clerk of the House ..... Charles J. Jackson Jr.

STATISTICS

Land Area (square miles) 47,233
    Rank in Nation 31st
Population 2,520,638
    Rank in Nation 31st
    Density per square mile 53.4
Number of Representatives in Congress 5
Capital City .... Jackson
    Population 202,895
    Rank in State 1st
Largest City .... Jackson
Number of Places over 10,000 Population ... 27

Missouri

Nickname . . . . The Show Me State
Motto . . . . *Salus Populi Suprema Lex Esto*
     (The Welfare of the People Shall Be
     the Supreme Law)
Flower . . . . Hawthorn
Bird . . . . Bluebird
Insect . . . . Honeybee
Tree . . . . Dogwood
Song . . . . *Missouri Waltz*
Stone . . . . Mozarkite
Mineral . . . . Galena
Entered the Union . . . . August 10, 1821
Capital . . . . Jefferson City

ELECTED EXECUTIVE BRANCH
OFFICIALS

Governor . . . . John Ashcroft
Lieutenant Governor . . . . Harriett Woods
Secretary of State . . . . Roy Blunt
Attorney General . . . . William L. Webster
Treasurer . . . . Wendell Bailey
Auditor . . . . Margaret Kelly

SUPREME COURT

Andrew J. Higgins, Chief Justice
William H. Billings
Charles Blackmer
Robert T. Donnelly
Albert Rendlen
Edward Robertson Jr.
Warren D. Welliver

GENERAL ASSEMBLY

President
   of the Senate . . . . Lt. Gov. Harriett Woods
President Pro Tem
   of the Senate . . . . John E. Scott
Secretary of the Senate . . . . Terry Spieler

Speaker of the House . . . . Robert F. Griffin
Speaker Pro Tem
   of the House . . . . Patrick J. Hickey
Chief Clerk of the House . . Douglas W. Burnett

STATISTICS

Land Area (square miles) 68,945
   Rank in Nation 18th
Population 4,916,686
   Rank in Nation 15th
   Density per square mile 71.3
Number of Representatives in Congress 9
Capital City . . . . Jefferson City
   Population 33,619
   Rank in State 12th
Largest City . . . . St. Louis
   Population 453,085
Number of Places over 10,000 Population . . . 51

Montana

Nickname . . . . The Treasure State
Motto . . . . *Oro y Plata* (Gold and Silver)
Flower . . . . Bitterroot
Animal . . . . Grizzly Bear
Bird . . . . Western Meadowlark
Tree . . . . Ponderosa Pine
Song . . . . *Montana*
State Ballad . . . . *Montana Melody*
Stones . . . . Sapphire and Agate
Fish . . . . Blackspotted Cutthroat Trout
Grass . . . . Bluebunch Wheatgrass
Entered the Union . . . . November 8, 1889
Capital . . . . Helena

ELECTED EXECUTIVE BRANCH
OFFICIALS

Governor . . . . Ted Schwinden
Lieutenant Governor . . . . George Turman
Secretary of State . . . . Jim Waltermire
Attorney General . . . . Mike Greely
Auditor . . . . Andrea Bennett
Supt. of Public Instruction . . . . Ed Argenbright

SUPREME COURT

Jean Turnage, Chief Justice
L.C. Gulbrandson
John C. Harrison
William Hunt
Frank B. Morrison
John C. Sheehy
Fred Weber

LEGISLATURE

President of the Senate . . . . Bill Norman
President Pro Tem
   of the Senate . . . . Chet Blaylock
Secretary of the Senate . . . . Bonnie Wallem

Speaker of the House . . . . John Vincent
Chief Clerk of the House . . . . Ed Smith

STATISTICS

Land Area (square miles) 145,388
   Rank in Nation 4th
Population 786,690
   Rank in Nation 44th
   Density per square mile 5.4
Number of Representatives in Congress 2
Capital City . . . . Helena
   Population 23,938
   Rank in State 5th
Largest City . . . . Billings
   Population 66,798
Number of Places over 10,000 Population 9

Nebraska

Nickname . . . . The Cornhusker State
Motto . . . . *Equality Before the Law*
Flower . . . . Goldenrod
Bird . . . . Western Meadowlark
Mammal . . . . White-tailed Deer
Tree . . . . Western Cottonwood
Song . . . . *Beautiful Nebraska*
Gemstone . . . . Blue Agate
Fossil . . . . Mammoth
Grass . . . . Little Blue Stem
Insect . . . . Honeybee
Rock . . . . Prairie Agate
Soil . . . . Soils of the Holdrege Series
Entered the Union . . . . March 1, 1867
Capital . . . . Lincoln

ELECTED EXECUTIVE BRANCH OFFICIALS

Governor . . . . Robert Kerrey
Lieutenant Governor . . . . Donald McGinley
Secretary of State . . . . Allen J. Beermann
Attorney General . . . . Robert Spire
Treasurer . . . . Kay Orr
Auditor of Public Accounts . . Ray A.C. Johnson

SUPREME COURT

Norman M. Krivosha, Chief Justice
Leslie Boslaugh
D. Nick Caporale
John T. Grant
William C. Hastings
Thomas M. Shanahan
C. Thomas White

UNICAMERAL LEGISLATURE

President of the
  Legislature . . . . Lt. Gov. Donald McGinley
Speaker of the Legislature . . William E. Nichol
Chairman of Executive Board,
  Legislative Council . . . . Chris Beutler
Vice Chairman of Executive Board,
  Legislative Council . . . . Shirley Marsh
Clerk of the Legislature . . Patrick J. O'Donnell

STATISTICS

Land Area (square miles) 76,644
  Rank in Nation 15th
Population 1,569,825
  Rank in Nation 35th
  Density per square mile 20.5
Number of Representatives in Congress 3
Capital City . . . . Lincoln
  Population 171,932
  Rank in State 2nd
Largest City . . . . Omaha
  Population 314,255
Number of Places over 10,000 Population . . . 12

Nevada

Nickname . . . . The Silver State
Motto . . . . *All for Our Country*
Flower . . . . Sagebrush
Bird . . . . Mountain Bluebird
Tree . . . . Single-leaf Pinon
Song . . . . *Home Means Nevada*
Animal . . . . Desert Bighorn Sheep
Metal . . . . Silver
Grass . . . . Indian Rice Grass
Fossil . . . . Ichthyosaur
Entered the Union . . . . October 31, 1864
Capital . . . . Carson City

ELECTED EXECUTIVE BRANCH OFFICIALS

Governor . . . . Richard Bryan
Lieutenant Governor . . . . Robert A. Cashell
Secretary of State . . . . William D. Swackhamer
Attorney General . . . . Brian McKay
Treasurer . . . . Patricia Cafferata
Controller . . . . Darrel R. Daines

SUPREME COURT

John C. Mowbray, Chief Justice
E.M. Gunderson
Charles E. Springer
Thomas L. Steffen
C. Clifton Young

LEGISLATURE

President
  of the Senate . . . . . Lt. Gov. Robert A. Cashell
President Pro Tem
  of the Senate . . . . Thomas R.C. Wilson
Secretary of the Senate . . . . . Janice L. Thomas

Speaker of the Assembly . . Byron "Bill" Bilyeu
Speaker Pro Tem
  of the Assembly . . . . Charles W. Joerg
Chief Clerk
  of the Assembly . . . . Mouryne B. Landing

STATISTICS

Land Area (square miles) 109,894
  Rank in Nation 7th
Population 800,493
  Rank in Nation 43rd
  Density per square mile 7.3
Number of Representatives in Congress 2
Capital City . . . . Carson City
  Population 32,022
  Rank in State 5th
Largest City . . . . Las Vegas
  Population 164,674
Number of Places over 10,000 Population 6

New Hampshire

Nickname . . . . The Granite State
Motto . . . . *Live Free or Die*
Flower . . . . Purple Lilac
Bird . . . . Purple Finch
Tree . . . . White Birch
Song . . . . *Old New Hampshire*
Insect . . . . Ladybug
Mineral . . . . Beryl
Rock . . . . Granite
Gem . . . . Smoky Quartz
Amphibian . . . . Spotted Newt
Entered the Union . . . . June 21, 1788
Capital . . . . Concord

ELECTED EXECUTIVE BRANCH
OFFICIALS
Governor . . . . John H. Sununu

SUPREME COURT
John W. King, Chief Justice
William F. Batchelder
David A. Brock
William R. Johnson
David H. Souter

GENERAL COURT
President of the Senate . . . . Vesta M. Roy
Vice President
   of the Senate . . . . George E. Freese Jr.
Clerk of the Senate . . . . Wilmont S. White

Speaker of the House . . . . John B. Tucker
Clerk of the House . . . . Carl A. Peterson

STATISTICS
Land Area (square miles) 8,993
   Rank in Nation 44th
Population 920,610
   Rank in Nation 42nd
   Density per square mile 102.4
Number of Representatives in Congress 2
Capital City . . . . Concord
   Population 30,400
   Rank in State 3rd
Largest City . . . . Manchester
   Population 90,936
Number of Places over 10,000 Population . . . 12

New Jersey

Nickname . . . . The Garden State
Motto . . . . *Liberty and Prosperity*
Flower . . . . Purple Violet
Bird . . . . Eastern Goldfinch
Tree . . . . Red Oak
Insect . . . . Honeybee
Animal . . . . Horse
Entered the Union . . . . December 18, 1787
Capital . . . . Trenton

ELECTED EXECUTIVE BRANCH
OFFICIALS
Governor . . . . Thomas H. Kean

SUPREME COURT
Robert N. Wilentz, Chief Justice
Robert L. Clifford
Marie L. Garibaldi
Alan B. Handler
Daniel J. O'Hern
Stewart G. Pollock
Gary S. Stein

LEGISLATURE
President of the Senate . . . . John F. Russo
President Pro Tem
   of the Senate . . . . Carmen Orechio
Secretary of the Senate . . . . John McCarthy

Speaker of the Assembly . . . . . Chuck Hardwick
Speaker Pro Tem
   of the Assembly . . . . John A. Rocco
Clerk of the Assembly . . . . Barbara A. Marrow

STATISTICS
Land Area (square miles) 7,468
   Rank in Nation 46th
Population 7,364,823
   Rank in Nation 9th
   Density per square mile 986.2
Number of Representatives in Congress 14
Capital City . . . . Trenton
   Population 92,124
   Rank in State 5th
Largest City . . . . Newark
   Population 329,248
Number of Places over 10,000 Population . . 110

New Mexico

Nickname . . . . The Land of Enchantment
Motto . . . . . *Crescit Eundo* (It Grows As It Goes)
Flower . . . . Yucca
Bird . . . . Roadrunner
Tree . . . . Pinon
Songs . . . . *Asi es Nuevo Mexico* and
                                O, Fair New Mexico
Gem . . . . Turquoise
Fossil . . . . Ceolophysis
Animal . . . . Black Bear
Fish . . . . Cutthroat Trout
Vegetables . . . . Chile and Frijoles
Entered the Union . . . . January 6, 1912
Capital . . . . Santa Fe

ELECTED EXECUTIVE BRANCH OFFICIALS

Governor . . . . Toney Anaya
Lieutenant Governor . . . . Mike Runnels
Secretary of State . . . . Clara P. Jones
Attorney General . . . . Paul G. Bardacke
Treasurer . . . . James B. Lewis
Auditor . . . . Albert Romero
Commr. of Public Lands . . . . Jim Baca

SUPREME COURT

William F. Riordan, Chief Justice
William R. Federici
Dan Sosa Jr.
Harry E. Stowers Jr.
Mary Walters

LEGISLATURE

President
  of the Senate . . . . Lt. Gov. Mike Runnels
President Pro Tem of the Senate . . Les Houston
Chief Clerk of the Senate . . . . Juanita M. Pino

Speaker of the House . . . . . C. Gene Samberson
Chief Clerk of the House . . . . Steve Arias

STATISTICS

Land Area (square miles) 121,335
  Rank in Nation 5th
Population 1,302,894
  Rank in Nation 37th
  Density per square mile 10.7
Number of Representatives in Congress 3
Capital City . . . . Santa Fe
  Population 48,953
  Rank in State 2nd
Largest City . . . . Albuquerque
  Population 331,767
Number of Places over 10,000 Population . . . 13

New York

Nickname . . . . The Empire State
Motto . . . . *Excelsior* (Ever Upward)
Flower . . . . Rose
Bird . . . . Bluebird
Tree . . . . Sugar Maple
Fruit . . . . Apple
Gem . . . . Garnet
Animal . . . . Beaver
Fish . . . . Trout
Fossil . . . . Sea Scorpion
Beverage . . . . Milk
Entered the Union . . . . July 26, 1788
Capital . . . . Albany

ELECTED EXECUTIVE BRANCH OFFICIALS

Governor . . . . Mario M. Cuomo
Lieutenant Governor . . . . (Vacancy)
Attorney General . . . . Robert Abrams
Comptroller . . . . Edward V. Regan

COURT OF APPEALS

Sol Wachtler, Chief Judge
Fritz W. Alexander II
Stewart F. Hancock Jr.
Judith S. Kaye
Bernard S. Meyer
Richard D. Simons
Vido J. Titone

LEGISLATURE

President of the Senate . . . . (Vacancy)
President Pro Tem
  of the Senate . . . . Warren M. Anderson
Secretary of the Senate . . . . Stephen Sloan

Speaker of the Assembly . . . . Stanley Fink
Speaker Pro Tem
  of the Assembly . . . . William F. Passannante
Clerk of the Assembly . . . . Francine Misasi

STATISTICS

Land Area (square miles) 47,377
  Rank in Nation 30th
Population 17,558,072
  Rank in Nation 2nd
  Density per square mile 370.6
Number of Representatives in Congress 34
Capital City . . . . Albany
  Population 101,727
  Rank in State 6th
Largest City . . . . New York
  Population 7,071,639
Number of Places over 10,000 Population . . . 86

North Carolina

Nickname . . . . The Tar Heel State
Motto . . . . *Esse Quam Videri*
(To Be Rather Than to Seem)
Flower . . . . Dogwood
Bird . . . . Cardinal
Tree . . . . Long Leaf Pine
Song . . . . *The Old North State*
Mammal . . . . Gray Squirrel
Gem . . . . Emerald
Fish . . . . Channel Bass
Insect . . . . Honeybee
Reptile . . . . Eastern Box Turtle
Rock . . . . Granite
Entered the Union . . . . November 21, 1789
Capital . . . . Raleigh

ELECTED EXECUTIVE BRANCH OFFICIALS

Governor . . . . James G. Martin
Lieutenant Governor . . . . . Robert B. Jordan III
Secretary of State . . . . Thad Eure
Attorney General . . . . Lacy H. Thornburg
Treasurer . . . . Harlan E. Boyles
Auditor . . . . Edward Renfrow
Supt. of Public Instruction . . . A. Craig Phillips
Commr. of Agriculture . . . . . James A. Graham
Commr. of Labor . . . . John C. Brooks
Commr. of Insurance . . . . James E. Long

SUPREME COURT

Joseph Branch, Chief Justice

Rhoda B. Billings   Harry C. Martin
James G. Exum Jr.   Louis B. Meyer
Henry E. Frye   Burley B. Mitchell Jr.

GENERAL ASSEMBLY

President
  of the Senate . . Lt. Gov. Robert B. Jordan III
President Pro Tem
  of the Senate . . . . J.J. Harrington
Principal Clerk of the Senate . . . . . Sylvia Fink

Speaker of the House . . . . Liston B. Ramsey
Speaker Pro Tem
  of the House . . . . John J. Hunt
Principal Clerk of the House . . . . Grace Collins

STATISTICS

Land Area (square miles) 48,843
  Rank in Nation 29th
Population 5,881,766
  Rank in Nation 10th
  Density per square mile 120.4
Number of Representatives in Congress 11
Capital City . . . . Raleigh
  Population 150,255
  Rank in State 3rd
Largest City . . . . Charlotte
  Population 314,447
Number of Places over 10,000 Population . . . 43

North Dakota

Nicknames . . . . The Flickertail State and
The Sioux State
Motto . . . . *Liberty and Union, Now and
Forever, One and Inseparable*
Flower . . . . Wild Prairie Rose
Bird . . . . Western Meadowlark
Tree . . . . American Elm
Song . . . . *North Dakota Hymn*
March . . . . *Spirit of the Land*
Stone . . . . Teredo Petrified Wood
Fish . . . . Northern Pike
Grass . . . . Western Wheatgrass
Entered the Union . . . . November 2, 1889
Capital . . . . Bismarck

ELECTED EXECUTIVE BRANCH OFFICIALS

Governor . . . . George A. Sinner
Lieutenant Governor . . . . Ruth Meiers
Secretary of State . . . . Ben Meier
Attorney General . . . . Nicholas Spaeth
Treasurer . . . . Robert Hanson
Auditor . . . . Robert Peterson
Supt. of Public Instruction . . . Wayne Sanstead
Commr. of Agriculture . . . . Kent Jones
Commr. of Labor . . . . Orville Hagen
Commr. of Insurance . . . . Earl Pomeroy
Tax Commissioner . . . . Kent Conrad

SUPREME COURT

Ralph J. Erickstad, Chief Justice
H.F. Gierke
Beryl J. Levigne
Herbert L. Meschke
Gerald W. VandeWalle

LEGISLATIVE ASSEMBLY

President of the Senate . . Lt. Gov. Ruth Meiers
President Pro Tem
  of the Senate . . . . Clayton Lodoen
Secretary of the Senate . . . . Leo Leidholm

Speaker of the House . . . . Roy Hausauer
Chief Clerk of the House . . . . Roy Gilbreath

STATISTICS

Land Area (square miles) 69,300
  Rank in Nation 17th
Population 652,717
  Rank in Nation 46th
  Density per square mile 9.4
Number of Representatives in Congress 1
Capital City . . . . Bismarck
  Population 44,485
  Rank in State 2nd
Largest City . . . . Fargo
  Population 61,383
Number of Places over 10,000 Population 9

Ohio

Nickname . . . . The Buckeye State
Motto . . . . . . *With God, All Things Are Possible*
Flower . . . . Scarlet Carnation
Bird . . . . Cardinal
Tree . . . . Buckeye
Song . . . . *Beautiful Ohio*
Stone . . . . Ohio Flint
Insect . . . . Ladybug
Beverage . . . . Tomato Juice
Entered the Union . . . . March 1, 1803
Capital . . . . Columbus

ELECTED EXECUTIVE BRANCH OFFICIALS

Governor . . . . Richard F. Celeste
Lieutenant Governor . . . . (Vacancy)
Secretary of State . . . . Sherrod Brown
Attorney General . . . Anthony J. Celebrezze Jr.
Treasurer . . . . Mary Ellen Withrow
Auditor . . . . Thomas E. Ferguson

SUPREME COURT

Frank D. Celebrezze, Chief Justice
Clifford F. Brown
Andrew Douglas
Robert E. Holmes
Ralph S. Locher
A. William Sweeney
Craig Wright

GENERAL ASSEMBLY

President of the Senate . . . . Paul Gillmor
President Pro Tem
  of the Senate . . . . Stanley Aronoff
Clerk of the Senate . . . . Martha Butler

Speaker of the House . . . . . . Vernal G. Riffe Jr.
Speaker Pro Tem
  of the House . . . . Barney Quilter
Legislative Clerk of the House . . . . . . Ty Marsh
Executive Secretary
  of the House . . . . Aristotle Hutras

STATISTICS

Land Area (square miles) 41,004
  Rank in Nation 35th
Population 10,797,630
  Rank in Nation 6th
  Density per square mile 263.3
Number of Representatives in Congress 21
Capital City . . . . Columbus
  Population 564,871
  Rank in State 2nd
Largest City . . . . Cleveland
  Population 573,822
Number of Places over 10,000 Population . . 150

Oklahoma

Nickname . . . . The Sooner State
Motto . . . . *Labor Omnia Vincit*
         (Labor Conquers All Things)
Flower . . . . Mistletoe
Bird . . . . Scissor-tailed Flycatcher
Tree . . . . Redbud
Grass . . . . Indian Grass
Song . . . . *Oklahoma*
Waltz . . . . *Oklahoma Wind*
Poem . . . . "Howdy Folks"
Stone . . . . Barite Rose (Rose Rock)
Animal . . . . American Buffalo
Reptile . . . . Mountain Boomer Lizard
Fish . . . . White Bass
Colors . . . . Green and White
Entered the Union . . . . November 16, 1907
Capital . . . . Oklahoma City

ELECTED EXECUTIVE BRANCH OFFICIALS

Governor . . . . George Nigh
Lieutenant Governor . . . . Spencer Bernard
Attorney General . . . . Mike Turpin
Treasurer . . . . Leo Winters
Auditor and Inspector . . . . Clifton Scott
Supt. of Public Instruction . . . . John Folks
Insurance Commr. . . . . Gerald Grimes

SUPREME COURT

Robert D. Sims, Chief Justice
John B. Doolin, Vice Chief Justice

Rudolph Hargrave	Marian P. Opala
Ralph B. Hodges	Hardy Summers
Yvonne Kauger	Alma Wilson
Robert E. Lavender	

COURT OF CRIMINAL APPEALS

Edgar Parks, Presiding Judge

Tom Brett	Hez J. Bussey

LEGISLATURE

President
  of the Senate . . . . . . Lt. Gov. Spencer Bernard
President Pro Tem
  of the Senate . . . . Rodger A. Randle
Secretary of the Senate . . . . Lee Slater

Speaker of the House . . . . Jim L. Barker
Speaker Pro Tem
  of the House . . . . Lonnie L. Abbott
Chief Clerk of the House/
  Administrator . . . . Larry Warden

STATISTICS

Land Area (square miles) 68,655
  Rank in Nation 19th
Population 3,025,290
  Rank in Nation 26th
  Density per square mile 44.1
Number of Representatives in Congress 6
Capital City . . . . Oklahoma City
  Population 403,213
  Rank in State 1st
Largest City . . . . Oklahoma City
Number of Places over 10,000 Population . . . 33

Oregon

Nickname . . . . The Beaver State
Motto . . . . *The Union*
Flower . . . . Oregon Grape
Bird . . . . Western Meadowlark
Tree . . . . Douglas Fir
Song . . . . *Oregon, My Oregon*
Dance . . . . Square Dance
Poet Laureate . . . . William E. Stafford
Stone . . . . Thunderegg
Animal . . . . Beaver
Fish . . . . Chinook Salmon
Insect . . . . Swallowtail Butterfly
Entered the Union . . . . February 14, 1859
Capital . . . . Salem

ELECTED EXECUTIVE BRANCH OFFICIALS

Governor . . . . Victor Atiyeh
Secretary of State . . . . Barbara Roberts
Attorney General . . . . Dave Frohnmayer
Treasurer . . . . Clay Myers
Supt. of Public Instruction . . . Verne A. Duncan
Labor Commr. . . . . Mary Roberts

SUPREME COURT

Edwin J. Peterson, Chief Justice
J.R. Campbell
Wallace P. Carson Jr.
W. Michael Gillette
Robert E. Jones
Berkeley Lent
Hans A. Linde

LEGISLATIVE ASSEMBLY

President of the Senate . . . . John Kitzhaber
President Pro Tem
of the Senate . . . . Charles Hanlon
Secretary of the Senate . . . . . Maribel Cadmus

Speaker of the House . . . . Vera Katz
Speaker Pro Tem of the House . . Rick Bauman
Chief Clerk of the House . . . . . Ramona Kenady

STATISTICS

Land Area (square miles) 96,184
  Rank in Nation 10th
Population 2,633,105
  Rank in Nation 30th
  Density per square mile 27.4
Number of Representatives in Congress 5
Capital City . . . . Salem
  Population 89,233
  Rank in State 3rd
Largest City . . . . Portland
  Population 366,383
Number of Places over 10,000 Population . . . 29

Pennsylvania

Nickname . . . . The Keystone State
Motto . . . . *Virtue, Liberty and Independence*
Flower . . . . Mountain Laurel
Game Bird . . . . Ruffed Grouse
Tree . . . . Hemlock
Dog . . . . Great Dane
Animal . . . . White-tailed Deer
Insect . . . . Firefly
Fish . . . . Brook Trout
Entered the Union . . . . December 12, 1787
Capital . . . . Harrisburg

ELECTED EXECUTIVE BRANCH OFFICIALS

Governor . . . . Richard L. Thornburgh
Lieutenant Governor . . William W. Scranton III
Attorney General . . . . Leroy S. Zimmerman
Treasurer . . . . R. Budd Dwyer
Auditor General . . . . Don Bailey

SUPREME COURT

Robert N.C. Nix Jr., Chief Justice
John P. Flaherty
William D. Hutchinson
Rolf Larsen
James T. McDermott
Nicholas P. Papadakos
Stephen A. Zappala

GENERAL ASSEMBLY

President of the
  Senate . . . . . Lt. Gov. William W. Scranton III
President Pro Tem
  of the Senate . . . . Robert Jubelirer
Secretary of the Senate . . . . . Mark R. Corrigan

Speaker of the House . . . . K. Leroy Irvis
Chief Clerk of the House . . . . . . John J. Zubeck

STATISTICS

Land Area (square miles) 44,888
  Rank in Nation 32nd
Population 11,863,895
  Rank in Nation 4th
  Density per square mile 264.3
Number of Representatives in Congress 23
Capital City . . . . Harrisburg
  Population 53,264
  Rank in State 10th
Largest City . . . . Philadelphia
  Population 1,688,210
Number of Places over 10,000 Population . . . 83

Rhode Island

Nickname . . . . Little Rhody
Motto . . . . *Hope*
Flower . . . . Violet
Bird . . . . Rhode Island Red
Tree . . . . Red Maple
Song . . . . *Rhode Island*
Rock . . . . Cumberlandite
Mineral . . . . Bowenite
Entered the Union . . . . May 29, 1790
Capital . . . . Providence

ELECTED EXECUTIVE BRANCH OFFICIALS

Governor . . . . Edward D. DiPrete
Lieutenant Governor . . . . Richard Licht
Secretary of State . . . . Susan L. Farmer
Attorney General . . . . Arlene Violet
General Treasurer . . . . Roger N. Begin

SUPREME COURT

Joseph A. Bevilacqua, Chief Justice
Thomas F. Kelleher
Florence K. Murray
Donald F. Shay
Joseph R. Weisberger

GENERAL ASSEMBLY

President
    of the Senate . . . . Lt. Gov. Richard Licht
President Pro Tem
    of the Senate . . . . William O'Neill
Secretary of the Senate . . . . . . Susan L. Farmer

Speaker of the House . . . . . . Matthew J. Smith
First Deputy Speaker
    of the House . . . . Donald Ferry
Reading Clerk
    of the House . . . . Eugene J. McMahon

STATISTICS

Land Area (square miles) 1,055
    Rank in Nation 50th
Population 947,154
    Rank in Nation 40th
    Density per square mile 897.8
Number of Representatives in Congress 2
Capital City . . . . Providence
    Population 156,804
    Rank in State 1st
Largest City . . . . Providence
Number of Places over 10,000 Population . . . 27

South Carolina

Nickname . . . . The Palmetto State
Mottos . . . . *Animis Opibusque Parati*
    (Prepared in Mind and Resources) and
    Dum Spiro Spero (While I Breathe, I Hope)
Flower . . . . Carolina Jessamine
Bird . . . . Carolina Wren
Tree . . . . Palmetto
Song . . . . *Carolina* and
    South Carolina on My Mind
Dance . . . . Shag
Stone . . . . Blue Granite
Dog . . . . Boykin Spaniel
Fruit . . . . Peach
Shell . . . . Lettered Olive
Beverage . . . . Milk
Entered the Union . . . . May 23, 1788
Capital . . . . Columbia

ELECTED EXECUTIVE BRANCH OFFICIALS

Governor . . . . Richard W. Riley
Lieutenant Governor . . . . Mike Daniel
Secretary of State . . . . John T. Campbell
Attorney General . . . . Travis Medlock
Treasurer . . . . Grady L. Patterson Jr.
Comptroller General . . . . . . Earle E. Morris Jr.
Supt. of Education . . . . Charlie G. Williams
Commr. of Agriculture . . . . Les Tindal
Adjutant General . . . . Eston Marchant

SUPREME COURT

Julius B. Ness, Chief Justice
A. Lee Chandler
Ernest A. Finney Jr.
George Tillman Gregory Jr.
David W. Harwell

GENERAL ASSEMBLY

President of the Senate . . Lt. Gov. Mike Daniel
President Pro Tem
    of the Senate . . . . Rembert Dennis
Clerk of the Senate . . . . Frank B. Caggiano

Speaker of the House . . . . . Ramon Schwartz Jr.
Speaker Pro Tem
    of the House . . . . W. Sterling Anderson
Clerk of the House . . . . Lois T. Shealy

STATISTICS

Land Area (square miles) 30,203
    Rank in Nation 40th
Population 3,121,820
    Rank in Nation 24th
    Density per square mile 103.4
Number of Representatives in Congress 6
Capital City . . . . Columbia
    Population 101,208
    Rank in State 1st
Largest City . . . . Columbia
Number of Places over 10,000 Population . . . 26

South Dakota

Nickname . . . . The Coyote State
The Sunshine State
Motto . . . . *Under God the People Rule*
Flower . . . . Pasque Flower
Bird . . . . Ringnecked Pheasant
Tree . . . . Black Hills Spruce
Song . . . . *Hail, South Dakota*
Mineral . . . . Rose Quartz
Gem . . . . Fairburn Agate
Animal . . . . Coyote
Fish . . . . Walleye
Insect . . . . Honeybee
Grass . . . . Western Wheat Grass
Entered the Union . . . . November 2, 1889
Capital City . . . . Pierre

ELECTED EXECUTIVE BRANCH
OFFICIALS

Governor . . . . William J. Janklow
Lieutenant Governor . . . . . Lowell C. Hansen II
Secretary of State . . . . Alice Kundert
Attorney General . . . . Mark Meierhenry
Treasurer . . . . David L. Volk
Auditor . . . . Vern Larson
Commr. of School
and Public Lands . . . . Sheldon Cotton

SUPREME COURT

Jon Fosheim, Chief Justice
Frank E. Henderson
E.W. Herts
Robert E. Morgan
Richard Sabers
George Weiss
Roger Wollman

LEGISLATURE

President of the
Senate . . . . Lt. Gov. Lowell C. Hansen II
President Pro Tem
of the Senate . . . . Mary A. McClure
Secretary of the Senate . . . . Joyce Hazeltine

Speaker of the House . . . . Donald Ham
Speaker Pro Tem
of the House . . . . Scott Heidepriem
Chief Clerk of the House . . . . Paul Inman

STATISTICS

Land Area (square miles) 75,952
Rank in Nation 16th
Population 690,768
Rank in Nation 45th
Density per square mile 9.1
Number of Representatives in Congress 1
Capital City . . . . Pierre
Population 11,973
Rank in State 9th
Largest City . . . . Sioux Falls
Population 81,343
Number of Places over 10,000 Population . . . 10

Tennessee

Nickname . . . . The Volunteer State
Motto . . . . *Agriculture and Commerce*
Flower . . . . Iris
Bird . . . . Mockingbird
Tree . . . . Tulip Poplar
Wildflower . . . . Passion Flower
Songs . . . . *When It's Iris Time in Tennessee;*
The Tennessee Waltz;
My Homeland, Tennessee;
My Tennessee; and *Rocky Top*
Stone . . . . Agate
Animal . . . . Raccoon
Insects . . . . Ladybug and Firefly
Gem . . . . Tennessee Pearl
Rock . . . . Limestone
Slogan . . . . Tennessee—America at Its Best
Entered the Union . . . . June 1, 1796
Capital City . . . . Nashville

ELECTED EXECUTIVE BRANCH
OFFICIALS

Governor . . . . Lamar Alexander

SUPREME COURT

Ray L. Brock Jr., Chief Justice
Robert E. Cooper
Frank F. Drowota III
William H.D. Fones
William J. Harbison

GENERAL ASSEMBLY

Speaker
of the Senate . . . . . . (Lt. Gov.) John S. Wilder
Speaker Pro Tem
of the Senate . . . . John R. Rucker
Chief Clerk
of the Senate . . . . . . Clyde W. McCullough Jr.

Speaker of the House . . . . . . Ned R. McWherter
Speaker Pro Tem
of the House . . . . Steve Bivens
Chief Clerk of the House . . . . . Bryant Millsaps

STATISTICS

Land Area (square miles) 41,155
Rank in Nation 34th
Population 4,591,120
Rank in Nation 17th
Density per square mile 111.6
Number of Representatives in Congress 9
Capital City . . . . Nashville
Population 455,651
Rank in State 2nd
Largest City . . . . Memphis
Population 646,356
Number of Places over 10,000 Population . . . 37

Texas

Nickname . . . . The Lone Star State
Motto . . . . *Friendship*
Flower . . . . Bluebonnet
Bird . . . . Mockingbird
Tree . . . . Pecan
Song . . . . *Texas, Our Texas*
Stone . . . . Palmwood
Gem . . . . Topaz
Grass . . . . Sideoats Grama
Dish . . . . Chili
Entered the Union . . . . December 29, 1845
Capital . . . . Austin

ELECTED EXECUTIVE BRANCH OFFICIALS

Governor . . . . Mark White
Lieutenant Governor . . . . William P. Hobby
Attorney General . . . . Jim Mattox
Treasurer . . . . Ann Richards
Comptroller of Public Accounts . . . Bob Bullock
Commr. of Agriculture . . . . Jim Hightower
Commr. of General Land Office . . Garry Mauro

SUPREME COURT

John L. Hill Jr., Chief Justice

Robert M. Campbell	C.L. Ray
Raul A. Gonzalez	Ted Robertson
Bill Kilgarlin	Franklin Spears
Sears McGee	James P. Wallace

COURT OF CRIMINAL APPEALS

John F. Onion Jr., Presiding Judge

Charles F. Campbell Jr.	Michael J.
Sam Houston Clinton	McCormick
Thomas G. Davis	Charles Miller
Wilbur C. Davis	Marvin O. Teague
	Bill White

LEGISLATURE

President
  of the Senate . . . . . Lt. Gov. William P. Hobby
President Pro Tem
  of the Senate . . . . Carlos Truan
Secretary of the Senate . . . . Betty King

Speaker of the House . . . . Gibson D. Lewis
Speaker Pro Tem
  of the House . . . . Hugo Berlanga
Chief Clerk of the House . . . . Betty Murray

STATISTICS

Land Area (square miles) 262,017
  Rank in Nation 2nd
Population 14,229,191
  Rank in Nation 3rd
  Density per square mile 54.3
Number of Representatives in Congress 27
Capital City . . . . Austin
  Population 345,496
  Rank in State 6th
Largest City . . . . Houston
  Population 1,595,138
Number of Places over 10,000 Population . . 151

Utah

Nickname . . . . The Beehive State
Motto . . . . *Industry*
Flower . . . . Sego Lily
Bird . . . . Seagull
Tree . . . . Blue Spruce
Song . . . . *Utah, We Love Thee*
Gem . . . . Topaz
Entered the Union . . . . January 4, 1896
Capital . . . . Salt Lake City

ELECTED EXECUTIVE BRANCH OFFICIALS

Governor . . . . Norman Bangerter
Lieutenant Governor . . . . W. Val Oveson
Attorney General . . . . David L. Wilkinson
Treasurer . . . . Edward T. Alter
Auditor . . . . Tom L. Allen

SUPREME COURT

Gordon R. Hall, Chief Justice
Christine M. Durham
Richard C. Howe
I. Daniel Stewart
Michael D. Zimmerman

LEGISLATURE

President of the Senate . . . . Arnold Christensen
Secretary of the Senate . . Sophia C. Buckmiller

Speaker of the House . . . . Robert Garff
Chief Clerk of the House . . . Carole E. Peterson

STATISTICS

Land Area (square miles) 82,073
  Rank in Nation 12th
Population 1,461,037
  Rank in Nation 36th
  Density per square mile 17.8
Number of Representatives in Congress 3
Capital City . . . . Salt Lake City
  Population 163,033
  Rank in State 1st
Largest City . . . . Salt Lake City
Number of Places over 10,000 Population . . . 22

Vermont

Nickname.........The Green Mountain State
Motto....................*Freedom and Unity*
Flower........................Red Clover
Bird......................Hermit Thrush
Tree.......................Sugar Maple
Song.......................*Hail, Vermont!*
Poet Laureate.................Robert Frost
Animal......................Morgan Horse
Insect........................Honeybee
Fish....................Brook Trout and
                            Walleye Pike
Soil.............Tunbridge Soil Series
Beverage..........................Milk
Entered the Union...........March 4, 1791
Capital........................Montpelier

ELECTED EXECUTIVE BRANCH OFFICIALS

Governor.................Madeleine Kunin
Lieutenant Governor...........Peter Smith
Secretary of State.........James H. Douglas
Attorney General...........Jeffrey Amestoy
Treasurer.................Emory A. Hebard
Auditor of Accounts......Alexander V. Acebo

SUPREME COURT

Frederic W. Allen, Chief Justice
Ernest W. Gibson III
Thomas L. Hayes
William C. Hill
Louis P. Peck

GENERAL ASSEMBLY

President of the Senate..Lt. Gov. Peter Smith
President Pro Tem
   of the Senate..............Peter F. Welch
Secretary of the Senate.....Robert H. Gibson

Speaker of the House..........Ralph Wright
Clerk of the House.........Robert L. Picher

STATISTICS

Land Area (square miles)..............9,273
   Rank in Nation.....................43rd
Population........................511,456
   Rank in Nation.....................48th
   Density per square mile...............55.2
Number of Representatives in Congress.....1
Capital City...................Montpelier
   Population.........................8,241
   Rank in State.......................5th
Largest City....................Burlington
   Population........................37,712
Number of Places over 10,000 Population....3

Virginia

Nickname................The Old Dominion
Motto................*Sic Semper Tyrannis*
                    (Thus Always to Tyrants)
Flower........................Dogwood
Bird..........................Cardinal
Tree..........................Dogwood
Song.........*Carry Me Back to Old Virginia*
Animal.......................Foxhound
Shell.........................Oyster
Beverage..........................Milk
Entered the Union............June 25, 1788
Capital.......................Richmond

ELECTED EXECUTIVE BRANCH OFFICIALS

Governor.................Gerald Lee Baliles
Lieutenant Governor.......L. Douglas Wilder
Attorney General...........Mary Sue Terry

SUPREME COURT

Harry Lee Carrico, Chief Justice
George M. Cochran
A. Christian Compton
Alex M. Harman Jr.
Richard H. Poff
Charles S. Russell
Rosco B. Stephenson
John Charles Thomas

GENERAL ASSEMBLY

President
   of the Senate....Lt. Gov. L. Douglas Wilder
President Pro Tem
   of the Senate...........Edward E. Willey
Clerk of the Senate........Jay T. Shropshire

Speaker of the House...........A.L. Philpott
Clerk of the House....Joseph H. Holleman Jr.

STATISTICS

Land Area (square miles).............39,704
   Rank in Nation.....................36th
Population......................5,346,818
   Rank in Nation.....................14th
   Density per square mile.............134.7
Number of Representatives in Congress....10
Capital City.....................Richmond
   Population.......................219,214
   Rank in State.......................3rd
Largest City.......................Norfolk
   Population.......................266,979
Number of Places over 10,000 Population...33

Washington

Nickname . . . . The Evergreen State
Motto . . . . *Alki* (By and By)
Flower . . . . Western Rhododendron
Bird . . . . Willow Goldfinch
Tree . . . . Western Hemlock
Song . . . . *Washington, My Home*
Dance . . . . Square Dance
Gem . . . . Petrified Wood
Fish . . . . Steelhead Trout
Entered the Union . . . . November 11, 1889
Capital . . . . Olympia

ELECTED EXECUTIVE BRANCH OFFICIALS

Governor . . . . Booth Gardner
Lieutenant Governor . . . . John A. Cherberg
Secretary of State . . . . Ralph Munro
Attorney General . . . . . Kenneth O. Eikenberry
Treasurer . . . . Robert S. O'Brien
Auditor . . . . Robert V. Graham
Supt. of Public Instruction . . . . Frank Brouillet
Insurance Commr. . . . . . Richard G. Marquardt
Commr. of Public Lands . . . . Brian J. Boyle

SUPREME COURT

James M. Dolliver, Chief Justice

James A. Andersen	Barbara Durham
Robert F. Brachtenbach	William C. Goodloe
Keith Callow	Vernon R. Pearson
Fred H. Dore	Robert F. Utter

LEGISLATURE

President
 of the Senate . . . . . Lt. Gov. John A. Cherberg
President Pro Tem
 of the Senate . . . . H.A. "Barney" Goltz
Secretary of the Senate . . . . Sid R. Snyder

Speaker of the House . . . . Wayne Ehlers
Speaker Pro Tem
 of the House . . . . John L. O'Brien
Chief Clerk of the House . . . . . . Dennis L. Heck

STATISTICS

Land Area (square miles) 66,511
 Rank in Nation 20th
Population 4,132,156
 Rank in Nation 20th
 Density per square mile 62.1
Number of Representatives in Congress 8
Capital City . . . . Olympia
 Population 27,447
 Rank in State 15th
Largest City . . . . Seattle
 Population 493,846
Number of Places over 10,000 Population . . . 36

West Virginia

Nickname . . . . The Mountain State
Motto . . . . *Montani Semper Liberi*
 (Mountaineers Are Always Free)
Flower . . . . Big Rhododendron
Bird . . . . Cardinal
Tree . . . . Sugar Maple
Songs . . . *West Virginia, My Home Sweet Home;*
 The West Virginia Hills; and
 This Is My West Virginia
Animal . . . . Black Bear
Fish . . . . Brook Trout
Entered the Union . . . . June 20, 1863
Capital . . . . Charleston

ELECTED EXECUTIVE BRANCH OFFICIALS

Governor . . . . Arch A. Moore Jr.
Secretary of State . . . . Ken Hechler
Attorney General . . . . Charlie Brown
Treasurer . . . . A. James Manchin
Auditor . . . . Glen B. Gainer Jr.
Commr. of Agriculture . . . . Gus R. Douglass

SUPREME COURT OF APPEALS

Thomas B. Miller, Chief Justice
W.T. Brotherton Jr.
Darrell V. McGraw Jr.
Thomas E. McHugh
Richard Neely

LEGISLATURE

President of the Senate . . . . Dan Tonkovich
President Pro Tem of the Senate . . . J.R. Rogers
Clerk of the Senate . . . . Todd C. Willis

Speaker of the House . . . . Joseph Albright
Clerk of the House . . . . Donald L. Kopp

STATISTICS

Land Area (square miles) 24,119
 Rank in Nation 41st
Population 1,949,644
 Rank in Nation 34th
 Density per square mile 80.8
Number of Representatives in Congress 4
Capital City . . . . Charleston
 Population 63,968
 Rank in State 1st
Largest City . . . . Charleston
Number of Places over 10,000 Population . . . 15

Wisconsin

Nickname . . . . The Badger State
Motto . . . . *Forward*
Flower . . . . Wood Violet
Bird . . . . Robin
Tree . . . . Sugar Maple
Song . . . . *On, Wisconsin!*
Rock . . . . Red Granite
Mineral . . . . Galena
Animal . . . . Badger
Wildlife Animal . . . . White-tailed Deer
Domestic Animal . . . . Dairy Cow
Fish . . . . Muskellunge
Symbol of Peace . . . . Mourning Dove
Insect . . . . Honeybee
Soil . . . . Antigo Silt Loam
Entered the Union . . . . May 29, 1848
Capital . . . . Madison

ELECTED EXECUTIVE BRANCH OFFICIALS

Governor . . . . Anthony S. Earl
Lieutenant Governor . . . . James T. Flynn
Secretary of State . . . . Douglas La Follette
Attorney General . . . . . . Bronson C. La Follette
Treasurer . . . . Charles P. Smith
Supt. of Public Instruction . . . Herbert J. Grover

SUPREME COURT

Nathan S. Heffernan, Chief Justice
Shirley S. Abrahamson
William A. Bablitch
William G. Callow
Louis J. Ceci
Roland B. Day
Donald W. Steinmetz

LEGISLATURE

President of the Senate . . . . Fred A. Risser
Chief Clerk
  of the Senate . . . . Donald J. Schneider

Speaker of the Assembly . . . . Thomas A. Loftus
Assembly Speaker
  Pro Tempore . . . . David E. Clarenbach
Chief Clerk of the Assembly . . . . Joanne Duren

STATISTICS

Land Area (square miles) 54,426
  Rank in Nation 25th
Population 4,705,767
  Rank in Nation 16th
  Density per square mile 86.5
Number of Representatives in Congress 9
Capital City . . . . Madison
  Population 170,616
  Rank in State 2nd
Largest City . . . . Milwaukee
  Population 636,212
Number of Places over 10,000 Population . . . 55

Wyoming

Nickname . . . . The Equality State and
                       The Cowboy State
Motto . . . . *Equal Rights*
Flower . . . . Indian Paintbrush
Bird . . . . Meadowlark
Animal . . . . Bison
Tree . . . . Cottonwood
Song . . . . *Wyoming*
Stone . . . . Jade
Entered the Union . . . . July 10, 1890
Capital . . . . Cheyenne

ELECTED EXECUTIVE BRANCH OFFICIALS

Governor . . . . Ed Herschler
Secretary of State . . . . Thyra Thomson
Treasurer . . . . Stan Smith
Auditor . . . . Jim Griffith
Supt. of Public Instruction . . . . . Lynne Simons

SUPREME COURT

Richard V. Thomas, Chief Justice
C. Stuart Brown
G. Joseph Cardine
Richard J. Macy
Walter C. Urbigkit Jr.

LEGISLATURE

President of the Senate . . . . Gerald Geis
Vice President of the Senate . . . John F. Turner
Chief Clerk of the Senate . . . . Ed Wren Jr.

Speaker of the House . . . . Jack Sidi
Speaker Pro Tem
  of the House . . . . Patrick Meenan
Chief Clerk of the House . . Herbert D. Pownall

STATISTICS

Land Area (square miles) 96,989
  Rank in Nation 9th
Population 469,557
  Rank in Nation 49th
  Density per square mile 4.8
Number of Representatives in Congress 1
Capital City . . . . Cheyenne
  Population 47,283
  Rank in State 2nd
Largest City . . . . Casper
  Population 51,016
Number of Places over 10,000 Population 8

District of Columbia

Motto . . . . *Justitia Omnibus* (Justice for All)
Flower . . . . American Beauty Rose
Bird . . . . Wood Thrush
Tree . . . . Scarlet Oak
Became U.S. Capital . . . . . . December 1, 1800

ELECTED EXECUTIVE BRANCH OFFICIALS
Mayor . . . . Marion S. Barry Jr.

U.S. COURT OF APPEALS FOR THE DISTRICT OF COLUMBIA
Chief Judge . . . . . . Spottswood W. Robinson III

DISTRICT OF COLUMBIA COURT OF APPEALS
Chief Judge . . . . William C. Pryor

U. S. DISTRICT COURT FOR THE DISTRICT OF COLUMBIA
Chief Judge . . . . Aubrey Robinson Jr.
U.S. Attorney . . . . Joseph E. DiGenova

THE SUPERIOR COURT OF THE DISTRICT OF COLUMBIA
Chief Judge . . . . H. Carl Moultrie

COUNCIL OF THE DISTRICT OF COLUMBIA
Chairman . . . . David Clarke
Chairman Pro Tem . . . . Frank Smith Jr.

STATISTICS
Land Area (square miles) 63
Population 638,333
   Density per square mile 10,132.3
Delegate to Congress* 1

*Committee voting privileges only.

American Samoa

Motto . . . . *Samoa-Muamua le Atua*
   (Samoa, God Is First)
Flower . . . . Paogo
Plant . . . . Ava
Song . . . . *Amerika Samoa*
Became a Territory of the United States . . 1900
Capital . . . . Pago Pago

ELECTED EXECUTIVE BRANCH OFFICIALS
Governor . . . . A.P. Lutali
Lieutenant
   Governor . . . . Faleomavaega Eni Hunkin

HIGH COURT
Robert Gardner, Chief Justice
Charles V. Ala'ilima, District Court Judge
F. Michael Kruse, Pro-Tem District Court Judge
Thomas W. Murphy, Associate Justice

LEGISLATURE
President of the Senate . . . . Letuli Toloa
President Pro Tem
   of the Senate . . . . Tuiasosopo Mariota
Secretary of the Senate . . . . Salilo K. Levi

Speaker of the House . . . Tuiafono P. Mata'utia
Vice Speaker
   of the House . . . . Frank Reed
Clerk of the House . . . . Wally Utu

STATISTICS
Land Area (square miles) 76
Population 32,395
   Density per square mile 419.0
Capital City . . . . Pago Pago
   Population 3,075
Largest City . . . . Pago Pago
Number of Villages 76

Guam

Nickname .... Pearl of the Pacific
Flower .... *Puti Tai Nobio* (Bougainvillea)
Bird .... *Toto* (Fruit Dove)
Tree .... *Ifit* (Intsiabijuga)
Song .... *Stand Ye Guamanians*
Stone .... Latte
Slogan .... *Where America's Day Begins*
Animal .... Iguana
Ceded to the United States
   by Spain .... December 10, 1898
Became a Territory .... August 1, 1950
Capital .... Agana

ELECTED EXECUTIVE BRANCH OFFICIALS

Governor .... Ricardo J. Bordallo
Lieutenant Governor .... Edward D. Reyes

SUPERIOR COURT

Paul J. Abbate, Presiding Judge
Benjamin J.F. Cruz
Ramon V. Diaz
Joaquin V.E. Manibusan
Peter C. Siguenza Jr.
Janet Healy Weeks

LEGISLATURE

Speaker .... Carl T.C. Gutierrez
Vice Speaker .... Joe T. San Agustin
Legislative Secretary ..... Elizabeth P. Arriola

STATISTICS

Land Area (square miles) 209
Population 105,816
   Density per square mile 506.3
Delegate to Congress* 1
Capital City .... Agana
   Population 896
Largest City .... Tamuning
   Population 8,862

---

*Committee voting privileges only.

Northern Mariana Islands

Tree .... Flame Tree
Flower .... Plumeria
Administered by the United States as a trusteeship
   for the United Nations .... July 18, 1947
Voters approved a
   proposed constitution .... June 1975
U.S. President signed covenant agreeing to
   Commonwealth status for the
   islands .... March 24, 1976
Became a self-governing Commonwealth
   .... January 9, 1978
Capital .... Saipan

ELECTED EXECUTIVE BRANCH OFFICIALS

Governor .... Pedro P. Tenorio
Lieutenant Governor .... Pedro A. Tenorio

COMMONWEALTH TRIAL COURT

Robert A. Hefner, Chief Judge
Herbert D. Soll

LEGISLATURE

President of the Senate ..... Ponciano C. Rasa
Vice President
   of the Senate .... Benjamin T. Manglona

Speaker of the House ..... Vincente M. Sablan
Vice Speaker of the House .... Juan B. Tudela

STATISTICS

Land Area (square miles) 184
Population 16,780
   Density per square mile 91.1
Capital City .... Saipan
   Population 14,549
Largest City .... Saipan

Puerto Rico

Nickname . . . . Island of Enchantment
Motto . . . . *Joannes Est Nomen Ejus*
(John Is Thy Name)
Song . . . . *La Borinquena*
Animal . . . . Coqui
Became a territory of the United States
. . . . December 10, 1898
Became a self-governing Commonwealth
. . . . July 25, 1952
Capital . . . . San Juan

ELECTED EXECUTIVE BRANCH OFFICIALS

Governor . . . . Rafael Hernandez-Colon

SUPREME COURT

Jose Trias Monge, Chief Justice
Carlos J. Irizarry Yunque
Antonio S. Negron Garcia
Francisco Rebollo Lopez
Hiram Torres Rigual

LEGISLATIVE ASSEMBLY

President
of the Senate . . . Miguel A. Hernandez Agosto
Vice President
of the Senate . . . . Sergio Pena Clos
Secretary
of the Senate . . . . . . Ramon Garcia Santiago

Speaker of the House . . . . . Jose Jarabo Alvarez
Vice President
of the House . . . . Samuel Ramirez
Secretary
of the House . . . . Jose Ramon Morales

STATISTICS

Land Area (square miles) 3,421
Population 3,187,570
Density per square mile 931.8
Delegate to Congress* 1
Capital City . . . . San Juan
Population 424,600
Largest City . . . . San Juan
Number of Places over 10,000 Population . . . 31

---

*Committee voting privileges only.

Virgin Islands

Flower . . . . Yellow Elder or Ginger Thomas
Bird . . . . Yellow Breast or Banana Quit
Song . . . . *Virgin Islands March*
Purchased from Denmark . . . . . March 31, 1917
Capital . . . . Charlotte Amalie

ELECTED EXECUTIVE BRANCH OFFICIALS

Governor . . . . Juan F. Luis
Lieutenant Governor . . . . Julio Brady

FEDERAL DISTRICT COURT

Almeric Christian, Chief Judge
David O'Brien

LEGISLATURE

President . . . . Derek M. Hodge
Vice President . . . . Eric E. Dawson
Legislative
Secretary . . . . Cleone Creque Maynard
Executive Secretary . . . . Eric Dawson

STATISTICS

Land Area (square miles) 132
St. Croix (square miles) 80
St. John (square miles) 20
St. Thomas (square miles) 32
Population 95,591
St. Croix 49,013
St. John 2,360
St. Thomas 44,218
Density per square mile 724.2
Delegate to Congress* 1
Capital City . . . . Charlotte Amalie, St. Thomas
Population 11,842

---

*Committee voting privileges only.

Federated States of Micronesia

Administered by the United States as a trusteeship
for the United Nations........July 18, 1947
Voters approved a
proposed constitution ....July 12, 1978
Effective date of constitution ....May 10, 1979
Capital ....Kolonia, Ponape

STATISTICS

Land Area (square miles)................271
  Kosrae District........................42
  Ponape District 134
  Truk District 49
  Yap District 46
Population 73,160
  Kosrae District 5,491
  Ponape District 22,081
  Truk District 37,488
  Yap District.......................8,100
Capital City ....Kolonia, Ponape
  Population 5,549
Largest City ....Moen, Truk
  Population 10,351

Marshall Islands

Administered by the United States as a trusteeship
for the United Nations........July 18, 1947
Voters approved a
proposed constitution .... March 1, 1979
Effective date of constitution ..... May 1, 1979
Capital...........................Majuro

STATISTICS

Land Area (square miles)................70
Population 31,042
  Density per square mile.............443.5
Capital City.......................Majuro
  Population........................8,667
Largest City .... Majuro

Republic of Belau

Administered by the United States as a trusteeship
for the United Nations........July 18, 1947
Voters approved a
proposed constitution ....July 9, 1980
Effective date of constitution ..January 1, 1981

STATISTICS

Land Area (square miles)...............192
Population 12,177
  Density per square mile..............63.4
Capital City.......................Koror
  Population 6,222
Largest City ....Koror

SUBJECT INDEX

(Page numbers in **boldface** indicate tables; a complete list of tables is on pages vi-ix.)

A

Acid rain, *see* Environmental and natural resource
    problems
Adjutants general
  Salaries, **58**
  Selection, methods of, **53**
Administration and management
  Archives and records management, 279, 280
  Developments in, 274-280
  Facility management, 277
  Fleet management, 276
  Organization, administrative
    Cabinet systems, **41**
    Executive branch, 45-50
  Personnel, 274, 275
    Administrative officials
      Salaries, **61**
      Selection, methods of, **56**
    Fair Labor Standards Act, 151, 274, 362, 428
    Garcia v. San Antonio Metropolitan Transit
      Authority, 151, 274, 362, 428, 429
    National League of Cities v. Usery, 151, 274
    Office of administrator: primary responsibilities,
      281
    Productivity improvement, 275
    Structure and functions, **284**
  Purchasing, 275, 276
    Administrative officials, salaries, **62**
  Risk management, 277
  Surplus property, 278, 279
  Telecommunications, 278
Administrative officials
  Length and number of terms, **51**
  Salaries, **58**
  Selection, methods of, **53**
  See also titles of individual officials
Age
  Of majority, **332**
  Minimum for specified activities, **332**
Agriculture
  Administrative officials
    Salaries, **58**
    Selection, methods of, **53**
  Elected state officials, terms, length and number of,
    51
Aid to local governments, 438-440
  By purpose, 438
  Individual payments, 438
  Miscellaneous programs, 439, 440
  State expenditures
    By state: 1978 to 1984, **442**
    Per capita by function and state: 1983, **443**; 1984,
      444
    Per capita distribution, **439**
    Percent distribution, selected years: 1974 to 1984,
      439
    Summary of payments: 1942 to 1984, **441**
Air pollution, *see* Environmental and natural
    resource problems
Alcoholic beverages, *see* Taxation and Tax revenue
American Federation of State, County, and
    Municipal Employees, et al. v. State of
    Washington, 150, 291, 292

Amusements, *see* Tax revenue
Archives and records management, 279, 280
Asbestos
  In buildings, state action on, **415**
  See also Environmental and natural resource
    problems
Assistance and subsidies, *see* Finances, state
Attorneys general
  Duties
    Advisory, **71**
    Antitrust, **72**
    Consumer protection, **72**
    Counsel for state, **73**
    Prosecutorial, **71**
    To administrative agencies, **73**
  Qualifications for office, **70**
  Salaries, **58**
  Selection, methods of, **53, 70**
  Subpoena powers, **72**
  Terms, length and number of, **51**
  To be elected 1986-87, **179**
Auditors
  Terms, length and number of, **51**
  To be elected 1986-87, **179**

B

Baker v. Carr, 76
Balanced Budget and Emergency Deficit Control
    Act, 429
Banking
  Administrative officials
    Salaries, **58**
    Selection, methods of, **53**
  See also Finances, state
Budget, state
  Administrative officials
    Salaries, **58**
    Selection, methods of, **53**
  Balanced budgets and deficit limitations:
    constitutional and statutory provisions, **246**
  Budgetary
    Practices, **220**
    Process, 29, 30
  Executive branch policy management, 48
  Gubernatorial powers, **37**
  Officials or agencies responsible for budget prepara-
    tion, review, and controls, **223**

C

Cabinet systems, 41
Cable Communications Policy Act of 1984, 428
California State Employees Association v. State
    of California, 291
Campaign finance laws, *see* Elections
Candidates for state offices
  Methods of nominating, **181**
Capital outlay, *see* Finances, state
Capital punishment, 399
Chief justice, *see* Courts

499

501

All-mail ballot, 178
Campaign finance laws
  Filing requirements, **185**
  Limitations on contributions
    By individuals, **194**
    By organizations, **190**
  Limitations on expenditures, **200**
Exit polls, 178
Funding of, **206**
Gubernatorial, 24, 25, **25**
Legislation, 176-178
Legislative districts, 176
  Bandemer v. Davis, 176
Nominating candidates for state offices, methods of,
  181
Polling hours, **209**
Primaries
  Election information, **183**
  Presidential, 178
  Republican Party of Connecticut v. Tashjian, 176
Recall of state officials, provisions for, **217**
State officials to be elected in 1986-87, **179**
Voting
  Elderly and handicapped, procedures for, 176, 177
  Gubernatorial elections, statistics for, **211**
  Registration for, 177, **208**
  Voter turnout
    For presidential elections, 1976, 1980, 1984, **213**
    In non-presidential election years, 1974, 1978,
      1982, **212**
Emergency management
  Administrative officials
    Salaries, **60**
    Selection, methods of, **55**
Employee retirement systems, finances of,
  305-307
  Benefit payments, 305
  Comparative statistics for: 1983-84, **314**
  Investments and assets, 306
  Membership and benefit operations of: last month
    fiscal 1983-84, **310**
  Membership size, 305
  Number and membership of by size-group: 1983-84,
    306
  Number, membership and monthly payments of:
    1981-82 to 1983-84, **308**
  Receipts and payments
    By state: 1983-84, **312**
    National summary: 1978-84, **309**
  Revenues, 306
Employment security administration, *see*
  Employment, state; Finances, state
Employment, state
  Average monthly earnings, summary: 1952-1984,
    295
  Classification and compensation plans, **286**
  Equal employment opportunity, 363
  For selected functions
    October 1983, **301**
    October 1984, **302**
  *Garcia v. San Antonio Metropolitan Transit
    Authority,* 151, 274, 362, 428, 429
  Holidays, paid, **288**
  Leave policies, selected, **287**
  Payrolls for selected functions
    October 1983, **303**
    October 1984, **304**
  Payrolls, monthly, summary of: 1952-1984, **295**

Personnel administration
  Office of administrator: primary responsibilities,
    281
  Structures and functions, **284**
Services
  Administrative officials,
  Salaries, **60**
  Selection, methods of, **55**
Summary of: 1952-1984, **295**
See also Compensation; Salaries
Employment, state and local
Employees
  Average earnings
    October 1983, **296, 299**
    October 1984, **296, 300**
  By function
    October 1983, **296**
    October 1984, **296**
  By individual states
    October 1983, **297**
    October 1984, **298**
  Payrolls
    October 1983, **296, 299**
    October 1984, **296, 300**
Energy resources
  Administrative officials
    Salaries, **60**
    Selection, methods of, **55**
  Administrative organization, 46
Environmental and natural resource problems,
  401-405
  Environmental quality, 401-404
    Air, 403, 404
      Acid rain, 403
      Asbestos in buildings, state actions on, **415**
      Toxins, 403, 404
    Land, 404
      Low-level radioactive waste
        Compacts, **411**
        Distribution by state: 1984, **410**
      Superfund sites, national priority list, **409**
      Underground storage tanks regulatory units,
        404, **412**
    Water, 402, 403
      Groundwater
        Policy development, status of, **406**
        Sources of contamination, **407**
        Types of contaminants, **408**
      Wastewater treatment works, alternate
        assistance, programs for, **414**
  Legislation
    Clean Air Act, 402, 403
    Comprehensive Environmental Response, Compen-
      sation, and Liability Act (CERCLA), 402
    Forest Resource Planning Act, 405
    Nuclear Waste Policy Act, 404
    Resource Conservation and Recovery Act (RCRA),
      402, 404, 428, **412**
    Right-to-know laws, 364, **413**
    Surface Mining Control and Reclamation Act
      (SMCRA), 404
  Natural resource concerns, priority ranking of, **403**
  Natural resources, 404, 405
    Coastal zone management, 405
    Forest resources, 405
    Interstate water agencies, 420, 421, **422**
    National wildlife refuge system, by state: 1984,
      416

502

Water resources, 404
Environmental protection agencies
  Administrative officials
    Salaries, **60**
    Selection, methods of, **55**
  Administrative organization, 46
Environmental quality commissions
  Names and functions, **417**
Equal Pay Act of 1963, 293
Equipment, *see* Finances, state
Executive branch
  Organization and issues, 45-50
  See also Governors
Expenditure, *see* Finances, state

F

Fair Labor Standards Act, 151, 274, 362, 428
Federal aid
  To child nutrition programs: fiscal 1983-84, **337**
  To education: 1983, **449**; 1984; **451**
  To health and hospitals, 385-387
    1983, **449**
    1984, **451**
  To highways, 226
    1983, **449**
    1984, **451**
    Fiscal 1985, **349**
  To public school systems: 1983-84, **333**
  To public welfare, 226
    1983, **449**
    1984, **451**
  To states: fiscal 1979-1984, **432**
Federal-state relations
  Developments in, 426-431
  Federal court decisions, 429, 430
  Federal legislation and regulation, 427-429
  Funding, 426, 427, 430
    Distribution of grants by region, **427**
Finances, state, 226, 227
  Administrative officials
    Employment
      October 1983: **301**
      October 1984: **302**
    Payrolls
      October 1983: **303**
      October 1984: **304**
    Salaries, **60**
    Selection, methods of, **55**
  Cash and security holdings, 227
    At end of fiscal year, national totals for selected
      years: 1970-84, **231**
  Debt
    Outstanding at end of fiscal 1983, **244**
    Outstanding at end of fiscal 1984, **245**
  Expenditure, 226
    Assistance and subsidies
      By state: 1983, **236**; 1984, **238**
      National totals: 1970-84, **230**
    By character and object
      By state: 1983, **236**; 1984, **238**
      National totals: 1970-84, **230**
    Capital outlay
      By state: 1983, **236**; 1984, **238**
      National totals: 1970-84, **230**
    Construction
      By state: 1983, **236**; 1984, **238**
      National totals: 1970-84, **230**

Corrections
  By state: 1983, **240**; 1984, **242**
  National totals: 1970-84, **230**
Current operation
  By state: 1983, **236**; 1984, **238**
  National totals: 1970-84, **230**
Debt redemption
  By state: 1983, **228**; 1984, **229**
  National totals: 1970-84, **230**
Direct expenditure
  By state: 1983, **236**; 1984, **238**
  National totals: 1970-84, **230**
Education
  By state: 1983, **240**; 1984, **242**
  National totals: 1970-84, **230**
  Per capita, by function and state: 1983, **443**;
    1984, **444**
  To local government: 1942 to 1984, **441**
Employment security administration
  By state: 1983, **240**; 1984, **242**
  National totals: 1970-84, **230**
Equipment
  By state: 1983, **236**; 1984, **238**
  National totals: 1970-84, **230**
Financial administration
  By state: 1983, **240**; 1984, **242**
  National totals: 1970-84, **230**
General
  By function: 1983, **240**; 1984, **242**
  By state: 1983, **228**; 1984, **229**
  National totals: 1970-84, **230**
Health and hospitals
  By state: 1983, **240**; 1984, **242**
  National totals: 1970-84, **230**
Highways
  By state: 1983, **240**; 1984, **242**
  National totals: 1970-84, **230**
  Per capita, by function and state: 1983, **443**;
    1984, **444**
  To local governments: 1942 to 1984, **441**
Insurance benefits and repayments
  By state: 1983, **236**; 1984, **238**
  National totals: 1970-84, **230**
Insurance trust
  By state: 1983, **228**; 1984, **229**
  National totals: 1970-84, **230**
Interest on debt
  By state: 1983, **236**; 1984, **238**
  National totals: 1970-84, **230**
Intergovernmental
  By function: 1983, **445**; 1984, **446**
  By state: 1978 to 1984, **442**; 1983, **236**; 1984,
    238
  By type of receiving government: 1983, **447**;
    1984, **448**
  National totals: 1970-84, **230**
  Per capita, by function and state: 1983, **443**;
    1984, **444**
  Summary of payments: 1942 to 1984, **441**
Land and existing structures
  By state: 1983, **236**; 1984, **238**
  National totals: 1970-84, **230**
Liquor stores
  By state: 1983, **228**; 1984, **229**
  National totals: 1970-84, **230**
Natural resources
  By state: 1983, **240**; 1984, **242**
  National totals: 1970-84, **230**

Terms, length and number of, **51**
To be elected 1986-87, **179**

U

Underground storage tanks
Regulatory units, 404, **412**
See also Environmental and natural resource
problems
Uniform state laws: 1984-85, 324-326
Acts being drafted for 1986-87, 326
Fraudulent Transfer Act, 324
Health-Care Information Act, 324
Land Security Interest Act, 324, 325
Land Transactions Act, 324
Law Commissioners' Model Insanity Defense and
Post-Trial Disposition Act, 324
Limited Partnership Act Amendments, 325
Personal Property Leasing Act, 325
Record of passage of, **327**
Rights of the Terminally Ill Act, 325
Securities Act, 325
Statutory Will Act, 325, 326
Trade Secrets Act Amendments, 326
Utilities, *see* Public utilities

V

Veto
Gubernatorial, 27, **37, 111**
Legislative, 28, 29
Override, **111**

Victims of Crime Act of 1984, 150
Voter
Registration information, 177, **208**
Turnout for presidential elections: 1976, 1980, 1984,
213
Turnout in non-presidential election years: 1974,
1978, 1982, **212**
Voting Accessibility for the Elderly and
Handicapped Act, 176

W

Wastewater treatment works
Alternate assistance programs for, **414**
See also Environmental and natural resource
problems
Water, *see* Environmental and natural resource
problems
Wildlife
National refuge system, by state: 1984, **416**
See also Fish and wildlife
Women
In the judicial system, 152
See also Comparable worth
Workers' compensation *see* Labor, workers'
compensation